Y0-BRG-711

Principles of
Modern Marketing

Principles of Modern Marketing

Stewart W. Husted
Indiana State University

Dale L. Varble
Indiana State University

James R. Lowry
Ball State University

ALLYN AND BACON
BOSTON • LONDON • SYDNEY • TORONTO

Copyright © 1989 by Allyn and Bacon
A Division of Simon & Schuster
160 Gould Street
Needham Heights, MA 02194

Marketing Director: Sandi Kirshner
Series Editor: Henry Reece
Developmental Editor: Hannah Rubenstein
Editorial Production Service: Karen Mason
Cover Administrator: Linda K. Dickinson

LIBRARY OF CONGRESS CATALOGING-IN-PUBLICATION DATA

Husted, Stewart W.
    Principles of modern marketing / Stewart W. Husted,
Dale L. Varble, James R. Lowry
        p.   cm.
    Includes bibliographies and indexes.
    ISBN 0-205-11575-6
    1. Marketing   I. Varble, Dale L. II. Lowry, James Rolf
III. Title
HF5415.H89 1989
658.8—dc19   88-25031

Printed in the United States of America

10 9 8 7 6 5 4 3 2 1   92 91 90 89

PHOTO CREDITS

CHAPTER 1/ p. 7—Dave Schaefer; **CHAPTER 2**/ p. 44—James L. Reynolds, p. 47—Paddy Mullen; **CHAPTER 3**/ p. 60—AP Wide World Photos; **CHAPTER 4**/ p. 95—Magnum, p. 97—Magnum; **CHAPTER 5**/ p. 120—Rob Nelson/ Picture Group, p. 131—James L. Reynolds, p. 134—Kulik Photographic, p. 136—James L. Reynolds; **CHAPTER 6**/ p. 155—Robert Harbison; **CHAPTER 8**/ p. 209—a) James L. Reynolds, b) Mark Antman/The Image Works, c) James L. Reynolds, p. 213—C&W Shields, Inc., p. 216—James Shaffer, p. 218—David Schaefer, p. 222—C&W Shields, Inc., p. 223—James Shaffer, p. 226—C&W Shields, Inc.; **CHAPTER 9**/ p. 240— James L. Reynolds; **CHAPTER 10**/ p. 264—Robert Harbison, p. 267—Bob Coyle, p. 269—a) Norman Prince, b) The Image Works, c) James L. Reynolds, d) Magnum, p. 279—James L. Reynolds; **CHAPTER 11**/ p. 288—Bob Coyle, p. 295—James Shaffer, p. 299—John Berens, p. 304—James Shaffer; **CHAPTER 12**/ p. 320—James Shaffer, p. 327—James L. Reynolds; **CHAPTER 14**/ p. 380—Bob Coyle, p. 384—James Shaffer, p. 391— C&W Shields, Inc., p. 394—James H. Pickerell, p. 396—Jim Shaffer, p. 397— Bob Coyle, p. 401 top—Mark Antman/ The Image Works, p. 401 bottom—James H. Pickerell; **CHAPTER 15**/ p. 427 top and bottom—Norman Prince, p. 430— Jack Spratt/The Image Works; **CHAPTER 16**/ p. 446—a) Bob Eckert-EKM/Nepethe, b) Bob Coyle; **CHAPTER 17**/ p. 481— Larry Mangino/The Image Works, p. 487—Alan Carey/The Image Works; **CHAPTER 18**/ p. 496—Frank Sitemann/ EKM-Nepenthe, p. 498—David Schaefer, p. 499—James Shaffer, p. 500—Joyce Bast, p. 510—Jan Pickerele, p. 517— David Shaefer; **CHAPTER 20**/ p. 552— Magnum; **CHAPTER 21**/ p. 582—C&W Shields, Inc., p. 587—Bob Coyle; **CHAPTER 22**/ p. 608—Andrew Popper/ Picture Group, p. 609—Norman Prince, p. 612—Bob Eckert/EKM-Nepenthe; **CHAPTER 23**/ p. 634—Bob Coyle, p. 646—Bob Coyle; **COMPREHENSIVE CASE 3**/ p. 675—Courtesy of Paws, Inc.

To my parents . . . John and Katheryn;
and Kathy, Ryan, and Evan

SWH

To Mary Ellen, Emily, Derek, Sarah, and Kathy

DLV

To Margaret, Stephen, Chip, and David

JRL

Brief Contents

Contents

Section Four
THE PRODUCT/ SERVICE PLAN 201

Chapter 23
ETHICS AND SOCIAL RESPONSIBILITY IN MARKETING   632

Preface

Several years ago, we conceived the idea for a new Principles of Marketing text. We wanted to write a marketing text with a different twist, one that did more than just repeat the approaches already taken by existing texts.

Our initial task as authors of *Principles of Modern Marketing* was to assist our publisher in the development of a marketing plan for our text. As in all marketing plans, our first step was to conduct a situation analysis. In other words, we evaluated the competition in this market and the factors that would influence the success of our text in the marketplace. Our analysis revealed that there were several high-quality texts that followed a rather standard, theoretical approach to teaching marketing principles. These texts combined the functions of marketing with the management of those functions.

Information from a survey of more than 200 marketing instructors, and several focus groups, revealed what was perceived by many to be a major weakness in existing marketing texts—the lack of *applied marketing*. An appropriate blend or balance of marketing theory and application was missing.

Armed with this information, we sought to find such a balance. Our goal was not to write a book that skimped on theory, but rather to develop a text containing theory that could be applied using an integrated pedagogical method.

The missing link soon became apparent. We discovered that no existing marketing text gave the marketing plan appropriate emphasis. In real-world settings, the importance of the marketing plan cannot be overemphasized. However, in textbooks on marketing, it is very much underemphasized. The marketing plan is the key link between theory and application.

WHY ADOPT THIS TEXT?

Principles of Modern Marketing is the first text to provide a true balance of theory and application in the comprehensive *marketing plan outline*. By including this seven-part marketing plan outline in the text and providing an overview of the components of a marketing plan in Chapter 2, the 4Ps are strongly reinforced for the students. This approach also helps them develop decision-making and other marketing management skills. In addition, we have included completed marketing plans in the Instructor's Manual for each of the four Comprehensive Cases appearing at the end of the text. Also included in the Instructor's Manual is an Extended Case and a completed marketing plan for it. (Details of the four Comprehensive Cases, as well as what is included in the Instructor's Manual, are discussed later in this preface.) We have provided comprehensive coverage of key topics, devoting at least two chapters to each of the 4Ps.

Each chapter of *Principles of Modern Marketing* was reviewed three times by separate groups of reviewers who worked hard to help us perfect our text plan. Students should enjoy reading the text and retain a high percentage of the material. Instructors will find a complete ancillary package, including instructor's manual, test bank, study guide, transparencies, videos, and the unique *The Modern Marketing Planner* software, a computer program that guides the student in creating a marketing plan.

STUDENT LEARNING AIDS

Principles of Modern Marketing was designed to make the study of marketing principles as rewarding as possible. Our state-of-the-art pedagogy includes:

Chapter Outlines	Each chapter is introduced by a chapter outline, which includes case titles, major chapter headings, and end-of-chapter features.
Learning Objectives	The learning objectives in *Principles of Modern Marketing* identify the knowledge and application skills the student should master after reading each chapter. A summary of each objective is provided in the Goal Summary section at the end of each chapter.
Introductory Cases/ The Case Continues	Each chapter opens with an introductory real-life case. The Case Continues feature extends the case, appearing at three or four junctures throughout each chapter. This feature serves a dual purpose: It extends the story into the chapter, encouraging students to continue reading, and it reinforces the text material it directly precedes. In addition, answers to the "Issues for Discussion" questions for each case are provided in the Instructor's Manual.

Three Kinds of Marketing Highlight Boxes

Appearing throughout the text are three kinds of boxes, including *Marketing in Action*, *Real People in Marketing*, and *The Rest of the Story*. These boxes link chapter content to real-world marketing people and events.

Margin Notes

Each chapter contains margin notes that highlight key concepts. Our intention when writing these notes was to amplify, rather than simply reiterate the text material. The margin notes provide an excellent additional "push" to the study process.

Goal Summary

As noted above, the Goal Summary section summarizes each learning objective.

Key Terms

Boldfaced key terms, appearing throughout each chapter, are listed at the end of the chapters and are cross-referenced to the pages in which they appear. Each boldfaced key term also appears in the glossary.

Check Your Learning

The Check Your Learning section consists of multiple-choice and true/false questions, with answers provided at the end of the book. This section provides students with quick feedback to help ensure that they are grasping key concepts. This feature was well received by reviewers and has proven successful in leading psychology texts.

Questions for Discussion and Review

Some questions in this section focus on reviewing chapter material, while others are more thought-provoking and can serve as catalysts for classroom discussion. Answers to each chapter's questions are provided in the Instructor's Manual.

Concluding Cases

Each chapter ends with a real-world case that asks students to analyze contemporary marketing problems and opportunities that occur in the operation of an organization. Cases are drawn from a wide range of organizations, including those in the service, consumer products, industrial, and nonprofit sectors. Again, the answers to the "Issues for Discussion" questions for each concluding case are provided in the Instructor's Manual.

Glossary

All key terms are defined in the glossary.

The Comprehensive Cases

Four comprehensive cases are provided at the end of the text. These may be used in conjunction with the marketing plan or read as discrete cases. They include nonprofit, industrial, consumer products, and retail organizations:

Case 1—Western Technical College
Case 2—Borg-Warner's Mechanical Seal Division: A Pulp Mill Market Plan
Case 3—Paws, Inc.—The Tale of Garfield
Case 4—Marsh—Retail Food Distributor

THE MARKETING PLAN

This text uses the marketing plan as a focal point to aid in the teaching and learning of marketing principles. It offers great flexibility as a teaching tool.

The instructor has a variety of options in deciding either how much or how little this feature will be used. If the instructor does not wish to assign students the task of developing a marketing plan, the plan outline can simply serve as a unifying theme throughout the book—providing a structure and a coherence to the various aspects of marketing. Students often experience difficulty in understanding how the different facets of marketing (for example, marketing research, consumer behavior, pricing, and promotion) interact in the real world of marketing management. The marketing plan outline gives students a very clear idea of what a marketing manager actually does.

As a second option, the instructor can direct the student to select one or more of the four Comprehensive Cases to use in developing the marketing plan. Completed marketing plans for the Comprehensive Cases—which include a consumer products company, an industrial firm, a nonprofit organization, and a retail company—are provided in the Instructor's Manual.

A third option is to provide the students with the Extended Case on Newbury Comics in the Instructor's Manual. A completed marketing plan for The Newbury Comics Company is also provided in the manual.

The Modern Marketing Plan software can be integrated into any of these approaches to teaching the marketing plan.

SECTIONS IN THE TEXT WHERE THE PLAN APPEARS	MARKETING PLAN PART, PAGE NUMBER, SAMPLE QUESTIONS
Section Three *Identification of Target Markets* (appears after Chapter 4)	**SITUATION ANALYSIS** (Part 2 of the Marketing Plan, p. 115) Describe your company's product or service. Is the size of the market increasing? Decreasing? How fast is the market changing? **MARKETING PLAN OBJECTIVES** (Part 3 of the Marketing Plan, p. 116) What is the organization's mission? Have the firm's resources been identified? Are the objectives of the marketing plan compatible with the firm's mission?
Section Four *The Product/ Service Plan* (appears after Chapter 7)	**MARKET SELECTION: TARGET MARKETS** (Part 4 of the Marketing Plan, p. 200) What are the characteristics of the market? Why were these target markets selected? Assess the potential of each market segment.

**MARKET STRATEGY
AND MARKETING MIX**
(Part 5 of the Marketing Plan, p. 200)
How will the product or service be positioned? What is the organization's strategy for implementing the marketing plan?

Section Five
The Price Plan
(appears after Chapter 9)

ACTION PROGRAM: Product/Service
(Part 6A of the Marketing Plan, p. 260)
What is the total product concept for this good or service? What is the breadth and depth of the firm's product/service modifications expected as it moves through the life cycle?

Section Six
The Distribution Plan
(appears after Chapter 11)

ACTION PROGRAM: Pricing
(Part 6B of the Marketing Plan, p. 316)
What is the overall pricing policy of the firm? How does the pricing structure compare to the competition? What is the target market's evaluation of price and its ability to purchase? Will there be significant demand at this price?

Section Seven
The Promotional Plan
(appears after Chapter 15)

ACTION PROGRAM: Distribution
(Part 6C of the Marketing Plan, p. 440)
What is the current distribution strategy and intensity? What (if any) new distribution channels should be added or eliminated this year? Why or why not?

Section Eight
*Strategic Planning
and Control*
(appears after Chapter 18)

ACTION PROGRAM: Promotion
(Part 6D of the Marketing Plan, p. 522)
What are the promotional objectives for the organization's product or service? What is the overall promotional strategy (push or pull) for the organization? Describe. What are the copy and media strategies? What is the role of sales promotion?

Section Nine
*The Broader Marketing
Perspective*
(appears after Chapter 20)

**BUDGETS, CONTROL,
AND ACCOUNTABILITY**
(Part 7 of the Marketing Plan, p. 572)
For your product or service, review what is to be accomplished and how much it will cost; who will do it; how it will be done and by when.

EXECUTIVE SUMMARY
(Part 1 of the Marketing Plan, p. 572)
Does the summary emphasize an action orientation?

THE SUPPLEMENTS PACKAGE

The Modern Marketing Planner by MarketWorks, Inc. is a unique, state-of-the-art, easy-to-use computer program that will guide students through the process of writing a marketing plan. The program features a data base of questions, notes, and guidelines for creating a marketing plan, along with a second glossary of marketing terms. A full-service word processing system with pull down command windows and help screens is built into the program. The program is available for IBM-PC and compatibles.

Instructor's Resource Manual,
> **by Charles Pettijohn, Southwest Missouri State University**
> This manual features:

- Comprehensive Chapter Outlines and Lecture Notes
- Chapter-by-chapter answers to each chapter's Questions for Discussion and Review section in the text
- Answers to each chapter's Introductory and Concluding Case "Issues for Discussion" questions
- Lecture Enrichment stories
- Student Involvement Exercises
- Completed marketing plans for the four Comprehensive Cases in the text.

In addition, the Instructor's Manual contains an Extended Case on The Newbury Comics Company, a Boston-based chain of five stores. Newbury Comics started selling vintage comic books and then moved rapidly into selling imported rock records and assorted goods for the youth market. The case focuses on the major strategic decision facing the company in 1985—when it had to decide whether or not to enter the compact disc market. A completed marketing plan for this case is also included in the IM.

Student Study Guide,
> **by Lee Neumann, Bucks County Community College**
> The Study Guide includes:

- Individual Chapter Summaries
- Key Chapter Concepts
- Key Terms Worksheets
- Pretest Section with true/false and multiple-choice questions
- Key Terms Crossword Puzzles
- Posttest, with column matching, fill-in-the-blank, and discussion questions
- Notes to Myself
- Answer Key

Test Bank,
> **prepared by James L. Finlay, Western Illinois University**
> Geared to meet a variety of testing needs, this Test Bank features a total of 2,300 test items with a mix of true/false, multiple choice, fill-in-the-blanks, and essay questions. The test items are keyed to individual learning goals and referenced to the text by page number.

Computerized Test Bank
> The Test Bank is available in IBM-PC, Apple II, and Macintosh versions for computerized test generation.

Transparencies

Two transparency packages are available to adopters. One package, consisting of 74 transparencies, was prepared specifically for *Principles of Modern Marketing*. Allyn and Bacon's generic package of 134 transparencies is designed for use in all principles of marketing courses.

Marketing Videos

A library of videos that can be used in the introductory marketing course are available from Allyn and Bacon publishers. Upon adoption of this text, contact an Allyn and Bacon representative for more information.

 KEY TOPIC COVERAGE

Ethics and Social Responsibility in Marketing

Recognizing the increasing emphasis upon and interest in ethical issues, both in business in general and specifically in the area of marketing, *Principles of Modern Marketing* offers a unique chapter, *Ethics and Social Responsibility in Marketing*, which gives students an ethical base from which to examine ethical dilemmas. Sections on *Ethical Theories, Demarketing of Resources, International Markets,* and *The Ethical Dimensions of the 4Ps*, offer a thoughtful framework for students and instructor alike.

International Marketing

The importance of international marketing can scarcely be overstated, particularly in view of current AACSB guidelines. Chapter 21 explores this key area in selected topics, such as *Multinational Corporations, Countertrade, International Competitive Environment, International Market Planning,* and *Implementing the International Marketing Plan.*

Marketing for Service and Nonprofit Organizations

This chapter differentiates between strategies for product and services marketing. It defines the nature of service and nonprofit organizations, examines the markets for them, and looks at how each uses the marketing mix. Selected coverage includes: *Characteristics of Services; The Marketing Mix for Services; Why is Nonprofit Marketing Different?;* and *Types of Nonprofit Marketing.*

 APPENDICES

The Mathematics of Marketing

This section provides extremely useful information on three areas of mathematics that marketers commonly use on the job: income statements, analytical ratios, and markups and markdowns.

Careers in Marketing

The *Careers in Marketing* appendix examines some common careers in marketing and gives suggestions about how to select the right marketing career and how to get a job by writing an effective resume and conducting a successful interview. Sections include:

- Selecting the Right Marketing Career: Formula for Vocational Choice
- Using the College Years to Your Best Advantage
- Writing the Resume and Letter of Application
- Interviewing for a Job/Accepting or Refusing a Job

 ## ACKNOWLEDGMENTS

A quality textbook requires a lot of quality help from many super individuals. This text is no exception. We would especially like to thank our Developmental Editor, Hannah Rubenstein, who practically dedicated her life to this project. Her hard work and many long hours on the text have given this book the polished look of a professional "classic." Other members of the Allyn and Bacon team who significantly contributed to the text were Karen Mason, Production Editor and Designer; Sandi Kirshner, Marketing Director; Beverly Peavler and Kathleen Shankman, Copyeditors; and Henry Reece, Marketing Editor.

Credit for assistance goes to several professional secretaries and office administrators at Indiana State University and Ball State University. They include Debbie Shake, Charlene Baker, Robin Beeson, Ruthetta Krause, and Sandra Marsh. Their help is especially appreciated. In addition, we would like to thank Jack Goebel, Dean of the School of Business at Indiana State, and Neil Palomba, Dean of the College of Business at Ball State, for their support and encouragement.

We are indebted to the authors of our ancillary package. These include Charles Pettijohn, Southwest Missouri State University, author of the Instructor's Manual and accompanying marketing plans for the Comprehensive Cases and the Newbury Comics Case; Lee Neumann, Bucks County Community College, Study Guide author; and James Finlay, Western Illinois University, who wrote the Test Bank.

Others providing assistance include Mary Ellen Varble and Kathy Husted. Kathy deserves special credit for completing our index during the hot summer of 1988. Credit and thanks are also due Hannah Rubenstein and Susan Lewis for their development work on the Newbury Comics Case, and to Bob Thompson for developing one of our Comprehensive Cases.

Finally, we would like to thank our many reviewers and focus group participants for their valuable feedback. They are listed here.

REVIEWERS

M. Wayne Alexander
Moorhead State University

James H. Berson
The Borough of Manhattan Community College of the City University of New York

Donna Bleck
Middlesex Community College

Howard W. Combs
Radford University

Eddie V. Easley
Wake Forest University

Jon Hawes
University of Akron

Edward Kirk
Vincennes University

Eric I. Kulp
Middlesex Community College

Paul James Londrigan
Mott Community College

Leslie E. Martin, Jr.
University of Wisconsin

Lee H. Neumann
Bucks County Community College

R. Vish Viswanathan
University of Northern Colorado

Robert J. Williams
Eastern Michigan University

Ralph D. Wray
Illinois State University

MARKETING RESEARCH CONTRIBUTORS

Jeff Totten
McMurry College

Tom Rossi
Broome Community College

Wm. Hannaford
University of Wisconsin

Linda Anglin
Mankato State University

Donald Anderson
University of North Dakota

Abraham Axelrud
Queensborough Community College

John Paxton
Wayne State College

Joseph Maglio
University of Wisconsin

R. E. Polchow
Muskingum Area Technical College

Alice Griswold
University of Dubuque

Jack Brinkley
Amarillo College

Diane Whiteford
Western Wisconsin Technical Institute

Debora Sheridan
Sioux Falls College

Allan Reddy
Valdosta State College

R. Arora
Bradley University

M. Edward Goretsky
George Mason University

E. T. Deiderick
Youngstown State University

Shane Premeaux
Northeast Louisiana University

Alan Graber
Morse School of Business

Robert Roe
University of Wyoming

James Walsh
Tidewater Community College

Thomas Ponzurick
Memphis State University

Jack Sheeks
Broward Community College

Maurice Clabaugh
University of Montevallo

Ned Bassler
Beaufort Technical College

William Willcutt
Oklahoma City University

Michael Loizides
Old Dominion University

D. A. Chase
Atlanta University

Don Kirchner
California State University

George Boulware
David Lipscomb College

Ken Lundahl
Jamestown Community College

Jeanne Conn
Horry-Georgetown Technical College

Hsin-Min Tong
Clarkson College

R. Vish Wiswanathan
Southern Illinois University

Scott Johnson
Mankato State University

Barbara Wiedeman
Spencer School of Business

Herbert Neal
County College of Morris

Athena Miklos
Hocking Technical College

T. Lynn Wilson
St. Leo College

Roger Abshire
University of Southern Mississippi

Bern Wisner
Central Oregon Community College

William Staples
University of Houston

John Lloyd
Monroe Community College

Mary Anderson
Frostburg State College

R. F. Gwinner
Arizona State University

Robert Ballinger
Siena College

Edna Johnson
Bowie State College

Russel Taylor
College of New Rochelle

Leonard Miller
College of Eastern Utah

Therese Riordan
St. John Fisher College

E. A. Prim
Macomb Community College

T. M. Rosania
Trenton State College

David Wheeler
Suffolk University

R. Spiller
California State University

Jay Close
Kentucky Wesleyan University

Margo Underwood
Crandall Junior College

Ralph Davenport
Sangamon State University

Louis Volpp
California State University

Clay Ferguson
*Chattanooga State Technical
Community College*

Bill Motz
Lansing Community College

Charles Goeldner
University of Colorado

Grant Thomas
Eastern Washington University

Carol Howard
Indiana University

Kenneth Maricle
Virginia Commonwealth University

Reed Holder
Nichols College

John Gubbay
Moraine Valley Community College

James McCullough
University of Arizona

Jeffrey Durgee
Rensselaer Polytechnic Institute

Edward F. Marecki
*Delaware Technical and
Community College*

James Bennett
Ithaca College

C. W. Forbes
Odessa College

Linda Delene
Western Michigan University

A. E. Reynolds
Gordon College

J. Peter Vernon
Monroe Community College

Thomas Lower
Stark Technical College

David Nemi
Erie Community College

Robert Lee
University of Northern Iowa

Anthony Muiderman
Hope College

J. R. Cosgrove
Fordham University

Steve Hutchens
Creighton University

Susan Harrison
Parkersburg Community College

Gilberto Delos Santos
Pan American University

Michael Landeck
North Texas State University

Jan Prashkner
Southern Seminary Junior College

Alfred Manduley
Manhattan College

Jack Atkinson
College of Alameda

H. Edward Saipher
Pace University

Sak Onkvisit
Northeastern Illinois University

Thomas Bertsch
James Madison University

Howard Combs
Radford University

A. C. Gross
Cleveland State University

Renee Wonser
North Dakota State University

John Brennan
Florida State University

Richard Immenhausen
College of the Desert

John Huse
Clark County Community College

George Lucas
Memphis State University

D. Ashton
University of Arkansas

William Layden
Golden West College

Robert Kosmidek
Champlain College

James Muldoon
State University of New York at Farmingdale

Ashok Kalburui
Keuka College

Lance Masters
California State University

Jim Wong
Lindenwood College

Leon F. McMullin
Lander College

John Milewicz
University of South Alabama

James Johnson
Lamar University

Karen Reed-Messing
Stonehill College

Frank McDaniels
Delaware County Community College

M. Alan Miller
Tennessee State University

Jack Ashmore
Bee County College

John Bartunek
Western Illinois University

Michael West
Maple Woods Community College

Stan Ricketts
Baptist College

M. Grabner
Milwaukee Area Technical College

Susan Friedlander
Broome Community College

William Rice
California State University

Charles Roman
Madonna College

Richard Stanish
Tulsa Junior College

Thomas Cook
University of Southwestern Louisiana

Harold Chapin
Central Connecticut State University

P. William Vaught
Middle Tennessee State University

Sanford Appleroth
York College

Royal Earle
Casco Bay College

Gail Miller
Westminster College

Sudhir Chawla
Angelo State University

*Principles of
Modern Marketing*

Section
One

Introduction

OUTLINE

CHAPTER 1

An Introduction to the Marketing Process

LEARNING GOALS

After reading this chapter, you should be able to:

1. Explain the meaning of the marketing concept.
2. Distinguish between marketing and selling.
3. Identify the elements in the exchange process.
4. Discuss the differences between a production orientation and a marketing orientation.
5. Explain the differences between a marketing orientation and a marketing-systems orientation.
6. Understand the importance of the marketing functions.
7. Identify the economic utilities that are created by marketing.
8. Distinguish between micro- and macromarketing.
9. Identify the macromarketing goals.
10. Explain why the study of marketing is important.

*A*n avid jogger, Jane was sometimes disappointed with the distance she logged on her daily course. With the new portable music system her husband gave her for Christmas, however, Jane found herself almost effortlessly gaining more ground.

A longtime commuter discovered that the soothing voice of Ray Charles, or the strains of Beethoven or Bach, made the tedious twice-daily train ride to and from his Chicago office and his suburban home a much more relaxing ritual.

Harvey's wife used to complain constantly about the loud music he played every night. Harvey finally gave up his favorite pastime to placate her. When a friend gave him a portable stereo system for his birthday, home was a happier place for everyone. Harvey could listen to music as long and as loudly as he pleased, and his wife's nerves no longer had to pay the price.

A unique electronic product, carefully designed and marketed, made a significant difference in the lives of the commuter, the jogger, and the lover of loud music (and his wife!). The person most responsible for this revolutionary product is Akio Morita, chairman of the Sony Corporation.

Recognizing the huge potential market for a personal stereo system, in 1979 Mr. Morita assembled a team of Sony specialists who designed, produced, and marketed the overwhelmingly popular Walkman in just six months.

The development of the Walkman involved a blending of established technologies by Sony's radio division. In the wake of organizational changes, several key radio division products—radio cassette recorders and tape recorders—had been shifted away from the radio division to the tape recorder division. This shift forced the worried radio division staff to meet day and night for a week in order to determine ways to sustain their sales and profitability. They had to find a new product to market to remain viable. Finally, a clever idea came to them. Why not take a Sony dictating unit that was already on the market, modify it, add

INTRODUCTORY CASE
THE SONY SIDE OF MARKETING

a pair of earphones, and create a personal stereo unit?

A major problem encountered in the Walkman's development was the size and clumsiness of the headphones. This was resolved when Masaru Ibuka, a co-founder of Sony, recalled that the research department was experimenting with new lightweight headphones. The new headphones were successfully substituted, and a new product was born. Today the Walkman is adding an entertainment dimension to many activities previously considered solitary and sometimes tedious.

Issues for Discussion
1. How can you determine whether there is an adequate market for a new product?
2. In the development of a new product, is it more important for a company to focus mainly on production problems or marketing ones?
3. How can you tell whether the Walkman produces consumer satisfaction?

Sources: Based on David E. Whiteside, Otis Port, and Larry Armstrong, "Sony Isn't Mourning the 'Death' of Betamax," *Business Week,* Jan. 25, 1988, p. 37; and Shu Ueyoma, "The Selling of the Walkman," *Advertising Age,* March 22, 1983, p. M–3.

■ A wide assortment of Walkman® models are available for many activities.
Source: Courtesy of Sony Corporation of America

Figure 1.1
Steps in the marketing process.

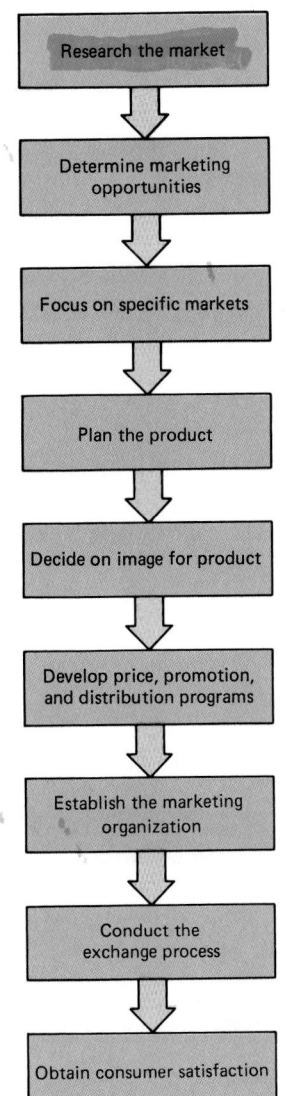

Research the market

Determine marketing opportunities

Focus on specific markets

Plan the product

Decide on image for product

Develop price, promotion, and distribution programs

Establish the marketing organization

Conduct the exchange process

Obtain consumer satisfaction

Marketing identifies the need for a good, communicates its benefits, and distributes it to the proper markets.

*O*rganizations that place primary importance upon consumer needs are called **marketing-driven organizations.** These organizations develop and distribute products that satisfy consumer needs. Sony, and many other companies—both domestic and foreign, for-profit and nonprofit—are marketing driven. To understand the orientation of these marketing-driven companies, you should understand the marketing concept, how it evolved, and the differences between marketing and selling. A marketing-driven organization must have the proper organizational structure to attain its marketing objectives. The study of the marketing structure and the activities within a particular organization is termed *micromarketing.* The study of marketing in the larger society in general is termed *macromarketing.*

This chapter begins by explaining what it means to be marketing driven. It defines *marketing* and then describes what the marketing concept is and how it develops. Next, it describes the marketing functions and their role in providing satisfaction, or utility, to consumers.

Marketing is studied at the level of the individual firm and at the level of the larger economic system. The chapter introduces both levels and ends with a discussion of why the study of marketing—at either level—is important. ■

THE MEANING OF MARKETING

Just what is marketing? The term *marketing* means different things to different people, but in both profit and nonprofit organizations, most managers agree that successful organizations are marketing driven. In this sense, we can say that marketing identifies the need for the good, communicates its benefits, and distributes it to the proper markets. A formal definition prepared by the American Marketing Association identifies marketing as the process of planning and executing the conception, pricing, promotion, and distribution of ideas, goods, and services to create exchanges that satisfy individual and organizational objectives.[1] In other words, marketing is a series of actions that results in the exchange of ideas, goods, and services that satisfy personal and organizational goals. To a businessperson, marketing means having the right product, at the right place, at the right time, at the right price, and at a profit. Figure 1.1 identifies the steps that are generally associated with the marketing process.

Sophisticated marketing systems help deliver comfortable standards of living to consumers in developed countries. The less-developed countries lack such systems. Their economies are generally based on agriculture that employs very primitive methods and tools. These countries' struggle for self-sufficiency is so great that the more sophisticated acts of trade are yet to be implemented. It is only when people in a country can provide for themselves and create a surplus that a system of middlemen develops to distribute the surplus. Trade then follows, which encourages the production of a greater variety of goods.

As consumers become aware of the availability of new goods and services, they cast the older goods aside and demand the newer ones. People in primitive civilizations may wash their clothes over rocks in a clear stream. But a higher standard of living arises when a washboard and a tub replace the rocks and the stream. An even higher standard is attained when the wringer washer replaces the washboard. For Americans, who have one of the highest standards of living in the world, washing drudgery has been almost completely eliminated by automatic washers with push-button controls and multiple washing cycles. Marketing has helped provide this high standard of living.

THE LOCKHORNS

"I HAVE NO CHOICE. WE LIVE IN A CONSUMER-ORIENTED SOCIETY."

The Exchange Process

The origin of marketing can be traced to the exchange process. An **exchange** occurs when something of value is given or received for something in return. An exchange involves a buyer and a seller, or two traders, the item to be exchanged, and some form of compensation for the item.

As a result of the exchange process, a transaction occurs. In a **transaction,** either the ownership of a good or the right to use it is transferred from seller to buyer. A videotape dealer may either sell or rent a Michael Jackson tape to customers. Although under rental agreements buyers may not actually obtain ownership of this tape, they have purchased the temporary right to use it.

We are all familiar with the merchandise transactions that occur when we exchange our money for a pair of Levi's at Sears or a box of Wheaties at Kroger's. Other types of transactions, perhaps less easily recognized, occur when something of psychological or social value is exchanged. For example, a college provides an education for a student in exchange for the required tuition. Members of the AFL-CIO receive collective bargaining representation in return for their monthly dues. A transaction should satisfy both buyers and sellers. When both parties believe they have gained from a transaction, they will continue to do business.

> *In a transaction, either the ownership of a good or the right to use it is transferred from seller to buyer.*

Acceptance of the Marketing Concept

We have already noted that most successful organizations are **marketing driven.** We could also say that these organizations have accepted the **marketing concept.**

In firms that have applied the marketing concept to the fullest extent, each department is responsive to consumer needs. This concept affects decision making in every area of a firm—not just in the marketing department. For example, the production department maintains the level of product quality that consumers want, and financial managers establish credit programs that help consumers buy.

A company that has adopted the marketing concept continually evaluates itself against three criteria (figure 1.2).

> *When fully implemented, the marketing concept affects decision making in every area of a firm.*

1. Do the decisions satisfy consumer needs?
2. Do all activities throughout the organization support marketing?
3. Is the organization achieving its primary objective by satisfying consumer needs?

IBM was not the first company in the computer field. Actually, it was a latecomer! IBM was, however, the first computer company to accept the marketing concept—to place consumers' needs first. It applied this concept by noting its customers' processing needs, designing the appropriate data processing systems for them, and

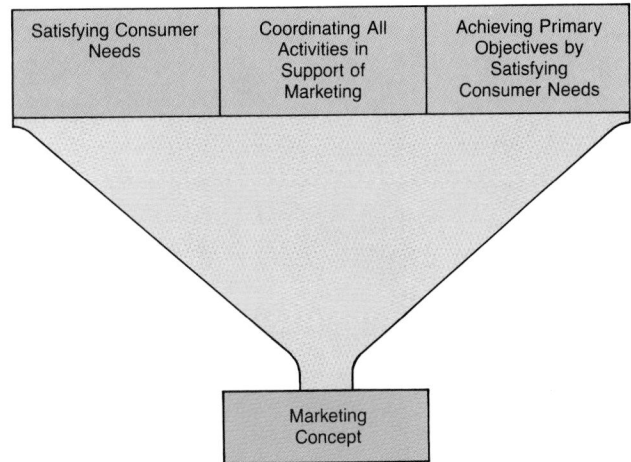

Figure 1.2
Adoption of the
marketing concept.

then training the customers' employees to run the system. IBM's Thomas J. Watson, Jr., remarked, "In time, good service became almost a reflex in IBM. . . . Years ago we ran an ad that said simply and in bold type, 'IBM Means Service.' I have often thought it was our very best ad. It stated clearly just exactly what we stand for. . . . We want to give the best customer service of any company in the world. . . . IBM's contracts have always offered, not machines for rent, but machines services, that is the equipment itself and the continuing advice and counsel of IBM's staff."[2]

An organization that puts the consumer first in decision making is a consumer-oriented one: McDonald's, for example, consistently stresses to its employees a program of "Quality, Service, Cleanliness, and Value" (Q, S, C, and V). If a store manager or franchisee frequently fails to meet the high standards in these areas, the company fires the manager or takes away the franchise.

To strengthen and reinforce its marketing activities, the Walt Disney theme parks have instituted an unusual program in which top management works to serve the visitors in the parks. For one week each year the managers leave their offices and handle tickets, sell Mickey Mouse hats, operate rides, sweep the grounds, and perform many other park activities. When they return to their desks, these executives are well aware of what it takes to satisfy the millions of visitors that pour through the parks' gates.[3]

**One way to satisfy
customer needs is to
communicate directly with
the consumer.**

GE's motto, ''We bring good things to life'' reflects their consumer orientation. In this ad, the company offers an extended 90-day warranty for its appliances.

Source: Courtesy of General Electric

At General Electric the marketing concept has evolved into a marketing philosophy that touches every aspect of the organization. About thirty years ago a chief executive of General Electric stated this philosophy by remarking: "Believe me, I recognize the risk I run when I make the statement that our definition of marketing is, in reality, so broad as to constitute a business philosophy. Perhaps I can make myself more clear by explaining that fundamental to this philosophy is the recognition and acceptance of a consumer-oriented way of doing business. Under marketing the customer becomes the fulcrum, the pivot point about which business moves in operating for the balanced best interest of all concerned."[4]

*M*anagers of consumer-oriented companies keep close tabs on their organizations' marketing activities.

Differences between Marketing and Selling

*S*elling follows production; much of marketing precedes it.

You may already have noticed that there is an important distinction between marketing and selling. The marketing process begins even before a good is produced, whereas selling occurs after its production. Through **selling,** an organization persuades consumers to purchase goods and services it already has available. In marketing, however, the needs of a specific market are identified—often through research—and then goods and services are developed to satisfy these needs. A classic example of the difference between selling and marketing occurred in the 1950s when the Ford Motor Company introduced the ill-fated Edsel. Without adequate marketing research, the company placed the Edsel model in its line so it would have an entry in the fast-selling, upper-medium-price class. The result was a sales disaster. In contrast, in the 1960s the firm patiently researched the market for the Ford Mustang and designed the car specifically to satisfy the needs of the growing number of two-car families and young married couples. This careful attention to marketing detail produced first-year sales higher than those for any other American car.

8 ❑

*M*r. Morita, Sony's chairman, knows very well that effective marketing means identifying and satisfying consumer needs. Shortly after the Walkman was developed, Mr. Morita assumed the role of the typical consumer and performed the first Walkman "use-test." To gauge consumer response to the tiny stereo package, Mr. Morita took it to a golf match and showed it to his friends. Using two sets of headphones, he

THE CASE CONTINUES

and another golfer listened attentively. As soon as they began to speak, they noted a problem. With the headphones on, neither could hear the comments of the other.

Mr. Morita recommended to his engineers that a special switch that temporarily cuts off the sound be installed in the unit. The switch would allow a listener to stop the music,

engage in conversation, and then turn the music back on. This feature was incorporated into the product and became known as the "hot-line" switch. To make the unit more user-friendly, several other minor features were added to the final design of the product. By adding these features, Mr. Morita demonstrated a keen appreciation for the importance of not just *selling* a finished product, but of creating and marketing a product that met consumer needs.

HOW A MARKETING ORIENTATION EVOLVES

IBM was the first computer company to accept the marketing concept. It is also one of the few companies that accepted the marketing concept early in its development. Most other organizations move in stages from a production, to a sales, to a marketing, to a marketing-system orientation. (See figure 1.3.) The historical development of U.S. business shows a similar progression.

❑ **Figure 1.3** Orientation of organizations.

	Production Orientation	Sales Orientation	Marketing Orientation	Marketing-Systems Orientation
Typical strategy	Lower cost	Increase volume	Build share profitability	Plan for long-term growth
Key operating systems	Plant income statements and budgets	Sales forecasts; results versus plan	Planning for the marketing activity	Strategic marketing plans that encompass the entire organization
Traditional skills	Engineering	Sales	Analysis	Analysis, planning, and department coordination
Normal focus	Internal efficiencies	Distribution channels; short-term sales results	Consumers and share of market	Consumers and long-term results
Typical response to competitive pressure	Cut costs	Cut price and sell harder	Conduct consumer research, plan, test, refine	Find market niche and serve it well
Overall mind-set	"What we need to do in this company is get our costs down and quality up."	"Where can I sell what we make?"	"What will the consumer buy that we can profitably make?"	"All departments of the company must focus on the consumer."

Source: Adapted from Edward G. Michaels, "Marketing Muscle," *Business Horizons*, May–June 1982, p. 72.

A marketing orientation is essential for many service organizations.

Source: Courtesy of Bermuda Department of Tourism

Production Orientation

*P*roduction-oriented companies focus on how best to make their products.

From the industrial revolution of the 1850s until 1930 most firms in the United States had a production orientation. They were concerned with lowering the costs of production by improving engineering and internal efficiency. For these firms, the decision to launch a new product was production oriented, not marketing oriented. For example, the availability of high-quality wheat and inexpensive water power led Charles A. Pillsbury to launch his milling company in 1869. He did not base his decision on the existence of growing markets or demand for convenient flour products. He could ignore marketing concerns because he operated in a seller's market—anything that could be produced could be sold. Even today, in less developed countries, the demand for goods tends to exceed the supply available, and many firms operating in these areas maintain a production orientation. In our country some small firms that lack marketing expertise continue to embrace a production orientation because they have a particular production skill.

Sales Orientation

*T*he Great Depression of the 1930s forced companies to focus on how best to sell products.

With the onset of the Great Depression of the 1930s, suppliers suddenly found themselves with large inventories and an excess of production capacity but only a trickle of demand. During that period, companies recognized that they needed a well-trained sales force to influence wholesalers and retailers to buy their products. The type of product that a company produced was determined by its manufacturing capability. If it could produce red bowling balls efficiently, it produced red bowling balls, and its salespersons were expected to persuade bowlers to buy them.

Unfortunately, for many firms a sales orientation produces marketing myopia, which eventually leads to their demise. **Marketing myopia** is the failure of a firm to recognize what business it is actually in. For example, the railroads experienced trouble because they focused on selling rail services and failed to understand that what consumers were buying was a more general service—transportation. The railroads were product-oriented rather than customer-oriented.[5] When a firm focuses too narrowly on the product it is selling and not broadly enough on recognizing and satisfying consumer needs, it eventually falls victim to market shifts that cause a loss in consumer demand for the product.

Marketing and Marketing-System Orientations

*M*arketing-oriented companies focus on making what consumers need and want to buy.

In the early 1950s the marketing era began. Companies became aware of consumer needs and established marketing research departments to learn more about them. Many manufacturers realized that the overall U.S. market could be divided into separate groups with similar needs, called **market segments**. It was in the 1950s that General Motors launched the sporty Corvettes, which were directed toward a young adult market. Appliance manufacturers, such as General Electric and Westinghouse, introduced and marketed the first built-in appliances for middle-class homeowners, who wanted modern kitchens. The increasing complexity of marketing caused companies to establish a marketing-manager position to coordinate selling, sales training, advertising, product development, and marketing research.

Consumer-goods companies, such as Procter & Gamble and Quaker Oats, were early arrivals in the marketing era. Perhaps they were forced into becoming marketing-oriented by their dependence on the fickle consumer. Companies could no longer depend on hyperbolic sales pitches to move their goods in an increasingly sophisticated society. They had to determine which products would best meet the needs of consumers. Keen competition from other consumer-goods companies kept these firms alert to new marketing opportunities.

Some firms—particularly those in industrial markets—continued to operate under a sales orientation. Until 1980, for example, Republic Steel's Industrial Products Division offered the same products as all of the other fabricators in the industry. Then, an analysis of its product line revealed that 3,000 of the 12,000 items the firm manufactured accounted for 95 percent of sales. The division dropped the slow-selling items and directed the remaining items to carefully defined markets. This action moved the division from a sales orientation toward a marketing orientation.

During the 1970s and the 1980s many organizations, such as IBM and General Electric, entered the marketing-systems era. The marketing-systems orientation extended the marketing orientation to encompass the entire organization.

Under the marketing-systems orientation, marketing is treated as a philosophy that touches each activity in an organization. The marketing manager is expected to develop strategic plans that provide for long-term growth and profitability by anticipating future changes in the market and developing innovative strategies to meet them. He or she must carefully consider how the total resources of a firm can be effectively used to meet the demands of an ever-changing market. Everyone in the

THE REST OF THE STORY

Adding Marketing Clout

In 1946, a Japanese physicist and a Japanese engineer founded a small electronics firm, Tokyo Tsushin Kogyo, with $600 in capital and about two dozen employees. The company originally concentrated on producing communications equipment for the reconstruction of Japan after World War II. A series of discouraging experiences with government purchasing officials, however, convinced the founders that they should abandon the specialized government market and pursue opportunities in the broader consumer market. Soon the small company was marketing the first tape recorder and tapes manufactured in Japan. These were followed shortly by the introduction of the world's first transistor radio.

In an effort to enlarge its consumer market, the company began marketing its products in the United States. One of the founders personally took charge of this operation and learned that Americans could not pronounce the company's name, nor did they associate it with any particular product. He realized that a company that markets worldwide should have a name that is readily recognized and easily pronounced. This prompted company officials to scratch their heads and to begin a search for a new name. They decided that three conditions had to be met for the new name. It had to be internationally acceptable, pronounced the same in all languages, and be short.

Numerous names were mentioned, carefully reviewed, and eventually rejected. Finally someone stumbled across the Latin word "sonus," which means sound. They noted that this word is similar to the English word "sonny," and the company was composed of a group of young men or "sonny boys!" The Latin and the English words were combined to create a brief corporate identification that was simple to spell and easy to pronounce in English. Now you know the rest of the story behind the search for a name that would add marketing clout to a small Japanese electronics firm. Today this small firm has become the worldwide giant—Sony!

Source: Adapted from Akio Morita, "Moving Up in Marketing by Getting Down to Basics," *The Conference Board Record*, December 1974, pp. 46–49.

Customers do not buy products; they buy benefits.

organization should understand that consumers are not buying products; they are buying *benefits*. That is, when consumers buy quarter-inch drill bits, what they really want is quarter-inch holes. The organization must make sure consumers understand why a product will generate the desired results.

AT&T illustrates the move to a marketing-systems orientation. Several years ago all the firm's new products resulted from its laboratory research, without regard to consumer needs. Furthermore, if an established product was selling well, the company sometimes delayed the introduction of promising new products. Eventually a marketing philosophy was adopted, however, and AT&T reorganized its Technologies subsidiary and created separate product divisions with each containing marketing, sales, and research and development departments. These divisions thoroughly study consumer needs before new products are developed. AT&T had been a production-oriented company, but now it is marketing-systems oriented.

IMPORTANCE OF THE MARKETING FUNCTIONS

Marketing functions are major economic activities that must be performed in the marketing system, in order for the marketing task to be accomplished.

Organizations may differ in their approach to marketing, but all perform certain important marketing functions. In order for computers in Silicon Valley in California; automobiles in Detroit, Michigan; and furniture in High Point, North Carolina, to reach their markets, specific marketing functions must be carried out. **Marketing functions** are those major economic activities that must be performed somewhere in the marketing system in order for the marketing task to be accomplished. These functions may be shifted among organizations and may be reduced or expanded in scope, but they cannot be totally eliminated.

A particular function is usually executed by the organization that can do it most economically and efficiently. For example, many retailers have shifted their consumer-financing function to a credit-card service. Self-service retailers, such as Kmart and Zayre, have reduced the scope of their selling function and shifted a portion of it to the consumer. In contrast, upscale full-service retailers, such as Gucci and Bonwit Teller, have expanded the scope of their selling function to include a variety of personal services.

The eight basic marketing functions are classified into the following general groups:

GROUPS	FUNCTIONS
Functions of exchange	Buying
	Selling
Functions of physical distribution	Transportation
	Storage
Facilitating functions	Marketing information and research
	Financing
	Standardization and grading
	Risk bearing

Marketers who pay careful attention to the buying function offer the proper assortment of goods to their customers and are generally successful in the marketplace. The selling function in marketing encompasses advertising, personal selling, sales promotion, and publicity. Transportation and storage activities make the goods available in the right place and at the right time. Marketing information and research help marketers to prepare competitive responses and to develop new products. The financing function is often necessary to complete a transaction. Execution of the standardization and grading function ensures that goods of established size and quality will be available to consumers. For example, the U.S. Department of Agriculture has adopted quality grades for beef. The dangers of product obsolescence and price declines, along with many other business risks, are associated with marketing, making risk bearing an important marketing function.

ECONOMIC UTILITIES

The efficient performance of marketing functions creates economic utilities.

Economists typically measure the value of a good or service by the utility, or satisfaction, that it creates. **Economic utilities** provide satisfaction and value to consumers. They include the utilities of form, place, time, information, and possession (figure 1.4). Consumers typically select and buy the goods and services that provide them with the greatest utility. The benefits derived from the utilities should exceed their costs to consumers. Consumers acknowledge the value of the utilities by patronizing the marketers that provide them.

The change in the form of a good is created by the production process and is called **form utility.** Manufacturing creates form utility when a sheet of steel becomes a can. Form utility creates the tangible product. In order for this product to reach the consumer, the utilities of possession, time, and place must be facilitated.

Economic utilities: form, place, time, information, and possession.

The performance of marketing functions generates utilities that increase the value of a good or service to consumers. **Place utility,** which creates value by transferring a good closer to the place of consumption, comes from the transportation function. A Maytag clothes washer assembled in Newton, Iowa, has no value to a consumer in Tampa, Florida, until it gets to Tampa. **Time utility,** which adds to consumer satisfaction by making the goods available at the time they are needed, is

☐ **Figure 1.4**
Creation of economic utilities.

Production	Marketing			
Production Function	Transportation Function	Storage Function	Selling Function	Selling and Financing Functions
Changes the form of a good and creates	Moves a good to the place of need and creates	Permits a good to be inventoried until needed and creates	Communicates the features and benefits of a good and creates	Facilitate the exchange process, often using financial arrangements and creates
= Form Utility	= Place Utility	= Time Utility	= Information Utility	= Possession Utility

created by the storage function. When a consumer goes to a Maytag dealer, he or she wants to compare and choose from several models, and the storage function makes that possible. The selling function creates **information utility,** which refers to the availability of knowledge about a good. By observing the promotions and sales presentations of a Maytag dealer, consumers learn about the features and benefits of the various Maytag models. The selling and financing functions provide **possession utility.** Selling brings about the exchange of a Maytag washer from dealer to consumer, and consumer financing arrangements facilitate the transaction.

THE CASE CONTINUES

Although new product development at Sony ordinarily takes one or two years, a herculean effort created the Walkman in fewer than six months. You'll recall that Sony's Radio Division badly needed a new product to sustain division sales. Sony provided consumers with valuable *form utility* by producing the only personal stereo package in a crowded market of complex stereo systems. Mr. Morita gathered ten individuals—from the production, product planning, design, advertising, sales, and export divisions of Sony—and formed a marketing-oriented project team. He assumed the chair-

manship of this group and empowered it to make all of the strategic decisions for the production and marketing of the unit.

The group met regularly to finalize the details of the product and to thrash out the elements of its marketing plan. Based on sales estimates, a production schedule was completed, and the cost structure and selling price were established. A promotional theme and a package design were chosen that would furnish consumers with the proper *information utility.* One of the last and

most controversial decisions of the team was to pick a name that would identify the product and have global acceptance. After much discussion, *Walkman* was chosen. Mr. Morita then had to convince all of Sony's overseas subsidiaries to adopt the same name for the product. This permitted the company to use the same packaging and promotional materials worldwide, facilitating *possession utility.* Publications throughout the world began writing about the tiny stereo unit, and because of a universal identification, Walkman almost became a generic term for a personal stereo, rather than a brand name.

MICRO- AND MACROMARKETING

Marketing is studied at two levels, which are usually identified by two terms borrowed from Greek—*micro,* which means "small," and *macro,* which means "large." **Micromarketing** refers to the marketing activities an organization performs in order to achieve its objectives. **Macromarketing** is concerned with the overall economic process that matches the supply of goods and services produced to the demand and, in turn, satisfies the goals of an economic system.

Micromarketing

*M*icromarketing relates to the way an organization carries out the marketing process.

Micromarketing relates to the way an organization carries out the marketing process identified in figure 1.1. In brief, this process begins with marketing research studies to determine the needs of potential customers. A good or service that satisfies these needs is designed and produced, and appropriate price, promotion, and distribution programs are selected. Then the product is sold to consumers. If the firm has carried out the process successfully, consumers are satisfied with the product.

BMW, the German luxury-auto maker, provides an example of how a micromarketing strategy develops. In the 1970s the company's initial promotional efforts in this country positioned the BMW as a sporty, high-performance automobile for younger drivers. The majority of its cars were priced between $20,000 and $30,000. More recently, however, an older and wealthier market has been purchasing more expensive luxury automobiles, such as Mercedes-Benz and Jaguar. To gain a larger share of this market, BMW, capitalizing on the quality image of its cars and a strong dealer organization, has introduced higher-priced models selling for well over $30,000. In addition, the company has begun sponsoring steeplechase events in Virginia, polo matches in Dallas, and downhill ski races at Western resort areas. These events target affluent consumers who do not spend their weekends wandering around automobile showrooms.

Micromarketing concerns not only firms that sell products but also organizations, such as colleges and charitable groups, that seek to market services or ideas. The admissions department of your college markets the school's programs to prospective students. Contacts with alumni, students, and others help college administrators determine what academic programs are needed. Through personal contact and a variety of promotions, such as college fairs and direct mailings, the admissions department tells prospective students about these programs.

Macromarketing

*T*he ultimate goal of a macromarketing system is to satisfy the needs of the public economically, efficiently, and fairly.

Macromarketing is concerned with the entire system used to distribute goods and services in a society. The goal of a macromarketing system is to satisfy the needs of the public economically, efficiently, and fairly. It may appear that there is little difference between studying macromarketing systems and studying economic systems. However, the study of macromarketing systems has a narrower focus. Economic systems attempt to allocate scarce resources among many competing activities of varying importance. Economic systems range from free market ones—such as that of the United States—to those that are completely planned and directed by the state—such as that of the U.S.S.R. Most systems contain elements of both types. Macromarketing systems include only the activities and institutions that move goods and services from producer to consumer.

MACROMARKETING GOALS

*S*pecific goals of a macromarketing system include maximizing information, choice, consumption, and satisfaction.

We have identified the ultimate goal of the macromarketing system as satisfying the needs of the public economically, efficiently, and fairly. Because such a general and idealistic goal is difficult to evaluate systematically, we will focus on a group of more specific macromarketing goals. They include maximizing the information, choice of goods and services, consumption, and satisfactions available to consumers.[6] When properly implemented, these goals enrich consumers' lives.

Maximizing Information.   A variety of promotional efforts are used to accomplish the first goal: communicating information to consumers. The Betty Ford Center for the treatment of drug and alcohol abusers markets its programs through the testimony of public figures such as Elizabeth Taylor and Mary Tyler Moore. The Advertising Council, a nonprofit organization of advertisers, has undertaken a campaign to inform the public about the United Negro College Fund. Since 1972, the Fund's donations have tripled compared with donations in its previous twenty-seven years.[7]

Maximizing Goods and Services.   By maximizing the choice of goods and services, marketers satisfy the demands of a large portion of society. The opportunity to choose permits consumers to select those goods and services that enhance and complement their personal lifestyles. In automobiles, for example, choices range from the simple and economical Chevrolet Sprint to the elegant and expensive Rolls Royce.

Consumers do pay a price for the availability of numerous choices. Firms that offer small quantities of many goods may be unable to achieve economies of scale—economies that occur when manufacturers produce hundreds of the same model of automobile, refrigerator, or personal computer each hour.

The proliferation of goods may even cause problems when the differences between goods in the same product class are minor. Are there really important distinctions between Tide and All detergents or between Winston and Marlboro cigarettes? Consumers may perceive the distinctions marketers make between such goods to be meaningless and may criticize the marketing process as wasteful.

Maximizing Consumption.   A frequently expressed opinion states that the primary goal of macro-marketing should be to generate demand, which will enhance consumption. For some, a satisfying lifestyle is created by the consumption of more and more goods and services. Furthermore, consumption raises the levels of production and employment. Thus, during business downturns we are confronted with appeals such as "You Auto Buy Now," and "Home Prices Will Never Be Lower." The hope is to stimulate consumption, with a resulting increase in employment.

Some people believe that a pattern of ever-increasing personal consumption is wasteful and perhaps immoral. They think that excessive personal consumption leads to a waste of the scarce resources needed to accomplish more important goals of society. For example, while other states were encouraging the use of their parks and natural resources, Oregon was discouraging their use in favor of preserving the beauty of its environment.

Maximizing Satisfaction.   Marketing generates a host of personal satisfactions. Your college admissions office marketed an educational program that is supplying you with useful skills and intellectual values. The marketing of a Bruce Springsteen concert provides you with information about musical entertainment. Adidas markets running shoes that help to satisfy your desire for recreation and physical fitness. Because each of us seeks different satisfactions, it is difficult to determine how well the macro-marketing system is meeting the goal of maximizing satisfaction. The best indication of success occurs when the majority of consumers express pleasure with their lifestyles.

 ## REASONS TO STUDY MARKETING

Clearly, marketing activities play an important part in the functioning of the U.S. economy. That in itself provides a good reason to learn more about marketing. Figure 1.5 lists several more specific reasons to study the subject.

❑ **Figure 1.5**
Reasons to study marketing.

1. To learn how firms create value and enhance our standard of living.
2. To learn how goods move from producers to consumers.
3. To better evaluate the efficiency of the marketing system.
4. To become more aware of the benefits of marketing.
5. To understand how the costs associated with marketing are incurred.
6. To appreciate the number of marketing institutions in the U.S. economy and the number of people they employ.
7. To learn about careers in marketing.

IBM, Harvard University, and the Mayo Clinic have attained outstanding reputations in their fields by creating and marketing superior goods and services. An important reason to study marketing is to learn how these and other organizations create, communicate, and supply us with value and so enhance our standard of living. A very practical reason for studying marketing is to become more familiar with how goods travel from the producer to you, the consumer. Studying marketing also helps us acquire information that permits us to evaluate the efficiency of the marketing system. Furthermore, it produces an awareness of the value, or benefits, derived from marketing activities.

Although much of the value that marketing creates is difficult to measure, those aspects that are measurable provide an indication of the importance of marketing in the business process and thus the importance of learning about marketing. Measurable factors include the cost of marketing and the number of marketing institutions, employees, and careers. The rest of the chapter describes these factors in more detail.

Costs of Marketing

The costs of marketing a product typically exceed the costs of producing it.

A classic study of distribution costs revealed that the costs of marketing a product are higher than the costs of producing it. The study indicated that marketing costs typically represent 59 percent of the total price of a product, while production costs account for only 41 percent.[8] Other research has shown that marketing costs frequently range from 40 to 60 percent of the selling price of a consumer good. These costs cover the performance of all of the marketing activities associated with the product.

If you have worked in retailing, you can easily understand why a hair dryer that costs $7.50 to manufacture carries a price tag of $15.00. The members of the distribution system for the hair dryer—manufacturer, wholesaler, and retailer—all have extensive marketing expenses that must be covered by the markups on their costs. The manufacturer who produces the dryer for $7.50 needs $1.50 more to pay for his or her marketing expenses. The wholesaler buys it for $9.00 and marks the price up another $2.00. The retailer purchases it for $11.00 and marks the price up another $4.00 to pay for its marketing expenses. Thus, $7.50 ($1.50 + $2.00 + $4.00) represents the marketing costs for the product. Since marketing costs consume so much of what people pay for goods and services, understanding how these costs are incurred constitutes a good reason to study marketing.

*J*ohnny Carson likes to poke fun at Cleveland, a lakeside metropolis known for its polluted river that caught on fire in the 1960s. Today, Cleveland is a vastly different city than the decaying community of the 1960s. The downtown has undergone a major renovation and is alive and vibrant with new stores and office buildings. Employment in the financial, educational, and health sectors has given the city a strengthened economic base. Cleveland's leading employer is no longer a manufacturer but a health care organization—the highly respected and praised Cleveland Clinic. With a staff of 9,000 workers, including 430 full-time physicians and 350 research institute employees, the clinic generates over half a billion dollars in revenue annually.

Clinic administrators recognize that they must always think in terms of the patients' needs. Thus, they have a strong marketing orientation. Just a little less than a decade ago, in 1980, the public affairs and corporate development staff—its marketing group—consisted of only four people. By 1988, the staff had increased to 80 individuals. The mission of this group is "to facilitate dynamic, mutually beneficial relationships between the Cleveland Clinic Foundation and its constituencies by providing staff support and counseling for marketing, strategic planning, corporate development, and two-way communication." To fulfill this mission, the marketing group is continuously looking for innovative pro-

MARKETING IN ACTION

A Clinical Approach

grams to satisfy the needs of its three major constituencies or markets: its own patients, referral patients from physicians outside the clinic, and health insurance programs, such as health maintenance organizations.

An important activity of the public affairs staff is to maintain and strengthen the relationships with the 35,000 doctors worldwide who direct their patients to the hospital for specialized medical help. An additional focus is to create an awareness of the clinic's many and varied services. About 230 newspapers and radio stations nationwide carry its articles and programs about health and medical care. The public affairs staff estimates that this publicity for the hospital is equivalent to over a million dollars worth of free advertising annually.

Another significant responsibility of staff members is to enhance the clinic's international reputation. The clinic continued relationships with many of the over 600 doctors in 62 countries who have been in residence at the hospital and with several thousand more who have participated in its varied medical education programs. An international center at the clinic serves foreign patients from 94 countries. The center makes the foreign visitor feel at ease by securing his or her airline and hotel accommodations, providing interpreters, and making doctors' appointments.

Outpatients and their families who want the finest accommodations while at the hospital can stay in the elegant penthouse suites on the 17th floor of the 348-room Clinic Center Hotel (cost = $750 to $1,000 a day). Those who want more modest priced accommodations can make reservations at the 196-room Clinic Inn, which features kitchenettes, allowing guests to prepare their own meals.

The marketing posture of the clinic is pushed by an active board of trustees that includes the chief executives of several major Cleveland businesses as well as key civic leaders. This governoring body determines the strategic direction for the hospital. Although it is composed of physicians, a number of these physician-managers also have master's degrees in business administration. These administrators are constantly considering ways to expand the clinic's services. To illustrate, a study of the clinic's geographic market indicated that a growing number of patients were coming from the southeast, particularly Florida—where many Midwesterners retire. As a result, the board established a satellite hospital in Fort Lauderdale, Florida. The administrators understand that in many respects the healthcare industry is similar to the automobile industry or any other consumer-goods industry. If you do not meet the needs of your markets by developing new products and providing quality service, soon you will not have any market to serve!

Number of Firms and Employees in the Marketing Structure

*M*ore than 4 million U.S. firms can be classified as marketing institutions.

The number and sales of wholesalers, retailers, and selected service organizations that are engaged primarily in marketing activities provide an insight into the importance of marketing in the U.S. economy. The U.S. Census of Business counts over 1,900,000 retailers, 400,000 wholesalers, and 1,800,000 selected service organizations—a total of 4,100,000 firms. This total does not include manufacturers with strong marketing orientations, such as IBM and GE, or supporting organizations such as financial institutions and transportation companies.

❑ Figure 1.6
Selected careers in
marketing.

Job title	Description
Advertising account executive	Liaison person between an advertising agency and its clients. The individual is employed by the agency to study the clients' promotional objectives and create promotional programs (including message, layout, media, and timing).
Credit manager	Supervisor of the firm's credit process, including eligibility for credit, terms, late payments, consumer complaints, and control.
Direct-to-home salesperson	Person who sells products and services to consumers by personal contact at the consumers' homes.
Fashion designer	Designer of apparel, such as beachwear, hats, dresses, scarves, and shoes.
Franchisee	Person who leases or buys a business that has many outlets and a well-known name. The franchisee normally operates one outlet and participates in cooperative planning and advertising. The franchisor sets rules for operating all outlets.
Life insurance agent (broker)	Person who advises clients on life insurance policy types available relative to their needs. Policies provide life insurance and/or retirement income.
Manufacturer's representative	Salesperson who represents several, usually small, manufacturers that cannot afford their own sales force. The representative normally deals with wholesalers and retailers. He or she determines needs and then displays, demonstrates, and describes products and services, often at the customer's place of business.
Marketing research project supervisor	Person who develops the research methodology, evaluates the accuracy of different sample sizes, analyzes data, and assesses statistical errors.
Retail buyer	Person responsible for purchasing items for resale. The buyer generally concentrates on a product area and develops a plan for proper styles, assortments, sizes, and amounts of the product. The buyer analyzes vendors on the basis of quality, style, availability, fit, flexibility, reliability, and price.
Sales manager	Supervisor of the sales force, responsible for recruitment, selection, training, motivation, evaluation, compensation and control.
Traffic manager	Supervisor of the purchase and use of alternate methods of transportation. This manager routes shipments and monitors securities.
Warehouser	Person responsible for storage and movement of goods within a company's warehouse facilities. The warehouser maintains inventory records and makes sure older items are shipped out before newer ones (rotating stock).
Wholesale salesperson	Seller representing a wholesaler to retailers and other firms.

Source: Reprinted from *Careers in Marketing,* published by The American Marketing Association, 1983, pp. 6–9.

*M*arketing workers make up more than a third of the U.S. work force.

Many people in the U.S. economy work in the marketing structure. The nearly 28 million employees in retailing (14.5 million), wholesaling (5 million), and selected services (8 million) give us a fair idea of the number of persons engaged in the field. To this number, however, we must add the marketing workers in a variety of other marketing-related enterprises, ranging from United Parcel Service to the American Red Cross. If we include everyone engaged in some form of distribution activity, we find that more than a third of the U.S. work force of over 100 million qualify as marketing workers.

Careers in Marketing

*T*he number and variety of jobs in marketing are increasing, especially in the service and nonprofit sectors of the U.S. economy.

The clothes you wear, the school you attend, and the textbooks you read were probably selected as the result of effective marketing programs by marketing professionals. The widespread application of the marketing concept has increased the number and variety of job opportunities in marketing—particularly in the service and nonprofit sectors. The *Dictionary of Occupational Titles and Supplements,* prepared by the U.S. Employment Service, lists nearly 20,000 different occupations.

Marketing helps nonprofit organizations accomplish their missions.

Source: Courtesy of United Negro College Fund, Inc.

Probably over a third of them are in the marketing and service fields. The types of marketing careers range from A to Z—account executive at an advertising agency to zoo marketing director. Appendix A provides an interesting overview of marketing careers, and figure 1.6 describes selected positions.

MARKETING IN SERVICE AND NONPROFIT ORGANIZATIONS

As mentioned, the service and nonprofit sectors offer many job opportunities in marketing. The fact that the service industries have created the great majority of new jobs has made service marketing even more significant than in the past. In 1988, nearly 75 percent of all workers were classified as service workers, and services are providing about 9 out of every 10 new jobs being created.

*M*arketers of services sell intangible rather than tangible products.

Service marketing involves intangible rather than tangible products. Like marketers of tangible goods, however, marketers of services can adopt a marketing orientation. Some service industries that have done so include those that provide health care, travel and recreation, computer software, and financial services. These marketers focus on consumers' needs. A marketing-oriented provider of financial services, for example, recognizes that consumers want, not a $100,000 annuity or a speculative stock issue, but financial security or capital appreciation.

Marketing is also applied in nonprofit organizations such as museums, educational institutions, and human-service agencies, including the March of Dimes and the Red Cross. Representatives of these agencies need to create programs for specific consumer groups. For example, the Metropolitan Museum of Art has a vice-president for development (a marketing position). For an exhibit entitled "Man and the Horse," this vice-president secured designer Ralph Lauren as a sponsor. Lauren's Polo clothing and perfume tied in well with the exhibit's theme and appealed to a group that might be expected both to like works of art that depict horses and to be able to afford them.[9]

THE CASE CONTINUES

In 1976, Sony invented the Betamax videocassette recorder, a high-resolution recorder which Sony claimed was far superior in picture quality to the emerging VHS systems on the market. But while few would dispute this claim about quality, by 1988 VHS sales worldwide had cornered 95% of the market, leaving Sony with a dramatically dwindling slice of the pie. VHS recorders are less expensive than Betamaxes, and thus captured the lion's share of the market.

Finally, in 1988, Sony announced that it too would introduce a line of VHS recorders. Many felt that Sony's decision to enter the VHS market was seriously overdue: "If they had

done it three years ago, they would have immediately become No. 3 instead of sinking to No. 14," said David Lachenbruch, editorial director of *Television Digest*.

While in 1988 the Betamax still dominated the market in some parts of the world, such as the Middle East and Singapore, Sony was clearly losing ground to the VHS manufacturers in most markets. But what finally turned Sony around, even more than its limited market for Betamaxes, was the clamour made by retailers, who wanted to offer a Sony package to customers—TV set, VCR, and camcorder.

Part of Sony's fear in entering the VHS market was that this move would signal an abandonment of the Betamax, thus endangering existing and future sales of a profitable product. But given their dilemma—attempt to garner a share of the VHS market and risk losing Betamax sales, or face the fallout from dissatisfied customers *and* the consequences of a missed opportunity— Sony decided to enter the fray. It is interesting to note that what really tipped the scales in this decision, according to Sony officials, was the need to offer consumers a complete package of video equipment. Thus Sony's decision was marketing-driven.

GOAL SUMMARY

1. **Explain the meaning of the marketing concept.** When an organization adopts the marketing concept to the fullest extent, all of its departments are responsive to consumers' needs. The organization bases its decisions on satisfying consumer needs, coordinates its activities in support of marketing, and achieves its primary objectives by being responsive to consumer needs.

2. **Distinguish between marketing and selling.** The marketing process begins even before a good is produced, while selling occurs after its production. Through selling, consumers are persuaded to buy the goods and services an organization already has available. In the marketing process the needs of consumers are identified and specific goods are developed to satisfy those needs.

3. **Identify the elements in the exchange process.** The exchange process, which is the basis for marketing, involves a buyer and a seller, the item to be exchanged, and a payment for the item. The process results in a transaction whereby either the own-

ership of a good or the right to use it is transferred from seller to buyer.

4. **Discuss the differences between a production orientation and a marketing orientation.** Organizations with a production orientation base decisions to launch new products on the production facilities available. Organizations with a marketing orientation base decisions to introduce new products on consumer needs.

5. **Explain the differences between a marketing orientation and a marketing-systems orientation.** Organizations with a marketing orientation segment the market and develop products to meet the needs of these segments. Organizations with a marketing-systems orientation go further by treating marketing as a philosophy that touches each activity in the organization.

6. **Understand the importance of marketing functions.** In order for goods to move from producer to consumer, certain important marketing functions must be carried out. Marketing functions are those

GOAL SUMMARY *(continued)*

major economic activities that must be performed somewhere in the marketing system in order for the marketing task to be accomplished. The performance of these functions may be shifted from one point to another within the system, but they cannot be eliminated.

7. **Identify the economic utilities that are created by marketing.** Place utility is derived from the transportation function, and time utility is created by the storage function. Information utility is provided by the selling function, and possession utility is accomplished through the selling and financing functions.

8. **Distinguish between micro- and macromarketing.** Micromarketing refers to the marketing activities an organization performs in order to achieve its objectives. Macromarketing is concerned with the entire system used to distribute goods and services in a society.

9. **Identify the macromarketing goals.** The ultimate goal of the macromarketing system is to satisfy the needs of the public economically, efficiently, and fairly. Specific macromarketing goals include maximizing information, choice, consumption, and satisfaction.

10. **Explain why the study of marketing is important.** An important reason for studying marketing is to learn how organizations create, communicate, and supply value. A practical reason for studying marketing is to learn how goods are moved from the producer to the consumer. Studying marketing gives us the ability to evaluate the efficiency of the marketing system and provides us with an awareness of the numerous benefits derived from marketing activities. Tangible evidence of the importance of marketing is provided by the cost of marketing, the number of marketing establishments and employees, and the variety of marketing careers.

KEY TERMS

Marketing-Driven Organizations, **p. 5**
Marketing, **p. 5**
Exchange, **p. 6**
Transaction, **p. 6**
Marketing Driven, **p. 6**
Marketing Concept, **p. 6**
Selling, **p. 8**
Marketing Myopia, **p. 11**
Market Segment, **p. 11**

Marketing Functions, **p. 12**
Economic Utilities, **p. 13**
Form Utility, **p. 13**
Place Utility, **p. 13**
Time Utility, **p. 13**
Information Utility, **p. 14**
Possession Utility, **p. 14**
Micromarketing, **p. 14**
Macromarketing, **p. 14**

CHECK YOUR LEARNING

1. Marketing begins to happen before a good is produced, whereas selling occurs after its production. **T/F**

2. The origin of marketing can be traced to (a) transactions, (b) selling, (c) the exchange process, or (d) the use of money.

3. For most companies a production orientation follows a sales orientation.   **T/F**

4. The Great Depression of the 1930s caused many companies to adopt a: (a) marketing-systems orientation, (b) sales orientation, (c) transaction orientation, (d) purchasing orientation.

5. The marketing functions of buying and selling are known as the functions of: (a) physical distribution, (b) exchange, (c) transaction, (d) purchasing.

6. Time utility is derived from the storage function. **T/F**

7. The marketing activities performed within an organization are referred to as: (a) micromarketing (b) metamarketing, (c) entrepreneurial marketing, (d) macromarketing.

8. As a proportion of the total price of a good, marketing costs typically are: (a) 1–20 percent, (b) 20–40 percent, (c) 40–60 percent, (d) 60–80 percent.

9. There are more wholesalers and service organizations than retailers in the United States.   **T/F**

10. About a third of the occupations listed in the *Dictionary of Occupational Titles and Supplements* are in the marketing and service fields.   **T/F**

QUESTIONS FOR REVIEW AND DISCUSSION

1. Define the key terms for this chapter that appear at the end of the goal summary.
2. Do a trip to the supermarket and the purchase of General Motors stock in the financial markets qualify as marketing? Explain.
3. What criteria determine whether an organization has adopted the marketing concept?
4. Are Japanese automobile manufacturers more marketing oriented than American ones? Discuss.
5. What is the difference between a marketing orientation and a marketing-systems orientation?
6. Is the selling function more important than the buying function in the marketing process?
7. Do the benefits received from economic utilities always exceed their costs to consumers? Discuss.
8. Should a study of micromarketing precede a study of macromarketing? Explain.
9. Is there a conflict between the macromarketing goal of having a pollution-free environment and the micromarketing goal of Inland Steel to be competitively priced?
10. What are the most important reasons to study marketing?

NOTES

1. "AMA Board Approves New Marketing Definition," *Marketing News,* March 1, 1985, p. 1.
2. Thomas J. Watson, Jr., *A Business and Its Beliefs* (New York: McGraw-Hill Book Company, Inc., 1986), pp. 29, 33.
3. Thomas D. Peters and Robert H. Waterman, *In Search of Excellence* (New York: Harper & Row, 1982), p. 167.
4. F. J. Borch, *The Marketing Philosophy as a Way of Business Life,* an address to the American Management Association, February 4, 1957.
5. Theodore Levitt, "Marketing Myopia," *Harvard Business Review* (Sept.–Oct. 1975), p. 26.
6. Frederick E. Webster, Jr., *Social Aspects of Marketing* (Englewood Cliffs, New Jersey: Prentice-Hall, 1974), p. 101.
7. Robert Garfield, "Who's the 2nd-Largest Advertiser?" *USA Today,* Sept. 14, 1984, p. 43.
8. Paul W. Stewart and J. Frederic Dewhurst, *Does Distribution Cost Too Much?* (New York: The 20th Century Fund, 1939), pp. 117–118.
9. Sandra Salmans, "The Fine Art of Museum Fund Raising," *The New York Times,* January 14, 1985, p. 1.

"*P*roductivity. Not Promises," describes the high-tech environment that is a hallmark of the Hewlett-Packard (H–P) Company. H–P, which was founded in 1945 in California's Silicon Valley, is a grandaddy among the more than 1,000 other computer-related companies residing in the Valley. Both of its founders—William Hewlett and David Packard—were engineering graduates from Stanford University. Technology has been the watchword of the company.

H–P's first product was an audio oscillator, a device for measuring sound waves. Walt Disney Studios ordered eight of these oscillators and used them in creating the unique sound system for the movie *Fantasia*. The company soon began producing a line of electronic testing devices such as those measuring the herbicide levels in food, and drug levels in athletes' blood. In 1968 H–P introduced its first minicomputer, which immediately found wide industrial application. Four years later the company began producing the versatile H–P 3000 computer, which generated strong sales. By 1984 there were more than 15,000 H–P 3000 systems at companies around the world. Through the years H–P had introduced several models of personal computers, but none of them had made a significant impact in the market.

In 1972 H–P produced the first hand-held calculator, appropriately called the "electronic slide rule." Although a marketing consultant advised against its production, the company introduced it anyway. The calculator sold exceedingly well despite a price of $395. Until Texas Instruments began selling a similar unit two years later, H–P had the entire market to itself. As more competitors came onto the scene, the price and profitability of hand-held calculators nosedived. This caused H–P to drop its low-priced units and concentrate on selling the higher priced ones used by engineers and financial analysts. H–P remained the leading marketer of hand-held calculators selling for $50 and more.

In 1984 H–P took a deep breath, expelled a wheeze sounding strangely like the word "marketing," and introduced three new products: a compact computer called the Portable and two printers named Laserjet and Thinkjet. These products were developed for the mass market, which H–P had previously abandoned. To explain its move back into this market, H–P president John Young indicated that the company was going to become more marketing-driven with the help of the personal computer group.

As a result of this new marketing focus, H–P began utilizing marketing strategies similar to those of consumer-goods companies such as Procter & Gamble and Gillette. In the past, H–P engineers employed two different methods to determine products and markets—ask co-workers what was needed or build a machine for one customer and then market it to others. This resulted in the production of a large number of tailor-made products that were directed to specific customers. This strategy permitted H–P to charge high prices for a differentiated product.

In the personal computer industry, however, a product that differs greatly from the IBM PC has a high probability of failure. The H–P 150 was rejected by retailers because it was not IBM-compatible even though the unit had more speed and memory than the IBM PC. It had a touchscreen permitting the operator to use the unit by pressing a finger against the monitor; however, it used a 3½-inch floppy disk rather than the IBM 5¼-inch disk. Originally there were only 25 software programs available on the smaller disk, while more than 5,000 were obtainable on the larger one. H–P engineers justified the use of the 3½-inch disk by declaring it was the better system.

Another reason for the failure of the H–P 150 related to the amount of gross margin (difference between cost and selling price) that a retailer could obtain on the unit. A small retailer could only expect to receive a 30 percent margin, while chains could anticipate about 40 percent. In contrast, dealers could realize nearly 45 percent margins on other personal computers because they could be sold with high-margined extras such as disk drives and monitors.

To overcome some of its previous marketing errors, H–P designed its new Portable model to be compatible with the IBM PC. The Portable carried a $2,995 price tag, which included a bundle of built-in hardware and software. Dealers were particularly pleased when H–P began offering better payment terms and larger quantity discounts. They benefited, too, from a doubling of the advertising allowances for ads that mentioned H–P products. As a result of improved dealer relations, the company increased the number of its full-line retailers from 350 to 750 and it stocked another 1,050 dealers with a portion of the line.

By 1987, computers and peripheral equipment accounted for over 65 percent of H–P's sales and profits. In 1987 nearly 10 percent of the company's output was sold to the U.S. government.

There have been other marketing-driven changes at H–P. Many of its industrial customers were prospects for both testing instruments and personal computers. In the past, H–P had two separate sales forces—one selling testing instruments and the other marketing computers. A sales force reorganization created a single sales force that now sells all H–P products rather than isolated machines. In order to create a brand family and gain greater consumer acceptance, H–P is giving names rather than numbers to its new products. The company hopes that Portable, Laserjet, and Thinkjet will become as readily identified among computer buyers as Cavalier, Corsica, and Corvette are among automobile purchasers. H–P is attempting to gain market share and to become a market leader by engineering its personal computer line for low-cost mass production. For many years, the company had followed co-founder David Packard's maxim that market share is not an object, but a reward. Today, the H–P marketing executives recognize that the personal computer industry, like the automobile industry, is a market-driven business and that only those producers with a dominant share will survive.

Issues for Discussion
1. Explain whether H–P has adopted the marketing concept.
2. How has H–P altered its marketing mix in an effort to become more marketing oriented?
3. What must H–P do in order to develop a marketing-systems orientation?
4. Identify several similarities between the marketing of cars and the marketing of personal computers.

Sources: Adapted from Bill Saporito, Jonathan B. Levine, "Mild-Mannered Hewlett-Packard is Making Like Superman," *Business Week,* March 7, 1988, pp. 110–114; "Hewlett-Packard Discovers Marketing," *Fortune,* Oct. 1, 1984, pp. 50–56; and Milton Moskowitz, Michael Katy, and Robert Levering, *Everybody's Business* (New York: Harper & Row, 1980), pp. 431–433.

Section Two

Assessing and Managing the Marketing Environment

OUTLINE

CHAPTER

2

Managing the Marketing Strategy

LEARNING GOALS

After reading this chapter, you should be able to:

1. List and define a marketing manager's general management activities.
2. Describe the characteristics of marketing plan objectives and outline the major sections of a marketing plan.
3. Describe the two basic types of marketing strategies used to achieve competitive advantage and the three generic marketing strategies used when firms lack a competitive advantage.
4. Describe the marketing mix.
5. Describe the skills needed to implement a marketing plan.
6. Define corporate culture.

Nautilus Sports/Medical Industries, a leading marketer of commercial fitness equipment, intends to fatten sales by muscling in on the $1.5 billion home exercise equipment market.

The move is part of a new strategy that capitalizes on consumer name recognition, expands the existing commercial product line and seeks new distribution channels.

Nautilus offered a home line from 1984 to 1986, but the effort was abandoned, reportedly because founder Arthur Jones was not interested in the home market. Ward International acquired Nautilus last year from Mr. Jones.

A major national retailer that carried the line said the products were "very successful because no other company has anything close to Nautilus' unique system. There's nothing else like Nautilus."

Nautilus built its name on exercise machines using progressive resistance motion.

Despite its name recognition, Nautilus faces competition in the highly fragmented home market.

"Nautilus home products might take away from the credibility of Nautilus in gyms," said Gene Callender, national sales manager—consumer products for Universal Gym Equipment, Cedar Rapids, Iowa. Universal is a high-end competitor in the commercial and home markets.

Nautilus and Universal hold a combined 50% share of the estimated $500 million institutional market separate from the home exercise market, according to a report by FIND/SVP, New York, a market research company. Although Nautilus would not reveal figures, industry sources suggested the company has annual revenues of about $100 million.

Because of overlapping product lines in home exercise equipment, market share is hard to calculate.

Currently, commercial sales account for about 95% of Nautilus' total revenues.

Nautilus will vie in the home market with fitness product marketers including Ajay Enterprises Corp. and Diversified Products Corp., as well as home gym marketers.

The line will be positioned as a supplement to club use.

"We have a company whose name is synonymous with fitness; yet it is marketed in a very small part of the market," said Stephen Thompson, Nautilus president-ceo. "We're primarily in just clubs and in strength-training equipment. Our major goal is to fill in the image we already have with new markets and products."

On October 30, Nautilus opened its first retail unit in Plano, Texas, a Dallas suburb, featuring the home line's five machines.

The home products will be available through Sears, Roebuck & Co.'s annual catalog to be dropped at the end of December. The line also is marketed through American Express Co. mailers. More major retailers will carry the line in the coming year.

"Our whole strategy is to market products based on the success of our commercial reputation," Mr. Thompson said. "The home products are a downsized version of commercial equipment. It's a product line positioned against a fairly knowledgeable exercise consumer."

Consumer familiarity has been a mixed blessing, Mr. Thompson said. "Frankly, I got tired of going into clubs without identifying myself and being told that the weight training equipment is 'just like Nautilus,' " he said. "There is the tendency to use our name generically, and we don't want that confusion."

To combat the problem, Nautilus named Michael & Partners to handle advertising and marketing.

Ad budget is under development, but initial placement has been limited to trade publications. The company still is formulating consumer ad plans.

Issues for Discussion
1. Describe the home gym market and its potential for Nautilus.
2. Recommend a marketing strategy for Nautilus in the home gym market.
3. What factors should be considered in market plan implementation and control at Nautilus?

Source: Jennifer Lawrence, "Nautilus Pumps Iron in Home Gym Market," *Advertising Age,* December 7, 1987, Copyright Crain Communications, Inc. All rights reserved.

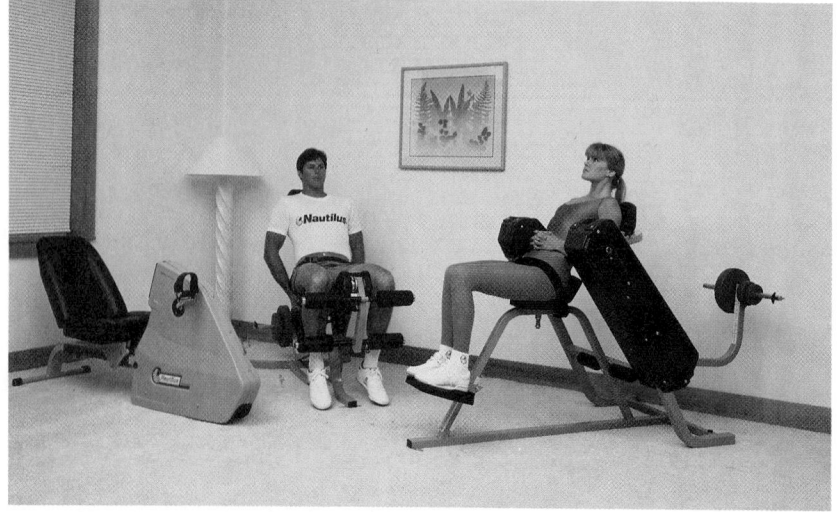

Illustrated are several home gym products created by Nautilus, including the Leg Extension/Leg Curl Machine and the Abdominal/Lower Back Machine.
Source: Courtesy of Nautilus

Marketing Nautilus to a new market—the home—could be a risky venture. To succeed, Nautilus needs a well-conceived plan—a blueprint for success—and a savvy **marketing manager**—the architect of the plan. The marketing manager is responsible for planning, implementing, and controlling the marketing activities for the firm. Whether creating strategies for new products or services, or for those already in the marketplace, these central management functions should always be performed.

One of the most important parts of the marketing process is creating the marketing plan. The **marketing plan** is a written document detailing the marketing strategy and the time frames in which the strategy is going to be implemented. To assemble a marketing plan, the marketing manager must assess the environment, set objectives, and formulate budgets, among a host of other activities. This chapter describes the parts of the marketing plan at length, including a discussion of its implementation. We end with a look at how the corporate culture affects the marketing plan. ■

THE MARKETER AS DECISION MAKER

A marketer does more than sell. A marketer can be the marketing manager or others in the company who perform the necessary steps to bring a product to the marketplace. Decision making is an essential part of the marketer's role. Consider the situation of marketers at Repro-Med Systems, Inc. Repro-Med developed an intravenous (IV) medication system to replace the suspended IV bottle.[1] The system, which contains a tiny pump, monitors the constant flow of medication and signals when the fluid runs out. Because it seems superior to the old system, the inexperienced marketer could mistakenly assume that marketing the product will go smoothly and easily. However, stumbling blocks to its successful marketing do exist. Government approval may be needed to sell the product, and acceptance by physicians and patients is uncertain. Loyalty to existing brands could be strong. Further, the company has limited financial and staff resources to market the product. Repro-Med executives, like marketers in general, face a situation in which they must make marketing decisions based on real conditions and then take appropriate action. Excellence in decision making and taking action leads to success in marketing.[2]

Marketers need to be good decision makers who will take action.

The Decision-Making Process

For a marketer, the decision-making process involves: (1) Identifying and defining the marketing goals; (2) collecting and analyzing information relevant to carrying out these goals; (3) forecasting or predicting the outcome of the goals in terms of key areas such as potential sales and profits; and, (4) taking action on a course determined by the above.

(1) *Identifying and defining the marketing goals.* With the organization's mission understood, the marketer asks, "What is our immediate task?" If the business is juvenile publishing, the marketer might identify the goal as that of increasing the sale of children's books by a certain percentage.

(2) In *collecting and analyzing information*, the marketer gathers and analyzes data that will provide the basis for making a decision about a course of action. This

can include an investigation of market opportunity, use of surveys, test market experiments, and information about competitors.

(3) In *forecasting,* the marketer predicts what a variable or group of variables will be at some future time in specified key areas such as potential sales and profit margins. Using various forecasting techniques, the marketer tries to determine the consequences, or outcome, of a course of action before committing resources to it. One technique nearly all firms use is called *trend extension,* a forecasting method that uses the firm's past experience to predict future outcomes. Forecasting is described in Chapter 7.

(4) After performing all of the above, the marketer must make a decision and take action.

An example of the Beef Industry Council's effort to inform and persuade the consumer that consumption of red meat is healthy.

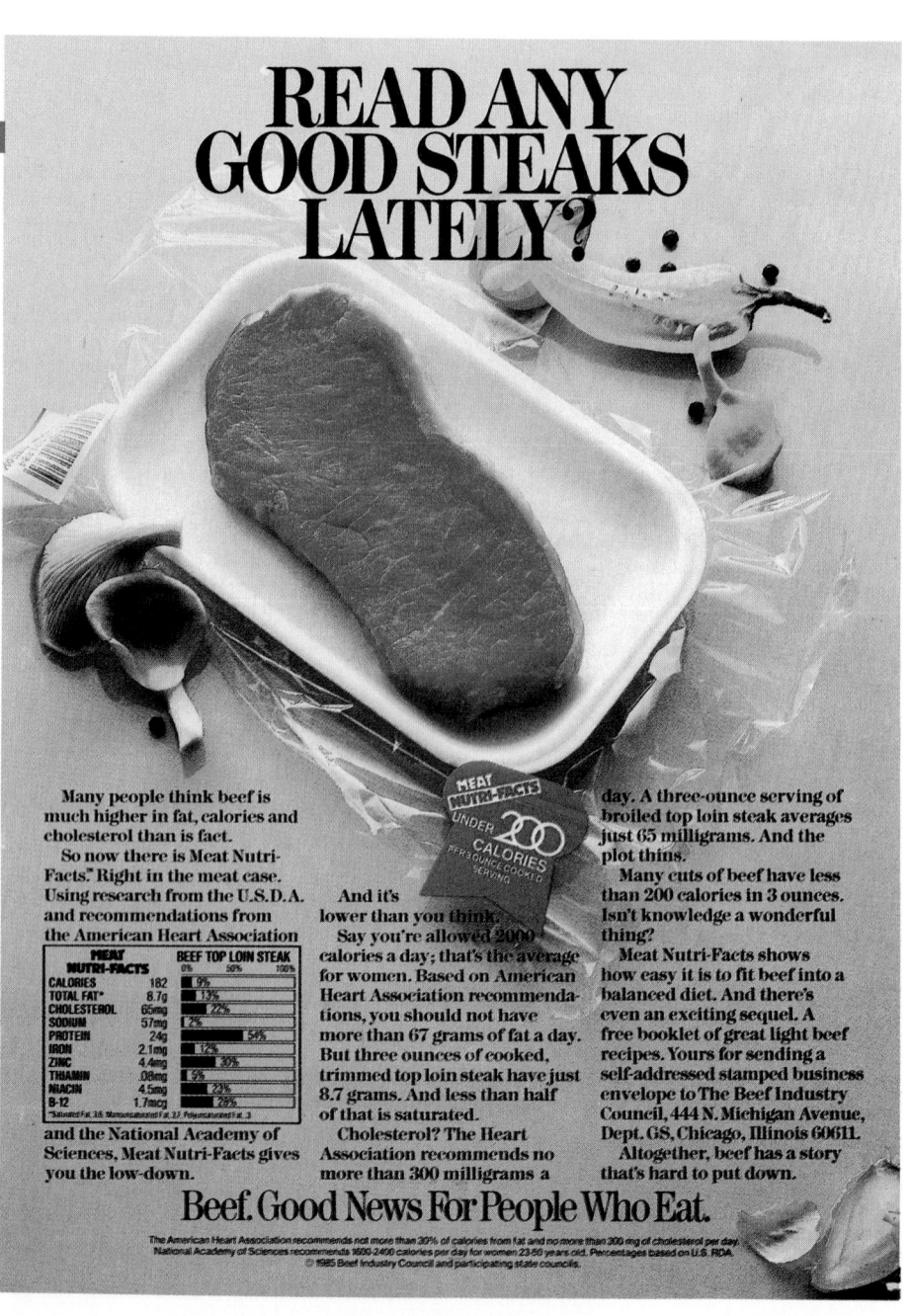

Source: Courtesy of Beef Industry Council

TAKING ACTION

*D*ecision making is only a mental exercise until decisions are acted upon.

Marketers must be action-oriented. Because of the uncertainty associated with decision making, some marketers may seem to engage in endless analyses, identification, and attempts at prediction. According to some analysts, however, America's best-run companies are managed by executives who emphasize doing and trying.[3] These managers collect, analyze, identify, and predict but go on to make decisions and take action within a reasonable period. Part of their ability to make informed timely decisions stems from their concentration on three key variables: the environment, the market, and the marketing mix.

 ## THE ENVIRONMENT, THE MARKET, AND THE MARKETING MIX

In planning their marketing strategy, marketers pay special attention to the following:

*E*nvironmental variables—external, uncontrollable factors.

(1) *Environmental variables.* In assessing the "climate" of the environment in which their products or services will be received, marketers must assess competitors' strengths and weaknesses, as well as try to predict their plans; the level of existing technology and its potential impact on product use; social and political factors that might affect how their good or service will be received; and a host of other *external* and *uncontrollable* factors. Although control of environmental variables is not possible in most instances, it is essential to identify trends and anticipate their effect on the goals in question. Environmental variables are discussed in Chapter 3.

*T*he market—all potential customers for a good or service.

(2) *Market variables.* The **market** consists of all potential customers for a good or service. Thus, when considering marketing variables, marketers consider existing and potential needs of consumers. What is the willingness and ability to purchase? Although the marketer cannot alter consumer characteristics, he or she can select the market most compatible with the firm's offerings and resources.

*T*he marketing mix—product, price, promotion, and distribution.

(3) *The marketing mix.* The **marketing mix** is the specific way in which four key variables are managed by the firm to satisfy the needs of its market and the organization. The marketing mix variables are considered the most controllable of all variables, and include *product, price, promotion,* and *distribution* (also called place). Marketers commonly refer to these as "the 4Ps." A key question the marketer must address is "What marketing mix should I use for the market selected?" or "What blend of product, price, promotion, and place should I use?" **Product** can be thought of as the *benefit* a buyer receives in exchange for money or other forms of trade: for instance, car repair, airline tickets, or a television set. **Price** represents the money (cost) necessary to obtain ownership or use of the product, or the *exchange value* of the product. The $57.80 price tag for a car repair, the $236 fee for an airline ticket, the price of a television set or a candy bar all represent examples of price. **Promotion** communicates information about the product by persuading or reminding people in the marketplace that the product exists. Personal selling, sales promotion, and advertising are key types of promotion. **Distribution** refers to the means of bringing the product to the consumer. Distribution questions include whether to sell Meaty Bone dog biscuits to supermarkets or pet shops, or both, and whether to sell only in the United States and Canada or worldwide.

The relationship between environmental, market, and marketing mix variables is shown in figure 2.1. The marketer uses the marketing mix variables to obtain the best possible fit between the market and the environment—one that moves the organization toward its objectives.

❏ **Figure 2.1**
Environmental market
and marketing mix
decision and action
areas.

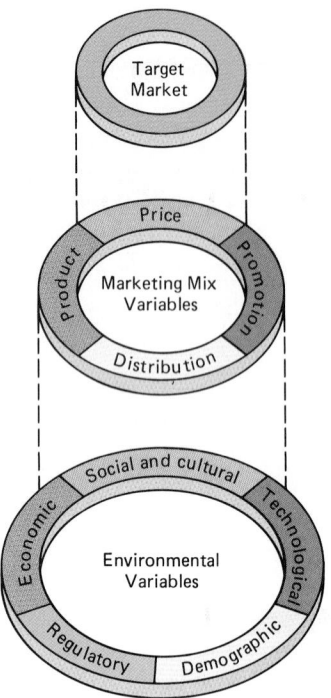

ORGANIZATIONAL MISSION

*O*rganizational mission
statements describe the
company's purpose.

Before taking any course of action, the marketer needs to understand the organization's overall goal, or **organizational mission.** Companies have mission statements that concisely answer the question: "What is our purpose, and for whom?" Or, put another way, the mission statement describes the essential nature of the company's business and what it seeks to accomplish. A well-defined mission statement reflects a company whose purpose is clear. All activities of the organization should support the overall mission of the organization. Thus, the marketing plan must support the company's mission.

THE MARKETER'S MANAGEMENT FUNCTIONS: PLANNING, IMPLEMENTATION, AND CONTROL

*M*arketing managers
plan, implement, and con-
trol marketing activities.

The marketer works within a framework of management functions that include (1) planning the marketing activities; (2) implementing or carrying through these plans; and (3) controlling performance.

In **planning,** the manager sets measurable objectives and creates strategies needed to achieve these objectives. **Implementing** involves functions such as staffing and communicating with personnel, allocating resources, and monitoring the day-to-day activities of the marketing plan. **Controlling** functions include monitoring the progress of the plan by comparing actual performance against standards, and taking corrective action when appropriate. Quantifying performance by using specific measurement techniques is an essential part of the controlling function. Figure 2.2 provides an overview of the activities involved in planning, implementing, and controlling.

☐ **Figure 2.2**
Marketing management framework for decision making and action.

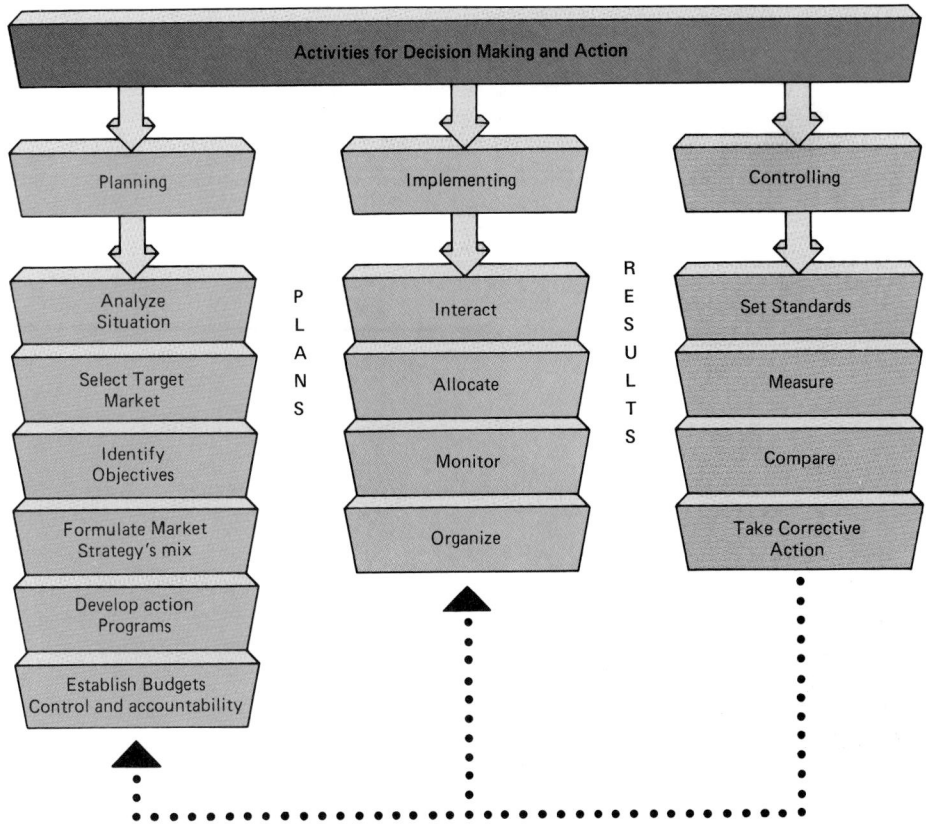

Planning means determining an efficient course of action.

When new executives took over at the Rayovac Corporation, the battery company's products had virtually disappeared from retailers' shelves because of distribution and packaging problems, dated advertising, and severe competition from Duracell and Eveready. Within the framework of the marketing management functions of planning, implementing, and control, Rayovac executives made the necessary decisions and took action to regain a respectable share of the battery market. They implemented distribution plans on the local level by providing employees with business cards that read, "I am an employee of Rayovac. I shop in your stores, and I'd like to see Rayovac batteries in your stores." To measure the effectiveness of the distribution plan and its implementation, the company monitored changes in the percentage of retailers carrying the batteries.

The management functions of planning, implementing, and controlling activities occur at all levels of an organization. Three levels most frequently identified are *corporate, division,* and *product/market.*

 ## LEVELS OF PLANNING

The marketing plan is set in the context of a relatively short time frame.

Companies create both short-term and long-term plans to achieve their objectives. Long-term strategic planning, performed at the corporate level, is usually viewed in larger time frames, such as five- and ten-year periods, and encompasses objectives for all areas of the firm. In this chapter, our discussion of the marketing plan is set in the context of short-term planning—for instance, one- or two-year plans. Short-term planning usually occurs at the product level rather than at the corporate or division level. The marketing manager of a clothing manufacturer, for instance, will plan at the product level. Top officers of a corporation will concentrate on planning the direction of the entire company rather than concentrate on creating a specific marketing plan for one or another good or service offered by the company. Similarly, the division manager concentrates on planning for the division as a whole. The company's overall strategic planning is described at length in Chapter 19.

	PLAN	IMPLEMENT	CONTROL
Corporate	Achieve world dominance in office automation	Expand computer and copier divisions	Compare market share with major competitors over five years
Division	Increase computer division growth by 50% over 2-year period	Increase computer model 1202 LANS sales by 75%	Compare sales now with sales in next two years
Product/Market	Increase sales of LANS by 100% over the next year	Target businesses with 100 to 500 employees	Compare sales now of LANS with sales at end of fiscal year

This grid demonstrates the interrelationships between the corporate, division, and product/market levels. This chapter emphasizes the marketing management functions at the product/market level. The next section provides an overview of the marketing plan.

THE CASE CONTINUES

ard International's corporate plan calls for Nautilus to expand into the home gym market. Successful expansion is unlikely to happen without market planning. The marketing manager has three sets of variables to consider when planning: these include variables in the environment, the market, and the marketing mix. Nautilus has already given some consideration to the following variables: two key fitness product competitors in the environment, Ajay Enterprises Corp. and Diversified Products Corp. have been identified (along with manufacturers in the home gym market); the market demand for home fitness products generates $1.5 billion in annual sales; distribution (a marketing mix variable) will take place in part through the Sears, Roebuck & Co.'s annual catalog and American Express. Additional information about the environment, the market, and the marketing mix will be used to flesh out the marketing plan.

THE MARKETING PLAN

The marketing plan describes how the marketing mix variables of product, price, promotion, and distribution will be used to attain the organization's objectives, usually within a year, in a specific market. Figure 2.3 shows an outline of a marketing plan.

Executive Summary

The **executive summary,** although it is the first section of the written marketing plan, should be written after all other sections have been completed. The summary,

❑ **Figure 2.3**
A marketing plan
outline.

Step	Summary
Executive summary	Overview of plan
Situation analysis 　Market analysis 　Internal analysis 　Environmental scanning	Describe past, present, and projected market in terms of revenue, expenses, and profits for industry competitors and company
Market selection	Identify group company will serve; describe in terms of revenue, expenses, and profit
Identify objectives	Specify what firm expects from serving market in financial and nonfinancial terms
Formulate marketing strategy and mix	Decide on most competitive way to serve market
Action programs	Develop ideas on most competitive ways to serve market into programs
Budgets, controls, and accountability	Fund programs and establish plan to see they are carried out

*T*he executive summary
provides an overview of
the marketing plan.

approximately one-page long, is often the most important part of the plan and may be the only part some executives read. The summary provides an overview of the entire plan, as illustrated in the following Devco Company executive summary:

Devco Company
Marketing Plan
Executive Summary

The 1991 marketing plan seeks a significant increase in Devco's revenues and net profit over 1990. The revenue target is $120 million, a planned 25 percent gain. Because of the declining residential mortgage interest rate and the decision by Stevens Builders, Inc. to withdraw from the residential market and build only in the commercial market, we believe this increase obtainable. The target gross margin is $18 million, a 25 percent increase over 1990, but no change as a percentage of revenue. To obtain these goals, ten new home styles will be added to those already offered. The prices on homes will increase 5 percent. The promotion budget will increase to $3.4 million or 2.83 percent of projected revenue. The advertising budget. . . .

The executive summary should be written specifically for the receiving executive. The summary should convey an action orientation. It should also concisely state the relationship of the plan to the organization's mission and the objectives it expects to achieve by some specific future date.

Situation Analysis

*S*ituation analysis determines the position of the
organization in the
environment.

A **situation analysis** is the process of gathering and examining information to determine the organization's past, present, and possible future position in the market. Market analysis, internal analysis, and environmental scanning are techniques used in situation analysis. Each provides different information.

TECHNIQUE	INFORMATION
Market analysis	Description of market
Internal analysis	Organization's strengths and weaknesses
Environmental scanning	Opportunities and threats

MARKET ANALYSIS

*M*arket analysis asks, "What is the company's market?"

The purpose of the market analysis is to define the company's market and identify demand. A description of the market includes:

Customers' needs, motives, and uses for the product.
The market's size in dollars and units and the size of market segments.
The products the company sells in the market, with their sales, prices, and gross margins.
Major competitors' sales, market share, and prices, strategies, strengths and weaknesses.

Analysis of market data should produce clues to trends developing in the market as well as factors that contribute to the product's success. Keys to success in the cosmetic market, for example, include large expenditures on promotions and wide retail distribution. In the prescription drug market, frequent personal contact with physicians and effective products contribute substantially to success.

INTERNAL ANALYSIS

*I*nternal analysis identifies strengths and weaknesses of the organization.

Internal analysis focuses on key features inside the company—its strengths and weaknesses. In searching for these, marketers concentrate on the customers in the market, their needs and uses of the product, and the marketing variables. They also look at the company's resources in terms of personnel, financial capability, and how the internal structure of the company will help or hinder their efforts.

Any element in the company that reduces customer satisfaction or impinges on the effectiveness of a marketing variable is a weakness. For instance, a high turnover rate among salespeople reduces the promotional effectiveness of companies that depend on salespeople, such as Allstate Insurance, and thus is a weakness. Identifying weaknesses allows the organization, through the marketing plan, to attempt to eliminate, reduce, or offset them. If Allstate has high employee turnover, analyzing its causes and formulating programs to reduce it would be in order.

Elements within the company that increase customer satisfaction or enhance the marketing variables are strengths. Identified strengths should be used in the marketing plan. The many types of insurance offered at Allstate, a strength, could serve in their company's marketing plan as the basis of innovative and aggressive programs to add new customers. Marketing programs at Allstate, for example, might stress the theme, "one-stop insurance service."

ENVIRONMENTAL SCANNING (EXTERNAL ANALYSIS)

*E*nvironmental scanning identifies trends that may influence the organization's marketing efforts.

Environmental scanning involves gathering and examining information about economic, social, political (including regulatory), technological, and competitive conditions in the environment to identify trends—particularly those that represent opportunities and threats. Identifying trends permits marketers to predict their impact on the organization and its marketing program. This in turn encourages preparation for change and decreases the need for hurried, poorly thought-out responses. For example, life insurance companies have observed the trend towards better health care and physical fitness and its life-lengthening effects. As a result, the insurance industry now offers a variety of insurance plans, many with lower premiums. Automobile manufacturers noted the increasing number of one- and two-person households with high incomes and created the Ford EXP for this market. Marketers at Hallmark Cards studied the increasing number of families with remarriages, and, as a result, introduced "new relationship" cards.[4]

Many organizations conduct scanning on an informal basis, a practice that often produces information that is piecemeal and inadequate.[5] To better meet marketing

❑ **Figure 2.4**
Sales growth influenced by opportunities and threats.

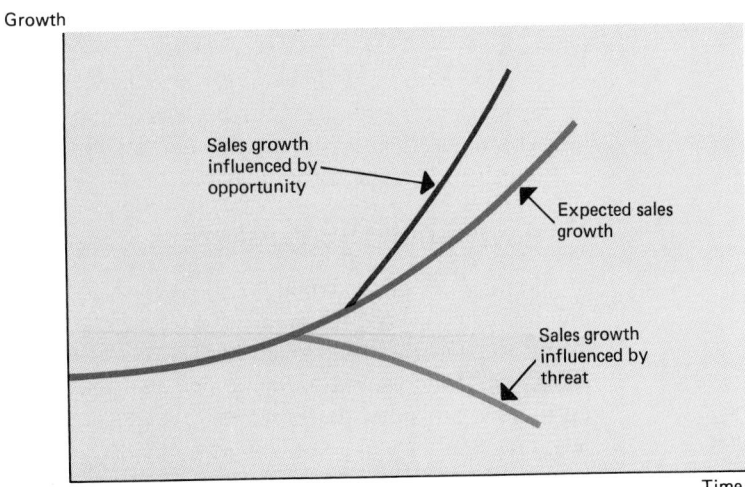

Source: From H. Ignor Ansoff, "Managing Surprise and Discontinuity Strategic Response to Weak Signals," in *Strategy & Structure = Performance.* Hans B. Thorelli, ed. (Bloomington, Indiana: Indiana University Press, 1977).

managers' need for information about the environment, some organizations have developed formal data collection procedures called marketing information and marketing research systems.

*M*arketers continuously monitor opportunities and threats in the environment.

Opportunities and Threats. A **marketing opportunity** is a circumstance in the market environment that provides an organization with a chance for advancement. A **marketing threat** is a circumstance in the market environment that could harm the organization. The small-arms industry, for example, faces threats of federal gun control, diminished hunting grounds and shorter hunting seasons, stiff competition from imports and foreign companies manufacturing in the United States, skyrocketing product liability costs, and highly restrictive import markets. Possibilities for growth for firms such as the Remington Arms Company, Smith & Wesson, and Colt Industries, Inc., therefore seem limited. In fact, heavy dependence on the small-arms market by any of these companies may mean small sales revenues. Possible relationships among growth, time, opportunities, and threats is graphically shown in figure 2.4.

*T*he organization can influence the environment, but only in a limited way.

Limits of Influencing the Environment. Instead of reacting to environmental forces, some companies work to change the environment in which they operate. These marketers attempt to influence government officials, public-interest groups, the news media, and other opinion molders in ways that would benefit their companies. The marketing theorist Phillip Kotler has termed this sort of marketing "megamarketing." He has suggested that in addition to managing the marketing variables, the environment should also be managed.[6] Although Kotler may be correct, there is a limit to how much marketers can influence the environment. Therefore, simply identifying trends remains an important part of market planning.

Market Selection: Target Markets

*T*he target market consists of individuals to whom the company intends to market a product or service.

The **target market** refers to the customers the organization intends to satisfy. In analyzing the market for batteries, Rayovac Corporation found that the average household uses twenty-six batteries a year, but heavy users, 20 percent of the total, use ninety-two batteries a year. Based on this information, the company selected the heavy users of batteries for its target market.

Marketers, like those at Rayovac, examine information from the situation analysis for market attractiveness to help them select a target market. Market attractiveness is measured by level of profitability in the market, presence or absence of government regulations, growth rate of the market, level of consumer sensitivity to price increases, availability of technology, and competitive forces in the market.[7]

Competitive forces in a market may include companies already offering products in the market, companies that may enter the market, suppliers who may demand more of the profit generated in the market, customers who may demand lower prices, and substitute products that may replace the product used to satisfy the market.

HOW SHOULD WE COMPETE FOR OUR CUSTOMERS?

Market selection depends on how the company competes. In the competitive environment, every firm seeks an advantage to find its customers. What a firm can do better than its competitors to satisfy customer needs constitutes its **competitive advantage.**[8] Such an advantage is deemed essential to a firm's survival. Why should customers patronize the firm? If no reason exists—if the firm has no competitive advantage—they will go to competitors instead.

Two basic types of competitive advantage exist: **low cost** and **product differentiation.**[9] To maintain low cost, all areas of the firm have to be cost conscious. The marketing plan should reflect the low-cost advantage by emphasizing low cost per unit and low price as an appeal to customers.

*C*ompetitive advantage—what the organization can do better than others.

*L*ow cost and differentiation produce competitive advantage.

Visions Cookware products are differentiated by highlighting toughness, clarity, and microwaveability in advertising illustrations.

MARKETING IN ACTION

Maintaining Competitive Advantage: Ivy Hill Packaging— Midwest Printing Plant

Ivy Hill Packaging—Midwest Printing Plant has created packages for Pfizer pharmaceuticals, Chanel products, CBS records, Digital Audio Disc Corporation (compact disc manufacturers), and many other products with which you are no doubt familiar. In 1975 Ivy Hill moved its midwest plant within a mile of one of the largest record-pressing plants in the United States. At that time, Ivy Hill's only clients were those in the music industry, and it therefore gained a sizable competitive advantage from its new location.

By 1980, however, the record industry, because of the growing popularity of cassette tapes and other forms of home entertainment such as VCRs, had fallen on hard times. How was Ivy Hill to survive? The plant's management decided it had to broaden its customer base to include companies outside of the music industry. Since these prospective customers were obviously widely scattered throughout the country, the plant's location was no longer necessarily an asset.

Thus, to garner new markets, other competitive advantages had to be developed. And once identified, these advantages had to be communicated to potential customers. After inventorying their strengths, managers at Ivy Hill came up with the following: (1) The plant's turnaround time was short—one week instead of the industry average of seven weeks. (Turnaround time is the time between receipt of an order and shipment of the order.) (2) The firm's library copied on film every order processed. If a customer wants a package identical to one ordered earlier, the film is pulled and the identical package produced from that film. (3) Still another advantage comes from the firm's use of a special coating that dries instantly and makes the stacking of recently printed materials possible. Previously a powder had been sprayed over the printing to dry it. The powder residue, however, created a sandpaper-like texture on the printed surface.

As Ivy Hill's competitors update their operations, these advantages may also be lost, so the search for new ones continues. A new seven-color press has been installed, for example, and for a time *it* will be a competitive advantage.

Source: Adapted from Jan Chait, "Ivy Hill Finds New Direction when Music Orders Play Out," *Terre Haute Tribune-Star,* May 25, 1986, p. C-12.

Product differentiation refers to the way marketers introduce variations in products that create perceived value for the customer. The Visions Cookware advertisement reproduced here identifies such differences.

Differentiation can be accomplished in numerous ways. Orville Redenbacher was innovative and astute in his understanding of how to market his popcorn. He took this mundane product, renamed it "Orville Redenbacher's Gourmet Popcorn," and cited great improvements in its lightness, fluffiness, and taste. The calculated use of the word "gourmet" appears designed to differentiate his popcorn and to appeal to an upscale segment of the popcorn-consuming market willing to pay a higher price.

Several large companies are known for their concentration on one marketing mix element over the others to differentiate their products: Procter and Gamble emphasizes promotion, General Motors emphasizes product, and Avon emphasizes distribution.

Most firms use several variables in the marketing mix to arrive at a competitive advantage. Even a minimal (perhaps only a perceived) difference gives the firm something to sell. Advertising is the primary vehicle for featuring these differences.

Changing variables in small ways may be thought of as *fine tuning*. A good marketing manager continually explores fine-tuning possibilities. Preferably, however, the product's competitive advantage is tangibly different from its competitors; optimally such a difference should be durable, easily perceived, and important to customers.

The search for competitive advantage is not without its ethical issues. Fabricating product differences can be misleading, unethical, and even unlawful. Controversies often arise over issues related to product differentiation. Kellogg's advertising of All-Bran as a high-fiber food that can help prevent cancer has generated such a controversy. Has the effectiveness of All-Bran in preventing cancer been substantiated? Has prevention been clearly defined? What type of cancer does it help prevent? Should the broad term *cancer* be used to stand for only this one type of cancer? Should Kellogg's be allowed to use the advertisement to differentiate its cereal?

Marketing Plan Objectives

*C*haracteristics of good objectives include compatibility, reasonability, measurability, and datability.

An early step in developing the marketing plan is identifying the major objectives to be accomplished. Clearly defined objectives have the following characteristics: compatibility, reasonability, measurability, and datability. To have *compatibility,* objectives must act in harmony with the organization's overall objectives and mission. An objective of Rayovac—increasing the number of retailers that stock its batteries—was compatible with the corporate goal of increasing market share. The greater the number of retailers stocking Rayovac, the larger the market share should be. A *reasonable* objective is one that the company has the resources—financial and otherwise—to achieve. Rayovac's objective of increasing the number of retailers that carried the brand within the immediate area of its plants was reasonable. Rayovac had the resources—plant employees—to carry out this plan. *Measurability* means management must be able to determine the extent to which the objective has been met. The goal of increasing the number of retailers carrying the Rayovac brand was measurable. *Datability,* or timeliness, means that each objective must specify the day by which it should be achieved. Typically, marketing plan objectives must be accomplished within a year.

When formulating the marketing plan, marketers typically update rather than develop entirely new objectives for each plan. In updating, the results of the previous year's marketing plan bear heavily on revised objectives. The new objectives of course take into account previous plans' failures and successes and also incorporate changes in the environment.

In determining objectives, marketers assess what is most significant to the firm and make these variables the basis of objectives. Because of its importance to the firm, **market share**—the firm's sales in relation to total industry sales—often serves as a basis for marketing plan objectives.[10]

*O*bjectives change with the environment.

The objectives must be closely examined in the light of internal and external environmental factors that would prohibit their attainment. After several years of research and development, for example, General Motors discarded its goals of marketing an electric car by the mid 1980s, because gasoline prices had stabilized. Boeing Aircraft dropped its commitment to the controversial SST (supersonic transport) as a result of complaints about the booming noise and because of the cutoff of development funds by Congress. At both General Motors and Boeing, the technology acquired in the initial stages of product development has been shelved, although they can be brought back if conditions change.

The Marketing Strategy and the Marketing Mix

*T*he marketing strategy matches company resources with marketing opportunities and threats to attain organizational objectives.

The **marketing strategy** is a carefully structured means of achieving the organization's objectives within the context of current trends, competition, and time frame. The core of the marketing plan matches available company resources with opportunities and risks in the selected market.

Figure 2.5 provides an overview of the home gym market profile, which will serve as the base of the marketing plan. Some areas in the figure are blank. A marketing manager would also experience gaps in data and could decide to obtain the information through research or proceed on the basis of assumptions. Proceeding on the latter course,

however, could prove very costly. Notice the market has been divided into two parts: male and female. It is quite common to divide a market into segments based on different responses to marketing efforts. Fitness

equipment product-knowledgeable consumers tend to purchase more expensive equipment. Men appear to have more product knowledge through their more frequent use of fitness equipment in institutional settings. For this and other reasons, males and females may respond differently to marketing efforts by Nautilus.

❑ **Figure 2.5** Home Gym Market Description

	FEMALE MARKET	MALE MARKET
Potential—$1.5 billion annually		
Size	$ _____	$ _____
Growth	_____ Percent	_____ Percent
Competition 1. Target market 2. Strategy 3. Marketing mix 4. Overall character	Ajay Enterprize Corp.	Diversified Products Corp.
Price	• Probably more price sensitive because of less product knowledge and lower incomes	• Increased knowledge of equipment increases willingness to purchase higher-priced models
Motive	Motives for purchasing home fitness equipment: fitness, to supplement club use and the desire for solitude.	
Benefits and product characteristics sought	• To condition stomach, buttocks, and upper thighs • Want lighter-weight equipment • Little interest in building bulk • Easy equipment storage • Attractiveness of equipment important • Ease of use important	• Want to build muscle bulk • Heavier equipment needed • Need equipment with slightly larger dimension • Want to condition upper torso, stomach, and legs
Unmet needs	• Product knowledge • Aesthetic equipment	• Specialized uses of equipment
Percent owners	_____ percent	_____ percent

Often, strategy development starts with creating a generic strategy. **Generic strategies** are basic strategies that apply to a general, recurring situation. Once the situation has been identified, a generic strategy can be selected. The generic strategy is then customized to the target market and the company. One general situation occurs when the firm lacks a competitive advantage.

GENERIC STRATEGIES WHEN THE FIRM LACKS A COMPETITIVE ADVANTAGE

A competitor may have a substantial competitive advantage. The marketing theorist, Wroe Anderson suggests three generic strategies to deal with this situation: emulate, deviate, and complement.[11]

Generic strategies built around the lack of competitive advantage include emulation, deviation, and complementation.

Emulation. Firms, as much as possible, imitate the behavior of the successful firm. In the brewery industry, Miller successfully introduced "lite" beer, and soon many other breweries, noting Miller's success, introduced their own light beers. More recently, Anheuser-Busch introduced "L.A." (low-alcohol) beer. Again, other breweries emulated the successful firm by introducing similar products. In an attempt to protect its competitive advantage, Miller sued Anheuser-Busch for using the word "lite." Use of another firm's strategy is not illegal but care must be taken not to infringe on brand names or otherwise patented or copyrighted material.

Deviation. The firm imitates the successful firm only in areas in which it cannot make improvements. If the products can be improved, the firm deviates and offers an improved product. Japanese firms are noted for their ability to improve on successful products.

Complementation. The firm may not attempt to imitate the successful firm at all but may instead try to develop products that can be used in conjunction with the other firm's successful product. For instance, Epson successfully sells printers for computers manufactured by various firms such as IBM and Apple.

To develop a strategy, a marketer may identify key factors in the market, environment, organization, and marketing variables that have been associated with success in the past. This process often occurs in the situation analysis.

The marketer then builds a strategy around the key success factors. If the company is well positioned with regard to these factors, then the core of the strategy is likely to emphasize their use. Conversely, when the company has a weak position, the strategy may center on changing or circumventing the factors. BASF Wyandotte executives, for example, realized brand recognition and distribution were key factors in the sale of antifreeze. Union Carbide dominated the market in recognition and distribution with its Prestone brands. BASF Wyandotte marketers decided not to challenge but to circumvent Union Carbide by manufacturing private brands (brands that carry individual retailers' company names). The firm now manufactures more than eighty private brands for companies like True Value Hardware. These companies all have excellent distribution networks.

One approach to discovering ways to use change, or circumvent key factors is the "what if" approach. Marketers can consider alternative scenarios reflecting a wide variety of market, organizational, environmental, and marketing mix variable factors by asking the simple question, "What if?" For example, executives of the Seattle Tool and Die Company may ask, "If the U.S. investment tax credit is reinstated, what will be the effect on our industrial equipment business and on our marketing program?" Similarly, Procter and Gamble executives may ask, "What if the advertising budget for Pringles potato chips is increased by 50 percent? Will sales increase significantly?"

*T*he marketing mix is a careful blend of marketing variables used to appeal to a specific target market.

THE MARKETING MIX

The marketing mix, a careful blend of product, price, promotion, and distribution, provides direction and structure to an organization's marketing program. The

BASF Wyandotte circumvented Union Carbide's Prestone brand dominance in recognition and distribution with the manufacture of private brands, such as True Value.

Figure 2.6
Marketing mix used to
achieve marketing plan
objectives.

Company	Marketing Objective	Marketing Strategy	Marketing Mix Factors Emphasized
Bosch (West German auto producer)	Increase use of electronic controls in autos.	Dominate auto electronic controls market.	Product
American Gas Association (natural gas utilities)	Increase natural gas consumption.	Increase use of current customers and encourage others to switch from electric to gas heat.	Advertising and price
Circus Circus Casino	Maintain revenue and profit growth rate.	Specialize in family market.	Price, product, and promotion
Humana, Inc. (integrated health care)	Increase market share.	Employ international medical experts. Offer innovative medical care.	Publicity advertising, product, and distribution
American Cancer Society	Reduce cigarette consumption.	Inform public of smoking hazards.	Advertising

marketing mix should achieve the organization's marketing objectives within the boundaries of its marketing strategy. Figure 2.6 illustrates the relationships among marketing objectives, strategy, and marketing mix for several organizations. Amway's marketing mix stresses personal selling of household products available only from the company's sales representatives. Conversely, Procter and Gamble's marketing mix emphasizes advertising. Its household products are available in stores everywhere.

Information from the situation analysis is used in arriving at the most appropriate marketing mix. When Hanes began marketing its L'eggs pantyhose, it chose to distribute the cleverly packaged product through supermarkets rather than through the traditional hosiery distribution channels of department stores and specialty stores. The company correctly believed that supermarket distribution was the key to the mass market.

Information may reveal that certain changes must be made in order to accommodate the environment. Textile companies that ignored the trend away from double-knit polyester and back to wools and worsted suffered marketing and financial setbacks. At one time the candy producer Hershey had a policy of not advertising its Hershey bar; but aggressive competitors with large promotional budgets eventually forced Hershey to move into mass advertising. Watchmakers who continued to produce only expensive mechanical analog watches long after the low-priced digital ones became popular lost market share and revenues.

A once-successful marketing mix may become dated, necessitating a change. For example, Magnavox once marketed high-priced television sets to upper-middle-income and high-income consumers through exclusive dealers. Today the company distributes medium-priced sets to middle-income consumers through a select group of dealers. Levi Strauss formerly sold its jeans through department stores and specialty stores. It has now included the general merchandisers Sears and J. C. Penney to its distribution system.

Marketers almost always must consider a **network of variables**—an interrelated set of variables—when they create or change a marketing mix. The executives of a company contemplating a price reduction in one of its products evaluate a network, including effects on competitors, on sales of its other products, on its image, on inventory, on suppliers, and on profit margins, among other factors.

Ultimately, the marketer must decide what will be done. After all the analysis (of environment, opportunities, competition, and other factors), and the manipulation of data, the time arrives to make decisions and take action.

THE CASE CONTINUES

*T*here are numerous strategies open to Nautilus to help it compete successfully in the home gym market. Given the information provided in the introductory case, a possible strategy is summarized in figure 2.7.

❑ **Figure 2.7** Nautilus Strategy for Entry into Home Gym Market

Strategy Summary:	Capitalize on company's name recognition and the uniqueness of the product to reenter and gain market share in the home gym market.
Market:	Product knowledgeable, primarily males (since they are most likely to have experience with fitness equipment).

Marketing Mix:

Product:	Downsized versions of commercial equipment.
Price:	Refrain from price competition since product is unique and market members are product knowledgeable and tend to purchase higher-priced equipment.
Promotion:	Promote product in trade publications for retailers and wholesalers to encourage retailers to stock products. Use consumer publications to persuade consumers to visit retailers and examine equipment. Promotion theme should emphasize effectiveness of equipment as supplements to club equipment, along with its safety, limited maintenance, and Nautilus's unique feature of variable resistance.

Marketing Plan Action Programs

*A*ction programs specify the what, why, when, who, and how of the plan.

A marketing plan's action program spells out the specifics of the plan: what, why, when, who, and how. As an illustration, consider another battery brand, Duracell, a competitor of Rayovac. The what, why, when, who, and how of a recent Duracell action program can be spelled out as follows:[12]

What: Win market share with a new, highly improved battery.

Why: Three newcomers have entered the U.S. battery market: Fuji, Panasonic, and Toshiba. Eveready and Rayovac have increased marketing efforts.

Who: Ogilvy and Mather, an advertising agency, will develop an advertising campaign and coordinate a heavy media schedule.

How: A nine-week prime-time television and print campaign with ads in twelve major consumer magazines will reach virtually all U.S. households more than thirty times.

In addition, a trade campaign in *Supermarket News,* a ten-percent savings rebate program, and a $250,000 Christmas sweepstakes will be used.

The company has developed a new "copper-top" battery that has a lifespan 30 percent longer than that of existing batteries.

When: Network television spots start in mid-October. The sweepstakes will run during the Christmas shopping season, when a large percentage of battery sales occur.

Paddy Mullen is Director of Marketing and Communications for the Leonard Morse Health Care Corporation in Natick, Massachusetts—a Boston suburb. The Leonard Morse Hospital, part of the corporation, was founded in 1890 and has 259 in-patient beds and forty departments.

Paddy, who is 29, grew up in New Jersey. After graduating in 1980 with a B.A. in American Studies from the University of Notre Dame in South Bend, Indiana, she worked for one and one-half years as a senate legislative aide in the nation's capital. Her next position was in Boston as Campaign Director for the American Heart Association, working in public relations and fundraising.

Once Paddy decided that her creativity could best be realized in a marketing position, she began to send out resumés. When responses were not forthcoming, Paddy settled on a unique tack. She decided to include a fake dollar bill, torn in half, with each resumé. In her cover letter, Paddy wrote to prospective employers that if they hired someone else, they would just be throwing their money away! She received many responses, including one from the Leonard Morse Hospital, where she has been for nearly five years. During the past two years, Paddy has been pursuing an M.B.A. degree in Marketing at night, which she'll soon complete.

Today, medical marketers, including Paddy, have their hands full. The healthcare industry has been hit from both sides. On the one hand, the Federal government has moved to force hospitals into healthcare cost containment. The insurance industry is also trying to keep its costs down. At the same time, technological advances in medicine have meant soaring costs for hospitals, and new medical procedures have resulted in fewer people requiring hospitalization. While in days past it was often difficult to find an available hos-

REAL PEOPLE IN MARKETING

Marketers in Medicine Mean Business

pital bed, today the national average occupancy rate for hospitals is 70 percent: some hospitals, of course, have higher rates, but many have far lower. "Today everything is driven to keep people out of the hospitals," Paddy says. "In addition, we have the additional liability of marketing for a hospital that is in the medical mecca of the world—Boston. Competition for patients is a fact of life for most hospitals today, and for a hospital in Boston, the competition is especially fierce."

"We're organized like any other corporation," Paddy says of Leonard Morse, "in that we have product line management. This means that I work with the clinical service administrators—mostly senior management people—who are in charge of areas such as Surgical operations and Emergency Medicine. From a marketing standpoint, I look at what they want to accomplish—the objectives they seek to fulfill, and then create and implement plans to achieve these objectives."

"As in any corporation, most objectives are financial or market driven, but as a healthcare provider

we always have the mandate to provide quality care and service. Every hospital's mission is one of social responsibility and all our programs must fall in line with this mission."

Paddy is always undertaking market research. "We do tons of it," Paddy says. "We hire research firms to do at least six big studies a year. For instance, one study investigated the feasibility of providing single-room maternity care. Through market research, we discovered that if we offered this service, we could get a significant proportion of the female population in our area to change their minds about their hospitals and come instead to ours."

"We study consumer behavior annually," Paddy added, noting that recently she hired a research firm to determine on what basis consumers choose physicians.

"We look at demographics—what kind of results we can achieve," Paddy continued, "and we investigate the financial implications—what the costs and benefits of a proposed service might be, and how it will affect the hospital overall."

Most importantly, Paddy stresses, "We define short- and long-term goals before getting into the plan. The most important thing you want to do as a marketer is to make sure that the powers that be in the hospital administration are behind the programs. This is absolutely key."

In addition to her work for the hospital, Paddy also serves as a consultant for several subsidiaries of the Leonard Morse Healthcare Corporation, providing her marketing expertise to medical groups and other hospitals. She is also a lecturer in marketing for the Healthcare Administration Program at nearby Simmons College in Boston. For marketers like Paddy and her colleagues, the healthcare industry's state of flux provides ample opportunities for creative market planning and implementation.

Budgets, Controls, and Accountability

Marketing plans have budgets. One of the purposes of the budget, of course, is to answer the question, "How much will it cost?" Furthermore, development of the budget may identify areas in the plan that need refinement or may reveal that the plan and the organization's resources have been incorrectly matched.

DEVELOPING THE MARKETING PLAN BUDGET

The marketing manager may have a limited role in determining the organization's budget. In many organizations, finance and accounting personnel do the budgeting. Marketing managers can try to ensure that the marketing plan is amply funded by keeping in close touch with those responsible for budget preparation. Even the best marketing plan, however, may not be fully funded if an alternative use of funds represents a better opportunity for the firm.

Once approved, the budget becomes the basis for controlling the action program. Marketing managers usually have the freedom to pursue marketing objectives in various ways as long as they stay within the budget. Once the allocation to marketing has been established, marketing managers allocate the funds to various marketing tasks.

CONTROL AND ACCOUNTABILITY

In the control process, results are compared with a standard and corrections in plans are made, if necessary. Effectiveness and efficiency are the criteria for evaluating marketers. Effectiveness refers to whether the goal has been attained, whereas efficiency refers to how well organizational resources have been used to attain the goal. Controls are built into marketing plans.

Accountability exists when a designated person has to answer when objectives are not achieved, when budgets are exceeded, when market share declines, and so on. It is impossible to be a marketer or a manager without having accountability. Control and accountability are the topics of Chapter 22.

Control and accountability should be the basis for accolades and changes for the marketing plan.

IMPLEMENTATION OF THE MARKETING PLAN

Creating the marketing plan is only part of the picture. To get the full value of the plan, it must not be filed and forgotten. It must be efficiently implemented. The four vignettes in figure 2.8 describe the possible interactions between the strategy embodied in the marketing plan and the implementation of the plan.

Superior implementation requires the application of four skills: interacting, allocating, monitoring, and organizing.[13]

Implementing involves interacting, allocating, monitoring, and organizing.

INTERACTING

A large part of marketing is influencing others. More often than not, the marketer must persuade others to respond rather than demand responses of them. For example, the marketer may need to persuade the sales force to show and discuss a particular product instead of other products. Major accounts may have to be persuaded to try the product; advertising agency personnel may be directed to develop a new creative theme; and accounting personnel may need to expand credit.

Possible interactions of the marketer with numerous others is shown in figure 2.9. Notice in the figure that many of the interactions involve persons outside the organization. Within the organization, the marketer interacts with nonmarketing as

Figure 2.8
Marketing plan
strategy and
implementation.

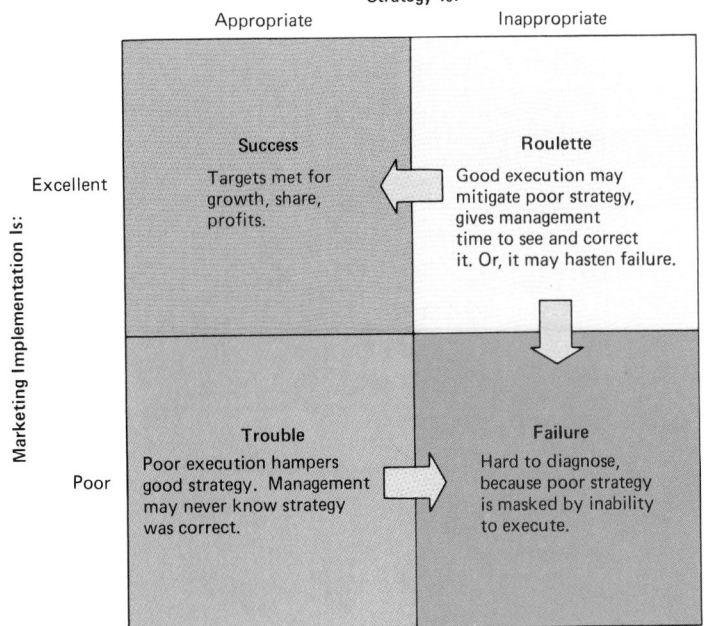

well as marketing personnel. The interests of the marketing manager do not always coincide with those of other individuals in and outside of the firm. Conflicts over control, money, and support are common. Figure 2.10 shows areas of possible conflict between marketing and other areas of business.

Figure 2.9
Interaction of marketer
with others inside and
outside the
organization.

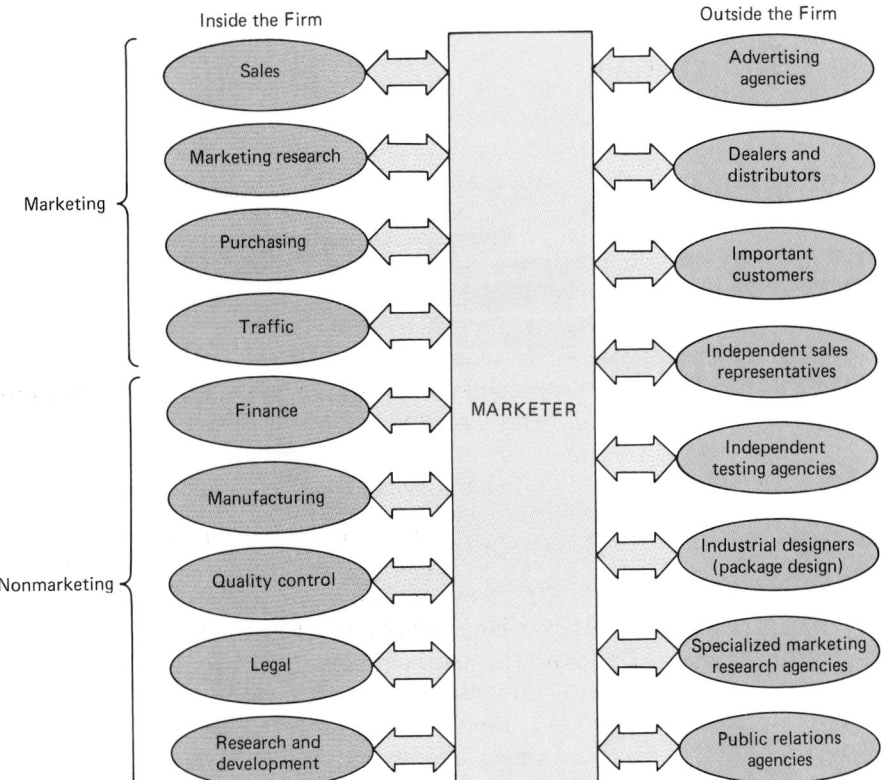

❑ **Figure 2.10**
Conflicts between
marketing and other
areas of business.

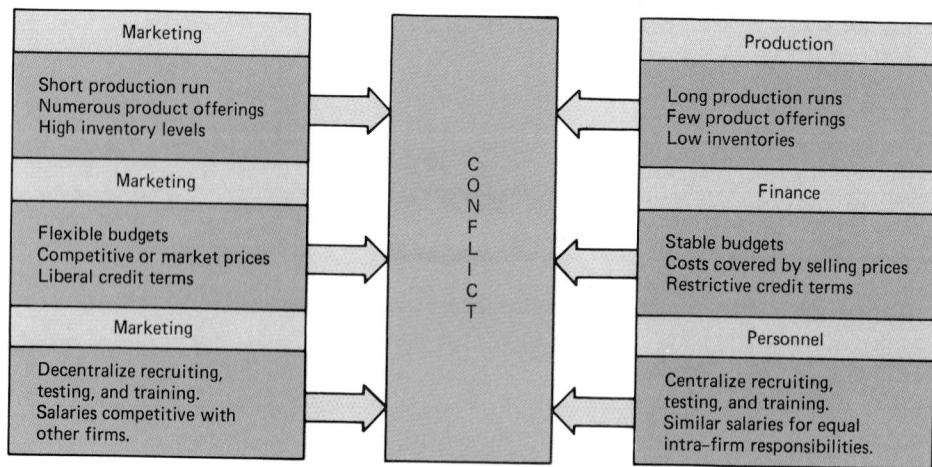

The purpose of allocating
is to divide available resources among tasks and
programs.

The ability to interact in a productive and persuasive manner with superiors within the firm, as well as with client companies is an essential part of effective implementation. Marketers must also be adept at allocating resources.

ALLOCATING

Allocating is the division of resources—time, money, and people—among tasks and programs. For example, the allocation process at Florida Power and Light Co. will determine how much money and management time should be devoted to publicity, as well as to other functions. Although allocation decisions about money do occur in budget development, the allocation of money continues beyond budgeting. The budget often establishes only the broad limits within which further allocation will take place. For example, having set its promotion budget, Hallmark Cards must decide how much to allocate to advertising, how much to broadcast media, how much to television, and so on.

At the most rudimentary level, allocation skills involve answering, "How much?" and "Is the amount too large or too small?" Monitoring the activity can help answer these questions.

MONITORING

*M*onitoring reads the
pulse of the company and
the market.

Monitoring requires the construction and maintenance of both formal and informal feedback systems. The objective of monitoring is the acquisition of timely information that will tell the marketer how the firm's actions are affecting the marketplace. Monitoring should be a measure of the marketer's "pulse." Feedback systems should be insulated from the possible corrupting effects of the politics that surround the situation. Thomas Watson, Jr., son of the IBM founder, recalls that in his first years with IBM everyone strived to make him look good because he was the boss's son. The politics of the situation were corrupting the monitoring system.

A more detailed discussion of monitoring appears in Chapter 20.

ORGANIZING

*I*mplementation requires
an organized structure.

The formal organization structure provides the mechanism for achieving some market plan objectives. However, the formal organization may also impede the marketing manager's effort to apply the marketing plan. Large size, bureaucratic structure, and other characteristics common to organizations may impede implementation. The best marketers can, when necessary, bypass the formal organization by developing informal network structures to help them efficiently implement their market plans.

THE REST OF THE STORY

Executive Strife Led to Carlson's Exit

Robert Carlson, President of United Technologies Corporation, was the victim of old-fashioned corporate backstabbing—wholly justified, according to his detractors, because of his allegedly poor business decisions.

Mr. Carlson joined United Technologies in 1979 as head of the Pratt & Whitney group. He struck some of his new colleagues as unsophisticated. He spent his entire business career, nearly thirty years, at Deere & Co., the Moline, Illinois, maker of farm equipment. Behind his back, some at United Technologies soon began referring to Mr. Carlson disdainfully as "Tractor Bob."

"Bob came in as an outsider," a Pratt & Whitney man says: "He wasn't an engineer in a division full of engineers, and he didn't know the aviation business in a division entirely devoted to aviation."

Carlson eventually became president. In the important aircraft-engine business, United Technologies' archrival is General Electric Co. Convinced that GE was developing jet engines that would rival United Technologies' in performance, Mr. Carlson quickly set about planning an unusual marketing offensive.

This was to trigger his downfall.

He decided to undercut GE by offering Pratt & Whitney's airline customers sweeping guarantees of low fuel consumption in three new engines the division was developing. If the new engines burned more fuel than Pratt & Whitney said they would, Pratt & Whitney would pay the difference.

Mr. Carlson even planned a kicker unheard of in the industry: If a customer was dissatisfied with the engines, Pratt & Whitney would take them back and refund the purchase price.

At the time few on United Technologies' corporate staff had any inkling of the Carlson initiative because he had been ignoring the headquarters' financial, legal, and public-relations staffs, continuing to work with his old colleagues at Pratt & Whitney.

Corporate staffers finally got wind of the project. About the same time, Mr. Harry Gray, Chairman of the Board, returned from vacation and was told of Mr. Carlson's plan. "When Harry heard of it," says a United Technologies official, "he went right through the roof."

Mr. Carlson's fate was sealed. Mr. Gray, says the United Technologies official, ordered the staff to build a case for ousting Mr. Carlson. "In a very traditional company, where ideas are approved by layer upon layer of management," the official says, "Carlson had committed the ultimate sin of not clearing the project. Worst of all, he hadn't cleared it with Harry."

Source: Adapted from William M. Carley, "Executive Strife, How Dissension Jolted United Technologies, Led to Carlson's Exit," *The Wall Street Journal,* May 20, 1986, p. 1. Reprinted by permission of *The Wall Street Journal,* © Dow Jones & Company, Inc., 1986. All Rights Reserved.

 ## CORPORATE CULTURE AND THE MARKETING PLAN

The corporate culture influences every element of marketing.

An organization's traditions, values, unwritten norms, management styles, and beliefs about and actions toward its customers, competitors, and the world make up its **corporate culture.**[14] The corporate culture exerts a powerful influence on every marketing action and every element of the marketing plan and its implementation and control. Delta Airlines employees are trained to work as a team to provide the best possible service. They may perform several tasks, such as working the ticket counter and helping with the baggage. Customer service is a significant part of Delta's marketing strategy.

At Pepsico, Inc., makers of the soft-drink Pepsi, the corporate culture is embued with a highly aggressive, "winning" philosophy. A basic aspect of its culture is its adversarial relationship to the Coca-Cola Company. Executives at Pepsico develop marketing plans with the intent of seizing market share from its competitors.

The corporate culture also influences the day-to-day operations of the organization. For instance, only present employees may be eligible to fill middle-level and top marketing positions. Entry-level marketing positions may be open only to college graduates with degrees in technical areas, such as engineering and chemistry, or to graduates from designated universities. Compensation may also be influenced. For instance, every marketer—even the worst—may receive a yearly salary increase. Such matters indirectly affect the marketing plan.

The marketing plan and its implementation must be consistent with the corporate culture. Plans that conflict with the corporate culture will either fail to win acceptance or will receive only minimal cooperation. Executives at Benco, Inc., a producer of plastic agricultural drainage pipe, invented a new drainage pipe that was up to 180 percent as efficient as existing pipe but that used only 67 percent as much material.[15] The orientation of the company, however, had emphasized high volume and low cost. Pricing had been cents-per-pound. The marketing plan for the new pipe called for a pricing theme that emphasized a value-added consumer orientation was not readily accepted. A **value-added consumer orientation** recognizes that the price a consumer is willing to pay depends on the benefits received from the product and not just the physical product itself. (The new pipe was 180 percent more efficient but had 67 percent less material.) Considerable change in the corporate culture was necessary for acceptance. Marketing managers can make their plans compatible with the corporate culture only if they understand the culture.

THE CASE CONTINUES

*T*he successful implementation and control of the marketing plan at Nautilus will require the use of interacting, allocating, monitoring, and organizing skills, and the continuous accurate reading of the corporate culture.

From 1984 to 1986, Nautilus offered a home gym line but then abandoned the effort. At the time, Nautilus was still owned by the system's inventor and company founder, Arthur Jones. Reportedly, the home line was abandoned due to his lack

of interest. Even under new ownership that is interested in the home gym market, the marketing manager must interact with others, especially top management, to obtain cooperation and maintain support for the marketing plan. The history of Nautilus indicates an emphasis on product design and promotion and less concern about marketing tasks. The

marketing manager will have to obtain the time, money, and personnel called for in the plan, and then properly allocate their use in order to prove the worthiness of the plan. Early results, gained from monitoring of the plan, may provide posi.ve feedback on the success of the plan to date. It has been shown that success encourages more support. Nautilus marketers will probably need to use both the formal and informal networks within the company to ensure the success of their plan.

MARKETING, THIS TEXT, AND YOU

Paddy Mullen, profiled in this chapter in a "Real People in Marketing" box (p. 47) has had extensive preparation and experience in marketing. Her successes, and those of many others mentioned in this text, are based on a solid understanding of the principles and practices of marketing.

Marketers like Paddy must be able to adapt to the highly competitive and continually changing business world of today. *Principles of Modern Marketing,* in addition to offering comprehensive coverage of the basic marketing concepts, emphasizes the marketing manager's tasks of planning, implementing, and controlling marketing activities. And because of the central importance of the marketing mix in all marketing programs, at least two chapters each are devoted to product, price, promotion, and distribution.

Principles of Modern Marketing is unique in its introduction of the elements of a marketing plan very early on in the text, as you've just seen, and in its presentation of a marketing plan exercise appearing at seven points throughout the text.

The relationship of the main parts of the marketing plan to the various chapters of this text are shown in Figure 2.11. Each section of the outline builds on the information provided in the chapters preceding it.

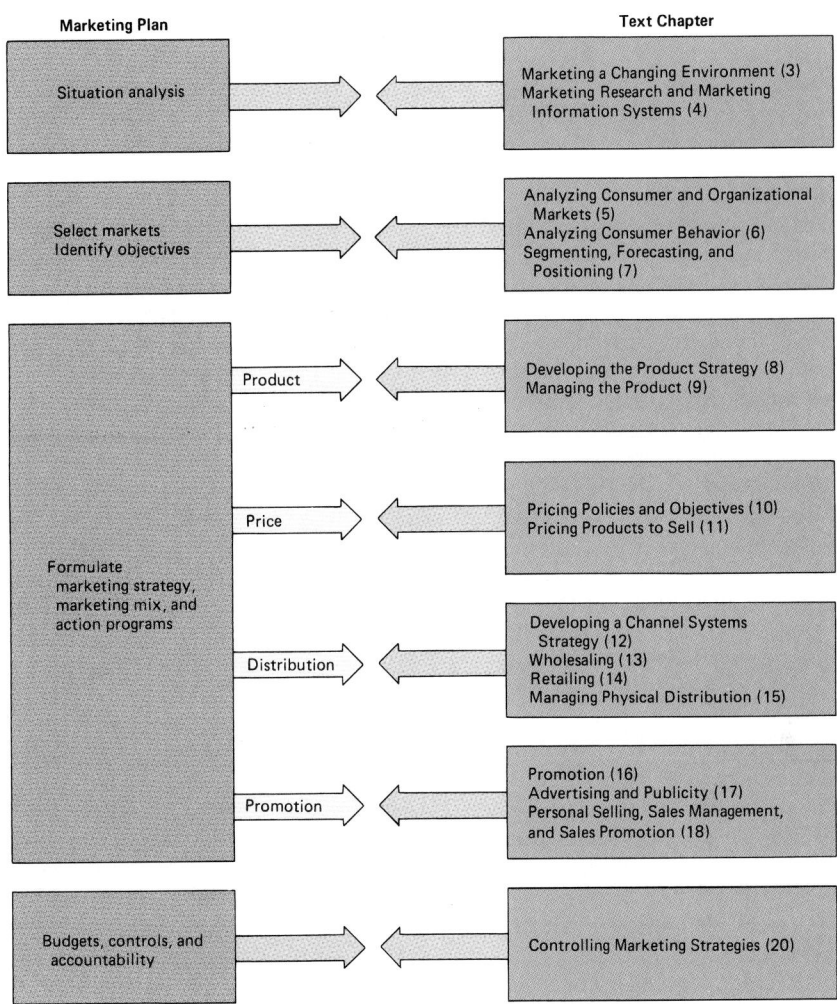

Figure 2.11
The marketing plan and text.

Marketing Plan

Situation analysis

Select markets
Identify objectives

Formulate marketing strategy, marketing mix, and action programs
- Product
- Price
- Distribution
- Promotion

Budgets, controls, and accountability

Text Chapter

Marketing a Changing Environment (3)
Marketing Research and Marketing Information Systems (4)

Analyzing Consumer and Organizational Markets (5)
Analyzing Consumer Behavior (6)
Segmenting, Forecasting, and Positioning (7)

Developing the Product Strategy (8)
Managing the Product (9)

Pricing Policies and Objectives (10)
Pricing Products to Sell (11)

Developing a Channel Systems Strategy (12)
Wholesaling (13)
Retailing (14)
Managing Physical Distribution (15)

Promotion (16)
Advertising and Publicity (17)
Personal Selling, Sales Management, and Sales Promotion (18)

Controlling Marketing Strategies (20)

If you choose to work on the marketing plan exercise, you will be able to apply marketing principles to a specific situation. We have provided four comprehensive cases at the end of the text from which you can choose as a basis for developing your marketing plan. Alternatively, you can select another company entirely—provided you are able to obtain the kind of detailed information needed to complete a marketing plan. As a third option, your instructor may assign his or her own case scenario on which to base your marketing plan.

The marketing plan exercise can be worked on individually or in groups. In preparing a complete, written marketing plan there are a few basic points to keep in mind:

- A sound marketing plan is based on facts and valid assumptions, not on guesses and hunches. Stick to factual information as much as possible.
- A marketing plan must have clear, achievable objectives. A plan that is unrealistic (for example, costs too much money, or requires manpower that the firm does not have) is no plan at all.
- A marketing plan must clearly state what is to be accomplished, who will do it, how it will be done, when it will be done, and how results will be measured.

When you have completed working on your marketing plan, you will have gained valuable hands-on experience in a central marketing function. In addition, you will have experienced the planning and decision-making process that is part of many business positions at all levels. All organizations, public and private, profit and not-for-profit must carefully develop their marketing plans, and each individual within the organization has a role to play in seeing that the firm's marketing plan is successfully carried out. Working through your marketing plan will provide you with skills that can be used in any business endeavor.

53

GOAL SUMMARY

1. **List and define a marketing manager's general management activities.** Marketers engage in planning, implementing, and controlling. Planning involves mapping out a course of action to attain organizational objectives. Implementing requires putting the plan into action by interacting, allocating, monitoring, and organizing. Controlling is a comparison of actual results to desired results and taking corrective action if necessary.

2. **Describe the characteristics of marketing plan objectives and outline a marketing plan.** Marketing plan objectives identify the goals of the marketing program. Marketing plan objectives should be (1) *compatible* with the organization's overall objectives, (2) *reasonable* in terms of the chances of their fulfillment based on company resources, (3) *measurable,* so that results can be monitored and evaluated, and (4) achievable within a specific time frame (*datability*).

   Marketing plan outlines vary in presentation, but a typical outline includes an executive summary, situation analysis (current market situation, internal analysis, external analysis), marketing plan objectives, market selection/target markets, marketing strategy and marketing mix, action programs (specifics of marketing mix implementation), and budgets, controls, and accountability sections.

3. **Describe two basic types of marketing strategies used to achieve competitive advantage and the three generic strategies marketers use when they lack a competitive advantage.** A competitive advantage stems from an organization's greater effectiveness in satisfying customers' needs. In developing a marketing strategy, the marketer would strive to obtain a competitive advantage through product, price, promotion, or distribution, or by some other means. *Low cost advantage* is achieved by emphasizing low cost per unit and low price as an appeal to customers. A *differentiation* strategy involves stress-ing differences in the product that will appeal to customers. Marketers who use a differentiation strategy rely heavily on promotional efforts to highlight differences (which in fact may be very slight).

   If the leading firm's offerings appear truly superior, the firm may choose to *emulate* the firm's marketing strategy. If improvements in the leading firm's product can be made, the firm may choose a strategy that *deviates* from competitors. A *complementation* strategy involves selling products that will complement the leading firm's offerings.

4. **Describe the marketing mix.** The marketing mix is the specific way in which the four key variables of product, price, promotion, and distribution are set for a given marketing program. The selected product is priced appropriately, promoted effectively, and distributed efficiently to meet the goals of the program.

5. **Describe the skills needed to implement the marketing plan.** Once the marketing plan is created, it must be implemented. Interacting with others, both within and outside of the company, is a central part of implementing the plan. Allocating resources involves assigning tasks, setting timetables, and creating budgets for the plan. Monitoring the results of the plan while it is being implemented is also crucial, so that if needed, modifications can be made. Finally, plans cannot be implemented in a vacuum. They require an organized structure. While the formal organization provides much of the structure needed to implement plans, marketers also use informal network structures to implement the plan. Making sure that the plan is supported by formal and informal structures requires superior organizing skill.

6. **Define corporate culture.** Companies have their own distinctive "cultures" that affect all aspects of their operation. Corporate culture consists of the company's shared values, traditions, beliefs, and long standing practices towards employees, customers, and competitors.

KEY TERMS

CHECK YOUR LEARNING

1. The time frame for a marketing plan is usually five or more years.   **T/F**
2. The last part of a marketing plan presented is the executive summary.   **T/F**
3. If an objective has the characteristic of measurability, management will be able to determine when the objective has been met.   **T/F**
4. Clearly defined objectives should possess: (a) compatibility, reasonability, measurability, and datability, (b) reasonability, measurability, datability, and obtainability, (c) reasonability, measurability, and obtainability, (d) obtainability, justifiability, measurability, and practicality, (e) none of the above.

5. It is illegal in the United States for an organization to imitate another organization's marketing strategy.   **T/F**
6. Planning is a continuous activity.   **T/F**
7. Marketing plans are always built from scratch.   **T/F**
8. Effectiveness in marketing management refers to the minimal use of an organization's resources in attaining an objective.   **T/F**
9. Budgets belong in the marketing plan.   **T/F**
10. Marketing managers must both compete and cooperate with other managers.   **T/F**
11. Corporate culture normally affects corporate strategy but seldom permeates to the marketing plan level.   **T/F**

QUESTIONS FOR REVIEW AND DISCUSSION

1. Define the key terms for this chapter that appear at the end of the goal summary.
2. What personal attributes—both positive and negative—influence your decision making?
3. What personal attributes does it take to be a good decision maker?
4. Is decision making learned or inherited?
5. Discuss how goals make a difference in the development of plans.
6. List the three management activities in which a marketing manager engages.
7. The executive summary serves what purpose in the marketing plan?
8. How can organizations influence the environment in which they operate? Should they?
9. Identify an opportunity that you have had. What risks were associated with it?
10. Identify a marketing strategy that an organization you know of seems to be employing. What is the competitive advantage involved?
11. What are the variables in the marketing mix?
12. What skills must a marketer have to successfully implement a marketing plan?

NOTES

1. "A Smarter Intravenous Delivery System," *Business Week,* October 7, 1985, p. 113.
2. Thomas J. Peters and Robert M. Waterman, Jr., *In Search of Excellence: Lessons from America's Best-Run Companies* (New York: Harper & Row, 1982).
3. Peters and Waterman, *In Search of Excellence.*
4. "New Markets, New Products," *Forbes,* July 30, 1984, p. 102.
5. Francis Joseph Aguilar, *Scanning the Business Environment* (New York: The Macmillan Company, 1967), p. 18.
6. Bernie Whalen, "Kotler: Rethink the Marketing Concept," *Marketing News,* September 14, 1984, p. 22.
7. Michael E. Porter, *Competitive Advantage* (New York: The Free Press, 1985), p. 8.
8. George Day, *Strategic Market Planning* (St. Paul: West Publishing Company, 1984), p. 25.
9. Porter, *Competitive Advantage,* p. 11.
10. Robert D. Buzzell and Frederik D. Wiersema, "Successful Share-Building Strategies," *Harvard Business Review,* January–February 1981, pp. 135–144.
11. Wroe Anderson, *Dynamic Marketing Behavior* (Homewood, Ill.: Richard D. Irwin, 1985), pp. 198–200.
12. Laurie Freeman, "Rayovac Back on Beam in Battery Market," *Advertising Age,* September 16, 1985, p. 47.
13. Thomas V. Bonoma, *Managing Marketing: Text, Cases, and Readings* (New York: The Free Press, 1984), p. 77.
14. Douglas J. Dairymple and Leonard J. Parsons, *Marketing Management: Strategy and Cases* (New York: John Wiley & Sons, 1986), p. 10.
15. *Harvard Business School,* Case 9–581–127. (Boston, MA: President and Fellows of Harvard College, 1981), pp 1–27.

*T*he Wall Street Journal, a national financially oriented daily newspaper—and for many years the *only* U.S. national daily paper—was first published in 1889. Over the years many changes have been implemented to keep pace with the ever-changing business environment. For most of its history, the *Journal* published only business and financial information. In 1980, however, a second section was added to the paper containing general interest stories, arts and entertainment coverage, and articles on personal finance.

Until the late 1970s, the *Journal*'s circulation was largely restricted to New York and other financial centers in the United States. Since that time, the subscriber base has grown both nationally and, with the introduction of international editions, internationally. The *Journal*'s circulation and advertising linage grew rapidly in the late 1970s and 1980. Circulation increased from 1,477,077 at the end of 1976 to 2,108,795 in 1983. Between 1979 and 1984, advertising linage rose by 36.8 percent.

The *Journal*'s environment continues to change—perhaps at a faster pace than ever. To sustain the *Journal*'s status as *the* financial newspaper in the United States and in the world, executives must successfully surmount many challenges. A host of newer national newspapers, including *USA Today, New York Times–National Edition, Investor's Daily,* and *Financial Times,* threaten to eat into the *Journal*'s market share. The publishing magnate Rupert Murdoch has even proposed a special U.S. edition of the British-based *Financial Times* to directly compete with the *Journal.*

A 1986 Simmons Market Research Bureau study of Media and Markets found the readership (the number of people who read a publication during the duration of the study period) for the *Journal* had declined and was less than that of *USA Today.* To capitalize on this finding, *USA Today* ran ads within the paper citing the study and proclaiming that "*USA Today*'s readership is the in-

dustry's largest." And to further ride the crest of the study's finding, the paper joined with General Mills in a promotion featured on GM products encouraging consumers to sign up for a free six-month subscription to the paper. While the response was high—450,000 people did sign up—*USA Today*'s bottom line was actually negatively affected by the promotion since the agreement between General Mills and the paper allowed General Mills to offer the subscriptions at prices far below the regular price. Nevertheless, *USA Today* and other national newspapers are gaining subscribers at the expense of the *Journal.*

It appears that the increased general news coverage the *Journal* instituted in 1980 must continue and expand for the *Journal* to keep up with its competitors. More coverage, however, requires more editorial staff, which in turn means higher operating costs. While revenue at the *Journal* grew 4 percent in 1987, profits dropped 13.6 percent. Cost cutting and cost containment appear probable in the next several years.

The general business climate also seems to be working against the *Journal.* The cost-cutting atmosphere in most U.S. businesses has reduced the ranks of middle managers, many of whom have received subscriptions to the *Journal*—paid for by the company—at work. The annual subscription fee, in excess of $100, has become a target of cost-conscious executives. Finally, the stock market crash of October 19, 1987 took its toll on the *Journal.* Advertising linage dropped 15 percent in two months and 2.3 percent for the year.

All is not doom and gloom, however. A 1986 nationwide poll by the *Los Angeles Times* found the *Journal* to be America's most trusted information medium. Another annual survey by *Fortune* once again found the

publisher of the *Journal,* The Dow Jones Corporation, at the top of all American corporations surveyed for quality of products and services.

From surveys and from the over 10,000 Letters to the Editor the *Journal* receives annually, executives learn about their market. A 1986 subscribers' survey provided the following information:

- Four out of 10 subscribers live in the 20 largest metropolitan areas in the U.S.
- There are *Journal* subscribers in nearly every community
- Thirteen percent live in California and 7 percent in New York
- Eighty percent are in business or the professions
- Forty percent hold management titles
- Forty-four percent work for small businesses
- Ninety percent are college graduates
- Thirteen percent are women
- Median age of readers is 47
- Readers have strong interest in personal financial information
- Readers have strong interest in mutual fund information

Based on this and other market research, *Journal* management identified several areas for possible action in the following year, including:

1. Provide the reader with a more timely and tightly edited newspaper by reorganizing and expanding the editing desks.
2. Group related stories and use more graphics, charts, and statistical summaries to enhance ease of use.
3. Increase coverage of daily developments and broad trends affecting readers' career goals, business decisions, and personal financial planning.
4. Permit inclusion of more late-breaking news by retooling pagination system.
5. Expand the *Journal*'s 154-city private delivery network (740,000 *Journals* were delivered by this

system in 1988) to increase speed and reliability of delivery.
6. Build more printing plants in overseas locations to speed overseas delivery.

Journal management will evaluate these identified goals and will select some or all of them to implement based on further study.

Issues for Discussion

1. Using the information provided in the case, complete a situation analysis of the *Journal.*

2. Describe what you think is the ideal *Journal* target market. Why?

3. Identify possible objectives that might be a party of a marketing plan.

4. What elements of the marketing mix can you identify in this case?

Sources: David Lieberman, "The Wall Street Journal Makes News of Its Own," *Business Week,* February 8, 1988, pp. 31–32; Warren H. Phillips, "A Report to The Wall Street Journal's Readers," *The Wall Street Journal,* January 16, 1987, p. 23; Van Wallach, "Journal Enjoys New Life as Multiple-Section Paper," *Advertising Age,* July 28, 1986, pp. s-26, s-27; and William F. Gloede, "USA Today Up, Journal Down In Study," *Advertising Age,* July 28, 1986, pp. 6, 63.

OUTLINE

CHAPTER 3

Marketing in a Changing Environment

LEARNING GOALS

After reading this chapter, you should be able to:

1. Identify the microenvironmental forces affecting marketers.
2. Distinguish among the macroenvironmental forces that influence marketing decisions.
3. Describe the factors giving rise to consumer purchasing power.
4. Understand how technology affects marketers.
5. Identify the major laws that affect marketing.

In 1954, Ray Kroc, then 52, was the owner of a small company that marketed a strange-looking multimixer milkshake machine. On his sales trips around the country, he had heard about the fantastic fast-food restaurant operated by the McDonald brothers, Maurice and Richard, in San Bernardino, California. Their little drive-in establishment had eight Multimixers whipping out forty shakes at once. Because other restaurants did not match McDonald's volume, Kroc made a special visit to observe this unique operation.

Kroc was both surprised and elated by what he saw. He was surprised by the stream of people who came away with bags of hamburgers, french fries, and milkshakes. He was elated because he could visualize similar restaurants nationwide, and all of them would be customers for his Multimixer.

To Kroc, the McDonald brothers had a winning combination. They stressed exceptional cleanliness and high value in their operations. Loose wrappers and empty paper cups were regularly removed from the premises. Their hamburgers contained a tenth of a pound of meat and sold for a mere fifteen cents. A sixteen-ounce milkshake was twenty cents, and a three-ounce bag of french fries retailed for ten cents.

Unable to contain his enthusiasm for the McDonald's operation, Kroc confronted the brothers and proposed that they rapidly expand their fast-food business. Kroc was astounded that they thoroughly enjoyed their present small-business status and did not want to change it. They equated more restaurants with more problems. In contrast, Kroc viewed expansion as an opportunity. Thus, he suggested that they allow him to establish McDonald restaurants throughout the country. Kroc visualized an extensive franchised operation whereby, for a fee, independent businesspersons could operate a McDonald outlet. After some difficult negotiation, a persistent Ray Kroc left San Bernardino with a signed contract.

INTRODUCTORY CASE

McDONALD'S . . . A CREATION OF ITS TIME

Well before the time of his death in 1984, Ray Kroc was hailed as the Henry Ford of the fast-food restaurant business. McDonald's restaurants brought mass production to an industry that had been built on individual service and small quantities. He developed an organization that contained specialists in every phase of the restaurant business. The company has been a leader in employee training programs and in upgrading the level of store supervision. Kroc realized that people would patronize a fast-food restaurant that offered good, fast service, and outstanding value.

The McDonald's chain grew rapidly because it satisfied an environmental climate that included working wives, an increasing number of youths, rising food prices, and a desire for convenience. Although numerous competitors arose to challenge McDonald's leadership in the fast-food industry, the company has remained the leader. In 1988, thirty-four years after Kroc's trip to San Bernardino, the fast-food giant celebrated the sale of its 70-billionth hamburger.

Over the years, the McDonald organization has spent hundreds of millions of dollars to create an image as a wholesome, fun place to eat. In the 1970s, a survey of school children revealed that Ronald McDonald, the corporate symbol, was readily identified by 96 percent of the respondents. Among all children's characters only one had a higher recognition factor—Santa Claus.

Issues for Discussion

1. How did microenvironmental forces affect the development of McDonald's?
2. What were the economic, social, and demographic factors that contributed to the great growth of McDonald's?
3. How will environmental factors change the fast-food industry in the future?

Sources: "McDonald's Reports 91st Consecutive Quarter of Record Sales and Earnings Increases," *News Release from McDonald's Corporation,* January 28, 1988, pp. 1–9; Robert Johnson, "McDonald's Combines a Dead Man's Advice with Lively Strategy," *The Wall Street Journal,* Dec. 18, 1987, pp. 1, 13; Ray Kroc with Robert Anderson, *Grinding It Out* (Chicago: Henry Regnery Company, 1977), pp. 5–11; Steve Raddock, "The Mammoth, Marvelous, Money Machine," *Marketing & Media Decisions,* Spring 1982 Special, pp. 111–118; and Milton Moskowitz, Michael Katz, and Robert Levering, *Everybody's Business* (New York: Harper & Row, 1980), pp. 128–131.

■ Ray Kroc built McDonald's into the world's top franchised chain.

*M*arketers at McDonald's and at other companies recognize that their decisions must reflect an accurate assessment of environmental factors that affect, or could affect, their businesses. They continually strive to identify and understand these factors. Microenvironmental forces are directly associated with a company's operations, and include suppliers, marketing intermediaries, competitors, and customers, among others. Macroenvironmental forces are broader conditions that affect society as a whole—economic conditions, social and cultural values, and technology are all macroenvironmental forces. Just what the many micro and macro environmental factors are, and how they are related to the marketing process, is the subject of this chapter. ■

MARKETERS RESPOND TO ENVIRONMENTAL FORCES

Microenvironmental forces, though smaller in scale than macroenvironmental forces, are just as important.

In 1984, after nearly forty years as a leader in consumer electronics, Sony announced that it would redirect its development efforts to products for business and industry. Akio Morita, Sony's chairman, expressed the belief that by 1990 half of the company's revenues would be generated by industrial products, which would be more profitable than consumer products. Competitive conditions and the lessening of brand loyalty among consumers were factors that forced this decision. In another instance, Coca-Cola, in response to consumers' concerns, introduced caffeine-free and sugar-free Coke. Alert marketers, such as those at Sony, Coca-Cola, and McDonald's, are aware of environmental conditions and respond to them.

Marketing managers are often confronted with conditions—both microenvironmental and macroenvironmental—over which they exert little or no control. What they can control is how they respond to these conditions in their planning process.

MICROENVIRONMENTAL FORCES

Micro, as you may recall from Chapter 1, means small. Thus, **microenvironmental forces** are the small-scale forces that directly affect the organization's marketing effort. These include the company's internal structure, suppliers, marketing intermediaries, competitors, and customers (figure 3.1). Keep in mind that small does not mean unimportant. In many ways the impact of microenvironmental forces on a company's marketing effort is as critical as the impact of the macroenvironmental forces present in the larger environment. However, the organization can probably exert more control over and react more promptly to the microforces. By working closely with company colleagues, a marketing manager can frequently maximize the positive effects of these forces and minimize those that are negative.

Internal Forces

Within the company itself, other departments, such as finance, accounting, production, research and development, and the organization's own distribution centers are considered microenvironmental forces, since the activities of all of these areas affect how the product or service is brought to the market. Lack of coordination or support in any of these areas will impinge negatively on the marketer's efforts.

❑ **Figure 3.1**
Types of
environmental forces
that affect marketing
management.

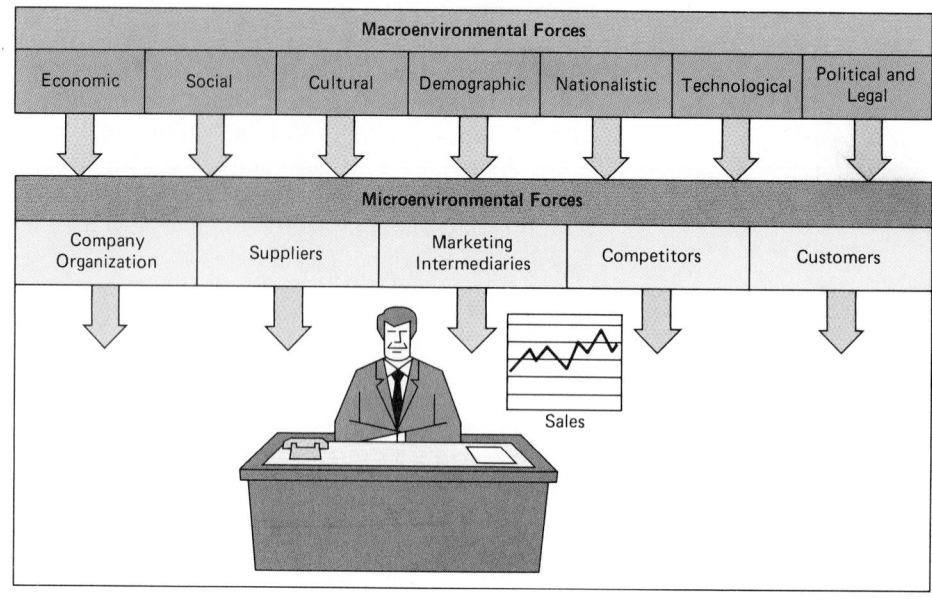

*C*ompanies seek long-
term contracts with sup-
pliers to establish closer
relationships with them.

Suppliers

Few companies are so completely independent that they manufacture all their own parts or products. Most companies use numerous suppliers to furnish the goods and services incorporated into the final product offering. For example, General Motors has nearly 30,000 automotive parts suppliers. Large retailers, such as Sears and Kmart, buy for resale thousands of items, including hardware, silverware, and underwear. A strong, friendly, long-term relationship between a firm and its suppliers helps the firm meet its marketing objectives.

Marketing managers should work closely with suppliers and carefully monitor their performance. The Ford Motor Company has nearly constant contact with its suppliers, who provide about half of its cars' components. This contact permits the giant automaker to obtain high-quality parts and dependable deliveries at the lowest prices. In the Sears organization, employees responsible for buying goods from suppliers—the buyers—are truly product marketing managers. They are responsible for monitoring the development, manufacturing, and movement of the product into the Sears stores.[1] Buyers in commercial firms continually rate the reliability of their suppliers, so the outstanding ones receive preference for future business. Companies often seek long-term contracts with a small number of suppliers in order to strengthen the suppliers' involvement with the firm and promote a stronger commitment to quality.

Marketing Intermediaries

*M*arket intermediaries
help move goods and
services from producers to
consumers.

Organizations often employ specialists, or marketing intermediaries, to assist in the performance of various marketing functions. These intermediaries help move goods and services from producers to consumers. They exist because of the efficiencies and economies they bring to the marketing process. Some marketing intermediaries take title to goods or resell them, and others simply aid in the performance of a particular marketing activity. Figure 3.2 shows the relationship between the important marketing functions and some significant marketing intermediaries. You can see from the figure that many different types of marketing intermediaries exist; the following discussion focuses on a few of the more prominent ones.

❑ **Figure 3.2**
Selected marketing
intermediaries and
their functions.

Marketing Intermediaries	Marketing Functions
Wholesalers Retailers Resident buyers Independent purchasing agents Advertising agencies Manufacturers' agents Sales agents Brokers Auction companies	Buying and selling
Trucklines Railroads Airlines Waterborne carriers Fast-freight agencies	Transportation
Public warehouses Distribution centers	Storage
Marketing research agencies Computer service bureaus	Marketing information and research
Banks Commercial finance companies Savings and loan associations Credit unions Credit checking agencies	Financing
Trade associations U.S. Bureau of Standards Manufacturers	Standardization and grading
Insurance companies Commodity speculators	Risk bearing

WHOLESALERS AND RETAILERS

The largest groups of marketing intermediaries are the wholesalers and retailers that buy and sell goods. Many wholesalers are small businesses; but a few are very large. Foremost-McKesson, for example, is the nation's largest drug and chemical wholesaler; it sells to more than 20,000 drugstores and almost 6,000 hospitals.[2] In retailing, too, several chains, such as Sears, J. C. Penney, and Kmart, operate hundreds of stores from coast to coast.

*E*very producer has certain types of wholesalers and retailers that can distribute its product most efficiently.

Every producer has certain types of wholesalers and retailers that can distribute its goods most efficiently. For example, General Motors uses the services of 10,000 automobile dealers. At times, however, the middleman that could serve a producer most efficiently is not available. When a producer is small and unknown, middlemen may refuse to handle its product. For example, the producer of an unknown brand of jeans may find it difficult to market them, because retailers would rather carry Levi or Wrangler. A producer may discover that a middleman carrying several brands of a particular product does not want to add another brand. For instance, a hardware wholesaler that sells and services both Lawn Boy and Toro lawn mowers probably does not want to add another line, such as Bolens or Snapper. This refusal may cause the producer to use a less desirable kind of wholesaler, such as one handling farm equipment. Sometimes these producers may decide to sell directly to consumers by mail order.

RESIDENT BUYERS

Resident buying firms are specialists that furnish buying assistance and central market information to retailers. Resident buyers are located in the central markets, such as New York and Los Angeles, which contain a large number of suppliers for the retail trade. Because of their location, resident buyers can furnish retailers in

Although most soft-drink companies are fervently pushing low-sugar and no-caffeine drinks, an upstart soft-drink company is doing things differently. To the nutritionists, this naughty firm has said "aw shucks," and is ardently promoting a cola called Jolt. This unusual drink, which has been on the market since 1986, has twice the caffeine of regular colas and uses 100 percent sugar—no artificial sweeteners or corn syrup—to sweeten it.

Jolt's label consists of a yellow lightening bolt slashing through its red-and-white logo. This dramatic label looks like something out of the Batman and Robin comic strip. Jolt exhibits some characteristics that are similar to Batman—both operate slightly out of the mainstream of society.

Jolt is a product of C. J. Rapp and his father, Joseph F. Rapp. The latter is a soft-drink industry veteran who operated a Canada Dry bottling plant in Rochester for several decades. C. J. Rapp, president, was 26 when the product was introduced.

Jolt is directed to a unique niche in the soft-drink market. C. J. Rapp contends that whoever thinks that soft drinks are meant to be a health food is completely off base. He strongly contends that a cola should have a lot of zip and zing. Rapp believes that over the years Coke and Pepsi have altered the tastes that consumers expect from a cola. He wants to bring back the jolting sensation that he believes was once the typical taste of a sparkling cola.

Industry analysts predicted that Rapp would receive a severe jolt when his new product did not survive in the marketplace. How, they insisted, can a drink that flaunts the environmental trends toward less sugar, caffeine, more fruit juice, and better nutritional values in general, be successful?

Rapp countered that he and his father spent $100,000 and experi-

MARKETING IN ACTION

A Jolt for Cola Lovers

mented with four formulas over six years in the development of the new cola. By farming out most of the company's production and marketing activities, the Rapps were truly operating on a shoestring when they started the company. There were no Jolt bottling plants, no Jolt trucks, no Jolt advertising programs, and only a few Jolt workers.

A year after its introduction, the astonishing success of Jolt was proving the analysts wrong. The cola was being distributed in 46 states and in Canada; and in the cities where it was being sold it was obtaining between a 1- and 6-percent share of the soft-drink market. In 1987, the Rapps introduced Jolt 25—so named for its calorie count. This low-calorie, high-kick product was created in response to consumer demand, and not as a concession to nutritionists. Jolt is now firmly established in the marketplace, and the Rapps are continuing to think of new ways to jolt America.

Sources: "Jolt to Provide Double the Punch at 25 Calories," *Knoxville, Tennessee Journal,* March 3, 1987; Richard W. Stevenson, "Jolt Cola's Contrary Strategy," *The New York Times,* August 20, 1986; Stephen W. Bell, "New Cola Pops Sugary Wallop," *Fort Wayne Journal Gazette,* June 23, 1986, p. 2C.

■ Jolt boldly proclaims its high sugar and caffeine content in its regular cola; for those who want fewer calories, there's the high caffeine and sugar/Nutra-Sweet blend version.
Source: Courtesy of The Jolt® Company, Inc.

outlying areas with important insights about changing market trends. Independent purchasing agents perform a similar function for wholesalers by locating the suppliers that offer the best values and thus provide a competitive advantage.

ADVERTISING AGENCIES

Advertising agencies help organizations to create and carry out promotional strategies designed to achieve their sales and promotional objectives. Large advertising agencies, such as Young & Rubicam and Grey Advertising, perform such a variety of marketing operations for their clients that they can be said to act as marketing consultants. If such an agency develops the wrong promotional campaign or furnishes improper marketing counsel, its client company may suffer losses in both revenue and image.

PHYSICAL DISTRIBUTION SPECIALISTS

Specialists that perform physical distribution activities include transportation companies that move the goods to market and public warehouses that store them until needed. Trucklines, railroads, airlines, and waterborne carriers supply transportation, as do fast-freight agencies such as United Parcel Service and Federal Express. Large companies often use public warehouses for all their storage needs. The goal of an organization in setting up its physical distribution system is to satisfy customers' time and place requirements while minimizing warehouse and transportation costs. The ability to deliver goods promptly and economically provides a basis for increased sales for the firm.

*A*n effective physical distribution system provides utilities of time and place while minimizing warehouse and transportation costs.

FINANCIAL SPECIALISTS

Financial specialists, such as credit and insurance agencies, play an important role in marketing transactions. Over 90 percent of all commercial exchanges involve some type of credit arrangement with banks, commercial finance companies, or other financial organizations. Since the late 1960s, credit card organizations, such as Visa and MasterCard, have become an important factor in financing the purchases of many consumers. Insurance companies, by assuming certain risks, protect marketing managers from unforeseen disasters and so provide a degree of certainty to an otherwise uncertain business environment.

Competition

Competition is one of the major forces in the marketing environment. It is so significant, in fact, that it is examined at length in Chapter 10. The goal of every marketer is to develop a unique good or service that has no close substitutes and that a consumer will insist on buying. Only a few products meet this exacting criterion. Marketing managers realize that competition for the consumer's dollar comes not only from competitors' brands, but also from a variety of other sources of gratification for the consumer. For example, movie theaters are competing with video rental centers for the entertainment dollars spent by consumers. Competition also occurs when a consumer weighs the purchase of a new stereo system against a vacation spent skiing in Colorado.

Customers

Customers are obviously a major factor in the marketing environment. Without customers there would be no marketing. Every company tries to satisfy one or more

A company's marketing effort is directed at satisfying the needs of specific customer groups.

customer groups, or target markets, with the proper assortment of goods and services. Most firms discover that a minority of their customers (such as 20 percent) account for a majority of their sales (such as 80 percent). Types of customers include the following:

> *Ultimate consumers,* who buy goods and services for their personal or family use (for example, you and your family members).
> *Commercial and service consumers,* who buy goods and services for office and service organizations (for example, Prudential Insurance Co., *The New York Times*).
> *Industrial consumers,* who buy goods and services for use in the production process (for example, General Motors, Dow Chemical).
> *Wholesale and retail consumers,* who buy goods and services for resale to others (for example, J. C. Penney, Macy's).

Chapter 7 discusses ultimate consumers and industrial consumers in more detail.

THE CASE CONTINUES

*M*cDonald's extraordinary success has been thoroughly planned and executed. The proper use of microenvironmental forces has contributed greatly to the McDonald's success. Independent suppliers and processors who are carefully chosen by the company prepare the raw products according to the company's strict quality specifications. When the products are ready for the restaurants, they are shipped to central distribution centers that are owned

by independent businesspersons. From these centers the products and supplies are delivered to the restaurants.

This system of distribution ensures high-quality products and efficient operations. Instead of making purchases from dozens of suppliers, McDonald's restaurant managers are

able to concentrate their purchasing with one major source. To ensure that its high-quality standards are continuously met, McDonald's employs agricultural experts, microbiologists, and food-processing specialists to inspect and monitor its supplies, processors, and distribution centers. In addition, the company has rigorously standardized its operating procedures for receiving, storing, preparing, and delivering a product to customers.

MACROENVIRONMENTAL FORCES

Macroenvironmental forces include conditions of the broader environment, such as economic conditions, social and cultural values, technology, political and legal factors, nationalistic forces, and demographic conditions. Tracking these forces permits marketers to develop goods and services that meet the needs of shifting markets. For example, a macroenvironmental trend—the tendency for people to live longer—has given rise to geriatric centers and health aids for the elderly. Another trend—the increase in numbers of women who hold managerial positions—has caused department stores to establish boutiques for women executives, including maternity executive clothing. As noted, macroenvironmental forces, though much broader in scope than microenvironmental forces, are not necessarily more important.

A firm that does not react rapidly enough to macroenvironmental factors may suffer fatal losses.

Sometimes firms do not react quickly enough to environmental factors. Kueffel and Esser, a major producer of slide rules, did not fully understand how the development of the microprocessor and its use in hand-held calculators would affect the slide-rule business. Today, the slide rule has taken its place next to buggy whips and high-button shoes. Marketers, to be good ones, must be aware of current trends and farsighted enough to envision long-range possibilities.

Economic Conditions

Changing economic conditions continually confront marketers. As the economy moves from boom to bust, the firm must alter its marketing mix. During a period of robust economic activity, for example, a consumer may be satisfied to buy a Ford from a limited assortment of models and pay the manufacturer's list price. When the economy weakens, the consumer—if he or she purchases a car at all—often seeks a particular model at a discounted price. Marketers should constantly reassess the strength of the economy in order to fine-tune their marketing strategies. Economic conditions include consumer purchasing power, inflation, employment, and other important trends.

PURCHASING POWER

*P*urchasing power includes income, wealth, and credit.

Consumers' **purchasing power** is composed of income, wealth, and credit—with income being the most important factor. **Disposable personal income,** which consists of the remainder of income after taxes, represents the bulk of the consumer's spending power. After expenditures for basic needs—such as food, shelter, and clothing—he or she is left with **discretionary income.** Marketers attempt to persuade the consumer to use this income for the purchase of Hobie Cat sailboats, BMW cars, Gucci shoes, and a host of other luxury goods.

A very early and important study of consumer income was conducted by Ernst Engel, a German statistician. In 1857, he formulated a set of laws that associated the following changes in expenditure patterns with increases in family income:

1.   A smaller percentage is spent for food.
2.   A constant percentage is spent for clothing, whatever the income.
3.   A constant percentage is spent for housing and household operations, whatever the income.
4.   A larger percentage is spent for other items, such as education, health care, and leisure.

In general, **Engel's laws** reflect the spending patterns of today's consumers.

An individual's **wealth** consists of all of his or her material possessions—such as home, automobile, furniture—and all claims and rights, such as stock certificates and life-insurance policies. The wide distribution of wealth in the United States has resulted in a high standard of living for many Americans.

Credit is the ability to exchange something of value now for a promise to pay in the future. In 1987, the average worker used almost $24.00 out of every $100 of disposable personal income to satisfy debts.[3] People who buy on credit redirect and accelerate spending or consumption, but they do not create additional purchasing power. By borrowing instead of accumulating savings to make a particular purchase, an individual advances his or her buying timetable, and, perhaps, buys something that could be afforded only through the use of credit.

INFLATION

During the 1970s and the early 1980s, the United States was confronted with a high level of inflation that pushed the cost-of-living index to an annual increase of over 12 percent. Fortunately, annual increases have eased to a range of 3 to 6 percent. **Inflation** reduces the purchasing power of money and increases the prices of goods to consumers. At the onset of inflation, consumers readily purchase goods in the belief that prices will be even higher in the future. Once into an inflationary period, however, consumers begin to reduce their purchases.

❑ **Figure 3.3**
Employment and
unemployment
trends—1950 to 1984.

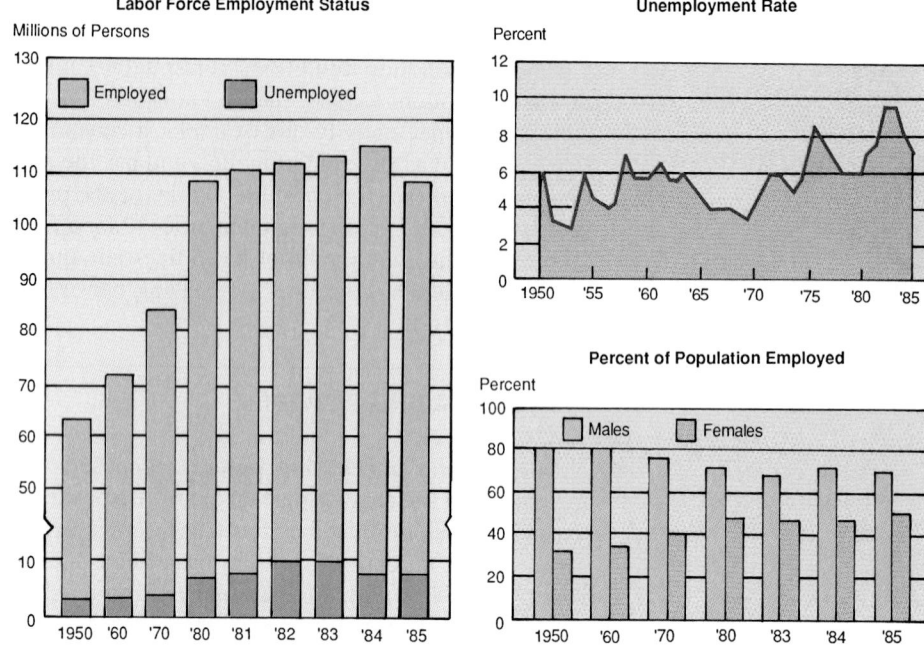

Labor Force Employment Status

Unemployment Rate

Percent of Population Employed

*Source: Statistical Abstract of the
United States: 1986* (106th ed.;
Washington, D.C.: Bureau of
Census, 1986), p. 386.

EMPLOYMENT LEVELS

Behind a country's economic health is its level of employment. As shown in
figure 3.3, in 1985 about 117.2 million persons—representing nearly 50 percent of the
population—were employed in the United States.

Working women represent a sizeable portion of today's work force. In 1950, only
28 percent of all workers were women; but by 1985 this percentage had increased to
44 percent. In 1950, only 25 percent of married women worked; but by 1986, 55
percent of all married women were employed.[4]

A high unemployment rate cuts into consumer spending power and makes a
marketing manager's job more difficult. In recent years, however, households containing two or more employed workers has lessened the impact of unemployment on
consumer expenditures.

OTHER TRENDS

*T*he United States'
economy has become
information-based
and international.

Several other important economic trends affect marketing. The United States
has moved from an agricultural economy to an industrial economy to an information
economy. U.S. workers are less frequently employed in factories and more frequently
employed in service and information-related jobs. Therefore, products and promotions must reflect this new economy.

In addition, the United States has moved from a national economy to a world
economy. What happens in places all over the world affects what happens in America.
And what U.S. companies once marketed only at home, they are now marketing
around the world. Consider the popularity of the commercial "I'd Like to Buy the
World a Coke." This commercial, with its catchy tune, was so popular that Coke
showed it every Christmas for a number of years. It highlights the fact that Coke
recognizes the international aspect of its market.

Still another important aspect of the economic climate involves time. Many
marketers during the 1970s considered only short-term gains. They focused all their
efforts on making one quarter's bottom line or earnings statement look better than
the last quarter's and ignored longer-term consequences of their actions. Many firms

□ Figure 3.4
Movement of households between states.

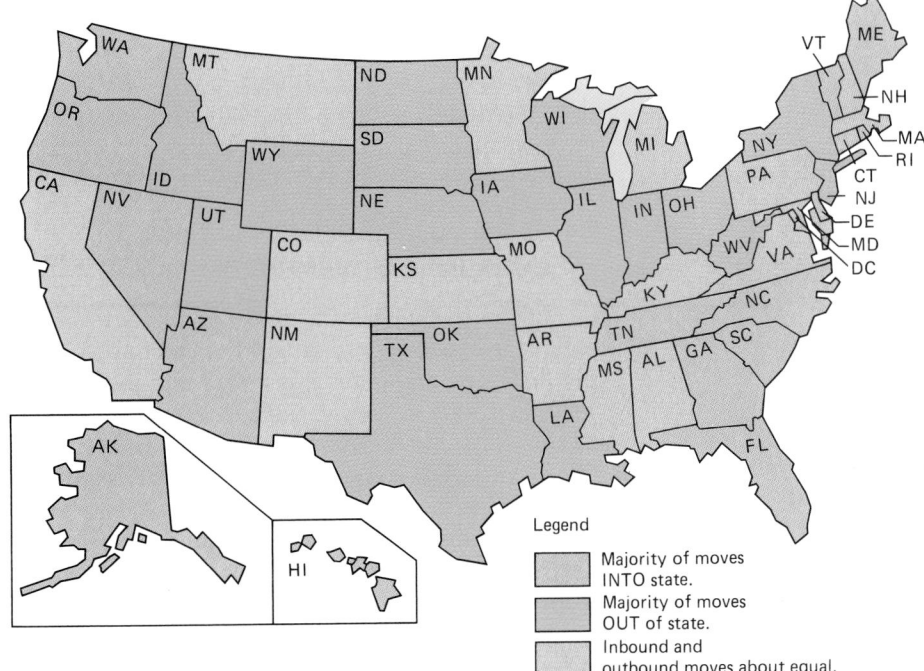

Legend

Majority of moves INTO state.

Majority of moves OUT of state.

Inbound and outbound moves about equal.

Source: 1987 traffic statistics of Allied Van Lines, Inc.

that followed this practice no longer exist. In planning a marketing approach, then, the marketer must ask not only what should be planned and marketed today but also what will be necessary in a few years.

America's economy is also moving geographically, from the North to the South and the Southwest. Marketers must be attuned to the fact that Americans are a mobile people who follow the best opportunities. More promotions and products must appeal to those who live in the South and Southwest (figure 3.4).

Social and Cultural Values

Social and cultural values that involve religious beliefs, the family, democracy, education, and free speech cannot be easily changed.

Certain social and cultural values, such as those involving religious beliefs, the family, democracy, education, and free speech, are basic to the fabric of U.S. society. Other values, such as current dress styles, are secondary. A society's basic values change very slowly over an extended period of time. Knowing that these basic values are nearly untouchable, marketers generally attempt to influence secondary values. Thus, realtors attempt to sell houses to apartment dwellers and designers create new fashions.

Social and cultural norms, or standards, often strongly influence consumers' actions. People with less income may feel uncomfortable shopping in a Sak's Fifth Avenue store, while those with more income may buy little from a Kmart. Certain social groups dress and act similarly. Businessmen commonly wear dark suits, silk ties, and wing tip shoes. The outfit for a successful businesswoman—at least in some corporations—often consists of a dark suit, a silk blouse, a scarf, and dark pumps. Truck drivers frequently prefer jeans, flannel shirts, leather boots, and wide-brimmed hats. We may not be a uniformed society, but sometimes our dress makes it appear that we are. Marketers need to keep these consumer differences and preferences in mind when they prepare product promotions.

Social and cultural trends currently of interest to marketers include the opening of new opportunities for minorities and women, the consumer movement, and heightened interest in physical fitness.

CIVIL RIGHTS AND WOMEN'S MOVEMENTS

The civil rights and the women's liberation movements have produced striking changes in U.S. society. Minority groups and women are finding doors open to them that were tightly closed a few years ago, and these new opportunities have resulted in broadened marketing opportunities for a variety of organizations. McDonald's and Coca-Cola are but two firms that have developed advertising campaigns specifically directed to Hispanics and blacks.

CONSUMER MOVEMENT

In the early 1900s, writer and crusader Upton Sinclair wrote, in *The Jungle,* about the shockingly unsanitary conditions of the meatpacking industry, sparking the first U.S. **consumer movement** and the passage of the Food and Drug Act of 1906. A resurgence of consumer activism occurred during the Depression of the 1930s, when one-fourth of the working population was out of work and could not afford to pay prevailing prices. Consumerist Stewart Chase's book, *Your Money's Worth,* helped to galvanize consumer activity. In the mid-1960s, homemakers in Denver, Colorado, picketed supermarkets to protest high food prices and fostered a third consumer movement. Ralph Nader's 1965 book, *Unsafe at Any Speed,* brought the issue of automobile safety to public attention.

As a result of these consumer movements, many producers have become much more aware of consumer problems and have developed enlightened solutions to them. Companies such as Ford Motors and the Chrysler Corporation have given their consumer relations departments more authority to deal with consumer complaints. Improved product quality, the open dating of perishable goods, and the unit pricing of food products by ounces or pounds are results of the consumer movement. Federal and state governments responded to consumerism by requiring clearer product warranties, passing consumer-credit protection acts, and taking other similar actions. By communicating with consumers, marketers obtain reactions to their products, promotions, and other marketing elements. The end result is to provide consumers with a better standard of living.

PHYSICAL FITNESS AND BETTER NUTRITION

The physical fitness trend has created several new industries and altered older ones. Racquetball clubs, body-building centers, sportswear, and running-shoe manufacturers have greatly benefited from this trend. In response to increased concerns about heart disease and cancer, the food industry now offers an ever-growing array

Pepper . . . and Salt

"It's not a rowing machine—it's what we call a boat."

Source: Reprinted from *The Wall Street Journal*—permission by Cartoon Features Syndicate

of sodium-free and sugar-free foods, natural cereals, and low-fat foods of every description. A new industry—cholesterol-testing, has emerged in response to new techniques measuring cholesterol levels in the blood.

LONG-TERM TRENDS

Marketers must recognize certain long-term trends in the U.S. society and culture in order to be effective. These include movements from the institution to the self, from hierarchy toward networks, and from either/or situations to options. Basically these trends mean that people in the United States are looking less to institutions and are depending more on themselves. Therefore, marketers must appeal to and promote individuals and not institutions.

*B*ecause people are coming to depend more on themselves than on institutions, marketers must appeal more to the individual.

Technology

One of the strongest macroenvironmental forces affecting the marketing effort is **technology**—technical methods for achieving practical purposes.

New and exciting technological developments have greatly affected the marketing programs of many companies. *Megatrends,* a best-selling book, enchanted readers by focusing on major events that are changing society. Many of these events have resulted from rapid advances in technology. Computer manufacturers, such as Commodore and Atari, have discovered that a computer whose introduction is delayed by a few months may be obsolete when it first appears on the market! People in the United States readily acknowledge that technology has a major influence on their lives.

Marketers must act and react quickly in response to new technology. Technical advances in many different fields, such as life science, biotechnology, and electronics, have spawned entirely new industries, altered older industries, and changed consumer lifestyles. For example, the introduction of the videocassette recorder (VCR) resulted in the growth of stores that specialize in the distribution of video cassettes. The VCR has been cited as a cause of declines in the audience for network television, movie attendance, and cable TV hookups.

*M*arketers must act and react quickly in response to new technology.

RESEARCH AND DEVELOPMENT

U.S. industry is now spending nearly as much money on research and development (R & D) as the federal government, which in the past provided the bulk of R & D funds (figure 3.5). In 1988, the total R & D outlays of businesses were expected to reach a new peak of $61.1 billion.[5] R & D expenditures as a percent of

❑ **Figure 3.5**
Sources of research and development funds expected for 1987.

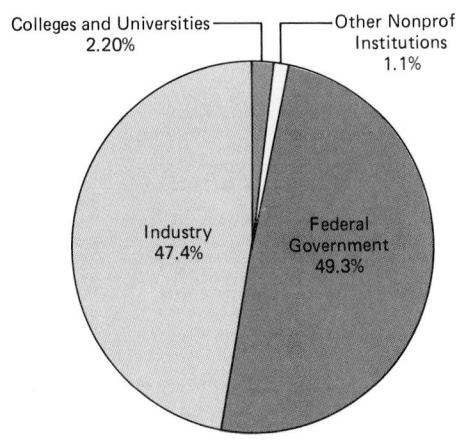

Colleges and Universities 2.20%

Other Nonprofit Institutions 1.1%

Industry 47.4%

Federal Government 49.3%

Source: Jules J. Duga and W. Halder Fisher, "Probable Levels of R & D Expenditures in 1987: Forecast and Analysis," Columbus Division of Battelle Memorial Institute, Dec. 1986, p. 6.

sales ranged from 0.42 percent in transportation services to 9.36 percent in the computer industry.[6] General Motors, the largest spender of R & D funds, has begun a major effort to integrate computers, software, robots, sensors, and telecommunication devices into automated manufacturing systems. These systems should reduce the costs of producing automobiles and permit the marketers of American cars to be more competitive with the Japanese. Marketers of industrial equipment should realize that the General Motors program could revolutionize the production process in a wide range of other companies.

HIGH-TECH/HIGH-TOUCH

The high-tech/high-touch trend injects the human element into high-tech applications.

Along with high technology has come a trend to emphasize warm, friendly feelings and the human element. Called **high-tech/high-touch,** it is a reaction to the nonhuman element of technology. It recognizes that, although computers and satellites can make it possible for us to do business with each other and be miles apart, we still have a need for close human interaction. Consider the factory with robots on its production lines and quality circles for its assembly-line workers. The high-tech

High-tech/high-touch.

high-tech to "Hi, Mom."

Ohio University is a leader in high technology. So it was no surprise that they knew exactly what they wanted in an integrated communications system. It would be based on fiber optics and meet their needs well into the next century.

Working together, we developed a system to serve the University's telephones and computer work stations in 110 buildings on the Athens, Ohio, campus. It can handle educational television, an energy control system, plus a security and fire detection system. It also has the growth potential to

link five regional campuses by microwave. Above all, it will give students and faculty unrivaled phone service, both local and long distance.

But Ohio University wanted more than just hardware and software. They wanted team players who knew how to make computer, communications and control systems work together, and who understood the need for continuing and conscientious service. Honeywell was the answer, because working together works. For more information, call 800-328-5111, ext. 1570.

Together, we can find the answers.

Honeywell

Source: Courtesy of Honeywell, Inc.

robots are countered by the high-touch interaction of the workers discussing solutions to common problems. As shown in the accompanying ad, Honeywell marketers clearly recognized that their high technology needed to appeal to the human element.

---

*A*re there too many fast-food restaurants chasing too few customers? By 1988, this question was being asked as intense competition resulted in several burger battles among McDonald's, Burger King, Wendy's and Hardee's. The battlefields were America's television screens, where consumers learned to heed messages such as "We do it like you do it," or watched the antics of "Mac Tonight" (a take-off on Mack the Knife).

The fast-food competition has broadened to include "gourmet"

THE CASE CONTINUES

hamburger shops, ethnic restaurants, and nutrition-conscious restaurants. All of these establishments are catering to the baby boomers who have grown up on a fast-food diet and still want its ease and convenience. Many consumers are looking for more variety and fresher, more nutritious and higher-quality foods than hamburgers, french fries, and shakes.

A major problem facing McDonald's is the decreasing supply of minimum wage teenage workers. There will be four million fewer teenagers in 1990 than in 1983. And although many older Americans—many of whom are retired—are increasingly filling these slots, McDonald's and other fast-food operators will continue to utilize technology, using more efficient equipment, to reduce costs and boost productivity. McDonald's is already known for producing automated hamburgers and french fries.

Political and Legal Factors

Our political and legal environment is constantly changing, and marketers must keep pace with these changes. As consumers, we "talk back" a great deal. There are organizations dedicated to holding down utility rate increases, maintaining social security payments, halting smoking, and thousands (probably millions) more. Consumer concerns are often transformed into laws, and these laws in turn alter the course of how companies conduct business. Public interest groups such as those led by Ralph Nader have galvanized consumers into action and have served as watchdogs for their interests.

Marketers do not operate in an entirely free environment. Government agencies, such as the Federal Trade Commission, the Food and Drug Administration, the Consumer Products Safety Commission, the Environmental Protection Agency, and the Office of Consumer Affairs all help to serve consumers' interests. These agencies cause marketers to take consumers' interests into account in their marketing programs.

For many years Braniff, with its brightly colored planes, was a major airline center in Dallas, Texas. Then, in 1978, the federal government deregulated the industry, and rough-and-tumble price wars broke out among the airlines. In 1982 Braniff suffered bankruptcy. For many months its hangar doors remained closed, although it finally obtained the funds to resume operations. Most government decisions do not push firms into bankruptcy, but many government actions do influence firms' marketing strategies.

Much government legislation that affects business is directed either to maintaining competition or to protecting consumers. In the early 1900s business regulation emphasized antitrust actions and the protection of competitors (figure 3.6); but in more recent years it has focused on guarding the rights of consumers.

❑ **Figure 3.6**
Early federal laws
affecting marketing.

Act	Date	Major Provisions
Sherman Act	1890	Forbids restraint of trade and creation of monopolies.
Clayton Act	1914	Prohibits price discrimination in commercial transactions, tying contracts between firms, and purchase of another company's stock where effect is to lessen competition.
Federal Trade Commission Act	1914	Prohibits unfair methods of competition; created the Federal Trade Commission (FTC).
Robinson–Patman Act	1936	Outlaws charging of different prices for the same goods to purchasers who are in competition; forbids suppliers to pay brokerage fees to "dummy" brokerage offices; prohibits promotional payments to a customer unless proportionally equal payments are made to the customer's competitors; forbids customers to knowingly receive from their suppliers price allowances that are unavailable to the customers' competitors.
Wheeler–Lea Act	1938	Allows the FTC to initiate action that prohibits false advertising of food, drugs, and cosmetics and halts business acts that cause injury to the public.

STATE LEGISLATION

*A*t the state level, unfair-trade and fair-trade laws have been used to protect small merchants from price competition.

At the state level, unfair-trade and fair-trade laws have been used to protect the small merchant from price competition from larger firms. **Fair-trade laws** granted manufacturers an exemption from antitrust legislation so that they could establish minimum resale prices for their goods. In 1975 Congress outlawed such laws in an attempt to reduce inflation. Since then, constant cries for their reinstatement have come from independent merchants.

Unfair-trade legislation prohibits retailers and wholesalers from selling below their cost (or below their cost plus a certain minimum markup, such as 6 percent at the retail level and 2 percent at the wholesale level). If a Thrifty drugstore located in a state that follows the 6-percent rule buys Pert shampoo at $2 a bottle from a wholesaler, then it cannot sell Pert for less than $2.12. In some states, certain items, such as milk, alcoholic beverages, and cigarettes, are covered by unfair-trade provisions. The provisions permit milk producers to recover their costs and encourages stable prices in alcoholic beverages and cigarettes, which discourage excessive consumption by these users who respond to price cutting.

FEDERAL LEGISLATION

*T*he most important pieces of early consumer legislation included two 1906 acts: the Pure Food and Drug Act and the Federal Meat Inspection Act.

Prior to the current consumer movement, the most important pieces of early consumer legislation included two 1906 acts: the Pure Food and Drug Act and the Federal Meat Inspection Act. The Pure Food and Drug Act was championed by an officer of the Department of Agriculture, who sought to eliminate the impurities in foods and drugs and to ensure their correct labeling. The Federal Meat Inspection Act was a response to a revealing book by author Upton Sinclair, who detailed the filth and harsh working conditions in meatpacking plants.

More than thirty years went by before Congress, in 1938, enacted additional consumer legislation—the Food, Drug, and Cosmetic Act, which updated the 1906 Pure Food and Drug Act and established the Food and Drug Administration (FDA).

The responsibility for ensuring that producers make truthful statements about their food, drug, and cosmetic items is unfortunately split between two government agencies. The FDA ensures that the labeling and packaging of these items is truthful, while the FTC, under the Wheeler-Lea Act, checks the advertising of these items for accuracy.

The consumer movement has caused the power of some federal agencies to be broadened.

The consumer movement has caused the power of some federal agencies to be broadened to include more consumer protection activities. In addition, Congress has enacted new consumer legislation: (1) to protect consumers against fraud and deception; (2) to guard their health and safety; and (3) to increase the amount of product information available to them.

In 1974, the FTC ordered direct sellers to provide customers who have made a purchase of over $20 with a three-day cooling-off period. During this time a customer can evaluate the purchase and cancel it, if desired. In 1975, the Magnuson-Moss Warranty and Federal Trade Commission Improvement Act was passed by Congress. Under this act, any product that sells for over $15 must contain an easy-to-understand warranty that indicates whether coverage under the warranty is full or limited. Because the FTC has the power to order advertisers to issue corrective advertising, advertisers check their ads more closely. In two highly publicized incidents, STP oil additive and Listerine mouthwash were cited by the FTC for misleading ads and were ordered to publish corrected ones. The FTC has declared its support for counter-advertising, advertising prepared by consumer groups to present the other side of a disputed product claim.

The FDA has been active in warning the public against food and drugs that may be harmful to their health. Under the Delaney clause, passed by Congress in 1958, the FDA must ban any product that shows a link with cancer. Because of this amendment, the producers of cyclamate, an artificial sweetener, and red dye no. 2, a food coloring, had to pull their products off the market.

In 1972, Congress created the Consumer Product Safety Commission (CPSC), which can ban or recall household products that present safety problems. The CPSC is responsible for checking the design, packaging, labeling, and operation of nearly 20,000 different consumer products made by nearly a million firms. As indicated in figure 3.7, the responsibility of the CPSC includes the administering of several

❑ **Figure 3.7**
Major acts administered by the Consumer Product Safety Commission.

Act	Date	Provisions
Flammable Fabrics Act	1953	Prohibits the sale of wearing apparel and fabrics that are highly flammable and dangerous.
Refrigerator Safety Act	1956	Prohibits the sale of refrigerators without a safety device that enables the door to be opened from the inside.
Federal Hazardous Substances Act	1960	To provide for the proper warning labels or the banning of any substances that may cause substantial injury or illness as a result of customary handling or use, including ingestion by children.
Poison Prevention Packaging Act	1970	Provides for special packaging to protect children from serious injury or illness resulting from the use or ingestion of household substances.
Consumer Product Safety Act	1972	Established the Consumer Product Safety Commission to set standards on certain products, require warning labels, and order product recalls.

❑ **Figure 3.8**
Major consumer credit
acts.

Act	Date	Provisions
Truth-in-Lending Act	1969	Provides for each consumer credit transaction a statement of the total finance charges in dollars and cents and in effective annual interest.
Credit Card Insurance Act	1970	Requires that credit cards be issued only in response to a request or application.
Fair Credit Reporting Act	1971	Protects the consumer from the use of inaccurate and obsolete information on his or her creditworthiness.
Fair Credit Billing Act	1975	Protects consumers against inaccurate and unfair billing practices by creditors.
Equal Credit Opportunity	1975	Prohibits discrimination by creditors on the basis of sex or marital status.
Amendments to Equal Credit Opportunity Act	1976	Expands the act to prohibit discrimination based on race, color, religion, national origin, age, or receipt of welfare benefits.
Holder-in-Due-Course Rule	1976	Provides consumers with a continuing right to raise claims against the misconduct of sellers against the credit contract has been passed to a third party.
Amendment to Truth-in-Lending Act	1977	Allows retailers to give discounts to customers who pay in cash rather than by use of a credit card.
Consumer Leasing Act	1977	Furnishes the consumer with the actual cost of a lease for personal property.
Fair Debt Collection Practices Act	1978	Prohibits creditors from using threats and undue pressure to collect debts.
Electronic Fund Transfer (EFT) Act	1978	Restricts organizations from requiring a consumer to establish an EFT account as a condition for the extension of credit and prohibits the issuance of unrequested EFT cards.
Amendment to Truth-in-Lending Act	1982	Clarifies credit terms through the use of model forms and reduces the number of disclosures required in the advertising of credit.
Credit Card Fraud Act	1984	Prohibits fraudulent use and counterfeiting of credit cards.

*T*he Truth-in-Lending Act
requires vendors to dis-
close the cost of their consumer finance charges in
both dollars and percent-
age terms.

important consumer protection laws. For marketing managers, the message of consumer legislation is clear: the cost of building safety into a product represents a
worthwhile long-term investment.

In 1969, Congress passed the Truth-in-Lending Act, which requires vendors to
disclose the cost of their consumer finance charges in both dollars and percentage
terms. Since then, several other significant pieces of credit legislation have been
enacted. As figure 3.8 shows, the purpose of these laws is to provide consumers with
more information about credit services and to protect them from unfair credit
practices.

Nationalistic Forces

International trade has made nationalistic forces an important component of the
marketing environment. We include in this category cultural differences that affect

The most exciting fast-food operation in the world was started in California by Maurice and Richard McDonald. In 1940, in San Bernardino they opened a drive-in restaurant which, in 1948, was converted to a self-service unit that was the forerunner of McDonald's as we know it today. Because of the success of this venture, they franchised six additional outlets on which they placed golden arches in order to create a single identity for all of the units.

Ray Kroc persuaded the McDonalds to permit him to become a McDonald franchisee and to franchise others throughout the country. Seeing the fantastic potential for fast-food eateries, in 1961, Kroc asked the brothers to sell out to him. They demanded the price of $2.7 million. As Kroc later commented, "I needed the McDonald name and those golden arches. What are you going to do with a name like Kroc?"

In the chicken carry-out business a situation similar to the McDonald story occurred. In 1955, the Kentucky Fried Chicken franchise chain was begun by 66-year-old Colonel Harland Sanders. In 1964, John Y. Brown, later the governor of Kentucky, purchased the organization;

THE REST OF THE STORY

The Tale of Two Spokespersons

and in 1974, he sold the operation to the giant distiller Heublein. Although Colonel Sanders was no longer a company official, he was retained by Heublein as a $200,000-a-year public relations figure. In contrast, when the McDonald brothers closed their deal with Ray Kroc, they completely dropped out of sight. What is the rest of the story regarding why the McDonalds never became spokespersons for the mammoth fast-food chain bearing their name?

Early in their negotiations, there was a personality clash between the reserved New England McDonald brothers and the flamboyant Chicago salesman, Ray Kroc. When Kroc built his first restaurant in Des Plaines, Illinois, he discovered that in order to store potatoes, he needed to modify the building plan and construct a basement. For legal reasons, he required written documentation from the McDonald brothers to alter the restaurant. Although Kroc made the alteration, the brothers refused to furnish him

with the required written statement. Kroc confided to his friends that the McDonalds acted as though they wanted him to fail.

In another incident, after the McDonalds had agreed to sell their organization to Kroc, they insisted at the last minute on retaining their original restaurant in San Bernardino. Kroc wanted this profitable outlet in order to generate necessary cash for the growing franchise chain. Kroc became extremely angry and disillusioned with the McDonalds when they would not budge from their position. Eventually, Kroc opened a restaurant directly across the street from the original one; and because he owned the McDonald name, the brothers were forced to rename their operation "The Big M." Kroc was greatly elated when he finally ran the brothers' restaurant out of business.

Sources: Adapted from Robert Johnson, "McDonald's Combines a Dead Man's Advice with Lively Strategy," Dec. 18, 1987, pp. 1, 13. Ray Kroc with Robert Anderson, *Grinding It Out* (Chicago: Henry Regnery Company, 1977), pp. 69, 70, 115, 116; and "The Burger That Conquered the Country," *Time*, Sept. 17, 1973, pp. 86, 87.

marketing efforts, as well as the tendency of nations to favor domestically made products.

U.S. marketers have often been accused of disregarding the customs of foreign cultures. The fast-moving pace of American businesspersons, for example, is out of place in South American countries. In Japan the need for a group consensus often delays decision making. Since the passage of restrictive legislation in 1977, under-the-table payments by U.S. businesspersons to foreign officials are illegal. Because such payments are a way of life in some foreign countries, this prohibition has placed Americans at a competitive disadvantage in some business dealings.

Nationalism encourages the development of stronger domestic industries, and this results in greater self-sufficiency. International events will probably cause nationalism to remain an important factor in overseas marketing activities. All countries seek a favorable balance of trade, which means that they want to export more goods than they import. Domestically produced goods are being heavily promoted in the

International events will cause nationalism to remain an important factor in overseas marketing activities.

United States for that reason—for example, TV commercials have featured Bob Hope, Carol Channing, and other celebrities flaunting "made-in-the-U.S.A." labels.

Demographic Forces

*D*emographic forces include age, race, sex, and population density.

Demography is the study of vital and social statistics. Macroenvironmental forces that have a demographic basis include age, race, density of population, and population of women versus men. Astute marketers look closely at the demographic aspects of the population and target their marketing accordingly.

For example, we know that the U.S. population is aging. Since 1972, its median age has risen to over thirty-one years, and median age will continue to rise as the post–World War II generation (the baby boomers) moves toward middle age. Because of better medical technology, nutrition, and physical conditioning programs, older people are living longer and are more active than their counterparts of a generation ago. Informed marketers are in tune with promoting products to this more mature audience. For example, some magazines target just the older citizen— such as *Modern Maturity*. And you have probably noticed that more and more advertising is aimed at mature consumers.

As noted, the 68 million baby boomers who were born between 1946 and 1962 form an important part of the aging U.S. population. Baby boomers who earn roughly $40,000 or more annually and who are in professional or management positions have often been referred to as Yuppies—young urban professionals.[6] These young consumers purchase in record numbers expensive foreign cars, gourmet hamburgers, home physical fitness equipment, and the like. By catering to the yuppies' desire to experience the good life and to display their wealth, marketers can reap large rewards (figure 3.9).

Race, as we pointed out earlier, is a factor in the marketing environment. Enlightened marketers realize that they should target their appeals and products to specific racial segments of the population, such as blacks and Hispanics.

The density of the population means the number of people living in a given area. Since 1980 rural growth has decreased while cities have continued to grow steadily.

❏ **Figure 3.9**
Characteristics of Yuppies.

A look at how the elite ranks of the baby boomers compare with the adult population at large.		
	U.S. Adult Population	Yuppies*
Cigarette smokers	36%	20%
American Express credit card holders	6%	21%
Gold AmEx card holders	2%	3%
Used cards within last three months	38%	70%
Foreign travel within last three years	11%	33%
Moviegoer within last year	44%	75%
'Involved in physical fitness'	31%	66%

Source: Simmons Market Research Bureau: "Study of Media and Markets"

*25–39 years old, earning more than $40,000 in professional or managerial positions.

Marketers must look at population density figures in order to analyze shifts in population and thus determine where marketing efforts should be strengthened or changed.

Still another demographic aspect of the marketing environment is the number of women versus the number of men in the population. Women in the United States form an important and a changing market. For example, they head up over 30 percent of all households. Marketers have realized that women outlive men, that they share housekeeping duties with their husbands, and that they work in increasing numbers outside the home. Marketing campaigns must be adjusted accordingly.

THE CASE CONTINUES

*B*ecause McDonald's deals with millions of customers and sells billions of burgers, it is broadly exposed to political and legal actions. Through the years McDonald's has encountered legal actions ranging from franchise litigation to building restrictions. In a celebrated case, McDonald's filed suit against a Los Angeles inner-city franchisee charging that he allegedly entered into another franchise contract with Popeyes Famous Fried Chicken, Inc. and violated a McDonald's agreement prohibiting involvement with another fast-food chain. In addition, McDonald's cited the refusal of this black franchisee to contribute the required amount to its advertising program. The franchisee countersued claiming that his wife owned the Popeyes outlets and that McDonald's advertising was not directed to inner-city residents. Another charge alleged that the company discriminated against blacks in awarding franchises. The case was finally settled when McDonald's purchased the four inner-city restaurants from the franchisee and both parties were able to declare a stand-off.

GOAL SUMMARY

1. **Identify the microenvironmental forces affecting marketers.** The major microenvironmental forces affecting marketers include the organization of the company, suppliers, marketing intermediaries, competitors, and customers.
2. **Name the macroenvironmental forces that influence marketing decisions.** Included among the most important macroenvironmental forces are economic, social and cultural, technological, political and legal, and demographic forces.
3. **Describe the factors that give rise to consumer purchasing power.** Consumer purchasing power is composed of income, wealth, and credit—with income being the most important factor.
4. **Understand how technology affects marketers.** Technology uses the results of science to create new products. Technology often involves impersonal or distant relationships. To counteract this, marketers need to develop marketing programs that emphasize human interactions.
5. **Identify the major laws that affect marketing.** The Sherman Act (1890) and the Clayton Act (1914) prohibit actions that would lessen competition or tend to create a monopoly. The Federal Trade Commission Act (1914) prohibits unfair methods of competition and created the Federal Trade Commission. The Robinson-Patman Act (1936) made it illegal to charge different prices for the same goods to purchasers who are in competition. The Wheeler-Lea Act (1938) halts unfair business acts that injure the public and prohibits the false advertising of food, drugs, and cosmetics.

KEY TERMS

Microenvironmental Forces, **p. 61**
Macroenvironmental Forces, **p. 66**
Purchasing Power, **p. 67**
Disposable Personal Income, **p. 67**
Discretionary Income, **p. 67**
Engel's Laws, **p. 67**
Wealth, **p. 67**
Credit, **p. 67**

Inflation, **p. 67**
Consumer Movement, **p. 70**
Technology, **p. 71**
High-Tech/High-Touch, **p. 72**
Fair-Trade Laws, **p. 74**
Unfair-Trade Legislation, **p. 74**
Nationalism, **p. 77**
Demography, **p. 78**

CHECK YOUR LEARNING

1. Microenvironmental forces are broad environmental forces that affect the decisions of marketing managers.   **T/F**
2. All of the following are microenvironmental forces except: (a) suppliers, (b) competitors, (c) customers, (d) legislation.
3. The time and place requirements of customers are satisfied mainly by (a) financial specialists, (b) physical distribution specialists, (c) wholesalers, (d) exchange specialists.
4. All of the following are major components of the purchasing power of consumers except: (a) income, (b) interest, (c) credit, (d) wealth.
5. The U.S. economy has moved from: (a) agricultural to industrial to information, (b) agricultural to information to computer, (c) handicraft to industrial to computer, (d) agricultural to handicraft to industrial.
6. U.S. industry spends nearly as much money on research and development than the federal government.   **T/F**
7. High technology appears to create a need for less human interaction.   **T/F**
8. Legislation that prohibits a retailer from selling Colgate toothpaste below the retailer's cost is: (a) the Federal Trade Commission Act, (b) the Robinson-Patman Act, (c) a fair-trade law, (d) an unfair-trade law.
9. The act that requires a bank to disclose the cost of its consumer finance charges in both dollars and percentage is the: (a) Fair Credit Reporting Act, (b) Truth-in-Lending Act, (c) Equal Credit Opportunity Act, (d) Fair Credit Billing Act.
10. Although Boeing Aircraft must disclose to its stockholders any under-the-table payments that it makes to foreign officials, these payments are lawful under the U.S. legal code.   **T/F**

QUESTIONS FOR REVIEW AND DISCUSSION

1. Define the key terms listed at the beginning of this chapter.
2. In the future, will suppliers be as important to companies as they are today?
3. Why would BankAmerica be considered a microenvironmental force for some organizations?
4. What is the significance of Engel's laws to marketers?
5. Provide three examples (that are not mentioned in the text) of cultural values that affect marketers' plans.
6. Why is a knowledge of high-tech/high-touch important to marketers?
7. How has deregulation of the banking industry affected the programs of bank marketing managers?
8. Provide examples of how consumer legislation has affected the marketing plans for the following products: Listerine, Delco car batteries, and Encyclopedia Britannica.
9. How does the responsibility for ensuring truthful advertising differ between the FDA and the FTC?
10. How does nationalism affect General Motors' approach to foreign markets?
11. What is the significance of an aging population to McDonald's, Columbia Pictures, and Levi Strauss?

NOTES

1. "Sears Buyer Is Now Product Marketing Manager: Swift," *Marketing News,* June 30, 1978, p. 1.
2. Milton Moskowitz, Michael Katz, and Robert Levering, *Everybody's Business* (New York: Harper & Row Publishers, Inc., 1980), p. 813.
3. *Statistical Abstract of the United States: 1987* (107th ed., Washington, DC: Bureau of the Census, 1986), p. 490.
4. *Statistical Abstract of the United States: 1987,* p. 382.
5. Jules J. Duga and W. Halder Fisher, "Probable Levels of R & D Expenditures in 1988: Forecast and Analysis," Columbus Division of Battelle Memorial Institute, Dec. 1987, p. 7.
6. Jules J. Duga and W. Halder Fisher, "Probable Levels of R & D Expenditures in 1987: Forecast and Analysis," Columbus Division of Battelle Memorial Institute, Dec. 1986, pp. 1, 21, 22, 24.
7. "The Year of the Yuppie," *Newsweek,* Dec. 31, 1984, p. 17.

On Chocolate Avenue, the main street in Hershey, Pennsylvania, the streetlights are shaped like Hershey kisses. For nearly one hundred years the dominant company in the city of Hershey has been the Hershey Foods Corporation, maker of the famous Hershey bars. Reese's, a maker of peanut butter cups, was another candy producer in Hershey, but in 1963 Hershey Foods acquired the company.

The founder of Hershey Foods, Milton Hershey, left school after the fourth grade. As a teenager, he served as an apprentice candymaker in Lancaster, Pennsylvania. At 19, he started a penny-candy operation in Philadelphia: it promptly failed. He then traveled to Chicago and entered the sticky business of making caramels. When this business collapsed, he moved to New York where he opened yet another business. It too quickly failed. Finally, Hershey went back to Lancaster and established the Lancaster Caramel Company. By 1884, this company was hailed as the world's largest caramel factory.

In 1900, Mr. Hershey sold his caramel business for $1 million and immediately began thinking about ways to put his new fortune to work. After considering several proposals, he decided to build a chocolate factory in his birthplace of Derry Church, Pennsylvania (renamed Hershey in 1906). By 1905, the factory was in production, and by 1911, Hershey was selling $5 million of chocolate annually.

Mr. Hershey's greatest inspiration occurred as a result of attending the 1893 World Exposition in Chicago. He noted the popularity of the chocolate-making equipment and the delicious chocolate it produced. At this time only the wealthy could afford to indulge in chocolate. Hershey reasoned that if he could produce inexpensive chocolate candy, customers would beat a path to his door. He believed that because of its rich taste, chocolate would remain a favorite confection of consumers. On the other hand, he felt that caramels

were just a fad. In 1921, Hershey introduced nationally the first Hershey bar, which was composed of pure chocolate and sold for only five cents.

Hershey's reliance on chocolate confections continued until 1973, when the company was jolted by a dramatic rise in the price of cocoa beans. This increase in the cost of its raw materials caused Hershey's earnings to drop by 30 percent. In 1976 and 1977, another steep rise in cocoa beans occurred. As a result of these price increases, the company fashioned a strategic corporate plan that would reduce its dependence on chocolate. The company, which was already making macaroni, added to its pasta line: today it is the second-largest macaroni producer in the country, just behind the Borden Corporation. In 1979, Hershey purchased the Friendly Ice Cream Corporation, which operates a chain of family restaurants. In 1985, the company purchased the firm that makes Luden's cough drops and Queen Anne chocolate-covered cherries. Although Hershey is continuing to diversify, its management does not see its chocolate sales falling below 50 percent of the total volume.

In the late 1960s, candy consumption hit a peak of twenty pounds per person annually. Then, several factors caused consumption to turn downward. In 1969, the five-cent candy bar disappeared forever. In the 1970s, a large number of new snack products that competed with chocolate appeared on the market. Another factor was the growing concern about nutrition and bulging waistlines. An additional factor was the graying of the population. Older individuals eat less candy than younger people. In 1982, chocolate and total confectionary consumption hit bottom at about sixteen pounds annually per person. Since then, it has been slowly rising again.

Hershey responded to its environment by introducing new products and positioning older ones to specific markets. The company introduced Take Five, a candy bar designed to appeal to the high-income market, in test markets. (After several years, the product was removed in 1986.) An old standard that has been heavily promoted to the mature market is Hershey Kisses. Skor, another product introduced in 1981, is a butter-toffee bar directed to the adult population. New Trail, initially a granola bar and now chocolate-covered, was designed for the adult market. In 1987, the company introduced Bar None, which features a chocolate wafer and peanut bar. Hershey also entered the packaged beverage market with premixed chocolate milk.

In order to compete effectively against other candy producers, the company needed to obtain greater product recognition and to presell consumers on the benefits of its products. In the early 1980s, a unique promotional opportunity came Hershey's way with the debut of the popular film "E.T., The Extraterrestial." The E.T. character followed a trail of Reese's Pieces. After viewing the film, large numbers of children wanted the candy. Hershey spent a million dollars promoting Reese's in connection with the movie's opening and continued to use the E.T. theme under an agreement with the film's producers.

With new product introductions and buyouts of other companies, Hershey is meeting its goal of becoming a diversified food and food-related company. Internationally, Hershey and several foreign firms have formed joint ventures that produce and distribute candy in foreign markets. Hershey has also granted certain foreign companies licensing agreements to produce Hershey products.

Perhaps one of the most unusual aspects of Hershey's operation is that a philanthropic organization receives nearly half of Hershey's profits. The Milton Hershey school owns 43 percent of the stock in Hershey's Foods. Mr. Hershey wanted to give boys and girls who had lost one or both parents, and who needed financial support, a family-like atmosphere for living and learning.

Issues for Discussion

1. Are microenvironmental forces as great a concern to Hershey as macroenvironmental forces? Explain.

2. Do you believe that Hershey's strategic corporate plan will be successful in our current environment? Discuss.

3. What other product lines do you believe Hershey could add?

4. Identify the three most important macroenvironmental forces that you believe will affect Hershey in the next ten years. How would you advise Hershey to react to these forces?

Sources: Adapted from "Hershey Chocolate Co. Vows New Bar None Bar," *Vending Times,* Dec. 1987, p. 14; N. R. Kleinfield, "Hershey Bites Off New Markets," *The New York Times,* July 22, 1984, p. 4F; Henry Altman, "Hershey's 'New' Ingredient," *Nation's Business,* June 1983, p. 42; and Gay Jervey, "New Hershey Bar Takes Aim at Mars," *Advertising Age,* Nov. 28, 1983, p. 2.

O U T L I N E

CHAPTER

4

Marketing Research and Marketing Information Systems

LEARNING GOALS

After reading this chapter, you should be able to:

1. Explain the role of information in marketing.
2. Discuss the nature of the marketing research process.
3. Describe how marketing problems are identified.
4. List the types of qualitative and quantitative research methods.
5. Explain the function of marketing information systems in marketing management.

Jay Mary has been in the food business for years, working in his family-owned chain of supermarkets. When in 1983 a national chain offered to buy out the company, which operated five stores in the Minneapolis–St. Paul area of Minnesota, the family accepted. Changes in consumers' lifestyles and increased competition from the national chains made the Mary company less and less profitable through the years, and Jay Mary, who was president by the time of the sale, had long considered moving from the supermarket business to the fast-food business. From his experience in the supermarket business, he knew that the proportion of people who ate out was on the rise.

Evidently, people juggling careers, family, and school—or various combinations—often require quick and convenient meals. The growing number of women in the work force and families' higher levels of disposable income have both made possible and encouraged the purchase of meals outside of the home.

Mary had read in industry publications that the fast-food industry was considered mature. Once an industry is mature, it is harder for new companies to enter the market. Still, the National Restaurant Association estimated that in 1983 fast-food restaurant sales exceeded $37 billion. This meant that there was plenty of demand, at least for the existing companies such as McDonald's, Burger King, Kentucky Fried Chicken, and the various pizza franchises. Sales in the chicken segment were approximately $4 billion and were predicted to increase by 20 percent in one year. With the exception of the Mexican foods segment, fast-food chicken products were demonstrating the most growth. Increases in these two segments were predicted to outpace other areas for the next several years.

Mary decided that if research indicated that people in the Minneapolis–St. Paul area liked hot-and-spicy

Cajun-style chicken, he would purchase a Popeyes Famous Fried Chicken and Biscuits, Inc. franchise, which sold this uniquely prepared food. Popeyes was the third-largest fast-food chicken company. Kentucky Fried Chicken, the market leader, controlled half of the market, having ten times more units than Popeyes. Church's was a distant second. The average sales of Popeyes' units of food was, however, twice the sales of a Kentucky Fried Chicken unit: $12,000 compared to $6,000 per week.

In 1983 Popeyes had about 400 restaurants in 30 states and in several foreign countries. The typical Popeyes' customer was supposedly upbeat, young, employed, and equally male and female and black and white. Marketers at Popeyes claimed that Popeyes' hot-and-spicy chicken had universal appeal. Since Popeyes' success, Kentucky Fried Chicken had introduced its own hot-

and-spicy chicken in 400 of its restaurants, most of which were in the South. Another hot-and-spicy chicken franchisor, Bojangles, had also entered the market since Popeyes came on the scene. Bojangles had been successful, but again in the South.

Although Mary was interested in purchasing a Popeyes' franchise, he had serious concerns about whether a sufficient number of people in the St. Paul–Minneapolis area would react favorably to the hot-and-spicy chicken. Unless he could comfortably predict that reaction would be positive, he would not undertake the venture.

From reading, Mary had determined that the most likely customers were those with children, of whatever age. From publications he also learned that families with working mothers also tend to eat out more frequently. A survey of one thousand adults yielded the following results concerning age, sex, amount spent, and frequency of eating at fast-food restaurants:

■ Known for its hot-and-spicy chicken, Popeyes continues to expand.
Source: Courtesy of Popeyes Famous Fried Chicken and Biscuits, Inc.

Amount Spent on Own Meal	Amount Spent by Sex	
	Male	Female
$4.00 +	27%	18%
$3.01 to 4.00	25%	19%
$2.50 to 3.00	28%	28%
Less than 2.50	19%	31%

Age	Frequency of Eating Out Per Month
18–24	8
25–34	5
35–49	4
50–64	3
65 +	3

Mary read that industry analysts claimed that fast-food companies have a bright future. However, they believed that these companies will have to keep their operations simple, controllable, and offer value and service to the customer.

Issues for Discussion

1. What kind of information and research does Mary need?

2. If Mary conducts a survey, what contact techniques and sample plan should he use?

3. Should open-end or closed-end questions be used? Does Mary have a need for a marketing information system at this time?

Sources: Elizabeth Rhein, "Popeyes Flexes Its Muscles," *Restaurant Business Magazine,* May 20, 1987; "Popeyes Spices the Competition," *Sales & Marketing Management,* September 12, 1983, p. 29; "Popeyes' Fried Chicken Is Hot—And Getting Hotter," *Sales & Marketing Management,* January 16, 1984, p. 24; Anna Solczynski, "Serving Up a Variety of Choices," *Advertising Age,* November 21, 1983, p. M10 + ; and Eileen Norris, "Popeyes Making a Name in the Chicken Game," *Advertising Age,* November 21, 1983, p. M23.

*M*arket research is an important part of the marketing process. Before introducing a product or service, well-prepared marketing managers use the scientific method of identifying questions—developing hypotheses—and then testing them by collecting and analyzing data. This chapter describes the marketing research process, from problem identification to data presentation, in detail. The two broad types of decisions marketers continually make—routine and nonroutine decisions—determine the kinds of information sought in the research process. The chapter ends with a discussion of marketing information systems, which help marketers make routine decisions. ■

THE ROLE OF INFORMATION IN DECISION MAKING

While shopping in a supermarket one day, Bruce F. Failing had a brainstorm. Why not put advertisements on shopping carts? Failing, a salesman for a company that manufactured food processors, was itching to start a business, and now he had an idea that felt right. But while he was eager to establish his own business, he felt that acting on intuition alone was too risky. Instead, Failing spent two years and a substantial amount of money conducting market research. At the end of that period, he felt ready to make a decision and founded the company Actmedia.[1]

❑ **Figure 4.1**
  Types of decisions.

Routine	Nonroutine
Characteristics: Made frequently, situation familiar. Example: Pricing of airline tickets.	Characteristics: Made infrequently, new situation. Example: A new product for First National Bank.

Need for Information Increases ⟶

Time to Make Decision Increases ⟶

Cost of Acquiring Information Increases ⟶

Was Failing better off spending those two years collecting information rather than starting his company sooner? What did the information he gathered tell him? We will begin to answer these questions by describing the types of decisions marketers make.

Types of Decisions

The role that information plays in decision making depends on the type of decision to be made. There are two general types of decisions: routine and nonroutine, as shown in figure 4.1. For decisions the marketer considers significant, the effort to acquire and use information generally increases.

ROUTINE DECISIONS

*S*ignificant routine and nonroutine decisions require information.

Routine decisions, although made repeatedly, may be very significant in terms of the organization's welfare. Pricing decisions are one such example. Airlines make pricing decisions almost daily, but the frequency with which they are made does not mean they are not significant—indeed, they strongly affect sales and profitability.

*S*etting prices on existing goods and services is an example of routine decision making.

The very nature of routine decisions often allows management to anticipate information they will need in the future and to collect it for this purpose. Information typically is used to modify previously made routine decisions. Since the marketer is familiar with the nature of the decision, alternatives and important variables have probably already been identified, but information on current conditions affecting each variable is needed. For instance, in pricing airline tickets, knowledge of competitors' prices is needed, and on a continuous basis. (A formalized procedure for collecting, storing, and retrieving information needed for routine decision making is called a *marketing information system.* Marketing information systems are discussed at the close of this chapter.)

NONROUTINE DECISIONS

Nonroutine decisions, when perceived as significant, usually generate uneasiness in the decision maker. Failing's decision whether to start a new company to sell ad space on shopping carts is a case in point. Decision makers in such situations normally seek information to improve their confidence, as well as the outcome of their actual decisions. Bankers have recently found themselves in such a situation. Deregulation has intensified competition for customers and made many previously routine decisions nonroutine. For example, before they introduce new products, bankers now want to know how their customers are likely to react.

*I*nformation typically plays a larger role in nonroutine decisions.

Information plays a much broader role in nonroutine decisions than in routine decisions. It may serve to identify key situational variables and alternatives. For

❏ **Figure 4.2**
Characteristics of
useful information.

Source: Reprinted with
permission of Macmillan
Publishing Company from
Marketing Research, 3/e, by
Donald S. Tull and Del I.
Hawkins. Copyright © 1984 by
Macmillan Publishing Company.

1.	Availability	—The information must be available when needed. Information provided at the end of next month is of little value in preparing a competitive bid due Friday.
2.	Relevance	—The information must fit the decision–making requirements. For example, it must be current, use appropriate units of measurement, and use appropriate definitions of classes.
3.	Accuracy	—The information must meet or exceed the accuracy level required for the decision.
4.	Sufficiency	—There must be enough information to make the decision.
5.	Benefits exceed cost	—The cost of gathering and processing the information should not exceed the value of the information to the organization.

example, Failing's research might have identified the willingness of supermarkets and advertisers to cooperate as a key variable. Information can form the basis for an estimate of probable outcomes. Even a clear definition of the decision to be made sometimes depends on gathering information.

Characteristics of Useful Information

*U*seful information is available, relevant, accurate, sufficient, and its benefits exceed its costs.

Whether it is used for routine or nonroutine decisions, useful information has certain characteristics. (See figure 4.2.) For example, it is available. Data that for some reason cannot be collected before the decision or that belong exclusively to a competitor lack availability and therefore are not useful, at least not until they are obtained. In considering data availability, then, two questions should be asked: Who has the data, and when, if ever, can the data be obtained?

Useful data are *accurate.* Accurate data can be described as data that are *valid* and *without error.* If the same mistake is made repeatedly, then the data are said to *lack validity.* Lack of validity indicates that there is *systematic error* in the gathering or analyzing of information. Data with random mistakes, where the amount or cause of error is different with each measurement, lack *reliability.* Reliability refers to the accuracy of the measurement techniques used in collecting data.

Keep the characteristics in figure 4.2 in mind as you read more about market research.

Decision Areas and Data Needs

All areas of marketing are open to successful data-gathering projects. Figure 4.3 shows some of the areas in which marketing managers find data necessary for formulating their plans. Since the marketing plan relies heavily on analysis of the market, it should come as no surprise that more companies engage in certain kinds of sales and marketing research than in any other kind of data gathering. More than ninety percent of the companies in the figure measure market potential, analyze market share, determine market characteristics, and analyze sales. Short-range and long-range forecasting and studies of business trends also receive considerable attention. In contrast, marketing managers appear to depend more on intuition—experience and personal feelings—to make decisions in the area of corporate responsibility.

Marketing managers can obtain information through marketing research and a marketing information system.

❏ **Figure 4.3** Decision areas with information needs.

		Total	Done by Marketing Research Department	Done by Another Department	Done by Outside Firm
Advertising research	Motivation research	47%	30%	2%	15%
	Copy research	61	30	6	25
	Media research	68	22	14	32
	Studies of ad effectiveness	76	42	5	29
	Studies of competitive advertising	67	36	11	20
Business economics and corporate research	Short-range forecasting (up to 1 year)	89	51	36	2
	Long-range forecasting (over 1 year)	87	49	34	4
	Studies of business trends	91	68	20	3
	Pricing studies	83	34	47	2
	Plant and warehouse location studies	68	29	35	4
	Acquisition studies	73	33	38	2
	Export and international studies	49	22	25	2
	MIS (management information system)	80	25	53	2
	Operations research	65	14	50	1
	Internal company employees	76	25	45	6
Corporate responsibility research	Consumers' "right to know" studies	18	7	9	2
	Ecological impact studies	23	2	17	4
	Studies of legal constraints on advertising and promotion	46	10	31	5
	Social values and policies studies	39	19	13	7
Product research	New product acceptance and potential	76	59	11	6
	Competitive product studies	87	71	10	6
	Testing of existing products	80	55	19	6
	Packaging research: design or physical characteristics	65	44	12	9
Sales and market research	Measurement of market potential	97	88	4	5
	Market share analysis	97	85	6	6
	Determination of market characteristics	97	88	3	6
	Sales analysis	92	67	23	2
	Establishment of sales quotas, territories	78	23	54	1
	Distribution channel studies	71	32	38	1
	Test markets, store audits	59	43	7	9
	Consumer panel operations	63	46	2	15
	Sales compensation studies	60	13	43	4
	Promotional studies of premiums, coupons, sampling, deals, etc.	58	38	14	6

OBTAINING INFORMATION THROUGH MARKETING RESEARCH

Conducting marketing research means gathering, recording, and analyzing marketing data systematically and objectively.

Marketing research is defined by the American Marketing Association's committee on definitions as the systematic and objective process of gathering, recording, and analyzing data for marketing decision making.[3]

Marketing research, by definition, must be an organized endeavor. Since data collected in market research serve as the basis of decisions, inaccuracies may lead unknowingly to undesirable and expensive outcomes. G. Heileman Brewing Company studied and introduced to the market its low-alcohol (LA) beer based on friends' reactions to the beer at backyard barbecues. Although G. Heileman's informal study may have produced worthwhile information, it cannot be called marketing research.[4]

To eliminate bias, the researcher must maintain an objective, detached approach—objective in seeking the facts, whether they seem favorable or unfavorable, and detached in refusing to allow possible personal gain or loss to color the research

Source: Courtesy of McGraw-Hill

results. Constant checking to ensure that the research plan is properly carried out also helps eliminate bias.

Sources of Marketing Research

*M*anagers decide whether to conduct research or hire independent research firms.

Managers must decide how they will obtain their marketing research. Most large consumer products manufacturers, such as Procter & Gamble, have their own research departments. Often, even organizations without research departments elect to do their own research, especially when it seems uncomplicated.

When the research requires intellectual detachment, special knowledge, or special equipment, and when the research project can be precisely defined, outside researchers may be employed.[5] Both large and small firms contract with independent research firms.

The independent research firms in the United States market alone receive over $1 billion a year in revenues. (See figure 4.4.) These companies are divided into categories based on what services they offer.[6] Research requiring large-scale, continuous data gathering has such high costs that the results are offered to any organization that wants to purchase them on a regular basis. Research firms that sell the same research results to several firms offer a **syndicated service.** A. C. Nielsen, for example, provides a syndicated service that tracks TV program ratings.

*S*yndicated services provide large-scale continuous data gathering.

❑ **Figure 4.4**
Worldwide expenditures for market research by independent research firms.

Source: Portion reprinted with permission from *Advertising Age* November 1, 1984, Copyright © Crain Communications, Inc. All rights reserved.

Market Research: Worldwide Expenditures				
(Prevailing year exchange rates, $ billion)	1988*	1983	1979	1977
North America**	2.0	1.4	1.1	.6
Europe	1.5	1.1	.8	.5
Asia/Oceania	.41	.3	.2	.15
Central/South America	.11	.08	.05	.04
Africa	.05	.04	.03	.02
Middle East	.03	.02	.02	.01
Total world market	4.1	2.94	2.20	1.32
	Source: Eileen Cole			

*Projections

**The U.S. represents approximately $1.3 billion of the 1983 total

Marketing research tailored to the needs of the purchasing organization is designated as **customized research.** Burke Marketing Service undertakes many customized research studies for clients. For instance, the Campbell Soup Company may contract with Burke to test market a new dehydrated soup. Burke would then market this product in several cities. Sales in these areas provide the data for projecting sales on a national level.

*C*ustomized research firms provide special data.

We can subdivide customized research firms into two categories: full and limited service. Full-service researchers conduct complete research projects. The advantage of employing such firms is their ability to act as the research department of the client firm. Limited-service firms specialize in some of the steps required to complete a research project—such as questionnaire design, interviewing, computer data entry, or statistical analysis. Such firms help clients to meet needs for specialized knowledge or equipment related to research projects.

There exist hundreds of small independent marketing research firms, many of which are listed in the American Marketing Association's *Directory of Marketing Research Organizations.* Many college and university faculty members also perform marketing research.

THE MARKETING RESEARCH PROCESS

Whether managers have marketing research done internally or by independent firms, they must be familiar with the marketing research process (figure 4.5). For the research to be objective, the process must proceed logically and in an orderly fashion. Evidence must be based on fact rather than emotion, and all conclusions must be supported.

*T*he marketing research process consists of clarification, refinement, and feedback.

Although presented here as a series of discrete steps, the marketing research process might better be thought of as consisting of *clarification, refinement,* and *feedback.* Each step clarifies and refines a situation until researchers achieve an objective understanding of the situation sufficient to lead them to the next step—and ultimately to a decision. Because the objective of marketing research should always be sufficient information to make a decision, not all the steps in the process have to

❏ **Figure 4.5**
The marketing research process.

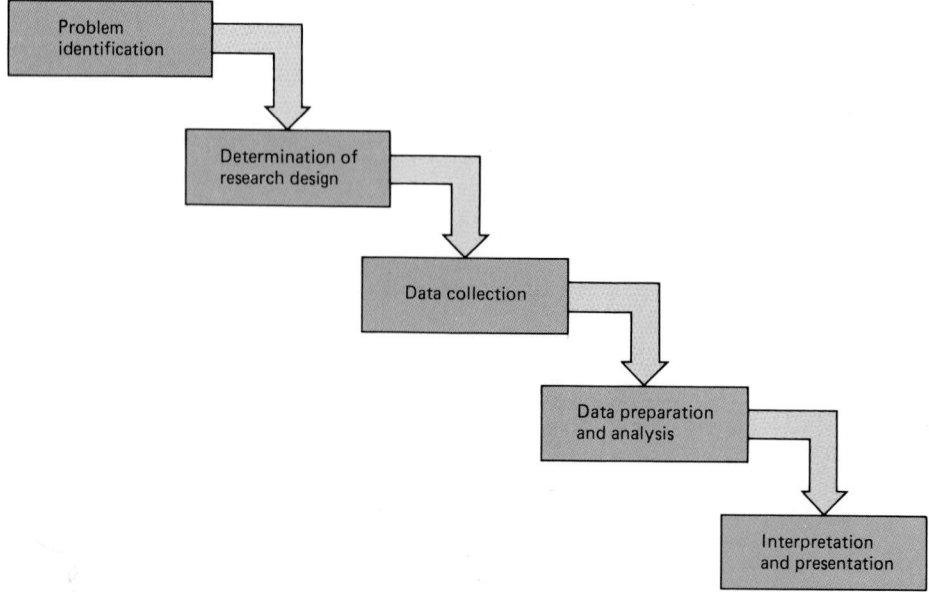

be carried out for every project. Many research studies end after the organization's records and library materials have been studied, for example.

Problem Identification and Research Objectives

*P*roblem identification means determining the reason for the research.

The goal of the problem identification phase of marketing research is to identify as precisely as possible the reason for the research. A well-defined problem gives direction to the research and aids in the formulation of research objectives.

According to William G. Zikmund, a **problem definition** indicates a specific marketing decision area that will be clarified by answering some research questions.[7] Albert Einstein noted: "The formulation of a problem is often more essential than its solution."[8]

Research objectives, also called research questions, specify what information will be sought. Concisely stated objectives increases the likelihood the research will be useful to the marketer. False conclusions may be drawn from research investigations that proceed with poorly or incorrectly conceived problem definitions or research objectives. Coca-Cola, for instance, based its decision to reformulate the taste of Coke on the information they obtained from certain research questions. Evidently, consumers were asked for their opinions about the taste of various formulations in taste tests. The research was too narrow in scope, however, because it failed to investigate consumers' strong emotional attachment to the original formulation. As a result, the decision to change Coke resulted in dramatic consumer protest.[9]

Recognizing a problem or an area for research is not the same as defining it. A marketing manager's awareness of a problem almost always develops from the realization that a departure from a norm or standard has occurred. The company president believes a problem exists because sales have declined (departed) from last year's sales (the standard). Thus the awareness of a problem depends on what the marketer's attention is focused on (such as sales or profits), what standard is used, and how the departure is perceived. The marketer must closely examine the elements of the comparisons being made to identify the problem. Care has to be taken, too, so that the marketer does not mistakenly identify a symptom of a problem rather than the problem itself. The fact that sales are down 30 percent is a symptom. The problem may be that a competing firm is winning market share.

The reason for the research exists as either a problem or an opportunity. In either case, decisions must be made. The inventor of a new product probably views the decisions necessary to successfully market it as responses to the challenges of opportunity. The president of a firm, on the other hand, may perceive only problems when the firm's annual sales have declined by 30 percent.

Exploratory Research

*E*xploratory research develops initial hunches and provides direction for further research.

Sometimes research is needed to clearly define the problem. In this case, exploratory research may help. **Exploratory research** is research intended to develop initial hunches or insights and to provide direction for any further research needed.[10] For instance, the director of Spectrum Industries, a sheltered workshop for persons with physical and mental limitations, asked a researcher for help in finding out why more work for his employees was not available. Since innumerable variables may have played some part in the problem, exploratory research to gain understanding and insight into the situation seemed advisable. Exploratory research takes a highly flexible approach. The marketer proceeds without a fixed plan, although a tentative guide may be used.[11] The nature and boundaries of the problem should develop during exploration. This type of research also provides information for establishing priorities when several problems are uncovered.

Researchers may conduct exploratory research by examining existing data—secondary data—or by collecting new data—primary data. The exploratory research should conclude in one of two ways: (1) a decision to forego further research can be made when sufficient information exists to solve the problem, or (2) a decision can be made to formulate a hypothesis that will require additional research efforts.

Hypothesis Formulation

A hypothesis (a tentative explanation) guides data collection.

A hypothesis differs from a problem statement in that a hypothesis focuses on the answer to a problem. **Hypothesis** is defined in various ways: a guess, an assumption, a tentative explanation, or a possible solution to a problem. To illustrate, here is a hypothesis to explain the increase in the sales of large General Motors cars: sales have increased because customers believe that gasoline prices will not increase dramatically in the next five years. We could offer many other hypotheses to explain the growth in General Motors' large-car sales. A testable hypothesis can be supported or refuted by empirical data. Thus, a hypothesis provides researchers with a guide to what data to collect—the data required to test the hypothesis.

To summarize, problem identification—the first step in research, and one of the most important and most difficult—determines what will be researched and how. The decisions that must be made to solve the problem determine what data must be obtained. A mistake made in problem identification usually means that all research efforts will be wasted until the problem is correctly identified.

Secondary Sources

*S*econdary data—data already collected—may be all that are needed.

Data that have already been collected, often for other purposes, are referred to as **secondary data.** Efficient researchers will always look to secondary sources of data first. The minimal cost and abundance of secondary data, combined with the speed with which they can be obtained, make them a first-choice alternative.

Secondary data generated from the organization's operation and residing within the organization—internal secondary data—are examined first. Such data include sales records, inventory levels, productivity records, and customer complaint records. For example, an investigation of Spectrum Industries' records could provide information on firms the company now serves, major customers, customers' locations, and type of business of customers. Internal secondary data have several advantages: they are more readily available than any other type of secondary data; knowledge of the data—their existence, accuracy, and so forth—are generally better known; and usually they are highly relevant to the organization's operations, problems, and opportunities.

Secondary data outside the organization—external secondary data—are more abundant than internal data. However, ascertaining what external secondary data are available, and where, presents the researcher with the biggest challenge in using secondary data. Sources of useful data include libraries, government agencies, nonprofit organizations, and a number of private sources. Besides developing a familiarity with these sources, researchers must develop a methodology for secondary data search.

LIBRARIES

An excellent place to start the search for secondary data is a good library. Locating a specific source in the library usually requires only a little time. Libraries, however, serve another very important purpose. For the researcher who does not know what secondary information (if any) is available, libraries provide some starting

Libraries offer a wealth of resources to the researcher of secondary data.

points.[12] Periodical articles can be located through indexes such as the *Business Periodical Index, The Wall Street Journal Index,* and the *Reader's Guide Index.* Computerized indexes are also available. To use one, the researcher enters key terms on a terminal, and the entries travel via phone line to the central computer. When the computer finds the key term in its files, it flags the reference and sends it to the terminal. Thus, the researcher receives a printout of all references in the file containing the key terms. Computerized searches usually are done quickly but for a fee. Many libraries also contain books, such as *The Source of Business Information* and *How to Use the Business Library,* that show researchers how to find secondary data for businesses.

GOVERNMENT

Government agencies constantly collect information and make it available for public use. The U.S. government collects more secondary information than any other organization or association—so much, in fact, that finding it requires use of the *Monthly Catalog of United States Government Publications,* available in large libraries. The *Statistical Abstract of the United States,* an annual publication, provides a good overview of available statistical data.

Governments constantly count and survey. Governmental data, therefore, tends to be statistical and demographic in nature. This data is especially valuable for determining market size and potential. For instance, the U.S. Bureau of the Census conducts a number of censuses. The *Census of Population* and the *Census of Business* (which covers manufacturing, wholesaling, and retailing) are two of the most widely used. The Department of Commerce also collects information, such as that found in the *County and City Data Book.* Information collected by state and local governmental agencies is usually not as widely available as that gathered by the federal government.

Before assuming that no governmental data exists, the researcher should always consider whether the problem situation is influenced by a governmental agency. Data usually exists if a permit, tax, license, or the like is required or if financing is provided or backed by a governmental unit.

NONPROFIT ORGANIZATIONS

Nonprofit organizations, such as trade, professional, and business associations, foundations, and university research bureaus, sponsor studies and collect data. The information they collect usually is not widely distributed, so researchers must make contact with the organizations to find out what data is available. An excellent source of associations' names and addresses is the *Encyclopedia of Associations,* found in most libraries.

PRIVATE SOURCES

Some businesses collect data as their primary activity or as a by-product of their main activity. For instance, the yellow pages of a telephone directory provide significant amounts of data, such as number of competitors and their locations. *Standard and Poor's, Value Line,* and other financial publications provide information on size, type, and even marketing strategies of specific businesses. Advertising media—newspapers, magazines, television and radio stations—collect information on the characteristics of their readers, viewers, and listeners in order to better serve their advertisers. Information from these sources is available for the asking, especially to potential advertisers.

"Survey of Buying Power," a special annual issue of the *Sales and Marketing Management* magazine, contains statistics on major markets throughout the United States. This is a very valuable source of annual, detailed data on specific markets. *Advertising Age* publishes estimates of companies' sales and market share—information that can be very useful in competitive analysis.

*J*ohn Grubb wanted to distinguish his San Francisco construction company, Clearwood Building Inc., from a host of competitors. So, in early 1983, he and his brother Robert started talking to Clearwood's customers: the architects and designers who hired their services.

What, the brothers asked their customers, were the worst features of Clearwood's competitors? The answer: Bad manners, workers who tracked dirt across carpets, and beat-up construction trucks, which high-class clients objected to having parked in their driveways.

Those seemingly small points were the signal for a repositioning. The brothers decided to make Clearwood the contractor of choice among the Bay Area's upper crust. The company bought a new truck and kept it spotless. Its estimators donned jackets and ties. And its work crews, now impeccably polite, began rolling protective runners over carpets before they set foot in clients' homes. In less than two years, Clearwood's annual revenue jumped to $1 million from $200,000.

Keeping an eye on the competition, of course, is a vital part of running any business. But the way it is

MARKETING IN ACTION

Quiz Customers for Clues about Competition

done is changing, particularly for small businesses. Increasingly, business owners are strengthening their ties to customers in the hope of gaining insights about competitors that they can turn to their advantage. "It's the difference between acquaintance and commitment," Robert Grubb says of the stronger links being forged.

The strategy of drawing closer to customers is a lesson some businesses are learning from Japan. There, tight bonds between suppliers and manufacturers have produced flexibility, cost savings and quality levels that translate into export advantages. But the approach is also spreading because the notion of strategic planning, long practiced by big U.S. companies, is percolating down to smaller concerns. Owners are taking a longer-term view of their companies and a more disciplined approach to analyzing the players in their markets.

Robert Grubb, for example, was studying strategic planning at business school when he began mapping competitive moves for Clearwood Building. He has since become president of DTM Products Inc., a Boulder, Colo., plastic injection-molding concern, where he is using a similar approach. "We are looking at the competition by focusing on the customer," he says.

In DTM's case, the current concern is foreign competition. One major customer, for instance, recently told the company that an Italian competitor had delivered a "beautiful" sample mold.

"We said, 'Look, we are committed to you guys as a team member,' " Mr. Grubb says. "Rather than being defensive, we say, 'That's great. What do you think the advantages are?' Through that kind of questioning, we can find out what they *can't* get overseas. We start realizing what we need to focus on in order to be their suppliers two, four, six, ten years from now."

---

*C*heck secondary data for availability, relevancy, sufficiency, and accuracy.

Secondary data offers several advantages, but it also has some disadvantages. Secondary data, like all data, should be questioned as to its accuracy. Did the people who collected it use techniques that ensure objective and unbiased results? Data collected by the U.S. Government Census Bureau and other government agencies can usually be accepted without question. Other sources of data require investigation of collection techniques. The researcher should at least examine the methodology used to collect the data; a description of methodologies usually appears at the beginning of a report. Finally, even though secondary research should be used first, it may lack the required completeness needed to achieve the research objectives. When secondary data is insufficient, the researcher turns to primary sources.

Primary Sources

*P*rimary data are original data collected specifically to solve the research problem.

Primary data consist of data collected from original sources specifically to achieve the research project's objectives. Since the researcher decides what data to collect and controls their collection, the accuracy of the data should be under the researcher's

Focus groups encourage participants to speak freely about their reactions to a good or service.

control. In collecting primary data, the researcher uses two basic types of research: qualitative and quantitative.

Qualitative Research Information-Gathering Methods

*Q*ualitative research provides insight but not statistical accuracy.

The objective of the research study determines whether qualitative or quantitative research will be used. If the researcher seeks insight into a situation (perhaps he or she is not completely satisfied with how the research problem has been identified or the hypothesis has been stated) or generally desires more understanding without requiring statistical accuracy, **qualitative research** will be used.

Research techniques aimed at the collection of qualitative information focus more on concepts and issues than on measurement and quantification. Three qualitative research techniques are *focus groups, depth interviews,* and *projection techniques.*

Focus groups. A focus group contains three to twelve people who have been selected because of their experience and knowledge of the research topic; for instance, they may be customers of a certain retail store, consumers of a particular product, or wholesalers of a category of products. Focus groups meet with a focus group leader, whose role is to occasionally pose questions about different aspects of the research topic to encourage group members to discuss the topic—give opinions, criticize, forecast, and generally express themselves.[13] The group atmosphere encourages and stimulates discussion; one person's observations bring out responses from others.[14] Focus groups have gained great popularity as a research method.

Depth interviews. In a depth interview, an interviewer and interviewee discuss the research topic at length. The interviewee is selected for his or her perceived knowledge or experience with the research topic. The interview has little structure; it is designed primarily to put the interviewee at ease. Usually it consists of general questions and lasts for approximately two hours. At the end of the interview, the researcher should feel confident that the interviewee has expressed all of his or her opinions, thoughts, facts, and attitudes on the research topic. Because of the time and cost associated with depth interviews, researchers usually complete only a few for each research project.

Projective techniques. Projective techniques require the researcher to create a set of stimuli that are intentionally vague but that include the research topic. The researcher then asks the respondent to react to the stimuli. Ideally, the respondent projects his or her true feelings, emotions, opinions, and attitudes into the vague situation. The objective of the technique is to obtain information that people normally would hesitate to give by depersonalizing the situation with vagueness rather than asking directly, "What is your opinion?" The classic illustration of the projective technique was a study conducted by Mason Haire to determine why people initially resisted buying instant coffee.[15] Haire gave grocery shoppers one of two grocery lists and asked them to describe the person who composed it. The only difference in the two lists was that one had "instant coffee" written down and the other had "brewed coffee." The shoppers described the person who included instant coffee on the list as lazy and indifferent to family needs. The person who bought brewed coffee was described as active, energetic, and concerned about family. Time has changed people's perceptions of instant coffee and instant coffee purchasers. Today's perceptions are probably very different.

Several methods have been developed to present stimuli in projective research. Word association, sentence completion, story completion, and cartoon interpretation are common techniques. For example, researchers frequently use word association to help select brand names for new products. Possible brand names are included in a list of words, and respondents are asked to give the first word that comes to mind when each word on the list is read. The researchers study the responses to determine what negative and positive connotations emerge most often.

Qualitative research provides information, insight, and knowledge that is impossible to obtain in any other way. However, since samples are usually small and the techniques limited, especially in the measurement of responses, different researchers may interpret the results differently. To overcome the limitations of qualitative research, quantitative research should be considered.

Quantitative Research: Research Design

*T*he research design is the master plan for collecting and analyzing data.

The researcher, having gained a better understanding of the research problem and having decided on research objectives and perhaps a stated hypothesis, may now want to conduct **quantitative research**—research in which the variables can be measured. The first step in conducting such research is creating an appropriate research design. The **research design** is a master plan specifying the methods and procedures for collecting and analyzing the needed information. It is a framework for the research plan of action.[16] The research design differs with the research objectives. Describing a situation calls for one type of research design, while determining cause-and-effect relationships requires another.

DESCRIPTIVE RESEARCH

*D*escriptive quantitative research describes the situation with numbers.

Most marketing research of a quantitative nature is descriptive. Descriptive research provides information concerning who, what, how, where, and when—sufficient information to solve many marketing problems. Understanding the characteristics of a phenomenon often allows the marketer to confidently predict some future aspect of the phenomenon. Gerber executives, for example, predicted decline in the sale of baby food, Gerber's product, based on data describing population, age, sex, income, and birthrate. If the marketer wishes to investigate a possible cause-and-effect relationship—for example, whether an improvement in the product's quality will increase unit sales—then a causal research design is more appropriate.

CAUSAL RESEARCH

Investigating cause-and-effect relationships requires a causal research design.

Causal research permits the researcher to examine the association among variables for the existence of a cause-and-effect relationship. Causal research studies use the **experimental research method,** a systematic scientific approach whereby the researcher manipulates a variable or variables and measures the resulting change in other variables.

Causal research can present problems to marketers, since identifying and controlling the many variables in marketing environments is often difficult, if not impossible. For example, test marketing, the causal research technique most often used by marketing managers, involves distributing a new product in a small market to determine whether it is likely to be accepted in the larger market. (See Chapter 8.) Its major advantage is that it allows marketers to test their new product or marketing plan under realistic conditions. But if competitors discover test marketing plans, they may attempt to sabotage the research by increasing their advertising, lowering their prices, and the like. As a result, the research may prove useless.

THE CASE CONTINUES

*J*ay Mary must decide whether or not to purchase a Popeyes' franchise. The fact that a major investment is at stake, the presence of considerable risk, and the nonroutine nature of the decision all call for marketing research, within reasonable limits. To get objective information uncolored by his own preferences, as well as to get the manpower, Mary may want to contract the job to an independent marketing research firm.

Mary, or the firm he hires, should look for secondary information first: it is less expensive and can be ob-

tained more quickly than primary information. A public library would have the *Franchise Opportunities Handbook,* an annual publication of the U.S. Department of Commerce. Recent information about Popeyes can be found here. Also available in libraries are reference guides indicating various sources of secondary data. For instance, *Marketing Information: A Professional Reference Guide,* by Jay L. Goldstucker and Dennis W. Goodwin (Georgia State University), contains a large section

on sources that contain information on franchising.

Information indicating whether hot-and-spicy chicken would appeal to Mary's market would most likely not be found in secondary sources. Mary should, however, contact the National Restaurant Association and other food-industry associations. He should also get recent back issues of the *Gallup Monthly Report on Eating Out.* This publication contains information on the "kinds of meals eaten and preferred, types of restaurants frequented and why, and other information."

Quantitative Research Data-Gathering Methods

Having decided on the type of data needed—descriptive or cause and effect—the marketer must decide on the research approaches. Two approaches are available: observation and surveys. Figure 4.6 shows a systematic method for deciding between the two approaches. To some extent, the choice depends on the type of data needed. Sometimes, however, marketers need data from both approaches.

OBSERVATION

Observation is best used to study frequent, discrete, and overt behavior.

Observation records a phenomenon at the time it occurs. Individual subjects, who may be aware or unaware of the research, do not directly interact with the researcher. Through observation, discrete, overt behavior or events can be recorded

❑ **Figure 4.6**
Choosing between the questioning and observation approaches.

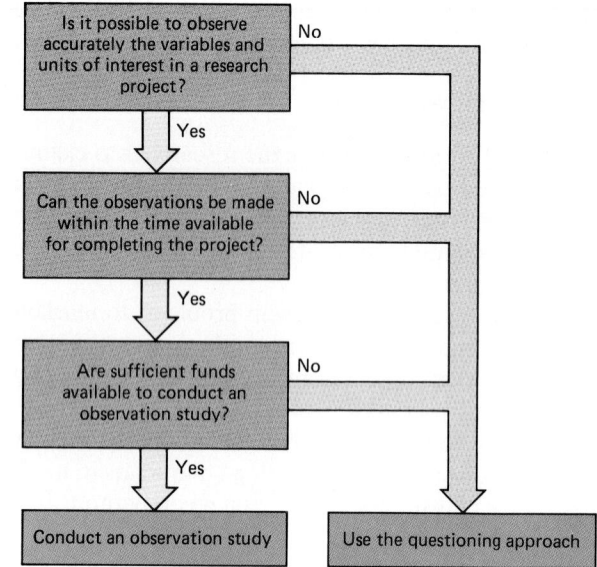

Source: A. Parasuraman, *Marketing Research,* © 1986, Addison-Wesley Publishing Co., Inc., Reading, Massachusetts. Page 208. Reprinted with permission.

either mechanically or by a human observer with minimum bias. A. C. Neilsen uses a mechanical means of recording when the TV is turned on and to what station it is tuned. Street traffic is mechanically measured by pressure-sensitive hoses placed across the street and connected to counters. Libraries use turnstyles to count the number of patrons. Traffic patterns in retail stores, on the other hand, usually require a human observer.

The observation method is used primarily with descriptive studies and works well if the event being observed occurs frequently. The event should require little interpretation—either it has occurred or it has not. Thus, the event must be physical in nature; changes in attitude, for example, cannot be observed directly.

SURVEYS

*S*urveys are the mainstay of primary marketing research.

Surveys are a means of gathering information through interviews. An example is the exit poll. Exit pollsters interview individuals immediately after they have experienced an event, such as a product test or a political election. Surveys can be applied to many different kinds of marketing problems, from product design to product disposal. Surveys have the additional advantage of allowing researchers to obtain information directly from the source rather than secondhand. Most marketing research that seeks primary data uses the survey approach.

Despite its many advantages, the survey method is not without disadvantages. Results depend on who was surveyed and how and what they were asked. A mistake in either area reduces the accuracy of the data. For instance, a marketer who asks

Source: © 1984 United Feature Syndicate, Inc.

❏ **Figure 4.7**
Data collection
techniques for full-
service research
companies.

Data Collection Techniques*			
	1986	1985	1984
WATS/centralized telephone	40%	39%	38%
Non-WATS telephone (local)	8	8	6
Central location/mall	19	17	19
Personal interview	12	12	14
Mail/diary	8	11	10
Focus group	8	8	6
Store audits/Scanner/Distribution check	1	1	2
Other marketing research	3	3	3
Other nonmarketing research	1	1	1

*Analysis of sales by type of study, by mean percentage

Source: Council of American
Survey Research Organizations
(CASRO), Financial
Compensation Research Survey.

an inappropriate question often receives an untruthful answer because the respondent either cannot or will not answer truthfully. The truthfulness of a response can be impossible to determine.

Researchers conduct surveys in person, by telephone, by mail, or through a combination of these techniques. Each technique offers advantages and disadvantages for a specific research project. Figure 4.7 shows how seventy-five members of the Council of American Survey Research Organizations (CASRO) used various interviewing techniques over several years.

*R*espondents can be
called, visited, or mailed
the questionnaire.

Personal Interviews.   Personal interviews involve face-to-face communication between the interviewer and the interviewee, usually on a one-to-one basis in the interviewee's home. Variations in the number of individuals involved and the interview location exist, but for comparison with other contact techniques, the two-party, at-home type is used. The advantages and disadvantages of the technique stem largely from the characteristics of face-to-face contact.

Personal interviews offer a variety of advantages to the researcher. One is that respondents seem more willing to spend time answering questions; they often devote as much as two hours to this type of interview. In addition, personal interviews give the best results when lengthy questionnaires are involved. Research on the aesthetics of product features relies heavily on personal interviewing because of the visual requirement. Personal interviews have a higher participation rate than mail questionnaires. Finally, the personal interview is especially useful in populations with high illiteracy rates.

*P*ersonal interviews overcome many communica-
tion problems but are
expensive.

The limitations of personal interviews include the respondent's loss of anonymity. When the interviewer is present the respondent is known—at least for the moment—and may alter his or her response because of the interviewer's presence. Sending interviewers over large geographic areas to interviews is costly both in time and transportation. Finally, control and supervision present problems for personal interviews. Each interviewer works alone most of the time. Thus, the dishonest interviewer can easily fill out the questionnaire without talking to the respondent or ask the respondent only a few questions and complete the rest of the questions alone. To verify that the interviews have been completed, research firms often call 10 to 15 percent of the respondents a second time.

Telephone Interviews.   Telephone interviews communicate solely by sound. Among all contact methods, they alone offer the advantages and disadvantages of sound-only communication.[17]

*T*elephone interviews provide data quickly, but not
everyone has a phone or a
listed number.

The speed of telephone interviewing in completing the data collection phase of a research project has been the primary reason for the popularity of the telephone contact method. Also important among the many advantages offered by telephone interviewing is its cost. The reduction in long-distance rates and the use of Wide

Area Telephone Service (WATS) have reduced the cost of telephone interviewing. The method is less expensive than personal interviews. The physical absence of the interviewer may also act as an advantage, because it may increase the willingness of the respondent to answer personal questions. While the interviewer's physical appearance usually does not affect the information obtained, articulation and voice characteristics do make a difference, and these are present in telephone interviews. Respondents who fear inviting strangers into their homes may also cooperate better in telephone interviews than personal interviews.

On the negative side, some members of the population do not have telephones, and many individuals have unlisted phones. To reach unlisted phones, researchers may use a random-digit dialing procedure. Here, the last four digits of the phone number are obtained from a random number table or a computer program. Finally, people hang up when calls become lengthy. Therefore, telephone interviews usually should last no longer than thirty minutes.

*M*ail questionnaires offer a low-cost way to reach respondents, but using them is time consuming.

Mail Collection.   Mail collection means sending a written questionnaire via delivery service (usually the U.S. Post Office) to the potential respondent and having the respondent return the completed questionnaire via delivery service. Variations exist; for example, researchers may hand out questionnaires with self-addressed stamped envelopes at shopping malls. Mail contact has advantages and disadvantages associated with written communication and the mail service.

A primary advantage of mail data collection has been its low cost. Mail questionnaires can reach widely dispersed populations more cheaply than personal and telephone interviews. Respondents may complete the questionnaires at their convenience and may answer more honestly because of the anonymity common in mail questionnaires. For instance, when asked what magazines they read, individuals may respond in personal interviews with such answers as *Time* and *Newsweek* but in anonymous mail questionnaires with answers such as *Playboy* and *Penthouse*.

Several weaknesses exist in the mail approach to data collection. Sending the questionnaires out, waiting for responses, and conducting follow-up mailings consume a considerable amount of time. If questions are not clearly stated, respondents must depend on their own interpretation. Finally, the response rate—the number of completed questionnaires returned divided by the number sent out—is often low. Response rate is crucial, since the researcher wants to discover as many views on the research topic as possible. Marketers have used various techniques to increase response rates, including direct incentives such as money accompanying the questionnaire.

Figure 4.8 reviews characteristics of the three survey contact methods.

❑ **Figure 4.8**
Typical characteristics of the three survey methods.

Source: Marketing, William Zikmund and Michael D'Amica. Copyright © 1984 John Wiley & Sons, Inc. Reprinted by permission of John Wiley & Sons, Inc.

	Personal	Mail	Telephone
Speed of data collection	Moderate to fast	Researcher has no control over the return of questionnaire	Quite fast
Respondent cooperation	Excellent cooperation	Moderate cooperation—poorly designed questionnaire will have low response rate	Good cooperation
Versatility of questioning	Very flexible	Highly standardized format	Moderate flexibility
Questionnaire length	Long	Varies depending on incentive	Moderate
Possibility for respondent misunderstanding	Lowest	Highest—no interviewer to clarify	Average
Influence of interviewer on answers	High	None	Moderate
Cost	Highest	Lowest	Low to moderate

Samples and Populations

*R*esearchers identify a population and then take a census or a sample of its members.

Surveys require contact with individuals. The marketer may contact everyone in the population—conduct a **census**—or take a **sample,** a group selected from the population. In either case, the population must be correctly identified. The **population,** or universe, consists of all elements, units, or individuals the researcher wants to study. For example, suppose a clothing manufacturer is considering the production of a line of clothing that is very easily put on. The manufacturer may be interested in the population of individuals who, because of physical ailments, have difficulty dressing. The population of interest can be difficult to identify, however. For example, what physical ailments make dressing difficult? A vaguely defined population may not include everyone it should, and as a result the research may be biased.

SAMPLING

*T*he sampling plan specifies the sample unit, size, and selection procedure.

When researchers use a sample, they want it to accurately represent the entire population. A representative sample is more likely produced from a good sampling plan. The **sampling plan** answers three primary questions: What are the sampling units (the entities to be sampled)? What is the sample size? What is the sample selection procedure?

The sampling units may be individuals, stores, city blocks, or the like. For instance, suppose researchers need to know the purchase rate of cola soft drinks. They might select individual consumers as the sample unit and conduct a survey of individuals. They might instead identify retailers selling cola as the sample unit. Or they might use city blocks and survey all individuals residing on selected blocks.

What should be the size of the sample? Should it be 25, 100, 500, 2,500, 50,000? The answer depends on how widely the characteristics in the population vary. The more the variation in the characteristic of interest, the larger the sample needs to be. Unfortunately the researcher seldom knows the variation; indeed, determining the amount of variation is usually the objective of the research. Larger samples normally seem preferable, since they increase the likelihood that whatever variation exists will appear in the sample. The method that will be used to analyze the data also affects sample size. For example, researchers may plan to use a statistical test like chi-square to evaluate the data they have collected. Such tests are reliable only if the sample is large enough. Practical aspects, such as the amount of time and money the researcher has, influence sample size as well. For most studies, samples of 400 to 500 are accepted as adequate by researchers and managers. An adequate sample size should produce a sample with characteristics proportionate to those of the population—a representative sample.

How individuals are selected to be a part of the sample is termed the sampling procedure. The choice of sampling procedure depends on the accuracy needed, cost, available information, research objectives, and other factors. Two general selection procedures exist: nonprobability and probability.

*N*onprobability samples are used primarily with exploratory research.

Researchers using **nonprobability sampling** procedures arbitrarily select the sample according to their own convenience or judgment. For exploratory research, or whenever insight and general understanding of a situation seem adequate as the bases for sample selection, nonprobability sampling works well. It usually consumes less time and money than probability sampling. It is, however, inappropriate to apply standard statistical testing to nonprobability samples. Types of nonprobability samples include the following.

Convenience samples include any population member who is readily available. Mall intercept studies, in which any individual passing by becomes part of the sample, are convenience samples.

Judgment samples include individuals who are known to have a common interest in a type of product. For example, surveying product opinion leaders with regard to a new product concept is an illustration of judgment sampling.

Quota samples divide the population into subgroups and include a certain number of individuals from each subgroup. The interviewer decides what members of each subgroup will be included.

*P*robability samples remove researcher bias from sample selection.

Probability sampling procedures give every member of a population a known, nonzero chance of being selected. Probability sampling prevents the researcher's bias from influencing selection, since the makeup of the sample is determined not by the researcher but by chance. Samples that do not perfectly represent the population because of probability sample selection are said to have sampling error.[18] Sampling error occurs because of chance and not bias. The following are some of the better-known types of probability samples.

In the **simple random sample,** each member of the population has an equal chance of being selected. To use this method, researchers must identify each member of the population and devise a method of randomly selecting a sample. For example, they might assign each individual a number and include in the sample those whose assigned numbers appear first in a random number table.

In the **systematic sample,** the researcher identifies the population as in random sampling, but then takes every *n*th item on a list of the population. Many telephone surveys employ systematic samples. If a sample of 100 is needed from a phone directory of 10,000 names, the researcher divides 10,000 by 100 and finds that one name per 100 is needed. Then the researcher chooses a random starting point within the first 100 names—say, the 67th name listed. The second name is the 167th (67 + 100); the third, the 267th; and so on.

The **stratified sample** contains randomly selected individuals from subgroups into which the population has been divided. The division is based on one or more characteristics. Assume, for example, that a sample from a population of males and females has to be taken and that females' opinions are expected to show greater variation. To take a stratified sample, the researcher can divide the population into two subgroups, males and females, and then select a random sample from each subgroup. The sample size would be larger for the female group since greater variation in their opinions is expected. Stratified sampling, then, is an efficient procedure where subgroups hold divergent opinions.

The **cluster, or area, sample** involves two stages: selecting a random sample of geographic areas, such as blocks, counties, or census tracts, and then taking a census or another sample from the randomly selected areas. Cluster sampling is an efficient sampling technique for researchers working with a large, dispersed population or a population whose members cannot be identified.

---

*T*o begin his primary research effort, Mary would probably conduct focus groups. Focus groups allow the researcher to discover in-depth reactions—such as respondents' feelings about competitors' brands. Physical proximity lets the researcher watch as well as listen to consumer reactions. If Mary were to

THE CASE CONTINUES

conduct a survey in the Minneapolis–St. Paul area, a telephone interview would be the quickest technique. Although Mary probably will do a telephone survey, a segment of the sample will have unlisted numbers or

be without telephones. Respondents also often have quirky and complicated responses to questions about food preferences, and telephone interviews are most effective when brief responses are desired. Other methods, such as taste tests, could also be used, although the expense would be considerable.

QUESTIONNAIRE CONSTRUCTION

Questionnaire construction requires posing the right questions correctly.

Questionnaires are standardized forms used to guide the interviewer or respondent in obtaining the desired data. The primary objective of a questionnaire is to elicit the desired information from the selected respondents. Therefore the researcher must decide early in the questionnaire construction process what data are to be obtained. Decisions based on the data and the research objectives serve as a guide. In short, the researcher should ask himself or herself, "How will the data from this question be used to make the decisions the marketing manager faces?" Posing this question helps eliminate the interesting but unnecessary questions that plague questionnaire construction. A more embarrassing and more costly problem develops from omission of questions needed to obtain critical data. Finding after a survey has been completed that additional questions should have been asked can mean conducting the survey a second time. The researcher and the marketing manager must work closely together to avoid such problems.

Form of Questions. **Closed-end questions** require respondents to choose among answers listed, such as multiple choice and dichotomous questions are examples of close-ended questions. From the researcher's view, closed-end questions save time in interpretation and tabulation. Closed-end questions do require careful construction, however, to ensure that all possible responses are included and appropriately worded. Respondents also like closed-end questions, since they usually require less time to complete.

Open-end questions allow respondents to answer in their own words. Essay questions are examples of open-ended questions. The answers to such questions reveal more and thus provide more insight about a topic than the responses to closed-end questions. This makes open-end questions especially useful in exploratory research. Open-end questions do present problems. Each answer is likely to be different from every other; therefore, if responses are to be classified, the researcher has to make a decision on how to categorize them. Open-end questions also tend to bias results toward respondents who express themselves fluently.

Question Wording. Wording a question is more an art than a science. Some rules do exist, however. For example, each question that asks for a comparison should include a standard of reference—imprecise words like *large, better,* and *regular* should be avoided. Instead of large, "Eighteen ounces or more" could be used. Each item should contain only one question, not two. Ambiguous wording—wording that can be interpreted in more than one way—should be avoided, as should leading, biased, and too-personal questions. A leading question implies the desirability of a response, for example, "Don't you prefer Mr. Y's pizza to Mr. X's pizza?" All questions should be clear and easy to understand. Figure 4.9 illustrates questions in which the rules were not observed.

Sequencing Questions. The lead questions in a questionnaire should create enough interest to encourage respondents to complete the questionnaire. Difficult or personal questions should be placed toward the end. Thus, at least some data will be obtained even if the respondent refuses to complete the questionnaire.

Pretesting. The length of the questionnaire and the types and lengths of questions vary with the method of contact. In addition, the questionnaire design influences the response rate. The only way to check whether the questionnaire will obtain the desired data without undertaking the complete survey is to conduct a trial run—a **pretest**—with a small representative sample.

❏ **Figure 4.9**
Illustrations of poorly
worded questions.

A "Questionable" Questionnaire

Suppose the following questionnaire had been prepared by a
summer camp director to be used in interviewing parents of
prospective campers. How do you feel about each question?

1. What is your income to the nearest hundred dollars?

> People don't necessarily know their income to the nearest
> hundred dollars, nor do they want to reveal their income that
> closely. Furthermore, a questionnaire should never open with
> such a personal question.

2. Are you a strong or weak supporter of overnight summer
    camping for your children?

> What do "strong" and "weak" mean?

3. Do your children behave themselves well in a summer camp?
    Yes ( )   No ( )

> "Behave" is a relative term. Besides, will people want to
> answer this? Furthermore, is "yes" or "no" the best way to
> allow a response to the question? Why is the question being
> asked in the first place?

4. How many camps mailed literature to you last April?
    This April?

> Who can remember this?

5. What are the most salient and determinant attributes in
    your evaluation of summer camps?

> What are "salience" and "determinant attributes"? Don't use
> big words.

6. Do you think it is right to deprive your child of the
    opportunity to grow into a mature person through
    the experience of summer camping?

> Loaded question. How can one answer "yes," given the bias?

Source: Philip Kotler, *Marketing Essentials,* © 1984, p. 68. Reprinted by permission of Prentice-Hall, Inc., Englewood Cliffs, New Jersey.

Accuracy of Data Collection

*D*ata collection is as important as research design.

Most often the weakest part of a research project is data collection. Data collection presents many opportunities for bias and inaccuracy. It is vital that the research design be implemented in data collection. However, the field force—the collectors of data—generally includes many individuals who have not been party to development of the research project and who may be unaware of or unconcerned about the precautions taken to obtain unbiased and objective data. Interviewers may unintentionally bias the data by leading the respondent. Occasionally interviewers are simply dishonest, making up responses and intentionally replacing individuals in the sample with individuals who can be more conveniently or easily interviewed. Clearly, the researcher must exercise extreme diligence in selecting, training, supervising, and controlling the individuals who help in data collection. Explicit instructions on handling callbacks, refusals, and other situations the interviewer will encounter should be given in advance of the interviews.

Data Preparation and Analysis

As the questionnaires are returned, the researcher checks to make sure the interviewers have correctly followed instructions and that the questionnaires have been completed. Each questionnaire must be checked for incomplete or ambiguous answers. The researcher verifies response accuracy and consistency, makes necessary

THE REST OF THE STORY

Retail Industry's Buy American Program

*W*hat do retail buyers think about the U.S. textile and apparel industry's Buy American campaign?

Not much.

In a national survey of retail buyers, the resounding answer was that imported merchandise provided better quality for the price than domestic apparel. Retail buyers also indicated that they were not willing to use Buy American promotional materials supplied by the industry.

Information was obtained from sixty-nine apparel retail buyers nationwide. The buyers were selected from three directories: *The 1984–1985 Directory of Department Stores, Directory of Discount Department*

Stores, and *Women's and Children's Wear Buyers.*

Overall, retail buyers indicated they were not promoting the Buy American campaign and that they were not willing to do so if such materials as hangtags and labels and point-of-purchase displays were available.

Statistical analyses identified salary as a factor in whether buyers would promote the Buy American campaign if materials were available.

High-salary earners were found to be less likely to promote the campaign than buyers with low salaries.

In addition, older buyers were more likely to be promoting the campaign than younger buyers.

The study showed that the main reason retail buyers purchased imported apparel was that foreign products were "better quality for the price," followed by higher markups and exclusive merchandise-private branding as reasons.

Source: Reprinted from *Marketing News,* published by the American Marketing Association, May 23, 1986, p. 8.

---

corrections, and decides whether some or all parts of a questionnaire should be discarded. In carrying out these tasks, the researcher attempts to maintain consistency and objectivity.

*S*hould tabulation be done by hand or by computer? Small samples and short questionnaires requiring little analysis can be done by hand, but computers allow extensive analysis of masses of data.

Upon completion of editing, the researcher can either tabulate the data by hand or enter it into a computer. Tabulation involves the counting of responses in each response category. Tabulation enables the researcher to describe the results and to examine relationships among key variables. Hand tabulation may be a reasonable alternative with a small sample, but it limits the amount of analysis possible. The use of a computer, of course, allows extensive analysis. For instance, the Statistical Package for the Social Sciences (SPSS), one of many software programs available, will run numerous statistical procedures. This and other software programs for data analysis require no programming skills.

Two relatively new computer procedures allow researchers to proceed directly from data collection to computer analysis. In one procedure, researchers present a questionnaire to respondents via personal computer, usually in a shopping mall. Respondents read the questions from the monitor screen and answer by striking the appropriate keys on the keyboard. As more portable computers become available, the use of computers to present questionnaires should become more widespread. A second procedure, used in telephone surveys, has the interviewer read the question from a monitor screen and enter the response on the keyboard.

Data Interpretation and Presentation

*I*nterpretation starts at the beginning of the research project.

Marketing managers who request research are seeking not raw data but answers to problems. Thus, researchers must present information and not masses of statistics. In other words, they must interpret the collected data.

Interpretation actually starts at the very beginning of a research project, with problem identification. The definition of the problem suggests important variables to be considered in the research. At this point, the researcher, working in close cooperation with the marketing manager, defines the decision criterion—what result will trigger a certain decision. For instance, a researcher studying the feasibility of a new product may focus on potential customers' attitudes toward the product concept. From experience, the marketing manager believes that a favorable response toward the concept from 75 percent of the respondents is necessary for the product's eventual success in the market. The decision criterion in this example is 75 percent favorable response. If 75 percent or more of the responses are favorable, the decision will be to go ahead with product development; if less than 75 percent of responses favor the concept, the decision will be to discard it. Many possible decision criteria exist.

Interpretation is the process of obtaining the most information from the data.

The researcher interpreting data has to be careful not to destroy valuable information. For instance, suppose the product concept receiving the greatest number of favorable responses is to be developed. But suppose this concept also received the greatest number of unfavorable responses. The researcher must acknowledge, not ignore, this fact. The researcher, having worked extensively with the problem environment and the data, should be able to help the marketing manager obtain the most—and the most objective—information possible from the data.

Good interpretation deserves good presentation. Presenting research results in terms the decision maker understands—that is, avoiding technical terminology—makes for a good start. The researcher should also try to anticipate the needs and expectations of the audience and the uses to which they will put the report. The uses of the report influence the amount of detail included. Giving adequate detail lessens the likelihood of misuse. The packaging of the research—the style of presentation, grammar, spelling, charts, visual aids, even the cover—may make the difference in acceptance or rejection by the decision maker.

The research must be packaged appropriately for the decision maker.

OBTAINING INFORMATION THROUGH A MARKETING INFORMATION SYSTEM (MkIS)

The MkIS helps managers to overcome the problem of information overload.

Managers of small organizations in small industries may effectively make day-to-day decisions by being alert to information and remembering it when they need it. As the organization or industry grows, however, the amount of information grows, too. Eventually, even being aware of it all becomes impossible. The solution to the overabundance of information, as well as information in the wrong form or the wrong place for quick retrieval, has been the development of the management information system. A subset of the management information system is the marketing information system. As mentioned earlier, a **marketing information system (MkIS)** is a formalized procedure for collecting, storing, and retrieving information pertinent to routine decision making.

The MkIS focuses on expediting an orderly flow of pertinent information.

A marketing information system is a framework for managing the information the marketing manager needs to effectively make day-to-day marketing decisions. Both internal and external information assumed to be useful for future decisions is continuously collected. The MkIS, anticipating common decisions, collects information about the current and future status of the market and the industry, about customers' reactions to market decisions, about competitors' reactions to the organization's decisions, and about the success or failure of plans the organization has implemented. Besides generating and collecting information, the MkIS analyzes, transforms (if necessary), sorts, classifies, stores, indexes, and retrieves. The system focuses less attention on the methods of gathering information and more on expe-

❏ **Figure 4.10**
An abbreviated MkIS.

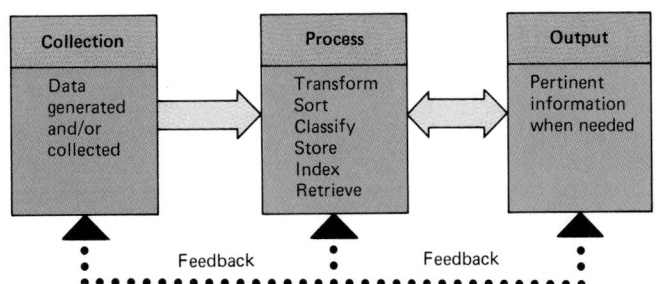

diting an orderly flow of information pertinent to marketing decisions. Figure 4.10 illustrates an abbreviated MkIS.

The organization must expend funds and effort to keep the MkIS operative, but it receives many benefits in return. Even the process of establishing an MkIS can prove beneficial. Developing the MkIS requires that the decision- and plan-making roles of various individuals be clarified so that each is supplied with the correct information. Accountability must be defined and assigned and a control process and procedures established. All this should result in better organization.

Other benefits are numerous. Because the MkIS anticipates common decisions, information is available instantaneously when the decision situation arises. The quality of information also improves, so fewer decisions are based on hunches, rumors, and unsubstantiated information. The MkIS, in providing day-to-day information, allows frequent comparison with budgets, plans, objectives, and standards, so potential problems should be detected early and corrections made before the operation is adversely affected. MkIS information also helps in planning. The information available through an MkIS can be used to build models of the market, the organization, or the like. Such models allow the decision maker to visualize more clearly the effect of various alternatives—to employ "what if" techniques.

*W*ith data from MkIS, "what if" scenarios can be studied.

Using the MkIS can present some difficulties. For instance, supermarket chains using scanners with computers generate daily reports on inventory levels, the effects of price changes, customer order size, and much more. This information can easily overwhelm a decision maker unless the MkIS has been designed correctly. Even with a well-designed MkIS, managers may be hesitant to use the information. For this reason, continuous training in using the MkIS effectively is needed.

THE CASE CONTINUES

*I*f Mary elects to conduct a mail survey, a questionnaire must be constructed. A decision to use open-ended or close-ended questions must be made. Unless the sample size is very small, an open-ended questionnaire involves tremendous work in editing and analyzing long and complicated responses. Carefully worded close-ended questions can more efficiently collect large amounts of data.

Mary will use a probability sample to eliminate researcher bias. One of the easiest probability samples to use is a systematic sample, perhaps from a telephone book. A stratified sample could be employed, using the variables Mary considers most likely involved in fast-food patronization (such as working mothers, families with children, age) as a base.

GOAL SUMMARY

1. **Explain the role of information in marketing.** Organizations face challenges and opportunities in carrying out the marketing function. In order to develop market plans, specific information on variables such as markets, competitors, and the environment is needed. The amount of information desired depends on the consequences and probability of making an incorrect decision. For routine decisions, information needs can be anticipated and continuously collected through a marketing information system. Nonroutine decisions, by nature more unexpected, require information that has not necessarily been collected previously; thus the need for marketing research.

2. **Discuss the nature of the marketing research process.** Marketing research is an organized, objective method of collecting, recording, and analyzing data for making marketing decisions. Any problem associated with marketing decisions can legitimately be the topic of marketing research. The marketing research process consists of a series of logical steps. Problem identification, the "must" first step, is followed by research design, data collection, data preparation/analysis, and interpretation/presentation. The marketing research process organizes the research. When carried out properly, it also helps to provide objective, unbiased data.

3. **How are marketing problems identified?** Defining the marketing problem is the most important but also most difficult task of the marketing researcher. Defining a problem often becomes a refining process. The researcher obtains information about the problem environment by utilizing situation analysis—internal sources of data. With the increased knowledge the researcher begins to make comparisons between the desired state and the actual state and to formulate the problem. An informal search for information outside the organization often increases the researcher's familiarity sufficiently to state the problem in specific terms. If not, the researcher will continue the exploratory research until a satisfactory problem statement or hypothesis develops.

4. **List the types of qualitative and quantitative research methods.** Qualitative research methods, such as focus groups, depth interviews and projective research, give the researcher insightful information. More exacting methods are necessary when the researcher wants to describe a population. Here, descriptive research is used. Usually surveys of samples are used to predict population characteristics. Even more exacting methods are used to obtain information indicating a cause-and-effect relationship. Causal research using carefully planned experiments, indicates cause-and-effect relationships.

5. **Explain the function of marketing information systems in marketing management.** A marketing information system's primary function is to expedite an orderly flow of information to help the marketing manager make day-to-day and other decisions that have been anticipated. A well-designed system, by anticipating information needs, provides information almost instantaneously when the decision situation arises. By providing data continuously, the marketing manager is able to make more frequent comparisons between results and objectives and to correct deviations before they become major problems.

KEY TERMS

CHECK YOUR LEARNING

1. The value of information generated by marketing research decreases as the risk associated with making a decision increases. **T/F**
2. Routine decisions are associated with marketing research, while nonroutine decisions are associated with marketing information systems. **T/F**
3. Independent marketing research firms should be employed to conduct marketing research when the research project can be precisely defined, specialized knowledge or equipment is needed, and intellectual detachment is sought. **T/F**
4. The marketing research process is: (a) synonymous with research design, (b) should always start with a clear definition of the problem, (c) helps to maintain objectivity in research, (d) both b and c, (e) both a and b.
5. A research design is the plan the researcher follows to obtain the needed information. **T/F**
6. Secondary information should be examined before primary information, and internal secondary information should be examined before other types of secondary data. **T/F**
7. The U.S. government collects a relatively small amount of data, but what it does collect is very accurate. **T/F**
8. To determine cause-and-effect relationships, a researcher conducts: (a) motivation research, (b) experimental research, (c) qualitative research, (d) quantitative research, (e) none of the above.
9. The observation method works best for collecting information on behavior. That is not overt. **T/F**
10. Telephone interviews rely solely on sound. **T/F**
11. A sampling plan requires decisions on all the following except: (a) sample size, (b) selection procedure, (c) the sampling units, (d) census information, (e) all of the aforementioned are always required.
12. A probability sample ensures representativeness. **T/F**
13. A major difference between the stratified sample and the quota sample is that the stratified sample allows the interviewer to select participants once the strata have been determined, while the quota sample does not. **T/F**
14. Questions that ask for personal information should be placed at the beginning of the questionnaire. **T/F**
15. In terms of bias and inaccuracy, data collection is one of the weakest parts of the marketing research process. **T/F**
16. Computer programming skills are necessary to analyze data. **T/F**
17. A marketing information system: (a) focuses on the future, (b) focuses on expediting information, (c) helps detect deviations from plans and objectives more quickly, (d) b and c, (e) all of the above.

QUESTIONS FOR REVIEW AND DISCUSSION

1. Define the key terms for this chapter that appear at the end of the goal summary.
2. Explain the services a marketing manager might purchase from different types of marketing research suppliers.
3. List the steps in the marketing research process.
4. What is exploratory research? Why is it used?
5. Why is problem identification so important in marketing research? What role do the researcher and the marketing manager play in problem identification?
6. Distinguish between the marketing research process and the research design.
7. How do secondary data differ from primary data? Is this difference significant to the decision maker?
8. Assume you were given the task of using word association to test how well consumers would accept the brand name *Sweetheat* for residential woodstoves. How would you go about the testing? What information would you expect to obtain?
9. When should quantitative research designs be used?
10. Why has the telephone interview gained popularity as a means of collecting data?
11. How would you go about selecting a probability sample from the student population at your college?
12. What does the researcher hope to learn from pretesting a questionnaire?
13. List some benefits of a marketing information system.

NOTES

1. "An Idea That Moves: Ads on Shopping Carts," *Business Week,* May 26, 1986, p. 97.
2. Charles D. Schewe and William R. Dillon, "Marketing Information Systems Utilization: An Application of Self-Concept Theory," *Journal of Business Research* (January 1978): pp. 67–69.
3. American Marketing Association, Committee on Definitions, *Marketing Definitions: A Glossary of Marketing Terms* (Chicago: American Marketing Association, 1960), p. 17.
4. Marj Charlier, "Heileman Again Goes to Battle, This Time to Capture the Low-Alcohol Beer Market," *The Wall Street Journal,* July 5, 1984, p. 15.
5. Bertram Schoner and Kenneth P. Uhl, *Marketing Research: Information Systems and Decision Making* (New York: John Wiley & Sons, Inc., 1975), p. 199.
6. William G. Zikmund, *Exploring Marketing Research* (Hinsdale, Ill.: The Dryden Press, 1982), pp. 79–81.
7. Zikmund, *Exploring Marketing Research,* p. 93.
8. A. Einstein and L. Infeld, *The Evolution of Physics* (New York: Simon and Schuster, 1941), p. 95.
9. Mitchell J. Shields, "Coke's Research Fizzles, Facts to Factor in Consumer Loyalty," *Adweek,* July 15, 1985, p. 8.
10. Donald S. Tull and Del I. Hawkins, *Marketing Research,* 3d ed. (New York: MacMillan Publishing Company, 1984), p. 32.
11. A. Parasuraman, *Marketing Research* (Reading, Mass.: Addison-Wesley Publishing Company, 1986), p. 120.
12. Lorna M. Daniells, "Sources on Marketing," *Harvard Business Review* (July–August 1982): pp. 40, 42.
13. Bobby J. Calder, "Focus Groups and the Nature of Qualitative Marketing Research," *Journal of Marketing Research* (August 1977): pp. 353–364.
14. Edward F. Fern, "The Use of Focus Groups for Idea Generation: The Effects of Group Size, Acquaintanceship, and Moderator on Response Quantity and Quality," *Journal of Marketing Research* (February 1982): pp. 1–13.
15. Mason Haire, "Projective Techniques in Marketing Research," *Journal of Marketing* (April 1950): pp. 649–656.
16. Zikmund, *Exploring Marketing Research,* p. 46.
17. Tyzoon T. Tyebjee, "Telephone Survey Methods: The State of the Art," *Journal of Marketing* (Summer 1979): pp. 68–78.
18. Henry Assail and John Keon, "Nonsampling vs. Sampling Errors in Survey Research," *Journal of Marketing* (Spring 1982): pp. 114–123.

Bryan Zindren, recently appointed development director at Gibault School, recognized quickly that he needed information about Gibault donors if he was to develop an effective program for giving. Gibault School was established many years ago by concerned Catholics to work with wayward teenage boys. The school has worked with Catholic organizations and various governmental agencies both for support and for referrals of boys who might benefit from attending the school. The school developed over the years a base of individuals who donated to the school. Some donors make regular contributions varying from as little as a dollar a month to substantial amounts. Other donors contribute irregularly—for instance, a single one-time contribution of $5–$10 at Christmas. Gibault, on a regular basis, conducts a direct mail campaign soliciting contributions. Although the direct mail approach has generated donations, it could be more effective by better targeting.

The reduced funding by government agencies of social programs has increased the importance of donors to Gibault. Bryan, therefore, decided to obtain the assistance of a student researcher at a local university. The student agreed to search the literature and advise Bryan on insights obtained from secondary data—especially as to possible questions for a mail questionnaire. The student returned two weeks later with the following report.

GIBAULT SCHOOL STUDY
This literature review focused on five major sources: government, firms, institutions, associations, and libraries. Within libraries visited, four types of publications were examined: books, periodicals, documents (government reports), and specialized collections (reporting services, microfilms and various published indexes). Computerized data bases, which are frequently useful re-

sources for marketing research, were not used because of the expense.

The research objective was to obtain pertinent literature about donor research, donor groups, and facilitation of design of a questionnaire, with possible question areas.

There have been numerous donor research studies conducted in the past that should be useful to Gibault. *Fundraising Management Magazine,* May, 1981, cites a study of people who contribute time and money to a variety of causes and projects. *The Journal of the Academy of Marketing Science,* Winter 1981, cites a study which investigated the relative efficiency of personality variables, organization-specific attitudes, and socioeconomic characteristics in grouping donors to the United Way. Socioeconomic variables were found to be most efficient in grouping donors.

The following references were especially helpful:

George Barna, "Profile of Attitudes of Christian Parochurch Group Donors," *Fundraising Management* (Feb. 1985), pp. 52–55.
Carl Bokal, *Charity U.S.A.* (New York: Times Books, 1979).
Mark Britto and Robert M. Oliver, "Forecasting Donors and Donations," *Journal of Forecasting* (Jan./Mar. 1986), pp. 39–55.
John A. Dunn, Jr. (ed.), *Enhancing the Management of Fundraising* (San Francisco: Jossey-Bass, 1986).
Richard F. Dye, Judith H. Hybels, and James Morgan, *Results from Two National Surveys of Philanthropic Giving* (Ann Arbor, MI: Survey Research Center, Institute for Social Research, University of Michigan, 1979).
William P. Freyd, "University Tries Creative Telemarketing," *Fund-raising Management* (Mar. 1987), pp. 64–68.
Linda J. Marks, "Rating Capacity Through Screening Sessions," *Fundraising Management* (July 1985), p. 26.

The following question areas should be considered when designing a questionnaire:

Demographics
Sex: Male, Female
Race: Black, White, Other
Geographic Region: Pacific, Mountain, West North Central, West South Central, East
Income: Over $35,000, $35,000, Less

Personality
Compulsive . . . . Noncompulsive
Introverted . . . . Extroverted
Dependent . . . . Independent
Liberal . . . . Conservative
Generous . . . . Nongenerous
Emotional . . . . Nonemotional
Uncaring . . . . Caring
Democratic . . . . Authoritarian
Follower . . . . Leader
High Achiever . . . . Low Achiever

Behavior Characteristics
Donation to Other Organizations: Religions, Education, Hospitals, Health/Welfare.
Tax Filing: Itemizer, Nonitemizer
Source of Knowledge About Gibault: Newsletter, Friends, Mass Mailings
Ownership: Stocks, Bonds, Real Estate, Life Insurance

Issues for Discussion
1. Have any important areas of secondary data been overlooked?
2. Have all the important topic areas been suggested? Should some of the topics be eliminated?
3. How useful will the explanation of personality variables be in researching donors?
4. Should the student be commended for excellent quality work?

MARKETING PLAN

STUDENT INSTRUCTIONS FOR MARKETING PLAN EXERCISE

This exercise is designed to acquaint you with the marketing plan and with the decisions required by the marketing manager or product manager. The exercise is focused primarily on an organization's product or product line. It is not designed to develop the company's strategic marketing plan or to illustrate the strategic marketing process.

The marketing plan exercise may be used in the following way: You may select one or more of the comprehensive cases provided at the back of the text. (Alternatively, your instructor may assign case material from another source). You will develop the marketing plan section by section, using the information you find in the cases. The questions will guide you in developing each part of the plan. Do not answer the questions with a sole "yes" or "no." Responses should be thoroughly developed in narrative form and should not appear as answers per se. In case a question/guideline is not applicable, it should be omitted from your plan. If needed information cannot be obtained, this should be stated in the narrative.

PARTS OF THE MARKETING PLAN
1. EXECUTIVE SUMMARY
2. SITUATION ANALYSIS (CURRENT MARKET SITUATION, INTERNAL ANALYSIS, EXTERNAL ANALYSIS)
3. MARKETING PLAN OBJECTIVES
4. MARKET SELECTION: TARGET MARKETS
5. MARKETING STRATEGY AND MARKETING MIX
6. ACTION PROGRAMS (SPECIFICS OF MARKETING MIX IMPLEMENTATION)
7. BUDGETS, CONTROL, AND ACCOUNTABILITY

MARKETING PLAN

PART 1 / EXECUTIVE SUMMARY

Note: The Executive Summary is written after the rest of the marketing plan has been completed. It appears first in the marketing plan because it may be the only part of the plan that the receiving executives have time to read. Guidelines for creating the Executive Summary appear on page 572.

PART 2 / SITUATION ANALYSIS
(CHAPTERS 2–4)

Current Market Situation
A. Describe your company's product or service.
B. What is the organization's current market situation?
  1. Sales in dollars? In units?
  2. Percent of the existing market for your product/ service?
  3. What percentages of the market do the largest competitors have?
  4. To what extent is there potential to enlarge the total market being served, e.g., expansion possibilities?
C. What trends are occuring in the market?
  1. Is the size of the market increasing? Decreasing?
  2. How fast is the market changing?
  3. Why has the market remained stable? Changed?
D. Does anything about the current market situation suggest changes in the marketing plan?

Internal Analysis
A. Analyze and describe the company's internal strengths.
B. Analyze and describe the company's internal weaknesses.
C. Have the firm's resources been identified?

continued to page 116

MARKETING PLAN

PART 2 / SITUATION ANALYSIS
continued from page 115

External Analysis (Environmental Scanning)
(CHAPTERS 2–4)
A. Describe important external conditions and/or trends in your industry. Do these conditions create opportunities for your product/service? Do these conditions pose threats to your product/service?
B. How should the organization compete? (Consider: If firm *does not* have a competitive advantage, *emulate, deviate, complement.*)
C. Does the organization have an obvious competitive advantage? If yes, what is it?
D. Can the organization develop a competitive advantage?
   In product?
   In service?
   In price?
   In distribution?
   In technology?
   In personnel?
   In _____ ?
   In _____ ?

PART 3 / MARKETING PLAN OBJECTIVES
(CHAPTERS 2–4)

A. What is the organization's mission?
B. What are the objectives of the marketing plan?
C. Are the objectives of the marketing plan compatible with the organization's mission?
D. Are the objectives of the marketing plan reasonable in relation to the firm's resources and abilities?
E. Can the objectives in the marketing plan be clearly measured?
F. Do the marketing plan objectives have a specified time frame in which they must be accomplished?

Section Three

Identification of
Target Markets

OUTLINE

Analysis of Marketing Opportunity: The Consumer and Organizational Markets

LEARNING GOALS

After reading this chapter, you should be able to:

1. Identify the major elements of a market as defined by marketers.
2. Define the various types of markets.
3. Describe the differences between the consumer and organizational markets.
4. Describe trends and dimensions of the consumer market and relate them to the marketing effort.
5. Relate types of buyers, purchase criteria, and types of buys in the organizational market to marketing efforts.

*M*ayflower Corporation engages in local, interstate, and international moving and storage of household and commercial goods. It also operates 3,700 route school buses with a daily passenger load of 275,000. Its fastest-growing business is transportation of computers, electronic equipment, and trade-show displays and exhibits, primarily for IBM and Control Data. Its wholesale appliance and home entertainment center serves Midwest retailers who need home appliances and home entertainment products quickly, safely, and efficiently.

Using 800 independent owner/operators, 700 independent agents, and 100 nonexclusive foreign independent agents, Mayflower serves as a common carrier of household goods to all fifty states and many foreign countries. Moving household goods accounts for 50 percent of its revenues. But when interest rates increase, houses do not sell as quickly and fewer people move. Mayflower has partially overcome this problem by contracting to move the employees of major corporations. Corporations are less sensitive to economic changes in moving personnel. Moving household goods still, however, is a very seasonal business.

The uncertainties of moving household goods, along with the major changes in the trucking industry as a result of deregulation, have prompted Mayflower to seek out other opportunities in other markets. Although the prospects for the trucking industry over the long run look favorable, deregulation has brought substantial changes. The Motor Carrier Act of 1980 deregulating trucking has brought substantial changes. Thousands of motor carriers have gone bankrupt since the passage of the Act. Most firms have improved financially, but industry experts predicted that failure in 1987 would continue, although at a much slower rate.

Deregulation allowed truckers to reduce rates. Rates were discounted from 10 to 30 percent with most being about 20 percent. With fuel accounting for 8 percent of revenues and wages representing 60 to 65 percent, discounts meant the end to some trucking companies. Some companies managed to survive by employing nonunion labor, which costs about 25 percent less than union labor. Other companies sought alternative opportunities. Rate discounting continues in the industry, but has not increased.

Deregulation has opened up markets by allowing truckers to compete for business where once they were denied by lack of appropriate government permits. Competition has increased the importance of marketing strategy, productivity, and technological improvements. In the business shippers market, several developments are in process. Large shippers are allocating shipments to a much smaller number of common and contract carriers.

Mayflower entered and is succeeding in the business shipper market of computers and electronic equipment. This part of its business has grown 20 percent annually. Mayflower convinced manufacturers that electronic equipment needs special handling in air-ride suspension vans used by household goods movers like Mayflower, rather than the steel spring trailers used by general freight common carriers. Quicker movement of goods has also been a selling point of Mayflower. Mayflower is adding to fleet size and sales force to penetrate the market even further.

To succeed in the business shippers' market will require innovation (such as expanded computerized information systems), cost competitiveness (such as wider tractors and twin trailers now allowed on the highways, improved load factors, and reduced unit cost), and improved service. Quality service along with price is an important consideration to shippers. Multimodal shippers argue that they can offer more services to shippers, including possibly one-stop shipping. Truck and rail combinations have already increased. Even with all of the above qualities, a trucker's fate depends somewhat on the shape of the economic cycle, for truck transportation is a derived de-

■ Mayflower has moved household goods for years. Large new markets include transporting school children and moving computers and appliances for the industrial market.

mand with business conditions determining the amount of demand.

To offset the seasonality of household goods moving and to be immune to economic cycles, Mayflower expanded into the transportation of school children. Mayflower offers to rid school boards of the headaches of school bus operations and at the same time, because of its expertise, reduce cost 10–15 percent. The potential for expansion in the market is considered very high. The public sector accounts for 80 percent of all school bus activities now.

For a company that wants to stay in the transportation business, maximize return on investment, and increase market share, has Mayflower successfully adapted to the deregulated environment? Is it moving into markets with good prospects?

Issues for Discussion
1. What markets does Mayflower serve?
2. What demographic, economic, and other trends in the consumer market would be of concern to Mayflower executives?

3. In serving the organization market, what should Mayflower executives consider?

Sources: Brian S. Moskal, ''Shakeouts and Mergers: Shippers Face Another Confusing Year,'' *Industry Week,* Jan. 26, 1987, p. 230; Brian Dumaine, ''Mayflower Makes Some New Moves,'' *Fortune,* March 4, 1985, p. 60; ''Trucking and Transport Leasing Industry,'' *Value Line,* July 5, 1985, pp. 278 and 285; ''Mayflower Corporation,'' *Standard & Poor's Corporation,* December 31, 1984, pp. 9204–9205; and ''Trucking,'' *U.S. Industrial Outlook 1985* (Department of Commerce, 1985), pp. 52–53 to 52–57.

*A*s we have seen in our Introductory Case, the Mayflower Corporation serves both *consumer* and *organizational* markets. In this chapter these two major markets are defined and profiled. We define the term *market* and introduce the steps marketers should follow in analyzing market opportunity. How do marketers select consumer markets? Some of the factors they consider are age, geographic location, income, living arrangements, and lifestyle. How do marketers select organizational markets? In the second portion of the chapter, we describe the nature and types of organizational markets, concluding with a discussion of buyer behavior in organizational markets. Chapter 6 describes buyer behavior in consumer markets. ■

 THE ANATOMY OF A MARKET

*M*arket = people with needs and ability to purchase.

A **market** is made up of all consumers and organizations that have both needs and the willingness and ability to make an exchange for the product, service, or idea that will meet those needs. Note that this definition includes both consumers, who buy for their own self-satisfaction, and organizations whose representatives buy so that the organization can produce a service, product, or idea for its customers. A market includes current as well as potential buyers. It is the marketer's responsibility, through the marketing plan, to keep current customers satisfied and to encourage potential customers to consider the firm's offering.

*U*nsatisfied needs – resistance = willingness to buy.

When the strength of their needs outweighs their resistance, potential buyers have a **willingness to purchase.** Willingness to engage in an exchange depends on the presence of unsatisfied needs, but also may be the result of marketing efforts. For instance, some people feel that advertising can sometimes create ''needs'' where none existed previously. Marketers generally do not attempt to evaluate the moral worthiness of a need (assuming that no ethical and legal codes are violated), preferring instead to let the potential buyer make the decision. Willingness is what the

THE REST OF THE STORY

Marketing Board Games—
It's Your Move

In 1935, the creators of a board game approached the Selchow & Richter Company about marketing their creation. The company's executives decided against the project, even though they recognized that it was unique. The company was uncertain about the size and composition of the market and the venture seemed too risky. This game requires players to buy and sell real estate. The purpose was to become wealthy (with play money) and at the same time drive the other players into bankruptcy.

The creators, undeterred, went to a second and competing company, Parker Brothers, who agreed to market the game. Monopoly became the best-selling board game for decades.

In 1982, creators of another board game approached Parker Brothers executives with their new product. They were turned down, since Parker Brothers was not convinced that a market of the necessary size and composition existed. The creators then went to another company and were again turned down. The third company they approached— Selchow & Richter—agreed to undertake the project. To play this game, participants move a marker several spaces with the roll of a die. Landing on a space, the player answers questions ranging from events and people in rock 'n' roll to facts about science. The rest you know. Trivial Pursuit became the best-selling board game of all time.

Source: John P. Tarpey, "Selchow & Richter: Playing Trivial Pursuit to the Limit," *Business Week,* November 26, 1984, p. 18; and James P. Forkan, "Game Marketers in Pursuit of Trivia Fans," *Advertising Age,* March 26, 1984, p. 52.

---

*A*bility to purchase = available resources + authority.

marketer evaluates. The marketer may try to increase willingness by attempting to reduce resistance. Easier credit and lower prices may, for instance, reduce the potential buyer's resistance.

Potential buyers must be able as well as willing to buy. To have the ability to exchange, the buyer must have both available resources and the authority to use them. Available resources, for most exchanges, means cash. For other exchanges, resources may be measured in terms of wealth, income, potential income, credit, commitment, or time. Sometimes potential buyers have resources but lack the authority to use them for the exchange. Examples of this situation include: (1) a child who has an allowance and wants to purchase bubble gum but must obtain the approval of a parent; (2) a person who wants to buy a new car but believes the approval of a spouse must be obtained; and (3) an office manager who wants to purchase a new office computer network, but must obtain approval from the organization's buying committee.

Analysis of Market Opportunity

*O*pportunities should be assessed in both established markets and new markets.

We might assume that marketing managers somehow know the market and the opportunities it offers without study. Often, however, this is not the case. The market for a new offering has to be clearly defined. What needs can the organization satisfy? Are those needs currently being met? If so, how? For example, when videocassette recorders (VCRs) first entered the market, they competed with video disk players. Both satisfied an entertainment need by allowing people to play prerecorded disks or cassettes, but VCRs met an additional need. They allowed people to record favorite TV programs for later viewing. Because VCRs satisfied more needs than video disk players, they were much more successful in their market.

Even for existing products, marketers should assess the market to make sure no opportunities have been overlooked. Arm & Hammer expanded its market for baking

❑ **Figure 5.1**
Analysis of marketing
opportunity.

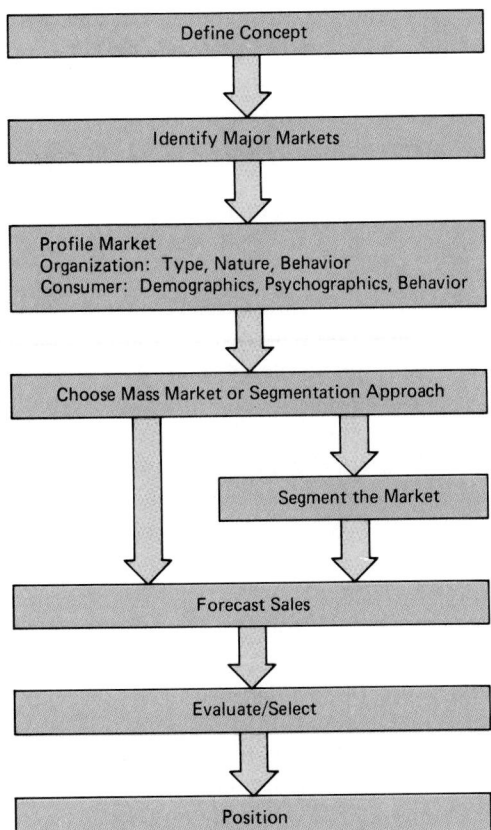

soda after recognizing the large deodorizing market. The company's advice to place a box of Arm & Hammer in the refrigerator, pour a box down the sink, and so on, expanded the product's market greatly. Markets usually also change in size or in some other way over time. Assessing the market permits executives to respond to changes with more appropriate market plans.

Analysis of market opportunity involves investigating and researching to locate the market with the highest potential for achieving the organization's objectives. Once the market has been identified, the marketing manager must develop a market plan that converts the market potential to sales.

One method of analyzing marketing opportunity is shown in figure 5.1. The analysis should, when completed, enable the marketer to respond effectively to the following questions:

1. To whom are we marketing this product/brand?
2. Why are we marketing to this group?
3. Why are we marketing in this way to this group?

*R*efining the market definition: marketers start with a general concept of the market, then identify major market types, then develop specific profiles of the markets.

A brief explanation of each element in figure 5.1 provides an overview of the process. The remainder of this chapter, along with Chapters 6 and 7, discusses the process in detail.

Define concept—An old cliché, "You cannot be all things to all people," is relevant to marketing. Because the organization cannot serve everyone, it must decide who to serve. The marketer's concept of the market supplies the initial perceptions of the market to be served. For example, Michelin executives' concept was to develop a superior way to satisfy the need for durable high quality car tires. Michelin became the worldwide leader in superior radial tires in the business. Michelin's initial concept—its starting point—was refined and developed.

Identify major markets—To clarify the market concept, the marketer may visualize the market in general terms. Identification of consumer and organizational markets often serves as a starting point. As more information becomes available, the major markets frequently are narrowed to more specific markets.

Profile the market—Who, more specifically, makes up the market, and why? In order to more precisely define a market in a way that permits building of a market plan, the marketer needs detailed information. Consumer demographics will supply much of the needed information to profile a consumer market. This important topic is covered in this chapter, followed by the characteristics of organizational markets.

Choose mass market or segmentation approach—How will the marketer cater to the market? Will it be treated as a homogeneous mass? Or will the marketer divide it into groups and serve only selected groups, with a market plan for each group?

Segment the market—If the market is to be segmented, what procedure should be used to divide it into groups? What variables are most effective in determining group membership?

Forecast—What sales can the company expect? The sales forecast is probably the most important factor in market selection.

Evaluate/select—With several markets available, what markets offer the most opportunity for the organization? Sales potential, competitors, growth rates, and organizational resources illustrate variables that enter into the evaluation and selection of markets. Since the analysis of market opportunity is a continuous process, evaluation and selection are also continuous. For this reason, the discussion of evaluation and selection is interspersed in Chapters 5, 6, and 7.

Position—How will the product and brand be perceived by the selected market, especially in relation to competing products and brands? The firm's efforts create the desired perceptions, referred to as positioning.

Segmentation, forecasting, evaluating, and positioning are discussed in detail in Chapter 7.

Selecting a market: marketers decide on a mass or segmented market approach, segment the market if necessary, forecast sales, and position their product.

Defining the Market

How a product, service, or idea is defined has an important effect on what market it will serve. For example, narrowing the product definition may narrow the market. The market for diesel motors of less than twenty-five horsepower is smaller than the market for diesel motors of larger size, and the market for diesel motors is smaller than the market for motors in general. Figure 5.2 illustrates a narrowing product definition.

A concept of the market may also develop along geographic and time dimensions. In other words, the market may be visualized as covering certain geographic areas and certain time periods. The marketer's concept of the market in terms of product, geography, time, and perhaps other dimensions regulates research activities. As the investigation proceeds, the marketer's concept of the market may change to reflect the information gathered.

Product, geography, and time are common elements in the marketer's concept of the market.

❏ **Figure 5.2**
A narrowing product definition.

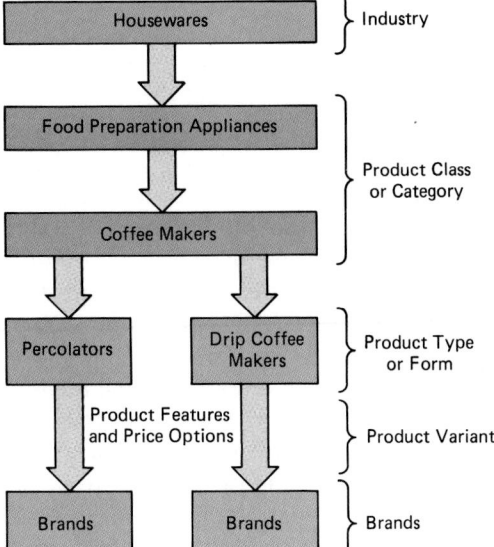

Identifying Major Markets

*C*onsumer markets purchase to satisfy personal needs.

Two commonly recognized market categories are consumer markets and organizational markets. The **consumer market** consists of all individuals who purchase for the sole purpose of satisfying their own personal or household needs. Each of us is a consumer. Obviously, the size of the consumer market is large.

*O*rganizational markets purchase to conduct operations.

The **organizational market** consists of all individuals within the organization who purchase goods or services the organization needs to produce a product, provide a service, promote an idea, or produce an income. In dollars, the organizational market is even larger than the consumer market. Note that the difference in consumer and organizational products does not lie with the physical nature of the product. The distinction is in how the product is used.

PROFILING THE CONSUMER MARKET: DEMOGRAPHICS

Several demographic elements, such as income and age, were introduced in Chapter 3 as macroenvironmental forces. Here, the discussion demonstrates how the marketer uses knowledge of the environment to identify and assess the viability of a market. The market's viability depends on the willingness and ability of its members to purchase the product. Determining willingness and ability to buy allows the marketer to estimate the size of the market and to decide on features needed in the marketing plan. In more specific terms, the marketing manager must answer the following questions:

Who will purchase the product?
Where will the product be purchased?
How will the product be purchased?
How much of the product will be purchased?

Population

*T*rends in population size indicate future potential and thus influence market plans.

The size of the population indicates, in the broadest terms, the potential market demand for consumer products and services. This is why marketing managers are excited about the market of China—its population is estimated at approximately one billion. Of course, since only some people in the population have both the willingness and the ability to buy, the size of the population is the upper limit to demand.

As general as population information is, it still is helpful. The rate of population growth, for instance, gives the marketer an idea of the future potential market. The U.S. population growth rate has decreased substantially since the 1950s, known as the baby-boom years, when the birth rate was very high. The birth rate per couple needed for zero population growth is 2.1, and the United States has been near this rate for several years. Thus, firms marketing items whose demand is tied to population size can no longer depend on an expanding population to increase sales. Sales increases will have to come from larger market shares. Types of products that typically depend on population growth for increased sales include staple products such as foods. Thus, Kellogg Company, for instance, must develop a strategy that will gain larger market shares for its breakfast cereals.

Population growth rates vary among nations. West Germany, for example, has a low growth rate, while Mexico has a high rate. In some countries, governments have used advertising campaigns to influence the rate of population growth.[1]

Age

*A*ge affects product consumption.

The age distribution of the consumer market is especially important in marketing some products. Soft-drink sales, for instance, depend on the youth market.[2] An organization that markets to a specific age group must be alert to changes in the group, especially changes in size. Educational institutions at all levels have learned the importance of shifts in the size of the age groups they serve. For example, the traditional age range of 5–22 of the student population is declining. Educational institutions, especially those of higher education, have learned to use marketing to attract more and better prepared students.

Shifts in the size of age groups provide varied marketing opportunities. The booming growth in the number of individuals over sixty-five (the senior-citizen market) has presented unique opportunities in cosmetics, recreation, and other product areas.[3]

Marketers can anticipate shifts in the size of various age groups by tracing the progress of individuals through the life cycle. The baby boomers of the fifties are now thirty-five to forty-five years old. Organizations marketing to this group, because of the large numbers of baby boomers, will have to consider adjustments in their marketing plans. In ten years, organizations that serve people forty-five to fifty-five years old will consider changes, because the baby boomers will then be in that group.

*T*he U.S. population is growing older.

The median age of the U.S. population is now in the early thirties. Projections indicate that the median age will increase to thirty-five by the year 2000. What does this mean for marketing? Perhaps less emphasis will be placed on youth, but greater emphasis on youthfulness—staying young.

Where We Live

*W*here people live makes a difference in the products they consume.

Knowing where the population lives helps marketers develop effective strategies. Managers of organizations that lack adequate resources to serve the national market may decide to operate on a regional, state, or local basis. National marketers, too, must be aware of geographic differences. Typically, they acknowledge such differences in their allocation of resources to advertising, sales force, inventory, warehousing, and other marketing areas.

Product use varies by geographic region. For instance, Cajun-type foods are popular in the lower Mississippi Valley region, snow blowers are popular in the North, and western-style clothing is popular in the Great Plains. Zip-code marketing, a technique employed by direct-marketing organizations, focuses on different geographic areas by zip-code designation, as described in the Marketing in Action feature on pages 128–129.

People are constantly moving from one area of the country to another and, within areas, from urban to suburban to rural regions. Almost 20 percent of the population moves each year. This movement makes it difficult for direct-mail marketers who want to keep their mailing lists up to date. Mobile people do, however, present a welcome opportunity for organizations in the communities to which they move. Moving disrupts buying habits and product loyalties, so new community members are more receptive to information presented by marketers.

*T*he populace constantly changes locations: interior to coast; North to South; city to suburb.

Shifts in population have tended to favor suburban areas; urban and rural areas have tended to lose population. Knowledge of population shifts helps in planning marketing facilities. Suburban growth, for example, has meant development of shopping malls and other facilities to accommodate the suburb dweller. It has also caused a shift in the demand for some products. For example, people who move from city to suburbs are more likely to need a clothes-washing machine, because fewer public laundry facilities are available in suburbs than in cities.

In the 1970s, an unusual shift in the population from urban and suburban to rural areas occurred. Several reasons seem to explain the shift: More jobs became available in rural areas as manufacturers established facilities there. The decision by General Motors to locate the Saturn automobile plant in Springhill, Tennessee, a rural area, is a good example. Also, many retirees moved to rural areas for environmental and other reasons, and many people moved to rural areas to escape the crime and other problems associated with cities. WalMart, aware of this movement, fared well by locating many of its discount stores in small-town America. Since 1980, however, urban areas have grown while rural areas have stabilized or declined in population.

The U.S. Commerce Department has defined three types of population areas for data gathering.[4] (See figure 5.3.) The Commerce Department–defined areas may cross political boundaries to describe the total market in a more useful way.

❑ **Figure 5.3**
U.S. population areas defined by U.S. Commerce Department.

Consolidated Metropolitan Statistical Area (CMSA)

These areas include large metropolitan populations of a million or more people that also meet certain other requirements. Examples include: New York, Los Angeles, Chicago, Houston.

Primary Metropolitan Statistical Area (PMSA)

PMSA are distinct major areas within CMSAs, such as an urbanized county or counties.

Metropolitan Statistical Area (MSA)

MSAs are freestanding urban areas with a minimum city population of 50,000 and a minimum total population of 100,000.

MARKETING IN ACTION

Zip It to Me

*E*ver wonder why you still keep getting mailings from American Express, even though you've applied for a card—and been rejected—several times already? The trouble is, one has absolutely nothing to do with the other. You're just another hapless victim of the Zip Code mailing syndrome.

Even in this sophisticated age of demographic and socioeconomic targeting, there are always going to be a few households that don't fit the pattern supplied by the majority of a particular Zip Code's residents. The sheer volume of data available for this level of geography is truly staggering. Companies that supply Zip Code statistics to marketers can now print out an endless stream of items designed to isolate even the most esoteric of customer or market profiles. Of course, there will always be a few who won't fit the mold.

Using New York City as an example, the variety of ethnic, racial, housing, and income data from three of its Zips paint a very diverse picture of neighborhoods that are sometimes only blocks apart. And even within these small areas, there is still plenty of diversity.

Brooklyn Heights—Zip Code 11201—has recently become a favor-

ite target of those companies looking for the epitome of today's young urban professional. Data for the area reveal a neighborhood that is roughly two-thirds white (65.7 percent), with almost half of its households containing only one person (48.2 percent). In addition, the largest age segment (25.4 percent) is between ages 25 and 34, and the households with incomes in excess of $30,000 comprise 22.3 percent of the Zip area.

Looking at these same characteristics for Manhattan's Chinatown district (Zip Code 10013), we see a racial split of 43 percent Asian versus 46 percent white, and a household demographic that shows 29 percent with three or more people. This leaves a considerable portion of smaller households in the area, but far fewer single-person households than in Zip 11201. The single-largest age segment is still the 25-to-34 group (25.0 percent), but the population over age 55 accounts for roughly a quarter of the total for the Zip. Income, on the other hand, shows the

biggest difference, with fully 44.2 percent earning between $5,000 and $15,000.

If we develop a simple customer profile based on these elements, each of these two Zips would produce a different norm. And from a marketing standpoint, even if you're not part of the norm, you're still part of the Zip Code.

Moving due north about six miles, just past the top of Central Park, we come upon the Morningside district of Manhattan. Here, the numbers show a third distinctive Zip Code subgroup, one that is 94.5 percent black, 3.9 percent Puerto Rican, and just 1.5 percent white. And while the 25-to-34 age group is still the largest, it accounts for only 13.2 percent of the Zip total. Children under age 13 make up a greater portion of the Zip population than they do in the other two areas, showing 19.1 percent versus Chinatown's 10.2 percent and the Heights' 13.1 percent. Household size leans toward the high end, with 37.9 percent consisting of three or more people. Single-person households, however, still account for a substantial percentage of all households (38.7 percent), but it should be noted that the New York metro area contains by far the most households

Income

*M*easurements of ability to buy include disposable and discretionary income.

Income statistics provide the marketing manager with measurements of ability to buy. As noted in Chapter 3, various definitions of income exist, each having associated statistics and each providing a different measurement of the ability to buy. Two of the most widely used to define markets are disposable personal income and discretionary income. **Disposable personal income** is income after taxes, and **discretionary income** is disposable income minus expenditures for necessities.[5] Marketers of luxury products and services—such as high-priced cars and cruises—frequently use discretionary income as a measure of the ability to spend.

Whether marketers are using disposable, discretionary, or some other income to demonstrate ability to buy, they pay particular attention to income distribution and changes in income.

INCOME DISTRIBUTION BY HOUSEHOLD

*A*merica's large middle-income group provides an excellent market.

The distribution of income by household in the United States for 1983 is shown in figure 5.4. The U.S. market has been and remains an especially good market of this type, more than 1 million at last count, making up nearly a third of all households in the metro.

Other characteristics, such as educational attainment, owner-occupied versus renter-occupied housing units, employment status, and even the number of bedrooms and bathrooms per housing unit, are available for all of America's nearly 17,000 Zips. But even with such highly specific data for these highly specific geographic areas, there are always a few who won't fit the marketer's profile—proving once again that marketing research is not yet the exact science that some would have us believe. But it's getting there.

As Seen By the Survey*
Different Zips make different blips

Zip Code: 11201

Name: Brooklyn Heights

Metro: New York

County: Kings (Brooklyn)

Educational attainment:
Did not finish high school—8,100 (25.5%)
Finished high school only—6,393 (20.1%)
Completed 1–3 years of college—4,702 (14.8%)
Completed 4 or more years of college—12,543 (39.5%)

Owner-occupied units:
2,983 (13.5%)

Renter-occupied units:
17,643 (79.6%)

Number of bedrooms:
0 or 1—12,410 (60.2%)
2—5,408 (26.2%)
3 or more—2,808 (13.6%)

Number of bathrooms:
1 only—17,050 (82.7%)
1½ or more—2,862 (13.9%)

Zip Code: 10026

Name: Morningside

Metro: New York

County: New York (Manhattan)

Educational attainment:
Did not finish high school—9,663 (60.7%)
Finished high school only—4,655 (29.3%)
Completed 1–3 years of college—1,020 (6.4%)
Completed 4 or more years of college—572 (3.6%)

Owner-occupied units:
145 (1.2%)

Renter-occupied units:
9,870 (78.8%)

Number of bedrooms:
0 or 1—4,053 (40.5%)
2—2,985 (29.8%)
3 or more—2,977 (29.7%)

Number of bathrooms:
1 only—8,801 (87.9%)
1½ or more—446 (4.5%)

Zip Code: 10013

Name: Chinatown

Metro: New York

County: New York (Manhattan)

Educational attainment:
Did not finish high school—8,429 (48.3%)
Finished high school only—2,754 (15.8%)
Completed 1–3 years of college—1,849 (10.6%)
Completed 4 or more years of college—4,405 (25.3%)

Owner-occupied units:
621 (6.6%)

Renter-occupied units:
8,155 (87.0%)

Number of bedrooms:
0 or 1—5,851 (66.7%)
2—2,400 (27.3%)
3 or more—525 (6.0%)

Number of bathrooms:
1 only—5,635 (64.2%)
1½ or more—423 (4.8%)

*Source: Sales & Marketing Management's 1985 Survey of Buying Power—Part II, Sales & Marketing Management; Sales and Marketing Management, November 11, 1985, p. 17. Reprinted by permission of Sales & Marketing Management.

❏ **Figure 5.4**
Income distribution by household, United States, 1986 (total = 89,479,000).

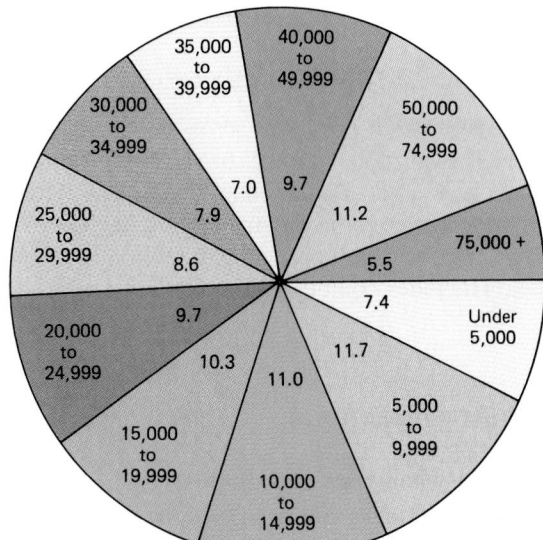

Source: Current Population Reports Consumer Income. Series P-60, No. 157. U.S. Bureau of the Census, 1986.

❑ **Figure 5.5** Income distribution by geographic area.

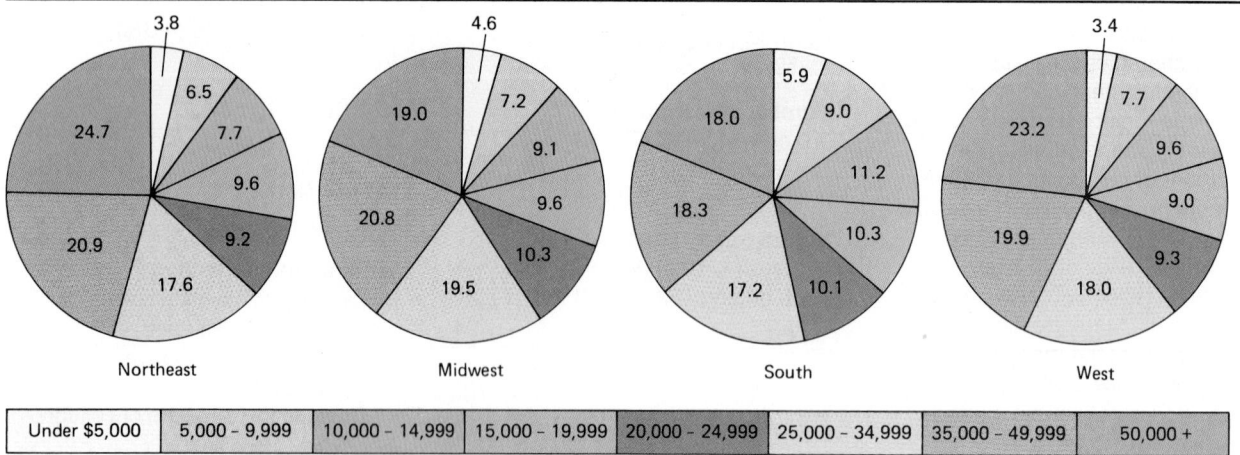

Under $5,000	5,000 – 9,999	10,000 – 14,999	15,000 – 19,999	20,000 – 24,999	25,000 – 34,999	35,000 – 49,999	50,000 +

Source: Current Population Reports, Series P-60, No. 159. U.S. Bureau of the Census, 1986.

because of the large number of middle-income households. The middle-income sector, as a percentage of the total, has decreased slightly in the 1980s. Governmental income redistribution policies have become more conservative in the 1980s, resulting in shifts from middle-income to lower-income classification for some households. In addition, the number of double-income families has increased, and many double-income families have entered the upper-income ranks. Research suggests that double-income families definitely tend to be spenders, not savers. In addition, their spending differs from that of single-income families in that they tend to use their incomes for products and services to give them immediate enjoyment.[6]

CHANGES IN INCOME LEVEL

A change in household income may boost willingness to buy even faster than it increases ability to buy.

Changes in household income influence willingness as well as ability to buy. An increase in income gives individuals more ability to purchase; furthermore, because of optimism generated by the higher income, their willingness to purchase frequently increases faster than their ability to purchase. This willingness to purchase is not spread evenly over all products and services. Engel's laws, discussed in Chapter 3, identify how expenditure patterns change as income increases. When income increases, individuals seem to adjust their consumption patterns upward rather quickly. When income decreases, however, they adjust consumption downward more slowly and to a lesser extent. This difference is described by the term **ratchet effect.**

INCOME DISTRIBUTION BY GEOGRAPHIC AREA

*B*ecause the people who live there earn higher incomes, some geographic areas make better markets.

Income distribution varies across the regions of the country. Figure 5.5 specifies income levels for four major U.S. regions. The *Survey of Buying Power,* an annual publication of *Sales & Marketing Management* magazine, is an excellent source of information on geographic distribution of income. *The Survey of Buying Power Index* also can be used as a more complete measure of the buying ability of a geographic market. The index combines three variables: income, population, and retail sales.

Living Arrangements

Consumers' willingness and ability to purchase are also affected by their living arrangements—household composition, the family life cycle, and lifestyle.

All family members often become involved in major purchase decisions.

HOUSEHOLD COMPOSITION

The number of households influences the number of purchases of products like refrigerators, dishwashers, clothes washers, and dryers. In 1987 there were over 90 million households in the United States, a 43 percent increase since 1970. The increase in number of households has not been equally shared by the two general types of households: family and nonfamily.

*T*he number of nonfamily households is increasing in relation to the number of family households, but family households still make up 70 percent of the total.

Family households are made up of individuals living together who are related by blood or marriage. Single-parent families have doubled since 1970. The high divorce rate and an increase in the number of unwed mothers has led to the increase. Single-parent families, commonly headed by a female, often have lower purchasing power. Family households account for 70 percent of the total households; nonfamily, 30 percent. However, **nonfamily households**—singles and nonrelated individuals living together—have increased in number by 85 percent since 1980. The nonfamily household is less stable than the family household. Instability reduces the willingness to invest in household items such as furniture. Nonfamily households spend more on items that can be moved easily, such as stereos and cars. They also spend more on travel and entertainment than family households.

*T*he decline in the average number of members per household has encouraged downsizing in products and packages.

The number of members in the average household has steadily declined, and this decline has meant that marketers have had to make adjustments. Cars and dwellings have been downsized, as have packages for food items. Many food products are now offered in single-serving containers. Changes in households have also led marketers to change promotional strategies; for instance, words such as *husband* and *wife* have been eliminated from many advertisements.

FAMILY LIFE CYCLE

The **family life cycle** traces the evolution of families from formation to final stage. The evolution is divided into stages according to age, family size, and marital status. Figure 5.6 outlines the life-cycle stages.

A family with young children buys different products than a retired couple.

The family's needs change as it moves through the cycle, as do its consumption motives and purchasing patterns. In the young-single and young-married-without-children stages, for example, incomes are usually high, as is optimism about the future. People in these stages enjoy their income through the purchase of cars, leisure activities, travel, and similar goods. With the arrival of children, a couple that had earned two incomes may choose to depend on only one income, and their purchases will be more oriented to child rearing. Organizations often form their marketing plans with a particular stage of the family life cycle in mind. However, differences do exist among families at the same stage of the life cycle.

❑ **Figure 5.6** Stages in the family life cycle.

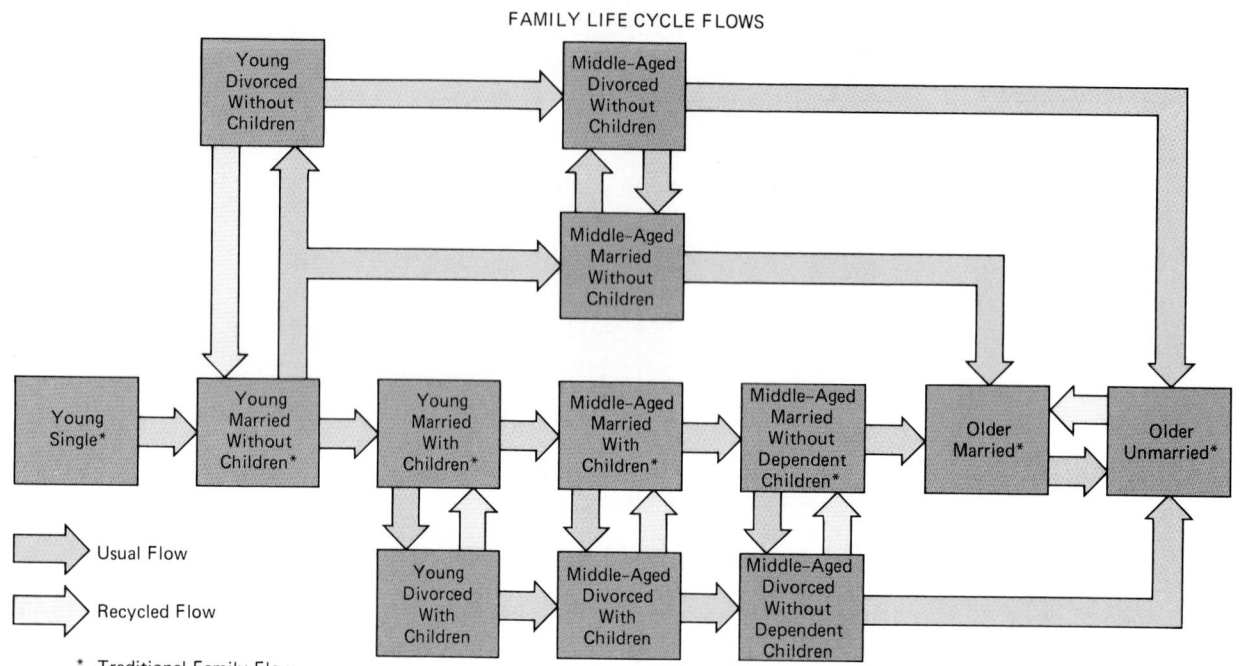

FAMILY LIFE CYCLE FLOWS

Usual Flow

Recycled Flow

* Traditional Family Flow

Source: Patrick E. Murphy and William Staples, "A Modernized Family Life Cycle," *Journal of Consumer Research,* June 1979, p. 17.

LIFESTYLE

Part of the difference in product purchase and use by families at the same stage in the family life cycle is attributed to lifestyle differences. Lifestyle as well as life-cycle stage affects purchasing behavior. In general, **lifestyle** describes a person's mode or manner of working and living. It is a composite of the individual's behavioral patterns and psychological makeup. Lifestyle research often focuses on activities, interests, and opinions (AIO).[7] This more restricted view of lifestyle is referred to as *psychographics,* which will be discussed in detail in Chapter 7.

Lifestyle information provides the marketer with a richer description of the market. Product selection, use of income, roles taken in the family, and leisure activities are all examples of lifestyle facets that the marketer may investigate. Lifestyle information has received its greatest application in the development of promotion programs (discussed in Chapter 16). The marketing department of a North Carolina hospital, in an attempt to widen their client base, identified nine different lifestyle groups. One of those they found was the "naturalist" group, whose members seek alternatives to regular healthcare. The group is comprised primarily of well-educated females who care about nutrition and fitness but not about sports. The hospital promoted its services to the naturalist by stressing its nutrition, diet, and nontraditional therapy programs. The hospital also sponsored a televised cooking show featuring the preparation of healthy meals, and began and used direct mail to distribute brochures on vitamins and nutrition tips. These promotional efforts, all targeted to the naturalist lifestyle, proved successful in attracting new clients to the hospital.

Changes in society have changed people's lifestyles. For example, the greater number of working women has changed the way women, men, and children live. The latchkey child—the child who, arriving home from school, must unlock the house because his or her parents are still at work—has become more common. Similarly, more men engage in meal preparation, grocery shopping, and other housekeeping activities. Organizations need to stay abreast of lifestyle changes in order to make effective marketing plans.

*M*ayflower executives should be alert to factors influencing the householder's willingness and ability to purchase moving services. Obviously the number of households is important. The number of households has continued to increase, but not dramatically. Nonfamily and single-parent family households have increased the fastest. Both nonfamily and single-parent family households tend to be smaller than family households; therefore, there would be less

to move. Income, especially of single-parent households, is also often less than that of two-parent families. The combination of smaller-size households and smaller incomes may result in moves being of the more economical U-Haul type.

The mobility of the population would also warrant Mayflower's attention. Since mobility decreases

with age, the increasing median age of the population would indicate a reduced market potential. The mobility of the population has decreased slightly to less than 20 percent of the population moving each year. Mayflower would want to be well represented in areas from which people are moving. It is the starting location from which moving companies are hired. Even the family life cycle and lifestyle would influence mobility and the quantity of household goods.

PROFILING THE ORGANIZATIONAL MARKET

Organizational markets consist of buyers who purchase products needed in their organizations' operation. Those who market to organizations must determine ability and willingness to purchase. Understanding the behavior behind organizational buying is important in determining willingness to buy, as it is with consumers. The behavior behind organizational buying, however, differs from consumer behavior.

Types of Organizational Markets

Objectives of organizations differ, and objectives influence buying behavior and thus willingness to buy. Based on objectives, we can distinguish three types of organizational buyers: industrial, governmental, and institutional.

INDUSTRIAL

*S*elling to industrial markets depends on understanding how they are attempting to make a profit.

For **industrial organizations,** willingness to buy often depends on the effect of the potential purchase on the income statement—the bottom line, or profit. Will the potential purchase reduce the cost of operation or increase sales? Economic criteria weigh heavily on the purchase decision. To sell more effectively to industrial buyers, marketers should know the strategy of the industrial concern. If, for instance, the strategy is to compete by selling a high-quality product at a higher price (the strategy used by Caterpillar Tractor Company), the emphasis in marketing should be on quality. On the other hand, if the price is determined by factors outside the industrial organization's control and the organization's strategy is to reduce cost (as is the situation with farmers), the emphasis in marketing should be on cost reduction and efficiency.

*P*roducers make a profit primarily from form utility; resellers from the time, place, and possession utilities.

Two subtypes of industrial organizations, producers and resellers, differ in how they make a profit. **Producers** make a profit primarily by creating and marketing form utility—for example, making products. **Resellers** make a profit primarily by creating time, place, and possession utility. They buy products and make them available to other buyers at the right time, place, price, and quantity. Marketing to resellers requires that demand for the product exists. Marketing efforts aimed at resellers thus normally include developing demand. Supermarkets are more apt to purchase Listerine mouthwash if the makers of Listerine invest heavily in advertising Listerine to consumers.

GOVERNMENT

*G*overnments provide a large market because they are involved in almost every kind of activity.

Government organizations have objectives such as maintaining order, providing at least minimal levels of service and standards of living, and maintaining political boundaries. To attain their many objectives, governments must be involved in just about every kind of activity; thus governments purchase just about every kind of product and service. The government market is large. In the United States, approximately 25 percent of the gross national product is purchased by the federal government. The willingness of governments to purchase depends on the policies and philosophies dominant at a particular time.

*B*ids and negotiations are typical in U.S. government markets.

Even though government objectives may be noneconomic, the purchase decisions necessary in achieving those objectives normally are economically oriented. In the United States, the federal government uses economic criteria in making purchase decisions. To reduce favoritism in supplier selection, it awards purchase contracts through competitive bidding. For example, the *Federal Supply Service (FSS),* created by the federal government to promote efficiency through centralized buying, purchases most of the nonmilitary products the federal government uses. FSS buys on the basis of low bid but must adhere to rules established by legislation that give favored treatment to some organizations. The 5 percent price edge for firms of less than 600 employees is one such rule.

To give every supplier an opportunity to bid, government agencies are normally required by law to advertise for the products and services they need. Local and state agencies usually advertise in the classified section of area newspapers. They also request bids from suppliers of record—firms that have previously supplied or bid on a similar product. The federal government announces most of its product and service needs in the *Commerce Business Daily.*

The PX or commissary stores found on military bases are part of the government market.

Government purchases are open to public scrutiny. That makes it easier to obtain information on government needs, but it also means that supporting documents to verify the purchase procedure and the purchase must be made available. Some executives supplying governments complain of the large amount of paperwork required. It is part of serving the market.

Foreign governments also make up a big market. For example, the Saudi Arabian governmental market expanded rapidly after the nation's petroleum income soared. Foreign governments have essentially the same objectives as the U.S. government, but purchase procedures vary. (International marketing is the topic of Chapter 21.)

*M*arketing to governments, especially foreign governments, may raise ethical issues.

Questions of ethics often arise in the organizational market because of the large purchases involved and the potential influence of a few individuals. The methods by which suppliers are chosen receive considerable discussion in relation to many foreign government markets. Based on the amount of discussion given to the topic, it would seem that marketers often use bribes, under-the-table payments, and other incentives to influence foreign decision makers. Of course, such practices are forbidden by U.S. law. Marketers may simply decline to market to some governments because the ethical standards acceptable to these governments are incompatible with the business practices required by U.S. law. The U.S. government also restricts the sale of military and advanced technological products to certain countries for reasons related to national security.

INSTITUTIONAL

*I*n institutional markets, ability and willingness to purchase are difficult to document.

The **institutional market** consists of organizations with objectives other than normal business goals, such as profit. These objectives include improving health, promoting a better quality of life, gaining acceptance of philosophical viewpoints, and many others. Just as objectives vary, so also do the organizations themselves— from temporary to permanent, from large to small, from unorganized to organized, from small product needs to large, and from substantial purchasing power to none. Information about the ability and willingness of this market to purchase is difficult to obtain except in a few well-established areas: health care, education, and religion. Thus, marketers may move into poorly charted markets when serving the institutional buyer. Many organizations, therefore, develop products and services that satisfy industrial or government markets and treat sales to institutions as a favorable by-product of marketing programs aimed at others.

Nature of Organizational Markets

Organizational markets—as distinct from consumer markets—are unique in several areas.

FEWER BUYERS

*T*here are fewer organizational buyers, but they spend more than consumers.

Although the organizational market contains fewer buyers than the consumer market, the average organization spends considerably more dollars in a year than the average consumer. The average dollar value of each purchase is also higher for the organization than for the consumer. Consequently, marketers are willing to spend more per organization to obtain business. For example, personal selling, an expensive technique, is more frequently used in organizational markets than in consumer markets.

CONCENTRATED GEOGRAPHICALLY

Personal selling can also be used in organizational markets because organizations that supply a particular type of good or service often can be found concentrated in

On-site sales visits pay off in the industrial market because of the large dollar amount per order and the geographic concentration of customers.

a relatively small geographic area. Examples include computer electronics in California's Silicon Valley and in the Northeast corridor; polymers in Akron, Ohio; steel in the Pittsburgh and Chicago areas; and automobiles in Michigan. Many industries, even those just named, are moving into new geographic areas. For example, we have already mentioned General Motors' decision to build a new auto plant in Tennessee. The markets remain only somewhat dispersed, however, so the cost of visiting each buyer still is less than in the very dispersed consumer market. The combination of geographic concentration and high sales per average buyer in the organizational market makes visiting the buyer's place of business practical.

DEMAND DIFFERENCES

Organizational market demand differs from consumer market demand in two respects: it is derived and it may be joint. The feature of **derived demand** comes from the fact that organizations purchase products and services only if their own products and services are in demand. Thus, demand in organizational markets is derived from demand for another product or service.

*O*rganizations buy if their products are in demand.

Derived demand has several marketing implications. The willingness of organizational buyers to purchase fluctuates widely depending on the organization's forecast of demand for its own products. An optimistic forecast leads to a greater willingness to purchase, while a pessimistic forecast may lead to a decision to depend on inventory and an unwillingness to purchase. Executives of firms that serve the organizational market may want to direct some marketing effort at the customers of the organizational market, to help the organizations stimulate demand. At the very least, marketers should have up-to-date information about their buyers' markets.

On the positive side, derived demand means that organizations willingly purchase products or services even if the prices increase, as long as they can either pass the increases on to their customers or absorb them without a major impact on their profit. Since neither passing the price on nor absorbing it represents as desirable an alternative as acquiring the item at a lower price, however, raising the price in an organizational market often means the purchaser will look to other suppliers with lower prices.

*P*romoting a brand to consumers may create demand for the brand with industrial buyers.

This is another reason marketers may want to direct some marketing effort at the customers of their organizational clients. If these customers become convinced that a particular product or service is better in some way than competing products and services, they may insist that the organizations they patronize use only these products or services. For example, General Motors promotes its auto parts to consumers with the slogan "Insist on genuine GM parts." Automobile repair shops and service stations may have to buy from General Motors to satisfy customers. Briggs

General Motors' advertising encourages consumers to insist on GM parts.

Source: Reprinted with permission from General Motors Corporation.

& Stratton, a producer of small gasoline engines, promotes its product to consumers even though it sells only to manufacturers.

Joint demand develops from the way in which many products are produced. The parts for products are often made by several organizations and assembled by still another organization. The demand for a particular firm's part depends on the parts produced by the other firms. If the other suppliers fail to supply parts, the demand for all parts is affected. For instance, the demand for Cummins diesel engines depends on suppliers providing the other parts needed to produce large, over-the-road trucks. Strikes and natural disasters can make joint demand considerations important.

Buyer Behavior in the Organizational Market

*O*rganizations tend to buy in a more organized and rational way than consumers.

Organizations do not make purchase decisions in the same way as consumers. The organization is often more organized and rational than the consumer. Organizations may also have professional buyers—trained individuals with expertise in buying. Many other individuals in an organization may also become involved in the purchase of products and services.

RESPONSIBILITY FOR BUYING

Who has the responsibility and authority to make a purchase decision depends on the type of organization and the product being purchased. Retailers and manufacturers, for instance, differ in this regard. Furthermore, infrequently purchased, expensive items are purchased differently than frequently purchased, inexpensive items.

*R*etail buyers may be responsible for both buying and selling or for buying only.

Retail Buyer. In larger department stores each department has a **retail buyer**, who normally is responsible for both buying and selling merchandise. Similar positions exist in chain stores (two or more stores centrally owned and managed). Chain-store buyers are responsible for purchasing designated products for all stores in the chain but usually do not have selling responsibility. When purchases for all stores in retailing or all units and divisions in a producer's organization are completed at one office, suppliers usually designate them "national accounts" and give them special attention. In smaller retail establishments, the owner or manager usually assumes buying responsibility.

Retail buyers are especially concerned with offering a balanced assortment of products—that is, sufficient types, models, and styles to meet target market demand. These buyers' willingness to purchase, therefore, depends on how the product fits into the retailer's overall offering. Levi Strauss & Co. uses a computer program called RIMS (Retail Inventory Management System) to help retailers control inventory and, of course, to sell Levi products. RIMS tracks inventory levels. Products with slow sales rates are pruned from the retailer's offerings and those with high sales rates are carried in greater quantity and kind.

*F*ormal buying committees must approve purchases in some companies.

Buying Committee. A **buying committee** is a group of individuals responsible for a purchase. Supermarkets and other resellers use buying committees to evaluate new products. A supplier makes a presentation on a new product to the committee, which decides whether the supermarket will carry the product. Since supermarkets are offered hundreds of new products a year, their buying committees have many decisions to make. In producer organizations, buying committees most frequently become involved with infrequent, unique, expensive, first-time purchases. The purchase of production equipment is an example.

*P*urchasing managers are responsible for a broad range of purchases.

Purchasing Manager. The person who fills the position of **purchasing manager** is typically employed by a nonretail organization. This individual is responsible for the acquisition of products and services, excluding financial and personnel services. Purchasing managers in large firms may be called purchasing agents. There usually are several such agents, and each may specialize in a particular type of product. The National Association of Purchasing Managers is an association devoted to the continued professional development of purchasing managers. This association certifies individuals who fulfill experience, education, and knowledge requirements as Certified Purchasing Managers (CPM).

*T*he buying center concept recognizes the roles of all individuals who influence the purchase.

Buying Centers. Purchasing managers often do not act alone; others influence what happens.[8] The **buying center** includes all individuals involved, formally and informally, in the purchase process (figure 5.7). Buying centers differ from buying committees in that buying committees function on a formal basis. They attend scheduled committee meetings, where they follow an agenda of business activities. Each person on the committee usually has a vote with which to reject or accept the product. Buying centers are much broader in scope. Their members are defined by function. **Users** may initiate the purchase process. They are also important in providing feedback about their past purchase satisfaction (or lack of it). **Gatekeepers,** knowledgeable about products, problems, functions, and possible suppliers, control

☐ **Figure 5.7**
Key buying center
participants.

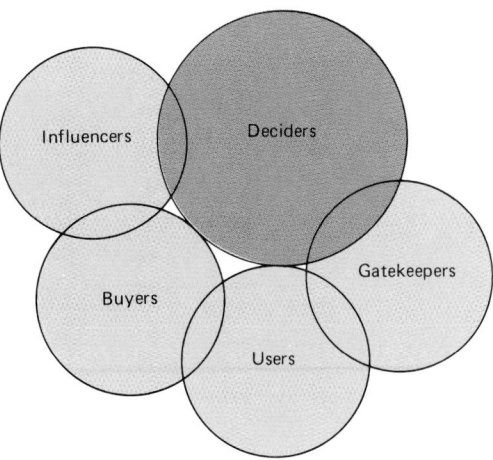

information. Gatekeepers, who are often purchasing managers, can determine which suppliers have access to the organization and its decision makers. **Influencers** are technical personnel and others who, by defining the criteria the purchase must meet, control aspects of the purchase. **Buyers** have formal authority to carry out the purchase function, although their authority is limited by other members of the buying center. **Deciders** are the individuals who make the final purchasing decision. The marketer should consider all individuals in the buying center in determining willingness to buy. The buying center concept emphasizes the importance of understanding the corporate culture in marketing to organizational buyers.

PURCHASE CRITERIA

*B*oth the item and the supplier are evaluated in most organizational buys.

In making purchase decisions, the organizational buyer has numerous criteria to use. Economic criteria receive special attention. Price, for instance, plays a major role. There are two common approaches to obtaining the "best" price. The purchaser may ask several acceptable suppliers to submit bids or may negotiate with a supplier to arrive at an acceptable price. In either case, the purchaser usually designates what specifications the product must meet. The purchasing organization generally evaluates the supplier on the basis of technological ability, consistency in meeting product specifications, overall quality, on-time delivery, and ability to provide the needed quantity. This evaluation is termed **vendor analysis.**

Because inventory is a major investment for most organizations, they keep close account of inventory levels. Some have found that by working closely with their suppliers, they can reduce the amount of inventory they must keep on hand. The Japanese have refined techniques for minimizing inventory level into a system called just-in-time (JIT) delivery. In this system, the vendor is expected to resupply the organization just before its inventory is exhausted. Any producer, whether using JIT or another approach, benefits from materials requirement planning (MRP).[9] MRP works backward from the production schedule to determine the quantity of materials and timing necessary to keep production running smoothly. Producers, especially those operating production lines, do not want to run out of a part they need to continue production. Thus, satisfying these producers means meeting scheduling as well as product requirements.

*F*riendship and other personal factors—psychological factors—also play a part in organizational buying decisions.

The long and complex nature of many organizational purchase decisions leads to extensive contact between buyers and sellers. Psychological factors emerging from their relationships influence the decision. In the buyer's mind, such considerations as friendship, trustworthiness, and other personal factors regarding vendors and salespeople may weigh heavily in the purchase decision, especially as more substantive differences between possible suppliers diminish.

❑ **Figure 5.8**
Types of buys.

	Purchase Stages						
	Awareness of Problem	Product for Problem	Search for Suppliers	Take Bids	Give Order	Buy	Evaluate
Full rebuy (Office supplies, raw materials)					Start ⟶	Stop	
Modified rebuy (New communication system)		Start ⟶					Stop
New task (Communications/ Data system)	Start ⟶						Stop

Source: P. J. Robinson, C. W. Faris, and Y. Wind, *Industrial Buying and Creative Marketing,* © 1967, p. 17, Allyn and Bacon.

(1) The stages involved in the purchase increase as problem familiarity decreases, solution cost increases.
(2) The number of individuals involved in the buying center increases as problem familiarity decreases.

TYPES OF ORGANIZATIONAL BUYS

*O*pportunity to sell may vary with the type of buy: full rebuy, modified rebuy, or new task.

The number of stages in a purchase decision varies with the familiarity of the problem and the cost of the solution. In general, familiarity decreases and cost increases across the three types of organizational buys—full rebuy, modified rebuy, and new task. Note in figure 5.8 that a full rebuy requires only a two-stage purchase decision, whereas a new task uses every stage in the process. A **full rebuy** is simply a reorder. Here, organizational personnel exhibit familiarity with the situation and confidence about the buy because of past experience and the type of product involved. The extreme example of a full rebuy occurs when the buyer agrees with the vendor to keep the product stocked in inventory. This is termed a *blanket order.* In a **modified rebuy,** organizational personnel show some familiarity with the situation but less than complete satisfaction with the previous buy. The individuals responsible for purchasing therefore launch an extensive search for a better product or service— a better buy. In a **new task** situation, the personnel lack familiarity with the situation and so must develop familiarity. Moving from full rebuys to new tasks usually means an increase in the number of individuals involved in the purchase. We can relate types of buys to the types of buyers described earlier as follows:

Retail buyers—full and modified rebuys.
Buying committees—new tasks.
Purchasing managers—full and modified rebuys; involved in new-task buying.
Buying centers—new tasks.

*T*he make, buy, or lease decision must be faced by buyers and sellers.

Buying is only one of three options available to the organization. The others are making and leasing. (See figure 5.9.) The first option, making the item, requires the most involvement from the organization. The firm usually selects this option either because it will need a large, continuous supply of the item and wishes close control

❑ **Figure 5.9**
Options for acquiring products.

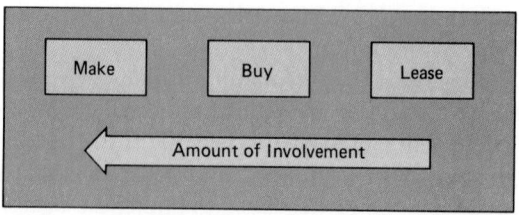

over supply or because no suppliers exist for the item. The option tends to be used less when the organization's market is expanding and more in contracting markets. In expanding markets, the organization needs all available resources to make its final product. In contracting markets, the organization may have unemployed resources that it can use to make items it needs and thus reduce costs.

Obtaining items by leasing requires the least involvement and the lowest expenditure of the organization. Firms whose need for a resource fluctuates often consider leasing, but any organization can use leasing as an option. Whether to make, buy, or lease often depends on external factors, such as income tax regulations.

Ability to Buy

*A*bility to buy varies with type of organization.

Ability to buy varies with the type of organization. In the government market, ability to buy depends on the tax base, the budget, and appropriations from other government units. Government information is generally open for public examination, and reports are periodically published on appropriations, budgets, and taxes. The trend has been toward a less active funding role for the federal government at the state and local levels. States have had to raise their tax rates to generate funds for products and services once supplied by the federal government.

Institutions depend on contributions, money-generating activities, and appropriations. Information on a particular sector of the institutional market can usually be found in publications associated with the sector. For instance, for information on the ability of higher education to buy, an excellent source is the *Chronicle of Higher Education,* which periodically reports on funding levels at institutions of higher education.

*P*roduction indicators are a measure of manufacturing activity in the United States.

An overview of the industrial market's ability to buy can be assessed from information such as production indicators and prices. A summary of these indicators can be found in the Business Week Index, a part of each issue of *Business Week* magazine. *Sales & Marketing Management* magazine publishes an issue entitled "Survey of Industrial Purchasing Power," which provides information on ability to purchase. Since the nation's economic health depends on what happens in the industrial sector, various governmental units collect information about this sector and make it available to the public. An excellent overview of major industries is the *U.S. Industrial Outlook,* published annually by the Department of Commerce. It includes projections for each industry. For information on specific companies, several sources exist: *Standard and Poor's, Value Line,* and *Everybody's Business* (described as a peep show of U.S. business) are examples.[10]

Much of the business information collected by government units is based on the **Standard Industrial Classification (SIC)** System. The purpose of the SIC is to provide a standard classification system for the collection, recording, and analysis of data. The SIC is a numeric system, and its four-digit level of detail is used most frequently. The first two digits designate the industry, the third digit the subindustry, and the fourth digit the product.[11] For example, consider the classification *SIC 2322.* The *23* represents the apparel industry; the second *2* represents male furnishings, work clothing, and the allied garments sector of this industry; and the last *2* represents underwear.

For information on countries, territories, and states within countries, the *Statesman's Year Book* and the *Europa Year Book* provide a good overview.[12] History, area and population, climate, constitution and government, budgets, energy and natural resources, industry, communications, justice, religion, education and welfare, and books of references serve as headings in the *Statesman's Year Book.* The *Europa Year Book* covers essentially the same topics, but in a more statistical fashion.

*M*ayflower serves several organization markets: the producer market when moving electronic equipment for IBM and Control Data, the government market when transporting students, and the reseller market when supplying appliances to retailers.

Transportation of electronic equipment is an especially attractive market because it's expanding. Electronic equipment often requires special trucking equipment, equipment that Mayflower already possesses. On the other hand, the trend for corporations to move their own

products may eventually mean that IBM and Control Data will do the same.

The government market (transportation of students) also has considerable potential since 80 percent of buses are operated by local school systems. Price will be an important criterion to school systems in making the decision to go with Mayflower. In addition, the school administration will expect the bus system to run smoothly and without com-

plaints. Even though school bus operations would seem to be immune to fluctuations in the economic cycle, appropriation levels to operate schools extends to the busing of students. The size and location of student populations (suburban, rural, or city) also influence the success of student transportation systems.

The reseller market, a large dollar volume market, fluctuates with consumer demand for appliances. With little need for special trucking equipment to transport appliances, market success depends heavily on pricing and scheduling.

GOAL SUMMARY

1. **Identify the major elements of a market as defined by marketers.** A market is made up of all consumers and organizations that have needs and the willingness and ability to make an exchange for the product, service, or idea that will meet those needs. The elements, therefore, are consumers or organizations with needs, willingness to satisfy the needs by making an exchange, and ability to engage in the exchange. Ability comes from available resources and the authority to use them to make an exchange.

2. **Define the various types of markets.** Two major types of markets exist: consumer and organizational. Consumer markets encompass all individuals who purchase products for their own self-satisfaction. Organizational markets include all purchasers who buy products to conduct their operations. Subtypes of organizational markets include industrial (producers and resellers), government, and institutional.

3. **Describe the differences between the consumer and organizational markets.** The organizational market differs from the consumer market in that it contains fewer buyers and these buyers are more geographically concentrated and tend to be better organized, more logical, and more economically oriented purchasers. Demand differences also exist; organizations purchase only if they can sell their product.

4. **Describe trends and dimensions of the consumer market and relate them to the marketing effort.** Dimensions of the consumer market mentioned in the chapter are population, age, geographic

location, income, and living arrangements. In the United States, marketers will have to work with a population that is stable in size, is increasingly older, and is shifting geographically to the South and West. Less emphasis should be placed on youth and more on youthfulness. Resource allocation decisions should be based on the geographical shifts in the market. The ability to buy is shifting with the population to the South and West. Since the market is stable in size, more emphasis should be placed on market share. More double-income households exist now than in the past, along with more single-parent and single-individual households. The number of individuals per household is fewer now than in the past. In spite of changes, families still make up most households. Lifestyle is changing along with household composition. More males are becoming involved in household duties and more females in activities previously associated with males. Marketing changes include downsizing products for smaller households, promoting all kinds of products using both male and female models, and improving the convenience of products and their purchase.

5. **Relate types of buyers, purchase criteria, and types of buys in the organizational market to marketing efforts.** Retail buyers make purchases of the full and modified rebuy types. The emphasis of the retail buyer is on having an adequate inventory from which the target consumer can make purchase choices. The buying committee, a group of people who make buying decisions, generally focuses on

GOAL SUMMARY *(continued)*

the new-task buy. An important concern is how the purchase influences the financial condition of the organization. Purchasing managers, usually found in nonretail organizations, complete full and modified rebuys on a routine basis. They also are involved in new buys. Price, quality, and service are a few of the criteria they consider. The buying center, made up of several individuals who influence the purchase process, primarily becomes involved in new-task buys. Each individual has a different set of criteria. A marketing planner must take into consideration the buyer, the criteria, and the type of buy.

KEY TERMS

Market, **p. 121**
Willingness to Purchase, **p. 121**
Consumer Market, **p. 125**
Organizational Market, **p. 125**
Disposable Personal Income, **p. 128**
Discretionary Income, **p. 128**
Ratchet Effect, **p. 130**
Family Household, **p. 131**
Nonfamily Household, **p. 131**
Family Life Cycle, **p. 131**
Lifestyle, **p. 132**
Industrial Organization, **p. 133**
Producer, **p. 133**
Reseller, **p. 133**
Institutional Market, **p. 135**
Derived Demand, **p. 136**

Joint Demand, **p. 137**
Retail Buyer, **p. 138**
Buying Committee, **p. 138**
Purchasing Manager, **p. 138**
Buying Center, **p. 138**
User, **p. 138**
Gatekeeper, **p. 138**
Influencer, **p. 139**
Buyer, **p. 139**
Decider, **p. 139**
Vendor Analysis, **p. 139**
Full Rebuy, **p. 140**
Modified Rebuy, **p. 140**
New Task, **p. 140**
Standard Industrial Classification (SIC), **p. 141**

CHECK YOUR LEARNING

1. A market is made up of all consumers who have the willingness to buy. **T/F**
2. An individual who has available resources has the ability to exchange. **T/F**
3. The difference in consumer and organizational markets rests on how the product is used. **T/F**
4. The population size tells the marketer how large the demand for a product is. **T/F**
5. Zip-code marketing is based on differences among consumers in different geographic locations. **T/F**
6. Families (a) are decreasing in numbers, (b) are the same as households, (c) with a double-income tend to use their income with current satisfaction in mind, (d) with a single-parent are increasing, but less rapidly than two-parent families, (e) experience basically the same needs through the life cycle.
7. Lifestyle changes in the last decade have been subtle and have had minimal influence on marketing plans. **T/F**

8. The three basic types of organizational markets are industrial organizations, resellers, and government. **T/F**
9. The U.S. federal government purchases about 50 percent of the products and services produced each year. **T/F**
10. The Federal Supply Service purchases most items on the basis of lowest bid. **T/F**
11. Organizational markets differ from consumer markets in all except which of the following: (a) the consumer market is more able to support the use of personal selling, (b) organizational buyers visit suppliers less frequently than consumers visit retailers, (c) organizational buyers' willingness to buy depends on the demand for their product or service, (d) the organizational market shows less price elasticity than the consumer market, (e) none of the above are exceptions.

QUESTIONS FOR REVIEW AND DISCUSSION

1. Define the key terms for this chapter that appear at the end of the goal summary.
2. Comment on the observation "Marketers generally do not attempt to evaluate the worthiness of needs."
3. What might a marketing planner for the March of Dimes consider in determining the ability of the market to exchange?
4. Under what conditions might ability and authority to exchange be separated?
5. Give two examples of consumer and organizational markets.
6. What are the marketing ramifications of zero population growth?
7. Of what significance to marketers is a geographic shift in population? an age shift?
8. If you were marketing fruit juice, how would you use information on household size, household income distribution, family life cycle, and lifestyle?
9. How does the industrial market's primary objective—making a profit—influence the way products are marketed to industrial firms?
10. Suppose you have been hired as a consultant by a small manufacturer of twelve-volt auto batteries who is considering marketing to the federal government. What suggestions would you make?
11. Why are salespeople more likely to be used in organizational markets?
12. How does a buying center differ from a retail buyer?
13. What does a purchasing manager do?
14. Distinguish between a full rebuy and a modified rebuy.

NOTES

1. See Adel I. El-Ansary, and Oscar E. Kramer, Jr., "Social Marketing: The Family Planning Experience," *Journal of Marketing* (July 1973): pp. 1–7; C. O. Fong, "Malaysian Integrated Population Program Performance: Its Relation to Organizational and Integration Factors," *Management Science,* January 1985, pp. 50–65; Kevin Higgins, "Marketing Enables Population Control Group to Boost Results," *Marketing News,* October 1983, pp. 12–13.
2. "The Graying of the Soft Drink Industry," *Business Week,* May 1977, pp. 68–72.
3. Rena Bartos, "Over 49: The Invisible Consumer Market," *Harvard Business Review* (January–February 1980): pp. 140–149; Betsy D. Gelb, "Exploring the Gray Market Segment," *MSU Business Topics,* pp. 41–46.
4. "Census Data to Reflect More Precise Geographic Definitions," *Marketing News,* January 21, 1983, p. 20.
5. E. Jerome McCarthy and William D. Perrault, Jr., *Basic Marketing* (Homewood, Ill.: Richard D. Irwin, 1984), p. 184.
6. "Changes Found in Attitudes, Shopping Behavior of the United States' Two-Income Couples," *Marketing News,* October 28, 1983, p. 12.
7. Joseph T. Plummer, "The Concept and Application of Life-Style Dimensions," *Journal of Marketing* (January 1974): pp. 30–34.
8. T. V. Bonoma, "Major Sales: Who Really Does the Buying?" *Harvard Business Review* 61 (May–June 1982): p. 114; Thomas V. Bonoma and Benson P. Shapiro, *Segmenting the Industrial Market* (Lexington, Mass.: Lexington Books, 1983).
9. James B. Dilworth, *Production and Operations Management,* 2d ed. (New York: Random House, 1983), p. 239.
10. Milton Maskowitz, Michael Katz, and Robert Levering, eds., *Everybody's Business: An Almanac* (New York: Harper & Row Publishers, 1982), p. 916.
11. U.S. Office of Management and Budgets. *1977 Standard Industrial Classification Manual.*
12. John Paxton, ed., *Statesman's Year Book* (New York: St. Martin's Press), p. 169; *Europa Year Book* (London: Europa Publications Limited), p. 3089.

The Pittsburgh Pirates, a professional baseball team, like many other sports teams, has found that marketing is necessary to increase its attendance figures. Dismal on-field performance in the mid-1980s led to low attendance at the Pirates' eighty-one annual home games. Rumors of a possible sale and shift in the team franchise—possibly to another city—had eroded fan enthusiasm. In addition to their disappointment over their team's standing, fans were concerned about ballplayers' high salaries and drug use. Since many more leisure-time activities than ever before were becoming available to Pittsburghers, some fans were finding their fun elsewhere.

Revenues decline directly with lowered attendance and indirectly when corporations become less willing to be sponsors. Season ticket sales are especially important to a pro baseball team. Ten thousand season tickets times eighty-one home games means 810,000 tickets sold. Walk-ups on the day of the game are also important. Walk-up sales, however, are influenced by the weather and other immediate events.

Pittsburgh represents a consolidated metropolitan area, so a large number of potential fans exist. Most professional baseball teams, including the Pirates, attempt to attract the family. A few, however, such as the Giants, focus on the eighteen- to thirty-five-year-old blue-collar males. The Oakland Athletics emphasize a family orientation by keeping prices in the $3 to $8 range. They have also targeted children in their give-away programs. For instance, during the 1985 season the A's offered a "workout kit" that included shorts, work-out jersey, warm-up top, warm-up pants, and a 50 percent-off coupon for Adidas shoes. The total retail value approached $100. Kids attending designated games received the items for the price of the admission ticket. Sponsors for the warm-up kit included J. C. Penney, the makers of Wheaties, Shell Auto Care Dealers, and the makers of Hostess cakes. The A's have sponsored tailgate parties for the first 10,000 fans at designated games. They have also included free BART (public transportation) tickets with tickets to an A's game.

The Chicago White Sox, too, has worked at its image to appeal more to families. In the early 1980s, the Sox had a following of rowdy fans. To be more appealing to attendees bothered by these fans' behavior, Sox administration instituted a policy of warning and, if necessary, removing offenders. At some games as many as 250 fans were evicted. Women and children no longer express fear of attending a Sox game. The Sox Club also refurbished Cominsky Park, added parking lots, upgraded the food, and saw to it that the ball park facilities were kept clean.

The Pirates celebrated their 100th season in 1987. By then, the team had been purchased by a private/public coalition inside the city, allaying fan fears. The marketing plan for 1987–88 centered on the centennial. Promotions were tied into its observance, with corporate sponsors such as Budweiser, Coca-Cola, and McDonald's participating. Despite the Pirates' last-place finish in the National League East in 1986, the strong marketing of the centennial and the new ownership arrangement saw attendance rocket up in 1987.

Few deny the very positive effect of a winning team on sales. Unfortunately, it is impossible to guarantee consistency when the product is an ever-changing sports team. "Our goal is to stay away from pennant hype," says Dick Hackett, VP-Marketing for the Milwaukee Brewers. "We feel it's more important just to sell the fun and excitement of coming to the ballpark." The Brewers' advertising theme is "Join us for fun in the summertime."

Some team executives have developed a range of expectations: 2 million fans in a winning season and 1.25 million fans in a losing season. Sports academicians have even suggested that teams might want to place less emphasis on winning when recruiting players and more on what fans want to see. For instance, if the fans want speedy hit and run players, they should be recruited even though power hitters might help the team more in winning.

Club executives also have made a greater effort to sell tickets in the off-season and to make more group sales. Sales forces have been beefed up. Efforts have also been made to reshape the image of players in general, to be more in line with fans' expectations. The Twins, for instance, send players to rural cities in Minnesota and North and South Dakota during the off-season. The White Sox have aired television commercials featuring their players.

Other professional ball team executives pay particular attention to in-park advertising space, radio and television advertising, and sponsorship contracts. Regardless of their method of choice, these days nearly everyone in the business agrees that marketing helps their attendance average.

Issues for Discussion

1. The Pirates' attendance skyrocketed in 1987—the year after they finished last place in the League. Why?
2. List some of the promotional activities used to market baseball games.
3. Discuss how baseball team marketers can use demographic elements such as age and income to identify markets.

Sources: Brian Moran, "Baseball Pitches Around Tight Budgets," *Advertising Age,* April 6, 1987, p. 4; Robert Raissman, "Root, Root for the Home Product," *Advertising Age,* April 4, 1985; Julie Liesse Erickson, "Players, Owners Polish Their Business Stance," *Advertising Age,* August 2, 1984, p. 8; Lynn Berling-Manuel, "Giants Weathering Bay City Blues," *Advertising Age,* August 2, 1984, p. 10; Jack Hofferkamp, "White Sox Give Image a Clean Sweep," *Advertising Age,* August 2, 1984.

OUTLINE

CHAPTER

6

Analyzing Consumer Behavior

LEARNING GOALS

After reading this chapter, you should be able to:

1. Explain why understanding consumer behavior is important to marketers.
2. Describe two consumer behavior models.
3. Discuss the role of the decision-making process in purchase behavior.
4. List psychological characteristics that influence the purchase and use of products.
5. Describe the effects of reference groups and culture on the behavior of consumers.

The Saturn Corporation is a wholly owned subsidiary of General Motors. Conceived in 1982, the original idea behind Saturn was to beat the foreign competition—as well as Ford and Chrysler—in the small-car market by using the very latest in manufacturing technology, including state-of-the-art robotics. The first cars are scheduled to roll off their very high-tech assembly lines in 1990. GM's chairman Roger B. Smith, in a *Business Week* interview, called the project "the key to GM's longterm competitiveness." Plans call for a $5 billion-dollar investment of the company's resources.

Saturn's initial goal was to be "cost-competitive with the lowest-priced imports." But although the cars have yet to be manufactured, GM executives have already had to alter their plans for this venture several times in response to unforeseen changes in the environment and in consumer buying patterns. By 1988 the Korean-made Hyundai and the Yugoslavian-made Yugo—both extremely low-priced subcompact cars—had been introduced. Manufacturers, especially in the U.S. where labor is more expensive, will be hard-pressed to undercut them. And the market for the lowest priced, smallest cars has changed a good deal in the short time since 1982. When Saturn was first formed, GM believed that gas prices were headed steadily upward. Instead, gas prices have fallen and consumers are again interested in the benefits larger cars offer. By 1988 the prototype for the Saturn had gotten larger and was targeted for the mid-

dle of the import market, where prices are a few thousand dollars higher.

In 1985, GM executives announced that 400,000 to 500,000 units would be manufactured annually. But by November of 1987, officials announced that only 1.7 billion will be spent for a "first-phase" plant, and only 250,000 cars will be turned out. These downsized plans underscore GM's concerns about the size of its market.

To attract buyers, Saturn plans to offer customers the opportunity to order cars through a computerized system. Customers can customize their orders by plugging in the exact specifications they want into a system linked directly to the manufacturing plant in Springhill, Tennessee. GM dealers with the highest "customer satisfaction" ratings will be first in line to receive a franchise to sell the cars. There is a good likelihood that separate Saturn dealer-

ships will be established in order to create an even more distinct image.

If the venture is in fact kept on track, no doubt millions will be spent on advertising to target the market the Saturn Company seeks. Buyer behavior will be of paramount concern.

Issues for Discussion
1. How does Saturn executives' understanding of buyer behavior influence product design, promotion, distribution, and pricing plans?
2. How might the consumer purchase decision process be used to facilitate successful marketing of Saturn cars?
3. How can Saturn executives differentiate their car from the other cars GM sells, such as Cadillacs, Chevrolets, and Pontiacs?

Source: William J. Hampton and James R. Norman, "General Motors: What Went Wrong," *Business Week,* March 16, 1987, p. 107; Ralph Gray, "Chevy, Pontiac Won't Be Saturn's Satellites," *Advertising Age,* January 28, 1985, p. 47; and Ralph Gray, "Eager Shops Ringing 'Round Saturn," *Advertising Age,* January 14, 1985, p. 3.

■ An early prototype of the Saturn. It continues to metamorphosize.
Source: Photo courtesy of Saturn Corporation

For the Saturn Corporation, and for all businesses, success depends heavily on buyer behavior. To effectively promote their offerings, marketers study buyer characteristics, for unless buyers' needs and wants are understood, the marketer stands little chance of persuading them to purchase. Our discussion of consumer behavior begins with an examination of several classic consumer behavior models, or explanations. Next, we investigate how groups, social class, and gender are involved in the purchasing process. In the following section, we examine the roles that motivation, perception, and cognition, all psychological characteristics, play in buying behavior. The chapter concludes with a look at the purchasing decision process. ■

Why do marketers need to understand buyer behavior? It might appear that, with advertising, personal selling, pricing, product design, and a number of other variables, marketers have the power to overcome buyers' resistance and manipulate them into product purchases. The advertisement shown here, part of a campaign by the American Association of Advertising Agencies (4As), attempts to demonstrate that buyers in fact think for themselves. They decide what their needs and wants are and what they will and will not purchase. Advertising does increase buyers' awareness and may even persuade some of them to seriously consider an organization's offering. The marketer's influence over buyers, however, is mitigated by the presence of several factors, including the existence of competing organizations, the individual buyer's self-interest, and the organization's limited resources.

Marketers are not in a position to force products on buyers; so they must understand buyers to successfully meet their product requirements. Understanding why people buy and use a product enables marketers to evaluate buyers' reactions

*B*ecause marketers cannot control consumers, they must understand why consumers think and act as they do.

According to this ad, while advertising increases our awareness, it does not control our ultimate decision to purchase.

Source: Reproduced by permission of the American Association of Advertising Agencies

DESPITE WHAT SOME PEOPLE THINK, ADVERTISING CAN'T MAKE YOU BUY SOMETHING YOU DON'T NEED.

Some people would have you believe that you are putty in the hands of every advertiser in the country.

They think that when advertising is put under your nose, your mind turns to oatmeal.

It's mass hypnosis. Subliminal seduction. Brain washing. Mind control. It's advertising.

And you are a pushover for it.

It explains why your kitchen cupboard is full of food you never eat.

Why your garage is full of cars you never drive.

Why your house is full of books you don't read, TV's you don't watch, beds you don't use, and clothes you don't wear.

You don't have a choice. You are forced to buy.

That's why this message is a cleverly disguised advertisement to get you to buy land in the tropics.

Got you again, didn't we? Send in your money.

ADVERTISING

ANOTHER WORD FOR FREEDOM OF CHOICE.

American Association of Advertising Agencies

to the firm's present marketing efforts and more accurately predict consumers' reactions to proposed marketing plans. Remember that the marketing concept as a philosophy rests on the idea of satisfying customers. What a firm has to offer must solve a buyer's problem—satisfy a need.

Consumer behavior consists of all of the activities in which people engage when buying and using products for personal and household (not business) use.[1] Much of the behavior that motivates buyers in consumer markets similarly motivates buyers in organizational markets. Organizational buyers, however, must satisfy specific needs of their organization. In addition, these buyers often receive training about products and purchasing procedures.

MODELS OF CONSUMER BEHAVIOR

Consumer behavior models explain consumer behavior by identifying variables that influence behavior and relating them to each other. Hundreds of variables could be included, in many combinations. Every individual—every marketing manager—may therefore have a unique model. Yet some models seem more logical than others and better able to effectively explain consumer behavior.

The Economic Man Consumer Behavior Model

*E*conomic man represents an ideal buyer who thinks exclusively in rational terms.

For years, economists have referred to a fictitious person called the "economic man." Economic man as a behavior model focuses on the economic variables that influence behavior. The model is structured on the concept of ideal consumer behavior, as defined by economists. It assumes that the individual's needs are unlimited, whereas resources are limited. Further, the individual has perfect information—all possible information on products, prices, and so on—and will act as a rational decision maker. The economic man maximizes need satisfaction with the limited resources he possesses. All decisions and all purchases are based on economic considerations and need satisfaction. For instance, if two sources of a desired product exist, the economic man will purchase from the lower-priced source. Super car dealers, who handle several competing brands and sell thousands of cars annually, continue to grow because they offer cars at lower prices than other dealers. Their customers, like the economic man, want the lower price. Marketers have used the economic man model as the basis for price reductions, two-for-one offers, coupons, and a number of other marketing practices. To some extent, the model does explain consumer behavior, but it is based on some questionable assumptions, such as the assumption that everyone has perfect information. In addition, the only variables it considers are economic.

The Psychoanalytic Model

*T*he subconscious plays a role in buyer behavior.

Some consumer behavior theorists analyze buyer behavior or motivation from the perspective of the **psychoanalytic model.** Based on the work of the Austrian physician and founder of psychoanalysis, Sigmund Freud (1856–1939), the psychoanalytic model assumes that subconscious forces influence the individual to behave instinctually as well as consciously and logically. And indeed, some behavior cannot be explained by logical economic principles alone. People are often unaware of why they purchase and use specific products.

❑ **Figure 6.1**
A model of consumer purchase behavior.

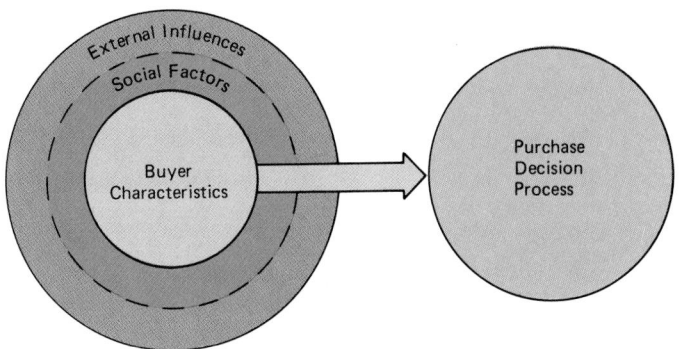

In terms of marketing, the psychoanalytic model suggests that the use of images evocative of sex and fantasy—symbols directed at the unconscious—will appeal to consumers. Products and advertisements are thus designed to appeal to subconscious desires. Because of the range of possible subconscious motivations to choose from, however, accurate explanations of consumer behavior are difficult to pin down with this model. There can be many explanations of the same behavior. The psychoanalytic model's importance lies in its acknowledgment of subconscious factors in buyer behavior.

A General Consumer Purchase Model

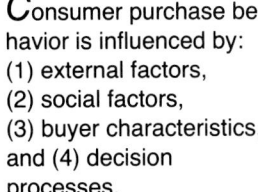

*C*onsumer purchase behavior is influenced by: (1) external factors, (2) social factors, (3) buyer characteristics, and (4) decision processes.

The strictly rational responses of the economic man model and the nonrational responses described in the psychoanalytical model are combined in a general consumer purchase model, illustrated in figure 6.1. This model depicts four areas of influence on buyer behavior: external influences, social factors (actually a part of external factors, but considered separately in consumer behavior because of their importance to buyer behavior), buyer characteristics, and the purchasing decision process.

Relevant external factors such as economic, political, legal, and technological conditions are all considered when creating the marketing plan, as we noted in Chapter two in our discussion of environmental scanning. Both the firm and the buyer are guided, in varying degrees, by external conditions. Thus the marketer pays particular attention not only to how external conditions affect the firm itself, but how they affect buyers.

Each market differs in buyer behavior characteristics. The general consumer purchase model guides market analysis by prompting the marketing manager to ask the right questions, such as *how is the purchase decision made, what influences the decision,* and *what are the characteristics of the people who make up the market?*

We now turn to an examination of social influences on consumer buyer behavior, buyer characteristics, and the purchasing decision process.

 ## SOCIAL FACTORS

*D*ecisions are influenced by interaction with others—individuals, small groups, and large groups.

Although the decision to purchase is ultimately made by the individual, interaction with others influences the decision process. As consumers, we may be influenced by an individual (a girlfriend or boyfriend, for example), a small group (the family, for instance), or a large group (such as the social class).

❏ **Figure 6.2**
Types of reference
groups.

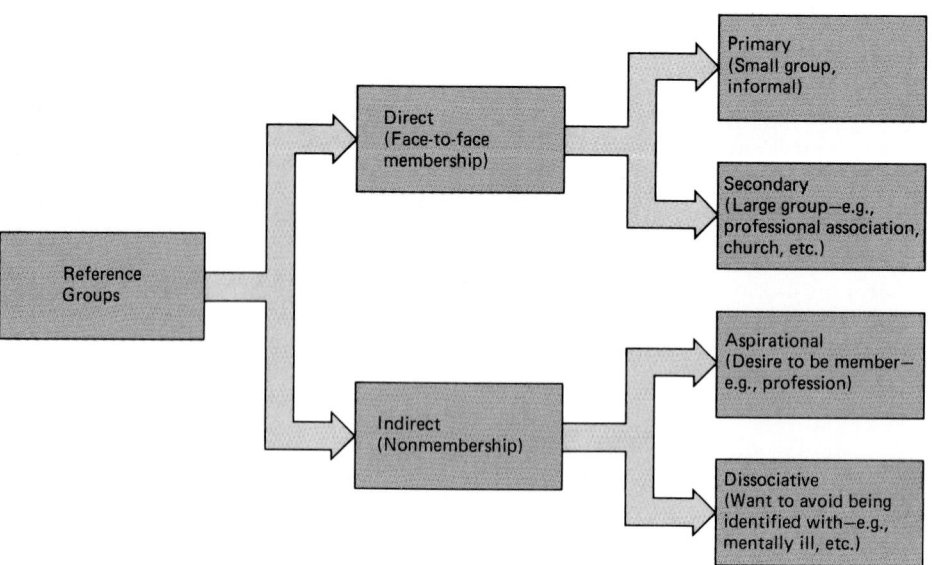

Reference Groups

*R*eference groups are made up of people with whom we identify.

Reference groups are all of the groups—large and small, formal and informal—that influence the purchasing behavior of an individual (see figure 6.2). Different reference groups exert positive or negative influence on individuals. Three broad categories of groups that at one time or another affect us all include: (1) *Membership groups.* These are groups that touch our lives directly and involve the people with whom we spend the most time. *Primary membership groups* include family, friends, coworkers, and others with whom we interact on a regular basis. *Secondary membership groups* include our church or synagogue affiliation, professional and leisure clubs, unions, and other groups we associate with on a less formal and consistent basis. (2) *Aspirational groups.* We are not only influenced by our friends and family, but also by groups to which we would like to belong, such as a successful baseball team or a famous rock and roll band. Our buying behavior can reflect these aspirations. (3) *Dissociative groups.* Sometimes, we will not purchase certain products or services because we associate their use with groups whose values or other characteristics we reject. A consumer may decide not to purchase an article of clothing, a particular car, or even a style of house because he or she associates that item with groups the consumer regards unfavorably.

Reference groups provide the marketer with valuable information with which to make decisions about how to market products or services. Knowing a group's habits, likes and dislikes, marketers can effectively target the right market for a product, and can tailor their advertising campaign accordingly.

Marketing and Reference Groups

*P*roduct visibility increases reference group influence.

The influence of reference groups on an individual's decision to purchase depends on the individual's susceptibility to reference groups, the strength of involvement with the group, and the cohesiveness of the group. In addition, the more conspicuous the consumption of the brand or product, the more reference groups influence the purchase.[2] For instance, a computer salesman whose market was farmers commented that a big problem in selling computers to farmers was the lack of visibility of the computers other farmers had purchased. The computer tended to be tucked away

This ad cleverly appeals to consumer behavior—on at least two levels. It appeals to parents' "sensible" values of "quality, durability, and outstanding value." At the same time, it demonstrates the power of reference groups by emphasizing the popularity of jeans among young boys.

WHEN HE ASKS FOR LEVI'S JEANS, MAYBE HE'S NOT BEING AS SENSIBLE AS YOU THINK.

He asks for a pair of Levi's jeans.

And you think, at last!—he's finally appreciating quality, durability and outstanding value.

While he thinks, "I knew she'd think that."

Because the truth is, Levi's jeans have become the most popular brand with boys today, bar none.

They simply love wearing them.

Which means they're not above saying *anything* to get you to buy them a pair.

Even the truth.

LEVI'S

Source: Courtesy of Levi Strauss & Co.

out of sight, unlike a new barn or a new tractor.[3] Thus one of the farmer's reference groups—other farmers—exerted little influence on purchasing behavior.

Marketers have successfully employed knowledge of reference groups in several ways. One strategy has been used to sell Izod clothing. Reference groups have long influenced the style of members' clothing, but most brand labels have not stood out sufficiently to gain reference group endorsement. Izod made it easy for reference groups to identify its product by placing the Izod alligator on the breast of the garment. No longer was it necessary to hunt for the label.

Party plans also use reference groups. What is a Tupperware party if not a gathering of a reference group? Still another use of reference groups has involved reference group opinion leaders. The idea is a simple one: identify the opinion leaders, convince them of the virtues of the product or brand, and let them communicate with the rest of the group. This concept, more commonly known as the two-step communication strategy, requires more work than it might at first appear to. Opinion leaders vary by product, by time period, and even by group. Identifying and communicating with them requires more than a simple approach. Cuisinart food processor executives believed that professional cooks were the opinion leaders in the cooking equipment market. Cuisinart thus appealed to this group when first entering the market. The professional cooks responded positively and Cuisinart then successfully moved into the general consumer market.

THE FAMILY

*P*eople belong to families of orientation and families of procreation.

The reference group that influences an individual's purchasing behavior and product usage more than any other is the family. Two types of families influence the individual. The family that one is born into, the *family of orientation,* probably does the most to socialize us in our youth. Much of our later behavior stems from values and attitudes learned in the orientation family. The value an individual places on money and the shopping habits he or she displays are areas typically influenced by the orientation family.

Another influence, the *procreation family,* is the family that one forms with a spouse. Day-to-day purchases almost always involve some element of concern for other members of the procreation family. "Will my spouse approve, will the children like it, is there enough money to buy this item and other items that family members want?"

*D*ecision making in the family has changed in recent years.

Marketers generally focus marketing efforts on the family decision maker. Thus, for a long time marketers have been interested in who in the family makes the decisions. The wife has traditionally been the main buyer for the family. Purchase of food, for example, has long been dominated by the female. Recently, family decision-making patterns have changed. The United States has more two-income families, more mothers working, and a shorter work week for some men. More decisions now than in the past are joint (syncratic) decisions involving both the male and female.[4] Vacation planning has traditionally involved joint decisions. Now, however, many families also decide jointly about investment planning and insurance, traditionally male-dominated areas. Conversely, men now take greater responsibility for purchasing food and home operation products.[5] Most such purchases are still made by women, however.

*C*hildren and youths influence family purchase and act as purchasers themselves.

Children, objects of family influence, also do their share of influencing of purchase decisions.[6] Very young children play a very limited role in this regard, although the presence of a child has some bearing on what products are purchased. As children get older, however, they assume a more active role. They learn how to propose, change, and finance product purchases within the family. By the time they are teenagers, they influence the purchase of automobiles as well as most other major consumer products. Youths also make purchases in their own right—they have money to spend. The proliferation of advertisements in teenage magazines, such as *Seventeen,* demonstrates two facts: teenagers make purchase decisions, and marketing managers are well aware of it.

ROLES AND STATUS

*W*hat people purchase may depend on the roles they play.

The typical buyer belongs to many groups, and in each group he or she holds a different position with regard to other members. Each position has a particular status and involves a particular role. The role, in turn, determines the activities a person in the position is expected to perform. For instance, a woman may be a mother, wife, corporate director of marketing, trustee of the church, soccer coach, and Girl Scout leader. Each role influences an aspect of her buying behavior. Products are often purchased to reflect the role and status of a position. Thus, as corporate director of marketing, the woman will buy professional clothing, while as soccer coach, she may prefer "sweats."

*F*our roles in product purchase: (1) decider, (2) purchaser, (3) user, (4) gatekeeper.

Four roles of interest to the marketer are those of *decider, purchaser, user,* and *gatekeeper.* The **decider** makes the purchase decision, so the marketer must convince the decider of the need and worthiness of the company's product if a sale is to take place. The **purchaser** physically carries out the purchase process. Ease and convenience are foremost in a marketer's mind when appealing to the purchaser. The **user** consumes the product and is primarily concerned with product characteristics. The **gatekeeper** establishes limits or boundaries within which the others must operate. For example, an organization's executive committee may be required to approve all purchase orders exceeding $5,000 in value. An individual may fill more than one of these roles; sometimes all four roles may be filled by one individual. To a marketer, knowing how the roles are distributed and who fills each role is important to deploying resources properly.

LARGE GROUPS

The large social group—the culture, subculture, or social class—may be so large that it is seldom thought of as a specific group. Although they exist as informal associations, large social groups do have a persistent, encompassing influence over all individual behavior, including purchase behavior.

CULTURES

*B*ecause a culture includes all the human-made elements in a society, its influence permeates the lives of its members.

A **culture** consists of the abstract and material elements made by human beings that distinguish one society from another. The abstract elements include *values* (goals the society holds as important), *attitudes* (predispositions to respond consistently to certain things in certain ways), and *norms* (rules of conduct); and the material elements include all the products used by a society. The culture of a society permeates the lives of its members. Cultural elements are learned and passed from one generation to the next.

Aspects of culture serve as determinants and regulators of purchasing behavior. For instance, human consumption of horse meat is accepted in some European cultures but is generally frowned upon in the United States. The marketer must consider the culture for which the market plan is intended. In the Persian Gulf region, for example, marketers who showed Afro hairstyles, the Muppets (especially Miss Piggy), or women improperly dressed according to Muslim standards in their advertising would harm their products' image. The offending material might be obliterated by a censor's black ink, and the product or brand might be associated with immorality. People of the Persian Gulf region may also be offended by advertisements depicting eating or drinking during the holy month of Ramadan and music and dancing during the Hajj period.[7]

A marketer should understand that cultural elements—values, for instance—exist because they are gratifying. As long as a value serves to satisfy the needs of a society, it will persist. Cultures do adapt to new needs, but change is gradual. Marketers, then, must become familiar with the culture and adapt to it. As the

America is made up of many different ethnic groups or subcultures, to which marketers attempt to appeal.

culture changes, they must be sensitive to the changes, so that they can continue to adapt.

Executives of organizations that serve two or more cultures must decide whether to use a single marketing strategy or a different strategy for each culture. Numerous firms, such as the Coca-Cola Company, have used a single crosscultural marketing strategy successfully. On the other hand, marketing literature is full of examples of firms that have attempted to use a standardized strategy and failed because of cultural differences. Chapter 21, International Marketing, discusses this subject in depth.

SUBCULTURES

Subcultures are groups that share elements of the overall culture but also have unique features.

Cultures with large populations tend to be sufficiently heterogeneous in their values, attitudes, and so on, to contain smaller, more homogeneous groups called **subcultures.** The subculture retains the elements of the larger culture but also has unique features of its own. This uniqueness presents the marketing manager with an opportunity to design a strategy specifically to satisfy the subculture. Subcultures have been identified based on nationality (German, American, Irish), religion (Jewish, Catholic, Muslim), geographic area (southern or western United States), and ethnic background (blacks, Asian Americans, Hispanics).

SOCIAL CLASSES

Social class is determined not only by income but by education, family background, and other variables.

In the United States, as in other societies, a social class system does exist. **Social classes** are groups separated by differences in authority, power, and social position. Figure 6.3 outlines the U.S. social class structure. Variables used in the United

❑ **Figure 6.3** The U.S. class system in the twentieth century—an estimate.

Class (and percentage of population)	Income	Property	Occupation	Education	Personal and Family Life	Education of Children
Upper class (1–3%)	Very high income	Great wealth; old wealth	Corporate heads, high civil and military officials	Liberal arts education at elite schools	Stable family life; autonomous personality	College education by right for both sexes
Upper-middle class (10–15%)	High income	Accumulation of property through savings	Managers, professionals, high-level executives	Graduate training	Better physical and mental health	Educational system biased in their favor—reflects upper-middle class values
Lower-middle class (30–35%)	Modest income	Some savings	Small business people and farmers, semiprofessionals, sales and clerical workers	Some college, high school	Longer life expectancy	Greater chance of college than working-class children
Working class (40–45%)	Low income	Some savings	Skilled labor, unskilled labor	Some high school, grade school	Unstable family life, conformist personality	Educational system biased against them; tendency toward vocational programs
Lower class (20–25%)	Poverty-level income	No savings	Highest unemployment	Illiteracy	Poorer physical and mental health, lower life expectancy	Little interest in education; high dropout rates

Source: Daniel W. Rossides, *The American Class System: An Introduction to Social Stratification,* p. 24. Copyright © by Houghton Mifflin Company. Adapted by permission.

States to determine social class may include occupation, income, source of income, education, family background, values, geographic location, type of dwelling, and others. Thus, although income is often mistakenly treated as the sole determinant of social class, it is only one factor among many.

Marketers continue to debate the value of social class information to marketing.[8] Some marketers argue that other variables, such as income, do a better job than social class in dividing up the market. On the other hand, individuals in the same social class do to some degree exhibit common patterns of behavior; usage of some products also seems to vary with social class.[9] The type of furniture people buy, for example, seems to vary by social class, with the lower class preferring "flashy" home furnishings; the middle class, functional furniture; and the upper class, elegantly designed or antique pieces. Product features and advertising have frequently been adjusted to social class differences. For example, Aprica Kassai, Inc., a Japanese firm, successfully markets a line of baby strollers in the $100-to-$300 price range to upper-class markets in the United States. Top artists and designers were commissioned to develop the stroller, and the vice-president of the company believes the primary appeal of the product is snob appeal.[10]

THE CASE CONTINUES

*C*ar buyers are significantly influenced by groups in their environment. Cars have high visibility, they act as status symbols, they have the potential for reflecting a person's values, and they are major investments. All of these qualities increase the role of others in purchase decisions.

The buyer's family probably will be included in the decision to pur-

chase a Saturn. The purchase is likely to be a joint decision made by both husband and wife. Children, especially teenagers, will exert influence. The high-tech electronic features will have appeal to this group.

Saturn's positioning in relation to

other cars will also influence the purchasing decision. Positioning it at the low end of the market, for instance, may elicit negative reaction. On the other hand, positioning Saturn above a foreign car such as high-end model Toyota would perhaps miss the large social class markets of the lower-middle class and the upper-lower class.

PSYCHOLOGICAL CHARACTERISTICS OF CONSUMERS

Psychological characteristics of the decision maker come into play in the purchasing decision process. As noted in Chapter 5, marketers consider both psychological and demographic characteristics when they analyze consumer markets. Demographic characteristics were discussed in Chapter 5. We now turn to the psychological factors of motivation, perception, learning, attitudes and beliefs. When the focus of research is on the psychological aspects of buying behavior, such research is termed **psychographics,** or lifestyle studies. The most ambitious psychographic study to date is the VALS system (value and lifestyle system). We discuss the VALS system in Chapter 7 on segmentation of consumer markets.

Psychological factors that affect the purchase and the use of products are listed in figure 6.4, along with demographic factors.

Buyer Characteristics	
Psychological	Demographic
Motivation Perception Learning Attitudes and Beliefs	Age Occupation Income Life Cycle

Motivation

What causes the consumer to move, to act, to purchase? The basic element that urges the consumer to activity is attributed to the consumer's needs. **Need** can be thought of as an imbalance within the consumer between an actual and a desired state of being. In short, a need is the lack of something perceived as useful. Needs are always in existence. They initiate action, however, only when they become activated, or aroused. *Motive* and *drive* are terms used to describe a need that has developed sufficient tension to direct a person to achieve need satisfaction in order to arrive at a state of equilibrium. A **motive** or **drive,** therefore, may be thought of as an energizing force that directs behavior toward a potentially need-satisfying goal. To illustrate, hunger always exists as a need. For a person who has just eaten a large meal, hunger is not an activated need. For a person who has skipped breakfast and had lunch delayed by an unscheduled meeting, hunger becomes a motive.

MOTIVATION AND MARKETING

A food company would find selling its product a difficult task if the market consisted of a group of people who had just finished a large meal. On the other hand, sales could be made more easily if the market consisted of people who had skipped breakfast and lunch. Marketing strategies must satisfy aroused needs to be successful. Therefore, studying needs and motives before developing a marketing plan seems sensible. Identifying these elements of consumer behavior, however, presents the marketer with a number of challenges.

The psychoanalytic theory of behavior suggests that a motive may rest in the individual's subconscious. If asked directly, then, an individual might not be able to explain the true motive behind a purchase. Projective techniques (mentioned in Chapter 4), although open to criticism with regard to accuracy, are often used to identify motives.

The task of motive identification is made more difficult by the existence of emotional motives. These motives deny a rational explanation. Nevertheless, marketers need to consider emotional aspects in their strategies. Product features that do not contribute to the functional aspects of the product may have a significant emotional impact on consumers. L'eggs panty hose is an illustration. The brand name "L'eggs" and the egg-shaped package clearly were not intended to satisfy the rational motives of panty hose purchasers.

MASLOW'S NEED HIERARCHY

A theory developed by the motivational psychologist Abraham Maslow helps marketers identify and work with consumers' needs. Maslow theorized that all people have needs of five general types: physiological, safety, social, esteem, and self-actualization (figure 6.5).[11] These five classes of needs have a hierarchial relationship, with physiological needs satisfied first, then safety, and so on. Maslow's structure is known as the **hierarchy of needs.**

□ **Figure 6.5**
Maslow's hierarchy of needs.

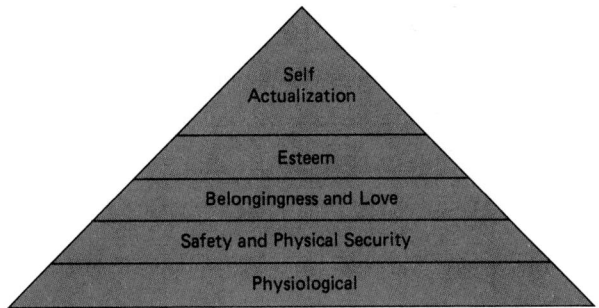

*P*eople focus attention on the need that is dominant at the moment.

The hierarchial arrangement means that the individual focuses attention on the dominant need, so marketers have to be alert to changes in the relative importance of needs. For instance, because of the high standard of living in the United States, many consumers within the U.S. population have dominant needs at the esteem and self-actualization levels. At another time or in another place, safety needs might dominate.

Note that companies selling such items as home alarm systems, life insurance, health-club memberships, and automobile tires have successfully emphasized safety to target markets that appear to be at the esteem and self-actualization need levels. This fact suggests that Maslow's theory, while helpful, does not provide all the answers. One problem with the theory is that the classes of needs are very general. Individuals may satisfy these needs in many different ways. Hunger for one person may lead to the purchase of a Snickers candy bar; for another it leads to the purchase of a vegetable juice drink at a health-food bar. Maslow's theory may also encourage oversimplification of the reason for a purchase. Hunger may be identified as the motive behind an individual's purchase of vegetable juice, for example, when in reality a set of needs led to the purchase—hunger, health concerns, and the influence of friends who drink vegetable juice. Maslow's theory does, however, emphasize that satisfied needs are not motivators and that individuals seem to have an unlimited supply of needs.

Perception

A motivated person is ready to act. How the person acts, however, is shaped by perception. **Perception** is the process of selecting, organizing, and interpreting stimuli of the world received through the five senses.[12] Two individuals standing near each other in an aisle at a grocery store may both be gazing at the display of detergents. One perceives Tide as an excellent brand and proceeds to put a box into the shopping cart. The other person never perceives Tide at all. This person thinks generic brands are the best value for the money and so walks past the Tide display to pick up a generic detergent. The moral: no two people perceive things exactly the same way. To a great extent, people perceive what they want to perceive in order to maintain their world view. Marketers' understanding of the subjective process of perception is essential to the development of an effective strategy.

*P*erception depends on: (1) stimulus factors, (2) the perceiver, (3) the surrounding environment.

Perception depends on three sets of factors—the stimulus, the individual, and the surrounding environment. Stimuli consist of bits of data that are capable of being sensed by the individual. Whether an object will be perceived depends on the characteristics of the factors that make up the object, such as weight, size, shape, color, odor, sound emitted, and taste. Factors related to the individual, such as experience, motivation, and expectation, also influence the degree of perception. A connoisseur of wine makes fine distinctions based on the stimuli present in the wines.

*T*he perception of value of a private brand, for instance, depends on other stimuli in the environment, specifically regional and national brands, and their price relationship to each other.

An occasional drinker of wine may find it difficult to tell the difference between an inexpensive California wine and the finest French brand.

The surrounding environment also affects perception. Other stimuli in the environment, their intensity, and their relationship to each other can distract, for example. Foods are often priced in three tiers: generic and private labels, regional brands, and major brands. The greater costs incurred by most major brands tend to make them higher priced. Generic and private labels have the lowest price, while regional brands are midpriced. As prices go up, the actual money difference between tiers may stay the same while the relative, or percentage, difference decreases. The perception of price difference also diminishes, usually to the detriment of generic and regional brand sales.[13]

SELECTIVE PERCEPTION

*T*o function in a stimulus-filled world, people perceive selectively.

The average person is pelted with thousands of stimuli in an average day, but most of these stimuli are ignored. The experience is similar to running outside into a rainstorm. The first few drops we notice, but after a minute or two the drops roll off without attracting our attention. Only a change in the intensity of the rainfall or the occasional drop that hits an eye receives attention. We simply cannot respond to every drop—to every stimulus. We must practice **selective perception** to have time to function.

*S*elective perception can occur at the point of exposure, in the organization and interpretation of the stimuli, or at the point of retention.

Selectivity in perception appears to occur at three points in the perception process. The first opportunity for selectivity develops at the point of exposure. **Selective exposure** means that individuals become aware of stimuli they wish to perceive—those that support their attitudes and beliefs about the world—and ignore other stimuli. A particular company's advertising, publicity, selling effort, and product may be tuned out while another company's is consistently tuned in. Perhaps only part of an advertising message is tuned out—for instance, the brand name. Alka Seltzer advertisements for a time used the phrase "I can't believe I ate the whole thing." People could remember the phrase but not the brand.

Buyers probably ignore most of the commercials aimed at them, just as they ignore most other stimuli. This means that dollars and effort are wasted by organizations trying to increase awareness of their products or services. To overcome selective perception at the point of exposure, some organizations resort to repetitiveness. Repeat the advertisement enough times, they believe, and eventually the buyer will pay attention. Perception at the point of exposure has also been found to occur if the stimulus (such as a particular commercial) is anticipated, if it can be associated with alternatives for satisfying current needs, and if its intensity is significantly different from that of surrounding stimuli. Marketers can take advantage of these findings by promoting the product when a need exists and using larger, louder, brighter stimuli—making the promotion different. PepsiCo, for example, departed from the traditional soft drink advertising format of upbeat music, dancing, and active sports when it introduced Diet Pepsi. The ads featured a series of sexy minidramas featuring a man and woman. An executive explained that to compete with seventeen other cola advertisers the company had to create advertising that was very different.[14]

A second form of selective perception is called **selective distortion.** Here, the individual, to make the received stimuli more consistent with his or her existing opinion of the world, organizes and interprets them in a way entirely different from what was intended. The individual's organization and interpretation may distort the reality of the situation. For instance, a consumer who has a very positive opinion of a particular brand of car may, upon hearing that the car was recalled because of a defect, interpret the recall as just another indication of the inept interference of the federal government in the activities of corporations.

Finally, **selective retention** means the individual, having become aware of the stimulus, tends to forget it unless it supports his or her views. A consumer may remember the especially desirable brands and the especially undesirable but forget all the others. It should also be noted that the buyer acts on only a small number of retained perceptions. Thus, even the individual who remembers the product may not buy it.

SUBLIMINAL PERCEPTION

*S*ubliminal perception—is it a hoax?

Receiving information at subconscious levels is referred to as **subliminal perception.** Subliminal transmission of data supposedly bypasses selectivity in perception. For example, a marketer might send a subliminal transmission by flashing information on a screen so quickly that the viewer was not consciously aware of seeing the information and so could not block it out. James Vicary, in a 1957 marketing research study in a New Jersey theatre, reported that sales of popcorn and Coca-Cola substantially increased when the words "Drink Coca-Cola" and "Eat popcorn" were alternately flashed on the screen for .003 seconds. Wilson Bryan Key popularized the technique with his book *Subliminal Seduction.* Over a million copies of the book were sold, primarily to college students.

Avoiding selective perception by sending subliminal directives would certainly give marketers an advantage in selling products and services, if it worked. However, according to a recent evaluation, "a review of the research literature on the use of subliminal stimuli in advertising and marketing show a range of conclusions—from disinterest to humor to outright disbelief. Some experts even contend that purveyors of [such] advertising techniques are con artists."[15] Another investigator, after conducting a comprehensive review of the literature on the topic concluded that "subliminal directives have not been shown to have the power ascribed to them by advocates of subliminal advertising."[16] In short, the effectiveness of subliminal techniques have not been supported by recent research findings.

Learning

For consumers, **learning** involves some change or modification from an earlier pattern of behavior to a new one, based on their experience in the market. Learning behavior is of interest to marketers as they try to analyze how customers develop new patterns of behavior in their purchase and use of products. Gillette marketers applied their knowledge of learning patterns when they promoted new shaving products in the Third World. Their promotion stressed teaching men the techniques and advantages of modern shaving equipment; their Third-World consumers learned to appreciate and buy Gillette's shaving product line. (See the Marketing in Action that follows.) As they attempt to guide the consumer's experience of learning about products, marketers generally apply one of two approaches to learning: the stimulus-response (S-R) approach or the cognitive approach.

THE STIMULUS-RESPONSE APPROACH TO LEARNING

*T*he stimulus-response theory focuses on drives, cues, responses, and reinforcement.

The **stimulus-response (S-R) theory** holds that learning is a series of responses to the external world. The elements of S-R theory consist of four items: drive, cue, response, and reinforcement.

Drive.   **Drive**—or motive—was discussed earlier in this chapter. The marketing manager who wishes to utilize drives in marketing plans has several tasks to perform. The most obvious is to determine what drives have relevance to the buyer. Once the drives have been identified, the marketer has to tell the consumer how it will satisfy

The market for blades in developed countries is stagnant. "The opportunities on the blade side really lie in new geography," says Roderick Mills, an executive vice president for Gillette's international business. "In the Third World, there's a very high proportion of people under 15 years old. All those young men are going to be in the shaving population in a very short time," he adds.

Tailoring its marketing to Third-World budgets and tastes—from packaging blades so they can be sold one at a time, to educating the unshaven about the joys of a smooth face—has become an important part of Gillette's growth strategy. The company sells its pens, toiletries, toothbrushes, and other products in developing countries.

The toughest task for Gillette is convincing Third-World men to shave. The company recently began dispatching portable theaters to remote villages—Gillette calls them "mobile propaganda units"—to show movies and commercials that tout daily shaving.

In South African and Indonesian versions, a bewildered bearded man enters a locker room where clean-shaven friends show him how to shave. In the Mexican one, a handsome sheriff, tracking bandits who have kidnapped a woman, pauses on the trail to shave every morning.

In other places, Mr. Mills says, Gillette agents with an oversized

MARKETING IN ACTION

Gillette Educates the Consumer

shaving brush and a mug of shaving cream lather up and shave a villager while others watch. Plastic razors are then distributed free and blades—which, of course, must be bought—are left with the local storekeeper.

Such campaigns win few immediate converts, acknowledges Robert King, director of international marketing, planning and administration. Mi-

gration of peasants to the city does more to boost Gillette sales. "If you slog around in the field all day, there's not much incentive to shave," he says. "If in the next generation, you move into the city and the older son gets a job as a counter clerk, he'll probably have to shave if not everyday, then every other day."

Source: Excerpts from David Wessel, "Gillette Keys Sales to Third World Tastes," *The Wall Street Journal,* January 23, 1986, p. 33. Reprinted by permission of *The Wall Street Journal,* © Dow Jones Company, Inc. 1986. All Rights Reserved.

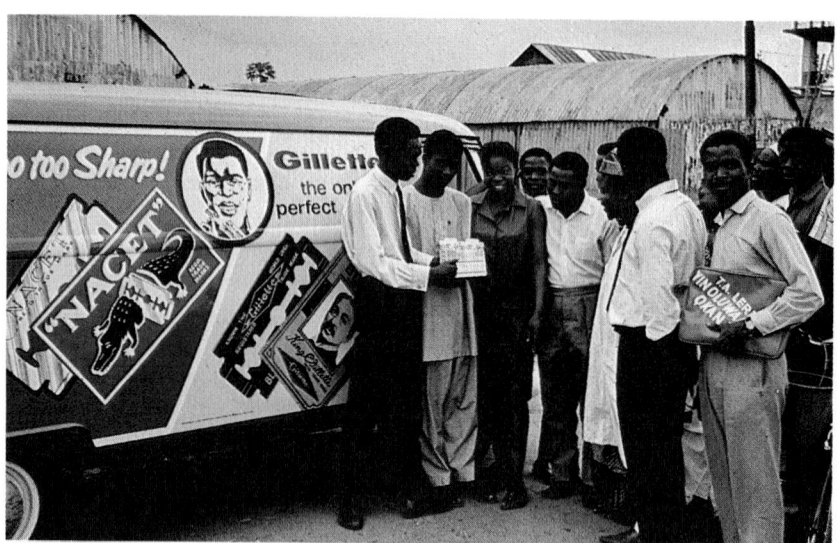

■ Gillette has increased its sales of razors and blades by public information programs in Third-World countries. Mobile education units move from village to village. *Source:* Photo courtesy The Gillette Company.

them. Consider the U.S. Navy recruiting slogan, "It's not just a job, it's an adventure." The Navy could have taken a very rational approach in communicating its offering: "We have jobs that pay $12,000 a year. Room, board, and training are provided." Instead, the Navy chose to appeal to two drives common in young people—to get a job and to lead an adventurous life.

Cue. A **cue** is any external stimulus that causes the consumer to think that a viable method for satisfying a need exists. Firms go to great lengths to incorporate the appropriate cues in their products and promotions. The sound a car door makes when it closes supposedly serves as an important cue to the consumer and therefore is of great concern to automobile manufacturers. The cues present in a Miller Beer commercial—the commercial's setting, participants, and the participants' activities—all seem to be important. The marketer, in developing the marketing plan, has to identify the specific cues it will use. Cues seem so important that competitors often copy successful ones. Thus the marketer may want to protect specific cues, such as brands and slogans. For instance, Prudential Insurance Company has legal protection through copyright of the slogan "Get a piece of the rock."

Response.   The **response** consists of the individual's effort to satisfy a drive based on the cues presented. One way of including responses in the marketing plan is to define what choices will be presented to the buyer. Retailers carefully consider the products they purchase for resale, because these products represent possible consumer responses.

Reinforcement.   **Reinforcement** is the reward or punishment that results from the response. Rewarded responses tend to be repeated, while punished responses tend to be repressed. **Shaping** is the process of supplying a series of rewards as reinforcement to develop more complex behavior over time. This process sometimes works in marketing a product. For example, the marketer may first give a free sample of the product; the sample package may contain a coupon for a substantial price discount; and each regular package may contain a coupon for a smaller price discount. The marketer hopes to shape the consumer's behavior in a series of steps: the consumer is meant to accept the free product, then buy the product at a substantial price reduction and then a small price reduction, and finally buy the product at full price—the desired behavior.

Marketers always want their customers to experience positive reinforcement. Because they want customers to be satisfied with their products, services, personnel, and so on, they must make customer service, customer relations, and similar variables a part of their marketing plans.

THE COGNITIVE APPROACH TO LEARNING

*C*ognitive theory focuses on people's ability to develop knowledge, rather than learning only from experience.

The **cognitive theory of learning** goes beyond the idea of simple response to a stimulus; it puts emphasis on human *cognitions,* or complex mental patterns based on past experience—thoughts, memories, and symbols. In the cognitive view, consumers do not simply react to a stimulus; they use their thoughts and memories to anticipate possible future consequences that might result from a stimulus. In this way, consumers may think ahead, calling on memories and associations to project how a newly advertised food may taste, or how a vacation experience may fill a complex need. Using the cognitive approach, marketers work from the basic stimulus-response pattern to a more complex accumulation of thought processes that they anticipate customers may experience in their buying behavior.

Attitudes

*A*ttitudes are learned and enduring.

An **attitude** is a learned, enduring predisposition to feel toward, act toward, or evaluate a particular object or idea in a certain way. Attitudes develop from experience and interaction with other individuals.

According to the multiattribute theory of attitudes, an attitude forms from the beliefs an individual holds about the attributes of an object or idea and the importance of each attribute.[17]

Attributes are the characteristics the buyer uses when thinking of the product. For a food item, attributes might include price, flavor, calories, status, temperature, and freshness. *Beliefs* are the individual's evaluations of attributes contained within

☐ **Figure 6.6**
Attitudes and behavior.

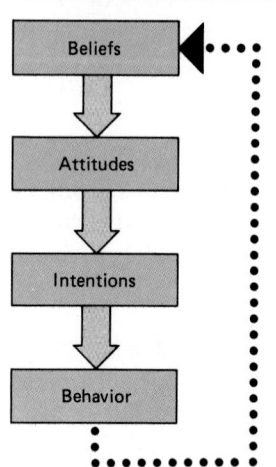

the product or brand. For example, John Hamyzsch believes Twinkies have just the right sweetness.

Attitudes put people in the frame of mind to move toward or away from an object or idea. When the object is the marketer's product or marketing mix, the attitude is of vital importance to the marketer. Favorable attitudes may lead to an intention to purchase and perhaps to an actual purchase. (See figure 6.6.) Marketers benefit in still another way from understanding attitudes. Attitudes, because of their enduring quality, provide consistency in the way people act. Among other things, this consistency allows marketers to forecast sales.

We should note that even people with a very positive attitude toward a product may not purchase it.[18] Attitudes represent one of several determinants of purchase. Others include motivation, financial ability, and situational factors. Thus, an individual with a very favorable attitude toward yachts does not automatically purchase one. The lack of financial means or the desire for other items represents a barrier to a yacht purchase.

ATTITUDE MEASUREMENT

To successfully develop or change attitudes in buyers, the marketer should know what attitudes buyers currently hold. Knowledge of current attitudes is all the more important because selective perception seems to function for the purpose of protecting and enhancing these attitudes. Because they are internal, attitudes do not permit direct measurements, so they must be inferred from information that can be obtained. The method most widely used to obtain information about attitudes in marketing has been the direct question approach in conjunction with rating scales. The **semantic differential,** a commonly used rating scale technique, is a good example. (See figure 6.7.) The individual whose attitude the marketer wants to determine is directly asked to respond to questions about the object. Rating scales attempt to quantify the strength of the attitude toward various features of the object. The semantic differential is always constructed with the scale anchored on each end by opposing descriptions, as shown in the figure.

☐ **Figure 6.7**
Example of semantic differential.

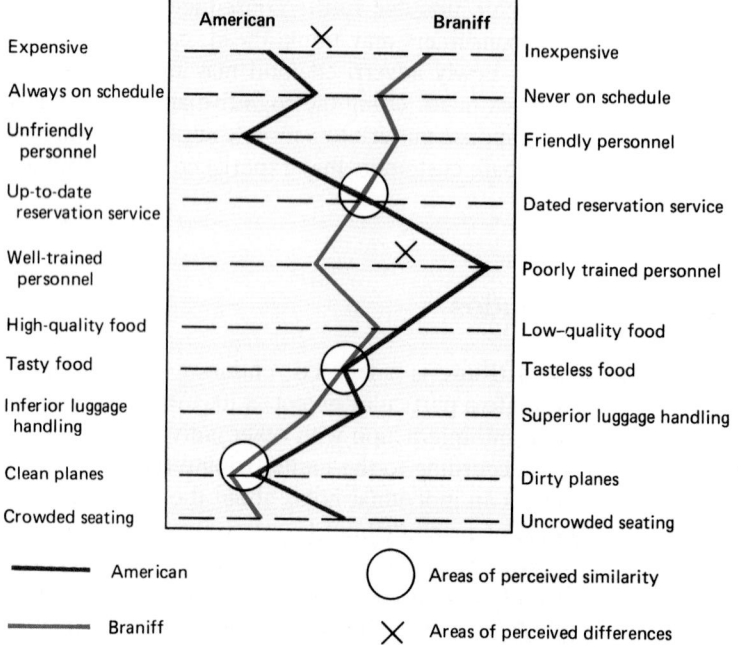

Source: Adapted from Martin Fishbein/Isek Ajzen, *Attitude, Intention and Behavior: An Introduction to Theory and Research,* © 1975, Addison-Wesley Publishing Co., Inc., Reading, Massachusetts. Reprinted with permission.

STRATEGIES TO CHANGE CONSUMER ATTITUDES

Marketers can adapt products to existing attitudes, attempt to change attitudes, or change both product and attitudes.

Marketers have three alternatives in working with the attitudes of the target market. Usually, the least difficult approach is to adapt the product or concept to existing attitudes, but the marketer can also attempt to modify existing attitudes to fit the idea or product. Indeed, the objective of marketing efforts is sometimes to change attitudes. Many nonprofit organizations find themselves in this position. Examples include attempts to change attitudes about smoking, drinking and driving, and wearing seat belts. Because of the enduring nature of attitudes, however, changing them represents a difficult undertaking. A third alternative is to change both consumers' attitudes and the organization's offering. Electric power companies have long encouraged home owners to use electric heat. Because it is more expensive than other forms of heating, however, many home owners have had a negative attitude towards it. The power companies have worked to change attitudes by stressing electric heat's cleanliness and efficiency.

Several specific marketing-plan strategies for changing attitudes are listed below. Beliefs, attributes, and the importance of attributes all serve as bases for strategy.[19]

Changing attributes, beliefs, and attribute importance should change attitudes.

Strategy 1: Identify key attributes and increase consumers' belief that the brand is strong in these attributes. Ford used this strategy in its "Quality is job one" advertisements. Quality, a key attribute for U.S. car buyers, has been perceived as low for U.S.-made cars. Ford wanted to change this perception.

Strategy 2: Make a key attribute more important. Assuming the firm is accomplished at providing the attribute, increasing the importance of the attribute may increase sales. Low-cholesterol margarines emphasize the importance of reducing cholesterol in the diet, for example. Price, value, health, safety, and risk are attributes that often lend themselves to this approach.

Strategy 3: Add a new attribute. Years ago, Procter & Gamble successfully used this strategy when it added fluoride to Crest toothpaste. Manufacturers of personal computer printers added an attribute when they produced a printer capable of near-letter quality as well as draft quality.

Strategy 4: Decrease the importance of attributes in which the product or brand is weak. A retailer with an out-of-the-way location may use the advertising slogan "A little out of the way, but far less to pay." Volkswagen of America's classic VW "bug" advertisements played down the less-than-rakish style of the "bug" with humor.

Strategy 5: Decrease consumers' beliefs about competitors' attributes. Comparative advertising may have this as its objective.

Marketers can also use intentions or behavior to change attitudes.

The marketing-plan strategy might also focus on using intentions or behavior to change attitudes. For instance, an intention strategy may involve offering a discount or rebate to encourage new people to buy with the hope that they will find the product better than they believed, change their beliefs (thus their attitudes), and continue to purchase, but without further incentives. Banks, in times past, used this strategy by offering gifts to people opening new savings accounts.

Behavior strategies focus on eliciting behavior. Behavior provides experiences through which the individual may form beliefs where none existed before or change beliefs. Household and personal product companies often offer samples of their new products, for example, to give people experience with the product before they form attitudes.

*T*he buyer's motivations, perceptions, and attitudes will all come to bear on the purchase decision. A buyer's motivation represents the reason for purchase. People with limited financial resources may buy a small car for efficient transportation. Others with the same limited resources may buy a large used car because their attitudes toward small cars are negative. Some purchases are motivated mainly by concerns for safety. Others are motivated by

status. Generally, purchases of the magnitude of a new car are made to satisfy several different needs. If the Saturn car is to satisfy the relevant needs of the market, marketers must understand these needs.

To Saturn marketers, consumers' perception—the organization and interpretation of incoming stimuli—means that the stimuli surrounding

the Saturn car must convey the intended message. In short, the car may be the best car manufactured, but if car buyers ignore it through selective perception, or perceive it in ways different than intended, the fact that Saturn represents the best car makes little difference.

Since the Saturn has not yet been produced, consumer perceptions are not formed. Marketers have the opportunity to create positive responses.

THE PURCHASE DECISION PROCESS

*B*uyers are decision-making problem solvers.

How does an individual decide whether to buy or not to buy a product or a brand? Through what process is the purchase decision made? The focus here is on *how* the decision is made rather than on what is purchased. Knowing how a decision is made allows the marketer to assist the decision maker and thus provides an opportunity to influence the purchase.

The buyer in the purchase decision process is perceived as a decision-making problem solver.[20] The approach implies that the buyer engages in rational, goal-oriented behavior.

Types of Decisions

*C*onsumers make routine decisions quickly with little effort.

The decision-making procedure varies in extent with the type of decision. A continuum based on decision type is diagrammed in figure 6.8. At the extreme left is the routine decision, the purchase decision that has been made repeatedly, with satisfactory results. New information that creates doubt in the decision maker, such as an unsatisfactory purchase or new technology, moves the decision to the right.

The type of decision depends in part on the involvement of the buyer. Routinized decision making has a mechanical element. The buyer makes the decision quickly, exerting little effort. The alternatives are familiar, and the buyer depends primarily on memory for information. The criteria to evaluate the alternative choices are well established in the buyer's mind. Buyers with preferred brands exhibit routine decision-making behavior. Purchases of cigarettes, beer, deodorants, shampoo, and similar products most often involve routine decisions. Routine decision making may also be used when the product generates low involvement. Potatoes and apples typically fall in this category.

In limited problem-solving situations, the buyer consciously thinks about the decision, or at least some parts of it. For instance, the introduction to the market of

❑ **Figure 6.8**
Purchase decision
continuum.

Routine Decision	Limited Decision	Complex Extensive Decision

• • • • • • • • Employment of Decision-Making Process • • • • • • • • ▶

☐ **Figure 6.9**
Procedure for making
complex decisions.

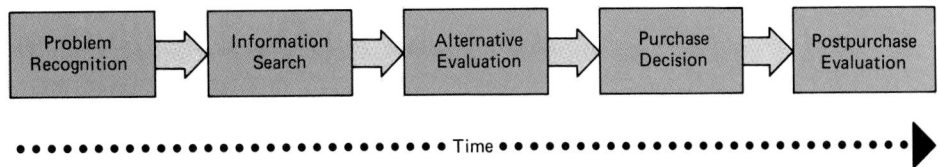

a new brand may stimulate the decision maker to rethink available alternatives. A medical study on carcinogens may prompt a reconsideration of what criteria should be used to evaluate products usually purchased as the result of routine decisions. The decision then becomes a limited decision requiring more deliberate decision making.

*C*omplex decisions require time, effort, and information.

Consumers purchasing homes, furniture, and computers tend to use complex problem-solving techniques. Here, the buyer follows a decision-making procedure that requires time and effort. The steps in the procedure, as shown in figure 6.9, are problem recognition, information search, evaluation of alternatives, purchase decision, and postpurchase evaluation.

Problem Recognition

*P*roblem recognition signifies a person's readiness to act.

Motives start the decision-making process; they initiate behavior and direct it to certain ends.[21] Several theories of what actually occurs when the buyer becomes aware of a problem have been proposed. One rests on the idea that some motives are internal and are caused by inner tension. These motives, whether physical or psychological, occur with little conscious thought. Hunger is an example of such a motive. Another explanation views motives as more conscious. The buyer supposedly compares the actual state of being with the desired state. Significant deviations give the buyer reason to act. A change in either the actual or the desired state may produce deviations. Depletion of the diet-cola supply (an actual state) may send the consumer to the supermarket to purchase another six-pack. Friends' or family members' comments about the dated style of an item of clothing (even though the consumer may have been satisfied with it) may lead the consumer to redefine the desired state. Problem awareness is necessary before any other step in the decision process. To be aware the individual must be aroused to act, have the energy to act, and have a sense of direction in which to act.

Information Search

*I*nformation search may enhance or modify problem awareness as well as uncover alternative solutions.

Aware of a problem, the individual seeks a remedy. Identifying possible remedies and evaluating and selecting one require information. Information may also serve to enhance or modify awareness. After opening the refrigerator door, the hungry individual may recognize that not just any food will satisfy that hunger—it has to be a dessert. The less knowledge and experience the consumer has in the situation and the greater the perceived risks, the more uncertain the decision maker will be, and the more intense will be the information search.[22] An individual purchasing a new personal computer, for example, desires more information than an individual purchasing a gallon of milk.

Purchasing milk is a routine decision. Here, remember, the individual relies almost entirely on internal information—existing knowledge. Additional information, if sought, will probably be gathered quickly from supermarket newspaper ads and in-store information, including product examination. American Cyanamid Company used knowledge of information gathering for a routine product purchase when faced with the decision of what to emphasize in advertisements of a household cleaner-disinfectant in the Brazilian market. Some marketers argued that the product's cleaning properties should be emphasized, but in-store observation of consumers making the brand choice decision found that nearly all collected information in the same way: They opened the bottle and smelled the product. The advertising campaign emphasized how nice the house would smell after the consumer had used the cleanser, and the campaign was a big success.[23]

In contrast, the personal computer purchase is an infrequent purchase with which the decision maker may have little experience. The decision-making task may generate a high degree of uncertainty and perceived risk. The consumer will probably turn to external sources—friends, colleagues, family, advertising, salespeople, and other sources—for information. For prices, design features, and availability information, the individual typically relies on market-dominated sources, such as advertising and salespeople. Information on social acceptability is gained from nonmarket sources.

*V*alue and cost are factors in information search.

The individual decision maker appears to view information acquisition in a very practical way.[24] He or she believes that the benefits derived from information should outweigh its cost, which can be economic, psychological, or physical. The decision-making consumer may not be willing to pay the physical and mental cost of driving in heavy traffic and looking for a parking place when searching for information about a product but may instead opt to request information by phone, mail, or from the most convenient retailer.

Decision makers may at times employ evoked sets, brand loyalty, national brands, and price to reduce their need for information. An **evoked set** is a group of brands, products, or stores that the buyer thinks of when the problem arises. The buyer looks for information only on items in the evoked set and usually also purchases from this set. National brands and medium-priced items substitute for information because the buyer perceives them as less risky. Similarly, brand loyalty reduces the need for information on a particular type of purchase.

Evaluation of Alternatives

*I*n evaluating alternatives, most consumers use specific criteria of varying importance, certain methods of evaluating each alternative, and certain methods of retaining or discarding alternatives.

The buyer, generally after collecting information, has several products or brands from which to select. How is the evaluation made? Naturally, individual consumers differ in their evaluation processes, but most include the following aspects:

- Evaluation criteria of varying importance
- Methods of evaluating each alternative
- Methods used to retain or discard alternatives

The evaluation criteria used and their importance affect product selection. For instance, some buyers may use price, maintenance information, and miles per gallon as criteria in purchasing a new car. Others may use style, resale value, and financing charges. Marketers should identify frequently used criteria and determine the importance of each criterion before formulating the marketing plan.

Methods used to evaluate alternatives vary. For instance, the buyer with two alternatives will probably use a different method of evaluating each than the buyer with two hundred alternatives. With two alternatives, a comparison of features of the two brands is possible. Many firms used comparison advertising, suggesting that the marketing managers of these firms expect buyers to compare a limited number of products or brands. With a large number of alternatives, the evaluation is more likely to rate each feature against the features of an ideal product.

The method used to discard or retain alternatives is also a part of the evaluation process. For example, the buyer may discard any alternative that fails to meet a certain criterion, as when a person shopping for a new suit rejects all suits that are not brown, blue, or gray. Another method involves evaluating alternatives and selecting the one that appears best overall. For example, the clothing shopper may select a suit that is olive green because it has the best cut, material, and stitching and is thus the best overall alternative.

Purchase Decisions

*P*urchasing usually involves a series of decisions.

The buyer ultimately must make a decision: select one of the evaluated alternatives, seek out additional alternatives, or postpone the purchase. The decision to purchase usually involves a series of decisions—for instance, decisions on price, size, color, quantity, and when and where to purchase. Some organizations have specialized in reducing the number of decisions to make deciding easier for the buyer. Consider, for example, the young man who lacks confidence in making wardrobe decisions. He may make one major decision, that being to shop at a men's clothing store that has established an image of "helping its customers to dress for the occasion." Similarly, many individuals turn their vacation planning over to a travel agent.

Postpurchase Evaluation

*D*oubts about whether the decision to buy was a good one give rise to cognitive dissonance.

The decision to purchase a certain item, especially one of value, immediately generates the ongoing question of whether the correct decision has been made and is being made in repeat purchases. An evaluation to answer the question may lead to an affirmative answer, a negative answer, or doubt about the answer. **Cognitive dissonance** is the psychological conflict resulting from incongruous beliefs and attitudes held simultaneously.

Cognitive dissonance occurs because each of the alternatives involves both weaknesses and advantages. The weakness of one alternative may be the strength of another, and vice versa. For instance, one car model has great gas mileage but poor acceleration. Another has great acceleration but poor mileage. If both mileage and acceleration are important to the buyer, either choice is likely to produce anxiety. Cognitive dissonance may also develop from weaknesses in the purchase decision process. Perhaps neither time nor information was available for alternative evaluation, for example.

Postpurchase evaluations are significant to marketers. Positive evaluations increase the probability of repeat purchases and brand loyalty. Negative or doubtful thoughts increase the probability that different alternatives will be considered next time the problem arises. Marketers have, therefore, attempted to reduce doubtful and negative postpurchase thoughts with assorted programs and techniques. For example, salespersons frequently assure buyers that correct decisions have been made, and some firms offer buyers free membership in product user organizations.

THE CASE CONTINUES

*U*sing their understanding of how consumers decide to purchase, Saturn marketers can organize the firm's marketing program. To begin, information describing the Saturn must be available. To be effective, the information must be properly placed so that buyers are likely to find it. Initially, information will be obtained through advertisements. As the purchase decision nears, the automobile dealer becomes more important in dispensing information.

Awareness of the criteria used by buyers in evaluating automobiles would also help Saturn officials. The Saturn design and marketing plan should incorporate this criteria. For instance, if safety is an important criterion, built-in safety features should be promoted. To ensure continued satisfaction and repeat purchases after a sale has been made, marketers can use newsletters, questionnaires, and discounts on parts, as well as a host of other enhancements to customer satisfaction.

GOAL SUMMARY

1. **Explain why understanding consumer behavior is important to marketers.** Consumers, along with industrial buyers, by their decision to purchase and use a product, determine the organization's marketing success. Since marketers cannot control consumers, it becomes essential that they understand consumers. With understanding, marketers can adapt strategies to consumers' thinking and behavior.

2. **Describe two consumer behavior models.** The economic man model, one of the earliest attempts to describe buyer behavior, focuses on economic issues, such as maximizing satisfaction with limited resources. It assumes that the consumer has perfect information and is a rational decision maker. Marketers use the economic model in pricing and other marketing decisions.

    The psychoanalytic model emphasizes the subconscious and emotional aspects of consumer behavior. It acknowledges that a particular purchase decision may be based more on emotion than on logic. Furthermore, the consumer may not be able to explain why the decision was made. Developers of promotional strategies often use the psychoanalytic model.

3. **Discuss the role of the decision-making process in purchase behavior.** Purchase behavior is considered to be goal directed. A purchase occurs because the individual has recognized a problem, searched for information, and evaluated alternatives. After the decision has been made, the results are evaluated. The goal of this process is solving a problem or satisfying a need. The marketer, by facilitating the consumer's decision making, may sell a product.

4. **List psychological characteristics that influence the purchase and use of products.** Many psychological variables may influence the purchase and use of products, but four seem especially significant: motivation, perception, learning, and attitudes. Motivation indicates the need behind the purchase. Perception describes the reception, organization, and interpretation of stimuli, including those relevant to the product. Learning occurs when purchase or use produces either a repeat purchase or the refusal to purchase again. Finally, attitudes indicate which products are held in favor and which are not.

5. **Describe the effects of reference groups and culture on the behavior of individuals.** Both reference groups and the culture at large represent social influences. Both may influence the individual's buying behavior. A reference group's influence tends to be greatest for products that are highly visible, such as clothing. Emulation plays an important role in reference group influence. Culture permeates our lives and exerts particular influence over behavior that involves values and norms.

KEY TERMS

Consumer Behavior, **p. 150**
Consumer Behavior Models, **p. 150**
Psychoanalytic Model, **p. 150**
Reference Group, **p. 152**
Decider, **p. 154**
Purchaser, **p. 154**
User, **p. 154**
Gatekeeper, **p. 154**
Culture, **p. 155**
Subculture, **p. 156**
Social Class, **p. 156**
Psychographics, **p. 157**
Need, **p. 158**
Motive, **p. 158**
Drive, **p. 158**
Hierarchy of Needs, **p. 158**
Perception, **p. 159**

Selective Perception, **p. 160**
Selective Exposure, **p. 160**
Selective Distortion, **p. 160**
Selective Retention, **p. 161**
Subliminal Perception, **p. 161**
Learning, **p. 161**
Stimulus-Response (S-R) Theory of Learning, **p. 161**
Drive, **p. 161**
Cue, **p. 162**
Response, **p. 163**
Reinforcement, **p. 163**
Shaping, **p. 163**
Cognitive Theory of Learning, **p. 163**
Attitude, **p. 163**
Semantic Differential, **p. 164**
Evoked Set, **p. 168**
Cognitive Dissonance, **p. 169**

CHECK YOUR LEARNING

1. The economic man model is based on what people should do according to economists.   **T/F**
2. The psychoanalytic model has been especially easy for marketers to use, since it focuses on rational, conscious behavior.   **T/F**
3. The gatekeeper in product purchases limits the alternatives open to the person making the purchase decision.   **T/F**
4. Cultures and social classes influence marketing in the following way. (a) A different marketing strategy is often required for each culture or social class. (b) The only effect of culture and social class is that they permeate the marketer's environment. (c) The predominant values that exist in each influence marketing. (d) Items a and c are correct. (e) All are correct.

5. A need is the lack of something perceived as useful.   **T/F**
6. To a marketer, emotional needs do not exist.   **T/F**
7. Perception is subjective.   **T/F**
8. Marketers have found efficient ways around selective perception.   **T/F**
9. Which of the following statements is correct? (a) Shaping is an application of the stimulus-response theory of learning. (b) It is possible to learn without changing. (c) Marketers who create a strong positive attitude about their product in consumers can be sure that the consumers will purchase the product. (d) Items a and b are true. (e) Items b and c are true.

QUESTIONS FOR REVIEW AND DISCUSSION

1. Define the key terms for this chapter that appear at the end of the goal summary.
2. Can marketers control buyer behavior?
3. Which model do you think offers the best explanation of buyer behavior: the economic man or the psychoanalytic model?
4. Based on your last purchase, how much time passed between problem recognition and purchase?
5. Find someone who has made a purchase recently involving an outlay of $250 or more. Ask that individual about each step of the decision-making process.
6. Compare the purchase of a new car with the purchase of a loaf of bread.

7. What is an evoked set?
8. Identify the evaluative criteria a person might use in selecting a university.
9. Discuss problems of applying Maslow's hierarchy of needs to a marketing situation.
10. Explain what is meant by selective perception.
11. Do you believe subliminal perception is effective in selling products? Why?
12. Have reference groups played an important role in the sale of personal computers? Explain.
13. Discuss how decision making is changing in the family, if at all.
14. Why does a person tend to purchase products compatible with his or her social class?

NOTES

1. James F. Engel and Robert D. Blackwell, *Consumer Behavior* (Hinsdale, Ill.: Dryden Press, 1982), p. 9.
2. David F. Midgley, "Patterns of Interpersonal Information Seeking for the Purchase of a Symbolic Product," *Journal of Marketing Research* (February 1983): pp. 74–83.
3. Ellyn E. Spragins, "Computers: How Ya Gonna Sell 'Em Down on the Farm?" *Business Week,* February 18, 1985, p. 144.
4. Brent Ritchie, "Joint Purchasing Decisions: A Comparison of Influence Structure in Family and Couple Decision-Making Units," *Journal of Consumer Re-*

search (September 1980): pp. 131–140.
5. "Large Numbers of Husbands Buy Household Products, Do Housework," *Marketing News,* October 3, 1980, p. 1.
6. George J. Szybillo, et al., "Family Member Influence in Household Decision Making," *Journal of Consumer Research* (December 1979): pp. 312–316.
7. Robin G. Marriott, "Ads Require Sensitivity to Arab Culture, Religion," *Marketing News,* April 25, 1986, p. 3.

NOTES *(continued)*

8. Charles M. Schaninger, "Social Class Versus Income Revisited: An Empirical Investigation," *Journal of Marketing Research* (May 1981): pp. 192–208; and Luis V. Dominquez and Albert L. Page, "Use and Misuse of Social Stratification in Consumer Behavior Research," *Journal of Business Research* (June 1981): pp. 151–173.

9. Patrick E. Murphy, "The Effect of Social Class on Brand and Price Consciousness for Supermarket Products," *Journal of Retailing* (Summer 1978): pp. 33–45.

10. Larry Armstrong and Judith H. Dobrzyorski, "Aprica Kassai: A Fast Ride into the United States with Status-Symbol Strollers," *Business Week*, January 21, 1985, p. 117.

11. A. H. Maslow, *Motivation and Personality* (New York: Harper and Row Publishers, 1954), pp. 80–106.

12. William L. Wilkie, *Consumer Behavior* (New York: John Wiley and Sons, 1986), p. 362.

13. "Panelists Offer Pricing Strategy Advice for Consumer and Industrial Products," *Marketing News,* February 1, 1986, p. 1.

14. "The New TV Ads Try to Wake Up Viewers," *Business Week,* March 19, 1984, p. 46.

15. "Subliminal Ad Tactics: Experts Still Laughing," *Marketing News,* March 15, 1985, p. 8.

16. Timothy E. Moore, "Subliminal Advertising: What You See Is What You Get," *Journal of Marketing* (Spring 1982): pp. 38–47.

17. Martin Fishbein and Isek Ajzen, *Attitudes, Intention and Behavior: An Introduction to Theory and Research* (Reading, Mass.: Addison-Wesley, 1975).

18. Joel Huber and John McCann, "The Impact of Inferential Beliefs on Product Evaluations," *Journal of Marketing Research* (August 1982): pp. 324–333.

19. Wilkie, *Consumer Behavior,* pp. 462–464.

20. Richard W. Olshovsky and Donald H. Granbois, "Consumer Decision Making—Fact or Fiction?" *Journal of Consumer Research* (September 1979): pp. 93–100.

21. James E. Engel, Roger D. Blackwell, and Paul W. Miniard, *Consumer Behavior,* 5th ed. (Hinsdale, Ill.: Dryden Press, 1986), p. 49.

22. Ibid.

23. "The Best Defense Is to Know What Customers Want and to Do It Better," *Marketing News,* February 1, 1985, p. 6.

24. Engel, Blackwell, and Miniard, *Consumer Behavior,* p. 68.

Not too many years ago many Americans would not consider eating fish. Now many of these same people eat fish on a regular basis. Fish sales have dramatically increased in the last several years. Fish consumption in 1988 rose to a record per capita consumption of 15.3 pounds.

Being health conscious has encouraged Americans to shift to low fat, low calorie fish in place of red meats. Fish also has gained gourmet status as many Americans, traveling abroad, sampled exotic fish preparations. According to the *Progressive Grocer,* a food industry publication, college students, possibly attuned to health issues because of their level of education, are 34 percent more likely to buy fresh fish and shellfish than the norm.

Several companies have increased their participation in the seafood business. Van de Kamp, for instance, has added a line of adult-oriented, lightly breaded, premium fish fillets called Van de Kamp Light. It is targeted to health-conscious 25- to 45-year-olds. The total frozen fish market represents about $800 million in retail sales in the United States.

Ralston Purina Company is also going into seafood on a large scale (pardon the pun). For instance, one of Ralston's products is a canned, boneless, and skinless salmon. Canned shrimp and canned crab are also being considered by Ralston.

Marketers at Ralston believe that if much of the fishy odor is eliminated and if it is made to look like tuna, people will buy almost any kind of fish.

And indeed, even the "underutilized" fish are selling well. Changing the name of "trash" fish species has increased demand. The grayfish is eaten by people who would not have considered eating the dogfish, even though grayfish *is* dogfish.

As demand goes up, so does price. Unfortunately, the availability of many species favored by American consumers has been curtailed because of fishing limits. This has triggered the development of "simulated" seafood products. Made with minced fish, colorings and flavorings, these products are fast becoming a hit with consumers, says the U.S. Department of Agriculture.

Surimi is an intermediary minced fish derived mainly from pollock. It can be shaped and flavored to taste like several kinds of seafood, including lobster and crab. The Japanese have produced it for nine centuries. The abundant amounts of pollock in U.S. waters are rapidly being "Americanized" as U.S. harvesters and processors increase their production.

The advantage of surimi is price. Surimi crab costs approximately $2 per pound, while at last count Alaskan King Crab cost $20 per pound. Seafood Management Corporation, a consulting firm, predicts that demand for surimi will increase fifteenfold by 1990.

Still, concern exists about the future of surimi sales. Fish purchasers have been motivated by health concerns. Any highly processed product (or one perceived as highly processed) goes against the philosophy of the health conscious. Will the trend away from many processed foods include surimi? Will the demand for all-natural foods grow or fade? These are recurring questions for many in the fish industry.

Issues for Discussion
1. What role will perception and attitudes play in surimi sales?
2. Do family and other reference groups enter into the decision to purchase fish?
3. Is the decision-making process involved in purchasing fish a complex type?
4. How might a marketer of surimi approach his or her market?

Sources: Stephen Bennett and Erin Sullivan, "Guide to Product Usage," *Progressive Grocer,* September 1987, p. 146; Mimi Sheraton, "Just Name Your Poison," *Time,* February 18, 1985, p. 92; Julie Franz, "Ralston Summons Salmon," *Advertising Age,* January 28, 1985, p. 6; "Van De Kamp's Lightens Up New Fish Pitch," *Advertising Age,* January 28, 1985, p. 24.

OUTLINE

CHAPTER

7

Segmenting,
Forecasting,
and Positioning

LEARNING GOALS

After reading this chapter, you should be able to:

1. Evaluate the different approaches a marketer can use in selecting and serving a market.
2. Outline the process of segmenting the market.
3. Identify sales forecasting methods.
4. Specify criteria for selection of a forecasting technique.
5. Explain positioning.

The Stroh Brewery Company is committed to becoming a broad-based beverage company and not just a seller of beer. "The dividing lines in the adult beverage industry are blurring as the consumer becomes more sophisticated and has more choices than just beer, hard liquor, or Coke and Pepsi," said John Bissell, senior vice-president of special products for Stroh.

Stroh has introduced several nonalcoholic malt beverages, coolers, and juice-added soft-drinks. With a flat domestic beer market, the company hopes to add profits with these nonbeer beverages.

In addition to wider choices offered consumers, other changes have occurred in relation to alcoholic marketing. Action groups have formed against alcoholic abuse, including TAAP (Total Alcohol Awareness Program), SUDS (Students Understand Drinking Sensibly), SADD (Students Against Drunk Driving), BADD (Bartenders Against Drunk Driving), and the most widely known group, MADD (Mothers Against Drunk Driving). Although MADD's focus is against drunk driving, Candy Lightner, founder of MADD, personally thinks alcoholic beverage marketers should do more, such as put warning labels on liquor bottles and "know your limit" information on beer containers.

Alcoholic beverage sales have also suffered from changing lifestyles that are tending toward health and physical fitness. And there appears to be a major change in U.S. taste away from the distilled spirits such as vodka, bourbon, and scotch to products perceived as having less alcohol and a more pleasant flavor. In 1985 the average age of the traditional bourbon or scotch drinker was over 40 and was perceived as a cigar-smoking male sitting in an overstuffed leather chair.

Among the nonalcoholic beers on the market are Clausthaler—a runaway hit in Germany and now sold in the U.S.—Guiness Import Company's Kalibar (popular with athletes), Moussy, a Swiss import,

Stroh's Barbican, Warteck (another Swiss import), and the G. Heileman Brewing Company's nonalcoholic Black Label.

Moussy uses the advertising slogan, "The drink to choose when you choose not to drink." Its advertising campaign is aimed primarily at people who are predisposed to beer. Warteck uses the slogan, "After tasting Warteck, you wonder why they put alcohol in it in the first place." Warteck, noted for its excellent flavor, is aimed at both the calorie and alcohol conscious.

The following gives the per capita consumption in gallons of both beer and nonalcoholic beverages for the years 1982–1986:

	Beer	Soft drinks
1982	24.4	35.7
1983	24.3	37.0
1984	24.0	38.9
1985	23.8	40.8
1986	24.1	42.1

Three markets have been suggested for nonalcoholic beer. These include small restaurants that lack liquor licenses or that want to serve a liquor-like beverage on a Sunday (where applicable); consumers who like the taste of beer but do not want to drink alcohol; and people who spend an evening out with friends who are obliged to "rent a seat" by buying a drink.

The question is, Will the nonalcohol beer market grow, and if so, how rapidly?

Issues for Discussion

1. Is there a nonalcoholic market segment in the beer market? If it exists, should Stroh attempt to serve it?
2. What sales forecasting techniques should Stroh's management use to predict sales of nonalcohol beer?
3. Can Stroh cultivate new customers with a nonalcoholic beer and retain its old customers?

Sources: Raymond Serafin, "Sundance Leads Stroh Away from Alcohol," *Advertising Age,* June 2, 1986, p. 24; Gary Jervey, "Nonalcoholic Beer Brands Come Ashore," *Advertising Age,* June 24, 1985, pp. 3, 93; Jack Rosenbaum, "MADD Spark Ignites Anti-liquor Activity," *Advertising Age,* August 15, 1983, M40–41; Ronald Alsop, "Liquor Concerns are Creating Fresh Ads for Baby-Boomers," *The Wall Street Journal,* June 21, 1984, p. 31; and Gary Jervey, "Distillers Snap Up New Schnapps Flavor," *Advertising Age,* July 1, 1985, p. 50.

■ Barbican is just one of the many nonalcoholic beverages The Stroh Brewery Company has introduced.
Source: Photo courtesy of the Stroh Brewery Company.

*E*very organization must decide which market it will serve. The pages ahead identify and discuss the different approaches to a market. When the needs of potential buyers are basically the same, the marketer takes a mass market approach. Many markets, however, are like the beer market. They consist of individuals with a diversity of needs and wants. When these needs and wants are diverse, the marketer uses a segmentation process to group individuals with like preferences. Both approaches are discussed in the chapter. Like Stroh's management, the marketer must also be able to forecast sales and position the product in the market. Forecasting and positioning are covered in the latter part of the chapter. ■

CHOOSING THE MASS OR SEGMENT MARKET APPROACH

The Mass Market Approach

In deciding on a market the marketing manager can select the total market, such as industrial or consumer. This approach is commonly referred to as a **mass market approach.** Marketing to the mass assumes that all individuals in the market have essentially the same product needs and will respond in a similar way to the firm's marketing plan. In other words, the market has homogeneity.

To use the mass market approach, the marketing manager divides the population into two parts: potential buyers and nonbuyers. A common mistake in dividing the population is excessive optimism about the size of the potential buyer group. To the question "Who is going to buy the automated machine to untie shoe strings?" the optimistic inventor answers, "Everyone!"

The mass market approach uses a single market plan to market the product to the potential buyer group. The market plan has an influence on the size of the immediate potential buyer group. For instance, the quantity demanded would increase, if the market plan called for a price of $10 instead of $50.

*T*he mass market approach assumes that all buyers' needs are identical.

Other conditions besides homogeneity encourage the marketer to use the mass approach. When an organization is the only one in the industry, mass marketing works. Purchasers, even though not completely satisfied, buy the organization's product. New products or regulated monopolies permit single-firm industries. The size of the organization also influences the use of the mass market approach. Large mass markets have more appeal to large companies with the ability to promote the product heavily and to produce enough of it to satisfy demand. A successful mass approach gives the firm the advantage of efficiency when economies of scale exist in the industry. (See figure 7.1.)

The Segment Market Approach

*I*f every buyers' needs are unique, the product should be customized.

Another option available when selecting a market is **segmentation.** The segmentation approach recognizes that not all buyers are the same. Even when people buy the same product, the needs they are satisfying with the product's purchase and use can be different. When every potential buyer seems to differ significantly in received benefits, extreme market heterogeneity exists. In such a situation, satisfying individuals in the market requires "customizing" the firm's offering. Talking with the

❑ **Figure 7.1**
The mass market.

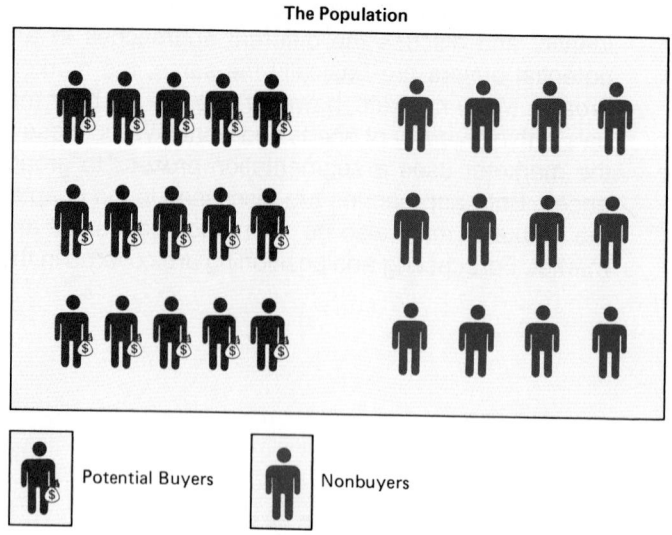

The Population

Potential Buyers   Nonbuyers

potential buyer, a representative of the organization determines the buyer's specific requirements, and the offering is structured to the individual buyer's needs. Construction of especially large manufacturing facilities takes a customized approach.

Although customizing leads to the greatest amount of satisfaction for the consumer, the benefits of standardization may be lost. The satisfaction of needs is usually less efficient, so the product costs more. To increase efficiency, individuals in the market with similar needs and response elasticity are grouped. People with similar **response elasticities** respond to marketing activities in the same way. For instance, individuals with the same response elasticity to advertising respond similarly to an advertising campaign. In grouping individuals, the manager strives to obtain the largest groups possible while maintaining homogeneity within groups and heterogeneity between groups. Segmentation, therefore, is defined as the process of identifying buyers who have similar needs and response elasticities. (See figure 7.2.)

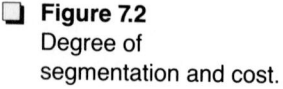

*G*rouping individuals with similar needs and similar responses to marketing— the objective of segmentation.

Reasons for Segmenting

*S*egment to serve the market better.

Several powerful reasons exist for segmenting. A diverse and changing market can be better satisfied, and communication and distribution within a market segment can be more focused and specific than with a mass market approach. The search for competitive advantage may force segmentation. Improved assessment of competitors

❑ **Figure 7.2**
Degree of segmentation and cost.

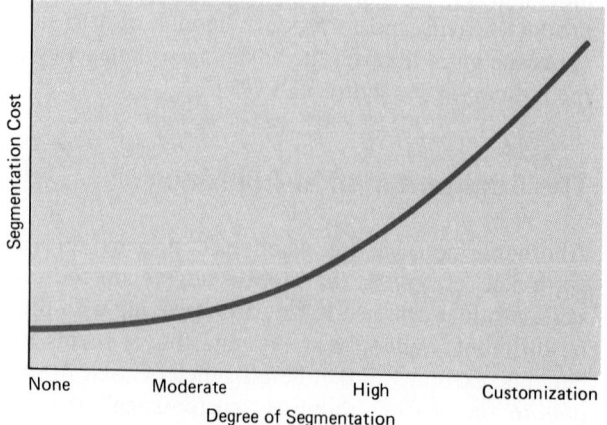

☐ Figure 7.3
Where to specialize—
production versus
market.

Conditions Favoring	
Production	Market
Homogeneous customer needs Economy of scale achieved at high levels of output. Large firm Few competitors Little possibility exists for differentiation of firm's offering	Diverse customer needs Economy of scale achieved at low levels of output. Small firm Many competitors Large potential for differentiation of firm's offering

in a market segment is possible, as is more precise knowledge of the market segment. Execution and control of the marketing plan specifically conceived for the segment should improve the marketer's overall efforts.

In general, the advantages of segmentation come from specialization in part of a market, while the advantages from the mass approach come from standardization in production. In deciding whether or not to segment the market, the marketing manager must answer the question: "How will the customers receive the most benefit, from production standardization or market specialization?" (See figure 7.3.)

SEGMENTING THE MARKET

The segmentation process involves several steps that culminate in the selection of the appropriate market segments (figure 7.4). These steps are identified and discussed in this section. Even though the steps provide a definite procedure for selecting segments, the selection of the most appropriate segments is the main objective, rather than following the procedure. The complexity of buyers makes segmentation a creative process rather than a plodding step-by-step procedure.

*C*riteria for successful segmentation: measurable; operational; substantial; and stable.

Four criteria for successful segmentation have been identified: a segment must be *measurable, operational, substantial,* and *stable*. Have the key variables—those that distinguish between response elasticities—really been identified and quantified? (Are they measurable?) Can those variables be identified in the market population? Does the firm have access to the identified segment group through communication and distribution channels? (Is the segment operational?) Is the market segment of sufficient size that the firm's sales will significantly exceed cost, even with the existence of competitors? (Is it substantial?) Will the segment exist tomorrow? Next year? (Is it stable?)[1]

Step 1. Identify the Total Market

To identify the total market, as discussed in Chapter 5, the marketer uses two criteria: willingness to purchase and ability to exchange. To evaluate the market in terms of these two criteria, the marketer might ask any of the following questions: Who will

☐ Figure 7.4
Segmentation process.

Steps
1. Identify the total market. 2. Select segmentation bases. 3. Determine specific variables within selected bases. 4. Assess potential of each segment. 5. Select the market segments.

❏ **Figure 7.5**
Segmentation base
hierarchy.

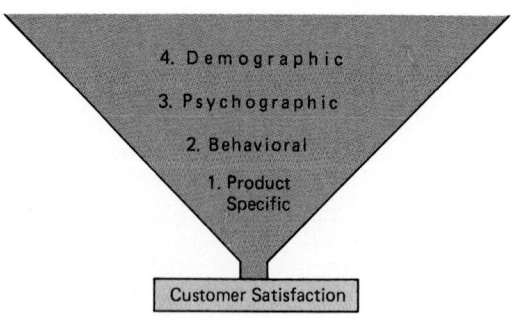

purchase the product? Why will they purchase? Where will the product be purchased? What quantity will be purchased?

Step 2. Select Segmentation Bases

Many variables can be used to segment a mass market: for example, age, educational level, income, occupation, geographic area, and a range of attitudinal variables. Rather than work with each one separately, a common approach is to group them into bases. A **base in segmentation** consists of variables that have common characteristics. Bases permit the manager to evaluate a group of variables at one time. Bases also suggest additional variables common to the base that may help segment the market. Finally, a manager may want to have each base represented by at least one variable when determining segments.

Variables in each of the bases in segmentation permit the marketing manager to infer probable response elasticity, but they do not measure it. The more closely the variables in a base conform to the actual characteristics of a group of potential buyers, the more accurately the base reflects customer satisfaction, which is the purpose of segmentation.[2] (See figure 7.5.) Common segmentation bases distinguish among demographic, psychographic, behavioral, and product-specific variables.

DEMOGRAPHIC BASE

*D*emographic variables are generally easily quantified.

Demographic variables include income, age, level of education, sex, and geographic area. "East coast on rye, west coast on wheat," for instance, recognizes regional food choice segments. Usually, demographic variables are more easily quantified than other types. In addition, governmental units often collect demographic data to describe the size and distribution of the population. These data can serve as a reference for the marketer.

PSYCHOGRAPHIC BASE

*P*sychographics describe mental characteristics.

A psychographic base consists of variables that attempt to describe the frame of mind of the market population. Sugar Free Jell-O targets the weight- and health-conscious, for instance. Examples of psychographic variables include attitude, interest, opinion, and values. Psychographic variables are usually more difficult to quantify and even to define than demographic variables. For instance, how does the marketer define attitude? Many definitions exist. Even more difficult, how does the marketer measure attitude? Despite these difficulties, psychographics may tell more about why the market is buying than demographics.

BEHAVIORAL BASE

*B*ehavioral base variables describe activities of individuals in the market.

Behavioral base variables include such items as work, hobbies, entertainment, shopping, and sports activities. To the extent that behavior can be related to product or service usage, behavioral variables make good segmentation variables.

COMPANY

Loctite Corporation, in existence for over thirty-five years, leads the market in its field of industrial adhesives and sealants. Sales growth, however, plateaued in the mid-1980s.

Loctite marketers decided to analyze the adhesive and sealants market, with emphasis on psychographic research. The executives knew the market for fasteners was much larger than the company's sales. Buyers of fasteners were satisfying a high percentage of their needs with traditional fasteners, such as screws, clips, and nuts and bolts rather than adhesives. Since engineers are the primary decision makers in the purchase of adhesives, sealants, and fasteners, a research firm was hired to conduct in-depth interviews with design, maintenance, and production engineers, both users and nonusers of adhesives.

RESULTS

Engineers who were nonusers of Loctite adhesives and sealants could be classified as risk avoiders. Nonusers did not want to risk the use of a nontraditional product.

Design engineers envision themselves as creative and innovative, but, like engineers in general, are risk avoiders. They prefer to see ads with charts, diagrams, and graphs where the impression of proven performance is conveyed.

Maintenance engineers envision themselves as fixers who keep the company running with creative solu-

MARKETING IN ACTION

Industrial Market Segmentation— Loctite Corporation

tions to maintenance problems. They are practical, "hands-on" types, and are uncomfortable with three-piece-suit types. They prefer ads that are photos of products instead of abstract graphs and diagrams explaining performance.

Production engineers envision themselves as oriented toward today's production. They want ads to communicate financial cost associated with use of the product advertised.

MARKET STRATEGY: SEGMENTATION USING PSYCHOGRAPHICS OF EACH TYPE OF ENGINEER

Loctite executives decided to segment the market based on the differences among engineers that were uncovered by psychographic research. The marketing mix, especially promotion, was designed with a specific type of engineer in mind. The ads Loctite created for production and maintenance engineering segments are shown here.

Source: Bob Donath, "What Loctite Learned with Psychographic Insights; Behavioral Research Proved the Key to a Strategic Decision," *Business Marketing,* July 1984, p. 100. Reprinted with permission from the July 1984 issue of *Business Marketing;* Copyright Crain Communications, Inc.

■ Loctite appeals to the maintenance engineer's segment with a product-in-use ad on the left; and to the design engineer's segment with detailed product information in the ad on the right.

Source: Loctite Corporation, 705 N. Mountain Rd., Newington, CT 06111

PRODUCT-SPECIFIC BASE

*P*roduct variables are excellent for segmentation since they are in close proximity to buyer satisfaction.

Product-specific variables are based on attributes, uses, or benefits of the product. Attribute variables include flavor, miles per gallon size, durability, color, and ingredients. Use variables include frequency, time, and amount. General Mills has found, for instance, that a heavy users' segment exists for cake mix. People in this segment use cake mix three or more times a month, have average annual incomes in excess of $20,000, have children at home, and are female between the ages of 25 and 54 years of age. They comprise 15 percent of all home bakers.[3]

❏ **181**

VALS

*V*ALS, segmentation by values and lifestyle.

Research continues to discover better segmentation variables, including the Values and Lifestyle (VALS) program developed at the Stanford Research Institute. **VALS** is a system for classifying American adults into nine distinct groups based on values and lifestyles. Values as used in the VALS program refer to a wide array of

❑ **Figure 7.6** VALS segmentation.

Percentage of Population (Age 18 and Over)		Consumer Type	Values and Lifestyles	Demographics	Buying Patterns
Need-driven consumers	4%	Survivors	Needs are survival and security, Lack confidence, Little-life satisfaction	Poverty-level income, Little education, Older, Median age = 65	Price dominant, Focused on basics, Buy for immediate needs
	7	Sustainers	Least satisfied with financial status, Angry, rebellious	Low income, Low education, Much unemployment, Live in country as well as cities, Median age = 30	Price important, Want warranty, Cautious buyers
Outer-directed consumers	38	Belongers	Conforming, conventional, Unexperimental, Traditional, formal, Nostalgic	Low to middle income, High school graduates, older, Median age = 57	For family, home, Middle and lower mass markets
	10	Emulators	Ambitious, show-off, Status conscious, Upwardly mobile, Macho, competitive	Good to excellent income, Youngish, Highly urban, Traditionally male, but changing	Conspicuous consumption, "In" items, Imitative, Popular fashion
	20	Achievers	Achievement, success, fame, Materialism, Leadership, efficiency, Comfort	Excellent incomes, Leaders in business, politics, etc., Good education, Suburban and city living, Median age = 42	Buys to give evidence of success, Top of the line, Luxury and gift markets, "New and improved" products
Inner-directed consumers	3	I-Am-Me	Fiercely individualistic, Dramatic, impulsive, Experimental, Volatile	Young, Many single, Student or starting job, Affluent backgrounds	Display one's taste, Experimental fads, Clique buying
	5	Experiential	Drive to experience directly, Active, participative, Person-centered, Artistic	Bimodal incomes, Median age = 26, Many young families, Good education	Will try anything once, Vigorous, outdoor sports, Action-oriented products
	11	Societally conscious	Societal responsibility, Simple living, Smallness of scale, Inner growth	Moderate to high incomes, Excellent education, Diverse ages and places of residence	Conservation emphasis, Simplicity, Frugality, Environmental concerns
	2	Integrated	Psychological maturity, Sense of fittingness, Tolerant, self-actualizing, World perspective	Good to excellent incomes, Age varies, Excellent education, Diverse jobs and residential patterns	Varied self-expression, Esthetically oriented, Ecologically aware, One-of-a-kind items

❏ **Figure 7.7**
Consumption differences in VALS segments (base = 100).

Source: T. C. Thomas and S. Crocker, *Values and Lifestyles— The New Psychographics* (Menlo Park, CA: Stanford Research Institute, 1981), pp. 24, 25

Lifestyle Categories	Carbonated Soft Drinks		Keep/Stay-Alert Aids	Contact Lenses
	Regular	Sugar-free		
Need-driven	112	50	167	50
Belongers	82	80	67	50
Emulators	171	90	200	112
Achievers	94	110	100	112
I-am-me	176	120	500	213
Experiential	94	150	67	150
Societally conscious	59	170	33	162

beliefs, hopes, desires, aspirations, and prejudices. The Stanford Research Institute, drawing from Abraham H. Maslow's needs hierarchy, describes the three primary consumer segments as need-driven, outer-directed, and inner-directed.

The *need-driven,* restricted by lack of money, spend out of need rather than choice or desire. The *outer-directed,* a significant part of the market, use other people as their guide to values and behavior. Generally they buy out of concern for what other people will attribute to the products they purchase. The *inner-directed,* enjoying some financial success, have shifted their attention to satisfying personal needs and resolving individual issues. The inner-directed group is growing rapidly.

Each primary segment has subsegments, and all segments are arranged in hierarchial order. Figure 7.6 is presented in hierarchial order and includes descriptions of values and lifestyles, demographics, and buying patterns.

VALS information helps marketing managers to select market segments, undertake more refined product development, define appropriate market positions for products, and develop better advertising. For instance, the difference in consumption patterns of the VALS segments can be seen in figure 7.7. Response elasticity of the three types of product areas do differ by segment. To successfully attract the segments described in VALS, however, the marketer should be able to reach them through advertising. Figure 7.8 indicates that differences do exist in media viewing habits. The large amount of information available in the VALS program obviously increases the probability of successful segmentation.

❏ **Figure 7.8**
Media viewing habits of VALS segments (base = 100).

Lifestyle Categories	TV Programs Watched Regularly			
	Comedies	Game Shows	Early Evening News (5-7 P.M.)	Late Evening News 10 P.M. or Later)
Survivors	67	233	126	93
Sustainers	195	225	87	115
Belongers	86	158	121	110
Emulators	152	108	79	88
Achievers	67	42	98	102
I-am-me	176	17	47	55
Experiential	138	42	72	90
Societally conscious	67	50	96	115

Lifestyle Categories	Magazine Readership*				
	Tabloids (*National Enquirer,* the *Star,* etc.)	Business Magazines (*Business Week, Fortune,* etc.)	News Magazines (*Time, Newsweek,* etc.)	General Sports (*Sports Illustrated,* etc.)	Literary (*New Yorker,* etc.)
Survivors	118	36	56	0	86
Sustainers	247	64	62	79	129
Belongers	129	100	74	68	57
Emulators	106	36	76	121	43
Achievers	53	186	129	100	100
I-am-me	100	100	132	195	71
Experiential	59	114	132	132	200
Societally conscious	47	157	147	110	200

Source: T. C. Thomas and S. Crocker, *Values and Lifestyles— The New Psychographics* (Menlo Park, CA: Stanford Research Institute, 1981), pp. 24, 25

*One or more of the last four issues

Step 3. Determine Specific Variables

*W*hat variable should be used to segment the market?

A number of variables have the potential for effectively segmenting a particular market. Managers seek to identify commonality of individuals in the market by way of the most efficient variables that influence product purchase and use. They search for the common threads that tie together individuals with the same response elasticity.[4]

Finding the common threads in order to define a segment of the market is often a common sense procedure. Examine the segmentation bases and use judgment to select the most viable base or bases to segment a market. Identify all possible variables in each base selected. Use judgment, experience, and previous research to select the most likely variables from the list, then research the variables' efficiency on part of the market. Variables selected by using common sense, because they seem logical, are said to have **face validity.** For instance, a manager of a credit union may use judgment in identifying a market segment with a high demand for loans. The common thread of this segment is obviously the need for money. The manager may decide that the target market will have the following characteristics: under 35 years of age (e.g., less likely to have achieved high salary level, less likely to have accumulated assets); married with family (the more dependents, the greater the need for money); and so on.

Another approach to identifying segmentation variables is to collect customer data on as many variables as practical and then use a statistical technique such as cluster analysis to identify the variables that are most effective. Cluster analysis "places variables or objects (or potential customers) into subgroups or clusters."[5] The objective of cluster analysis is to assign each potential customer to a cluster in such a way that he or she is more closely associated with potential customers in that cluster than with customers in any other cluster.

Step 4: Assess Potential of Each Segment

*P*otential of a segment should be considered in both the short and long run.

Once the most efficient variables for segmentation have been identified, the market segments are determined. If many segments exist, the marketer may want to determine the potential of all segments, but that decision will likely be based on the organization's resources and strategy. Commonly, a limited number of segments are selected for an in-depth analysis of potential. **Potential** refers to the possible short- and long-term net benefit to the organization from serving the market segment.

To estimate the potential of a segment for an organization, the overall potential should be determined, the firm's market share should be forecast, a budget developed, and ultimately a projected net profit determined. The overall potential of a segment depends upon the number of potential buyers in the segment and their purchase rate. Thus to determine overall potential, the size of the segment in numbers of potential buyers must be known, or at least estimated, and the buyer purchase rate must be calculated. Both the annual purchase rate and purchases over the length of time the product will be available to the market should be known.

Annual Segment Potential (Usually in Dollars)	=	Number of Potential Buyers × Estimated Annual Rate of Purchase per Buyer
Total Segment Potential (Usually in Dollars)	=	Number of Potential Buyers × Estimated Purchases of Buyer Over Total Time Product Offered

❑ **Figure 7.9**
The segmentation
approach and degree
related to costs.

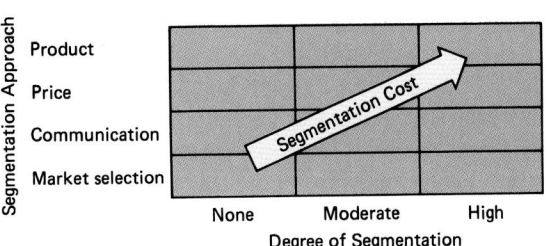

Source: Reprinted by permission of the publisher, from *Segmenting the Industrial Market,* by Thomas V. Bonoma and Benson P. Shapiro. (Lexington, Mass.: Lexington Books, D. C. Heath and Company). Copyright 1983, D. C. Heath and Company

Both measurements of potential are helpful. Annual segment potential indicates what potential exists in any one year; total segment potential indicates potential longevity.

A firm's own activities and those of competitors will affect benefits received from serving a market segment.

The organization's market share forecast must account for the existence of competitors. Rarely will competitors be absent. Therefore, an analysis of each competitor's strengths and weaknesses is necessary to allow the manager a basis for estimating the market share the firm can command. The firm's own market plan also influences the size of market share. Formulation of a market plan, at least in general terms, is essential to forecasting market share.

In order to determine net potential of a segment, the cost and expenses of serving the segment are needed. In general, the lowest cost approach to segmentation is simple market selection, and the highest cost approach is developing a specialized product (figure 7.9). A developed budget provides the cost and expense information. The process of developing a budget includes identifying cost and expense items and estimating the amount of each.

Step 5. Select the Market Segments

Each market segment will represent different opportunities for the firm—selection of segments is necessary.

The net benefit developing from each market segment—determined by subtracting budgeted cost and expenses from estimated firm sales—provides most of the information a marketer needs to order the segments from most to least desirable. At this point, the manager should recheck the criteria of a good market segment: measurable, operational, substantial, and stable.[6]

UNDIFFERENTIATED AND CUSTOMIZED STRATEGIES

The marketing manager can choose from several methods in approaching the market. Already discussed in some detail at the beginning of this chapter was the mass market approach, more specifically referred to as the **undifferentiated strategy.**[7] Recall that this approach treats all buyers in the market as identical. Thus, only one marketing plan is required. The opposite of the undifferentiated approach is the customized approach to the market, in which every buyer in the market is considered unique. The basic marketing plan is loosely formulated. Product description and price range, for example, remain general until the characteristics of the specific individuals who will comprise the market have been identified.

Between the undifferentiated and customized approaches lie two approaches based on segmentation—the concentrated strategy and the differentiated strategy.

CONCENTRATED STRATEGY

Two strategies based on segmentation: concentration and differentiation.

After successfully identifying the segments in a market, if the marketer decides to use the firm's resources to approach only one of those segments, then a **concentrated strategy** is being employed.[8] Campbell's with its easy-to-prepare soups, General Mills with cake mixes, and Ore-Ida with frozen potatoes are all examples of successful concentration strategies. With these products, these companies all focus on segments of the market that want easy-to-prepare foods. The Harlequin Press also uses a concentrated approach. Its product, romance novels, is sold primarily to married females, average age of thirty-five years, and probably high school graduates.

*C*oncentrated strategy—serving only one segment.

In marketing parlance "finding a niche" has several attractions. It enables a small organization to develop expertise—a competitive advantage—with very few resources and perhaps dominate the market segment. Royal Crown Cola could have used a concentrated strategy successfully in the 1960s. Royal Crown introduced Diet Rite Cola three years before any other firm had a diet soft drink. "Instead of concentrating all its resources on fortifying that niche, Royal Crown dissipated itself by maintaining its regular cola, now a loser. From a leadership position, the firm fell to less than 4 percent of diet cola sales."[9] Concentration also seems attractive if most of the total market sales develop from the selected segments. Unfortunately marketers sometimes overlook the fact that a single segment that generates a large percentage of the total market will have attracted competition. The term used to describe the oversight is **majority fallacy.** The organization that uses a concentration approach also runs the risk that the market will shift and revenues will tumble, as they did for Levi Strauss & Company when the jeans market shifted.[10]

*T*he majority fallacy—the biggest market segment is the best.

DIFFERENTIATED STRATEGY

*D*ifferentiated strategy—serving more than one segment.

Selecting two or more market segments to serve is a **differentiated strategy.** This approach to the market recognizes the heterogeneity of the market and at the same time the need for efficiency in production and marketing. Each market segment requires a market plan. Procter & Gamble, General Motors, and numerous other organizations use this approach. The approach requires more organizational resources if all segments that make up a market are served.

---

*P*eople in the beer market do seem to have different needs and different response elasticities. The nonalcohol beer (NAB) market would appear to satisfy one group existing in the beer market. To identify the NAB market segment, any of the segmentation bases might be used, although the demographic and psychographic bases appear most applicable.

THE CASE CONTINUES

Specifically the NAB consumer tends to be younger than the typical beer drinker, and it is hypothesized that the NAB drinker is more likely to be female. Psychologically, NAB con-

sumers seem to be concerned about personal health and fitness issues. They may also be weight conscious. They may be against drunk driving, but not against drinking.

In making the decision to serve the NAB market, Stroh's management needs to consider whether the segment is measurable, operational, substantial, and stable.

 ## FORECASTING SALES

Selecting and developing a market depends upon the current and future size of the market. A marketing manager considers a market in three ways—its market potential, sales potential, and sales forecast. The market potential for a product, also referred to as industry potential, is a measurement of the maximum total sales for all firms in an identified market.[11] Sales potential of a firm represents the maximum sales in a served market for a single firm. The **sales forecast** represents the estimated future sales of a firm employing a designated marketing plan with anticipated environmental conditions. Figure 7.10 indicates one way the relationship between market and sales potential can be visualized.

*M*arket potential = maximum total sales for all firms in a market.

❏ **Figure 7.10**
Market potential sales.

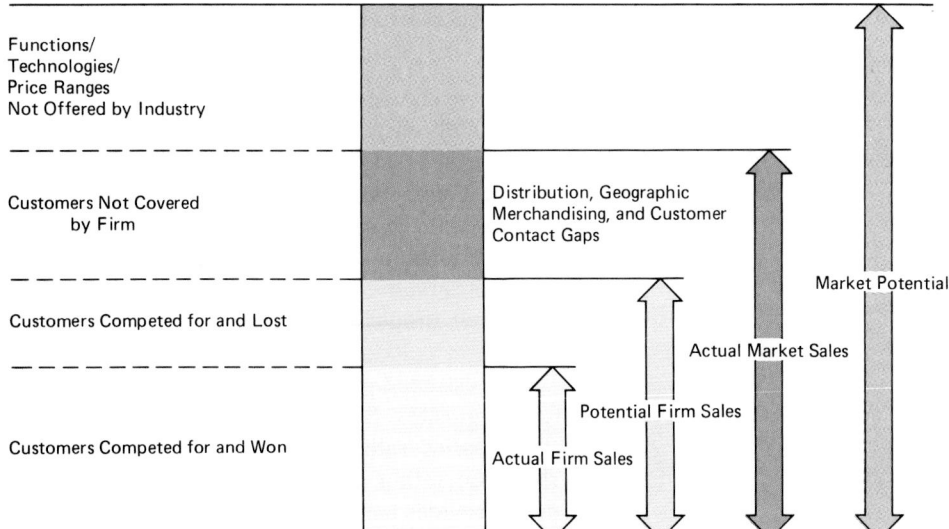

*F*orecast—the basis of many plans.

A sales forecast serves as the foundation for several plans within an organization. Since the level of marketing effort influences the amount of sales, the general parameters of the marketing plan are usually developed before sales are forecast. The details of the plan may, however, depend upon the sales forecast. The sales forecast also serves as the foundation for production schedules, staffing plans, financing requirements, budgets, and control procedures. Sales forecasts play an important role in operating an organization. Short-term forecasts (a year or less) have the most influence on marketing plans since marketing plans tend to be formulated on an annual basis. Long-term forecasts (periods greater than a year) influence strategy.

All forecasting methods are methods of prediction. The techniques of forecasting can be qualitative or quantitative. If a prediction is based on a person's judgment, the method is qualitative. If the information used to generate the prediction is based on manipulating numbers such as past sales volumes, the method is quantitative.

Qualitative Forecasting Methods

JURY OF EXECUTIVE OPINION

*E*xecutive opinion—a quick method, more accurate for short-term general type forecast.

Constructing a jury of executive opinion by querying executives provides information from individuals with a broad perspective on major factors influencing sales. Besides being quick and simple, the technique has the advantage of involving individuals who are responsible for achieving the sales. The group should consist of well-informed, experienced executives.

Predictions based on a jury of executive opinion are more accurate for short time frames (a year or less). In addition, aggregate predictions have higher accuracy. Accuracy suffers if the executive has to break down the prediction into product style, model, territory, customer type, or other small units.

Since the selection of executives influences the prediction, executives from several functional areas should be included. Executives outside the organization can also add perspective to the predictions. The predictions can be improved over time if the assumptions of the executives are written down. Tracking both assumptions and predictions helps eliminate inappropriate assumptions from the process and identifies executives whose predictions differ widely from actual sales. The jury of executive opinion is used widely as a supplement to other forecasting methods because of its convenience and low cost.

SALES FORCE COMPOSITE

*S*ales force composite—
more accurate in short-
term and when biases of
salespeople are known.

A **sales force composite** is a sales forecast developed from sales representatives' predictions. The sales force is in a good position to know market conditions because it meets with customers every day. Customer outlook and concerns are common topics of conversations between customers and salespeople. In using a sales force composite managers should recognize that salespeople tend to be optimistic. On the other hand, if the sales force works on a quota salary system (where a salesperson earns additional income for sales in excess of the quota), the forecast may intentionally be conservative. Sales representatives should know that the sales manager will review their predictions. This will encourage the salesperson to be as accurate as possible.

The restricted perspective of most sales representatives limits the utility of sales force composites. Salespeople tend to see the narrow day-to-day activities in their own territories, rather than broad economic and market issues, and they tend to take a short-run rather than a long-run perspective. Thus, the sales force composite usually provides a more accurate short-term than long-term forecast. It is also more accurate when market and economic conditions are stable. The sales force composite lends itself to forecasts for smaller breakdowns within the organization: divisions, geographic areas, products, and customer types. Since the information for composite forecasts is collected in small units, product by product or customer type by customer type, predicting sales for these units is relatively simple.

SURVEY OF BUYER INTENTIONS

*I*f buyers plan their purchases, a survey of buyers
can be a reasonably accu-
rate technique.

What customers say they will be buying provides the information for a forecast based on the survey of buyer intentions. Normally, the time and expense involved in surveying all customers are too great, so a representative sample is taken.

The buyer intention approach works best if the market has well-defined characteristics and tends to be concentrated, and if buyers typically formulate purchase plans based on an assessment of their requirements.[12] The technique also works best with established products and with customers who have experience with the product.

The survey of buyer intentions does not work as well with new products. It is also limited by the inability or unwillingness of customers to articulate their buying intentions. The short-term perspective of customers is a limitation if long-range forecasts are being compiled. Finally, carrying out a survey is a costly endeavor.

Quantitative Forecasting Methods

*Q*uantitative forecasting
techniques—based on
numbers indicating what
people have done.

Quantitative methods analyze numbers to uncover relationships that can be used for predicting sales. They depend upon extrapolating relationships that existed in the past and projecting them into the future. Past relationships must continue to exist in the future if predictions based on these relationships are to be accurate. Any sharp changes in behavior from past to future impair accuracy. Since extrapolation underlies most quantitative forecasting methods, and it is impossible to know with certainty that the future will be like the past, the wise manager supplements quantitative methods with qualitative techniques. Such techniques, which are based on expert opinion and experienced judgment, can often detect sharp changes in relationships.

TIME SERIES ANALYSIS

*T*ime series—how sales
have behaved over time.

The marketer uses time series analysis to show the change in sales over time. The interval on which the analysis is based can be long or short. Figure 7.11 graphs the annual sales of the Harvest Company each year for seventeen years (1970 to 1987). Thus, the graph shows a sales **trend,** which is a long-term movement either

❑ **Figure 7.11**
Graph of the Harvest Company's annual sales.

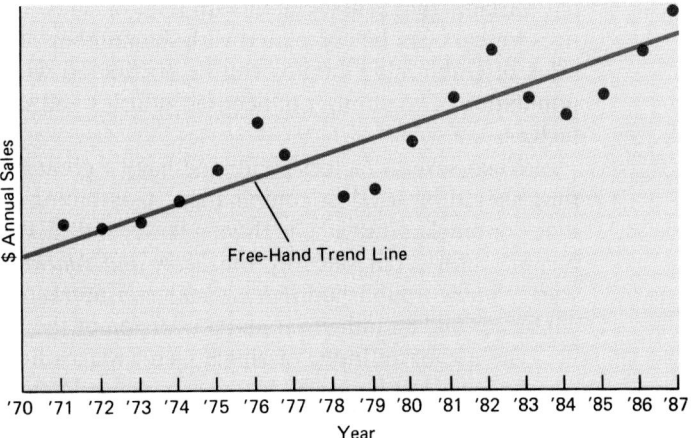

upward or downward. In this case, the trend is upward, a steady increase in the company's sales over time.

If the monthly sales volumes for each of the seventeen years were plotted, the graph would show much wider fluctuations in sales. The graph would then depict a **season,** an undulating short-term movement usually measured annually.

Graphing monthly sales volumes for the Harvest Company only for 1978 and 1979 would most likely show sales declining, despite the fact that the long-term trend is upward. Extending the period of the graph to five years, 1977 to 1982, would show sales declining and then rising. The graph would then depict a **cycle,** which is an undulating long-term movement.

Basing a prediction of 1988 sales on the trend line in figure 7.11, we could expect the sales figure to be slightly higher than the 1987 trend sales. Note that actual sales in 1987 are higher than the 1987 trend sales. The trend line does not account for all the variation in sales from year to year. Seasonal and cyclical factors as well as **erratic factors** consisting of random variables also influence sales. The relationship between sales and time can be expressed in the following equation:

$$Y = F(T, C, S, E)$$

Sales = Function (Trend, Cycle, Season, Erratic Factors)

To fit an equation to historical sales, the least squares method or regression is commonly used. Refer to a statistics book for an explanation of regression analysis.

MOVING AVERAGES

*M*oving averages—forecasting by using the average of current sales periods.

The moving average method of forecasting is a variation of the time series method. Rather than use all available data in the projection, the moving average selects a specified number of periods to consider. Even though more periods of data become available, the number of periods remains constant. The most up-to-date periods are included and the oldest are discarded. The effect is to give the most recent data more weight in the projection. Many variations to the basic time series method exist. All have the same advantage: they are simple to employ, and they provide precise output.

CORRELATION ANALYSIS

*C*orrelation analysis—depends on discovery of a relationship between sales and at least one other variable.

With the time series analysis the forecaster attempts to discover a relationship between sales and time. With correlation analysis the forecaster attempts to discover a relationship between sales and a factor other than time. A **market factor** can be any variable that is associated with level of sales. For example, sales of replacement tires for cars can be correlated with the number of licensed vehicles. The volume of sales of children's vitamins can be correlated with the number of children in the population. The number of licensed vehicles and the number of children are market factors.

When several factors combined have a greater association with sales, naturally they should be used in combination. Combining factors produces a market factor index or **market index.** The Buying Power Index (BPI), a combination of population, income, and retail sales by the *Sales and Marketing Management* magazine, is a widely known published index. *Sales and Marketing Management* publishes both a consumer and an industrial market version of the BPI.

A leading series factor predicts sales.

The use of an index or single factor makes little difference to a forecaster, but whether the **leading series factor** can be used does make a difference because it has predictive potential. A factor developing concurrently with sales is a leading series factor if it actually has a greater relationship with future sales than current sales. Consider replacement car tires again. The sale of new cars should be a leading indicator of replacement tires. The higher the sales of new cars in a given year, the higher the sale of replacement tires in two to three years.

How does a marketer identify factors that have a high correlation with sales? Often it is simply a matter of experience or common sense as in the replacement tire example. Identification can also be facilitated by statistical procedures. Consult a statistics or forecasting text for explanations of factor identification procedures.

COMPUTER-AIDED QUANTITATIVE TECHNIQUES

*F*orecasting has improved with the aid of the computer.

In forecasting, modeling a market has been employed for a number of years. The model, a series of equations, attempts to identify factors, their relationship to sales, their relationship to each other, and their interactive effect (how, when working together, they influence sales). Input-output models are one example of such models. Because the models become quite complex, computers, although not absolutely essential, are a valuable aid.

Selection of a Forecasting Method

*U*se more than one forecasting technique.

With so many methods of forecasting available, the marketer should not rely only on one. Changing conditions in the business environment should preclude reliance on only one method. Furthermore, the use of several methods allows for comparison of results. Significant differences between results should encourage the marketing manager to investigate the difference.

In recent years forecasting scholars have focused on selection of the appropriate forecasting techniques. The result has been the development of procedures that aid in selection. Box-Jenkins, a computerized procedure, is just one example.

*C*riteria for evaluating forecasting techniques: accuracy, cost, precision, the time horizon, and technique requirements.

Basic criteria for evaluating forecasting methods include the time horizon, accuracy, cost, precision, and the requirements of the technique. The **forecast time horizon** refers to whether a short- or long-term forecast is desired. Some methods work better with one time horizon. Time series methods work well with a short-term forecast, for example. **Forecast accuracy** is a measurement of how close the projection comes to the actual sales. Typical benchmarks for accuracy are 90 percent and 95 percent. **Forecast precision** refers to the width of the range of the forecast. Often, rather than providing a single figure as a forecast, a range is given. An illustration of a range forecast: optimistically, sales may be as high as twelve million units and pessimistically, as low as eight million units. If precision were to increase, the four million units difference between optimism and pessimism would be reduced. Each forecasting method has different requirements. The time series analysis techniques require a minimum number of periods of data, for instance.

Forecasting Sales for New Products

The lack of a history makes new product forecasting difficult.

Forecasting sales is more challenging for new products than for established products because there is no experience with the product on which to draw and there are no sales records. The lack of sales records makes it difficult to use quantitative techniques. If the marketer wishes to use them, sales records have to be generated. Two methods are common: finding a close substitute product and using the substitute sales records, or conducting a test market to generate sales figures. When neither of these two approaches has merit, the alternative is one of the qualitative forecasting techniques.

THE CASE CONTINUES

*S*troh's management could use quantitative or qualitative techniques to forecast nonalcohol beer sales. For new products, time series, correlation analysis, or other quantitative forecasting methods that depend on a sales record could obviously not be used, unless a substitute for Stroh's

NAB sales was found. Using total sales of NAB on the market may provide a viable substitute. Of the qualitative techniques, only a jury of executive opinion has the potential for accurately forecasting NAB.

Salespersons would not be able to provide information for accurate forecasting since they would have no experience with a new product, and customers are likely to give little thought to the purchase of NAB and their estimates would probably not be accurate.

 ## POSITIONING

*P*ositioning—shaping customers' perception of a product or brand.

A marketer forecasting the size of a market realizes that the chosen marketing strategy influences the organization's sales. One strategic aspect influencing the organization's sales is how the manager positions the product. **Positioning** is the process of shaping the way customers perceive the firm's product. Brands may be positioned as well as products. Procter and Gamble works to have each of its brands occupy a different position: Cheer is for washing in all temperatures, Dash is for low-suds concentrated cleaning power, Bold has fabric softener, and so forth.[13] Positioning actually occurs in the customer's mind. Whether or not a marketing manager attempts to position a brand, the customer probably has some perceptions of its attributes and how it compares to other brands. The manager wants to create and maintain a desired position. Positioning requires management to think about the answers to the following questions:[14]

1.   What role should positioning play in the marketing plan?
2.   To whom should we sell?
3.   What benefits do we stress in promotion?
4.   How much should we charge?
5.   Where should we sell?
6.   Where should we advertise?

Positioning is determined by the combination of marketing signals perceived by individuals in the market. The signals come from the advertising media, promotions, packaging, and pricing. They must all reinforce each other to avoid confusion.

Positioning and the Marketing Plan

*I*s positioning to be a major part of the strategy, as "un-cola" was to 7-Up?

The activities required to position a brand successfully are part of developing a marketing plan. The "desired" position may even be a part of the overall marketing strategy. Successful positioning first requires a decision on how positioning will be used in the strategy. Will it be a major part? For instance, in its "un-cola" advertising campaign, 7-Up gave positioning a major strategic role. Does the strategy require the brand to be repositioned? Taco Bell tried attracting working women in downtown locations through repositioning.[15] Working women perceived Taco Bell's food as "too heavy" and "too spicy" and therefore avoided Taco Bell for lunch. To attract them, Taco Bell added a light salad to its menu. In promoting the new salad, Taco Bell successfully repositioned itself in the mind of working women. Customers

The Five-Minute Personal Pan Pizza® enabled Pizza Hut to reposition its lunch image as one of quick service.

Source: Used by permission of Pizza Hut.

□ **Figure 7.12**
Focal points for
positioning.

Focal Point	Example
Product Class	Tylenol, aspirin free
Competitors	Pepsi, taste test
Attributes	Canon Micrographics, making very best out of a small thing
Price/ Quality	Kmart, the savings place
Use or Application	Arm & Hammer Baking Soda, eliminates odors
Product User	Charlie, young, active lifestyle

Source: Adapted from David A. Aaker and J. Gary Shonsby, "Positioning Your Product," *Business Horizons,* May–June 1982, pp. 56–62

perceived Pizza Hut as a place to eat only if a long lunch hour was available. Pizza Hut developed the five-minute, Personal Pan Pizza® and repositioned itself in consumers' minds. Repositioning often requires changing the benefits offered to customers as well as the advertising.

A second requirement for successful positioning is choosing a focal point. (See figure 7.12.) The choice of a focal point depends on how the marketer wants the buyer to perceive the product and distinguish it from its competitors. Typically the focal point is selected only after examining the market and the current position that the product or brand occupies.

*R*epositioning may be necessary but risky.

Frequently, repositioning a brand may have detrimental effects. The brand may lose its distinctiveness, and buyers may begin to feel that it is replaceable by other brands. Clarity may also suffer from repositioning. Buyers have "fuzzy" perceptions about the brand when clarity is lost. For instance, both Corvette and Thunderbird were introduced as sports cars. Mention Corvette and people still think of it as a sports car because Chevrolet has never repositioned the Corvette. Thunderbird has been repositioned several times, from sporty to luxurious, from "sleek" to "fat," and back to streamlined. Mentioning Thunderbird may evoke several different perceptions in a group of buyers.

Position Mapping

*P*osition mapping—our product in relation to other products. How will it be perceived?

In examining the market, the objective is to match the firm's market offering to the market's needs. Research can identify the elements that customers use in formulating perceptions. The relative importance of these elements should also be studied. An alternative to research is to rely on executive experience with the market to identify perceptual elements and to assess their importance.

Once the elements have been identified, a process known as **position or perceptual mapping** helps to locate the various competing organizations. Figure 7.13 illustrates a position map for automobiles. Each of the competing brands is located on the position map based on research findings or executive opinion. The labels on the vertical axis in figure 7.13 imply that an automobile cannot provide good gas mileage and at the same time have "a touch of class." This evidently is the way the market views cars.

The closer the brands are to each other, the more willing the buyer would be to switch among them. Thus, the center of the position map usually represents the largest market. The perimeter usually represents the smallest potential market but the greatest opportunity for uniqueness.

The Position of an Organization's Brand

*W*hat position is the best?

The position of an organization's brand like Pontiac on the position map in figure 7.13 should immediately generate questions in the marketer's mind. Is the brand in

❑ **Figure 7.13**
Two-dimensional
position map with
competing brands of
autos located.

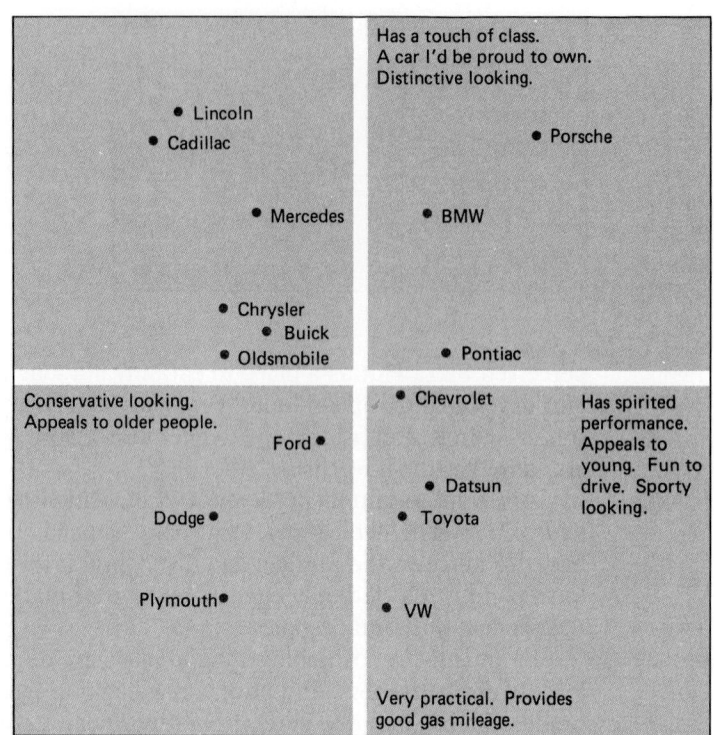

the desired position? If not, is it because the brand does not possess the necessary qualities, or have those qualities been improperly conveyed to the market? Will attempting to reposition the brand result in a loss of sales that derive from the current position while failing to gain offsetting sales? What elements of the marketing mix should be used to gain a desired position?

Determining what position the brand should have requires an evaluation of competitors' strengths and weaknesses as well as their positions. The ideal would be to identify an area on the position map that is void of competitors but still represents a large market. Such areas normally do not exist. The manager is therefore left with assessing the organization's strengths and weaknesses and attempting to position the brand in an area that will provide the greatest competitive advantage.

THE CASE CONTINUES

*A*ny time a company introduces a new product, there is some concern about how the product should be positioned in relation to the firm's existing products. Stroh's management probably would not want nonalcohol beer to take sales away from the firm's regular beer. Worse still would be the creation of an unfavorable perception of Stroh's regular beers by the consumer. For example, perception of Stroh's beer as being weak could lead to loss of sales.

Several of the existing NAB brands have already been positioned—Kalibar as a drink for the young, active consumer, and Warteck as a very flavorful beverage for the calorie conscious.

GOAL SUMMARY

1. **Evaluate the different approaches a marketer can use in selecting and serving a market.** Two general approaches exist for the marketer to use. Every person in the market can be treated as having the same needs—the mass or undifferentiated approach. The undifferentiated approach to the market generally results in cost savings from high-volume production and long production runs. Alternatively, differences in individuals can be recognized. Assuming that every individual is unique results in a customized approach. Grouping individuals with similar response elasticities results in the segment market approach. An organization may select one group to serve, in which case it is concentrating, or it may serve several or all groups, each with a different marketing plan, in which case it is differentiating the market.

2. **Outline the process of segmenting the market.** These are the steps in the market segmentation process: identify the total market, select a segmentation base or bases, identify specific segmentation variables, determine the potential of each segment, and select the market segment or segments the firm will serve.

3. **Identify sales forecasting methods.** Forecasting methods are of two general types: (1) qualitative methods, which depend on someone's judgment about the future, and (2) quantitative methods, which depend on projecting numerical relationships into the future. Three often-used qualitative methods are jury of executive opinion, sales force composite, and survey buyer intentions. Three widely known quantitative methods are time series, moving average, and correlation analysis.

4. **Specify criteria for selection of a forecasting technique.** Although more than one forecasting technique should be used to permit comparison of results, enough methods exist that the marketer must make a decision on which techniques to use. Criteria that help in making this decision include the time horizon involved, the accuracy of the technique, cost, precision, and requirements of the method.

5. **Explain positioning.** Positioning is the process of shaping the way customers perceive the firm's market offering. A firm's market offering may be positioned against competitor offerings, against the product class, by use or application, by product user, or by several other focal points. Position can take a major role in strategy, as with 7-Up's "uncola."

KEY TERMS

Mass Market Approach, **p. 177**
Segmentation, **p. 177**
Response Elasticities, **p. 178**
Base in Segmentation, **p. 180**
VALS, **p. 182**
Face Validity, **p. 184**
Potential, **p. 184**
Undifferentiated Strategy, **p. 185**
Concentrated Strategy, **p. 185**
Majority Fallacy, **p. 186**
Differentiated Strategy, **p. 186**
Sales Forecast, **p. 186**
Sales Force Composite, **p. 188**

Trend, **p. 188**
Season, **p. 189**
Cycle, **p. 189**
Erratic Factors, **p. 189**
Market Factor, **p. 189**
Market Index, **p. 189**
Leading Series Factor, **p. 190**
Forecast Time Horizon, **p. 190**
Forecast Accuracy, **p. 190**
Forecast Precision, **p. 190**
Positioning, **p. 191**
Position or Perceptual Mapping, **p. 193**

CHECK YOUR LEARNING

1. The more homogeneous a market the more probable an organization will use a: (a) concentrated approach, (b) differentiated approach, (c) segmented approach, (d) undifferentiated approach, (e) customized approach.
2. The cost of serving a market increases with segmentation. **T/F**
3. All but one of the following are reasons for segmenting a market. Which one is not? (a) improved distribution, (b) economies of scale, (c) better execution and control of the marketing plan.
4. Identifying the segmentation base or bases is the first step in the segmentation process. **T/F**
5. The "majority fallacy" refers to the selection of a segment by majority vote of top administrators. **T/F**

CHECK YOUR LEARNING *(continued)*

6. Which of the following is not a criterion suggested for use in selecting a market segment? (a) reputable, (b) measurable, (c) stable, (d) substantial, (e) all of the above should be used.
7. Differentiated marketing requires fewer organizational resources than undifferentiated marketing if the total market is covered.   **T/F**
8. At least a generalized marketing plan should be prepared before forecasting sales.   **T/F**
9. Which of the following forecasting techniques does not depend upon historical data? (a) time series, (b) correlation analysis, (c) jury of executive opinion, (d) all of them depend on historical data, (e) none of them depend on historical data.
10. Sales force composite forecasting technique works best for a long-run forecast.   **T/F**
11. In time series analysis, sales is a function of all the following except: (a) erratic factors, (b) trend, (c) cycle, (d) season, (e) competitive action.
12. In correlation analysis a leading market factor is any variable that has a greater relationship with future sales than present sales.   **T/F**

13. Which of the following is not a basic criterion for evaluating a forecasting method? (a) time horizon, (b) accuracy, (c) precision, (d) all of the above are criteria, (e) none of the above are criteria.
14. Positioning refers to the marketer's efforts to influence how the customer perceives the product, service, or offering of the firm.   **T/F**
15. A product is positioned in the customer's mind even without the influence of the marketer.   **T/F**
16. The focal point for positioning includes: (a) price/quality, (b) product user, (c) competitors, (d) all of the above, (e) only a and b.
17. The position map shows the location of positioning focal points.   **T/F**
18. Brands located near each other on a position map are the most likely substitutes for each other in the buyer's mind.   **T/F**
19. A company should position its products in the largest market segment in order to obtain maximum sales.   **T/F**

QUESTIONS FOR REVIEW AND DISCUSSION

1. Define the key terms for this chapter that appear at the end of the goal summary.
2. As a consumer, would you prefer that marketers segment the market or take an undifferentiated approach in attempting to serve your needs?
3. Comment on the statement, "The more commodity-oriented the product, the greater the probable use of a mass market approach."
4. Nyquil Cough Syrup—describe its market segment.
5. Identify possible segmentation variables for cough syrups.
6. What role do segmentation bases play in the segmentation process?
7. Identify at least one variable from each of the bases: demographic, psychographic, behavioral, and product-specific.
8. How is cluster analysis typically used in the segmentation process?
9. What criteria should be used to evaluate potential segments?
10. Distinguish between market potential and a sales forecast.
11. What role does a sales forecast play in an organization?
12. What differences exist between a jury of executive opinion and time series forecasting?
13. Can a product such as salt be positioned?

NOTES

1. David W. Cravens, Gerald E. Hills, and Robert B. Woodruff, *Marketing Decision Making,* rev. ed. (Homewood, Ill.: Richard D. Irwin, 1980), p. 177.
2. Terry Elrod and Russell S. Winer, "An Empirical Evaluation of Aggregation Approaches for Develop

ing Market Segments," *Journal of Marketing* (Fall 1982): pp. 32–34.
3. Patrick E. Murphy and Ben M. Enis, *Marketing* (Glenview, Ill.: Scott, Foresman and Company, 1985), p. 203.

NOTES *(continued)*

4. Thomas Kinnear and James R. Taylor, *Marketing Research An Applied Approach,* 2d ed. (New York: McGraw-Hill Book Company, 1983), p. 525.

5. "Cake," *Advertising Age,* September 27, 1984, p. 44.

6. Cravens, Hills, and Woodruff, *Marketing Decision Making,* p. 177.

7. This terminology originally appeared in Phillip Kotler, *Marketing Management* (Englewood Cliffs, N.J.: Prentice-Hall), pp. 151–154.

8. For specific application, see Ronald H. King and Arthur A. Thompson, Jr., "Entry and Market Share Success of Brands in Concentrated Markets," *Journal of Business Research* (September 1982): pp. 371–383.

9. "Authors Chronicle Strategies of Winners and Losers," *Marketing News,* June 20, 1986, p. 11.

10. "Levi's: The Jeans Giant Slipped as the Market Shifted," *Business Week,* November 5, 1984, pp. 79 & 82.

11. Thomas C. Kinnear and Kenneth L. Bernhardt, *Principles of Marketing* (Glenview, Ill.: Scott, Foresman and Company, 1986), p. 222.

12. Richard Rippe, Maurice Wilkinson, and Donald Morrison, "Industrial Market Forecasting with Anticipation Data," *Management Science* 22 (February 1976): pp. 639–651.

13. "Positioning Reigns for Consumer or Industrial Products," *Marketing News,* May 9, 1986, p. 14.

14. "Sacrifice is the Penance Paid for Effective Positioning," *Marketing News,* November 23, 1984, p. 3.

15. "Spotting Competitive Edges Begets New Product Success," *Marketing News,* December 21, 1984, p. 4.

Larry Bird came to Terre Haute from nearby French Lick to attend Indiana State University and to play basketball. In some respects Larry never left. Although he has played for the Boston Celtics since 1979, Terre Haute people still ardently follow Larry's basketball career. And Larry continues to contribute to Terre Haute life. In 1987 he and several friends who are local businessmen bought a former Sheraton Inn, renovated it, and turned it into the Boston Connection Hotel.

The Boston Connection has an obvious theme—Larry Bird. It also highlights the entire Boston Celtics team. From his years as a professional basketball player, Larry understands what it takes to be comfortable and entertained on the road. All 109 rooms have first-quality furnishings and decorations. All have extra-length mattresses, remote-controlled televisions, and complimentary, luxury bath accessories. Three basic room types are available: king-size bed with recliner, king-size bed with sofa sleeper, and twin beds. The Larry Bird Suite and "coaches' suites" offer deluxe accommodations, including separate living and sitting rooms and wet bar. As one travel writer put it, "When you check in at Larry Bird's Boston Connection, you can expect the same kind of excellence in accommodations, food, and service that you expect from Larry Bird on the basketball floor."

Each of the four floors is named for a different team. The first floor is the Boston Celtics floor; the Indiana State University Sycamores take the third. The hotel gift shop is crammed with Larry Bird and Celtic memorabilia, including tee-shirts, hats, posters, sweaters, and pennants. Once past the front desk, it's usually the first stop for visitors.

The hotel has several restaurants, including the MVP Club, the Boston Garden, and the Bird Nest Lounge. The MVP Club, offering fine dining, is home to Larry Bird's Most Valuable Player trophies, including a monumental Waterford crystal trophy.

The MVP Club is open to hotel guests and members of the community who pay initiation and annual fees. The walls of the Boston Garden Room are lined with childhood photographs of Bird, old uniforms, and even a basketball hoop. The Bird Nest Lounge features Celtic games carried via cable on three giant screens. Restaurant and Lounge employees wear black and white striped basketball official shirts.

Hotel manager Glen Ankney estimates that 90 percent of the hotel's bookings Monday through Thursday are for people on business trips to the area, or for those traveling through Terre Haute on their way to other business destinations. Many use the Boston Connection because it appeals to the sports enthusiast in them. Other customers who are not sports enthusiast, Celtic fans, or Larry Bird fans come for the quality facilities, according to Ankney. On weekends, the clientele changes. Then, as much as 90 percent are tourists and families who are traveling.

As an independent hotel, The Boston Connection is not affiliated with a reservation network. All reservations must be made directly. To encourage local businesspeople to book their visiting clients, participating secretaries of the firms receive $1.25 per room reserved. Referred to as "Larry Connectors," the secretaries are themselves the subject of various promotions, including Larry Bird autographed basketballs and parties.

The Boston Connection staff works to encourage visiting athletic teams to stay at the Boston Connection. Most of these teams come to compete with the Indiana State University teams. Some play against the Rose-Hulman Institute of Technology, an engineering school. Other teams are sponsored by sports pro-

motion associations—for example, "Miss Softball America."

The Boston Connection's most significant promotion comes from free publicity generated by the fantastic interest in Larry Bird. Stories about the player often mention the hotel. Manager Ankney estimates that the exposure received from such publicity would cost the Boston Connection millions of dollars in paid advertising.

By quality and price, the Holiday Inn is the Boston Connection's closest competitor. Both firms are at the top of the Terre Haute hotel market. The Holiday Inn offers an enclosed indoor swimming pool and 230 rooms. The Signature Inn, with its lower rates, has successfully appealed to the business market, according to Mr. Ankney. In all, twenty hotel firms offer 1500 rooms, with new hotels entering the market.

Over 100 restaurants compete for customers in Terre Haute, ranging from dinner theater establishments to fast food restaurants, and from American to Mexican cuisine. Both the Boston Garden Room and the MVP Club offer an American menu. The Garden Room has a family orientation, but Mr. Ankney believes the restaurant has had only limited success in attracting them, especially those from the upper-lower- and lower-middle-class socioeconomic groups. Unfortunately, most of Vigo county's population of 110,000 fall into these two groups. It may be that the exclusive image of the MVP Club has spilled over onto the Garden Room.

The Boston Connection vacillates between being completely booked and experiencing vacancies, the latter occurring most frequently on weekends and especially on Sunday nights. Most hotels have slow periods—the average occupancy rate in the U.S. is 67 percent.

Like Bird, the staff and management of the Boston Connection are willing to work to move from "good" to "excellent" in order to increase bookings and revenues from the restaurants and lounge operations. The question of course is just how to do it. Should the Boston Connection appeal to different groups than those they currently attract, increase emphasis on a particular group currently served, or do something else? According to an industry report, "Older citizens constitute a fast-growing segment of the population," and hotels are expected to launch more programs targeted to them. The weekend trip is also emerging as a strong factor in pleasure travel, replacing stays of longer duration.

Issues for Discussion

1. Should the Boston Connection appeal to other groups of customers? If so, describe them.

2. What can the Boston Connection do to take more of the business market away from local competitors?

3. Describe the market segments to which each of the Boston Connection's features might appeal (The MVP Club, Boston Garden Room, Bird Nest Lounge, Larry Bird/Boston Celtics gift shop, three types of rooms, and individual team-designated hotel floors).

Sources: Visitor's Guide to Terre Haute, Indiana (Terre Haute Convention and Visitors Bureau, 1988); *Terre Haute Area 1987 Buyers Guide and Membership Directory* (Terre Haute Area Chamber of Commerce, 1987); "Hotels and Motels," *U.S. Industrial Outlook 1988* (U.S. Department of Commerce), pp. 64-1 to 64-4; Gordon Edes, "Suite Dreams," *Los Angeles Times,* November 30, 1987, p. B-1; Frank Deford, "A Player For The Ages," *Sports Illustrated,* March 21, 1988, pp. 46–65; *Terre Haute, Indiana The Faces The Places* (Terre Haute Area Chamber of Commerce), no date given; and Itinerant Travel Writer, "A Stay in Boston—The Boston Connection," *Indiana's Great Southwest,* Spring/Summer 1988, p. 13.

MARKETING PLAN

PART 4 / MARKET SELECTION: TARGET MARKETS (CHAPTERS 5–7)

A. Describe the firm's target market or market segments. Consumer? Organizational?
B. What are the characteristics of the market? (If *Consumer market*—age, geography, income, lifestyle; if *Organizational market*—market characteristics and buyer behavior.)
C. Why were these target markets selected?
D. How does your product or service meet the needs of your target market(s)?
E. Assess the potential of each market segment.
F. Describe the purchase decision behavior of your target markets.
G. If applicable, what is the sales forecast for your product/service/idea?
H. If known, is this market(s) a departure from last year? Explain the rationale for the change, if any.

PART 5 / MARKETING STRATEGY AND MARKETING MIX (CHAPTERS 5–7)

A. Does your product or service have a competitive advantage? If yes, explain your broad marketing strategy (put in the context of current trends, competition, and time frame).
B. What is the organization's strategy for implementing the marketing plan? Concentrated? Differentiated? Expand.
C. How will the product or service be positioned?
D. What is the organization's marketing mix (brief description)?
   1. Product
   2. Price
   3. Promotion
   4. Distribution
E. If known, how will the current marketing plan differ from the most recent plan? Why do changes seem necessary?

Section Four

The Product/ Service Plan

OUTLINE

CHAPTER

8

Developing the Product Strategy— Consumer and Industrial Markets

LEARNING GOALS

After reading this chapter, you should be able to:

1. Define the total product concept.
2. Explain product line and mix.
3. Discuss the importance of product classification schemes as they relate to market plans.
4. Distinguish between consumer and industrial goods.
5. List the categories of industrial goods.
6. Discuss the role of branding and packaging as they relate to product strategy.
7. Explain warranties from a consumer's and a marketer's viewpoint.

*P*olaroid Corporation has recently introduced two new products: Palette and Autoprocess System. Palette produces instant slides from graphic displays on computers. Six million computer owners may develop a need for Palette. Autoprocess System allows the user of a 35mm camera to develop slides within five minutes. Palette has received favorable ratings in the industry. It is one of the most complete systems available.

Palette and Autoprocess represent Polaroid's first major move away from the consumer amateur photography market. Both new products have been developed for the industrial-commercial market, and Polaroid executives anticipate even more products suitable for that market. Polaroid's Product development research has focused on the imagery industry, especially in the electronics and optical technologies, which hold the most promise for industrial-commercial users.

Polaroid is also said to have changed from a product-oriented to a market-oriented company. Executives at the company once believed that an innovative product could always be sold. The strategy was to develop the product first, then consider selling it. This strategy worked with the instant Polaroid cameras until competitive products improved— fast film processing and easy-to-use 35mm cameras. Unit sales of Polaroid cameras and film peaked in 1979. Profits peaked in 1980 and declined in 1981, 1982, and 1983.

The company lost between $250 and $300 million on Polarvision, the instant home movie camera that was discontinued in 1980. Thus Polaroid's more recent approach has been to find out what the market wants and needs, then develop a product to fulfill the need. With Autoprocess, company executives wanted to make the product proprietary, usable only in a Polaroid, but research results indicated more film would be sold to the industrial-commercial market if the new product

was compatible with any 35mm camera. Industrial-commercial purchasers also wanted high picture quality at a reasonable price. Polaroid now has good quality pictures at a competitive 46 cents per slide.

Robert Delahunt, Polaroid's vice-president of worldwide industrial marketing, made a comment underscoring the company's new respect for the market: "What really counts is that the market perceives and understands that we will support these products." To be successful, Polaroid must communicate the intrinsic benefits of instant photography to the consumer and industrial-commercial markets. In the future, industrial market sales are projected to represent one-third of the company's total sales.

Polaroid is not forgetting the consumer market. In 1983 the company entered the blank videotape business and by 1987 held close to 10 percent of the market. A large percentage of the blank videotape sales are to individuals who use the tapes in home VCRs. Products sold to the

amateur photographer are now considered a part of the conventional package goods market and package goods testing techniques are being used.

Issues for Discussion
1. Why the change in focus at Polaroid to less dependency on the consumer market?
2. Will marketing to the industrial market require a different strategy for Polaroid?
3. Should Polaroid associate its brandname with new products or establish a new identity for each new product?
4. How much will labeling, packaging, and warranties influence Polaroid's success?

Sources: "Product Comparison," *Info World,* March 21, 1988, p. 54; "The Second One Hundred Leading National Advertisers," *Advertising Age,* Nov. 23, 1987; Gary Jervey, "Polaroid Develops Marketing Orientation," *Advertising Age,* January 30, 1984, p. 4; "Polaroid Sharpens Its Focus on the Marketplace," *Business Week,* February 1, 1984, pp. 132–136; Gary Jervey, "Polaroid Crows, Kodak Mum on Instant Market," *Advertising Age,* May 14, 1984, pp. 55–56; Stephanie Flory, "Polaroid Aims to Be Among Top Three Blank Tape Vendors," *Merchandising,* April 1984, p. 9.

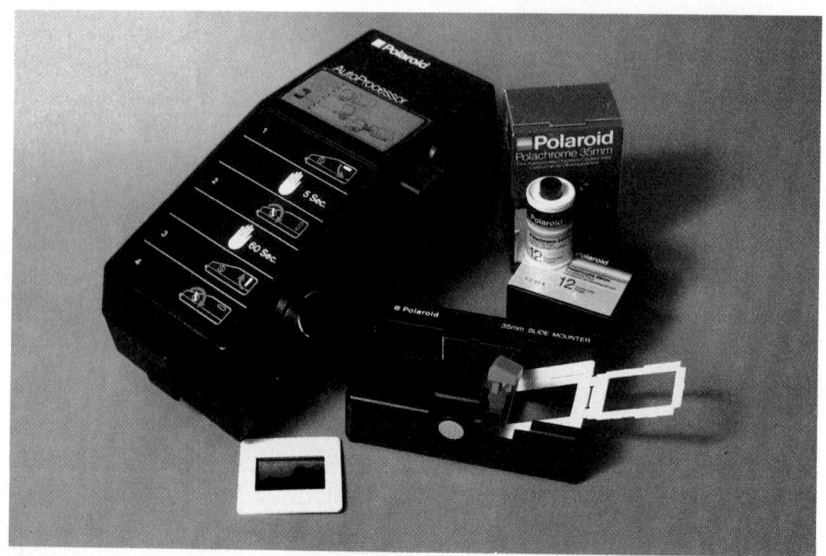

■ The Autoprocess is a compact and easy-to-use system.

*P*olaroid Corporation, successful for many years, finds it necessary to reevaluate its products and markets. In the pages ahead, we give careful consideration to the nature of a product and to the decisions a marketing manager must make in managing products. For most of its corporate lifetime, Polaroid concentrated on the instant photography amateur market—a consumer market. Recently, company executives decided to enter the industrial market, a fundamental shift in direction. The chapter distinguishes between consumer and industrial goods. It presents a system for classifying consumer goods according to consumer purchase behavior and industrial goods according to their function in the production process. The discussion of products will emphasize the marketing ideas and strategies associated with each class of goods. To market a product successfully, companies like Polaroid must make numerous decisions about branding, labeling, packaging, and warranting their products. We conclude with a discussion of the advantages and disadvantages associated with each decision, the strategies available to the marketer, and the marketer's responsibilities to the consumer. ■

WHAT IS A PRODUCT?

A product satisfies customer needs.

A **product** is a bundle of tangible and intangible benefits that a buyer receives in exchange for money or other consideration.[1] A physical good, a service, and a concept, alone or in combination, all qualify as products. A product performs functions. A computer, for example, adds, subtracts, multiplies, and processes information. A product provides satisfaction. With a computer, this includes prestige of ownership, time saved through its use, and pride generated from the speed and accuracy of its work.

A product is more than a physical thing.

A product may actually pass through several stages as it proceeds along its path to the customer. (See figure 8.1.) To illustrate, a washing machine may be manufactured by Whirlpool, branded and sold by a Sears store, and serviced by a Sears service firm. Several companies in several locations contribute to what the consumer perceives as simply the product.

The plan of the marketer determines which elements in the equation in figure 8.1 will be emphasized. For instance, the marketer may decide to emphasize intangibles such as service and brand instead of the physical product. From an individual firm's perspective, a product by definition is limited to the customer need satisfaction offered by the firm. Farsighted managers consider how the product will be transformed by other organizations before it is ultimately consumed.

❑ **Figure 8.1** Total product concept.

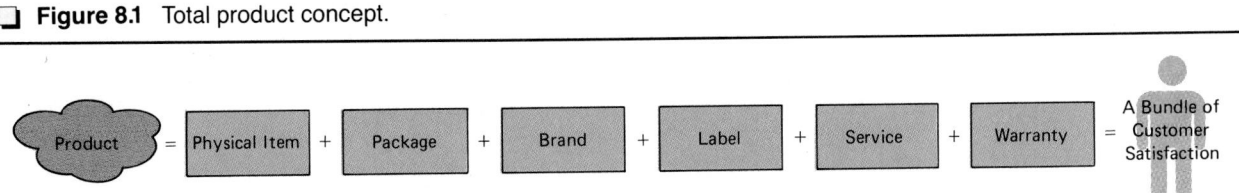

Beatrice Foods has a large number of products in its product mix.

Source: Photo courtesy of Beatrice/Hunt-Wesson, Inc., Operating Company of Beatrice Companies, Inc.

 ## THE PRODUCT ITEM, LINE, AND MIX

Each unique product offered for sale by an organization is a **product item.** A product is unique if the seller lists or identifies the product and distinguishes it from all other products sold. The product item is usually differentiated by brand, size, price, material, or some other characteristic. Fisher brand salted mixed nuts in a 16-ounce pull-top can is an example of a product item for Beatrice Foods.

Product items, when grouped, become **product lines.** The marketer groups product items into product lines because they have qualities in common. They may have similar physical or functional characteristics. To Beatrice Foods, Samsonite luggage is one such product line. Items may be grouped because their purchasers have characteristics in common: age, income level, leisure-time interests, or the like. Items may also comprise a product line because they have similar outlets for distribution, specialty stores, for example, or discount department stores. The use of product lines reduces the number and magnitude of decisions the marketer must make because decisions are for the entire line instead of each separate product item.[2]

The number of product items in a line is referred to as the length of the line, or by wholesalers and retailers as assortment. Champion International Corporation's paper line has a greater length than its building materials line because the paper line has more products. (See figure 8.2.) All product lines considered together are a company's **product mix.** The number of lines in the product mix is the width, or variety, of the mix.

*T*he composite of the product line attracts customers.

The length of each product line and the number of lines are major policy decisions, as is the composite of each line. The **composite of a line** refers to the variety of the product items included in the line. When considering the composite of a product line, the marketer should account for such factors as the need to balance risk, to offset cyclical and seasonal sales declines, to capitalize on product attributes, and to recognize the purchasing habits of customers. The composite of General Electric's home appliance line, for example, consists of refrigerators, dishwashers, air conditioners, garbage disposals, and clothes washers and dryers. GE's numerous products balance risk. If a new product fails, the company still has other successful products. Likewise, the seasonal sales swings of air conditioners tend to be offset by the sale of other products in the line.

❑ **Figure 8.2**
Illustration of product mix—Champion International Corporation.

Product Line	Product Line	Product Line
Paper	**Building Materials**	**Packaging**
Coated printing, publication, and packaging papers Label papers Uncoated papers printing, writing, cut-size, envelope converting, business forms and related products Bleached paperboard Milk and juice cartons Ovenable paperboard packaging Specialty packaging closures Bleached hardwood pulp Bleached Kraft market pulp Wood chemicals and associated products Newsprint Dielectric electronic communication papers Business and specialty papers	Softwood plywood Softwood lumber Reconstituted wood structured panels	Linerboard corrugating medium Kraft paper corrugated shipping containers Multiwall bags, shopping bags, Inflatable, dunnage bags Compactor bags Sugar packets Gift wrap and box wrap Wood chemicals and associated products Packaging equipment

• • • • • • • • • • • • • • • • • Product Mix Width • • • • • • • • • • • • • • • • •

Seeking an advantage, a firm may decide to use long lines and a wide product mix. Related products can stimulate demand for each other. The "one-stop shopping" slogan used by Sears and other retailers embodies the concept of stimulating demand. Production and marketing economies may also be realized from a wide product mix, thereby giving the firm a cost advantage. On the other hand, a small product mix reinforces an image of specialization that some organizations desire. A small mix requires fewer resources to implement as well.

MARKETING MANAGEMENT AND PRODUCT CLASSIFICATION

Classifying products alerts the marketer to various types of available strategies. Knowledge of the successful strategies associated with each classification contributes significantly to successful product management.

The consumer/industrial classification is a classification of goods based on the buyer's reason for purchase. Goods purchased to provide pleasure or satisfaction directly to the consumer are called **consumer goods.** Goods purchased for the purpose of producing for sale another product or service are **industrial goods.** The purchasers of industrial goods include manufacturers, retailers, wholesalers, brokers, individuals, and others who buy goods in order to produce other goods to sell. Note that the identical product can be an industrial good and a consumer good. A drill bit purchased by a manufacturer of machine tools is an industrial good. The same bit purchased by a homeowner building a deck is a consumer good. (See figure 8.3.)

Consumer goods give pleasure or satisfaction; industrial goods are goods purchased by organizations for use in other products or for company operations.

Consumer Goods

Consumer goods include a broad spectrum of products. The consumer goods category is further subdivided based on the type, amount, and frequency of consumer shopping behavior.[3]

❑ **Figure 8.3**
Goods classification for
marketing strategy.

CONVENIENCE GOODS

Little effort is expended in buying convenience goods.

Convenience goods consist of items frequently purchased with a minimum of effort immediately upon the consumer's discovery of a need. Convenience goods are routinely purchased at the nearest location. Examples include shampoo, newspapers, and milk.

The convenience goods marketer will increase sales by following several rules of thumb. First, make the product readily available in many locations. Second, presell the product with extensive advertising. Third, maintain high point-of-purchase awareness and brand recognition with an attractive, eye-catching package; large, well-designed product displays; and point-of-purchase brand advertising.

Convenience goods that are purchased routinely and frequently are *staple* items. Once the consumer has found an acceptable product or brand, the purchase requires little thought. Location and image of the retailer are factors in staple goods purchase. Many package goods can be classified as staples, such as bread, breakfast cereal, motor oil, and gasoline.

Convenience goods like candy that are purchased on sight without previous planning are classified as **impulse goods.** The importance of sight in the sale makes visual appeal critical. Location in convenient and heavily trafficked areas is also important.

In an emergency almost any good becomes a convenience good.

When a good is needed immediately because it is necessary and consumers spend little time considering the purchase, the good is an **emergency good.** What normally would be a staple might become an emergency good if the consumer runs short. Milk, eggs, and other cooking supplies often become emergency goods if the consumer runs out. Emergency goods are usually purchased at the most convenient location even though the price may be higher and the service less than at the customary place of purchase. Infrequently purchased items may also be emergency goods. Automobile repairs obtained on a trip are an emergency purchase.

Retailers as a group are quite important in the sale of convenience goods, but the individual retailer is less so since wide distribution provides the convenience that consumers demand. Retailers typically carry the same brands and are unlikely to promote convenience goods. Promotional efforts, therefore, are up to the manufacturer.

SHOPPING GOODS

*S*hopping goods are pur-
chased by comparison.

"**Shopping goods** are goods that the customer, in the process of selection and purchase, characteristically compares on such bases as suitability, quality, price, and style."[4] Unsure of what they want, consumers compare competing goods in competing stores. They shop. The purpose of shopping is to gather information.

Shopping goods firms locate near their competition to reduce the effort required of the consumer. On the other hand, the fact that the consumer will expend effort tells the marketer that the good does not have to be sold in every possible outlet. Shopping goods tend to be higher priced and less frequently purchased than convenience goods. Examples of shopping goods include furniture, cars, and clothing.

Homogeneous shopping goods are those that the consumer perceives as essentially the same and buys based on the lowest price.[5] Even though the manufacturer and retailer try to make the product and service unique, price sells the product. Television sets and washing machines are considered examples by some consumers.

*C*onsumers perceive dif-
ferences in heterogeneous
shopping goods.

Heterogeneous shopping goods are those that consumers perceive as different in quality and attributes.[6] Examples are dishes and furniture. Brands typically are less important with heterogeneous goods than homogeneous goods. Because heterogeneous goods are perceived as unique, manufacturers and retailers have more freedom in pricing. At the same time, the consumer expects greater assistance at the point of purchase.

**Consumers' purchase
behavior differs
according to type
of goods.**

a) Milk purchases are typical of convenience product purchases. Little time and
effort is expended in making the purchase.

b) Clothing often is a shopping good, with the
consumer going from retailer to retailer before
making a purchase.

c) Reebok or Nike? The consumer who treats the
purchase as a specialty good purchase knows his
or her preference.

❑ **Figure 8.4**
Marketing mixes—
consumer goods
classes.

Marketing Variables	Convenience Goods	Shopping Goods	Specialty Goods
Advertising	Manufacturer	Manufacturer/Retailer	Manufacturer/Retailer
Number of retailers	Many	Few	Restricted
Price/Unit	Low	Relatively high	High
Retailer's image	Of little importance	Considerable importance	Important
Channel length	Long	Short	Very short

SPECIALTY GOODS

*N*o substitutes accepted for specialty items.

In some cases, consumers make the purchase decision before making the purchase trip. When they insist on a certain brand name, consumers are in the market for a **specialty good.** A specialty good is one for which the consumer plans the purchase rather than shopping for it. Since the consumer is willing to expend considerable effort in acquiring a specialty good, location and the number of retailers are less important than for the other types of consumer goods. A retailer of specialty goods is eager to gain the right to distribute a particular manufacturer's brand. The retailer may be the single representative of the manufacturer in a local market, such as a Magnavox retailer. In turn, the manufacturer, aware of the brand loyalty of consumers to specialty goods, is usually very particular in selecting retailers and insists that the retailer maintain inventory and standards of management.

Retailers themselves may have specialty status. In such a case the consumer insists on buying a good from a certain retailer. Many consumers accord specialty status to Ethan Allen furniture stores. The product brand loses significance in the consumer's mind when the retailer has specialty status because the consumer trusts the retailer to provide the correct good. (See figure 8.4.)

Over time, shopping goods and even convenience goods may become specialty goods with consumers insisting on certain brands. Most marketing managers consider the possibility of a brand becoming a specialty good when they develop marketing plans. Magnavox and Ethan Allen furniture are examples of shopping goods that developed into specialty goods.

CONSUMER GOODS: PROBLEMS OF APPLICATION

A product's classification depends on the behavior of a majority of the selected market.

Recall that the classification of consumer goods is based upon the behavior of consumers: shopping effort, frequency of purchase, and other associated purchase behavior. A given product might simultaneously be classified as a shopping, specialty, and convenience good, depending on the behavior of different consumers. For the classification of goods to be useful in suggesting marketing strategy, the marketer must observe the behavior of the majority of consumers in the target market.

The degree of effort consumers are willing to expend on the purchase of goods increases from convenience goods to shopping goods to specialty goods; however, a product will not necessarily fit neatly into one of the categories. The behavior of a consumer buying a new Buick, for example, may define the car as a shopping good and a specialty good. The consumer may shop at several Buick dealers, but insist on a Buick.

The three categories of consumer goods discussed so far all suppose at least some effort on the part of the consumer to make a purchase based on prior knowledge of the good. The marketer should be aware of a fourth category that is now gaining acceptance, the unsought goods category.

Unsought goods are of two sorts: (1) goods of which consumers have no prior knowledge and (2) goods for which consumers are unaware of their own need. In figure 8.3 unsought goods are attached with dotted lines. A new product is an example of the first kind of unsought good. Clearly, consumers can make no effort to purchase a good until they become aware of it. The success of a new product, therefore, depends on the establishment of awareness through a well-aimed mix of promotional efforts.

With the second kind of unsought good, where consumers are aware that a good exists, but unaware that they need it, a different marketing approach is called for. Heavy amounts of personal selling are required to sell a product where the product is known but the need is not fully developed. Encyclopedias are an example; personal care products, another. With the other categories of consumer goods, the initiative lies with the purchaser; with unsought goods it lies with the seller.

Industrial Goods

Recall that industrial goods are goods purchased for use in the production of other goods. Unlike consumer goods, which are classified according to consumer behavior, industrial goods are classified according to the function of the good in the production of a finished product.

CLASSIFYING INDUSTRIAL GOODS

Although the classification of industrial goods is based on the production function the goods perform, the marketer must understand the behavior of the industrial purchasers in each class in order to market industrial goods effectively. Seven classes of industrial goods have been identified. This textbook, for example, incorporates products (and services) from all seven classes, and its appearance in college bookstores depends on the contributions of diverse sectors of the U.S. economy.

1. **Supplies** consist of items that facilitate the production of products and services but do not become part of the finished product. The pens used in editing the manuscript of this book are an example of supplies.
2. **Raw materials** include such items as farm and natural products. The wood pulp used to manufacture the paper is a raw material.
3. **Processed materials** are used in production but do not become an identifiable part of the product. The film used in printing is a processed material.
4. **Component parts** need little if any additional processing, are ready for assembly, and become part of the physical product. Paper is a component part of this text.
5. **Accessory equipment** does not become part of the finished product but does facilitate an organization's operation. Office machines (typewriters, word processors) are pieces of accessory equipment.
6. **Installations** are major capital investments used to produce a firm's products and services. The four-color press used in printing is an installation.
7. **Services** are intangibles needed and used by an organization in conducting its operation. An example of services is the repair of any of the accessory equipment or installations used to produce this textbook.

MARKETING INDUSTRIAL GOODS

*D*evelop a marketing mix from purchase behavior.

In a diversified, modern economy numerous firms and sectors produce the industrial goods that ultimately comprise the consumer product. Thus, marketing industrial goods is a complex and challenging process. Understanding the purchase behavior associated with each class of industrial goods assists the marketing manager in developing a marketing plan, and especially a marketing mix, based on purchase behavior. Common purchase behaviors for all seven product categories appear in figure 8.5.

❑ **Figure 8.5** Purchase behavior— industrial products.

Product Type	Examples	Purchase Frequency	Purchase Decision	Supplier Characteristics	Price	Special Consideration	Number of Suppliers
Supplies	Brooms, cleaning agents, fuel filters, grease, typing ribbon, equipment parts	Frequently	Routine	Dependability wide assortment	Lite effort to negotiate price except for large quantity items	Supplies that may interrupt production process if shortage occurs. Downtime expensive	Many
Raw materials 1. Natural raw materials	Coal, iron ore, lumber	Frequent except for contracted large volume items	Routine except for large volume items	Dependability	Negotiated contracts	Promotion not usually factor in purchase. Supply is limited.	Few large firms
2. Farm products	Wheat, corn, cotton, milk	Frequent except for contracted items	Routine except for large volume items	Collectors and graders. Product handling/storage important	Price lite impact in short run on purchase. Contract for large quantity items	Supply limited in short run. Supply expandable in long run	Many
Process materials	Abrasives to smooth, stamped auto parts, tannic acid in leather production, potassium benzoate in Diet Coke	Annual contracts common	Engineers, production managers, and purchasing agents may all play a role	Continuous supply important, usually from producer, but wholesalers provide emergency supplies	Price an influencing factor in purchase	Supply continuity. Suitability and quality of product important	Many
Component parts	Goodyear tires, Honeywell thermostats	Long-term contracts common	Engineers involved, product must meet specifications	Reliable, consistent quality producer. Suppliers evaluated carefully	Must be competitive	Buyer may work closely with supplier to insure quality control and reliability of supply. Suppliers may seek original equipment market (O.E.M.) and after-market. Brands can be effective marketing tool.	Several
Accessory equipment	Calculators, fork-lifts, portable drills, hand tools	Item usually expected to last for more than one year	Purchasing agent usually responsible, careful, but not extensive; deliberation	Wholesalers (industrial distributors)	Important as quality features and service	Normally standardized items	Several to many
Installations	Stamp presses for Toyota, draglines for Amax Coal	Infrequently purchased long-lived investments	Often a committee decision	Usually a producer. Technical expertise, important as is installation, training, repair	Important but usually not deciding factor	Affect of purchase on profitability and on human factors (unemployment—the status derived from purchase)	Few
Services	Financial, legal, consulting, office machine repair, janitorial	Frequent to infrequent	When professional service involved normally management decision. Nonprofessional service purchasing agent or personnel	Reputation of supplier often important	Important but may not be deciding factor	Buyer may decide to provide own services if demand is consistent	Few to many

❑ **Figure 8.6**
Marketing mixes—
industrial goods
classes.

Marketing Variable	Service	Installation	Accessory	Raw Material	Components	Supplies
Personal selling	Little to important	Very important	Important	Of less importance	Important	Of less importance
Distribution	Wide	Limited	Limited	Wide	Limited	Wide
Price/unit	Low–medium	High	Low–medium	Low	Low	Low
Sellers/image	Low–high importance	High	Medium–high	Low	Low–high	Low
Channel length	Short	Very short	Short/medium	Medium/long	Short/medium	Medium/long

*E*lements of a marketing mix for component parts based on purchase behavior.

Purchase behavior differs significantly across categories. Figure 8.6 specifies possible marketing mixes for each class of industrial goods based on the purchasing behavior associated with each one. The supplies category of industrial goods, for example, is similar in some respects to the convenience goods category of consumer goods. Items like paper clips, pens, and file folders are purchased routinely and frequently from many sources. The marketer of supplies will therefore develop a marketing plan including, among other components, wide distribution, low unit price, and general convenience to the purchaser.

Purchase behavior associated with the component parts category is quite different. Here the buyer is interested in long-term contracts and wants to work closely with the supplier to insure quality control and a reliable supply. These elements in the buyer's behavior tell the marketing manager that personal selling is important in the marketing mix, that distribution will be limited to a few major buyers, and that the channel of distribution will be short—the producer will work directly with users of the components. Since initially the purchaser may work with several qualified suppliers the price must be competitive. The price per unit is likely to be low, as figure 8.6 indicates. Finally, to be a qualified supplier the producer must insure that the product meets specifications. The supplier also has to provide a continuous and

---

*P*olaroid Corporation's concentration in the consumer market with a consumer product—instant development film and cameras—has made the name Polaroid familiar nationwide. Note that Polaroid also sells the camera to businesses and organizations, and when sold to them it is an industrial product. However, with the Polaroid camera, instant film development was more convenient, easier to use, and provided immediate feedback to the photographer, all features with greater appeal to the consumers than organizations. Initially, consumers shopping for a camera would consider Polaroid along with other cameras. Later as the nation became familiar with the name, Polaroid became a specialty

THE CASE CONTINUES

good to large numbers of buyers who knew that they wanted an instant development camera. Recent changes in the camera market, including developments in non-instant cameras, have decreased Polaroid's sales. Using Polaroid Corporation's engineering and technical ability to develop products for the industrial market (where they had never been applied) seems a logical way to increase sales revenue.

For Polaroid Corporation to market industrial products, the marketing strategy will necessarily be different from the one used in the consumer

market. For the most part, products marketed by Polaroid to the industrial market are likely to be classified as accessory equipment. As such, the purchaser will be different. Purchasers in the industrial market generally have more product knowledge and tend to be more rational in their purchase decisions. Price, quality, features, and service are important in the sale of accessories. Mr. Delahunt, the vice-president of worldwide industrial marketing, has recognized the importance of conveying to the market the fact that Polaroid will support its products. When compared to consumer products, less advertising and more personal selling will be needed to market the Palette and Autoprocess.

consistent quality of product. The more difficult it is to meet the product specifications and to provide a continuous and consistent quality product, the more important the supplier's reputation in successfully marketing the product.

In summary, the marketing manager devising a marketing mix for a component parts marketing plan, where contracts are involved, would emphasize personal selling, make sure the products meet specifications, insure a consistent quality and a continuous supply, and be prepared to deal directly with the user at a competitive price.

PRODUCT IDENTIFICATION

*B*rands identify and differentiate.

Organizations use a number of techniques to identify their products and services: brand names, symbols, color, features, and distinctive packaging. Successful product identification differentiates the product from other products in the purchaser's mind. Differentiated products offer the marketer more latitude in developing a marketing mix. Prices, promotion, and distribution can be unique to the successfully identified product.[7] One approach to identifying the product is simply to brand it.

Brands

Consumers are very accustomed to seeing brands. Ivory, Caterpillar, Hertz, One-Hour Martinizing, and Sunkist are a few of the thousands of brands we recognize. Brands are so familiar that they are taken for granted. The organization must, however, decide on whether to brand.

A **brand** is a name, term, sign, symbol, or design (or a combination of them) that is intended to identify the goods or services of one seller (or group) and to differentiate them from those of competitors.[8] If the brand can be vocalized, it becomes more specifically a brand name. Examples include Pontiac, Olympus, Blistex, and Bounce. When part of the brand is a recognized symbol but is not actually a name, it is called a brandmark. Examples include the Florida Orange Growers' tree, Ralston-Purina Company's red and white checkerboard square, and Vantage cigarette's red, white, and blue target. (See figure 8.7.)

*L*egal protection is given to trademarks, service marks, trade names, and copyrights.

Trademarks, service marks, and trade names have legal protection. To have legal protection, a brand must be registered with the U.S. Patent Office. No other similar brands can exist or an organization must be able to establish that it was the first to use the brand. To signify registration, the brand is followed by the small letter ®. To signify a trademark, the brand is followed by the small letters ™. Trademarks such as NutraSweet indicate products. Service marks such as the NBC network peacock

❏ **Figure 8.7**
Examples of branding terms.

Source: Courtesy of Chrysler Corporation.

symbol indicate services. Trade names such as Ford signify the legal name of an organization.

One other term commonly associated with brands is copyright. A copyright is the exclusive right to reproduce, sell, or publish the matter and form of literary, musical, or artistic work. The designation for copyright material is a small ©. Although an organization usually has a trademark for its product, it will also protect the other artistic work in its commercials with a copyright (for example, "Where's the Beef?").

A sample of generic products.

Consumer arguments against branding—higher prices, proliferation of brands, and confusion.

Benefits of Branding to the Customer

The issues of whether or not to brand and whether branding benefits the customer have been discussed for many years. A large percentage of consumer products sold each year carry a brand. Still, products are sold quite successfully without brands. **Generic brands** and products without brands have gained in popularity and percentage of the market in recent years.[9] With generic brands, brand identification is minimized. Each retailer has its own brand of generics. For example, Cost-Cutter is Kroger Company's generic brand. Generic brands are most common for staple goods such as paper towels, canned vegetables, and dog food. Generic drugs, on the other hand, are unbranded. Generic items compete with branded products that physically are very similar.

To some consumers the slight difference in generic and brandname alternatives may be unimportant or offset by the much lower price.[10] The purchaser of the generic product believes the value is better. One of the arguments against branding from the customer's point of view is the "assumed to be higher price" of the branded product. This logic says that obtaining customer recognition of a brand requires promotion, promotion requires money, and money comes from a higher priced product. Another argument against branding rests on the premise that brands increase in number without really adding any benefit. Thus, the customer gains nothing and grows confused by the large number of brands.

Actually, branding provides several benefits to the customer. The brand symbolizes a certain level of quality. If customers have purchased a company's brands before, they are likely to perceive that a different product from that company will have the same quality even if the product is unfamiliar. Generally, brands make shopping more efficient. When a desired brand is distributed through one type of store, the shopper soon recognizes the need to shop there. When the brand is distributed by many different stores, the shopper does not have to evaluate the store. The brand itself establishes quality level. Finally, there are psychological rewards associated with brands, the status of owning and wearing designer label clothing, for instance.

Seller benefits of branding—more promotional freedom, more pricing freedom, and more repeat purchases.

Benefits of Branding to the Seller

The most obvious benefit to the seller of branding a product is that it helps to escape some of the rigors of competition. Successful branding with customer recognition gives the seller more options in pricing. The price can be below, above, or the same as that of competitors.

Branding also aids in promotional efforts. A brand enables the seller to create an image different from other brands. The image may be the only significant difference in what are otherwise homogeneous products from different companies. Promotion of a successful brand also has an indirect but positive influence on the sales of other corporate products and the corporate image overall.

One of the most important benefits of branding is that satisfied buyers make repeat purchases. Brand-loyal customers tend to stabilize market share for an organization. When the market share is stable, it usually means that the company can plan better and use resources more efficiently. Since repeat purchases are more routine purchase decisions, they do not require as much of the marketer's selling time. A successful brand eventually builds additional volume. With volume, economies of scale can be realized and the price can be reduced for the buyer.

Factors Influencing the Decision to Brand

Success at branding is far from guaranteed. Marketers look for the existence of the following factors before branding:

1. Product quality should be easy to maintain.
2. Customers should consider the corporate product a good buy for the money.
3. The product should be easy to differentiate from competitors' products either pyschologically or through product features.
4. Money should be available for initial promotion.
5. The difference between product cost and selling price should be sufficient to allow for the continued expense of promotion.
6. The demand for the product class and the corporate share of the product class should be sufficiently large to support the branding efforts.
7. Finally, the brand must be readily available to the customer once customer recognition is obtained. Wide distribution and desirable locations within outlets are essential.

Customer Reaction to a Brand

Customers react differently to a brand over time. First, during the awareness stage the customer becomes aware of the brand's existence. Awareness is achieved through advertising, couponing, sampling, and other promotional efforts of the organization. Companies offering new brands of soaps, deodorants, and shampoos often achieve customer awareness by distributing free samples to the desired market. People who use and like the sample are more likely to buy the new product.

Once customers are aware of the brand, satisfied with it, and inclined to buy it again if it is available, their reaction to the brand is at the preference stage. The organization owning the brand can be competitive in the industry when its products are at this stage. For many consumers, Coca-Cola has been at this stage for years.

Coca-Cola is at an even more desirable stage with other consumers. They will accept no alternative. This stage of consumer acceptance is called brand insistence or brand loyalty. The firm has a monopoly with customers who insist on the brand. Organizations obviously prefer brand insistence, but few ever achieve it for very long with a very large segment of the market.

Promotion and marketing strategies are aimed at moving customers from no knowledge of the brand to brand insistence. At any point along the way, the customer may evaluate the brand and decide to reject it.

Who Will Do the Branding?

*R*etailers and wholesalers brand products, too.

A product may be branded at any point in the channel of distribution—from the manufacturer up to, but not including, the ultimate user.[11] Thousands of brands are owned by manufacturers. These brands are referred to as **manufacturer or national**

brands. When the manufacturer brands the product, a marketing effort all the way to the ultimate user is required. Involvement in distribution, pricing, and promotion is typically required of the manufacturer to make a national brand competitive.

When a retailer, wholesaler, or other channel member besides the manufacturer brands the product, such brands are **private or distributors' brands.** With the proliferation of chain stores, distributors' brands have become more popular. Examples include Sears with its DieHard, Kenmore, and Craftsman brands and IGA (Independent Grocer's Alliance) with its many brands. Owners of private brands can profitably use the brands to establish the image of the organization. Private brands also allow more control over the sale of the products. In addition, private brands normally have higher markups than national brands and are sold for a lower price. The price advantage is possible because the producer of the private label sells it to the brander for less than the national brand. The private brand owner, like the national brand owner, also assumes more marketing responsibility—product image, availability, price, and quality.

The competition between private and national brands continues to be intense.[12] The marketing literature refers to this competition as the "battle of the brands." National branders have developed multiple brands and distribution systems to offset the private brands. Low-priced national brands, "fighting brands," have been developed and distributed through discounters to compete with the low-priced private brands.

Selection and Protection of a Brand

*B*rand name selection: there's more to it than most people suspect.

Selecting a brand name and mark is a very significant decision because both influence the customer's awareness, perceptions, and acceptance of the product. Hotpoint is an excellent name for kitchen ranges, for example, but how would consumers perceive a Hotpoint air conditioner or Levi's business suits?

Examining the processes used by large manufacturers suggests an organized method for selecting a brand name.[13] The obvious first step is to identify the objectives the brand name is to meet. Should the brand name describe an attribute or function of the product? Should it be easy to read? Should it, perhaps, evoke an attribute of the potential consumer? (See figure 8.8.) When there is more than one objective, the relative weight of each should be determined.

Once the objectives have been determined, brand name alternatives should be generated. Brainstorming, suggestions from customers and executives, computer simulations, and other techniques are available for generating alternatives. The alternatives then need to be screened. Ideally, a large number of names will be generated, and screening at this stage will reduce the number to less than a half dozen. The screening should be based on how well the name meets the designated objectives.

With the remaining names, research of the desired customers should be instituted. Information on which names the customers prefer as well as their opinions

❏ **Figure 8.8**
Characteristics of good brand names.

Characteristic	Example
Easy to pronounce, spell, and read	Life — cereal
Short and simple	Joy — detergent
Easy to recognize and remember	Avon — cosmetics
Suggestive of product benefits	Butterball — turkeys
Unique	Huggies — diapers
Applicable to foreign markets	Exxon — petroleum
Undated by time	Betty Crocker — foods

and images of each one should be obtained. Some of the names can be eliminated at this point. The remaining names may be excellent but already in use. A trademark search should be conducted. If more than one name remains, a final brand name should now be selected.

If the selection of a brand name has been successful, it should serve well for years. Brand name changes are expensive. They add promotional costs and can lose customers. Nissan Motor Corporation executives estimate that changing Datsun to Nissan may have cost as much as $150 million.[14] Small businesses can lose customers from a name change, too. A small independent retailer located in a regional enclosed mall originally had a shop called the Bath Boutique. She decided to change locations within the mall, change the name to M. L. Tanners, and expand the line of products to include gifts. Since she gave little promotional support to the changes, many of her original customers did not realize she had not gone out of business even after as long as a year.

*U*nprotected brand names eventually become a part of the language as generic names.

To protect a brand name legally from use by others, the brander must follow certain guidelines. Without protection eventually anyone can use the brand name legally. In such a case the brand becomes a **generic name** for the product. The public refers to the entire product category by the brand name, and the brand name no longer designates only the brander's version of the product. Examples of generic names include shredded wheat, nylon, aspirin, zipper, scotch tape, and kerosene. The owner of a brand, of course, wants the public to think of the owner's brand when it thinks of the product, but not to the extent of asking for the product by the brand and then willingly accepting any brand.

Based on the **Lanham Act** (1946) a brand owner may protect a brand by taking steps to continually remind the public that it is a brand name:

1. Always capitalizing the brand name when used in sentences or phrases.
2. Always using the brand name in conjunction with the generic product name.
3. Always following the brand name with the symbol ® or ™.
4. Always notifying people who use the brand name in a generic fashion that they have done so.

In order to be legally protectable under the Lanham Act, the brand name must not contain words in general use, such as sugar or car.

Branding Policy Decisions

Heinz uses a family brand strategy. The Heinz name and label are prominent on each of Heinz's products.

The decision to brand generates other related decisions. Will the brand name be limited to one product or applied to several? If a company applies a brand to only one product, it is following an individual branding policy. If it applies a brand to more than one, it is using a family branding policy. The company must also make decisions about the quality level of a brand and the image it is intended to convey.

THE FAMILY BRAND DECISION

*F*amily branding is used if promotional efficiency is desired.

A **family brand** is the application of a single brand name to several related products. Heinz, Libby's, and Campbell's are examples. Using a family brand has several advantages. Promotional expenditures on any one product tend to stimulate demand for all products under the umbrella of the family brand name. New products are more easily introduced using a family approach to branding. The reputation of the family brand name paves the way for customer acceptance of a new product.[15] Also, customers are familiar with the family brand and equate the quality of the new product with the quality of the family of products. Retailers and wholesalers tend to equate the promotional support and demand for the family brand with support and demand for the new item. However, since the new item is equated with the family in the minds of customers, it will tarnish the family brand name if it does not provide equal value (or better).

THE INDIVIDUAL BRAND DECISION

*I*ndividual branding is used if internal competition, shelf space, and multiple market segments are desired.

When a separate brand name is assigned to each item in the product line rather than a common name for the entire line, the brand is an **individual brand.** International Shoe, Procter & Gamble, and Lever Brothers employ an individual branding strategy. Individual branding can be used successfully with dissimilar products.

Under the individual branding policy, one brand competes for sales with other brands in the organization. Executives prefer losing sales to another of their own brands rather than losing to a competitor. Retailer shelf space, which is so critical to the sale of consumer products, may be obtained more easily. Retailers frequently allocate shelf space on the basis of brands, so the more brands a company has, the more shelf space for its products.

A refinement of individual branding is the *multibrand* approach, when a corporation uses several brands for each market segment. For instance, Lever Brothers has Caress, Dove, Lifebuoy, and Lux bath soaps. The multibrand approach helps a company saturate the market. Each brand can be a different price, quality, and image level.

When a very successful brand serves as a basis for product innovations, a *brand extension* has occurred. Procter & Gamble extended its Tide brand laundry detergent and created liquid Tide.

QUALITY AND IMAGE DECISIONS

*S*electing quality level for a brand can make a difference.

In the initial stages of product and brand planning a quality level is determined. The quality of a brand cannot be an afterthought partly because it is difficult to change in production and in the minds of customers.[16] Based on market information, the quality level should be set before the product is introduced.

Image is partially determined by quality, and, like quality, it is difficult to change once it is established in the customer's mind. Like quality, image should be based on market information. What criteria do consumers use to evaluate a brand? The market is seldom narrow enough for one image to satisfy all. Procter & Gamble has Tide and Dreft brands because, among other reasons, a detergent like Tide—strong enough to clean tough stains from work clothing—is perceived as too harsh on more delicate clothing. Dreft has a more delicate image.

THE LICENSING DECISION

*L*icensing involves renting brands to others.

Occasionally a brand owner will find that the name itself is the valuable asset. In such situations the brander may decide to license the use of the brand name to other organizations. Many examples exist: Budweiser Beach Towels, E. T. shirts, and Cabbage Patch dolls. **Licensing** allows another firm to use the brand legally. Generally, a royalty for use is paid to the brand owner.

Source: © 1986 United Feature Syndicate, Inc.

*B*rands seem to be less important in the industrial market than in the consumer market, but Polaroid is sure to brand products intended for the industrial market. All of the issues are in favor of branding—product identification and the ability to maintain consistency of quality and resources to advertise. Indeed, the two products developed to date for that market have brand names. The selection process used to arrive at

THE CASE CONTINUES

Palette and Autoprocess were not made public. The two names do seem to have desirable characteristics. Palette (taken from the artist's palette) would connote the many possible colors and the artistic designs of computer graphics being captured on a slide. Even though Palette and Autoprocess identify the products, the Polaroid name proba-

bly will be prominently displayed. In effect, a combination of individual and family brand strategy is used. With the recent failure of Polarvision, executives at Polaroid must be concerned about the effect of a second product failure affecting Polaroid's good reputation. Because the industrial market also desires high quality, the association with the Polaroid name, not known for high quality in photography, may also be a mistake.

LABELING

*L*abels provide information to the customer.

Often thought of as a part of the package, **labels** provide information to the buyer and others, satisfy legal requirements, and help to identify the brand owner. The extent to which each of the purposes is served varies with the product. Bananas have a small brand sticker affixed to each bunch, for example, Chiquita. Eggs and many other products have a grade label in addition to brand and buyer information.

One of the most important purposes of labels is to provide information to the purchaser. Typical information includes content, instruction on use, warning of possible dangers, where to write or call for additional information or to lodge complaints, guarantees and warranties, and disposal of product and package instructions. The question in many a marketer's mind is how much and what information should be provided. Too little information may result in less than complete consumer satisfaction. Too much may simply be ignored.[17]

*U*PC provides information to the seller.

Retailers and distributors also benefit from label information. Initially, they do a better job of selling and keeping track of the product if the right information is provided. The Universal Product Code (UPC)—the familiar black and white bars on food packages—identifies the manufacturer and the specific product (brand, size, etc.). When read with a scanner, the UPC enables quick data entry into a computer. Once the code is entered, the computer matches the information identifying the product with previously stored information about it such as price and inventory. Flashing the price on the checkout screen for the consumer to see, the computer simultaneously reduces the inventory level by one unit. Retailers benefit from less labor cost in stocking shelves, better records on product turnover, and greater control over inventory. For consumers UPC means faster checkouts and fewer checkout errors. However, some consumers have resisted the use of scanners for UPC checkouts because the retailer may not price every item individually but only post the price on the shelf.[18] Consumers feel that having shelf prices alone leaves room for possible confusion, and they fear that a higher price will be charged at the checkout lane.

Legal Requirements

*W*hat information must the seller supply?

Several federal laws require specific information on certain types of products. The most noteworthy is the Fair Packaging and Labeling Act (1966). This act pertains primarily to cosmetics and kitchen items. Mandatory information on processed food

**Information on labels often
includes the brand, the
UPC, directions on use,
and for many products, a
list of ingredients.**

labels include ingredients and weight or volume information. Ingredients must be listed in order of their amount in the product—from most to least. As of July 1, 1985, sodium content had to be listed if the label disclosed other nutritional information. The act also encourages industries to design and adopt voluntary labeling standards. For example, the food industry might want to adopt standards on the use of the word *natural* because the Federal Trade Commission, the Food and Drug Administration, and the Department of Agriculture have not legally defined natural. Any food company is free to use the adjective to describe ingredients or a food production process.

Identification

The product's label should be eye-catching with good use of color, graphics, and photographs. The label can play an important role in making the organization's product unique and in selling it—a "silent salesperson."[19] Philip Morris Inc. considered legal action against British American Tobacco (BAT). Why? Because Philip Morris's cigarette package of their Brazilian brand Free features a red-and-blue stripe on a white background and a gold heraldic emblem. BAT's Galaxy brand has essentially the same package. The copycat Galaxy confuses the consumer, according to Philip Morris representatives.[20]

 PACKAGING

*T*he package serves as
more than simple product
protection.

A **package** is the container or wrapping of the product. Finding a container would seem to be an easy marketing task. Often, however, the package is more than a container; it can be a reason for buying the product. For example, Avon Products, Inc. has successfully sold after-shave lotion and other products in unique bottles. Since the company periodically changes bottle design, the bottles have become collectors' items, with many collectors buying directly from Avon. The marketer can depend on the package to make the product unique, differentiate it from competitors, and attract the buyer's attention. The Jack Daniels distillery uses a square bottle for its bourbon so the consumer can distinguish it even in the dark from other bourbon bottles that are round.

Good Package Design

Packages, as already indicated, may serve multiple functions. No single package has to incorporate all of the functions at the same time. What makes a good package depends upon the target market, the environment, and the objectives of the firm. In particular, the package functions are important in determining a good design. The package functions are referred to collectively as the package concept.

Packaging serves five basic functions. First, and most important, it must protect the product. Many university design and engineering classes have as class assignments the design of a package that will protect a fragile product under specified conditions. For instance, students must design a package using less than five cents worth of material that will protect an egg from damage in a fall of twenty feet onto a concrete floor. Such assignments are informative and good learning experiences but fail to match the varying conditions under which most packages must protect the product. The package may have to protect the product during shipment, storage, stocking, and use (after opening and closing) as well as protect from moisture and temperature changes.

Whoever hatched up the egg was indeed a Great Creator, but he didn't know the first thing about packaging. One look at the egg will tell you he believed—like all package designers and manufacturers—that packages are designed for products.

Well, that's scrambled thinking. Packages really should be designed for consumers. Of course, the package must preserve and protect its product. But ideally, packaging is positioning. A great package positions and promotes its product to a specific, targeted consumer segment.

Now let's take a hard-boiled look at the sad and sorry package that is the egg.

All in all, eggs have a thoroughly bad image. Eggs are obsolete, marketing-wise.

We can forgive the Great Creator His mistake. After all, Modern Marketing Research didn't exist back then. Segmentation studies and delta matrices and multidimensional perceptual mapping hadn't been invented. It's no wonder the egg is not the package it's cracked up to be. But put *today's* top package designers to work, and look what happens to the old-fashioned egg!

Now *that's* great packaging in an eggshell.

MARKETING IN ACTION

Egg-o-Mania

❏ A package designer can suggest changes and improvements even for the egg, a great package.

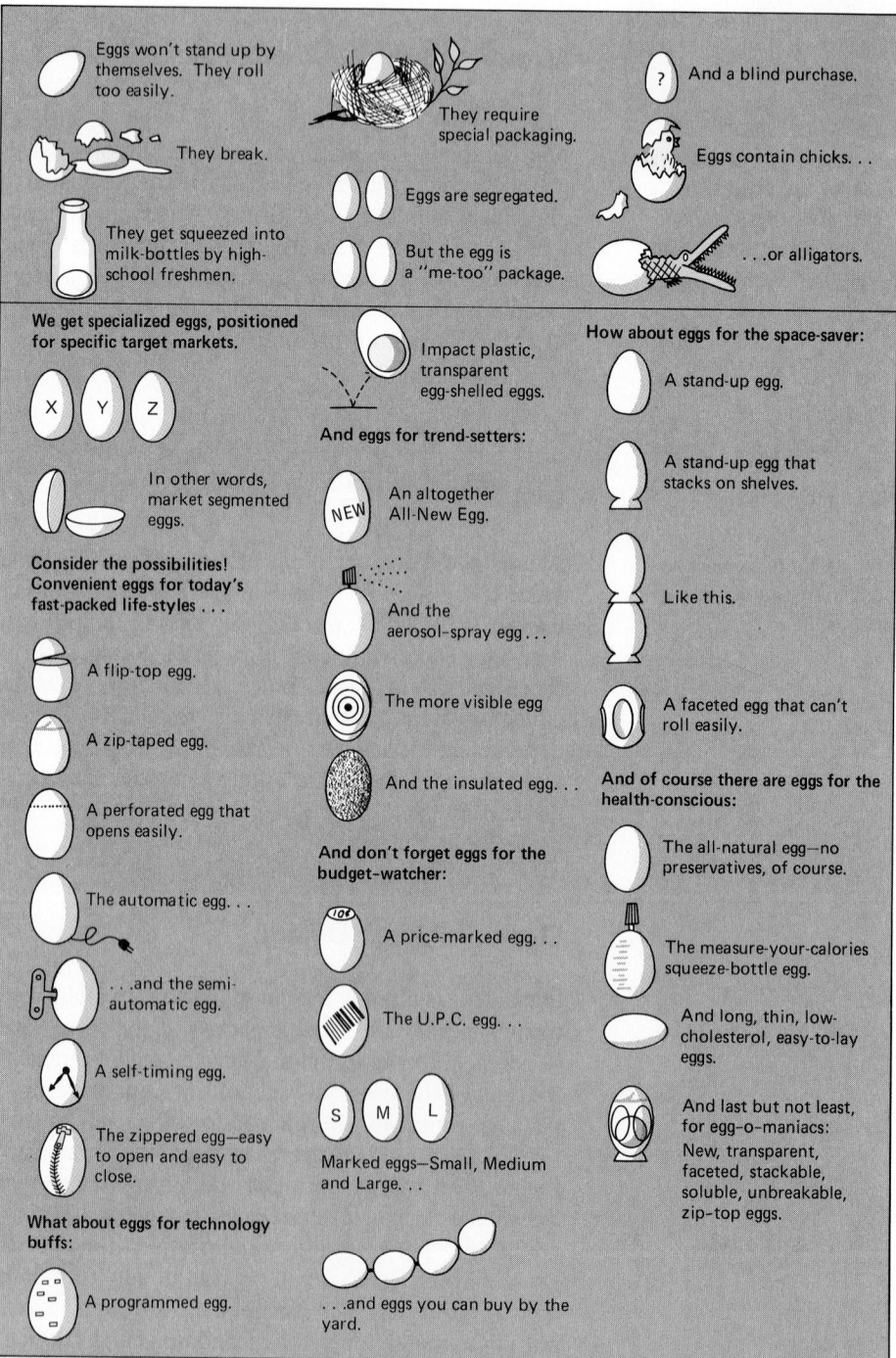

Source: Artwork originally created and drawn by Robert Pliskin, The First Team Inc., New York, N.Y.

*T*he package must serve wholesalers, retailers, and consumers.

Second, the package should help sell the product. As the product moves through the channel of distribution, the package must help sell it at each stage—to the wholesaler, retailer, and consumer. From the retailer's point of view the package and information should enable the consumer to purchase without sales help. The package should prevent shoplifting (e.g., blister packages for small valuable items). The package should shelf, stock, and store easily in a minimum amount of space. Consumers are interested in size, shape, color, material, and ability to examine or see the product. Consumer advocates emphasize the visibility of the product as an important aspect of the package. The Canadian method of packaging bacon with one strip fully visible is said to be preferred to the U.S. method, where strips overlap and only the lean is visible. If the package is to help sell the product, it must help establish and maintain the desired image of the product.

*E*ven for ketchup, the package is important.

Heinz marketers, for instance, realized that ketchup users evaluate ketchup quality by thickness. The Heinz advertising slogan, "The slowest ketchup in the West," was verified by demonstrating Heinz ketchup against other brands oozing through coffee filters and dribbling down plates. Consumers have to shake, whack, and coax Heinz ketchup from its glass container. An inconvenient container—an apparent marketing nightmare—actually enhanced the image of the brand.[21] In short, the package needs to be compatible with the rest of the marketing mix.

The third function of packaging is economy, that is the package should be economical in the sense that it satisfactorily completes all functions expected of it at minimum cost. Considering packaging cost alone and not total distribution costs is normally a mistake. Low package cost may be offset by higher shipping, storing, and sorting costs, and by more damage to the product.

*S*afety and ecology are a part of the package design.

Fourth, a package should be convenient, especially for the consumer. It should be convenient to open and close, to handle in use, to store, and to discard. The plastic containers of most liquid dish detergents are a good example. Ivory Liquid dish detergent is sold in a plastic container. If dropped, it will not break. Slightly constricted in the middle, the container will not slip out of soapy hands. A slight pull on the top opens the container and a push closes it. The plastic does not leave a rust stain on counter tops or fall apart if dropped in water. Its upright design requires little storage space, yet a slightly larger base than top gives it stability.

"Say good-bye to America's favorite can of motor oil," a recent advertisement of Quaker State trumpeted. Quaker State is changing to plastic bottles because the do-it-yourself consumer prefers the convenience of plastic bottles.

The fifth function a package should perform is that it should meet social concerns. Product safety continues to be a major concern of society. Childproof and pilferage-free containers for drugs and foods have become a necessity. Clearly distinguishable packages for different types of products to avoid mistaken use are also a concern. Other societal concerns include excessive use of packaging materials, thereby needlessly depleting natural resources; excessively costly packaging, making many products too expensive for people of lower incomes; deceptiveness in packaging (e.g., half-full containers); and the health and environmental hazards created by improper disposal of packages. It should be pointed out that a package is not absolutely necessary, at least not for all products. The sale of unpackaged foods—bulk foods—was common at one time. There has been renewed interest in the purchase of some items without packages.[22] Products of particular interest for bulk purchase include dog food, grains, nuts, and sugar.

Developing a Good Package Design

*R*esearch is the only way to design a good package.

After the package concept is determined, marketers will either develop themselves or have a package design specialist develop several alternative designs. The best of the alternatives will be prototyped. Each prototype will be subjected to a series of tests: engineering tests to determine protective ability, ability to withstand wear and tear, ease of fill, and cost; consumer tests to determine how consumers open and close, handle, store, and dispose of the package; visual tests to determine how quickly the product is recognized, its uniqueness, and the image it conveys. Based on the tests, a design will be chosen.

Other Packaging Decisions

There are some advantages to packaging the entire product line in the same basic package. Economies in materials and packaging machinery are achieved. Product line packaging has more visual impact on the consumer, and it allows the product line to dominate shelf space. Campbell Soup Company, for instance, packages all of its canned soup in essentially the same container so a shopper walking down the grocery aisle sees a mass of red and white labels.

*C*onvenient multipacks sell more products.

Multiple packaging can sell more products. Twin, tri, quad, and six packs are naturals for selling some products. Automobile spark plugs frequently are individually wrapped and multiple packed using the number of motor cylinders to determine the number of plugs in the multiple package.

Will the package be designed for reuse? Some packages like soft drink bottles are designed for reuse as a container for the same product. Other packages are designed for secondary use. Kindergarten, day care, and church school staffs are especially creative at finding secondary uses for packaging materials as artwork or gifts for Mom and Dad. Many secondary uses are unintended, but some are designed into the package.

*"P*aper bottles" are another example of technology improving packaging.

The frequency of package change is also a factor in package management. Changes in the product or in promotional strategy may be sufficient reason for redesigning the package. Changes in packaging materials and technology also offer reasons to change the package. The aseptic "paper bottle" consists of aluminum foil between laminates of paperboard and plastic, using new technology to create an airtight container. The paper bottle is less expensive to make and fill than cans and bottles. The product does not have to be refrigerated, extending the shelf life up to six months. Consumers have readily accepted the paper bottles for fruit drinks such as Hi-C and Capri Sun because they are convenient. There is some question, however, whether consumers will accept the paper bottle as a milk container.

When the package loses its effectiveness as a sales aid, change is almost essential. Avon changes its packages regularly. Avon executives realize that the package may be as much a part of the purchase decision as the product itself.

The manufacturer of Capri Sun fruit drinks uses aseptic packages as the basis of a marketing strategy.

The Tylenol package addresses many of society's package concerns, especially safety.

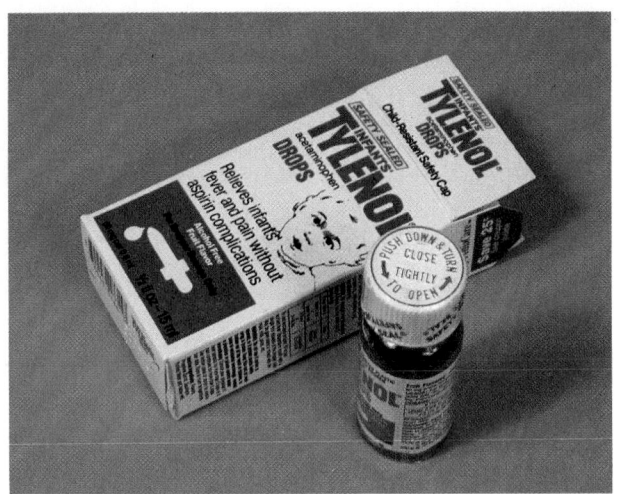

 PRODUCT SAFETY AND WARRANTIES

*P*roducts should safely satisfy the need for which they were made.

Consumers rightfully expect products to function properly and fulfill the needs and purposes for which they were promoted and purchased. Likewise, consumers expect products to be safe.

Product Safety

Safe products and safe use of products is the desired goal. If a product is unsafe, ascertaining responsibility only establishes fault. Retribution based on determination of liability may compensate for damages, but it does not correct them. Designing safe products, very much a marketing concern, has been an elusive goal. Childproof medicine containers have been effective in reducing the number of child poisonings but have also been described as peopleproof. Air bags in cars seem to increase safety, but their installation may drive the price of cars up substantially. Although some disagreement exists on the definition of safe products, safety should be designed and manufactured into a product wherever possible. The package and label should be designed to reduce accidental and incorrect use. Warnings and instructions for correct use should be prominently displayed. Manufacturers and marketers do have product liability—responsibility for injuries and damages caused by their products.

Warranties and Guarantees

*W*arranty is protection against malfunction.

A **warranty** is an assurance that a product is not defective or will not malfunction during a specified period of time. Warranties are considered a part of the product under the total product concept. For consumers, warranties reduce both monetary and nonmonetary purchase risk. Warranties also establish the product's integrity in the consumer's mind.

Holiday Inns Inc. found that offering a money-back **guarantee** on accommodations helped improve its service and helped gain a second chance with unhappy customers. A guarantee is a company's commitment that it will compensate customers if they are dissatisfied with a product or service. Holiday Inn promotes the warranty program with the advertising slogan, "No excuses, guaranteed."[23]

The 7-70 warranty, one more reason why a consumer should purchase a Chrysler product, according to Chrysler representatives. No other auto manufacturer offers a warranty for as long.

Legally, written warranties must be easy to read and understand.

In consumer surveys warranties have ranked near the bottom of the list of purchase considerations. Still, many retailers do a brisk business in extended warranties sold separately—Sears, for example. A warranty may be the deciding difference in a purchase decision when two brands seem physically alike.

The confusion and deceptive practices surrounding warranties led to the passage of the **Magnuson-Moss Warranty Act** (1975). The act empowered the Federal Trade Commission to regulate written warranty practices of products costing more than $15. The producers or sellers do not have to offer written warranties, but if they do, the Magnuson-Moss Act specifies that they must be easy to read and understand,[24] they must be available for inspection before purchase, and an informal consumer complaint procedure must be established. The warranty itself must indicate whether it is a full or limited warranty, who the warrantor is, what is covered in the warranty (the total item or specified parts), whether the warranty is to repair or replace, and if it includes labor.[25] The obligations of the purchaser must also be specified. The decision to provide a warranty is a marketing strategy decision.[26] It depends on the total concept of the product developed by the organization. The warranty decision should be clearly communicated to the target market and to the organization's personnel.[27]

A cassette tape explaining the warranty and maintenance schedule is presented to buyers of new Cadillacs, and Armstrong World Industries prints an 800 toll-free number on the surface of its floor coverings. When the customer calls Armstrong to find out how to remove it, a representative gives instructions on how to keep the floor cover under warranty as well as how to remove the phone number.

THE CASE CONTINUES

*T*he total product concept that marketing-oriented companies use means that labeling, packaging, and warranties are thought of as part of the product. They are emphasized more in the consumer market but must also be considered in the industrial market. Since Polaroid executives made a decision to make Autoprocess compatible with other producers' 35mm cameras, packaging especially becomes important. Polaroid's package must compete on the retailer's shelf with other brands.

The package for both Autoprocess and Palette equipment needs to protect the product, as all packages must. In the industrial market, product protection may be even more important. For film sold in the industrial market, the label with appropriate instructions on use and disposal are especially important, since the incorrect use of the product may result in

damage to the user's product or service. Clear instructions for use of Palette and Autoprocess must make each "user friendly." Labels attached to the products should make all switches and processes self-explanatory. Warranties are also important to Polaroid in the industrial market. Again, because the user may have considerably more at stake in gained or lost business, warranties accompanied with reliable and quick service enter in the purchaser's product decision.

GOAL SUMMARY

1. **Define the total product concept.** In this chapter we have seen that a product is more than a physical item. It may include the package, label, warranty, and more. In fact, a physical item may not be present at all; the product may be a service or even a concept.

2. **Explain product line and mix.** Seldom does a firm sell a single product item. Usually several products are offered. When the product items are grouped into categories based on similarities of the product, the categories are referred to as lines. All product lines together comprise the product mix.

3. **Discuss the importance of product classification schemes as they relate to market plans.** An infinite number of possible product strategies exist. To provide a marketer with a set of guidelines to limit the possible strategies being considered, products have been categorized. Examples: consumer goods and industrial goods.

4. **Distinguish between consumer and industrial goods.** The classification into consumer and industrial categories is based on how the good is used: if for pleasure, a consumer good exists, and if for producing an industrial good exists. Consumer and industrial goods are marketed differently.

5. **List the categories of industrial goods.** Industrial goods have been grouped into seven categories based on the product's use and behavior of purchaser at time of purchase. Supplies do not become a part of the product nor are they involved directly in the production of the product. Raw materials become a part of the product after considerable processing; when purchased they exist in the unprocessed state. Processed materials are used directly in the production of a good or service but do not become a part of it. Component parts become a part of the finished product; however, they have been processed before purchase. (The purchasing firm may have only to assemble them into a finished product.) Accessory equipment facilitates an organization's operation and production of products. Installations are major capital production equipment and are directly employed in production. Services consist of intangibles needed by a firm. Examples: janitorial and legal.

6. **Discuss the role of branding and packaging as they relate to product strategy.** Brands are a way of identifying a good with a particular seller—the brand owner. Branding, when successful, leads to repeat purchases. Once customers become familiar with a brand, they can have some confidence that the quality level will be consistent from one purchase to the next. Some sellers do not brand because of the inability to control quality, and some think too much promotion is required. Branding has been criticized for increasing the price. The decision to brand means several other decisions have to be made, including quality level and the employment of family or individual brands. Packages are needed to protect some items. They also may help to sell the item. Users of an item may look for a convenient-to-use package in making a purchase. Economically, packages have an impact. Manufacturers spend millions of dollars on packaging equipment and materials each year. The cost of the package is a major consideration to the manufacturer in package selection. Society is also concerned about the expense and safety of packages.

7. **Explain warranties from a consumer's and a marketer's viewpoint.** Even with a good physical product, a good brand, an excellent package, an informative label, some potential purchasers need assurances of product reliability. Warranties, when clearly written and communicated, can provide assurance. The Magnuson-Moss Act regulates warranty use.

   It should be clear that as a marketer, you have to work with the total product concept.

KEY TERMS

KEY TERMS *(continued)*

CHECK YOUR LEARNING

1. A product as defined by most marketers would be: (a) a physical item, (b) a bundle of customer satisfaction, (c) a brand, package, and warranty, (d) a physical item plus service.

2. The product mix: (a) means the ingredients that go into the product, (b) includes the product item but not the product line, (c) consists of all the products and services offered by an organization, (d) contains products that are closely related.

3. Which of the following lists is most likely to be considered as consisting of all convenience goods? (a) milk, gasoline, emergency car service, and vegetables, (b) milk, dishes, emergency road services, and frozen vegetables, (c) dishes, milk, and frozen vegetables, (d) milk, gasoline, frozen vegetables, and dishes.

4. In the industrial goods category: (a) goods are used for the purpose of providing pleasure or satisfaction to the ultimate consumer, (b) demand depends upon the demand for other goods and services, (c) promotion depends less on personal selling than in the consumer goods category.

5. In the marketing of component parts: (a) reliability of supply is not a factor since the purchaser buys from several suppliers, (b) identifying the producer on the part is futile, as the part becomes unidentifiable in the finished product, (c) price is unimportant, (d) consistency of quality is essential.

6. In the purchase of installations: (a) price is unimportant if the bottom line looks good, (b) status conveyed by the product is unimportant, (c) the buyer prefers to work with a wholesaler rather than the manufacturer, (d) the decision is normally made by the purchasing agent.

7. A brand: (a) is the same as a brand name, (b) with legal protection is called a trade mark, service mark, or trade name, (c) gives the organization something to promote, (d) both b and c are correct.

8. Branding proponents believe customers' benefits include: (a) assurance of top quality, (b) greater shopping efficiency, (c) assurance of top quality but at higher prices, (d) both a and b above, (e) both b and c above.

9. A national brand: (a) is distributed throughout the United States, (b) is owned by large national distributors, e.g., Sears and Kmart, (c) is promoted more heavily than a private brand, (d) if low-priced and intended to compete with the private brand, is called a fighting brand, (e) allows the retailer more control over product image, availability, price, and quality.

10. In selecting a brand name: (a) the person who conceived the product idea will usually have the best suggestion for a brand name, (b) the more unique the name, the easier it will be to protect, (c) the primary criterion should be that it is easy to remember, (d) none of the above are correct.

11. The five objectives of good package design are: (a) convenience, protection, societal concern, sellability, and economy, (b) convenience, protection, societal concern, storage, and visibility, (c) societal concern, storage, economy, convenience, and accessibility, (d) all of the lists are incorrect.

12. Product safety: (a) from a marketing point of view, emphasizes what should be done after an unsafe incident has occurred, (b) is usually lacking because of misuse by consumers; therefore, product liability lies with the consumer, (c) can be improved by product, package, and label design, (d) all of the above.

13. The Magnuson-Moss Warranty Act: (a) requires manufacturers to provide written warranties, (b) requires the manufacturer to establish a formal consumer complaint procedure, (c) covers only full warranties, (d) specifies that the warrantor must clearly state what is covered in the warranty.

QUESTIONS FOR REVIEW AND DISCUSSION

1. Define the key terms for this chapter that appear at the end of the goal summary.
2. Describe a total product.
3. Distinguish between a product item, line, and mix.
4. Give two examples each of industrial and consumer goods.
5. Highlight the features of a marketing mix for a shopping, convenience, and specialty good.
6. What consumer behavior would be expected of a person interested in purchasing a shopping good, for example a man's suit?
7. Select the best industrial goods category for the following goods: wheat, a robotic controlled arc welder, marketing research, transistors, cutting oil, and thumb tacks and paper clips.
8. Discuss the benefits of brand names to the customer.
9. What conditions would tend to discourage an organization from branding a product?
10. Identify some of the policy decisions with regard to branding once the decision to brand has been made.
11. Take a label from a product that you have purchased recently. What functions does the label serve? How well does it serve the functions of a label?
12. Find two packages, one that you think is especially good and one that you think is especially bad. Evaluate each, telling why you like or dislike it as a package.
13. What are the legal requirements of warranties from the marketer's perspective of product safety?

NOTES

1. Lawrence Ring, Derek Newton, Neil Borden, and E. Ralph Biggadike, *Decisions in Marketing* (Plano, Texas: Business Publications, Inc., 1984), p. 291.
2. Earl L. Bailey, ed., *Product Line Strategies,* The Conference Board, New York Report No. 816, 1982, pp. 6–23.
3. Marvin A. Jolson and Stephen L. Proia, "Classification of Consumer Goods—A Subjective Measure?" *Marketing: 1776–1976 and Beyond* (Chicago: AMA Association, 1976), pp. 71–75.
4. Philip Kotler, *Marketing Essentials* (Englewood Cliffs, N.J.: Prentice-Hall, Inc., 1984), p. 189.
5. E. Jerome McCarthy and William D. Perrault, Jr., *Basic Marketing,* 8th ed. (Homewood, Ill.: Richard D. Irwin, 1984), p. 293.
6. McCarthy and Perrault, *Basic Marketing,* p. 294.
7. J. Morgan Jones and Fred S. Ziefryden, "An Approach for Assessing Demographic and Price Influences on Brand Purchase Behavior," *Journal of Marketing* (Winter 1982), pp. 36–46.
8. *Committee on Definitions, Marketing Definitions: A Glossary of Marketing Terms* (Chicago: American Marketing Association, 1960), pp. 8–10.
9. K. L. Granzin, "An Investigation of the Market for Generic Products," *Journal of Retailing* (Winter 1981): pp. 39–55.
10. Robert H. Ross and Frederic B. Kraft, "Creating Low Consumer Product Expectations," *Journal of Business Research* (March 1983), pp. 1–9.
11. K. B. Rotzall, C. H. Patti, and R. P. Fisk, "Store Brand and National Advertiser: A Historical Perspective with Contemporary Options," *Journal of the Academy of Marketing Sciences* (Winter/Spring 1982): pp. 146–155.
12. Joseph A. Bellizzi, Harry F. Krueckeberg, John R. Hamilton, and Warren S. Martin, "Consumer Perceptions of National, Private and Generic Brands," *Journal of Retailing* (Winter 1981): pp. 56–70.
13. James U. McNeal and Linda M. Zeren, "Brand Name Selection for Consumer Products," *MSU Business Topics* (Spring 1981): pp. 35–39.
14. "A Worldwide Brand for Nissan," *Business Week,* August 24, 1981, p. 104.
15. Edward M. Tauber, "Brand Franchise Extension: New Product Benefits from Existing Brand Names," *Business Horizons,* March–April 1981, pp. 36–41.
16. Carl McDaniel and R. C. Baker, "Convenience Food Packaging and the Perception of Product Quality," *Journal of Marketing* (October 1977): pp. 57–58.
17. Dennis L. McNeill and William L. Wilkie, "Public Policy and Consumer Information: Impact of the New Energy Labels," *Journal of Consumer Research* 6 (June 1979): pp. 1–11; and John A. Miller, "Labeling Research: The State of the Art," *Marketing Science Institute* (Cambridge, Massachusetts: Report No. 78–115, 1978).
18. Frederick W. Langrehr and Virginia B. Langrehr, "Shoppers' Acceptance of Item Price Removal: A Trend and Store Type Analysis," *AMA Educators' Proceedings* (Patrick E. Murphy et al. eds.), 1983, pp. 231–235.

NOTES *(continued)*

19. George Miaoulis and Nancy D'Amato, "Consumer Confusion and Trademark Infringement," *Journal of Marketing* (April 1978), pp. 48–49.

20. Laurel Wentz, "Philip Morris May Sue BAT in Brazil," *Advertising Age,* April 23, 1984, p. 55.

21. Betsy Morris, "Thwack! Smack! Sounds Thrill Makers of Hunt's Ketchup," *The Wall Street Journal,* April 27, 1984, p. 1.

22. Linda Savage Ruhe, "The Battle of the Bulk," *Advertising Age,* May 3, 1984, p. 39.

23. John Koten, "Aggressive Use of Warranties Is Benefitting Many Concerns," *The Wall Street Journal,* April 5, 1984, p. M44.

24. John C. Lehman, L. Lee Manzer, James W. Gentry, and Hal W. Ellis, "The Readability of Warranties," in John C. Crawford and James Lumpkin eds., *Proceedings of the Southwest Marketing Association, 1983,* pp. 19–22.

25. Robert E. Wilkes, "Limited Versus Full Warranties: The Retail Perspective," *Journal of Retailing* (Spring 1981): pp. 65–77.

26. Fred W. Morgan, "Marketing and Product Liability: A Review and Upgrade," *Journal of Marketing* (Summer 1982), pp. 69–78; and Karl A. Boedecker and Fred W. Morgan, "The Channel Implications of Product Liability Developments," *Journal of Retailing* (Winter 1980): pp. 59–72.

27. C. L. Kendall and Frederick A. Russ, "Warranty and Complaint Policies: An Opportunity for Marketing Management," *Journal of Marketing* (April 1975): pp. 36–43.

*C*ampbell Soup Company is the nation's third largest manufacturer of cans. It has been selling soup in cans carrying the red-and-white label with gold medallion, the cherished corporate symbol, since 1897. The company promotes canned soup in general rather than Campbell's brand. Campbell controls 80 percent of the canned soup market, and private-label brands manufactured by H. J. Heinz Co. control 10 percent.

Campbell executives have decided to phase out the tin soup can. "The can isn't as user friendly as it used to be," states Anthony Adams, Campbell's director of marketing research.

As sold by Campbell, soup is not just the physical item, but also includes the package, brand, and label. Before Mr. McGovern, Campbell's president and chairman, took over, Campbell emphasized products compatible with existing production facilities, an approach that produced sluggish profits. Campbell's decision to develop a new package reflects an emphasis for providing customer satisfaction by knowing and meeting consumer preferences.

Campbell executives do not want to do anything to change consumers' routine for buying soup. They don't want to muck up that good, solid, conservative image consumers and retailers have grown to rely upon. Offering a dud package as a substitute for the tin can could be disastrous.

In changing from the can as a container, Campbell would expect to make a large investment in new installation goods. Revamping production facilities could cost $100 million or more. The change would also likely mean the raw and processed materials purchased by Campbell would change from those needed to make a tin can to those needed to produce some other type container.

Currently the company uses a family brand policy with all canned soup bearing the Campbell trade name. Any miscues on packaging may influence sales negatively on the whole line of soups. Campbell is also interested in attracting a new market—people who have shunned canned soup, particularly convenience-minded singles. Many young consumers associate cans with preservatives and artificial ingredients. A new brand name may reach the young market more efficiently. Attitudes concerning cans are hard to dispel. Since Campbell, not just the can, may be associated with the attitude, a new brand may be appropriate.

Packaging objectives of protection, societal concerns, economy, sales, and convenience are important to Campbell. Convenience, however, bears special concern. The major competitive advantage of a can's extended shelf life has been eroded by technological advances.

Plastic is now nearly impervious to air. A can of soup now seems inconvenient. The consumer must use a can opener, mix the condensed soup with water, heat the mixture, and then clean several utensils.

A leading contender of possible containers, a plastic microwavable bowl capped by an easy-open top, has fared well with consumers in a San Francisco test market.

Aseptic packages, also, present a number of advantages over cans and possibly will dominate the market in the future. Another possible successor to the metal soup can is a plastic container shaped just like a metal can.

Issues for Discussion
1. As a convenience good producer, what marketing consideration do Campbell executives have to keep in mind?
2. Do you think Campbell should market soup in a new container under a different brand name?
3. What factors should Campbell have considered in the decision to change to a new package?
4. Establish a list of criteria for Campbell to use in deciding on what package to use.

OUTLINE

CHAPTER

9

Managing
the Product

LEARNING GOALS_____

After reading this chapter, you should be able to:

1. Describe the stages in the product life cycle (PLC).
2. Discuss the product life cycle as it relates to marketing management.
3. Describe the new product development process and each of its stages.
4. Recognize the importance of the adoption and diffusion processes and be able to distinguish between them.
5. Identify the organizational forms developed for new product management.

*B*lack & Decker, a noted marketer of products for the do-it-yourself market, acquired the General Electric Company's small home appliance business in 1985 for $300 million. B&D had enjoyed a 50 percent market share in the worldwide market for power tools, but the recession of the early 1980s and competition, especially from the Japanese, forced changes in manufacturing and marketing at B&D and led to the GE acquisition. Makita of Japan, for instance, offered competitive power tools at a lower price, and in a very short time its market share was nearly equal to B&D's.

B&D executives realized that the company could not stand still and ride on past successes. In 1982 B&D lost $77 million, primarily due to the sale and write-off of McCullough chain saws. Losses had increased to $158.4 million in 1985 with plant shutdowns and other cost-saving measures, but then swung back to a 1987 profit of $55.6 million. The profits came about in part due to the closing of six plants and the elimination of 2,000 jobs, and the simultaneous turnaround in power tool sales.

The GE acquisition allowed B&D to combine its technical and manufacturing abilities—mainly in motor design and cordless appliances—with GE's sales and distribution know-how. One hundred household appliances from GE were added to B&D's 500 products to make up the B&D product mix. Executives believe the B&D brand name is strong enough to support almost any consumer gadget, but retailers are not so sure. The GE name has been an asset in selling at the retail level, but will a woman buy a B&D mixer? The Dustbuster Cordless vacuum sweeper, however, has been very successful for B&D. Still, B&D is known in the hardware, not in the houseware, sections of most stores.

B&D has designed a hair dryer for men—men know the B&D name.

However, research indicates that there is also high name recognition among women. Four models of the hair dryer called Black Tie have been test-marketed. More new products—in both the power tool and small appliance divisions—are to be developed and backed by extensive advertising. The GE acquisition helped accelerate B&D's new product development. In the past, the marketing of household appliances assumed a short life cycle: designed to do a specific job, produced in large volume, promoted extensively but briefly, and then ignored. B&D is out to break this mold.

Issues for Discussion
1. Black & Decker management seems to be emphasizing the development of new products. Why do you think a profitable firm would be so interested in new products?
2. How can B&D increase the probability that the consumer will buy its new small appliance products?
3. If you were in charge of B&D, how would you organize B&D for product management?

Sources: Joseph Weber and Laurie Brann, "Black and Decker Sees a Perfect Fit," *Businessweek,* February 8, 1988, p. 27; Christopher S. Eklund, "How Black and Decker Got Back in the Black," *Business Week,* July 13, 1987, pp. 86, 90; Francine Schwadel, "Black and Decker's New Ideas Include Men's Hair Dryers," *The Wall Street Journal,* September 14, 1984.

■ Black & Decker's cordless electric mixer—one of hundreds of small home appliances the company hopes will be used in the home.
Source: Photo courtesy of The Black & Decker Corporation

Black & Decker executives have developed a successful company with successful products. They realize, however, that products do not last forever—the product life cycle forces decisions upon management. In the pages ahead we will examine the product life cycle and discuss the marketing decisions managers must make due to this cycle. The consumer power tool market, Black & Decker's primary market, has reached saturation. Many products in the market have reached maturity. Technology and competition reduce market share for even the best products and new products have to be developed to meet the needs of changing markets. We will see how products are developed, concluding with a discussion of both product adoption and product diffusion. ■

INTRODUCTION

*T*iming is a big part of product management.

This chapter is about product management, but by necessity it also considers the dimension of time. All variables of the marketing mix have a time dimension, but time is especially important in product management. International Business Machines, Communication Satellite Corporation, and Aetna Life and Casualty, the partners in a firm called Satellite Business Communications, have invested over a billion dollars in the firm but have not seen a profit and may not for many years. Satellite business systems technology is said to be too far ahead of the market's needs.[1] Some patterns and cycles have been identified that make managing products less difficult.

THE PRODUCT LIFE CYCLE

A product passes through a series of stages while on the market.

The **product life cycle** refers to stages a product progresses through while on the market. The time period required for the product to move through all the stages is the product's life. The start of the first stage is the introduction of the product to the market, its birth, followed by growth, maturity, decline, and finally its death. In each stage the level of product acceptance and purchases by customers in a market changes. The life cycle concept is applied to whole classes of products, product forms, or designs, and to individual brands.

The measure of a product's age or its position in the life cycle depends on three variables: time, sales, and profit.[2] (See figure 9.1.) Sales are determined by other variables such as the market served and the competition. Likewise, profit is influenced by cost and other variables.

The marketing mix will usually need to be adapted to each stage of the product life cycle. The target market, competition, and even environmental conditions change as the product passes through the life cycle.

❑ **Figure 9.1**
Product life cycle
stages.

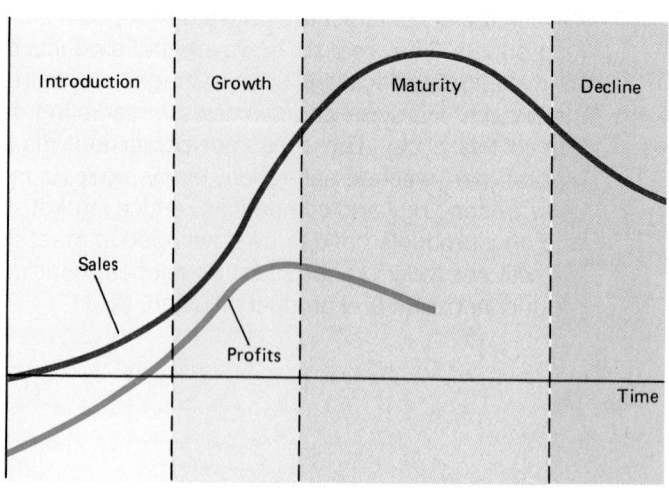

Stages of the Product Life Cycle

Four stages have been identified in life-cycle theory: introduction, growth, maturity, and decline. (See figure 9.1.)

*S*ales volume determines the stage in the product life cycle.

The movement of a product from one stage to the next depends more on sales trends than time. One product may pass through the growth stage very quickly, for instance, Cabbage Patch dolls and other toys; another, such as TV sets, may require years.

INTRODUCTORY STAGE

The **introductory stage** begins when the new product first becomes available for sale, and it ends when sales start to increase rapidly. An example of a product/ service in the introductory stage is videotext. Videotext is computer-to-computer communication that allows consumers to shop, pay bills, make reservations, and leave messages via their computers. Several conditions typify this stage: (1) sales are low because the product is new, and most consumers are unaware of its existence; (2) undetected technical and marketing problems may surface; (3) losses are much more likely to occur than profits; (4) costs are high in relation to revenue because of research and development, initial marketing, and other start-up costs.

*I*ntroductory stage objective—stimulation of demand.

In the introductory stage management must be future-oriented and willing to assume risk. A product that is unproven in the market requires large expenditures to secure distribution because retailers are concerned about volume, margins, and promotional support of the product. Promotional expenses are also high because the product's merits and benefits must get widespread exposure to establish customer awareness. In the introductory stage the price of the product is high in hopes of offsetting the risk by speeding recovery of dollars invested. The most important objective in this stage is stimulating demand for the product.

The length of time the product stays in the introductory stage varies with the product. Expensive, complex, and uniquely new products stay in the introductory stage a longer time. Products like Crest with tartar control formula, however, which are low in cost, easy to use, and require little change in purchasing and usage habits, pass through this stage rapidly.

GROWTH STAGE

*G*rowth stage objectives—meet demand and prepare for competition.

The **growth stage** is marked by rapidly increasing industry sales. The robotics industry, which develops robots to perform tasks, is now in the growth stage in the

United States. The first company to put a product on the market will usually dominate the market in the growth stage, especially if it has developed a strong marketing strategy in the introductory stage.

Demand may be so strong in the growth stage that shortages of the product actually develop. Buoyed by demand, profits increase well into the growth stage, but even though firms welcome this development, it can cause them to overextend capacity and to fail to control costs—both expensive strategic errors. Enticed by favorable profit margins, competitors enter the market and expand production capacity. High profits cause firms already in the market to expand capacity as well. Eventually, capacity overtakes demand, and firms are left to cover their fixed capital investments in the face of steady or even shrinking demand for the product. At this point, profits peak and begin to decline.

Consider the example of high technology home health care, a service item that provides care of seriously ill patients outside the hospital with complicated treatments such as intravenous therapies. Profit margins before taxes are reported to be as high as 25 percent, and the industry's annual growth rate is nearly 40 percent. Still, industry analysts predict that many firms will fail because there are too few patients to support all the companies in the market.[3]

When production capacity outstrips demand and competition becomes intense, companies respond by reducing prices and improving the quality of their product. They also seek new markets and new channels of distribution. All of these efforts require them to improve their marketing techniques. In an attempt to obtain brand loyalty, promotional campaigns can stress the uniqueness of the firm's brand. To erode brand loyalty to other firm's products, companies can stress product similarity and a lower price. Total industry dollars spent on promotion remain relatively stable throughout the growth stage. As a percentage of sales, however, promotion declines because sales are increasing.

MATURITY STAGE

*M*aturity stage objectives—contain cost and increase or maintain market share.

Industry sales grow slowly at the beginning, peak, and then start to decline in the **maturity stage.** The consequences of the decision to expand capacity made in the growth stage are most likely to occur during this period. As competitive pressures intensify, the weaker firms in the market may drop out or merge. However, the well-entrenched and well-managed firms remain very profitable. Product managers keep a close eye on the product, the marketing mix, and the environment. Since most products on the market are in the maturity stage, most marketing managers work with mature products. Cost containment must be emphasized since much of the revenue generated will be used to support the development of new products and to offset losses of products in the introductory stage.

Growth in sales has to be achieved by increasing market share, since industry sales have leveled off. Even though the best product features and customer appeals have already been discovered, competitors and the firm itself continue efforts to come up with fresh promotional and product features. For instance, in addition to emphasizing that its vinegar is 100 percent natural, Heinz U.S.A. recently started a campaign to promote Heinz vinegar to clean automatic drip coffee makers. Differences among brands often diminish, however, and customers may perceive little difference. Psychological image and style differences are emphasized as the functional differences diminish. Some manufacturers sell private or distributor labels along with the generic products to increase sales.

DECLINE STAGE

*D*ecline stage objective—adjust to decreasing sales volume

In the **decline stage** sales for the industry continue the downward movement that began in the maturity stage. Sales may move downward very slowly or drop precipitously. Social trends, governmental regulation, advances in technology, and

Even with a seemingly mundane product such as vinegar, awareness of product differences can alter the consumer's purchase decision. Heinz executives think consumers are more inclined to purchase a natural vinegar, Heinz's brand.

PICK THE VINEGAR THAT ISN'T MADE FROM PETROLEUM.

It may sound incredible, but the fact is, many other white vinegars start with petroleum. That's right. Petroleum.

But not Heinz.

For over 110 years the Heinz recipe for vinegar has been 100% natural. Our white vinegar is made from sun-ripened corn. Our cider vinegar is made from real apples.

No additives, no preservatives. Absolutely nothing artificial.

So next time, make sure your vinegar is really all natural. Make sure it's Heinz.

Heinz
WHEN YOU KNOW THE DIFFERENCE.

© 1987. H.J. Heinz. Co.

Source: Courtesy of Heinz U.S.A.

foreign competition are major reasons for the decline. For example, Ethyl Corporation, producer of the lead additive to gasoline, has been searching for new products and businesses since the U.S. government decided to phase out leaded gasoline. Likewise the future of the U.S. clothespin industry is reported to be on the line because less expensive clothespins are available from China and other countries. New products capable of fulfilling the need replace the old.

Large drops in sales in the decline stage force traumatic adjustments—closing plants, releasing or retraining employees, and refinancing debt among others, whereas gradual sales declines allow for gradual adjustments. Marketers may trim marginal styles and models from the product line as well as marginal distributors and national accounts. Price competition usually continues, but deep price cuts are less likely than in the maturity stage. Fewer competitors exist, and those that do operate conservatively. Companies with strong brands often continue to make a profit until almost the end by catering to individuals who resist change. There comes a time, however, when a manager will look at the opportunity costs of continuing the product, find they are too high, and decide to take the product off the market.[4] With the fierce loyalty developed over time by managers and the nostalgia of the good old days held by some distributors and customers, taking a product off the market may not be a simple economic decision.

❑ **Figure 9.2**
Shape and length of
product life cycle.

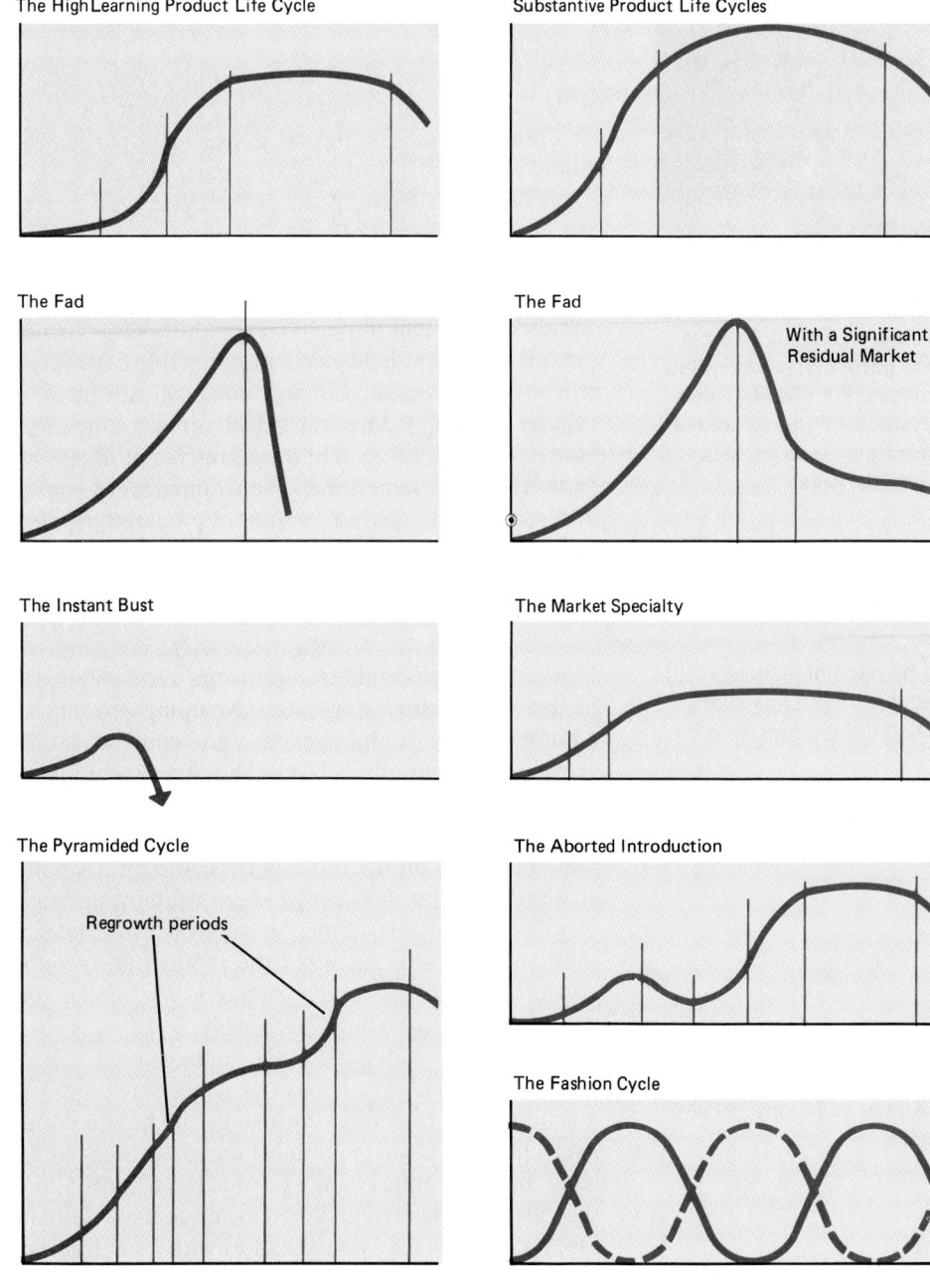

The High Learning Product Life Cycle

The Missing Link and Other Low Learning Substantive Product Life Cycles

The Fad

The Fad

With a Significant Residual Market

The Instant Bust

The Market Specialty

The Pyramided Cycle

Regrowth periods

The Aborted Introduction

The Fashion Cycle

Source: Chester R. Wasson,
*Dynamic Competitive Strategy
and Product Life Cycle,* 3rd ed.
(Austin, TX: Austin Press, 1978),
p. 13

Shape and Length of the Product Life Cycle

*N*ot all product life cycles
are the same.

*T*he Rubik's Cube with its
huge but short-lived de-
mand is typical of the com-
pressed product life cycle
of fads.

The product life cycle varies considerably in both length and shape for different products. (See figure 9.2.) The life cycle described in the preceding pages, the traditional cycle, is most typical for a product form such as the dial telephone.

As shown in figure 9.2, the shape of the cycle varies. **Fads,** for example, have short life cycles. In 1981, consumers purchased millions of Rubik's Cubes. Only three years later sales dropped to almost zero. The Hot Sox Company has capitalized on fads, producing such creations as toe socks and fishnet anklets.[5] The company's products become popular quickly, but just as quickly lose their appeal. Thus, Hot Sox frequently introduces new items to its product line and retires older ones. For

Children and adolescents are particularly susceptible to fads. For a while, combs positioned "just so" out of teenagers' jean pockets, were the rage.

each item introduction is rapid, growth is steep, maturity is short, and decline is precipitous.

Fashions have short recurring life cycles. Manufacturers make men's neckties wider and wider for several years, narrower for several more, then wider again. The acceptance of a style like wide ties for a particular period of time is its life cycle. Many products, including skirts, hats, and cars, have a fashion cycle.

The length of the product life cycle also varies. Some products move through the cycle faster than others—for instance, pet rocks as compared to peanut butter. Although there is variation, life cycles do seem to have shortened.[6] The pace of technological advancement has reduced the life of many products.[7] For example, the rapid development of personal computers has virtually eliminated stand-alone word processors. Hand-held calculators capable of differentiating and finding integrals are still quite expensive, but technological advances will enable their price to drop rapidly. When it does, they will replace current, more limited models. Parallel research and development programs result in several companies developing similar products at the same time. The willingness of some managers to ignore patent laws and produce "knock-off" copies of patented products also shortens life cycles.

Marketing Management and the Product Life Cycle

*T*he pace of technological advancement has shortened the product life cycle.

Market strategy should change as the cycle changes. For instance, critical to success in the introductory stage are developing product awareness in the target market, communicating product benefits, and convincing customers to try the product. Free samples, trial periods, rebates, and other techniques are used to gain awareness and communicate product benefits. During the growth stage, developing competitive advantage by differentiating and positioning the product increases the probability that the firm's product and not a competitor's will be purchased. In the maturity stage refinements in the product, in strategy, and in cost control provide some of the elements of value customers have grown to expect. Reminder promotion to insure that customers do remember the product plays an important role. Market segmentation to satisfy customers better is useful. In the decline stage, efficiency and continued cost control weigh heavily.

*F*lexibility is needed to offset unpredictability of the product in the product life cycle.

Figure 9.3 summarizes the management responses at different stages in the product life cycle. The market manager may not be able to predict the length of time a product will remain at each stage of the life cycle or even the shape of the cycle itself, but that is not essential. Flexible strategy and an understanding of the underlying forces creating change provide the essentials of success. For example, although the videodisc was originally predicted to have tremendously large markets and a long life, the product life cycle was short with a small sales volume. The RCA Corporation

❑ **Figure 9.3**
Product life cycle characteristics and responses.

Source: Peter Doyle, "The Realities of the Product Life Cycle," *Quarterly Review of Marketing,* (U.K.), Summer 1978, p. 5

	Introduction	Growth	Maturity	Decline
Characteristics:				
Sales	Low	Fast growth	Slow growth	Declining
Profits	Negligible	Peak levels	Declining	Low or zero
Customers	Innovative	Mass market	Mass market	Laggards
Competitors	Few	Growing	Many rivals	Declining number
Responses:				
Strategic focus	Expand market	Market penetration	Defend share	Productivity
Marketing expenditures	High	High (declining %)	Falling	Low
Marketing emphasis	Product awareness	Brand preference	Brand loyalty	Selective
Distribution	Patchy	Intensive	Intensive	Selective
Price	High	Lower	Lowest	Rising
Product	Basic	Improved	Differentiated	Rationalized

and Pioneer Video, Inc. both adjusted first by reducing price and promotional efforts in the videodisc market to develop profitable positions and eventually by dropping out of the market when profits evaporated.

THE CASE CONTINUES

*B*lack & Decker executives have developed a successful company with successful products. Nevertheless, they realize that products do not last forever, and that product life cycles force decisions on them. Many of the products in the con-

sumer power tool market have reached maturity. Competition, which may have access to newer or more efficient technology, reduces market

share for even the best products. Thus, new products must be developed to meet the needs of changing markets. The power tool division of B&D is expected to come up with a dozen new products each year. That number will probably grow.

 ## NEW PRODUCTS

A new product may be different from all other products or it may simply replace existing but similar products.

When a firm phases out a product, it should not have a negative effect if adequate preparation has been made for a new product. What is a new product? A **new product** might be truly unique and satisfy a need that has gone unsatisfied, for instance, medication to prevent heart disease. A product is also considered new when it substitutes for considerably different existing products, such as herbicides for tillage equipment in crop production. In no-till farming, the farmer uses herbicides to control weeds and plants and grows the crop without tilling. A product is new if it simply replaces existing but similar products, such as word processors in place of typewriters. In the office, both serve the same functions—typed communication. Even imitative products, the "me-too-products" new to the company but not to the market, are new products.[8]

New is used in a relative sense. One way to visualize the different meanings of newness is shown in figure 9.4. Notice that a continuous innovation requires only a small amount of change in the product and in customer behavior. A discontinuous innovation, on the other hand, requires the creation of a previously unknown product and new behavior patterns on the part of the consumer. To determine newness, therefore, marketers ask: Is the product perceived as new to the target market? How much change in consumer behavior will be required? Is the product new to the

---

❑ **Figure 9.4**
Range of product newness.

Continuous	Dynamically Continuous	Discontinuous
Involves alteration of existing product	Involves creation of new product or alteration of existing one	Creation of previously unknown products
Little disruption of habits, behavior and consumption patterns	Disruption of habits behavior and consumption patterns, but does not require new	Requires new consumption and behavior patterns
Examples: Plaque prevention toothpaste Low-alcohol beer Annual new car changeovers	Examples: Electric toothbrush Electric knives Dodge Caravan	Examples: Computers Gene splicing Television Copying machines

Source: Adapted from Thomas S. Robertson, *Innovative Behavior and Communication.* (New York: Holt, Rinehart, and Winston, Inc., © 1971), p. 7

company in any way, such as form, function, or style? An old product marketed to a new target market would be new to the market and to the company. The Federal Trade Commission limits to six months, starting with the introduction to the market, the time a company can promote a product as "new."

*S*hould a new product be acquired or developed?

Organizations have two avenues open for obtaining new products. They can develop them internally or acquire them. Acquisition means the product concept will become the property of the organization. Licensing means the acquiring organization has limited rights to the product concept such as the right to produce the product or sell the product in specified geographic areas. The licensee usually must maintain product quality and pay a royalty fee. Acquisition of the rights to a product saves product development time. Development of a new product is usually a lengthy process. In addition, development is usually expensive. It also may require knowledge that personnel in the firm lack. The executives of many organizations, however, believe that if a product concept isn't developed internally it can't be much good. Because executives emphasize new product development, the following pages will discuss it in detail.

New Product Development Process

*T*he product development process increases the success of new product development.

New products have a considerable risk of failing in the market.[9] Products that fail are costly to the company. They not only tarnish the company image but also represent large investments in time, money, and talent. The development of a single new product may require years and consume large amounts of talented employee time. To increase the chances of developing successful new products and avoid wasting company resources, new product development should be an organized and controlled process synchronized with the company's overall business strategy. The objectives of the process are to develop successful new products quickly and efficiently by generating and developing only viable new product ideas. Product ideas with a destiny for failure must be eliminated as quickly as possible to keep costs down.

The **product development process** is more likely to be used when management perceives risk as high—when the product is not one the firm has previously marketed. At any point management may be so convinced the product will be successful that intermediate development steps are dropped and the product goes to national commercial distribution. On the other hand, management may conclude the product will not succeed and drop it completely. Eight stages make up the development process: idea generation, screening ideas, concept development and testing, marketing plan development, business analysis, product development, test marketing, and commercialization (figure 9.5).

IDEA GENERATION

*I*dea generation systematically keeps those ideas flowing.

New product development starts with an idea—many ideas—but only a few are good enough to become successful products. The source of the ideas is not particularly important, but their generation cannot be left to chance. Product **idea generation** results best from a systematic organization that maintains an ongoing search, stimulates idea sources, and records and makes the ideas available to the company when needed. At the very least, management needs to be open to suggestions for new product ideas.

The type and source of ideas will vary to some extent with the way management defines what the company is and what it should be. For example, in response to the U.S. government's edict to separate local telephone operations into independent companies, AT&T management shifted its focus from the telephone business to the information business. Now that AT&T is an information company, the type and

❑ **Figure 9.5**
The product
development process.

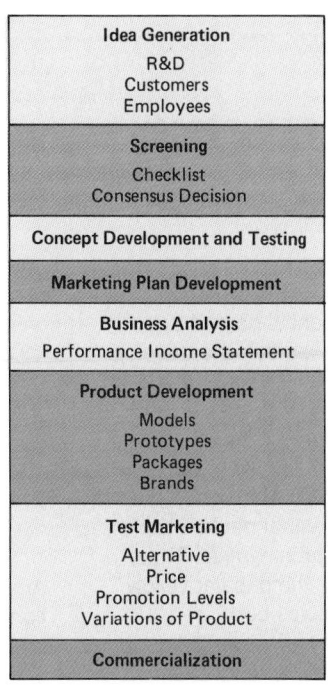

Idea Generation
R&D
Customers
Employees

Screening
Checklist
Consensus Decision

Concept Development and Testing

Marketing Plan Development

Business Analysis
Performance Income Statement

Product Development
Models
Prototypes
Packages
Brands

Test Marketing
Alternative
Price
Promotion Levels
Variations of Product

Commercialization

source of ideas for new products will be different from what they were when it was just a telephone company.

Ideas result from someone trying to solve a problem or to satisfy a need more completely or more efficiently.[10] Pillsbury Company, for instance, has developed a microwave pizza line because a large number of consumers now use microwaves.

*I*nternally, employees are a good source for ideas.

Internally, a company has several sources of ideas. For technically oriented companies the research and development department generates many ideas. Production employees and salespeople have good ideas that they obtain from producing the product or hearing customers' requests and complaints.[11] Quality circles, a Japanese concept in which groups of employees from the same area meet regularly to define, analyze, and solve problems, are a source of ideas for new products. Brainstorming sessions and incentive or reward systems for product suggestions are some of the other techniques companies use to generate ideas internally. With brainstorming, a problem area is defined and in a freewheeling atmosphere participants are encouraged to generate as many ideas, logical and wild, as possible. Criticism of ideas is discouraged. In general terms the techniques focus on a problem, establish openness and participation, encourage many diverse ideas, and allow participants to build on each other's ideas.[12] Sometimes good product ideas result from problems within the company, for instance, the problem of what to do with production waste and by-products, or the need for more complete utilization of manufacturing facilities or distribution networks. Sawdust, a by-product of lumber mills, has been developed into several products. Composite board and fuel for power plants are two examples. Poultry processors sell feathers to animal feed processors for animal feed, and to clothing manufacturers, who use the feathers as filling for coats and vests.

*E*xternally, ideas come from customers and others outside the firm.

Externally, companies can look to consumers and industrial buyers of their products for suggestions and to independent inventors, patent attorneys, consultants, industry publications, and competitors' products. Consumers, for instance, have a way of finding new uses for products to solve their needs more completely. Examples include Avon's Skin-So-Soft Bath Oil as an insect repellent, Preparation H to smooth wrinkles on the face and to shrink puffiness under the eyes, and denture tablets to clean toilet bowls.[13] Upon investigation marketers may get ideas for possible new products from consumers' uses. They may also decide to update the instructions and warnings on the existing product's label.

There is at least one American company that actually keeps an open mind regarding mistakes and even off-beat, wild ideas. This management philosophy leads to hundreds of new product ideas. And it certainly has been important in the growth of a company that has forty-five major product lines.

That the company was founded on a mistake may have something to do with its attitude. In 1902 a doctor, a lawyer, a butcher, and two railroad employees each put down $1,000 to sell a mineral—they thought it was corundum—to grinding wheel manufacturers. The mineral turned out to be worthless and the company, surviving through many difficult years, turned to making sandpaper. This firm, still a leading manufacturer of this product today, has operations in forty-nine countries, thirty-seven with manufacturing.

Here are some examples of mistakes that were turned into product opportunities:

THE REST OF THE STORY

Mistakes Make Millions

1. In 1970 a scientist named Spencer F. Silver was trying to develop a super-strong adhesive, but instead came up with a very weak one. Several years later another company scientist, Arthur Fry, put some of Silver's weak glue on a piece of paper that marked his place in a church hymnal. Thus, Post-it Notes, the popular yellow stick-on note was born.
2. A fabric protector was accidentally discovered when a chemist spilled some liquid on her tennis shoes. She soon discovered that her shoes repelled dirt and water. Today we know the product as Scotchgard brand fabric protector.
3. In the early 1940s company scientists were working with synthetic fibers they hoped could be bonded to produce a useful, non-woven product. Three times the project was close to getting the axe. But given a fourth opportunity, the researchers developed a yarn to produce a ribbon about 3/8-inch wide. That was the beginning of the decorative ribbon business. Nonwovens have since formed the basis for such products as surgical and protective face masks.

These stories are about one of America's most successful corporations—Minnesota Mining and Manufacturing Company, better known as 3M.

Source: Adapted from "3M's Aggressive New Consumer Drive," *Business Week,* July 16, 1984, p. 118; Milton Moskowitz, Michael Katz, and Robert Levering, *Everybody's Business* (New York: Harper & Row, 1980), p. 937.

SCREENING

*S*creening involves separating ideas with potential from the rest.

The objective of **screening** is to separate ideas for new products with potential from those without. Screening eliminates a number of ideas obtained from the idea generation stage. Because screening is the least expensive of the steps in the development process, successful screening is critical in reducing the cost of product development. On the other hand, screening can be very expensive if it eliminates product ideas with high potential. Some marginal product ideas pass to the next stage because of management's fear of eliminating good products at this stage. (See figure 9.6.)

To improve the effectiveness of screening, it is often systematized. The individual presenting the idea may be requested to write it up on a standard form. The form should be simple so it does not discourage people from submitting ideas. A brief description of the product, target market, competition, and a broad estimate of market size typically make up the entries on the form.

A checklist is a method of systematically screening product ideas.

A committee of people from different functional areas then reviews the idea. They may simply discuss its advantages and disadvantages and based on consensus decide whether or not to continue the development process. They may use a checklist approach to evaluate the idea on the basis of a list of criteria. Typically, the checklist covers a wide range of criteria. Some of the criteria concern the nature of the company. For example, is the new product idea compatible with the company's current product offering? Does the company have the expertise, facilities, and capacity to produce the new product? Are current channels of distribution adequate

☐ **Figure 9.6**
Sample checklist for
rating product ideas.

Criterion	Weight	Excellent	Good	Marginal	Poor	Weight X Rate
		2	1	0	−1	
Market leadership	15	X				30
Complement current target markets	5		X			5
Sales volume	16	X				32
Company image	8			X		0
Patent protection	8	X				16
Social impact	8				X	−8
Competitive strength	10		X			10
Complements current production	10			X		0
Complements current technology	10		X			10
Complements current distribution channels	10			X		0
	100				Total Score	95

for the product or will new ones have to be developed? Will the product meet financial objectives? Other criteria concern the market for the product. For example, what is the product's target market? How large is the market? Is the product unique or does it resemble existing products? What is its competition?

The review committee evaluates the new product idea for each of the criteria on the checklist, usually on a scale of zero (lowest) to ten (highest). If the committee weights the criteria, the weight is multiplied by the score that the product idea has received for each item on the checklist. These subtotals are summed, producing a total score. This total is compared to a previously established standard to determine if the product idea is continued.

CONCEPT DEVELOPMENT AND TESTING

Concept development—decisions about product features.

Concept development requires that the product idea be visualized in product form. A new deodorant, for instance, could be a product in stick, roll-on, or aerosol form. Among other things, the dimension, shape, features, and function of the product are visualized. Each of the visualized forms is described on paper.

Concept testing involves gathering information about customers' reactions to the descriptions of the new product and recording their preferences. Focus groups, in-store polling, and other qualitative research techniques are used to get the information. Respondents may be asked to react not only to the concept features, but also to expected use, price, etc. Both final customers and wholesaler and retailer intermediaries should be involved in testing the concept.

Concept testing—potential customer's reaction to product features.

Trade-off analysis is a method of testing concepts that presents respondents with mutually exclusive attributes. For instance, respondents are asked to select between a combination of service levels and price levels. How much price reduction would be required to offset a service reduction or how much service increase would be necessary to offset a price increase? The answer to what the respondent is willing to trade ultimately determines the product concept.

THE REST OF THE STORY

Velcro Takes Hold

The "touch fastener," or "hook-and-loop fastener," which you may know best as the Velcro brand fastener, wasn't invented in the 1970s. Furthermore, it did not develop from an organization's R&D department, or from customer complaints, or employee suggestions. An inquisitive Swiss inventor, probably after taking a hike through the country, decided to examine a cocklebur under his microscope. A tiny little hook terminated each extension from the cocklebur's center. Over forty years ago, George deMestral decided the little hooks could be synthesized and made into some sort of fastener. Thus the touch fastener was invented.

Other creative individuals have found hundreds of ways to use the touch fastener. The space shuttle has 1,200 square inches of Velcro in its cargo bay and flight deck areas. Velcro has replaced string on shoes. It is used to anchor removable uphol-stery and seat cushions on furniture. It is also used in bloodless bull fights. The spears are tipped with the Velcro hooks and the bull fitted with the loop material.

Do you have any creative ways to use the touch fastener? Velcro USA, a subsidiary of Velcro Industries NV, a Dutch company, might be interested.

Source: Kevin McManus, "That Funny Ripping Noise? It's Music," *Advertising Age,* April 15, 1985, p. 60. Copyright © Crain Communications, Inc.

MARKETING PLAN DEVELOPMENT

Development of a tentative marketing plan utilizes the information generated in concept development and testing. All aspects of a marketing plan are developed—objectives, target market, price, distribution, promotion, and product. A forecast of sales, even though it cannot be fully accurate, will also be prepared at this point.[14]

BUSINESS ANALYSIS

Does the idea look good on paper?

Business analysis refines the information developed in screening, concept development and testing, and marketing plan development and adds new information. Business analysis remains a pencil-and-paper activity where qualitative evaluation and quantitative analysis are both required.[15] A qualitative evaluation must be made of the information about customer preferences gathered in the concept development and testing stage. In addition, quantitative analysis is required of information about the market potential of the new product as well as its growth rate, competitive strengths, and compatibility to other areas of the organization.

Will the idea achieve financial objectives?

The business analysis will come together in a pro forma income statement, a rough break-even projection, and a return-on-investment projection. The decision to continue a new product ultimately depends on sales revenue and cost. In addition to the pattern of sales, incremental sales have to be determined. Incremental sales are equal to total product sales minus cannibalized sales—sales the product takes from the firm's existing products. Product ideas that look favorable on paper continue in the process.

PHYSICAL PRODUCT DEVELOPMENT

Going from descriptions and drawings to the physical product constitutes **physical product development.** Research and development and engineering are heavily involved, but marketing management also has a role. R&D and engineering personnel make the pilot models, the prototypes, and run laboratory tests, attempting to translate the concept into a workable product. Product development has become faster with the introduction of the computer-aided design and manufacturing programs now on the market. Marketing helps determine if a project is technically

The Wonder Winder is a product used to store flexible cord. An early prototype is shown here on the left. After market reactions and suggestions, the final prototype was handmade and is shown here on the right.

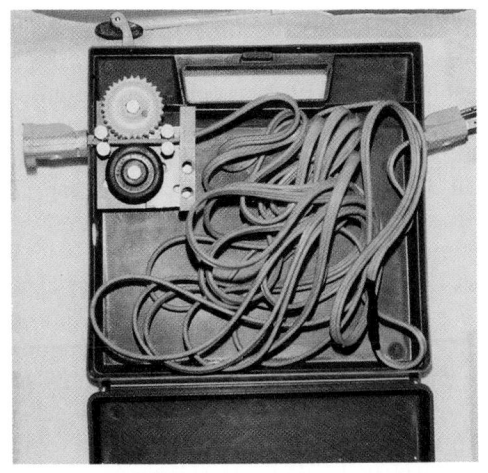 

Source: Photos courtesy of Wonder Winder, Box 1442, Terre Haute, Indiana

feasible by establishing how the product is likely to be used, including the incorporation of safety features. The key attributes visualized for the product must also be designed into the product. Marketing can help clarify the key attributes for engineering and R&D. Marketers insure that the consumer orientation continues to be a focal point as the product takes form. Engineering personnel evaluate the product technically by testing it physically and checking manufacturing cost. At the same time marketing personnel are busy determining an appropriate brand name, package, and price, and making sure that both tangible and intangible features are considered and included. Focus groups, target market surveys, and other market research techniques with the physical product give the marketer additional information.

A computer firm, producing software for children, founded a grade school in Provo, Utah, supplied it with computers, and now tests software at the school. Both marketers and engineers adjust, refine, and reformulate as results come back from their tests.

TEST MARKETING

The introduction of the product in specific and limited geographic areas to assess customer and dealer reaction is called **test marketing.** Test marketing allows the organization to observe the product in an authentic marketing environment and find out whether it will sell without going to the national market. For Benihana of Tokyo the product was a line of frozen foods, and test markets in New York City and Los Angeles did find that the product would sell.

Besides being less expensive than national distribution, test markets provide an opportunity to determine weaknesses that still have not been discovered in the product or the marketing plan and to make necessary adjustments. It is best to make adjustments now because mistakes or weaknesses that remain undetected at the point of national distribution can cost a new product potential customers. Customers who try the product and find it lacking are often unwilling to try it again.

Using several different test markets, managers can test alternative approaches to marketing the new product. Especially if managers are unable to reach a decision about such things as price, promotional focus, package design, or advertising copy, test markets provide the opportunity to gauge customer response to each alternative in preparation for entry into the national market. For example, Monet Jewelry, a New York City marketer of costume jewelry, wanted to see if TV advertising could be used successfully to promote a new jewelry product. The costume jewelry market makes little use of TV advertising, and the test market Monet used did not support it for Monet's new product, either.[16]

*A*lternatives to a full test market.

Test markets are quite useful, but they are not without problems. Obviously, they must be well designed and planned if they are to yield the desired information, but even when they are, it may not be forthcoming.[17] In addition, test marketing provides information and opportunities to competitors. Seeing a company's new product and its promotional strategy in a test market, competitors can use both to develop their own. Furthermore, competitors can take action to upset the results of test marketing, for instance, by offering coupons or increasing the advertising for their own, similar products.

Another problem with test markets is their expense. A traditional, full-fledged test can cost $2 million or more.[18] The time required to complete a test may also be lengthy if customer's initial and subsequent reactions are to be obtained. Because of the expense and time required for test marketing, some organizations have adopted alternative techniques.[19] The simulated test market is one example. A sample of customers from the desired market are invited to an experimental store where new products are displayed. They are given a sum of money and told they may either keep it or buy products.[20] Another variation is the sales wave experiment. Consumers are given a new product to use in their homes. They then have the option of purchasing the product or competing products at reduced prices. A third alternative or supplement to a full test market is the use of a computerized model to simulate the market and the market's reaction to the product. The success of this technique depends on how accurately the model reflects the market, but it has some advantages. Besides keeping the product from the scrutiny of competitors, the computerized model simulation can provide very quick feedback to different marketing alternatives.

In part because of these problems, companies have become more selective in their use of full test markets. Procter & Gamble, for instance, has shortened the test market period for most of its new products, especially those not considered to be technological breakthroughs. When a company believes that a product is sure to be a success, it may not use test markets at all. For highly perishable products like fashion or fad items, test marketing would take too long and the market would be missed. When high fixed production costs are involved, as with many industrial products, test marketing is impractical. (See figure 9.7 for an overview of when to use test marketing.)

The decision to go commercial must be made after test marketing. It is an easy decision if the product does especially poorly or well, but several conditions make the decision more difficult. Initial sales may be high but repeat purchases small. Initial sales may be high but the frequency of purchase less than expected. Both initial and repeat purchases may be marginal, or cannibalization may be much more predominant than expected. The test market can be continued, or the product can be sent back for adjustments, dropped, or advanced to commercialization.

❑ **Figure 9.7**
When to use text marketing.

Source: Joseph P. Guiltinan and Gordon W. Paul. *Marketing Management Strategies and Programs*, p. 203. Copyright © 1985 by McGraw-Hill Book Company

Factors Favoring Test Marketing
1. Acceptance of the product concept is very uncertain.
2. Sales potential is difficult to estimate.
3. Cost of developing consumer awareness and trial is difficult to estimate.
4. A major investment is required to produce the product at full scale (relative to the cost of test marketing).
5. Alternative prices, packages, or promotional appeals are under consideration.

Reasons for Not Test Marketing
1. The risk of failure is low relative to test-marketing costs.
2. The product will have a brief life cycle.
3. Beating competition to the market is important because the product is easily imitated.
4. Basic price, package, promotional appeals are well established.

COMMERCIALIZATION

*M*anagement decides to market the product.

The prime reason that firms use a systematic process to develop a new product is the large capital investment required to produce and market it. When, after considerable testing, refining, adjusting, and retesting, managers finally decide that the product will be successful, they plan and launch full-scale production and marketing programs. This is the **commercialization** stage of new product development. In this stage, the company must risk capital for production facilities, for promotion to acquaint the sales force, intermediaries, channel members, and customers, and for inventory to fill the channels of distribution have to be made.

*T*he roll-out strategy—introduction of the product to successively larger markets.

Fine tuning the marketing program and the product itself continues in the commercialization stage. Decisions about when and how to introduce the product have to be made. The appropriate time to introduce the product is when the economy and customer attitudes and desires are favorable to its purchase.[21] If the time seems inappropriate, introduction is delayed until more favorable conditions develop.

When conditions are favorable, an appropriate strategy for introducing the product is chosen. One option is the roll-out strategy, a region-by-region introduction of the product. New regions where the product is introduced typically have a common boundary with a region where the product is already established. Anheuser-Busch rolled out LA, its low-alcohol beer, for instance, with initial distribution in 65 percent of the United States market. A limited introduction allows time to gear up the production and marketing facilities for larger markets and continues on a contiguous basis until national distribution is achieved. A problem with the roll-out strategy, however, is that it allows competitors to develop their own products before national distribution is obtained. Many large companies that have the capacity, therefore, often prefer to use an instant national distribution strategy.

THE NEW PRODUCT—SUCCESS OR FAILURE?

*O*ops! The product failed!

Even after the expenditure of considerable time and money in developing a new product, it still may fail. Failure, of course, is relative. It may be defined from one extreme as organizational bankruptcy to the other as narrowly missing the established objectives of reasonable profit.[22]

Product failure has numerous causes. Occasionally, a key executive favors a product concept and pushes it through the development process even though there is little evidence that it is likely to succeed. Much more often, however, market demand for the product is overestimated. Other reasons for failure include poor market timing, incorrect positioning in the market, incorrect pricing, failure to continuously analyze customers' needs and attitudes, and competitors' moves.[23]

PRODUCT ADOPTION

With so much effort involved in the development of new products, their success would seem assured, but the potential customer has the final say. Product adoption, the regular use of the product, has two elements: the adoption process and the diffusion process.

Adoption Process

The individual's evaluation and decision to use the new product is referred to as the **adoption process** (figure 9.8). Everett Rogers conducted the landmark studies on

❏ **Figure 9.8**
The adoption process.

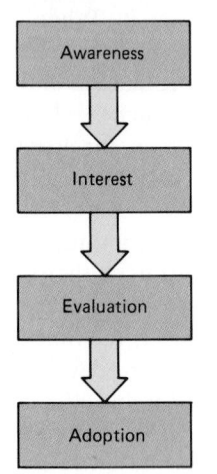

*E*ffective promotion and the adoption process.

the adoption process.[24] He discovered that individuals go through a series of steps: awareness, interest, evaluation, trial, and adoption or rejection. In the *awareness* stage individuals learn of the product's existence. In the *interest* stage, individuals perceive some possibility that the product will satisfy their needs based on their knowledge of the product, and they seek more information about it. In the *evaluation* stage, individuals use the information at hand (perhaps seeking additional information if what they have is incomplete or conflicting) to compare the product with its alternatives. They seek the alternative with the most potential for satisfying their needs. *Trial* usage of the product with the highest potential either confirms the evaluation or refutes it. Confirmation leads to regular use of the product—*adoption*. At any one of the stages in the adoption process, the individual may decide to reject further consideration of the product.

Rogers's research on the adoption process is significant to the marketer because it demonstrates that products are not adopted instantaneously. Time is required, and different individuals require different amounts of time to adopt a product. To aid the individual and to speed the process, several techniques are helpful. For instance, in less than five years Johnson & Johnson started producing toys and became the number two seller in the one-to-three year age category by developing a strategy that took into account the adoption process. Heavy television promotion to gain awareness was too expensive with the small size of the target market. Consequently, the company decided to go directly to the parents with a toy-of-the-month club offer. Each toy, designed to stimulate the child's skills and attention, is sent with a booklet explaining what the toy does for the child. The booklet generates interest. To help the parent through the evaluation stage, Johnson & Johnson policy allows the child to play with the toy at home before the parent has to make a decision to purchase.[25]

Extensive use of promotion can build widespread awareness quickly. Individuals trust different promotional forms and different sources of information at different stages in the adoption process. Advertising can convey information about product attributes, the need-satisfying ability of the product, and evaluation criteria that the consumer might use. Personal selling seems to be effective when the individual is in the evaluation stage and near the decision to purchase. Samples and simulated trials encourage initial purchase decisions at the trial stage since both reduce the risk to the potential buyer. Assuring quality by presenting a quality product for the price and by providing guarantees also helps reduce the buyer's perceived risk and encourage adoption.

Diffusion Process

*T*he diffusion process classifies purchasers into: innovators, early adopters, early majority, late majority, and laggards.

The adoption process focuses on the individual; the **diffusion process** focuses on the market. The diffusion of innovation is the acceptance of the innovation by individuals in the market. Individuals require different amounts of time to decide to adopt a new product. The study of diffusion considers the differences among individuals and classifies them based on how quickly they adopt. It also considers the communication about the product between individuals. Rogers developed five categories of adopters: innovators, early adopters, early majority, late majority, and laggards.[26] Note that all of the groups eventually do adopt the product. Nonadopters are not considered in Rogers's taxonomy. The categories are based on the normal distribution, with innovators as the first 2.5 percent to adopt. They are two standard deviations from the mean. See figure 9.9 for the categories of innovation adoption.

INNOVATORS

*I*nnovators influence others and the product's success.

Of all the adopter categories, the innovators have received the most attention from marketers. They are thought to be critical in the diffusion of the product to the

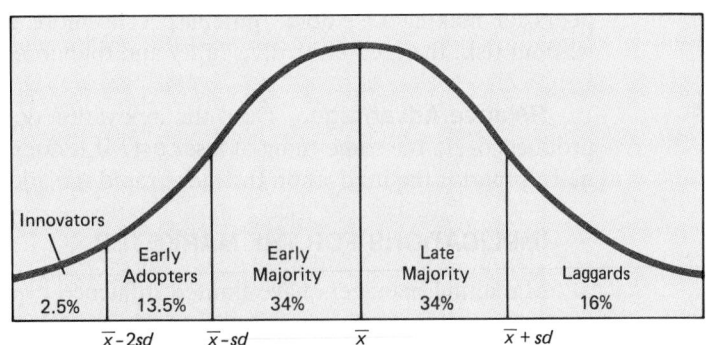

□ **Figure 9.9**
Categories of innovation adopters.

Source: Reprinted with permission of The Free Press, a Division of Macmillan Inc. from *Communication of Innovations: A Cross Cultural Approach* by Everett M. Rogers with F. Floyd Shoemaker. Copyright © 1984 by The Free Press

rest of the market. Innovators seem to purchase the product almost as soon as it is placed on the market. Other potential buyers wait to gain from the innovators' experience and wait for more information in general. The key role of the innovators encourages the marketer to identify and appeal to them. Unfortunately, the first adopters of one product are not the same for other products. They do, however, have similar characteristics. When compared to later adopters, they tend to be more mobile in jobs and residence, have more income and higher social status, and be younger and better educated. They also rely more on informal information sources— group affiliations—than do later adopters.[27]

DETERMINANTS OF THE RATE OF ADOPTION

*T*he five factors that influence adoption rate—communicability, compatibility, simplicity, divisibility, and relative advantage.

Some products are adopted more rapidly than others. By studying an innovation's characteristics, the rate at which a product will be adopted can be estimated. Rogers and Shoemaker have identified five characteristics as significant influences on the rate of adoption: communicability, compatibility, simplicity, divisibility, and relative advantage.[28]

Communicability.   Communicability is the ease with which the results of using the product can be discussed with others. Since visible results are easier to communicate, the more tangible the results, the more rapid the adoption.

*T*he less the product user has to change, the faster the adoption.

Compatibility.   The compatibility of an innovation refers to the amount of change its use requires. The more an innovation requires learning new concepts and changing attitudes and habits, the less compatible it is and the longer it requires for adoption. The DuPont Company, for instance, produces and sells a herbicide, Glean, which is especially toxic to weeds, requiring as little as a tablespoon to rid an acre of weeds. Most farmers use a much greater quantity of herbicide, and they have been slow to change their habits and attitudes. The results of using Glean do not appear immediately—the weeds stay healthy and green for nearly two weeks before turning brown. DuPont is still trying to educate farmers to Glean's unique mode of action. The executives of Radiation Technology Inc. have been trying for years to convince consumers and executives that foods should be irradiated to prolong shelf life. However, most consumers' attitudes toward radiation prevent easy acceptance of irradiation.

Simplicity.   If the innovation and the way in which it functions are easy for the ordinary individual to understand, adoption will progress rapidly.

Divisibility.   Can the innovation be divided, sampled, or used on a trial basis to minimize the initial risk of the adopter? Buyers do not want to lose financially by the decision to purchase nor do they want to be embarrassed or ridiculed by their peers for making a "stupid" purchase. The more easily the product can be tried without risk, the greater its divisibility and the more quickly adoption will occur.

The greater the advantage of purchase, the faster the adoption.

Relative Advantage.   Does the innovation do something better than existing products or do the same thing at less cost? If it does, it has relative advantage. The more superior the innovation the more rapid the adoption.

IMPLICATIONS FOR THE MARKETER

Marketing managers have limited influence over the five characteristics. Even so, they should consider the degree to which an innovative product embodies each characteristic and evaluate the impact each will have on the rate of adoption. Then, managers can take action to lessen the impact. If nothing can be done, the marketing strategy should reflect the anticipated adoption rate.

THE CASE CONTINUES

There is every indication that Black & Decker will be successful in developing new products based on the GE line. Top management seems very supportive of new product development. B&D has successfully developed and marketed new products— including the Dustbuster. The firm has familiarity with all phases of new product development from idea generation to commercialization.

To increase consumer acceptance and purchase of new products, Black & Decker can employ the concept of product adoption. B&D develops awareness of its new products by advertising campaigns at the time of introduction. These campaigns in-

crease interest by promoting potential benefits, such as that cordless appliances are easier to use. Consumers can be encouraged to evaluate the product by trial low introductory prices. Most importantly, B&D tries to develop new products that are better than what's already on the market; that are simple and easy to use and are what people want.

 ## ORGANIZING FOR PRODUCT MANAGEMENT

New products require special attention.

Managing products presents many opportunities and challenges to the organization. Since developing new products requires a different focus from managing an existing product through its life cycle, different organizational forms have been created to handle the two processes. Separating responsibility for new products from that for existing products means that the new products will receive the time and devotion they deserve, and that the high risk associated with new product development will not overly restrict development. Marketing personnel assigned to new product development become accustomed to working with risk. They devise methods to reduce it rather than ignoring it or limiting the development of new product concept.[29]

Organizational Forms for Developing New Products

There is no one best organizational structure for product development. In fact, different organizational forms are sometimes used in conjunction with each other. (See figure 9.10.) More important than the type of form is the continuing commitment and long-term support from top management.

□ **Figure 9.10**
New product
development
organization.

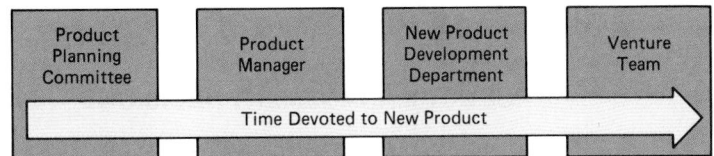

PRODUCT-PLANNING COMMITTEE

A committee that approves product concepts, prepares budgets, and makes plans for the further development of new product ideas is a **product-planning committee.** The committee, which consists of managers from the functional divisions, seldom performs developmental tasks like generating new product concepts, developing the product, or determining the marketing strategy. Instead, the committee approves or disapproves of the developmental efforts of other units in the company.

Product-planning committees are sometimes criticized for being slow to make decisions. They also tend to be conservative, steering away from products that may have high potential but that also carry large risks. On the positive side, a favorable decision from the product-planning committee usually means that the product will receive support from all the functional divisions since their managers are represented.

PRODUCT MANAGER

*P*roduct managers
specialize.

Companies with many varied products assign an individual to plan and coordinate complete programs for a brand, product, product line, or market. These individuals, referred to as **brand, product, or market managers,** specialize in a particular area. Although they do have responsibility for price, distribution, and promotion as well as the product, they have a promotional orientation. Usually they work only with existing products, but some companies assign new product concepts to product managers for development. If they can somehow find the time to devote to a new product concept and overcome their promotional orientation, they can be very effective planners. Occupying staff positions, they also must persuade other executives to cooperate.[30]

NEW PRODUCT DEVELOPMENT DEPARTMENTS

A special department which has sole responsibility for product development is the **new product development department.** The head of this department reports to a top executive. The department personnel guide the product concept through the various stages of product development to commercialization. After market introduction, the product is turned over to another department. Because the development of new products is a permanent full-time activity of the department, expertise and experience in product development are definite advantages of this organizational form.

VENTURE TEAM

*V*enture teams are treated
as a new company.

The **venture team** is a select group of individuals representing the functional areas who devote all of their time to a particular product concept that has high market potential.[31] The venture team operates like an independent entrepreneur. All the tasks of product development—finance, production, distribution, and market strategy—are performed as if the venture team were a separate new company.

Managing the Product and the Product Mix

PRODUCT MANAGEMENT DECISIONS

Successful development of a new product propels it into the product life cycle. If the decision to commercialize a new product was correct, its adoption by buyers will be rapid, and its diffusion through the market extensive. Therefore the product will progress quickly through the introductory and growth stages of the product life cycle.

At this point, product management decisions come into play. How should the company manage the product as it progresses through the life cycle? One possibility is to allow it to move through the cycle essentially unchanged. Another possibility is to modify it as it passes from the growth stage to maturity and then begins its decline in an effort to lengthen its life.

*S*tretching the success of a product through modification.

Product Modification Decisions. If the product has shown a profit and good return on investment an attempt will be made to prolong its life by modifying it even though modification is expensive.[32] How can a product be modified? Its function, style, and quality can be changed. Style changes are intended to make the product more attractive to potential buyers. Functional modifications include changes in versatility, convenience, or safety of the product. Quality modifications include changes in durability, speed, and consistency of performance. The Leica M4P range finder camera of today is based on the Leica design introduced in 1954. Apple Computer Inc. has successfully modified its Apple II design with new technology.[33] All successful modifications depend upon the change being possible, buyers believing the alteration has been accomplished, and a sufficient number of buyers desiring the modification.

*W*hen and how to take a product off the market.

Deletion Decisions. When and how should a product be removed from the organization's offerings? The decision on when to remove a product should be made systematically by evaluating the performance of the product, the condition of the market, and the impact of competition in relation to the organization's objectives.

How should a product be removed from the market? Where there are no legal restrictions, removal can be abrupt. Abrupt elimination of an old product is sometimes paired with the introduction of a new product that satisfies the same buyer needs. When buyers have other alternatives, abrupt elimination works well. When alternatives are difficult to find or buyers show loyalty to the organization's product line, not just the product, other techniques should be used. A phased-out elimination, for instance, could be used with a gradual reduction of variations in the product, location, inventories, and promotion. Price may also be raised gradually. Phased-out elimination has a buyer orientation and allows the organization to generate profit as long as possible.

PRODUCT MIX DECISIONS

*W*hat does the firm have to offer? Should it be different?

The decision to eliminate a product alters the product mix. Will top management want to add other products? Management's perceptions of the firm and of what its offering should be in the future influence the mix. Some marketing managers would like to see their organizations in the forefront of product offerings and thus support continuous innovation in order to add new products. Other managers have more limited views. They may see their organization as the source of a single product dominating the market. Other managers may want to have a limited offering of products—a limited line. Successful limited line managers can engage in line stretching. With success, the limited line manager may decide to switch strategies to offer more products to satisfy buyer requests and to discourage competition. To offer more products, the manager may engage in line stretching and filling.

Stretching a line often occurs along the price and quality dimensions. Stretching a line requires a sequential addition of products to the line. For instance, if the present product offering is medium-priced, a new product may be offered at a price just above or just below the present price. Filling holes in the product line is also a strategy marketing managers employ. In filling, the range of product offerings in the line is considered. If gaps in the line exist, the marketer may offer new products to fill the gaps. For instance, if the present range of products extends from high quality to low quality, with no products offered at medium quality, a gap exists and the addition of a medium quality seems reasonable. Both stretching and filling may keep out competition, satisfy dealers and customers, use excess capacity, and result in extra profit.

THE CASE CONTINUES

The jury is still out on B&D's ability to successfully market small appliances. GE was number one in the business when it sold out to B&D after 75 years. GE found it impossible to make a decent profit against cutthroat competition, such as that posed by Sunbeam. B&D management needs to make decisions on which products the company will keep and which will be eliminated. To make better, more informed decisions, including those about product deletion, B&D probably has developed a structure that allows an individual or department to stay in close contact and be responsible for a product or market, a product management or market manager organization approach.

GOAL SUMMARY

1. **Describe the stages in the product life cycle.** The stages in the product life cycle are phases the product passes through while on the market. The stage that the product occupies at the moment depends on how long it has been on the market and on its sales. In the introductory stage the product has just been launched in the market, little if any direct competition exists, and potential buyers may not be aware of its existence. In the growth stage product sales increase rapidly, competition increases, and potential purchasers see the product as a viable alternative for satisfying their needs. In the maturity stage sales peak, competition is intense, and the price declines. At this time distribution firms are evaluated and encouraged with sales promotions and other forms of promotion. In the decline stage sales fall, weaker firms drop out of the market, and the product is eventually phased out.

2. **Discuss the product life cycle as it relates to marketing management.** The product life cycle forces a marketing manager to make decisions about strategy. The marketing strategy has to be adjusted to changes that occur as the product passes through the life cycle. The marketing mix, for instance, is al-

tered with the changing environmental conditions of each stage in the cycle. Competition, for example, increases from introduction to maturity. The marketer making decisions on price will need to take into account the increased competition.

3. **Describe the new product development process and each of its stages.** The new product development process consists of a systematic procedure for developing new products that are compatible with the organization's overall goals and that have a high probability of satisfying the potential customers' needs and wants. The steps in the process include idea generation, idea screening, business analysis, product development, test marketing, and commercialization. Idea generation is intended to identify a means of satisfying a consumer need or delivering a customer benefit. Many ideas are needed since most ideas, when examined closely, fail to deliver the necessary benefits or satisfactions to the consumer and/or fail to meet organizational objectives. The purpose of product screening is to identify and retain for further development those ideas with potential as viable products. Business analysis, product development, and test marketing all are means of refining the

GOAL SUMMARY (continued)

product and the marketing strategy. If refinement seems impossible, the product idea is eliminated from further development.

4. **Recognize the importance of the adoption and diffusion processes and be able to distinguish between them.** The adoption process refers to the procedure that individuals use in becoming aware and eventually deciding to adopt or not adopt a product. Marketing decisions are significantly influenced, since marketing can sometimes aid the individual's

progression through the process. Diffusion is the process by which an innovation spreads through a group. By understanding the process, marketers are in a better position to encourage diffusion of their organization's innovation.

5. **Identify the organizational forms developed for new product management.** Several alternative forms are available. Some of the more popular include: product managers, venture teams, and new product development departments.

KEY TERMS

Product Life Cycle, **p. 235**
Introductory Stage, **p. 236**
Growth Stage, **p. 236**
Maturity Stage, **p. 237**
Decline Stage, **p. 237**
Fads, **p. 239**
Fashions, **p. 240**
New Product, **p. 241**
Product Development Process, **p. 242**
Idea Generation, **p. 242**
Screening, **p. 244**
Concept Development, **p. 245**

Concept Testing, **p. 245**
Business Analysis, **p. 246**
Physical Product Development, **p. 246**
Test Marketing, **p. 247**
Commercialization, **p. 249**
Adoption Process, **p. 249**
Diffusion Process, **p. 250**
Product-Planning Committee, **p. 253**
Brand, Product, or Market Manager, **p. 253**
New Product Development Department, **p. 253**
Venture Team, **p. 253**

CHECK YOUR LEARNING

1. The product life cycle concept is based on the observation that products pass through stages that influence the amount of sales.   **T/F**
2. Even though the product passes through stages in its life, the marketing mix should remain the same in order to provide consistency and stability to the market.   **T/F**
3. The clothespin is most probably in the maturity stage of the product life cycle.   **T/F**
4. Like other products, fads have life cycles, except that they are very short.   **T/F**
5. The product life cycle: (a) is approximately the same length for all products, (b) is best when it is short from a management point of view, (c) means that sooner or later every firm, if it wants to continue in business, will need new products, (d) is such that a marketer always knows a product's stage in the cycle.
6. For a product to be new, it must satisfy a need that has gone unsatisfied.   **T/F**
7. The product development process is more likely to be used when the marketer is not familiar with the product type or product market.   **T/F**

8. The business analysis stage of product development requires that a model be built to determine production cost and the market's reaction for a sales forecast.   **T/F**
9. Test marketing is intended to answer one basic question, "Will the product sell?"   **T/F**
10. The first stage in the diffusion process is awareness followed by interest.   **T/F**
11. In the trial stage of product adoption individuals attempt to confirm or refute their previous evaluation of the product.   **T/F**
12. The study of diffusion of innovation focuses on how an innovation spreads through a market or group. **T/F**
13. The rate of adoption: (a) is unaffected by how much people talk about the product, (b) is increased if the product is more complex because people are more interested, (c) is increased if the product can be tried with little or no risk, (d) is increased if people have to learn new concepts to use the product.
14. Many firms have organization forms that separate new products from existing products so that new products receive the needed time and attention.   **T/F**

CHECK YOUR LEARNING (continued)

15. Product-planning committees should not have a heavy representation of individuals from top management.   **T/F**
16. Venture teams operate as if they were independent companies.   **T/F**

17. Product management: (a) should focus on new product development, (b) should start with the overall strategy and objectives of the firm, (c) should ignore the diffusion process since little can be done about it anyway, (d) all of the above.

QUESTIONS FOR REVIEW AND DISCUSSION

1. Define the terms for this chapter that appear at the end of the goal summary.
2. Why is it so important that marketers understand the product life cycle concept?
3. Explain what the marketing mix might be for a product in the maturity stage.
4. List and briefly define the steps in the product development process.
5. Describe a procedure appropriate for concept development and testing of an idea for a new soft drink made out of soybean milk.
6. List the stages in the adoption process.

7. Using the determinates of the rate of adoption, assess the rate of adoption for audio digital disc players.
8. Why is the organizational structure important to the success of new and existing products?
9. How would you go about determining the stage of the product life cycle for a specific product?
10. You have developed a new industrial stamping press for stamping out metal parts. Would you test market it? Why or why not?
11. How do fads and fashions differ?
12. You are in the cookware business. Generate a number of good ideas for new products.

NOTES

1. John Marcom, Jr., "Satellite Company's Technology Is Too Far Ahead of Market's Needs," *The Wall Street Journal,* May 3, 1984, p. 27.
2. George S. Day, "The Product Life Cycle: Analysis and Application Issues," *Journal of Marketing* (Fall 1981): pp. 60–67.
3. Jennifer Bingham Hall, "High-Tech Home Health Care Is Showing Promise, But Some Big Problems Remain," *The Wall Street Journal,* April 18, 1984, p. 33.
4. Paul W. Hamelman and Edward M. Mazze, "Improving Product Abandonment Decisions," *Journal of Marketing* (April 1972): pp. 20–26.
5. Sarah Oates, "Holes in Your Socks? Don't Worry, You Have the Foot Fashion," *The Wall Street Journal,* May 5, 1984, p. 31.
6. William Qualls, Richard W. Olshovsky, and Ronald E. Michaels, "Shortening of the PLC—An Empirical Test," *Journal of Marketing* 45, no. 4 (Fall 1981): pp. 76–80.
7. Susan Frakes, "High Speed Management for the High-Tech Age," *Fortune,* March 5, 1984, pp. 62–67.
8. "New Product Strategy: How the Pros Do It," *Industrial Marketing,* May 1982, pp. 49–60.

9. Booz, Allen, and Hamilton, Inc., *New Product Management for the 1980's: Phase I* (New York: Booz, Allen, and Hamilton, 1981): p. 3.
10. James H. Myers, "Benefit Structure Analysis: A New Tool for Product Planning," *Journal of Marketing* (October 1976): pp. 23–32.
11. Eric Von Hippel, "Get New Products From Customers," *Harvard Business Review* (March–April 1982): pp. 117–122.
12. Glen L. Urban and John R. Hauser, *Design and Marketing of New Products* (Englewood Cliffs, N.J.: Prentice-Hall, 1980), pp. 190–195.
13. Ronald Alsop, "Why Some Patients at Dr. Shea's Clinic Smell of Mayonnaise," *The Wall Street Journal,* April 13, 1984, p. 234.
14. William L. Moore, "Concept Testing," *Journal of Business Research* (September 1982): pp. 279–294.
15. Edward M. Tauber, "Forecasting Sales Prior to Test Market," *Journal of Marketing* (January 1977): pp. 80–84.
16. "Test Marketing," *Sales & Marketing Management,* March 10, 1986, p. 89.
17. Jay E. Klompmaker, G. David Hughes, and Russell I. Haley, "Test Marketing in New Product Develop-

NOTES *(continued)*

ment," *Harvard Business Review* (May–June 1976): pp. 128–138.

18. Klompmaker, Hughes, and Haley, "Test Marketing," p. 89.

19. Eleanor Johnson, "Testing Time for Test Marketing," *Fortune,* October 29, 1984, pp. 75–76.

20. Alvin J. Silk and Glen L. Urban, "Pre-Test Market Evaluation of New Packaged Goods: A Model and Measurement Methodology," *Journal of Marketing Research* (May 1978): pp. 171–191.

21. Derek Abell, "Strategies Windows," *Journal of Marketing* (July 1978): pp. 21–26.

22. Jeremy Main, "Help and Hope in the New-Products Game," *Fortune,* February 7, 1983, pp. 60–64.

23. See David S. Hopkins, "New Product Winners and Losers," Research Report Number 773 (New York: The Conference Board, 1980), pp. 12–20; J. Hugh Davidson, "Why Most New Consumer Brands Fail," *Harvard Business Review* (March–April 1976): pp. 117–122; Glen L. Urban and John R. Hansen, *Design and Marketing of New Products* (Englewood Cliffs, N.J.: Prentice-Hall, 1980), pp. 42–46.

24. Everett M. Rogers and F. Floyd Shoemaker, *Communication of Innovation: A Cross-Cultural Approach* (New York: The Free Press, 1971), pp. 135–157.

25. John Koten, "Novel Promotion Plan Helps Johnson & Johnson Toy Sales," *The Wall Street Journal,* April 26, 1984, p. 31.

26. Rogers and Shoemaker, *Communication of Innovation,* p. 182.

27. Elizabeth Hirschman, "Innovativeness, Novelty Seeking and Consumer Creativity," *Journal of Consumer Research* (December 1980): pp. 283–295; Richard W. Olshovsky, "Time and Rate of Adoption of Innovations," *Journal of Consumer Research* (March 1980): pp. 425–428.

28. Rogers and Shoemaker, *Communication of Innovation,* pp. 135–157.

29. David W. Nylen, "New Product Failures: Not Just a Marketing Problem," *Business,* September–October 1979, pp. 4–6.

30. Richard T. Hise and J. Patrick Kelly, "Product Management on Trial," *Journal of Marketing* (October 1978): pp. 28–33.

31. Don T. Dunn, Jr., "The Rise and Fall of Ten Venture Groups," *Business Horizons,* October 1977, pp. 32–41; William W. George, "Task Teams for Rapid Growth," *Harvard Business Review* (March–April): pp. 71–80.

32. Ben M. Enis, Raymond LaGarce, and Arthur E. Prell, "Extending the Product Life Cycle," *Business Horizons,* June 1977, pp. 45–56.

33. Richard A. Shaffer, "Next Apple Computer Blends Old Design, New Techology," *The Wall Street Journal,* March 23, 1984, p. 19.

Lean Cuisine frozen entree line of products has been a product success for the Stouffer's Corporation. Lean Cuisine development actually started in 1967 when Stouffer began investigating lifestyles of the health- and diet-conscious consumer segment. Lifestyle is a person's mode of living, which reflects a person's needs, motives, perceptions, attitudes, the products purchased, and how products are used and consumed.

One survey of 1,800 adults found that household food buyers could be classified into one of four groups based on life-style information. *Hedonists,* who make up 20 percent of the population, want good tasting, convenient, and inexpensive food. They do not worry about sugar, cholesterol, salt, calories, or preservatives. Young males dominate the group. *Don't Wants* represent 20 percent of the population. They willingly sacrifice taste, convenience, and money to avoid preservatives, sugar, cholesterol, and calories. These health-oriented individuals seek nutrition and usually are not weight conscious. They are older, with half being over fifty, have no children at home, live in large urban areas, and are better educated. The *weight conscious* make up 33 percent of the population, worry primarily about cal-

ories and fat, but also are concerned about cholesterol, sugar, and salt. Taste, nutrition, and preservatives are not of particular importance. Convenience, however, is important. Many are women employed full-time. Their incomes are higher than average. *Moderates,* who comprise 25 percent of the population, are average in every respect.

After several years of studying the health and diet conscious consumer, as well as those who needed to diet, observing exercise trends, and consulting with physicians on dieter needs, Stouffer's was ready to develop a product. Data in hand, Stouffer's established the characteristics the product must have, including texture, flavor, and portion size. The product was then developed, tested in experiments and consumer surveys, test marketed, and finally put on the market.

Pleased with the success of Lean Cuisine, which indicated that Stouffer's interpreted the market successfully, the company would like to develop other successful products. The firm has a pizza product called French Bread Pizza. One of the distinguishing characteristics of the product is its French bread crust.

Stouffer's had to reeducate the public on pizza crust and change consumers' attitudes to acceptance of a bread crust pizza. They did this very successfully. Another product, Italian Sandwiches, was marketed for a time, but dropped when volume was not high enough to support the dedicated production equipment (dedicated equipment can only be used for the production of the one product).

Issues for Discussion

1. Discuss the use of lifestyle information as the basis for developing new products.

2. How might consumer lifestyle influence the life cycle and the management of a product?

3. Based on the information in the case, what new product ideas can you visualize that Stouffer's should develop into products?

4. What steps in the new product development process were employed by Stouffer's and mentioned in the case? What steps, if any, would you suggest they use that were not mentioned?

Source: Anna Sobczynski, "Reading the Consumer's Mind," *Advertising Age,* May 3, 1984, pp. M–16, M–17; and "Research on Food Consumption Values Identifies Four Market Segments: Finds Good Taste Still Tops," *Marketing News,* May 15, 1981, p. 17.

MARKETING PLAN

PART 6A / ACTION PROGRAM: PRODUCT/SERVICE (CHAPTERS 8 AND 9)

A. What is the total product concept for this good or service?
B. What is the breadth and depth of the organization's product/service mix?
C. How does the organization's product assortment differ from that of the competition?
D. If known, does the product mix/product line or service mix differ from the previous year? If so, analyze the competition's likely reaction and how (if at all) you will respond.
E. If applicable, describe the package (size, color, label, etc.). Will the package create any unusual distribution problems that will affect the optimum distribution system?
F. Are any product modifications expected as the product moves through the product life cycle? Describe. Any service modifications expected? Describe.
G. How is the product or service positioned or repositioned?
H. Are any warranties or guarantees offered? What are their provisions?
I. What is the test marketing process for your product? Your service?

Section Five

The Price Plan

OUTLINE

CHAPTER

10

Pricing Policies and Objectives

LEARNING GOALS

After reading this chapter, you should be able to:

1. Explain the importance of price to consumers and the firm.
2. Identify the factors that allow a marketer some control over price.
3. Differentiate between profitability, volume, competitive and social price objectives.
4. Compare and contrast from a marketing point of view one-price and flexible-price policies.
5. Define full-line psychological and life-cycle pricing.

*P*ierce Gonzales, owner and manager of the Book Center in Denver, Colorado, wonders how to combat the discounter threat. During the last twenty years, the largest chains, including discount chains, have taken as much as a third of the $6 to $10 billion retail book market. Some publishers sell more than one half of their books to chains. Chains have worried the independents but the real threat to survival is seen coming from discount chains. Crown Books, a national discount bookstore chain, has rapidly expanded into the Denver area. The largest book discounter in the United States, Crown has expanded at a rate of thirty-five stores a year and expects to continue at the same pace for several more years.

A typical independent bookstore may carry upward of 20,000 titles. The average independent operates on a net profit margin of 3 to 5 percent on annual sales of $150,000. The Book Center, an independent, will probably survive but will lose the best-seller business on which it depends. Best-sellers sell quickly and easily, thereby supporting the large inventory of slow moving titles.

Crown advertises heavily and emphasizes price. Crown's advertising slogan "If you paid full price, you didn't buy it at Crown Books" is especially upsetting to Gonzales and other independent bookstore operations. It implies that the independent bookstores have been ripping off customers. Crown's marketing efforts have created price resistance among consumers. Consumers have become bargain hunters. Gonzales finds customers bartering and asking what the store will take for a book. The discount chains have made its customers think that prices should be lower.

Luckily, Gonzales is not alone in facing the problem of discounters. Independent booksellers across the nation have recognized the problem. In fact, the Mountain Plains Booksellers Association, headquartered in Denver, was formed to organize cooperative efforts against the problem.

The Association's efforts include advertising in newspapers, autograph parties with authors, newsletters, catalogs, window stickers identifying "full service" bookstores, a directory, and book fairs.

The Booksellers Association recently made plans to initiate a computerized order service to pool the tiny orders of individual shops. The order service should enable small bookstores to obtain the same discounts as the large chains. Independents usually purchase from publishers at 40 percent off the list price, but large chains qualify for discounts of 45 to 50 percent. Gonzales thinks the Association may also be able to help reduce the cost of transportation. Whatever the Association decides to do, however, should be carefully considered from a legal standpoint. Crown has already brought suit against the Northern California Booksellers Association for alleged anticompetitive acts.

Gonzales sees several possible alternatives to the discounter problem. The Book Center could emphasize the full service approach including sponsoring adult reading groups, children's story hour, poetry readings, stocking an extensive inventory of backlist literature, and providing special ordering and gift wrapping. The Book Center could become active in the Association to obtain help in promotion and perhaps lower cost. Alternatively the Book Center could try to compete head-to-head with discounters by lowering prices and adopting their other tactics.

Issues for Discussion
1. How would you describe the pricing environment in which the Book Center operates?
2. What should be the price objectives of the Book Center?
3. How do the Book Center's and other firms' price policies influence the pricing of books?

Sources: Madalynne Reuter (ed.), "B. Dalton Discontinues Pickwick Discount Chains," *Publishers Weekly,* July 4, 1986, p. 13; Steve Weiner, "Independent Bookstores Improving Services and Marketing to Survive," *The Wall Street Journal,* June 7, 1984, p. 5; and Brian Moran, "Pickwick Adds to Discount Book Threat," *Advertising Age,* July 30, 1984, p. 28.

■ Discount chain bookstores attract a higher volume of potential customers, which ultimately threatens the survival of the smaller independent bookstore.

*P*ierce Gonzales has some important pricing decisions to make. One decision is the establishment of pricing objectives for the Book Center. Should the objective be to maximize profits, to increase market share, to increase volume, or something else? We will look at several possible objectives, what they mean and when they might be used. Gonzales must also make decisions about the price policies to use at the Book Center. Apparently, book-buying consumers have decided that book prices should be negotiable. Gonzales may select a flexible-price or one-price policy; the chapter considers the advantages and disadvantages of each. Gonzales must also formulate policies on complementary and psychological pricing. The chapter describes these as well. ∎

INTRODUCTION

The marketer decides on the price of the items that the organization offers to customers. Answering the key question "What price do we charge?" requires thought and information because price affects the purchaser and the firm. The decision must be made within the context of the marketer's understanding of price in relation to customers, the organization, the competition, and the economy. Therefore, before we actually price an item (which is done in the next chapter), we will develop an understanding of the perceptions of price and its role. With a general understanding of price, the marketer can make decisions on pricing objectives and policies. Then the price can be set and adjusted when necessary.

THE IMPORTANCE AND CHARACTER OF PRICE

The **price** of a product or service is the money or other goods or services exchanged for the ownership or use of the product or service.[1] Although the common term is price, other terms may be used, such as rent, offering, contribution, tuition, and so forth. (See figure 10.1.) Price represents the exchange value of a good or service. Either as buyers or sellers our willingness to make an exchange depends upon the value we attach to the product. As buyers the more value we perceive in a product, the more we are willing to pay for it. As sellers the more value we perceive, the more we ask in payment. The **value** of an item, therefore, is what it can be exchanged for in the marketplace. For example, bicycling enthusiasts would pay a higher price for a Fuji 18-speed, customized, sealed-bearing mountain bike with an oval-shaped chain wheel than they would for a single-speed, twenty-inch Huffy. The seller would also ask a different price; under $100 for the Huffy and approximately $1,000 for the Fuji. Value derives from **utility**—the ability to satisfy. The more utility a product has, the more worth it has and the more satisfaction it will give.

Two very similar products may have very different prices. For example, the Heath Company sells an unassembled personal computer at a lower price than IBM sells its essentially the same, but assembled, computer. Why the price difference? First, the Heath computer requires assembly. Second, it is possible to examine the IBM

*A*n IBM-PC and a Heath-PC sell at different prices for a number of reasons.

❑ **Figure 10.1**
Price—What we call it.

	The Meaning of Price	
Alternative Terms	What Is Given by Buyer	What Is Received by Buyer
Price	Money/goods/service	Most physical merchandise
Tuition	Money/service	College courses, education
Rent	Money/goods/service	A place to live, or use of equipment for a specific time period
Interest	Money/goods/service	Use of money
Fee	Money	Professional services: for lawyers, doctors, consultants
Fare	Money	Transportation: air, taxi, bus
Toll	Money	Use of road or bridge, or long-distance phone rate
Salary	Money/goods	Work of managers
Wage	Money/goods	Work of hourly workers
Bribe	Money/goods	Illegal actions
Commission	Money/goods	Sales effort

Source: From *Principles of Marketing* by Thomas C. Kinnear and Kenneth L. Bernhardt. Copyright © 1983 by Scott, Foresman and Company. Reprinted by permission.

computer at conveniently located retail outlets. Third, the IBM is a better known and widely accepted brand so its purchase produces less psychological risk. Fourth, after-sale reassurance, service, and "hand-holding" are more readily available with IBM.

Importance of Price

PRICE AND THE PURCHASER

*P*rice serves the buyer as well as the seller.

Price influences purchase behavior in several ways. For instance, price forces purchasers to assign priorities to needs. With a limited ability to buy, consumers and organizations use their resources to obtain the most possible satisfaction. Price, therefore, restricts consumption. The restrictive effect of price lessens overindulgence and waste. For example, many natural resources in America, such as the forests and water, have been used frivolously because they seemed to be free. On the other hand, the prices of some necessities, like housing in New York City, may be so restrictive that they leave some people without the basic essentials of life.

Price may also serve to alert the consumer to quality differences. A $15 Timex wristwatch and a $500 Rolex differ in quality. Even if potential purchasers have a limited knowledge of watches, they look for and expect more quality in the Rolex.

Finally, price may serve as an indicator of social standing. For example, a Volkswagen and a Rolls Royce have functional differences, but probably not to the extent that the difference in their prices suggests. The price of the Rolls Royce may well be worth every penny to the purchaser, not for the functional aspects of the car, but because it helps identify the purchaser's social standing.

PRICE AND THE ECONOMY

*P*rices influence the direction of economic activity.

In a free enterprise economy, price serves as a clearing mechanism in the market. If the quantity of a product demanded is greater than the quantity supplied, prices normally go up, and only those purchasers willing and able to pay the higher price obtain the product. If the quantity supplied is greater than the quantity demanded, prices normally fall, bringing in more purchasers.

Excess supply forces price down.

To earn a profit, a firm must cover costs with revenue. The cost of producing a product is, therefore, a basic factor in determining its price. Price, in turn, can influence costs. A high or low price affects the quantity of a product that is likely to be sold, and this quantity can make a difference in a company's costs. If, for instance, a firm's pricing decisions encourage it to produce a large quantity of a product, it can realize efficiencies in production and thereby reduce its costs. Prices also serve to allocate resources—land, labor, capital, and entrepreneurship—to the highest bidder. For example, to attract scarce resources away from other industries, a firm may have to pay higher prices for them. This process can shift resources from one sector of the economy to another.

The long-term supply of a product also depends on its expected price in the future. A low current price, such as the price of corn and soybeans in the mid-1980s, generally leads to low price expectations in the future. Production is normally curtailed when price expectations are low and increased when price expectations are high. Low prices, on the other hand, encourage expansion of demand. To the extent that consumption becomes habit-forming, a rise in consumption when prices are low may continue even if prices rise in the future. When gasoline prices are low for an extended period, people purchase large cars, which use more fuel than small cars. They find it difficult to cut gasoline consumption when prices go up.

*P*rices influence us psychologically.

Finally, prices have an important bearing on the psychology of the populace.[2] Spiraling medical costs in the United States, for instance, have caused people to think differently about medical treatment: who is entitled and who should pay. During periods of high inflation or deflation, forced adjustments in employment, savings, and spending patterns generate psychological and political unrest. Prices, whether given in dollars, francs, pesos, or another currency, affect how the populace relates psychologically to the present and the future. As the perceptions of the value of a currency become more favorable, the currency becomes more valuable, and the economy and outlook of the country are also perceived more favorably.

PRICE AND THE FIRM

Price is the most important factor influencing the marketing program.[3] The price a firm asks for its products influences the level of consumer demand. If a firm's products are in high demand, its competitive position will be stronger, its share of the market will be greater, and its revenues and profits will be higher. Thus, price is an integral part of a firm's efforts to meet its objectives.

In some organizations price serves as the basis of the marketing program. Consider, for instance, retail discount merchandisers such as Kmart and Wal-Mart. They have developed their marketing programs around price. Retail stores with a prestige image, such as Saks Fifth Avenue or Neiman-Marcus, also employ price as a key factor in their marketing programs.

*P*rices and marketing strategy need to be compatible.

Price should be compatible with the rest of the marketing strategy. When promotion is emphasized, as with cosmetic products, price must be sufficiently high to provide a gross margin to cover promotion and other cost. When distribution is direct from the manufacturer to the ultimate consumer, as with Amway, a direct distributor of detergent and other household products, the selling price has to provide a gross margin that will cover the cost of direct marketing.

Price is the most flexible variable in the marketing mix because it can be changed more quickly than other variables. Usually all that is required is an announcement that the price has been changed. Changes in product design, promotion, and distribution, require more effort.

To make demand less sensitive to price, marketers often spend considerable time with product design, branding, packaging, personal selling, advertising, and other marketing variables. They strive to create an environment in which their brand, and only their brand, will be demanded.

The Ability to Control Price

A marketer's control over price varies with the type of market.

Before marketers price a product, they must assess whether and to what extent their firms can control price. **Administered pricing,** the firm's ability to control price, depends on the type of market in which the firm operates. There are four types of price markets: pure competitive, monopolistic competitive, oligopolistic, and pure monopoly. Except for the pure competitive market, marketers can set price in all of the price markets, but they can fully control price only in the pure monopoly market.

THE PURE COMPETITIVE MARKET

*T*iming transactions is the marketing focus in the pure competitive market.

A **pure competitive market** consists of many buyers and sellers exchanging a nearly identical product. Corn, cotton, soybeans, and other agricultural commodities exchange in a nearly pure competitive market. The market, rather than the selling firm, establishes price, which is largely a function of supply and demand. If supply is high relative to demand, commodity prices drop. If supply is low, they rise. A cotton broker, for example, cannot control price because, within a given grade, all cotton is the same. Buyers will simply refuse to purchase at the higher price and take their business to brokers selling at the market price.

In pure competitive markets, price fluctuations result from expectations about the future level of supply. The marketing strategy of both buyers and sellers involves forecasting and attempting to time sales and purchases to coincide with favorable price levels.

THE MONOPOLISTIC COMPETITIVE MARKET

*C*reating and maintaining product uniqueness permits some pricing freedom.

Monopolistic competitive markets contain many sellers trading slightly different products. A company uses **product differentiation** by varying the function, style, quality, service, or packaging of its product from that of the competition. Firms can use product differentiation to move products out of a normal exchange of identical products in a pure competitive market, and into a more restricted market where they can avoid competing on the basis of market price alone. Natural Pak Produce, for example, created a monopolistic competitive market by developing a new agricultural product. They sell a specialty winter tomato that is sealed in an airtight package with

These products sell in
markets with different
competitive structures.

a. Produce: pure competition

b. Computers: monopolistic competition

c. Automobiles: oligopoly

d. Postal service: monopoly

a moisture absorbent, permitting the tomato to be stored for a month at the peak of ripeness. Natural Pak tomatoes have the quality of fresh summer tomatoes instead of the lack of taste and fibrous texture of winter tomatoes.[4] In this way they avoid the pure competition that exists for the more standard but relatively tasteless commercial tomatoes.

Companies using product differentiation stress the differences between their products and those of their competitors in their promotional campaigns. The personal computer industry is a case in point. The IBM PC has the greatest name recognition, but numerous other firms manufacture PCs. Many of the competing PCs are compatible with the IBM, and their compatibility is a definite selling point, but their manufacturers stress their differences as well. Leading Edge, for example, claims full compatibility with IBM but stresses that its product is easier to use.

Differences in purchasers' perceptions of competing products allow the marketer a degree of control over price in a monopolistic competitive market. Purchasers choose a product because they perceive it to be different from the products of its competitors and will buy it even though it is not the same price. Marketing strategy, therefore, plays an important role in monopolistic competitive markets where identifying, creating, and enhancing the perceptual difference purchasers have about competing products permit the company to set a price different from that of competitors. If the strategy of creating perceptual differences is very successful, the market fragments into segments and becomes several smaller markets. For a time, at least, each firm may have a market segment to itself, allowing a degree of control over price. General Mills' Bisquick is still the only brand in its segment. General Mills has completely satisfied the buyers in the segment with a good product at a low price.

OLIGOPOLISTIC MARKET

'Watch thy competitor!" is an axiom of marketers in oligopolistic markets.

An **oligopolistic market** is a market served by relatively few sellers. In the years before foreign competition, the American automobile industry had only four manufacturers and was an oligopoly. Barriers to market entry (investment, technology, or regulation) restricted the number of manufacturers selling cars. Buyers varied in number from many in some markets to few in others. Prices charged by individual sellers differed to the extent that their marketing strategies differed. The more unique the strategy and product, the more the seller can deviate from the average price in the market and obtain the desired level of sales. Since customer purchases depend on the marketing strategy and the price offered by the seller, marketers in oligopolistic markets devote considerable time to developing strategy and observing competitors.

PURE MONOPOLY

'How sweet it is!" Freedom to set price, but for government regulators.

A **pure monopoly market** is a market supplied by only one seller. Before divestiture AT&T was a monopoly in the long-distance telephone lines market. When patents or secret technical knowledge limit the numbers of producers to one, the seller has the freedom to establish the price provided the market desires the product. The seller may charge the highest price the market will bear. Sometimes, however, the seller may charge a lower price in order to serve the market better, to lessen the chance of government regulation, or to reduce the likelihood of competitors entering the market. When a monopoly exists because of regulation, as in the case of electric utilities, the price level depends on the seller's ability to convince the regulator to accept the price.

THE CASE CONTINUES

The Book Center operates in a monopolistic competitive market. Hundreds of independent book sellers and several chains exist. The Book Center, like other book sellers, has the ability to make its offering to the public unique by virtue of providing services, such as gift wrapping, po-

etry readings, special ordering, children's story hour, and title selection. Thus, within limits, Gonzales can adjust the selling price to the store's requirements. Operating on a profit

margin on sales of 3 to 4 percent, the Book Center manager must carefully weigh the impact of each pricing decision on other areas of the firm. Consumers have made it known to all book sellers that price is important because so many have purchased from low-price sellers.

DETERMINING WHAT PRICE TO CHARGE

Using a pricing procedure to determine what price to charge encourages the marketer to give pricing decisions the emphasis they deserve. The procedure outlined in figure 10.2 should be used in its entirety when setting the list price that final consumers are expected to pay. Once the environment is understood and pricing objectives and policies are determined, pricing an item would entail a quick review of steps 1 through 3, an estimate of cost and demand—steps 4 and 5, and concentration on step 6—setting the price. Steps 1, 2, and 3 are discussed in detail in this chapter, and the rest of the steps are discussed in the following chapter.

STEP 1: EVALUATING ENVIRONMENTAL FACTORS

Product price is set within the context of competitive and economic factors.

The competitive and economic environments influence price. Earlier the different types of competitive environments were discussed. At that time the issue was a

❑ **Figure 10.2**
Procedure for setting price.*

Stage 1: Environmental and administrative actions

Step 1
Evaluating environmental factors
Step 2
Selecting pricing objectives
Step 3
Establishing pricing policies

Stage 2: Action to establish a specific price

Step 4
Estimate cost and review cost-based pricing
Step 5
Estimate demand and review demand-based pricing
Step 6
Selecting a pricing method and setting the price
Step 7
Decide on discounts and allowances
Step 8
Adjust the price when necessary

*Steps 1–3 are discussed in this chapter.
Steps 4–8 are discussed in the next chapter.

In a pure competitive market competitors seldom react to a firm's price change.

In a monopolistic competitive market, competitors will react to a firm's prices if they perceive loss of customers and sales.

*M*onitor competitors' price to anticipate competitors' reaction to a price change.

marketer's ability to administer price. Now the focus is on competitors' price behavior. What prices do competitors charge? What is the price range? How do competitors react to price changes? What technique for establishing price has each competitor adopted? These are typical questions that the marketer would like to answer from analyzing the type of market and monitoring the prices of individual competitors. Analyzing the type of market in which the firm operates provides clues about the reactions that can be expected from competitors. Is the market most similar to a pure competitive, monopolistic competitive, oligopoly, or monopoly? Competitors in each market usually react differently to pricing strategy of other firms.

In a pure competitive market, a price change by a competing firm would stimulate little, if any, reaction from competitors because all firms can sell their product at the market price. If a Florida orange grower agreed to sell oranges at less than the market price, other growers might laugh in amazement. However, they would have little reason to take a pricing action of their own, since possible increases in quantity sold would only be offset by lower profits in an industry with similar costs. In a pure competitive market producers do best to sell their product at the higher market price. Likewise an orange grower who sets a price higher than the market would receive good luck wishes from fellow growers, but no money from buyers. The market price is the highest possible price at which the product will be exchanged.

In a monopolistic competitive market, firms have differentiated their products. As long as a competitor perceives that its customers are remaining loyal, it is not likely to react to a company's price reductions. If the company's price lures customers away from competitors, they will probably react. To lure customers away from competitors the price saving offered to the customer has to outweigh the customer's nonprice reasons for buying from another company.

In an oligopoly market, a price reduction will normally be met with quick reaction from competitors, an equal or greater reduction. Exxon would not watch a competitor reduce the price of gasoline without also reducing its price. Since purchasers basically perceive all gasoline as the same, Exxon would lose its customers if it failed to meet price reductions.

Since a monopoly market lacks direct competitors, the only reaction of a competitive nature to a price reduction would be from the manufacturers of substitute products. How they may react cannot be accurately generalized.

Identifying the type of market gives an initial indication of possible competitors' actions with regard to the company's price. Executives operating companies in

This competitive ad stresses more value for the same price.

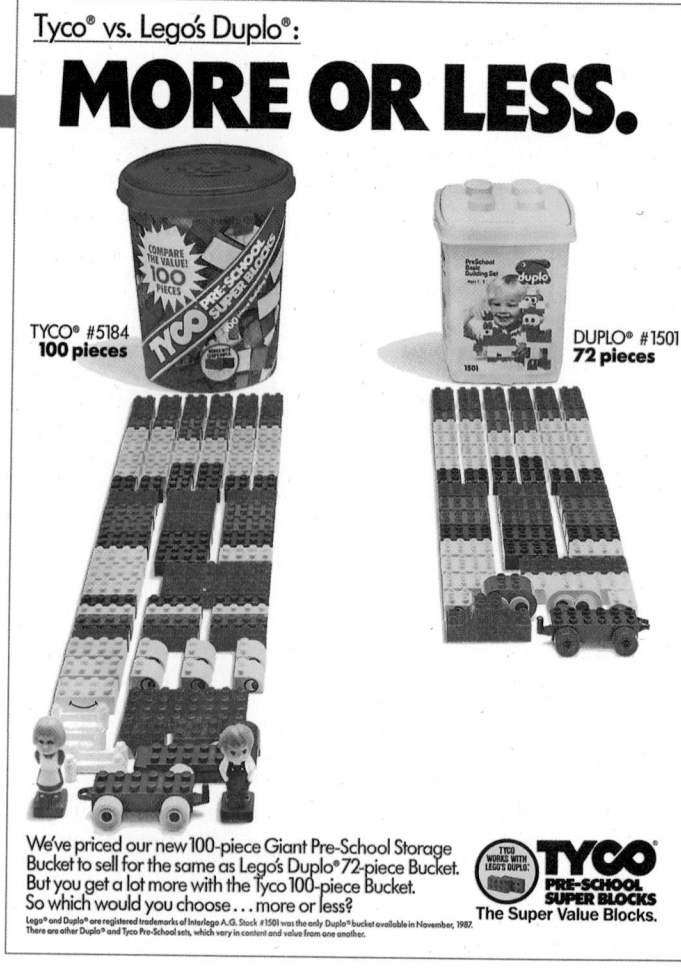

Tyco® vs. Lego's Duplo®:

MORE OR LESS.

TYCO® #5184
100 pieces

DUPLO® #1501
72 pieces

We've priced our new 100-piece Giant Pre-School Storage Bucket to sell for the same as Lego's Duplo® 72-piece Bucket. But you get a lot more with the Tyco 100-piece Bucket. So which would you choose...more or less?

Lego® and Duplo® are registered trademarks of Interlego A.G. Stock #1501 was the only Duplo® bucket available in November, 1987. There are other Duplo® and Tyco Pre-School sets, which vary in content and value from one another.

TYCO
PRE-SCHOOL
SUPER BLOCKS
The Super Value Blocks.

Source: Courtesy of Tyco® Toys, Inc.

monopolistic competitive and oligopoly markets, however, need to know how individual competitors will react. For this reason, they are constantly monitoring their competition.

The marketer has several ways to monitor competitor prices. Retailers, such as department stores, review the advertisements of competitors for price information. They may also use comparison shoppers. Comparison shoppers, often the employees of firms specializing in gathering information about competing businesses, pose as shoppers and visit retailers to acquire price and other information.

Industrial firms monitor competitors' prices by asking salespeople to report price information, by acquiring price lists from syndicated service firms, and by conducting marketing research. Since negotiated prices are common in industrial markets, information about the exact selling price may be impossible to obtain.

Even reasonably accurate information about competitors' prices can serve the marketing manager as a starting point for setting price. If the firm's offering is unique and of better quality than the competitions', the manager may set a higher price.

Competitive information on price also helps the marketer to anticipate a competitor's reaction to price, which is important because it will influence the success of the price change. If a major competitor adjusts its price to meet a firm's price change, the success of the price change in attracting customers to the firm may diminish.

*A*uto industry firms react quickly to price.

In the auto industry competitors react quickly to price change. For instance, General Motors cut its annual interest rate on car finance loans from 9 to 2.9 percent on Thursday. On Friday Chrysler cut its rate to 2.4 percent, and the same day Ford matched General Motors' rate. The following Wednesday American Motors cut its

"Let's hold out for 'buy one, get one free.'"

rate to zero. In less than a week after General Motors' initial reduction, all the American car manufacturers had cut their finance rate. General Motors' executives must have reasoned that they would sell more cars even if competitors responded quickly because more people would buy cars. Competitors also behave differently with changes in the economy, usually becoming more price competitive during deflationary periods. (See figure 10.3.)

 ## STEP 2: SELECTING PRICE OBJECTIVES

Price objectives state what the firm wishes to accomplish with its price. Executives may develop volume, profitability, competitive, and social price objectives.

Profitability Pricing

As an objective, maximizing profits does not mean charging the highest possible price.

Profitability pricing focuses on the ability of price to affect profit. One of the most common forms of profitability pricing is maximization of profit. **Maximization of profit** is achieved when the cost of producing an additional (or last) unit of a product is just less than or equal to the revenue gained from the sale of that unit (marginal cost ≤ marginal revenue).

Recall from the discussion of the product life cycle in Chapter 9 that during the introductory and growth stages of the cycle profits rise, but, as a product moves through the maturity stage, they decline. That is, each additional unit of the product sold yields a smaller profit than the unit before. At some point, the cost to produce one additional unit will equal the revenue gained from the sale of that unit, and no profit will be earned for the firm. In order to maximize its profit, the firm should stop producing the product at this point.

❑ **Figure 10.3**
Pricing and company
objectives.

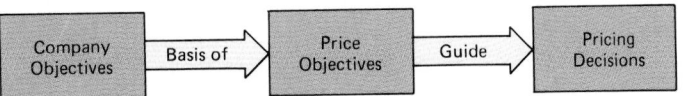

*W*ith ROI objectives, profit in relation to dollars invested is the measure of success.

The problem with the maximization of profit form of profitability pricing is that marketers seldom have enough information to decide exactly how many units of sales they can get to reach the level of production that will maximize profits. Therefore, many executives adopt a return on investment objective. **Return on investment (ROI)** objectives measure profitability in terms of the amount of money invested. The simplest ROI formula divides investment into profits.

$$\text{ROI \%} = \frac{\text{Profit}}{\text{Investment}}$$

An ROI objective must specify a particular level of return. For instance, Harvest Company's ROI objective specified the targeted goal of a 20 percent annual return, meaning that the company's managers expected to achieve a $.20 return for every dollar the company invested for a year. Refer to target return on investment in Chapter 11 for an illustration of how ROI objectives are used to establish a specific price.

'*S*atisfactory ROI" is a popular pricing objective.

Some marketing managers prefer to use targeted ROI objectives in conjunction with sales objectives. First they emphasize the obtainment of specified ROI goals, but once these goals are achieved, their interest shifts to increasing sales or perhaps to increasing market share. It was found that "satisfactory return on investment" was the most popular pricing objective.[5]

Volume Objectives

When managers adopt volume objectives, their goals are related to the level of sales. Sales are necessary but do not assure profits, hence profit and sales objectives do differ. Volume objectives stated in terms of dollars are simply referred to as sales objectives. Sales levels relate to price through the price/quantity relationship.

As price decreases from P_1 to P_2 (shown in figure 10.4) the quantity demanded increases from Q_1 to Q_2. If the percentage reduction in price is less than the percentage increase in quantity, the price change results in a dollar increase in sales. This concept, termed price elasticity of demand, is discussed in the next chapter.

*W*hat share of the market is the firm serving? Should it be serving? If pertinent questions, then market share objectives are needed.

Volume objectives also take the form of market share goals. An organization's **market share** is its percentage of total industry sales:

$$\text{Market Share \%} = \frac{\text{Organization's Sales}}{\text{Industry's Sales}}$$

The company with the largest market share normally has a more widely known and favorable public image, for example, Caterpillar Tractor Corporation. Market share also correlates with ROI so companies with a high market share tend to have a high ROI.[6]

❑ **Figure 10.4**
Price/quantity relationship.

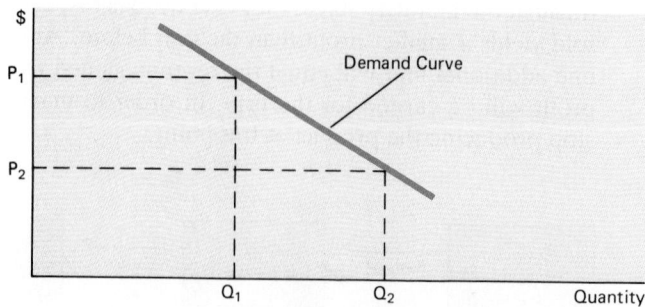

☐ **Figure 10.5**
Competitive responses
to pricing action.

Competitive Reactions	Pricing Actions		
	Stable Prices	Price Reductions	Price Increases
1. Maintain current prices	No change	Hold the line	Hold the line
2. Follow competitor's actions	• No change • Follow the leader	• Meet price decreases • Follow the leader	• Meet price increases • Follow the leader

3. Challenge competitor's actions
  By pricing actions
  By nonprice actions
	• Increase or decrease prices
	• Increase advertising and sales promotions
	• Introduce new brands
		• Exceed price cuts
		• Initiate price war
		• Increase advertising and sales promotions
		• Introduce new brands
			• Exceed price increases
			• Increase advertising and sales promotions
			• Introduce new brands

4. Outflank competitor's	Establish a pricing niche	Establish a pricing niche	Establish a pricing niche

Source: From Henry Assael,
*Marketing Management: Strategy
and Action* (Boston: Kent
Publishing Company, 1985), p.
458. Copyright © 1985 by
Wadsworth, Inc. Reprinted by
permission of Kent Publishing
Company, a division of
Wadsworth, Inc.

Competitive Objectives

*W*hat should the price be
in respect to competitors'
price: above, at, or below
market?

Competitive objectives focus on competitors' behavior as the basis of determining price. Prices can be above, below, or at competitors' prices. When a firm's prices are higher than competitors' prices, the product must be perceived to have greater value. IBM can price its personal computer above the market and sell it because the market perceives IBM to have a high-quality, well-serviced, and widely distributed product. Pricing "at" market or "with" a competitor indicates a more conservative position. Management may not want to provoke a pricing battle by pricing below market, nor does it have enough confidence in the firm's offering to price above the market. (See figure 10.5.)

*T*o safely price below
competition the firm must
have lower costs.

A firm can price below market when its production is efficient, or it is willing to accept a lower profit margin, or is willing to let its product be perceived as less valued than its competitors' products. The ability to maintain a cost advantage while selling a product that is equally valued in the market puts an organization in a very desirable position. Prices can be at levels that make it difficult for competitors to survive. Toyota, Honda, and Nissan were in such a position when exporting to the U.S. automobile market. Their costs were several thousand dollars less per car than the costs of U.S. producers. The establishment of "voluntary" import quotas helped domestic auto producers to survive.

Competitive price objectives may use a specific competitor, as do the NBC and CBS TV networks in selling national advertising time, a select group of competitors, or the industry average as a reference point.[7] All require data that are difficult to collect. As much as possible, firms keep price and cost data from competitors.

Social Pricing

*P*rices established primarily to encourage or dis-
courage consumption are
based on social objectives.

Social pricing objectives attempt to accomplish social goals. Businesses and charitable and social organizations may have social pricing objectives. Planned Parenthood, for instance, bases charges on need and on the ability to pay. Many churches and other organizations sponsor activities or special functions at which they pass the hat, asking those present to contribute no prescribed amount. It does not matter that the giver perceives the contribution as a charitable donation. It is still the price of attendance.

❏ **Figure 10.6** Pricing objectives.

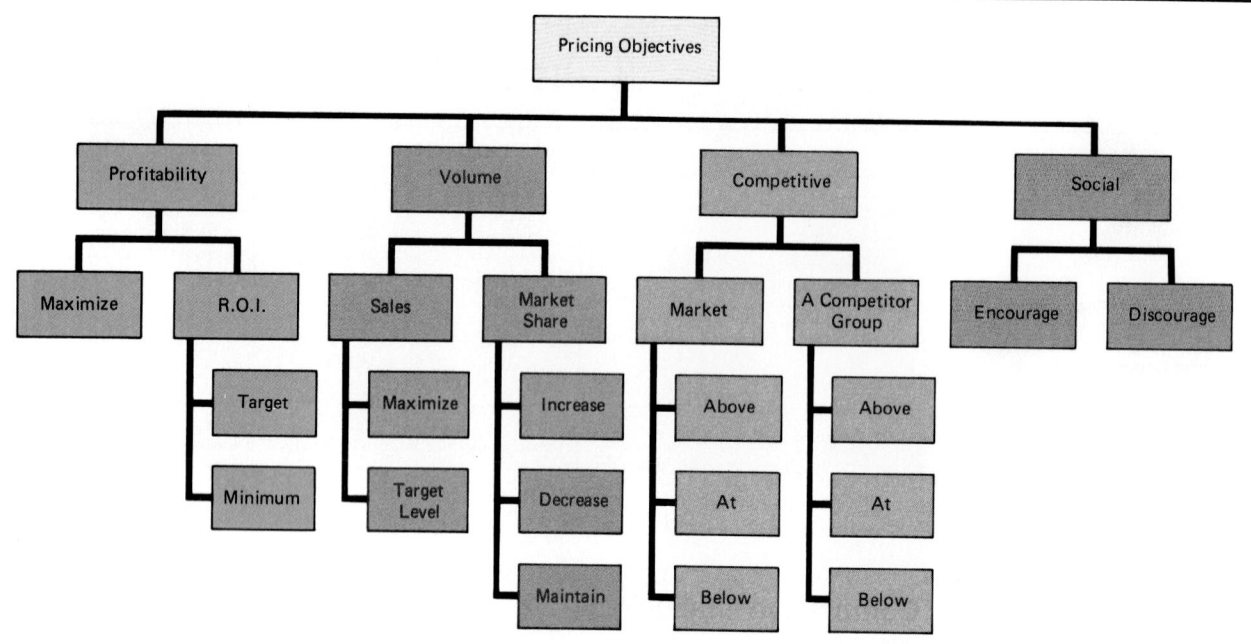

In some respects social pricing objectives are related to volume objectives, in that they are frequently intended to encourage or discourage consumption. For instance, the YWCAs and the YMCAs price programs at or below their cost to encourage participation. Programs to teach toddlers and young children to swim are a case in point. The low student/instructor ratio necessary for safety and instruction requires a substantial fee per student to cover cost. However, fees are kept low to increase participation and ultimately to reduce the number of drowning victims.

An organization may have several different pricing objectives. In one market the objective may be based on profitability and in another market, volume. Objectives can coexist compatibly if they are carefully constructed. (See figure 10.6.)

THE CASE CONTINUES

*W*hen selecting a price objective for the Book Center, Gonzales must consider the overall firm objectives. If the overall objective is to be the headquarters of the local literary society and to serve as a warehouse of knowledge, the pricing objectives are likely to be more social in nature. On the other hand, if the overall objective is to dominate the local book market, a volume objective, market share, or targeted sales level seems more reasonable. With a 3 to 4 per-

cent profit margin on net sales of $150,000, a profit objective seems most appropriate for the Book Center. There are insufficient resources and volume to promote an overall objective of market dominance. With the current volume and profit margin very close to the industry average, it does not appear that the firm has had a social objective—although it

could possibly adjust to a social objective. Finally, Gonzales may feel the overall objective is simply to be competitive; therefore, a competitive pricing objective would be adopted. Certainly the discount chain operators have emphasized the competitive side of selling books. Still, management should not be forced into certain objectives by competitors but should adjust desired objectives and sharpen techniques for achieving them.

STEP 3: ESTABLISHING PRICING POLICIES

*P*rice policies—guidelines for setting price.

Price policies establish the rules to help an organization achieve its pricing objectives. To develop the rules one must understand the behavior and psychology of buyers and sellers. For instance, a buyer may want to negotiate in order to obtain the product at the lowest possible price. The marketing plan may include policies on negotiation of price as well as other policies.

Price Negotiability

Because of the typical interchanges between buyer and seller, a policy on price negotiability plays an important role. Basically a seller has two options—refuse to negotiate or negotiate. Few U.S. retailers are willing to negotiate price with consumers. Retailers in many other countries do, however. Manufacturers, wholesalers, and other nonretailing firms in and out of the United States frequently negotiate.

ONE-PRICE POLICY

*T*ransaction efficiency is increased when a one-price policy is used.

A seller, such as Safeway Supermarkets, offering the same price to all customers uses a **one-price policy.** A one-price policy is more efficient than negotiation. To complete a transaction, negotiation requires time of both the buyer and seller. Reimbursement for the time spent in negotiation requires a higher selling price. Many American customers dislike negotiating, feeling they lack the appropriate skills. Many also believe that a negotiated price may depend more upon social status than negotiating skill. Even if sellers adopt a one-price policy, they may have to adjust price unless the initial price is exactly right. If enough customers decide not to purchase at the initial price, the price adjustment is downward. All customers would then be expected to pay the adjusted price.

A FLEXIBLE-PRICE POLICY

A **flexible-price policy** means the seller is willing to negotiate price. When trade-ins or items with a high unit price are involved, negotiation is quite common. Homes, vehicles, and furniture are examples. Sellers may also use a negotiated price as a promotional tool.[8] A West Coast Honda cycle dealer, for instance, advertises, "We will trade for almost anything!" As purchasers, industrial, wholesale, and retail firms commonly negotiate prices.

Complementary Pricing

*C*omplementary products considered as a unit should be priced as a unit.

A complementary product is used in conjunction with another product, for example, cameras and film, razors and blades, and shoes and shoelaces. **Complementary pricing** means that the products used together are considered as a unit when establishing the price of each item. Often this results in one of the products carrying a low price to encourage consumption of the other product. For instance, manufacturers of both razors and blades frequently price the razors low (or even give them away) in order to sell the blades.

Full-Line Pricing

A product as part of a line should be priced accordingly.

Pricing the full product line requires the marketer to consider all the products in the line when pricing an individual product. The objective is to maintain compatibility between products and to have a complete customer offering. A company with a low price image, such as Kmart, would be violating the rules of compatibility if it suddenly decided to offer high-priced, one-of-a-kind, Paris-designed clothing. But Kmart executives may very wisely offer higher-priced clothing if they perceive that their target market desires a higher quality product. It would help complete the line.

PRICE LINING

Price lining commonly occurs at the retail level. First, retailers use a cost plus pricing method (that is, they add a fixed percentage to the cost of the goods to arrive at the price) to generate prices for hundreds of very similar items. Then, instead of offering each item at a different price, retailers determine the most popular price points. For instance, J. C. Penney women's better dresses have primary price points at $29.99, $39, $44, $49, $54, $58, and $68.[9] The price points constitute a price line for the retailer. If the firm adheres to price lining, every product should carry one of the price points. J. C. Penney does not strictly follow price lining. Its prices cluster around the seven primary price points. Price lining aids the retailer in purchasing merchandise. For instance, if the dress buyer at J. C. Penney wants to sell a dress for $44 and uses a markup of 40 percent the product should cost $31.43.

$$\$31.43 + (\$31.43 \times 40\%) = \$44$$

All items that the retailer purchases must be able to provide an adequate markup at one of the price points.

Offering products at too many prices may be confusing.

Price lining reduces consumer confusion by reducing the number of prices consumers have to consider.[10] For example, even though J. C. Penney did not adhere strictly to price lining in a recent catalog, it offered approximately 100 different styles of dresses at only twenty-five prices.

Selection of price points requires special care on the part of the retailer. Incorrect price points can reduce sales. Price points only a few dollars higher than those of competitors may label the store in the market as "out of line on prices." Price lining may also give a competitor an opportunity to slightly undercut each price point. Instead of $46 the competitor might price the same dress at $41. Price lining can also present problems when price changes from inflation or deflation are frequent. The retailer must decide whether to offset inflation by changing the price to the next highest price point, buy lower quality goods, or allow the price to remain unchanged and accept less profit.

STANDARD UNIT PRICING

Unit pricing makes price comparisons easier.

Standard unit pricing occurs when the price per standard unit is given as well as the total price of the item. For example, in most supermarkets, consumers can choose among several brands and package sizes of corn flakes, each carrying a price per ounce as well as a total package price. Unit pricing most frequently occurs with food items at the retail level. Unit pricing facilitates comparison shopping by making it easier for consumers to compare prices. Its use by consumers, however, is less than expected. The well-educated, upper-middle-class consumer uses unit price information the most.[11]

Psychological Pricing

Price has psychological dimensions, and they should influence the price set. For instance, price and product quality have a psychological dimension. There may even be a psychological dimension between the acceptability of a price and whether the price ends with an even or odd number.

Standard unit pricing makes price comparison shopping easier.

PRESTIGE PRICING

High price and high quality may be one and the same to some customers.

Prestige pricing, a type of psychological pricing, considers the tendency for people to think that a product has to be expensive to be high quality. In other words, people tend to judge quality by price,[12] especially with new and complex products and products that they evaluate subjectively. Audio digital disk players, for example, are relatively new, and they are complex enough that most consumers do not understand how they work. Therefore, consumers use price to judge quality. Jewelry and other products where esthetic and other subjective criteria play a major role in the decision to buy have a perceived price-quality relationship. The subjective criteria are difficult to evaluate. Price becomes an indication of quality. Tiffany's, a chain of exclusive jewelry shops, uses prestige pricing. Since many services are intangible and therefore difficult to evaluate, price may be used to evaluate service quality. The attorney that charges the most may be perceived as the best.

Many years ago home hair permanents were marketed for $.25. Even though $.25 was a phenomenal buy, sales were disappointing. After careful consideration the price was raised substantially, whereupon sales increased severalfold. The market had evidently evaluated the product by its price. At $.25 people thought the product was inferior and were unwilling to take the chance of damaging their hair. The backward bending demand curve in figure 10.7 signifies that consumers are more willing to buy at high prices. Such curves reflect buyer psychology.

❑ **Figure 10.7**
Backward-bending demand curve.

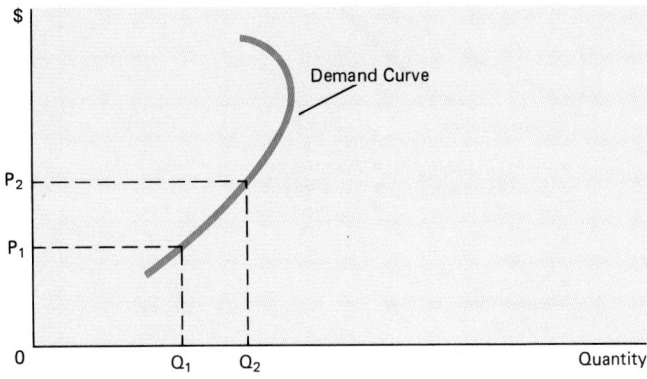

ODD-EVEN PRICING

A price ending in an odd number may seem lower to some customers.

Odd pricing is setting a price that ends in an odd number like $4.95 rather than an even number like $5. Although originally intended to force the cashier to make change and thus ring the sale up on the cash register, odd-even pricing is believed to have a psychological foundation. Supposedly the odd price results in more sales because psychologically it is more pleasing. The customer thinks the price is "better." However, research on the effectiveness of odd pricing in increasing sales has produced inconclusive results.[13]

Life-Cycle Pricing

As a product advances through the life cycle, its pricing often changes. Figure 10.8 shows typical price strategies for each stage of the life cycle. A firm has at least two strategies available in each market, penetration and skimming. With **penetration pricing** the product price normally covers cost and a small profit margin. Occasionally, however, the objective is to obtain a foothold in the market even if it initially requires selling at cost or below. Japanese companies reportedly priced at or below cost to enter several U.S. markets. Republic Airlines entered the Atlanta market with a low fare, attempting to obtain volume by attracting passengers from the strong competitor, Delta Air Lines. A low price encourages mass numbers of customers to buy the product. In the case of a new product, the firm penetrates the market and establishes strong customer loyalty before competitors can organize. The firm depends heavily on volume sales to generate a reasonable total profit. Competitors are thwarted because of the difficulty of generating sufficient volume to obtain economies of scale.

Conditions favoring penetration pricing include the willingness to undertake substantial risk, resources to promote the product, and a belief that a significant portion of the market is willing to buy the product but will resist a high price.[14]

❑ **Figure 10.8**
Life-cycle pricing.

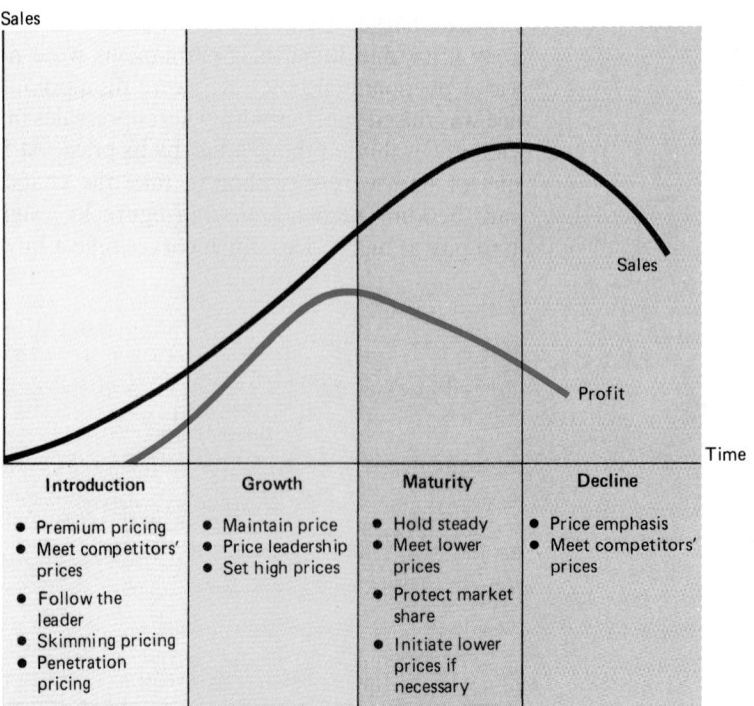

Source: William Lazer and James D. Culley. *Marketing Management Foundations and Practices* (Boston: Houghton Mifflin Co., 1983), p. 549. Adapted by permission.

*E*veryone has their price: sell to the high payers first.

In a **skimming** strategy, the marketer views the market as layered. The top layer consists of potential customers with the resources to purchase and a strong desire for the product. The strategy develops around satisfying one layer at a time, starting with the top. Therefore, the introductory price is high with a large per-unit profit margin. Once the top layer has purchased, the firm reduces the price and opens the market to another layer. The procedure may continue until either the mass market is opened or competition strengthens and forces abandonment of the strategy. McNeil Subsidiaries introduced Tylenol using a skimming strategy. Bristol-Meyers noted the success of Tylenol in the market and introduced its own nonaspirin pain reliever, Datril—acetaminophen equal to Tylenol in quality but lower in price. Polaroid's pricing of the original Land Camera is another example of a skimming strategy. The camera was originally priced high. When the market was saturated at the high price, Polaroid lowered the price and added new features to the camera.

The skimming strategy reduces the investment payback time since high profit margins generate profits early. Since demand at the high price is less, the manufacturer has time to develop more and better production facilities to maintain quality. Skimming also may be used if the firm sells a unique product and educating customers to its use takes time. A large part of the market is also considered to be insensitive to price. They will buy even at a high price. On the other hand, high profit margins encourage competition to enter the market.

---

*E*vidently book sellers, including the Book Center, have had a one-price policy. Consumers now, however, have indicated a desire to negotiate price. The Book Center may want to change its policy to a flexible-price policy. If not, promoting the virtues of a one-price policy should be considered.

THE CASE CONTINUES

The discounters' policy of competing on the basis of price has resulted in a lower price for the best-sellers.

Price consciousness by consumers has influenced the publishers' pricing policies. Publishers have pro-vided a standard 40 percent discount off suggested retail list price for all retailers. In addition, a discount up to 10 percent is available for large orders, so a large chain may obtain a total discount as large as 50 percent. The book sellers' association's computerized order service was designed to obtain larger discounts available from the publisher.

GOAL SUMMARY

1. **Explain the importance of price to consumers and the firm.** Price serves the consumer in a number of ways. It can alert the consumer to quality differences in products. It may help to distinguish the purchaser's social standing. It may also force consumers to assign priorities to needs. For businesses, price is one of the marketing variables managers have an opportunity to control. Price level also influences competitive position and profitability of a firm.

2. **Identify the factors that allow a marketer some control over price.** The more competitive a market, the less price administration is possible. Competition increases with greater number of competitors and less uniqueness of product.

3. **Differentiate between profitability, volume, competitive, and social price objectives.** Profitability focuses on the measurement of the difference between revenue and cost, that is, profit—profit in total dollars, as a percentage of sales or as a percentage of investment (ROI). Volume focuses only on revenues generated or unit output. Volume level in dollars or the organization's volume compared to the industry's volume (share of the market) are common volume objectives. The focus is on the competition prices—above, at or below market levels—with competitive pricing objectives. With social objectives, price may be flexible to encourage or discourage the use of the product.

GOAL SUMMARY (continued)

4. **Compare and contrast from a marketing point of view one-price and flexible-price policies.** Both policies establish how the marketer works with price and the purchaser. With a one-price policy the marketer expects the customer to accept the price marked on the product or not to purchase. The time spent with the customer discussing price is minimal. Often the sale involves self-service. When using a one-price policy, the price marked on the item is usually lower than the initial price under a flexible-price policy. If some give and take negotiation over price does not occur when high-unit value items and trade-in items are involved, sales may be lost.

5. **Define full-line, psychological, and life-cycle pricing.** Full-line pricing requires the marketer to consider all the products in the product line when pricing an individual item. By considering all products, items are more likely to have prices that reflect the value and position in the product line. All prices that buyers expect for products offered for sale can also be covered. Psychological pricing means the marketer should think about the buyer's perceptions of price. A high price, for instance, is often perceived as a high quality product. Life-cycle pricing, the pricing of the product by stage in the product life cycle, helps to insure that the price is current with market conditions.

KEY TERMS

Price, **p. 265**
Value, **p. 265**
Utility, **p. 265**
Administered Pricing, **p. 268**
Pure Competitive Market, **p. 268**
Monopolistic Competitive Market, **p. 268**
Product Differentiation, **p. 268**
Oligopolistic Market, **p. 269**
Pure Monopoly Market, **p. 270**
Price Objectives, **p. 273**
Maximization of Profit, **p. 273**

Return on Investment (ROI), **p. 274**
Market Share, **p. 274**
Competitive Objectives, **p. 275**
Social Pricing Objectives, **p. 275**
One-Price Policy, **p. 277**
Flexible-Price Policy, **p. 277**
Complementary Pricing, **p. 277**
Prestige Pricing, **p. 279**
Odd Pricing, **p. 280**
Penetration Pricing, **p. 280**
Skimming, **p. 281**

CHECK YOUR LEARNING

1. Price is a statement of perceived value.   **T/F**
2. Since price is extremely important, marketers attempt to make the rest of the marketing mix compatible with price.   **T/F**
3. In general, marketers work to make the market more sensitive to price.   **T/F**
4. The factors of production that price allocates are land, labor, and capital.   **T/F**
5. Which type of market exists when the following conditions prevail: prices can be administered, each competitor controls a very small share of the market, the price is unregulated, and slight differences exist in products? (a) monopolistic competitive,

(b) pure competitive, (c) monopoly, (d) oligopoly, (e) none of the above.
6. Price objectives are compatible with the objectives of the rest of the firm if they are derived from the overall goals of the organization.   **T/F**
7. Pricing policies determine pricing objectives.   **T/F**
8. An objective of pricing below competitors will be successful if the firm has and can maintain greater efficiencies than its competitors.   **T/F**
9. Social pricing should not generate a profit.   **T/F**
10. Given the following information about a four-company industry, what is the market share of Company C: Company A sales $200,000, profit $1,500; Com-

CHECK YOUR LEARNING *(continued)*

pany B sales $350,000, profit $21,000; Company C sales $400,000, profit $25,000; Company D sales $300,000, profit $20,000? (a) 6 percent, (b) 33.6 percent, (c) 5 percent, (d) 28 percent, (e) none of the above.

11. A one-price policy is more expensive to use than a flexible-price policy.   **T/F**
12. Complementary pricing combines two products and treats them as one.   **T/F**
13. Psychologically, the price of a product is never too low.   **T/F**
14. Odd-even pricing does make a difference in sales, according to the research that has been conducted.   **T/F**
15. A backward bending demand curve signifies: (a) a greater willingness to buy at higher prices, (b) fewer available products at lower prices, (c) the existence of a monopoly, (d) a product in the introductory stage of the life cycle, (e) none of the above.
16. A penetration pricing strategy attempts to increase competition by lowering price.   **T/F**

QUESTIONS FOR REVIEW AND DISCUSSION

1. Define the key terms for this chapter that appear at the end of the goal summary.
2. List the ways price is important to a firm.
3. In your own words define what selling price means.
4. Assuming that you have just been hired as marketing manager for a firm operating in a pure competitive market, what functions of your job would you emphasize?
5. Briefly discuss the four general types of pricing objectives.
6. If you were asked to select a single factor as the most important in price objective selection, what would it be? Why?
7. Calculate annual ROI when revenue is $200,000, investment is $500,000, and profit is $30,000. Do you think this would be an acceptable ROI for most companies? Why?
8. As a firm's market share increases, its ROI also frequently increases. Why?
9. When should standard unit pricing be used?
10. How would you explain the relationship between price and quality?
11. Compare penetration and skimming pricing strategies.

NOTES

1. Eric Berkowitz, Roger Kerin, and William Rudelius, *Marketing* (St. Louis: Times Mirror/Mosby College Publishing, 1986), 284; and David L. Kurtz and Louis E. Boone, *Marketing* (Chicago: The Dryden Press, 1984), p. 368.
2. C. P. Rao and G. E. Kiser, "An Evaluation of Consumer Inflation Psychology and an Assessment of Income Effects," *Proceedings: Southern Marketing Association,* 1977, Henry Nash and Donald Robin, eds., pp. 13–16.
3. Louis E. Boone and David Kurtz, "Pricing Objectives and Practices in American Industry," A Research Report, 1979. See also, Barbara Coe, "Perception of the Role of Pricing in the 1980s Among Industrial Marketers," *AMA Educator's Conference Proceedings,* Patrick E. Murphy et al., eds., pp. 235–240.
4. Christopher S. Eplund, "Will a Tomato by Any Other Name Taste Better?" *Business Week,* September 30, 1985, p. 105.
5. Saeed Samiee, "Pricing Objectives of U.S. Manufacturing Firms," in *Proceedings: Southern Marketing Association,* Robert S. Franz, Robert M. Hopkins, and Alfred G. Toma, eds. (New Orleans: 1978), pp. 445–447.
6. Robert D. Buzzell and Frederik D. Wiersema, "Successful Share-Building Strategies," *Harvard Business Review* (January–February): pp. 135–144.
7. Sarah Stiansen, "Greyhound, Trailways in Price Battle," *Advertising Age,* May 7, 1984, p. 1.
8. James R. Krum, "Variable Pricing as a Promotional Tool," *Atlanta Economic Review* (November–December, 1977): pp. 47–50.
9. *J. C. Penney Fall and Winter Catalog,* 1986.

NOTES *(continued)*

10. Eric N. Berkowitz and John R. Walton, "Information Needs for Comparative Pricing Decisions," *AMA Educator's Conference Proceedings,* Patrick E. Murphy et al., eds., 1983, pp. 241–246.

11. Bruce F. McElroy and David A. Haker, "Unit Pricing Six Years After Introduction," *Journal of Retailing* (Fall 1979): pp. 44–57.

12. Lee Adler, "To Make the Right Pricing Decision Try One of These Research Techniques," *Sales and Marketing Management,* December 1978, p. 96.

13. Zarrel V. Lambert, "Perceived Prices as Related to Odd and Even Price Findings," *Journal of Retailing* (Fall 1975): pp. 13–22, 28.

14. Gary M. Erickson, "New Product Pricing: An Investigation of Marketing Conditions That Lead to Penetration and Skimming Strategies," *AMA Educator's Conference Proceedings,* Patrick E. Murphy, et. al., eds., 1983, pp. 222–225.

*D*ynascan, a producer of cordless phones, CBs, and short wave radios had to work hard in 1984 to survive in a volatile market. In the first quarter of the year, the company had losses of $4.7 million because of write downs on cordless units in inventory.

When AT&T's monopolistic control as supplier of U.S. telephones was broken by the courts, other manufacturers came forward with their versions of telephones. One of the most innovative phones was the cordless. Sales were initially terrific. In 1982, 1983, and 1984, sales were 2 million, 4.7 million, and 6 million units respectively. Entrepreneurs entered the market producing phones faster than consumer demand could absorb them. Six-and-one-half million cordless phones were imported (virtually all cordless phones are made in other countries) in 1984. There was also approximately a three million unit carryover inventory from 1983. However, there was a trend of declining profits on factory sales. At the June, 1984, consumer electronics show, over 200 companies displayed products; only seventy-five were expected to survive for one year.

The market for cordless phones was not considered to be saturated, but perhaps was a narrower market than originally thought. At the end of 1984, seven to eight million cordless phones were estimated to have been installed. Approximately 20 percent of cordless phones purchased by consumers at the time were returned because of poor reception caused by interference from other phones. There are an estimated 70 million residential and 40 million business access phone lines in the United

States. In heavily populated areas, interference between five-channel cordless phones was likely. To resolve the problem, the FCC promised to double the number of available channels, to ten by January of 1984.

By mid-1984 the FCC finally installed the five new channels. The inventory of five-channel phones was large, but many manufacturers went immediately to big production runs of ten-channel phones. Retailers were hesitant to purchase them, fearing they would not be able to sell a new ten-channel phone for $100 when the five-channel was selling for $39.95. Many retailers waited for the right opportunity to buy liquidated inventories at rock-bottom prices. Retailers were also looking to "copycat" cordless manufacturers—copying existing products and selling them at a lower price. Retailers are normally allowed a 40 percent discount off list price. In one survey, most retailers were expecting to purchase cordless phones to sell in the list price range of $79.95 to $249.95, with most of the action between $139 and $149. Several manufacturers watched their prices of $135 to $150 in 1980 drop to $75 and $80 in 1983, and to $50 and less in 1984.

Rumors in the industry indicated that most people believed the shakeout in manufacturers would be at the low price end.

Other manufacturers had already taken a marketing and price position. For instance, AT&T, which did not at the time sell a cordless phone, had

designed a program to educate consumers to realize that what they pay for in phones from AT&T really gives them an advantage over the cheaper models produced by other manufacturers. GTE basically took the position that is was not bothered by competition in the phone market; low price or otherwise, GTE executives believed its good products and market knowledge gave it an advantage. Quality, dependability, and service were emphasized by GTE. Uniden Corporation, the 1984 cordless industry leader, set out to scramble its price-oriented strategy by offering consumer rebates from $10 to $60. Jack Nicklaus became the featured spokesman in Uniden's several million dollar advertising campaign. The company also offered co-op advertising, ads, and announcer—a prepared script, point-of-sale materials, counter cards, and a shelf talker. Retailer support programs were extensive. Dynacan also spends extensively on promotion.

Issues for Discussion

1. Can Dynascan Corporation management administer price in the cordless phone market?
2. What advice would you give Dynascan executives about appropriate pricing objectives?
3. Should Dynascan have any pricing policies?

Sources: Marilyn Sibirski, "New Frequencies Offer Hope for Cordless Phone Revival," *Merchandising,* June 1984, pp. 103 and 109; Richard Edel, "Cordless Phones Dial *T-R-O-U-B-L-E*," *Advertising Age,* June 7, 1984, pp. 30–32; and Crystal Nix, "Price Wars and Overproduction Spur Shakeout in Phone-Making Industry," *The Wall Street Journal,* August 2, 1984, p. 10.

OUTLINE

CHAPTER 11

Pricing Products to Sell

LEARNING GOALS

After reading this chapter, you should be able to:

1. Explain the range that a firm uses in establishing price.
2. Describe the types of cost and cost-based pricing methods.
3. Discuss the role of price elasticity and total revenue in setting price.
4. Utilize marginal and break-even analysis in pricing a product.
5. Discuss discounts and allowances as adjustments to price.
6. Explain the philosophy on which the laws pertaining to pricing are based.

*T*he Jeans Company has always strived to provide the best products for the money. Through the years the company has improved the durability, stylishness, and comfort of the clothing it sells. In fact, the company has tried to develop clothes that fit people of all sizes and shapes—at a price that fits.

The company is known widely for jeans. Company executives watch the jean market carefully for changes in style, fabric, and demand. Alerted to impending changes in the market, the company acts swiftly to stay ahead of their close competitors.

Changes in America's work, workforce, and demographics between now and the year 2000, have not escaped The Jeans Company executives' attention. Total manufacturing jobs, where a durable jean would be more in demand, continue to decline in relation to service and technical jobs, where a jean is less likely to be worn. In the next decade, six million more jobs are projected in the most skilled occupations—executive, professional, and technical—compared to only about a million new jobs in the less-skilled and laborer categories.

Another big change noted is the shift in the age of the U.S. population. The proportion of population from sixteen- to twenty-four-years-old will shrink from 30 percent in 1988 to approximately 15 percent in 2000. The sixteen- to twenty-four-year-old age group buys more jeans than any other age group. As individuals grow older, fewer jeans are bought. With age, the physique often changes. Finding jeans that fit discourages many older buyers. For the mature market, jean manufacturers long ago went to fuller cut jeans. They also manufactured pleated stretch-waist jeans. For men, however, the pleated stretch-waist loses the ''macho'' look of a jean, and thus demand has failed to develop.

The question is how to satisfy the mature male market thirty-five-years-

old or older with a jean product. One alternative would be to market a jean made from material that stretches, but retains the look of denim. The material is about 20 percent more expensive than regular denim.

Projected cost for a pair of stretch denim jeans is $5.25 in material and $3.75 in labor. Overhead production costs will total $1,750,000 per year, and marketing and administrative overhead costs will come to $750,000 per year.

Examples of relationships between demand and price are:

Price	Units
$14.25	600,000
16.50	525,000
18.75	375,000
21.25	175,000

The Jeans Company's prices on men's jeans run from $14.25 to $32.00, depending on the style and material. Retailers will normally add from 40 percent to 80 percent to the cost of jeans in arriving at the selling price to consumers.

The Jeans Company does offer some discounts and allowances that influence the final price to the buyer. To promote their products, the company employs an advertising allowance. Usually the program reimburses the retailer for 50 percent of the cost of an advertisement, provided that a certain quantity of the product has been bought and that other conditions are met.

The Jeans Company also prepays transportation if certain conditions are met. Its freight policy divides orders into three categories: orders of 200 units or more, orders of less than 200 units, and orders for overruns and irregulars.

The freight is prepaid by The Jeans Company on orders of 200

units or more if the following conditions are met: the merchandise is purchased at full price; the merchandise is first quality; the merchandise ordered is offered and available; and the order is to be delivered at one time to one destination. All orders less than 200 garments will be shipped collect with no freight or transportation charges allowed. All orders for manufacturer's overruns and irregulars will be shipped FOB distribution center, no freight allowed.

Issues for Discussion

1. Given the information in the case, what cost- and demand-based pricing method would be most appropriate for pricing the stretch denim jean?

2. With regard to setting price, what information can be gained from break-even analysis in this situation?

3. Should The Jeans Company use discounts and allowances to sell the stretch denim jeans?

4. Should The Jeans Company use markdowns, rebates, and promotional pricing? What legal issues would The Jeans Company need to be concerned about?

■ The price of jeans, how much should it be?

he Jeans Company could use costs in setting a price for its new stretch denim jeans. In the pages ahead we will discuss the cost-oriented pricing methods available to The Jeans Company.

The Jeans Company's marketers should also consider demand for their company's product in arriving at the price to be charged. Demand in pricing and its limitations are described. We will examine break-even analysis as a procedure in pricing, and we will calculate The Jeans Company's break-even point at several selling prices. The Jeans Company executives may also want to allow departure from the set price with discounts and allowances. The Jeans Company has used both in the past. The reasons for adjusting price and the ways to do it, as well as the legal aspects of price, will be discussed in detail. ■

INTRODUCTION—THE PRICE RANGE

In pricing a specific item, the marketer can normally choose among a range of prices. The upper limit of the range—the ceiling—is the point at which demand for the product is nonexistent. The lower limit of the range—the floor—is determined by costs. (Occasionally a product will be sold below cost, but generally not for extended periods.)

Demand and costs determine the price range.

The range may be very broad or narrow depending on competition, cost pressure, and other forces. (See figure 11.1.) A broad range allows marketers more flexibility, but they still must choose the specific price that best achieves the organization's objectives within the range. Some marketers start with cost as a reference point and work up; others start with demand and work down. Both cost and demand should be considered before a price is set.

In Chapter 10 we introduced an eight-step procedure for establishing price, and we discussed the first three steps: (1) evaluating environmental factors, (2) selecting pricing objectives, and (3) establishing price policies. These steps provide the marketer with necessary background information. Steps four through eight comprise a procedure for setting the actual price.

Figure 11.1
The price range.

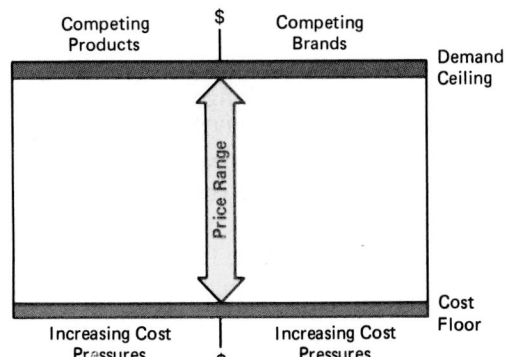

STEP 4: ESTIMATE COST AND REVIEW COST-BASED PRICING

In cost-based pricing the objective is to set a price above the floor determined by cost and sell the product. For years, employee-relocation companies like Merrill Lynch Relocation and Equitable Relocation Management have insured that their costs were covered with the simplest of approaches. They charged their corporate customers for the purchase and sale of the homes of transferred employees on a flexible cost-plus basis. The arrangement permitted the relocation companies to take their cost, whatever the amount, and add a fixed percentage for profit. Most organizations would not find the situation so easy. Just determining their costs can be a problem.[1] With the help of an accountant a marketer can usually project product cost, but several types of costs exist: total cost (TC), average total cost (ATC), fixed cost (FC), variable cost (VC), average variable cost (AVC), and marginal cost (MC). Therefore, the marketer must be familiar with the various types of costs to make the best pricing decisions.

Total Cost

*T*otal sales revenue in excess of total cost equals profit.

The **total cost** includes all costs associated with all units of the product. Total cost must be lower than total revenue to produce a profit.

$$\text{Total Revenue} - \text{Total Cost} = \text{Profit}$$

Companies like Bechtel Engineering, the international construction company, that produce and sell single units (large buildings, highways, and other custom-made products) can set their prices on the basis of total cost. For firms that market many units of a standardized product, average total cost is more useful in determining price.

Average Total Cost—Target Margin on Sales Pricing

Average total cost represents total cost divided by the number of units.

$$\text{Total Cost/Quantity} = \text{Average Total Cost}$$

Because of economies of scale, average total cost falls until the economy of scale volume is obtained, but then it begins to increase. This is illustrated in figure 11.2.

Many manufacturers realize that they can reduce average cost by increasing the volume of production. To obtain higher volume in anticipation of lower average cost, manufacturers sometimes price products low. For example, suppose that Sony marketing executives are trying to price a wide-screen TV set, and they are working with the cost structure illustrated in figure 11.2. Marketing research suggests that the market might demand up to 400,000 units per year of the product if it is priced no higher than $800 per unit. Sony's average total cost declines up to 300,000 units, but at that point, economies of scale cease to operate, and average total cost begins to rise. Sony executives must decide how to price their wide-screen TV set in order to maintain annual sales of 300,000, the point at which average total cost is lowest. If the competitive environment is such that Sony could project annual sales of only 100,000 units, the company must charge a minimum of $800 per unit in order to cover its costs. However, Sony's objective is to sell 300,000 units per year so, in order

□ Figure 11.2
Average total cost
curve.

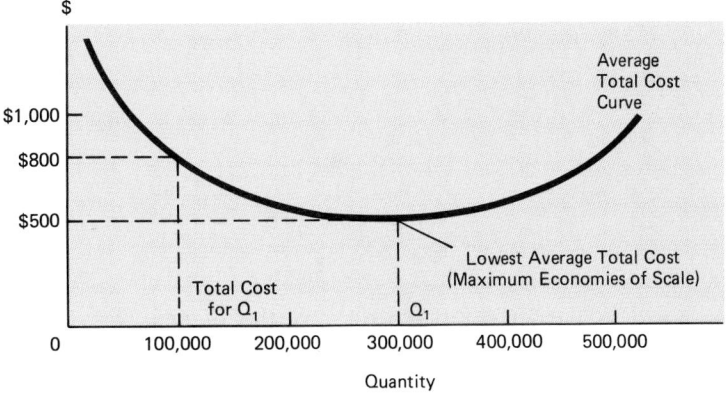

*E*fficient firms keep total
cost low in relation to the
quantity produced.

to meet its goal, it should price its TV set somewhere below $800, the price at which demand drops off, but above $500, the price at which it will just cover its costs.

Firms use **experience curve pricing** if they initially price low to obtain volume in anticipation of a lower average total cost. The organization obtaining a volume close to the lowest average cost has a definite advantage over other companies, as already illustrated.[2] It can pass on the cost advantage to customers by offering a low price, or it can price with competitors and make a larger profit.

*T*arget margin on sales
pricing uses average cost
to set a price for a desired
profit margin.

A technique for deriving selling price that uses the average total cost is the **target margin on sales.** The company chooses the profit margin it wants to make on each dollar of sales and calculates price as follows:

$$\text{Price} = \frac{\text{Average Total Cost}}{100\% - \text{Profit Margin Desired }\%}$$

*A*ccurate cost estimates
and expected sales vol-
ume are essential to target
margin on sales pricing.

There is a danger in using average total cost to derive price. Companies calculate average total cost for projected volumes of production in order to determine the maximum volume at which they can realize economies of scale. However, the volume that will yield the lowest average total cost might not necessarily be the volume that the company will actually sell.

Suppose Nike, the shoe manufacturer, has an average total cost of $6.50 per pair of shoes, and it wants a profit margin of 10 percent on each dollar of sales. The selling price would be $7.22.

$$P = \frac{\$6.50}{100\% - 10\%} = \frac{\$6.50}{90\%} = \$7.22$$

Nike's average total cost of $6.50 per pair of shoes is based on a volume of production of 800,000 units, the total cost of which is $5,200,000. Suppose Nike decides to produce 800,000 units in order to take full advantage of economies of scale.

$$\frac{\$5,200,000 \text{ Total Cost}}{800,000 \text{ Quantity}} = \$6.50 \text{ Average Total Cost}$$

Nike then prices each pair of shoes at $7.22 in order to realize a 10 percent profit on each pair of sales.

$$\$6.50 \text{ Average Total Cost} + \$.72 \text{ profit} = \$7.22$$

If Nike actually sells all 800,000 pairs, it will reach its target margin on sales, earning a total of $5,776,000 (800,000 × $7.22) for a profit of $576,000 ($5,776,000 −

$5,200,000). However, if Nike sells only 400,000 units, it will suffer a substantial loss of $5.78 per unit, or $2,312,000 total.

$$\frac{\$5,200,000 \text{ Total Cost}}{400,000 \text{ Quantity}} = \$13 \text{ Average Total Cost}$$

$ 13.00 Average Total Cost Per Unit
−   7.22 Revenue Per Unit
$ 5.78 Loss Per Unit

The $5.78 loss assumes that the total cost remains the same for 800,000 and 400,000 units. The fixed cost remains the same, but the variable cost diminishes. Fixed and variable costs are discussed next.

Fixed, Variable, and Marginal Costs

*F*ixed cost—a function of time—cannot be altered quickly.

To obtain a better understanding of the refinements of cost pricing, other types of cost have to be considered. **Fixed costs** remain the same regardless of the quantity of output. Equipment and fixture costs are examples of fixed costs. Even when the output is minimal, fixed costs are the same as when the output is at full capacity. Figure 11.3 illustrates how fixed costs behave with changes in output. From the standpoint of fixed costs, a firm prefers to operate near capacity because fixed costs are spread over more units.

*V*ariable cost—a function of output.

Total variable costs are a function of the quantity of output. Direct labor and materials are examples of variable costs. As the output increases, variable costs increase. For instance, with variable costs per unit at $1.50 and production levels at 100,000 units and 250,000 units, total variable costs would be $150,000 and $375,000 respectively, as shown in figure 11.4. The **average variable cost** is the total variable cost divided by quantity.

A marketing manager should set a price at least high enough to cover the variable cost. In the long run, of course, all costs must be covered.

TARGET RETURN ON INVESTMENT PRICING

*T*arget ROI pricing requires fixed and variable cost, quantity, investment, and target ROI desired.

The **target return on investment** pricing method uses both fixed and variable costs. The method establishes the price required to achieve a desired rate of return on investment. The formula used:

$$P = \frac{(ROI\%) \, I}{Q} + \frac{FC}{Q} + AVC$$

Where:

❑ **Figure 11.3**
   Total fixed cost.

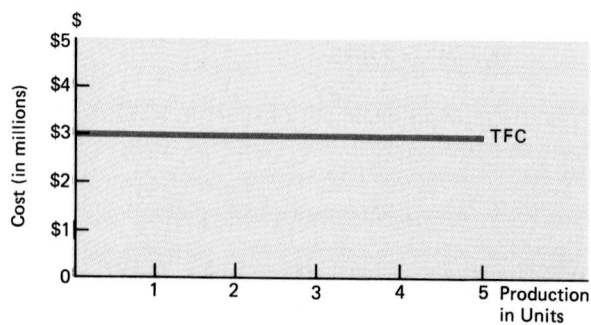

❏ **Figure 11.4**
Total variable cost.

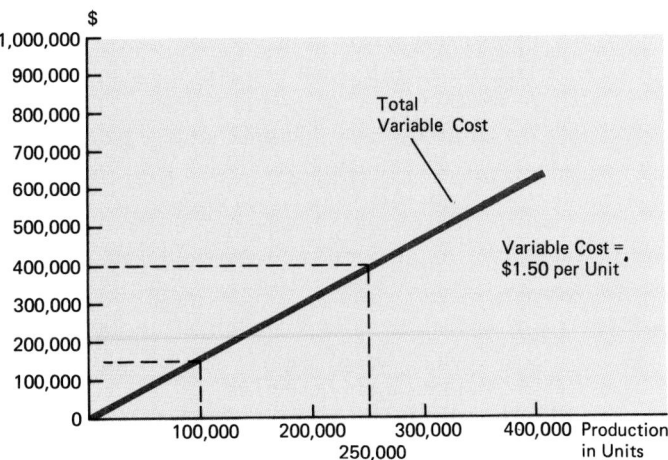

ROI = return on investment desired;
  I = investment;
 FC = fixed cost;
  Q = expected sales quantity; and
AVC = average variable cost

If General Motors, desiring a 25 percent ROI before taxes, invests $50,000, has a fixed cost of $20,000 and a variable cost of $50 a unit, and expects to sell 5,000 units, the selling price would be $56.50.

$$\$56.50 = \frac{(.25)\,\$50,000}{5,000} + \frac{\$20,000}{5,000} + \$50$$

The accuracy of the target ROI method depends on the accuracy of the estimate of sales. Therefore, after determining the price, the marketer should ask whether the number of estimated units can be sold at that price. The number of units actually sold must equal or exceed the number used in the formula to obtain the targeted ROI.

Source: Ladies' Home Journal.
Reprinted by permission of
Orlando Busino.

INCREMENTAL COST PRICING

*T*he incremental method ignores overhead cost.

The **incremental cost method** of pricing uses only the variable costs of direct labor and materials to determine the price. The technique emphasizes the incremental cost of producing additional units. Overhead is not directly considered in the calculation. The equation is:

$$(DL + DM) + M (DL + DM) = P$$

Where:

DL = direct cost of labor
DM = direct cost of materials
M = the desired markup percentage

Automobile mechanics often use this method. They know the amount of direct labor time required from published time study references. They also know the cost of the parts to repair the car and their labor rate. Thus, if a car repair requires three hours of labor at $25 an hour and $50 worth of parts, and if the mechanic uses a markup of 150 percent, the price is $350.

$$(\$25 \cdot 3 \text{ hrs.} + \$50) + 150\% (\$75 + \$50) = \$350 \text{ (plus tax)}$$

This method considers fixed-cost overhead only indirectly, usually by including it as a factor in the markup percentage. By using this kind of markup over variable-cost increments, the producer assumes that the more material and time consumed in the production job, the greater the share of overhead costs that job should carry in the price. For some businesses this may work out in the long run; however, in many situations the small or unfamiliar jobs are likely to take up a disproportionately greater share of overhead costs, which this pricing method would not adequately cover.

PRICING SERVICES

Marketers of services often use direct labor and overhead costs as a basis for establishing price. The materials required to provide the service are usually minimal; therefore, the material cost is ignored. Consider the public accountant, for example. The end result of the accountant's work may be a few sheets of figures. The material cost (the paper) has little relevance to establishing the price. The accountant must charge for time and overhead.

*T*he conversion cost method emphasizes value added to the material.

In order to set a price for services, the accountant may use the **conversion cost method,** which considers direct labor and overhead. The formula used:

$$(DL + OH) + M (DL + OH) = P$$

If direct labor is $250, overhead $100, and markup 40 percent, the selling price is $490. Direct labor is usually determined by multiplying job hours by hourly rate. Overhead costs are all job-related costs other than direct labor and materials. To determine overhead cost for a job, the overhead rate is commonly multiplied by the direct labor cost. One method of arriving at the overhead rate is:

$$\text{Overhead rate} = \frac{\text{Total annual overhead}}{\text{Total annual direct labor cost}}$$

The technique may distort actual costs for production involving high direct-material-consuming products.

THE REST OF THE STORY

$436 Claw Hammers

■ Who would pay $436 for an ordinary claw hammer?

A $436 price for a claw hammer seems out of line, but yes, it has happened. Perhaps someone was in desperate need of a claw hammer and only one was available within miles? No. There were hammers available in local retail stores and the need was not one of desperation. Several were purchased at the price. Would you say the hammers were not ordinary hammers, perhaps antiques or made of special metal and wood, or perhaps a unique new innovative design? No, the hammers contained ordinary metal and wood, nothing special. They were of recent vintage and not antiques. It is true the hammers functioned well enough to pound nails or other items, to extract bent nails, and as pry bars. All of these functions are functions performed by ordinary hammers. The hammers were ordinary claw hammers that typically sell for $7.

Who would have the nerve to ask such an outrageous price for an ordinary claw hammer? Gould Simulation systems sold the hammers. How did they arrive at the $436 selling price? Why not $4,130 or $44,612?

Gould accountants followed a widely used accounting procedure in which the manufacturer's overhead costs for an entire contract are divided by the number of items being supplied in the contract. Each hammer's share of the overhead cost was $333. To the $333, the cost of acquiring the hammer, plus inspection, packaging, and handling costs of approximately $8 were added to arrive at total cost, since Gould did not manufacture the hammers but purchased them from another supplier. Because Gould used a cost-plus method of arriving at the price, the costs were multiplied by a profit margin of about 13 percent and this was added to the cost to arrive at the $436 selling price.

Who would pay $436 for an ordinary claw hammer? Maybe you have guessed by now—the U.S. Military. Since the U.S. Navy had a contract covering numerous items, the overall sum of the contract was evaluated rather than individual items. The contract price, once accepted, was paid. Some items in the contract should have been underpriced, based on the fact that they bore less overhead cost than they rightfully should have. And now you know the rest of the story.

Source: Defense Budget Project: U.S. Senate, Committee on Governmental Affairs, Staff Investigation, *Congressional Record,* May 15, 1984, H-3922-24.

RETAILER AND WHOLESALER PRICING

Retailers and wholesalers, who set the price on hundreds of items for resale, use a simple approach to pricing. The only cost they consider in establishing the price of the item is its cost to them.

$$\text{Item Cost} + \text{Markup \% (Item Cost)} = \text{Selling Price}$$

The local hardware store may carry several thousand items. It would be cumbersome to price each item using direct labor, overhead, and other costs. Markups are explained in more detail in the appendix of this text.

MARGINAL COST

Marginal cost (MC) represents the cost associated with the last unit of output. Thus, if total costs increase from $650,000 to $650,001.50 when output increases from 100,000 to 100,001 units, the marginal cost is $1.50, as shown.

$$MC = \frac{\text{Change in Total Cost } (\Delta\ TC)}{\text{Change in Quantity } (\Delta\ Q)} = \frac{\$650,001.50\ -\ \$650,000}{100,001\ -\ 100,000} = \$1.50$$

❑ **Figure 11.5**
Marginal cost and
average total cost
relationship.

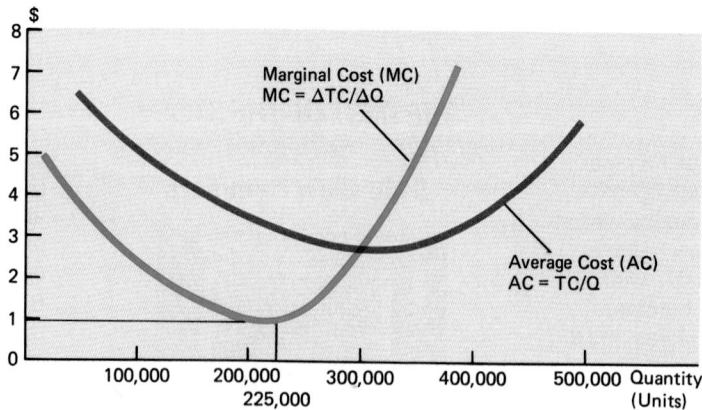

Recall that the average total cost equals the total cost divided by total quantity. Thus, after the increase in output, the average total cost would be:

$$\frac{\$650,001.50}{100,001} = \$6.50$$

The marginal cost decreases as the output expands from zero, and increases when inefficiencies enter the production process. In figure 11.5, the marginal cost declines to the lowest amount, one dollar, at 225,000 units. As inefficiencies cause the marginal cost to increase, the average cost continues to decline until the marginal cost exceeds the average cost. The average cost is always at a minimum where the marginal and average cost lines intersect.

STEP 5: ESTIMATE DEMAND AND REVIEW DEMAND-BASED PRICING

*D*emand establishes the upper limit of the price range.

Demand determines the ceiling of the price range. Will the market purchase the projected quantity at the established price? The price at which the market refuses to purchase the projected quantity is the price ceiling. Some firms use a hit-and-miss approach, hoping they will be lucky enough to select a price that permits the desired sales. Other firms use marketing research to estimate the price ceiling.[3] For instance, at an anniversary party for Pampers, Procter & Gamble recently revealed that a 1961 test market in Peoria, Illinois, indicated that parents liked the idea of a disposable diaper, but that most were unwilling to pay the price of ten cents per diaper. After six months, P&G pulled the product from the test market. In 1962, the price was cut to six cents a diaper, and the product was test marketed in Sacramento, California. The demand was sufficient for Procter & Gamble to introduce Pampers at that price.[4] Still other firms use the product life cycle or other variables to forecast quantities demanded.

The marketing manager uses demand to estimate three types of revenue: total, average, and marginal revenues. **Total revenue** is the total money received from the sale of the product. **Average revenue** is the total revenue divided by units sold. **Marginal revenue** is the revenue received from the last unit sold. The responsiveness of total revenue to a price change is especially helpful in setting the price.

Price Elasticity of Demand

*P*rice demand elasticity—
how price changes affect
total sales revenue.

The **price elasticity** of demand is an index measuring the effect of a change in price on the quantity of demand for a product. If the price is reduced by a certain percentage, will demand for the product increase by a larger percentage (elastic demand), a smaller percentage (inelastic demand), or the same percentage (unitary demand elasticity)? The formula for price elasticity is:

$$\frac{(\text{Original Quantity} - \text{New Quantity})/\text{Original Quantity}}{(\text{Original Price} - \text{New Price})/\text{Original Price}} = \frac{Q\%}{P\%} = \text{Price Elasticity Index}$$

For the sake of simplicity, negative signs are ignored in the division. To illustrate, assume Motown Records decides to reduce the price of a cassette tape from $7.95 to $6.45 with the expectation that sales volume will go from 3.5 million to 5.75 million units.

$$\frac{(3.5 - 5.75)/3.5}{(7.95 - 6.45)/7.95} = \frac{2.25/3.5}{1.50/7.95} = \frac{64.28\%}{18.86\%} = 3.4$$

A price elasticity index of 3.4, substantially greater than 1.0, indicates that Motown's cassette tapes are very price elastic. A drop in price of 18.86 percent yields a much larger rise in demand, 64.28 percent.

Substitutability is a factor in determining price elasticity. The more substitutes consumers can find for a product or brand, the more sharply demand will fall relative to a rise in price.[5] For instance, if Procter & Gamble raises the price of Tide, consumers can substitute any one of a number of cheaper brands of laundry detergent. Electricity, on the other hand, is price inelastic because it has no substitutes.

The nature of customer needs also influences elasticity. Necessities like medical services are inelastic; people suffering from kidney disease are not likely to decide against treatment from one time to another because the price has risen. Luxuries like cruise tickets are price elastic, and so are some conveniences. A person can ignore the need for a new Dustbuster for a long time.

Price elasticity is a useful index for the marketer because it indicates the responsiveness of total revenue to price changes. See figure 11.6 for other possible effects of price changes on total revenue, assuming a traditional demand curve. When the price elasticity equation yields a value greater than one, demand is elastic with respect to price. If the marketer decides to raise the price, total revenue will fall because the percentage decrease in demand will be greater than the percentage increase in price. A lower level of sales will produce less total revenue, and this will not be offset by the increase in price per unit. If, on the other hand, the marketer decides to lower the price, total revenue will increase because the higher volume of sales will compensate for the lower unit price. When demand is highly elastic, a company may capture a larger share of the market if it lowers its prices slightly, especially if competitors do not react. Marketing research suggests that demand for motor homes is elastic with respect to price. Total revenue will increase if prices are reduced.

❑ **Figure 11.6**
Price elasticity and the possible effects of price change on total revenue.

Elasticity of Demand		
Price Elasticity Greater Than One	Price Elasticity Less Than One	Price Elasticity Equal to One
Price increase → Total revenue decreases	Total revenue increases	Total revenue remains same
Price decrease → Total revenue increases	Total revenue decreases	Total revenue remains same

When the price elasticity equation yields a value less than one, demand is inelastic with respect to price. In this situation, the marketer's decision to increase the price of the product will produce an increase in total revenue. Since demand for the product will not fall significantly as the price rises, the percentage increase in price will offset the percentage decrease in demand. However, if the marketer decides to decrease the price, total revenue will decrease because demand will not rise enough to offset the effect on revenue of the lower per-unit price. Natural gas is inelastic; a drop in price will not induce enough of a rise in demand to make up for the lower price.

Marketers interested in total revenue should consider price elasticity in conjunction with cost. At some point increases in demand and total revenue in an elastic situation may be more than offset by lower profit margins. `

Price elasticity also focuses on and along the demand curve. Shifting the whole demand curve is an alternative way of increasing total revenue and can sometimes be accomplished with promotion. Shifts in the total demand curve are considered in a later chapter.

Pricing to Maximize Revenue

*D*emand schedule is the relationship between quantity and price.

When the objective is to maximize total revenue, the marketer attempts to identify the price that generates the largest total sales revenue. Since the total revenue equals the quantity times price per unit—which for a price range becomes a **demand schedule**—the marketer must have at least a general picture of the demand schedule. Several possible demand schedules are shown in the top section of figure 11.7.

As can be seen, demand schedules take different shapes and different locations with regard to price and quantity. Demand schedule D_1 in figure 11.7 has perfect inelasticity; regardless of the price charged the quantity demanded remains the same.

❑ **Figure 11.7**
Demand schedule illustrations.

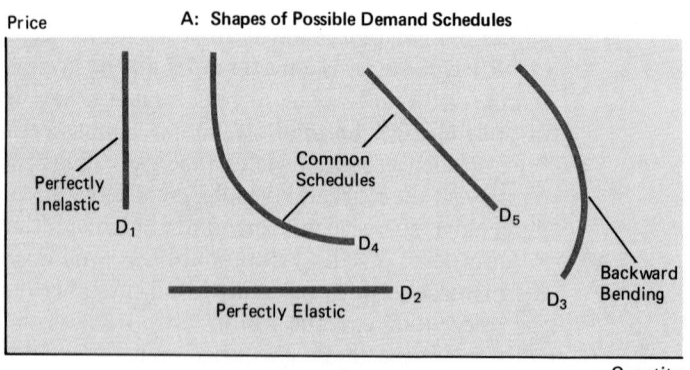

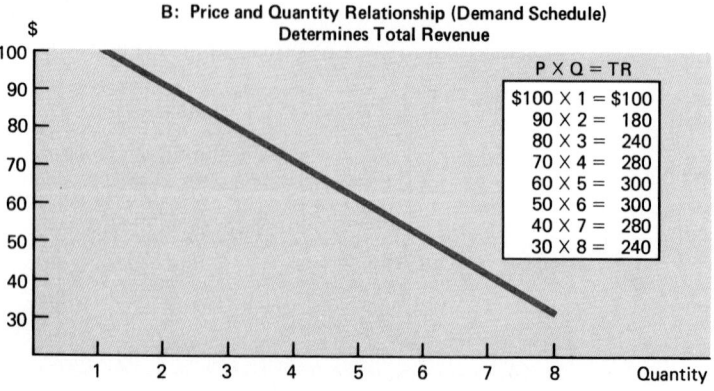

Schedule D_2 has perfect elasticity; a slight increase in the price destroys all demand for the product. Schedule D_3, the backward demand curve, reflects customer perceptions about the relationship between price and quality. As the price increases, the quantity demanded increases because customers perceive that the product has greater quality. Eventually, however, customers reduce their demand for a product as the price increases, as shown in the top half of schedule D_3. Schedules D_4 and D_5, common or traditional demand schedules, have neither perfect elasticity nor perfect inelasticity. An increase in the price causes a decrease in the quantity demanded. Schedules D_4 and D_5 occur more frequently than D_1, D_2, or D_3.

> *V*alue pricing—what's it worth to the buyer.

A marketer desiring to maximize sales with the demand schedule in the bottom half of figure 11.7 would set a price between $50 and $60 a unit, since total revenues are maximized between those prices.

Value Pricing

Value pricing is a method of setting price that requires the marketer to assess how much the product is worth to the buyer. The technique focuses on the buyer's perception of value and not the seller's cost. Buyers' perceptions of value are based on the benefits they expect to receive from the purchase and use of the product. Sellers should therefore analyze the benefits of their products.

A product used in two different markets may have two very different prices.

Benefits will differ with different uses and markets. For instance, in humid areas homes with painted exteriors sometimes become covered with mildew. To remove the mildew a homeowner may visit a paint store and buy a gallon of mildew remover, which sells for approximately $8. The benefits of removing the mildew are well worth the price to many homeowners. Common household bleach sells in supermarkets for $1.50 a gallon, and its effects on mildew are exactly the same as the mildew remover. Bleach manufacturers could sell their product in paint stores for $1.50. They realize, though, that homeowners perceive considerable benefits from the removal of mildew so they price each gallon at $8.00 and call it mildew remover.

THE CASE CONTINUES

*T*o set a price for the stretch denim jean, The Jeans Company marketing executives have both cost- and demand-based alternatives available.

Based on available information, however, none of the cost-based methods can be used by The Jeans Company executives to set a price. More information is needed. Addi-

tional information for each method is included in the chart below.

Since The Jeans Company produces hundreds of variations by style and material in jeans, and would likely know the direct material and la-

bor costs, the incremental cost method is an appropriate method for The Jeans Company to use in pricing the new stretch denim.

Possible demand-pricing methods include maximizing revenue and value pricing. With the consultant's prediction of sales at the specified prices, company executives could price to maximize sales. The price per unit multiplied by unit sales projected by the consultant gives the estimated sales in dollars. For the price $16.50, sales are $8,662,500. Of the four prices, the $16.50 price produces the largest dollar sales. Value pricing should be considered. If the stretch denim does allow for a better fit, its value to the consumer should be greater. Research to determine the increased value would be needed to use value pricing.

Method	Additional Information Needed
Total Cost	Unit quantity
Target Margin on Sales	Unit quantity and desired Profit Margin
Target Return on Investment	Investment, ROI, and unit quantity
Incremental Cost	Markup percentage desired on direct labor and material
Conversion Cost	Markup percentage desired on direct labor and overhead and overhead rate

The marketer who analyzes market opportunities may discover numerous ways besides charging a higher price to build the perception of value in the buyer's mind. Japanese automakers, for instance, have succeeded in establishing a reputation for quality. Although the Japanese have been reluctant to charge higher prices than U.S. automakers, apparently consumers would accept a higher price because they perceive a benefit from quality.

STEP 6: SELECTING A PRICING METHOD AND SETTING THE PRICE

Cost establishes the minimum price that is acceptable. The marketer can employ several different kinds of costs. (See table 11.1.) Each of the cost-based methods of pricing employs different combinations and types of cost, so each method should be used with caution. Are the costs accurate, does the method emphasize some products by ignoring part of their cost, and can the product be sold in the quantity desired at the price are all relevant questions. The biggest limitation to cost-based pricing is that it does not consider demand.

Demand-based pricing focuses on the market.

Since the marketing concept focuses on the purchaser, especially the consumer, marketing management readily accepts the demand-oriented price. In fact, **demand backward pricing,** which starts with the consumer and works backward to the producer, is a recommended method. Demand-based pricing does, however, require accurate information that is often difficult to obtain. There are many types of demand and not all assume the classic schedule. Pricing based on the demand schedule also ignores cost.

Cost, Demand, and Revenue Relationships

Using marginal analysis and break-even analysis, the marketer arrives at the selling price by considering the cost, demand, and revenue.

Maximizing Profit—Marginal Analysis

Marginal analysis results in profit maximization.

Marginal analysis looks at the effects on total revenues and total costs of selling one additional unit. It is based on the idea that an organization should continue to

❏ **Table 11.1** Cost structure for firm.

(1) QUANTITY Q	(2) TOTAL FIXED COST TFC	(3) TOTAL VARIABLE COST TVC	(4) AVERAGE VARIABLE COST AVC	(5) TOTAL COST (TFC + TVC = TC) TC	(6) AVERAGE COST (AC = TC/Q) AC	(7) MARGINAL COST (PER UNIT) MC
1	$100	$ 52	$152	$152	$152	$152
2	100	72	36	172	86	20
3	100	84	28	184	61	12
4	100	100	25	200	50	16
5	100	135	27	235	47	35
6	100	180	30	280	47	45
7	100	224	32	324	46	44
8	100	296	37	395	50	72

❏ **Table 11.2** Profit maximization.

(1) QUANTITY Q	(2) PRICE P	(3) TOTAL REVENUE TR	(4) TOTAL COST TC	(5) PROFIT (TR − TC)	(6) MARGINAL REVENUE MR	(7) MARGINAL COST MC	(8) MARGINAL PROFIT (MR − MC)
1	100	100	152	− 52	100	152	− 52
2	90	180	172	+ 8	80	20	+ 60
3	80	240	184	+ 56	60	12	+ 48
4	**70**	**280**	**200**	**+ 80**	**40**	**16**	**+ 24**
5	60	300	235	+ 65	20	35	− 15
6	50	300	280	+ 20	0	45	− 45
7	40	280	334	− 54	− 20	54	− 74
8	30	240	396	−156	− 40	62	−102

Best price = **70**
Best quantity = **4**

produce and market a product as long as the marginal cost is less than the marginal revenue. Production should stop when the cost of the last unit equals or exceeds the revenue from sales.

Table 11.2 shows that profits are maximized when the marginal revenue is closest to the marginal cost. The greatest amount of profit results from a price of $70 with four units sold. Marginal revenue and cost intersect at another point, when the product is priced at $100 and only one unit is produced, but this intersection occurs before any profit and would not be selected.

Although marginal analysis is theoretically sound, it requires information that is difficult to obtain. Many firms, therefore, use break-even analysis.

Break-Even Analysis

Break-even analysis identifies the level of sales at which the firm has neither a profit nor a loss. If sales do not reach this level, the firm will sustain a loss. If they exceed this level, the firm will make a profit. If sales equal this level, the firm will break even. The following procedure yields the quantity of sales that will provide the break-even revenue.

CALCULATING BREAK-EVEN QUANTITIES AND CONTRIBUTION MARGIN

To break even on a product, a firm's revenue from sales must equal the variable cost plus the fixed cost of producing the product.

Break-Even Revenue = Variable Cost + Fixed Cost

To make a profit, a firm's total revenue from sales must exceed its break-even revenue. Total revenue is defined as price per unit (P) times quantity sold (Q):

Total Revenue = P × Q

To find the quantity of sales at which total revenue equals break-even revenue, substitute total revenue for break-even revenue in the formula for break-even revenue:

$$(P \times Q) = \text{Variable Cost} + \text{Fixed Cost}$$

Recall that total variable cost (assumed to be constant per unit) is defined as cost per unit (C) times quantity sold (Q):

$$\text{Variable Cost} = C \times Q$$

To find the quantity of sales at which total variable cost is at the break-even point, substitute the definition of total variable cost in the formula for break-even revenue and solve the equation for Q:

$$
\begin{aligned}
(P \times Q) &= (C \times Q) + \text{Fixed Cost} \\
PQ &= CQ + \text{Fixed Cost} \\
PQ - CQ &= \text{Fixed Cost} \\
Q(P - C) &= \text{Fixed Cost} \\
Q &= \frac{\text{Fixed Cost}}{P - C} = \text{the break-even point in units} \\
P - C &= \text{the Contribution Margin}
\end{aligned}
$$

The contribution margin consists of the amount the price can contribute to fixed costs after all of the variable costs have been paid. For instance, if Nike has $5 worth of material in a new style of shoe and $3 of labor with no other variable costs, the total variable cost per pair is $8. If the shoe sells for $8, there is a zero contribution margin, and the firm cannot cover any of its fixed cost. If the price cannot be raised, Nike should discontinue the style. If the price can be raised to $10, the contribution margin would be $2 per unit ($10 − $8 = $2). If fixed costs were $1,000,000 the firm would need to produce and sell 500,000 pair.

$$\frac{\$1,000,000}{\$2} = 500,000$$

*B*reak-even analysis combined with a demand schedule is more informative than break-even alone.

Break-even analysis does not determine the best selling price. It allows the marketer to compute the quantity that will have to be sold in order to break even if a specific price is selected. Therefore, the marketer should test several prices. Let's consider prices of $7, $5, and $3 for a product with a fixed cost of $125,000 and a variable cost of $2.25 per unit.

$$Q = \frac{\$125,000}{\$7.00 - \$2.25} = 26,316 \text{ units}$$

At a unit price of $7, the firm will have to sell 26,316 units to earn the break-even revenue of $184,212 (26,316 × $7). Substituting $5 for $7 in the equation yields a break-even quantity of 45,455 units and a break-even revenue of $227,275. Substituting $3 gives 166,667 units and $500,001.

The break-even analysis as presented assumes that an unlimited quantity can be sold at the price selected. Obviously this assumption is untrue, and therefore the quantity demanded at each possible price should be estimated. Both quantity demanded and the break-even at each price would then allow selection of best price.

A Final Review and Set the Price

At this stage in the price-setting process the information has been collected and analyzed, but a review of the three main factors (demand, cost, and competition) usually precedes the final decision on price. Will the product be purchased at the identified price? In what quantity? How much total revenue will be generated? What perceived benefits are the buyers receiving? Is there sufficient value? Is the price sufficient to pay all of the costs and achieve the profit objective? How will the competition react to the price set? Why? Precise answers to these questions are usually not possible. At best, the answers are interpretations of subjective data. Because of this subjectiveness, pricing remains an art instead of a science.

STEP 7: DECIDE ON DISCOUNTS AND ALLOWANCES

Steps one through six of the pricing procedure result in the **base or list price,** which is the price that the company quotes to buyers. Discounts and other adjustments are made to the list price.

Offering Discounts

Discounts are reductions from the list price. The seller may offer a discount as payment to the buyer for services performed in distributing the product or for other purposes.

FUNCTIONAL (TRADE) DISCOUNTS

*F*unctional discounts encourage firms to participate in distributing the product.

Trade discounts encourage wholesalers, retailers, and others to participate in distributing the product. **Trade or functional discounts** are payments for performing marketing functions. Usually the more services performed, the larger the discount. The manufacturer may work from the final price the customer is expected to pay back through the channel of distribution, allowing a reduction for each level. For instance, a Firestone tire may be listed at $69.95 at the retail level. In other words, Firestone expects the consumer to pay $69.95 for the tire. How much do the wholesaler and retailer who distribute and sell the tire pay for it? Firestone may discount the price 30 percent to the retailer and 15 percent more to the wholesaler. Thus the retailer pays $48.97 for the tire.

$69.95 − 30% discount ($21.00) = $48.97

The wholesaler receives an additional 15 percent discount and therefore pays $41.62 for the tire from Firestone.

$48.97 − 15% additional discount ($7.35) = $41.62

The retailer and wholesaler receive a discount off the consumers' price.

Source: Photo courtesy of International Business Machines Corporation

Although Firestone sells the tire to the wholesaler for $41.62, the wholesaler has the freedom to select a price at which to sell the tire to the retailer.

The manufacturer's policy on the amount of reduction at each level in the channel influences the willingness of channel members to participate. A manufacturer allowing a larger reduction than others will find members of the channel more eager to carry the product and perform the marketing functions.

Another way of arriving at discounts occurs when the manufacturer adds a percentage to the cost of producing the product to cover other expenses and profit. For example, Bristol-Meyers, marketers of Clairol hair products, may use the cost of production plus 100 percent. Each company that resells the product likewise adds a percentage to the cost of acquiring it in order to determine the selling price. The manufacturer, in pondering the price to charge the final customer, may anticipate these add-on percentages. Thus, Clairol managers, pricing a new hairstyling mousse that will sell through retail stores like Peoples Drug, may anticipate the selling price to the final customer by estimating that Peoples and other stores add 40 percent to the price at which they acquire the styling mousse. If Clairol sells the product to Peoples for $12 a case and Peoples adds 40 percent, the selling price to the final customer anticipated by Clairol executives is $16.80 ($12 + $12 (.40)). The question that any manager who is pricing a product must ask is, "Will enough customers buy the product at this price to make the production and the sale profitable?"

QUANTITY DISCOUNTS

Quantity discounts are offered to buyers who purchase large quantities. There are two types, noncumulative and cumulative, and a seller may offer one or both.

*N*oncumulative quantity discounts may encourage overbuying.

Noncumulative discounts are offered when the purchase invoice specifies a minimum amount or more. The noncumulative discount encourages the placement of single large orders. From the seller's perspective large orders can reduce costs by increasing the size of the production run. Order processing, marketing, and transportation costs can also be less.

For a buyer, noncumulative discounts offer the obvious advantage of a lower price but also present several possible disadvantages. Buyers looking to the discount sometimes overbuy, tying up working capital in inventory. Buying large quantities from one seller may also mean that other sellers' products cannot be purchased. The buyer becomes dependent upon one seller.

*C*umulative quantity discounts encourage buyer loyalty.

Cumulative discounts are granted to the buyer who purchases a minimum amount or more in a specified period of time. Cumulative discounts encourage buyer loyalty. The IGA supermarket manager who offers customers $20 worth of free groceries if they purchase $20 or more for ten consecutive weeks is offering a cumulative discount at the consumer level. Sellers reduce their marketing cost and sell more products by offering cumulative discounts. Buyers obtain a lower price but inadvertently may forego shopping elsewhere for the product, where it may even be sold for less.

Sellers need to use quantity discounts carefully despite their advantages. The Robinson-Patman Act prohibits quantity discounts that discriminate among like buyers.[6] Quantity discounts may also have a negative effect if they tend to load up the buyer with a large inventory. Buyers with large inventories do not reorder frequently. Thus, quantity discounts can produce cycles in sales.

SEASONAL DISCOUNTS

Seasonal discounts should really be called "out of season discounts." Offered most often before the high volume selling period rather than after, seasonal discounts encourage purchases when the demand is low and help the supplier to obtain sales during slack periods. Manufacturers therefore can continue production in the off-season at a higher level of capacity than would be possible without seasonal discounts. When producing in anticipation of the season without purchase commitments, the manufacturer can continue high levels of production but must accept the risk associated with speculating that the seasonal sales will develop as expected. Seasonal discounts allow the manufacturer to shift the storage function to the buyer when the immediate acceptance of the merchandise is a condition of a seasonal discount.

Sears stimulates sales of air conditioners and furnaces by use of seasonal discounts.

CASH DISCOUNTS

*C*ash sales are aimed at increasing quickness of payment rather than sales.

The typical company expects to place an order for merchandise, receive the merchandise, receive a bill (invoice), and then pay. Cash with the order is not required. In rare cases when the buyer has a poor credit record or none at all, cash on delivery (COD) is required. The terms of sale, including payment information, are included as a part of the invoice sent to the purchaser. **Cash discounts** are price reductions given to buyers who pay the invoice within a specified number of days. Typical cash discount terms are 2/10, net/30. The buyer has ten days after the invoice date to pay and thereby qualify for a 2 percent discount (2/10).[7] If more than ten days pass, the buyer must pay the total invoice amount in a maximum of thirty days (net/30). After thirty days the seller considers the account overdue and may ask the buyer to sign an interest-bearing note. Other cash discount terms include 3/10, n/30, 2/10, ROG (Receipt of Goods is starting date), and 2/10, 60 extra (buyer has sixty extra days to take the discount).

Missed cash discounts are expensive.

Buyers should make every effort to take advantage of cash discounts. The annual interest rate associated with cash discount terms usually exceeds the cost of borrowing to pay the invoice. For example, the terms 2/10, n/30 have an interest rate of 36 percent.

Offering Allowances

Like discounts, **allowances** reduce the list price of a product. Customarily, they are rewards for providing services, but they may function as an incentive to purchase. Trade-in allowances typify the purchase incentive kind of allowance.

PROMOTION ALLOWANCES

Promotion and advertising allowances reward the purchaser for assistance in promoting the product.

Promotion allowances reward the purchaser for assisting in promoting the product. They often reduce the price of merchandise by supplying free units in addition to those purchased. Buy ten—get two free for hanging the product's banner across your store front. Promotional allowances are given for all kinds of promotion programs but especially in exchange for the use of point-of-purchase material, special displays, and shelf space.

ADVERTISING ALLOWANCES

Advertising allowances require the purchaser to cooperate in advertising programs such as those featuring the seller's product in newspaper advertisements. Advertisements co-sponsored by the buyer and seller are referred to as cooperative advertisements. Both sellers and buyers stretch their advertising budgets through cooperative efforts since they receive the benefits of advertising while sharing the cost.

TRADE-IN ALLOWANCES

Trade-in allowances encourage the buyer to purchase by giving compensation for the product already owned. Trade-ins are more prevalent for high-value, durable items, as in the automobile industry. Business firms tend to purchase more up-to-date equipment when cost saving justifies the investment. A trade-in allowance helps provide the justification.

Determining Transportation Allowances

Transportation costs can make a product more expensive. Several arrangements for paying for them have evolved.

UNIFORM DELIVERED PRICE

Delivered price the same to all buyers.

With the **uniform delivered price** the seller pays all transportation costs as a matter of policy. The delivered product is the same price to all buyers regardless of

❑ **Figure 11.8**
   Zone pricing.

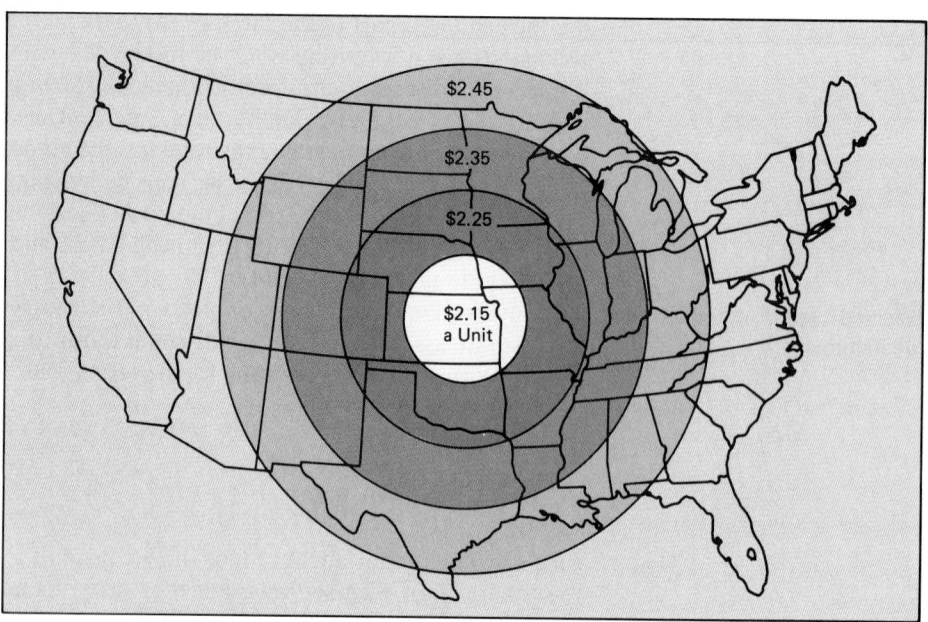

their geographic location in the market. A higher selling price covers the transportation expense for the seller. The uniform delivered price works well as a policy if the marketer desires to cover the entire market at one price—for promotional or other purposes. Transportation costs, however, have to be low as a percentage of total selling price. Therefore, items with a high unit value that are not bulky are most suited to uniform delivered price.

ZONE PRICING

Under **zone pricing** the seller pays the actual transportation charge, billing the buyer the average amount that has been established for the buyer's zone. The price plus the transportation charge is the same for all buyers in the same zone. Zone pricing is used when transportation costs represent a large enough percentage of the total price that charging the identical price throughout the market would overcharge close buyers. (See figure 11.8.)

BASE-POINT PRICING

Base-point pricing allows the seller to charge the buyer for transportation costs from the nearest designated base location even if the item is shipped from a different location. For example, if USX (formerly United States Steel) has a single base point in Gary, Indiana, and ships an order from its Pittsburgh plant to a customer in Denver, the customer pays freight from Gary even though the shipment is from Pittsburgh. If the shipment is from a Denver plant, the customer also pays freight from Gary.

Base-point pricing has several effects. Customers pay phantom freight (charges for freight service never received) if they are located near the factory from which the product is shipped, but which is not a base point. The Denver-to-Denver situation above is an example. On the other hand, buyers may pay for less freight service than they actually receive if they buy from a factory more distant than the base point. The Pittsburgh-to-Denver situation above is an illustration. If all sellers use the same base point, they eliminate competition. All buyers pay the same price regardless of factory location.

The above discussion assumes a single base point. Multiple base points are also possible. The buyer's freight charge is calculated from the nearest base point. The legality of both single and multiple base point pricing is often argued in the courts in terms of how individual firms apply this pricing method.

FREE-ON-BOARD PRICING

*F*OB—The seller loads the product, but it is then the buyer's responsibility to assume the transportation costs.

Free-on-board pricing (FOB) means the buyer has the responsibility for paying transportation costs from a designated point. Free-on-board factory, for example, means that the seller accepts only the responsibility for loading the merchandise on the transportation carrier. Ownership of the merchandise passes to the buyer at the factory. The owner of the merchandise must file a claim for recovery of any damages that may occur in transit.

Free-on-board terms are easily altered by replacing the word *factory* with other terms, for instance, FOB destination, FOB Kansas City, and FOB port of entry. In all the examples the buyer becomes the owner and pays transportation from the designated point.

When transportation costs are a significant portion of the overall cost of the merchandise, FOB is the preferred method of pricing. Buyers pay their actual transportation costs, not an average charge, which may be larger or smaller than the actual cost. FOB factory pricing does, however, tend to restrict the geographic size of a seller's market. Buyers in distant locations purchase from firms near them because transportation costs are lower.

THE CASE CONTINUES

*U*sing break-even, we might want to test the four prices for stretch denim jeans used by the consultant for break-even quantities.

$$\frac{\text{B.E.}}{\text{(units)}} = \frac{\text{Fixed cost/}}{\text{unit price}} - \frac{\text{variable}}{\text{unit cost}}$$

Price

$14.25:
526,316 units = $2,500,000/14.25 − 9
$16.50:
333,333 units = 2,500,000/16.50 − 9
$18.75:
256,410 units = 2,500,000/18.75 − 9
$22.00:
192,308 units = 2,500,000/22.00 − 9

The highest price, $22, provides the lowest break-even point, and at first glance would seem to be the best price. The consultant's unit sales projections at the four prices indicate that at $22 only 175,000 units would be sold less than the

break-even point. Obviously, $22 should not be selected as the selling price.

Subtracting break-even for each price from the consultant's projection, the $16.50 price has the greatest difference.

Price	Consultant's Unit Sales Projection	Break-even	Difference
$14.25	600,000	526,316	73,684
16.50	525,000	333,333	191,667
18.75	375,000	256,410	118,590
21.25	175,000	192,308	− 17,308

Is $16.50 the best price? To determine the answer, calculate the total profit.

$8,550,000 − $7,900,000 = $650,000
8,662,500 − 7,225,000 = $1,437,500
7,031,250 − 5,875,000 = $1,156,250

The price of $16.50, based on maximizing sales and total profit objectives, is the best price of the four for the stretch denims.

As to discounts and allowances from the $16.50, The Jeans Company does not use a consumer list price, therefore, trade or functional discounts would not apply. Company officials may want to determine the price at which retailers would offer the stretch denim to consumers. Retailers add from 40 percent to 80 percent to their cost. The price to the consumer, therefore, would be $23.10 to $29.70.

$16.50 + 40% (16.50) = $23.10
$16.50 + 80% (16.50) = $29.70

By paying transportation cost on orders of 200 units or more, The Jeans Company does offer a noncumulative quantity discount. Advertising allowances are also offered, but products such as stretch denim are not singled out for special allowances and discounts.

FREIGHT ABSORPTION PRICING

To extend the boundaries of the geographic market, sellers offer **freight absorption pricing.** That is, they agree to pay all transportation costs in excess of those the buyer would owe with a purchase from a nearer seller. The seller does not increase the price of the product but subtracts the freight from profit margin. Sellers make less per shipment when they absorb freight, but their total profit may be greater, especially when they have high fixed operating costs.

STEP 8: ADJUST THE PRICE WHEN NECESSARY

Circumstances force price changes even if the initial price was well chosen. With increased demand, reduction of supply, or higher cost, the price will be adjusted upward if possible. Reduction in a price occurs for the opposite reasons, but also for promotional reasons.

Should the price be changed? Even if the answer is a definite yes, resistance can develop from customers. They may delay purchase or substitute other products or brands. To lessen the reaction of customers, marketers use one or more of the following techniques:

1. Adopt delayed quotation pricing. By waiting until the last possible minute to quote a price, marketers can include up-to-date costs. When costs are rising rapidly and unpredictably, including the most recent cost may mean the difference between profit and loss.
2. Write escalator clauses into contracts. Escalator clauses increase the price of a product or service in proportion to increases in costs as measured by an index. A common form of escalator clause is the cost of living allowance found in labor contracts (COLA).
3. Unbundle goods and services and price them separately. Unbundling goods and services means selling them in parts instead of pricing them as a unit. Funeral homes are required by the FTC to sell caskets, flowers, embalming, etc., separately. The funeral service has been unbundled.
4. Reduce discounts. The company reduces the discounts (cash, trade, and quantity, for example) given to purchasers.
5. Attempt to sell the higher margin products and markets. The company focuses on products and customers that generate high profit.
6. Increase minimum order size. Small orders, per dollar of sales, are more expensive to complete. They may be eliminated by the company.
7. Reduce product quality, features, or service.[8] To maintain profit margins without increasing the price, the company may reduce the quality, features, or service of products.

Price reductions may also meet resistance. Wholesalers and retailers who have large inventories of the product see the value of their inventory diminish when the manufacturer lowers the price. Customers may also have misconceptions, believing that the firm is having financial problems or that the quality of its product or service is less.

Markdowns and Rebates

*R*ebates and markdowns both reduce price but are used differently.

At the retail level price reductions are called **markdowns.** Expressed as a percentage, markdowns are calculated by subtracting the new price from the original price and

Toys "Я" Us rebates to reinforce its lower-price image and to promote sales.

dividing the difference by the new price. Retailers have policies regarding the amount and timing of markdowns. They also try to reduce the total number of markdowns by wise buying and by more promotion of products with slow rates of sales.

For wholesalers and manufacturers downward price changes are simply called reductions. If they are short-term, they are sometimes called **rebates.** Rebates can also apply at the consumer level. To obtain the rebate, the consumer pays the original price and then applies for the rebate. Since rebates are perceived as temporary, they encourage immediate purchase, and they make restoration of the original price easier. Rebates also provide a promotional theme—price reductions.

Promotional Pricing

*P*romotional pricing—reductions to encourage people to buy.

Price reductions appeal to a large segment of the market. To capitalize on the appeal—to motivate people to shop and purchase—firms may reduce the price on a product even though the item is selling well. The firm expects to sell other items at full price by attracting customers with the reduced item. The promoted item generates traffic through the retail store.

The strategy of reducing the price on an item to generate traffic is called leader pricing. When the reduction brings the price below cost, the strategy is loss leader

3 Way, Your Way!
Create your own pizza
with any 3 toppings
ONLY
$8.39
Large Round or
Thick Pan Pizza

AN EXTRA
$1.75 OFF
3 Way, Your Way! Large Round
or Thick Pan Pizza
Limit 1 coupon per customer, per visit. Not good on other
specials. This coupon good on $8.39 offer only.
Offer Good 3/21/88-5/22/88
#5622 **Papa Gino's**

Save an extra $1.75 with
our 3 Way, Your Way!
Coupon above

Papa Gino's expects to sell other products in addition to
its "3 Way, Your Way" promotionally priced pizza.

Source: Courtesy of Papa Gino's

Bait and switch—illegal
promotional pricing that
employs deception to sell
full, high-priced products.

pricing. To be effective, leader items should be widely recognized brands, purchased frequently, for which people know the usual selling price.

Bait-and-switch pricing is an unethical and illegal form of promotional pricing. The firm advertises a product at a very low price (the bait) with no intention of selling it. The potential customer finds either that the product is not available or that it is available but that the salesperson denigrates it. In both situations the salesperson suggests a different product (the switch), which is more expensive, of course.

To protect purchasers, the Federal Trade Commission requires that firms advertising products have in stock a sufficient number of units to satisfy demand or to state in the advertisement the limited number available.

LEGAL ASPECTS OF PRICING

In the free enterprise economy of the United States a competitive business environment is preferred. Because the nature of price makes it susceptible to manipulation and trickery, several guidelines exist for businesses to follow. Sellers who conspire to establish prices are considered to be violating the premises of the competitive system and the provisions of anti-trust law. General Cinema Corporation's General Cinema Beverage of Washington, D.C., Inc., was fined $1 million when executives pleaded guilty to conspiring to fix the price of cola soft drinks in Washington.[9] Sellers who provide misleading price information, discriminate against some of their customers, or unfairly compete are also violating the premises of the economic system. Otherwise, businesses are generally free to establish their own prices.

Legal Price Issues—Consumers

Deceptive pricing information to mislead consumers
violates the law.

The competitive economic system protects the consumer from unreasonable prices. The consumer has to be able to depend on accurate information from the seller. Consumers, for instance, expect the seller's list price to be correct. The government and the business community consider companies to be unethical if they falsely report

❑ **Figure 11.9**
Pricing actions the FTC
considers to be
unethical.

Should not advertise:
1. In a price comparison, a product of less quality than the comparison product.
2. A price below quoted retail when the retail price has not been established.
3. A price below regular retail when no sales have been made.
4. Implied sale of product for special price because of unusual event when it did not occur.
5. As two articles for price of one when not true.
6. As a one-cent sale when not true.
7. As factory or wholesale price when not the same paid by retailer.
8. As a price markdown when product was artificially marked at high selling price in order to mark it down.

*C*harging consumers a
high price is usually not
illegal.

*C*harging competing buy-
ers different prices for like-
grade and quality products,
is generally illegal.

their list prices as high to create the illusion that they are offering substantial discounts.

The **Wheeler Lea Amendment** to the Federal Trade Commission Act gives the FTC power to stop "unfair or deceptive acts in commerce." Figure 11.9 contains some of the pricing and promotion actions the FTC considers unethical. In each of the situations listed, a false or misleading reference point encourages the prospective customer to conclude that the price of the offered product is superior and therefore the product should be purchased. For example, item 1 in figure 11.9 identifies the practice of promoting an item by comparing its price to the price of an item of much lower quality without informing the consumer of the difference.

The law does not prohibit a seller from establishing a very high price. On the other hand, supposedly to protect competition, some states have minimum price limits. Approximately one half of the states have **unfair trade practice acts.** Such acts restrict wholesalers and retailers from establishing prices that are too low.[10] The price, most often, must cover the cost of the item to the seller plus a minimum markup.

Legal Price Issues–Businesses

The primary premise of the legal system with regard to price is to protect and promote competition. Competitors are not allowed to collude to fix prices, for example. To illustrate, the Justice Department recently filed a lawsuit against five of the biggest U.S. companies that buy and sell hops, charging them with fixing prices. Hops are an essential ingredient in beer.[11] Although at one time many states enacted resale price maintenance laws or fair trade laws, which permitted price fixing if the brand owner requested that the brand be sold at a set price, federal legislation made the state laws illegal in 1975.

Federal laws also prohibit predatory pricing, defined as selling a product near, at, or below cost with the intent or result of injuring or eliminating competitors. Predatory pricing may force weaker, smaller competitors to withdraw from the market. A spokesperson for the Dixie Brewing Company, for example, claims that Dixie will lose market share if the Miller Brewing Company continues to price Milwaukee's Best $.60 a case below the cheapest beer in the market. Dixie officials have filed complaints with the Justice Department.[12]

A very significant federal act, the **Robinson-Patman Act,** makes most price discrimination illegal. **Price discrimination** exists when the seller sells a like grade and quality product to like buyers at different prices with the effect of injuring competition. The act does not cover consumers. A firm can sell to different consumers at different prices and be within the law. Wholesalers, retailers, and other firms are covered by the act as buyers. The act specifies competing "like" buyers, who have generally been defined by the courts as buyers performing the same functions in distributing the product. A wholesaler and retailer would not be like buyers, but two wholesalers performing the same function would be. Competing buyers are defined as buyers who vie for the same customers. Since buyers in different markets are generally not competing, charging them different prices is legal.

Price discrimination laws cover products of like grade and quality. The definition of like grade and quality is, however, open to question. Does a different brand label on the same physical item make a product different? The Borden Case in the mid-1960s was based on that question. The court held that a different brand label did not by itself make the product a different grade and quality but found that no injury to competition had been evident. Changing only the brand label and not the physical product may, however, subject the seller to unnecessary legal risk.

Not all price discrimination is illegal. When the seller can prove that the difference in price has resulted from a difference in the cost of servicing the buyers,

*P*rice differences are legally acceptable if the difference is less than the proven cost difference in serving the buyers.

discrimination is legal. The price difference has to be equal to or less than the cost savings. The seller must also be able to prove the difference in cost. The seller may charge different prices in order to meet competition. The price difference should reflect a defensive, not an offensive, effort to meet competitors' prices.

Discounts and allowances generally do not violate the Robinson-Patman Act if they are made available to all buyers on a proportionally equal basis. A promotion allowance of one free item for every ten purchased should be within the legal limits of the Robinson-Patman Act if offered to all buyers. Even the smallest buyer needs to be able to qualify. Although the allowance for a large quantity purchaser would be greater in total, the proportion of one to ten would be the same for all buyers.

---

*T*o sell merchandise in excess supply, The Jeans Company changes prices by using terms such as "overruns and irregulars." If the inventory of a product becomes too large, the item may be classified as an overrun

THE CASE CONTINUES

item and a price break given to retailers.

Since The Jeans Company prepays transportation on orders of 200

units, the company is in effect giving a quantity discount. Apparently the Robinson-Patman Act has not been violated by the quantity discount given. Evidently all retailers are large enough to qualify for the discount.

GOAL SUMMARY

1. **Explain the range that a firm uses in establishing a price.** In determining a product's price, firm managers often work from two reference points. The upper reference point (the ceiling) is a function of demand; the lower point (the floor) is a function of cost. Some managers prefer to start with cost, others with demand, but ultimately both have to be considered in order to arrive at the best price within the range.

2. **Describe the types of cost and cost-based pricing methods.** Several types of cost are commonly referred to—total cost, average total cost, total fixed cost, total variable cost, average variable cost, and marginal cost. All of the average costs are computed by dividing the relevant total cost by total quantity. Total fixed costs do not change with quantity; total variable costs do change with quantity. On a per-unit basis, variable costs are treated in two ways: (1) constant, not changing with quantity, and (2) changing, because of economies of scale. Changing variable costs decrease initially with quantity and then increase. Marginal costs are the costs associated with one additional unit. Starting from zero units, as quantity increases, marginal costs decrease, but eventually increase with large quantities.

   Cost-based pricing methods use either total cost or variable costs. For instance, the incremental cost method uses the variable costs of direct labor and material. Retailers and wholesalers use the cost of the item, a variable cost.

3. **Discuss the role of price elasticity and total revenue in setting price.** Total revenue pricing depends on the demand schedule. A marketer interested in the largest total revenue would select that price on the demand schedule where the price multiplied by the quantity produces the largest revenue.

   Elasticity is a measure of the relationship between the quantity demanded and the price as the price changes. If demand for a product is elastic with respect to price, then if the price increases, the total revenue declines. Knowledge of elasticity allows the marketer to anticipate the impact of various prices on total revenue.

4. **Utilize marginal and break-even analysis to price a product.** Marginal analysis considers the equality of marginal cost and revenue. The price that maximizes total profit is the one where MC = MR. The break-even point occurs when the sales revenue equals the total cost. Break-even may be used as an aid in setting price by determining the break-even point in units at a given price and then comparing the break-even in units with the amount of expected demand at that price. The price would be unacceptable if the expected demand is less than the break-even point.

5. **Discuss discounts and allowances as factors in the price that the buyer pays for a product or service.** A company's selling price is determined first before discounts and allowances are considered. The selling price, sometimes called the list price, is

GOAL SUMMARY *(continued)*

the price the buyer is expected to pay if the buyer does not receive credit for an allowance or discount. Normally, discounts are reductions in the list price earned by the buyer. Discounts may be earned for early payment of invoices, large quantity purchases, buying out of season, and helping distribute the product.

Allowances also have the effect of lowering the price. With allowances the buyer normally receives credit for an activity or product. The credit can be used to reduce the price of the item, to purchase additional items, or for a cash rebate. Common allow-

ances include those for promotion, advertising, and product trade-ins. Allowances may also be given for transportation.

6. **Discuss the philosophy on which laws pertaining to pricing are based.** A number of laws have been passed to encourage and maintain a competitive environment. The philosophy is that both the customer and the individual firm should be assured, over the long run, of the best possible price. The customer should always have the opportunity to purchase from many different firms. Firms should have the opportunity to compete under fair conditions.

KEY TERMS

Total Cost, **p. 290**
Average Total Cost, **p. 290**
Experience Curve Pricing, **p. 291**
Target Margin on Sales, **p. 291**
Fixed Costs, **p. 292**
Total Variable Costs, **p. 292**
Average Variable Cost, **p. 292**
Target Return on Investment, **p. 292**
Incremental Cost Method, **p. 294**
Conversion Cost Method, **p. 294**
Marginal Cost **(MC)**, **p. 295**
Total Revenue, **p. 296**
Average Revenue, **p. 296**
Marginal Revenue, **p. 296**
Price Elasticity, **p. 297**
Demand Schedule, **p. 298**
Value Pricing, **p. 299**
Demand Backward Pricing, **p. 300**
Marginal Analysis, **p. 300**
Break-Even Analysis, **p. 301**

Base or List Price, **p. 303**
Discounts, **p. 303**
Trade or Functional Discounts, **p. 303**
Quantity Discounts, **p. 304**
Seasonal Discounts, **p. 304**
Cash Discounts, **p. 305**
Allowances, **p. 305**
Trade-in Allowances, **p. 305**
Uniform Delivered Price, **p. 305**
Zone Pricing, **p. 306**
Base-Point Pricing, **p. 306**
Free-on-Board Pricing (FOB), **p. 307**
Freight Absorption Pricing, **p. 308**
Markdowns, **p. 308**
Rebates, **p. 309**
Bait-and-Switch Pricing, **p. 310**
Wheeler Lea Amendment, **p. 311**
Unfair Trade Practice Acts, **p. 311**
Robinson-Patman Act, **p. 311**
Price Discrimination, **p. 311**

CHECK YOUR LEARNING

1. Costs are more important than demand in determining selling price.   **T/F**
2. Which of the following costs decrease because of the economies of scale? (a) average fixed, (b) average variable, (c) marginal, (d) b and c, (e) a, b, and c.
3. A firm should not continue to operate if the price is less than the average cost.   **T/F**
4. Calculate the price using the target margin on sales method for the following: average total cost $10 and a 15% profit margin is desired. (a) $28.57, (b) $200, (c) $15.38, (d) $66.67, (e) none of the above.
5. The incremental cost method of pricing tends to emphasize sales of low overhead products.   **T/F**
6. When elasticity has a value greater than one, a

price increase will: (a) decrease the quantity demanded, (b) increase total revenue, (c) decrease total revenue, (d) both a and c, (e) both b and c.
7. A marketer should increase the price if the objective is to increase total revenue.   **T/F**
8. All demand-based pricing methods depend upon knowledge of the demand schedule.   **T/F**
9. Marginal revenue based on the classical demand curve first increases and then decreases as quantity increases.   **T/F**
10. It is possible for marginal revenue to equal marginal cost without maximizing profit.   **T/F**
11. In break-even analysis contribution margin is equal to the selling price minus total cost.   **T/F**

CHECK YOUR LEARNING *(continued)*

12. Calculate the break-even if variable cost per unit is $2.50; fixed cost, $150,000; selling price, $5; and expenses, $1 per unit. (a) $60,000, (b) 100,000 units, (c) $30,000, (d) $100,000, (e) 60,000 units.
13. The theme behind U.S. laws that pertain to pricing is the assurance of a competitive environment. **T/F**
14. Unfair trade practice acts make it illegal to reduce the selling price below a certain level. **T/F**
15. Based on the doctrine of buyer beware, the FTC allows a retailer to quote a fictitious list price and then show a discount from it to entice consumers to buy. **T/F**
16. State fair trade laws passed since 1975 make it le-

gal for the manufacturer of a product to set the retailer's selling price. **T/F**
17. Which of the following is a defense against price discrimination? (a) Products are not of like grade, (b) The difference in price represents an offensive effort to beat competition, (c) The difference in price is less than the difference in cost, (d) Both a and c, (e) There are no defenses.
18. Rebates are generally perceived as temporary, thus encouraging immediate purchase. **T/F**
19. Which of the following is not legally acceptable? (a) price skimming, (b) bait-and-switch pricing, (c) promotional pricing, (d) prestige pricing, (e) none are acceptable.

QUESTIONS FOR REVIEW AND DISCUSSION

1. Define the key terms for this chapter that appear at the end of the goal summary.
2. If you were asked to establish the price of a product, would you use a cost or demand method? Why?
3. Describe the conditions that would most likely prevail when a narrow range exists between demand and cost.
4. How do average cost and marginal cost differ?
5. How do the economies of scale influence pricing?
6. Average variable costs may not be constant. Why?
7. Why would a firm's managers want to continue to operate the firm if price per unit were below average cost?

8. Discuss the targeted return on investment pricing method.
9. Demand-based pricing is compatible with the marketing concept. Tell how.
10. State in your own words the fundamental rule of marginal analysis pricing.
11. If variable costs are $7.50 a unit and fixed costs are $14,000, what would be the best price? Discuss. What other information would be helpful?
12. Discuss why functional discounts are given.
13. What are the advantages and disadvantages of quantity discounts to the buyer?
14. Identify three laws discussed in the chapter and briefly explain how they affect pricing decisions.

NOTES

1. "Employee-Relocation Companies' Pricing," *The Wall Street Journal,* October 8, 1986, p. 37.
2. Arthur A. Thompson, Jr., "Strategies for Staying Cost Competitive," *Harvard Business Review* (January–February 1984): pp. 413–428.
3. D. Frank Jones, "A Survey Technique to Measure Demand Under Various Pricing Strategies," *Journal of Marketing* (July 1975): pp. 75–77.
4. "Disposable Diaper Pioneers Remembered," *Terre Haute Tribune-Star,* September 15, 1986, p. A8.
5. Kent B. Montoe and Albert Della Bitta, "Models for Pricing Decisions," *Journal of Marketing Research* (August 1978): pp. 413–428.
6. Asho K. Rao, "Quantity Discounts in Today's Market," *Journal of Marketing* (Fall 1980): pp. 44–51.
7. Michael Levy and Dwight Grant, "Financial Terms

of Sale and Control of Marketing Channel Conflict," *Journal of Marketing Research* (November 1980): pp. 524–530.
8. Norman H. Fuss, Jr., "How to Raise Prices—Judiciously—to Meet Today's Conditions," *Harvard Business Review* (May–June 1975): p. 10.
9. "General Cinema Corporation," *The Wall Street Journal,* October 16, 1986, p. 53.
10. Michael J. Houston, "Minimum Markup Laws: An Empirical Assessment," *Journal of Retailing* 57, *No. 4* (Winter 1981): pp. 98–113.
11. Robert Taylor, "U.S. Sues 5 Firms That Buy, Sell Hops in Price-Fixing Case," *The Wall Street Journal,* July 24, 1984, p. 2.
12. Robert Reed, "New Miller Beer Faces Price Fight," *Advertising Age,* April 9, 1984, p. 1.

GREYHOUND BUS LINES FACES PRICE AND ROUTE WARS

The future for bus lines does not look favorable. Greyhound Bus Lines, Inc.'s (G/H) ridership fell to 31 million in 1986—down 50 percent from 1976. Further declines in ridership may well be expected as a result of continuing changes in the environment.

The Bus Regulatory Reform Act of 1982 presented both challenges and opportunities to the industry. Bus companies now operate under a large measure of freedom—they can go anywhere and charge what the market will bear. A very competitive industry now exists. Fare wars are a fact of life. With the deregulation of the airline industry, the bus industry has found that it must also compete for passengers with airlines. Often airlines offer equal or better fares than those offered by bus lines.

Since deregulation, hundreds of applications for new bus companies have been filed. Most of these new companies serve the charter and tour markets—a highly flexible and profitable market. Twenty percent of G/H revenues are derived from charters and tours. Small bus companies use this part of the business to support their efforts to obtain profitable regular routes.

Greyhound and Trailways control a majority of the regular route market. They have both the experience to serve this segment and the impetus to do so. The largest source of revenue in the bus line market is for regular route ridership. There are opportunities, however, for the small companies to take G/H routes.

Cost competitiveness is essential in an unregulated industry. To generate revenue and profits, the costs of a bus line company must rival competitors' costs. New and small bus companies generally have lower costs, especially for labor. G/H drivers are unionized and receive higher salaries per year than the average driver. The chief executive officer of Greyhound has let it be known that in future contract negotiations, the drivers will have to make wage concessions to make G/H more cost competitive.

G/H has attempted to meet the challenge of falling ridership by, among other things, increasing its advertising budget. Fares have also been reduced in select markets. Fares for college students, senior citizens, Hispanics and blacks are offered at reduced rates. Together, these groups constitute the bulk of the bus passenger market. G/H has also focused on smaller cities lying 50 to 150 miles from metropolitan areas. It is in these areas that G/H can compete with airlines in travel time and fares. G/H is taking an aggressive position.

A profitable, scheduled route from Buffalo to New York City that has been serviced primarily by G/H is now offered by a second company—Blue Bird of Elsor, New York. Blue Bird needs $1.80 per mile (about $700) to cover the cost of a trip to Buffalo. The company is now charging $30 per seat—its break-even point is $20. G/H now charges $50. Most of Blue Bird's business to date has been in charters and tours.

Issues for Discussion

1. If you were in charge of pricing for G/H, what price would you set for the Buffalo to New York City route? Why?

2. Would you price differently to each segment of the market?

3. Would you use demand- or cost-based pricing?

Sources: Based on J. Hurlock, "How an Ace Mechanic Wants to Fix Greyhound Lines," *Business Week,* January 12, 1987, pp. 45–46; C. V. Oster and C. K. Zorn, "Impact of Regulatory Reform on Intercity Bus Service in the United States," *Transportation Journal,* Spring, 1986, pp. 33–42; Jeff Blyskal, "Leave the Driving to Adam Smith," *Forbes,* August 1, 1983, pp. 100–101; Luis Ubinas, "Bus Concerns Lose Business to Airlines," *The Wall Street Journal,* September 6, 1984; John Maes, "Bus Lines Work to Brake Ridership Decline," *Advertising Age,* July 12, 1984, pp. 30–31; and "Deregulation Will Take Bus Lines on a Rough Ride," *BusinessWeek,* July 11, 1983, pp. 66–68.

MARKETING PLAN

PART 6B / ACTION PROGRAM: PRICING
(CHAPTERS 10 AND 11)

A. What is the overall pricing policy for the organization?
B. What are the organization's pricing objectives?
C. How is the pricing structure for this product or service? Is it different from last year's level?
D. How does the pricing structure for the product or service compare to that of the competition?
E. What is the target market's evaluation of price and its ability to purchase? Will there be significant demand at this price? What is the estimated effect of lowering or raising the price of the product or service?
F. What is the competition's likely reaction to our pricing structure for the product or service at this price level?
G. What (if any) price promotions (sales, discounts, allowances, etc.) will be used during the year? How do these compare with those of the competition?

Section Six

The Distribution Plan

OUTLINE

CHAPTER

12

Developing a Channel Systems Strategy

LEARNING GOALS_____

After reading this chapter, you should be able to:

1. Explain the rationale for the use of middlemen.
2. Identify the various factors that influence the selection of a particular channel system.
3. State the different kinds of channel systems.
4. Identify the different types of vertical marketing systems.
5. Discuss the different types of channel-mix strategies and their intensities.
6. Explain how a channel captain emerges in a channel system.
7. Examine the types and causes of channel conflicts.

INTRODUCTORY CASE

AN EVOLVING SEARS

Franklin D. Roosevelt once suggested that the best way to convince the Russians of the superiority of American life would be to send them thousands of Sears catalogs. Since its founding by Richard Warren Sears in 1886 as a mail-order business, the giant retailer has stocked an array of merchandise that strongly appeals to middle-class Americans. Although mail-order distribution has been extremely successful for Sears, the use of this particular marketing channel was not applauded by everyone. Rural merchants who felt the sting of catalog competition made slurring references to Sears as "Rears and Soreback" or "Shears and Rawback." Despite these cutting remarks, Sears prospered. In the early 1900s an increase in farm prices added to the income of Sears' key customers—the farmers. In 1913, the beginning of parcel-post service by the U.S. Post Office permitted the shipment of larger packages and boosted Sears' revenues.

To ensure the quality of its goods, Sears established a company testing laboratory. Other retailers in the early 1900s purchased the stock items of large manufacturers for resale. In contrast, Sears dealt mainly with small and medium-sized manufacturers who would produce goods according to the company's specifications. In some instances, Sears obtained an ownership interest in a supplier in order to assure itself of a continuous supply of quality goods. Today, Sears remains part-owner of several suppliers, including De Soto, a paint company; Armstrong Rubber, a tire maker; and Universal-Rundle, a plumbing fixture producer.

During the decades of the 1920s, Sears' management recognized that improved roads and the greater use of automobiles were causing farmers to increase the number of trips that they made to town. As a result, in 1925 Sears built its first store in an attempt to capture a greater share of the spending of the newly mobile farmers and their city-dwelling cousins. Soon Sears' stores became a familiar sight in the downtowns of many American communities. After World War II, Sears executives noted a further dramatic increase in the use of automobiles and the growth of suburban home sites. This prompted the company in the 1950s to construct its stores in freestanding neighborhood locations where there was ample parking. The advent of large, regional shopping centers in the 1960s and 1970s convinced Sears management to join with other retailers and become shopping-center tenants.

While Sears was adapting its stores to changing purchasing patterns, its catalog operation was undergoing a dramatic alteration, too. As the population moved from the country to the city, the Sears catalog began focusing more on attractive apparel and less on farm supplies. Another aspect of the post-World War II years was the consumers' desire for convenience and time-saving shopping. These factors eventually changed the Sears' mail-order operation to more of a telephone-order system. Today, nearly 80 percent of catalog shoppers who use the 300 million Sears' catalogs distributed annually place their orders by phone. Although Sears has passed its one-hundredth anniversary, it continues to explore the use of new distribution systems, such as videotex and videodiscs, in order to serve consumers better.

Issues for Discussion

1. What environmental considerations have influenced the channel systems that have been adopted by Sears?

2. What types of vertical marketing systems are used by Sears?

3. Explain why Sears should be considered a channel captain.

Sources: Adapted from Steve Weiner, "They Buy Their Stock When They Buy Their Socks," *Forbes,* March 7, 1988, pp. 60–67; Tom Mahoney and Leonard Sloane, *The Great Merchants,* 2d ed. (New York: Harper & Row Publishers, 1966), pp. 221–243; Milton Moskowitz, Michael Katz, and Robert Levering, *Everybody's Business* (San Francisco: Harper & Row Publishers, 1980), pp. 308–314; Bernard Wysocki, Jr., "Sears, Facing an Array of Nagging Problems, Moves to Reorganize," *The Wall Street Journal,* Dec. 27, 1978, pp. 1 and 17; and Steve Weiner and Frank E. James, "Sears, a Powerhouse in Many Fields, Now Looks into New Ones," *The Wall Street Journal,* Feb. 10, 1984, pp. 1 and 7.

■ Sears provides a video check for catalog order pickup.

The type of channel system marketers use is influenced by the objectives of the system and various environmental considerations. Channel systems range from very short ones, which are composed only of producers and consumers, to quite lengthy ones, which include producers, agents, wholesalers, retailers, consumers, and a variety of other marketing specialists. Because of the nature of the goods and their markets, the channels for industrial goods differ from those for consumer goods. In order to foster greater cooperation among the members of a channel system, vertical marketing systems are established. After carefully observing their markets, suppliers choose either an intensive, selective, or exclusive distribution strategy. If marketers decide to use an exclusive channel mix, they should study the legality of the arrangement thoroughly.

Although channel members attempt to work together, conflicts do occur. A channel captain or leader, who provides direction and discipline to the other channel members, frequently emerges in a channel system. This chapter addresses all of the above subjects and several additional ones that relate to the development of channel strategies. ■

FUNCTIONS OF MARKETING CHANNELS

IBM uses a variety of marketing channels to reach its customers.

When mighty IBM initially explored the possibility of marketing its PCjr computer through Kmart, IBM's 1,500 independent retailers quickly vented their collective feelings to IBM. If Kmart became a direct competitor, the independents feared that their prices and profit margins would fall. Because of the independents' grumblings, an IBM spokesperson resolutely declared that IBM had no plans to expand its marketing channels to include mass merchandisers such as Kmart.[1] Some observers of IBM suggest that its refusal to market the PCjr through mass merchandisers led to the unit's failure in the marketplace. To market its other computers, IBM selects the most effective channels for placing a particular machine in the hands of its customers. Sears Business Systems Centers are important marketers for the IBM personal computer. To market its larger computers, IBM uses a direct sales force that understands the data processing needs of its commercial, government, and educational customers.

Some distribution channels are very short—such as when IBM sells a mainframe computer directly to the Chase Manhattan Bank. Other channels are very long—such as when a small canner of vegetables sells through food brokers to grocery wholesalers to grocery retailers to ultimate consumers. Selection of the proper channel of distribution is a key aspect of a properly conceived marketing plan.

A **marketing channel or channel of distribution** is a group of organizations or individuals assisting the flow of goods and services from producer to consumer. A marketing channel is always composed of a producer and a consumer and frequently includes one or more marketing intermediaries. Although the goods and the title to them usually move together, there are some exceptions. In some instances, the title moves but the good does not. For example, the title to real property may move through several hands while the property remains on the same site. In another instance, a good may move, but the title does not. When a consumer leases a car, its title remains with the leasing party. A lease conveys a temporary ownership right to the user of the property.

*M*iddlemen are marketing intermediaries, but not all marketing intermediaries are middlemen.

Marketing intermediaries comprise all of the specialists who aid in performing the marketing functions. These include middlemen and facilitating agencies. **Middlemen** are wholesalers or retailers in a marketing channel who assist in transferring a good and its ownership rights. **Facilitating agencies** are the transportation firms, financial institutions, and other organizations that are not directly involved in the exchange process but assist in accomplishing it. From the preceding definitions, you can ascertain that although middlemen are marketing intermediaries, not all marketing intermediaries are middlemen.

RATIONALE FOR THE USE OF MARKETING CHANNELS

Marketing channels and the middlemen within them are often criticized for being wasteful and nonproductive. However, the critics are wrong because the services of channels and their middlemen make marketing more efficient and economical. The sorting process and the web of relationships among producers and consumers explained in the next two sections will clarify the value of marketing channels.

Sorting Process

*I*n the sorting process, middlemen resolve the differences between the amount and kinds of goods produced and purchased.

The **sorting process,** which relies on the use of middlemen, resolves the differences between the amount and kinds of goods produced and purchased (figure 12.1). Manufacturers generally produce small assortments of goods in large quantities, but consumers want large assortments in small quantities. An assortment is a collection of goods that either complement each other or provide some other value to a target market. The sorting process includes sorting out, accumulating, allocating, and assorting.[2]

*A*ccumulation creates economic benefits associated with the handling of large quantities of goods.

Sorting out involves establishing standards and placing goods into classes that are based on these standards. For instance, a hardware manufacturer may divide wrenches into two classes, those of high quality that meet the standards of the industrial market, and those of lower quality appropriate for the do-it-yourself trade. By sorting output, the manufacturer creates homogeneous supplies that customers can readily specify and order. Accumulation occurs when a large inventory of goods in a particular category is gathered, like wrenches for the do-it-yourself market. This inventory comes from either a single manufacturer or several different manufacturers. The accumulation of an item can take place with the manufacturer, wholesaler, or retailer, depending on the item's perishability, the availability of storage space, and the ability to finance inventories. Accumulation creates economic benefits associated with the handling of large quantities of goods.

Allocation, also called breaking bulk, takes place when a large quantity is divided into smaller units for purposes of resale. Allocation occurs when the wrench manufacturer distributes thousands of wrenches to its sixty hardware wholesalers for the do-it-yourself market. The sixty wholesalers allocate hundreds of wrenches among nearly 200 hardware retailers. In turn, each retailer sells wrenches individually to its do-it-yourself customers.

Assorting is the process of putting together a variety of different goods that will appeal to a particular market segment. A hardware wholesaler brings together from many different manufacturers a variety of hardware items that should be carried in a hardware store. A hardware retailer selects from the wholesaler's inventory an assortment of items that will have strong customer appeal.

☐ Figure 12.1
The sorting process.

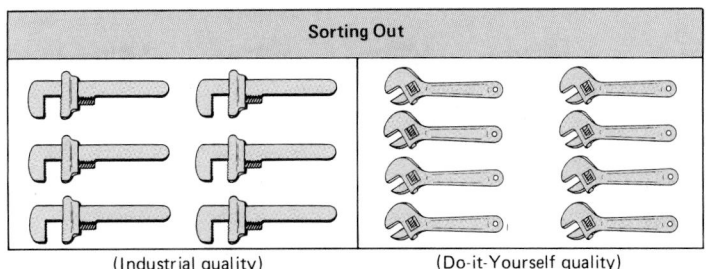

Sorting Out

(Industrial quality)   (Do-it-Yourself quality)

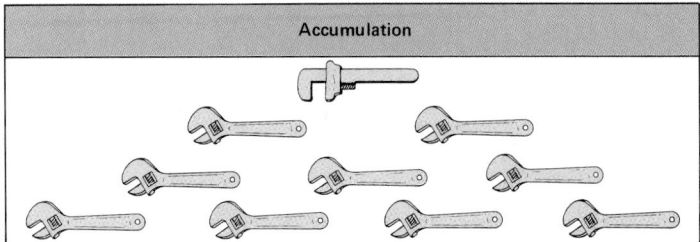

Accumulation

(From different manufacturers)

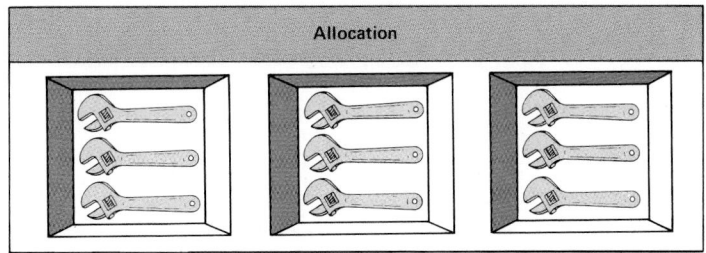

Allocation

(Smaller units to many stores)

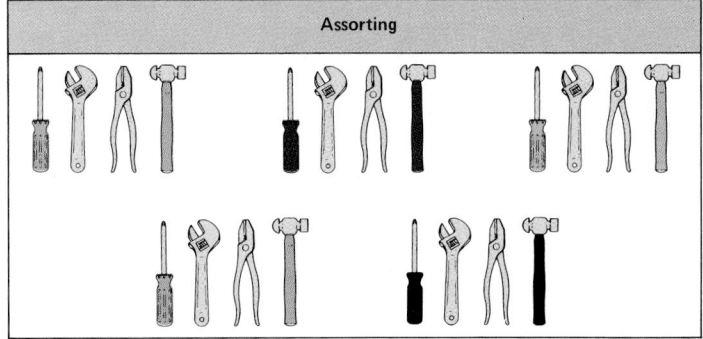

Assorting

(Variety of items from different manufacturers)

Web of Relationships

*D*irect transactions between producers and consumers create a much larger number of relationships than when a middleman is interposed between them.

The **web of relationships** consists of the many direct transactions that occur among producers and consumers when a middleman is not present in the marketing process. These direct transactions create a much larger number of relationships between producers and consumers than occur when a middleman is interposed between them. This concept is illustrated in figure 12.2, which shows the transaction process with and without the presence of a middleman. A total of twenty-five transactions takes place when five producers sell to five consumers ($5 \times 5 = 25$). However, when five producers sell to five consumers through a middleman, only ten transactions occur

❏ **Figure 12.2**
Web of relationships
with five producers and
five middlemen.

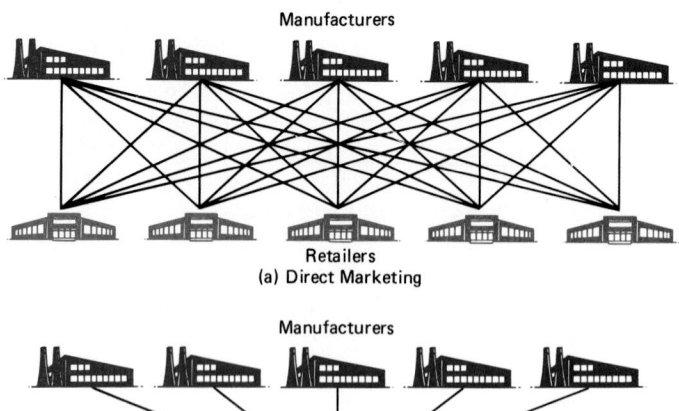

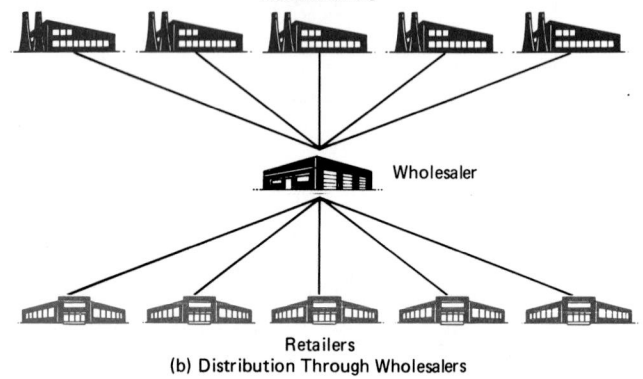

❏ **Figure 12.3** Web of relationships with ten producers and ten middlemen.

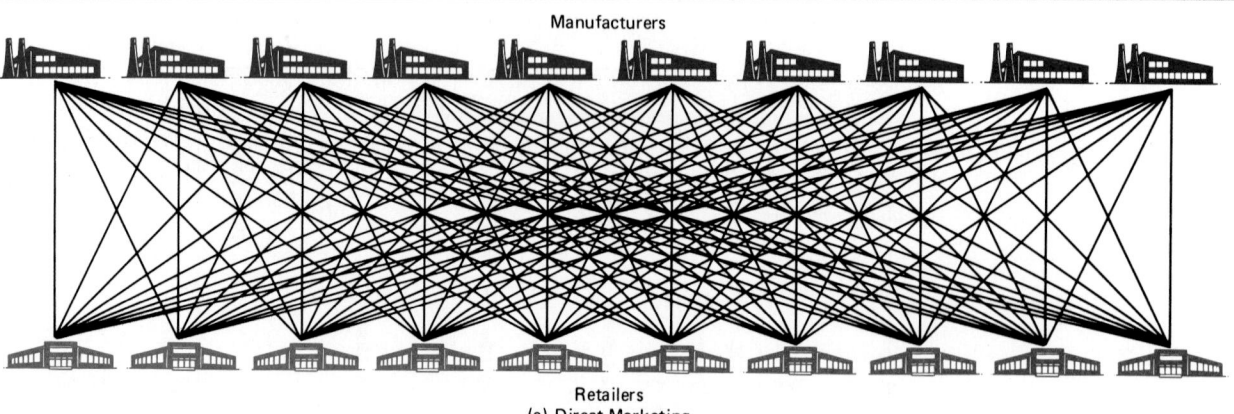

(5 + 5 = 10). This significant reduction in transactions means that marketing functions are executed more efficiently. Instead of making sales, financial, transportation, and storage arrangements with each consumer, a producer deals only with a limited number of middlemen. The middlemen contact consumers, offering them an assortment of goods and performing the marketing functions that would otherwise be performed by the producers.

*T*he use of middlemen produces significant economies and efficiencies when a large number of producers and consumers are present.

The importance of the middleman can be demonstrated more dramatically as the demand for a good increases and more middlemen are employed. Let us assume that the number of producers and consumers engaged in transactions increases from five to ten (figure 12.3). When ten producers make direct contact with ten consumers, 100 transactions take place (10 × 10 = 100). With a middleman inserted between the ten producers and ten consumers, only twenty transactions occur (10 + 10 = 20). When the number of producers and consumers doubles from five to ten, the number of direct transactions rises from twenty-five to 100—a fourfold increase. However, when the number of producers and consumers doubles but a middleman is used, the number of transactions grows from ten to twenty—only a twofold increase. Thus, a middleman can provide significant economies and efficiencies as the number of producers and consumers increases.

OBJECTIVES OF A CHANNEL SYSTEM

Harry and David of Medford, Oregon, want you to purchase their succulent apples, pears, and other delights through their Fruit-of-the-Month Club. Hershey wants you to buy and eat its confections. Both companies seek the same end—consumption of their products—but they employ different marketing channels to obtain these results. Harry and David sell directly to you via mail order; Hershey uses wholesalers and retailers. A channel system that uses middlemen has the same objectives as one that moves a product directly into consumers' hands: (1) to direct a good swiftly and efficiently to its target market, (2) to control the marketing program, and (3) to minimize the cost of exchange.

Hitting a Target Market

A channel system should deliver a good efficiently to its target market.

A major objective of a marketing channel system is to deliver a good to its target market as inexpensively as possible. Before an effective channel system can be established, the producer should carefully identify the markets it wants to serve. Some products have numerous targets; others, only a limited number. Producers of convenience goods, such as candy bars, cigarettes, and ballpoint pens, are anxious to have their products reach a large segment of the population. These producers use many different types of middlemen in an effort to contact all potential customers. The Automotive Parts and Accessories Association calculates that there are twenty-two marketing channels for automotive parts, used to reach over 540,000 wholesalers and retailers.[3] In contrast, in the heavy electrical equipment industry the huge transformers manufactured by Westinghouse and General Electric have a single key market—electric utility companies. The marketing channel is quite short—goods move directly from producer to consumer.

Controlling the Marketing Program

Another key objective of most manufacturers in making marketing channel decisions is to maintain control of a product's marketing program. A manufacturer who

☐ **Figure 12.4**
Factors in channel
selection.

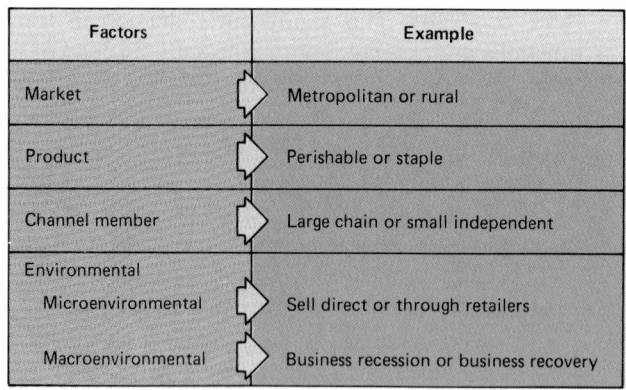

Factors	Example
Market	Metropolitan or rural
Product	Perishable or staple
Channel member	Large chain or small independent
Environmental	
Microenvironmental	Sell direct or through retailers
Macroenvironmental	Business recession or business recovery

A key objective in making channel decisions is to maintain control of a product's marketing program.

generates a product idea and develops it into a commercial success is understandably reluctant to lose control over the product as it passes through the channel systems. However, antitrust statutes prohibit the seller of a good from dictating the precise conditions under which a buyer can resell or use a good. This means that when the title to a good is transferred, most of the seller's control over the good ends. To thwart this loss of control, some producers operate their own channel system. Others tie their marketing intermediaries closely to them through administered and contractual arrangements.

Minimizing the Cost of Exchange

*A*n important objective for most channel systems is to minimize the cost of exchange.

A final important objective for most channel systems is to minimize the cost of exchange. The advertising of some retailers claims, "We save you money because we buy directly from manufacturers." However, short distribution channels are not necessarily the most cost-effective. It depends on the nature of the goods exchanged and their market. For example, the exchange of convenience goods and low-priced staple shopping goods through a long channel that includes middlemen is more cost-effective than their direct exchange through a short channel. This is because the middlemen assemble an assortment of goods from many suppliers, generally deal in large quantities and provide numerous specialized marketing activities and services. On the other hand, for higher-priced shopping and specialty goods, a short, more direct channel is often the lowest-cost method of distribution. (See figure 12.4 for a list of the factors involved in channel selection.)

THE CASE CONTINUES

*S*ears is America's largest middleman, generating sales of over $50 billion from its merchandising activities. In order to perform the sorting process at the stage between its suppliers and its retail stores, Sears has a network of ten huge distribution centers, and the company's catalog operations are served by another seven distribution centers.

In 1980, after a period of indecision, Sears executives decided that the company should serve the broad

center of the middle-income group. The giant retailer, however, experienced difficulty in obtaining the proper cooperation from all elements in its channel systems.

At the regional and store levels, managers were making merchandising decisions without informing headquarters. This caused store in-

ventories to grow too large and the wrong merchandise to be ordered. In its central buying organization, Sears' buyers became too chummy with suppliers and the result was purchases that did not make good business sense. These problems caused Sears to centralize much of its decision making and to develop more effective controls so that all elements in its channel systems would be working toward the same objectives.

Direct selling is often used in industrial markets.

FACTORS IN CHANNEL SELECTION

In general, if a company decides to use a short channel of distribution, it will have numerous contacts with its customers and a relatively high selling cost per customer, but it will be able to maintain close control over its marketing program. On the other hand, the decision to use a long marketing channel reduces the number of contacts with customers as well as the selling cost per customer, but the company loses at least some control over the marketing of its products. The selection of a particular channel system is strongly influenced by a number of factors: the nature of the market, the nature of the product, and the nature of the environment.

Market Factors

*T*he market to which a product is directed affects a company's marketing-channel decisions.

Whether a product is directed toward the consumer market, the industrial market, or both affects a company's marketing-channel decisions. Wholesalers and retailers are often used to distribute to consumer markets. Direct selling is frequently the method used to tap industrial markets.

The geographic extent of a market is a major factor determining the kind of channel to use. When the market for a good is concentrated in a large metropolitan area, such as Boston or Houston, a short channel is appropriate. A market that is scattered over a wide, sparsely populated area, such as Wyoming or Montana, usually employs longer channels.

A market's ethnic makeup also affects the decision on which type of channel to use. For example, Los Angeles, with its huge concentration of Hispanics in one area allows suppliers to this market to use short distribution channels such as producers to retailers to consumers.

A certain segment of the consumer market prefers to purchase directly from producers. Many consumers feel that direct purchase gives them the lowest prices and the widest selection.

Product Factors

A product's attributes greatly influence the type of channel that will be used.

A product's attributes greatly influence the types of channels that will be used in its distribution. Perishable goods and fashion merchandise, which often have a short life cycle, generally use short marketing channels. The following types of goods also employ short marketing channels: (1) specially designed goods, such as escalator or elevator installations designated for a single user; (2) expensive items, such as fine jewelry and elegant furs; (3) bulky and inexpensive products, such as concrete blocks and coal (due to their high cost of handling); and (4) personal services because the production and distribution of a service usually occur at the same time.

*L*ong channels are common for staple convenience goods.

*T*he stage in a product's life cycle affects its channel selection.

Long channels are commonly used for staple convenience goods such as gum, candy, and health and beauty aids. These goods are mass produced and distributed in quantities too large for individual retailers to buy.

The stage in a product's life cycle is often an important consideration in the selection of distribution channels. During the introductory and growth stages of their products, some manufacturers choose to sell direct—perhaps by mail order—in order to retain close control over their marketing efforts and to establish a market for their products. Once a product has an established market, middlemen express a greater interest in handling it.

When a product reaches the maturity and saturation levels in its life cycle and sales stabilize, producers often use several channels in an effort to obtain greater market representation. When the blue jeans market reached maturity, major jeans producer Levi Strauss added the Sears and J. C. Penney stores to its distribution system in order to broaden its market coverage.

When a product reaches the decline stage and its sales fade, large retail chains usually drop it from their inventories. This often forces the manufacturer to distribute the product through wholesalers because they are able to locate small segments of the market that still want the product.

Environmental Factors

MICROENVIRONMENTAL INFLUENCES

*M*icroenvironmental influences on channel selection involve managerial decisions.

Microenvironmental influences on channel selection relate to the managerial decisions that are made within a firm. The size of a producer has an impact on its choice of a distribution channel. Many small- and medium-sized firms rely on long channels because they lack the managerial, financial, and marketing resources to market directly to consumers. For example, small canneries producing limited quantities of fruits and vegetables often use a series of middlemen—food brokers, wholesalers, and retailers—to reach consumers. When companies are too small to develop effective marketing programs, they frequently permit middlemen known as manufacturers' agents and sales agents to act as their marketing arms and maintain contacts with wholesalers and retailers.

Very large firms are in a better position to market directly through short channels of distribution. Certain retailers like Sears and Kmart purchase directly from suppliers in order to obtain their goods at the lowest possible prices. The massive size of these retailers permits them to perform the wholesaler's function. Sometimes, large retailers use their immense market power to obtain certain price, promotion, product, or place concessions from their suppliers, but this can lead to problems. For instance, the courts admonished the huge Federated Department Store chain for pressuring its suppliers to halt shipments to the low-priced Burlington Coat retail chain.

*P*roducers with strong marketing, management, and financial capabilities can more readily assume the functions of marketing intermediaries.

Another factor in a firm's choice of a distribution channel is the desire to control its marketing program. One way for the producer to obtain such control is to shorten the marketing channel and perform some or all of the functions of a marketing intermediary. Producers with strong marketing, management, and financial capabilities will be able to assume these functions successfully; others will experience difficulty. Cost as well as control influences the decision to market directly. A manufacturer like Procter & Gamble that produces a complete product line often sells directly to retailers without going through wholesalers. When a company spreads its total marketing costs over a broad product line, the marketing expenses for each product are relatively low.

A company with established product lines generally uses its customary marketing channels for its new products. When the Ralston-Purina Company introduces a new cereal, the company relies on the same distribution channels that handle its other foods. Occasionally, however, a company will find that its usual marketing channel is closed to a new product because middlemen have long-standing commitments to their present suppliers and are reluctant to stock a competing line. One of the reasons that Coleco, the toy manufacturer, dropped its home computer was its inability to obtain a strong network of retail stores to handle the product.

*P*roducers may use nontraditional channels as the most effective way to market their goods.

Producers sometimes develop nontraditional channels because they view them as the most effective means for marketing their goods. Coca-Cola plans to use its soft-drink delivery system to distribute videocassettes from its Columbia Pictures unit to supermarkets.[4]

In some instances, management recognizes the shortcomings of a particular distribution policy and takes steps to remedy it. When Radio Shack introduced its personal computers, it used its chain of audio equipment stores to market the new product. However, personnel in the audio stores were unable to cope with the complexities of computers so Radio Shack management established a separate chain of computer stores.

MACROENVIRONMENTAL INFLUENCES

*M*acroenvironmental influences on channel selection involve social, economic, and political considerations.

Social, economic, and political considerations comprise the macroenvironmental influences that affect the selection of marketing channels. Do the poor pay more? is a question that social activists and politicians frequently ask. Generally they do pay more for goods because the large chains shy away from unprofitable ghetto locations. This leaves small independent merchants to serve these areas, and they, because of their size, procure their goods through an extensive and often expensive channel system.

Another social reality—the aging of our population—is providing new marketing opportunities for some channel members. Already, there are mail-order retailers and in-home sellers who cater to the elderly confined indoors.

When business recessions occur and unemployment rises, numerous consumers switch from higher-priced to lower-priced goods and from full-service department stores to self-service discount stores. A channel development of the early 1980s recession was a great growth in off-price stores such as T. J. Maxx and Marshall's and factory outlets such as Swank factory stores.

An upward turn in the economy encourages the growth of channel members that can siphon off the discretionary income that becomes available. Specialty retailers, such as the gourmet chocolate chip cookie stores of Famous Amos and Mrs. Fields and the prestige car dealerships of BMW and Mercedes, expand rapidly during strong economic periods.

Political forces occasionally cause alterations in marketing channels. In some states such as New Hampshire and Pennsylvania, liquor can be purchased only through state-operated stores. Other states, such as Ohio and Michigan, require retailers to purchase beer only from wholesalers within their county.

 ## STRUCTURE OF CHANNEL SYSTEMS

*I*f we could buy direct from producers, there would be no need for complex marketing channels.

If all of us were able to go directly to the Cincinnati plant of Procter & Gamble or the Battle Creek plant of Kellogg's to purchase our food products, there would be no need for complex channels of marketing intermediaries. However, to facilitate a more orderly and cost-efficient marketing of goods, elaborate channel systems have evolved. We will categorize them into consumer, industrial, and other channel systems.

Channels for Consumer Goods

*T*he shortest marketing channel is a direct producer-to-consumer one.

As illustrated in figure 12.5, channels for consumer goods range from very simple producer-to-consumer channels to those involving several middlemen.

PRODUCER TO CONSUMER

If you have ever stopped at a farmer's roadside market and purchased some homegrown corn, you have used a direct producer-to-consumer channel (P–C). By selling and delivering merchandise to your home, direct sellers provide you with significant place and possession utility. Amway, Avon, Electrolux, and Encyclopedia Britannica are several of the largest and best-known direct-selling organizations.

❑ **Figure 12.5**
Channels for consumer goods.

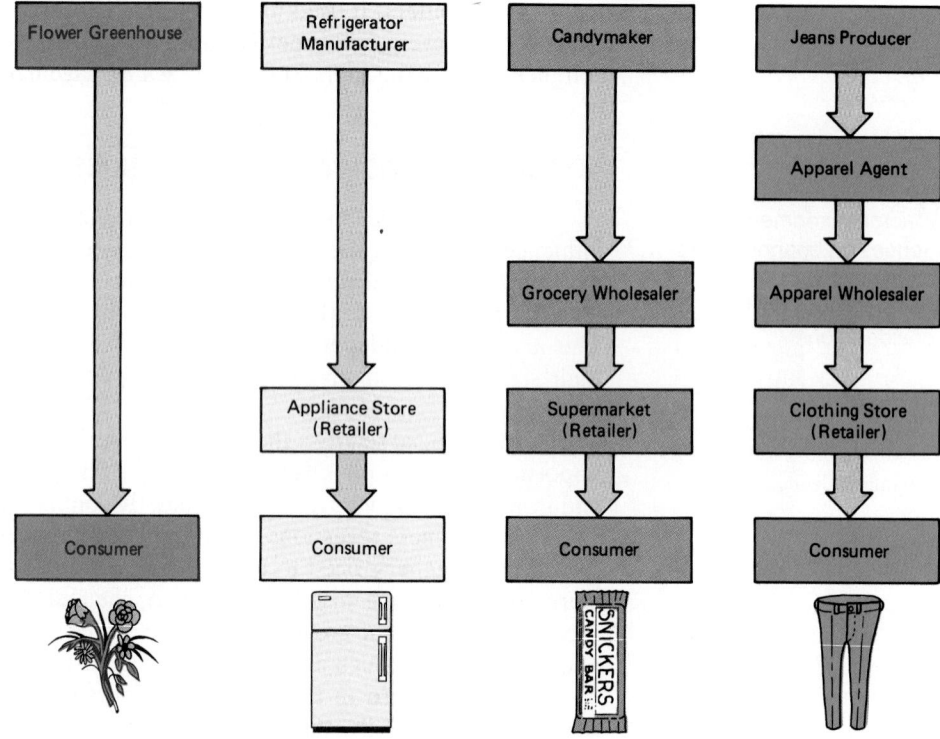

*T*here are frequently no middlemen between the producer and the consumer of personal services.

The production of personal services—hair styling or investment counseling—is not easily separated from their distribution so marketing them seldom involves middlemen. In the case of Michael Jackson, Bruce Springsteen, and other performers, however, an agent may serve as a middleman between the artist and the ticket purchasers. The short P–C marketing channel typical of the personal service industry permits a producer to respond rapidly to the fickle wants of customers.

PRODUCER TO RETAILER TO CONSUMER

The producer-to-retailer-to-consumer channel (P–R–C) is commonly used for numerous shopping and specialty goods. Retailers handling bulky and expensive items like furniture and automobiles customarily purchase them directly from manufacturers. The P–R–C channel is frequently used in the apparel industry, where manufacturers must have orders from retailers before they begin production. Producers store and deliver the goods to retailers, who then develop selling programs and financial arrangements to market the goods to consumers.

PRODUCER TO WHOLESALER TO RETAILER TO CONSUMER

*W*hen markets began expanding across wide areas, producers turned to wholesalers to contact potential retail customers.

As the population moved from the eastern seaboard areas of Boston, New York, and Philadelphia across the Appalachians into Ohio, Kentucky, and Indiana, the producer-to-wholesaler-to-retailer-to-consumer channel (P–W–R–C) developed to move goods from eastern producers to midwestern markets. The scattering of markets across a wide expanse made it difficult for producers to contact all of their potential retail customers directly so they turned to wholesalers to represent them. Today, convenience goods and low-priced shopping goods, such as food, hardware, and health and beauty aids, are distributed through the P–W–R–C channel. In this channel, producers often promote the goods extensively; wholesalers break bulk and provide storage and delivery; and retailers offer assortments to consumers.

PRODUCER TO AGENT TO WHOLESALER TO RETAILER TO CONSUMER

Agents or brokers are often used in industries, such as agriculture and apparel, where many small producers lack the capability to market their products. By bringing wholesalers in contact with numerous small producers, agents perform a valuable service. A channel system develops that moves goods from producer to agent to wholesaler to retailer to consumer (P–A–W–R–C). For example, in the Seventh Avenue garment district in Manhattan, there are over 3,800 small apparel manufacturers who use agents extensively.

Channels for Industrial Goods

Retailers are not usually present in industrial channels.

Channels for industrial goods develop for the same reasons as the channels for consumer goods: to move products efficiently into the hands of their users. Because industrial goods are often produced for very specialized markets, short channels are frequently used. As noted in figure 12.6, industrial channels do not usually include retailers. At the industrial level, sales are generally in large quantities, and transactions are few. Producers sell directly to their customers, usually businesses and institutions.

PRODUCER TO INDUSTRIAL USER

Installation goods and services are almost always marketed directly from producers to industrial users (P–IU). Processed materials, component parts, and accessory equipment are frequently distributed in this manner, too. Cincinnati Millicron uses a direct channel to supply the Ford Motor Company with new robotic machine tools. Geographically concentrated markets, custom-designed products, or a need for technical services make a P–IU channel the most appropriate one.

PRODUCER TO INDUSTRIAL DISTRIBUTOR TO INDUSTRIAL USER

Industrial supplies, such as paints, waxes, and small tools, are generally marketed through a producer-to-industrial distributor-to-industrial user channel (P–ID–IU).

❑ **Figure 12.6**
Channels for industrial goods.

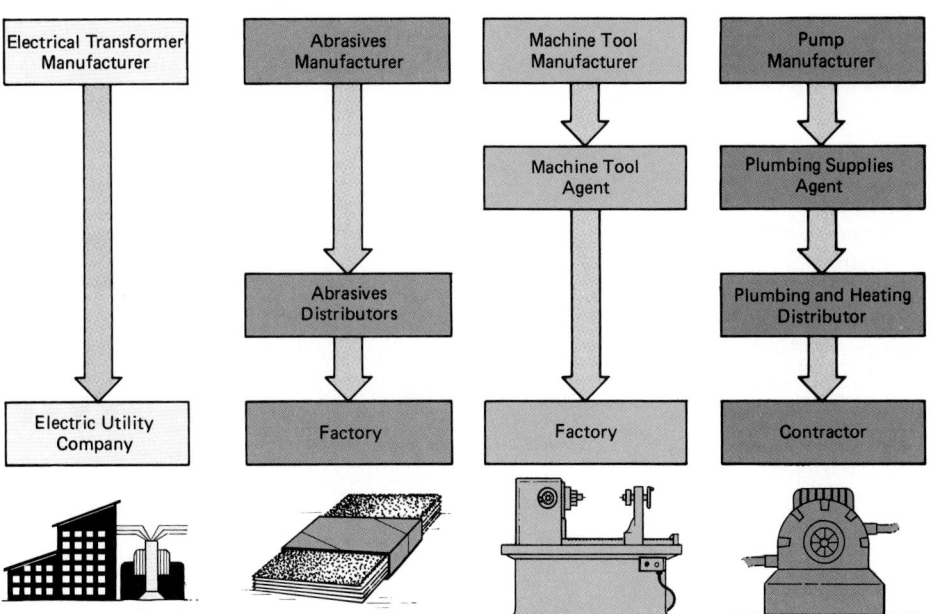

The **industrial distributor** is the equivalent in industrial markets to the wholesaler in consumer markets. This middleman takes title to the goods and performs the sorting process for industrial customers. In every major metropolitan area, industrial distributors service the local machine shops and factories by handling abrasives, V-belts, hoses, saws, and portable and stationary tools.

PRODUCER TO AGENT TO INDUSTRIAL USER

The producer-to-agent-to-industrial user channel (P–A–IU) is sometimes used for marketing agricultural products, such as corn or grain, to industrial customers. For example, Anheuser-Busch, Miller, and other brewers need a continuous supply of grain for conversion into malt. They use agents to locate numerous sources of this grain and negotiate its purchase.

PRODUCER TO AGENT TO INDUSTRIAL DISTRIBUTOR TO INDUSTRIAL USER

*T*he role of an agent is to match sellers with distributors having access to the proper markets for goods.

The lengthy producer-to-agent-to-industrial distributor-to-industrial user channel (P–A–ID–IU) is often used when it is necessary to provide marketing assistance to small manufacturers or importers with limited marketing expertise. The role of an agent is to match producers with distributors that have access to the proper markets for the goods. These agents generally specialize in a particular line of goods, such as electronics or automotive supplies, and know the capabilities of the distributors in their fields.

Other Channel Systems

The recycling of certain wastes and the increased growth of service industries have given rise to a variety of different channel systems.

REVERSE CHANNELS

When aluminum cans or old newspapers are sent back to producers for reprocessing, a **reverse marketing channel** develops. The goods to be reprocessed often move from consumer to middleman to producer, as depicted in figure 12.7.

*T*he development of a channel system for waste goods is directly related to the value placed on the goods by reprocessors.

The degree of development of a channel system for waste goods is directly related to the value that reprocessors place on the goods. For example, the channel for old newspapers is fairly well established and frequently follows the path of consumer to nonprofit organization (church or Boy Scouts) to broker to paper mill.

❑ **Figure 12.7**
Reverse marketing channel.

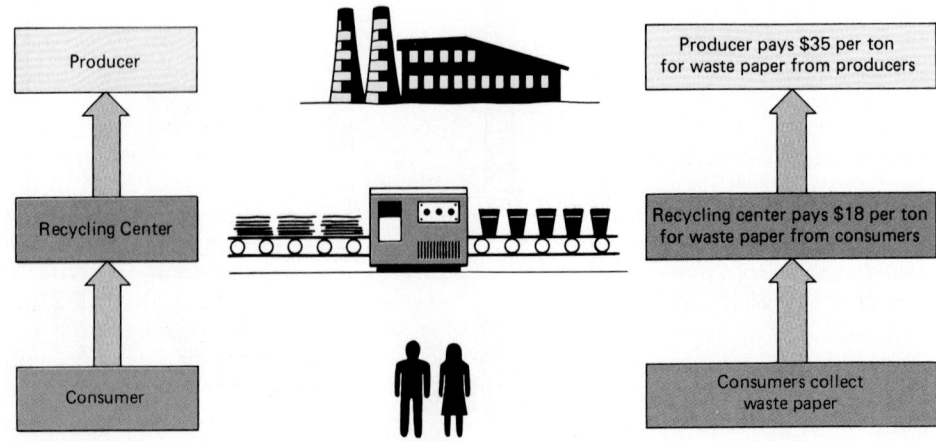

AMI is both a healthcare provider and a middleman in the channel system.

Source: Courtesy of American Medical International

CHANNELS FOR SERVICES

Although most services are marketed through a direct producer-to-consumer channel, middlemen are playing an increasingly important role in some service channel systems. In the health-care field the number of health maintenance organizations (HMO) has increased significantly in the last ten years.[5] Through their benefit programs, employers act as middlemen and enroll their workers in HMO programs. Another health-care organization that acts as both a service provider and a middleman is the ambulatory care clinics that are found in many metropolitan areas. These clinics handle minor medical emergencies and refer serious conditions to hospitals. Although middlemen have been customarily associated with the marketing of physical goods, they are becoming increasingly important in the marketing of services, too. (We will discuss the role of wholesalers in the service industries more extensively in Chapter 13.)

THE CASE CONTINUES

Never content to sit on its catalogs, Sears, in 1981, established its Business Systems Centers to market computers and other office products to small businesses that would not ordinarily buy electronic office equipment in a conventional Sears store. In another development, Sears announced the start-up in small communities of limited-line stores handling mainly paint and hardware. These stores will attract consumers who want to make home repairs. This is a logical move because most individuals do not want to take the time to drive to a gigantic full-line Sears store in a large community to buy only these few items.

Sears uses a variety of channel systems to reach its retail customers. A relatively short channel is from supplier to mail order distribution center to consumers. A longer and the most widely used channel by Sears is from supplier to store distribution center to store to consumer. The Sears-owned distribution centers should be considered as units in its channel system because they function as wholesalers.

Although we have been discussing Sears' merchandising activities, the company is in the financial services industry, too. Its Allstate insurance business uses a short marketing channel that consists of producer to consumer. Unlike many insurance companies that use independent agents, the Allstate salespersons are company employees. In contrast, its Coldwell Banker real estate organization uses agents in its marketing channels.

≡ VERTICAL MARKETING SYSTEMS

If each member in a channel system adopted separate marketing objectives and established different marketing mixes, chaos would develop in the marketing process. Confusion would result if the manufacturer emphasized the quality of a product; wholesalers featured its extended warranty; and retailers stressed its low price. For this reason, one of the channel members often emerges as a **channel captain** or leader to integrate and coordinate the objectives and policies of all the other members. Because the channel captain directs the operation of the entire channel system, the captain is the most important member. When the channel members at different levels in the marketing process are linked tightly together in a centrally controlled marketing effort, a **vertical marketing system** (VMS) is formed.[6] Vertical marketing systems can be administered, contractual, or corporate.

Administered Systems

*I*n an administered VMS, the strongest member in the marketing channel exercises a degree of control that is accepted by the other channel members.

In an administered VMS, the member in the marketing channel wielding the greatest economic power and influence exercises control over the channel. Although the other members are independent businesses, they agree to this control because it is in their best interests. Examples of administered VMSs at the different levels in a channel system include Zenith at the manufacturer's level (expects Zenith dealers to vigorously adhere to its marketing programs); Super Valu food distributors at the wholesale level (offers special promotional and pricing deals to grocery retailers and negotiates low prices from suppliers); J. C. Penney at the retail level (contracts with suppliers for a large proportion of their output). Figure 12.8 shows that of the three types of VMSs, the administered system is the least controlled and exhibits the least amount of cooperation among the channel members.

Contractual Systems

Contractual VMSs involve legal agreements that bind together the members of a channel system. This type of VMS is more tightly controlled than the administered

❑ **Figure 12.8**
Degree of control in vertical marketing systems.

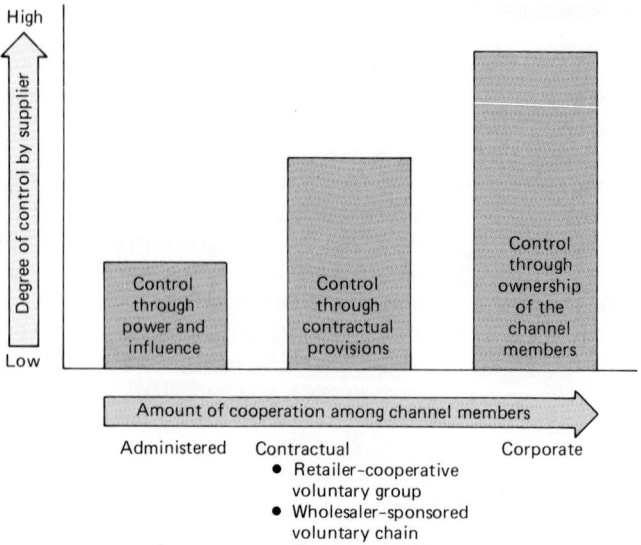

system. The three formats of contractual VMSs include the retailer cooperative voluntary group, the wholesaler-sponsored voluntary chain, and the franchise operation.

RETAILER COOPERATIVE VOLUNTARY GROUP

True Value hardware stores and the Associated Food Stores of New York resemble centrally owned and operated retail chains, but in reality they are retailer cooperatives. A **retailer cooperative voluntary group** is composed of a group of retailers who join together and establish their own distribution center, which takes the place of a wholesaler in the channel system, in order to gain operating efficiencies and economies. Each cooperating retailer owns a share of the operation and benefits from the buying power of the group. Although this type of cooperative is customarily found at the retail level of distribution, it exists at the wholesale level, too.

WHOLESALER-SPONSORED VOLUNTARY CHAIN

The major difference between a retailer-cooperative group and a wholesaler voluntary chain is in the ownership of the wholesaling facilities.

A **wholesaler-sponsored voluntary chain** is created by a wholesaler who organizes a group of independent retailers into a centrally controlled channel system. With a large group of retailers as captive customers, the wholesaler sponsor is able to buy in large amounts and obtain generous quantity discounts from suppliers. The major difference between a retailer cooperative group and a wholesaler-sponsored voluntary chain is in the ownership of the wholesaling facilities. In the former, the retailers own the wholesaling facilities; in the latter, the wholesaler does. Voluntary chain operations include the IGA food stores and Sentry Hardware.

Franchise Operation.   A successful franchise operation is the product of a vigorously controlled contractual arrangement. Under a franchise agreement, a franchisor licenses an independent businessperson (franchisee) to conduct business using the franchisor's name and operating methods. The major benefit the franchisor offers the franchisee is a particular franchising concept that the latter is expected to follow closely. Because of this requirement of uniformity, all of the units in a franchised chain, such as McDonald's, Holiday Inn, or Midas Muffler, offer similar goods and services and operate under similar business formats.

Corporate Systems

The most tightly controlled VMS is a corporate channel system, in which a single corporation owns and operates the channel units at each level in the system. Ownership allows control over the channel system to be vigorous and continuous.

Vertical integration can be either forward or backward.

When a corporation establishes a VMS, the process is called vertical integration. Forward integration occurs when a tire manufacturer, such as Goodyear or Firestone, operates its own wholesale distribution centers and retail stores. In this instance, a manufacturer owns the distribution facilities that are ahead of it in the channel system and thus achieves a closer link to the ultimate consumer. Backward integration takes place when a retailer, such as Sears or Kmart, moves backwards in the channel system and operates its own wholesaling and, perhaps, even manufacturing facilities.

HORIZONTAL MARKETING ARRANGEMENTS

To obtain the advantages associated with large-sized operations, channel members on the same level of distribution sometimes form close working relationships that

☐ **Figure 12.9**
Horizontal marketing
arrangements at the
wholesaler and retail
levels of distribution.

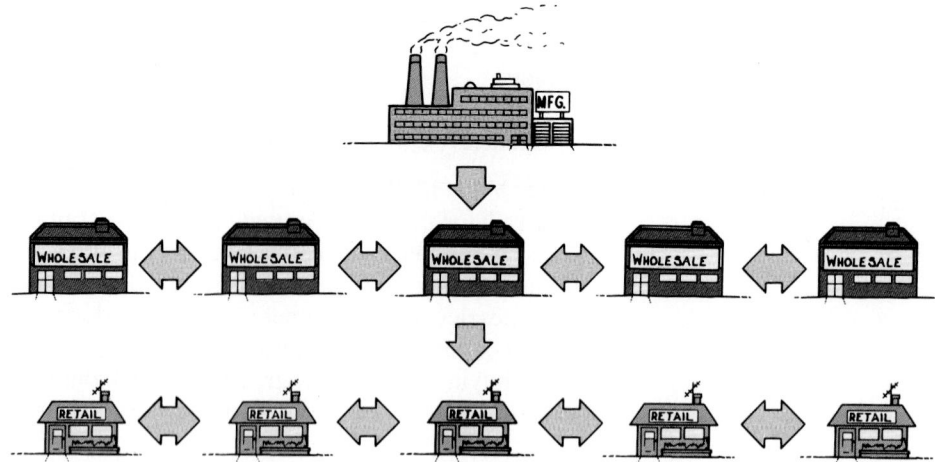

A manufacturer with a
strong channel system
may elect to resell the
products of other manufacturers through the system.

are known as **horizontal marketing arrangements** (figure 12.9). At the retail level, all of the White-Westinghouse appliance dealers in a city may pool their orders and purchase in truckload lots from the manufacturer. Then, they promote their offerings through the use of a single newspaper ad that lists the participating dealers.

In recent years, cooperative marketing arrangements between manufacturers have increased. For example, an efficient, technically competent manufacturer will produce a particular good and sell it to another manufacturer for resale under the second manufacturer's label. If the second manufacturer already has a strong channel system developed, this is an easy, low-risk method of introducing a new product line. This mutual marketing arrangement between companies is called **symbiotic marketing**.[7] Many videocassette recorders are made by a handful of Japanese manufacturers that includes Sony, Sanyo, and Matsushita, but they are marketed under nearly three dozen different labels including Sylvania, RCA, and Zenith.[8]

 ## CHANNEL MIX: STRATEGY AND INTENSITY

Snickers candy bars and Wrigley chewing gum are widely sold where they can be bought on impulse—in grocery stores, hardware stores, service stations, and theaters. In contrast, for an elegant and expensive product like a Rolls Royce or a Ferrari, a few dealers cover a very broad market. For example, there are no Ferrari dealers at all in the state of Montana. Manufacturers should first identify the proper markets for their goods and then adopt either an intensive, selective, or exclusive distribution strategy (figure 12.10).

☐ **Figure 12.10**
Channel mix: Strategy
and intensity.

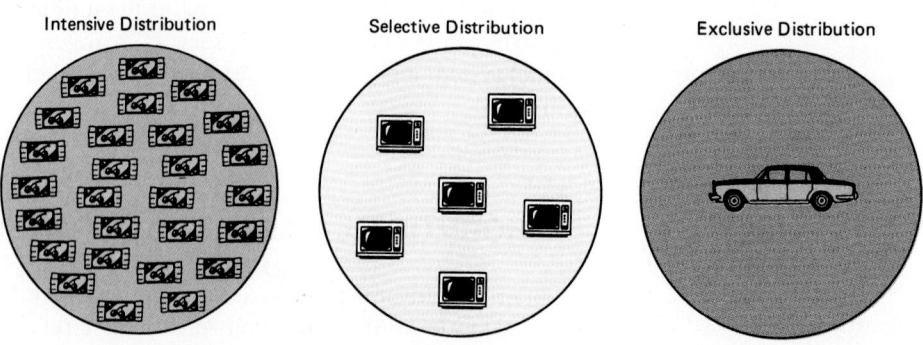

Intensive Distribution

Producers of convenience goods generally follow a strategy of **intensive distribution** in which they use all possible types of outlets to sell the goods. This strategy ensures that impulse (candy), emergency (flashlight batteries), and regularly purchased staple items (shampoo) are always available to consumers. These items are purchased frequently, require no services, and are low priced. Intensive distribution is successful only when a wide variety of wholesalers and retailers are involved in handling the goods.

Selective Distribution

*U*nder the 80-20 principle, 80 percent of a firm's sales is accounted for by 20 percent of its customers.

In a strategy of **selective distribution,** a limited number of carefully chosen middlemen in a particular trading area stock a line of goods. Knowing that consumers will shop around and even go great distances to find certain goods, producers of shopping and specialty goods frequently adopt a policy of selective distribution. This provides a middleman with a territory that is relatively free of competitors handling the same goods. Because of the 80-20 principle—80 percent of a firm's sales are accounted for by 20 percent of its customers—producers who are selective in their choices of middlemen usually increase their sales and profits. Palm Beach suits, some TV sets, and Florsheim shoes are marketed at the retail level in this manner.

Sony uses a policy of selective distribution.

Source: Sony Corporation of America

The Century Furniture Company—like certain producers of high-priced shopping and specialty goods—employs a policy of exclusive distribution.

Source: Century Furniture Company

Exclusive Distribution

Under a strategy of **exclusive distribution** a middleman agrees to perform certain specific marketing activities for a producer in return for an exclusive sales territory. The agreement between producer and middleman is usually a written contract that specifies the responsibilities of both parties in regard to inventory levels, amount of advertising, product training, product warranties, prices and terms, and customer service. In some instances, middlemen actively compete to become the exclusive dealer for a highly desirable good. When General Motors introduced the Saturn and announced that a new dealer network would market the advanced-technology, subcompact car, hundreds of prospective dealers immediately besieged the company.

 LEGALITY OF DISTRIBUTION ARRANGEMENTS

The right to choose a customer was affirmed by the U.S. Supreme Court in the famous Colgate case of 1919.

Because businesspersons are subject to a maze of laws and regulations, there are times when they may wonder whether they have the right to sell to anyone. Actually, the U.S. Supreme Court affirmed the right to choose a customer in the famous Colgate case of 1919. The Court's decision established the right of producers to sell to the middleman of their choice as long as there was no intent to create a monopoly.

If the provisions of an exclusive distribution contract are not clearly and carefully stated, they may violate federal anti-monopoly statutes—either the Sherman Antitrust Act, the Clayton Act, or the Federal Trade Commission Act. Three of the

REAL PEOPLE IN MARKETING

C. B. Vaughan, Jr.: A Channel Captain

C.B. Vaughan, Jr. is described by associates as a "tremendous competitor, someone who wants to be number one." His somewhat brazen style, by now the company's trademark, has worked both for and against CB Sports: For every American skier who feels part of the CB "cult," there is probably a retailer who would prefer to not carry the CB logo.

As a downhill racer, Vaughan set a world speed record of over 106 mph in Portillo, Chile, in 1963. The following year he was clocked at 109 mph. He was bypassed, however, when the U.S. Ski Team selected its 1964 Olympic squad, the same year both Billy Kidd and Jimmie Heuga were on the team. Vaughan doesn't seem bitter now, but the disappointment lingers.

"I thought I should have made the team," he recalls. "(But) if I can't be the greatest ski racer, maybe I can be the best ski designer."

In managing the company from its $5,000 beginning in 1969 to sales of $35 million this season, Vaughan has always tried to keep his hand on all facets of the company, with varying degrees of success. While CB Sports' gear is praised by most dealers, the firm has been criticized for a looseness of organization.

"CB's design talents can be seen in his skiwear," said one of the company's large East Coast retailers. "But someone has to work alongside him and clean up the production mess he leaves behind."

Vaughan's recent move to tighten the management ranks at CB Sports will partially rectify the production problems, and, he hopes, leave him time to continue designing skiwear.

"It's very satisfying to work with a research and development team, designing and marketing a product; that's really what keeps me interested in the business—the creative aspect," said Vaughan, who regularly attends sizing sessions at his Bennington plant, trying on most of the clothing before giving it the final o.k. Indeed, Vaughan works so closely with his merchandising staff that one CB worker commented, "Nothing goes into production until he's checked it again and again."

He is also choosy about where his lines are sold in the United States. When the company started, retailers such as Saks and Bloomingdale's were eager to carry the product, and did, at one time, have accounts with CB. But Vaughan soon pulled his clothing out of those stores.

"We do sell to Nordstrom's and Dayton's, but in a lot of cases we don't understand the philosophy of the larger retailers," Vaughan said. "We want our product in selective stores. And we aren't interested in having our clothing displayed in every ski shop across America."

"I view these [current] years as a time to get revved up for another level, another challenge," said Vaughan, who has met athletic challenges, even outside skiing, notably the New York City Marathon. "The reason CB Sports is so important to me is the thirst and challenge for success. When I lose that desire or I no longer think that we can maintain our uniqueness and authenticity, then it's time to change and move on to something else."

Source: Marianne Bhonslay, "C. B. Races for the Big Time," *Sportstyle,* November 26, 1985, p. 21. Reprinted by permission.

important provisions of an exclusive distribution agreement, as identified in figure 12.11, relate to exclusive dealings, exclusive territories, and tying contracts.

Exclusive Dealing

In **exclusive dealing** a producer prohibits its middlemen from handling competing products. If a producer that holds a dominant share of a particular market attempts

❏ **Figure 12.11**
Important provisions of an exclusive distribution agreement.

Provisions	Examples
Exclusive dealing	Only Exxon products sold here
Exclusive territories	This offer available only to residents of Richland County
Tying contracts	These scarce diamond-tipped drill bits are available only when you buy this power drill

to keep its middlemen from stocking competitive goods, the courts would probably rule this restriction illegal. Exclusive dealing is also illegal when a large producer imposes this restriction on a small middleman. On the other hand, the Supreme Court has declared that exclusive dealing is generally legal under the following conditions: (1) the producer has a small market share; (2) the producer wants to ensure a customer a sufficient supply of a good that is vital to his or her trade; or (3) there is no trend toward concentration in the industry.[9]

Exclusive Territories

The prevailing sentiment of the courts is that competition among middlemen carrying the same brands in a geographic area benefits consumers.

In order to provide middlemen with a substantial market and a strong incentive for promoting a product line, manufacturers furnish them with exclusive territories. A producer grants an **exclusive territory** when it selects a single middleman to handle its goods in a designated geographic area. The prevailing sentiment of the courts has been that competition among middlemen carrying the same brands in a geographic area is healthy and beneficial to consumers. In a 1977 decision, however, the Supreme Court ruled that GTE Sylvania was within its legal right when it refused to permit one of its TV dealers to sell in another dealer's assigned territory. In other instances, the courts have ruled that the use of exclusive territories is legal when they are granted by new firms or small ones or when they do not interfere with free competition.

    The alcoholic beverage industry makes significant use of exclusive territories. As a result of aggressive lobbying, all the states except Indiana and Virginia have legislation that grants beer wholesalers exclusive territories. The advocates of exclusive territories in Indiana argue that the number of beer wholesalers in Indianapolis decreased from sixteen to four since the right to exclusive territories was repealed in 1979.[10] Opponents of exclusive territories cite a study indicating that the average price for a six-pack of beer is higher in states with exclusive territories—19 percent higher in Ohio, 21 percent higher in Michigan, and 31 percent higher in Kentucky.[11]

Tying Contracts

To obtain additional sales, a manufacturer may employ a **tying contract,** which links the sale of one item with another. In some cases, a tying contract requires that a middleman buy a less desirable item in order to obtain a highly desirable one. The courts usually consider these contracts to be in violation of the antitrust laws. However, the courts accept tying agreements when a company is small, just getting started in business, or using exclusive dealers that are expected to handle its complete line.

Guidelines for Legality

The rule of reason analysis in antitrust cases requires that the positive and negative effects of business practices be weighed.

In the GTE Sylvania case of 1977, the Supreme Court stressed the desirability of applying the rule of reason in antitrust cases. This requires that the positive and negative effects of business practices be carefully weighed. When the effects are positive and stimulate competition, the practice should be considered legal. When the effects are negative and restrain competition, the activity should be judged illegal.

    In the mid-1980s the U.S. Justice Department drafted nonbinding guidelines to support the legality of most marketing restrictions that producers place on their middlemen.[12] The purpose of the guidelines is to convince the courts that exclusive distribution agreements and their nonprice restrictions—exclusive dealing, tying contracts, and exclusive territories—do not usually limit competition.

THE CASE CONTINUES

As a sophisticated retailer and a channel captain, Sears understands the meaning of intensive, selective, and exclusive distribution in regard to its overall operations. Some Sears stores sell candy bars and cartons of soft drinks in convenient locations within the store. Sears is also one of the retailers that handles Levi jeans on a selective basis. By working closely with its suppliers, Sears has developed its own exclusive roster of brands, such as DieHard batteries, Weatherbeater paints, and Cheryl Tiegs sportswear.

Although Sears has occasionally experienced some problems in its supplier relationships, the legality of its overall distribution arrangements have not been questioned. This is because once the goods reach a Sears distribution center, they are placed into a vertical marketing system that is owned mainly by a single corporation.

Multiple Distribution

Products that are sold to both industrial customers and the ultimate consumer often use multiple marketing channels to reach the desired markets.

Many companies use **multiple marketing channels,** that is, more than one channel to reach either the same, or, perhaps, different target markets. Producers of items like personal computers and typewriters, which are sold to both industrial users and consumers, often use multiple marketing channels to reach their different markets. The microcomputer software industry uses at least ten marketing channels for software as it moves from the developer to both industrial and personal consumers.[13] The service sector of the consumer market also uses multiple distribution.

Five conditions give rise to multiple distribution, all of which reflect the need to reach different customers differently:[14]

1. the diverse needs of small and large customers
2. the different responses that consumers make to promotions
3. the different reactions that consumers have to price levels
4. the legal factors that determine the use of a policy of multiple distribution
5. the inability of a company to market all the goods that it produces

TRANSSHIPPING

Transshippers move products in an unauthorized manner from an area of low prices to one of high prices.

Transshipping is the unauthorized movement of goods intended for an area where they sell at low prices to one where they sell at higher prices (figure 12.12). In the soft-drink industry, bottlers under contract with Coca-Cola or Pepsi are given exclusive territories and told not to compete with each other. Some bottlers, however, sell to transshipping distributors who buy cases of Coke or Pepsi from low-cost bottlers and resell them to retailers in territories where the costs—and wholesale prices—of bottlers are higher. It has been estimated that over five million cases of soft drinks are transshipped into New York City annually.[15] In another example,

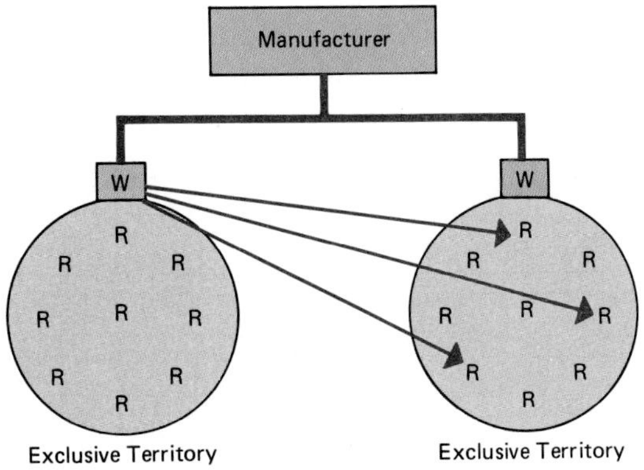

❑ **Figure 12.12**
Transshipping.

IBM discovered that unauthorized resellers were purchasing small quantities of a low-memory IBM personal computer, upgrading it with non-IBM memory, and reselling it at a discount price. To end this transshipping practice, IBM threatened to terminate any dealer who sold to unauthorized dealers.[16]

GRAY MARKETS

*F*luctuations in the world currency markets aid the gray-market importers.

A thriving gray market has created concern and confusion for numerous middlemen handling cameras, perfume, automobiles, and other imports. The **gray market** is a form of transshipping whereby goods are brought into this country by importers who have not been appointed by foreign producers as their official distributors. Fluctuations in the world currency markets often permit these importers to bring gray-market goods into the United States at cut-rate prices. In the automobile market, it was estimated that in a recent year gray-market dealers imported 25,000 foreign cars, such as Mercedes-Benzes, BMWs, and Porsches, and sold them at prices that greatly undercut the legitimate dealers.[17] In 1988, the Supreme Court legitamized the gray markets by upholding the rights of discounters to import trademark goods without going through the producer's authorized distributors.

EMERGENCE OF A CHANNEL CAPTAIN

Because the drawing of a vertical channel system usually shows a manufacturer as the first link, you might assume that the manufacturers always direct and control the systems. Although large producers like IBM and Procter & Gamble generally command their channel systems, sometimes strong middlemen dominate. In the hardware and grocery fields, Sentry Hardware, the IGA organization, and other wholesalers manage their channel systems by forming retailers into voluntary chains.

*I*n the past, when both manufacturers and retailers were smaller, wholesalers were more dominant in channel systems.

In the past, when manufacturers and retailers were smaller, wholesalers dominated channel systems more than they do today. In retailing, the huge chains, such as Kroger, Kmart, and Sears, control their channel systems. Because of their closeness to consumers, retailers are in an excellent position to develop marketing programs and captain the channel systems. In fact, a reason for the passage of the Robinson-Patman Act in 1936 was to stop large retailers from pressuring grocery suppliers into making unjustified price concessions.

Knowing both the capabilities of foreign manufacturers and the wants of domestic retailers, importers and exporters have been able to assume leadership in channel systems that span the oceans. Some of these specialists establish a complete marketing program for a good, including its specifications and brand name, and select an appropriate foreign manufacturer to produce it.

*C*hannel power allows one channel member to exert a leadership role over the other channel members.

Channel power is the ability of one channel member to get another member to do what the latter would not otherwise have done. A number of sources of economic and social power allow channel captains to emerge.[18] (See figure 12.13.) As highlighted in figure 12.14, the expressions of such power include rewards, coercion, expertise, identification, and legitimacy.[19]

☐ **Figure 12.13**
Emergence of channel captains.

Situations Where Manufacturer Emerges as Channel Captain	Situations Where Wholesaler Emerges as Channel Captain	Situations Where Retailer Emerges as Channel Captain
Manufacturer to consumer	Wholesaler-sponsored voluntary chain	Retailer-cooperative voluntary group
Large manufacturer to small middlemen to consumer	Small manufacturer to large wholesaler to retailer to consumer	Small manufacturer to large retailer to consumer
Forward integration	Importers and exporters	Backward integration
Franchisor		

Sears is a channel captain.

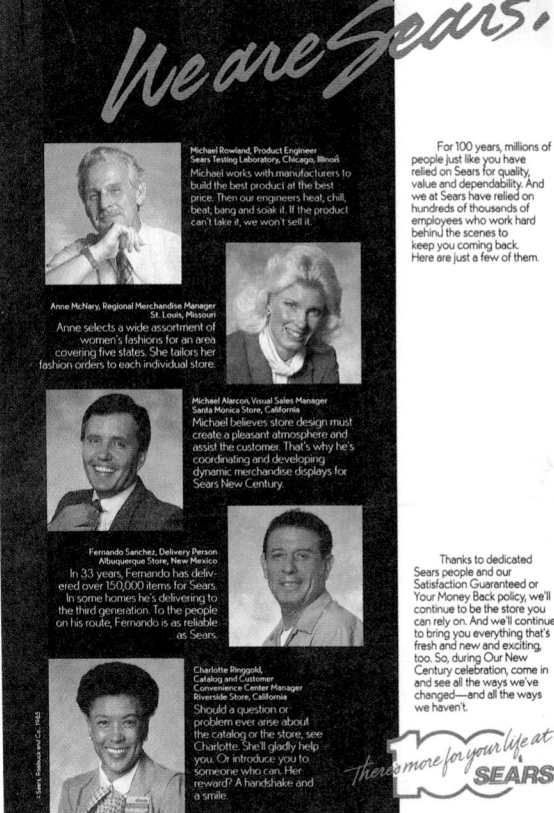

Source: Sears, Roebuck and Co.

 CHANNEL CONFLICTS

*T*he three basic types of channel conflicts are horizontal, intertype, and vertical.

Similar to the conflicts that happen within a family, conflicts take place among the members of a channel system. Wherever there is a linkage between channel members, discord can occur. The three basic types of conflicts are horizontal, intertype, and vertical.[20]

Horizontal conflicts involve competition between similar organizations, such as J. C. Penney and Sears, on the same organization level. These conflicts occur when two or more firms direct their offerings to the same market. Although the channel leader may not be directly involved in a horizontal conflict, the leader is affected because any disputes within the channel system weaken the efficiency of the entire system.

In intertype conflicts different kinds of middlemen on the same level of distribution compete against each other. An example would be a 7-Eleven convenience store competing against a Safeway supermarket for the sale of convenience food items. This competition develops because several different middlemen can meet certain consumer needs, such as convenience or cost savings.

A vertical channel conflict takes place when one channel member perceives another on a different level of distribution to be engaged in behavior that is preventing

❑ **Figure 12.14**
Bases for channel power.

Rewards — Result of channel members' believing that another member can produce rewards, such as higher profit or greater market share, for them.

Coercion — Based on the premise that channel members will receive punishment, such as reduced margins or loss of an exclusive territory, if they do not follow the directions of the channel leader.

Expertise — Exercised when the channel members feel that another member has special knowledge in areas such as inventory planning and store layouts.

Identification — Refers to the channel members' belief that by identifying with another member certain benefits will be gained.

Legitimacy — Derived from the belief of channel members that another member has the legitimate right or authority to exert dominance over them.

*M*ost of us would probably say that Sears and J. C. Penney have very similar channel systems. They both manage massive mail-order businesses and huge chains of general-merchandise stores that stretch across the country. However, the two organizations had strikingly different beginnings. The following paragraphs relate the rest of the story that caused J. C. Penney and Sears to develop differently.

SEARS

In 1886, twenty-three-year-old Richard Warren Sears was a $6-a-week railroad station agent in Minnesota when he purchased and resold a shipment of watches that a local jeweler refused to accept. Later, he added jewelry and diamonds to the offerings of his new business; and in 1887, he issued his first catalog. It was directed primarily to the nation's largest consumer group—farmers and small-town residents—who composed nearly 72 percent of the population.

Sears was a handsome, mustached young man with outstanding charm and a dynamic personality. The ethical standards of business were not too high in the 1800s, and Sears was quite comfortable in using excessive adjectives and sky-igh claims to promote his goods. He enjoyed receiving orders and then worrying about how to obtain the merchandise to fill them.

In 1925, Sears officials noted the growing number of metropolitan centers that were drawing its rural customers away from mail-order sales.

THE REST OF THE STORY

A Tale of Two Channels

As a result, Sears finally opened its first retail store! This initial unit of what was to become a mammoth retail store chain was housed in a corner of Sears' Chicago mail-order plant.

J. C. PENNEY

The retailing organization that became the legend of James Cash Penney evolved in a completely different manner from the Sears-Roebuck Co. J. C. Penney was the twenty-seven-year-old son of a Baptist minister when, in 1902, he and two partners opened a small dry-goods store in Kemmerer, Wyoming. This establishment was named the Golden Rule store in keeping with Penney's strong belief that you should "do unto others as you would have them do unto you." The store was mainly stocked for the coal miners and sheepherders who populated the area.

Penney's first retailing job was clerking in a general store in his hometown of Hamilton, Missouri. In this position, he worked many long, hard hours that placed a strain on his health. Following doctor's orders, he moved to Colorado where he bought a butcher shop in the small community of Longmont. Unwilling to provide his biggest customer—a hotel cook—with a weekly bottle of whiskey in return for the hotel's meat purchases, the fledgling butcher failed. Completely broke, Penney went to

work at $50 a month in a Longmont store. Because Penney proved to be an outstanding worker, the two men who owned the store invited him to become a partner in a new store in Kemmerer, Wyoming. It was this Kemmerer store that inaugurated the very successful J. C. Penney chain. By 1913, there were forty-eight units in the chain and seventy-five years later the organization included over 1,500 department stores, nearly 400 drug stores, and over 1,800 catalog sales centers in all fifty states, Puerto Rico, and Belgium.

By 1960, Penney executives were concerned that increased spending by two-income families and the need for time-saving shopping were altering the buying habits of consumers. Catalog shopping was becoming a way of life for urban consumers' buying and Penney officials wanted to obtain a share of this growing business. These factors influenced the giant retailer to purchase the General Merchandise Company, a Milwaukee catalog house, and develop a mail-order operation that would rival its giant competitor, Sears. Today, there are over 1,800 Penney catalog sales centers. Now, you know the rest of the story—how two merchants initially employed different channel systems but, because of environmental factors, eventually came to use similar channel systems.

Sources: Adapted from Tom Mahoney and Leonard Sloane, *The Great Merchants* (New York: Harper & Row Publishers, 1966), pp. 221–243 and 259–272, and *The Illustrated J. C. Penney* (New York: J. C. Penney Company, Inc., undated), pp. 6–12.

or impeding achievement of certain goals.[21] For example, a wholesaler may note that, because a retailer fails to advertise sufficiently, sales are lower than expected. If left uncorrected, a vertical channel conflict can seriously weaken or destroy a channel system.

Although vertical channel conflicts have numerous causes, they can be divided broadly into two categories: attitudinal and structural. Attitudinal conflicts result from the ways that channel members absorb and process information about a channel and its environment. They arise from disagreements about channel roles, expectations, perceptions, and channel communications. For example, if a manufacturer informs a middleman that it is the exclusive dealer in an area and then the manufacturer adds other dealers in the same area, a dispute is inevitable.

*S*tructural difficulties refer to a clash of opposite interests within a channel system.

Structural difficulties refer to a clash of opposite interests within a channel system. These clashes occur among channel members because of the differences in their objectives, desire for independence, and use of scarce resources. For example, manufacturers who attempt to control the pricing of their goods through the use of suggested retail prices often find themselves in conflict with the retailers in the channel. Discord in the channel frequently occurs when a scarce product, such as the original Cabbage Patch doll, is allocated by a manufacturer to its middlemen.

---

*S*ears uses several channels of distribution to move its goods into the hands of consumers: full-line retail stores, specialty stores, and catalog stores. By using a Sears catalog, a consumer is able to send an order to a mail-order distribution center or telephone it to a local catalog office. To bolster the competitive advantage of its catalog channel system against the more than 4,000 other catalog houses, Sears has developed specialogs that appeal to particular markets.

THE CASE CONTINUES

Because of Sears' close relationship with its 12,000 suppliers, the company has had minimum involvement with transshippers and gray markets. Sometimes, however, even the best of supplier relationships can turn sour. In an unsuccessful court case, the inventor of a quick-release socket wrench claimed that Sears should pay him royalties because the retailer had taken his idea and sold $172 million worth of a similar

wrench. Other vertical conflicts between Sears and suppliers have centered on the amount that Sears pays for its goods. Some small suppliers that are dependent on Sears for their livelihood have complained that the giant retailer places undue pressure on them to reduce their prices. The increase in the sales of foreign goods has caused some importers to emerge as channel captains. Because of its massive buying power, however, Sears remains the channel captain in its dealings with foreign suppliers.

GOAL SUMMARY

1. **Explain the rationale for the use of middlemen.** One rationale is the sorting process, which relies on the use of middlemen to resolve the differences between the amount and kinds of goods produced and purchased. Another rationale is the web of relationships that refers to the many direct transactions that occur among producers and consumers when a middleman is not present.

2. **Identify the various factors that influence the selection of a particular channel system.** The selection of a particular channel system is strongly influenced by market, product, and environmental factors.

3. **State the different kinds of channel systems.** Channel systems can be short, producer-to-consumer systems, or long, producer-to-agent-to-wholesaler-to-retailer-to-consumer systems. The channels for industrial goods are usually shorter than those for consumer goods. Other types of channels include reverse channels of distribution and channels in the

service industries.

4. **Identify the different types of vertical marketing systems.** The vertical marketing systems include administered, contractual, and corporate systems.

5. **Discuss the different distribution strategies as they relate to the intensity of distribution.** A company that follows a strategy of intensive distribution uses all possible types of outlets to sell goods. With selective distribution, a limited number of carefully chosen middlemen in a specified trading area stock a line of goods. Under exclusive distribution, a middleman agrees to perform certain specific marketing activities for a producer in return for an exclusive selling territory.

6. **Explain how a channel captain emerges in a channel system.** The emergence of a channel captain is determined by a number of economic and social sources of power. The bases for power include rewards, coercion, expertise, identification, and legitimacy.

GOAL SUMMARY *(continued)*

7. **Examine the types and causes of channel conflicts.** Horizontal channel conflict involves competition between similar organizations on the same level of distribution. Another kind is an intertype conflict where different kinds of middlemen on the same level of distribution compete against each other. A third type is a vertical conflict wherein one channel member perceives another on a different level of distribution to be engaged in behavior that is preventing it from attaining certain goals.

KEY TERMS

Marketing Channel or Channel of Distribution, **p. 321**
Marketing Intermediaries, **p. 322**
Middlemen, **p. 322**
Facilitating Agencies, **p. 322**
Sorting Process, **p. 322**
Web of Relationships, **p. 323**
Industrial Distributor, **p. 332**
Reverse Marketing Channel, **p. 332**
Channel Captain, **p. 334**
Vertical Marketing System, **p. 334**
Retailer Cooperative Voluntary Group, **p. 335**
Wholesaler-Sponsored Voluntary Chain, **p. 335**

Horizontal Marketing Arrangements, **p. 336**
Symbiotic Marketing, **p. 336**
Intensive Distribution, **p. 337**
Selective Distribution, **p. 337**
Exclusive Distribution, **p. 338**
Exclusive Dealing, **p. 339**
Exclusive Territory, **p. 340**
Tying Contract, **p. 340**
Multiple Marketing Channels, **p. 341**
Transshipping, **p. 341**
Gray Market, **p. 342**
Channel Power, **p. 342**

CHECK YOUR LEARNING

1. In a marketing channel the title to the goods and the goods always move together.   **T/F**
2. Although middlemen are marketing intermediaries, not all marketing intermediaries are middlemen. **T/F**
3. The sorting out process would probably be a major activity of: (a) a manufacturer of office supplies, (b) a manufacturer of elevators, (c) an automobile dealer, (d) the ultimate consumer.
4. A typical objective of a channel system is: (a) minimizing exchange costs, (b) establishing shorter marketing channels, (c) developing effective sales training programs, (d) lobbying for less government regulation.
5. In the channel selection process, geographic concentration would be viewed as: (a) a product factor, (b) a market factor, (c) an environmental factor, (d) managerial factor.
6. A microenvironmental influence on the channel selection process is: (a) a Sunday Blue Law, (b) a decision to use wholesalers, (c) an economic downturn, (d) a ghetto location.
7. In the marketing of large mainframe computers, industrial distributors are commonly used to sell and service the units.   **T/F**
8. An agent's proper role is to match the small producers of electronic components with electronic supply distributors.   **T/F**
9. In a VMS, the Goodyear organization is an example of: (a) an administered system, (b) a contractual system, (c) a cooperative system, (d) a corporate system.
10. By marketing through a limited number of carefully chosen middlemen within a particular trading area, the Whirlpool Corporation is following a strategy of exclusive distribution.   **T/F**
11. For a small producer all of the following would be important elements in an exclusive distribution agreement except: (a) requiring a retail price of $49.95, (b) insisting that a dealer handle only the producer's goods, (c) designating a particular county as the dealer's territory, (d) requiring that product A must be purchased with product B.
12. According to the Colgate case of 1919, IBM can choose whomever it wants for its customers.   **T/F**
13. When cases of Coca-Cola are moved in an unauthorized manner from an area where they sell at low prices to an area where they can be sold at high prices, the activity is called: (a) gray marketing, (b) transshipping, (c) pirating, (d) cross transporting.
14. Because of its closeness to customers, Kmart is in a weak position to captain a channel system.   **T/F**
15. IBM may obtain channel power from all of the following bases except: (a) coercion, (b) identification, (c) rationality, (d) legitimacy.
16. Intertype channel conflicts involve competition between similar organizations, such as Sears and J. C. Penney, on the same level of distribution.   **T/F**

QUESTIONS FOR REVIEW AND DISCUSSION

1. Define the key terms for this chapter that appear at the end of the goal summary.
2. What are the differences between marketing intermediaries and middlemen?
3. Is the sorting process more important in a longer marketing channel than in a shorter one? Explain.
4. Do Procter & Gamble, Whirlpool Appliance, Apple Computer, and Mercedes Benz have the same objectives for their channel systems?
5. What do you believe is the most important factor that determines the type of channel system used for Rolex watches? For IBM mainframe computers? For Coleman tents? For Jack Daniels bourbon?
6. Are the channel systems for industrial goods more carefully analyzed and planned than for consumer goods?
7. How can a vertical marketing system and a horizontal marketing arrangement be used jointly and effectively in marketing Sony TV receivers?
8. Under what conditions would the manufacturer of a product that is normally categorized as a consumer convenience good follow a policy of selective distribution? Of exclusive distribution?
9. Of the three provisions that are often contained in many exclusive distribution agreements, which one is the most anti-competitive?
10. Do transshippers and gray-market vendors benefit consumers or harm them in the short run? In the long run?
11. Is a horizontal conflict more threatening to the health of a channel system than a vertical conflict?

NOTES

1. "IBM Rules Out Selling its PCjr in Kmart Stores," *The Wall Street Journal,* September 28, 1984, p. 2.
2. Wroe Alderson, *Marketing Behavior and Executive Action* (Homewood, Ill.: Richard D. Irwin, Inc., 1957), pp. 201–211.
3. "Automotive Aftermarket Is Confronted with Turbulent Times," *Marketing News,* February 18, 1983, p. 24.
4. "Coke Plans to Enter Frozen-Food Business Within a Few Months," *The Wall Street Journal,* September 28, 1984, p. 43.
5. Elizabeth Chappell White, "HMO's Keep Profession on Its Toes," *Advertising Age,* November 8, 1984, p. 20.
6. Bert C. McCammon, Jr., "Perspectives for Distribution Programming," in *Vertical Marketing Systems,* Louis P. Bucklin, ed. (Glenview, IL: Scott, Foresman, 1970), p. 43.
7. Lee Adler, "Symbiotic Marketing," *Harvard Business Review* (November–December 1966): p. 59.
8. "How to Tune in to Videorecorders," *Business Week,* April 25, 1983, p. 132.
9. Anthony J. Greco, "The Retail Dealers' Agreement Act: An Unwise Background Vertical Restraint," *Enterprise,* University of Cincinnati, 2, no. 3, (Spring 1983): p. 20.
10. Greg Charleston, "Beer Baron Law: Wholesalers, Retailers Battle Over Beer Territory Rule," *Indianapolis Business Journal,* April 4–10, 1983, p. 7.
11. Grant M. Monahan, "A Beer Baron by Any Other Name . . . ," *Indianapolis Business Journal,* December 3–9, 1984, p. 5.
12. Andy Pasztor, "Justice Department Guidelines Support Most Marketing Restrictions by Makers," *The Wall Street Journal,* January 24, 1985, p. 14.
13. Jeffrey Tarter, "Micro Software Industry Faces Clogged Distribution Channels, *Mini-Micro Systems,* February 1984, pp. 131–140.
14. Robert E. Weigand, "Fit Product and Channels to Your Markets," *Harvard Business Review* (January–February 1977): pp. 104–105.
15. John Koten, "Bootleggers Plague Soft-Drink Industry by Utilizing Differences in Bottlers' Cost," *The Wall Street Journal,* March 13, 1979, p. 10.
16. Mark Helper, "IBM Using All Distribution Channels to Buckshot Approach to Marketing," *Electronic News,* December 6, 1982, p. 62.
17. Jacqueline Tears, "Gray Market a Thorn to Foreign-Car Franchises," *The Fort Wayne Journal-Gazette,* June 3, 1984, p. 9.
18. Louis W. Stern and Adel I. El-Ansary, *Marketing Channels* (Englewood Cliffs, N.J.: Prentice-Hall, Inc., 1977), p. 286.
19. Stern and El-Ansary, *Marketing Channels,* pp. 288–292.
20. Bruce Mallen, "Conflict and Cooperation in Marketing Channels," *Reflections on Progress in Marketing,* L. George Smith, ed. (Chicago, IL: American Marketing Association, 1964), p. 65.
21. Stern and El-Ansary, *Marketing Channels,* p. 282.

The mid-1980s were bust years for the personal computer industry. With approximately 400 computer retailers biting the dust in 1985, and hundreds of others leaving the field in 1986, Apple Computer severed its contracts in 1986, with about 600 of its 2,600 U.S. outlets that were authorized to sell its products. These eliminated dealers were generally the weaker stores offering deep discounts, which drove down Apple's prices. Contributing to the emergence of a variety of marketing channels for personal computers was the general oversupply of retail sellers.

Value-added resellers, who are known as VARS in the trade, are newer links in a channel system for personal computers. These resellers have increased their market share by combining very competitive pricing, sales offices without the extra expense of showrooms, after-the-sale service, and a genuine concern for their customers. VARS assemble and sell complete computer systems, often built from the products of several different companies.

As a response to the changing personal computer industry, authorized computer retailers are embracing new marketing strategies. In a 1986 poll of its franchisees, MicroAge found 87 percent of its sales were to businesses, 10 percent to education and government buyers, and only 3 percent to walk-in customers. This caused MicroAge to recommend to their franchisees that they deemphasize the use of fancy showrooms and utilize more spartan sales offices. MicroAge officials cautioned, however, that showrooms won't disappear because they provide an attractive controlled environment conducive to closing a sale.

Many computer retailers, recognizing that walk-in traffic has turned to a dribble, have reorganized their sales forces according to specialized markets such as educational institutions, banking, governmental sales, and desk-top publishing. These markets represent the final link in a channel system. The factors that determine the particular markets that a retailer seeks include the kinds of businesses in the area, the types of computers handled (e.g., Zenith is strong in government and Apple is often preferred by educators), the kinds of training programs prepared by the producers, and the expertise of the salespeople.

A channel system that is similar to one that employs VARS has been established by retailers who purchase computer hardware from a number of different suppliers and then place their own brand name on all the components. This practice of private branding has been followed by Entree and Inacomp, two large computer retailers. When the private-branded computer systems are successfully received by customers, they generate dealer loyalty and repeat business.

To obtain maximum exposure for its computers in a minimum period of time, Atari decided to introduce its products in computer stores and later place them in mass-merchandising units such as Sears and Kmart. To gain the greatest advantage from its entry into mass merchandising, Atari dropped its prices and offered models that were slightly different from those handled by the computer stores.

Certain computer manufacturers have established channel systems that are in conflict with their conventional dealer organizations. In order to tap new markets, these producers have bypassed their dealers and are using mail-order sales and national account representatives to sell directly to educational institutions and other major users. Some dealers do not believe that producers who use these short channels will succeed. They point to the extensive amount of personal service that is necessary after a computer purchase has been made.

Observers of the computer industry cite the difficulty that manufacturers experience in attempting to establish their own dealer organization. IBM is one corporation that recognizes that it is too expensive to operate their own retail stores. Some manufacturers, such as AT&T, have tried it and failed. Today, about 25 to 30 percent of AT&T's total personal computer sales are generated from computer stores. Most of the remainder of the sales come from AT&T's direct sales force, which contacts corporate, government, and other institutional users.

Zenith computers are marketed through a channel system that includes wholesalers. The vast majority of its North American wholesalers were recruited from the ranks of its consumer electronics channel. Reasons for using these particular wholesalers include their known financial strength, promotional capability, and dealer support. The Zenith computer staff provided these wholesalers with a business plan and trained their newly employed salespeople. As a result, these salespeople recruited nearly 1,300 dealers to handle Zenith computers.

The gray market for computers has generated a channel system that produces frowns from authorized dealers. IBM halted the sales of its computers to International Computer Systems of Miami because the thriving seven-store chain was disposing of about one million dollars of IBM units to gray marketers. An estimated 10 percent of IBM computers are sold through the gray market. Other sources of IBM machines that find their way to unauthorized marketers include corporations, universities, and other large purchasers that obtain them at deep discounts of 30 to 40 percent or more. These large buyers are able to resell the computers profitably at an amount that is less than the price that a small buyer would pay to IBM. The gray marketers include mail-order houses, computer dealers, and other electronics retailers. They typically offer the computers to their customers for discounts of 10 to 20 percent below the manufacturer's suggested price.

Some analysts of the computer scene declare that only three types of computer retailers will survive in the industry shakeout. One type is the franchised dealers such as Computerland, MicroAge, and Entree. Another is the financially solvent corporate operations that include BusinessLand, CompuShop, and Sears Business Systems. A third type is the independent specialty retailers who offer outstanding service and retain a loyal customer base.

Issues for Discussion

1. What are the objectives of a channel system for personal computers?
2. What factors have caused a variety of marketing channels to develop in the personal computer industry?
3. Can you identify any channel captains in the personal computer industry? Explain.

4. What specific actions can IBM take to attempt to eliminate the gray market for its computers?

Sources: Adapted from Kevin T. Higgins, "Computer Industry Adopts Leaner, Market-Driven Distribution System," *Marketing News,* April 11, 1986, p. 5; Anthony Ramirez, "Blue vs. Gray: IBM Tries to Stop the Discounters," *Fortune,* May 27, 1985, p. 79; and Michael W. Miller, "Apple to Reduce Its 2,600 U.S. Outlets by 600 Stores in Bid to Help Marketing," *The Wall Street Journal,* April 7, 1986, p. 4.

OUTLINE

Wholesaling

LEARNING GOALS

After reading this chapter, you should be able to:

1. Define the terms *wholesaling* and *wholesaling transactions.*
2. Explain how the broad, intermediate, and narrow concepts of wholesaling differ.
3. Identify the marketing functions that wholesalers perform for manufacturers.
4. Identify the marketing functions that wholesalers perform for retailers.
5. Describe the various kinds of merchant wholesalers.
6. Distinguish between limited-function wholesalers and functional middlemen.
7. Discuss the nature of integrated wholesaling.
8. Explain how cooperatives engage in wholesaling activities.
9. Explain the usefulness of trade shows and central markets.
10. Explain how wholesaling is performed in the service industries.

SUPER VALU IS SUPER WHOLESALER

*S*uper Valu Stores, Inc., headquartered in a Minneapolis suburb, is the nation's largest wholesaler, supplying over 2,300 independently owned supermarkets. The president of Super Valu has stated that the company wants the people who run supermarkets to get rich. Of course, by supplying them with the merchandise to sell and get rich, Super Valu will also prosper. Although the company operates some retail food stores, more than 85 percent of its sales and earnings are generated by its wholesale grocery operation.

For an aggressive individual with some retail experience and a chunk of capital, Super Valu will add the necessary merchandising assistance and develop a strong independent food store. By operating sixteen efficient grocery warehouses, the company is able to provide its retailer-customers with the economies of a large-scale operation that rivals a chain such as Kroger or Safeway. As part of its service to retailers, Super Valu selects store locations, designs stores, finances equipment, stocks shelves, trains personnel, and prepares advertising.

An executive of Super Valu believes that the large grocery wholesalers are truly channel captains who drive the retail grocery market rather than merely supply it. He points out that capable wholesalers with large staffs of management and merchandising specialists have the resources to make independent retailers better merchandisers.

A key factor in the success of Super Valu is its skillful warehousing operation. The carefully designed warehouses are run extremely efficiently with warehouse employees operating mechanical pallet jacks rather than automated equipment. Through the use of industrial engineering and advanced computer modeling, Super Valu has been able to greatly increase its storage density. A computer assigns shelf positions to the incoming merchandise and indicates the order in which the workers select cases for delivery. To

accommodate additional items in a warehouse, a computer simulation program develops designs that alter the building's layout. Over a year, a warehouse may experience six to ten major or minor alterations. With a rapid stock turnover of about 1.5 times a month, proper warehouse layout and order handling are very important to Super Valu.

Two of Super Valu's most significant services to retailers are its store design and its site selection program. Company architects use a computer-aided design system that has over 100 different store layouts programmed into it. A retailer can choose a particular format and then make the necessary adjustments to accommodate his or her special store needs. In site selection, the wholesaler has thirty individuals who are continuously seeking the best locations for retail stores. When an outstanding location is found, the company's SLASH (Site Location Analysis Strategy Heuristic) team performs a complete marketing study. This includes details on the potential customer base, the type of competition, and market shares of the competition.

Super Valu provides additional aid to retailers through the use of retail

counselors. These individuals roam retail stores looking for situations that need improving. If an area, such as produce or meats, needs particular attention, a specialist comes from the central office to resolve the problem. When Richard Niemann's three stores in Illinois began losing sales to a warehouse competitor, the Super Valu consultants recommended that his stores be operated as discount supermarkets. Niemann adopted the discount format and sales rebounded vigorously.

Issues for Discussion
1. Will it become more difficult in the future for smaller grocery wholesalers to survive?
2. How can limited-function wholesalers compete against service wholesalers such as Super Valu?
3. Why is it useful for a wholesaler, such as Super Valu, to operate some retail stores?

Sources: Adapted from Jan Parr, "Leader of the Pack," *Forbes,* Feb. 8, 1988, pp. 35–36; Bill Saporito, "Super Valu Does Two Things Well," *Fortune,* April 18, 1983, pp. 114–117; Frank W. Campanella, "Wholesale Success," *Barrons,* October 17, 1983, pp. 71–72; and Wendy Kimbrall, "Super Valu's Stores Lead Grocery Charge to Warehouse Market," *Advertising Age,* September 24, 1984, pp. 4, 88.

■ Skillful warehousing is critical to Super Valu's success.
Source: Photo courtesy of Super Valu Stores, Inc.

*I*n this chapter we enter the world of wholesaling, seeing exactly how it fits into marketing channel systems. We first define just what *wholesaling* and *wholesale transactions* are, and then identify *broad, intermediate,* and *narrow* views of wholesaling. The relationship of wholesaling intermediaries to manufacturers and retailers is explained. There are four major classifications of wholesaling intermediaries—merchant wholesalers, functional middlemen, integrated wholesaling operations, and cooperatives and voluntary groups—and this chapter describes each classification and its subclasses. Of course, new forms of intermediaries constantly develop in response to changing market conditions. An important change in the U.S. market has involved a shift toward service industries; this chapter describes several providers of wholesaling services in these areas. A discussion of new developments in wholesaling concludes the chapter. ■

UNDERSTANDING WHOLESALING

Who is the country's largest wholesaler? Is the annual volume of retail sales greater than the annual volume of wholesale sales? Are the majority of the sales of wholesale establishments made to retailers? Learning the correct responses to these questions will furnish you with some interesting insights into the field of wholesaling. Wholesaling receives scant attention from the media and at first may not appear to offer exciting career choices. Although there are over 5.8 million workers in the wholesaling industry, only a handful of colleges offer courses in wholesaling. In the curriculum of most business schools, a student's lone exposure to the field comes from a single chapter in a marketing textbook. Certainly, wholesaling is not as dynamic as the information technology field or as exciting as the automobile industry, yet it plays a vital role in the efficient distribution of goods in our economy.

Wholesaling Defined

*W*holesaling includes all transactions in which a buyer purchases goods for resale or for use in making other products.

Wholesaling includes all transactions in which a buyer purchases goods either for resale or for use in making other products.[1] Wholesaling includes sales to retailers, commercial and industrial users, institutions, and government agencies but does not usually involve sales to the ultimate consumer.

Wholesale Transactions

*T*he most important difference between retailing and wholesaling transactions is the motive of the purchaser.

When you hear the term *wholesaling* mentioned, you probably think of low prices, large quantities, and a warehouse operation. You may believe that all three factors must be present. Although these help us to distinguish between retailing and wholesaling transactions, however, the most important difference is the motive of the purchaser (figure 13.1).

The phrase "I can get it for you wholesale" is frequently used to mean "I can get it for you at a low price." Most wholesale transactions involve prices lower than those found on similar goods at retail. There are, however, numerous exceptions to

❑ **Figure 13.1**
Definition of a
wholesale transaction.

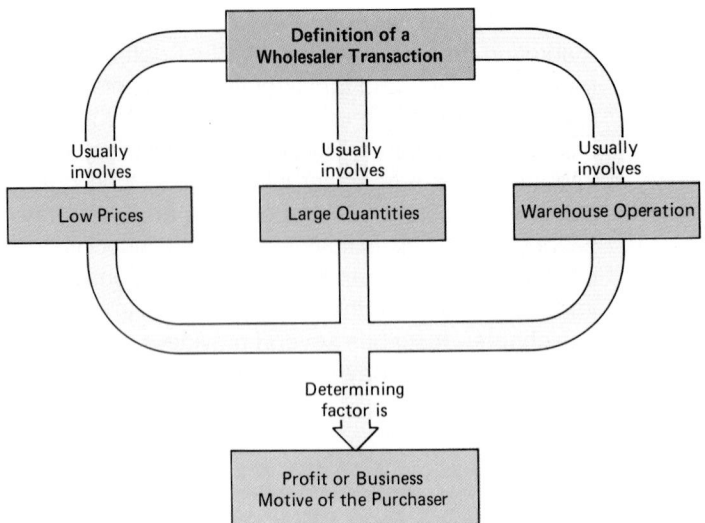

Low prices, large quantities, and method of operation do not adequately distinguish a wholesale transaction from a retail one.

Computers provided by wholesalers help pharmacists to reorder stock.

Source: Courtesy of McKesson Drug Company

this rule. For example, an operator of a small service station may buy a few cases of Zerex antifreeze from a tire, battery, and accessories (TBA) wholesaler, which also provides many marketing functions for the small operator. Because of the small quantity of antifreeze involved, processing the transaction is expensive for the wholesaler, who must sell the Zerex at a high price in order to cover expenses. The operator then passes the high price on to his or her customers. On the other hand, a mass merchandiser such as Kmart assumes many of the marketing functions and purchases Zerex by the truckload from the manufacturer at a very low price. As a result, Kmart can offer Zerex to consumers at a price lower than the one the TBA wholesaler charges its service station customers.

Wholesale transactions are generally assumed to involve large quantities. As noted in Chapter 12, one function of a middleman is allocating, or bulk breaking. Television and appliance wholesalers buy their goods in truckload quantities and then allocate them in smaller units to retailers. The retailers, in turn, sell them one at a time to consumers. Sometimes, however, wholesalers sell in small quantities, too. A pharmacist's customer may request a drug that is out of stock. When this occurs, it is not unusual for a drug wholesaler to rush the single item to the drugstore.

The motive of the purchaser, as noted, determines whether a transaction is a wholesale or a retail one. Low prices, sales in large quantities, and method of operation are not sufficient to make this distinction. **Wholesale transactions** must have a profit or business motivation. A wholesale transaction occurs when a purchasing agent at Eastman Kodak buys new tires for the company's fleet of cars. The cost of the tires is a business expense and is reflected in the selling price of Kodak products. A buyer at Macy's who purchases Polo shirts for resale to the department store's customers wants to procure them at the lowest possible price so the markup on them will cover expenses and profit. The incentive for both of these purchases is profit. In contrast, when you buy tires for your car and purchase Polo shirts, you are buying for your personal use. Transactions involving sales to the ultimate consumer for their personal or family use are designated retail transactions.

It is important to know whether a transaction is a retail or a wholesale one for legal reasons involving the Robinson-Patman Act and the retail sales tax laws. The Robinson-Patman Act prohibits wholesalers from selling at different prices to buyers that are in direct competition. The retail sales tax laws require collection of a tax on all retail purchases.

☐ Figure 13.2
Broad, intermediate,
and narrow views of
wholesaling.

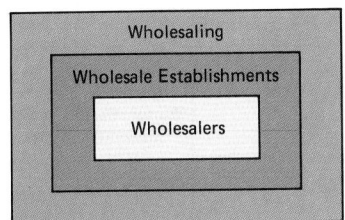

Conceptions of Wholesaling

You can better understand the field of wholesaling and its complexity if you know who performs wholesaling transactions. A study of these transactions leads to a formulation of broad, intermediate, and narrow views of wholesaling, as shown in figure 13.2.

BROAD VIEW

*U*nder the broad view, wholesaling encompasses all transactions that are made for business or profit.

Under the broad view, wholesaling encompasses all transactions made for business or profit reasons. These include sales from any source to industrial concerns, government agencies, retailers, and other wholesale enterprises. The following types of transactions qualify as wholesaling in this view: Ford truck sales to the U.S. Postal Service, Levi Strauss sales to J. C. Penney, Acme food broker sales to Super Valu wholesaler, John Deere tractor dealer sales to farmer Bob Brown, and Xerox sales to Aetna exporters. Because this concept of wholesaling includes all commercial buyer-seller relationships, it is the broadest view of the wholesale trade. Since the types of wholesale transactions are so numerous and so varied, the annual volume of wholesale sales is much greater than the annual volume of retail sales, as shown in Table 13.1.

INTERMEDIATE VIEW

*U*nder the intermediate view, only the transactions that take place in whole-sale establishments are considered part of wholesaling.

Under the intermediate view, only transactions that take place in wholesale establishments are classified as wholesale transactions. A wholesale establishment is a separate place of business that conducts such transactions. Although these establishments are often owned by wholesalers who are specialists in wholesale trade, they may belong to manufacturers, retailers, farmers, and others. However, manufacturers, retailers, farmers, and others who engage in wholesaling frequently do not have separate establishments for conducting their wholesale business. Figure 13.3 identifies three important types of wholesale establishments and their customers.

The intermediate view of wholesaling is important because the most complete information on the wholesale trade is based on the activities of wholesale establishments. The data, which include statistics on volume of sales and number of employees, are collected from wholesaling establishments by the Bureau of the Census and other divisions of the U.S. Department of Commerce. The census defines a wholesale

☐ Table 13.1 Total Retail and Wholesale Transactions

YEAR	SALES OF RETAIL ESTABLISHMENTS (IN BILLIONS)	SALES OF WHOLESALE ESTABLISHMENTS (IN BILLIONS)	WHOLESALE SALES AS PERCENTAGE OF RETAIL SALES
1977	700	1,258	180%
1982	1,039	1,998	192%

❏ **Figure 13.3** Percentage distribution of sales of wholesale establishments by class of customer.

Type of Wholesale Establishment	Farmers for Farm Use	Builders and Contractors	For Export	Retailers and Repair Shops	Wholesalers	Household Consumers and Individual Users	Industrial Users, Manufacturing and Mining	Institutional, commercial, and professional users, etc.	Federal, State, and local government
Merchant wholesalers	5.2	4.5	9.8	28.0	24.8	1.6	15.0	8.9	2.2
Manufacturers' sales branches	.7	2.4	3.1	32.5	22.6	.6	24.5	11.3	2.3
Agents, brokers, commission merchants	4.5	1.6	6.9	19.7	37.5	.3	19.6	8.1	1.8
Total, all types	3.6	3.5	7.3	28.6	25.5	1.1	18.6	9.6	2.2

establishment as one that derives over 50 percent of its business from wholesale transactions. In contrast, when over 50 percent of an establishment's business is accounted for by sales to the ultimate consumer, the operation is considered a retail business. A recent U.S. *Census of Wholesale Trade* listed over 400,000 wholesale establishments, which generated nearly $2 trillion in sales.

NARROW VIEW

*U*nder the narrow view, the scope of wholesaling is limited to transactions performed by wholesalers.

The narrow view limits the scope of wholesaling to transactions performed by wholesalers. A wholesaler is a type of wholesaling intermediary that purchases goods from suppliers and resells them to other commercial enterprises. As we have noted, many different types of organizations, such as manufacturers, retailers, and farmers, engage in wholesaling, but they are not wholesalers and are not classified as part of the wholesaling industry. The narrow view of wholesaling, which is held by many consumers, does not include all the wholesaling channels available to marketers, nor does it reveal the total picture of wholesale trade in the United States. It does, however, help us to focus on the nature of the wholesalers' functions. Understanding these functions is useful because certain operating data collected by trade associations and the *Census of Wholesale Trade* are applicable only to them.

THE CASE CONTINUES

*S*uper Valu executives are very aware that wholesaling involves more than purchasing large quantities of goods from a producer and reselling them in smaller units to retailers. A Super Valu official refers to the firm as a retail support company, and he becomes visibly annoyed when it is called a wholesale operation. Retail support means moving small retailers into larger, more competitive stores that will purchase

more goods from Super Valu. The purpose of each wholesale transaction that Super Valu has with a retailer is to help him or her conduct a profitable business.

The large scale of operations and merchandising expertise of Super Valu permits it to service and perform marketing functions for small

retail chains as well as independents. For example, the Pantry Pride stores in Miami were being supplied by their own chain store warehouse, but Super Valu purchased the warehouse and is now supplying the stores. The wholesaling transactions occurring when Super Valu sells from its facilities to retail food stores correspond to the narrow view of wholesaling (wholesale transactions performed by wholesalers).

FUNCTIONS OF WHOLESALING INTERMEDIARIES

Many independent supermarket operators can wave an electronic wand over the labels of the products on their shelves and reorder goods automatically, thanks to the grocery wholesalers that provide this cost-saving innovation. Wholesalers, recognizing their own need to keep customers, often use such means to help retailers implement their managerial, financial, and marketing strategies. Of course, providing these services may involve high costs, which threaten the existence of small, thinly financed wholesale establishments. For example, a large wholesaler with $250 million in sales can invest $250,000 in computer software programs and easily spread the costs over its numerous accounts. A small wholesaler with a sales volume of only $5 million is unable to justify a similar expenditure. This partly explains why the number of wholesalers serving the supermarket industry declined in the ten-year period between 1974 and 1984 from nearly 1,000 to about 400.

Chapter 1 described the eight basic marketing functions inherent in the marketing process. These functions include: buying, selling, transportation, storage, marketing information and research, financing, standardization and grading, and risk bearing. Wholesaling intermediaries frequently perform these functions, along with other marketing services, in their role as a critical link between manufacturers and retailers.

Functions Performed for Manufacturers

*W*holesaling intermediaries create efficiencies by purchasing in large quantities from manufacturers, breaking bulk, and reselling in smaller units to their customers.

Many manufacturers depend on wholesaling intermediaries to establish efficient distribution systems for their goods. Although some consumers equate manufacturing with large-scale organizations, such as General Motors and General Electric, in reality the great majority of manufacturing enterprises are relatively small. These smaller firms need the variety of services that wholesaling intermediaries can economically perform. These services are shown in figure 13.4. Wholesaling intermediaries create buying efficiencies by purchasing in large quantities from

❑ **Figure 13.4**
Functions that a wholesaling intermediary can perform for manufacturers.

In the area of buying:
  • Creates buying efficiencies by purchasing in large quantities.
  • Buys on a regular basis from manufacturers, permitting long production runs.
In the area of selling:
  • Acts as an extended sales arm for a manufacturer.
  • Can obtain orders that a manufacturer could not afford to obtain.
  • Reduces the selling costs of manufacturers by using computer-to-computer reordering procedures.
  • Can introduce new products to the retail market rapidly and effectively.
In the area of physical distribution:
  • Can reduce physical distribution costs through truckload-lot purchases.
  • Uses storage space more efficiently than a manufacturer.
  • Provides manufacturers with specialized facilities close to their markets.
Other Functions:
  • Informs manufacturers about the needs of ultimate consumers.
  • Advises manufacturers on a variety of marketing problems.
  • Reduces manufacturers' capital needs and provides financial assistance.
  • Performs the standardization and grading function, particularly with agricultural and imported goods.
  • Reduces the risks of manufacturers by buying goods before there is an established market for them.
  • Reduces size of manufacturers' inventories and the associated risks of price and product changes.
  • Offers numerous value-added services to customers.

manufacturers, breaking bulk, and reselling in smaller units to their customers. Often, wholesaling organizations carry a wide range of products, which permits them to economically call on even small retailers. Thus, they are frequently able to obtain orders that a manufacturer could not afford to obtain.

Many manufacturers of consumer goods do not have adequate sales forces to call on all of their customers. For example, the U.S. food industry includes about 360,000 producers and 150,000 food stores. Even many large producers with wide lines of products, such as General Foods and Beatrice, find it impossible to contact all of their potential customers on a regular weekly basis. They depend on the 38,000 grocery wholesalers that service the grocery retailers. Some wholesaling intermediaries help to reduce the selling costs of manufacturers by using computer-to-computer reordering procedures. For example, E. J. Brach and Sons, the Chicago-based candy manufacturer, annually processes over 25,000 computer-to-computer purchase orders.[2]

Industrial distributors frequently offer their customers value-added services, ranging from automated ordering systems to product customizing for very specific markets. Value added is indicated by the difference between the value of a good or service as it enters the channel system and its value as it leaves the system. For example, one Celanese Chemical distributor uses a divided tank truck that holds four or five different chemicals, allowing a customer who needs several small orders of different chemicals to be served in one trip.[3] Steel distribution centers offer a wide range of metal processing.

Functions Performed for Retailers

*W*holesaling intermediaries accumulate a variety of goods from numerous manufacturers in order to sell a complete assortment to retailers.

Every retailer deals with some type of wholesaling intermediary. Small retailers depend on wholesalers to provide them with a variety of goods to satisfy their customers, and large retailers who buy directly from manufacturers frequently use wholesalers to satisfy certain specialized merchandising needs and to provide fill-in items. Wholesaling intermediaries accumulate a variety of goods from numerous manufacturers so that they can offer a complete assortment to retailers. By maintaining inventory records on their retailer customers and rapidly replenishing any stocks that are low, the intermediaries render a valuable service to retailers.

Because of their continuous association with a variety of retail establishments, wholesaling intermediaries gain a broad perspective on the merchandising requirements of retailers. Since they assemble a variety of goods from many different manufacturers, they have available what retailers want in the quantities wanted and

A Super Valu planner discusses store remodeling with one of its client retailers.

Source: Photo courtesy of Super Valu Stores, Inc.

☐ **Figure 13.5**
Functions a
wholesaling
intermediary can
perform for retailers.

> In the area of buying:
> - Assists retailers in developing and implementing their merchandise buying plans.
> - Screens available products and accepts those with best sales potential.
> - Passes on savings from buying in quantity and truckload lots to retailers.
>
> In the area of selling:
> - Accumulates from numerous manufacturers complete assortments of goods for retailers.
> - Can rapidly replenish retailers' inventories.
> - Assists retailers with sales training and promotional efforts.
>
> In the area of physical distribution:
> - Reduces size of retailers' inventories and the associated risks of price and product changes.
> - Provides specialized storage facilities for retailers.
> - Assembles assortments of goods, minimizing the retailers' transportation costs.
>
> Other functions:
> - Passes on information about general market conditions to retailers.
> - Finances retailers through credit purchases.
> - Provides retailers with extensive accounting help.
> - Inspects and grades goods prior to their sale to retailers.
> - Provides retailers with prompt adjustments and product guarantees.

at the time wanted. They also frequently provide retailers with information on store operating procedures and management, including suggestions on site selection, interior design and layout, displays, and promotions. Without trade credit from wholesaling intermediaries, it is doubtful whether small, marginally financed retailers would be able to secure adequate operating funds. The wide range of services provided by wholesaling intermediaries to retailers is listed in figure 13.5.

THE CASE CONTINUES

*S*uper Valu has become a successful and prosperous wholesaler by doing the things that it does best—servicing manufacturers and retailers. Super Valu purchases in large quantities from manufacturers; racks, stacks, and repacks the goods in its warehouse; and sells them in smaller quantities to retailers. Manufacturers benefit by the wholesaler's efficient warehousing and transportation operations. Super Valu examines every detail of the distribution process for a good as it moves from

the producer through the Super Valu warehouse to retailers. The wholesaler knows as much about the movement of canned salmon from a cannery in the Pacific Northwest to a supermarket in Pittsburgh as a fisheries biologist knows about the travels of the live salmon upstream in the Columbia River.

Super Valu has offset the advantages that chains have over independent retailers by supplying the

independents with strong lines of goods and services. The giant wholesaler furnishes them with low prices, outstanding locations, sophisticated operating systems, and sometimes even complete stores. When Super Valu officials learn that a chain, such as A & P or Kroger, is closing its operations in a market, they rush to the area and evaluate the available sites. Then, they purchase the best sites and resell them to independent retailers who become Super Valu customers.

TYPES OF WHOLESALING INTERMEDIARIES

In your own community, you can see many different types of retailing facilities—ranging from small gift boutiques to giant department stores. Are you aware, however, that there are many kinds of wholesaling intermediaries, too? Some of them are very small, one-person agencies, and others are very large organizations that employ thousands of workers, such as Super Valu, the Fleming Company, and Wetterau. Super Valu has a total annual sales volume of over $6.5 billion, the Fleming Company over $5.5, and Wetterau generates over $3 billion.

REAL PEOPLE IN MARKETING

A Dynamic Wholesaler

*H*ope's Specialty Foods is a creation of a dynamic young lady who is inflamed with the entrepreneurial spirit. This gourmet food wholesaling organization was formed in 1981 by Hope Klayman, a woman who had a longtime dream to operate her own business. Hope got into wholesaling by being at the right place at the right time and tasting the right product. One evening, she and her husband, Mark, ventured into Joe's Restaurant in Reading, Pennsylvania, to try its famous mushroom dishes—consisting of mainly soups and sauces. The owner sadly declared to the Klaymans that he was experiencing great difficulty in marketing his mushroom soup to food stores. Mark replied that he could understand the difficulty because he had experienced similar problems in his role as a pizza salesman for his father's pizza company. Hope impulsively made an offer that Joe could not refuse—she would become the distributor of his products. Joe immediately accepted!

The first step for Hope in this new venture was to taste test some of Joe's soups in her kitchen. After assuring herself she was offering a quality product, she contacted the owner of a local cheese shop and asked for an order. Because Joe's soups were well known to the proprietor, he readily bought a case. Her initial success caused her to develop a marketing strategy that consisted of using phone books and road maps to identify all the cheese shops in the surrounding area. When convincing these shops, she would take a thermos of hot soup and use it for product sampling. With thermos and order book in hand, she obtained orders from twenty stores within two weeks.

Because Hope was the master wholesaler for Joe's products, she

■ Hope Klayman is a gourmet food wholesaler.

was able to establish the prices and order quantities and to sell the products anywhere. Her first business problem was discovering that a 19 percent gross margin was inadequate to cover costs and permit growth. As a result, she immediately increased the margin to around 30 percent.

Hope truly started her business on a shoestring. Her initial investment was only $240 and this paid for the opening of a checking account, files, maps, and invoices. Her greatest expense was for gasoline for the family car that was used for sales trips and deliveries. She soon realized, however, that she needed a larger delivery vehicle so she obtained a $7,000 loan and bought a new van.

With the addition of two gourmet brands of mustard, Hope began an

expansion of her product line. She shortly had thirteen delivery routes that included a variety of customers ranging from specialty food outlets to a bookstore. The addition of customers and product lines caused Mark to join his wife's business and assume responsibility for about 80 percent of the deliveries. By establishing a network of manufacturers' agents in numerous markets, such as Atlanta, Detroit, and Hawaii, the Klaymans greatly expanded their fledgling business. To make the line attractive to agents, a 10 percent commission on initial orders and a 5 percent commission on reorders was established.

By the end of 1983, the Klaymans had 247 retail customers and were handling 324 products that included spices, jelly beans, French cider, and New Zealand honey. The food products came from twenty-four manufacturers and one food broker that represented five small producers. Although sales were increasing, further growth was prevented by a lack of storage space. This was resolved when Mark's father rented them a portion of the warehouse that he used for his pizza business in Philadelphia. As a result, Hope was able to move imported products to storage more rapidly and provide faster delivery to customers. Low operating costs and an aggressive selling approach—Hope does not refuse small orders—has contributed to a continuous increase in the sales of Hope's Specialty Foods. By 1987, Hope had 1,875 customers and was handling 1,460 products.

Sources: Adapted from "A Tasty Distribution Company," *In Business,* July/August, 1983, p. 14; and a conversation with Hope Klayman.

□ Figure 13.6
Types of merchant
wholesalers.

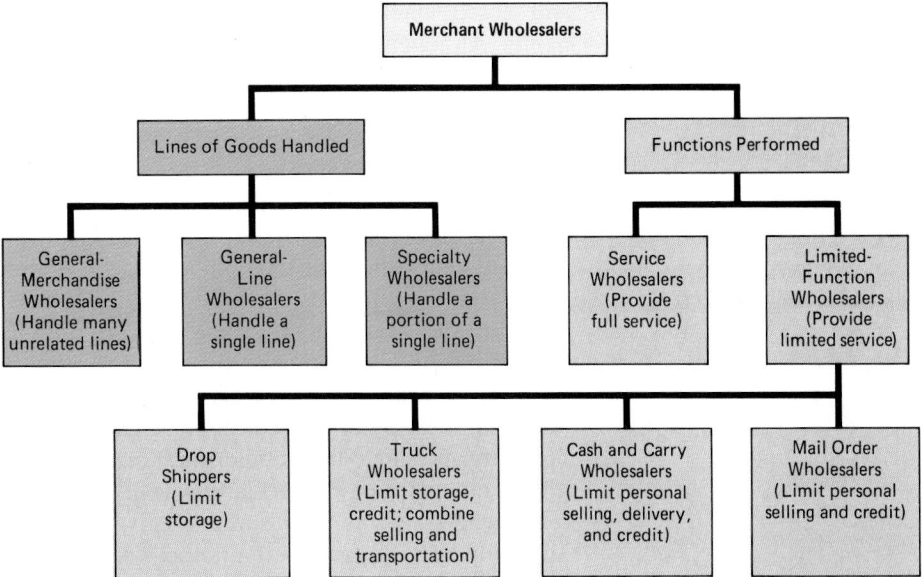

*T*he major classifications of wholesaling intermediaries include merchant wholesalers, functional middlemen, and integrated wholesaling operations.

This section examines four distinct classifications of wholesaling intermediaries and several subclasses. The major classifications are merchant wholesalers, functional middlemen, integrated wholesaling operations, and cooperatives and voluntary groups. Although most of the wholesaling intermediaries described under these classifications are those listed in the U.S. Census classifications, there are numerous variations of these types, too. Customers' needs generally determine the functions performed by wholesaling intermediaries. New forms of intermediaries constantly develop in response to changing market conditions and as a means to increase the efficiency of distribution channels.

Merchant Wholesalers

A merchant wholesaler in a particular trade may be called a jobber, a distributor, a supply company, or a mill house.

A **merchant wholesaler** is an independent middleman that buys goods, takes title to them, assumes all risks for them, and resells them, mainly to retailers or industrial users. When you hear the term *wholesaler,* you probably envision a merchant wholesaler. Perhaps, you have heard this type of middleman in particular trades called by other names, such as jobber, distributor, supply company, or mill house. Merchant wholesalers can be categorized according to the lines of goods handled and the functions performed (figure 13.6).

LINES OF GOODS HANDLED

*M*erchant wholesalers may carry broad, narrow, or moderately balanced lines of goods.

Some wholesalers carry very broad lines of goods, some very narrow lines, and others moderately balanced lines. **General merchandise wholesalers** handle a wide variety of unrelated goods, which may range from aspirin to aprons. Because their customers are rural general stores, small variety stores, and small department stores, these wholesalers carry many of the nonperishable lines these retailers typically sell, including home furnishings, housewares, hardware, apparel, and health and beauty aids.

General-line wholesalers limit their merchandise offering to a single line, such as groceries, hardware, drugs and beauty aids, or plumbing and heating equipment. Within its line, such a wholesaler handles a wide selection of items. For example, a hardware wholesaler may carry light hardware, builders' hardware, tools and cutlery, and closely allied goods such as small appliances, glassware, sporting goods, and paints. Although most general-line wholesalers are local businesses, some—such as McKesson Corporation, a drug wholesaler with fifty-two distribution centers—operate nationwide.

In the industrial market, general-line wholesalers are often called **general-line distributors.** They handle broad lines of industrial products, such as chemicals or electrical supplies and apparatus. The largest general-line distributor for mining and industrial supplies is Fairmont Supply Company. This distributor sells over 165,000 different items valued at $50 million, from four hundred manufacturers, and delivers to over ten thousand customers in thirty-eight states.[4]

Specialty wholesalers confine their offerings to a narrow grouping of goods in a general line. For this reason, they are sometimes called short-line distributors. In the grocery business, some specialty wholesalers limit their stock to candy, tobacco, and cigarettes; others, to coffee, tea, and spices; and still others, to frozen foods. Specialty and single-line retailers that carry deep assortments in only a few lines are important customers of specialty wholesalers. A disadvantage associated with specialty wholesalers is their small size, which causes them to have proportionately higher operating expenses than other wholesalers. In the industrial market, similar wholesalers called **specialty distributors** restrict their line to a narrow product category, such as abrasives or power-transmission equipment.

FUNCTIONS PERFORMED

The scope of the operations of merchant wholesalers reflects the needs of their markets. Merchant wholesalers can be broadly categorized as service (or full-service) wholesalers and limited-function (or limited-service) wholesalers.

Service Wholesalers.   Service wholesalers perform many or all of the marketing functions for their customers. Although buffeted by competition from many other wholesaling intermediaries, these wholesalers have managed to survive and even retain a relatively stable share of the total wholesale trade. Most general merchandise, general-line, and specialty wholesalers furnish a broad array of services to their clienteles and thus are classified as service wholesalers. Because of the numerous services they offer, their operating expenses as a percentage of sales are generally over 10 percent, which is higher than for most other wholesaling intermediaries.

An unusual type of service wholesaler is the service merchandiser, or rack jobber. At first, such firms furnished supermarkets with nonfood items, such as housewares, records, magazines, and health and beauty aids. Today, service merchandisers supply discount, drug, and hardware stores, too. A service merchandiser warehouses its goods, places display racks in stores, stocks the racks with goods, prices the goods, and bills the retailer only for the goods sold from the racks. Sav-A-Stop of Jacksonville, Florida, with three major distribution centers and 180 regional warehouses, is the largest service merchandiser in the country. It credits its success to its tremendous buying power.

Limited-Function Wholesalers.   **Limited-function wholesalers** restrict their performance of marketing activities and thus reduce their operating costs. Types of limited-function wholesalers include drop shippers, truck wholesalers, cash-and-carry wholesalers, and mail-order wholesalers.

Drop shippers generally operate from an office and do not take physical possession of the goods that they resell. Sometimes called **desk jobbers,** they mainly deal in bulky commodities, such as coal, lumber, and building materials. Here, the elimination of physical handling can result in considerable economies. Although they buy and sell on their own account, drop shippers act mainly as negotiators between

*M*ost general merchandise, general-line, and specialty wholesalers are service wholesalers, which perform many or all of the marketing functions for their customers.

*L*imited-function wholesalers, which perform few marketing functions, include drop shippers, truck wholesalers, cash-and-carry wholesalers, and mail-order wholesalers.

THE REST OF THE STORY

IGA—An A-1 Organization

*I*f you live in any of the forty-six states that have IGA food stores, you may be familiar with the red and while IGA logo. Perhaps you believe that IGA operates about the same as the grocery giants, Safeway and Kroger. Although IGA is the third largest food retailing organization in the country, it is not a corporate chain. This relates the rest of the story about the IGA operation.

In 1926, J. Frank Grimes was an unknown accountant who served as a partner in a Chicago accounting firm that specialized in handling wholesale grocery accounts. In viewing the records of his wholesaler clients, he grew appalled at the number of small independent food stores being swept away by corporate chain stores. Gathering together a small group of independent retailers, Mr. Grimes led the delegation to Poughkeepsie, N.Y., which was the home of W. T. Reynolds & Company, a grocery wholesaler. The Reynolds company wanted to organize a wholesale venture with the independents so they could effectively combat the threat of the growing chains. At the first meeting of the group in

Poughkeepsie, sixty-nine of them pledged to join a new independent movement that would be named the Independent Grocers Alliance (IGA).

The IGA system is actually a layer of three independent operations: retailers, wholesalers, and a headquarters staff. In the IGA system, the 3,300 IGA retailers are the key to the distribution operation. These retailers are independents that have an extensive investment of time and money in their businesses. Servicing these independents are thirty-three IGA authorized wholesalers, which operate fifty-seven distribution centers. Unlike the chain-store warehouses of Safeway and Kroger, the distribution centers of the IGA wholesalers are not part of the same close-knit corporate chain. Each wholesaler is independently owned in the same manner that IGA stores are independently owned. In Chicago, the IGA headquarters staff of

about 100 represents the administration, but not the ownership, of IGA. The organization is actually owned by the IGA wholesalers and their elected members sit on the IGA board of directors. A key function of the headquarters staff is to serve as the public and trade relations arm of the system. Another function is to provide staff specialists for almost every aspect of retail operations: dry groceries, meats, produce, bakery, frozen foods, and dairy. Others specialize in areas such as store development and equipment, advertising, promotion, public relations, training, management development, food science, and quality control.

Now, you know the rest of the story! By forging an alliance of independent grocery wholesalers and retailers, J. Frank Grimes in 1926 created an organization that has become one of the nation's leading food merchants.

Sources: Adapted from "The IGA Story," published by IGA, Inc., undated, pp. 1–16; "An Inside Look at IGA with President Bill Olsen," *Chain Store Age Supermarket,* Dec. 1980, pp. 22–23.

---

buyers and sellers. Their method of operation drops their costs to a relatively low 4 to 5 percent of sales.

Truck wholesalers or wagon distributors, combine the selling and transportation functions by using driver-salespersons to contact retailers and other institutions. Because truck wholesalers use their trucks as warehouses, they must restrict their offerings to a limited line of goods. They usually sell for cash but occasionally extend credit and may even take telephone orders. The stock of truck wholesalers is generally limited to perishable or semiperishable goods, such as candy, bakery goods, dairy products, and fruits and vegetables.

Customers of **cash-and-carry wholesalers** pick the goods from warehouse shelves, place them on carts, and wheel them to a checkout counter, where they pay cash. The customers use their own trucks to carry the goods back to their businesses. As their name indicates, these wholesalers do not offer credit or delivery, and they curtail some selling activities, too. This type of wholesaler evolved in the late 1920s as a response to the growing competitive threat of grocery chains such as A & P and Kroger. Cash-and-carry wholesalers usually handle grocery products, office supplies, auto supplies, hardware, and electrical goods. Because they restrict the

☐ **Figure 13.7**
Types of functional
middlemen.

```
┌─────────────────────────┐
│   Functional Middlemen   │
└─────────────────────────┘
│
│  ┌─────────────────────┐
├──│   Manufacturers'    │
│  │      Agents         │
│  │ (Sell only portions │
│  │ of several producers'│
│  │  outputs in assigned │
│  │     territories)    │
│  └─────────────────────┘
│
│  ┌─────────────────────┐
├──│  Export and         │
│  │  Import Brokers     │
│  │ (Specialize in      │
│  │ certain goods from  │
│  │  a few countries)   │
│  └─────────────────────┘
│
│  ┌─────────────────────┐
├──│      Brokers        │
│  │    (Negotiate       │
│  │    sales on a       │
│  │   transaction       │
│  │      basis)         │
│  └─────────────────────┘
│
│  ┌─────────────────────┐
├──│       Food          │
│  │      Brokers        │
│  │  (Handle food       │
│  │  products and       │
│  │   resemble          │
│  │ manufacturers'      │
│  │     agents)         │
│  └─────────────────────┘
│
│  ┌─────────────────────┐
├──│    Commission       │
│  │    Merchants        │
│  │   (Deal in          │
│  │  specific lots      │
│  │    of farm          │
│  │  commodities)       │
│  └─────────────────────┘
│
│  ┌─────────────────────┐
├──│     Auction         │
│  │    Companies        │
│  │   (Deal in goods    │
│  │ requiring physical  │
│  │    inspection)      │
│  └─────────────────────┘
│
│  ┌─────────────────────┐
├──│   Selling Agents    │
│  │   (Sell all of      │
│  │    several          │
│  │   producers'        │
│  │    outputs)         │
│  └─────────────────────┘
│
│  ┌─────────────────────┐
├──│      Export         │
│  │    Management       │
│  │    Companies        │
│  │  (Used by small     │
│  │ producers who       │
│  │ want to market      │
│  │    overseas)        │
│  └─────────────────────┘
│
│  ┌─────────────────────┐
└──│  Manufacturers'     │
   │  Export Agents      │
   │ (Provide selling    │
   │ assistance on a     │
   │  short-term basis)  │
   └─────────────────────┘
```

services they offer, they have been successful in keeping their costs below 9 percent of sales. Most of their customers are small retailers seeking the lowest-priced goods and others needing fill-in items.

Mail-order wholesalers sell through catalogs and accept both mail and telephone orders. They eliminate the personal selling activity and often restrict the use of credit. These wholesaling intermediaries serve small retailers, industrial firms, and institutional users that may be too small to be regularly visited by salespersons. The processing of numerous small orders causes the operating costs of mail-order wholesalers to be relatively high.

Functional Middlemen

The term **functional middlemen** is applied to wholesaling intermediaries that do not acquire title to the goods they sell and seldom perform all of the wholesaling functions (figure 13.7). Most of these intermediaries engage solely in bringing buyer and seller together. Based on whether they provide continuous or noncontinuous representation for their principals, these middlemen are divided into two major classifications, agents and brokers. The major difference between brokers and agents is that brokers are used on a transaction basis rather than over a long continuous term. It has been estimated that there are over 50,000 agents alone, many employing numerous salespeople. The key operating features of the major types of functional middlemen are shown in figure 13.8.

MANUFACTURERS' AGENTS

Manufacturers' agents—sometimes called **manufacturers' representatives**—generally establish continuous contractual relationships with several noncompeting producers and handle the goods of these producers in certain designated territories. A producer often uses several manufacturers' agents, each selling only a portion of the producer's output. To maintain uniformity in its marketing policies, producers who use several agents retain pricing authority and control of their marketing efforts rather than relinquishing them to individual agents.

Manufacturers' agents are generally employed by small producers that have production skills but lack financial and marketing capabilities. Manufacturers' agents are compensated by sales commissions, which normally range from 6 to 7 percent of sales, depending on the nature of the product, competition, territory, and sales effort required.

SELLING AGENTS

Selling agents act as the marketing arms of producers and sell the producers' entire output. They are responsible not only for selling the goods but for a complete range of marketing activities, including pricing, credit arrangements, promotion, product planning, and marketing research. Selling agents, which usually represent several small noncompeting producers in a similar line, are able to offer their customers a wide assortment of goods in that line. Agents generally maintain long-term contracts with their principals.

Because they handle the entire output of a manufacturer, selling agents are free to sell the goods wherever markets are available and to negotiate the best price with customers. A significant difference between representation by a manufacturers' agent and by a selling agent is that a producer can use several manufacturers' agents but only one selling agent. Selling agents are compensated on a commission basis, with rates ranging between 2 and 10 percent of sales.

❑ **Figure 13.8**
Features of major
functional middlemen.

Features		Manufacturers' Agents and Food Brokers	Selling Agents	Brokers	Commission Merchants	Auction Companies
	Relationship with principal	Continuous	Continuous	Transaction	Transaction	Transaction
	Stocks and inventory	No	No	No	Yes	Yes
	Provide credit	No	Yes	No	Some	No
	Offers delivery	Some	No	No	Yes	No
	Represent seller or buyer	Seller	Seller	Seller or buyer	Seller	Seller
	Anticipate customer needs	Yes	Yes	Some	Yes	Some
	Variable selling expense	Yes	Yes	Yes	Yes	Yes

BROKERS

You probably know a local real estate broker, and you may know a stockbroker in your community, but you probably do not know any merchandise brokers. Although generally unknown to the public, merchandise brokers are numerous. Their primary activity is to negotiate a sale between buyers and sellers. **Brokers** do not take physical possession of the goods, have only limited pricing authority, and do not maintain continuous contractual relationships with their principals. Brokers may represent either buyers or sellers, but the vast majority represent sellers. Since brokers perform only a negotiating function, their operating expenses as a proportion of sales generally run only 3 to 4 percent.

FOOD BROKERS

A specialized form of broker that more closely resembles a manufacturers' agent than a traditional broker is the **food broker.** These wholesalers represent both large and small producers in the grocery industry on a continuous contractual basis. In 1980, a study by the Arthur D. Little consulting firm revealed that 50 percent of all processed foods were distributed by such brokers.[5] For their services, food brokers receive a commission ranging from 3 to 5 percent of wholesale, depending on the product and volume.

COMMISSION MERCHANTS

Commission merchants are used by their principals to sell specific lots of goods. They deal mainly in agricultural commodities that must be sent from small local markets to large central ones. Although they usually do not take title to goods, these merchants often take physical possession of them. Because they deal in large quantities, they are able to maintain operating expenses of about 5 percent of sales.

AUCTION COMPANIES

"Going once, going twice, going three times, sold," is the cry of the auctioneer. You are probably familiar with retail auctions at which household goods and antiques are sold. At the wholesale level, **auction companies** are an important method of selling tobacco, livestock, fur, and used cars. Auctions are particularly useful in the sale of goods that require physical inspection for an accurate evaluation of their qualities. The operating expenses of auctions generally average about 3 percent of sales.

INTERNATIONAL BROKERS AND AGENTS

As the world becomes a global village, with each country dependent on others for certain goods, exporting and importing become more important (see Chapter 21). Many types of functional middlemen handle foreign goods. Three of the most important are export and import brokers, export management companies, and manufacturers' export agents.

Export and Import Brokers.   **Export and import brokers** bring buyers and sellers together and may represent either party. These brokers sell single lots of goods and do not have a continuous relationship with their principals. Often, they specialize in a particular line of goods from a limited number of countries. Cotton, wool, sugar, coffee, and other bulky commodities are often sold through brokers, for example. Knowledge of foreign trading procedures and markets is an important advantage offered by this type of broker.

Export Management Companies.   **Export management companies (EMC)** are used by producers who want to market overseas but are too small to support their own international operations. By handling the goods of several noncompetitive producers of complementary products, an EMC can offer a complete line of goods in a specialized field. To accomplish its primary purpose—selling the goods of its principals in foreign markets—the EMC often selects the distribution channels, promotional activities, and credit arrangements for the goods. The EMC operates on a continuous contractual basis as the foreign marketing department of its principal. Some EMCs, such as the Marshall International Trading Company, which does business in 120 countries through eighteen worldwide offices, take title to goods they sell in addition to acting as functional middlemen.[6]

Manufacturer's Export Agent.   A **manufacturer's export agent (MEA)** provides a basic selling service for its principals and has only a short-term relationship with them. A principal would use only one EMC, but it would probably use several MEAs to obtain adequate representation in various foreign markets. In its relationship to principals, the MEA operates similarly to the manufacturer's agent, whereas the EMC is akin to the selling agent.

THE CASE CONTINUES

*B*y concentrating on a full line of grocery products, Super Valu has found a particular niche in grocery wholesaling and has developed a strong reputation as a full-service grocery wholesaler. The company traces its origin back to 1926 when Winston and Newell Company (which later became Super Valu), was formed from two major grocery wholesalers, B. S. Bull & Company, and Newell & Harrison Company. Although Super Valu could choose to develop a specialty wholesaling operation and supply fast-food chains and other dining establishments, its management has refused to enter this business. Another business that Super Valu has not pursued is cash-and-carry grocery wholesaling. With over sixty years of outstanding experience as a full-service grocery wholesaler, Super Valu wants to stick with this type of operation where it is an acknowledged leader.

Super Valu deals with a variety of other middlemen in its buying activities. Brokers provide the wholesaler with seasonal fruits and vegetables. Food brokers sell a variety of dry groceries, including some well-known national brands to Super Valu. Manufacturers' agents, selling agents, and producer-cooperatives are additional sources of supply for the giant wholesaler.

❑ **Figure 13.9**
Activities and channels
in integrated
wholesaling.

Chain-Store Warehouse		Manufacturers' Sales Branch	
Activity	Channel	Activity	Channel
Manufacturing ⇨	Manufacturer	Manufacturing ⇨	Manufacturer
Wholesaling ⇨	Chain-store warehouse	Wholesaling ⇨	Manufacturers' sales branch
Retailing ⇨	Retail unit in chain	Retailing ⇨	Business customers

Integrated Wholesaling Operations

General Electric and Sears operate wholesaling facilities, but they are not merchant wholesalers. General Electric is a manufacturer and Sears is a retailer. Both have integrated wholesaling activities into their primary operations in order to obtain distribution efficiencies and control in their channel systems (figure 13.9).

CHAIN-STORE WAREHOUSES

*B*y operating their own wholesaling facilities, retailers integrate backward in the channel system.

Perhaps you have driven on a freeway in a major city such as Atlanta, Boston, or Dallas and spotted a huge, one-story building with many loading docks. A sign on the building may have identified it as a Kmart, Safeway, Walgreen, Sears, or J. C. Penney operation. The building is probably a **chain-store warehouse** owned by a retailer and operated as a wholesaling facility. Because of the wide variety of goods that they purchase and the large number of stores that they operate, chain-store organizations can perform the sorting process as economically as merchant wholesalers. By operating their own wholesaling facilities, retailers integrate backward in the channel system—that is, they incorporate activities closer to the production end of the system.

MANUFACTURERS' SALES BRANCHES

A manufacturer establishes a sales branch by integrating forward in the channel system.

When you see an office building with the letters IBM on it or a warehouse with the name Goodyear, you are probably looking at a **manufacturer's sales branch,** a wholesaling unit operated by a manufacturer. A manufacturer establishes a sales branch by integrating forward—that is, toward the retailer—in the channel system. There are two types of manufacturers' sales branches—those with stock and those without stock. Most IBM branches consist of a sales office without stock. In contrast, the Goodyear units contain both sales offices and a stock of tires.

Manufacturers' sales branches without stock are important in industrial marketing and operate much like drop shippers. Those with stock operate in much the same way as specialty wholesalers. Manufacturers' sales branches are generally located in the major urban areas, where their salespersons can contact prospective customers with high buying potential. Because sales branches perform fewer functions than wholesalers and have larger order sizes, their operating expenses are generally lower.

Public Warehouses. Manufacturers who operate sales branches without stock sometimes use public warehouses as distribution centers. Goods are sent in truckload or carload lots to these warehouses and are shipped to customers in smaller quantities. A **public warehouse** is an independently owned storage facility that for a rental fee provides space and sometimes a variety of marketing services to businesses.

Walgreen chain-store warehouses are highly automated.

Source: Photo courtesy of Walgreen Company

Such warehouses sometimes specialize in a particular line of goods, such as grain, cotton, or frozen foods.

Cooperatives and Voluntary Groups

*C*ooperatives are owned and operated by their members. Voluntary groups are associations of independent organizations.

The members of a cooperative own and operate the business for their own benefit. Collective action is substituted for private endeavor. In the wholesaling industry, a prominent type of cooperative is the producer cooperative. Similar to cooperatives are voluntary groups such as retailer-cooperative voluntary groups and wholesaler-sponsored voluntary chains. These groups bind independents together so they can obtain operating economies.

PRODUCER COOPERATIVES

Producer cooperatives are important in the agricultural industry, where they market such well-known brands as Sunkist, Ocean Spray, and Land O'Lakes. Cooperatives, or co-ops, accumulate, grade, process, and distribute the goods produced by their farmer members and often sell farm supplies to their members, as well. Cooperatives market members' goods at the best prices obtainable and procure supplies for members by buying in bulk at low prices. Farmer co-ops market about 30 percent of all crops sold and handle nearly 27 percent of all supplies farmers buy.[7] Any profits generated in a cooperative are returned to the members in the form of patronage dividends. In a recent year, the giant Land O'Lakes co-op generated over $2 billion in sales.

VOLUNTARY GROUPS

Retailer-cooperative voluntary groups are formed when independent retailers bind together to establish a wholesaling facility that serves its retailer-members. Ace Hardware is such a group. These organizations have been developed by independent retailers as a means of surviving against the onslaught of chain-store competition. Wholesale-sponsored voluntary chains, such as IGA food stores, are similar to retailer-cooperative groups, but they are established by wholesalers. The wholesalers are motivated by a desire to preserve their customer base of independent retailers. Chapter 12 contained a more complete discussion of these organizations.

OTHER BUYER-SELLER CONTACTS

Sellers participate in trade shows and visit central markets to make contact with prospective buyers.

In order to make contact with prospective buyers, sellers often participate in trade shows and go to central markets. Because of the specialized nature of these events, the contacts they foster are often quite productive.

Trade Shows

At the beginning of the buying period for an industry, industry associations—such as the National Housewares Manufacturers Association and the Automotive Service Industry Association—frequently sponsor trade shows. In 1986, more than nine thousand trade shows with ten or more booths were held, and they generated expenditures of $10 billion for space rentals, exhibits, shipping, and other items. More than 37 million people attended one or more industrial trade shows during 1986. The major reasons that exhibitors enter trade shows is to introduce new products, make new sales contacts, take orders, train salespersons, find new dealers and distributors, and develop an image.[8] Compared with the cost of $229 for an average industrial sales call, the cost to reach prospects at a trade show is relatively low—only a little more than $100.[9]

Central Markets

A **central market** is a major marketplace for a line of goods, such as furniture or apparel. Central markets usually contain giant exhibit malls called merchandise marts where sellers can keep their products on permanent display. Wholesalers and retailers visiting a central market can compare the offerings from various suppliers and learn about new products and trends. The famous twenty-one-story Merchandise Mart in Chicago is the largest mart in the world—equivalent in size to over forty Kmarts!

WHOLESALING INTERMEDIARIES IN THE SERVICE INDUSTRIES

Although our discussion has focused on the wholesaling of tangible goods, such as appliances and food products, wholesaling functions are performed in the marketing of services, too. Some intermediaries that perform these functions are listed in figure 13.10. The activities of some of these intermediaries are examined in the following paragraphs.

❑ **Figure 13.10**
Examples of wholesaling intermediaries in the service industries.

Financial Intermediaries	Healthcare Intermediaries	Cultural Intermediaries	Social Service Intermediaries
• Investment banking companies • Wholesale banks • Correspondent banks • Factors • Reinsurers	• General hospitals (referrals) • Employers' medical benefit programs • Hospital-cooperative voluntary groups	• Marketers of instructional materials • Branch library systems • Major museums	• Salvation Army Red Shield Stores • United Funds

Financial Intermediaries

*I*nvestment banks, wholesale banks, correspondent banks, factors, and reinsurers are among the service businesses that perform wholesaling functions.

The job of financial wholesaling intermediaries is to efficiently allocate the funds of savers to investors. These intermediaries include investment banking companies, wholesale banks, correspondent banks, factors, and reinsurers.

Investment banking companies, such as Goldman Sachs, buy large stock or bond issues from companies seeking funds, divide the issues into smaller amounts, and sell the smaller issues either to individual investors or to brokerage houses, which resell them to their customers. The investment banker bears all the risks of possible fluctuations in the price of the security from the time it is issued by the corporation until the time it is sold by the banker. The banker performs another important marketing function by furnishing the issuer with information about the prospects of selling the issue.

Some banks are reducing their emphasis on consumer banking and engaging in wholesale banking, which involves dealing with corporate customers. The Bankers Trust New York sold its eighty branch banks, which had $900 million in deposits, and became a wholesale bank handling only corporate accounts. The four core businesses of wholesale banking consist of trust service, corporate finance, money and securities, and commercial banking.[10]

In a correspondent banking system, large correspondent banks act as wholesalers to smaller banks. The smaller banks carry deposits with the larger banks and receive various financial services from them. Smaller banks use this arrangement because they can purchase certain services from larger banks more economically than they can produce them. The services of correspondent banks include sharing portions of their loan portfolios with smaller banks, clearing smaller banks' checks, and providing useful banking information.

Another example of wholesaling in the finance field involves the sale, or factoring, of a company's accounts receivable to a financial institution. The buyer of the accounts maintains a credit department, which checks the accounts' creditworthiness. In the home mortgage field, the sale of outstanding mortgages to other institutions constitutes wholesaling. A bank may finance the mortgage on your home and then sell it at a discount to a government agency, such as the Government National Mortgage Association (Ginnie Mae), which deals in mortgage loans.

In the insurance industry, reinsurers supply a form of wholesaling services. Insurers assume a risk when they provide insurance coverage. Reinsurance is the shifting of a part of the risk from the original insurer to another one, called the reinsurer. That way, no single insurer bears the total loss brought on by a major disaster. In the reinsurance field, the sorting process begins with the selection of an acceptable risk, which is accumulated by one insurer and then allocated to reinsurers. Another wholesaling service in the insurance industry is provided by companies that sell insurance in bulk to banks and other corporate middlemen. For example, Old Republic, a Chicago insurer, offers title and mortgage protection insurance to banks and other corporate middlemen unable to underwrite their own insurance.[11]

Healthcare Intermediaries

*H*ospitals that refer patients to other hospitals are acting as wholesaling intermediaries.

The healthcare field provides several examples of wholesaling activities. When a general hospital refers a patient to a hospital that specializes in the treatment of the patient's illness, the general hospital is performing the role of a wholesaling intermediary. Under the medical benefit programs offered by most employers, physicians and employers are members of a hospital's distribution channel and patients are the final consumers of the hospital's services.

Because of overcapacity and rising operating expenses, hospitals are taking a variety of steps to contain their costs. One of these steps involves cooperative ventures. Ranging across the South from the Carolinas to Oklahoma is the Sun Alliance, a voluntary group of thirty large nonprofit hospitals that make joint purchases and share operating information. This operation resembles a retailer-cooperative voluntary group and was established to combat the competition of profit-making hospitals.[12]

Cultural Intermediaries

Your school may offer certain courses on videotapes prepared and marketed by other organizations, such as the Nebraska Educational Television Council for Higher Education. As a student who views the videotapes in class, you are the ultimate consumer of this creative service. The distribution of the material can be thought of as a wholesaling service.

*B*y operating branch units throughout a city, metropolitan libraries, with their central acquisition and processing operations, engage in wholesaling activities.

By operating branch units throughout a city, a metropolitan library engages in wholesaling activities. The central library selects new books and purchases them. Upon their delivery to the central library, the new books are allocated to the appropriate branches. Some libraries operate bookmobiles that provide moving branches for those unable to come to a library. This service involves the sorting process inherent in distribution systems.

Museums sometimes accumulate large collections of art from numerous sources and then allocate portions of the collections to other museums. Fine Art Acquisitions, Ltd., a private purveyor of art, owns three art galleries and also markets through independent galleries in several cities. The firm operates as both wholesaler and retailer by commissioning new works and then selling signed and numbered prints at about $500 each.[13]

Social Service Intermediaries

In order to help support its activities and to aid the less fortunate, the Salvation Army operates Red Shield stores throughout the country. Processing the donated clothing sold in these stores entails a wholesaling operation. When donated articles arrive at the Red Shield store in Anderson, Indiana, or any other store in Indiana, for example, they are sent to a warehouse in Indianapolis, where they are inspected, sorted, and priced. From Indianapolis the processed articles are allocated to Red Shield stores throughout the state. In many cities, the Salvation Army is a member of the United Fund organization, which serves as a fund raiser and fund distributor to various social service groups.

*A*lthough the United States has moved from an industrial to a service economy, the need for wholesaling activities continues.

As indicated in this section and throughout this chapter, the performance of wholesaling functions is necessary for the distribution of goods and services. Although the United States has moved from an industrial to a service economy, the need for wholesaling activities continues. In the service industries these activities are present, but they take a variety of forms and often go unrecognized as wholesaling operations.

 ## NEW DEVELOPMENTS IN WHOLESALING

In the 1800s and the early 1900s, wholesalers were important marketing intermediaries serving small manufacturers and retailers. During the 1920s, the growth of large retailing chains, such as Sears and Woolworth, and giant manufacturers, such as General Electric and Firestone, reduced the importance of wholesalers. The retailing chains constructed chain-store warehouses and the large manufacturers established sales branches to perform the wholesaling functions. In recent years,

*T*rends in wholesaling include an increase in the number of multi-unit wholesalers, shifts in the market shares of various product-line wholesalers, an emphasis on value-added services, increased use of catalog selling, and establishment of computerized reorder systems.

independent wholesalers have adopted numerous innovative approaches and have regained some of their former strength in the channel system. In the 1972–1982 period, wholesalers experienced a 228 percent sales increase, while manufacturers' sales branches posted a large, but more modest, 145 percent gain.[14] The sales of wholesale establishments are now growing at about the same rate as the sales of retail establishments.

A recent trend in wholesaling has been an increase in the number of multi-unit wholesalers—wholesalers that operate several establishments. This development has paralleled the growth of multi-unit retailers and manufacturers. For example, Bearings, Inc., of Cleveland—a wholesaler of bearings, lubricants, and power transmission equipment—operates 131 distribution centers in twenty-five states and Canada. A wholesaler of this size can achieve economies of scale in buying, transportation, order processing, and selling.

Although total wholesale sales have been increasing in recent years, the number of wholesale establishments has increased only modestly. The average establishment, however, has been growing in size. Numerous mergers have created larger establishments, while some small, inefficient wholesalers have failed. Some wholesalers have diversified by acquiring wholesaling firms in other merchandise lines. Wholesalers in the petroleum field have been particularly active in acquiring wholesaler operations in other areas.

Shifts in consumer tastes and the composition of the population have contributed greatly to changes in the wholesaling industry. Although the number of electrical goods wholesalers has been increasing, for example, the total sales of these wholesalers have been declining. Perhaps small wholesalers have survived in this area because they furnish a wide range of services to customers. A reduction in the number of small variety stores and rural general stores has resulted in a decline in the sales of wholesalers that handle piece goods (cloth fabrics), notions (miscellaneous small items), and apparel. Farm-product wholesalers and petroleum wholesalers have decreased in number, although the sales of each of these types of wholesalers have been increasing.

Customers of wholesalers have tended to concentrate their purchases with a single wholesaler and to develop a close working relationship with that firm. This tendency has contributed to a decrease in the number of wholesalers but an increase in the average size of wholesale establishments. Attempting to increase efficiency, McDonald's restaurants are experimenting with a policy of purchasing all of their supplies for a particular product from one wholesaler.

❑ **Figure 13.11**
Share of wholesale sales by product line for 1948 and 1982.

Product Line	1948 (% share)	1982 (% share)	Change (%)
Motor vehicles and automobile equipment	4.4	21.1	7.7%
Furniture and home furnishings	1.9	2.1	.2
Lumber and construction materials	4.3	3.3	(1.0)
Metals and minerals, except petroleum	9.3	6.6	(2.7)
Electrical goods	6.6	7.7	1.1
Machinery, equipment, and supplies	10.5	17.0	6.5
Piece goods, notions, and apparel	9.9	3.6	(6.3)
Groceries and related products	26.5	18.6	(7.9)
Farm products, raw materials	18.4	9.9	(8.5)
Petroleum and petroleum products	8.2	19.1	10.9
Totals	100.0%	100.0%	

The changing patterns in wholesaling between 1948 and 1982 can be illustrated by the shifts in market shares of various product-line wholesalers (figure 13.11). These wholesalers fall into three categories: share gainers, share maintainer, and share losers. Four important fields in which wholesalers gained market share are (1) motor vehicles and automobile equipment; (2) electrical goods; (3) machinery, equipment, and supplies; and (4) petroleum and petroleum products. The one which maintained market share was furniture and home furnishings. Wholesalers who lost market share were concentrated in: (1) lumber and construction materials; (2) metals and minerals; (3) piece goods, notions, and apparel; (4) groceries and related products; and (5) farm raw materials.[15]

In order to establish a niche in the market and maintain a continuous association with their customers, many wholesalers are emphasizing value-added services. In the relationship between manufacturers and industrial distributors, service has always been an important factor. Uncertain deliveries and seemingly unjustified price increases have caused purchasers of industrial goods to seek the help of distributors in lessening the effects of the authoritarian selling practices of certain original equipment manufacturers. These purchasers greatly value the loyalty of distributors and consider them part of their purchasing strategies.

Another development in wholesaling is the increased use of catalog selling. Some customers are willing to forego services in order to obtain lower prices and a greater variety of goods. Certain industrial distributors have developed successful mail-order businesses by offering high-quality goods that do not require the distributors to provide installation or technical assistance.

Progressive wholesalers are becoming essential links in vertical marketing systems by establishing with their customers computerized automatic reorder systems to reduce selling costs. In the retailing industry, the National Retail Merchants Association has established standards for electronic purchase orders (EPO) and electronic vendor invoices (EVI). The EPO/EVI system allows a retailer's computer to communicate directly with a vendor's computer, reducing manual entries and creating operating economies.

The wholesaling industry includes about seventy trade associations. Many of them are very active in conducting management development programs for their members. Through these programs, wholesalers are developing greater managerial expertise in promotion, accounting, credit management, and inventory control. At association meetings successful wholesalers share the strategies of their success with others, who can then adopt the strategies in their own organizations.

THE CASE CONTINUES

Super Valu has integrated backward into food processing through its Preferred Products, Inc., and has integrated forward into retailing with its Cub Food stores and several other ventures. Since buying the Cub warehouse organization in 1980, Super Valu has expanded to over twenty Cub stores with a goal of operating 100 stores by 1990. By supplying the Cub operation from a Super Valu distribution center, the center assumes the role of a chain-store warehouse.

Whenever Cub moves into a market, such as Minneapolis or Indianapolis, conventional supermarket chains scramble to remain competitive. In some cases, Super Valu's retail activity conflicts with its wholesale operation. In Minneapolis, an independent owner of four stores that are supplied by Super Valu declared that Cub decreased the market share of each of his stores by 10 to 15 percent, but he still refused to change suppliers.

Super Valu is engaged in wholesaling in the service field through its SUVACO insurance subsidiary, which is a reinsurer. The purpose of this operation is to provide stable, comprehensive insurance programs to grocery retailers and to overcome the periodic price and coverage instabilities that are faced by supermarket operators.

GOAL SUMMARY

1. **Define the terms *wholesaling* and *wholesaling transactions.*** Wholesaling includes all transactions in which a buyer purchases goods either for resale or for use in making other products. Although low prices, large quantities, and warehousing operations are often associated with wholesaling, the key attribute of a wholesaling transaction is the business or profit motive of the buyer.

2. **Explain how the broad, intermediate, and narrow concepts of wholesaling differ.** Wholesaling in the broad view encompasses all wholesale transactions made for business or profit reasons. The intermediate view includes only the wholesaling transactions that take place in wholesale establishments. The narrow view limits the scope of wholesaling to transactions performed by wholesalers.

3. **Identify the marketing functions that wholesalers perform for manufacturers.** Wholesalers act as an extended sales arm, introduce new products into the retail market rapidly and effectively, create buying efficiencies by purchasing in large quantities, reduce physical distribution costs through large-lot purchases, perceive the needs of ultimate consumers, reduce manufacturers' capital needs, perform the standardization and grading function, and reduce manufacturers' risks by taking title to goods.

4. **Identify the marketing functions that wholesalers perform for retailers.** Wholesalers accumulate a variety of goods from numerous manufacturers, understand the merchandising requirements of retailers, have on hand what is wanted in the quantities wanted at the time wanted, gather information about general market conditions, allow purchases to be made on credit, inspect and grade goods prior to sale, and reduce risks through the storage of goods and the use of product guarantees.

5. **Describe the various kinds of merchant wholesalers.** By lines of goods handled, merchant wholesalers are categorized as general merchandise, general-line, and specialty operators. By functions performed, merchant wholesalers are classified as service wholesalers and limited-function wholesalers.

6. **Distinguish between limited-function wholesalers and functional middlemen.** Limited-function wholesalers take title to goods but restrict their performance of marketing functions, moving them either backward to manufacturers or forward to retailers. Functional middlemen do not acquire title to the goods they sell and seldom perform even all of the wholesaling functions.

7. **Discuss the nature of integrated wholesaling.** Large retailers often operate chain-store warehouses that handle a variety of goods, service a large number of stores, and perform the sorting process as economically as a merchant wholesaler. This type of wholesaling is considered backward integration in a channel system. A manufacturer's sales branch operates like a wholesaler but is owned by a manufacturer. It represents forward integration in the channel system.

8. **Explain how cooperatives engage in wholesaling activities.** Producer cooperatives accumulate, grade, process, and distribute the goods of their members. Retailer-cooperative voluntary groups are formed by independent retailers that band together to establish their own wholesaling business. Wholesaler-sponsored voluntary chains are similar to the retailer co-ops but are established by wholesalers.

9. **Explain the usefulness of trade shows and central markets.** Trade shows and central markets bring buyers and sellers together. Exhibitors attend trade shows to introduce new products, make new sales contacts, take orders, train salespersons, find new dealers and distributors, and develop an image. Central markets are trade centers at which buyers and sellers converge.

10. **Explain how wholesaling is performed in the service industries.** Wholesaling in the service industries serves the same purpose as in other industries, even though it is sometimes harder to recognize. For example, investment banking companies buy large issues of stocks and bonds from a company, divide the issues into smaller amounts, and sell them either to individual investors or to brokerage houses, which in turn resell them. In the banking business, large correspondent banks act as wholesalers to smaller banks. In the insurance industry, reinsurance arrangements are a form of wholesaling. Large museums accumulate art or other displays from numerous sources and then allocate portions to other museums.

KEY TERMS

Wholesaling, **p. 353**
Wholesale Transaction, **p. 354**
Merchant Wholesaler, **p. 361**
General Merchandise Wholesaler, **p. 361**

General-Line Wholesaler, **p. 361**
General-Line Distributor, **p. 362**
Specialty Wholesaler, **p. 362**
Specialty Distributor, **p. 362**

KEY TERMS *(continued)*

Limited-Function Wholesaler, **p. 362**
Drop Shipper or Desk Jobber, **p. 362**
Truck Wholesaler or Wagon Distributor, **p. 363**
Cash-and-Carry Wholesaler, **p. 363**
Mail-Order Wholesaler, **p. 364**
Functional Middlemen, **p. 364**
Manufacturers' Agents or Manufacturers' Representatives, **p. 364**
Selling Agent, **p. 364**
Broker, **p. 365**
Food Broker, **p. 365**

Commission Merchant, **p. 365**
Auction Company, **p. 365**
Export and Import Broker, **p. 366**
Export Management Company (EMC), **p. 366**
Manufacturer's Export Agent (MEA), **p. 366**
Chain-Store Warehouse, **p. 367**
Manufacturer's Sales Branch, **p. 367**
Public Warehouse, **p. 367**
Producer Cooperative, **p. 368**
Central Market, **p. 369**

CHECK YOUR LEARNING

1. Which of the following factors most effectively distinguishes a wholesale transaction from a retail one? (a) prices, (b) quantities, (c) operating facilities, (d) motivation of the purchaser.
2. A farmer who buys a tire for a farm wagon is engaged in a wholesale transaction.   **T/F**
3. The wholesaling transaction that takes place when a farmer sells his sweet corn to a grocer reflects the following concept of wholesaling: (a) broad, (b) intermediate, (c) narrow, (d) none of the above.
4. The Robinson-Patman Act prohibits a wholesaler from charging different prices for goods of similar quantity and quality to a Safeway store and a Kroger store that are in direct competition.   **T/F**
5. In general, if a manufacturer cannot afford to obtain orders from certain prospective customers, then wholesaling intermediaries cannot afford to obtain orders from them either.   **T/F**
6. When an electronics distributor buys printed circuit boards from a manufacturer and then attaches connectors and switches before selling the upgraded product, the service rendered is called: (a) product development, (b) value added, (c) symbiotic marketing, (d) functional changes.
7. Most large food producers, such as General Mills and Kellogg's, do not use wholesalers because they have large sales forces that are able to contact all their customers on a regular basis.   **T/F**
8. Wholesaling intermediaries usually perform all the following functions for retailers except: (a) screen products for sales potential, (b) provide specialized storage facilities, (c) offer marketing research, (d) provide suggestions for promotions.

9. A type of wholesaler that carries many nonperishable lines, such as home furnishings, housewares, hardware, and apparel, is known as a: (a) general merchandise wholesaler, (b) general-line wholesaler, (c) specialty wholesaler, (d) retailing wholesaler.
10. Drop shippers combine the selling and transportation functions by employing driver-salespersons who contact retailers and other institutions.   **T/F**
11. A functional middleman that represents several noncompeting producers, acts as their marketing arm, and sells their entire output is known as a: (a) manufacturer's agent, (b) selling agent, (c) broker, (d) commission merchant.
12. Export management companies are used mainly by large manufacturers who want to market overseas but do not want to employ their own sales forces. **T/F**
13. An IBM sales office has many characteristics in common with a drop shipper.   **T/F**
14. A major motivation for the formation of wholesaler-sponsored voluntary chains is the preservation of a customer base of independent retailers.   **T/F**
15. A type of bank that acts as a wholesaler to smaller banks is known as a(n): (a) mutual savings bank, (b) wholesale bank, (c) investment bank, (d) correspondent bank.
16. Under the medical benefit programs of most employers, physicians and employers are members of a hospital's distribution channel and the patients are the final consumers of the hospital's services. **T/F**

QUESTIONS FOR REVIEW AND DISCUSSION

1. Define the key terms for this chapter that appear at the end of the goal summary.
2. Is the purchase of a typewriter for use in an attorney's office a retail or a wholesale transaction? Would your answer be the same for a purchase made by a college student? Explain.
3. When most individuals think of a wholesaling transaction, do they think of its taking place in the context of the narrow, intermediate, or broad view of wholesaling?
4. Are advertisements that state "You save because we buy direct and eliminate the wholesaler" likely to be correct?
5. Are the services that wholesalers provide to retailers more important than the ones they provide to manufacturers?
6. Would you expect the general merchandise, general-line, or specialty wholesaler to experience the greatest decrease in number in the future?
7. What are the differences between manufacturers' agents and selling agents?
8. Why does a food broker resemble a manufacturer's agent more closely than it resembles a merchandise broker?
9. Isn't it confusing and incorrect to classify chain-store warehouses and manufacturers' sales branches as wholesaling establishments? Explain.
10. If cooperatives can perform wholesaling activities efficiently, why don't we eliminate all profit-making wholesalers and use only cooperatives?
11. In addition to the ones in the text, provide some examples of wholesaling in the service industries.

NOTES

1. Theodore N. Beckman, William R. Davidson, and W. Wayne Talarzyk, *Marketing,* 9th ed. (New York: Ronald Press, 1973), p. 288.
2. "Computer-to-Computer Ordering Passes Test by Wholesale Grocers' Association," *Marketing News,* November 9, 1984, p. 38.
3. Margaret Price, "Distributors: No Endangered Species," *Industry Week,* January 24, 1983, p. 49.
4. Maury Bates, Jr., "From A (Abrasive) to W (Wrenches) and 165,000 Indispensible Items in Between," *Conoco 83,* no. 2, pp. 18–19.
5. Sandra Salmans, "Brokers, Middlemen of Food," *The New York Times,* April 23, 1982, D-1.
6. John D. Daniels, Ernest W. Ogram, Jr., and Lee H. Radebaugh, *International Business: Environments and Operations,* 3d ed. (Reading, Mass.: Addison-Wesley Publishing Co., 1982), p. 386.
7. "The Golden Years Are Gone for Farm Co-ops," *Business Week,* July 23, 1984, p. 159.
8. Thomas V. Bonoma, "Get More Out of Your Trade Shows," *Harvard Business Review,* January–February 1983, p. 76.
9. Information from the Trade Show Bureau, New Canaan, Conn.
10. "Wholesale Banking's New Hard Sell," *Business Week,* April 13, 1981, pp. 82–83.
11. Jill Andresky, "Discipline Is All," *Forbes,* July 16, 1984, p. 50.
12. Abigail Trafford, "Hospitals: A Sick Industry," *U.S. News & World Report,* March 18, 1985, p. 40.
13. Jeffrey A. Trachtenber, "The Imagemakers," *Forbes,* December 31, 1984, p. 101.
14. Price, "Distributors"; and U.S. Bureau of the Census, Statistical Abstract of the United States: 1987 (107th edition), Washington, D.C., 1986, p. 764.
15. Ronald A. Michman, Stanley D. Sibley, and Lynn Harris, "Wholesaling: A Neglected Area," in *Marketing: The Next Decade,* ed. David M. Klein and Allen E. Smith (Boca Raton, Fla.: Southern Marketing Association, 1985), p. 168.

A "big Makro" refers to a huge stock of goods in a giant warehouse rather than a plump hamburger in a sesame seed bun. Makro self-service wholesale centers of nearly 200,000 square feet are doing business in Washington, D.C., Philadelphia, Atlanta, and Cincinnati; and more are planned for major metropolitan areas that contain over one million residents. The Makro Self-Service Wholesale Corp. is a subsidiary of a Netherlands-based company that operates about forty other large wholesale centers in Europe, Africa, and South America. In Europe, where there are no small wholesalers, the concept of huge, self-service centers has been very successful.

Makro centers supply their customer base of retailers, small businesses, and professional groups with more than forty-five major categories of products. Before establishing an operation in the United States, Makro's research department conducted, over a period of eleven years, extensive marketing surveys.

The general public is not admitted to a Makro center, and customers must show a business license or professional credentials to obtain a free Makro "passport" that permits them to shop in a center. Passports are only issued to individuals who plan to resell the goods or use them in the operation of a business or other organization. In each center's trading area, there are at least 35,000 to 40,000 "passports" outstanding. This represents about three percent of the eligible market. Makro basically views itself as a secondary supplier to small businesses.

A Makro center is unique because of its mammoth size and its offering of both food and nonfood items. Each center stocks nearly 10,000 food items and about 25,000 nonfood items. Some suppliers were initially hesitant about selling to Makro, but the wholesaler ultimately was able to attract most national suppliers.

A major feature of a Makro center is a repacking facility that provides smaller quantities of goods at nearly the same unit price that other wholesalers offer for larger quantities. Makro establishes the item count per pack to fit the needs of the majority of its customers. For example, if most customers want to buy six jars of mustard rather than eight, then the count is adjusted.

Because of its self-service, self-delivery, and cash-sales policies, the operating costs and personnel requirements at Makro are minimized. A typical center employs only 225 workers who keep the center open six days a week for at least seventy hours.

The major customer groups for Makro are in the food service industry, which includes grocery stores, restaurants, caterers, convenience stores, associations, and clubs. A second important market are the general merchandisers, fashion retailers, specialty retailers, and other small independents. This group patronizes Makro for additional supplies rather than for its major lines. For example, a shoe retailer may use Makro to fill out its line and as a supplier of all of its cleaning materials, stationery, and other paper goods.

Although each center has an ultimate sales goal of $100 million, the first-year objective is a more modest $60 million. In order to attain this, a center requires at least 25,000 active customers—those who shop at the warehouse more than once a year. To provide information to its customers about stock additions and special savings, the wholesaler issues semimonthly circulars.

Issues for Discussion

1. How does a Makro center differ from other cash-and-carry wholesalers?
2. Why would some suppliers hesitate to sell to a Makro center?
3. Will the large Makro-type centers eventually displace the smaller cash-and-carry wholesalers?
4. Would there be any advantages for a full-service wholesaler to operate on the same large scale and to carry a similar mix of food and nonfood items as Makro?

Sources: Adapted from "Dutch Firm Expands No-Frills Idea to U.S. Self-Service Wholesale Centers," *Marketing News,* October 2, 1981, p. 1; Jo-Ann Zbytniewski, "The Big Makro Attack, Self-Service Wholesaler Offers Acres of Items," *Progressive Grocer,* November 1981, pp. 73–78; and "Makro Scores with Campaign Aimed at Small Businesses in Urban Areas," *Marketing News,* April 15, 1983, p. 11.

OUTLINE

CHAPTER

14

Retailing

LEARNING GOALS_____

After reading this chapter, you should be able to:

1. Discuss the importance of retailing in our economy.
2. Explain how new forms of retailing develop.
3. Relate how retailers develop their management strategies.
4. Identify the different types of retailers.
5. Explore the trends in retailing.

Wal-Mart Stores, Inc., is one of the nation's fastest-growing chains of discount stores. In recent years, the chain has been experiencing compounded annual growth rates near 40 percent, while other large retailers have averaged 10 percent. Its 1987 sales reached nearly $15.9 billion and security analysts were predicting that by 1990 its sales might surpass Kmart, making it the number two general merchandise retailer in the country. How it became what it is, is a tribute to Sam M. Walton, an Arkansas retail executive, who carefully created and nurtured the enterprise. The discount chain is composed of nearly 1,150 units that operate mainly in small communities in the South and Midwest.

Sam Walton obtained his initial baptism in retailing as a management trainee in a J. C. Penney store. Then, in 1945 he bought and operated a franchised Ben Franklin variety store in Newport, Arkansas. Five years later he lost his lease and moved to Bentonville, Arkansas, where he started Walton's 5 and 10, which eventually grew to a chain of fourteen stores. In 1962, he opened his first Wal-Mart store. This was a large warehouse-type structure—similar to a Kmart—that handled a broad general merchandise selection ranging from windshield wipers to disposable diapers.

Although a Wal-Mart store looks much like any other discount establishment, its operating strategy has been carefully conceived and implemented by its management. Other than the vision and persuasive character of Sam Walton, the success of the discount chain has been credited to Walton's ability to exploit opportunities in the retail market. Noting that Kmart, Target, and other large discounters were locating in urban centers, Walton decided to build his stores in rural communities and offer to small-town consumers brand-name goods at discount prices. To maintain its small-town culture, all of the ten regional vice-presidents live near Wal-Mart headquarters in Bentonville and are flown by a company jet to their regions each Tuesday and returned each Thursday evening.

Although they are responsible for corporate policy, the firm's top management never loses touch with the operating units. Each company executive must spend at least one week a year working in a store, doing tasks such as stocking shelves and processing customer transactions. In addition, corporate executives frequently visit both their own and their competitor's stores in order to discuss the health and direction of the company with store personnel and to stay abreast of industry developments. These executives get involved in merchandise selection, too. Each year they can choose a favorite item and be its champion by making suggestions as to how to better display or promote it.

An important cost advantage that separates Wal-Mart from many of its competitors is its distribution system. The discounter orders in large quantities directly from suppliers and uses its own highly automated warehouses and fleet of delivery trucks. Store managers phone their orders into a central computer each week; the goods are shipped from suppliers to one of seven warehouses; the goods are then sorted and sent onto the stores in Wal-Mart trucks. This centralized distribution helps the discounter to control its shipping and inventory costs.

To encourage good employee relations, all of the nearly 185,000 part-time and full-time employees of Wal-Mart are called associates and participate in a stock-purchase plan and a profit-sharing arrangement. At its Saturday morning meetings of top and middle managers, store clerks who have developed unusual displays resulting in increased sales may be cited for their outstanding contributions. Mr. Walton credits his two-year stint at J. C. Penney as making him aware of the importance of employee participation in a business.

Issues for Discussion
1. Could the Wal-Mart discount stores be considered a modern version of the older rural general stores?
2. Could Wal-Mart have been more successful and expanded more rapidly by becoming a franchisor and then franchising stores nationwide?
3. What type of shopping center would be the best kind for Wal-Mart to locate in? What would be the advantages and disadvantages to Wal-Mart of locating in a center?

Sources: Adapted from a personal conversation, Wal-Mart, April 1988; Lorraine Chichowski, "Small-Town Roots Make Wal-Mart Big," *USA Today,* March 8, 1985, pp. 1B–2; "Small-Town Hit," *Time,* May 23, 1983, p. 43; and Lynda Schuster, "Wal-Mart Chief's Enthusiastic Approach Infects Employees; Keeps Retailer Growing," *The Wall Street Journal,* April 20, 1981, p. 19.

■ Wal-Mart sells for less.

Sam Walton obviously has a truly outstanding knowledge of retailing. This giant industry includes nearly 2 million stores and employs about 15 million workers. While you have nearly daily contact with one or another aspect of the industry, how well do you understand how retailing works? In this chapter, we examine the nature of retailing and summarize several theories of retail development. We explain how different kinds of retailers evolved and describe retail management strategies, including the components of the retail marketing mix. Retailers can be classified in several ways, and the chapter describes these classifications in detail. We also look at the types of locations available to retailers and why certain locations are preferred over others. We conclude with a review of trends in retailing today. ■

NATURE OF RETAILING

You may think of Macy's in New York as a giant department store that sponsors a Thanksgiving parade, Nieman Marcus in Dallas as an elegant purveyor of fashionable apparel, and L. L. Bean in Freeport, Maine, as the largest catalog seller of sporting goods in the world. In all cases you are right, but behind these organizations' highly visible exteriors lie very carefully conceived merchandising strategies that draw customers to their establishments. Whether a retailer is large or small, it depends on the continuing patronage of loyal customers to generate sales and earnings. Only by serving the needs of customers with the appropriate goods and services can retailers, such as Macy's, Nieman Marcus, and L. L. Bean, survive and grow. Retailers serve producers, too, by linking them with ultimate consumers.

Retailing includes all activities that involve selling to the ultimate consumer. Most retail sales are made by retailers in retail establishments. Manufacturers, wholesalers, farmers, and government agencies also sometimes sell to the ultimate consumer, however, and retail sales are made through telephones, vending machines, and computers, too. A **retailer** is a marketing intermediary who takes title to the goods and who sells primarily to ultimate consumers. Sears, Tiffany's, the Avon lady, and the Good Humor man qualify as retailers. A **retail establishment** is a separate place of business from which sales are made mainly to ultimate consumers. Many retailers operate retail establishments, but retail facilities may be run by nonretailers, too. An Army post exchange and a farmer's market are examples of retail establishments that are not operated by retailers.

The terms *retailing*, *retail establishment*, and *retailer* may be differentiated by the number of retail transactions they cover. *Retailing*, the most inclusive term, covers all sales made to the ultimate consumer. Next is *retail establishment*, which includes all of the different types of establishments that sell to the consumer, whether or not these establishments are run by retailers. Finally, the most narrow term, *retailer*, refers to the marketing intermediary who makes the sale to the consumer.

Retailing is important in several ways. One is its size. With nearly 2 million stores—one store for every 121 persons—the United States is truly a nation of shopkeepers. The 18 million U.S. retail workers represent nearly 15 percent of the nation's work force. The sales of all retail establishments amounted to about $1.5 trillion in 1986, which accounted for over 34 percent of the gross national product.[1] (See figure 14.1.) By providing us with everything from refrigerators to oil paintings, retailers improve our standard of living.

*R*etailers serve consumers by offering appropriate goods and services, and they serve producers by linking them with ultimate consumers.

*R*etailing is important because of its size, because of the utilities it provides, and because it gives many people the opportunity to develop management skills.

❑ **Figure 14.1** U.S. retail sales as a percentage of the gross national product (billions of dollars).

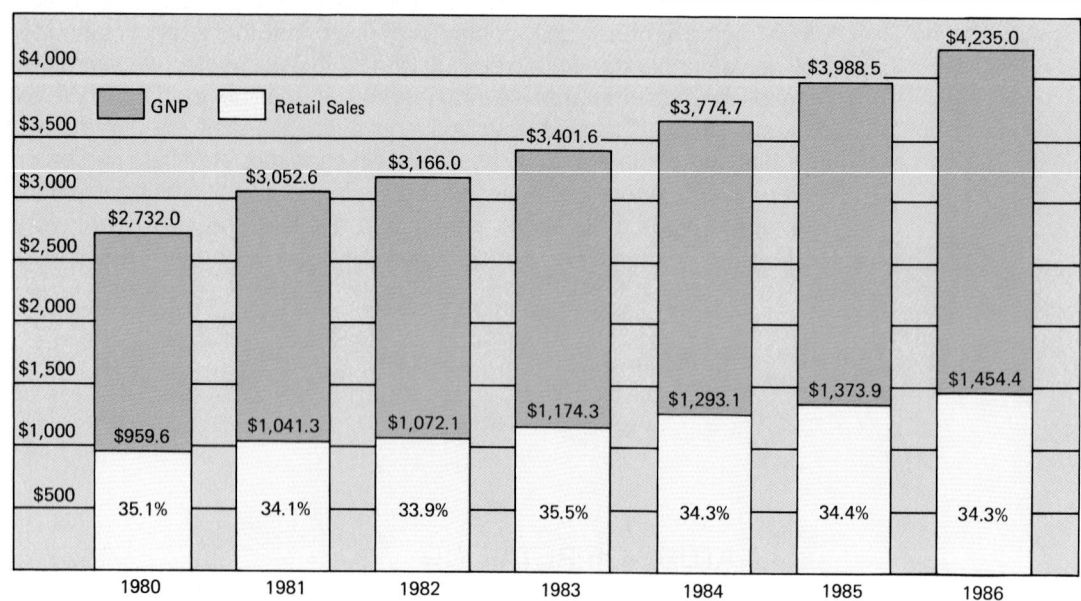

Source: U.S. Bureau of the Census, *Statistical Abstract of the United States: 1988* (108th edition). Washington, D.C., pp. 410, 737.

Retailing furnishes place, time, information, and possession utilities or satisfactions. When your family's twenty-year-old refrigerator finally dies on a 90° July day, you immediately begin searching for an adequate replacement. By having on hand a variety of models at the time you need them, appliance retailers provide place and time utilities. A store's advertisements and salespersons supply information utility. You obtain possession utility by making the proper credit arrangements and purchasing the good.

Retailing gives many individuals the opportunity to develop their managerial skills. Nearly 20 percent of all retail employees have some type of supervisory assignments. Some of these individuals will eventually establish their own retail businesses. Most retail establishments are independent businesses, and the smallest of them, which are frequently family owned, are often referred to as Mom and Pop operations. Because the financial, training, and government requirements are minimal, retailing is an easy field to enter. Unfortunately, according to Dun & Bradstreet statistics, it is also an easy field in which to fail. Failures in the retail industry represent about 20 percent of all commercial and industrial bankruptcies in the United States.[2]

 DEVELOPMENT OF RETAILING

*T*he wheel-of-retailing, dialectic, and general-specific-general theories help to explain the development of retailing institutions.

In response to a changing environment, new forms of retailers periodically appear on the business scene. As shown in figure 14.2, supermarkets developed in the 1930s, discount stores in the 1950s, and furniture warehouse showrooms in the late 1960s. The wheel-of-retailing, dialectic, and general-specific-general theories have been proposed to explain the development of retailing institutions. The retailing life cycle provides additional insights into the various phases in the development of retail establishments.

□ **Figure 14.2**
Development of
several retail
institutions.

Source: Bert C. McCammon, Jr.,
"The Future of Catalog
Showrooms: Growth and Its
Challenges to Management"
(Marketing Science Institute
working paper, 1973), p. 3.

Retail Institutions		Date of Innovation	Maturity	Approximate Number of Years to Reach Maturity
	Department stores	Mid 1860s	Mid 1960s	100 years
	Variety stores	Early 1900s	Early 1960s	60 years
	Supermarkets	Mid 1930s	Mid 1960s	30 years
	Discount department stores	Mid 1950s	Mid 1970s	20 years
	Fast-food service outlets	Early 1960s	Mid 1970s	15 years
	Home improvement centers	Mid 1960s	Late 1970s	15 years
	Furniture warehouse showrooms	Late 1960s	Late 1970s	10 years
	Catalog showrooms	Late 1960s	Late 1970s	10 years

Wheel-of-Retailing Hypothesis

According to the **wheel-of-retailing hypothesis,** new types of retailers emerge as low-price, limited-service, low-margin, and low-status operators in inexpensive facilities. Their customers are price-conscious individuals in lower income groups. Over time, these retailers improve their status by offering higher-priced goods, more attractive decor, and more services—all of which require higher margins. This turn of the wheel attracts middle- and higher-income patrons. (See figure 14.3.)

The wheel effect can be seen in the evolution of department stores, which began as plain, bargain-priced establishments. The forerunner of the fashionable Macy's department store was aptly named the Haverhill Cheap Store. The development of supermarkets, discount stores, and many other retailing types also conforms to the wheel hypothesis. Perhaps the trading-up by retailers over time simply reflects their understanding of the market and their ability to adapt to it. As the mass market grows more affluent and demands better goods, low-priced merchants upgrade their stocks, stores, and status. As a result, nonprice competition replaces price competition. This creates a void in the low-price end of the market, which is eventually filled by new low-price, low-margin competitors.

□ **Figure 14.3**
Wheel-of-retailing
hypothesis.

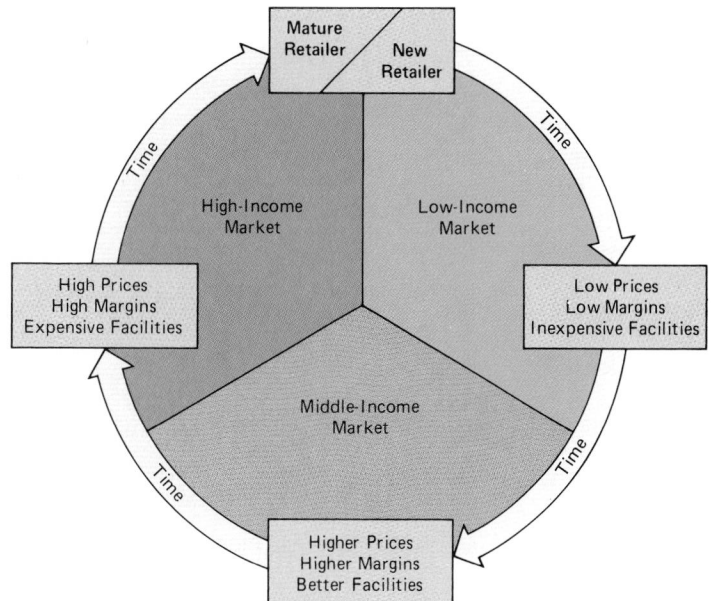

Source: James R. Lowry, *Retail Management* (Cincinnati: South-Western Publishing Co., 1983), p. 14.

REAL PEOPLE IN MARKETING

The Right Guy

*I*f one word were used to describe Guy Kumagai, a Kinney Shoe store Manager-Trainer and Hawaiian Market Manager in Hilo, Hawaii, the word would be "involved."

He came to Kinney thirteen years ago as a part-timer during summer vacation from high school. "It was either find a job, or go pick pineapples." He went full-time after graduation and in 1978 checked into his first store as manager of the old Hawaii Kai store, now closed. He met and married his wife Cora Sue while both were part-timers; she works as a legal secretary and is the mother of their two daughters.

Guy managed the Kauai store for two years before coming to his present store, Kaiko'o Mall, Hilo, on the big island of Hawaii. It is the largest-volume store in the Hawaiian market and has been the training ground for practically every Kinney store manager in the state.

Guy was named Manager-Trainer in 1982. One of his trainees is managing the Kauai store and another was named "Assistant Manager of the Year" for the entire Pacific Division earlier this year. To be a good trainer you have to be a good manager. Fourteen no-deficiency audits (the last ten in a row) and four Inventory Achievement Awards (1981–1984), plus a variety of league sales trophies hanging on Guy's wall attest to his success.

In November 1983 he was named market manager (area supervisor) of the ten Hawaiian Kinney stores, the only such position in the Kinney Shoe Division. This was done to give the division—which also includes the San Diego area—a closer supervision of its two main markets, separated as they are by 2,500 miles of the Pacific Ocean.

"My duties are mainly personnel and merchandise," says Guy. "I act as a link between the Hawaiian stores and the mainland office." He adds, "I think it gives these manag-ers a closer involvement with the Kinney company by having a supervisor with them at all times." Guy visits about four stores a month under normal circumstances, "but if I can get in more visits, I'll do it. We keep in close touch because the mainland needs to be aware of our unique merchandising needs. Departments 23 and 4, we need them all year round, and there are local items that get hot, like that patent wedge thong last Christmas, if we can jump on them. That shoe was the number one seller in the division for six weeks."

Yes, Guy has been a successful Kinney Manager, and by his own admission, it was "wake up, go to work, come home, wake up, go to work, come home, wake up, go to work, Kinney, Kinney, Kinney. At one point, my personality was really boring. I knew I had to get involved in more things. But it all would have to tie in."

Developing people for his market is an important involvement for Guy, and he is always sending out lines to attract the right kind of potential Kinney associate. "Take DECA (Distributive Education Club of America)," he says. "I am as active as possible in trying to make a worker out of a distributive education student." He holds talks with high school students and invites DECA advisors to come to his store. The local community college will have a group tour of his store now and then to see how Kinney runs. "It's fun because you watch kids start to understand what retailing is all about. The ones with drive will ask questions, and those are the ones we want."

Source: "Personality Plus . . . Guy Kumagai," *Kinney World,* April 1985, p. 20. Reprinted by permission.

■ Good managers make good trainers at Kinney.

Dialectic Hypothesis

The **dialectic hypothesis** of retail development adapts the belief of the German philosopher G. W. Hegel (1770–1831) that existing institutions are continually challenged by new and opposite kinds of institutions. He reasoned that an existing thesis (stated proposition) is always confronted by an antithesis (its opposite proposition). This interaction produces a synthesis, which has characteristics of both the established thesis and the contrasting antithesis. Later, after the synthesis has become established, it is challenged by a new antithesis. The development of the retailing industry shows the relevance of the dialectic hypothesis to the establishment of new modes of retailing.

Because of the large number of retailers and their need to be responsive to consumers, competition in the retailing industry is intense. Changes in the industry are often responses to competitive challenges, and the dialectic approach considers the effects of these challenges. For example, the catalog discount showroom can be thought of as a synthesis resulting from a thesis—the conventional mail-order house—and an antithesis—the discount store.

General-Specific-General Hypothesis

The **general-specific-general hypothesis** postulates that retailing has tended to move from general merchandise assortments to specific or limited lines, and then back to general merchandise lines. A look at the history of retailing reveals that as a town grew, general stores were superseded by limited-line stores, which in turn were followed by department stores. This theory also recognizes that the size of the community is a key determinant of the types of retailers that locate there. As a community expands, specialized stores offering deep assortments replace general stores with their broad but shallow selections. When the community attains the status of a major metropolitan area, it can support department stores, which provide both depth and breadth in many merchandise lines.

Although none of these three hypotheses completely explains the development of all forms of retailing, the hypotheses do provide insights into why new forms of retailing emerge. These insights can help retailers that wish to undertake an innovative retailing strategy to determine whether their innovations will succeed. Because the hypotheses have a historical context, they allow retailers to make managerial judgments based on past patterns.

Retailing Life Cycle

*E*ach of the four stages of the retailing life cycle—innovation, accelerated development, maturity, and decline—requires its own type of marketing strategy.

As mentioned, the retailing life cycle, which for retail institutions is somewhat akin to the product life cycle, offers further insights into the development of retailing businesses—insights that help retailers develop an appropriate marketing strategy. The **retailing life cycle** includes four stages—innovation, accelerated development, maturity, and decline. In the innovation stage, few competitors exist, sales grow very rapidly, and profits are modest. During the period of accelerated development, competitors arise, sales continue to grow, and profits are high. At the maturity stage, many direct and some indirect competitors appear, sales growth slows, and profits moderate. At the point of decline, the number of direct competitors decreases and the number of indirect ones increases, sales growth halts, and profits almost disappear. A retailer that in the 1970s reached the decline stage is the closed-door discount store, which required its patrons to purchase a membership card and be associated with the government. Department stores took a century to attain maturity, as figure

❑ **Figure 14.4**
Stages in the retail life
cycle.

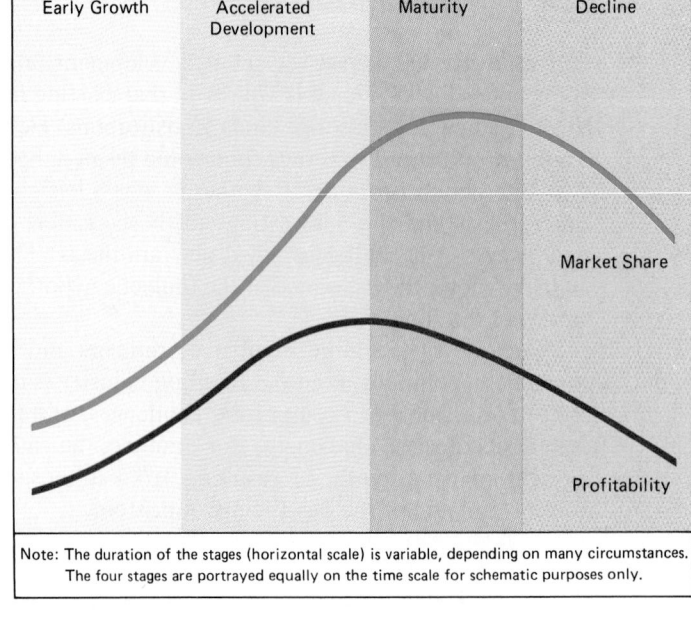

14.2 indicated, whereas furniture warehouse showrooms reached this stage in only a decade.

By carefully analyzing their retailing operations, merchants can determine the life-cycle stage that fits their organization. Knowledge of the apppropriate actions to take at each stage allows management to make decisions that will enhance sales and profitability. As shown in figure 14.4, the profitability of a retail institution peaks at the end of the accelerated development stage, and market share peaks during the maturity phase. Retailers that see their institution in the decline stage should take steps to either phase out the business or reposition it in the marketplace. For example, the S. S. Kresge variety store chain remained a viable organization until the 1950s, when discount stores began making inroads into its traditional markets. By 1960, the Kresge organization had recognized that variety stores were in the decline stage while discount stores were in the accelerated development phase. As a result, Kresge's management decided to switch its retailing emphasis from variety stores to discount stores—even changing the corporate name to Kmart Corporation. With over 3,700 stores, Kmart has surged past J. C. Penney to become the nation's second-largest retailer.

 RETAIL MANAGEMENT STRATEGIES

Many small retailers are more product driven than market driven. They expect consumers to purchase whatever goods they offer for sale. These retailers seldom conduct marketing research studies to determine consumer needs. Not too many years ago, large retailers, such as Macy's and the May Company, attempted to satisfy the needs of all consumers by offering a grab bag of goods ranging from budget-basement items to high-priced apparel. Today, enlightened retailers perform extensive consumer surveys to learn about their customers' tastes and wants. As a result of this research, retailers can identify specific target markets. Macy's for example, which now focuses on a stylish, upper-middle-income customer, has been transformed from a "grim warehouse" to "New York's ultimate loft."[3]

Successful retailers establish marketing strategies that position them as primary suppliers to a target market.

If a store does not satisfy the needs of a particular market segment, it will not survive. Successful retailers establish marketing strategies that position them as primary suppliers to a target market. This position involves providing consumers with emotional or psychological reasons to buy, in addition to rational ones. In developing their marketing strategies, retailers employ the appropriate marketing mix and emphasize the attributes that will create the desired store image and operating efficiencies.

Store Image

Consumers patronize stores in which they feel comfortable and in which they find goods that support their self-images.

When a consumer warmly refers to a particular retail establishment as "my store," that establishment has probably nurtured an appealing image. A **store image** is a set of attitudes that consumers hold as a result of their evaluations of the store attributes that they consider important.[4] Consumers patronize the stores in which they feel most comfortable and in which they find goods that support their desired self-images. It is doubtful whether the wealthy patrons of chic Nieman Marcus are also customers of the self-service Kmart stores. Store image studies tell retailers whether their merchandising efforts are reaching the proper target markets. This information permits a retailer to either accept and strengthen the image or to alter it to a more favorable one.

Each type of retailer has a bundle of attributes that creates its image. The image of an elegant women's apparel store results from one set of attributes, and the image of a food supermarket results from quite another. Research on store image reveals that, for many retailers, nine elements typically interact to produce an image.[5] These include the following:

1. *Merchandise*—quality, selection or assortment, styling or fashion, guarantees, and pricing.
2. *Service*—salesclerk service, self-service, ease of merchandise return, delivery service, and credit policies.
3. *Convenience*—general convenience, locational convenience, and parking.

Source: Drawing by Charles Addams; © 1986 The New Yorker Magazine, Inc.

4. *Promotion*—sales promotions, advertising, displays, symbols, and colors.
5. *Clientele*—social-class appeal, self-image congruency, and store personnel.
6. *Physical facilities*—store layout, architecture, aisle placement, elevators, lighting, and uniformity of operation in a multi-unit organization.
7. *Store atmosphere*—atmosphere and congeniality, customers' feeling of warmth, acceptance, and ease.
8. *Institutional factors*—conservative or modern projection of the store and the attributes of reputation and reliability.
9. *Post-transaction satisfaction*—merchandise in use, returns, adjustments, and overall consumer satisfaction with the purchase and the store.

To properly assess their store images, retailers must know their customers' characteristics as well as their stores' qualities. This is because the income, age, sex, lifestyle, and attitudes of customers affect their perceptions of retailers.

Patronage Motives

By reviewing the relationship between types of stores and types of goods, retailers can gain insights into useful marketing strategies. In Chapter 8 we discussed the three types of consumer goods: convenience, shopping, and specialty. We can use these categories to identify specific types of retailers, too. We do this by classifying retailers according to patronage motives. **Patronage motives** are factors that consumers perceive to be controlled by the retailer and that cause consumers to purchase at a particular retail establishment.[6] They are the same factors that contribute to the development of a store image.

A **convenience store** is accessible to the consumer and offers frequently purchased goods, abundant parking, and rapid checkout. A **shopping store** is patronized by consumers conducting a search to compare the offerings of several stores. Because they handle an extensive selection of goods, these stores often generate traffic from a wide geographic area. A **specialty store** is the preferred store of a loyal customer group willing to travel great distances to patronize it.

By cross-classifying the types of stores with the types of goods, we can identify nine types of consumers, as shown in figure 14.5. Most likely, only three or four consumer groupings contain many potential purchasers of a particular product from a particular type of store. Through careful study, each retailer can determine the segments that represent its largest potential groups of customers and can develop the appropriate market strategies to appeal to these segments.

❏ **Figure 14.5**
Consumer characteristics related to types of stores and types of goods.

Source: Reprinted from *Journal of Marketing,* January 1963, pp. 53–54, published by the American Marketing Association. Louis Bucklin, "Retail Strategy and the Classification of Consumer Goods."

		Type of Good		
		Convenience	**Shopping**	**Specialty**
Type of Store	Convenience	Prefers to buy the most readily available brand at the most accessible store	Compares brands and chooses one from the selection available at the most accessible store	Buys a favorite brand from the most accessible store that carries it
	Shopping	Indifferent to the brand, but shops different stores to obtain the best service and/or prices	Compares both store services and features of the different brands	Has a strong preference for a brand, but shops different stores to obtain the best service and/or prices
	Specialty	Prefers to shop at a specific store but is indifferent to the brand to be purchased	Prefers to shop at a specific store, but compares brands and chooses one from the selection available	Has a strong preference for a specific store and a specific brand

*T*ypes of goods, stores, and customers can be cross-classified to provide knowledge about who is likely to shop where for what goods.

The usefulness of figure 14.5 in developing marketing strategy can be illustrated with reference to the market for black-and-white television receivers. When these sets were introduced in the early 1950s, most consumers were uncertain of their quality. This uncertainty caused them to select a well-known brand from a store that offered outstanding service and warranty protection. These consumers fit into the specialty store–specialty good group. In the late 1950s, as the popularity of television grew, more brands became available; department stores, appliance stores, and furniture stores began stocking television receivers; and consumers began comparing the offerings of several stores before making a purchase. These consumers were in the shopping store–shopping goods group. As the prices of black-and-white television receivers dropped to $60 and $70 in the 1970s, many consumers began viewing them as convenience goods. This caused supermarkets and drugstores to begin handling the sets. Consumers who purchase the units from these stores fall into the convenience store–convenience good category.

Developing a Retail Marketing Mix

Retailers must tailor their marketing mix to meet their organizational objectives, which may include market dominance, fashion leadership, price leadership, and long-term growth. The planning process that leads to the proper retail marketing mix and strategy is diagrammed in figure 14.6. The marketing mix of Zayre's, a low-price

☐ **Figure 14.6**
Planning the retail marketing strategy.

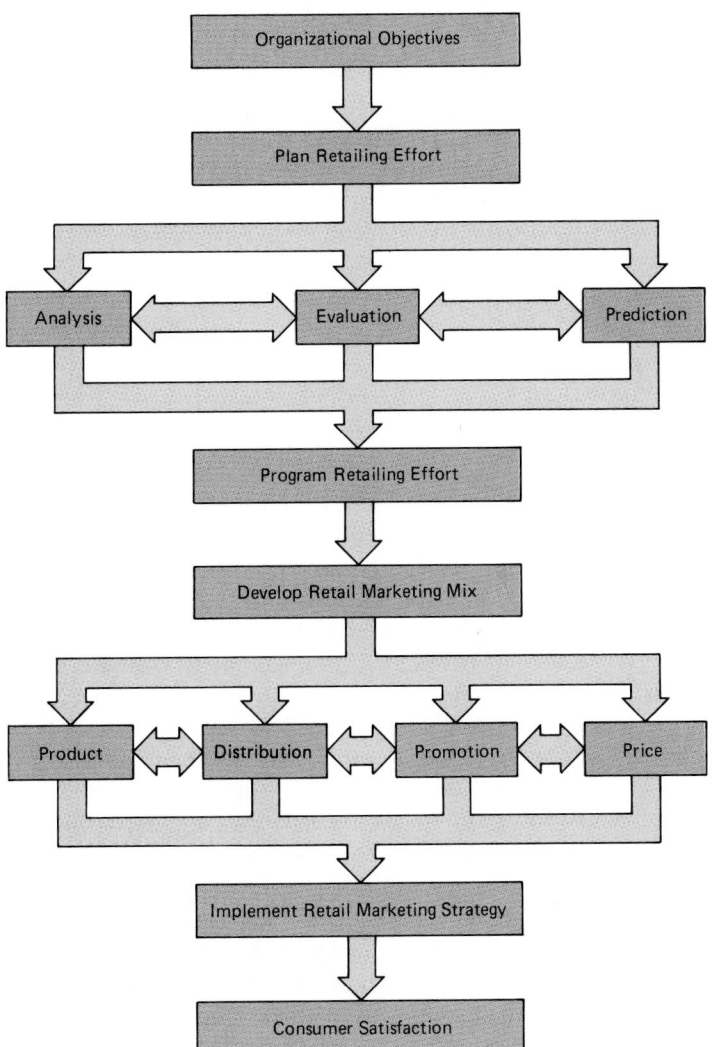

❑ **Figure 14.7** Breadth and depth of stock.

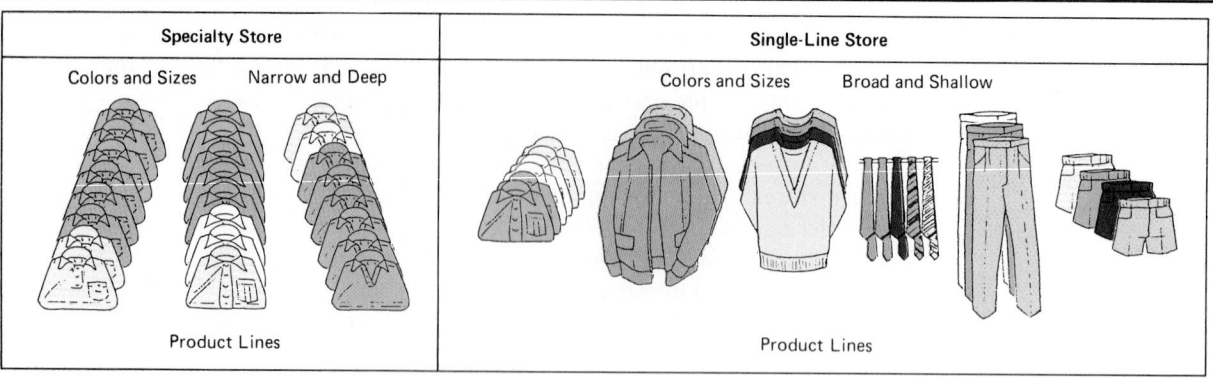

Specialty Store	Single-Line Store
Colors and Sizes Narrow and Deep	Colors and Sizes Broad and Shallow
Product Lines	Product Lines

mass merchandiser, differs greatly from that of New York's Bloomingdale's, which caters to affluent, trendy customers. Because of the intangible nature of their offerings, service retailers, such as travel agents and insurance agents, develop mixes that are different from those of retailers of tangible goods.

The four P's of marketing—product, price, promotion, and distribution (place)—are the major decision elements in a retailer's marketing mix, but each element is expressed somewhat differently than in a manufacturer's mix. In a retailer's marketing strategy, the four P's have the following meanings:

> *Product*—depth and breadth of merchandise assortments, including national brands and private brands.
> *Price*—level of prices and methods of pricing and credit arrangements.
> *Promotion*—types of advertising, in-store promotion, displays, and personal selling.
> *Distribution*—location and method of operation.

The four P's of marketing, though expressed somewhat differently in a retailer's marketing mix than in a manufacturer's mix, are still key components.

PRODUCT

Without the proper assortment and variety of goods and services to meet the requirements of its target market, a retailer will soon close its doors. Conversely, Horchow's, a specialty mail-order house, has a group of loyal customers who buy its expensive and stylish goods, even though it offers no elegant store or attentive salespeople.

A major consideration for a retailer is to determine the proper depth and breadth of offerings.

A major consideration for a retailer is to determine the proper depth and breadth of product offerings (figure 14.7). A specialty shop, such as a shirt shop, generally features great depth of stock in shirts but little breadth in complementary lines such as pants and jackets. In contrast, a single-line store that handles a related line of goods, such as a men's apparel store, usually provides a great breadth of merchandise—many different products, such as shirts, pants, shoes, and jackets—but limited depth in any one type.

The availability of goods is an important product consideration, too. Consumers want high-fashion goods, such as evening wear and dresses, when they are in vogue, and they want staple goods, such as penny loafers and white dress shirts, available all the time. To assure adequate selections, many retailers employ sophisticated, computerized inventory control systems.

In recent years, people in the United States have altered their buying patterns and have begun to purchase Japanese cars and cameras because of their high quality and overall value. In apparel, too, they are seeking outstanding values. Today's consumers are willing to pay more for a good, such as a Harris Tweed sportscoat or a Pendleton skirt, if it offers high quality and durability. Numerous merchants handling men's and women's apparel are benefiting from this trend by stocking higher-priced merchandise that provides fashion and durability.

DISTRIBUTION (PLACE)

A 100-percent location for a particular retailer is the best site based on the target customer, merchandise lines handled, competition, and traffic flows.

A **100-percent location** for a particular retailer is the best site based on the target customer, merchandise lines handled, competition, and traffic flows. For example, two of the major criteria for a Burger King location are that about 16,000 cars pass daily and that the trading area consist of nearly 7,000 households. Most retailers cannot obtain a 100-percent location, so they accept a less desirable site and compensate by focusing on lower prices, extensive advertising, or unique product offerings. Large chain retailers conduct elaborate computer and mathematical analyses to identify outstanding locations. Small retailers use license plate checks by relating a license number to a particular locality, traffic counts, sales-receipt analyses by obtaining a customer's address on the receipt, and consumer interviews in making decisions on location.

The proper store layout can contribute significantly to a retailer's success. Each area within a store has different characteristics and is suitable for different classes of goods. For example, the areas with the most desirable space characteristics are those that generate the most customer traffic and are usually near the entrances, elevators, and escalators. Department stores generally place high-margin impulse goods, such as fragrances and costume jewelry, in these areas. Fine furs, silverware, and other expensive specialty goods, which require special display and storage facilities, can be located in the more remote areas of the store.

*B*y blending the proper visual, aural, taste, and touch components, a retailer can create the desired store atmosphere.

A store's **atmospherics** contribute greatly to its image and to the kinds of customers it attracts. By carefully selecting and blending visual, aural, taste, and touch components, a retailer can create the desired store atmosphere.[7] When you enter a self-service, warehouselike store that uses drab metal shelving and has plain concrete floors, you probably associate the atmosphere with low price and low quality. On the other hand, when you view a tastefully decorated store with plush carpeting, custom display cases, and numerous well-dressed salespersons, you perceive an elegant retailer offering high-quality merchandise.

PROMOTION

*P*romotional objectives may include generating immediate sales, creating a favorable image, generating more traffic, and providing information about new goods or changes in the store.

Large retailers, such as Marshall Field's and Filene's, have extensive advertising departments. Their artists, copywriters, and production specialists prepare advertising for newspapers, radio, magazines, direct mail, and television. Small retailers often rely on the media's advertising department or advertising agencies to prepare their ads. When a retailer's promotional objective is to generate immediate sales, its advertising message must communicate its sales appeal clearly and forcefully. Other

A tasteful decor projects an elegant retailer.

promotional objectives include creating a favorable store image, generating more store traffic, providing information about new goods, and informing shoppers about changes in the store.

Through the use of attractive in-store displays, which often feature extravagant use of color and animation, retailers draw attention to their product lines. Supermarkets effectively use displays at the ends of their aisles to increase sales of a variety of impulse goods. By participating in highly visible community projects, retailers can generate a great amount of favorable publicity. Macy's receives excellent consumer response from the telecast of its annual Thanksgiving Day parade, for example. Other forms of retail promotion include samples, coupons, premiums, and trading stamps.

PRICE

A store's prices furnish a clue to the quality of its goods and to the number of services it provides.

A retailer's pricing strategies should reflect the expectations of its target market. Discount stores (Caldor and Wal-Mart) maintain low prices, general merchandisers (Sears and J. C. Penney) employ market-level pricing, and high-fashion retailers (Bonwit Teller and Nieman Marcus) charge high prices. A store's prices furnish a clue to the quality of its goods and the number of services it provides. Retailers that maintain high prices and have very few sales events are associated with high-quality merchandise and a wide range of services. Those with low prices and numerous sales promotions are identified with lower-quality goods and limited service.

To cover their operating costs and to realize a profit, retailers mark up their goods a specified amount above cost. Various product lines are associated with typical markups; for example, many items of furniture are marked up 100 percent. Certain market and competitive factors may prevent retailers from obtaining a desired markup. In these cases, they may resort to the use of a customary price, such as 30 or 35 cents for a candy bar, or the price "that the traffic will bear," which is the upper limit that consumers will pay. Although most retailers purport to charge everyone the same price, some retailers, such as automobile dealers, vary their prices by accepting trade-ins. Drugstores and supermarkets are among the retailers that employ a strategy of leader pricing. These retailers charge very low (leader) prices on high-demand goods, such as toothpaste and milk, to attract customers into their stores. They expect that once customers are in the store, they will make additional, unplanned purchases.

THE CASE CONTINUES

*S*am Walton is a key participant in the wheel-of-retailing effect. The Wal-Marts, Kmarts, and other discount stores have changed from the bargain barn type of operation to a more upgraded one. The stores are attracting a larger number of middle-income patrons than they did in the 1960s. The dialectic approach to retail development may help to explain the origins of the Wal-Mart organization. Sam Walton understood the variety store business (thesis) and he knew the advantages of self-service,

central checkouts, spartan decor, low prices, and operating style of a supermarket (antithesis). By blending together the two forms of operation, he created Wal-Mart (synthesis).

Sam Walton methodically developed a retail mix strategy that appealed to a target market of small-town consumers who had been previously ignored by other discount re-

tailers. To instill a consistent low-price image for Wal-Mart, Sam Walton attempts to keep his prices lower than competitors'. As part of his marketing strategy, he limits sales events to only thirteen annually—refusing to bombard consumers with sales on selected merchandise once or twice a week. In order to generate traffic and attract crowds, he uses a series of exciting promotional activities, such as Army paratroopers landing in a Wal-Mart parking lot and "Western Days."

□ **Figure 14.8** Classifications of retailers.

Merchandise Lines		Ownership and Control	Type of Operation	Retailer Concentrations
General merchandise retailers General stores Department stores Departmentized specialty stores Discount stores Catalog discount showrooms Hypermarches	Limited-line retailers Single-line stores Supermarkets Convenience food stores Furniture warehouses Building supply centers Specialty retailers Service establishments	Independents Chains Quasi-chains Wholesaler-sponsored voluntary chains Retailer-cooperative voluntary chains Franchise oganizations	Mail-order houses Direct sellers Automatic merchandisers Electronic shopping systems	Planned shopping centers Neighborhood centers Community centers Regional centers Specialty centers Central business districts Secondary shopping districts Neighborhood shopping districts String-street locations

TYPES OF RETAILERS

Several general classifications of retailers can be identified. These classes are based on merchandise lines, type of operation, type of concentration, and ownership and control (figure 14.8).

Merchandise Lines

*R*etailers may stock either general or limited lines of goods.

Depending on how a retailer perceives the needs of its market, it may stock either a general offering or a limited line of goods. In some instances, a retailer starts with a limited line and then expands it to satisfy the broad needs of many customers. In other instances, a retailer begins business by handling numerous general lines and then reduces its offerings, focusing on the needs of a particular market segment.

GENERAL MERCHANDISE RETAILERS

General merchandise retailers range in size from the small Northern Commercial general store in Fort Yukon, Alaska, to the massive Marshall Field department store in Chicago. They also include discount stores, catalog discount showrooms, and hypermarches.

General Stores.   In rural, sparsely populated areas, such as many areas in the western United States, general stores are the primary trading centers. These small nondepartmentalized operations stock staples, such as food, hardware, and apparel, that allow their patrons to maintain a satisfactory level of living between visits to an urban community. Better communications, improved transportation systems, and more demanding consumers have contributed to a decrease in the number of general stores.

*E*ach department within a department store is a profit center that seeks to closely control its inventories and selling expenses.

Department Stores.   The giant department stores offer consumers an array of stylish goods in a stimulating environment. During the Christmas season, the flagship stores of Macy's and Marshall Field generate over $1 million in sales daily.

A department store is a large departmentalized establishment that carries a wide variety of shopping and specialty goods, including apparel, cosmetics, home furnishings, and furniture. Each department within a store is a profit center that seeks to closely control its inventories and selling expenses.

Department stores developed after the Civil War as a result of a number of changes in U.S. society, including urban growth, establishment of trolley service to the central city, increased personal incomes, diversification of small existing stores,

☐ **Figure 14.9**
Top ten department
store organizations.

1986 Rank	Company/Division (headquarters)	Units	Sq. Ft. (000)	Volume (000,000)
1.	Dillard's (Little Rock)	115	15,588	$1,851.4
2.	Nordstrom (Seattle)	53	5,098	1,629.9
3.	Macy's (New York)	22	7,710	1,575
4.	Dayton Hudson (Minneapolis)	37	7,791	1,566.3
5.	Macy's (New Jersey)	24	6,550	1,440
6.	Macy's (California)	25	5,682	1,335
7.	Foley's (Houston)	37	8,003	1,107.0
8.	Bloomingdale's (New York)	16	4,269	1,050.0
9.	The Broadway (Southern California)	43	7,459	1,045
10.	Saks Fifth Avenue (New York)	44	N/A	1,005

Source: Reprinted from STORES
magazine, Copyright © National
Retail Merchants Association,
1987.

Department stores anchor the giant regional shopping malls.

*D*iscount stores work by turning over their stock many times annually and accepting a low profit on the sale of each item.

and textile manufacturers' aggressively seeking new outlets for their goods. Although department stores originated in downtown areas, the growth of the large suburban shopping malls has shifted the bulk of the sales of many such stores to their suburban units.

Department stores provide consumers with a wide range of services, such as credit, delivery, alterations, adjustments, gift wrapping, telephone orders, and fashion shows. Because of these numerous services, the markup on goods is greater than in stores that offer only limited services. Realizing that they cannot compete on price with self-service discount stores, department stores such as Bloomingdale's and Macy's have closed their bargain basements and have added upscale boutique departments offering gourmet foods, housewares, wines, books, art works, and delicatessen foods. These departments attract the upper-middle-income consumers that will purchase the better goods throughout the store. Department stores account for nearly 10 percent of total retail sales and employ about 11 percent of all retail workers. Figure 14.9 lists the top department store organizations.

Departmentized Specialty Stores.   Departmentized specialty stores are similar to department stores, but they restrict their lines mainly to men's, women's, and children's clothing. By focusing their merchandising and promotional efforts on apparel, they are able to introduce new designs rapidly and make strong fashion statements. East Coast-based Sak's Fifth Avenue and Texas-based Nieman Marcus have developed marketing strategies to position themselves as fashion leaders in their regions.

Discount Stores.   Rather than offer the 200,000 or more items available in a department store, discount merchants stock about 40,000 to 50,000 items of the best-selling soft and hard goods. Discount stores work by turning over their stock many times annually and accepting a low profit on the sale of each item. In contrast, conventional retailing involves fewer stock turns and a higher profit on each item sold. Discount stores are characterized by self-service, central checkouts, practical fixtures and decor, few customer services, and low prices. Over a period of nearly thirty years, discount-store executives, noting the increase in consumer incomes, have altered their operations from disheveled bargain barns to neatly organized and decorated stores. In fact, Zayre's and Hill's prefer to be known as department stores. The major discount merchants are identified in figure 14.10.

Catalog Discount Showrooms.   Catalog discount showrooms combine the features of a mail-order house and the low prices and limited selections of a discount store. Catalog discount showrooms contain catalogs, order forms, and several counter clerks who immediately fill customers' orders from inventories located in

Source: Reprinted by permission from *Discount Store News*, July 20, 1987 issue, p. 27. Copyright © Lebhar-Friedman, Inc., 425 Park Avenue, New York, NY 10022.

☐ **Figure 14.10**
Top ten discount store organizations.

1986 Rank	Company or Division	Sales (in millions)	Store Count Units	
			Jan. 1987	Projected Dec. 1987
1.	Kmart (Troy, Mich.)	22,107	2,204	2,244
2.	Wal–Mart (Bentonville, Ark.)	10,200	980	1,100
3.	Target (Minneapolis, Minn.)	4,355	246	319
4.	Zayre (Framingham, Mass.)	3,046	362	387
5.	Price Club (San Diego, Calif.)	2,590	34	39
6.	Service Merchandise (Nashville, Tenn.)	2,527	300	314
7.	Toys "R" Us (Rochelle Park, N.J.)	2,270	295	370
8.	Best Products (Richmond, Va.)	2,142	194	194
9.	Bradlees (Braintree, Mass.)	1,900	162	172
10.	Ames (Rocky Hill, Conn.)	1,888	321	348

adjacent stockrooms. These discounters keep expenses low by handling only rapidly selling goods, using inexpensive warehouse shelving, and minimizing the number of employees. By discounting brand-name housewares, cameras, watches, sporting goods, jewelry, and other fast-moving goods that typically carry high margins, the showrooms have attracted a price-conscious target market.

Hypermarches.   The self-service hypermarche, or superstore, offers both hard and soft goods and food products. The concept for these giant retail emporiums originated in France in the 1970s and then moved to Canada and the United States. In order to attain adequate sales volume, these stores, which range in size from 50,000 to 200,000 square feet or more, generally locate in major metropolitan areas such as New York, Minneapolis, and Detroit. Fred Meyer, Inc., based in Portland, Oregon, operates several superstores, some as large as 200,000 square feet. They handle everything from groceries and prescription drugs to sporting goods, apparel, and other general merchandise items. Compared with a traditional supermarket, a hypermarche usually has twice the traffic, triple the sales volume, and four times the number of different products.[8]

LIMITED-LINE RETAILERS

Single-line and specialty shops developed to offer depth in a narrow product line. Although the distinction between these two types of stores is often blurred, they may be differentiated by the breadth of the lines of goods they handle.

*B*y focusing their attention on one line, single-line retailers establish close ties to their suppliers and become very sensitive to market changes.

Single-Line Stores.   **Single-line stores** handle a broad assortment of goods in a basic line, such as men's apparel, women's apparel, hardware, groceries, or drugs. These stores range in size from large supermarkets and building supply stores to small drugstores and gift shops. Because they focus their attention on one line, single-line retailers establish close ties to their suppliers and become highly sensitive to market changes. Promotions, sales training, merchandise selection, and inventory control are simpler for single-line stores than for general merchandise stores.

Some retailers that are basically single-line stores have added other lines to offer one-stop shopping and to increase their profitability. The strategy of adding nonrelated offerings to a traditional merchandise line is called **scrambled merchandising.** For example, the People's and Osco drugstore chains sell housewares, hardware, underwear, and a host of other items. The stores often prominently display these items so that consumers who come to the stores to fill prescriptions will make additional, unplanned purchases. The unplanned nature of these purchases means that no price comparisons have been made. Higher prices can be charged, resulting in more generous gross margins for the stores. To attract additional customers, these stores often use promotional pricing on selected items.

Supermarkets stress sales of impulse and convenience goods.

Supermarkets have adjusted their offerings to the upscale consumer.

A typical independent supermarket contains 19,000 square feet and generates $5.5 million in annual sales; a typical chain unit averages 31,000 square feet and produces $9.4 million annually.

Supermarkets. A major type of single-line store is the supermarket, a large, departmentalized food establishment that maintains low prices, promotes extensively, limits customer services, features self-service, and employs central checkouts. The supermarket is a product of the depression years of the 1930s. Entrepreneurs developed the concept of the supermarket by moving into vacant buildings—factories, warehouses, and dance halls—using Coke cases and boards for shelving, placing open food cartons on the shelves, and employing a central checkout system.

The 13,100 items in a typical independently owned supermarket and the nearly 16,500 items in a chain-operated supermarket include a variety of nonfood items, such as health and beauty aids, housewares, and soft goods. In some Kroger stores, over 60 percent of the space is allocated to nonfood items. A typical independent supermarket contains 19,000 square feet and generates over $5.5 million in annual sales while a typical chain supermarket averages nearly 31,000 square feet and produces about $9.4 million in annual sales. Because of competitive pressures, both independents and chains have a profit margin of about 1 percent of sales. In order to satisfy convenience-oriented consumers, capture a greater share of total food expenditures, and obtain higher gross margins, supermarket operators have expanded their prepared food selections by offering freshly baked goods, delicatessen items, and salad bars.

To accommodate their many and varied offerings, new supermarkets may contain 40,000 to 50,000 square feet of space. Because stores of this size need larger markets, major chains, such as Safeway, Kroger, and A&P, have been closing their older, cramped stores in small communities and focusing on clusters of bigger stores in large urban areas. When these chains locate a large number of stores in a metropolitan area, they gain not only a larger market but also the ability to spread their promotional expenses, inbound freight costs, and staff salaries among several stores.

Convenience Food Stores. As supermarkets got larger and checkout lines got longer, consumers sought faster and more convenient service. These needs spawned the convenience food store, which resembles both the older neighborhood grocery store and the modern supermarket. These small, self-service stores offer a limited selection of about 3,000 fast-moving, staple items, such as bread, milk, soft drinks, cigarettes, and beer. Some stores have added carry-out foods, freshly baked goods, and even post-office boxes. The typical customer is a male who spends fewer than five minutes and less than three dollars in the store. Neighborhood locations, fast checkouts, long hours, and ample parking explain why these stores are convenient.

MARKETING IN ACTION

Going Bananas

he Banana Republic is not a tiny country carved out of the African jungle; it is a retailer offering safari-style apparel. This offbeat retail operation is the product of Mel and Patricia Ziegler. The Zieglers began their business by purchasing their unusual inventory in army and navy surplus stores in countries throughout the world. Mel is a writer and Pat is an artist, so they combined their talents and wrote and illustrated a striking catalog promoting their safari clothing. The entertaining catalog can almost be viewed as a travelogue to various parts of Africa.

Although most new entrepreneurs begin one business at a time, the Zieglers opened a retail outlet at the same time that the catalog was in preparation. Banana Republic stores now dot California and are found in several large cities such as Dallas, Boston, Chicago, and Miami.

A problem for the Zieglers was to create a market for their type of goods since there was no evident demand for them. The Zieglers used their catalog to develop the proper context for the firm's unique offer-

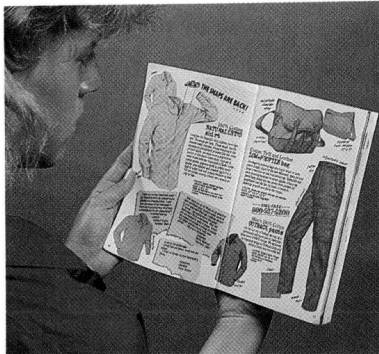

Illustration is used effectively to market Banana Republic catalog products.

ings. They carefully selected the type of clothing to be featured in the catalog and the way the clothing was presented in an effort to project the proper image for their business.

Because they were purchasing surplus merchandise, the Zieglers had difficulty maintaining an adequate inventory of fast-selling goods. Sometimes the goods that were bought had the correct styles, but the fabric was too old. In other cases, the sizes and shapes of the garments did not fit America's youthful consumers. For these reasons the Zieglers developed a number of resources that would produce goods to their specifications.

As the Banana Republic has become better known, its offerings have been expanded into nonapparel lines. Stores now handle a variety of travel books, specially designed luggage, and a distinctive line of shoes and boots. Although in 1988 the Zieglers resigned from the company that is now owned by The Gap, the present management is counting on the fashion-conscious to continue to enjoy the safari look.

Source: Adapted from Judy Kinsey, "Business as Usual for Entrepreneurs," *Advertising Age,* December 13, 1984, p. 35.

For this convenience, you may pay 15 to 20 percent more than you would in a supermarket. Leading convenience store chains include 7-Eleven, Li'l General, Majik Market, and Stop-N-Go.

Furniture Warehouses and Building Supply Centers.   Furniture warehouse showrooms and building supply centers are relatively recent retailing forms that have successfully applied mass merchandising techniques to fields that have traditionally featured full service, high markups, and slow turnover of merchandise. Because of their large scale of operation and extensive advertising, these retailers generally locate in large urban communities. The medium-priced, brand-name furniture that is displayed in attractive room settings in the giant stores of Levitz and Wickes strongly appeals to the middle-income market. The huge building supply centers of Lowe's and Furrow offer a wide selection of discount-priced materials, including lumber, paint, hardware, and electrical and plumbing supplies.

Specialty shops carry only one segment of a line of goods but provide many styles, colors, and sizes in this segment.

Specialty Shops.   **Specialty shops** differ from single-line retailers in that they carry only one segment of a line of goods but provide many styles, colors, and sizes in that segment. Because of their limited offerings, the most successful specialty shops direct their merchandising to a particular target audience. Examples of outstanding specialty shops include The Gap stores, Fannie May candy shops, and The

Limited, which received its name from limiting its assortment to young women's sportswear. Most specialty retailers handle shopping goods, although some carry an exclusive line of specialty goods. Contributing to the growth of both single-line and specialty retailers has been the development of shopping malls. In large malls, these stores are situated between the major department store tenants and benefit from the flow of pedestrian traffic that they generate.

In service retailing, it is important to closely match the level of service with demand because, unlike tangible goods, services cannot be stored.

Service Establishments. Because of the specialized nature of their offerings, most service retailers, such as beauty salons and theaters, are specialty operations. Retail service establishments are generally small enterprises whose success depends on particular abilities or techniques possessed by their operators. These establishments include self-service laundries, physical fitness centers, income tax preparation services, and motels. Because the seller of a service often is its producer as well, there is usually no need for marketing intermediaries in its distribution channel. The consumer, by assisting in the creation of the service (as in a self-service laundry) or by cooperating in its production (as in a photographic studio), often actively participates in generating the service. Since their offerings are greatly influenced by the performance of their employees, it is difficult for service retailers to obtain uniform quality and provide a consistent level of service. It is important for service retailers to closely match the level of service with demand, because, unlike tangible goods, services cannot be stored. The empty theater seats on the night of a performance cannot be stored and added to the seating capacity for a future performance.

THE CASE CONTINUES

*S*am Walton is hailed by many as a retailing genius. In 1940 he graduated from the University of Missouri with a major in economics. His initial work experience at J. C. Penney and in the variety-store industry should have pointed him toward a career in conventional retailing. These early assignments in general merchandise stores did, however, prepare him to enter the maverick discounting business in 1962. After all, a discounter is a general merchandise retailer that maintains low operating costs and stresses low prices. Prior to opening his first discount store, Walton had employed a price-cutting strategy on brand name goods in his variety stores and had noticed an appreciable increase in sales.

Sam Walton realized that the buying power of large mass merchandisers permitted them to keep their prices below those of most small single-line and specialty retailers. Knowing that most rural communities contained only small merchants, Walton decided to locate his discount stores in these communities. He believed that larger stores could be placed in towns smaller than anyone had thought possible. Today, Wal-Mart stores reflect the general merchandise background of Sam Walton and his belief in providing customers with good values at low prices.

Ownership and Control

*B*ased on the type of ownership and control, retailers can be broadly classified as chains and independents.

A successful retailer with adequate managerial and financial resources often tries to obtain economies of scale in operations by establishing a chain. Other retailers are content to remain independent and devote all of their effort to one unit.

Based on the type of ownership and control, retailers can be broadly classified as chains and independents. Some organizations, such as franchises and voluntary chains, have features of both classifications.

INDEPENDENTS

The landscape of retailing in the United States is dotted with small independent merchants, which constitute over 80 percent of all retailers and account for over 50 percent of retail sales. These merchants often operate a single store, buy in small quantities, pay high prices for their goods, do little advertising, and charge high prices to consumers. Because the large suburban shopping malls seek leases with financially strong chains, independent merchants often have to be satisfied with secondary locations. In small towns, however, independents line the downtown streets and are often the major retailers. A crucial problem for the independents is their inability to obtain the cost-lowering economies of scale available to the large chains.

CHAINS

*C*hain-store organizations are multi-unit operations that handle similar goods, have similar images, and are under the same ownership and control.

Chain-store organizations are multi-unit operations that handle similar goods, have similar images, and are under the same ownership and control. During the 1920s, enterprising merchants applied the mass production strategies of standardization and division of labor to retailing. The use of these techniques greatly expanded the role of chain organizations in the U.S. economy. In 1919, only 5 percent of retail sales volume was generated by chains, but by 1929 the percentage had increased to nearly 30. Chains now account for about 45 percent of retail sales. Initially, independents attempted to persuade consumers not to purchase from the chains intruding into their markets. When this failed, they tried to slow the growth of chains through restrictive legislation at the state level. Finally, noting that the legislative action was not working, some independents adopted many of the features of the corporate chains and formed their own quasi-chains.

As you walk through a shopping mall, you encounter names such as Sears, The Limited, The Gap, and Woolworth. Shopping mall developers choose chain retailers as tenants because of their merchandising skill, ability to generate traffic, and financial strength. An outstanding attribute of chains is their ability to purchase in large quantities at the lowest possible prices from suppliers. Another is their ability to spread operating costs and risks over a large number of units. To obtain efficiencies in operations, chains standardize their operating procedures and employ specialists for major activities such as buying, finance, personnel, and promotion. Perhaps the greatest disadvantage of chains is their bureaucratic organization which often inhibits innovation and prompt responses to local situations and competition.

QUASI-CHAINS

Quasi-chains possess many of the operating characteristics of corporate chains but are made up of units owned by independent retailers. Wholesaler-sponsored voluntary chains and retailer-cooperative voluntary chains, which were discussed in Chapters 12 and 13, are important forms of quasi-chain organizations. Another significant type of quasi-chain is the franchise organization, briefly mentioned in Chapter 12.

*F*or the privilege of operating a franchise, the franchisee pays to the franchisor several fees, such as an initial franchise fee, annual royalty fee, and an annual advertising fee.

Franchise Organizations.   McDonald's, Midas Muffler, and Manpower Temporary Services are well-known franchise organizations that run nationwide operations through networks of independent merchants. A **franchise** is a contractual relationship between an initiating organization and independent businesspersons, who are required to follow a carefully prescribed method of operation. The initiating organization, or **franchisor,** may be a manufacturer, wholesaler, or a franchise specialist. The independent businessperson who accepts the terms of the franchise agreement is known as a **franchisee.**

In a franchise agreement, a franchisee obtains the right to use the decor, trademarks, products, and other features identified with the franchise. In addition, the franchisee receives managerial assistance, training, and promotional support from the franchisor. For these privileges, the franchisee pays the franchisor several fees, which generally include an initial franchise fee, an annual royalty fee, and an annual

THE REST OF THE STORY

The Prince of Pizza

Thomas Monaghan's father died when he was four. As a result, he was moved in and out of numerous foster homes and orphanages. At one point, he was sent to a house of detention—"for running away to play basketball"—as he observed. Although Tom did not have a role model or much guidance, he was an extremely enterprising young man. By the time he was fourteen, he was supporting himself on a work farm. At seventeen, Tom attempted to get his life together by entering a seminary. This experience was short-lived because he was expelled for wrongful conduct, including pillow fights and talking during study hall.

After straining to get through high school, Tom joined the Marine Corps. During his tenure in the Marines, he began reading and studying self-help books. These books gave him a more positive and enlightened outlook. As a result of this newly acquired self-confidence, Tom decided he would explore the various avenues to riches. When an oil speculator promised him wealth, he took three years of hard-earned savings and entrusted them to the individual.

Unfortunately, Tom never saw his savings nor the speculator again.

In 1960, Tom and his brother borrowed $900 so they could purchase a small pizza parlor in Ypsilanti, Michigan, near the Eastern Michigan University campus. The next year, in order to obtain full control of the operation, Tom traded his Volkswagen for his brother's share. Tom soon expanded the number of pizzerias through both personal ownership and franchises. He noted that college students and military personnel were large consumers of pizza, so he concentrated his pizza stores in college towns and near military bases.

Unlike Pizza Hut or Godfather's Pizza, you won't find chairs and tables in any of Tom's stores. He secured a unique niche in the pizza business by offering free home delivery from a limited menu of moderately priced pizzas and soft drinks. An additional feature of his service is guaranteed delivery within thirty minutes or $3.00 off the price of your pizza. Tom claims to sell more than half of all the home-delivered pizzas in the country.

Although he is now quite successful, Tom has not forgotten his humble beginnings. He attempts to attend church daily, does not drink or smoke, and jogs five and one-half miles each morning. One of his indulgences has been the purchase of the Detroit Tigers baseball club—a ballclub he's admired since childhood. He also funded a Catholic mission in Honduras—right next to one of his pizza franchises.

Thus, the rest of the story is that Tom Monaghan, a homeless boy with great determination, became the successful operator of the country's largest home-delivery pizza chain—Domino's Pizza.

Sources: Adapted from Wendy Zellner, "Tom Monaghan: The Fun-loving Prince of Pizza," *Business Week,* Feb. 8, 1988, p. 90; Richard Behar, "Domino Theories," *Forbes,* February 13, 1984, pp. 124–128; and "Domino's Pizza: How It Became the No. 2 Chain," *Business Week,* August 15, 1983, p. 114.

advertising fee. A McDonald's franchisee pays 11.5 percent of sales in fees; 8.5 percent of this amount represents a lease payment for the building and equipment and 3 percent covers the royalty fee. An additional 4 percent of sales is collected for promotional activities. McDonald's and other popular fast-food franchisors usually insist that a businessperson invest from $200,000 to $400,000 in a franchise; many of the characteristics of a McDonald franchise are listed in figure 14.11. Nearly 500,000 retailers, which generate close to $600 billion in sales, are involved in some aspects of franchising.[9]

Type of Operation

Consumers' desire for convenience, their need to save time, and their willingness to buy from limited assortments have helped nonstore retailers make more sales.

Consumers who want convenience, need to save time, and are willing to buy from limited assortments can buy from nonstore retailers, such as mail-order houses, direct sellers, and automatic merchandisers. Such establishments are generating an increasing number of retail sales transactions. As interactive computer-cable television systems become more popular and economical, electronic in-home shopping will increase as well.

□ **Figure 14.11**
Characteristics of a
McDonald's franchise.

Characteristics of a McDonald's Franchise

MCDONALD'S CORPORATION
1 McDonald's Plaza
Oak Brook, Illinois 60521
Licensing Department

Description of Operation: McDonald's Corporation operates and directs a successful nationwide chain of fast food restaurants serving a moderately priced menu. Emphasis is on quick, efficient service, high quality food, and cleanliness. The standard menu consists of hamburgers, cheeseburgers, fish sandwiches, French fries, apple pie, shakes, breakfast menu, and assorted beverages.

Number of Franchisees: 1,700 in the United States

In Business Since: 1955

Equity Capital Needed: *Conventional Franchise—* $140,000 minimum from nonborrowed funds and ability to acquire outside financing for an additional $160,000 to $220,000.

Business Facilities Lease—$60,000 from nonborrowed funds.

Financial Assistance Available: None

Training Provided: Prospective franchisees are required to complete a structured training program which includes approximately 12–18 months of in-store training (on a part-time basis) and 4 weeks of classroom training.

Managerial Assistance Available: Operations, training, maintenance, accounting and equipment manuals provided. Company makes available promotional advertising material plus field representative consultation and assistance.

MAIL-ORDER HOUSES

In the late 1800s, Sears & Roebuck and Montgomery Ward started the first mail-order operations to serve rural consumers who were unable to make frequent trips to the city. The establishment of a nationwide railroad system, rural free delivery, and, in 1913, parcel-post service—which allowed the post office to deliver small packages directly to homes—contributed to the development of the mail-order business.

In recent years, mail-order retailing has shifted from general merchandise operations, such as Sears and J. C. Penney, to specialty houses, such as L. L. Bean, Land's End, and Horchow. Some organizations—such as Harry and David, which specializes in the shipment of fresh fruits, and Williams-Sonoma, which offers high-quality housewares—focus on very narrow product lines. Computerized mailing lists

Specialty catalogs offer a convenient alternative and unusual assortments of product lines to very specific markets.

allow the catalog specialists to target their mailings to very specific markets. Telephone ordering, with purchases charged to credit cards, has made this type of retailing truly convenient for consumers. In order to participate in the growth in catalog selling, many department stores, such as New York's Bloomingdale's and Cleveland's Higbee's, send their customers a dozen or more catalogs annually.

A major advantage of mail-order retailing is its low operating expenses. A major disadvantage is the need to make buying and pricing decisions far in advance.

Low operating expenses are a major advantage of mail-order selling. Catalog retailers keep expenses low by operating from warehouses and employing unskilled clerks. However, a serious problem for mail-order merchandisers is that they must make buying and pricing decisions long before their catalogs reach prospective customers. Thus, they cannot respond quickly to changes in the market. Another difficulty is the necessity of offering liberal adjustment and guarantee policies because of the inability of customers to inspect the goods prior to purchase. In spite of these disadvantages, however, about 12,200 mail-order houses, which employ approximately 103,000 workers and account for about 1 percent of retail sales, have been established.

DIRECT SELLERS

Direct sellers, or in-home sellers, trace their origin to the Yankee peddlers of the late 1700s, who sold pots, pans, knives, spices, and small household goods from packs strapped to horses. Today, the largest direct sellers, such as Amway and Avon, generate sales of over $1 billion annually. Although direct selling represents under 1 percent of total retail sales, it is an important method of distribution for some product lines, such as encyclopedias and insurance.

A limit to direct selling is its high cost. But direct selling permits marketers to obtain better control over their total marketing program.

A limit to direct selling is the high cost that results from shipping and selling in small quantities and from paying direct salespersons, who often receive between 30 and 50 percent of a product's selling price. Of course, some savings result from operating without a store or warehouse. Direct selling is used most effectively when a thorough explanation of the goods' hidden benefits is required. In addition, some consumers enjoy the convenience and personalized service provided by this form of selling. Direct selling permits marketers to obtain better control over their total marketing program.

Increases in the number of working women have affected direct selling in several ways. Fewer part-time salespersons are available. Working women are in general more sophisticated consumers who are less likely to accept the type of peer pressure often found in direct selling. In addition, it is more difficult to find target buyers at home, and these consumers are more likely to buy from direct-mail sellers.

Some people have tended to view direct sellers as unprincipled individuals who use hard-sell tactics on prospective buyers. Many communities where this attitude prevails have enacted Green River ordinances (patterned after a Green River, Wyoming, law), which forbid direct selling without the invitation of the householder. At the national level, the Federal Trade Commission has adopted a "cooling-off period" rule that allows consumers who buy from a direct seller to cancel their orders within three days after purchase.

AUTOMATIC MERCHANDISERS

Automatic merchandisers operate many of the vending machines that provide consumers with a variety of impulse goods ranging from coffee to cosmetics. These merchandisers furnish consumers with a high degree of place utility by locating their machines in high-traffic areas where other types of retailers cannot possibly fit. In a recent year, soft drinks, hot beverages, cigarettes, candy, and snacks accounted for nearly 80 percent of the $15 billion in sales produced by vending machines. This $15 billion represents about 1.5 percent of total retail sales.[10] In the service industry, a unique type of vending unit is the automatic bank teller, which enables bank customers with special cards to obtain around-the-clock banking services.

MARKETING IN ACTION

CompuServe—Direct to You

You have probably shopped in a number of different shopping malls, but have you ever shopped the Electronic Mall? This unusual mall is available to subscribers of CompuServe Information Service, an on-line data library. The Electronic Mall is a fascinating joint venture between CompuServe and L. M. Berry, publishers of the Yellow Pages for phone books. By subscribing to the mall service, consumers are able to purchase goods, request information and catalogs, or send electronic mail to more than 100 merchants in eleven different product categories. Among the "tenants" in this unique mall are Waldenbooks, Bloomingdale's by Mail, Sears, and Stark Brothers Nurseries.

After the mall's first few months of operation, research by the A. C. Nielsen Company revealed that the mall generated an acceptable 2.1 percent response and purchase rate. Later research indicated a response rate closer to 3 percent. Because the average response rate for direct mail and catalogs is only 1.5 percent, the higher rate for the electronic mall is particularly impressive. The research

indicated, too, that the potential market for the mall are all households with personal computers and modems. These households represent an upscale market with an average annual income of $44,000.

Retailers who are tenants of the mall are billed to join the service, and they receive an additional billing each time their goods are ordered. Shoppers who pay about $12 an hour to use CompuServe receive the mall service along with hundreds of other videotex offerings.

In 1988, CompuServe's total subscriber roster topped 400,000 with about 5,000 to 7,000 new subscribers being added monthly. The company claims that it has about 42 percent of all subscribers to on-line services. The CompuServe subscribers have an assortment of exciting services available to them. In addition to the Electronic Mall, another on-line shopping service is Comp-U-Store. This service offers discount home shopping on over 60,000

name-brand consumer products. In the field of financial transaction services, on-line banking, New York Stock Exchange quotations and transactions, and a discount stock brokerage service are available to subscribers. In the area of travel, the ABC Worldwide Hotel Guide, the Official Airline Guide, and the TWA airline reservation service are offered. For those desiring information on health and family, there is a recipe data base called the Electronic Gourmet, an Internal Revenue Service data base of tax tips, questions, and publications, and Healthnet, which permits a discussion of sports medicine, nutrition, and other health interests with physicians. The preceding examples are only a few of the varied and distinctive on-line offerings that are provided directly to consumers by the nation's largest electronic information service.

Sources: Susan Spillman, "CompuServe Opens Electronic Mall Service," *Advertising Age,* March 4, 1985, p. 74; and Melissa Calvo, "CompuServe Reaches Major Membership Milestone," *InfoWorld,* January 6, 1986, p. 3.

Convenience and lack of competition permit automatic merchandisers to obtain high margins on the goods vended.

The convenience factor and the lack of competition permits automatic merchandisers to earn high margins on the goods vended. A major problem for these merchandisers is their high operating costs, which average about 20 percent more than those of conventional retailers. These costs are the result of supplying small quantities of goods to many scattered units and maintaining the units. In addition, the units are exposed to theft and destruction because of their highly visible locations.

ELECTRONIC SHOPPING SYSTEMS

Interactive electronic shopping networks, called videotex systems, link home computers, cable or satellite TV, consumer credit cards, and home-delivery parcel service. These systems allow consumers to shop directly from their homes. With an interactive home computer, a consumer can communicate directly with retailers' computers. After viewing on a television screen the types of goods available, the consumer can order goods by punching the appropriate computer keys. The transaction can be charged to a credit or debit card. (The use of a debit card requires the presence of an electronic funds transfer system, which immediately debits, or deducts, the amount of the transaction from the cardholder's bank account and transfers it to the retailer's account.) The purchase can be sent to the consumer's home by the use of a home delivery system such as United Parcel Service.

*A*s electronic shopping systems decline in cost, their use should greatly increase.

The use of electronic shopping systems should greatly increase as their cost decreases. Already the Home Shopping Network (HSN) is offering discount merchandise through a number of cable TV stations. HSN is not interactive like videotex; it is identified as a teletext system. Consumers usually place their orders to HSN by phone rather than by computer. Federated Department Stores is participating in the Comp-U-Card electronic shopping service. Through its data bank, this service offers subscribers a choice of 30,000 products. In some cities, Comp-U-Card operates an all-electronic shopping service, an interactive system that permits consumers to use their home computers to access the service's data base and place orders directly. Another interactive electronic shopping service is Trintex, which is owned by CBS, IBM, and Sears.

THE CASE CONTINUES

*S*am Walton could not abide being an independent merchant; his aggressive spirit led him to form a discount store chain. Evidently, chains have been a way of life for Walton. His first variety store eventually blossomed into a chain of fifteen stores. The Wal-Mart organization has grown both by adding new stores and by buying other discounters. In 1980, Wal-Mart bought the Kuhn chain in the Southeast and immediately added 116 variety and discount

stores. By 1986, there were nearly 900 Wal-Mart stores in twenty-two states spread across the south from Florida west to New Mexico and into the north as far as Iowa and Nebraska.

Although the Ben Franklin variety store that Walton once operated was a franchised unit, he chose not to franchise the Wal-Mart concept. Walton must have reasoned that the ad-

vantage of total organizational control would more than offset the rapid expansion that would be possible through franchising. Walton knew the potential from mail-order houses and direct sellers, but these organizations did not fit into his scheme of operation. Over the last three decades, Sam Walton has admirably demonstrated that he knows how to sell general merchandise at low prices and generate a respectable profit.

Retailer Concentrations

Some retailers, such as discount stores and furniture stores, can operate successfully in free-standing sites; others, such as newsstands, must locate in the middle of pedestrian traffic in order to succeed. Deciding which locational strategy is best for a particular retailer is often difficult. Among the alternative locations available are planned shopping centers, central business districts, secondary shopping districts, neighborhood shopping districts, and string-street sites.

PLANNED SHOPPING CENTERS

*S*hopping centers are classified according to size and location, as well as goods offered and other factors.

Since about 1950, the construction of planned shopping centers has converted many former meadows and pastures into huge retailing complexes. In some cities, large suburban shopping centers—which now number over 26,000—have replaced the downtowns as the hub of retailing activity.[11] As shown in figure 14.12, the centers are often classified by the number and types of stores that they contain.

Neighborhood Shopping Centers.   The smallest type of retail center and the most prevalent one is the **neighborhood shopping center.** These centers often contain fewer than a dozen convenience-goods stores, such as a drugstore, hardware store, and dry cleaner. These small stores surround a supermarket, which is usually the major traffic generator. The centers are usually constructed as strips of stores

❑ **Figure 14.12**
Classifications of
shopping centers.

	Neighborhood	Community	Regional
Number of Stores	Fewer than 12	20 to 50	Minimum of 50
Major Store	Supermarket	Small Department or Discount Store	Two or More Department Stores
Trading area Population	5,000 to 20,000	20,000 to 100,000	100,000 to 1,000,000 or more
Driving time to center	5 to 10 minutes	10 to 20 minutes	20 to 60 minutes
Design of center	Strip	Strip or u-shape	Enclosed mall

with generous parking areas in front, and each generally serves from 5,000 to 20,000 consumers, who live within a five- to ten-minute drive.

Community Shopping Centers.   A larger shopping complex is the **community shopping center.** Such a center may contain from twenty to fifty limited-line stores, which handle a variety of convenience and shopping goods. These smaller stores often cluster around the center's focal point, a department or discount store of moderate size. A community shopping center usually serves between 20,000 and 100,000 consumers, who reside within a ten- to twenty-minute drive. Community shopping centers often can be identified by their design—generally either a long strip or a U-shape.

Regional Shopping Centers.   The largest type of planned center is the **regional shopping center,** which consists of at least fifty limited-line stores positioned between two or more department stores. The major department stores draw traffic, which benefits the other tenants in the center. This type of center serves from 100,000 to 1,000,000 or more consumers, who may drive twenty to sixty minutes to get to it.

Most regional shopping centers, such as beautiful Lenox Square in Atlanta and the vast Woodfield Mall in suburban Chicago, feature enclosed malls, which may contain two or three levels of stores and restaurants. To enhance their attractiveness, these malls feature numerous promotional events, controlled temperature and

*R*egional shopping centers feature the large, enclosed malls with which most Americans are so familiar.

Shopping malls are designed to attract consumers.

humidity, and striking decor. A major function of the marketing director of a mall is to coordinate the advertising and other promotional events for all of the mall's tenants.

In many medium-sized cities, such as Fort Wayne, Indiana, and Mansfield, Ohio, regional shopping centers have replaced the downtown as the primary shopping area. Similarly, the growth of attractive regional shopping centers in many suburban communities has caused many shoppers to desert the retailers in the older, decaying downtowns. In order to reverse this condition, some cities, such as Milwaukee, St. Louis, and Philadelphia, have developed inviting downtown malls by closing streets, demolishing old buildings, and constructing arcades to connect the major department stores. Ample parking, good transportation systems, excellent security, and a captive market of office workers have contributed to the success of these malls.

Specialty Shopping Centers.   Recently, specialty shopping centers positioned to appeal to a specific target market have developed. These enclosed centers, which may concentrate on high-fashion goods, international fashions, or off-price goods, are much smaller than regional centers and usually lack a large department store as an anchor. Their concentration on a unique offering draws patrons from long distances. Florida's Bal Harbour center, which contains Cartier, Ted Lapidus, and Gucci shops, typifies a high-fashion mall. The Mayfair-in-the-Grove mall in affluent Coconut Grove, Florida, houses the elegant shops of international retailers. Shoppers at the Eastgate Consumer Mall in Indianapolis can visit the stores of a Burlington Coat Factory Warehouse, The Front Row, The Outletter, Cub Foods, and other off-price merchants. In New Orleans, the old Jax Brewery has been renovated and converted into an attractive gift and food gallery.

CENTRAL BUSINESS DISTRICTS

Until about 1950, the **central business districts (CBD),** or downtowns, contained the largest concentrations of retailers in U.S. cities. The CBD was the hub of a city, with all major streets leading to it. Then, street congestion, deteriorating downtowns, population shifts to suburbs, and the development of suburban shopping centers reduced the commercial strength of many CBDs. Even today, however, the flagship store of most multi-unit department store organizations is located in the CBD. Lazarus in Columbus, Ohio and Rich's in Atlanta fit this pattern. CBDs are homes for numerous apparel stores, furniture stores, service establishments, and other specialty shops, too. In large urban communities, such as Minneapolis and Seattle, many CBD retailers are developing marketing strategies directed at workers employed in the downtown area. Through the concerted efforts of municipal governments, CBD merchants, and private developers, many CBDs are being redeveloped in an effort to attract tourists and conventioneers in addition to local residents.

OTHER RETAILER CONCENTRATIONS

*S*econdary shopping districts, neighborhood shopping districts, and string streets are other retailer concentrations.

Retailers that handle convenience items, such as food and drugs, and shopping goods, such as audio and video components and apparel, frequently locate in secondary shopping districts. These districts are beyond the primary shopping areas so they have some disadvantages of convenience and accessibility, but their locations still generate adequate traffic. These districts often develop at the intersection of a major artery leading to a major shopping complex. The strategy of retailers at such sites is to intercept shoppers before they reach the larger shopping area.

Some retailers seek out neighborhood shopping districts. These unorganized clusters of retail buildings lie along well-traveled streets adjacent to residential areas. Food and drug stores, self-service laundromats, branch banks, and other convenience establishments often gravitate to these districts. Because of their neighborhood location, the retailers in these districts generally have close personal contact with the local residents and cater to their needs.

Certain heavily traveled streets in cities achieve reputations for being the habitats of particular types of retailers. These so-called string-street locations often have nicknames, such as "automobile row" and "franchise lane," that identify their retail character. By clustering their establishments together, the retailers on these streets facilitate the search process of consumers.

TRENDS IN RETAILING

*T*he future of retailing should include both functional and institutional changes.

The future of retailing should include both functional and institutional changes. Functional changes affect the performance of retailing activities, such as transaction processing, physical distribution, and inventory control. Institutional changes refer to the development of new forms of retailing. Because functional changes can be accomplished within established types of retailing organizations, they are the easiest and safest for retailers to initiate. The high risk of failure associated with completely new forms of retailing makes established retailers very hesitant to begin innovative ventures. This may explain why, in the 1950s, Sears did not build discount stores and why, in the late 1960s, it shunned the catalog discount showroom business.

The functional and institutional changes that will occur in retailing will be the result of economic, social, governmental, and technological events. Retailers must be constantly alert to the critical events that will produce changes in our fast-paced society. Several of these events that should affect retailers in the future are discussed in the following paragraphs.

Changes in Income Levels

Some observers have expressed concern that the growth of the service industry is creating large numbers of unskilled jobs, such as fast-food server and motel clerk, that pay low wages. In the long run, this trend could have the effect of reducing the number of middle-class consumers. The increasingly large elderly population cuts into the number of middle-class consumers, too, since many senior citizens must subsist mainly on Social Security payments. On the other hand, many members of the baby-boom generation earn high incomes, which they eagerly spend on expensive goods and services. The number of families with two or more incomes has been increasing, too. Growth in both the lower- and higher-income markets has contributed to extremes in the types of retailers that are developing. At one end of the spectrum are large, low-price, self-service retailers, and at the other end are small, specialized, high-price establishments. Low-price mass merchants include those in the following product categories: food (Cub stores), furniture (Levitz), building supplies (Lowe's), and general merchandise discount clubs (Price Club). Small, specialized, higher-price retailers include cookie merchants (Famous Amos), gourmet hamburger restaurants (Chili's), elegant clothiers (Gucci), and sellers of fine leather goods (Coach Leatherware).

Convenience and Time Savings

Because consumers continue to want convenience and time savings, new forms of retailing will develop to meet these needs. Already over the past decade the importance of catalog shopping has increased greatly. Talking vending machines are being developed that accept credit cards and will permit the vending of many new items, ranging from mixed drinks to computer software. As consumers become more familiar with computers and as the prices of home computers and subscriptions to database networks decline, convenient electronic shopping should gain wider use. In the future, Sears, J. C. Penney, and other catalog merchandisers may primarily use electronic catalogs, whose pages are illustrated on computer screens.

Productivity

*P*roductivity, which measures the efficiency with which a business provides goods and services, is often expressed as a comparison of output to input.

The heightened interest in manufacturing productivity is carrying into retailing. Productivity measures the efficiency of a business in providing goods and services and is often expressed as a comparison of output to input. The common measures of productivity in retailing are: (1) sales per square foot of selling space, (2) sales per worker, and (3) size of average customer transaction. In an effort to obtain greater productivity, retailers are using more effective layouts, attempting to increase the size of each transaction, reducing the number of workers, instituting more cost controls, and employing the latest computer technology.

Growth of Services

The growth in consumer expenditures for services is causing many retailers to expand their service offerings. Many large retailers, such as J. C. Penney and Macy's, already provide travel, financial, and other personal services to their customers. Perhaps in the future these merchants will offer health-care and educational services, too. If this occurs, a consumer might have his broken arm treated at Bloomingdale's health-care center or obtain her B.S. in business administration from Marshall Field University.

Increased Interest in Fashions

More effective worldwide communication and transportation systems have produced a greater awareness of fashions. Many consumers insist that the stores they patronize carry the latest fashions and are willing to pay the price for them. Fashion also plays a role in the selling of appliances, toys, homes, aerobic exercising, and many other products. When a new fashion appears, retailers must immediately stock it in order to maintain their competitive edge. This surge in fashion awareness caused J. C. Penney to employ Halston to design a line of women's wear. St. Laurent, Givency, Calvin Klein, and other designers are profiting by licensing their names to manufacturers, who can then produce designer-label apparel. Because of the higher profit margins that designer goods bring, department stores and specialty apparel retailers are stocking these goods and seeking exclusive lines for their stores.

Diversification

Noting opportunities for growth, some merchants are diversifying into new aspects of retailing. Federated Allied Stores Corporation, a department store group, has expanded its presence in specialty retailing through operation of several groups of stores, including Ann Taylor and Catherine's Stout Shoppes. The Dayton Hudson department store group operates a discount organization, Target; an audio specialty store, Lechmere; and a specialty apparel merchandiser, Mervyn's. F. W. Woolworth Co.

operates Woolworth variety stores, Kinney Shoes, The RX Place, Frugal Frank's, Foot Locker, Little Folks Shop, Susie's, and several other specialty-store groups.

By establishing exacting specifications for their product lines, contracting for production of the lines, and checking continually on quality, many retailers have immersed themselves in the manufacture of their goods. On the other hand, some suppliers have formed their own retailing operations. Lancaster Colony, Phillips–Van Heusen, and Glidden are among the manufacturers that operate retail establishments. Because they are tied closely to the retail market and understand the retailing industry, both retailers and their suppliers will look to retailing for new opportunities and challenges in the future. These organizations will direct their resources to activities that promise the highest rate of return on their capital investment. In some instances, new retailing ventures that have a high potential for success will be started. In others, conventional operations that have been successful will be copied.

Retailers and their suppliers will direct their resources to activities that promise the highest rate of return on their capital investment.

THE CASE CONTINUES

*B*y locating their stores primarily in small towns, Wal-Mart has been protected from some of the more blistering price-cutting competition. Recently, however, Wal-Mart has been expanding into larger cities where there are numerous established discounters. For example, the company has a store in Springfield, Missouri, which has a population of over 200,000. At the other extreme, Wal-Mart is developing stores of 25,000 to 30,000 square feet for rural communities that several years

ago were deemed too small to support a discount store.

Sam Walton is a careful observer of retailing trends. After noting the success of discount membership clubs that sell only to businesses and individual groups, he has opened similar operations called Sam's Wholesale Clubs in cities of a

half million or more population. These clubs operate from a 100,000 square foot warehouselike building and follow the Wal-Mart philosophy of selling identifiable name-brand merchandise at low prices. In another trend-setting move, Wal-Mart purchased a satellite communications system that links all stores and distribution centers with its general offices. When a new retailing trend fits the pattern of the Wal-Mart organization, you can bet that Sam Walton will vigorously pursue it.

GOAL SUMMARY

1. **Discuss the importance of retailing in our economy.** With nearly 2 million stores, 15 million workers, and sales of over $1 trillion annually, retailing is a gigantic industry in the United States. Since 20 percent of all retail employees hold some form of supervisory assignment, the retailing industry is considered a major developer of managerial talent. Through transportation, storage, selling activities, and credit service, retailing furnishes us with place, time, information, and possession utilities, or satisfactions.

2. **Explain how new forms of retailing develop.** Under the wheel-of-retailing hypothesis, new types of retailers emerge as low-price, limited-service, low-margin, low-status operators in inexpensive facilities. Over time, these retailers improve their status by offering higher-priced goods, more attractive decor, and more services—all of which require higher profit margins. The dialectic hypothesis assumes that an older thesis is always confronted by an antithesis and that this interaction produces a synthesis. The general-specific-general hypothesis postulates that

GOAL SUMMARY *(continued)*

the retailing industry has developed from general merchandise assortments to specific or limited lines and then back to general merchandise lines.

3. **Relate how retailers develop their management strategies.** Knowing that consumers patronize the stores in which they feel most comfortable, retailers attempt to develop appealing store images for their target markets. As part of their marketing strategies, retailers develop a marketing mix that consists of the four P's of marketing: product, place, promotion, and price.

4. **Identify the different types of retailers.** Retailers can be classified by merchandise lines into general merchandise and limited-line operations. By ownership and control, retailers can be categorized as independents, chains, and quasi-chains. When

retailers are grouped according to type of operation, the major groups are mail-order houses, direct sellers, automatic merchandisers, and electronic shopping systems. Based on location, retailers are classified as occupying planned shopping centers, central business districts, secondary and neighborhood shopping districts, and string-street locations.

5. **Explore the trends in retailing.** The future of retailing will be molded by economic, social, governmental, and technological events. Changes in retailing will be both functional and institutional. Some future changes may be based on shifts in income levels, desire for convenience and time savings, increased productivity, growth of services, increased interest in fashion, and diversification by retailers and their suppliers.

KEY TERMS

Retailing, **p. 381**
Retailer, **p. 381**
Retail Establishment, **p. 381**
Wheel-of-Retailing Hypothesis, **p. 383**
Dialectic Hypothesis, **p. 385**
General-Specific-General Hypothesis, **p. 385**
Retailing Life Cycle, **p. 385**
Store Image, **p. 387**
Patronage Motives, **p. 388**
Convenience Store, **p. 388**
Shopping Store, **p. 388**
Specialty Store, **p. 388**

100-Percent Location, **p. 391**
Atmospherics, **p. 391**
Single-Line Store, **p. 395**
Scrambled Merchandising, **p. 395**
Specialty Shop, **p. 397**
Franchise, **p. 399**
Franchisor, **p. 399**
Franchisee, **p. 399**
Neighborhood Shopping Center, **p. 404**
Community Shopping Center, **p. 405**
Regional Shopping Center, **p. 405**
Central Business District, **p. 406**

CHECK YOUR LEARNING

1. The term that includes all sales made to the ultimate consumer is: (a) retailer, (b) retail establishment, (c) retailing, (d) retail store.
2. The dialectic hypothesis of retail development recognizes that changes in the retailing industry are often responses to competition.   **T/F**
3. In retailing, *place* refers to both location and method of operation.   **T/F**
4. All of the following are typical promotional objectives of retailers except: (a) to generate immediate sales, (b) to create a favorable store image, (c) to provide information about new goods, (d) to support a trade association's promotional campaign.

5. A type of store that developed after the Civil War as a result of urban growth, trolley service to the central city, and other factors was the: (a) general store, (b) department store, (c) specialty shop, (d) supermarket.
6. Discount stores work by obtaining a modest number of stock turns annually and accepting a modest profit on the sale of each item.   **T/F**
7. The typical convenience food store customer is a woman who spends about five minutes and five dollars in the store.   **T/F**
8. The operations of a travel agency and a beauty salon are classified as being: (a) single line,

CHECK YOUR LEARNING *(continued)*

(b) departmentized specialty, (c) specialty, (d) limited categories.

9. Independents at first attempted to slow the growth of chains by promoting restrictive legislation at the state level. **T/F**

10. Which of the following is not one of the fees usually paid by a franchisee to a franchisor? (a) initial franchise fee, (b) annual royalty fee, (c) annual training fee, (d) annual advertising fee.

11. Because direct sellers operate without a store or warehouse, their expenses are generally lower than those of conventional retailers. **T/F**

12. Green River ordinances have been enacted to restrict the operations of: (a) mail-order houses, (b) direct sellers, (c) automatic merchandisers, (d) franchisors.

13. The type of shopping center that usually serves between 20,000 and 100,000 consumers, who reside within a ten- to fifteen-minute drive, is the: (a) neighborhood center, (b) community center, (c) regional center, (d) specialty center.

14. A busy thoroughfare that contains Ford, General Motors, Chrysler, Toyota, and Honda dealers is known as a string street. **T/F**

15. Changes that affect the performance of retailing activities, such as transaction processing and inventory control, are called: (a) functional, (b) administrative, (c) institutional, (d) vocational.

16. All of the following are common measures of productivity in retailing except: (a) sales per worker, (b) size of average customer transaction, (c) sales per advertising dollar, (d) sales per square foot of selling space.

QUESTIONS FOR REVIEW AND DISCUSSION

1. Define the key terms for this chapter that appear at the end of the goal summary.

2. Do you believe there are too many retailers in the United States? How would you determine the proper number of retailers—the number necessary to serve consumers?

3. Which theory of retail development best explains the introduction of the food supermarket? the catalog specialty house?

4. Explain how a retailer can extend its life cycle.

5. Do you think low-income consumers view the image of the elegant Nieman Marcus store differently than high-income consumers?

6. Relate the differences between the marketing mixes of Kmart and J. C. Penney.

7. Are the differences between department stores and discount stores disappearing?

8. Based on merchandise lines, what types of retailers are the following: florist shops, women's apparel stores, bowling alleys, furniture stores, and family clothing stores? Provide reasons for your answers.

9. Wouldn't it be beneficial for all independents to operate as franchisees in a franchise organization?

10. How do the mail-order operations of sixty years ago differ from those of today?

11. Why won't electronic shopping systems appeal to everyone?

12. What are some reasons for the revitalization of central business districts in large urban areas?

13. Is productivity in retailing as important as it is in manufacturing? Explain.

NOTES

1. U.S. Bureau of the Census, *Statistical Abstract of the United States:* 1988 (108th ed.), Washington, D. C., 1987, pp. 407, 737.

2. *The Dun & Bradstreet Business Failure Record* (Dun & Bradstreet, Inc.: 1987), pp. 8–9.

3. Milton Moskowitz, Michael Katz, and Robert Levering, *Everybody's Business* (San Francisco: Harper & Row Publishers, 1980): p. 330.

4. Dan L. Jones, Richard M. Durand, and Robert A. Dreves, "The Use of a Multi-Attribute Model in a Store Image Study," *Journal of Retailing* 52 (Summer 1976): p. 25.

NOTES *(continued)*

5. Jay D. Lindquist, "Meaning of Image," *Journal of Retailing* 50 (Winter 1974–1975): pp. 31–32.

6. Louis Bucklin, "Retail Strategy and the Classification of Consumer Goods," *Journal of Marketing* 27 (January 1963): pp. 53–54.

7. Phillip Kotler, "Atmospherics as a Marketing Tool," *Journal of Retailing* 48 (Winter 1973–1974): pp. 48–64.

8. Walter J. Salmon, Robert D. Buzzell, and Stanton G. Cort, "Today the Shopping Center, Tomorrow the Superstore," *Harvard Business Review* 52 (January–February 1974): pp. 89–98.

9. U.S. Bureau of the Census, *Statistical Abstract of the United States:* 1988 (108th ed.), p. 742.

10. Statement from the National Automatic Merchandising Association, Chicago, Ill., July 16, 1985.

11. Information received from the International Council of Shopping Centers.

*O*n October 27, 1858, Rowland Hussey Macy, a former Nantucket whaler, opened a small dry-goods store on Sixth Avenue in New York. Because he had failed in three previous retailing ventures, he looked forward to success in this one. His store stocked ribbons, laces, embroideries, artificial flowers, feathers, handkerchiefs, cambric flouncings, hosiery, and gloves. On the first day he sold $11.06 and in the first thirteen months of business he recorded sales of $90,000.

Beginning in 1866, Macy kept adding stores piecemeal until the business eventually occupied the ground space of eleven stores. By 1877, the small dry-goods store had been transformed into a full-fledged department store handling a selection of items ranging from toilet goods to musical instruments.

In 1902, Macy's moved to a new nine-store building at Herald Square. A series of building additions in the 1920s and 1930s resulted in the retailer encompassing the entire city block. These additions allowed Macy's to claim that its floor space of 2,012,000 square feet made it the world's largest store. Today, over 400,000 different items from all over the globe are stocked in Macy's 168 selling departments.

The early Macy's store sold only for cash and was oriented to the thrifty middle-class market that was developing in this country. Macy was one of the first merchants to use typographic devices to gain attention, and his outlays for advertising were a robust 3 percent of sales while most retailers were spending only 1 percent. In its promotions, Macy's latched onto a slogan that it used for many years—even painting it on the store roof: "It's Smart to Be Thrifty." By 1950, the image of Macy's was one of a retailer that provided a wide variety of merchandise and services to the broad middle-income group.

During the 1950s, low-priced discounters, such as E. J. Korvette and Caldor, began siphoning business away from the medium-priced department stores. Macy's reacted to this vigorous competition by lowering its prices and strongly promoting its bargain basement. By trading down, Macy's began losing its mainstay, middle-class customer base. By 1960, the combination of an older inner-city store, harsh price competition, and an erosion of its middle-income market gave rise to a confused, lackluster Macy organization.

In the early 1970s, Bloomingdale's, which had been a stodgy department store unit in the Federated Department Store group, suddenly came alive under new management and blossomed into a trendy, high-fashion department store. This awesome competitor—only twenty-five blocks north of Macy's—left the giant retailer dazed and without direction. In 1974, Macy's brought in Edward S. Finkelstein from its California division as president. He was the third president in three years, and his mission was to restore glamour and excitement to a decaying institution. Finkelstein completely renovated Macy's, changing it from a virtual warehouse into a giant theater of style and taste. Showrooms were made airier; aisles were widened; departments were rearranged; and unprofitable departments were dropped and new trendy ones were added. A hallmark of Finkelstein is "The Cellar," which replaced the dreary bargain-basement tables of budget dresses and sportswear. "The Cellar" is a block-long row of unusual and delightful shops including a gourmet food area, a 19th century English pharmacy, and a pottery.

By the 1980s, Macy's had regained its stature as a finely tuned, adventuresome department store. Macy's has been steadily upgrading from moderate-priced goods to more high-fashion and designer labels. Through its promotions and displays, Macy's is communicating that it provides excellent value and full assortments at all times. Both the new upscale younger customers and the faithful older patrons of the store appreciate this approach. Today, Macy's is a vital, contemporary store with a clientele that is rooted in the middle-income group. As the store continues to improve its image, its customer base is broadening into a more affluent market.

Issues for Discussion
1. What are the major attributes of Macy's image?
2. How has the retail marketing mix for Macy's changed over the years?
3. What are the retailing trends that will affect Macy's in the future? How do you believe Macy's will react to these trends?

Sources: Lisa Anderson, "2 Giants Battle for the '80s," *Women's Wear Daily,* April 11, 1983, pp. 1, 4, and 6; James O'Hanlon, "This Is Show Biz," *Forbes,* February 20, 1978, pp. 71–73; and Tom Mahoney and Leonard Sloane, *The Great Merchants,* 2d ed. (New York: Harper & Row Publishers, Inc., 1966), pp. 149–169.

OUTLINE

CHAPTER

15

Managing Physical Distribution

LEARNING GOALS_____

After reading this chapter, you should be able to:

1. Explain the importance of physical distribution to the U.S. economy.
2. Describe the total cost approach and the cost trade-off approach to establishing physical distribution objectives.
3. List the elements of physical distribution.
4. Discuss the differences in types of storage facilities.
5. Distinguish between traditional inventory methods and the just-in-time approach.
6. Explain how modern technology is reducing materials handling costs.
7. Compare and contrast the five major modes of transportation.

_I_ f you are into gourmet cooking, you've probably heard of Williams-Sonoma. This thirty-two-year-old company, based in San Francisco, California, did $137 million in sales in 1987. Its products are high-quality cookware and serving equipment and other household articles for the home and garden. These products are sold through the company's mail-order and retail outlets.

The company also owns twenty-six Pottery Barn stores, five Hold Everything stores, and two Gardener's Eden stores. These divisions also provide mail-order services.

While some large companies are still decentralizing their distribution operations, Williams-Sonoma redesigned its distribution system and returned to a centralized approach. In the summer of 1984, the company moved its distribution operation from California to Memphis, Tennessee, commonly referred to as "America's Distribution Center." This relocation was completed after a careful year-long study of mail-order shipments by zip code. Findings revealed that only 20 percent of its shipments went to points west of the Mississippi. Thirty percent went to the East Coast, where there is a heightened awareness of gourmet cooking, 30 percent to the Midwest, and the rest to the South.

A further consideration in studying relocation was Williams-Sonoma's desire to align the growth of its kitchen stores—58 as of 1988, with plans for 100—where its mail-order business is.

While this may seem self-defeating, Robert Early, vice-president and head of distribution, claims, "For every dollar of mail-order lost (to retail) we gain $7 in (retail store) sales." In other words, people spend more in the stores. Williams-Sonoma believes it has reached the core of its over 3 million customers and that mail-order sales will continue to fall below retail store sales. Thus the company is projecting its greatest growth in the retail stores.

Issues for Discussion
1. What sort of cost trade-offs did Williams-Sonoma consider when developing its distribution system?
2. What types of transportation modes is Williams-Sonoma likely to use in distributing its product?
3. What types of storage facilities is Williams-Sonoma likely to use? Will they be the same for all products?
4. Name some technological advances that would make the job of materials handling easier for Williams-Sonoma.

Sources: Conversation with Williams-Sonoma corporate headquarters, May 1988; and Joan Feldman, "Return to the Future," _Handling and Shipping Management,_ April 1986, pp. 53–56—Reprinted with permission from _Handling and Shipping Management,_ April 1986 issue. Copyright © 1986 Penton Publishing, Cleveland, Ohio.

Williams-Sonoma is building its future by opening retail cookware stores in malls across the United States. A strong distribution system is needed to support these stores and mail-order operations.
Source: Photo courtesy of Williams-Sonoma

_I_ t is not enough for a company to simply select the best channels of distribution for its products. Although this helps establish an overall plan for distribution, other decisions must also be made. With so many customers and so many products, Williams-Sonoma must operate an effective and efficient physical distribution system that moves its products to consumers. Marketing managers must consider who will store and transport these goods and how much they will pay for these services. Other parts of the system include order processing, inventory control, protective packaging, and materials handling. This chapter explains the relationships among these components and suggests how companies like Williams-Sonoma make decisions in this increasingly important area of marketing. ■

THE NATURE OF PHYSICAL DISTRIBUTION

Physical distribution is the handling and moving of goods within organizations and through the channels of distribution. It involves all the activities closely related to the transportation and storage of goods. The process of physical distribution is nothing new, but the concept of an integrated physical distribution system, which involves coordinated management of all related activities, has been around only since the advent of computers in the late 1950s.

Importance and Costs of Physical Distribution

*P*hysical distribution creates time and place utility.

The importance of physical distribution should not be underestimated. Physical distribution is a major contributor to the marketing concept because it can decrease costs and increase customer satisfaction. It is physical distribution that creates the time and place utility so important to us in receiving the products that we want, when we want them, and where we want them. The end result is added value in the goods we purchase.

*P*hysical distribution provides a greater variety of goods and broadens the area of competition.

Physical distribution adds to the variety of goods available. There would be few Shetland wool sweaters sold or worn, for example, if everyone had to travel to Scotland to buy one. Similarly, consumers can purchase an L. L. Bean knapsack at the same price anywhere in the United States, even though these products are made in and distributed from Freeport, Maine. Thus, physical distribution not only provides a greater variety of goods, but it also broadens the area of competition.

*P*eople perceive physical distribution as customer service.

The physical distribution process also greatly influences customers' perceptions of the quality of a firm's service. A landmark study by LaLonde and Zinszer reported that physical distribution comes closest to what people perceive as customer service.[1]

Physical distribution costs are high, often 5 to 30 percent of the total costs of goods. Distribution costs vary according to the type of business. For instance, a real estate agency incurs few distribution costs, because it primarily moves paper (contracts, leases, records, and the like) and office supplies. In contrast, a manufacturer like Westinghouse incurs larger distribution costs because of the many supplies and products it moves and stores in diverse geographic areas. Storage and transportation are the highest distribution costs. According to one study conducted for the National Council of Physical Distribution Management, transportation costs for both manufacturing and merchandising goods account for an average of 44 percent of total distribution costs. In total, physical distribution costs in the United States annually amount to over $650 billion, approximately 21 percent of the gross national product.[2]

Because of high costs, management must make every effort to reduce expenses. Cost savings in physical distribution can have a tremendous impact on profits. If costs can be minimized and higher profits earned, the savings may be passed on to consumers in the form of lower prices. This can give a firm a distinct competitive edge in the marketplace.

Objectives of Physical Distribution

*T*he most important objective is minimizing total costs while maximizing customer service.

Although physical distribution has several objectives, none is more important than minimizing total costs while maximizing customer service.[3] This two-part objective, however, is not as simple to achieve as it might appear. Balance between the two parts is essential. Because physical distribution activities are interrelated, satisfying one part of the objective may affect the other unfavorably. For example, if an effort is made to increase the amount of service, then an increase in cost can be expected. Conversely, if a decision is made to reduce the cost of a physical distribution activity, a reduction in customer service can be expected.[4] The key to this decision is found in the marketing concept. Marketers need to find out what types of service and how much service customers need.[5] With this knowledge, they can decide on a reasonable compromise between cost and service.

Marketers can use two related approaches in evaluating costs: the total cost approach and the cost trade-off approach.

*T*wo major approaches to evaluating distribution costs: (1) total cost approach and (2) cost trade-off approach.

TOTAL COST APPROACH

In order to achieve maximum customer service at the lowest cost, the total cost of all components in the physical distribution system must be examined. The idea implied in the **total cost approach** is to consider all component costs as a whole rather than what might be saved on an individual component.

For example, consider a decision made by the distribution manager for an office machine manufacturer. The manager must select the least expensive method for distributing 500 typewriters to a southern wholesaler. He selects rail as the mode of transportation because it is less expensive. However, by selecting rail he ignores the fact that he now incurs additional distribution costs that other transportation modes might have avoided. For instance, few rail lines can deliver freight directly to the user. Thus, the shipment must be off-loaded and sent by truck to a warehouse or distribution center, where it must be broken down and possibly stored before being put back on a truck for ultimate delivery. Thus in this case (each situation will be different), the savings made by selecting rail would be offset by other costs. Air transportation, therefore, may be the best choice in this situation, because total costs are lower due to reduced inventory handling. Table 15.1 illustrates the total cost concept by showing specific annual costs for moving office machines from Chicago to southern markets.

❏ **Table 15.1** Annual costs to a manufacturer for transporting office machines from Chicago to Atlanta.

COST CATEGORY	MODE OF TRANSPORTATION		
	Air Freight	**Rail**	**Truck**
Transportation	$ 842,621	$ 734,953*	$ 755,482
Inventory management	401,178*	622,739	622,739
Order processing	NR	NR	NR
Packaging	72,491	50,684*	52,364
TOTAL	$1,316,290	$1,408,376	$1,430,585

*Lowest cost in each category
NR = Not relevant

❑ **Figure 15.1**
Cost related to
customer service.

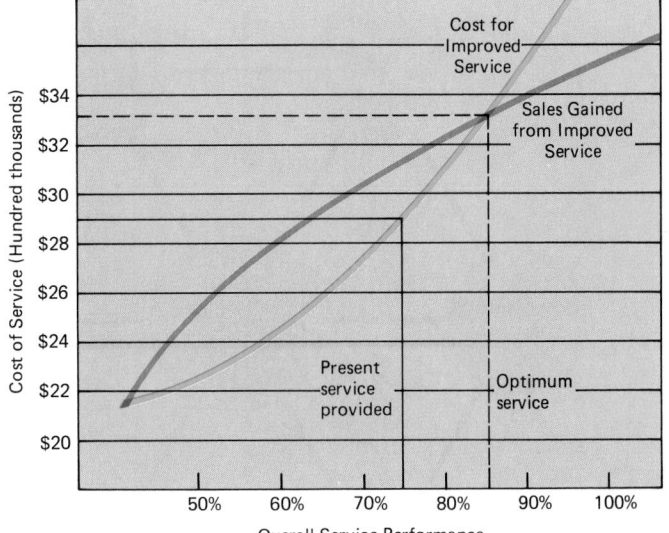

Source: Reprinted from *Traffic
Management Magazine,*
September 1982.

COST TRADE-OFF APPROACH

The **cost trade-off approach** supports the primary objective of the total cost
approach. It recognizes that changing the components of a physical distribution
system can create a conflicting cost structure. For example, if better protective
packaging were used to ship goods, the cost of packaging would increase. At the
same time, there would be a corresponding decrease in the costs of materials handling, because less labor and time would be required to repair shipping crates, and
fewer goods would be damaged. Distribution managers face cost trade-off decisions
each time they change a component in the overall physical distribution system.

Ultimately, managers must choose what level of customer service they want to
offer. Once the decision has been made, a set of written standards should be established. Like all standards, they are used to measure results and to facilitate the
control process. Standards developed for this purpose should relate to time, loss,
damage, and reliability.

*U*p to a point, extra sales
from increasing service
more than offset increased
costs.

Although lowering costs is important in physical distribution, managers are
learning that the additional cost of providing customer service often yields more sales
and profits. Figure 15.1 illustrates the general relationship between cost and customer
service. The figure shows that up to a certain level the extra sales from increasing
customer service more than offset increased costs. Past that point, however, extra
costs exceed the extra sales.

ELEMENTS OF THE PHYSICAL DISTRIBUTION SYSTEM

*T*o achieve maximum efficiency, a system must be
designed that integrates a
wide variety of distribution
activities.

According to the National Council of Physical Distribution Management (NCPDM),
physical distribution includes a broad range of integrated activities concerned with
the efficient movement of finished goods and raw materials.[6] In order to achieve
maximum efficiency, a system that integrates these activities must be designed. These
activities include the following.

1. Order processing
2. Warehousing and storage

❑ **Figure 15.2**
Major components of a
physical distribution
system.

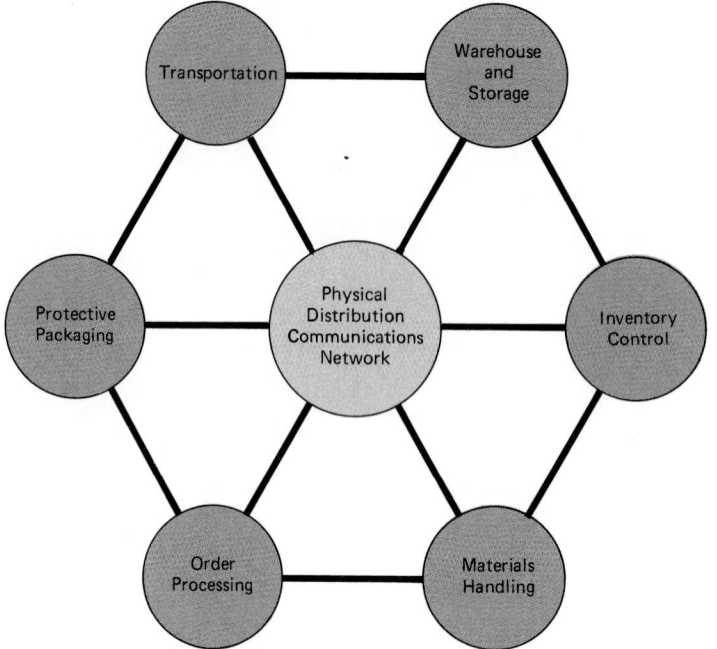

Source: Samuel C. Certo, Max E.
Douglas, and Stewart W. Husted,
Business, 2d ed. Copyright ©
1987 by Allyn and Bacon, Boston.
All rights reserved.

*W*arehousing, inventory,
materials handling, protective packaging, distribution
communications, and
transportation are the core
of the physical distribution
process.

3. Inventory control
4. Materials handling
5. Protective packaging
6. Distribution communications
7. Transportation

This chapter focuses on the management of these activities, with primary emphasis on warehousing, inventory, materials handling, protective packaging, distribution communications, and transportation. Most experts consider these activities
to be the core of the physical distribution process. (See figure 15.2.)

---

*W*illiams-Sonoma fully understands the importance of physical
distribution and its relationship to
customer service satisfaction. To
maximize customer service and minimize costs, the company uses the
total cost approach. Each compo-

THE CASE CONTINUES

nent—warehousing, order processing, protective packaging, inventory
control, and others—is considered
as a whole when making decisions
regarding the physical distribution

system. Furthermore, managers
must remember that some trade-offs
will occur anytime a component is
changed. For example, the use of
computerized forklifts represent an
increased cost, but order processing
time will be reduced, thus saving
money on this component.

Warehousing

Companies cannot manufacture goods in every location where the goods are demanded. Furthermore, they cannot exactly predict demand. For these reasons, they
must be able to store goods. Storage not only reduces transportation and production
costs but it helps companies coordinate supply and demand.[7] Storage space is maintained by various middlemen at or near central market locations.

*S*torage facilities perform four functions: (1) hold and protect stock, (2) consolidate goods, (3) break bulk, and (4) mix product lines.

Goods are stored in three major types of facilities: private warehouses, public warehouses, and distribution centers. These facilities perform four major functions: (1) holding and protecting goods in stock until needed; (2) consolidating goods from several sources; (3) breaking bulk and transloading into smaller quantities desired by customers; and (4) mixing broad product lines (when manufactured at different locations) according to customer orders.[8]

PRIVATE WAREHOUSES

Private warehouses are owned or leased by a company for its exclusive use. The largest users of private warehouses are retail chain stores.[9] Manufacturers may use regional private warehouses, enabling them to stock a full line of goods. Sometimes unique hazards or characteristics associated with the products they store force companies to use private warehousing facilities. Such is the case for chemicals, munitions, and petroleum products.

*G*oods are stored in three major types of facilities: (1) private warehouses, (2) public warehouses, and (3) distribution centers.

PUBLIC WAREHOUSES

Public warehouses are owned and operated by private contractors and are available to all users. Companies that need space can lease it as required and avoid the capital investment of buying and maintaining warehouses. Many public warehouses are specialized (refrigerated, for example) and offer a variety of services. One specialized service, **bonded storage,** involves storing goods such as tobacco and liquor in a duty-free zone until all state and federal taxes or U.S. customs duties have been paid. Public warehouses may also offer office and display space; marketing information systems; inventory level maintenance; local delivery; unpacking, testing, assembling, repacking, stenciling, and price marking; and securing of goods.[10]

IBM distribution centers consolidate products for quick shipment.
Source: Photo courtesy of International Business Machines Corporation

DISTRIBUTION CENTERS

One of the latest developments in physical distribution is the **distribution center,** which focuses on collecting goods from other plants and suppliers and moving them out as soon as possible. Normally, a company builds from one to fifteen centers in central locations across the country. One important requirement for a distribution center location is proximity to major transportation modes, such as interstate highways, railroads, and airports. Examples of companies that operate their own distribution centers include Rubbermaid (Wooster, Ohio), Montgomery Ward (Kansas City), Toyota (San Francisco), Pabst Brewing (Perry, Georgia), and IBM (Mechanicsburg, Pennsylvania).[11]

Inventory Planning and Control

A major component of any physical distribution system is inventory control. Planning for the proper levels of inventory is a major concern for the distribution manager. If inventory levels are allowed to go too high, carrying costs can balloon. On the other hand, if inventory is allowed to get too low, high restocking and production costs can result.[12] In addition, companies that run out of stock—a condition known as a **stockout**—risk losing sales and customer goodwill.[13]

The traditional approach to inventory control assumes that large stocks are needed to act as buffers against possible interruptions in production. Thus, the key to inventory management is knowing when and how much to order. The level at which reordering is required is known as the **stock point** or reorder point. In addition to the basic stock kept to meet average demand, a **safety stock** is kept as insurance against unexpected variations, demand and lead time.

*T*he key to good inventory control and management is knowing when and how to order.

❑ **Figure 15.3**
The EOQ model.

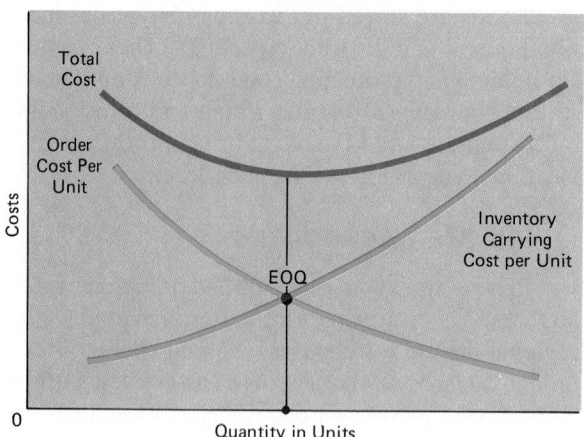

The economic order quantity (EOQ) model identifies the order size that minimizes the total cost of ordering and carrying inventory.

How much inventory to order at any time is guided by the **economic order quantity (EOQ) model.** This model identifies the order size that minimizes the total cost of ordering and carrying inventory. Figure 15.3 illustrates the trade-off between ordering costs, which decrease as inventory increases, and carrying costs, which increase with the addition of extra inventory. Ordering costs are expenses associated with purchasing, data processing, and receiving. Carrying costs, on the other hand, are associated with the cost of storage, handling charges, property taxes, insurance, and other areas related to maintaining inventory. At the order quantity identified by the EOQ point, total inventory costs are minimized, as shown in the figure.

The factors and costs described in the EOQ model can be expressed as a mathematical formula.

$$\text{EOQ} = \sqrt{\frac{2\,(\text{Annual demand in units} \times \text{Cost of placing order})}{\text{Annual holding costs as \% of value} \times \text{Cost per unit}}}$$

Since the 1981–1982 recession, a renewed effort has been under way to increase product quality and productivity. Today that means investing in major improvements in managing inventories. Rather than building inventories on overtime and depleting them on idle time, physical distribution leaders such as General Motors are once again borrowing techniques from the Japanese. This time, U.S. companies are learning much from just-in-time practices and technologies. The **just-in-time (JIT) concept** means "buying and producing in very small quantities just in time for use."[14] The original idea, called "Kanban," was developed by Toyota to meet precise demands for various vehicle models and colors with minimum delay.

The just-in-time concept— buying and producing in very small quantities just in time for use.

In Japan, JIT is characterized by scientific precision. On average, Japanese manufacturers keep auto parts inventories down to $200 per car. U.S. automakers carry inventories of $700 to $1,000 per car but expect to cut inventories by 20 to 30 percent when JIT techniques are fully implemented. By 1984, Detroit's efforts had accounted for 3 percent of the nation's JIT inventories.[15]

JIT is also having an effect on purchasing practices and, consequently, on quality (see table 15.2). A widely accepted practice in the United States is to have several suppliers for every part. In contrast, JIT encourages purchasing from one supplier. This practice allows the manufacturer to build a stronger relationship with the supplier and enhances the supplier's ability to contribute to the product's design and quality.

Perhaps the ultimate JIT facility is Buick City in Flint, Michigan. GM invited suppliers to build warehouses surrounding its new plant and provided them with engineering and managerial help to improve their own inventory cost controls. GM

☐   **Table 15.2**   The effect of JIT purchasing practice on quality.

PURCHASING ACTIVITIES	JIT PRACTICE	EFFECT ON QUALITY
Lot size	Purchase in small lot-sizes with frequent deliveries	Fast detection and correction of deliveries
Supplier evaluation	Suppliers evaluated on ability to provide high-quality products	Suppliers put more emphasis on product quality
Supplier selection	Single source in close geographical area	Frequent on-site visits by technical people; rapid and better understanding of quality requirements
Product specification	Fully specify only essential product characteristics	Suppliers have more discretion in product design and manufacturing methods, which results in specs that are more likely to be attainable
Bidding	Stay with same suppliers; do informal value analysis to reduce bid price; no annual rebidding	Suppliers can afford cost of long commitment to meet quality requirements, and they become more aware of buyer's true requirements
Receiving inspection	Vendor certifies quality; receiving inspections are reduced and eventually eliminated	Quality at the source (the supplier more effective and less costly)
Paperwork	Less formal system; reduced volume of paperwork	More time available for purchasing people to devote to quality matters

Source: Richard J. Schonberger and Abdolhussein Ansari, " 'Just-in-Time' Purchasing Can Improve Quality." *Journal of Purchasing and Materials Management* 20 (Spring 1984): pp. 2, 7. Reprinted by permission.

will use similar practices to manufacture its new Saturn line of autos, to debut in 1991. The accompanying Marketing in Action feature discusses this new phenomenon in further detail.

Distribution Communications

The concept of a fully integrated communications network within the physical distribution system has recently become a reality. Such communications networks take on many forms, but their common denominator is the use of the computer to process data and to provide marketing information.

A **channel system** is one technique used to integrate the communication network. Channel systems (pioneered by the McKesson Corporation in the mid-1970s) place computer terminals in customers' offices. McKesson uses its system to allow

*C*hannel systems link customers and distributors through computer systems.

Buick City, General Motors' highly publicized manufacturing and assembly complex, was completed in the summer of 1985. It's an integrated operation that will produce virtually all major components of the automobile, from blank steel to engines, transmissions, and axles. The first cars to roll off Buick City's assembly lines were Buick LeSabres and Oldsmobile Delta 88s.

Located in Flint, Mich., fifty-seven miles from Detroit, Buick City is truly a just-in-time facility. On average, only about four hours' worth of parts are on hand, reflecting GM's intense efforts to keep inventories to the absolute minimum.

A "flow-through" terminal adjacent to the Buick site supplies parts to the nearby assembly areas on an

MARKETING IN ACTION

Buick City: A JIT Showplace

as-needed basis throughout the day. The terminal, owned and operated by Leaseway Transportation Corporation, handles about three-quarters of all the parts that go into the Buick City cars. The 150,000-square foot high-rise facility features such technological advances as automated loading/unloading equipment, laser bar-code scanners, automated guided vehicle systems, and high-rise stacker cranes. Eaton-Kenway designed the automated handling portions of the terminal.

GM's goal is to have only five major carriers haul the inbound parts

shipments from the vendor companies to the terminal. These shipments will stay in the terminal for less than twenty-four hours before they are shuttled to the plant. Leaseway, which provides this shuttle service, expects to make 234 deliveries *daily.* This represents 2.3 million pounds of parts a day, moving in 1,500 specially designed reusable containers.

"You need very good customer relations to make this work," says Leaseway Vice President Martin J. Kelly, adding that his company views itself as a "partner" with GM in the Buick City venture.

Source: Adapted from Francis J. Quinn, "No Room for Error," *Traffic Management,* vol. 23, no. 5 (1984): p. 34. A Cahners publication. Copyright © September 1984.

its 15,200 drugstore customers to punch their orders into small hand-held devices. Each order is instantly relayed to one of McKesson's two data centers, where the order is assembled for local delivery. Besides providing instant ordering, the channel system helps customers to better manage their inventory, analyze costs, control quality, develop marketing plans, and electronically seek advice.

The company supplying the computer system stands to increase sales or otherwise benefit. In fact, the company that places the first system in a market often becomes the runaway leader and is hard to displace. Examples include American Hospital Supply, which placed order-taking terminals in hospital supply rooms, and American Airlines, which placed the Sabre System on the desks of travel agents. American Hospital has grown to a $3.4 billion-a-year operation, and American Airlines gained a 12- to 20-percent market share. Competitors filed—but did not win—antitrust suits against both companies.

Most channel systems also provide competitors' products' prices, but a few, such as American Hospital Supply, do tie customers to a single supplier. The trend is to lightly "tilt" the data provided to the customer in favor of the supplier. For instance, General Foods' system takes information collected by bar-code scanning equipment at supermarket checkout counters and transforms it by adding economic and demographic information about the store's local market. By allowing supermarket managers access to General Foods' terminals, the company hopes to become these grocers' market analyst and thus gain valuable access to scanner data. In turn, the grocer can learn which items should be put on sale to boost business the most and can obtain other valuable marketing information.

The computerized communications process is also valuable in selecting the best mode of transportation, controlling outbound shipping and inbound receiving, and carrying out many other functions, such as those listed in figure 15.4. The accom-

MARKETING IN ACTION

Fleet Management—Frito-Lay Style

■ Frito-Lay uses computers to manage its national physical distribution network.

Source: Photo courtesy of Frito-Lay, Inc.

*F*rito-Lay, the snack food manufacturer, recently introduced computers to assist the management of its private truck fleet (700 tractors and 1,600 trailers). These computers support a national physical distribution network of twenty-seven traffic centers and regional warehouses, and several single product plants.

A linear mainframe computer is used to determine each product's lowest landing cost (the total cost of producing, storing, and transporting an item to its user). This system downloads figures from actual invoices in order to deal in facts, not assumptions. The mainframe is also used for nationwide vehicle scheduling activities and maintenance management. For example, the mainframe creates a monthly Fleet Maintenance Report (FMR), which produces summary statements on total parts and labor expenses. Each report breaks down costs by vehicle and facility. This information helps

Frito-Lay determine replacement schedules.

The latest use of computers is in the placement of IBMPC computers at the desk of each distribution staff member. Each microcomputer is plugged into the mainframe for greater flexibility. In addition, micros are installed on fleet vehicles. This system enables drivers to record all functions which they are now required to report daily for log-keeping purposes. At the end of a run, drivers remove a module from the micro and later download it into a PC at the vehicle terminal. In addition to routine logging records, the computer monitors engine and road speeds. This system has more than paid for itself in accurate verification of driving performance and reduced fuel costs.

Source: Adapted from Jack W. Farrell, "Fleet Management—Frito-Lay Style." Adapted from *Traffic Management Magazine,* July 1985.

panying Marketing in Action feature gives a closer look at how one company, Frito-Lay, uses microcomputers to manage its private transportation fleet. However they are used, computers are playing a major and increasing role in the physical distribution strategies of most companies.

❏ **Figure 15.4**
Distribution functions handled by computerized communication process.

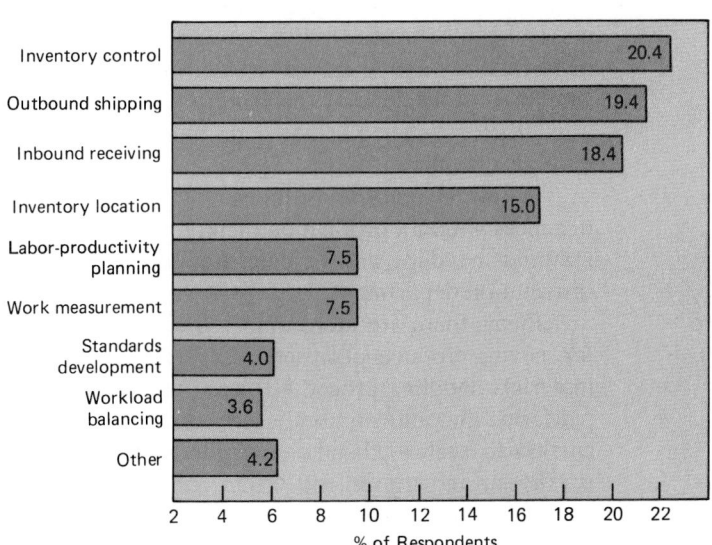

Function	% of Respondents
Inventory control	20.4
Outbound shipping	19.4
Inbound receiving	18.4
Inventory location	15.0
Labor-productivity planning	7.5
Work measurement	7.5
Standards development	4.0
Workload balancing	3.6
Other	4.2

% of Respondents

Source: Reprinted from *Traffic Management Magazine,* July 1985.

Computer technology is widely used by companies such as Leaseway Transportation, to coordinate the components of complicated distribution systems.

Source: Courtesy of Leaseway Transportation.

Protective Packaging and Materials Handling

*O*ver 40 percent of all goods shipped need protective packaging.

The preparation of goods for shipping is often referred to as *industrial packaging.* Over 40 percent of all goods shipped require protective packaging, which costs more than $55 billion annually.[16] Because proper packaging can greatly reduce the cost of shipment, much research and testing has been conducted in this area.

A variety of packaging choices exist—steel drums, wooden boxes, plastic shrink-wrap, fiber boxes, and paper and cloth bags, for example. A key to choosing the proper protective packaging is coordination. For example, regulations in the truck, air, and rail industries require proper classification of goods, and this classification in turn controls how the goods will be packaged. The packaging decision process should also consider how the product will be warehoused and how the packaging will affect the customer. Furthermore, managers must consider requirements related to materials handling.

Materials handling includes all the activities involved in moving products short distances within a production facility, warehouse, or retail store. Responsibility for materials handling may be delegated to the production department or to a physical distribution department.

*P*allets and forklifts are the most common type of materials handling devices.

Today, there are more than 300 different types of mechanical devices available for moving products of varied sizes, shapes, and weights. The most common type of materials handling procedure uses pallets and forklift trucks. Pallets are portable platforms that allow a number of boxes to be stored or moved as a group. Forklift trucks can easily load and unload goods on pallets. This process, called **unit loading,** is efficient and convenient. Other common types of materials handling equipment include roller and wheel conveyors, automated drag lines, hand and platform trucks, cranes, and tow trains.

Proper protective packaging can greatly reduce the cost of handling and shipping. These packages of coffee are shipped in cardboard boxes marked *fragile*.

In recent years, an all-out effort has been made to improve the materials handling process. Experts believe that productivity in this process can be increased 15 percent without replacement of any existing equipment or buildings. This would reduce total costs by as much as $1 billion annually.[17] Part of this saving would come from better utilization of existing space. In order to obtain the maximum use of height, for example, it is necessary to utilize a system of racks and bins. With this system a storage space can be designed as a "cube." Most cubes are filled to approximately 25 percent capacity; however, it is desirable to achieve 60-percent space utilization.[18] One way to do that is to use mezzanines, or floors situated between two main ones.

Mezzanine use is common in many warehouses where order processors (or *pickers*) often work in the same area as stockers. To prevent its pickers and stockers from bumping into each other, the Berton Company, a wholesale merchandiser in Commerce, California, designed a three-level mezzanine of controlled-flow conveyors for zone (stationary) stocking and picking. This simple step produced a 20-percent labor savings, and Berton predicted it would recover its costs in five years.[19] It should be recognized that although mezzanines are ideal for picking, they are not recommended for bulk storage. Distributors that need greater bulk storage should explore the use of lifts and other materials handling devices that will maximize the heights at which goods can be stored.

In order to speed the materials handling process, distributors have developed coding systems to facilitate location, identification, and retrieval of goods. This approach has been revolutionized by the use of bar-coding systems similar to those found in supermarkets. According to the National Industrial Distributors Association, roughly one-half of its members currently use such systems. **Bar codes** can be read by fixed-position or hand-held optical scanners, perhaps attached to forklifts. Another example of improved distribution communications is the use of FM radios or other electronic devices to send messages directly to pickers.

The combined use of computers and communications devices is rapidly automating the warehouse. Montgomery Ward operates one such warehouse. This twenty-five-acre facility houses a fully automated storage and retrieval system (ASRS) that includes an optical scanner, wire-guided order picking trucks, and automated guided vehicles.[20]

*B*ar-coding systems, which facilitate location, identification, and retrieval of goods, are used in approximately one-half of all warehouses.

Mechanical lifts are often used for loading trucks, planes, and rail cars.

Williams-Sonoma's distribution center is located in Memphis near the International Airport. The distribution center contains 450,000 square feet and 24,000 pallet locations. Williams-Sonoma's numbered receiving lines are like those at other distribution centers, where an inspection of the quantity and type of goods received from vendors is conducted. However, its system of stock location and control is not common. Logisticon supplies Williams-Sonoma with a hardware and software

THE CASE CONTINUES

system that includes computer terminals installed on forklifts.

Forklift drivers use the terminals to find out what their next task is, where stock is located, and how much of a given type exists. At the end of the day, the Logisticon system allows managers to print out reports on driver performance; for example, the time it takes to replenish stock, and whether that performance meets company standards.

Between the time Williams-Sonoma receives goods from vendors and subsequently ships them to customers, it uses a variety of packaging techniques. The company saves a lot of money ($.43 versus $1) on glasses by skin-packaging sets of glasses onto cardboard that can be cut to fit goods. In addition, a lot of products are being placed in a shrink tunnel to reduce the size of box needed. A computer selects the shipping proper sized cartons, based upon the total cube and weight of each item in the order.

Transportation[21]

*T*ransportation is the most expensive element of physical distribution.

Transportation is the movement of goods from one location to another. It accounts for more dollars than any other element in the physical distribution mix and comprises approximately 20 percent of the U.S. GNP. The importance of transportation goes far beyond having cars or airplanes available when we wish to go somewhere. It means having less expensive goods because of economies of scale, made possible by many goods being produced at one location and transported to nearby stores. It means having a superior national defense system, greater competition, and a higher standard of living. In short, it means the survival of our economy.

TYPES OF CARRIERS

*C*ommon carriers include airlines, railroads, truck lines, and buses.

Carriers can be classified legally as common, contract, or private. **Common carriers** offer regular services to the general public. They haul the vast majority of small shipments in the United States and will carry just about anything along specified routes. Common carriers include airlines, railroads, truck lines, and buses.

Beginning in late 1977, the federal government started deregulating common carriers. The first to be deregulated was the airline industry, and cargo airlines, such as Flying Tiger, were freed of regulation. Then, in 1980, the *Motor Carrier Act* and the *Staggers Act* gave the truck and train industries more freedom by allowing them to negotiate rates and services in establishing fares and routes.[22]

As a result of deregulation, the transportation industry has been drastically altered. More freedom is bringing more competition and risk. It's interesting to note, for instance, that since deregulation the number of common carrier trucking firms had doubled to 32,000 by 1985. Perhaps the greatest alteration is the formation of "supertransportation" companies formed by expansions and mergers. For example, CSX, the result of a 1980 merger of Seaboard Coast Line and the Chessie System, now owns several different companies, which can deliver goods by truck, rail, barge, or pipeline. Whether such systems will be profitable in the long run, no one knows; however, it's clear that shippers have benefited from better services and lower costs.

*I*ndependent truckers and charterers are examples of contract carriers.

Contract Carriers offer their services for hire by individual contract. Chartered planes and buses and independent truckers are examples of contract carriers. Because contract carriers are subject to fewer regulations, price rates vary depending on the individual circumstances.

Private carriers provide their own transportation fleets to move their products. Exxon, for example, owns a fleet of supertankers and trucks to move petroleum

Private carriers provide transportation for their own products.

products to the market. This form of transportation is very economical for large companies that can afford to buy and maintain transportation equipment.

SELECTING MODES OF TRANSPORTATION

As previously discussed, transportation companies are making sizable investments in computer-based technologies designed to meet the needs of shippers. One part of this investment involves the development of software designed to help managers evaluate various transportation possibilities.

For example, Navistar (formerly International Harvester) developed its Focus program to help current and potential customers make the right purchase decision. A Navistar sales manager visits potential customers and programs detailed information about operating characteristics of the customer's business into a portable Focus minicomputer. Focus processes the data and produces generic vehicle and component specifications that will best serve the customer's needs.

Criteria for selecting transportation modes include speed, cost, flexibility, capacity, and frequency.

Regardless of the evaluation method they use, shippers must be concerned with several factors when selecting a transportation mode. These factors are not independent of one another; overlapping and interdependence are common.[23]

1. *Speed.* The amount of time needed to move a product from one location to another is of considerable importance. This includes the time necessary for pickup and delivery, handling, and so on. Speed is the factor most closely related to customer service. Furthermore, certain products, such as flowers or other perishable items, must be shipped by the fastest carrier.
2. *Cost.* As mentioned earlier in this chapter, decision makers must make trade-offs when considering cost—the amount that must be paid to shippers for their service. Distributors must decide if the extra service provided by one mode of transportation is worth the additional cost, for example.
3. *Flexibility.* A distributor must decide what modes of transportation will be needed to get products to their final destination. Many locations are inaccessible to certain modes of transportation, such as planes or barges.
4. *Capacity.* The ability of a transportation mode to handle the size and special requirements of a shipment must be considered. For example, many chemicals require special tanks that can be carried only by barge, truck, or train. Rail must be used if the chemicals are in large bulk and if the route is not close to a waterway.
5. *Frequency.* How many times delivery can be made during a specified time can be very important during seasonal peaks and for companies using JIT.

MODES OF TRANSPORTATION

Using the criteria just discussed, the manager selects from the following major modes of transportation: rail, truck, pipeline, waterway, or air. Each mode offers advantages, as shown in figure 15.5.

Figure 15.5
The advantages of the five modes of transportation.

	Railroads 34%	Trucking 25%	Pipelines 24%	Waterways 16%	Air freight 2%
Speed		•			•
Flexibility		•			
Capacity	•		•	•	
Frequency	•	•	•		•
Cost	•	•	•	•	

Percentage of total freight

Piggyback systems offer transportation companies
maximum flexibility.

THE THOROUGHBRED AND THE PIGGY.

Riding "piggy-back" isn't child's play. In the railroad business it means moving trailers and containers on flatcars. That's serious business.

In true Thoroughbred fashion, Norfolk Southern is constantly improving our piggyback services to meet customers' changing needs. We've enlarged our intermodal terminals by as much as 40%. We've added side-loading equipment to speed up handling. We're currently "stretching" over 800 trailers to 48 feet in length.

Just recently, we launched a new type of piggyback service which for the first

time offers double-stack containerized service between the West Coast and Atlanta. This service enables a customer to double the amount of containerized freight he can ship on railroad cars.

These piggyback improvements and innovations are among the reasons our intermodal traffic is growing 15% annually.

Our customers appreciate the way The Thoroughbred and the piggy work together. It's one of the many reasons we enjoy the reputation as "The Thoroughbred of Transportation." And we intend to keep that reputation.

NS NORFOLK SOUTHERN

Source: Courtesy of Norfolk Southern Corporation.

Railroads are the back-
bone of the U.S. transportation system.

Rail.   Railroads are the backbone of America's transportation system. Nearly 500 companies offer rail service on a network of approximately 185,000 miles of railroad line (down from the peak of 254,000 miles in 1906).[24] Goods commonly hauled by rail include metallic ores, motor vehicles, pulp and paper, and primary forest products. Coal, chemicals and related products, and grain account for 43 percent of total rail tonnage. Railroads have a good record for transporting goods over long distances with minimum damage. Railroads offer low rates for hauling heavy, bulky freight such as commodities and merchandise shipped in large quantities. Shipping in full carloads (CL) enables manufacturers to pay much lower rates than shipping in less-than-carloads (LCL). Shippers of less-than-carloads find that goods take longer to reach markets because of increased handling. The average rail car moves fifty-eight miles per day.[25]

Because railroads no longer serve many small communities, goods designated for these areas must be transferred to other modes of transportation at the end of the rail line. To be competitive, railroads offer a variety of innovative services to meet this need. In response to competition from trucking, for example, railroads introduced **piggyback** service for hauling truck trailers on flatcars (TOFC) to locations close to customers.[26] Today the use of TOFC/COFC (cars on flatcars) is a growing practice with tremendous potential (due partially to the elimination of economic regulations in 1981 by the Interstate Commerce Commission). It currently accounts for approximately 8 percent of total rail revenues.[27]

Motor Transport.   Trucks are the second-largest mode of transportation and the fastest growing. Motor transport has the advantage of being able to deliver goods quickly almost anywhere there are roads. A truck can transport goods from New York City to Los Angeles in approximately 72 hours. The average length of haul is 301 miles, compared with 587 miles for rail.

Trucks move many types of goods. More than 70 percent of all meat and dairy products, textiles and leather products, apparel and related products, fabricated metal products, industrial machinery, and transportation equipment are transported by trucks. Furthermore, trucks are relatively inexpensive; truck shipping rates are lower than LCL rail rates.

Trucks are limited only by the weather and the size of the shipment. Although special trucks have been designed to hold liquids, perishable goods, and livestock,

A variety of cargo trucks
deliver many types of
goods to stores and homes.

❏ **Figure 15.6** The pipeline network.

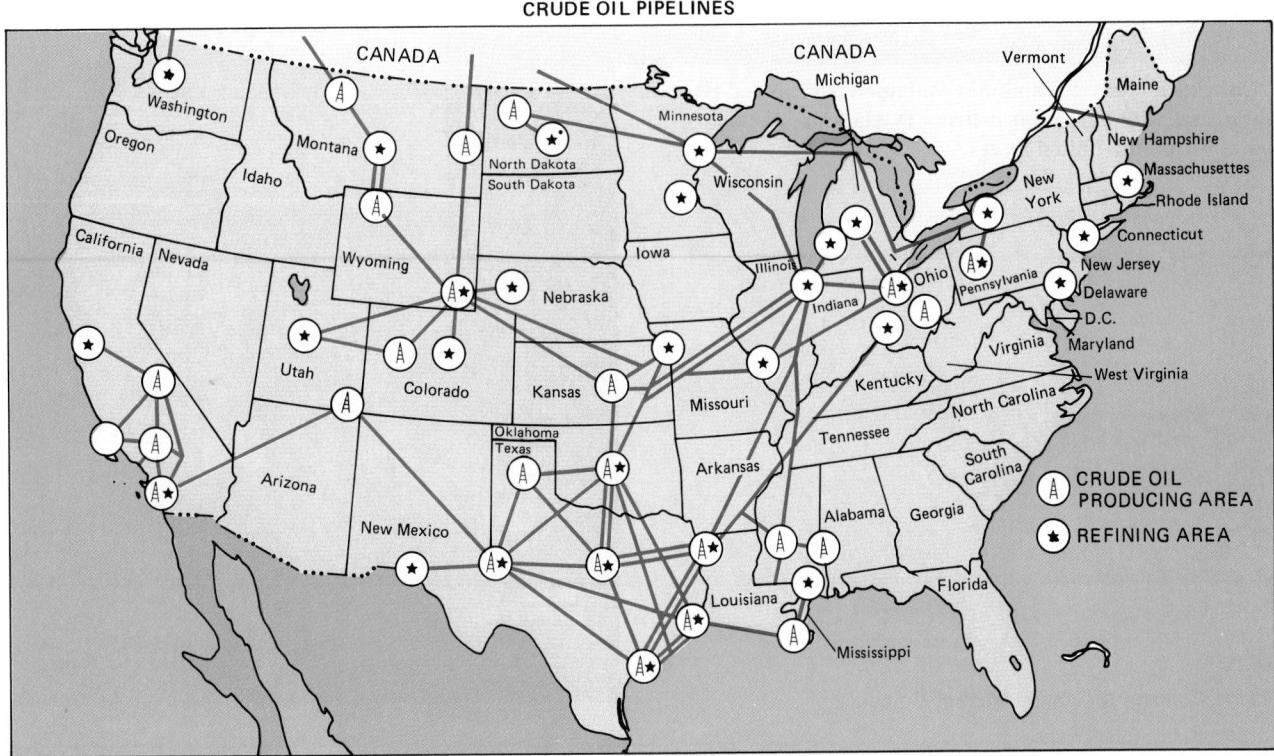

CRUDE OIL PIPELINES

CRUDE OIL PRODUCING AREA

REFINING AREA

Source: Reprinted with permission of Macmillan Publishing Company from *Introduction to Transportation,* by Donald Bowersox. Copyright © 1981 by Macmillan Publishing Company.

trucks are still limited in the delivery of heavy, bulky items. In addition, each state has strict laws regulating the weight of the loads trucks can transport on its highways. However, in 1981 the Supreme Court ruled that states could no longer forbid the hauling of tandem, or double, trailers. This ruling has made trucks more flexible in hauling large quantities of goods.

Pipelines. Pipelines are a relative newcomer to the field of transportation. Although they account for approximately 24 percent of all ton-miles moved in the United States, they account for only 2 percent of all revenues. Best known is the Alaskan pipeline, which carries millions of barrels of crude oil to ships for transport to the United States and international markets. The total U.S. pipeline system comprises over 300,000 miles. See figure 15.6 for a map of the crude oil pipeline network.

Pipelines were specifically designed to transport liquids and natural gas.

Pipelines were specifically designed to transport liquids and natural gas. Later, renewed interest in coal as an energy source led to the development of slurry pipelines, which carry powdered coal mixed with water thousands of miles to areas of major usage and to port cities for export.[28] Pipelines lack flexibility and speed, but when linked with other modes of transportation, they offer continuous delivery unaffected by weather.

Domestic waterways are used primarily for the transport of raw materials and other products for which delivery speed is not crucial.

Waterways. It would be hard to overestimate the historical importance of waterways as a mode of transportation. Indeed, they were the major mode of transportation up to the mid-1800s. Waterways within the United States comprise a transportation network of over 25,000 miles, divided into domestic inland (rivers and canals), Great Lakes (including the St. Lawrence Seaway), and domestic ocean (ocean travel between U.S. port cities). Domestic waterways are used primarily for

"Fishyback" service combines containerized rail and truck shipments with barges for delivery to Alaska and other ports within the United States.

Source: Courtesy of Crowley Maritime Corporation.

the transport of raw materials and the transport of products for which delivery speed is not crucial.

Today, ships and barges are the major vehicles of water transport, and together they provide the cheapest form of transportation available. The 2,343-mile St. Lawrence Seaway, completed in 1959, enables most ships to enter the Great Lakes to serve the U.S. industrial and agricultural heartland. Ships and barges are hampered only by winter ice and occasional spring river flooding. Engineers and scientists have proposed a plan to melt ice on the St. Lawrence waterway system, but environmentalists and many others strongly oppose the plan. Another way around the ice problem has been proposed by General Dynamics. This firm wants to build a fleet of gigantic submarine supertankers to ferry liquified natural gas beneath the Arctic ice cap to the east coast of North America and to Europe.

The early 1970s witnessed a major advance in coastal and transoceanic shipping with the advent of the **intermodal system,** whereby ships were redesigned to handle containerized freight, or conex. **Containerization** involves consolidating many items in a single container that is sealed at origin and not opened until it arrives at its destination. Containerization cuts down on damage and pilferage of goods—both major disadvantages of water transportation. It also enables ships and barges to link more efficiently with trucks and railroads. Containerized truck and rail shipments can be carried in barges or ships, resulting in what is called **fishyback** service. Another name for ships carrying loaded railroad cars is **seatrains.** Alaska depends heavily on fishyback service to deliver many of its goods to market.

*A*ir transportation is divided into three categories: U.S. mail, freight, and express.

Air Transport.   The newest of the U.S. transportation systems is air transport. This mode of transportation can be divided into three categories: U.S. mail, freight, and express. Items commonly shipped by air include fresh flowers, perishable food, such as lobsters from Maine, emergency replacement parts, high value items, and overnight mail. The air transport system offers a fast but expensive means of transportation. Air freight accounts for less than 2 percent of all goods shipped. However,

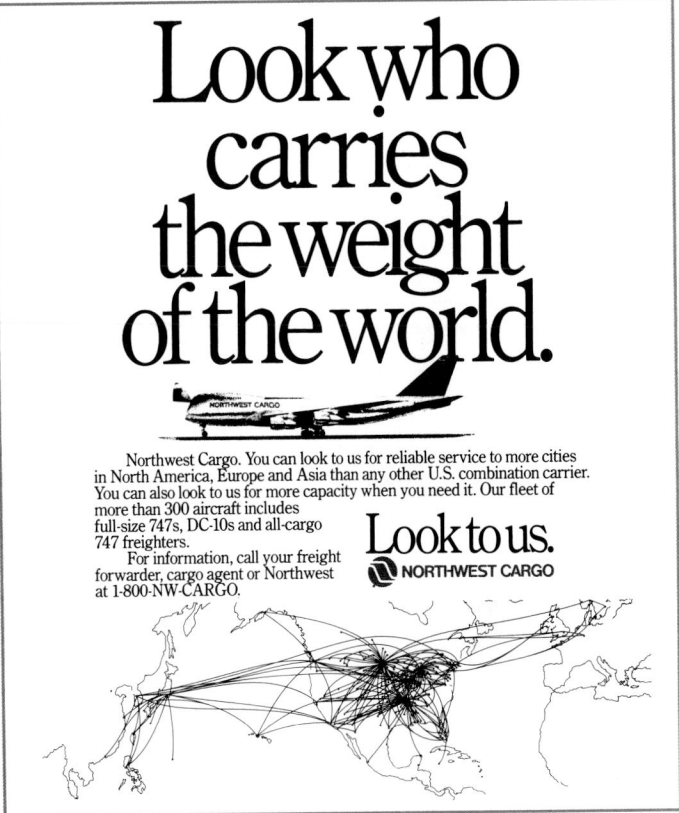

Air freight shipped by Northwest Orient Cargo and other carriers accounts for less than 2 percent of all goods shipped.

Source: Advertisement from 1986 advertising campaign promoting Northwest Airlines' cargo services.

with the use of wide-body cargo planes and increased exporting (35 percent of the value of International commerce moves by air), the tonnage is growing. Over 90 percent of the air cargo volume is carried by passenger airlines. The rest is carried by all-cargo airlines, such as Flying Tiger, Seaboard, World Airlines, and Airlift International. Although all-cargo airline services have slowly increased, the opposite is true in the air express business.[29] The Rest of the Story feature on page 434, provides more detail on this interesting and fast-growing industry.

Other Transportation Modes and Services.   In addition to the major modes just discussed, other supplemental carriers and third parties may be involved in the transportation process. For example, when sending smaller packages, the physical distribution manager might use the services of bus lines, the U.S. Postal Service, or carriers such as United Parcel Service (UPS), Federal Express, Purolator Courier, and others. The bus lines are suitable for frequent, scheduled trips to cities across the country. The mail service and private package carriers provide door-to-door service, but the packages they deliver must meet strict size, weight, and packing restrictions.

*F*reight forwarders and shippers' associations consolidate many small shipments.

The most commonly used third parties are freight forwarders and shippers' associations. **Freight forwarders** consolidate the small shipments of many shippers. In addition to assembling and consolidating the shipments, freight forwarders assume responsibility for their transportation. By assembling full train carloads or full truckloads, freight forwarders offer their customers the advantage of lower cost. **Shippers' associations** are groups of members that consolidate and distribute freight for themselves on a not-for-profit basis. The purpose of such associations is to secure the benefits of shipping in full carloads or truckloads.

*I*n the 1960s, a young Yale University student named Fred W. Smith submitted an economics paper that received only the grade of "C." As legend has it, the paper outlined a company equipped with a network of trucks, airplanes, and computers so sophisticated that it could "absolutely, positively" guarantee that a package shipped in one day would get to the recipient the next. In 1971, after a tour of duty as a Marine in Vietnam, Smith re-read the paper and decided to found a company called Federal Express. Although Federal Express processed only eighteen packages during its first night of operations in April of 1973, it created a new industry, and by 1987 the company was moving 179 million packages annually and doing over $3.2 billion in business.

Much of the appeal of this industry rests on the ease and reliability of the physical distribution system. The overnight-delivery industry created a market where there had been none. Indeed, stories now abound about the overuse of the service. Some people have admitted sending express packages and letters to colleagues in the same office building merely to catch their attention.

Each package is picked up by one of 20,000 courier vans, returned to a station, and then flown by one of Federal Express's 100 jets operating out of 90 airports. From there, the package goes to a central sorting center in Memphis, Tennessee, where over 4,000 part-time workers (mostly college students) unload,

THE REST OF THE STORY

The C Paper That Made an AAA Business

handle, sort, and reload an average of 800,000 packages between midnight and 2:00 A.M. (the record is more than one million in one night!). The packages are then flown to their destinations—the service covers 99 percent of the United States—and delivered to priority locations by 10:30 A.M. the next day.

Today it's hard to argue with Fred Smith's astute assessment of an industry that could succeed. He was right on target and on time with the creation of a new service, which he achieved with exceptional execution. And although analysts now wonder if Federal Express is growing too fast, most concede that Smith's plans for future expansion into small communities and international markets—in 1988 Federal Express served 89 foreign countries—makes more than good sense.

Sources: "The Man in the Pilot's Seat," *Fortune,* August 17, 1987; "An Industry that Keeps Promises—Overnight," *U.S. News & World Report,* October 22, 1984, pp. 53–54; Federal Express Corporation, *Annual Report,* 1987.

■ Federal Express depends on aircraft to offer speedy delivery at a comparatively higher cost per shipment.
Source: Photo courtesy of Federal Express Company

Williams-Sonoma shipped over 2 million mail-order packages in 1987 and over 700,000 pieces (a piece can be up to 48 units) to its retail stores. It uses United Parcel Service (UPS) for 90 percent of its mail-order shipments. The balance is divided between the U.S. Post Office, Federal Express, and common carriers. Of the 90 percent UPS business, about two-thirds are put into the UPS system by using a piggyback freight forwarder. Williams-Sonoma would like to close an exclusive mail-order deal with Federal Express for all

shipments because of its reliability, use of automation, and reduction in transit time.

Piggyback freight forwarders to local delivery systems are used almost exclusively for the delivery of retail store merchandise. All retail shipments arrive at the stores on Tuesday, meaning a staggered shipment schedule from Memphis. This gives the merchandise department

time to evaluate weekend sales to see what the stores need before cutting the shipping orders.

Eventually, Williams-Sonoma hopes to merge its retail and mail-order shipments. With the rapid expansion of the retail stores, the company is thinking about the use of ten- to twelve-day shipment points. That clustering would enable Williams-Sonoma to offer carriers more volume and truckloads of shipments more often during the year rather than having to rely on LTL transportation.

GOAL SUMMARY

1. **Explain the importance of physical distribution to the U.S. economy.** Physical distribution creates the time and place utilities that are important to consumers. In addition, it adds to the variety of goods available and broadens the area of competition. Economically, transportation costs alone account for 20 percent of the U.S. GNP.

2. **Describe the total cost approach and the cost trade-off approach to establishing physical distribution objectives.** The total cost approach considers the components of the physical distribution process as a whole rather than individually. This approach is designed to yield maximum customer service at the lowest cost. The cost trade-off concept recognizes that changing the components of a physical distribution system can create a conflicting cost structure.

3. **List the elements of physical distribution.** The elements of physical distribution include: (1) order processing, (2) warehousing and storage, (3) inventory control, (4) materials handling, (5) protective packaging, (6) distribution communications, and (7) transportation.

4. **Discuss the differences in types of storage facilities.** Goods are stored in three major types of storage facilities: (1) private warehouses (owned and operated by companies for their private use), (2) public warehouses (owned and operated by private contractors for use by others), and

(3) distribution centers (which collect and assemble goods from other plants and suppliers and move them on as soon as possible).

5. **Distinguish between traditional inventory methods and the just-in-time approach.** The traditional approach to inventory operates on the theory that large stocks are needed to act as a buffer against possible interruptions in production. In contrast, the JIT concept involves buying and producing in very small quantities just in time for use.

6. **Explain how modern technology is reducing materials handling costs.** Materials handling includes all the activities involved in moving products short distances within a production facility, warehouse, or retail store. Today, computers and other electronic devices are being used to automate storage facilities. For example, computerized coding systems are used to facilitate location, identification, and retrieval of goods. Another example involves the use of radio and other electronic devices to send messages to pickers and to guide automated vehicles to specified locations.

7. **Compare and contrast the five major modes of transportation.** According to the evaluative criteria given in the text, the best transportation modes for the following evaluative criteria are: airplane (speed), water (cost and capacity), pipeline (frequency), and truck (flexibility). The worst transportation modes for the following criteria are: pipeline (speed, flexibility, and capacity), water (frequency), and airplane (cost).

KEY TERMS

Physical Distribution, **p. 417**
Total Cost Approach, **p. 418**
Cost Trade-Off Approach, **p. 419**
Private Warehouse, **p. 421**
Public Warehouse, **p. 421**
Bonded Storage, **p. 421**
Distribution Center, **p. 421**
Stockout, **p. 421**
Stock Point, **p. 421**
Safety Stock, **p. 421**
Economic Order Quantity (EOQ) Model, **p. 422**
Just-in-Time (JIT) Concept, **p. 422**
Channel System, **p. 423**
Materials Handling, **p. 426**

Unit Loading, **p. 426**
Bar Code, **p. 427**
Transportation, **p. 428**
Common Carrier, **p. 428**
Contract Carrier, **p. 428**
Private Carrier, **p. 428**
Piggyback, **p. 430**
Intermodel System, **p. 432**
Containerization, **p. 432**
Fishyback, **p. 432**
Seatrain, **p. 432**
Freight Forwarder, **p. 433**
Shippers' Associations, **p. 433**

CHECK YOUR LEARNING

1. Which of the following is not a reason physical distribution is important: (a) it provides a better product, (b) it increases the variety of products available, (c) it broadens competition, (d) it increases customer satisfaction.
2. If the number of warehouses is increased, the cost of inventory also increases.   **T/F**
3. The total cost approach is based on: (a) minimizing the cost of each component, (b) equalizing all physical distribution costs, (c) minimizing the total physical distribution costs, (d) none of the above.
4. All of the following are major functions of warehousing except: (a) holding and protecting goods, (b) consolidating goods, (c) mixing product lines, (d) all of the above are functions of warehousing.
5. Safety stock is the amount of stock normally stored to meet average demand.   **T/F**
6. The EOQ model identifies the order size that mini-mizes the total cost of ordering and carrying inventory.   **T/F**
7. The most commonly used materials handling devices are the: (a) forklift and pallet, (b) crane and conveyor, (c) forklift and platform truck, (d) hand truck and conveyor.
8. Transportation costs comprise approximately 20 percent of the U.S. GNP.   **T/F**
9. Which of the following types of carriers offers its services for hire on a charter basis? (a) common, (b) private, (c) intermodal, (d) contract.
10. Which of the following is a factor in evaluating transportation modes? (a) speed, (b) flexibility, (c) frequency, (d) all of the above.
11. The least expensive mode of transportation is motor vehicles.   **T/F**
12. Freight forwarders are nonprofit associations that consolidate and distribute freight for members.   **T/F**

QUESTIONS FOR REVIEW AND DISCUSSION

1. Define the key terms for this chapter that appear at the end of the goal summary.
2. Explain how physical distribution broadens the area of competition.
3. What is the difference between product packaging and industrial packaging?
4. Using the criteria given in your text, select the best mode of transportation for each of the following and explain your choices:
   a. Coal from Indiana to be shipped to New York.
   b. Chemicals from New Orleans to be shipped to St. Louis.
   c. Natural gas from Houston to be shipped to Chicago.
   d. Horses from Kentucky to be shipped to Miami.
   e. A computer part from Mechanicsburg, Pennsylvania, to be shipped to Knoxville, Tennessee.
5. Explain how physical distribution adds value to products, and give examples.
6. What are some of the services offered by a public warehouse? Why are bonded warehouses needed?
7. What types of costs can result from stockouts?
8. Explain how a warehousing operation can effectively cut costs.

NOTES

1. Bernard J. La Londe and P. H. Zinszer, *Customer Service: Meaning and Measurement* (Chicago: National Council of Distribution Management, 1976).

2. National Council of Physical Distribution Management, *Measuring and Improving Productivity in Physical Distribution,* 1984, p. 7.

3. William D. Perault, Jr. and Frederick A. Russ, "Physical Distribution Service: A Neglected Aspect of Marketing Management," *MSU Business Topics,* Summer 1974, pp. 37–45.

4. Harvey N. Shycon and Christopher R. Sprague, "Put a Price Tag on Your Customer Servicing Levels," *Harvard Business Review,* July–August 1979, pp. 71–78.

5. Robert E. Sabath, "How Much Service Do Customers Really Want?" *Business Horizons,* April 1978, pp. 26–32.

6. Charles A. Taft, *Management of Physical Distribution and Transportation* (Homewood, Ill.: Richard D. Irwin, Inc., 1984), p. 9.

7. Kenneth B. Ackerman and Bernard J. La Londe, "Making Warehousing More Efficient," *Harvard Business Review,* April 1980, pp. 94–102.

8. James C. Johnson and Donald F. Wood, *Contemporary Physical Distribution and Logistics* (Tulsa, Okla.: PennWell Books, 1982), p. 356.

9. Ronald H. Ballou, *Basic Business Logistics* (Englewood Cliffs, N.J.: Prentice Hall, 1978), pp. 158–201.

10. Gerry O. Paltino, "Public Warehousing: Supermarkets for Distribution Services," *Handling and Shipping,* March 1977, pp. 59–61.

11. Francis J. Quinn, "Montgomery Ward Distribution Center Stresses Materials Handling, Efficient Traffic Controls," *Traffic Management,* May 1980, pp. 51–57.

12. Hal F. Mather, "The Case for Skimpy Inventories," *Harvard Business Review,* January–February 1984, pp. 40–42, 46.

13. Taft, *Management of Physical Distribution and Transportation,* p. 18.

14. Brian S. Moshal, "Just in Time: Putting the Squeeze on Suppliers," *Industry Week,* July 9, 1984, pp. 59–63; Richard J. Schonberger and Adbohossein Ansari, "Just-In-Time Purchasing Can Improve Quality," *Principles of Purchasing and Materials Management,* Spring 1984.

15. Vivian Brownstein, "The War on Inventories Is Real This Time," *Fortune,* June 11, 1984, pp. 20–24.

16. Taft, *Management of Physical Distribution and Transportation,* p. 261.

17. "How Merchandiser Cut Costs 20%," *Handling and Storage Management,* October 1984, pp. 3–4.

18. Milton J. Ellenbogen, "Logistics in the Warehouse," *Industrial Distribution,* September 1984, p. 39.

19. Brownstein, *The War on Inventories Is Real This Time,* p. 23.

20. Taft, *Management of Physical Distribution and Transportation,* p. 285.

21. Samuel Certo, Max Douglas, and Stewart Husted, *Business,* 2d ed (Boston: Allyn and Bacon, 1987), pp. 315–318. This section is adapted from the author's materials included in this text.

22. "Deregulation of Railroads to Create Competitive Pricing, Better Service," *Marketing News,* May 1, 1981, p. 9.

23. James M. Daley and Zanell V. Lambert, "Toward Accessing Trade-Offs by Shippers in Carrier Selection Decisions," *Journal of Business Logistics* 2 (1980): pp. 35–54.

24. *Transportation Facts and Trends,* 15th ed. (Washington, D.C.: Transportation Association of America, 1979), p. 31.

25. *Transportation Facts and Trends,* p. 43.

26. "ICC Adapts Rules Exempting Railroad Piggyback Service from Regulation," *Traffic World,* March 2, 1981, pp. 50–51.

27. *Piggyback: The Efficient Alternative for the 80s,* a report by Booze, Allen, and Hamilton, Inc., for TransAmerica Interway, Inc., New York, March 1980, p. 4; "Total Transportation: Just Around the Corner," *Traffic Management,* August 1983, pp. 70–71.

28. Martin T. Farris and Donald L. Schrock, "The Economics of Coal Slurry Pipelines—Transportation and Non-transportation Factors," *Transportation Journal,* Fall 1978, pp. 45–47.

29. "Express Delivery Services," *Traffic Management,* September, 1984, p. 79.

Sherwin-Williams was founded in 1873. It was the originator of quality ready-mix paints and today is the world's largest paint company. In 1979, the company brought in a new president, John G. Breen, to revive the ailing paint giant. A major focus of the turnaround was the distribution operations. The distribution system at that time was expensive and outmoded and in desperate need of restructuring. Breen hired a new management team for distribution, headed by Distribution Operations Director Dick Morreale.

Morreale quickly established several goals for his operation: reduce costs of distribution, improve customer service, and increase productivity. In order to meet these goals, Morreale employed several key employees to strengthen his management team. These individuals were needed to add flexibility and technical expertise at Sherwin-Williams' six distribution centers. These distribution centers were the heart of reorganization efforts. In addition, eight satellite warehouses (a mixture of public and leased space with no order/entry capability) are used.

Achieving higher customer service sometimes requires a balancing act and is not always practical. Dutch Boy, acquired by Sherwin-Williams in 1980, was a classic case. "It proved that high costs of providing the fastest service possible doesn't alone build sales," said Mr. Morreale. "They had organized, equipped, and staffed for same-day delivery, but sales did not grow as a result. Consequently, cost-per-order-delivered was staggering. They were paying premium price for transportation."

"Of course the best level of service is not an easy thing to determine," Gene Ivnik, director of technical services admitted. "We're constantly testing it. We get to 96 percent product availability, we don't hear much. But when we drop to 92 or 93 percent, you'd think an earthquake hit."

Sherwin-Williams believes that the key to closely watched service levels is timely and accurate information. To assist with this function, the company has developed a database-driven system called CSS (Customer Service System). This system generates the reports needed to monitor unveiled orders accurately and has provided the base for building additional distribution control systems.

The process begins with customer orders being collected by the regional computers and passed on to the host computer in Cleveland. The computer processes the orders by the customer's assigned truck pool number and individual stop number (orders for several locations are pooled on one truck and taken off at individual stops) and then compiles all orders for the Transportation and Distribution Report. This report lists all orders for a particular organized day.

From this report the distribution managers plan their next day's picking and shipping activities to optimize their scheduled outbound trucking capacity. For example, if more than 40,000 pounds of orders are on hand for a particular pool truck run, the center manager can decide to hold the order for a day or two, send it LTL, or try to build another pool load. If a certain pool load looks light, the manager can pull an order ahead from the next week—after checking with the store—or he or she can add some private-label or dealer-label shipments that normally go by common carrier.

In order to achieve other goals, Sherwin-Williams chose its Garland, Texas, distribution center to pilot its new distribution approach. The Garland center covers a territory stretching up to Wyoming and east to the Mississippi. It serves a significant portion of Sherwin-Williams' more than 1,400 retail outlets and 365 Kmart stores. Until the reorganization, a basic pick, pack, and ship method was used. This system wasted much time, as pickers were required to collect orders. Far too much time was spent walking the length of the center.

By instituting batch picking (selecting items within a "floating zone"), conveyor lines on four levels of mezzanines were used to collect customer orders from a particular zone. The zone "floats" as the flow of orders varies with the arrival of each wave of pool trucks. "In addition, batch picking does not require a lot of fancy equipment," says Mr. Morreale. "But we're here to make money for the company, not spend it. You really have to guard against 'over-equipmenting' yourself. That's the way you become the low-price distributor."

The system used to pick orders within the warehouse is only part of Sherwin-Williams' changed distribution philosophy. It also has overhauled transportation purchasing.

Most of Garland's shipments are carried by Contract Transportation Services, the company's trucking subsidiary. Meanwhile, use of outside carriers, either common or contract, is now handled on a centralized basis, rather than allowing each center to negotiate on its own. The company obviously is taking advantage of its business volume leverage to obtain discounts. It has also reduced the number of carriers with whom it does business. At Garland that meant reducing from eighteen outside carriers to four.

"The beauty of our area physical distribution," says Dick Morreale, "is that when you save the company a dollar, it goes right to the corporate profit. You'd have to sell about $35 worth of paint to get the same $1 profit."

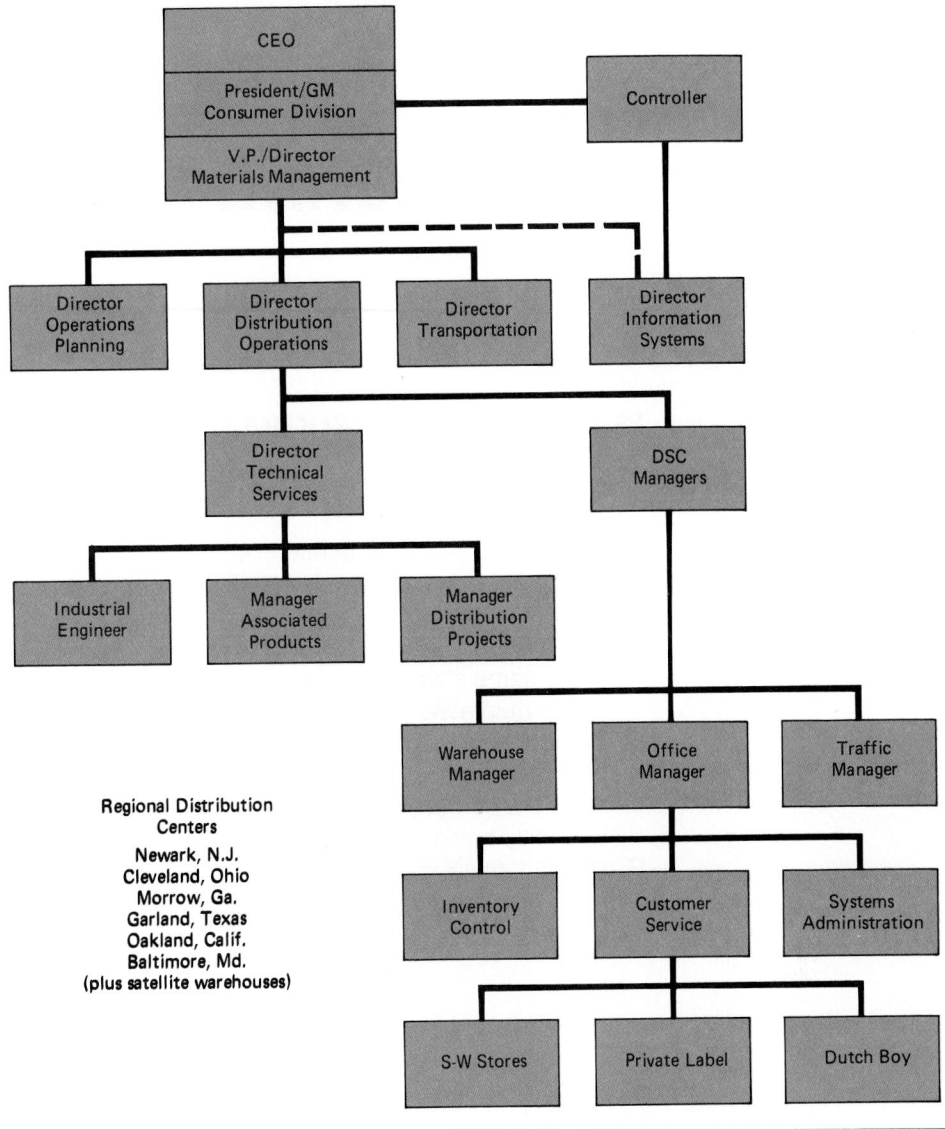

□ **Figure 15.7**
Distribution operations
at Sherwin-Williams.

Regional Distribution
Centers

Newark, N.J.
Cleveland, Ohio
Morrow, Ga.
Garland, Texas
Oakland, Calif.
Baltimore, Md.
(plus satellite warehouses)

Source: "Distribution Operations
at Sherwin-Williams," *Handling
and Shipping Management,*
November 1981, p. 25.

Issues for Discussion

1. Has Sherwin-Williams used a to-tal-cost approach to physical distribution? Explain your answer.
2. What trade-offs do you think Sherwin-Williams made when implementing its new distribution system?
3. Why would Sherwin-Williams need to use public and leased warehouses

to process its goods?
4. Explain how the EOQ model could be used by Sherwin-Williams.
5. What materials handling techniques did Sherwin-Williams utilize?
6. What advantages does Sherwin-Williams have in owning its own trucking company?

Sources: Patrick Gallagher, "A Fresh Coat for Sherwin-Williams," *Handling & Storage Management,* November 1981, pp. 31–35; Joan M. Feldman, "A Second Coat for Sherwin-Williams," *Handling & Storage Management,* October 1984, pp. 53–56.

MARKETING PLAN

**PART 6C / ACTION PROGRAM:
DISTRIBUTION**
(CHAPTERS 12, 13, 14, AND 15)

A. What is the current distribution strategy and intensity?
B. How will the organization's distribution objectives be met?
C. How effective are the current distribution channels? Will these same channels allow the achievement of this year's marketing objectives?
D. What (if any) new distribution channels should be added or eliminated this year? Why or why not?
E. Does the competition use any distribution channels not presently being used by this organization?
F. What (if any) expected future developments could affect how, what, when, or where consumers will purchase this product?

Section Seven

The Promotional Plan

OUTLINE

CHAPTER

16

Promotion

LEARNING GOALS_____

After reading this chapter, you should be able to:

1. Distinguish between marketing communications and promotion.
2. Describe the communications process.
3. Identify the criteria effective promotional objectives should meet.
4. Distinguish between push and pull strategies.
5. List the methods of estimating a promotional budget and explain each.
6. Identify the elements of the promotional mix.
7. Discuss the factors that influence the promotional mix.

While civic causes and cultural events have long been the accepted darlings of corporate sponsorship and philanthropy, controversial social issues by contrast have been taboo. Johnson & Johnson consumer product companies recently shattered that taboo by establishing "Shelter Aid," a nonprofit organization, to help women and their children who experience domestic violence. "We saw absolutely nothing controversial about helping women and children," a Johnson & Johnson spokesperson said.

For years, Johnson & Johnson had been providing personal-care products for distribution at domestic violence shelters. In May of 1986, the firm began discussing with NCADV (National Coalition Against Violence), how they could increase their participation. Plans were made to wage a promotional campaign to raise money for a network of new shelters, to establish a hotline, and to increase public awareness for the issue.

The effort to form Shelter Aid brought together a diverse collection of Johnson & Johnson subsidiaries (which normally function as distinct companies) and the NCADV. The Burson-Marsteller public relations agency and OLM Associates, a promotional agency, were involved in the execution. At the root of the promotions is Johnson & Johnson's conviction that it bears a responsibility to its consumers and the community.

Through market reserach, Johnson & Johnson learned just how deeply women care about domestic violence. When 300 women were asked to rank a set of issues on which they cared most about, domestic violence topped the list. They further found that many women had either experienced such violence directly, or knew someone who had.

Issues for Discussion
1. In your opinion, what are the dangers to companies of promoting social issues?
2. How can companies like Johnson & Johnson benefit from promotional campaigns that are tied to social, civic, or cultural causes?
3. What type of promotional campaign would you suggest for promoting Shelter Aid?

Source: Personal Products Co., Johnson & Johnson Company; and Laurie Peterson, "Promotion Goes Behind Closed Doors," *Adweek's Marketing Week,* January 25, 1988, pp. 1 and 4.

SUPPORT SHELTER AID™ WHEN YOU BUY THESE PRODUCTS

SHELTER AID
A safe home when home isn't safe

Help fund the only national toll-free domestic violence hotline

1-800-333-SAFE

Stayfree® Maxi-Pads	$0.00
Stayfree® Mini-Pads	$0.00
Sure&Natural™ Maxishields	$0.00
Carefree Panty Shields®	$0.00
o.b.® Tampons Slender Regular	$0.00
Assure &Natural™ Breathable Panty Liners	$0.00

1-800-333-SAFE
National Toll-Free Domestic Violence Hotline
• Domestic violence occurs every 15 seconds
• Domestic violence is the single largest cause of injury to women
• Domestic violence involves children 50% of the time

■ The above illustrates advertising copy used by Johnson & Johnson to promote Shelter Aid.
Source: Courtesy of Personal Products Co., Johnson & Johnson Co.

*I*n order to earn profits, marketers must thoroughly understand the fundamentals of marketing communications and promotion. Their tasks include setting promotional objectives and corresponding strategies and making plans to implement the promotional mix of advertising, personal selling, sales promotion, and publicity. Choosing among these elements requires familiarity with the product's characteristics, the target market, the product life cycle, and the promotional strategy. This chapter discusses these concepts and reviews a variety of techniques for developing the promotional budget. ■

MARKETING COMMUNICATIONS AND PROMOTION

Since 1902, when the company was founded, Minnesota Mining & Manufacturing (3M) Company has focused on new product ideas. As one might imagine, this can be a marketer's nightmare. 3M's biggest marketing problem has been the difficulty of promoting so many high-quality products. For example, in the early 1980s, 3M introduced a new suntan lotion called "Mmm, What a Tan." The product failed in the marketplace because 3M did not support it with a sufficient advertising budget. The lotion was water-repellent—an advance at the time—but consumers were not made aware of this property. 3M also lost its market leadership in audio tapes. Sony, Maxell, and TDK advertised their tapes more heavily, cut prices, and distributed to discount outlets. Because of these factors, 3M stopped manufacturing audiotapes.[1] As the saying goes, "What we have here is a failure of communication"—marketing communication.

*C*onsumers must be made aware of products and their benefits, and channel members must be kept informed.

The example proves the point that potential customers must be made aware of products and their benefits if they are to make purchases. However, it may not be enough to promote products just to consumer and industrial users. Members of the marketing channel are often essential to promoting and should be included in the promotional process. Therefore, it is necessary that communications be developed to keep them informed. In addition, as populations and the geographic scope of markets grow, the number of potential customers increases. Distance becomes a problem as more products are sold in international markets. Thus, the promotion of products to culturally diverse and distant markets becomes increasingly important. Finally, during times of economic decline, effective promotion is necessary to maintain high standards of living and employment.

Promotion and the Promotional Mix

*M*arketing communications involves an exchange of information; promotion usually involves a one-way information flow.

Marketing communications is the exchange of information between individuals (such as marketers and customers) involved in the marketing process. It involves not only word-of-mouth communication, but all forms of messages dealing with the buying and selling process. For example, a sales manual developed by a sales manager for his or her sales force is a form of marketing communication. A customer writing a letter to a manufacturer to complain about a product is also engaging in marketing communication. Later in this section the fundamentals of marketing communications will be discussed.

❑ **Figure 16.1** Innovative promotions.

Type of Innovative Promotion	Examples	Company
Sales Promotion	Postage Stamps	7–Eleven
Advertising	Walking Billboards	New York Ice Cream Co.
Sales Promotion	Grocery Cart Infant Safety Belts	Pepsi
Advertising	Commercials during Theater Movies	Canteen
Sales Promotion	Talking Displays	Anheuser-Busch
Advertising	Glow-in-the-Dark Truck Panels	Champion Spark Plugs
Sales Promotion	Clothing	Coca-Cola
Advertising	Laser Sky Writing	Stone Mountain Park
Advertising	Magazine Pop-ups	*Business Week*
Publicity	Americas Cup Sponsorship	Grant, Amway, *Newsweek*

At this point, however, we need only distinguish between marketing communications and promotion. **Promotion** is the communications means used by sellers to persuade or remind potential buyers that a product or service exists. Except in personal selling, promotion usually involves a one-way flow of information about goods or services that attempts to inform or persuade buyers or remind them to act. Marketers should listen to buyers first and then respond by developing products that satisfy customers' needs and wants. Only then has the time come to start promoting the product. Figure 16.1 lists some innovative promotions.

How marketers communicate with their customers depends on the promotional tools they use. These elements (discussed in Chapters 17 and 18) are often called the **promotional mix** and include a variety of promotional activities, including the following:

*T*he promotional mix includes advertising, personal selling, sales promotion, and publicity.

> **Advertising:** "Any paid form of nonpersonal presentation and promotion of ideas, goods, or services by an identified sponsor."[2]
> **Personal selling:** A promotional presentation by a seller using an interpersonal, verbal communication (one-on-one approach) with a prospective buyer.
> **Sales promotion:** "Those marketing activities, other than personal selling, advertising, and publicity, that stimulate consumer purchasing and dealer effectiveness."[3]
> **Publicity:** Nonpersonal stimulation of demand for a good, service, or business unit that is transmitted by a mass medium at no charge.

Table 16.1 compares these promotional elements. The complete range of promotional tools that make up the promotional mix will be discussed in later chapters.

A promotional strategy can focus on individuals, groups, or organizations. Promotion targeted at these audiences is designed to directly or indirectly influence their perception about a good, service, or idea. For example, Wendy's may wish to develop a promotion aimed at senior citizens and others who seek value in their meals. The message could say that there is more hamburger in a Wendy's patty. Of course, this was the message in the popular TV commercial, "Where's the beef?" Or Wendy's could send a message about its sponsorship of an anti–child abuse campaign to communicate the idea that it is a civic-minded organization. The goal of the latter message would be to improve the company's image rather than to

❑ **Table 16.1**   Characteristics of promotional elements.

	NATURE OF COMMUNICATION	ADVANTAGES	DISADVANTAGES
Advertising	Mass/nonpersonal	Standard message that can be controlled; relatively inexpensive per contact	Lacks direct feedback; overall expense can be high
Publicity	Mass/nonpersonal	No cost; message is more believable	Lacks direct feedback; marketer has no control of message
Personal Selling	Personal	Message tailored to the customer; direct feedback	High cost per contact
Sales Promotion	Mass/nonpersonal	Standard message; quick to gain attention	Lacks direct feedback; message is not constant

*T*he ultimate purpose of a business promotion is to sell more products by increasing demand for them.

promote a specific product. Of course, an improved image could, over a period of time, lead to additional patronage.

Regardless of which audience or message is chosen, the ultimate purpose of a business promotion is to sell more hamburgers or other products by changing the demand for them. This change occurs as the result of informing, reminding, and/or changing customers' behavior patterns or attitudes by persuasion.[4] Figure 16.2 illustrates a change in demand from an economic standpoint. With the help of promotion (other nonprice factors can have the same effect), a company hopes to increase a product's sales volume at a given price.[5] In other words, promotion attempts to make

Magazine ads, like this Dole promotion, help build brand loyalty.

Source: Courtesy of Dole Frozen Desserts

❑ **Figure 16.2**
Changing demand
pattern created by
promotion.

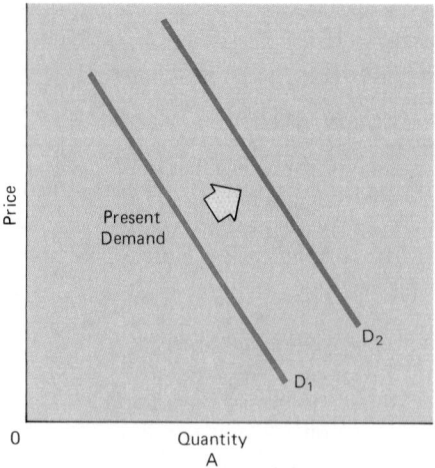

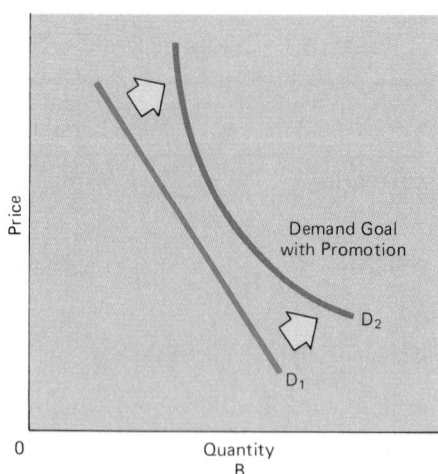

the demand curve (see figure 16.2) increasingly price insensitive (inelastic) at high prices and increasingly price sensitive (elastic) at low prices. Thus, the demand curve shifts to the right (a) and in effect increases the size of the market and creates a new demand curve (b).

It should be kept in mind that promotion can be used by individuals, groups, and organizations. These may include nonprofit organizations or individuals trying to promote an idea or service. For instance, when you graduate, you will aim appropriate elements of promotion—such as personal selling, direct mail, and possibly classified advertising in professional journals or employment directories—at your target market of prospective employers. The Toronto Knights of Columbus designed a promotional campaign to recruit priests. The organization's promotional tools included billboard advertisements and publicity. Promotional campaigns, even when they have different ultimate goals, may use the same promotional tools, though the proportions may vary.

THE BENEFITS OF PROMOTION

*P*romotion can help an organization introduce a new product, create brand loyalty, enhance buyer satisfaction, secure product distribution, build a positive image, or gain a marketplace "voice."

Promotion can do many things for a firm. First, it can help new products. For example, if Dole introduces a new frozen juice bar, consumers will become aware of it through a series of TV advertisements, magazine ads, coupons, samples, product displays, and other promotional tools. Promotion can also help create brand loyalty. Proper promotion can enhance buyer satisfaction with a product by pointing out its benefits and the social status associated with the brand, thus adding to the product's value.[6]

Other benefits include helping the firm secure distribution for its products, build a positive image, and gain a "voice" in the marketplace. Promotion is often the key to whether a retailer or wholesaler stocks a product. Understandably, middlemen prefer to stock products that they can turn over quickly and that will use a minimum of their promotional budgets. Finally, promotion gives a firm the opportunity to keep the public aware of such things as new product technology and features. General Motors, General Electric, and many other firms over the years have given consumers looks into the future of their industries with informative TV commercials, news and news photos, and trade shows.

The Fundamentals of Marketing Communications

A "commonness" must be
established if messages
are to be fully understood.

The word *communication* is derived from the Latin word *communis*. The meaning of this word, "common," is of utmost importance to marketers. In order to

Advertisements often give us a look at future product technology and features.

communicate, the marketer must establish a commonness with some individual or group of people. In other words, the marketer's message and its meanings must be fully understood.

The process of communicating is illustrated in figure 16.3. This model reflects the research of Bernard Berelson, Wilbur Schramm, R. A. Bauer, and Otto Kleppner, who were among the first to propose that communication was best understood as an exchange between the sender (seller) and the receiver (buyer).[7] The simplest form of communication is interpersonal. Here, a **message** is sent from one person to another.

❏ **Figure 16.3**
The communications process.

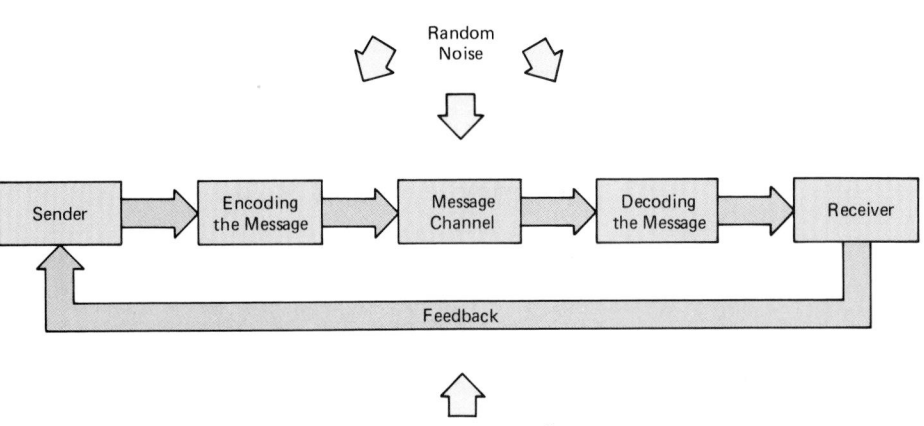

*C*omponents of interpersonal communication include a message, a medium of transmission, a sender, a receiver, encoding and decoding processes, and feedback. Noise may interfere with communication.

Since personal selling is interpersonal in nature, we will use it to illustrate the communication process. Suppose that David Hewett is a new salesperson at a large Atlanta furniture store. One of David's first customers, Karen, asks the location of the store's commodes. Thus, a message is sent by voice (the **medium of transmission**) from the **sender** (a customer) to the **receiver** (David). Other transmission options may include body language, facial expression, appearance, gestures, laughter, and writing. However, for this or any message to have meaning, it must first be coded into a series of signs or symbols. This process is called **encoding.** To encode her message, the customer could have used pictures or given a detailed description of what she was seeking to purchase.

During the transmission of a message, its accuracy can be greatly influenced by random **noise,** a condition that can affect all or part of the communications process. In our example, considerable random noise is being generated by other customers and salespeople, cash registers, passing outside traffic, and other interrupters.

To understand this customer's message, David (the receiver) must convert it into recognizable concepts and ideas. This process is called **decoding.** Once David has decoded the message, he must give a response in the form of **feedback.** This response will indicate whether the message has been understood, or correctly decoded. In this case David decodes the word *commode* as representing a plumbing fixture found in a bathroom. Since David lacks a *frame of reference* similar to Karen's and has had limited experience in the furniture business, he has failed to recognize that a commode is also a not-so-common French name for a small chest. The response to David's feedback reply is immediate, and luckily, it takes the form of laughter. Thus, we can see that the communications process can be viewed as a circular exchange that does not have to be spoken, as figure 16.3 has shown.

*M*ass communication messages are impersonal and group directed.

Now we can examine the similar but more complex *mass marketing communications model.* Here, the sender is an organization that wishes to reach a potential market. The goal of the sender is to inform, persuade, or remind an audience about a product or idea. The sender's message will be impersonal in nature and directed to a group rather than an individual. The format for the message can be either verbal or nonverbal symbols. One problem for marketers is encoding message content so that it is understandable to many individuals. This problem is illustrated in the accompanying cartoon, which depicts the decoding of symbols seen by highway motorists.

An element of the mass media—radio, TV, newspapers, magazines, books, billboards, or some other—serves as the medium of transmission. As in interpersonal communication, the message must be decoded by the receiver. Once again, noise can play an important part in whether the message is properly transmitted or even heard. To overcome this problem, many TV and radio advertisers, for example, schedule commercials during times when small children are in bed.

*F*eedback from mass communication is usually delayed and indirect.

Finally, the sender will begin to receive feedback. Unlike the feedback in interpersonal communications, the feedback received from mass communications may

Pepper . . . and Salt

□ **Table 16.2**   Examples of the communications process in marketing.

	PERSONAL SELLING	MAGAZINE ADVERTISING	SALES PROMOTION (SPECIALTY ADVERTISING)	PUBLICITY
Sender **Encoding**	IBM salesperson Spoken words; gestures; demonstration; appearance	Del Monte Copy and illustrations in color ad for pineapple.	Pilot Life Insurance Copy and logo	Levi Strauss Words written about Levi's sponsorship of "ride and run" sports events; Levi's banner at events.
Medium	Salesperson	*Better Homes and Gardens; Southern Living; Ladies Home Journal*	Desk calendar	*Business Week*—news article.
Receiver	Buyer at Computerland	A consumer reads the ad at home.	A consumer sees the message daily as he sits at his desk.	Readers across the nation.
Decoding	Steps in demonstration hookup for IBM PC not understood	The consumer likes the recipe included with the ad.	The consumer develops a positive image of the company.	Readers, participants, and spectators develop positive image of Levi's.
Feedback	Buyer asks salesperson to demonstrate again	Consumer purchases more pineapple required in the recipe.	The consumer increases his life insurance coverage.	Consumers purchase more jeans; no formal research conducted.

□ **Figure 16.4**
Decision sequence for developing promotional programs.

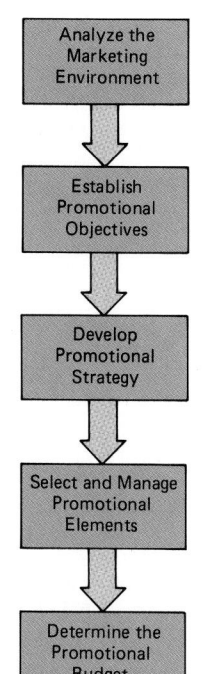

take the form of increased sales or the redemption of coupons or rebates. Instant feedback is available now in homes where cable services such as QUBE exist. With QUBE, viewers can respond immediately to advertisements and other messages they see on their TV screens by pressing hand-held computer devices. Further examples of the communications processes in mass marketing are illustrated in table 16.2.

 PROMOTIONAL OBJECTIVES, STRATEGIES, AND PLANS

Before establishing a promotional strategy and a plan to implement it, a firm must identify sound objectives. These objectives should be based on an analysis of the marketing environment as discussed in Chapter 3. By first establishing objectives, the firm can develop standards that will help it measure the success or failure of the promotion. Figure 16.4 illustrates the decision-making sequence for establishing objectives, strategies, and plans.

Establishing Promotional Objectives

Effective promotional objectives are actually nothing more than the responses an organization expects from its promotion. Of course, these objectives should be tied to an overall organizational plan and objectives. (Figure 16.5 shows the relationship between promotional objectives and other objectives.) Although the need for objectives may seem clear, lack of objectives is a leading promotional deficiency. Therefore, effective management of the promotional process requires a clear knowledge and understanding of the promotional objectives to be reached.

The choice of promotional objectives influences the types of promotion desired. For example, when the Clorox Company wanted to introduce a modified form of its

MARKETING IN ACTION

Fiero Workers Receive Valuable Interpersonal Communications Feedback

*A*t the General Motors Fiero plant in Pontiac, Michigan, fifty volunteer workers were directly involved in the interpersonal communications process between producers and consumers. This unusual customer service program was begun in 1984. Each worker followed five Fiero buyers for a year by surveying them with phone calls every three months. Calls were made on the worker's time, usually from home, and Pontiac paid the phone bill.

Feedback received from consumers was sent back to the plant where problems may have originated. In addition, it was sent to service experts who educate dealers about repairs. Feedback was primarily used at the plant where problems were isolated and corrected immediately. Normal feedback is processed in six to twelve months, and thus corrections take considerably longer.

Considering the low cost of implementing the program ($15 to $20 per worker in phone bills), the benefits were high. One problem that was quickly discovered was that windshields were cracking in the upper corner. The problem was isolated to some window tabs which were creating excessive pressure on the glass. Another program benefit was the positive press and publicity generated. The message from this communication was clear . . . General Motors wanted to build quality autos.

Unfortunately, the initial success of this program (first-year sales of 102,000) was short-lived. In March of 1988, Pontiac announced plans to quit making the car in September, 1988. Decreased demand for two-seat cars, high consumer insurance rates, and poor performance were the reasons given for the decision to discontinue the Fiero.

Source: "A GM Plant With a Hot Line Between Workers and Buyers," *Business Week,* June 11, 1984, p. 165.

---

existing bleach product, it wanted to create mass awareness (an objective) of that product. Likely choices to suit this objective are the promotional elements of advertising, sales promotion, and some publicity. Supplementing each of these elements involves its own set of subobjectives. Other objectives may include increased product knowledge, preference conviction, and the primary objective of stimulating demand.

For these objectives to be effective, they should meet the following five criteria:

1. They should be measurable and should be written in concrete terms.
2. They should be based on sound research and should identify a well-defined target audience.

☐ **Figure 16.5**
Relationship of promotional objectives to other objectives.

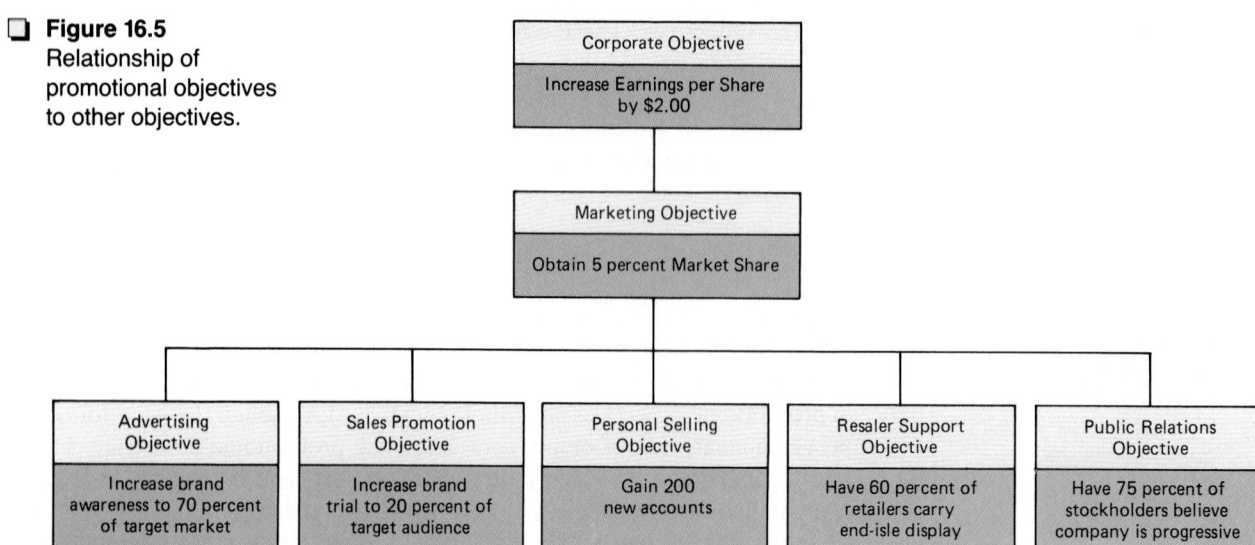

Source: Adapted from James Engle, Martin Warshaw, and Thomas Kinnear, *Promotional Strategy,* Copyright © 1979 by Richard D. Irwin, Inc.

THE REST OF THE STORY

Promotion Produces Sweet Results

*F*or seventy years one of America's great companies refused to use advertising to promote their products. The company founder, Milton S. Hershey, insisted that quality was the best kind of advertising.

For years this strategy worked, and the company was the number one manufacturer of candy. However, after World War II, candy stores and tobacco shops disappeared, and candy started being sold on the shelves of supermarkets. Of course this required the preselling of candy products with advertising. In addition, with the introduction of TV, more Americans were staying away from movie theaters. The result was

a nosedive in candy sales for Hershey.

Finally after slipping to number two in candy sales, the company selected an ad agency and ran their first consumer ad on July 19, 1970. The ad, a full page for Hershey syrup, ran in 114 newspapers. Two months later, ads appeared on the radio and TV. Since 1970 Hershey has become a heavy hitter in advertising circles. Promotional spending rose to $137 million, or 8.8 percent of

sales in 1982, from $76 million, or 6.5 percent of sales in 1979.

Although Hershey advertises today, the company is careful about the kind of promotion directed to children. Nevertheless, Hershey is committed to a major advertising program and to regaining its number one market share. For more information on Hershey and its current marketing strategy, see the concluding case in Chapter 3.

Sources: Milton Moskowitz, Michael Katz, and Robert Levering, *Everybody's Business* (Harper & Row Publishers, 1980), p. 42; "Hershey: A Hefty Ad Budget Has Profits Flying High," *Business Week,* February 13, 1984, p. 88.

---

3. They should be realistic.
4. They should reinforce the overall marketing plan and relate to specific marketing objectives.
5. They should be reviewed periodically and changed as necessary.[8]

Developing the Promotional Strategy

A promotional strategy is like a general's overall battle plan. It tells in broad terms how a firm will use promotion to secure an advantage over the competition, to attract buyers, and to capitalize on its resources. In other words, a firm's objectives indicate where it wants to go, and its strategy describes how it will get there—how it will accomplish its objectives. This requires a specific promotional budget and plan for selecting and managing the promotional elements.

Two major types of promotional strategies are used in business. The first is called a **push strategy.**[9] This strategy places primary emphasis on personal selling at all stages of the product's progress through the marketing channel; however, personal selling is often supplemented with advertising and other promotional efforts. For example, when the Fellows Corporation introduces a machine cutting tool, its sales force will provide wholesalers with equipment displays, trade advertising, special allowances, and certainly a strong sales pitch. These wholesalers, in turn, will visit and heavily promote the machine tools to industry. Thus, as you can see in figure 16.6, the product is forced, or "pushed," through the channels of distribution. This strategy can be used for both consumer and industrial goods.

The push strategy is usually most successful when the manufacturer offers a high-quality product with unique features. These attributes give salespeople a way to attract and hold attention. In addition, marketers of higher-priced or high-volume products often use the push strategy because these types of products provide higher margins and thus allow the use of more personal selling. The higher margins can usually be passed on to resellers, along with special contest prize incentives or premiums.[10]

By advertising in popular women's magazines, Clorox creates a mass product awareness for its new liquid product.

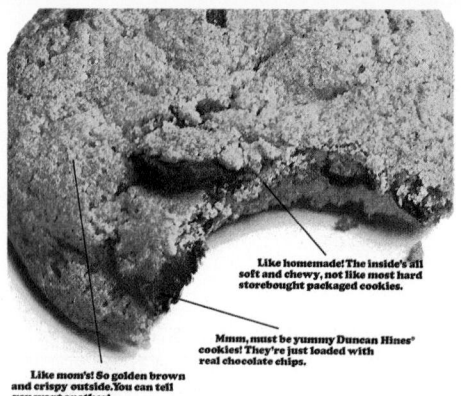

Like homemade! The inside's all soft and chewy, not like most hard storebought packaged cookies.

Mmm, must be yummy Duncan Hines® cookies! They're just loaded with real chocolate chips.

Like mom's! So golden brown and crispy outside.You can tell you want another!

One taste'll tell you

...Duncan Hines
Chocolate Chip Cookies taste
crispy, chewy like mom's.

Procter & Gamble used a pull strategy of heavy advertising to promote their newest Chocolate Chip cookies.
Source: Courtesy of Duncan Hines.

☐ **Figure 16.6**
Push and pull promotional strategies.

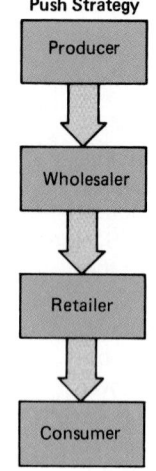

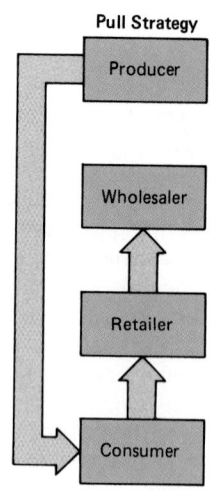

The opposite of the push strategy is the **pull strategy,** which tries to stimulate consumer demand for a product through heavy advertising. Supposedly, consumers will see or hear a promotion that will cause them to visit their retailer and "demand" a product. This strategy uses less personal selling, and salespeople often become little more than order takers. Besides advertising, various sales promotion techniques are commonly integrated into the promotion. For instance, when Procter & Gamble introduced its brand of chocolate chip cookies, it offered free trial samples and coupons to homes across the country.

Most consumer marketers use a combination of push and pull strategies. In a combination strategy, salespeople push the products, while extensive advertising and sales promotions attempt to produce a pull effect. Such combinations require extensive promotional expenditures.

THE CASE CONTINUES

The population focus of the J&J promotional strategy was women and children subject to abuse in the home. This form of social marketing (promoting ideas and causes) was used to create mass awareness of the problem of domestic abuse and to measurably increase sales and profits. In order to accomplish their objectives, the company selected a promotional mix of personal selling, advertising, sales, promotion, and publicity.

The sensitivity of the cause—domestic violence—prompted J&J to move forward cautiously. The company first tested the concept with key retail accounts to determine whether they understood the issue, and, more important, if they would give a program to aid victims of domestic violence retail support. In approach-

ing these retailers, J&J chose to use roundtable sessions with a 10-minute video that mixed clips from a television documentary on the subject with interviews of battered women and their children. The video explained the program and how public relations and support materials for Shelter Aid might work. Finally, using a "push strategy," J&J appealed for retail support—and got it. The video underwent about twelve revisions as the program and creative execution evolved. It was used to sell the program internally to J&J employees and to sell it to the industry. Another version was used for publicity. Actress Lindsay Wagner was selected as the celebrity spokesperson.

Shelter Aid was launched in June of 1987 with a "Call to Action" conference in Washington, D.C. The event was attended by several hundred leaders of national and local womens, civic, religious, community, etc., organizations.

The J&J salesforce was already in the field "pushing" the promotion. Representatives from local shelters went on sales calls to brief retailers on the situation in their communities. Retailers were offered a one percent discount on purchases of participating rebate brands when they featured the nine participating J&J products, the Shelter Aid logo, and the hotline number. J&J supplied the ad slicks. The rebate was refunded in the form of a tax-deductible check in the retailer's name, to be used as a donation to shelters.

Planning the Promotion

Short- and long-range plans must be developed to specify the promotional elements to be used.

Once the promotional strategy has been established, the firm can develop a set of short- and long-range plans that specify the promotional elements to be used. Promotional plans should reveal how organizational resources are to be allocated among the elements and what results are expected. This information will help the marketer to determine the promotional mix and to coordinate the promotional elements. The elements of the promotional mix are discussed in detail in the last section of this chapter.

One company, Johnson & Johnson, developed a novel promotional plan to sell toys. Its long-range plan was to become a leader in marketing young children's toys. This part of the plan was accomplished within five years and without the cost of TV advertising. (The company now ranks second behind Fisher Price.) The direct-marketing approach selected used the promotional activities of direct mail, magazine advertising, packaging, and word-of-mouth promotion through nurseries and physicians. Parents were urged to sign up their newborns to receive a learning toy by mail every six weeks until the child was three. This promotional plan resulted in high sales and profits, both of which the company planned for by carefully defining the target audience and establishing objectives, budget, and measurement techniques for its promotional plan.[11]

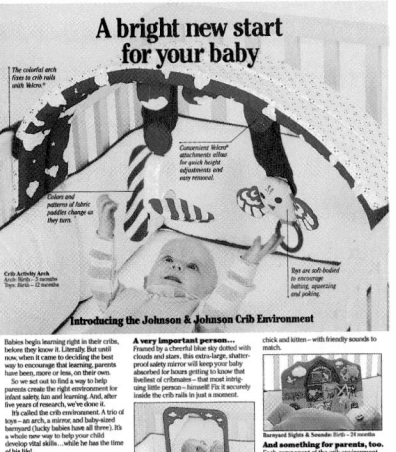

Johnson & Johnson developed a promotional strategy, consisting of magazine ads and other direct marketing activities, to sell education toys.

Source: Courtesy of Johnson & Johnson

DEVELOPING THE PROMOTIONAL BUDGET

It is never easy to determine the size and allocation of a firm's promotional spending budget; however, guidance can be found in the overall marketing plan. The marketing plan usually specifies an appropriation, or approved amount, that can be spent for the entire function. Decision makers—often the product manager in cooperation with the advertising/promotion manager—must then allocate the amounts that can be spent for advertising, sales promotion, and publicity.[12] In addition, the budget can be further broken down by sales territory, customer, and so on.

Factors That Influence the Promotional Budget

Factors that influence the size of the promotional budget: objectives, product class, economic conditions, stage in life cycle, channels of distribution, and previous expenditures.

Many major factors influence the size of promotional budgets. Some of these include the following:[13]

1. *Objectives.* The use of specific objectives can provide direction in the establishment of a budget. An objective that will take a greater effort to accomplish probably will require a greater expenditure. For example, the objective of increasing market share for a product from 10 percent to 15 percent should normally require more funds than the objective of increasing market share from 10 percent to 12 percent.
2. *Product class.* Different kinds of products require different amounts of promotion. For example, convenience goods like cigarettes and soft drinks require a great deal of promotion because of their intensive distribution and the heavy use of advertising to presell them. Shopping goods like automobiles, TVs, and even long-distance phone service require even heavier promotional efforts because of the intense competition in these markets. By contrast, specialty goods usually have obtained considerable brand loyalty and thus require less promotional effort.

❏ **Table 16.3** Major determinants of the allocation decision: external.

FACTOR	IMPACT ON ALLOCATION	
	INCREASE ADVERTISING	INCREASE SALES PROMOTION
Stage in brand life cycle		
Introduction	X	
Growth	X	
Maturity		X
Decline		X

Source: Excerpted from Roger A. Strang, "Major Determinants of the Allocation Decision External," in *The Promotional Planning Process* (New York: Praeger Publishers, 1980), p. 94. Copyright © 1980 by Roger Strang. Reprinted by permission of the publisher.

Effect of inflation on budget must be evaluated.

Promotional spending will likely be greatest during introductory stage.

Intensive distribution policy requires greater promotional budget.

3. *Economic conditions.* Many firms cut back on promotion as a whole or switch their dollars from advertising to sales promotion when the economy is performing poorly. Another economic factor to be considered is inflation, which can drive costs up.

4. *Stage in the product's life cycle.* Except for products that die quickly, most products go through the product life cycle. As previously discussed, the product life cycle involves marketing decisions related to all aspects of the marketing mix. The amounts spent on promotion are usually greatest during the introductory and growth stages. At the decline stage, price appeals are used more and promotional spending, less (see table 16.3).

5. *Channels of distribution.* The size of the promotional budget often depends on the length of the distribution channel. If the channel includes several middlemen, the producer usually must promote more aggressively. This is because middlemen who distribute convenience goods often fear they will be helping their competitors if they supplement the producer's promotions. When an exclusive distribution policy is followed, the producer can count on more support, since the retailers do not want to lose their exclusive rights to sell the product. Specialty and shopping goods are often promoted in this manner.

6. *Previous expenditures.* Many firms view their promotional budgets in terms of how much was spent last year. This amount may be based on the absolute amount available or on how much the competition spent last year.

Methods of Estimating the Promotional Budget

Several methods of estimating budgets are available to the marketer. Some of the more common ones include the following:[14]

Arbitrary allocation is based on experience and judgment—and often on how much the firm can afford.

1. *Arbitrary allocation.* Most organizations that promote are small, nonmanufacturing firms. Such firms usually do not have a promotional budget of the kind we have discussed. Instead, they tend to have advertising and sales budgets. These budgets are often based on the experience and judgment of marketing and advertising or store managers. Sometimes, how much promotion the firm can afford is the basis for a manager's budget decision. It is very difficult to determine the effect of promotional tools when the arbitrary approach is used.

2. *Percentage of sales.* The percentage of sales method is the most popular for estimating the promotional budget. Historical precedent plays an important role in guiding marketers who use this approach. One executive cited in a recent study stated that product managers "project dollar and unit sales for the

*T*he promotional budget is often based on a fixed percentage.

year (and) then decide whether they are going to spend more or less than the year before.'' The budgeted amount is often a fixed percentage of expected sales.[15]

The percentage of sales approach can also use past or forecasted sales figures applied to an industry average to determine the promotional budget. For example, suppose that in the auto industry an average 0.5 percent of net sales is spent for promotion. If Chrysler's sales last year were $14 billion, it would set its promotional budget at $70 million (0.5% × $14 billion) if it used this budgeting method.

Although this method is simple and easy to apply, it has its drawbacks. For one, it assumes that sales are the cause of promotion rather than the result, whereas the opposite is true. In addition, the percentage selected is often too small or too large, because it is based to some extent on a historical percentage that may not reflect present conditions.

*S*pending at the same level as competitors assumes that all competitors share the same marketing situations and goals.

3. *Competitive parity.* Some firms try to spend at the same level as their competitors. This approach assumes that all competitors share the same marketing situations, and it fails to consider that the firms' promotional objectives may differ significantly. Furthermore, a firm must remember that the competitor it seeks to copy may be using the same strategy.

Most firms do take into account their competitors' allocations, but most use them more as guides to determining levels of spending for specific promotional elements than as determinants of overall allocation. One practical reason for this practice is a lack of accurate data on competitors' promotional spending.

*T*he soundest method for creating a promotional budget involves developing specific objects and subobjectives and placing a dollar value on each.

4. *Objective and task.* Probably the most defensible method for determining the promotional budget is the objective and task method. This approach assumes nothing and requires the marketer to develop specific objectives and subobjectives. An analysis must be completed for each objective so the nature and size of the promotional activities (tasks) required can be determined. The sum of the amounts "built up" for each of these activities becomes the firm's promotional budget.

Despite its soundness, this method has not gained wide acceptance. One study suggests two possible reasons. The first and main reason may be that the focus in promotional planning is on established brands rather than new brands. With new brands marketers may have little information on which to base an allocation decision. A second possibility is greater involvement in the allocation decision by senior management. Recently, more marketers have been reporting restrictions by senior management on their planning efforts.

THE CASE CONTINUES

*T*o further promote Shelter Aid, J&J bought space for a three-page freestanding newspaper insert. Each insert included facts about domestic violence, the hotline number, and $3.95 worth of coupons that would generate a five-cent donation for each coupon redeemed, to shelters nationally. Additionally, for a six-month period, for each proof-of-pur-

chase seal submitted for Stayfree and Medipren, an additional five cents was donated.

Through Lindsay Wagner's connections, a public service announcement was produced as well as a tie-

in with an episode of the television show, "Cagney and Lacy," that had a storyline that dealt with domestic violence. Before the show premiered, it was screened before several hundred celebrities, members of the press, and concerned people working in the field of domestic violence. It was followed by a panel discussion on domestic violence.

FACTORS THAT INFLUENCE THE PROMOTIONAL MIX

The promotional mix, introduced earlier in this chapter, is composed of two or more coordinated elements meant to promote a product. Each promotional element includes a mix of promotional media. For example, advertising includes radio, newspaper, TV, magazines, and other promotional media.

    The promotional mix varies according to product characteristics, such as whether the product is being sold to consumers or industrial users. Other influencing factors include the product life cycle stage, target audience, and type of strategy chosen.

*T*he promotional mix varies with product characteristics, life cycle stage, target audience, and type of strategy chosen.

Product Characteristics

*P*ersonal selling plays an important role in the promotion of industrial products.

Industrial producers usually place a high degree of importance on personal selling and relegate other promotional elements to lesser roles. Figure 16.7 illustrates the relative importance of promotional elements in consumer versus industrial markets. This is not to say that advertising does not play an important role in industrial markets, for research indicates that personal selling performance increases about 25 percent when supported by advertising. The same is true of some consumer products, such as automobiles, diamonds, and appliances. These products usually have one or more of the following characteristics: they have high value or cost; they require demonstration; they are infrequently purchased; or they are technical in nature.

Target Market Analysis

An analysis of the target market to ascertain its size and geographic distribution will reveal important information about what type of mix is needed. For example, if a product is not used over a wide geographic area or if it is used by a relatively small number of consumers, then personal selling and local or regional advertising could be a good choice. This promotional mix is common in the selling of farm and dairy products.

*A*dvertising is the best promotional element for reaching large numbers of people.

    Firms that sell to relatively small numbers of customers can afford to use personal selling, but firms that market to many consumers distributed across the country cannot. That is why Wendy's, Pepsi, Philip Morris, Warner-Lambert, Bristol-Myers, and others rely so heavily on advertising in their mix.

❑ **Figure 16.7**
Relative importance of promotional tools.

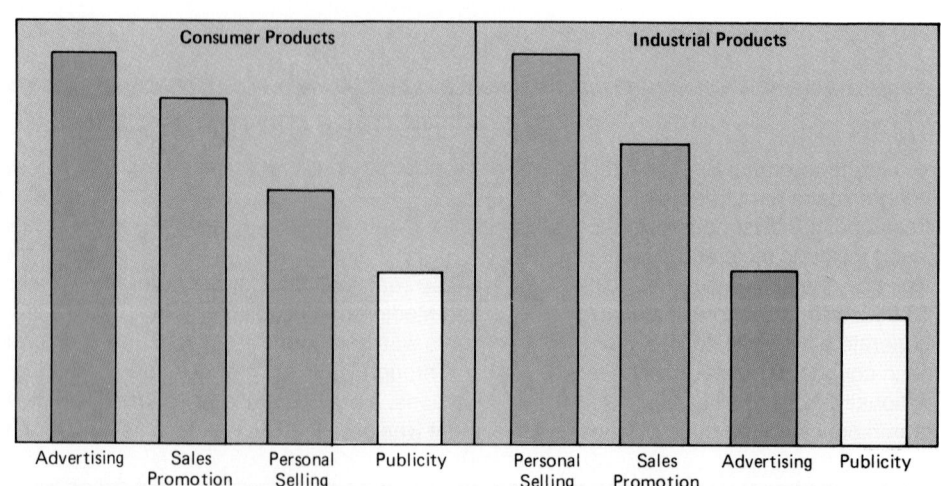

Source: Philip Kotler, *Principles of Marketing,* Third Edition, © 1986, p. 500. Adapted by permission of Prentice-Hall, Inc., Englewood Cliffs, New Jersey.

❑ **Figure 16.8** Projected promotional activities used over the life cycle of cellular phones.

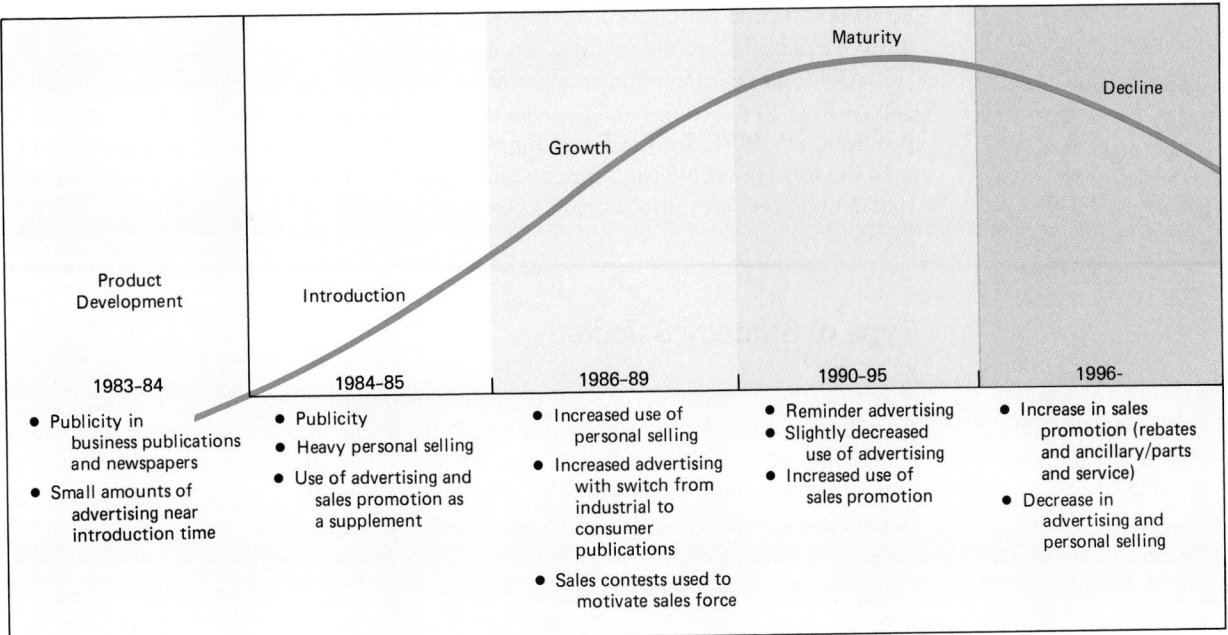

Stage of the Product Life Cycle

The promotional mix changes over the product's life cycle.

As noted in previous chapters, the marketing mix changes over a product's life cycle. Of course, this includes the promotional mix, which changes as promotional objectives change.

Let's examine how one product might evolve through the life cycle (see figure 16.8).[16] Cellular phones were first developed in the early 1980s. In the developmental stage, the promotional mix consisted largely of publicity and some advertising as the phones neared market entry. The publicity element was especially important, because feature articles were published in *The Wall Street Journal, Business Week,* and other influential publications. The objective of these elements was to develop awareness and to stimulate demand among innovators to adopt.

In 1984 the product was introduced in the marketplace. The objective at this stage was to continue developing interest, to stimulate general trial and adoption, and to gain distribution penetration in eight major metro markets. The continued use of publicity and the heavy use of personal selling were the mainstays of the promotional mix. They were supplemented by some advertising and sales promotion activities like trade shows. This mix was chosen because of the product's high price ($3,000) and technical nature and the need to demonstrate the product.[17]

During the growth stage, the price was cut to $1,500 and additional services were offered. This change in price caused an increase in sales in the industrial market, and consequently a few consumers started purchasing the phones for their autos. At this point, the amount of advertising was increased, and some advertising was switched from industrial to consumer publications. In addition, trade deals and sales promotions in the form of sales contests were used to motivate salespeople to sell more. The objective at this stage was to develop brand preference and to hold and gain distribution.

The maturity stage could bring more deep price cuts. (It is estimated that the phones will cost less than $250 by 1990.) This strategy could mean that many more consumers will be able to afford the phones. Manufacturers may increase their sales promotion efforts and slightly decrease their advertising. Their general objective will be to hold brand preference for replacement units and to continue sales growth as more users buy a second or third phone.

Although cellular phones are nowhere near the decline stage at this point, we can assume that as sales start to decline, a corresponding decline will occur in the promotional effort. Some advertising will still be used, but most sales promotion will take the form of rebates and free ancillary parts or service. Recent research indicates that more firms are emphasizing sales promotion in the later stages of a product's life cycle.

Type of Strategy Selected

*P*ush and pull strategies require different promotional mixes.

Whether the firm selects a push or a pull strategy has a definite influence on the promotional mix. As previously discussed, firms that choose the push strategy use a sales staff to force the product through the distribution channels. At the other extreme, firms that use a pull strategy place heavy emphasis on advertising to attract buyers to a product and to encourage them to demand it.

THE CASE CONTINUES

*E*very promotional campaign must be evaluated. While there are many standards for measuring the success of campaigns, the bottom line is how well the campaign objectives have been met. In this case, the J&J campaign was a success by every measurable standard. By the end of the campaign in 1988, nearly $1.5 million was raised for the hotline and shel-

ters and an average of 5,000 calls a month are received on the hotline.

In addition, market share of Stayfree experienced its highest period-to-period share increase in seven years after newspaper coupons appeared with the appeal, "Help

women and their children find a home when home isn't safe."

Finally, by public relations standards, the campaign was also a stunning success. During the active campaign more than 1,000 stories in the press generated an estimated 167 impressions, or number of persons reading the stories, according to Burson-Marsteller's calculations.

GOAL SUMMARY

1. **Distinguish between marketing communications and promotion.** Marketing communications is the exchange of information between individuals involved in the marketing process. Promotion, except for personal selling, usually involves a one-way flow of information about goods or services that attempts to inform or persuade buyers or remind them to act.
2. **Describe the communications process.** Communication is an exchange between a sender and a receiver. The simplest form of communication is interpersonal; here, a message is sent from one person to another. For example, in personal selling, the

salesperson sends an encoded message. The receiver decodes the message and then provides feedback to the sender that indicates whether the message was understood. Often, noise interferes with the transmission and reception of a message.

In the more complex marketing communications model, the process is similar; however, the sender is usually an organization and the message is impersonal and formatted in either verbal or nonverbal symbols. An element of the mass media serves as the medium of transmission.

GOAL SUMMARY *(continued)*

3. **Identify the criteria effective promotional objectives should meet.** Effective promotional objectives should meet the following criteria: (1) be measurable and written in concrete terms, (2) be based on sound research and identify a well-defined target audience, (3) be realistic, (4) reinforce the overall marketing plan and relate to specific objectives, and (5) be periodically reviewed.

4. **Distinguish between push and pull strategies.** The push strategy places primary emphasis on personal selling to push the product through the marketing channel. The pull strategy tries to stimulate consumer demand and so uses heavy advertising.

5. **List the methods of estimating a promotional budget and explain each.** There are four major methods of estimating a promotional budget: (1) arbitrary (based on experience and personal judgment), (2) percentage of sales (based on past or estimated sales applied to a fixed percentage), (3) competitive parity (based on what major competitors are spending), and (4) objective and task (based on the development of specific objectives and subobjectives).

6. **Identify the elements of the promotional mix.** The elements of the promotional mix include advertising, sales promotion, personal selling, and publicity.

7. **Discuss the factors that influence the promotional mix.** The following factors influence the selection of the promotional mix: (1) product characteristics, (2) target market analysis, (3) stage of the product life cycle, and (4) type of strategy chosen.

KEY TERMS

Marketing Communications, **p. 445**
Promotion, **p. 446**
Promotional Mix, **p. 446**
Advertising, **p. 446**
Personal Selling, **p. 446**
Sales Promotion, **p. 446**
Publicity, **p. 446**
Message, **p. 449**
Medium of Transmission, **p. 450**

Sender, **p. 450**
Receiver, **p. 450**
Encoding, **p. 450**
Noise, **p. 450**
Decoding, **p. 450**
Feedback, **p. 450**
Push Strategy, **p. 453**
Pull Strategy, **p. 454**

CHECK YOUR LEARNING

1. *Marketing communications* and *promotion* are synonymous terms.   **T/F**
2. All of the following are objectives of promotion except: (a) reminding, (b) informing, (c) encouraging, (d) persuading.
3. Which of the following elements of the promotional mix is free? (a) advertising, (b) sales promotion, (c) personal selling, (d) publicity.
4. One benefit of promotion is that it provides a firm with a "voice" in the marketplace.   **T/F**
5. The word *communication* comes from a Latin word meaning "to talk."   **T/F**
6. A message is decoded once it is converted into recognizable concepts and ideas.   **T/F**
7. All of the following are criteria for a promotional objective except: (a) must be measurable, (b) must be written, (c) must be realistic, (d) must be general.

8. A push strategy uses advertising to force the product through the marketing channel.   **T/F**
9. All of the following strongly influence the promotional budget except: (a) competitive parity, (b) product class, (c) objectives, (d) stage in product life cycle.
10. Which of the following budget estimation methods is the most defensible? (a) percentage of sales, (b) arbitrary allocation, (c) objective and task, (d) competitive parity.
11. The percentage of sales method is the most popular for estimating promotional budgets.   **T/F**
12. The competitive parity method assumes that sales are the cause of promotion rather than the result. **T/F**
13. At the maturity stage of the product life cycle, the amount of sales promotion generally (a) decreases,

CHECK YOUR LEARNING *(continued)*

(b) stabilizes, (c) increases, (d) is not used.

14. In industrial markets, personal selling performance increases about 50 percent when supported by advertising.   **T/F**

15. All of the following affect the promotional mix ex-cept: (a) product life cycle, (b) target audience, (c) media selected, (d) type of strategy selected.

16. Firms using a pull strategy will place a heavy emphasis on sales promotion.   **T/F**

QUESTIONS FOR REVIEW AND DISCUSSION

1. Define the key terms for this chapter that appear at the end of the goal summary.

2. Explain why promotion is important to the marketing mix.

3. Compare and contrast interpersonal communications and mass communications.

4. How can nonprofit organizations use promotion? Give at least five examples.

5. Discuss some ways in which a firm can benefit by using promotion.

6. Using a TV commercial of your choice, give an example of how the message is sent and received. What role does noise play in the transmission and reception of the message?

7. Explain why it is important that promotional objectives be measurable.

8. Why do many firms use a combination of push and pull strategies?

9. What factors influence the development of the promotional budget?

10. Discuss how the product life cycle affects the elements used in a promotional strategy and the amounts budgeted for each element.

11. Which budgeting method is the most defensible for estimating a promotional budget? Explain why it is not a popular method.

12. Explain how a promotional mix might be selected for a product of your choice.

NOTES

1. "3M's Aggressive New Consumer Drive," *Business Week,* July 16, 1984, p. 114.

2. Committee on Definitions, *Marketing Definitions: A Glossary of Marketing Terms* (Chicago: American Marketing Association, 1963), p. 9.

3. Committee on Definitions, p. 20.

4. B. C. Cotton and Emerson M. Babb, "Consumer Response to Promotional Deals," *Journal of Marketing,* July 1978, pp. 109–113.

5. Robert G. Brown, "Sales Responses to Promotions and Advertisements," *Journal of Advertising Research,* August 1974, pp. 33–40.

6. *How Advertising Works in Today's Marketplace: The Merrill Study* (New York: McGraw-Hill, 1971), p. 4.

7. Wilbur Schramm, "How Communications Work," in *The Process and Effects of Mass Communications* (Urbana, Ill.: University of Illinois Press, 1960), p. 6.

8. Richard E. Stanley, *Promotion* (New York: Prentice-Hall, 1977).

9. Michael Levy, John Webster, and Roger A. Kerin, "Formulating Push Marketing Strategies: A Method and Application," *Journal of Marketing,* Winter 1983, pp. 25–34.

10. Michael Levy and George W. Jones, Jr., "The Effect of Changes in a 'Push Strategy' in a Marketing Channel Context," *Journal of the Academy of Marketing Science,* Winter 1984, p. 107.

11. "Novel Promotion Plan Helps Johnson & Johnson Toy Sales," *The Wall Street Journal,* April 26, 1984, p. 31.

12. Marvin Harper, Jr., "The Marketing Communications Budget," *Printer's Ink,* June 26, 1959, p. 87.

13. William M. Kincaid, Jr., *Promotion* (Columbus, Ohio: Charles E. Merrill Co., 1981), pp. 167–168.

14. David L. Hurwood, "How Companies Set Advertising Budgets," *The Conference Board Record,* March 1968, pp. 34–41.

15. Roger A. Strang, *The Promotional Planning Process* (New York: Praeger, 1980), pp. 38–39.

16. Colin Leinster, "Mobile Phones: Hot New Industry," *Fortune,* August 6, 1984, pp. 108–113; Kevin Higgins, "Marketing Blitz Launches Cellular Phone War," *Marketing News,* March 1, 1985, p. 1.

17. Alan J. Dubinsky, Thomas E. Bany, and Roger A. Kerin, "The Sales–Advertising Interface in Promotional Planning," *Journal of Advertising* 10, no. 3 (1981), pp. 35–41.

*F*ounded in 1802 as a manufacturer of gunpowder, DuPont is known today as America's number one producer of chemicals, synthetic fibers, and gel explosives. DuPont inventions include such well-known names as nylon, rayon, Teflon, SilverStone, Corfam, Freon, and Lucite.

The company is organized along four major lines of business. The fiber business produces carpet and apparel threads like Orlon and Dacron, and accounts for over 33 percent of DuPont's sales. The second major division is the specialty products, which include Raindance car wax, film, cookware coatings, Remington firearms and ammunition, and explosives. These products account for 28 percent of total sales. Plastics, artificial resins and synthetic rubbers contributed 22 percent, and the remaining 17 percent comes from petrochemicals and additives for agricultural feeds. To manufacture these products (a grand total of 1,700) the company has eighty-seven plants in twenty-seven states. Most products are sold to other manufacturers in the U.S. and overseas. International sales account for 33 percent of DuPont's total sales and 40 percent of its profits.

Because DuPont sells most of its products directly to manufacturers, the consumer doesn't see company fibers until they are woven into clothing and carpets. Therefore, over the years DuPont has not been known for its consumer marketing skills. Now, faced with increased competition from Asian nations and a fear of decreased brand loyalty for products made with DuPont fibers, DuPont is reawakening to the role that consumer-oriented promotions can have.

In 1983 DuPont elected to budget approximately $100 million for promoting products in its fiber division. This represented a 15 to 20 percent increase over the previous year. As the director of industry fibers put it, "A lot of our products are maturing, and we have to be better marketers." To stimulate demand, DuPont focused its efforts on a series of aggressive sales promotion activities. These included giving away more than 50,000 home computers to consumers who bought carpets made with its fibers, sponsoring a tennis tournament at Hilton Head, and awarding honeymoon trips to Acapulco, along with suitcases made of DuPont fibers, in a sweepstakes to cash in on the $91 million a year bridal market for luggage. In addition, rebates were used following the sweepstakes and computer giveaways.

Another big market for DuPont is the denim jeans business. Although penetration of this cotton stronghold will be difficult, DuPont hopes to catch its competitor, Celanese, who claims to have captured a 10 percent market share with its Fortrel E.S.P. Polyester stretch yarn. To counter, DuPont planned and implemented a two-week $1 million TV ad blitz stressing the comfort of jeans made with its Lycra fibers.

Issues for Discussion

1. Is DuPont truly marketing its products, or is it merely offering consumers gimmicks? Explain your answer.
2. Is it really necessary for companies like DuPont to promote their products to consumers? Discuss.
3. Identify the promotional strategy and mix used by DuPont.
4. Can brand loyalty be created for DuPont's products? How?

Sources: Adapted from Ronald Alsop, "DuPont Steps Up Promotions to Prove Its Selling Ability," *The Wall Street Journal,* December 1, 1983, p. 31; and Milton Moskowitz, Michael Katz, and Robert Levering, *Everybody's Business* (New York: Harper & Row, 1980), p. 603.

OUTLINE

17

Advertising and Publicity

LEARNING GOALS_____

After reading this chapter, you should be able to:

1. Explain why advertising is important to our economy.
2. List and explain the uses of advertising.
3. Discuss the steps in managing an ad campaign.
4. Explain how AIDA is used to develop the advertising message.
5. List the major media used to advertise a good, service, or idea. Know their characteristics and major advantages and disadvantages.
6. Explain the purpose of advertising agencies.
7. Discuss the role of publicity in the promotional mix.

*T*he 1984 Olympics in Los Angeles proved to be the most successful Olympic Games, both in sports for our athletes and in profits for our businesses. Never before had the Olympics been such a commercial venture. Thirty corporations paid from $4 million to $15 million each to become official Olympic sponsors. The total sponsorship package was worth $127 million, or 34 percent of the Games' budget. In addition, ABC-TV paid $225 million to broadcast the Games, and an additional fifty firms pledged to return 10 percent of their wholesale revenues from product sales tied to the Olympics.

Not to be outdone, the 1988 Winter Olympics held in Calgary, Canada carefully imitated the 1984 Summer Olympics marketing plan. Calgary organizers also signed lucrative corporate-sponsorship deals and a rich TV pact with ABC for a record $309 million. Corporate sponsors signed up for $67 million in exclusive rights to use Olympic trademarks associated with the Winter Games and another $120 million to the International Olympic Committee (IOC) to link their names to the games in Calgary and Seoul.

The IOC's program offers a unique technique for the nine international sponsors to market their products throughout the world and to enhance their image. In addition, many sponsors liked a provision that allows 1988 sponsors first crack at sponsorship rights to the 1992 Olympics in France and Spain. This opportunity will allow the sponsors a chance to carefully evaluate the success of their advertising campaigns and other promotions. If sales and profits increase, then they have a jump on their competition in repeating their success. The nine international sponsors included Eastman Kodak ($15.5m), Visa International ($14.5m), Federal Express ($14.5m), Brother ($14.5m), Panasonic ($14.5m), Phillips ($14.5m), Coca-Cola ($13m), 3M ($12m), and *Time* ($7m).

Issues for Discussion
1. Do you think the Olympic sponsorships are worth the high cost that corporations pay for them?
2. How many advertisements and other Olympic promotions can you recall from the 1988 Winter or Summer Olympics?

3. Would you purchase a product because its producer was an Olympic sponsor?

Sources: Adapted from "In Olympics Business Also Goes for the Gold," *U.S. News & World Report,* June 25, 1984, pp. 73–74; Walecia Konrad, "Will Corporate Sponsors Get Burned by the Torch?," *Business Week,* February 1, 1988, p. 93; Patrick McGeehan, "Visa, Kodak Big Winners in the Olympics," *Advertising Age,* February 1, 1988, pp. 1, 74.

■ The Brother International Corporation and eight other International sponsors provided U.S. teams with monetary and/or product support.
Source: Courtesy of Brother International Corporation.

The advertising campaign is an important element in a successful promotional plan. Ad campaigns are usually supported by various sales promotions during the later stages of the product life cycle and heavily implemented during key product phases. This chapter discusses the management of an advertising campaign and explains the nature and types of publicity that accompany the campaign. Among our topics are budget setting, message development, and selection and scheduling of media. As our Introductory Case continues in the chapter, you'll see how some Olympics sponsors planned their campaigns to fully realize the benefits of being associated with the Games. ■

 ## ADVERTISING

The overall goal of advertising is to increase sales.

Marketing is credited by many for making us a generation of choices. However, despite having so many choices, we would still be at square one if it weren't for advertising. As previously discussed in Chapter 16, **advertising** is any paid and impersonal presentation of products or ideas by an identified sponsor. The overall goal of advertising is to increase profits, but it must do much more. Advertising usually makes us aware of our choices by informing, persuading, and reminding us of their potential benefits and availability. Thus, advertising is an important and heavily used element in the promotional mix.

The Importance of Advertising

Advertising is vital to the stimulation and growth of the economy.

The importance of advertising should not be underestimated. Not only is advertising important for the more obvious promotional reasons, but it also plays a vitally important role in the stimulation and growth of our nation's economy. More advertising money is spent per person in the United States than in any other nation, according to *Advertising Age*. For example, during the 1982 recession, the top 100 U.S. advertisers increased their ad expenditures by 15.2 percent. Total spending by these leaders was $17.1 billion.[1] Procter & Gamble alone spent $1.4 billion on advertising in 1986, and Philip Morris continued to narrow the gap by spending $1.3 billion. The U.S. government was ranked thirty-third. Table 17.1 lists ad expenditures for the top twenty-five U.S. advertisers. It is interesting to note that ad expenditures vary not only from company to company, but also from industry to industry.

Ad expenditures vary from company to company and industry to industry.

Uses of Advertising

Advertising has many purposes. A few major ones include:

Advertising can reach more people at less cost than personal selling.

1. *Reaching prospects.* As a mass media tool, advertising can reach far more people far less expensively than a sales force. Such is the case with consumer goods, where it is not practical for a salesperson to call on every consumer. Furthermore, it is sometimes difficult for salespeople to make calls on top executives. Nearly everyone from housewife to corporate executive reads magazines or newspapers, listens to the radio, or watches TV almost daily.

❑ **Table 17.1** Leading national advertisers.

RANK	COMPANY	AD SPENDING	RANK	COMPANY	AD SPENDING
1	Procter & Gamble Co.	$1,435,454	15	J. C. Penney Co.	496,241
2	Philip Morris Cos.	1,364,472	16	Pillsbury Co.	494,877
3	Sears, Roebuck & Co.	1,004,708	17	Ralston-Purina Co.	478,031
4	RJR Nabisco	935,036	18	American Telephone &	
5	General Motors Corp.	839,000		Telegraph	439,919
6	Ford Motor Co.	648,500	19	Kraft Inc.	437,952
7	Anheuser-Busch Cos.	643,522	20	Chrysler Corp.	426,000
8	McDonald's Corp.	592,000	21	Johnson & Johnson	410,672
9	Kmart Corp.	590,350	22	American Home	
10	PepsiCo Inc.	581,309		Products Corp.	395,718
11	General Mills	551,561	23	Kellogg Co.	374,142
12	Warner-Lambert Co.	548,726	24	Coca-Cola Co.	370,379
13	BCI Holdings	535,852	25	General Electric Co.	354,250
14	Unilever N.V.	517,746			

Source: Reprinted with permission from *Advertising Age,* September 24, 1987, p. 1. Copyright © Crain Communications, Inc. All rights reserved.

*A*dvertising attracts interested prospects.

*R*apid exposure encourages new product innovation.

2. *Preselling a product.* When combined with personal selling, advertising can acquaint prospects with a company and the merits of its products and attract interested prospects to make inquiries.
3. *Introducing new products.* Through the use of advertising, millions of people can quickly be exposed to messages informing them about a new product. This rapid exposure encourages new product development, which is necessary if business is to prosper.

Sara Lee and others try to presell their products by using various advertising messages that acquaint prospects with the merits of their products.

Source: Courtesy of Kitchens of Sara Lee

*S*ales are generated by advertising in off-periods.

4. *Reducing sales fluctuations.* Many businesses produce products for which demand varies significantly from season to season and even from month to month. At times, companies can't operate efficiently because of personnel, inventory, and financial changes; advertising is then used to generate trade in such off-periods. For example, Toro recently featured a successful ad campaign to generate summer and fall sales of snowblowers by offering partial-to-full refunds if snowfall didn't amount to a predetermined number of inches.

*A*dvertising is used to improve company image.

5. *Building goodwill.* To improve their image and build a positive reputation, companies use advertising to inform the public of their various public service projects or to tell the public about their organizations.

Types of Advertising

*P*roduct advertising can be primary or selective.

There are two basic types of advertising. **Product advertising** is designed to promote a product or product line. It can be aimed at the ultimate user or channel users. **Institutional advertising** is designed to promote an image or goodwill message for a company, industry, organization, or government.

*P*rimary advertising stimulates demand for a class of goods.

Product advertising can be primary or selective. The aim of primary advertising is to stimulate demand for a class of goods without particular regard to brand. This form of advertising occurs in the introductory or **pioneering stage** of advertising. Sometimes this type of advertising is so basic that it merely explains what a product is or how it works. For example, initial ads for men's engagement rings, such as DeBeers, informed consumers that breaking traditions was acceptable in order to stimulate demand for the product.

*S*elective advertising persuades customers to purchase a specific brand.

The aim of selective advertising, on the other hand, is to persuade consumers to purchase a specific brand. This type of advertising is commonly found in newspapers and magazines and on radio and TV. The ads are for products like Cartier perfume, the Chevrolet Corvette, and Westin hotels, which are in the growth and maturity stages of the product life cycle. Selective advertising is conducted during the **competitive stage** of advertising and accounts for the largest share of advertising dollars spent.

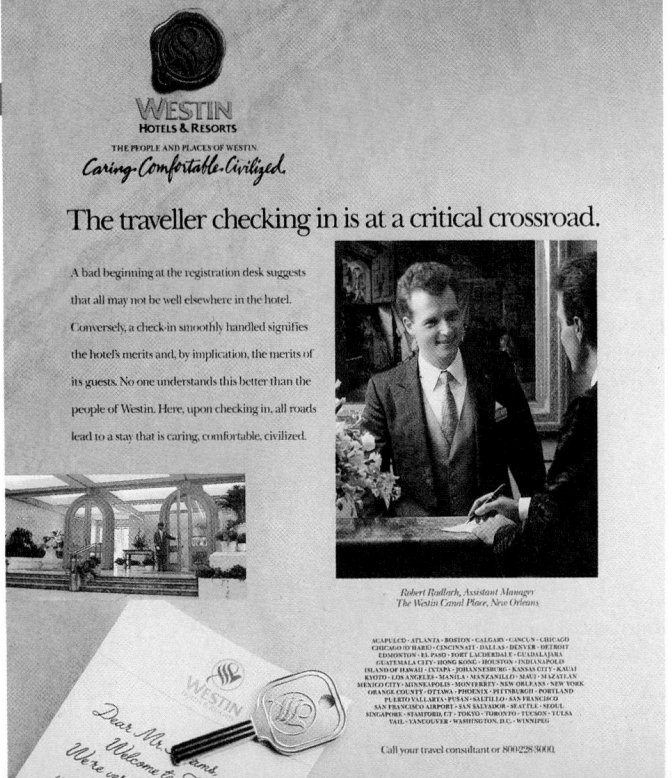

Services can be advertised. This Westin ad illustrates selective advertising.

Source: Courtesy of Westin Hotels & Resorts.

*M*adison Avenue used to think it ungentlemanly to knock a competitor in public. Advertisers referred to rivals only as "other leading brands" or, more often, ignored them. Advertising practitioners believed what they'd learned in Sunday school: If you can't say something nice about someone, don't say anything.

No longer. In one of its ad campaigns, struggling Seven-Up Co. brags that its lemon-lime soda doesn't contain caffeine. The company doesn't explain what, if anything, is wrong with caffeine but notes that most other soft drinks have it. Drackett Co. has told homemakers to use its Vanish toilet-bowl cleaner because, the company claimed, other brands could wreck plumbing. Pillsbury Co.'s Totino's pizza contends that the crust on other frozen pizzas "tastes like cardboard," while another pizza marketer once ran TV commercials saying its rivals made their cheese from a substance that is "the main ingredient in some glues."

MARKETING IN ACTION

Comparative Ads Are Getting More Popular, Harder Hitting

This is what might be called the Don Rickles school of advertising, where nothing scores as well as a put-down. The guiding principle: Don't tell consumers why they should buy your product. Try to persuade them *not* to buy your competitors'.

"Comparative advertising is becoming more hard-hitting," says Jeffery Edelstein, a director of broadcast standards and practices at American Broadcasting Cos. "Competitors are taking each other by the throat."

Comparative Advertising is a relatively recent development. Only a decade ago it was prohibited by two of the three television networks and frowned on by advertising and broadcast-industry self-regulatory codes.

One of the first companies to try comparative ads was Avis Rent A Car System in the mid-1960s. Its "We try harder" campaign helped the floundering concern become a strong competitor of Hertz Corp. The most important breakthrough for comparative ads came in 1971 and 1972, when the Federal Trade Commission began pressuring the television networks to allow ads that named competitors.

Savin Business Machines compared its copiers with Xerox Corp.'s and prospered. Helene Curtis Industries showed its shampoo against five others and said in ads, "We do what theirs does for less than half the price." Without naming Warner-Lambert Co.'s Listerine, Procter & Gamble Co.'s Scope mouthwash referred to it as the brand that gave users "medicine breath."

Then, in 1979, the FTC formally endorsed comparative advertising and said that ads disparaging other

This Virginia Slims ad illustrates the retentive stage of selective advertising. Its objective is to reinforce the idea that the product is still around.

products weren't necessarily illegal. "Comparative advertising, where truthful and nondeceptive," the FTC said, "is a source of important information to consumers and assists them in making rational purchase decisions."

Even the sharpest critics of comparative advertising have softened their views. Ogilvy & Mather, a leading ad agency, strongly opposed it for many years but changed its position in late 1980, after acknowledging that comparative advertising had been effective in some instances. Coca-Cola Co. criticized such advertising when rival Pepsi-Cola Co. used it but then employed taste comparisons to introduce a new wine.

Comparative advertising now is a widely accepted marketing device, particularly for brands that don't lead their categories. Most comparative advertisements are relatively mild, with claims that a particular product works or tastes better or is otherwise more effective than another. Put-down ads, in contrast, suggest that rival brands are unwholesome or even dangerous.

Norcliff-Thayer Inc., a Revlon Inc. subsidiary, took the put-down approach to market its Nature's Remedy laxative with advertising that described rival Ex-Lax as containing "an artificial chemical." Coca-Cola, in ads for Minute Maid lemonade, blasted General Foods Corp.'s Country Time as the "no-lemon lemonade." Raisin growers advised mothers: "There are a lot of 'extras' in most manufactured snacks . . . things you may not want your kids to eat."

Many ads of this type "make specific claims about a competitor's product having negative attributes that the consumer might not be aware of," says Richard Kurnit, a New York advertising lawyer. Some marketers believe such tactics make consumers skeptical about an entire product category; beverage sources say powdered lemonade sales went flat after Minute Maid's attack on Country Time.

Another risk: legal or regulatory challenges from the targets of comparative ads. Most companies protest first to the broadcasting networks in the hope that they'll drop the ads. Last year ABC received 131 such challenges and upheld 30% of the protests.

Complaints also are heard by the advertising industry's self-regulatory body, the National Advertising Division of the Council of Better Business Bureaus. Among the ads modified or dropped after it began to investigate them were ones from Minute Maid, Nature's Remedy laxative, and the California Raisin Advisory Board.

Increasingly, companies are taking their gripes directly to federal courts. The Drackett attack on toilet-bowl cleaners was blunted by competitors' lawsuits, and Pillsbury is now in court defending its pizza advertising. Plaintiffs sometimes want more than a halt of the ads in question. Gillette Co. and its ad agency, J. Walter Thompson, once paid $4.3 million to Alberto-Culver Co. after running ads saying its shampoos left hair too oily.

Source: Bill Abrams, "Comparative Ads Are Getting More Popular," *The Wall Street Journal,* March 11, 1982, p. 25. Reprinted with permission of *The Wall Street Journal,* © Dow Jones & Company, Inc. (1982). All rights reserved.

Comparative ads make specific brand comparisons.

Often product advertising campaigns become comparative in nature. Comparative advertising makes comparisons among specific brands and now occurs in approximately 35 percent of all TV commercials. Although comparative ads may be popular now, this hasn't always been the case. Only in 1971–1972 did the Federal Trade Commission state that comparisons might lead to better products and lower prices, and it did not formally endorse this position until 1979. The final breakthrough for advertisers was the abolition of comparative advertising guidelines by the National Association of Broadcasters in 1981.[2] See the Marketing in Action for more examples of this form of advertising.

Ads that remind or reinforce the idea that a product is still around are another form of selective advertising. These ads occur during the **retentive stage** of advertising and attempt to maintain market share of popular products like Virginia Slims, with its commonly used reminder, "You've come a long way, baby." Unlike ads in other advertising stages, these ads do not tell you what Virginia Slims are, nor do they give you reasons why you should smoke them, or why they are better than the competition.

Institutional advertising can also be retentive. For instance, after the Tylenol scare Johnson & Johnson successfully attempted to convince the public that it was a reliable company with safe and effective products. Several other forms of institutional advertising also attempt to build goodwill. These include patronage, public relations,

Many states, like New York, use institutional advertising to promote business and tourism.

If you think New York State goes all out for a birthday, you should see what we do for business.

In terms of size and success, the celebration was uniquely New York.

And New York State can offer those same dimensions to your business. What other state has more capital? Or more Fortune 500 companies?

For that matter, what state has more colleges, museums, plays? Millions of acres of wilderness and parklands? Even spectacular sports teams? All for an unsurpassed quality of life.

What's more, New York State is continuing to cut taxes by billions of dollars. Combined with unequalled loans and financial assistance, our business benefits are one-of-a-kind. And that's something to celebrate.

To find out why New York State is a better place to do business, mail this coupon to:
New York State Department of Commerce, One Commerce Plaza, Box A, Albany, NY 12245 (518) 473-1720

Name
Title
Company
Address
City _____ State ____ Zip ____
Phone ( )

NEW YORK ♥ BUSINESS

Source: Courtesy of New York Department of Economic Development.

and public service ads. To encourage continued patronage, J. C. Penney in Terre Haute, Indiana, took out ads in a local newspaper to announce its new location and store hours. As a public relations gesture, a local Ford dealer advertised that free coffee and donuts were available to travelers on a Labor Day weekend. McDonald's is another company that has extensively used institutional advertising to promote over 100 of its Ronald McDonald Houses, a public service.

*I*nstitutional advertising is popular in promoting state tourism and economic development opportunities.

Cities, states, and nations often use institutional advertising to promote their images and to attract business and tourism to their areas. For example, Virginia sponsored its popular "Virginia Is for Lovers" campaign, Bermuda promoted "Bermuda Now," and Kentucky featured a series of ads touting "Kentucky & Co.—The state that is run like a business."[3]

THE CASE CONTINUES

*O*nce a corporation is selected as an official sponsor, the firm will normally spend an additional $30 to $40 million on promotional campaigns. For example, Coca-Cola staged a chorus of about 50 children singing "Can You Feel It" for the opening Winter ceremonies. The song, written by Coke specifically for the opening ceremonies, was used again in Coke commercials. Visa introduced an ad campaign the summer before the Olympics to increase product awareness. Its theme was "Pull for the Team." In contrast, Federal Express sponsored a sound and light show to fete the day's winners using

a backdrop of laser graphics and Calgary office towers. Many of these campaigns featured both product (see the Brother ad at the beginning of the Case) and institutional ads.

Besides being official 1988 Olympic sponsors, many companies signed on to sponsor the less expensive U.S. Olympic team or a specific team such as the ski or skating teams. For example, Miller Brewing was one sponsor of the Olympic Training Center; Budweiser, Kmart,

and Sure deodorant sponsored the U.S. hockey team; and Campbell's soups sponsored the U.S. Figure Skating Team. Campbell's developed a print ad campaign featuring Olympic skating star Debbie Thomas. The campaign, "Go for the Gold," used a bronze ($1), silver ($2), and gold ($3) refund theme.

It should also be noted that a number of companies such as Sears' Discover Card tried to cash in on the Olympics without being official sponsors. Discover Card used an Olympic theme in their ads which ran in popular magazines like *Sports Illustrated.*

❑ **Figure 17.1**
The steps of
advertising planning.

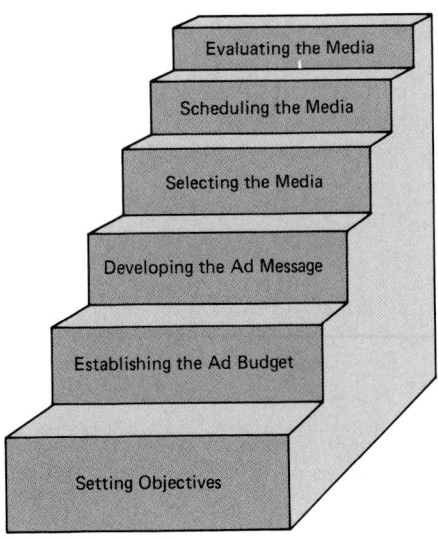

MANAGING THE ADVERTISING CAMPAIGN

*A*d campaigns must be
based on marketing plans.

Management of the advertising campaign must be based on decisions related to the overall marketing plan. After reviewing the plan, advertising objectives must be set, budgets established, messages developed, media selected and scheduled, and the campaign results evaluated. (See figure 17.1.)

Setting the Advertising Objectives

*O*bjectives must be developed for each ad campaign and advertisement.

Although the overall marketing strategy determines advertising objectives, the marketing manager still must develop specific objectives for each ad campaign and each ad. Many of the purposes of advertising discussed previously can be transformed into advertising objectives designed to inform, persuade, or remind consumers. Once established, these objectives determine the type of advertising needed. For example, if the objective of an ad is to inform the public of a price change, then product advertising is needed. On the other hand, if the objective is to improve a company's image, then institutional advertising is required.

*D*AGMAR is a method of
turning ad objectives into
measurable goals.

Russell H. Colley, in his book, *Defining Advertising Goals for Measured Advertising Results* (DAGMAR), states that advertising objectives should be written in communications terms if any meaningful measurement of results is to take place. His method of turning advertising objectives into specific measurable goals is called DAGMAR. Colley defines an *advertising goal* as "a specific communications task to be accomplished among a defined audience to a given degree in a given period of time."[4] In total, Colley lists fifty-two possible advertising objectives.

A good advertising objective should specify the following:

1. What is to be accomplished and how much is to be accomplished? This should include some type of bench mark for comparison purposes. For example, an advertiser might want to increase market share from 15 percent to 20 percent.
2. Who is the target market or segment? For example, if the product is sports cars, the target market might be recent college graduates.
3. What is the time frame for accomplishing the objectives? For instance, from April to June might be the best time frame for a local Chevrolet dealer to run a Corvette ad aimed at graduating seniors.

Establishing the Advertising Budget

*O*bjective-and-task is the best method for establishing an ad budget.

The advertising budget is the dollar amount that represents a company's total expenditures for planned advertising activities over a specified period of time (usually a year). Chapter 16 discussed four methods for determining the promotional budget and six factors influencing the budget. The same four methods are used for the advertising budgeting, and once again the *objective-and-task method* is considered to be the best. *Competitive parity, percentage of sales,* and the *arbitrary approach,* however, are still more commonly used.

*T*he ad budget must contain items directly related to ad campaign effectiveness.

In order to evaluate the advertising appropriation effectively, the marketing manager must be certain that the budget contains only those items directly related to the effectiveness of the advertising campaign. These items include:

1. paid advertising space and time in all recognized medias;
2. literature intended to perform a selling function, such as brochures, circulars, catalogs, and package inserts used for advertising, not for directions on product use;
3. the salaries and operating expenses of the advertising department;
4. fees paid to advertising agencies, writers, artists, and other ancillary services;
5. mechanical costs involved in the preparation of advertising material such as photography, typography, artwork, engravings, radio transcriptions, TV films, etc.[5]

Developing the Advertising Message

Planning the best message to be communicated is the next step in managing the advertising campaign. Once the objectives are established and the budget set, marketing planners must develop the campaign's creative strategy. Much of this work is handled by advertising agencies and coordinated by the company's advertising department. Creation of the message, copy, and illustrations is accomplished by teams of copywriters and art directors who actually write and design the TV commercials and print ads you see each day.

*A*IDA signifies the sequence consumers go through in the persuasion process.

If the advertising message is to succeed, it must accomplish four tasks: it must first attract *attention,* then create and hold *interest,* stimulate *desire,* and finally obtain *action.* These tasks are referred to as the **AIDA** *concept.* The acronym signifies the sequence that the ad takes the consumer through in the persuasion process.

ATTRACTING ATTENTION

*H*umor is increasingly used in ads to attract attention.

Every day you pick up a magazine or newspaper, listen to the radio, or watch TV, but you miss most of the messages in the ads before you. Why? Because nothing in the ad attracted your attention. Several devices can be used to attract your attention. They include the use of cartoons, larger ads, color, key location points (back cover), celebrities, testimonials, bold headlines, humor, special effects, music, and others. Let's examine three of the more popular attention getters.

After a period of serious ads during the 1970s, advertisers began to loosen up in the 1980s with a bit of humor. Inspired by the success of the clever Federal Express and Miller Lite commercials, an increasing number of companies now attempt to draw attention to their products or services by being funny. A recent survey of 500 TV ads by McCollum Speilman & Company found that tongue-in-cheek commercials substantially outscored two other popular kinds of ads, "celebrities" and "real people." The funny ads were, on average, more memorable and more persuasive than the other two types.

Volkswagen once used humor to express its absolute confidence in the VW bug. A magazine ad was designed that displayed the word "Lemon" in a headline over a photo of the auto. In fine print below that, the ad explained that VW inspectors had rejected the car because of a scratch found in the glove compartment. A VW ad pictures the entire lineup of VW products. The copy reads, "The Smartest way to spend $40,000: Buy them all."[6]

*S*pecial effects are increasingly used in TV ads to attract attention.

Special effects, aided by high-powered computers, have become widely used during the 1980s. However, according to Video Storyboard Tests Inc., people often don't remember the message in ads with special effects. Furthermore, their studies find little enthusiasm for high-tech computer animation in commercials. People instead prefer the "warm, fuzzy, Walt Disney-type characters" in ads. Despite this preference, companies continue to spend large sums to generate eye-catching, high-tech ads. For example, ads for Timex wristwatches made actual ticking watches look gargantuan. The ads featured ballerinas twirling across the watch faces and joggers running on them. In some commercials a watch even functioned as a boat dock or an elevator door.[7]

*O*ne of every three ads features a celebrity.

Approximately one of every three TV commercials features a celebrity. The reason? Surveys by Gallup & Robinson, Inc. claim that celebrity ads are very effective in grabbing viewers' attention. For example, the Hertz Corporation claimed a 36 percent boost in car rentals after introducing its classic campaign featuring O. J. Simpson sprinting through airports to reach his rental car. Sales for Restonic mattresses increased from $22 million to $35 million after Steve Allen and Jayne Meadows endorsed the product.[8]

*C*elebrity advertising can cause special problems.

Celebrity advertising also has its dangers. Because of FTC guidelines, most advertisers seek celebrities who will verify in writing the products they endorse. This has been a special concern since the FTC brought charges against singer Pat Boone for endorsing Acne-Satin, a product he claimed his daughter Debby used.

Other problems can also arise. For example, in 1984 Vanessa Williams was the reigning Miss America with promotional contracts for both American Greetings Corporation and the Gillette Company. Then, seven weeks before the 1985 pageant, nude photos of Williams appeared in a men's magazine. American Greetings had already scheduled ads in seven women's magazines to promote the Miss America $100,000 Scholarship Sweepstakes. Fortunately, the company had time to pull five of the ad features. Gillette was not as fortunate. Although it was able to pull its store displays, a photo of Williams adorned its annual report.

CREATING AND HOLDING INTEREST

Once a person is attracted to an ad, a relationship must be established between what attracted the individual in the ad and the actual product or service. When no relationship exists, the individual moves on.

Z, L, and S ad layouts are easy for the reader's eyes to follow.

In addition, ad layouts for magazines and newspapers can also be arranged so that the reader's eyes move smoothly through the ad. Arrangements can be designed in patterns such as Z, L, or S, or similar layouts that look right to the reader.

STIMULATING DESIRE

In order to stimulate desire, the advertiser must know and understand how the customer thinks, behaves, and makes decisions. Various appeals to logic, the emotions, or economic concerns, among others, can be used to convince customers that they should make a purchase and that the product advertised can satisfy their needs.

*E*motional needs are strong motivators in stimulating desire.

Emotional needs are strong motivators in stimulating desire. For example, Malcolm MacDougall, president of fifty-five C&B advertising agencies, claims, "We want the people we're talking to to relate our product to their lives." Slogans often talk about feeling (Maxwell House), touching (Cannon Mills, AT&T), and sharing

(Hershey, E&J Gallo Winery). Soft sell is the rule, and a product's purported emotional benefits are stressed over its functional ones. For example, a recent Cannon commercial shows a fast-paced montage of happy people—a father reading a story to his two daughters, a mother cuddling an infant, kids and a puppy frolicking under a garden hose. The slogan is sung four times in the commercial: "Cannon touches your life." The products themselves—sheets, towels, and blankets—are mentioned only once. "A towel is an insignificant thing until you relate it to a person's involvement with it," says Jerry Siaro, creative director of Cannon's agency, N. W. Ayer. "It's what you get out of it, the way it makes you feel."[9]

OBTAINING ACTION

Coupons within an ad are designed to stimulate immediate demand.

A fair amount of advertising attempts to stimulate immediate action. Inserts found in the Sunday newspaper often offer coupons for various fast-food chains. These coupons are usually good for a limited period of time, thus stimulating immediate action. Other ads might attempt to sell the customer over a period of time. For example, Ford used direct-mail advertising to attract executives and professionals into showrooms. Over 14,000 people borrowed Thunderbirds for full-day test drives as a part of Ford's VIP promotion. The effect was a 200 percent sales increase.[10]

Selecting the Media

The media are any avenues used to stimulate demand for a product.

In advertising, the term *media* refers to any avenue used to stimulate demand for a product. Included are TV, newspapers, radio, magazines, direct mail, outdoor, or any other vehicle used to expose an ad message to a target market. Table 17.2 illustrates the expenditures in the media for national advertising in 1986. Network TV has the largest share, followed by spot TV, magazines, and newspapers.

The media planner must develop a **media plan.** This includes the media to be used and a time schedule for advertisements to appear, and it is a crucial element in

❏ **Table 17.2** National advertising expenditures by media (in billions).*

MEDIA	1986	1985	PERCENT CHANGE
Magazine	$ 5,120	$ 4,928	3.9
Newspapers	3,660	3,636	0.7
Newspaper supplements	413	401	3.0
Business publications	2,157	2,115	2.0
Farm publications	166	181	(8.3)
Network TV	8,600	8,313	3.5
Spot TV	7,785	7,044	10.5
Cable TV networks	543	469	15.8
Network radio	570	443	28.7
Spot radio	1,458	1,440	1.3
Outdoor	675	685	(1.5)
TOTAL	$31,147	$29,655	5.0

*This table represents ads placed by national advertisers. It does not include all other ads, such as classified ads. Adding all unmeasured (local) ads together, newspapers are the number one advertising medium.
Source: Reprinted with permission from *Advertising Age,* September 24, 1987, p. 166. Copyright © Crain Communications, Inc. All rights reserved.

❑ **Figure 17.2** Media characteristics.

Media	Advertising Media					
	Newspaper	Television	Direct Mail	Radio	Magazines	Outdoor
Media						
Expenditures (% of total advertised)	27%	21%	16%	7%	6%	1%
Characteristics	Most popular mass media; used heavily by retailers	Fastest growing media	Includes letters, catalogues, postcards, folders	Experiencing strong comeback in the 60s and 70s	Renewed popularity as alternate media; designed for special markets	Oldest medium; includes billboards, skywriting, lasers, etc.
Advantages	General appeal; lowest cost per thousand; short placement lag time	Maximum reach and frequency selectivity; product demonstration ability	Can be personalized; very selective	Low cost for spots and production; demographic selectivity; universal availability	Demographic and geographic selectivity; longer life, color pictures, inserts	Cost; geographic selectivity; longer life
Disadvantages	Expensive for advertisers; short life span; possible clutter	High absolute cost; clutter and noise level; length of production time	Very expensive per thousand; limited reach	Clutter; low reach; short life of messages	Delayed reach and frequency; early closing dates; clutter	Reach; frequency

Source: Samuel C. Certo, Max E. Douglas, and Stewart W. Husted, *Business,* 2d ed. Copyright © 1987 by Allyn and Bacon, Boston. All rights reserved.

*T*he media plan must consider: (1) type of product, (2) target market characteristics, (3) general media characteristics, (4) specific media characteristics.

successful promotions. In developing the media plan, the marketer must consider the type of product to be advertised, the characteristics of the target market, the characteristics of the various media, and the characteristics (size, audience, and costs) of specific newspapers, radio stations, magazines, and so forth.

For example, if Bristol-Myers wanted to develop a media plan for Clairol hair-coloring, it might consider some of the following. The product is such that its use can be demonstrated. The target market for the product is a mass market including mostly women users of all ages. The product is especially suited for advertising on TV and in women's magazines, but it could be advertised in other media as well. For example, it could be advertised on the "Days of Our Lives" soap opera and in *Ladies Home Journal, Woman's Day,* and *McCall's.* These four media vehicles would provide the desired **reach** (number of potential viewers or readers) and **frequency** (number of times the average person is exposed to the message). In addition, the media planner must consider the cost-effectiveness of these media vehicles. This information can be obtained from the Standard Rate and Data Service and similar services that provide the data needed to calculate the cost-per-contact (usually calculated per thousand) for readers, viewers, or listeners. Much of this information is fed into computers where sophisticated programs provide an analysis and make the initial media mix selection. The following sections discuss ad media and their characteristics. (See figure 17.2.)

*C*omputers often analyze and select the initial media mix.

NEWSPAPERS

*N*ewspaper advantages: (1) reach large portions of local market, (2) relative low contact cost per thousand, (3) contain special interest sections.

Most adults read the newspaper. Studies indicate that over 70 percent of adult Americans who have read a newspaper within the last week are regular newspaper readers.[11] Newspapers are the most widely used advertising media, and because of their local emphasis, retailers use them heavily. This type of local advertising is called *retail advertising.* In contrast, *USA Today,* America's first and only national newspaper, sells national advertising space to producers. The paid circulation of *USA Today* is 1.42 million, making it the third largest daily. Thus far, *USA Today* has sold its fourteen available ad pages to over 750 national advertisers.[12]

America's 9,205 newspapers offer many advantages for advertisers. Their general appeal means they reach large portions of a local market or metropolitan area. Another is their relatively low contact cost per thousand. Newspaper advertising is much less expensive than TV advertising. In addition, newspapers are timely: some small newspapers appear weekly, but most are dailies. Their special interest sections such as entertainment, business, sports, and family pages are effective in reaching a target market. For example, within twenty-four hours of the start of the 1987 football strike, rival entertainment groups (movies, theater, concerts, and other sports, including college football) were placing ads in the sports sections of newspapers to attract disgruntled professional football fans.

*N*ewspaper disadvantages: (1) expensive for national advertisers, (2) harder to reach individual target markets, (3) short life span, (4) often cluttered with other ads.

There are also disadvantages to using newspapers as an ad medium, and most of them represent the flipsides of the advantages just enumerated. Newspaper ads can be very expensive for national advertisers because the newspaper charges them the more expensive general rates, rather than the cheaper rates charged local retailers. It is for this reason that many national advertisers use **cooperative advertising** because they can share costs with the local retailer who features their products. Newspapers' general appeal makes it harder to reach individual target markets. Their short life span means that ads do not last as long, and their special interest sections make for possible clutter (especially on Wednesdays and Fridays).

TELEVISION

*T*elevision is the fastest-growing media.

Television is the second most popular advertising media. According to A. C. Nielsen figures, the average U.S. family watched 49 hours and 48 minutes of TV per week in 1987, or more than 7 hours per day. Average American adults spend four hours and twelve minutes watching TV daily. However, viewers are likely to be tuned to nonnetwork stations. In 1974, the big three networks had a 91 percent audience share. By 1984, that share had slipped to 74 percent. A study by the BBDO advertising agency predicts that the figure will fall to 65 percent by 1990.[13] Figure 17.3 gives a breakdown by type of television advertising.

One reason for the decline has been the introduction of over 5,000 cable systems in the United States. One of the first cable systems with advertising was Ted Turner's national cable super station, which he set up in Atlanta and beamed by satellite to other parts of the country.

*U*ses for TV advertising are growing.

Some advertisers such as Procter & Gamble are even producing their own cable programming so they can better match their commercials with audiences. For example, commercials for Pampers or Ivory Snow interrupt *What Every Baby Should Know,* a magazine-style cable show for young parents. Furthermore, cable producers

❑ **Figure 17.3**
Local and national television advertising.

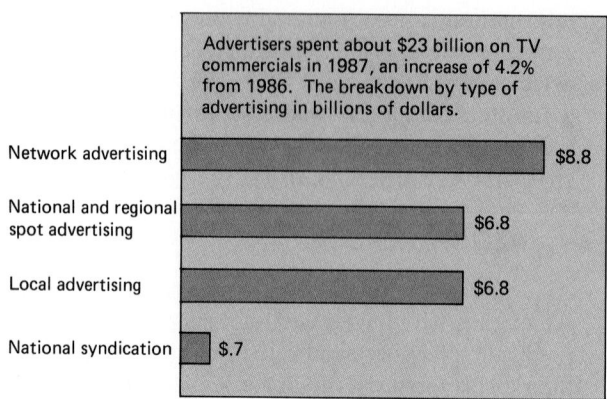

are experimenting with all advertising stations, such as Cableshop, which gives advertisers up to six minutes each to promote their products.

An additional use of TV is in its infancy. Movie studios are beginning to experiment with the sale of advertisements to be placed on movie videocassettes. One of the first featured Pepsi before the start of "Top Gun." If movie producers don't catch you that way, they may do so by plugging products in films. For example, MGM's *2010* includes a futuristic Pan Am commercial that the airline will use in its own marketing. Who can forget E.T. downing Reese's candy or the Russian tank in *Red Dawn* racing up to the McDonald's golden arches. Each of these and scores of other products will flash on TV screens for years to come.

*T*elevision advantages: (1) maximum reach and frequency, (2) demographic selectivity, (3) product demonstration capabilities.

Television offers both maximum reach and maximum frequency. In addition, TV can be demographically selective, which means it is relatively easy to reach a target market. For example, GM can advertise its trucks during westerns and police shows, which are viewed primarily by male audiences. Marketing research indicates that this type of selective advertising can yield increased sales. Finally, TV has superior capabilities of demonstrating products because of its visual dimension.

*T*elevision disadvantages: (1) high absolute cost, (2) clutter and noise level, (3) time required to make commercials.

The major disadvantage of TV is its high absolute cost; however, its comparative cost is quite low. Some network shows, such as CBS's *60 Minutes,* which is a leader in weekly ratings, can command as much as $175,000 per thirty-second spot. The average cost per thirty-second prime time spot in 1987 was $121,860. Some of the most expensive spots in the history of television were those run during the concluding episode of *M*A*S*H*,* where a thirty-second spot cost $450,000. The cost of a 1988 Super Bowl spot was as high as $650,000 per thirty seconds. As these figures indicate, many local advertisers or small companies simply cannot afford to buy TV time. In addition, commercials are often jammed back to back. Viewers frequently leave the room to get a snack, or ignore the commercial by talking to one another, or use their remote control to blip it out. Furthermore, it takes time to prepare TV commercials, and this can be a disadvantage for national advertisers because they may miss a timely event that they could use to their advantage.

DIRECT MAIL

*T*he purpose of direct mail is to obtain immediate orders or inquiries from customers.

Direct mail is the third most commonly used advertising medium. It includes letters, catalogs, postcards, folders, and other methods. The purpose of direct mail is to obtain immediate orders or inquiries from customers.

Direct mail advertising is very expensive. The cost is calculated per thousand pieces and includes the cost of printing, purchasing mailing lists ($25 to $50 per 1,000 names for one-time use), and the cost of postage. A highly specialized mailing list would have limited reach but could yield many eager buyers for a new product. For example, a mail-order camping company like L. L. Bean may get good results from buying a mailing list from *Field & Stream* magazine, a publication read by many hunting and fishing enthusiasts. In order to increase the possibility of an order, the frequency or number of mailings could be increased.

*L*ess-expensive "shared mail" is a growing trend for many advertisers.

A trend in direct mail is *shared mail* (cooperative mail). This industry is dominated by Advo-Systems, which in 1986 had more than 16,000 companies (two-thirds are small business) using their services. Even the retailing giants like Kmart and J. C. Penney are shifting to shared mail because it is competitive with newspaper advertising rates and it provides a much heavier saturation of an area than most newspapers. For example, Advo-Systems will bundle a circular promoting Kmart's weekly specials and a bunch of cents-off coupons and then mail the package—at inexpensive third-class postal rates—to nearly every home in a given area.[14]

RADIO

*R*adio has shown tremendous recent growth.

Like magazines, radio has made a strong comeback after a sharp decline in popularity during the 1950s. Today there are more than 4,500 AM stations and 4,000

FM stations. AM stations can broadcast at greater distances and, in addition, are more suitable for car radios. FM stations feature clearer reception and fuller tones and are more suitable for stereo systems. Together they take in over $6.7 billion in advertising revenues a year.

*R*adio advantages: (1) inexpensive rates for local advertisers, (2) demographic selectivity, (3) universal availability, (4) high message frequency.

Many advertisers feel that radio is undervalued for the size of audience it can reach. Because there are so many local radio stations in existence, all competing for the same advertising dollars, local spot times are rarely sold out. Cost benefits have made radio especially attractive to local advertisers, who account for two-thirds of radio advertising revenues. These benefits come not only from the lost costs for spots, but also from negligible production costs.

Like TV, radio is demographically selective. Radio advertisers can select market segments and broadcast their commercials on the stations that appeal to the people in a particular segment, such as talk shows or Spanish programming.

Other advantages include radio's universal availability and its high message frequency. People wake up to radio alarm clocks and listen to radio as they shop at their local mall. From joggers with earphones to rush-hour commuters (100 million of them have car radios), everyone listens to the radio. Such flexibility means that radio can offer multiple channels of programming to listeners twenty-four hours a day, seven days a week. Thus, radio is a popular media-mix element for supplementing local newspaper ads or for regional or national advertisers who need to support their magazine ads.

*R*adio disadvantages: (1) clutter, (2) low reach, (3) short life of messages, (4) repetition required.

Some of the more important disadvantages of radio as an advertising medium include lack of visual image, clutter, low-reach capabilities, and the short life of messages. Clutter is usually more of a problem on AM stations than on FM, but the amount of clutter depends on the time and the station. Another problem stems from radio's high degree of selectivity. An advertiser promoting a product with universal appeal must purchase time on several stations to attain the same coverage as on TV. Finally, because it is of an audio and not visual nature, a radio ad is best suited for simple messages that do not require product demonstration. In radio, repetition is not only possible but necessary.

MAGAZINES

*M*agazines are the oldest American advertising medium.

Magazines, the oldest U.S. advertising medium, are getting a new lease on life as more advertisers see alternatives to beat the increasing costs of TV spot time. Currently, over $5 billion is spent annually on magazine advertising. This popularity is obvious at the newsstands, where every month new magazines designed for specific market segments in sports, psychology, art, fitness, computers, food, and music are showing up. Furthermore, magazines like *Time, Newsweek,* and *Business Week* among others publish special geographic and demographic editions.

*M*agazine advantages: (1) demographic selectivity, (2) geographic selectivity, (3) longer life of message, (4) repeated exposure, (5) attractive graphic options.

Magazines offer special unique advantages to the advertiser. They are demographically and geographically selective. They have a longer life than newspapers, and they provide repeated exposure. It is not uncommon, for example, for a patient to sit in a doctor's waiting room and read an issue of, say, *Life* magazine that is three or four months old. Its large color ads stay attractive and readable for some time. Magazines offer a number of attractive graphic options such as centerfolds, bleeds (a picture that covers an entire page), and inserts.

*M*agazine disadvantages: (1) clutter, (2) delayed reach, (3) delayed frequency, (4) early closing dates.

The major disadvantage of magazines as an ad medium can be traced to the fact that they come out periodically (usually once a week or once a month). Magazines such as *National Geographic* are often read months after they are received. Thus, they have delayed reach and frequency, which often date the ads. A related disadvantage is the early closing dates. Monthly magazines often have a closing date for ads eight weeks ahead of the cover date. Clutter is also a disadvantage. With so many ads on a page, some popular magazines often resemble catalogs.

Maguzine advertising is frequently coordinated with a
sales promotion, such as the contest explained in this ad.

Source: Courtesy of the Campbell Soup Company.

OUTDOOR ADVERTISING

Outdoor advertising is a $1 billion industry that includes billboards, portaboards,
hot-air balloons, blimps, skywriting, neon signs, and a new technique using lasers.
Don't confuse outdoor advertising with signs or on-premise advertising (sales promotion) placed by proprietors to identify their businesses. The two are different.

*T*wo most basic types of
outdoor advertising:
(1) poster panels,
(2) painted bulletins.

The two basic types of outdoor advertising that account for most of the advertising revenue are the *poster panel* and the painted bulletin. Poster panels are the
billboards we are most used to seeing, the ones that dot our interstates and major
roads. They measure 12′3″ × 24′6″ and are designed to accommodate sales messages
printed on posters by the advertiser. The posters are distributed by an outdoor
agency, meaning one that specializes in outdoor advertising. Manufacturers of beer,
cigarettes, automobiles, and soft drinks commonly use this type of billboard, which
has experienced fourfold growth since 1970, when tobacco ads were banned from the
airwaves. According to the Federal Highway Administration, over 500,000 billboards
were lining U.S. roads in 1985. This represented a 50 percent drop from the more
than one million billboards counted in 1966, the year the Highway Beautification
Act was passed. The Act was not renewed in 1986 and billboards again are on the
rise.

*T*he tobacco industry is
responsible for the growth
surge in outdoor
advertising.

Painted bulletins are another type of billboard that usually measure 14′ × 48′
and are produced individually by artists from designs provided by the advertiser.
They are becoming more common in large cities such as Los Angeles, where they
are used to advertise Las Vegas shows, records, and premier movie runs.

**Marlboro has successfully
used lifelike painted billboards to promote
cigarettes.**

Another rapidly growing outdoor medium is called inflatables. These product
replicas come in two forms: *portaboards* and hot-air balloons. Portaboards are in-
flatable advertising pieces in the shape of characters or corporate products (soda pop
and beer cans, liquor bottles, and cigarette packs are among the more popular).
They appear as giant billboards inflated with cold air and fastened to the ground
with stakes or water ballast. Coppertone, for instance, uses such billboards at

beaches across the country. By contrast, hot-air balloons rise to the occasion and contain a three- to four-person gondola. Currently over 1,000 hot-air balloons carry commercial messages in the United States. Many of these are also giant replicas of products or characters such as a pair of Levi jeans or Planter's Mr. Peanut.[15]

*M*ajor advantage of outdoor advertising: repetition; major disadvantage of outdoor advertising: lack of visibility.

The main advantage of outdoor advertising is the repetition it offers. People usually have set driving patterns and they pass the same billboard every day on their way to work. A disadvantage can be the lack of visibility if the billboard is in an area that is not well lighted at night.

Scheduling the Media

*M*edia schedules are commonly developed around seasons or expected economic developments.

The media schedule is the culmination of media planning. The schedule reflects the number of advertisements to appear in each medium, their size or length, and the times they are to appear. Because every advertiser has different objectives, there is no such thing as an ideal schedule or one that will work for every advertiser. Schedules do follow certain patterns, however, and are commonly developed around seasons or expected economic developments.

The advertiser has several scheduling strategies from which to choose. For example, Apple Computers used a **blitz** schedule to introduce its Macintosh personal computer. Apple bought multiple-page ad space in several magazines and continued the ads in consecutive issues. In other words, Apple spent large sums of its advertising budget in one shot. Another strategy, **pulsing,** calls for fairly regular intermittent bursts of advertising separated by short periods of relative or complete inactivity. **Flighting,** another strategy, is similar to pulsing except the concentrated ad bursts do not have the regularity associated with pulsing. These strategies are popular with advertisers because they can take advantage of seasonal demand for their products. Pulsing and flighting cost less than the alternative strategy of continuously advertising at an even rate over a given period.

Evaluating the Advertising Campaign

*S*ales cannot be the only measure of an ad's success.

The ultimate goal of any advertiser is to measure an ad's direct effectiveness in increasing customer sales. However, sales alone are not the best measure of effectiveness, and its sole use as a measure can be very misleading. Reasons for this vary, but basically it is very difficult to isolate the effect of any single advertisement or campaign from the remaining effects of previous efforts or from the effects of other elements of the promotional mix.[16] Thus, evaluation focuses on other aspects of the ad or campaign such as the accomplishment of advertising objectives; a comparison of advertisements to determine the best copy, illustrations, or layouts; or a comparison of media and media plans to determine their strengths and weaknesses.

The tests and measurements used to evaluate the effectiveness of ads are part of the marketing communications effort called **copy testing.** This effort is usually divided into pretesting and posttesting.

PRETESTING

*P*retesting helps select the best appeals, ads, media, and eliminates mistakes.

Testing done prior to an advertising campaign is called **pretesting.** The purpose of pretesting is to select the best appeals, ads, media, and so on, and to limit or eliminate possible mistakes. There are numerous pretests available to researchers. Some of the more common ones include:

1. **Focus-Group Interviews.** This method, previously discussed in Chapter 4, assembles a group of prospective consumers and a group leader. The group is

shown several advertisements and asked to react (individually and as a group) to all or parts of each. For example, Levi Strauss used the focus-group technique to determine the type of ad campaign to conduct for its proposed new line of men's suits. Levi was especially interested in the types of appeals necessary to attract a specific market segment.

2. **Portfolio Tests.** These tests are used exclusively for magazine print ads. The idea is to present a respondent with a portfolio (folder) of ads. The interviewer asks the respondent to recall as much about the ads as possible. When all of the questions are asked, a recall score is calculated. This score is normally expressed as a percentage of respondents who remember the brand advertised and so on. From these scores, researchers get a pretty good idea whether an ad will stand out and its message be remembered.

3. **Physiological Testing.** Laboratory tests are designed to measure a consumer's involuntary responses to specific ad elements. These tests appeal to many advertisers because of their objectivity (the responses cannot be distorted); however, their high cost discourages others from using them. Various tests performed might measure a person's heart beat, blood pressure, eye movement, or even perspiration while reading or viewing an ad. Their purpose is to measure how well an ad can attract attention.

POSTTESTING

Posttesting is conducted after an ad or campaign has run in the media. There are many types, but two of the most popular are recognition tests and recall tests.

*T*he Starch Readership Survey is commonly used to measure ad recognition.

1. **Recognition Tests.** The most commonly used recognition test is the Starch Readership Survey. Hundreds of newspapers and magazines use this service to evaluate the readership of ads tested. Researchers from the Starch organization interview sample respondents (100 to 300 per issue) and ask questions

Dole uses the Starch Readership Survey to determine the percentage of readers who note, associated, or read most of the ad.

Source: Courtesy of Starch Intra Hooper and The Dole Company

about ads within publications that respondents claim to have read. From the questioning, readers are classified into three groups: those who noted the ad, those who associated the ad with a brand, or those who read most of the ad (half or more). The group totals are then expressed as percentages of all readers. The scores are reported to advertisers on a computer printout and on copies of magazines with special labels attached that indicate, by sex, the readership scores on each ad element.

*R*ecall tests are effective in determining the ability of an ad to be noticed and retained.

2. **Recall Tests.** These tests differ from recognition tests in that respondents are not shown an ad. Instead, they are asked to remember which ads they read or viewed. Recall can be aided or unaided. For example, in aided recall the interviewer might ask, "Can you recall an ad for a stereo recently?" By contrast, in unaided recall, respondents might be asked if they can recall any ad that they have seen recently. Unaided recall tests are not used frequently because results are usually vague and of little help to advertisers unless their campaigns were blockbusters. Regardless of which test is chosen, recall tests are effective in determining the degree to which an ad is noticed and retained.

THE CASE CONTINUES

*A*ll of the 1988 Olympic sponsors managed their own advertising campaigns. The advertising objective of most sponsoring companies was to create awareness and goodwill. For example, Brother International believes strongly in the Olympic "spirit" and what the Olympics stand for . . . the pursuit of excellence. It is that feeling that every athlete who qualifies to represent their country for the Olympics, is a "gold medal winner," even before the Olympics. An Olympic gold is just the "icing on the cake." To support this spirit, Brother International corporation, U.S.A., worked with the U.S. Olympic Organizing Committee to raise money for the team and supplied the U.S. Olympic Training Center with typewriters and word processors.

The advertising campaign budgets usually ranged from $7 million to over $100 million. To communicate

their Olympic message, sponsors select a media mix of TV, radio, magazines, and newspaper ads. Two 1984 sponsors, Buick and Fuji Film, used two different forms of outdoor advertising. Buick used its seventy-foot hot-air balloon with the Olympic emblem on one side and the Buick hawk on the other. Fuji Film used a blimp to advertise that it was the official film of the Olympics. Most scheduled advertising began a year before the Olympics on a fairly continuous basis. Once the actual games neared, advertising blitzes were used.

In the case of the Olympics most advertising was pretested and posttested. An *Advertising Age* poll conducted just prior to the 1988 Winter Games showed that Olympic spon-

sorships seemed to be paying off. More than half of the people polled recalled advertising that mentioned a company's status as an Olympic sponsor or supplier, though only 36 percent could name a specific company. Visa International and Kodak had the highest recall rates. The recall helped verify for Visa that their campaign was at least partially responsible for a 17 percent increase in charges for the 3rd quarter of 1987.

Survey respondents (46%) also indicated that a company's Olympics sponsorship raises their opinion of the company, while 50 percent said sponsorship does not affect their opinion. When asked whether they would be inclined to buy a specific brand or product because its maker is an Olympics sponsor, 37 percent said they would and 61 percent said they would not.

 ## ORGANIZING FOR ADVERTISING MANAGEMENT

Advertising is an important and highly specialized activity. For most retail and manufacturing companies the advertising effort begins with an internal advertising department, which is assisted by a variety of outside organizations including media staff, photographers, commercial artists, printers, ad agencies, and suppliers. Thus, unlike most other marketing activities, advertising can be integrated into several outside organizations.

Advertising Departments

Usually a company will choose to work with an advertising agency, thus enabling the company to keep its staff small and save costs. By using an agency, the advertising department has at its disposal a variety of specialists whom the department can use as needed. The advertising department then is responsible for doing overall planning, setting objectives, establishing a budget, selecting an ad agency, supervising, serving as liaison between the company and the agency, and making the important "final" decisions.

*R*etail ad departments are most likely to be involved in ad production.

It is possible for an advertising department to take an active role in the production of ads, but this occurs primarily in local retail advertising. Retail ads must usually be prepared quickly so they can stress availability and price. In addition, it is extremely important that all elements of advertising be coordinated with in-store displays and other promotions. Occasionally, smaller retailers use ad agencies, but retailing giants like Sears and J. C. Penney use them regularly.

Advertising Agencies

Advertising agencies are independent companies that specialize in all phases of preparing and executing client advertising. An advertising agency that offers a wide range of services is called a **full-service agency.** Young & Rubicam, the nation's largest ad agency, provides market research, media planning, package design, account management, copy and art layout, media placement and monitoring, public relations, and many other services. Young & Rubicam's clients have included Kentucky Fried Chicken, Sanka, Xerox retail stores, and Band-Aids. Often an agency will work with a client from the time of product conception through each stage in the product life cycle.

*M*ost ad agencies no longer use a 15 percent media commission.

According to the Association of National Advertisers, 43 percent of ad agencies still charge the traditional 15 percent media commission or a variation of this plan. For example, if the J. Walter Thompson agency buys $120,000 worth of advertising

☐ **Table 17.3**   Top ten advertising agencies.

RANK	AGENCY	GROSS INCOME		BILLINGS	
		1987	1986	RANK	1987
1	Young & Rubicam	$735	$628	(1)	$4,906
2	Saatchi & Saatchi Advertising	694	610	(2)	4,609
3	BBDO Worldwide	537	445	(3)	3,664
4	Ogilvy & Mather Worldwide	529	460	(4)	3,663
5	McCann-Erickson Worldwide	513	428	(5)	3,418
6	Backer Spielvogel Bates Worldwide	499	371	(6)	3,330
7	J. Walter Thompson Co.	483	471	(7)	3,222
8	Lintas: Worldwide	418	325	(8)	2,787
9	D'Arcy Masius Benton & Bowles	371	334	(10)	2,494
10	Leo Burnett Co.	369	305	(12)	2,462

Notes: Dollars are in millions. U.S.-based agencies are ranked by worldwide gross income and billings.
Source: Reprinted with permission from *Advertising Age*, March 14, 1988, p. 1. Copyright © Crain Communications, Inc. All rights reserved.

on the TV show *Dallas* for a client, it will pay CBS $102,000. The $18,000 difference is the 15 percent commission granted by CBS to the agency. The agency will then charge the client $120,000 and keep the difference as compensation. In addition, the client will be charged for expenses incurred in outside services such as commercial production costs and photography.

Some agencies charge expenses plus a standard 17.65 percent markup on outside services and a fee for agency staff time spent on work not related to media. Other agencies use combination plans and alternate systems. Because of the diversity of payment plans offered, advertisers must be aware of what services they are paying for and the exact method of payment.[17] See table 17.3 for a list of the top ten U.S. ad agencies and their total billings.

PUBLICITY

Publicity, the fourth type of promotion available in the promotional mix, is the "nonpaid commercially significant news or editorial comments about ideas, products, or institutions."[18] In other words, publicity is free. If Polaroid buys space in a magazine to tout the features and benefits of a new camera, that is advertising. However, if an astronaut returning from a space shuttle flight offers reporters Polaroid photographs from his mission in space, that is publicity.

*P*ublicity can be oral, written, or action oriented.

Publicity can be oral, written, or action oriented. For example, the senior economist for Hilliard Lyons, a regional brokerage firm, regularly speaks at free investment clinics throughout the Midwest. Kroger prepares written press releases to publicize new store openings or to inform the public of new services such as in-store banking, restaurants, florists, or even photo shops. This technique yielded numerous news releases and a feature article in *Fortune* magazine. Or take the case of an airline that provides free transportation for a child and his family to another part of the country so the child can receive life-saving surgery. Or consider McDonald's, which provides the child's family with free shelter at a nearby Ronald McDonald House.

This form of nonpersonal promotion serves to stimulate demand for a good, service, or business. It can be generated by the company or by word of mouth. One example is the publicity recently generated by corporations not only sponsoring athletic teams and participants, but actually creating their own athletic events as well. Take Bordens, which put up $1 million to create an old-timers' baseball game to promote Cracker Jacks, or Manufacturers Hanover Trust, which created corporate challenge races in cities across the country. Imagine the publicity generated when rival bank teams were required to wear numbers bearing the Hanover name. The races were a success not only in bringing out hordes of racers, but also in generating prospective customers in cities where the Hanover name is little known.

Publicity can be good or bad, and, unlike advertising, it can be difficult to control. McDonald's initially received negative publicity from a community near San Diego. The chain had made plans to open as usual after a shooting incident claimed the lives of twenty-two people at a local restaurant. Quick thinking by McDonald's executives rapidly changed the negative publicity to positive when they announced that the store would be torn down and made into a shrine, as requested by the community.

*P*ublicity and PR work together at relatively low costs.

Publicity is a part of the larger concept of **public relations (PR),** or the process by which a business obtains goodwill and promotes a positive image. Publicity and public relations often work together to contribute significantly to mass selling that can be relatively low in cost, and in some cases more effective than advertising. Take, for example, the Indiana Pacers basketball team, which in 1983 drew an average 4,800 fans per home game. In 1984, Ray Compton, the new head of marketing and

7-Eleven and Lite beer sponsor a local United Cerebral Palsy sports event in order to promote a positive image.

promotions for the Pacers, began a combined PR and publicity program that increased attendance to over 10,000 per game in 1984. For opening night, the Pacers threw a pre-game party where they put on a laser light show and suggested that fans wear tuxedos to the game. About 4,000 fans did wear tuxedos, and 17,096 showed up to see the Pacers. Other games have featured pop concerts and the Indianapolis Symphony Orchestra.

Establishing Publicity Objectives

Because publicity is a tool of public relations, objectives can be clearly defined and stated. Examples include: (1) conducting a press conference to announce a new product offering; (2) creating a positive image about a company by releasing information about company involvement in the local United Way drive; (3) preparing a press release to announce the promotion of key employees; (4) inviting the public out to meet a celebrity; or (5) introducing a new logo or slogan by writing a magazine article on the company's history. All of these possible objectives and many more must be tailored to the company's overall marketing and promotional plan.

Managing Publicity

*P*ublicity budgets usually reflect costs for related but indirect costs.

Once the objectives are established, budgets must be considered. Because publicity is free, budgets usually reflect costs for related but indirect expenditures. For instance, McDonald's had to budget for the cost of containers to collect money for the Ronald McDonald House. Hills retail store chain had to budget for the cost of having football star Herschel Walker appear at new store openings. These things are not free, but the newspaper articles and word-of-mouth promotion are.

The next management step is to put the publicity plan into action—carefully selecting a message and a media or special event to carry the message. This is very important because many publications receive hundreds of press releases and use only a very small percentage. Therefore, the publicist must produce well-written, newsworthy releases or develop events that are of interest to the general public. Furthermore, the publicist must be aware of which media are most appropriate for which types of publicity.

*M*easurement of publicity effectiveness is difficult.

Finally, the publicity generated should be evaluated for its effectiveness. As in sales promotion, exact measurement is sometimes difficult because of the integration of publicity into the overall promotional campaign. The easiest form of evaluation is simply to keep a clippings book of all publicity that is actually published with a notation of when and where it appeared. Then a cost-of-space check can be used to determine what the cost would have amounted to if space had been purchased. A similar step can be used for TV and radio. A return card can be sent to stations, requesting information on when and how often a spot is played. Other methods of evaluation include conducting surveys or checking to see if there has been an effect on sales and profits. Needless to say, better ways of measuring the effectiveness of publicity need to be developed.

THE CASE CONTINUES

*A*nheuser-Bush, an Olympic sponsor, began preparing for its 1984 Olympic promotion three years in advance. The first step was to hire Fleishman-Hillard, a public relations firm, that created the award-winning Budweiser Olympic Art Program. Six former Olympic champs were commissioned to create abstract paintings using the tools of their sport. For example, Wilma Rudolph, field and track star, created designs with running shoes oozing wet pigment; and Bill Russell, former basketball great, dribbled a ball down a ten-foot, white cloth that bad been dunked in paint, blending colors with his fancy footwork.

The collection of paintings was unveiled at a press conference held at a prestigious New York art gallery and then auctioned off at a $100-a-plate luncheon at the Waldorf Astoria. Proceeds ($86,500) from the luncheon and paintings were donated to the U.S. Olympic Committee. Additional funds were raised from the sale of limited-edition lithographs and posters.

The second phase of the campaign consisted of a national tour with one or more of the athletes present with the original collection. The tour included shopping malls, sports arenas, college campuses, and other high-traffic locations. Each stop included autograph sessions and media interviews. Phase three of the campaign was an extension of the national tour in which Budweiser distributors were allowed to rent the collection or reproductions and lend the collection to interested groups for display. For an extra fee, the athletes could be booked for personal appearances. The PR firm even produced a sales promotion brochure to presell the extension tour.

Other sales promotion materials and publicity included press kits, videotapes of the athletes in competition, photos of the "artists" at work, and extensive media coverage from print and electronic media, including "Good Morning America," the "Today Show," *People, Sports Illustrated,* and *The Wall Street Journal.* The total budget for this highly successful publicity and sales promotion effort was $60,000.

GOAL SUMMARY

1. **Explain why advertising is important to our economy.** Advertising is important to the American economy because it helps stimulate growth by encouraging consumers to buy products. Furthermore, advertising is a major industry that employs thousands and annually contributes around $40 billion into our economy.

2. **List and explain the uses of advertising.** Advertising has the following uses: (1) reaching inaccessible prospects, (2) preselling a product, (3) introducing new products, (4) reducing sales fluctuations, and (5) building goodwill.

3. **Discuss the steps in managing an ad campaign.** An effective ad campaign must be based on the overall marketing plan. After reviewing the plan, advertising objectives must be set, budgets established, messages developed, media selected and scheduled, and the campaign results measured and evaluated.

4. **Explain AIDA, which is an acronym that stands for Attention, Interest, Desire, and Action.** This concept represents the sequence a consumer goes through in the persuasion process. Advertisers use AIDA as a guide in developing effective ad copy, illustrations, and layout.

5. **List the major media used to advertise a good, service, or idea. Know their characteristics and major advantages and disadvantages.** The major media used in advertising are newspapers, TV, radio, direct mail, magazines, and outdoor advertising. An advertiser should thoroughly understand the advantages and disadvantages of each because they will affect the cost and determine the frequency and reach of every ad.

GOAL SUMMARY (continued)

6. **Explain the purpose of advertising agencies.** The advertising department in most companies needs specialized assistance in implementing its advertising plans. Advertising agencies can provide a wide range of service such as market research, media planning, package design, account management, copy and art layout, media placement and monitoring, and public relations.

7. **Discuss the role of publicity in the promotional mix.** Publicity is the free promotion that a company receives in the form of news and magazine articles, TV editorial comment, or word-of-mouth comment. Organizations try to generate positive publicity as a part of their public relations programs to build goodwill and to supplement other efforts to stimulate demand for a product or acceptance of an idea.

KEY TERMS

Advertising, **p. 467**
Product Advertising, **p. 469**
Institutional Advertising, **p. 469**
Pioneering Stage, **p. 469**
Competitive Stage, **p. 469**
Retentive Stage, **p. 471**
AIDA, **p. 474**
Media Plan, **p. 476**
Reach, **p. 477**
Frequency, **p. 477**
Cooperative Advertising, **p. 478**
Blitz, **p. 482**

Pulsing, **p. 482**
Flighting, **p. 482**
Copy Testing, **p. 482**
Pretesting, **p. 482**
Focus-Group Interviews, **p. 482**
Portfolio Tests, **p. 483**
Physiological Testing, **p. 483**
Posttesting, **p. 483**
Recognition Tests, **p. 483**
Recall Tests, **p. 484**
Full-Service Agency, **p. 485**
Publicity, **p. 486**
Public Relations (PR), **p. 486**

CHECK YOUR LEARNING

1. Advertising is any paid, personal, or impersonal presentation of products or ideas by an identified sponsor.   **T/F**
2. Advertising can be used for all of the following purposes except: (a) introducing new products, (b) reducing sale fluctuations, (c) creating demand, (d) building goodwill.
3. Institutional advertising is used for: (a) public service, (b) patronage, (c) public relations, (d) all are correct.
4. All of the following are examples of advertising stages except: (a) retentive, (b) initial, (c) pioneering, (d) competitive.
5. DAGMAR is an acronym used for establishing advertising budgets.   **T/F**

6. AIDA is an acronym used to develop the advertising message.   **T/F**
7. All of the following are advertising media except: (a) radio, (b) laser lights, (c) coupons, (d) bus placards.
8. A scheduling strategy calling for fairly regular, intermittent bursts of advertising separated by a short period of relative or complete inactivity is called: (a) pulsing, (b) blitzing, (c) flighting, (d) continuous.
9. Unaided recall tests are popular because of the specific information they give researchers.   **T/F**
10. Most advertising agencies still charge the traditional 15 percent media commission.   **T/F**
11. The easiest way to evaluate publicity is to keep a "clippings book."   **T/F**
12. Public relations is a tool of publicity.   **T/F**

QUESTIONS FOR REVIEW AND DISCUSSION

1. Define the key terms for this chapter that follow the goal summary.
2. Explain why ad expenditures vary so much, not only from company to company, but from industry to industry.
3. If all advertising were prohibited, what impact would that have on our economy? Which industries would be most affected? Which would be affected least?
4. Give a current example of each medium that illustrates the use of advertising.
5. Identify the characteristics of a good advertising objective.
6. Discuss the value of celebrities and testimonials in advertising.
7. Take an ad of your choice and discuss whether you believe the ad uses the AIDA concept.
8. Compare and contrast the advantages and disadvantages of each major type of media.
9. What considerations must be made when developing a media plan?
10. List different types of advertising not discussed in your text. What are the advantages and disadvantages of each?
11. Which advertising media would you select for the following products? Why?
    a. Izod shirt
    b. Xerox copying machine
    c. Allstate auto insurance
    d. Camel cigarettes
    e. Pacific Tanning Salon
12. Discuss the importance of evaluating the effectiveness of advertisements.
13. Discuss the current trend in compensation for advertising agencies. Why is this occurring?

NOTES

1. Marion L. Elmquist, "100 Leaders Parry Recession with Heavy Spending," *Advertising Age,* September 8, 1983, p. 1.
2. Bill Abrams, "Comparative Ads Are Getting More Popular, Harder Hitting," *The Wall Street Journal,* March 11, 1982, p. 25.
3. Sam Certo, Max Douglas, and Stewart Husted, *Business, 2d ed.* (Boston: Allyn and Bacon, 1988), p. 320.
4. Russell H. Colley, *Defining Advertising Goals for Measured Advertising Results* (New York: Association of National Advertisers, Inc., 1961), p. 6.
5. Louis Kaufman, *Essentials of Advertising* (New York: Harcourt Brace Jovanovich, 1980), p. 11.
6. John Koten, "After Serious '70s, Advertisers Are Going for Laughs Again," *The Wall Street Journal,* February 23, 1984, p. 29.
7. Ronald Alsop, "Ad Firms Turn to Computers to Enliven TV Commercials," *The Wall Street Journal,* August 16, 1984, p. 25.
8. "The Big New Celebrity Boom," *Business Week,* May 22, 1978, pp. 79–80.
9. Bill Abrams, "If Logic in Ads Doesn't Sell, Try a Tug on the Heartstrings," *The Wall Street Journal,* March 8, 1982, p. 27.
10. Meg Cox, "Ford Rushes Thunderbird With VIP Plan," *The Wall Street Journal,* October 17, 1977, p. 37.
11. *American Newspaper Publisher Handbook,* 1979.
12. Myron Magnet, "Can Cathie Black Pull *USA Today* Out of the Red?" *Fortune,* September 3, 1984, pp. 98–101.
13. William MacDougall, "Why People Are Turned Off By Television," *US News & World Report,* February 13, 1984, pp. 49–50.
14. Bill Abrams, "Newspaper Publishers Want Distributors of Job Mail to Pay Higher Postal Rates," *The Wall Street Journal,* August 15, 1984, p. 29.
15. "Advertising That Really Takes Off," *INC.,* April 1984, p. 37.
16. Jagdish A. Sheth, "Measurement of Advertising Effectiveness: Some Theoretical Considerations," *Journal of Advertising* 3, no. 1 (1974): pp. 6–11.
17. "The 15% Media Commission Is on the Way toward Becoming a Relic in Ad Agency Cooperation Plans," *Marketing News,* June 10, 1983, p. 6.
18. James F. Engle, Martin R. Warshaw, and Thomas C. Kinnear, *Promotional Strategy* (Homewood, IL: Richard O. Irwin, Inc., 1979), p. 30.

CONCLUDING CASE
A CELEBRITY MALPRACTICE?

Johnny Unitas became a legend too soon. As the Baltimore Colts' blue-chip quarterback of the 1950s and 1960s, he played before a man who could throw a football 60 yards was worth a fortune. While O. J. Simpson signed a million-dollar contract with Hertz in the 1970s, Johnny U. in retirement was left with outfits like First Fidelity Financial Services Inc. of Hollywood, Florida, a second-mortgage broker that paid him a mere $7,000 for an endorsement. Four years later that deal may wind up actually costing Unitas money. First Fidelity is bankrupt, its founder is in jail after a fraud conviction, and Unitas has a dubious new trophy: the first pro-football player ever sued for advertising a bum product. Call it a charge of celebrity malpractice.

The radio copy Unitas read was innocuous enough: "I know what it's like to put your name on the line and make it count. That's where my friends at First Fidelity come in." But some listeners seemed to take him at face value. This week a federal judge in Miami is scheduled to hear a suit by two investors who say they relied on the endorsement. "They invested their money based upon the belief that someone like Unitas . . .

would not be involved in misrepresentation," says their lawyer, Fred A. Schwartz. "A celebrity has some obligation to . . . make sure he is not being used in a scheme of fraud." His two clients want Unitas to refund their $78,000 plus interest.

Through lawyer Ken Ryskamp, Unitas argues that the suit is a "nuisance" action. "There is nothing in the law to require an endorser . . . to go through the books to make sure the product he is putting his picture on is sound." Indeed, another rule seems at play: when a company collapses, its investors look for a defendant who possesses the metaphorical "deep pockets."

Celebrity malpractice is not an unknown concept. In 1978 the Federal Trade Commission announced that it would go after stars who made false claims in their ads. Its best-known target was singer-actor Pat Boone, until then assumed to be as spotless as his white bucks; he agreed to stop advertising an acne cream which, to his surprise, had the same facial efficacy as shoe polish. In another FTC claim, former astro-

naut Gordon Cooper agreed to discontinue advertising an automobile gas valve that did not deliver the promised fuel economy. Such actions have led agents and lawyers to insist on indemnification clauses, forcing the advertiser to bear any fines that their clients incur. Celebrities want to be trusted—but only up to a point.

Issues for Discussion
1. Can celebrities successfully "sell" products that don't meet consumer standards or needs?
2. How many current celebrities and the products they endorse can you name? Does the length of this list tell you anything about the effectiveness of celebrities in commercials? Explain.
3. Do you think the large amounts of money paid to celebrities is wisely spent, or do you think the money could be put to better use in other types of promotional efforts?

OUTLINE

Personal Selling, Sales Management, and Sales Promotion

LEARNING GOALS

After reading this chapter, you should be able to:

1. Identify the primary roles of the salesperson.
2. Distinguish between retail selling and industrial selling.
3. Explain the steps of the selling process.
4. Explain the process of sales management and identify the duties of the sales manager.
5. Explain the purpose of sales promotion and list major sales promotion tools.

*W*inning Ways is a privately owned company with annual sales of about $40 million. The company manufactures a line of men's and women's activewear under the Winning Ways and Street Smart labels. Winning Ways is also the licensee through its Sports Apparel Division for Wilson brand sportswear. Faced with tough competition, Winning Ways must continually strive to implement new approaches to sell clothing to retail customers.

The Winning Ways national sales force consists of fifty sales representatives from fourteen rep organizations. National sales manager, Gary Markham, claims "our line can be very strong, but if our salespeople are weak, our line won't get placed." Therefore, Markham planned a four-day sales meeting to show the company's new product line, to win acceptance of the marketing strategy behind the line, and to reward performance for the past year. An agenda was planned with input from the sales reps. Input was received from surveys that had been sent to each rep requesting identification of pertinent topics for the agenda.

The meeting was held at the Mariner's Inn at Hilton Head Island, South Carolina, a site that many sales reps recommended as an excellent meeting facility. This location provided Winning Ways with the facilities needed to have fashion

shows and several concurrent breakout groups. In addition, excellent dining and recreation facilities were located on-site or nearby on the island. Keeping to the theme that "all work and no play makes Johnny (or Sally) a dull person," an afternoon was set aside as "tee time" for golf, tennis, volleyball, swimming, or beachcombing.

Issues for Discussion
1. Do you believe that sales training is an important task for the sales manager? Explain your answer.
2. Why do you believe Winning Ways uses independent sales reps rather than employ its own sales force?
3. How would you motivate the sales reps for Winning Ways?

Source: Rayna Skolnik, "Four Big Days with Winning Ways," *Sales & Marketing Management,* July 2, 1984, pp. 60–68.

◼ Product lines must be effectively introduced to the sales force for successful sales results to occur.

*A*lthough many companies have separate marketing and sales staffs, the two should be inseparable. As the sales manager for Winning Ways implied, it doesn't matter how good your product is if you don't have a good sales force to sell it. This chapter reviews the various kinds of personal selling and the responsibilities of various types of salespeople. A close look is also given to the process of how a salesperson makes a sale. The functions of the sales manager are examined, including how he or she sets sales goals, recruits, trains, motivates, and evaluates the sales force. Finally, the use of sales promotions to supplement both the personal selling effort and advertising is discussed. ◼

THE NATURE OF PERSONAL SELLING

As previously discussed in Chapter 1, it is no accident that many of America's top executives come from a sales background. These individuals have learned to communicate to others their ideas about their companies and products. At the same time, they are selling themselves as valuable employees and future corporate leaders. Once at the top, the job of personal selling never stops. For example, do you think Lee Iacocca (CEO of the Chrysler Corporation), who started as a Ford salesman, will ever stop selling his products and the Chrysler Corporation as long as he is at the helm?

Communication on a personal level is what selling is all about. The salesperson must be able to communicate the features and benefits of the product for the purpose of making a sale. Although it is important to persuade someone to make an immediate purchase, the role of the salesperson must go beyond closing the sale. The salesperson must also be a consultant to the customer and assist the customer in making the right buying choice. Many times this will result in a sale, but sometimes the salesperson will suggest that the buyer postpone the purchase. It is just as important that the salesperson build goodwill and attempt to get the customer to return. This cannot be accomplished if the customer is sold something he or she does not need or will not find satisfying.

Selling can be a most rewarding and essential career. There are an estimated eight million salespeople in the United States. They are found in both retail and industrial selling. Many people in the selling profession earn incomes significantly higher than other workers with comparable levels of education and experience, and this high cost per contact is one reason why selling is the most expensive element in the promotional mix. Not only is income generation important to the salesperson, but according to one study, the typical salesperson involved in industrial selling generates enough business to keep thirty-one factory workers steadily employed.[1] Furthermore, many other businesses and employees rely on the salesperson. These include wholesalers, retailers, banks, advertising agencies, advertising media, transportation and storage companies, and many more. As you can see, the salesperson is vital to our economy.

The Role of the Modern Salesperson

The role of the salesperson has changed dramatically in recent years. No longer just a peddler of merchandise, today's salesperson has many roles and cannot afford to be the fast-talking, hard-driving stereotype of a salesman. The primary roles include gathering marketing intelligence, solving customer problems, locating and maintaining customers, and providing support services.

GATHERING MARKET INTELLIGENCE

Gathering information is very important to any business, but unfortunately it is often overlooked. All salespeople should strive to learn as much about their competition and their products as possible. In addition, new product uses, customer complaints or special satisfactions, and ideas for new products and services should also be reported to management.

Salespeople must listen carefully to customers before assisting in the solving of problems.

SOLVING CUSTOMER PROBLEMS

The specialty advertising profession calls its salespeople counselors. This is a very appropriate title because it implies that the salesperson is available to provide advice, opinions, and information that eventually will lead to the satisfaction of needs. In other words, part of every salesperson's role is to listen and ask appropriate questions that will assist customers in solving their business-related problems.

LOCATING AND MAINTAINING CUSTOMERS

Salespeople must devote considerable amounts of time to searching for new accounts, developing new orders from present accounts, and maintaining goodwill with existing customers.

PROVIDING SUPPORT SERVICES

Once a sale is made, a multitude of tasks remain. Some of these include: finding financial assistance, arranging delivery, providing technical assistance and liaison for service, and providing training.

Types of Selling

*C*lassifications of personal selling: retail and industrial selling.

Personal selling—a one-on-one promotional presentation by a seller to a prospective buyer—is often classified according to the market in which the product will be sold. There are two major classifications of personal selling, retail selling, and industrial selling.

RETAIL SELLING

Approximately 55 percent of the personal selling force in the United States is involved in **retail selling**—the sale of products for personal, nonbusiness use to the consumer. Many of these salespeople are retail clerks (2,500,000) who provide the one-to-one selling found in retail settings. These individuals usually do little more than cashier and therefore are often paid a minimum wage.

*R*etail stores are reducing their number of salespeople.

The current trend in retailing is to reduce the number of these salesclerks and replace them with other forms of promotion. Retailers claim that shopping in the future will be "characterized by price value promotion, smaller selections of merchandise, store layouts designed to increase sales, and signs and displays instead of salespeople."[2] The result will be more self-service stores characterized by fast, efficient, central or area checkouts. The masters of merchandising such as Sears, J. C. Penney, and Montgomery Ward have already moved in this direction.

Not all retail salespeople are clerks. Many retail selling jobs require a great deal of product knowledge and a high degree of personal selling skill. Take, for example, a department store salesperson who sells major appliances, men's suits, women's furs, or even furniture. This individual usually earns a commission and is a vital part of the store's profit picture.

*D*irect home selling has been on the rise.

The decline of in-store services has resulted in the growth of retail selling outside the store, or direct home selling. Related to the old door-to-door selling practice, where a salesperson goes from house to house presenting products, in-home selling relies on a sales force of neighbors and friends who sell products from companies such as Amway, Mary Kay, Tupperware, and Avon. This popular form of retail selling is successful because salespeople are "invited" into homes at convenient times. The sales presentation often resembles a social event, with friends and neighbors gathered for fun and refreshment. People don't seem to mind buying from

Many department store chains have recently installed central checkouts in order to reduce labor costs.

friends, but hesitate at the high pressure techniques often used by strangers operating from door to door.

A variation of retail selling is the selling of services to consumers. This area continues to increase steadily and will provide many career opportunities. For example, many more salespeople will be needed who are knowledgeable about insurance, real estate, investment securities, advertising media, and other areas.

*S*elling of services will be a major growth area.

INDUSTRIAL SELLING

In contrast to retail selling, **industrial selling** is one of the highest paid professions in America today. Industrial salespeople sell products used to make other products and/or for a firm's operations to buyers for use in business and industry. The field of industrial selling is opening up increasingly to women. For example, in 1971 only 2 percent of the salespeople in the life insurance industry were women. Today, women constitute an estimated 15 percent of all salespeople.

*W*omen constitute a growing number of salespeople.

The job of industrial salesperson involves selling to purchasing agents, middlemen, and manufacturers and institutions. Examples of products sold might include merchandise for resale, such as Nike jogging shoes to shoe stores or the materials sold to Nike to manufacture the shoes. Examples of different types of selling will be discussed later in the chapter.

TELEMARKETING

Another type of selling that can be used in both retail and industrial settings is telemarketing, which uses the telephone as the medium for marketing the message.

Telemarketing magazine defines **telemarketing** as "the discipline that puts advanced telecommunications technology to work as part of a well-organized and well-managed marketing program. It uses sophisticated management information systems and emphasizes the use of personal selling skills to help companies keep in close contact with their customers, to increase sales, and to enhance business productivity, all while reducing costs."[3]

Although the telemarketing approach to selling has been around for some time, it has just recently reached a sophisticated, professional level. Suddenly it has become the rage because of the pressure exerted by the skyrocketing costs of field sales. *U.S.*

REAL PEOPLE IN MARKETING

**Joyce Bast—
Top-of-the-Line
Sales Representative—
Allyn and Bacon Publishers**

*J*oyce Bast is one of a growing number of female sales representatives working in practically every industry. In Joyce's field of college textbook publishing, many women are building successful sales careers.

The responsibilities of a textbook sales representative are many and varied. Joyce's primary goal is to sell textbooks to professors at the eighty colleges and universities in her territory of Western Michigan and Northwest Indiana. Joyce combines on-site sales work with telemarketing to reach these schools.

Joyce's job involves selling and promoting all new, revised, and backlist books published by her company. In addition to selling, she also scouts for new textbook authors, submitting manuscripts for publication consideration. Joyce's performance each year is measured by the total sales dollars generated in her territory as well as by the number of authors signed to write for her company as a result of her manuscript leads.

Most instructors select or "adopt" new textbooks during the spring for use in their fall classes. In a busy month during the adoption season, Joyce can visit as many as three schools in a single day. In addition to

selling at each school, Joyce must also service her accounts by checking with instructors who use her textbooks as well as with the bookstores that carry them to solve problems that may be brought to her attention and to insure that her customers are satisfied.

As an undergraduate, Joyce was an English major with a History

minor. After graduation, she worked for several years as a flight attendant. A good friend in publishing was instrumental in convincing Joyce that a selling job in textbook publishing was right for her. "I thought that selling would fit my personality," Joyce remarks. "I didn't want anything that was routine in terms of hours or location."

Joyce has a definite strategy in mind when she meets with her clients, although like all savvy salespeople, she won't reveal the exact nature of her approach. She's learned a great deal from the professors with whom she's worked: "Professors are a very interesting group of people. I've learned a lot from them that has helped in my personal and professional development."

In 1988, Joyce was elected to both the Leader's Club and the President's Club—the highest sales awards given by her company. Entrance to the President's Club is given to the salesperson with the greatest increase in dollar volume over a three-year period. To belong to the Leader's Club, a sales representative must be among the top five company salespeople in increased sales for the year. Not a bad way to crown the ten years Joyce celebrated with the company in 1988!

News & World Report predicts that by the year 2000, 8 million jobs will be available selling by telephone. Marketing managers are using the new tool to:

Telemarketing is used to: screen and qualify incoming sales leads, generate sales leads, and call present customers on a regular basis.

1. screen and qualify incoming sales leads before passing them on to salespeople in the field;
2. generate sales leads by calling prospects identified from suitable directories or mailing lists;
3. call present customers on a regular basis to take orders, offer additional service, or determine customer satisfaction.[4]

Types of Salespeople

Tasks conducted by salespeople include: (1) order taking, (2) order getting, and (3) supporting.

Salespeople can be classified according to the types of tasks they perform: (1) order taking, (2) order getting, and (3) supporting. Most salespeople will be involved in all three, but the degree of involvement will vary according to the type of sales job.

MARKETING IN ACTION

Telemarketing

*P*icture this: Long rows of "communicators" sit in glass-encased booths, headphones to their ears, push-button telephones and computer terminals in front of them. In call after call, they repeat the same message, reading from a script on the computer screen. A supervisor glides about the room, wordlessly scanning computer printouts that measure productivity in something called "throughput" per hour.

This is computerized telephone marketing at its most sophisticated. It is not to be confused with non-computerized telephone sales, which consist of calling names on a sheet of paper. The communicators, or telephone sales representatives, work for one of a handful of fully-automated telemarketing service bureaus that find and refine sales leads, and even sell products and services to both new and existing customers. Their sales pitch, a "branched" script, leads the sales rep through a spiel that takes its direction from the prospect's responses.

Computerized telemarketing takes the mystery out of sales, allowing you to judge precisely who is selling how much and for what

reasons. It allows you to control how your product is presented, to measure responses to various sales pitches, and to change an unproductive approach quickly and systematically. The greatest drawback is its expense. Until recently it was limited almost entirely to Fortune 500 companies selling expensive items or political organizations raising funds and recruiting members.

Although the price of telemarketing services won't decline—thanks to rising labor and telephone costs—telemarketers predict that escalating costs of personal sales visits—now put at close to $200—will bring the service within reach of many small businesses. According to Aldyn Mc-Kean, president of Aldyn McKean Associates, a telemarketing consulting firm in New York, the cost of telemarketing "is increasing much less rapidly than the cost of face-to-face sales."

Telemarketing seems to work best in conjunction with other marketing

strategies. As a complement to direct mail, it can increase customer response anywhere from 2 percent to 20 percent. McKean insists that, for a given list of sales prospects, telemarketing can produce five to six times the response of direct mail.

The services are provided by companies such as Salesnet, in Hartford, and Campaign Marketing Group, in Washington. These companies typically charge $60 an hour, compared with $35 to $40 an hour for non-computerized telemarketing. They make eight to 10 consumer calls per hour and six to eight business calls. Beyond the hourly fees, you can expect to spend at least $15,000 to develop and test a telephone marketing strategy. If you don't already have a good list of sales prospects, you will have to invest in that too. Nevertheless, some small companies are using less sophisticated forms of computerized telemarketing while waiting for the cost of full service to fall.

Source: Reprinted from the May 1983 issue of *Venture,* For Entrepreneurial Business Owners & Investors, by special permission. © 1983 Venture Magazine, Inc., 521 Fifth Ave., New York, N.Y. 10175

ORDER TAKERS

*O*rder takers are essential to keeping repeat customers.

The typical retail clerk is an order taker. Responsibilities in this job are limited to answering customer questions, writing sales invoices, checking credit, handling adjustments and complaints, completing the sale, and other routine tasks after the customer becomes interested in a good or service through prior promotional efforts.

Order takers are essential to keeping repeat customers. The order taker must keep in close contact with customers and fill their product needs quickly. In addition, it is sometimes necessary for the order taker to train the customer in how to use a product and to provide service assistance as needed. This type of position is an excellent opportunity for a new salesperson to learn a company and its products, and it is found not only at the retail level of selling, but also at the manufacturing and wholesaling levels. These positions are often the lowest paying sales jobs because they require no creative selling duties and little if any travel.

ORDER GETTERS

*O*rder getters are used to generate sales not otherwise likely to occur.

Salespeople involved in order getting are involved in the **creative selling process.** In other words, they must aggressively seek out their customers and then use a well-organized sales presentation to motivate a customer to make a purchase. Order getters are employed to generate sales that would not be likely to happen otherwise. For example, a salesperson for the Clark Equipment Company would have to locate a prospective customer, explain why a Clark forklift would be more beneficial than one made by Hyster or another competitor, and then close the sale. In the process the salesperson might make recommendations to a customer who is seeking ways to cut materials handling costs. Making such recommendations is an important part of the salesperson's function because they may very well generate future sales, even though they may not lead to an immediate sale.

An order getter can either be part of a company sales force or an independent sales representative. Smaller manufacturing companies often employ **manufacturer's representatives** to sell to wholesalers, distributors, dealers, and sometimes to the ultimate consumer. These independent sales reps are often used as order getters for new products.

Order getters must be knowledgeable about their products and the industries in which they are selling because their responsibilities include many nonroutine selling tasks like problem solving and counseling. This often requires intense sales training and a higher degree of education (usually college).

*S*maller manufacturing companies often use manufacturer's representatives.

SUPPORT PERSONNEL

*S*upport personnel attempt to build goodwill by providing product information and post-purchase service.

Sales personnel involved in the support of the sales force must assist the salesperson in all feasible ways. These salespeople usually do not make sales but attempt to build goodwill with current and prospective customers by providing product information and post-purchase service.

There are two primary types of support salespeople, technical salespeople and missionary salespeople. **Technical selling** is often done by experienced scientists who work with customers and their technical staffs. For instance, International Minerals and Chemicals Corporation, Inc. employs technical salespeople with Ph.D.'s in such areas as animal or poultry science to help sell feed and pharmaceuticals to farmers. Other companies like Lockheed employ aerospace engineers to work with government agencies like NASA or the Air Force to design new space systems.

*T*wo primary types of support salespeople: (1) technical salespeople, and (2) missionary salespeople.

Missionary selling is conducted to supplement the personal selling done by middlemen. The missionary salesperson periodically contacts both wholesalers and retailers to check their stocks, arrange displays, provide advice on selling, and to inform the customer about new products. Usually any orders that result are given to wholesalers to fill. For its cereals and various other lines, General Mills needs aggressive selling beyond what the wholesaler can provide. Therefore, the company employs a sales force of missionary salespeople to call upon wholesalers and retailers.

THE CASE CONTINUES

*W*inning Ways is a clothing manufacturer that must use personal selling along with other elements in its promotional mix. Rather than employ a staff of salespeople, Winning Ways uses independent manufacturer's representatives. These individuals sell the Winning Ways product line along with other manufacturers' lines. Their job is to communicate, in an oral presentation, the features

and benefits of the clothing line to middlemen, who in turn will sell the clothes to consumers. Additional roles include gathering marketing intelligence, solving customer problems, locating and maintaining customers, and providing support services.

The Winning Ways reps are involved in industrial selling because

they are selling products that will be resold to consumers. By contrast, retail salespeople will sell the Winning Ways line directly to the consumer. While the primary task of the rep is to get orders, these salespeople will also take orders and provide service support to their customers. Occasionally they will benefit from sales leads passed on to them from the use of telemarketing.

❑ **Figure 18.1**
Seven stages in
selling.

Seven stages in selling

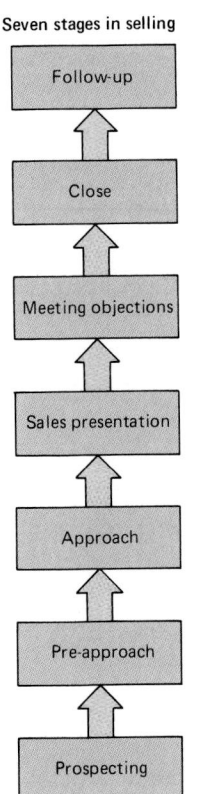

*T*he purpose of the preapproach is to qualify
prospects.

THE SELLING PROCESS

The creative selling process is normally associated with seven steps (figure 18.1). Although these steps can vary according to the salesperson and the type of merchandise sold, they usually occur in the following sequence: (1) prospecting, (2) preapproach, (3) approach, (4) sales presentation, (5) meeting objections, (6) close, and (7) the follow-up.

As salespersons proceed through each step, they draw closer to the achievement of their sales goal: to sell a product by first analyzing the needs of a prospective buyer and then to translate those needs into reasons to purchase a product. As basic as this idea may seem, many salespeople are never trained in the selling steps necessary to accomplish this goal. On the other hand, some companies like IBM, Xerox, General Electric, and NCR spend millions annually training their sales forces. These companies realize that salespersons thoroughly trained and motivated will exhibit an exemplary performance in the selling process.

Prospecting

In the first step of the selling process, the salesperson attempts to locate potential customers. **Prospecting** is the systematic approach to developing new sales leads. Every salesperson loses customers for a variety of reasons ranging from death to a firm's going out of business or simply switching the account to another company. Some studies reveal that the average company loses 15 to 20 percent of its customers annually.[5] Salespeople must continue to seek new customers or risk a decline in their sales.

The concept of old customers constantly leaving and being replaced by new ones is illustrated by the ferris wheel concept presented in figure 18.2. The popular sales trainer and consultant, Joe Girard, uses it to illustrate the relationship between prospecting and the loss of customers due to attrition.

During the prospecting phase of the selling process, many salespeople use the **cold canvass** approach to finding customers. They call on prospects without appointments or without advance knowledge of the needs or financial status of the prospect. This technique can be combined with telemarketing to eliminate unnecessary sales calls. Cold canvassing works best where products have widespread demand such as life insurance. Many new insurance salespeople will search the births and marriages section of the newspaper for leads.

Preapproaching Prospects

The purpose of the preapproach is to qualify a prospect. **Qualifying** is the procedure followed to determine if prospects need a product, whether they have the authority to buy, and whether they have the money to pay for it. In addition, it is to the advantage of the salesperson to learn as much as possible about prospects. For example, what are their likes and dislikes, brand preferences, and working schedules?

The following list of questions can serve as guidelines for further qualifying prospects. Such guidelines will help prevent salespeople from wasting time on unnecessary calls.

1. Does the name represent a customer who is already buying from you? If so, is there a chance of increasing her business?
2. Is the name a former customer? If so, do you know why she stopped buying from you? Should you try to get her back?

❑ **Figure 18.2**
The "ferris wheel" concept of prospecting.

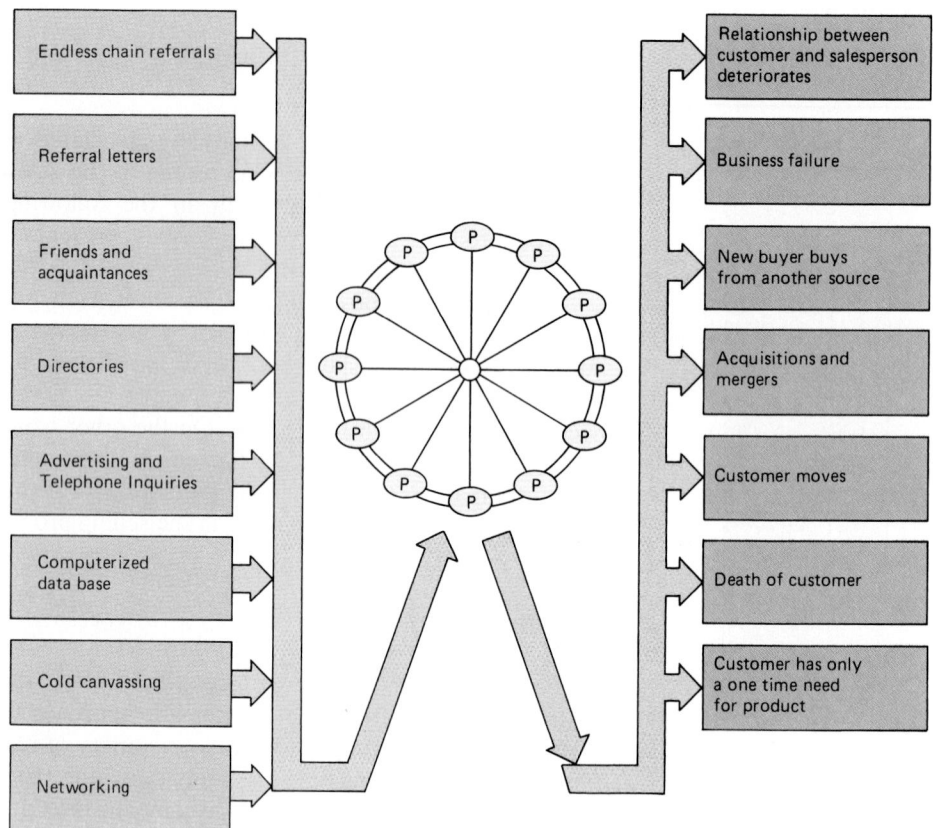

3. Does the name represent a user of your type of product? Is it one who now buys from your competitors? How much does she buy from them? At what prices? What terms?
4. If it is a name that represents a company you've never heard of, what product lines and services does it handle? Who uses its products?
5. What is the company's primary industry? Is it also engaged in other businesses? Does the name represent a main operation, headquarters, branch, service, or a subsidiary?
6. What is the company's sales volume? The number of employees?
7. What is the company's credit rating? (Note: The Dun and Bradstreet *Reference Book* is one excellent source of credit information.)
8. Does the company sell to the government? To a prime contractor?
9. Who are the company's main known suppliers? (Some of them might be your acquaintances or customers who can give you additional information or help in contacting the company.)
10. Are there other sources that might offer direct or indirect assistance, such as an advertising agency, banker, accountant, etc.?[6]

Approaching the Customer

*R*apport established between the prospect and salesperson often determines the success or failure of a sales call.

The **approach** represents the initial contact with the prospect. Approaching prospects can be simple if the salesperson has previously developed a relationship with them. This relationship or rapport often determines the success or failure of the sales call.

Because the prospect is often busy, the first few minutes are very important. A good salesperson quickly learns to avoid doing anything that might annoy the prospect. Although various approaches can be used, one of the best is to get the prospect's attention by engaging him or her in a social conversation.

Presenting the Product

If the approach is successful, the salesperson gets to make the **sales presentation,** which is the attempt to make a sale by persuasively communicating with the prospect. Some salespeople use a **canned presentation** (also referred to as a black-box approach). A canned presentation is prepared in advance and stops only to allow the prospect to make directed responses. It is based on the theory of stimulus-response, and thus the key to success is finding the correct response on which to make the sale.

A needs assessment is often the first step in the sales presentation.

Another popular technique used to make the sales presentation is the **need-satisfaction approach.** Manning and Reece refer to this approach as the "consultative sales presentation."[7] It begins with discovering the needs of the prospect by completing a needs assessment. This involves asking a series of questions and then participating in a dialogue with the prospect. Once this process is completed, the salesperson must select and recommend the product that will provide maximum satisfaction. Finally, the salesperson must communicate to the prospect through persuasion, information, or reminders, the satisfaction the product will provide.

*V*oice communication, combined with visual demonstration, dramatically increases retention rate.

Words alone will not usually sell a product. A study reported in *Sales & Marketing Management* magazine claims that if you use the voice alone in making presentations, you can expect only a 10 percent retention rate. However, when you combine voice with an appropriate visual demonstration, the retention rate increases dramatically. Actually, many products require an effective sales demonstration.

Salespeople use a variety of sales aids to demonstrate product performance. These include article reprints, brochures, models, video disks and cassettes, and other audiovisuals. Of course, the best aid is the product itself. Whenever possible, salespersons should involve their prospects and try to get them to visualize ownership. (See figure 18.3.)

❑ **Figure 18.3**
The consultative sales presentation.

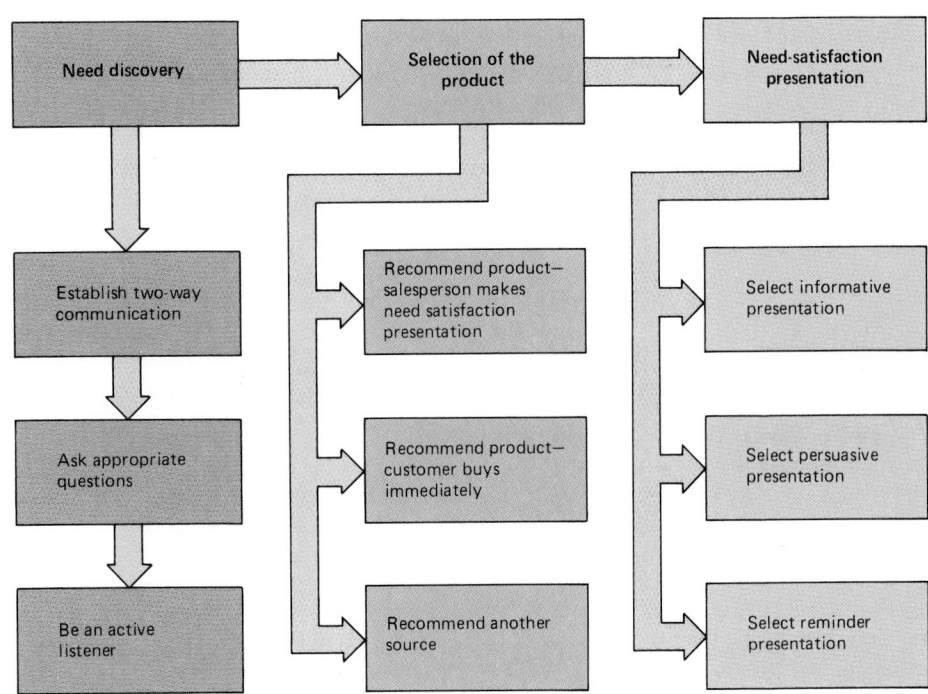

Handling Objections

*C*ustomer reservations are usually expressed in questions or strong objections.

*M*ost customers object to:
(1) product,
(2) salesperson, and/or
(3) price.

Few selling situations occur without some sales resistance. Almost every prospect (in an order-getting situation) will have some reservations about a product, usually expressed as questions or strong objections. Therefore, it is essential at this point in the sales process for salespersons to listen intently as prospects explain why they are resisting.

Most prospects will object to the need for the product, to the product itself, to the salesperson or company selling it, or to the price. Although each of these objections has its own best strategy for overcoming the resistance, the important things to remember are to find some point of agreement and never allow any anger to surface. If possible, the salesperson should try to anticipate the prospect's resistance and insure that the objection is fully understood and validated.

Closing the Sale

*W*hen closing, a salesperson must focus on the prospect's greatest points of interest.

The close, or getting the prospect to say yes, is the goal of every salesperson. The salesperson must recognize the various closing clues and be careful not to oversell. A salesperson with a good close will quickly focus on the prospect's greatest points of interest and will attempt a trial close as soon as verbal or nonverbal clues are recognized. A **trial close** is used to test the readiness of the prospect to buy (this can come early in the presentation). The **assumptive close** is closely related to the trial close, except it takes for granted that the prospect is going to make a purchase by making a statement like, "Will this be cash or charge?" Another popular close is the **summative close.** This close takes the customer's main points of interest and reviews those benefits point by point.

Regardless of the type of close used, the salesperson should remain confident and reassure the prospect that the buying decision is a wise one. Furthermore, since every selling situation is unique, the salesperson must not get too confident. Like any skill, closing skills need constant practice.

Following Up the Sale

*P*ost-purchase follow-up allows excellent sales quotas.

Unfortunately, too many salespeople end a sale with the close. However, every good salesperson knows that new and old accounts need servicing and that eventually the customer will need to make another purchase. The effective salesperson follows up a sale to insure that delivery and installation were satisfactory, that credit was arranged if necessary, and that all promises were kept. In addition, a follow-up visit can be used to determine if additional accessory equipment is needed. This is called **suggestive selling.** In any event, the follow-up is an ideal time to cement a relationship and to insure future sales.

THE CASE CONTINUES

*W*inning Ways is very aware of the importance of the personal selling process. In order to stress this, management conducted four sessions on selling. Attendees were split up for breakout sessions, one each to view the men's and women's lines, one on making the sales presentation, and one on handling ob-

jections. Each session was scheduled to run four times so that everyone could attend each one.

In addition, sales reps were asked to list three to five elements of pre-call preparation that make the call successful. Next, the reps listed

problems they incur in preparing for the call and making the presentation. Finally, they viewed a videotape of the national sales manager making a presentation that was deliberately wrong. The reps then critiqued the tape for errors and viewed another taped presentation that was very polished.

MANAGING THE SALES FORCE

Developing and operating a sales force are the responsibility of the sales manager. **Sales management** is the process of planning, organizing, directing, and controlling the personal selling effort. The sales manager must carefully establish the objectives for the personal selling effort; recruit the sales force; match the sales force to territories; provide the proper and appropriate compensation, motivation, and training; and evaluate the sale results and sales force. Each of these responsibilities will be discussed in the following sections.

Establishing Sales Objectives

*S*ales objectives are often set in the form of sales quotas.

A good manager always sets objectives, and the sales manager should be no exception. Objectives for the sales force are often stated in the form of sales quotas. Quotas should be stated in precise, measurable terms and be based on the sales forecast for a specific time. In addition, the sales manager should consider market potential, or the amount of sales that can be made in a specific geographic area by all competitors. The sales that one particular company might make in an area are called its *sales potential*. The sales manager uses a combination of market potential, sales potential, and judgment to divide the total sales forecast among salespeople's territories to establish sales quotas.[8]

A sales forecast is derived from: (1) market potentials, (2) sales potentials, and (3) judgment.

Sales objectives can be stated for the total sales force or for each salesperson. Further breakdown of the sales forecast might include quotas established by

❏ **Figure 18.4**
Use of computers in corporate sales.

Applications
Entering Orders
Checking Order Status
Checking Inventory
Preparing Forecasts
Planning and Scheduling
Territory Management
Account Management
Reporting Expenses
Reporting Sales Calls
Analyzing Customer Requirements
Preparing Bids for Proposals
Managing Leads
Computer-based Training

Personal Applications
Word Processing
Spreadsheet Analysis
Database Management
Electronic Mail

Percentage of 160 Reporting Companies

Operational   Planned
Pilot Program   Not Planned

A survey of major corporations that are computerizing their sales forces show how computers are being used in the sales process, and how well computers were integrated into the company's business.

Source: The Conference Board, *InfoWorld,* November 17, 1986, p. 43.

Willy Loman, the downtrodden protagonist of "Death of a Salesman," was obsessed with the importance of being liked.

But modern marketing experts say it is even more important for salespeople, and their managers, to be well organized. "We'll give you the fact there's a little black magic to sales. But as soon as you say sales management you need organization," says Terry Beers, a Carlisle, Mass., management consultant.

Thus, the computer is playing a growing role in the glad-handing, backslapping world of salespeople—whether as computerized nags that remind the peddler to write a note to a customer or as analytical tools that let a manager trace a salesperson's weekly progress.

Computers are replacing card files of contracts, black books of appointments and file folders of hot prospects. They are forcing salespeople to prepare sales scripts for each call. Computer programs provide instant customer information.

MARKETING IN ACTION

Better Than a Smile: Salespeople Begin to Use Computers on the Job

Some even are designed to let salespeople do quick psychological profiles of purchasing agents and figure out how best to sell to them. And they make it harder for a salesman to spend hours currying old cronies at existing accounts by letting him and his manager analyze how he spends time.

CAN'T LIVE WITHOUT IT

"I wouldn't try to manage a sales office without it," says Charles B. Mitchell, a copier sales manager in Savin Corp.'s Dallas branch. Using a personal-computer program called Sell! Sell! Sell! since last winter, he says he does a better job critiquing salespeople. He can show them graphs that prove their lower sales reflect too few sales calls. Client contacts are up because the com-

puter spews out letters and even holiday greetings. And new employees produce faster because they follow the software's training program. Best of all, revenue is up because the computer keeps records of when customers' copier contracts expire, and it makes sure Savin salespeople are there to make a pitch. "We aren't losing the customers who said to us, 'Not now, but come back in six months,' " says Mr. Mitchell.

Still, getting salespeople to accept computers is often a hard sell. "They are the least automated of all major business functions," says David Toub, market manager for a Digital Equipment Corp. sales-management program. "Sales people are widely distributed and nontechnical."

Software suppliers say many salespeople worry about losing autonomy when all their records are easily available to the sales manager; they regard the machines as virtual management spies. Others resent having to learn often abstruse computer codes or even learn how to

---

customer, product, or territory. For example, a salesperson for Sony might have a monthly quota of selling a minimum of fifty-five Walkman radios to Kmart, which is but one part of a $125,000 quota (415 units) for this product. This same salesperson could also have a total sales quota for all products.

*A*ctivity quotas are used to insure that essential sales activities are performed.

In addition to sales volume quotas, some companies use activity quotas designed to guarantee that essential sales activities are performed. Activities that might be used as a basis for quotas include the number of calls, orders, presentations, service calls, demonstrations, and collections.

Another type of quota is the expense quota. Sales managers must review past expense records to determine the appropriate quota amount for such items as travel and entertainment expenses. Any expense quota used should have a close relationship to the salesperson's sales budget. See the Marketing in Action and figure 18.4 to see how sales managers use computers to keep records on orders, quotas, expense records, and so forth.

Recruiting the Sales Force

*J*ob analysis determines the job requirements.

A major responsibility for the sales manager is recruiting and selecting the sales force. This process begins by performing a *job analysis* to determine the requirements

type. And computerizing doesn't work well unless salespeople put all their customer records into the computer and stop keeping memos on random slips of paper.

"You have to be committed to using the system. You can't do it both ways," says James Beutel, a sales representative in Digital Equipment's Wilmington, Del., office who, predictably, likes the Digital sales software.

A TRAUMATIC SWITCH

But for companies with low-tech sales forces, the switch can be traumatic. Norton Co., a Worcester, Mass., abrasives maker, keeps price and inventory information on a computer and urges salespeople to use their computers to obtain it. Steven Saylor, manager of information services, says some of the company's most senior salespeople prefer to call headquarters for information rather than use computers, and Norton still lets them. But, he adds, "We can't afford to maintain duplicate systems forever."

To avoid traumas, many companies move cautiously. Monsanto Co.'s polymer products unit is providing its sales force with computers for checking on customer orders. But

Russel C. E. Sprague, director of commercial information systems, says, "We don't expect them to become computer jocks. We don't want them sitting at the terminal for an hour." To accommodate poor typists, Monsanto had Digital Equipment modify the sales package so salespeople can get along by typing two-letter codes rather than full words.

Even when salespeople adapt to computerization, expanded reporting systems may hold corporate risks, says Elizabeth Towne, an account executive with United Research Corp., a Morristown, N.J., consulting firm that advises large companies on boosting sales. She says newly automated sales managers may overemphasize numbers of sales calls and forget about the quality of the customer. Moreover, there's a risk that a company will simply try to automate outmoded systems—what she calls "paving the cowpath."

SALES ARE PICKING UP

Despite such risks, computer sales to sales departments are picking up. Thoughtware Inc., based in Coconut Grove, Fla., says it sold 18,500 copies of Sell! Sell! Sell! in just six months. Producers of software

estimate that there are more than 50 sales-oriented programs available for personal computers and dozens more for larger systems.

There are commanding financial reasons for companies to try to improve sales-force productivity. The average industrial-products salesperson makes $36,000 a year and calls on three to eight customers daily, according to *Sales & Marketing Management* magazine, a trade publication. Excluding compensation, the average sales call cost $102, the magazine says. Ms. Towne says that most sales representatives spend only 35% of their time actually selling, with another 35% traveling. "We find the selling portion of the day can be increased to as much as 50% with better management," she says. Computers help reduce paperwork, make better information available faster and make it easier to focus on the best leads.

Source: William M. Bulkeley, "Better Than a Smile: Salespeople Begin to Use Computers on the Job" *The Wall Street Journal,* September 13, 1985, p. 210. Reprinted by permission of *The Wall Street Journal,* © Dow Jones & Company, Inc., 1985. All rights reserved.

of the job. From the job analysis, the sales manager must develop job specifications and job descriptions. *Job specifications* are the specific qualifications needed for the job such as the amount of education and experience required, desirable personality traits, and other requirements. Often qualifications are determined by studying the traits of successful and unsuccessful salespeople. By contrast, the *job description* states the duties and responsibilities for a specific job. The job description is often a basis for developing ad copy to announce job openings.

Once the sales manager knows the necessary job specifications, a search can begin for the best candidates. The search will seek candidates from a variety of sources: company personnel, advertising in newspapers or in trade and professional journals, competitors, educational institutions, customers, employment agencies, and the recommendations of friends. From these sources, the sales manager develops a list of applicants for various sales openings.

Selection step process: (1) application, (2) screening, (3) personal interview, (4) testing, and (5) physical exam.

The selection process includes several steps. Once the application is completed, it is screened to see whether the applicant meets the qualifications required for the job. If those qualifications are met, the applicant is then invited for a personal interview. The interview should be a time of sharing information. The sales manager has the responsibility to provide the applicant with complete and honest information about the job. On the other hand, the applicant has the responsibility to honestly share information about his or her background, plans for the future, and other

The job interview should be a time of sharing information.

Geographic area is the primary method of assigning territories.

relevant facts. The sales manager should verify all information obtained at the interview by checking references.

Some companies will also require psychological tests. These tests are but one additional device to aid the sales manager in the selection process and are commonly used to measure many of the personality traits found in successful salespeople. If the applicant is acceptable to this point, then the final step is normally the physical exam. The purpose of the exam is to see if there are any health-related problems that could prevent future success.

Matching the Sales Force to Territories

Once the sales force has been selected, it is extremely important to assign each salesperson a definite territory and see that territories are properly organized to avoid duplication of effort. **Sales territories** are normally the geographic areas in which salespeople work. The chief factors in determining the size of a territory are the number of customers and prospects, the frequency with which sales reps must call on old customers, and the number of daily calls they make.[9]

Assigning territories by geographic area has its advantages and disadvantages. One common error of sales managers is to assign too large a geographic area to some sales reps. For example, one medium-sized aluminum products company assigned a sales rep the entire states of Texas and Louisiana. The sales rep had to spend weeks on the road before returning home. Needless to say, situations like this are not good for morale or family life.

Another common error of sales managers is trying to overmanage employees. For instance, a company assigned one of its sales reps a territory in northern Florida; however, to maintain close contact with the sales manager, the sales rep was forced to work out of the Atlanta office. This required a five-hour drive just to get to the territory!

Most reps will start out with a small territory and be promoted to larger territories. However, this does not necessarily mean a larger geographic area. For example, a rep may initially be assigned the southern half of Illinois and then be promoted to an assignment in Chicago, which could have more customers and require less driving and overnight time.

Although the primary method of assigning territories is by geographic area, some companies use other methods within a specific area. For instance, the McGraw-Hill Book Company assigns sales reps on the basis of customer type. McGraw-Hill is organized into several divisions. Its Gregg Division has sales reps who call on teachers in the secondary and postsecondary markets, and its Collegiate Division reps call on professors at four-year (as opposed to two-year) colleges and universities.

Procter & Gamble uses still another method. It assigns sales reps according to product line. For example, it is possible to have seven sales reps calling on one grocery store. Each rep sells a different line of goods such as beverages, paper products, soaps, breakfast foods, health and beauty aids, and others. Procter & Gamble and other large, multi-product companies believe that there are too many details to remember about too many different products. Therefore, each sales rep is expected to specialize and to be an expert in his or her individual product line.

Training the Sales Force

Even though it can be expensive, training the sales force is an important investment in a company's future. (See table 18.1.) Most large companies employ sales training managers. These individuals are primarily responsible for conducting a **training needs analysis,** which indicates problem areas for their sales force. Once the training manager understands the company's sales training needs, he or she develops sales

❑ **Table 18.1** Average cost of sales training per salesperson

Type of Company	TRAINING COST INCLUDING SALARY*		PERCENT CHANGE	MEDIAN TRAINING PERIOD (WEEKS)	
	1986	1987	1986–1987	1986	1987
Industrial products	$27,525	$27,569	+ 1.6%	17	22
Consumer products	19,320	22,500	+16.5%	19	22
Services**	20,460	30,000	+46.6%	14	27

*In addition to salary, covers such items as instructional materials prepared, purchased, and rented for training program; transportation and living expenses incurred during training course; instructional staff; outside seminars and courses; and management time spent with salesperson when it is a part of the training budget.
**Includes insurance, financial, utilities, transportation, retail stores, etc.
Source: Sales & Marketing Management. Copyright © 1988/"Survey of Selling Costs," Feb. 22, 1988, p. 49. All rights reserved. Reprinted by permission.

and sales management courses, visual materials, product newsletters, and sales manuals and also conducts a variety of courses for the sales reps and sales managers. In most cases, the sales training manager trains the field sales managers who, in turn, train their sales force. In other instances, companies employ outside consultants to conduct specialized training.

TYPES OF TRAINING

*T*ype of training needed varies according to employee level.

The needs analysis usually uncovers a variety of training needs. The type of training needed varies according to the level of the employee. For example, new salespeople need an intensive employee orientation course in company policy, procedures, products, and basic salesmanship techniques. This instruction is often followed by several weeks in the field with an experienced sales rep or the sales manager. (See table 18.2.)

❑ **Table 18.2** Sites most frequently used for sales training

Location	PERCENTAGE OF COMPANIES CONDUCTING TRAINING AT THIS LOCATION		
	Industrial Products	Consumer Products	Services*
Home office	75%	60%	67%
Field office	88	80	89
Regional office	13	20	44
Plant locations	22	13	0
Central training facility (away from home office)	38	0	33
Noncompany site (hotel, restaurant, club)	0	0	22

*Includes insurance, financial, utilities, transportation, retail stores, and others.
Note: Length of time should not necessarily be considered cumulative because not all training programs include all locations.
Source: Sales & Marketing Management. Copyright © 1988/"Survey of Selling Costs," Feb. 22, 1988, p. 49. All rights reserved. Reprinted by permission.

Sales training managers must spend considerable time preparing sales education courses on the latest company products and promotions.

Source: Photo courtesy of Univar Corporation.

*R*ole playing is the most popular method of teaching the sales presentation.

An experienced salesperson (usually a minimum of two years' experience) will receive training in advanced selling techniques, new product information, telephone selling, human relations, customer service, effective listening, and other areas. For example, when General Motors salespeople were having difficulty selling small cars, GM conducted training courses to persuade 5,000 salespeople that compact cars were here to stay and that they must know more about the technical details of their cars. The result was a 75 percent sales increase in Chevette sales the following year.[10]

Sales managers must also be trained. Common sales management courses include coaching techniques, training methods, proposal writing, and employee evaluation techniques.

Although many sales managers prefer that the sales training manager conduct training for a company, the sales manager must be taught the importance of follow-up and reinforcement. If skills taught in the classroom are not practiced, the training sessions are wasted. Sales managers are much more likely to support a concept if they are involved in the development stage of the training.

TRAINING TECHNIQUES

Training techniques and methods vary widely. For example, the most popular method for teaching the sales presentation is role playing. Other popular methods include on-the-job training, simulations, case studies, lectures, audiovisuals, demonstrations, sales manuals, and others.

The sophistication of training will depend largely on the size of the company and the size of the training budget. Xerox, for example, has a large training facility in northern Virginia, where up to 900 trainees can be housed. The facility includes conference rooms of all sizes, closed-circuit TV capacity, production studios, a reference library, recreation and food service facilities, and much more. Fourteen companies are now even licensed to grant college degrees.

Motivating the Sales Force

Every sales manager has the task of inspiring salespeople to perform at their highest levels. Many people are self-motivated, but all have periods when they need additional motivational support. The ideal support from sales management comes in the form of promotions, responsibility, recognition, enhancing the enjoyment of work, and other intrinsic motivators. Thus, the sales manager should first establish a positive organizational climate before trying to implement various extrinsic motivational programs such as sales contests, bonuses, and prizes.

COMPENSATING THE SALES FORCE

*C*ompensation plans include: (1) straight salary, (2) straight commission, (3) commission with draw, (4) bonus, (5) combination.

The compensation that a salesperson receives plays a tremendous role in affecting attitudes and behavior, which are the basis for organizational climate. Compensation plans are monetary rewards that must be tailored to the needs of the sales force and those of the company and should meet certain basic criteria. These criteria include providing stable earnings and incentives to increase sales volume and profits and providing management control of the salesperson's activities. Compensation plans should be easy to understand, simple and inexpensive to administer, and fair to all as well as competitive with other plans in the industry and the area.[11]

Figure 18.5 provides the average compensation and travel and entertainment expenses for sales personnel at different levels and in different industries.

Straight Salary. Salespeople on straight salary have the benefit of security and stability. This method of payment provides a regular income but fails to provide

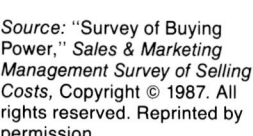

Figure 18.5
Salespeople's average 1987 compensation.

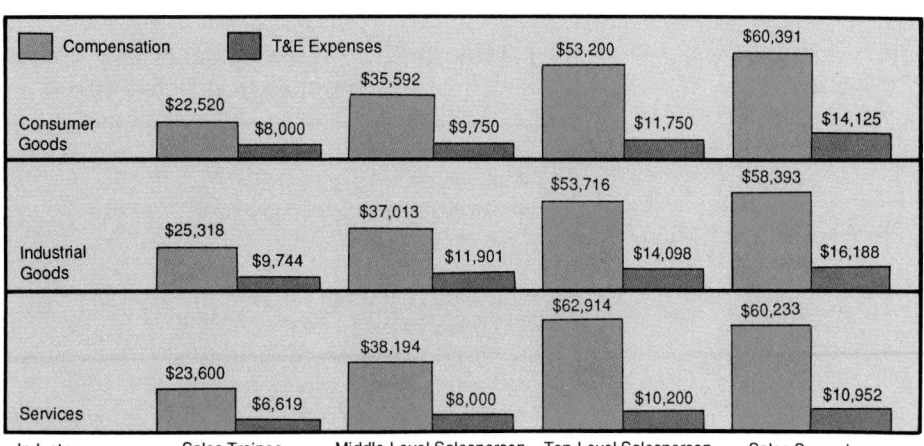

NOTES: Compensation includes base salary, commission, and bonus. **T&E Expenses** include travel, entertainment, food, and lodging.

the extra incentive that is often necessary for success in sales. Straight salary is most appropriate for those salespeople who perform routine selling tasks such as retail salesclerks or those who perform many nonselling duties.

Straight Commission.   Various types of brokers, agents, and manufacturer's representatives are normally paid a straight commission. The purpose of this plan is strictly to reward sales performance. The straight commission provides little security. For example, in 1984, Merrill-Lynch and other brokerage firms began demanding more productivity from their brokers and started terminating the lowest performers, many of whom were earning over $80,000. The standard commission for a broker is 35 percent to 40 percent with no salary.[12]

Commission with Draw.   Many salespeople sell seasonal products and would have little income were it not for the **draw account,** which helps salespeople through tough selling times. Draw accounts enable salespeople to increase their pay by accepting an advance against future commissions. The draw must be paid back when sales return to higher levels.

Bonus.   The bonus plan provides an extra incentive for reaching preestablished quotas. For example, one publisher gave a $250 bonus to any salesperson who could sell an additional 1,000 copies of two texts by a certain date. This type of compensation is often combined with other compensation plans.

Combination.   Although several combinations of the above plans are possible, the most popular is the combination of salary and commission. This method is successful because it capitalizes on the advantages of each while avoiding the weaknesses of both. In addition, it allows for the greatest range of earnings and gives salespeople more security.

PROVIDING INCENTIVES

*M*ost companies offer sales incentive programs.

The use of extrinsic motivators is very popular in the selling field. Studies by *Sales & Marketing Management* magazine indicate a growing number of consumer goods and service companies offer incentive plans. The most commonly used incentives are merchandise, cash, and travel. Although many companies mix different types of incentives, there is a trend towards separating cash incentives and noncash awards. More and more sales managers believe that travel and merchandise are more

□ **Table 18.3** How one company estimates the payoff from incentive travel.

Anticipated sales without program	$114,000,000
Anticipated net profit @ 5%	5,700,000
Actual sales with program (115%)	131,100,000
*Net profit @ 5%	6,555,000
Increased sales	17,100,000
*Increased net profit	855,000
Gross travel incentive costs	429,000
Subtract cost of money (revenue from	
deferral of award costs)	(20,592)
Subtract goodwill value	(1)
Net travel incentive costs	408,407
Incentive costs ÷ sales	.0031
Incentive costs ÷ increased sales	.0238
**Incentive costs ÷ total net profit	.0623
**Incentive costs ÷ net profit increase	.4776

*Due to fixed costs (overhead) being amortized over anticipated projections, actual net profit was $8,088,863, or 6.17%; increased net profit was $2,388,863.
**Corrected for actual net profit, these figures would drop to .0505 and .1710, respectively.
One anonymous (but real) sales manager figures that every 24¢ he spends on his incentive program should give him $1 in added sales.

effective motivators. (See table 18.3.) Furthermore, more sales managers are trying to match programs to specific products or objectives rather than tie incentives to total sales volume. Many incentive programs are also passed on to distributors, reps, and even field sales managers.[13]

Any good incentives program must be simple and well planned. For example, planners should develop contest themes, design and produce motivational mailings, and devise a system for keeping track of points. Most executive sales managers handle all of these duties in-house; however, some seek help from travel agencies, catalog companies, premium and incentive reps, and ad agencies.

Clairol designed a simple and well-planned incentive program. The purpose of the program was to maintain Final Net's number one place in the market. A two-tiered contest involving 400 field salespeople and 100 regional and national account managers was developed. To qualify for prizes, salespeople had to place a certain number of Final Net displays in retail outlets for each month of the ninety-day contest. Sales managers had to meet volume sales quotas to qualify for their monthly prizes as well as grand prizes at the conclusion of the contest. One goal of the program was to insure that everyone had an equal chance of earning an award, thus quotas varied according to the territory. The results were very gratifying to management. More than 90 percent of the sales force qualified, and sales soared above precontest expectations.[14]

Evaluating the Sales Force

Measuring the performance of the sales force is too important to be left to informal methods. Unfortunately, many sales managers rely on subjective techniques. These

Many companies offer an incentive program to motivate their sales force or dealers to sell more products. This ad is an example of an incentive program, as offered by Sony Corporation.

Imagine what they could have done
if they'd had the Sony incentive program.

The Sony incentive program will inspire your employees, dealers and your sales to new heights.
That's because, when given a choice, more people would rather work for a Sony than any other brand of consumer electronics.
So find out what the Sony incentive program can do for you. Contact Murray Singer, National Incentive Sales Manager, 9 West 57th Street, New York, New York 10019. Or call (212) 418-9431.
Because when it comes to building sales and morale, the Sony incentive program just might be the eighth wonder of the world. **SONY**
THE ONE AND ONLY™

© 1985 Sony Corporation of America. Sony is a registered trademark of Sony Corporation. The One and Only is a trademark of Sony Corporation of America

Circle No. 138 on Reader Service Card

Source: Sony Corporation of America.

are inevitable, but they are subject to personal bias and are often incomplete. They can lead to an inaccurate and unbalanced picture of important sales performance activities.

QUANTITATIVE MEASURES

*T*ime and duty analysis are the two most popular quantitative measures for evaluating salespeople.

Quantitative measures rate a salesperson's efforts by frequency calculations that are compared to predetermined standards. The two most popular quantitative measures are time analysis and duty analysis. **Time analysis** provides a detailed account of how much time a salesperson allocates to each job activity. This often explains why sales results are unusually good or bad. **Duty analysis** is often performed in conjunction with time analysis and focuses on the content of the sales call. "This is normally accomplished by comparing the relationship between what the salesperson does when making a sales call and the results reported. Relationships measured include the number of items mentioned and the number sold per call; the number of items mentioned and sold to the number of selling appeals; and the number of selling methods."[15]

QUALITATIVE MEASURES

*Q*ualitative measures of effort rate how well salespeople carry out sales activities.

Qualitative measures of effort rate how well salespeople carry out the sales activities quantitatively. Qualitative measures are important because they influence a salesperson's selling. For example, sales managers must appraise a salesperson's individual characteristics such as temperament, persistence, personal appearance, cooperativeness, resourcefulness, and many others. Of course, these factors must be evaluated on the basis of the sales manager's observations and experience and are subject to personal bias.

*R*ankings and ratings are the two most common forms of qualitative evaluation.

The two most common forms of qualitative evaluation are *rankings* and *ratings*. Rankings measure the salesperson's performance in relationship to other salespeople in the company. Ratings, on the other hand, measure the salesperson's results against standardized levels of performance. Checklists are often used where numerical values are applied. A scale of one to ten is very common.

*S*alespeople should be evaluated on performance factors over which they exercise control.

According to the *Small Business Report,* "Regardless of the type of sales performance measure used, salespeople should be judged on those performance factors over which they exercise control. Sales volume, costs, profit margins, etc., can be affected considerably by outside factors beyond the sales force's control, such as increased competition, high interest rates, or economic downturns.

However, one of the most important sales skills that should be measured is the ability of the salesperson to adjust to these uncontrollable factors while maintaining sales results. While this particular criterion is difficult to measure, a formal approach to measuring efforts will point to whether the responsibility for poor performance lies with the salesperson because efforts are falling short of the reasonably established standards."[16]

SALES PROMOTION

*T*he purpose of sales promotion is to move products through channels of distribution.

Long a stepchild in promotional planning, **sales promotion** has increasingly become a major element. Although sales promotion is a catchall of activities not classified as advertising, personal selling, or publicity, its purpose remains that of moving products through channels of distribution. This is done by providing a variety of promotional tools to stimulate the sales force, the middleman, and the consumer.

*S*ales promotion accounts for 64.4 percent of the average promotional budget.

Expenditures for sales promotion often equal or surpass advertising during a product's maturity stage.[17] Overall expenditures for sales promotion have exceeded those of advertising in recent years and have been growing at a 12 percent annual rate from 1975 to 1985. During 1986 the growth rate slowed to 5 to 10 percent. Sales promotion expenditures exceeded $100 billion in 1987 and account for 64.4 percent of the entire promotional budget, according to Donnelly Marketing.

Objectives of Sales Promotion

*S*ales promotion operates at three levels:
(1) salesforce,
(2) middleman, and
(3) consumers.

Sales promotion has three general goals: (1) supporting the sales force and its merchandising efforts, (2) gaining the acceptance and active support of middlemen in marketing the product, and (3) increasing the sale of the product to the consumer.[18] In order to maintain a good sales promotion program, it is necessary to operate at all three levels. At the trade level, middlemen must be offered merchandise allowances, trade shows, free merchandise, cooperative advertising, dealer sales contests, visual merchandising assistance, and more. Consumers, on the other hand, can be stimulated by the use of coupons, samples, premiums, rebates, trading stamps, contests and sweepstakes, and demonstrations. The sales force is usually motivated by bonuses, sales contests, and even inspirational sales rallies.

In order to accomplish these goals it is often necessary to use several sales promotion activities. Some common objectives of these activities include:

1. encouraging people to try a product,
2. assisting the sales force in gaining more (and better) shelf space and displays,
3. countering the competition's sales promotion,
4. increasing the product's use,
5. increasing the inventories of middlemen,
6. educating the sales force and consumers regarding product features or improvements,
7. smoothing out seasonal sales fluctuations.

Sales Promotion Methods

POINT-OF-PURCHASE DISPLAYS AND DEMONSTRATIONS

80.7 percent of all consumer buying decisions are made at the point of purchase.

Once consumers have entered a store, **point-of-purchase (POP) displays,** demonstrations, and other forms of visual merchandising can be very effective in making them aware of a product or reminding them of its existence. Supermarket studies have revealed that 80.7 percent of all brand purchase decisions are made at the point of purchase.[19] Attractive displays should be located near where the purchase is actually made. Besides displays, POP includes signs, posters, price cards, streamers, racks, and others. Often the manufacturer provides POP displays, such as those for Timex watches, L'eggs, or Esquire shoe polish. Demonstrations often complement displays during holidays and special events. For example, at Christmas it is often common to see demonstrations of small appliances such as microwave ovens and popcorn poppers. In addition, more than 75 grocery stores in 33 states have added computerized information stations that carry co-op advertising from retailers and manufacturers. They also dispense coupons and recipes. In total, $10.8 billion was spent on POP in 1986.

SAMPLING

Samples are the most effective way to introduce new products.

Samples are small, trial-size products distributed to consumers free of charge during a product's introductory stage. Samples of established products are also distributed to dislodge an entrenched market leader. Although samples are the most effective way to introduce new products, the distribution process of mail or in-store handouts is very expensive. For example, S. C. Johnson & Sons spent $12 million for samples of its new Agree shampoo.

A growing number of shoppers appear to be persuaded by samples. According to the Point of Purchase Advertising Institute, only 19 percent have a specific purchase in mind when they walk in a store (down from 35 percent in 1977). For example, Pathmark stores asked consumers to compare their current diaper brand with Pampers. Sales during the promotion increased tenfold and continued running ahead of previous levels. Overall, retailers and manufacturers claim that sales volume increases as much as five to ten times during a product demonstration and 10 to 15 percent thereafter. Point-of-purchase promotions are generally most effective when reinforced on the spot with coupons.

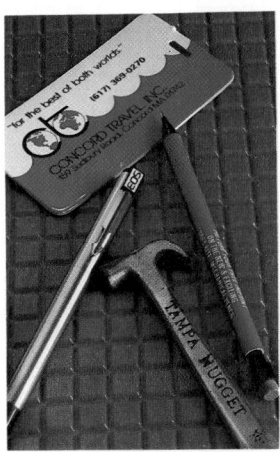

SPECIALTY ADVERTISING

Advertising specialties are available in a wide variety of items to promote a company's image.

According to the Specialty Advertising Association International, **specialty advertising** is imprinting useful articles of merchandise with an advertiser's message and distributing them without obligation to the recipient.[20] First used in 1845 by an insurance agent who distributed calendars to his clientele, specialty advertising has grown to annual billings of over $3 billion and now represents an estimated 15,000 articles of merchandise. These articles are classified as advertising specialties and include baseball hats, glasses, advertising calendars, playing cards carrying the company name, or business gifts such as a set of golf balls bearing the company logo. The repeated exposure of the advertising message without added cost is just one of the major advantages of using specialty advertising. Imprinted calendars, for example, keep the advertiser's name before the client (and perhaps others) throughout the year.

Unlike advertising that uses the mass media, specialty advertising is aimed at smaller target groups in order to solve specific internal or external client problems. Some basic objectives of specialty advertising include: introducing new products and services, opening new accounts, building an image, motivating employees, and promoting new facilities. This merchandise is distributed by a network of 3,300 specialty advertising counselors or distributors (some of whom hold exclusive franchise rights to specialty items).

PREMIUMS AND TRADING STAMPS

*P*remiums are designed to encourage a change in consumers' purchasing behavior.

A **premium** is a piece of merchandise that is either offered as a free gift or sold for a small fee to cover its cost. This type of promotion is designed to encourage a change in consumers' purchasing behavior. Towels in boxes of laundry soap, toys in boxes of cereal, and the exchange of "premium" cigarette box tops for gifts are all examples of premiums. Banks often offer premiums to customers who open new accounts or deposit large sums of money. A California bank once offered free luxury cars to people who deposited one million dollars.

*T*rading stamps are used to build customer loyalty to a retailer.

Trading stamps, such as those offered by S&H Green Stamps and Top Value, are similar to premiums. Consumers collect the stamps from a retailer when they purchase merchandise and can exchange the stamps at a redemption center for additional merchandise. Trading stamps have traditionally been used to build customer loyalty to a retailer; the customer keeps coming back to accumulate more stamps. At the peak of the stamp craze in 1969, nearly three-quarters of Americans found stores handed out stamps from 400 companies. Twenty have survived. However, consumer groups have recently attacked trading stamps because they add to the cost of goods and they are difficult to collect and redeem, so they are no longer as popular as they once were. The newest version of stamp collecting is just making its way into American stores. Sperry & Hutchinson Co., makers of S&H Green stamps, relies on a "Gift Saver Card" and computerized registers. When an order is totaled, the clerk inserts the card into the terminal and the correct number of stamps is added. Customers seem to appreciate not having to paste any more stamps.

COUPONS

Manufacturers offer price breaks through **coupons.** Commonly distributed by newspapers, magazines, and direct mail, coupons offer cents off the retail price and

Polaroid cameras are offered as a free gift to dealers who use Polaroid cameras to display nonrelated product lines. Cameras are also given as gifts to customers who purchase dealer products.

Source: Courtesy of Polaroid Corporation, prepared by Charnas Advertising, Manchester, CT.

CHAPTER 18 PERSONAL SELLING, SALES MANAGEMENT, AND SALES PROMOTION ☐ **517**

are redeemed at the point of purchase. The redemption rate varies from 2 percent to 33 percent, depending on the value of the coupon. In 1985, U.S. consumers redeemed 6.49 billion coupons, saving $2.24 billion.

Like trading stamps, coupons have recently come under attack. Although coupons continue to grow in popularity, some consumer groups claim that they actually cost consumers more money. They argue that if the five-cent retailer handling charge and the coupon promotional costs were eliminated, consumer products would cost much less. Also they argue that consumers often purchase products they do not need because of the coupons. One large supermarket chain apparently agrees. Foodland, a Maryland chain, has decided to quit accepting coupons.

Coupons are coming under attack from consumers.

CONTESTS AND SWEEPSTAKES

Contests and sweepstakes involve the customer in games of chance or skill, and they are popular sales promotion activities. *Reader's Digest* and Publishers Clearing House are famous for their annual sweepstakes. Contests like McDonald's "Monopoly" and Kodak's "Snapshot Game" pay cash to contest winners.

Although contests and sweepstakes attract many new customers (20 percent response rate), they must be open to everyone, meaning that customers do not have to make a purchase to enter. Many professionals enter, and sometimes there are lawsuits over rule interpretations. In Pepsi's 1981 "Spell Pepsi Spirit" contest, for example, people advertised in the paper for key letters needed to win. In some cases Pepsi refused to pay, claiming that some of the key letters were obtained outside the contestant's region, which was against the rules. The "winners" complained bitterly and countered that Pepsi dealers had not displayed contest rules. Needless to say, the lack of contest pretesting can cause many legal and/or marketing problems (illegal in some states).

Contests and sweepstakes must be pretested.

TRADE SHOWS AND EXHIBITS

Trade shows are a relatively low-cost promotional method used as a pushing strategy. A sale (versus a contact) generated by a trade show is much more expensive as compared with a sale by traditional industrial sales calls. Aimed primarily at channel middlemen, such as wholesalers and retailers, trade shows offer manufacturers the opportunity to exhibit and sell their various lines. For some industries such as agriculture, publishing, furniture, fashion, and toys, trade shows are very important.

Trade shows are the fastest growing promotional segment in marketing. Growth is expected at an 8 percent annual rate through 1991. Part of this success is due to the extension of trade shows and exhibits into consumer markets. For example, exhibits such as the Atlanta Home Show, the Detroit Auto Show, and the Indianapolis RV Show offer retailers the chance to combine sales promotion and personal selling as major promotional elements supplemented by advertising and publicity.

Trade shows are the fastest growing promotional segment in marketing.

Evaluating Sales Promotion

Few attempts are made to measure effectiveness of sales promotion.

Like other elements of the promotional mix, sales promotion should be evaluated to measure its effectiveness. Yet studies by Strang and others indicate that sales promotion receives little attention and the few evaluations attempted are usually superficial.[21] There are several explanations for this. The most common is that many sales promotion efforts are so closely tied to personal selling, advertising, and publicity that no measurement of their individual effects is possible.

If specific objectives for sales promotion efforts are established (as discussed earlier), then effective marketing research tests can be used to measure the results.

For example, consumer focus groups can be used to reveal what types of individuals responded to the promotion and whether or not they eventually made a purchase. In addition, it is necessary to pretest promotions such as premiums and contests to determine whether they are appropriate.

THE CASE CONTINUES

*L*ike all large corporations, Winning Ways uses a national sales manager to manage its sales force. Gary Markham, sales manager, has recruited a sales force of independent sales reps and brought them to Hilton Head to provide further training and motivation.

While the trip to Hilton Head is an incentive in itself, Markham used a sales contest to award the top salespeople for the year. The climax of the selling season was the awarding of prizes at a festive banquet and the announcement that the winner of next year's "Frequent Seller" award would win a ten-day Caribbean cruise for two aboard the QE2. To be eligible, the rep must sell the highest percentage of quota, or above, and open 110 new accounts by June 30.

To assist the Winning Ways sales force in securing sales, the company purchases space at various trade shows. Companies, like Winning Ways, annually spend over $25 billion on trade shows (approximately $400 per qualified lead) to improve their image and to develop sales leads for their salespeople, thus lowering the average cost of a sales call. To attract customers to their exhibit booths, a variety of sales promotion techniques are often used. For example, drawings may be held for merchandise or trips, specialty advertising items such as pens, bags, note pads, or even samples of company products may be given away.

GOAL SUMMARY

1. **Identify the primary roles of the salesperson.** The primary roles of the salesperson include gathering marketing information, solving customer problems, locating and maintaining customers, and providing sales support services.
2. **Distinguish between retail and industrial selling.** Retail selling includes approximately 55 percent of the total selling force in the United States. This type of selling is primarily of an order-taking nature. The typical retail clerk answers consumer questions, writes sales invoices, checks credit, handles adjustments and complaints, and does other routine tasks. In contrast, those involved in industrial sales sell to manufacturers, middlemen, and professionals. These individuals are as much consultants as they are salespeople so they are much better paid than retail salespeople.
3. **Explain the steps of the selling process.** The creative selling process has seven steps. Although these steps can vary according to the salesperson and the type of merchandise, they usually occur in the following sequence: (1) prospecting, (2) preapproach, (3) approach, (4) sales presenta-

tion, (5) meeting objections, (6) close, and (7) the follow-up.
4. **Explain the process of sales management and identify the duties of the sales manager.** Sales management is the process of planning, organizing, directing, and controlling the personal selling effort. The sales manager must carefully establish the objectives for the personal selling effort; recruit the sales force; match the sales force to territories; provide the proper and appropriate compensation, motivation and training; and evaluate the sales results and sales force.
5. **Explain the purpose of sales promotion and list major sales promotion tools.** Sales promotion is any activity not classified as advertising, personal selling, or publicity. Its purpose is to move products through the channels of distribution. This is accomplished by providing a variety of promotional tools to stimulate the sales force, the middleman, and the consumer. Sales promotion includes such tools as point-of-purchase displays, sampling, specialty advertising, premiums, trading stamps, coupons, and trade shows and exhibits among others.

KEY TERMS

Personal Selling, **p. 496**
Retail Selling, **p. 496**
Industrial Selling, **p. 497**
Telemarketing, **p. 497**
Creative Selling Process, **p. 499**
Manufacturer's Representative, **p. 500**
Technical Selling, **p. 500**
Missionary Selling, **p. 500**
Prospecting, **p. 501**
Cold Canvass, **p. 501**
Qualifying, **p. 501**
Approach, **p. 502**
Sales Presentation, **p. 503**
Canned Presentation, **p. 503**
Need-Satisfaction Approach, **p. 503**
Trial Close, **p. 504**
Assumptive Close, **p. 504**

Summative Close, **p. 504**
Suggestive Selling, **p. 504**
Sales Management, **p. 505**
Sales Territories, **p. 508**
Training Needs Analysis, **p. 508**
Draw Account, **p. 511**
Time Analysis, **p. 513**
Duty Analysis, **p. 513**
Sales Promotion, **p. 514**
Point-of-Purchase (POP) Displays, **p. 515**
Samples, **p. 515**
Specialty Advertising, **p. 515**
Premiums, **p. 516**
Trading Stamps, **p. 516**
Coupons, **p. 516**
Trade Shows, **p. 517**

CHECK YOUR LEARNING

1. Today's salesperson must sometimes be a consultant to the consumer.   **T/F**
2. All of the following are roles of the salesperson except: (a) fixing products, (b) gathering marketing intelligence, (c) solving customer problems, (d) providing support services.
3. Telemarketing can be used to screen and qualify incoming sales leads.   **T/F**
4. Which of the following types of salespeople are used to supplement the efforts of middlemen? (a) technical salespeople, (b) manufacturer's reps, (c) missionary salespeople, (d) retail salespeople.
5. There are normally seven steps associated with the creative selling process.   **T/F**
6. Studies indicate that salespeople can expect an annual customer attrition rate of: (a) 5–10%, (b) 10–15%, (c) 15–20%, (d) 20–25%.
7. The canned approach is also called the need-satisfaction approach.   **T/F**
8. The key to handling an objection is learning to listen.   **T/F**

9. Which type of close is used to test the readiness of the customer to buy? (a) assumptive close, (b) trial close, (c) summative close, (d) none are correct.
10. Intrinsic motivators include such things as sales contests, bonuses, prizes, and others.   **T/F**
11. Which of the following compensation plans is normally paid to brokers and agents? (a) straight salary, (b) straight commission, (c) bonus, (d) combination.
12. The most commonly used incentives are cash, merchandise, and travel.   **T/F**
13. Which of the following evaluation measures provide a quantitative measure of a salesperson's performance? (a) time analysis, (b) ratings, (c) duty analysis, (d) a and c.
14. All of the following are examples of sales promotion except: (a) displays, (b) hot-air balloons, (c) specialty advertising, (d) trade shows.
15. Samples are most effective when distributed during the product's growth stage.   **T/F**

QUESTIONS FOR REVIEW AND DISCUSSION

1. Define the key terms for this chapter that follow the goal summary.
2. Why do you think so many top corporate executives have sales backgrounds?

3. Explain why the role of the modern salesperson is different from the stereotype of past years.
4. What trends in retail selling have you noticed recently? Be specific and give examples.

QUESTIONS FOR REVIEW AND DISCUSSION *(continued)*

5. Explain why the use of telemarketing is rapidly growing as an integral part of marketing programs.
6. Explain the role of support personnel.
7. Discuss the importance of qualifying a prospect.
8. What is meant by the ferris wheel concept?
9. Distinguish between the canned presentation and the need-satisfaction approach.
10. Explain the various ways a sales manager can establish sales objectives.
11. List the sources from which a sales manager can attempt to recruit a sales force.
12. Discuss the importance of sales training and list some of the types of training most salespeople need.
13. Discuss some techniques a sales manager can use to motivate a sales force.
14. Compare and contrast quantitative and qualitative sales performance evaluation.
15. How would you structure a sales promotion effort for an athletic team at your school? How would you generate publicity for the team?

NOTES

1. Charles A. Kirkpatrick and Frederick H. Russ, *Effective Selling,* 7th ed. (Cincinnati: South-Western, 1981), p. 3.
2. Steve Weinter, "Many Stores Abandon 'Service With a Smile,' Rely on Signs, Displays," *The Wall Street Journal,* March 16, 1981, p. 1.
3. "The Telemarketing Glossary of Terms," *Telemarketing,* December 1983, p. 34.
4. Earl Hitchcock, "Suddenly Marketers Are Calling Up America," *Sales & Marketing Management,* June 4, 1984, pp. 34–36.
5. Gerald L. Manning and Barry L. Reece, *Selling Today* (Dubuque, Iowa: Wm. C. Brown Publishers, 1984), p. 233.
6. "Qualifying Prospects—Where Do You Find Them?" Reprinted by permission from *American Salesman* magazine, November 1975. Copyright © 1975 by the National Research Bureau, Inc., 424 N. Third St., Burlington, Iowa 52601.
7. Manning and Reece, *Selling Today,* p. 279.
8. Richard E. Stanley, *Promotion* (Englewood Cliffs, N.J.: Prentice-Hall, 1977), p. 276.
9. Frederick Russell, Frank H. Beach, and Richard H. Buskirk, *Selling* (New York: McGraw-Hill, 1982), p. 526.
10. "Learning How to Sell Small Cars," *Business Week,* March 27, 1975, pp. 124–126.
11. Stanley, *Promotion,* p. 285.
12. Scott McMurray, "Brokerage Firms Push Salespeople to Produce More or Face Penalties," *The Wall Street Journal,* June 19, 1984, p. 31.
13. "Getting a Kick from Experience," *Sales & Marketing Management,* September 10, 1984, pp. 92–98; and Al Urbanski, "Good Times or Bad, Motivators Rage On," *Sales & Marketing Management,* April 2, 1984, pp. 110–111.
14. "Clairol Bends the Rules and Brings in Sales," *Sales & Marketing Management,* April 2, 1984, pp. 110–111.
15. "Sales Performance Reports," *Small Business Report,* August 1983, pp. 31–34.
16. "Sales Performance Reports," p. 34.
17. Roger A. Strang, "Sales Promotion—Fast Growth, Faulty Management," *Harvard Business Review* (July–August 1976): pp. 115–124.
18. Stanley, *Promotion,* p. 310.
19. Russ Bowman, "Sales Promotion," *Marketing and Media Decisions* (January 1987): p. 78.
20. "The Case For Specialty Advertising," Specialty Advertising Association International, 1980.
21. Strang, "Sales Promotion," p. 120.

*M*iles Laboratories, manufacturer of the well-known Alka-Seltzer, wanted to stimulate consumer interest in their analgesic/gastrointestinal remedy. The solution to their problem was an eventual award-winning sales promotion (winner of the 1986 Reggie Award) tied into another company's product, the *Better Homes and Gardens'* "Hot and Spicy Cookbook." By purchasing Alka-Seltzer, the consumer received a free recipe booklet. The objective of the promotion was to increase factory shipments of displays of Alka-Seltzer by 15 percent and to increase the number of displays installed by 5 percent.

To generate interest within the grocery trade, Miles offered the stores end-aisle displays, designed in the form of kitchen ranges to tie in with the kitchen/cooking theme. Tear-off pads were used to publicize the offer and promote mail-in orders. The Miles sales force gave store managers and buyers a promotional tube resembling the Alka-Seltzer bottle, which included a copy of the recipe booklet, bibs printed with the "Alka-Seltzer to the Rescue" slogan, and a chili spoon with a burned-out hole in the middle.

To support the sales promotion campaign, Alka-Seltzer dropped a freestanding insert in the Sunday and food day editions of newspapers, alerting the public to the in-store displays. In addition, a television campaign was launched to further encourage retailer support. While the total cost of this promotion has not been made public, according to Leading National Advertisers, Miles spends about $20 million annually in media support.

The success of the promotion was easy to measure. Display shipments were requested at a rate 20 percent higher than seasonal norms, and a total of 10,000 displays were actually placed in supermarkets nationwide. For *Better Homes and Gardens,* the payoff was similar. Not only were the 775,000 familiar red plaid recipe booklets scooped up quickly, but mail orders for two additional cookbooks were also strong.

Miles has had success with several joint promotions. In 1987, they again teamed up with H & R Block for a tax time sweepstakes. Like the first sweepstakes, the winner received $5,000, a trip for two to the Bahamas, and free tax-return preparation for life. Along with the sweepstakes, the promotion included tax-tip brochures, point-of-purchase displays, 25-cent coupons for Alka-Seltzer (distributed to 34 million households). Alka-Seltzer samples were placed in the 7,500 H & R Block offices. The sales promotion effort was supported with a 30-second TV spot that aired through April 15—the tax deadline.

Issues for Discussion

1. Discuss the role of the Miles Laboratories sales force in obtaining the maximum value from Alka-Selzer sales promotions.

2. Explain why it is important that sales promotions be supported with advertising campaigns.

3. What are the hazards or unique problems that can result from joint promotionals?

Source: Adapted from Laurie Freeman, *"Better Homes and Gardens'* Recipes Spice up Alka-Seltzer's Interest," *Advertising Age,* April 27, 1987, pp. 3–4, 6. Copyright © 1987 by Crain Communications, Inc. Reprinted with permission.

MARKETING PLAN

PART 6D / ACTION PROGRAM:
PROMOTION (CHAPTERS 16, 17, AND 18)

A. What are the promotional objectives for the organization's product or service?

B. What is the overall promotional strategy (push or pull) for the organization? Describe.

C. How much money is allocated for the promotional budget? How will it be divided?

Advertising	$ _____
Personal Selling	$ _____
Sales Promotion	$ _____
Publicity	$ _____

D. Will an advertising agency be responsible for developing the advertising plan? If so, what is their role in determining overall copy and media strategy?

E. What are the advertising objectives for the product or service?

F. What are the copy and media strategies for this product or service? How does the advertising differ from any competitors?

G. How will the effectiveness of advertising be evaluated?

H. What is the role of personal selling in the promotional mix? What is the ratio of advertising spending to personal selling spending? Does this ratio reflect the importance given to personal selling in the overall promotional strategy? Explain.

I. What is the role of sales promotion? What is the ratio of advertising expenditures to sales promotion expenditures? Does this ratio reflect the importance given to sales promotion in the overall promotional strategy? Explain.

J. What types of sales promotion will be used? How will each be used? Analyze the competition's reaction and how, if at all, you will respond.

K. What are the objectives of the public relations program? Who will handle the PR function?

Section Eight

Strategic Planning and Control

OUTLINE

CHAPTER

19

Strategic Marketing

LEARNING GOALS_____

After reading this chapter, you should be able to:

1. Describe a mission statement for an organization.
2. Evaluate opportunities.
3. Contrast organization strategy, marketing strategy, and annual marketing plans.
4. Discuss the fundamental concepts and purpose of portfolio analysis.
5. Explain the PIMS Model.

*T*he Kroger Company, a Cincinnati-based retail food chain, has been in business for over a hundred years. Based on revenues, Kroger is the second-largest food retailer in the United States, just behind Safeway. Kroger has 1,300 supermarkets, 735 convenience stores, and 40 food plants. For many years Kroger concentrated its efforts in the Midwest. Later it expanded to the East, and more recently the company has expanded into other geographic areas. But Kroger does not always expand—sometimes it withdraws from markets.

Kroger claims to provide convenient, competitively priced, quality food for consumers. It has prided itself on being the nation's most innovative grocer. In keeping with its purpose, Kroger has instituted in some markets one-stop shopping, 24-hours-a-day store hours, and additional services and products. Its in-store floral shops make it the nation's biggest florist.

Kroger's activities during the mid-1980s have been criticized because they seemed to show a lack of strategic planning. During this period, the company's decisions were not always easy to explain. First, Kroger aggressively expanded by acquisition into the sunbelt. The Dillon Company's food-related stores were acquired in the southwestern United States for $607 million. At the same time, Kroger decided to withdraw from the Pittsburgh, Washington, Kansas City, and Minneapolis markets. Supposedly the decision to withdraw was based on slow market growth, rising employee wages, and strong competition for market share.

Market trends made success difficult for Kroger. Population growth had slowed in some markets and stopped entirely in others. Food price inflation, which was rampant in the 1970s, was only 2 or 3 percent a year in the mid-1980s. Passing higher costs on to consumers by price increases was always tough, but it has become nearly impossible

for any grocer. The market trends have led grocers to lower prices in order to raise sales. Kroger competed aggressively on the price front. Its profit margin and those of other grocers dropped.

Kroger also battled another trend. With inflation, consumers turned to generic and low-priced private brands. The company was already positioned to benefit from the increase in private brand sales. Kroger had more manufacturing facilities than any other grocer and greatly expanded production to include plants for peanut butter, crackers, candy, coffee, and many other dry goods. Price stability, however, changed consumers' purchases away from the private brands to national brands; away from Kroger corn flakes to Kellogg's corn flakes, for example. Kroger executives have been forced to seek other, new ways to use the production facilities. The company, for example, makes the bread for Stouffer's French Bread Frozen Pizza.

What happened in Pittsburgh illustrates Kroger's challenge in some markets. The company had lagged at third or fourth place in the market for years, with little hope of improvement. In fact, it was at a competitive disadvantage against nonunion independents and superwarehouse

stores. Seventy-five percent of its employees were unionized, and most were at the senior level. With Kroger's emphasis on customer service, the situation became impossible for the company when the clerks' and meatcutters' union refused to grant Kroger concessions it had given a competitor. The result: forty-five stores were closed in Pittsburgh. In markets where Kroger has closed its retail stores, it sometimes supplies the independents that replace its stores from its distribution and manufacturing facilities. Kroger has obtained concessions in its labor contracts with unions in Denver, Nashville, and Michigan.

In markets like West Virginia, Kroger granted wage increases even though a wage freeze was more in line with some executives' thinking. The West Virginia market is one of Kroger's best markets, however, and the company wished to consolidate its position there.

Kroger has sought a greater share of new and old markets, basing many of its decisions on market research. New and remodeled stores may contain new departments such as seafood, deli, gourmet foods, baked goods, drugs, health foods, and even insurance and banking services. Approximate annual advertising is $175 million. Still, when competitors moved into the Indianapolis and Memphis markets, Kroger managed to retain market share only by launching price wars. It sold bread,

■ Kroger executives changed the company structure to benefit from market changes.
Source: Photo courtesy of Kroger

for example, in Indianapolis at five loaves for $1 and a gallon of milk for $.99.

Because of Kroger's competitive stance in Indianapolis, the Minneapolis-based SuperValu Stores, Inc., the nation's largest food wholesaler, decided to eliminate one of the four big warehouse-type Cub chain stores it had planned to build in Indianapolis. SuperValu executives think Kroger overreacted and reduced prices far more than necessary to remain the price leader in the Indianapolis market.

Issues for Discussion
1. Does Kroger seem to lack a strategic plan? Explain your answer.
2. Describe some of the market trends that have effected Kroger.
3. What do you think determines Kroger's management decisions to continue allocating resources in some markets while dropping out of others?

Sources: Based on *The Value Line Investment Survey* (New York: Value Line, Inc.), Feb. 26, 1988, p. 1511; *Standard Corporation Description* (New York: Standard and Poor's Corporation), Nov. 5, 1987, p. 5207; Rikki Danielson, "Kroger Dodging Volleys from All Sides," *Advertising Age,* April 18, 1985, pp. 20 and 22; and Julie B. Solomon, "Aggressive a Century, Kroger Is Retrenching to Stem Fall in Profits," *The Wall Street Journal,* May 31, 1984, pp. 1 and 18.

*K*roger has been criticized for lacking a strategic marketing plan. If the company lacks direction because there is either no plan or a poorly designed one, the fault lies with the company's management. In the chapter ahead, we define corporate strategic plans—the company's overall strategic plans—and strategic marketing plans—the objectives and plans for implementation for a defined business within a company. We chart how top officers and unit managers form their strategies. You'll learn what a strategic business unit is, and understand the nature of organizational objectives. Several models for strategic market plans are presented. ■

MARKETING AND ORGANIZATIONAL PLANS

*M*arketing plans are part of a bigger picture.

As we discussed in Chapter 2, plans within organizations exist at several levels. The marketing plan is always part of a bigger picture. **Corporate strategic plans** involve broad strategies at the highest level for the entire corporate organization. Such plans have an external orientation and a commitment to specific actions, with an evaluation of the probable consequences to the whole organization. At a more concrete level, **strategic marketing plans** encompass the marketing aims for a defined business within the corporation (a corporation may contain several businesses). Formulated with a long-range perspective, plans at this level require assessment of current trends that will affect the business. At the most concrete level, **marketing plans** are the tactical action plans that were presented in Chapter 2; they show how all the elements of the marketing mix will interact and be managed for a specific time period. Their emphasis is on forecasts of revenues, costs, and capital needs for the coming period, usually a year.

*M*arketing plans must be compatible with strategic plans.

Recall from Chapter 2 that a marketing plan focuses primarily on implementing a strategy as it relates to the selected market. Most of this text has focused on what goes into developing the components of an annual marketing plan. But such a plan will not be realistic unless the planner has developed it to show how it will achieve the objectives of the strategic marketing plan for that business. The strategic marketing plan in turn must show how its strategies will fulfill the organization's overall

❑ **Figure 19.1**
Differences among
levels of planning.

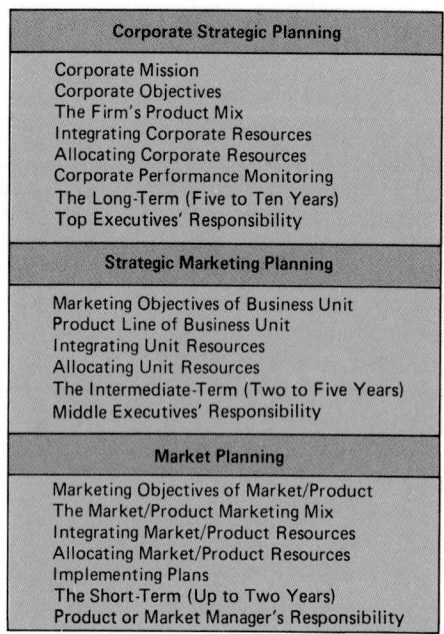

strategic plans. Each plan must be compatible with the broader plan at the next higher level. The most common levels of planning are shown in figure 19.1. This chapter is devoted primarily to strategic marketing planning and corporate strategic planning.

DEVELOPING THE CORPORATE STRATEGIC PLAN

A corporate strategic plan focuses on the organization's mission statement, including its principal objectives. The plan then goes on to specify how the company's resources will be distributed and how its performance will be monitored. The elements that combine to form a corporate strategy are discussed below.

Organization Mission

The mission statement provides a unifying, common thread.

As discussed in Chapter 2, the organization's **mission statement** defines the enduring purpose, vision, or aim of the whole organization in a way that will distinguish it from all other organizations.[1] The mission statement answers the question "Who are we and what do we do?" For example, a mission statement for the University of Akron, in figure 19.2, answers the question "Who are we?" with "We are a provider of distinctive educational opportunities." It then goes on to specify "What do we do?" with "We create a learning environment; we create and discover knowledge . . . " and so on.

The mission statement serves to tie together the organization's people, strategies, and programs. From an understanding of the mission statement, each member of the organization should have a good idea of the role that organization seeks to play in society, and also a clear sense of his or her own contribution. The organization's image is likely to become identified with the mission statement. In turn, the organization's ability to communicate "what we're known for" (its image) may depend on its ability to publicize its mission statement. The University of Akron at

❏ **Figure 19.2**
Mission: The University
of Akron.

Mission
The University of Akron maintains a commitment to: ● Provide learning opportunities to the full spectrum of students. ● Create and discover knowledge through basic and applied research. ● Create a learning environment that emphasizes a full collegiate experience for each student, leading to opportunities for cognitive, social and personal development. ● Provide a forum for the examination of ideas and concepts and the generation of scholarly dialogue within the established principles of academic freedom. ● Encourage opportunities for interdisciplinary study and research. ● Prepare career-oriented persons for professional leadership roles in regional, national and international organizations and institutions. ● Offer appropriate educational and professional services to its various publics within available resources and established continuing education and outreach philosophies. ● Maintain its firmly established tradition of concern for the higher educational and cultural needs of our area.

Source: General Bulletin, The
University of Akron.

one point turned to large-scale athletics in order to publicize its larger educational mission and overcome an image that its president once characterized as "the largest unknown university in the country." Even a well-known company like General Electric must clearly emphasize its mission statement. GE does this by using the slogan, "We bring good things to life," in its advertising. A slogan like this calls everyone's attention to the GE mission of helping people in society.

*T*he mission statement reflects an organization's values.

The mission statement reflects the values of the organization. In recently established organizations, the values reflected are usually those of an entrepreneurial nature. F. Kenneth Iverson, pioneer of minimill steel making in the United States, has always cherished self-reliance. Self-reliance as a value shows up not only in the mission statement of Iverson's firm, the Nucor Company, but also in the arrangement of the corporation as well, which is primarily decentralized. Individuals or activities at odds with the company's values usually have to be reevaluated. For example, there is concern at the University of Akron that big-time athletics—instituted to bring attention to the school—will result in undesired changes in the university's values— away from academics to sports.

In developing a mission statement, a company considers its history, distinctive competencies—what it does best—and its environment.[2] An organization seldom

The NCR Corporation advertises its mission statement in leading business publications.

STAKEHOLDERS

NCR

We believe in building mutually beneficial and enduring relationships with all of our stakeholders, based on conducting business activities with integrity and respect.

NCR's Mission: Create Value for Our Stakeholders

EMPLOYEES

NCR

We respect the individuality of each employee and foster an environment in which employees' creativity and productivity are encouraged, recognized, valued and rewarded.

NCR's Mission: Create Value for Our Stakeholders

Source: Courtesy of NCR
Corporation

can divorce itself completely from its past image, its accomplishments, and its mistakes. It can only attempt to conceive of and act upon its best image of itself. An organization's statement is also designed to focus on what it does best—its competitive advantage—and not simply on its basic competency. While AT&T might have the competency to produce and market TV sets, it has no distinct advantage over other firms here; for this reason AT&T's mission statement and corporate image emphasize a broader communicative role for the company.

Environmental threats and opportunities are also a major consideration in deciding how broad or how specialized the company's mission should be. The Ball Corporation would have a very restrictive mission in today's environment if it focused too narrowly on supplying the nation's home canning needs, since so few households now can their own food.

A very broad statement of purpose, on the other hand, can take away from the unifying effect that can come from a good mission statement. An organization that tries to be all things to all people might have products, programs, and strategies that go off in opposing directions in pursuit of every possible customer need. If so, its company resources and management skills might become stretched too thin. Thus Levi Strauss executives broadened the mission statement too far when they defined the firm very generally as a consumer products company. When Levi Strauss tried to manufacture and sell a diverse line of products outside the firm's garment business, their resources were stretched too thin and they suffered financial losses. Redefining the company as a *garment business* helped focus efforts on the organization's strengths, leading eventually to a recovery.

*M*ission statements connect the organization to society.

Thus the actual mission statement should neither be too broad or too narrow in stating the organization's purpose. Figure 19.3 illustrates the range from narrow to broad purposes. Narrowly stated mission statements do focus attention, and thus improve the manageability of an organization's activities. Yet they may make executives blind to the significance of environmental changes. Many bank executives, for example, thought of their institutions as protectors of customers' money instead of financial service firms. They therefore restricted their business hours and services to customers. When alternative financial institutions became available, banks lost customers. What has happened in the U.S. banking system is but one example of how technology and customer needs can severely sap an organization's vitality.

An organization's mission must be reviewed and updated periodically since the ever-changing environment soon dates most mission statements. The March of Dimes, for instance, with its mission to aid polio victims and encourage polio research, was a thriving organization, but with the discovery of a vaccine a decision had to be made. The vaccine meant that aid to polio victims and the need for polio research would both diminish considerably. If the March of Dimes executives had failed to change the mission, the organization would have been forced to follow a reduction plan. Instead, the organization changed its mission to that of reducing

❏ **Figure 19.3**
Broad and narrow
purposes.

Source: From *Marketing,* by
Patrick E. Murphy and Ben M.
Enis. Copyright © 1985 by Scott,
Foresman and Company.
Reprinted by permission.

Mission Statements

Organization	Short Term/Narrow	Long Term/Broad
Penn Central	Railroad	Transportation
General Electric	Electrical equipment	"Creating business"
Xerox	Copying	Automated office
Singer	Sewing	Aerospace
Schlumberger	Oil-well drilling	Data collection and processing
Sears	Retailing	Consumer services
Libbey-Owens-Ford	GM supplier	Export, aerospace, and architectural glass
Utilities	Power generation	Real estate, fish hatcheries
Banks	Lending money	"Information in motion"

❑ **Figure 19.4**
Common topics for
organization
objectives.

Topic	Example
Profit	At least 10 percent profit should be obtained on annual sales.
Volume	The church will have 350 members by the end of the calendar year.
Growth	The hospital will increase patient admittance by 10 percent in each of the next five years.
Employees	Employee turnover will be less than the industry average.
Creditors	The credit rating will be maintained at the highest level.
Customer Satisfaction	Customer complaints will be less than one per $100,000 in sales.

birth defects and aiding birth defect victims. Philip Morris changed its mission when federal legislation restricted cigarette advertising. Executives of the company decided that the firm should diversify into nontobacco products, notably Miller beer. The Singer Company faced stagnation as the sewing machine market matured and Japanese companies entered the low-price end of the market. Singer no longer produces or markets sewing machines. Its mission has changed.

In summary, mission statements express an organization's relationship to society. They are long term; they unify; they identify products and services; they identify the needs the organization must satisfy; and they give direction to organizational activities.

Organization Objectives

Objectives develop from the benefits that a company hopes to obtain.

Organization objectives stress benefits the organization wants to obtain as a result of actions taken. Objectives statements should stimulate action. Organization objectives focus on numerous topics. (See figure 19.4.)

Objectives come from the concerns of those who benefit from the organization's operation—the stakeholders. Stakeholders include investors, creditors, employees, suppliers, customers, and others. Investors' concern for return on their investment leads to organization objectives such as, "ROI of 20 percent annually." Consumers' concerns for value and quality lead to organizational objectives such as, "The best value and quality product available." The objectives selected are at least partially determined by the magnitude and durability of the concerns of the various stakeholders.

The fact that an organization can have many different objectives means that conflicts are likely because reaching one objective may jeopardize the achievement of another. For instance, attaining the objective of increasing employee benefits may simultaneously reduce profits. Organization objectives serve as guides for the marketer in developing marketing objectives, programs, and strategies. Objectives may be stated in quantitative or qualitative terms, but they will be more acceptable if they are realistic, consistent, specific, and measurable. Figure 19.5 highlights features to include in stating objectives.

Resource Allocation

Resource allocation is a necessary part of strategy.

All organizations have limited resources. The strategy at the organization level must therefore include guidelines on resources allocation. Resources are allocated in three general areas: corporate development, shared resource programs, and marketing units. Corporate development includes major capital expenditures such as General

❑ **Figure 19.5**
How to tell a good objective.

In order for the managerial purposes of objectives to fulfill their purpose, they should meet five specifications.

1. An objective should relate to a single, specific topic. (It should not be stated in the form of a vague abstraction or a pious platitude—"we want to be a leader in our industry" or "our objective is to be more aggressive marketers.")
2. An objective should relate to a result, not to an activity to be performed. (The objective is the result of the activity, not the performance of the activity.)
3. An objective should be measurable (stated in quantitative terms whenever feasible).
4. An objective should contain a time deadline for its achievement.
5. An objective should be challenging but achievable.

Consider the following examples:

*   Poor: Our objective is to maximize profits.
    Remarks: How much is "maximum"? The statement is not subject to measurement. What criterion or yardstick will management use to determine if and when actual profits are equal to maximum profits? No deadline is specified.
    Better: Our total profit target in 1985 is $1 million.

*   Poor: Our objective is to increase sales revenue and unit volume.
    Remarks: How much? Also, because the statement relates to two topics, it may be inconsistent. Increasing unit volume may require a price cut, and if demand is price inelastic, sales revenue would fall as unit volume rises. No time frame for achievement is indicated.
    Better: Our objective this calendar year is to increase sales revenues from $30 million to $35 million; we expect this to be accomplished by selling 1 million units at an average price of $35.

*   Poor: Our objective in 1984 is to boost advertising expenditures by 15 percent.
    Remarks: Advertising is an activity not a result. The advertising objective should be stated in terms of what result the extra advertising is intended to produce.
    Better: Our objective is to boost our market share from 8 percent to 10 percent in 1984 with the help of a 15 percent increase in advertising expenditures.

*   Poor: Our objective is to be a pioneer in research and development and to be the technological leader in the industry.
    Remarks: Very sweeping and perhaps overly ambitious; implies trying to march in too many directions at once if the industry is one with a wide range of technological frontiers. More a platitude than an action commitment to a specific result.
    Better: During the 1980s our objective is to continue as a leader in introducing new technologies and new devices that will allow buyers of electrically powered equipment to conserve on electric energy usage.

*   Poor: Our objective is to be the most profitable company in our industry.
    Remarks: Not specific enough. By what measures of profit—total dollars, or earnings per share, or unit profit margin, or return on equity investment, or all of these? Also, because it concerns how well other companies will perform, the objective, though challenging may not be achievable.
    Beter: We will strive to remain atop the industry in terms of rate of return on equity investment by earnings a 25 percent after-tax return on equity investment in 1985.

Source: Arthur A. Thompson, Jr. and A. J. Strickland, *Strategic Management: Concepts and Cases* (Homewood, Ill.: Business Publications, Inc.), pp. 24–25. Copyright © 1984.

Motor's Saturn plant. Such expenditures tend to improve or expand the organization. Shared resource programs are those that all divisions use jointly, such as R&D facilities. The departments responsible for implementing marketing also need resources. The guidelines for resource allocation in marketing usually depend on how closely sales respond to increased expenditures—the sales responsiveness curve—and on how well each profit center of the business is doing.

SALES RESPONSIVENESS CURVE

Corporations use the **sales responsiveness curve** in order to observe the relationship between marketing expenditures and sales. It is most often shown as an S-shaped curve and labeled "sales curve." As seen in figure 19.6, a small allocation of resources to marketing has a negligible influence on sales (point x), but a very large allocation of resources is also wasteful (point y). Sales do not increase appreciably after a certain level of allocation is reached. Thus, too small or too large an allocation should generally be avoided. An optimum expenditure (point z) will do the most for sales and profits.

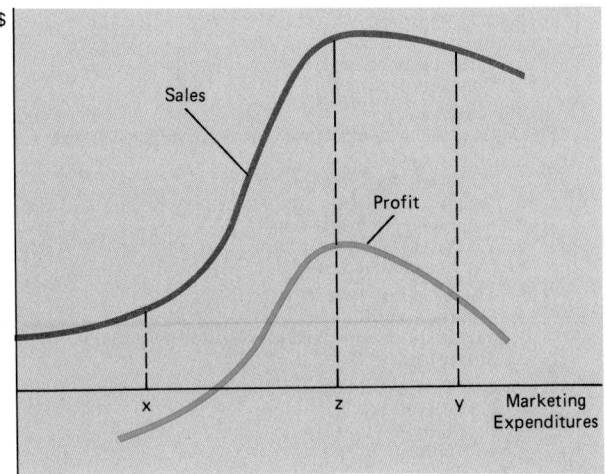

STRATEGIC BUSINESS UNIT

*A*n SBU is an operating entity within an organization.

The large size of some organizations often requires that a smaller unit, the strategic business unit (SBU), be used to narrow the scope of a marketing manager's perspective. A **strategic business unit (SBU)** is an identifiable part of an organization large enough and homogeneous enough to exercise control over most strategic factors affecting performance.[3] It may be viewed as a separate business and is often a designated profit center. An SBU includes such functions as production, distribution, management, and sales.

Small businesses may have only one SBU, but larger organizations usually have several. Firms organize SBUs on any one of a number of bases—product, product line, customer type, or distribution. Marathon Petroleum, for instance, separates distribution from other functions and views it as a separate business.

The next sections discuss evaluation techniques, strategy development, and resource allocation for SBUs.

STRATEGIC MARKETING PLANS

Strategic marketing plans match the resources and abilities of the organization at the SBU level with the opportunities available to achieve objectives and fulfill the mission as well as the risks involved in doing so. Strategic marketing plans have a two- to five-year orientation. An organization depends on its strategic plans to survive in a competitive environment.

Figure 19.7 presents a format that strategic marketing planning can take. The strategic marketing plan maps out the path for the SBU. The plan will include all important assumptions and judgments made during the planning process as well as any anticipated contingencies. The work to develop a strategic plan centers on six focal areas: the *planning situation, situation assessment, situation summary, strategic decisions, financial summary,* and *contingencies.* Several of the areas have already been discussed in chapters on environmental monitoring (Chapter 3), on analyzing opportunities (Chapter 5), and on market segmentation (Chapter 7). Here we discuss how these issues come together in strategic planning.

❏ **Figure 19.7**
Strategic marketing
plan.

A. Planning Situation
  1. Business definition
  2. Performance assessment in terms of prior objective
  3. Corporate guidelines
B. Plan Overview
  One-page summary of situation, strategy, and forecast results
C. Situation Assessment
  1. Market analysis and segmentation
  2. Competitor analysis
  3. Major trends in environment
  4. Internal capabilities and current position in served markets
  5. Cost and profit analysis
D. Situation Summary
  1. Planning assumptions
  2. Market attractiveness and business strength analysis
  3. Strategic issues
E. Strategic Decisions and Action Programs
  1. Business strategy
    ● Objectives
    ● Thrust
    ● Supporting functional strategies
  2. Key programs
    ● Strategy elements
    ● Resource requirements
    ● Timing and responsibilities
  3. Discarded options
F. Financial Summary
  1. Performance
  2. Risks
  3. Validity test
G. Contingencies

The Planning Situation—Defining the Business

The purpose of a business definition is to specify the present or prospective scope of an SBU's activities.[4] Just as mission statements define the organization's purpose and direction, a well-thought-out business defines the purpose and scope of the business. SerVend International, Inc., for instance, defines its business as manufacturing and marketing high-quality, self-service ice and beverage dispensers.[5] The image that develops around the business definition should instill a sense of direction in individuals within the SBU. The business definition establishes the boundaries of business activities and provides the basis for a detailed analysis of strategy.

Marketers become involved in developing the business definition because the market that the business intends to serve is part of the definition. SerVend, for example, has identified its market as consisting of convenience stores, miniature delis, bakeries, and other outlets with a self-service approach to soft drink sales. The business definition also identifies the types of product or service to be offered and customer needs most likely to be satisfied. SerVend designed a small ice dispenser requiring limited space on the cluttered counters of convenience stores. Because a primary function of a business definition is to establish direction, consensus on the business definition is essential.

*M*ethods of defining a business: customer function, customer segment, and technology.

Business definitions usually develop in three dimensions: customer function, technology, or customer segment.[6] Figure 19.8 illustrates all three dimensions of a business as applied to Federal Express, showing that they operate simultaneously.

*A*ffordable and available legal service—Hyatt's business definition.

A good example of a business definition oriented toward customer segment is seen in the statement by Joel Hyatt, founder of Kansas City-based Hyatt Legal Services, a chain of no-frills, low-cost legal clinics: "I was challenged to make legal services available and affordable to people who did not have access to legal counsel."[7] Hyatt Legal Services has been so successful that it has grown to over 175 offices and

□ **Figure 19.8**
Three-dimensional
business definition—
Federal Express.

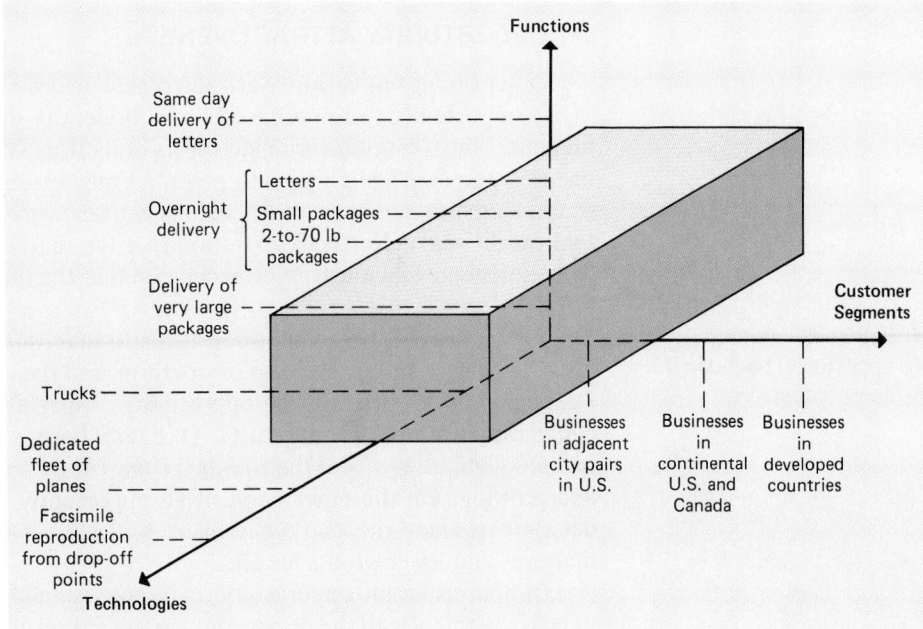

handles 20,000 new cases a month. Hyatt Legal Services, the largest U.S. law firm
based on number of cases, has made Joel Hyatt, still in his thirties, millions of
dollars.

The Situation Assessment—Monitoring the Environment

*E*nvironmental awareness
is important to all planners.

Throughout this book, and specifically in Chapters 2 and 3, we have emphasized the
importance of keeping abreast of changes in the environment. Larger organizations
usually have a formal procedure for monitoring the environment. Either they assign
the function to a department or to a particular position, which may be filled by the
organization's economist, librarian, or strategic planner. Smaller organizations, and
even some larger ones, depend on top executives to read the environment and alert
the rest of the firm to environmental change. For instance, James F. Beré, chairman
and CEO of Borg-Warner, diversified his smokestack company into communication
and other services long before the trend to services became generally apparent.
Regardless of the arrangement made for monitoring the ever-changing environment,
the task is always challenging. The process, which has been compared to reading a
crystal ball, might seem frustrating, but the marketer should remember that it is the
environment from which all threats and opportunities arise.

*"M*ake hay while the sun
shines"—an old adage
recognizing a strategic
window.

Which of the hundreds of changes occurring in the environment will serve the
organization? Opportunities encompass a number of environmental conditions that
have the potential for providing benefits to the organization. As the combination of
environmental factors changes, opportunities appear and disappear. Strategists refer
to the time element associated with an opportunity, the point when the right combination of factors exists, as the **strategic window.**[8]

To evaluate the strategic window, the marketer should answer three questions.
First, how attractive is the opportunity given the prevailing environmental conditions? Second, what will be required of the organization to take advantage of the
opportunity? Third, does the organization have the ability to capitalize on the
opportunity?

OPPORTUNITY ATTRACTIVENESS

Determining **opportunity attractiveness** involves assessing the benefits and costs of the opportunity to the organization. To identify the potential of an opportunity, marketers must estimate critical aspects of its size. What is client, patient, member, or sales potential? High growth potential may offset limited present benefits. For example, marketing consultants and executives from other organizations repeatedly told executives of Xerox Corporation that the market for copying was either small or nonexistent. Obviously, Xerox decided that the market existed and that it would grow.

*N*utraSweet—an attractive opportunity because it had few competitors.

The nature of the competition helps to determine an opportunity's attractiveness. The fewer and weaker the competitors and the longer the competition remains weak, the more attractive the opportunity. Aspartame (NutraSweet) was an especially attractive opportunity for G. D. Searle because it was protected by patent, it had few competitors, and the size of the market for low-calorie sweeteners was large and growing. On the other hand, if an opportunity faces intense competition, the decision to enter the market is likely to result in reduced prices, smaller profit margins, and lower profits for all.

In appraising an opportunity, marketers should examine the structure of the industry within which the opportunity exists. As an example of opportunity analysis, Porter identifies four sources of pressure on an opportunity related to industry structure—*suppliers, new entrants, substitutes,* and *buyers*—any one or all of which could draw away profit. (See figure 19.9.) If, for example, the sources of the supplies needed to produce a product viewed as an opportunity are concentrated enough to

❏ **Figure 19.9** A scheme for analyzing opportunity through industry structure.

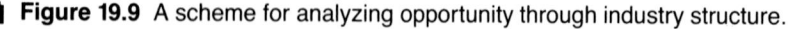

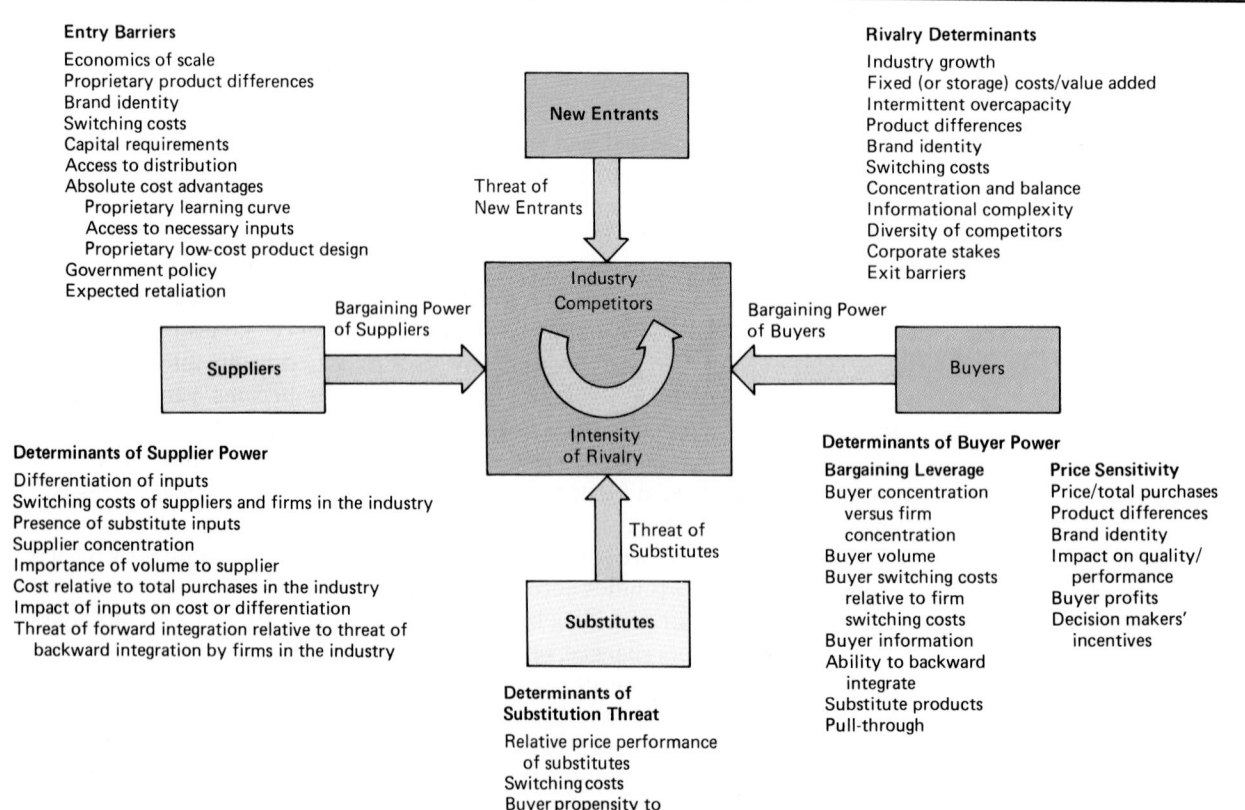

Source: Reprinted with permission of The Free Press, a division of Macmillan, Inc., from *Competitive Advantage: Creating and Sustaining Superior Performance,* by Michael E. Porter. Copyright © 1985 by Michael E. Porter.

drive up the costs of raw materials, an opportunity should be considered less attractive. On the other hand, if other supplies can be substituted, concentration is less of a problem, and an opportunity becomes more attractive. Similarly, if buyers can readily find substitutes for the product, its attractiveness as an opportunity is less. On the other hand, barriers to the entry of competing products in the market increase the attractiveness of an opportunity. The marketer should weigh the elements of industry structure singly and in combination to arrive at a comprehensive evaluation of opportunity attractiveness.

OPPORTUNITY REQUIREMENTS

Opportunities are available to everyone, but only some are prepared.

Seldom can an organization exploit opportunities without effort. What investment will the organization have to make? Nestlé's freeze-dried decaffeinated coffee, Taster's Choice, did not require a large investment. Nestlé's already had the production, distribution, and sales resources and marketing know-how to produce and market the coffee.

High cost can often lessen an opportunity's attractiveness. From another viewpoint, however, high initial cost can limit the number of competitors and thus make the opportunity more attractive. Searle invested several years and thousands of dollars in the new pharmaceutical, aspartame, in order to obtain approval from the U.S. government to sell the product. This involved years of testing to receive government approval. Such testing is desirable from the consumers' point of view, but it discourages competition by raising an entry barrier—an increase in the investment of time and money needed to enter the market.

The primary question concerning **opportunity requirements** comes down to "What is needed to competitively take advantage of the opportunity?" Some organizations find it's a full line of products, or government approval, or other requirements. The chairman and CEO of General Electric believes it is necessary for General Electric to perceive competition in global, not domestic, terms in order to compete. Regardless of the requirements needed to capitalize on an opportunity, there must be a match between the requirements and the organization's resources and position in the market.

CAPITALIZING ON OPPORTUNITIES—ORGANIZATION ABILITIES

Does the organization have what it takes to take advantage of an opportunity?

Does the organization have what it takes to capitalize on a market opportunity? To answer this question, the marketer can use the data obtained from monitoring the environment and from evaluating an opportunity's requirements to derive an overall assessment of the organization's market position. Market position is a key element in determining whether the firm can capitalize on an opportunity. Figure 19.10 lists some common checkpoints in assessing position, including market factors, competitive strength, financial and economic factors, technological expertise, and sociopolitical factors. Marketers should use the checkpoints to analyze the position of their particular firms (right column of figure 19.10) in relation to conditions prevailing in the market at large (left column of figure 19.10).

Any of the elements in the checkpoints may be the key to success in a given situation. Continental Airlines lacked the financial strength, for example, to support its expanded route system. The company was eventually reorganized under Chapter 11 of the bankruptcy law with a smaller route system. Kraft, on the other hand, has a strong position in the market because of its good relationship with food distributors. Although its success is not ensured, it is enhanced since it has primary supermarket freezer space for its cheeses. Likely to succeed are companies such as Coca-Cola and Miller Brewing, which have developed light beers and caffeine-free soft drinks in response to changing attitudes toward alcohol and caffeine. *The greater the compatibility between the opportunity and the organization's abilities and position, the more likely the company will be to succeed if it exploits the opportunity.*

❑ **Figure 19.10**
Factors contributing to
market attractiveness
and business position.

Attractiveness of Your Market	Status/Position of Your Business
1. Market Factors	
Size (dollars, units, or both)	Your share (in equivalent terms)
Size of key segments	Your share of key segments
Growth rate per year:	Your annual growth rate:
Total	Total
Segments	Segments
Diversity of market	Diversity of your participation
Sensitivity to price, service features, and	Your influence on the market
external factors	
Cyclic nature	Lags or leads in your sales
Seasonality	
Bargaining power of suppliers	Bargaining power of your suppliers
Bargaining power of customers	Bargaining power of your customers
2. Competition	
Types of competitors	Where you fit, how you compare in terms of
Concentration	products, marketing capability, service,
Changes in type and mix	production strength, financial strength,
	management
Entries and exits	Segments you have entered or left
Changes in share	Your relative share change
Substitution by new technology	Your vulnerability to new technology
Degrees and types of integration	Your own level of integration
3. Financial and Economic Factors	
Contribution margins	Your margins
Leveraging factors, such as economies of scale	Your scale and experience
and experience	
Barriers to entry or exit (both financial and	Barriers to your entry or exit (both financial and
nonfinancial)	nonfinancial)
Capacity utilization	Your capacity utilization
4. Technological Factors	
Maturity and volatility	Your ability to cope with change
Complexity	Depths of your skills
Differentiation	Types of your technological skill
Patents and copyrights	Your patent protection
Manufacturing process technology required	Your manufacturing technology
5. Sociopolitical Factors	
Social attitudes and trends	Your company's responsiveness and flexibility
Laws and government agency regulations	Your company's ability to cope
Influence with pressure groups and government	Your company's aggressiveness
representatives	
Human factors, such as unionization and	Your company's relationships
community acceptance	

Source: Derek Abell and John
Hammond, *Strategic Market
Planning: Problems and
Analytical Approaches,* © 1979,
p. 214. Reprinted by permission
of Prentice-Hall, Inc., Englewood
Cliffs, New Jersey.

THE CASE CONTINUES

*A*lthough at first glance the information about Kroger's operation seems to confirm the contention that Kroger lacks a strategic plan, the evidence actually supports the opposite. First a quasi mission statement is evident in the material presented: "Kroger seeks to provide convenient, competitive, quality food for consumers." Second, organizational objectives are implied. Withdrawal from a market can be interpreted as the failure to achieve the organization's objectives in that market. Finally, the evaluation of opportunities, a major part of strategic planning, appears to be an ongoing process at Kroger, as evidenced by changes in customer offerings and ongoing market research.

The Situation Summary—Evaluating Marketing Attractiveness and the Business Strengths of SBUs

*H*as the organization effectively capitalized on opportunities? The portfolio analysis provides a measure.

An SBU's potential in the market largely determines the amount of resources it will receive from the corporate resource pool. To analyze the strength of SBUs, it is useful for corporate managers to think of them as a **portfolio,** that is, as a collection of separate investments, and to evaluate them according to their potential through some method of **portfolio analysis.**[9] Portfolio analysis provides a way to measure how effective the organization has been. It also helps to identify possible needed action.

THE PORTFOLIO MATRIX

*C*ash flow = funds available.

Cash Flow.   The decision on what to do with a product rests heavily on cash flow. Net **cash flow** equals cash generated by the product minus expenses requiring cash.

Net Cash Flow = Cash Revenue − Cash Expenses

Executives focus on cash flow because it represents funds available for immediate use. Positive cash flow means that funds are available to carry out a marketing strategy. Negative cash flow means that funds will have to come from other sources, such as other SBUs, stockholders, charitable contributions, and creditors. Executives prefer to use cash flow to carry out their marketing strategies rather than other sources of funds such as selling stock or increasing debt.

To some extent, cash flow is a function of market growth and market share. Therefore, it is useful for executives to analyze each SBU in terms of these two variables.

*F*unds are required for fast market growth, but this reduces the cash that's available.

Market Growth and Market Share.   One of the best known methods for evaluating SBUs was developed by the Boston Consulting Group, Inc., a nationally known management consulting firm. This model allows the marketer to locate each SBU in the company's portfolio on a matrix. Figure 19.11 applies the portfolio matrix model to some products of the Coca-Cola Company. The vertical axis, market growth rate, represents the annual growth rate of the industry in which an SBU is located.

❑ **Figure 19.11**
A portfolio matrix for the Coca-Cola Company.

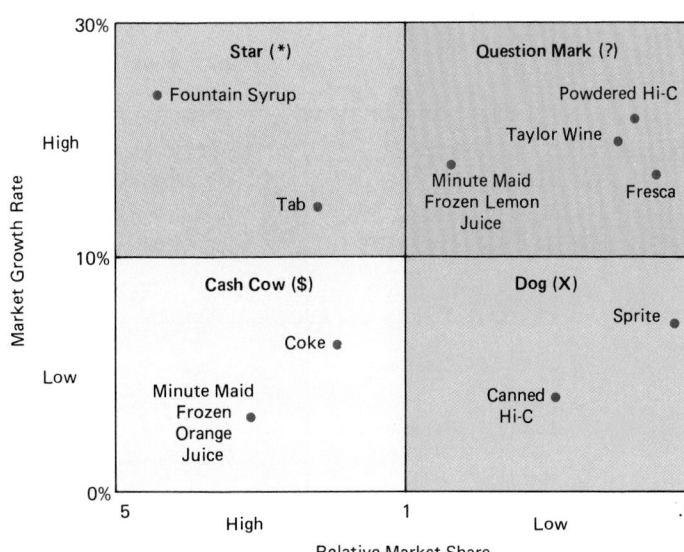

Source: Reprinted from Burke & Weitz, "The Use of the BCG Portfolio Model in Strategic Marketing Decision Making: An Empirical Investigation," p. 470, 1979 AMA Proceedings, published by the American Marketing Association.

The horizontal axis, relative market share, is the ratio of the SBU's sales to the sales of the largest firm in the industry.

The divisions between high and low growth rate and high and low market share produce four quadrants, which the Boston Consulting Group has named stars, cash cows, dogs, and problem children. The position of an SBU (or a product) in one of the quadrants reflects market performance and, therefore, the attractiveness of the products located in the quadrant.[10]

*S*tars: products with potential that are doing well.

Stars.   In figure 19.11, the Coca-Cola Company's fountain syrup is a star. It is located in a rapidly growing industry, and it has a rapidly growing share of the industry's market. The rapid growth rates of stars require that the company continually allocate cash to them to keep ahead of demand.

Often, stars are opportunity breakthroughs for a company. Their high market shares signify a market with a developed but unsatisfied need. The fact that they enjoy a high market share shows that the company recognized the need before most competitors and was able to combine the ingredients necessary to satisfy customers in the market.

*C*ash cows: successful products in their prime.

Cash Cows.   For the Coca-Cola Company, Minute Maid Frozen Orange Juice is a cash cow. It is located in a slow growing industry, but it has a high market share. Consequently, cash cows generate much more cash than they need, some of which can be channeled to other SBUs in the company's portfolio.

What happens to cash cows? Since they are usually at the maturity stage of the product life cycle, they cannot be expected to continue forever. The goal of the marketer is therefore to maintain their position for as long as possible. Upgrading the product or revitalizing its marketing plan are helpful strategies in this regard.

*D*ogs: products with limited growth and likely problems.

Dogs.   Dogs have a low share of a low-growth market. They may generate enough cash to sustain themselves but hardly any positive cash flow. The outlook for a dog is dismal. To transform a dog into a cash cow requires increasing its market share, a difficult, expensive, and often futile undertaking.

*P*roblem children: products with potential that have failed to do well.

Problem Children.   Problem children, also called question marks, are products with a small market share so they don't produce much cash. On the other hand, they are located in rapidly growing industries so they have the potential to do better, but they require resources from the parent organization just to maintain their position in the market.

☐ **Figure 19.12**
Portfolio matrix and resource allocation direction.

The low market share of problem children may mean that management was late in spotting an opportunity and entering the market or that the company failed to implement effectively. Low market share may also result from adept competitors putting together a better product and marketing plan.

MARKETING STRATEGIES, RESOURCE ALLOCATION, AND PORTFOLIO ANALYSIS

Once the marketer positions each of the company's products on a matrix, the task is first to decide the direction in which to allocate resources and, second, to develop a marketing strategy. Resources can be directed toward *growth, maintenance, harvesting,* and *divestment.* The location of a product in one of the quadrants of the portfolio matrix (star, cash cow, question mark, or dog) will point toward a direction for resource allocation. (See figure 19.12.) However, any direction can be chosen for any of the matrix cells. Particular marketing strategies are associated with each resource direction.

Going for it even though risk may be high with growth: new venture or diversification strategies.

Growth Strategies.   The objective of the growth strategies is to increase the sales and profit generated from the SBU. Four generic strategies can increase sales: the penetration strategy, the market development strategy, the product development strategy, and the diversification strategy. (See table 19.1.)

When Florida Orange Growers promoted orange juice as more than a breakfast drink, they used a penetration strategy. They attempted to gain a large market share with an existing product in an existing market. The University of Akron's move to big-time athletics to gain recognition for all the university's programs is also a penetration strategy. The U.S. Post Office, in offering Express Mail as guaranteed overnight delivery service, used a market development strategy—offering a new product in an existing market. Promoting Vaseline as a protector of shoes and leather is an example of a product development strategy—promoting an existing product in a new market. BIC manufacturing and selling cigarette lighters in addition to pens illustrates diversification—a new product and market. Figure 19.13 lists factors to consider in selecting from among the growth strategies.

Maintenance Strategies.   Maintenance strategies stabilize a product. Segmentation, balance, and retention are all maintenance strategies.

Segmentation may be selected when a marketer is interested in either growth or maintenance. Marketers may decide to focus on only part of a market when they enter a new market because the total market may be too large or expensive to pursue. In the market segment they can develop the skills and reputation to compete in a larger market. BIC, for instance, produces only disposable razors and blades. The firm has not entered the nondisposable razor and replacement blade market. However, if the decision were made, the transition would be smooth because BIC now has the reputation and skills necessary to compete in the larger razor and blade market.

Segmentation also works to maintain sales in a very competitive market. A company can often serve a niche or segment more efficiently and thus protect its

❑ **Table 19.1**   Product/Market matrix.

	EXISTING PRODUCT	NEW PRODUCT
Present market	Penetration strategy	Market development strategy
New market	Product development strategy	Diversification strategy

❑ **Figure 19.13** Factors to consider in selecting a growth strategy.

Strategy Position	Competition	Product	Distribution	Market Knowledge	Intercompany Functional Relationships	Untapped Market Potential	Typical Marketing Objectives
Market penetration	Well known and well established	Often at maturity stage of life cycle with no anticipated changes	Existing relationships unchanged	Extensive and based on considerable experience	Well established and unchanging	Somewhat limited due to product life-cycle stage and market maturity	Stabilize market share; stabilize ROI
Market development	Often new due to move into new markets	Product has potential but not in present market	May require new channels of distribution, new relationships	Sometimes minimal due to move into new markets	May change to accommodate new markets, mostly within marketing area	Must be considered good enough to move into new markets	Increase sales; increase market share; maintain ROI; increase awareness
Product development	Usually well known and well established	New product developed for an existing market	Usually can maintain existing channel relationships	Extensive and based on considerable experience	May change in production, engineering, and R&D because of new product	Must be considered good enough to warrant expense of new product	Increase sales; increase ROI; create awareness; maintain or increase market share
Diversification	May be totally new because of new product and new market	Often totally new and in early stages of life cycle, but might not be if product introduced into an established program	May require completely different channels, new relationships	Often very minimal due to new products in new markets	May change in both production and marketing sides of organization	Must be considered very good to warrant expenses of new product introduction into new market	Achieve higher ROI; increase awareness; increase sales

Source: David W. Cravens, "Marketing Strategy Positioning," in Robert W. Haas and Thomas R. Wotruba, *Marketing Management Concepts: Practice and Cases,* © 1983, Business Publications, Inc.

sales. Timken, in the steel industry, has competed successfully by serving the steel bearing and specialty steel markets.

*B*alance strategy: don't rock the boat.

Executives employ the balance strategy to keep profits at present levels by controlling cost and maintaining sales. This strategy is primarily applied in long-established industries where desired product characteristics and competitors are well known. In these industries, control overshadows planning as an activity, and firms are content with their operations. Steel and the primary metals industries have used this strategy. Complacency appears to be the major weakness of the balance strategy.

*M*arket retention or penetration: limit risk by making few changes.

The market retention strategy focuses on retaining market share. This strategy differs from the balance strategy in that desired product characteristics are subject to change, and competitors seek to improve their positions in the market. Product adaptations, promotion programs, distribution, and pricing all play an important role in retaining market share. The annual marketing plan is the focal point of planning. Automobile manufacturers have used the market retention strategy.

*N*eed money? Harvest.

Harvesting Strategies.   With a harvesting strategy, marketers attempt to squeeze every dollar of profit possible from the product. Market share may deliberately be allowed to decrease. Product quality may be reduced and promotion costs may be cut, allowing momentum to carry the product. Lifebuoy soap has been harvested for years with few resources used for promotion and other support.

As a strategy, harvesting works well for companies with high market share. Managers usually refrain from this strategy with products classified as stars. Harvesting is best applied to products that can produce a badly needed cash flow or increase short-term earnings.

Exit barriers hinder the effectiveness of a harvesting strategy. They discourage marginal competitors from leaving an industry, and a harvesting strategy is unlikely

MARKETING IN ACTION

Cone Mills

*C*one Mills, located in Greensboro, North Carolina, started turning out denim for farmers' overalls in 1891, following with corduroy in 1927. In 1987, Cone had sales in excess of $750 million. With over 11,000 workers and 119 plants, Cone Mills is one of the five or six largest employers in North Carolina.

Cone Mills used to be known as a company that persistently made the strategic choice not to diversify. Their fortunes ebbed and flowed with the changing demand for denim and corduroy. As the world's largest denim producer, the company simply toughed out the downcycles. After World War II, for instance, demand for denim was high. With the advent of the motorcycle toughs, with jeans as their trademark, a drop-off in demand occurred. In the 1960s, the hippie movement brought a resurgence of demand, with denim serving as both a uniform and as an anthem of the times.

Beginning in the early 1980s, the picture for American textile manufac-

turers began to change radically as foreign imports gained a steadily increasing share of U.S. markets. The impact has been devastating. By 1988, imports from China, Korea, and Hong Kong, among other countries, accounted for more than half of the domestic apparel and textile market. In 1981, fourteen of the largest American textile companies were publicly owned. In 1988, just three survived—Springs Industries, Fieldcrest Cannon, and WestPoint Pepperell.

In 1983 Cone was the object of a hostile takeover, which they averted with a leveraged buyout in March of 1984. While they still have not diversified outside textiles, their new policy is one of flexibility in product offering and manufacturing capability. They have broadened their prod-

uct line with several new cloths, including chamois cloth shirting fabric, soft-filled sheeting, and different colored denims. They are now prepared to shift production to meet changing product demand. If the market for denim falls, they shift production to another cloth that is in demand.

Cone is still very vulnerable to market shifts and foreign competitors, but its new policy of flexibility has helped the company. The years 1986 and 1987 were two of the best years in its history. Nevertheless, Cone strongly supports the enactment of the Textile and Apparel Trade Act restricting foreign imports. The Act was vetoed in 1986; an override attempt failed in 1987. The House of Representatives passed an amended Act in 1988 and it went on to the Senate, pending action.

Sources: Cone Mills Public Relations Department, May 1988; and Richard Levin, *The Executive Illustrated Primer of Long-Range Planning* (Englewood Cliffs, N.J.: Prentice-Hall, 1981), pp. 35–36.

---

to be successful until they do leave. Their presence may require a company to spend more for promotion and to reduce its prices to remain competitive. The high value of distribution networks is an example of an exit barrier. Marketers in marginal firms dislike losing their investment in the channel network by exiting the industry.

Divestment Strategies. Divestment allows a company to discontinue the expenditure involved in producing a particular product. Two possible approaches to divestment are liquidation and unit sale. Termination by liquidation means that assets are sold piece by piece. A unit sale is the sale of the entire unit, including the total production and distribution facilities, to a single buyer who will continue to produce the products in that unit. Piecemeal liquidation is usually a last resort since it generates fewer resources than a unit sale.

Limitations of Portfolio Analysis

*P*ortfolio matrix analysis and other techniques may improve strategies, but insightful, creative managers with good judgment are still needed.

Portfolio analysis can help the marketer develop strategy, but it has its critics. Some think it oversimplifies a highly complex process. An SBU's success depends on more than market share, growth, and cash flow. Even if success was highly dependent on market share and growth, each has to be determined for the SBU in question. Furthermore, portfolio analysis implies that increasing market share always has a positive effect. Beyond a certain point, however, market share may have a detrimental effect on profits. Likewise, cash flow should be kept in perspective. It is necessary, but it does not substitute for profits. Finally, portfolio analysis may really be more of a diagnostic tool than a guide for marketing strategy. It helps in identifying the problem, but it does not tell the marketer what to do about it.

The Financial Summary—Assessing the Risk

Will the marketing strategy have the intended impact on sales, market share, return on investment, profit, and other objectives? Marketing strategies should be evaluated before they are implemented in order to assess their impact on the achievement of objectives.

PIMS MODEL

PIMS is the acronym for Profit Impact of Marketing Strategy, a computerized approach to risk assessment. The project was started by General Electric and then taken over by the Strategic Planning Institute of Cambridge, Massachusetts. The institute uses a computer to analyze strategic position and the prospects of individual businesses. The computer compares data about the company and its strategy with a data base containing information about similar companies operating under similar conditions. Hundreds of companies are included in this data base, which is updated frequently.

*P*IMS, a method of evaluating what makes a good strategy.

❏ **Figure 19.14**
Summary of strategy factors influencing business success.

1. **Investment intensity.** Technology and the chosen way of doing business govern how much fixed capital and working capital are required to produce a dollar of sales or a dollar of value added in the business. Investment intensity generally produces a negative impact on percentage measures of profitability or net cash flow, i.e., businesses that are mechanized or automated or inventory-intensive generally show lower returns on investment and sales than businesses that are not.
2. **Productivity.** Businesses producing high value added per employee are more profitable than those with low value added per employee. (Definition: value added is the amount by which the business increases the market value of the raw materials and components it buys.)
3. **Market position.** A business's share of its served market (both absolute and relative to its three largest competitors) has a positive impact on its profit and net cash flow. (The served market is the specific segment of the total potential market—defined in terms of products, customers or areas—in which the business actually competes.)
4. **Growth of the served market.** Growth is generally favorable to dollar measures of profit, indifferent to percent measures of profit, and negative to all measures of net cash flow.
5. **Quality of the products and/or services offered.** Quality, defined as the customers' evaluation of the business's product/service package as compared to that of competitors, has a generally favorable impact on all measures of financial performance.
6. **Innovation/differentiation.** Extensive actions taken by a business in the areas of new product introduction, R&D, marketing effort, and so on generally produce a positive effect on its performance if that business has strong market position to begin with. Otherwise usually not.
7. **Vertical integration.** For businesses located in mature and stable markets, vertical integration generally has a favorable impact on performance. In markets that are rapidly growing, declining, or otherwise changing, the opposite is true.
8. **Cost push.** The rates of increase of wages, salaries, and raw material prices and the presence of a labor union have complex impacts on profit and cash flow, depending on how the business is positioned to pass along the increase to its customers and/or to absorb the higher costs internally.
9. **Current strategic effort.** The current direction of change of any of the above factors affects profit and cash flow in ways that are frequently opposite to that of the factor itself. For example, having strong market share tends to increase net cash flow, but getting share drains cash while the business is making that effort.

Source: S. Schoeffler, "Nine Basic Findings on Business Strategy," *Pimsletter* no. 1, The Strategic Planning Institute, Cambridge, Mass., 1977.

PIMS allows executives to receive reports on the effectiveness of present marketing strategy and consequences of possible marketing strategies. PIMS is both diagnostic and prescriptive.

PIMS data have been instrumental in helping the Strategic Planning Institute identify major strategy influences on a firm's profitability. For instance, a 10 percent difference in market share is associated with a 5 percent pretax difference in ROI.[11] Although market share makes a difference in ROI, its influence is less than one might conclude from studying the portfolio matrix. The Strategic Planning Institute has identified eight other influences accounting for some of the successes or failures of businesses. (See figure 19.14.)

VISUALIZING RISK

*A*ssessing risk is a part of strategy evaluation.

Many marketers do not have access to PIMS or hesitate to use it. They may be satisfied with visualizing the risk of a marketing strategy. Visualizing risk is an attempt to foresee the strategy's possible wins and losses, what factors may increase or decrease the wins and losses, and the probability of those factors occurring.

The amount of risk that executives willingly allow an organization to assume varies considerably from organization to organization—and even from one executive to the next. The risk of a marketing strategy is a function of environmental and organizational factors. Since neither set of factors can be measured precisely, risk becomes perceived risk. Generally the more and the greater the changes required of an organization to implement strategy, the greater the perceived risk. The University of Akron's move, for example, from the National Collegiate Athletic Association's division I-AA to I-A is considered potentially risky. It will be the first university to make the move. The university also asked the football coach, who had a winning record but lacked a national reputation, to step aside, and it hired a coach with a national reputation. More athletic scholarships, more attendance at athletic events, and most of all, winning athletic teams will be required to make the strategy work.

A product development strategy requires fewer changes than a diversification or new venture strategy and is generally considered less risky. Procter & Gamble's development of soft-centered cookies, for example, was less risky than Frederick W. Smith's pioneering work to develop Federal Express in a new market, overnight package delivery.

THE CASE CONTINUES

*T*he amount of effort Kroger management puts into a market can be explained in several ways. It appears that Kroger executives have defined each market (Pittsburgh, Kansas City, etc.) as an SBU. Using portfolio analysis, each market could be located on a matrix by Kroger's market share and growth of the market, as shown in figure 19.15. Kansas City, Minneapolis, Pittsburgh, and Washington markets were terminated. Their location on the matrix as low market share and growth markets indicated that termination was a viable

□ **Figure 19.15** A portfolio analysis for the Kroger Company.

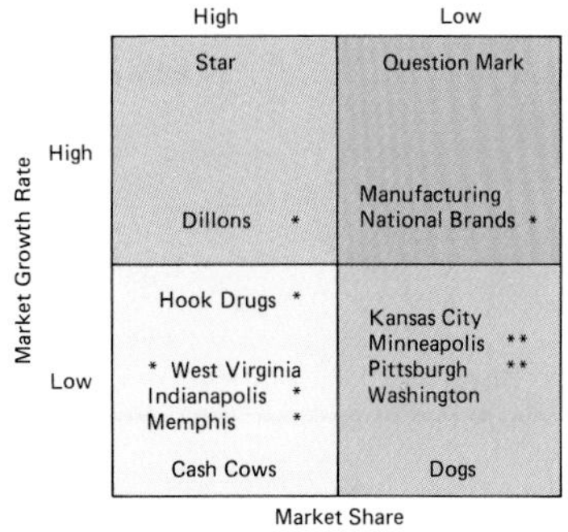

strategy. Hook Drugs, in conjunction with the 630 SupeRX stores that Kroger already owned, should position Hook in the cash-cow position, a reasonable purchase for Kroger. With population increasing in the southwestern United States and food sales growing, the number of stores in the Dillon chain should give Kroger a good share of the market. Dillon appears to be a star. The manufacturing for national brands is definitely a question mark. The success of manufacturing for other companies is still to be proven as a viable business venture.

GOAL SUMMARY

1. **Describe a mission statement for an organization.** Mission statements have a long-term, broad perspective! They focus on what the organization is uniquely qualified to do and on how these capabilities benefit its target markets. To create a mission statement, managers often first identify the issues relevant to their target markets that the organization is able to and wants to satisfy. Do their target markets have a need for transportation, communication, entertainment, etc.? Managers may then examine each issue for durability, ability to unify and give direction, and compatibility with the interests, values, and resources of the organization.

2. **Evaluate opportunities.** At any point in time, organizations can potentially take advantage of hundreds of opportunities. To best match opportunities with resources to develop strategic plans, evaluate the opportunities and the organization's abilities. Opportunity evaluation proceeds under two general headings: assessment and requirements. Assessment considers factors such as the size of the market, the growth potential, competitors, and their strategies. Opportunity requirements focus on what resources will be needed to develop the opportunity successfully. An organization's capabilities encompass items such as location, personnel, expertise, technology, and production.

3. **Contrast organization strategy, marketing strategy, and annual marketing plans.** Each type of plan represents an activity occurring at different levels, with organization strategy at the highest level and the annual marketing plan at the lowest. Organization strategy outlines the paths the organization will follow in achieving goals in the environment. Marketing strategy develops the procedures for obtaining marketing objectives within the context of the organization strategies and in cooperation with the other functional areas. An annual marketing plan specifies how the objectives in the marketing strategy will be achieved. The annual marketing plan focuses on the interaction of the market and the marketing mix variables.

4. **Discuss the fundamental concepts and purpose of portfolio analysis.** The organization's collection of products and/or strategic business units (SBUs) is referred to as its portfolio. Portfolio analysis is a process of evaluating and classifying the products or SBUs into categories based on their current and potential contribution to the organization. Several variables have been used to evaluate the portfolio. The Boston Consulting Group uses market growth and market share to assess probable cash flow and to classify products. The purpose behind portfolio analysis—of classifying SBUs by potential contribution—is to develop optimum marketing strategies.

5. **Explain the PIMS model.** PIMS stands for *profit impact of marketing strategy*. PIMS is a computer-assisted tool for analyzing risk. It includes a data base containing information about the operations of several hundred companies. Analysis of the data base allows generalizations about effective marketing strategy. For member organizations, PIMS can evaluate the probable outcomes of current and alternative marketing strategies.

KEY TERMS

Corporate Strategic Plans, **p. 527**
Strategic Marketing Plans, **p. 527**
Marketing Plans, **p. 527**
Mission Statement, **p. 528**
Organization Objectives, **p. 531**
Sales Responsiveness Curve, **p. 532**
Strategic Business Unit (SBU), **p. 533**

Strategic Window, **p. 535**
Opportunity Attractiveness, **p. 536**
Opportunity Requirements, **p. 537**
Portfolio, **p. 539**
Portfolio Analysis, **p. 539**
Cash Flow, **p. 539**
PIMS, **p. 544**

CHECK YOUR LEARNING

1. A mission statement should be internally oriented. **T/F**

2. A mission statement and organizational self-image are closely related. **T/F**

CHECK YOUR LEARNING *(continued)*

3. Organization objectives should have an external orientation. **T/F**
4. A strategic plan is the road map the organization will use to obtain its stated objectives. **T/F**
5. An opportunity requirement is the investment necessary to take advantage of an opportunity. **T/F**
6. Strategic marketing centers on the marketplace and involves all aspects of an organization's strategy. **T/F**
7. Portfolio analysis requires that each item in the portfolio be evaluated in much the same way that a person would evaluate financial holdings. **T/F**
8. Positive cash flow gives the manager funds to invest. **T/F**
9. Which one of the following is not a criticism of the product portfolio analysis as developed by the Boston Consulting Group? (a) it is a guide for developing marketing strategy, (b) it is basically a diagnostic tool, (c) cash flow is overemphasized, (d) market share is overemphasized, (e) all of these are valid criticisms.

10. The major advantage of PIMS is that the impact of a potential strategy can be determined before it is implemented. **T/F**
11. Regarding the relationship of risk to management philosophy: (a) it has no place in the development of marketing strategy, (b) it is essentially the same in all organizations, (c) risk is often perceived as change, (d) as risk increases, the importance of marketing decreases, (e) all of these are correct.
12. Which of the following strategies would generally be associated with the highest risk and the greatest need for marketing? (a) new venture or diversification, (b) growth, (c) market/product development, (d) market penetration, (e) all are equally associated.
13. Balance strategies are typically found in mature markets. **T/F**
14. In the market retention strategy, management emphasizes control more than marketing. **T/F**
15. Federal Express is a good illustration of market development strategy. **T/F**

QUESTIONS FOR REVIEW AND DISCUSSION

1. Define the key terms for this chapter that appear at the end of the goal summary.
2. Is it necessary that an organization have a mission? Why?
3. Do mission statements for profit- and nonprofit-making organizations differ? In what respect?
4. Why is it essential that marketing objectives be compatible with organization objectives?
5. What purpose do objectives serve?
6. Name opportunities that are currently available to service organizations.
7. What factors would you use to evaluate the requirements of an opportunity?
8. Because we live in the United States, we are most familiar with opportunities here. What suggestions can you make for increasing our awareness of opportunities in other countries? For evaluating those

opportunities?
9. Why is it necessary to develop a strategic marketing plan for each SBU?
10. Do you agree with the important position given cash flow in the portfolio matrix model of the Boston Consulting Group?
11. Name a product that you think is a cash cow. A problem child. A dog. A star.
12. Which type of product do you think would be easiest to manage: cash cow, dog, problem child, or star? The most challenging? The most fun? The greatest opportunity?
13. What advantages does PIMS have over the portfolio models?
14. Should growth underlie all acceptable marketing strategies?

NOTES

1. John A. Pearce III, "The Company Mission As a Strategic Tool," *Sloan Management Review* (Spring 1982): pp. 15–24.

2. R. E. Stewart, J. K. Allen, and J. M. Cavender, *The Strategic Plan* (Palo Alto, Calif.: Stanford Research Institute, 1973).

NOTES *(continued)*

3. William K. Hall, "SBU's: Hot New Topic in the Management of Diversification," *Business Horizons* 21, no. 1 (February 1978): pp. 17–25.

4. George S. Day, *Strategic Market Planning* (St. Paul, MN: West Publishing Company, 1984), p. 16.

5. Paul Vincent, "Cool Profits Down South," *Indiana Business,* October 1986, p. 67.

6. Derek F. Abell, *Defining the Business: The Starting Point of Strategic Planning* (Englewood Cliffs, N.J.: Prentice-Hall, 1980), p. 207.

7. Sandra D. Atchison and Bruce Nussbaum, "Hyatt: A 'Mission' to Make Legal Services Affordable," *Business Week,* January 21, 1985, p. 70.

8. Derek F. Abell, "Strategic Windows," *Journal of Marketing* (July 1978): p. 21.

9. Philippe Haspeslagh, "Portfolio Planning: Uses and Limitations," *Harvard Business Review* (January–February 1982): pp. 58–73.

10. George S. Day, "Diagnosing the Product Portfolio," *Journal of Marketing* (April 1977): pp. 29–38.

11. *The PIMS Program* (Cambridge, Mass.: The Strategic Planning Institute, 1977).

*E*xecutives of Canon, Inc., a noted Japanese manufacturer of photography products, business machines, and optical equipment, believe that Canon can continue to grow and become a major force in the U.S. office automation market, which is the largest in the world. The market encompasses all kinds of office products, including copiers, typewriters, facsimile transceivers (fax), and computers. It has plants in Japan, the U.S., Europe, and Taiwan.

Just a decade ago Canon was a successful but struggling camera maker. It is now the world's largest maker of copiers and a major producer of 35mm cameras. It has surpassed Xerox in U.S. copier sales and is gaining on IBM in electric typewriter sales. Canon's president has stated that the company's objective is to be a serious contender with IBM in the office automation market. Other company executives question the credibility of this objective, suggesting it is more a dream than a real possibility. Three-fourths of Canon's revenues are generated from business machine sales, however, and this apparently has given Canon's president confidence to take on the giant IBM.

Canon's motto could easily be "patience." The president's philosophy is to look ahead in a market, prepare for changes, and when the market does change, move in. The company's marketing strategy of quality, timely products (their facsimile transceivers, or "faxes," are a case in point), a good reputation, and excellent marketing implementation has served Canon well.

In the copier market, Canon developed a high-quality, less-expensive process for copiers. When the market appeared ready, Canon initiated the personal-copier market by reducing the price and putting critical parts in a cartridge, replaceable by consumers. With aggressive advertising, Canon has been able to maintain a 90 percent share of the U.S. personal-copier market. Executives at the company expect the price to drop eventually to the level where students can own one.

Until as recently as thirteen years ago, Canon had tried one strategy after another with little success. The current strategy seems to be working, but will it continue? Sluggish growth was predicted for 1988. Most of Canon's most successful products rely on optics (copiers, faxes, cameras), where it has its technical strength. Personal computers require minimal optical technology, and Canon's market share is correspondingly small. Still, Canon expects the computer in the 21st century to use optical chips as key parts. Canon is researching these chips and at the same time is working on integrated circuits. Company executives are looking ahead in the market and are preparing to move when it changes.

Issues for Discussion
1. Does the fundamental process of developing organizational mission statements and objectives differ for Canon—a Japanese firm with a large presence in the U.S.—than for a U.S. firm? Explain.
2. Describe and evaluate Canon's corporate strategy.

Sources: Information based on "Standard Corporate Descriptions," New York: *Standard and Poor's Corporation,* July 30, 1987; "The Value Line Investment Survey," New York: *Value Line,* February 26, 1988, p. 1553; and Leslie Helm and Rebecca Aikman, "A Japanese Slugfest for U.S. Turf," *Business Week,* May 13, 1985, pp. 98–102.

OUTLINE

Controlling Marketing Strategies

LEARNING GOALS

After reading this chapter, you should be able to:

1. Identify and briefly describe the major elements of a marketing control system.
2. Describe the objectives of attitude tracking, sales analysis, and market share analysis.
3. Distinguish between natural and functional cost and between contribution-margin and full-cost analysis.
4. Identify the fundamental concept of efficiency analysis.
5. Explain marketing audit.

*I*n the early 1980s, competitors took part of Procter & Gamble's (P&G) market share in three vital businesses: dentifrices, diapers, and detergents. In the diaper business, Kimberly-Clark introduced Huggies as a counter to P&G's Pampers. Huggies saw a steady increase in its market share in the U.S., as did low-priced private brands.

Luvs were P&G's initial counter to Huggies, but instead of garnering part of the Huggies' market, Luv sales came at the expense of Pampers sales. P&G's market share began to rebound only when it introduced Blue Ribbon Pampers, with their leak-proof waists and leg bands. The introduction of Ultra Pampers—thinner than other disposables and containing a chemical that turns to gel when damp (absorbing wetness)—continued to lift P&G's market share.

P&G's fortunes were much the same in the Japanese market as in the U.S. P&G dominated the Japanese market until Japan's Uni-charm Corporation introduced a diaper containing a granulated polymer gel and won a large share of the market. P&G took the idea of using the gel in Ultra Pampers from Uni-charm. Although the polymer-to-gel concept was not patent-protected, it took three years before P&G introduced its Ultra Pampers.

The dentifrice and detergent markets in Japan and the U.S. during the early 1980s were an instant replay of the diaper market. To that point, P&G had dominated both markets: the company then saw market share decline when competitors developed equal or superior products, which they aggressively marketed.

P&G's basic marketing strategy had been to rely on research to develop superior products to sell at premium prices, while supporting them with promotion and intense distribution. With competitors gaining ground, P&G found itself straying from this strategy and instead chasing the competition with lackluster, me-too products.

Thus, for a time at least, P&G was said to have lost its technological and marketing edge in the U.S. and Japanese markets. In addition, P&G was slow in adapting to local markets. The same marketing strategies used in the U.S. were used in Japan. This led to several problems, including the alienation of wholesalers and retailers who reacted to price cutting and misguided advertising.

P&G's CEO has rejuvenated the aging corporate culture of the company by implementing new business procedures and by reinstituting successful strategies. Each division now has a cost-education team composed of executives and blue-collar employees. In the past, P&G relied on volume alone to hold costs down. Now, efficient manufacturing and marketing is stressed. The company has also adopted a regionalized market strategy—the first major household products company to do so. The regional manager tracks product sales, market share, and other regional market variations. He or she then develops market-specific strategies to improve sales. Finally, P&G has refocused on its long-time successful strategy of relying on research to develop superior products, which are then aggressively marketed.

In the diaper market, P&G continues to improve its Pampers and Luv brands. Improvements are guided by consumer opinion. The company has similarly used consumer opinion to improve its products in the dentifrice and detergent markets.

Although P&G can claim to have regained leadership in each of these three important categories, analysts say that the company no longer can expect to *dominate* categories as it once did in disposable diapers—when it commanded more than 75 percent of the market. Competitors will not sit back and let P&G take sales. Wholesalers and retailers have grown more independent in their dealings with the company. Food industry consolidation at the retail and wholesale levels has left firms larger and more willing to use their size. Retailers have found new muscle in information generated by computerized checkout scanners. With data from these scanners, retailers can assess product needs on a neighborhood-by-neighborhood basis.

Both wholesalers and retailers are also using new techniques to evaluate products, such as direct product profitability, or DPP. DPP allows the direct handling cost of a product to be measured from the time the product is received until it is purchased by the consumer. Some high-volume products have had such high handling costs that retailers are reducing space allocated to them.

Fortunately, P&G's new thin Pampers require one-half the space for a

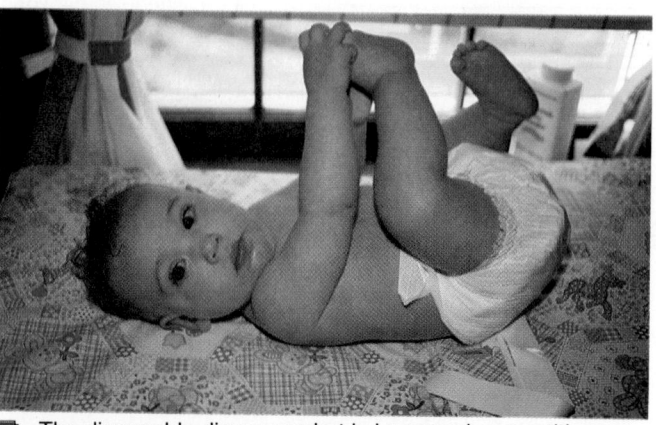

■ The disposable diaper market is large and competitive.

box of the same number of diapers as Huggies. While in the past P&G had oriented itself to supermarket sales, the company has taken steps to secure greater distribution through drugstores by meeting with executives from drugstore chains. Finally, to keep in touch with consumers, P&G operates a consumer hotline.

Issues for Discussion
1. What details from the case show that P&G regularly evaluates its marketing performance? Where are there signs of an attempt to gain control over critical aspects of the marketing program?
2. Where is there evidence that P&G has done some systematic market analysis?
3. Since P&G can no longer rely on volume alone to hold down costs, what moves have they made to improve efficiency?
4. In view of P&G's response to a shifting competitive environment, does the company's future marketing efforts seem likely to need less systematic monitoring, or more?

Sources: Bill Saporito, "Luv That Market," *Fortune,* August 3, 1987, p. 56; Nancy Giges, "Toothpastes Challenging P&G's Crest," *Advertising Age,* May 4, 1987, pp. 2, 110; Laurie Freeman, "P&G Hops on Regional Trend," *Advertising Age,* April 20, 1987, pp. 1, 96; Jeffrey A. Trachtenberg, "They Didn't Listen to Anybody," *Forbes,* December 15, 1986, pp. 168–170; Zachary Schiller, "How P&G Was Brought to a Crawl in Japan's Diaper Market," *Business Week,* October 13, 1986, pp. 71–74; Faye Rice, "The King of Suds Reigns Again," *Fortune,* August 4, 1986, pp. 130–133; and Laurie Freeman, "P&G Back on Track as Earnings Rocket," *Advertising Age,* July 14, 1986, pp. 3, 77.

*L*ike every organization, Procter & Gamble has to evaluate its performance constantly. No businessperson, including the marketing manager, likes to have programs result in surprises. Thus, at each step, marketers should know what is happening in their marketing programs and why. When problems occur, they should know what they can do about them. A well-designed marketing control system provides this information. Marketing control systems are used to measure and evaluate performance. In the pages ahead, we explain the elements of a control system. We look at how marketers identify standards, measure and evaluate actual results, and take corrective action. We describe the methods used to analyze markets, and conclude with a discussion of the most comprehensive marketing control system—the marketing audit. ■

 ## MARKETING CONTROL SYSTEMS

Marketing control is the process of monitoring marketing performance and identifying problems that arise from unsatisfactory performance levels. Results are compared against standards and, when necessary, corrective action is taken. Figure 20.1 presents the sequence of the marketing control process.

❏ **Figure 20.1**
Elements of marketing control.

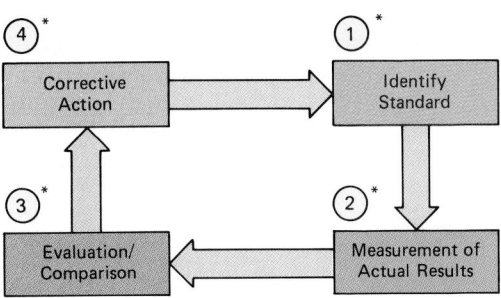

*Monitor the Environment

The control system should operate at all levels in the organization. For top management, the control system focuses on strategy. For middle and lower management, the focus shifts from strategy to a more tactical orientation.

This chapter emphasizes control in relation to marketing strategy and tactics. To understand marketing strategy and tactics, a broader perspective on the company helps. The marketer can gain this perspective by answering questions such as:[1]

1. Why is the company successful, given competitors' patterns of doing business?
2. What traits or characteristics has the company followed regularly?
3. To what strategic posture do these traits and characteristics lead?
4. What critical factors make a difference in the success of the strategy?
5. Are the critical factors likely to change? How much? In what direction? When?

*S*trategic control focuses on markets and products.

At the *marketing strategy level,* control frequently takes on a product or market orientation. That is, either the product or market serves as the basis for the identification of standards, the measurement and evaluation of results, and the designation of corrective action. Answers are sought to questions such as: What markets did we seek? What markets do we have? How did we attempt to serve the market? How do we serve the market? Are we serving market segments? Should we serve market segments? What characteristics and traits have we attempted to give our product? What characteristics and traits does it have in the market's opinion?

*T*actical control focuses on the day-to-day activities.

Control at the *tactical level* focuses on daily and monthly activities. Is the sales force effective? Is each individual salesperson performing adequately? Has an advertising campaign been effective? Are designated retailers distributing the product efficiently? The data collected by accounting departments are useful in tactical control. Although marketers occasionally tend to downgrade the significance of tactical control because it frequently relies on the more limited perspective of accounting, it is necessary in the operation of an organization. For this reason, we present several examples of tactical control in this chapter. At both the strategic and tactical levels control should tell the marketer about effectiveness (are the goals being achieved?), efficiency (what and how many resources are being used to achieve the goals?), and contributing environmental causes.

*C*ontrol begins with the planning process.

Control should begin at the planning stage and permeate every level of the marketing organization. For instance, international competition forced many U.S. companies to increase the quality of their products. Many executives mistakenly attempted to improve quality by hiring more inspectors to inspect the product once it was produced. Experience has shown, however, that product quality is improved more effectively by quality control throughout the production process, starting with raw materials. Marketing control is also more effective if it is included in the planning process. Waiting to consider the control process until results are in is usually too late.

THE MARKETING CONTROL PROCESS

To design a marketing control system, a knowledge of the fundamentals of the marketing control process is essential. The marketing control process involves the identification of standards, the measurement and evaluation of results, and corrective action.[2]

Identifying Standards

*T*he same performance can be acceptable with a low standard; unacceptable with a high standard.

The only way to analyze performance is to compare it with a standard. **Standards** are expected levels of achievement. An exceptionally high standard (high expecta-

THE REST OF THE STORY

Herb Campaign Wasn't a Whopper

*D*on't expect to see Burger King Corporation's geeky pitchman, Herb, ever again.

In four months, the second-seeded fast-food chain sank $40 million into a campaign centered around a mythical nerd who'd never eaten at Burger King.

Horn-rimmed Herb, portrayed by actor Jon Menick, grabbed headlines in more than 5,000 newspapers.

He was interviewed on "Entertainment Tonight," "Today," and "PM Magazine."

He did a stint on MTV.

And he drew a flood of 500 letters to Burger King headquarters in

Miami—more than any other Burger King campaign.

What Herb didn't do was sell hamburgers.

Burger King's average unit sales rose a paltry 1 percent in January 1986, compared with January 1985. And company executives were peeved.

Upon unveiling the bizarre campaign, Burger King officials boasted sales would jump 6 percent. Com-

pany spokeswoman Joyce Myers blamed the shortfall on:

The overall fast-food industry doldrums.

An unexpected $80 million ad counterattack from rival McDonald's Corporation for its new McD.L.T. dream patty.

"We're certainly disappointed. But the whole industry is soft," Myers said at the time. "Who knows how we would have done without Herb?"

Source: Copyright © 1986, USA TODAY. Excerpted with permission. From Susan Spillman, "Herb Campaign Wasn't a Whopper," p. B1.

tions) may often produce the response "We are not doing very well." On the other hand, an exceptionally low standard (low expectations) may often produce the response "We are doing very well," even though the performance is the same with both standards. Identification of appropriate standards, therefore, is paramount to a successful marketing control system.

Standards can be based on perfection or on what seems practically possible.

There are two types of standards: comparative and ideal. *Ideal* standards evolve from the marketer's perception of how the program, system, policy, or campaign would work if perfection were achieved. Ideally, every potential customer should be aware of the company's product. Surprisingly, more agreement on what constitutes perfection exists than one might expect. Generally, organizations at the top of their industry have a greater tendency to use ideal standards.

Understandably, most standards are of the comparative type. *Comparative standards* are based on the performance of a competitor, industry averages, or previous organizational achievements. To illustrate, last year 30 percent of the potential customers were aware of the company's product; this year 40 percent should be aware.

Environment affects performance, and likewise should influence the standard.

Standards should be established within an environmental context. For example, the possibilities for achievement when the economy is in a downturn will not be the same as when it is expanding. The manager should devise standards for different levels of economic activity, competition, and other variables to reflect the dynamic nature of the organization's environment. Performance evaluation should be sufficiently flexible to incorporate the dynamic nature of the environment.

Measurements of Results

Objectives establish how performance is measured.

In order to compare standards with performance, performance must be known. Measuring performance is not achieved by happenstance. How does the sales manager know what the performance of an outside salesperson in a distant territory has been in a particular week? If the sales manager wants an accurate assessment of performance, he or she needs to follow a system that measures and compares in the same units that objectives are specified. The sales manager will want to know how

❑ **Figure 20.2**
Possible performance
measurements.

Effectiveness Standards	Efficiency Standards

Sales:
    Total Sales
    Percentage Increase in Sales
    Market Share
    Sales by Geographic Area
    Sales by Sales Territory
    Sales by Channel of Distribution
    Sales by Product/Service
    Sales by Market Segment
    Sales by Salesperson
	Cost:
	    Total Cost
	    Cost by Geographic Area
	    Cost by Sales Territory
	    Cost by Channel of Distribution
	    Cost by Product/Service
	    Cost by Salesperson
	    Cost Per Dollar of Sales

Market Satisfaction:
    Perceived Product Quality
    Perceived Value
    Brand Loyalty
    Quantity Purchased
    Rate of Repeat Purchases
    Number of Documented Complaints
	Effectiveness-Efficiency Standards
	Profits:
	    Total Profits
	    Profits by Geographic Area
	    Profits by Sales Territory
	    Profits by Channel of Distribution
	    Profits by Product/Service
	    Profits by Salesperson
	    Profits Per Dollar of Sales

the actual compares to the objectives: actual sales to expected sales, actual sales calls to expected sales calls, and actual contacts to expected new contacts.

Standards that are stated in terms of goals without consideration of the costs to obtain them are termed **effectiveness standards.** Profit organizations express effectiveness standards in terms of sales or market satisfaction, as shown in figure 20.2. Standards that focus on the use of resources are called **efficiency standards.** Figure 20.2 shows various cost-related measurements.

Evaluation of Results

Comparison of the standard with actual results is the first step in evaluation. When results deviate significantly from standards, the manager should examine the situation. For example, the performance of a salesperson who generates only $100,000 in sales in a territory with a $400,000 sales quota shows a significant enough deviation to merit further evaluation.

*U*nderstanding why the gap exists between performance and standards is an important part of control.

Once the deviation has been noted, the manager should determine why it developed in order to take appropriate action. Possible reasons for the low figures generated by the salesperson may include his or her inadequate performance, and/or changes in customer demand and in the competitive environment. The manager should examine each to determine its contribution to the deviation.

When a deviation signals the need for closer examination of a situation to determine underlying causes, the iceberg principle comes into play. The **iceberg principle** refers to those situations where 90 percent of the information pertaining to a situation lies below the surface. Like real icebergs, which only project about 10 percent of their mass above water level, many business and marketing problems need careful analysis to be fully understood. In the sales quota situation that follows, sales below quota illustrate only the tip of the iceberg. They are symptoms of a much larger problem.

*A*n index standardizes performance for easier comparisons.

To facilitate examination, marketers often reduce data to a common base called a **performance index.** Performance indices make comparisons easier because data are transformed to a base of 100. To illustrate, consider a company with three salespeople. At the end of the year, sales are:

	Sales
Salesperson 1	$100,000
Salesperson 2	175,000
Salesperson 3	205,000

One way to calculate a performance index is to total sales and divide by three, generating the mean.

$$\frac{\$480,000}{3} = 160,000$$

Obtain the performance index based on the mean by dividing each salesperson's sales by the mean. The results are:

	Index
Salesperson 1	63
Salesperson 2	109
Salesperson 3	128

Using the mean as the standard, determine the deviation from the standard by subtracting 100 from the index.

	Index	Deviation
Salesperson 1	63	− 27 (63 − 100)
Salesperson 2	109	+ 9 (109 − 100)
Salesperson 3	128	+28 (128 − 100)

As shown, the deviation of the first salesperson is 27 percent below the mean.

Another way of calculating a performance index uses the sales quota for each salesperson as the base. For instance, consider the three salespeople again.

*M*ultiple measures are less misleading than single measures.

	Sales	Sales Quota	Index
Salesperson 1	100,000	100,000	100 (100,000/100,000)
Salesperson 2	175,000	160,000	109 (175,000/160,000)
Salesperson 3	205,000	225,000	91 (205,000/225,000)

Subtract 100 from the index to obtain the deviation as a percentage. In the illustration the third salesperson has fallen below the quota. Salesperson three has a larger quota, it is true, but at this point the question is performance in relation to quota.

Many other indices can be constructed such as those based on selling cost and profit. One example for the three salespeople is shown. Divide sales by selling cost to obtain the sales per dollar of selling cost. Add the sales per dollar of selling cost for all three salespersons and divide by three to obtain the average. The index shown is based on the average.

	Selling Cost	Sales	Sales per Dollar Selling Cost	Index
Salesperson 1	$10,000	$100,000	$10.00(100,000/10,000)	111(10/8.98)
Salesperson 2	20,000	175,000	8.75(175,000/20,000)	97(8.75/8.98)
Salesperson 3	25,000	205,000	8.20(205,000/25,000)	91(8.20/8.98)

*B*eware—performance can be manipulated if evaluation is confined to a single operating period.

Numerous other analytical and diagnostic techniques can be used to arrive at the causes of deviations. The results of a single operating period are sufficient to make an evaluation about the short run, but not the long run. In the short run, performance measures can be manipulated. For instance, a salesperson may make his or her performance look better in an operating period by convincing purchasers to buy earlier than normal. Manipulation is more difficult when evaluation concentrates on trends in performance measured over several periods.

Corrective Action

Corrective action: change standard, change strategy, or do nothing.

Having located the cause of the deviation, marketing managers must make a decision. Should they take corrective action? They may decide to change the standards if they find that the environment has changed appreciably, even if they believe that the element being controlled, for example strategy, is still the most appropriate. Taking corrective action may stem from the belief that the original action was incorrect or that conditions have changed to the point that the original action no longer is the most appropriate. Inaction results when the person is completely overwhelmed by the situation or believes the deviation is only temporary.

Contingency plans are plans developed at the same time as the action plan. They anticipate that deviations might occur because of environmental changes. Causes for deviations must be anticipated when developing contingency plans. Contingency plans are considered an indication of good management.

Monitoring the Environment

Control systems are established for activities that will take place in the future. Thus, they require assumptions about the future environment. These assumptions must be written down for later reference and use in the control system. The environment should be monitored as the marketing activity unfolds to determine if the assumptions are valid. Invalid assumptions help explain deviations from standards.

THE CASE CONTINUES

*T*here is ample evidence in the introductory case that P&G has a marketing evaluation/control system. Although specific standards do not appear in the case, the fact that executives at P&G believe performance should be better indicates that standards do exist. For the Pampers brand, market share and profit margins serve as the basis of performance standards. It is also obvious that P&G personnel and others have measured the company's performance by product market share.

Furthermore, the performance deviations apparently were significant enough to spur P&G into developing a new strategy to regain market share for diapers, dentifrices, and detergents. Knowledge of the changing relationship between P&G and wholesalers and retailers is evidence that P&G monitors the environment.

Finally, P&G's efforts to control costs include the participation of executives and nonexecutives alike. Control systems design needs to include the participation of the individuals evaluated.

Market Analysis

The three methods of analyzing the market are attitude tracking, sales analysis, and market share analysis.

ATTITUDE TRACKING

Customer attitudes reflect satisfaction with the organization's marketing practices.

Attitude tracking attempts to measure market satisfaction through the study of consumer attitudes. Generally, the change in attitudes is considered to be as important as the level of attitudes. Many corporations that sell services—restaurants, for example—continuously survey customers, commonly through the use of response cards (figure 20.3). Customers are encouraged to complete the response forms, and management periodically reviews them. Besides close scrutiny of specific comments on the forms, the percentage of forms containing negative customer statements and

❑ **Figure 20.3**
Restaurant comment card.

> TO THE CUSTOMER:
> You can help us serve you better. Please tell us how we rated. THANK YOU!
> Rating scale: 4 = Excellent   3 = Good   2 = Fair   1 = Poor (Circle your choice.)
>
> • Courteous Service   4   3   2   1   • Meal Value   4   3   2   1
> • Prompt Service   4   3   2   1   • Atmosphere   4   3   2   1
> Menu Items: • Restaurant
> • Sandwich   4   3   2   1   Cleanliness   4   3   2   1
> • Potato   4   3   2   1   • Overall Dining
> • Salad Bar   4   3   2   1   Experience   4   3   2   1
>
> Time _____ Date _____   Location _____
> COMMENTS/SUGGESTIONS _____
> _____
> _____
> _____
>
> Name _____
> Address _____
> City _____   State _____ Zip _____

those containing positive statements are calculated. The number of response forms and percentages are compared to previous periods to determine change.

Some organizations devote more resources to attitude tracking than others. For instance, in the broadcast industry the various rating services such as Nielsen and Arbitron provide data on audience reaction to TV and radio programming. The data has a competitive orientation—Which station is doing the best programming?

SALES ANALYSIS

A popular approach to control, **sales analysis** goes beyond the mere reporting of sales. Current sales have traditionally been perceived as a barometer of marketing performance. Current sales represent an absolute measure. In other words, the worst a company can do is to have no sales. The higher the current sales, the better the organization is perceived to be doing.

*S*ales by geographic area, customer type, and product type provide in-depth information.

Obviously a summary sales figure fails to convey a complete message on the success of an organization's marketing program.[3] To be fully useful, sales figures are broken down, most commonly at the level of geography, product, channel of distribution, and target market. A breakdown of sales figures is only possible if sales data are kept for a particular level. For instance, to break down total sales into geographic regions, the sales associated with each region had to be recorded previously.

*D*ifferences in sales may exist in different geographic areas.

The **geographic sales analysis** approach breaks sales figures into geographic areas. This approach is useful because organizations often allocate resources based on geographic regions, and market potential also varies geographically.

Figure 20.4 illustrates a typical geographic sales analysis, which allows the marketing manager to compare percentages across regions. For instance, the Mid-

❑ **Figure 20.4**
A geographic sales analysis.

Region	Resources Allocated		Sales Potential		Actual Sales	
	$	%	$	%	$	%
Northeast	544,269	11.5	898,511	12.6	871,555	14.0
Southeast	309,951	6.6	533,027	7.5	522,366	8.4
Midwest	741,617	15.8	986,366	13.8	907,456	14.5
Midsouth	560,345	11.9	984,066	13.8	698,686	11.2
Plains	768,538	16.4	1,103,148	15.4	1,014,896	16.3
Southwest	825,221	17.6	1,237,468	17.3	1,051,848	16.8
West	69,219	1.5	105,658	1.5	90,866	1.5
Northwest	878,366	18.7	1,293,699	18.1	1,086,707	17.4
TOTAL	4,697,526	100	7,141,943	100	6,244,380	100

❏ **Figure 20.5**
A product sales
analysis for Walt
Disney Production's
major lines.

Source: The Value Line
Investment Survey: Ratings &
Reports (New York: Value Line,
Inc., March 11, 1988), p. 1757.

Walt Disney Productions Major Lines* Revenues (in millions)				
Major Lines	1985	1986	1987	1988
Parks	$1,257	$1,524	$1,834	$2,000
Motion Pictures	320	512	876	970
Consumer Products	123	130	167	195

west region received 15.8 percent of the company's resources, had 13.8 percent of the sales potential, and realized 14.5 percent of the company's sales. The question, "When compared to other regions, how has the Midwest region fared?" would probably be in the back of the marketing manager's mind. After analysis of regional results, most managers would break down each region into smaller geographic areas, perhaps by state, city, and county.

Organizations with multiple products break down sales by product line. For instance, Walt Disney Productions has three major types of products. From the revenue dollars listed in figure 20.5, it is evident that executives at Walt Disney Productions have successfully developed strategies to revitalize the motion picture line. After several money-losing films in the early 1980s, Walt Disney Productions has had substantial success with *Three Men and a Baby* and *Good Morning Vietnam*. **Product sales analysis** draws attention to product lines that have performed successfully, as well as to those that need attention.

To add even more detailed information, product sales analysis is carried out at the brand level (a competitive orientation). This is illustrated by the Quaker Oats cold cereal line in figure 20.6. The major brands of Quaker Oats would receive primary attention from marketing management. Cap'n Crunch, supported with a heavy promotional outlay, retained its share of the market in pounds and dollars. Life, however, was adversely affected by competition and, as a result, lost market share.

Oh's were introduced in 1986 as the first all-family cereal. Halfsies were dropped from the line in 1985. The brand was introduced in 1983 to stay with the industry that introduced several new brands for the child segment.

Channel of distribution sales analysis breaks down sales by distribution channels when multiple channels are used. A typical analysis is shown in figure 20.7. As with all sales analyses, channel of distribution analysis provides insight into what has occurred. For the firm in figure 20.7, a shift in sales from the more direct channels to the indirect channels has occurred. The shift may have been part of the marketing strategy, or it may have developed from other sources. With the information in figure 20.7, the marketing manager would investigate further to determine the reason behind the shift.

❏ **Figure 20.6**
A product sales
analysis within a
product line for Quaker
Oats' cold cereal
products (in millions).

Source: John C. Maxwell, Jr.,
"Cereals Report Crisp Gains,"
Advertising Age, September 28,
1987, p. 88.

Quaker Oats Cold Cereal Share of Market in Pounds and Dollars						
Brand	1984		1985		1986	
Cap'n Crunch	2.7 lbs.	$3.2	2.6 lbs.	$3.1	2.6 lbs.	$3.1
Life	2.4	2.2	2.0	1.9	1.8	1.7
100% Natural	1.5	1.4	1.5	1.4	1.3	1.2
Corn Bran	0.8	0.6	0.6	0.6	0.6	0.6
Oh's	—	—	—	—	0.5	0.6
Halfsies	0.2	0.3	—	—	—	—
Others	0.9	0.9	0.6	0.7	0.3	0.2
Total	8.5 lbs.	$8.6	7.3 lbs.	$7.7	7.1 lbs.	$7.4

❑ **Figure 20.7**
A sales analysis for
channels of distribution
($ in millions).

CHANNELS OF DISTRIBUTION (In millions)				
Channel	1988		1989	
	Sales	% of total sales	Sales	% of total sales
National Accounts	$518	24.2%	$512	21.8%
Retail Distribution	632	29.5	536	22.9
Wholesale Distribution	953	44.5	1240	52.9
Broker Distribution	38	1.8	56	2.4
Total	$2141	100%	$2344	100%

Customer segment sales analysis helps answer the question, "Who is buying and using the company's products?" Often a relationship exists between the type of distribution channel and the market segment since a particular channel tends to serve specific markets.

MARKET SHARE ANALYSIS

*M*arket share is a competitive measure.

Few marketing executives are comfortable comparing performance only with the previous year's results. Knowing how the organization is performing in relation to competitors provides another desirable type of measurement. A marketer may think that sales potential exists at a certain level but may lack the resources or ability to prove the potential. On the other hand, competitors' actual sales are usually considered hard evidence. Thus, the objective of **market share analysis** is to ascertain how the firm is performing compared to other firms in the industry.

An organization's market share is calculated by dividing organization sales by industry sales. The formula is deceptively simple.

$$\text{Market Share} = \frac{\text{Organization's Sales}}{\text{Industry's Sales}}$$

To determine market share correctly, the time period has to be established. The time period makes a difference in that natural fluctuations in the organization's sales may not coincide with fluctuations in industry sales. Annual market share is the most common method of measurement, but quarterly and monthly market share figures are also calculated in large industries such as the auto industry. In addition, the industry has to be carefully defined. Again with autos, the industry could be viewed as foreign and domestic, domestic only, subcompacts, compacts, medium size, full size, or all sizes. The more narrowly the industry is defined, the larger the organization's market share.

*T*o increase sales, increase market share or increase the total market.

Figure 20.8 illustrates market share data in the U.S. wine market. A marketing executive probably would make the general observation that total U.S. market growth has been less than 3.6 percent. How does this percentage of growth compare with other years? How does it compare with beer and other alcoholic beverages? If the increase in total market growth is unusually low or high, the marketer would then turn to market analysis to determine why. Perhaps the number of people in the prime wine drinking age is declining. With the total market growing less than 3.6 percent annually, increases in a firm's volume will have to result from taking sales from competitors.

The growth in domestic wine sales has increased while import sales have decreased. Why the better performance by domestic wines? Is it a better image? Better distribution? Better price? Again, further examination is necessary. During the period under examination, the value of the dollar had declined, thereby making domestic wines inexpensive.

E&J Gallo accounts for one-fourth of the total U.S. wine market, and its share is increasing. Is this evidence of marketing strategy that is working? Heublein has

❑ **Figure 20.8**
U.S. wine market: Top
ten companies (in
millions of gallons).

	Top Ten Companies (Sales in Millions of Gallons)		
	1984	1985	1986
E & J Gallo	142.0 gal.	152.5 gal.	168.8 gal.
Vinters Int'l	49.9	57.0	62.0
Canandaigua	19.5	31.0	45.0
Almaden	25.9	23.8	24.3
Heublein	21.5	20.8	20.3
Franzia	14.3	16.2	18.6
Monarch	13.0	13.2	13.5
Guild	10.5	9.7	11.1
Sebastiani	6.0	6.6	5.2
Lamoni	3.6	3.7	5.1
Total Domestic	412.0 74.3%	441.0 76.3%	486.3 81.7%
Imports	142.4 25.7%	136.7 23.7%	108.7 18.3%
Total	554.4 100%	577.7 100%	595.0 100%

Average annual % growth 595−554.4/2=3.6%

Source: John C. Maxwell, Jr.,
"Wine Industry Stays Cool,"
Advertising Age, May 25, 1987,
p. 50.

lost market share in each of the years shown. Is this evidence of a marketing strategy that should be carefully reexamined?

MARKET SHARE, BREAK-EVEN ANALYSIS AND POTENTIAL STRATEGY CHANGES

Market share information is frequently combined with *break-even analysis* to assess the practicality of potential strategy changes. Frequently, a strategy change involves a change in cost; thus a break-even analysis will be calculated to assess the effect of the strategy change on the break-even point. The new break-even point is then compared to market share. To illustrate, suppose that Monarch Company executives in figure 20.8 were considering a new strategy. They calculate the break-even analysis of the new strategy and find that in order to reach the break-even point, Monarch's market share would need to be 5 percent. However, with a current market share of 2.3 percent, an increase to 5 percent is unlikely.

THE CASE CONTINUES

*F*airly strong evidence exists that P&G uses attitude tracking, sales analysis, and market share analysis in an overall market analysis system. The new versions of Pampers, for instance, were based on criteria that parents said were important in the purchase of diapers. P&G operates a consumer hotline. In the area of sales analysis, P&G executives seem to possess data on sales of Pampers, Luvs, Liquid Tide, and other P&G products—sales analysis by product. The use of regional managers means that P&G can also analyze sales by geographic area. All the references to market share made in the case tell us that P&G executives analyze market share statistics.

Marketing Cost Analysis

*M*anagers have to spend money effectively and efficiently in order to make money.

Executives of any type of organization—profit, nonprofit, industrial, consumer, service, or product—should think in terms of resource expenditure as well as sales. To generate sales, resources have to be expended. Have these resources produced a net gain for the organization?

Figure 20.9
Natural and functional
cost accounts of
Harvest, Inc.

Harvest, Inc.				
Natural Account	Functional Accounts			
Promotion	Personal Selling	Publicity	Advertising	Sales Promotion
$1,125,000	$500,000	$125,000	$400,000	$100,000

Figure 20.9
Natural and functional
cost accounts of
Harvest, Inc.

Cost analysis focuses on the income statement to determine if the organization gained from its expenditure of resources.[4] A part of cost analysis is the classification of cost from natural to functional accounts.

NATURAL AND FUNCTIONAL COST ACCOUNTS

Functional cost accounts identify specific reasons for expenditures.

Accounting records are usually maintained in **natural cost accounts**—a general classification of expenditures, such as rent, salaries, promotion, and supplies. Although natural accounts serve the accountant very well in showing the big picture without distracting detail, they fail to serve the marketer as well. A marketer needs more detail to analyze cost adequately. **Functional cost accounts** classify costs more specifically according to the reasons for which the expenditures were made. (See figure 20.9.)

Each functional account can be broken down into even smaller accounts, the purpose being to increase the manager's understanding of the company's operation. Typically, breakdowns are made on the basis of product, geographic area, and customer type. Figure 20.10 presents some of the functional breakdown for Harvest, Inc.

COST DISTRIBUTION

The marketer classifying cost has two tasks. The first task is to identify meaningful categories. For instance, customer types may be chosen, as illustrated in figure 20.10: consumer/industrial, large/small, frequent purchase/infrequent purchase, and so forth. Trade associations sometimes design categories that are useful because they allow a company to compare its results with the industry.

Cost may be assigned on a proportional basis.

The second task is distribution of cost to the various cost categories. Direct costs, the easiest to categorize, are obviously attributable to the performance of the marketing function. All the illustrations in figure 20.11 represent direct cost. Traceable common costs are costs that are associated with the marketing function but that

Figure 20.10
Typical functional cost
accounts of Harvest,
Inc.

Harvest, Inc.					
Product					
Advertising $450,000		Model 1546 $150,000	Model 1550 $250,000		Model 1554 $50,000
Geographic District					
Personal Selling $500,000	District I $175,000	District II $200,000	District III $75,000		District IV $50,000
Media					
Advertising $400,000	Radio $130,000	Television —	Direct Mail $225,000	Magazine —	Newspaper $45,000
Customer Type					
Sales Promotion $100,000	=	Consumer $40,000	+		Industrial $60,000

☐ **Figure 20.11**
Full cost approach of
Harvest, Inc.

Harvest, Inc.		
	Product A	Product B
Sales	$1,500,000	$2,000,000
Cost of Goods	1,000,000	1,400,000
Gross Margin	500,000	600,000
Direct Marketing and Other Variable Marketing Cost	200,000	300,000
Contribution Margin	300,000	300,000
Fixed (Overhead) Cost	220,000	280,000
Net Profit	80,000	20,000

have to be assigned to categories by an indirect technique since they are common to all categories but specific to none. Many bases for distributing traceable common costs exist, such as ton miles, square feet, cubic feet, kilowatt hours, and miles. Transportation costs, for instance, could be distributed to product categories based on ton miles (one ton of product shipped one mile).

Transportation Cost for the Year $ 560,000
Total Ton Miles   3,000,000
Product A Ton Miles   600,000

$$\frac{600,000}{3,000,000} = 20\% \text{ of Total Ton Miles Attributed to Product A}$$

Transportation Charged to Product A
$20\% \times 560,000 = \$112,000$

Nontraceable common costs, however, cannot be assigned using logical criteria.

COST ANALYSIS AND THE INCOME STATEMENT

What has been the contribution of a product, division, and so forth, to an organization's overall objectives? One technique for assessing the contribution is the income statement. When the manager considers only traceable costs on the income statement, the technique is referred to as the **contribution-margin approach.** (See figure 20.12.) The resulting income statement is incomplete in that nontraceable costs do not appear. The resulting contribution figure is the amount that can be applied to covering nontraceable cost and planned profit.

*C*ontribution margin =
revenue − traceable cost

The **full-cost approach** requires that *all* costs be assigned. The bottom line on the income statement is net profit (or loss). The full-cost approach, also known as the profit-center approach, must be used when management wants to evaluate each center in terms of net profit. Figure 20.12 illustrates the additions necessary to the contribution-margin approach to arrive at the full-cost approach. In the figure the contribution margin of products A and B are equal. However, product A is more profitable. The difference is obviously due to the difference in assigned nontraceable costs (overhead costs). Many arguments grow out of overhead cost assignments. The

☐ **Figure 20.12**
Contribution margin.

	Product A	Product B
Sales	$1,500,000	$2,000,000
Cost of Goods	1,000,000	1,400,000
Gross Margin	500,000	600,000
Traceable Cost	200,000	300,000
Contribution Margin	300,000	300,000

executive responsible for product B (figure 20.12) would probably argue that overhead costs are not within his or her control and therefore should not be included in the evaluation or should be divided equally between products A and B.

Both the contribution-margin approach and the full-cost approach appear to emphasize the short run—a year or less. American managers have been criticized for paying too much attention to short-run profits and neglecting the long-run development of their organizations. Profits, in the short run, should be considered in control, but not to the detriment of the long-run development of the organization.

*E*valuation should encompass both short- and long-run contributions to objectives.

Benefit/Efficiency Analysis

The organization's resources may produce a net benefit for the organization—but how efficiently? Were resources as productive as possible? **Benefit/efficiency analysis** attempts to determine how efficiently resources have been deployed. Two common benefit/efficiency techniques are ROI and ratio analysis.

RETURN-ON-INVESTMENT (ROI)

The dollar amount of net profit a firm generates may be the first step in arriving at how well the firm actually performed. Dollar amounts, however, can be misleading. For instance, if someone told you that you could make $50,000 a year, you'd probably be excited. However, if the method involved investing $1 million at a 5 percent annual interest rate, your excitement would quickly disappear. **Return-on-investment (ROI)** allows the company executives to decide whether they should continue to be excited about net dollar profits.

ROI represents a measure of net profit per dollar invested. A simplified equation to calculate ROI is:

$$\frac{\text{Net Profit}}{\text{Investment}} = \text{ROI}$$

*R*OI is a measure of the efficient use of invested money.

Whether ROI has been calculated before or after taxes should be stated. Either is correct. Before-tax calculation perhaps provides a better reading since it is less affected by tax law changes. Still, after-tax ROI may be more important to investors.

RATIO ANALYSIS

*P*ercentage trend analysis shows how costs are changing over time.

Percentage Analysis.   Several valuable relationships for evaluation derive from the income statement. Sales are the reference point (the base) in a **percentage analysis.** Figure 20.13 demonstrates common percentages a marketing manager would consider.

In figure 20.13 the gross margin percentage of 31.43 percent means that thirty-one cents out of every dollar sold is used to pay expenses and meet profit objectives. As the gross margin percentage becomes smaller and smaller, the firm will find it

❑ **Figure 20.13**
Percentage analysis of Harvest, Inc.

Harvest, Inc.			
Sales	$3,500,000	100%	
Cost of Goods	2,400,000	68.57	
Gross Margin	1,100,000	31.43	(1)
Selling Expenses	500,000	14.29 ⎱	(2)
		⎰ 28.58%	
Other Operating Expenses	500,000	14.29 ⎰	(3)
Net Profit	100,000	2.86	(4)

more difficult to pay expenses and meet profit objectives. Therefore, management desires to maintain or increase the gross margin percentage.

The selling expense ratio indicates the percentage of each sales dollar necessary to pay selling expenses—advertising, personal selling, and other marketing expenses. It is found by dividing selling expenses by sales. Each identifiable selling expense can be broken out for further percentage examination. Lumping all expenses together and dividing by sales results in the operating ratio. For Harvest, Inc., the percentage is 28.58 percent.

$$Productivity = \frac{Output}{Input}$$

Productivity. **Productivity** measures the relationship between output (results) and input (resources). For each unit of input, how many units of output were obtained? Productivity, therefore, requires that output be divided by input. In the percentage ratios already discussed, costs (input) were divided by sales (outputs). Many possible productivity ratios, such as number of customer complaints per salesperson, sales volume per advertising dollar, dollar sales per sales call, completed interviews per research interviewer, and dollar sales per inquiry, are valuable to the marketer.

THE CASE CONTINUES

The desire to improve efficiency at P&G seems to be stronger now than in the past. Competitive pressures have apparently reduced margins by forcing P&G's volume and price down. P&G executives, to improve margins, are working on restoring volume and price, but are also attempting to improve efficiency. Cost-

reduction committees made up of both executives and other personnel have been formed to resolve these problems.

The method used to evaluate products such as Pampers at P&G

should provide data on whether the product is making an adequate contribution. P&G probably uses both the contribution-margin approach and full-cost approach to evaluate products. For instance, diapers have typically accounted for 20 percent of P&G's profit. Any amount less than 20 percent would be disappointing.

 MARKETING AUDIT

The marketing audit is a detailed evaluation of marketing in the organization.

A **marketing audit,** the ultimate control system in marketing, is a systematic, unbiased examination of an organization's marketing philosophy, programs, and results. The entire marketing operation is studied in a marketing audit. This includes problem, potential problem, and nonproblem areas.

Auditors should develop an audit plan and follow it carefully throughout the audit.[5] In conducting a marketing audit, the auditor often starts by formulating a series of questions about each area included in the audit.[6] Figure 20.14 lists focal areas of the marketing audit within which questions can be formulated. By carefully developing a set of questions, the auditor will cover every aspect of the organization's marketing operation. By obtaining answers to the questions, the auditor secures numerical and evaluative information. Such data, when properly organized, presents both a detailed and overall picture of marketing as employed by the organization. The information should also suggest possible changes.

Audits may cover all areas of an organization's marketing operation in detail, or focus on specific areas. Typical areas considered in audits are shown in figure 20.14.

❏ **Figure 20.14**
Focal points of a
marketing audit.

A. Facts About the General Environment
1. Technology
2. Political-Legal
3. Sociocultural
4. Economic-Demographic

B. Facts About the Market
1. Trends
2. Competition
3. Industry Practices

C. Facts About the Purchaser/Consumer
1. Interest in Product/Service
2. Who Motivates, Who Makes Purchases
3. Brand Awareness
4. Frequency of Purchase/Use
5. Product/Service Characteristics Liked—Disliked

D. Facts About Supply and Distribution
1. Main Trade Channels Customers Use
2. Trends and Efficiencies in Trade Channels
3. Main Supply Channels
4. Trends and Efficiencies in Supply Channels
5. Firms that Facilitate Supply and Distribution
(transportation, advertising, etc.)

E. Facts About the Organization/Company
1. Formal Organizational Structure
2. Skills and Knowledge Pool
3. Financial Resource Pool
4. Interface Between Divisions and Departments

F. Facts About Marketing Strategy
1. Marketing Objectives—What Are They, Are They
Appropriate
2. Strategy—What Is It, Does Firm Have Resources to
Implement

G. Facts About Marketing Systems
1. Marketing Information Systems, Marketing Research,
Marketing Intelligence
2. Marketing Planning System
3. Marketing Organization Systems
4. Marketing Control Systems

H. Facts About Marketing Efficiency
1. Profitability Analysis
2. Productivity Analysis
3. Cost Analysis

I. Facts About Marketing Functions and Subfunctions
1. Product
2. Price
3. Distribution
4. Promotion: Personal Selling, Advertising

J. Facts About Competition
1. Number of Competitors
2. Strengths and Weaknesses of Competitors
3. Trends in Competitive Environment

Who Should Conduct the Audit?

*A*uditors should have
enough time to do the job,
and they should be
objective.

Self-audits, conducted by an organization's marketing executives, have the advantage that the executive is familiar with the marketing operation and can complete the audit more quickly. However, the executive's bias might influence the results of the audit. To avoid this, other executives, who should be less biased, could conduct the audit. In either case the responsibility of conducting an audit would infringe on the executives' other responsibilities.

To obtain even more objectivity in the audit, outside auditors can be used. Outsiders may require more time to familiarize themselves with the marketing operation, but they often specialize in conducting audits and are thus more efficient because of their expertise.

When to Conduct an Audit

*U*ndertake audits when high energy levels, time, and employee trust exist.

Executives often wait to conduct a marketing audit until the marketing operation is saddled with problems and is under stress from not achieving its objectives. However, times of stress generate mistrust in employees, demand attention, and command energy. Successful audits also require these elements. A marketing audit cannot be successful when competing with other problems. Regularly scheduled audits, when the organization has the resources to devote to the process, produce good results.

Marketing Control and Evaluation

Perhaps the real lesson to be learned from the brief review of marketing control processes in this chapter is that many methods exist and that none of them are flawless, just as no single perfect measurement of performance exists. This should not leave a feeling of frustration but an awareness that control needs to be carried out using more than one method or measurement.

THE CASE CONTINUES

*N*o mention is made of P&G's having conducted a marketing audit. The size of P&G's operation, however, would support a full-time marketing audit department. Outside auditors employed periodically would provide a different perspective on P&G's operation. In view of the diversity and competitiveness of the markets in which P&G operates, frequent audits would seem warranted. In the most competitive markets, perhaps audits performed even as frequently as annually or biannually might be justified. Information that P&G executives seem to have at their disposal—market size, company strengths and weaknesses, and distribution channel changes—are typical products of a marketing audit.

GOAL SUMMARY

1. **Identify and briefly describe the major elements of a marketing control system.** Marketing control systems have five elements: identifying standards, measurement of results, evaluation/comparison, corrective action, and monitoring the environment. Standards should be established as a part of the strategy, plan, or policy. (If standards are not stated, they have to be identified.) Measurement of results requires that what has been done must be quantified. Measurement is much easier if standards are stated in quantifiable terms. Comparison of results and standards highlight deviations that may require corrective action. The control system requires constant monitoring of the environment. (Environmental factors influence results.)

2. **Describe the objectives of each: attitude tracking, sales analysis, and market-share analysis.** The objective of attitude tracking is to keep abreast of market opinion concerning the organization's products or quality of service, and the organization itself. Sales analysis should uncover where a company's sales originate: by product characteristics, geographic region, etc. Information about the origin of sales combined with potential sales allows assessment of how well the market is served. Market-share analysis provides information on the firm compared to other firms in the same industry.

3. **Distinguish between natural and functional cost accounts and between contribution-margin and full-cost analysis.** Natural cost accounts are more

GOALS SUMMARY *(continued)*

general accounts that accountants use to obtain an overall view of an organization's operation. Functional accounts break down natural accounts into categories based on why the expenditures were made. The categories are frequently based on product, geographic area, and distribution channel. Functional accounts provide the marketer with the more detailed information needed to make marketing decisions. The contribution-margin approach considers only traceable cost in the evaluation. The full-cost approach considers all costs, traceable and non-

traceable. Profit is the bottom line.

4. **Identify the fundamental concept of efficiency analysis.** ROI, ratio analysis, percentage analysis, and productivity are all types of efficiency analysis. All are based on analysis from a per-unit perspective. Productivity, for instance, is calculated on the basis of output per unit of input.

5. **Explain what a marketing audit is.** A marketing audit is a detailed, systematic, unbiased study of marketing in an organization.

KEY TERMS

Standards, **p. 554**
Effectiveness Standards, **p. 556**
Efficiency Standards, **p. 556**
Iceberg Principle, **p. 556**
Performance Index, **p. 556**
Contingency Plans, **p. 558**
Attitude Tracking, **p. 558**
Sales Analysis, **p. 559**
Geographic Sales Analysis, **p. 559**
Product Sales Analysis, **p. 560**
Channel of Distribution Sales Analysis, **p. 560**
Customer Segment Sales Analysis, **p. 561**

Market Share Analysis, **p. 561**
Natural Cost Accounts, **p. 563**
Functional Cost Accounts, **p. 563**
Contribution-Margin Approach, **p. 564**
Full-Cost Approach, **p. 564**
Benefit/Efficiency Analysis, **p. 565**
Return-on-Investment (ROI), **p. 565**
Percentage Analysis, **p. 565**
Productivity, **p. 566**
Marketing Audit, **p. 566**

CHECK YOUR LEARNING

1. Performance indices make comparison easier because individual statistics are converted to a base of 100 by dividing the individual statistic by the mean. **T/F**

2. Attitude tracking provides quicker feedback to an organization than sales figures. **T/F**

3. Attitude tracking provides general information about changes in the market but lacks detail about reasons for changes. **T/F**

4. Sales analysis breaks down general sales into parts, giving the marketer information on the sources and changes in sales. **T/F**

5. Sales analysis by channel, although intended to give information on the performance of each channel, may reflect changes in markets, prices, and other causes. **T/F**

6. Sales analysis is (a) always carried out on a customer basis, (b) intended to provide information on the sources and changes of sales, (c) easily completed even if dollar amounts of sales is the only information recorded, (d) all of the above, (e) none of the above.

7. Natural cost accounts classify costs according to the reason for which the expenditure was made. **T/F**

8. The marketing manager has control over direct and indirect cost. **T/F**

9. Advocates of the full-cost approach essentially believe that ultimately the bottom line must be positive, regardless of the size of the contribution margin. **T/F**

10. The gross margin percentage is calculated by dividing gross margin by cost of goods sold. **T/F**

11. The marketing audit assesses marketing philosophy as well as market size, product image, and other factors. **T/F**

12. Listing questions about areas to be covered is an approach often used in conducting an audit. **T/F**

13. By definition marketing audits are comprehensive and always cover all areas of an organization's marketing operation. **T/F**

14. The best time to conduct a marketing audit is when the organization has failed to achieve objectives and generally is having problems. **T/F**

QUESTIONS FOR REVIEW AND DISCUSSION

1. Define the key terms for this chapter that appear at the end of the goal summary.
2. Discuss the relationship between standards of performance and actual performance.
3. Identify the marketing standards at the college in which you are enrolled. Categorize each as either an ideal or a comparative standard. The college public relations office or press relations office can be of help in identifying the standards.
4. Explain how you would measure the results of a local retailer's advertising program.
5. What is the iceberg principle?
6. Given the following information, develop a performance index.

	Sales	Cost
Division I	$450,000	$200,000
Division II	700,000	450,000
Division III	625,000	400,000

7. Comment on the statement: "A good manager does not need contingency plans."
8. Try to find a restaurant that uses response or comment cards. Take one of the cards and analyze it. What attitudes is management tracking?
9. From current publications, find information on a company's market share. Analyze the commentary about the market share. Has the market share increased or decreased? Why?
10. In examining an organization's records, you see an account labeled "rent." Is this a natural or a functional account?
11. Which approach do you think is best, contribution-margin or full-cost? Why?
12. Obtain an organization's annual income statement. Calculate the net profit percentage, cost of goods sold, and gross margin.
13. Marketing audits should be conducted semiannually by each organization's marketing executives. Comment.

NOTES

1. *Perspectives of Corporate Strategy.* (Boston: The Boston Consulting Group, 1968), p. 42.
2. Subhash Sharma and Dale D. Achobal, "STEM-COM: An Analytical Model for Marketing Control," *Journal of Marketing* 46 (Spring 1982): pp. 104–113.
3. J. Irwin Peters and Robert O'Keefe, "Marketing and Customer Analysis for Sales Management," *The Journal of Personal Selling and Sales Management* (Spring–Summer 1981): pp. 44–48; Ed Weymes, "A Different Approach to Retail Sales Analysis," *Business Horizons* (March–April 1982): pp. 66–74.
4. Patrick M. Dunne and Harry E. Walk, "Marketing Cost Analysis: A Modularized Contribution Approach," *Journal of Marketing* (July 1977): pp. 83–94.
5. Alice M. Tybout and John R. Hauser, "A Marketing Audit Using a Conceptual Model of Consumer Behavior: Application and Evaluation," *Journal of Marketing* (Summer 1981): pp. 82–101.
6. Hal W. Goetsch, "Marketing Audit Questions," *Marketing News,* March 18, 1983, Section 1, p. 14.

*E*astern Airlines, like other airlines, has had its share of problems since the industry was deregulated in 1982. In 1982 and 1983, the company experienced considerably more losses than profits. For instance, in 1982 Eastern's revenues reached $3.8 billion, but the company was in the red.

In early 1983, Eastern faced stiff competition, had labor union problems, faced accusations of using little marketing, and had a huge debt. Eastern's sales growth lagged behind the industry average, and bankruptcy seemed a distinct possibility. Still, CEO Frank Borman remained optimistic about the airline's future. Eastern's executives had forecast 1983 revenues to grow by 9 percent, and for 1984 by 18 percent, while industry analysts predicted 6 percent and 10 percent respectively. Eastern's managers had been criticized for excessive focus on the long term; airplanes were still being added to the fleet even though the company was plagued with excess passenger capacity. According to many critics, not enough attention was being paid to quarterly earnings.

At that time, Eastern's strategy was simple—cut costs and increase yield. Here, yield is the average price per mile the customer is charged. If Eastern could have boosted yield by just one-tenth of a cent, revenue would have increased by $26 million. If the number of miles per passenger flying increased by just one percentage point, revenue would have

increased by $40 million. Marketing efforts were to help in establishing both. A Kansas City hub was to be established. Eastern managers badly wanted to stop reacting to competitors' activities and develop a marketing plan.

Two years later, in the spring of 1985, Eastern had made some changes. Frank Borman had reorganized Eastern to make it more responsive to changes in the marketplace. Labor union problems had lessened. The new hub at Kansas City was established. Losses at the Houston Hub had been reduced by cutting flights. Eastern had also met competition from People Express by pricing its full service New York-to-Florida routes only a few dollars above People's no-frill flights.

In 1986, Eastern lost money. When the International Association of Machinists (IAM) refused to accept pay cuts for its pilots and flight attendants to avoid a takeover, Eastern was acquired by Texas Air. Frank Borman was replaced by acting CEO Joseph Leonard who froze expansion plans and launched a drive to slash operating costs by a minimum of $100 million annually. Revenue collected per passenger mile dropped 12 percent. The drop was attributed to fare wars and public fears of a possible strike, and concerns about the possible collapse of the company.

In 1988 the Federal Aviation Administration (FAA) undertook a safety inspection of Eastern equipment. Soon thereafter, Eastern filed a $1.5 billion lawsuit against its own pilots and machinists, charging that they had deliberately tried to drive the value of Eastern down in order to purchase it themselves. Rumors flew about a Chapter 11 bankruptcy reorganization that would move Eastern's assets to Texas Air.

Issues for Discussion

1. In the last years of Borman's regime, what approach might management have taken for monitoring the effects of its efficiency reorganizations, or the effects of competitive fare cuts? What kinds of criteria and what kinds of data would be used?
2. After the Texas Air takeover, and following the new regime's cost-cutting drive, what approach might management have taken to analyze relationships between the 12 percent revenue drop that occurred and the possible contributing factors—for example, fare wars, strike or bankruptcy fears, or perceived service drop due to cost cuts?

Sources: Jo Ellen Davis and Pete Engardio, "Showdown Time at Eastern," *Business Week,* February 8, 1988, pp. 20–21; Pete Engardio, "Why Eastern is Backing Off from a Union Showdown," *Business Week,* October 12, 1987, pp. 108–109; and Pete Engardio, "Is Eastern Giving Lorenzo a Lesson in Cost Cutting?" *Business Week,* August 18, 1986, pp. 38–39.

MARKETING PLAN

PART 7 / BUDGETS, CONTROL, AND ACCOUNTABILITY (CHAPTER 20)

A. For your product or service, review
   1. What is to be accomplished and how much will it cost?
   2. Who will do it?
   3. How will it be done, and by when? (Often, this section of the marketing plan is presented in table form.)
B. How will results be measured? (Think about sales analysis, market share analysis, and cost analysis, etc.) What information is needed for comparison of actual and planned results?
C. Who will be responsible for monitoring and controlling the marketing plan? Who is accountable for significant deviations from the plan?

PART 1 / EXECUTIVE SUMMARY

As noted, the executive summary is written after the rest of the marketing plan has been completed. It appears first in the marketing plan and serves as a summary for top-level management. The summary should present an overview of the main points and highlights of the plan and should be one to two pages.

A. Identify the executive(s) to which the marketing plan will be submitted.
B. Is the relationship between the organization's mission, objectives, and strategy and the marketing plan clearly expressed?
C. Does the summary emphasize an action orientation?

Section
Nine

The Broader
Marketing
Perspective

OUTLINE

CHAPTER

21

International Marketing

LEARNING GOALS_____

After reading this chapter, you should be able to:

1. Explain why international marketing is important to the U.S. economy.
2. Discuss factors a firm must evaluate when operating in an international marketing environment.
3. Explain why protectionism is a barrier to international marketing efforts.
4. Compare the available alternatives for organizing an international marketing effort.
5. Modify a marketing plan for an existing good or service to be exported to an international market.
6. Identify the decision-making steps for determining whether to engage in international marketing.

The H. J. Heinz Company has operated abroad since 1905. Its international sales in 1987 accounted for more than one-third of its total $4.6 billion sales. Historically, Heinz soups, ketchup, and other food products have been marketed in Great Britain, Australia, New Zealand, and a few other nations, mostly in Europe.

While maintaining a 50 percent domestic share for ketchup sales in retail stores and 60 percent in restaurants, Heinz also produces over 3500 other products. In Great Britain, the Heinz brand is so strong that most people believe it is a British company. Of course, Heinz is the source of such British delicacies as "beans on toast" and "spaghetti on toast." Soup is also popular in Great Britain, where Heinz held a 65 percent market share. Approximately 14 percent of Heinz's total revenues are from Great Britain. Until 1969, Heinz made twice as much money overseas as it did in the United States.

Heinz was founded in 1869 by Henry J. Heinz, the first of nine children born to two German immigrants. In that year Heinz formed a partnership with a friend to sell food in bottles. The company, which made horseradish, sauerkraut, pickles, and vinegar, went bankrupt in 1875. Heinz then started a new company and made a priority of repaying his previous debts. By 1900, Heinz was one of the nation's top businesses. It was number one in pickles, ketchup, mustard, and vinegar. In total, Heinz made over 200 products. After building one of America's premier businesses, Heinz died in 1917 at age seventy-five.

Today, led by an Irish chairman, Anthony J. F. O'Reilly, Heinz is expanding its operations into the less-developed nations of Africa, Latin America, and Asia. O'Reilly states, "Much of our planning stems from an awareness that we serve only 15 percent of the world's population. There's huge potential to expand our markets to the remaining 85 percent."

Issues for Discussion

1. What types of risks will Heinz incur by seeking new markets in less-developed nations?

2. Do you think there is an Asian market for Heinz's best-selling ketchup? How would you market this product in Korea?

3. Do you think a goal of $1 billion in sales from Third World nations by 1990 is unrealistic? Explain your answer.

Sources: Based on *H. J. Heinz Annual Report,* 1987; Carol Hymorvity, "Heinz Sets Out to Expand in Africa and Asia, Seeking New Markets, Sources of Materials," *The Wall Street Journal,* September 27, 1983, p. 35; Bill Saporito, "Heinz Pushes to Be the Low-Cost Producer," *Fortune,* June 24, 1985, pp. 44–54; and Julia Michaels, "Heinz Reveals Third World Plan," *Advertising Age,* June 16, 1986, p. 59.

■ "Beans on toast" is a popular British delicacy that is provided by Heinz products.
Source: Courtesy of the Heinz Company

The H. J. Heinz Company exports Heinz food products around the world and imports many raw food materials to make its successful products. Like many manufacturers, Heinz has decided to expand its international markets to include Asia, Latin America, and Africa. This chapter explains why it is important that companies like Heinz attempt to market their goods and services overseas. It also describes the process by which a company determines whether—and how—to market internationally. After evaluating the economic, sociocultural, political-legal, technological, and competitive environments, the company decides whether to enter a foreign market. It must then decide how to enter—through exporting, joint venture, licensing, contract manufacturing, or direct investment. The marketing plan may require changes to suit the new marketing environment. Finally, the plan must be implemented. ■

 ## THE IMPORTANCE OF INTERNATIONAL MARKETING

*I*nternational trade is of increasing importance to the United States.

The marketing of American goods and services internationally is of increasing importance to the U.S. economy. Each year more and more U.S. companies are trading with foreign nations. This exchange of products among nations is called **international trade.** The marketing activities performed to facilitate this trade are called **international marketing.** Once a minor element in this country's economy, international trade now plays a major role. Between 1960 and 1980, imports plus exports rose from 10 percent of the GNP to 24 percent.[1] However, by 1987 this figure declined to 14 percent as a result of decreased exporting. Figure 21.1 illustrates the U.S. trade deficit, 1980–1990.

A major concern for any nation that engages in international trade is its **balance of payments,** which represents the difference between the expenditures made to foreign nations and the receipts taken in from foreign nations during a given time. This balance of payments consists of eight major categories. Three are receipts (inflows) and five are expenditures (outflows). Inflows include receipts from exports, entering tourists, and investment income. Outflows include expenditures for imports, exiting tourists, foreign investments, foreign aid, and military expenditures.

❏ **Figure 21.1**
U.S. trade deficit (in billions of dollars)

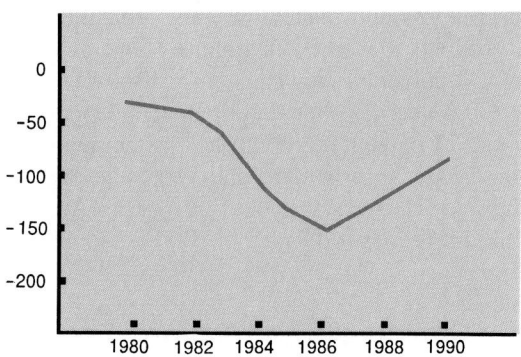

A little over a decade ago, the trade balance was virtually even. By 1987 the plunging U.S. trade deficit had reached $171.2 billion. The current shrinking trade gap could prove to b e atrend or a two-year blip. The outcome depends on future policies developed by major industrial nations, including the U.S.

☐ **Table 21.1**   U.S. trading partners for 1986 (in billions of dollars).

COUNTRY	U.S. EXPORTS	U.S. IMPORTS
Canada	$141.4	$68.7
Japan	26.9	84.5
West Germany	10.6	26.1
United Kingdom	11.4	16.0
Mexico	12.4	17.6
China	5.1	5.2
South Korea	6.4	13.5

Recently Americans have focused on another balance: America's **balance of trade,** or the differences between its exports and imports. **Imports** are the goods and services purchased by a country from foreign countries, while **exports** are goods and services sold by a country to foreign countries. In 1971, although it was the world's leading exporter, the United States began to experience periodic trade deficits. By 1987 the U.S. trade deficit was $171 billion—more than 50 times the 1973 figure. Table 21.1 illustrates the U.S. trade picture with our major trading partners.

To finance the unprecedented trade deficit, U.S. firms borrowed heavily from abroad and made the United States a debtor nation in 1985 for the first time since 1914. In the short run, the transformation to a debtor nation has little impact. However, if trade deficits continue at the 1987 rate, the nation could be faced with a foreign debt so large that it could be paid only by sharply reducing the American standard of living.[2]

Fortunately, a restructuring of many U.S. businesses and a weakened dollar are leading a drive to strengthen American exports. Because the export revival is rooted in industry-by-industry overhauls (cheaper and leaner labor force, better equipment, and sounder management practices), the U.S. can now produce less expensive goods. This trend is expected to last through the early 1990s. Furthermore, small and midsized firms are suddenly finding that they can compete. In 1988, 39,000 American manufacturers—about one in ten—exported their goods. The top 250 U.S. multinational companies accounted for 85 percent of exports.[3]

On the brighter side, international marketing has brought us many high-quality, attractively priced goods. For example, the Japanese export several million cars to the United States each year. These cars provide us with a greater choice in our selection process and makes the U.S. auto industry more competitive. Other imported products we enjoy in quantity and at often less-expensive prices include clothing (30 percent), electronic goods (60 percent), shoes (84 percent), costume jewelry (30 percent), photo equipment (16 percent), bicycles (42 percent), power hand tools (27 percent), and musical instruments (28 percent).[4] The percentages in parentheses are approximate and represent the import as a percentage of U.S. consumption. Thus, as you can see, we as Americans have come to rely on the availability of these products.

Why Do Companies and Nations Engage in International Marketing?

A country achieves an absolute advantage when only it can supply a product or when it can produce the product at a lower cost than any other country.

Nations trade for a variety of reasons. Some trade because of the absolute advantage they enjoy. A country achieves an **absolute advantage** when it is the only country that provides a product or when it can produce the product at a lower cost than any other country. Hong Kong, for example, currently has an absolute advantage in producing many toys, because it can produce them at a lower cost than other countries. An absolute advantage can result from a nation's resources, labor, technology, or climate. Hong Kong receives its advantage from a cheap labor force. An absolute advantage can also result when a country enjoys a monopoly in the world market. The United States, for example, has an absolute advantage in oil drilling bits, because it is the only nation that produces this equipment. Even the Soviet Union has to purchase oil drilling bits from the United States, since it lacks the advanced technology needed to produce them. Theoretically, each nation should specialize in and export those products for which it has an absolute advantage and should import other products it needs.

Most nations, lacking an absolute trade advantage, develop a comparative advantage by specializing in products they can supply more efficiently than they could supply other products.

Few nations have absolute advantages. However, they can and do internationally market their products. These countries use their **comparative advantages;** they specialize in those products that they can supply more efficiently and at a lower cost than they could supply other items. Because the United States is a leader in technology and rich in resources, for example, it has a comparative advantage in the manufacturing of computers and other high-technology goods, automobiles, electrical machinery, aircraft, and weapons. However, comparative advantage is not constant. The United States has lost its comparative advantage in some manufacturing areas.

By concentrating on what they can do best, nations are better able to utilize their natural resources, technology, labor, and climate to produce more efficiently. Products in which a country enjoys an advantage will most likely be exported. On the other hand, nations are more likely to import the products in which they lack an absolute or comparative production advantage.

 ## MULTINATIONAL CORPORATIONS

Multinational corporations must have marketing strategies keyed to the world market.

Multinational corporations operate in several countries and often have a substantial share of their total assets, sales, or labor force in foreign subsidiaries. There is no stereotypical multinational corporation. These firms vary in size, philosophy, investments, motives, locality, and many other respects. However, corporations that engage in multinational trade must have production and marketing strategies keyed to the world market.

Sometimes, countries invite foreign companies to operate within their boundaries, providing that the companies agree to follow government regulations. Many multinationals began originally as exporters but later found themselves hampered by trade restrictions, foreign exchange problems, and high transportation costs. In order to compete, they eventually put down manufacturing roots in foreign countries. Manufacturing is often coordinated by a local management staff supervised by parent company officials.

As we face the questionable economic times of the 1990s, multinational corporations are expected to continue doing well because of their access to growing global markets. Corporations such as General Motors are confident that moves into foreign countries will yield long-range profits. One study indicated that more than a third of the profits earned by the top 100 U.S. multinationals came from overseas. Some companies with products in the maturity stage, such as Bristol-Meyers, Coca-Cola, and Polaroid, are finding real advantages in marketing internationally. Coca-Cola, selling in 155 countries, has obtained as much as 46 percent of its sales and 63 percent of its earnings from foreign countries. Increasing that amount is the company's main goal. Faced with domestic losses, Polaroid was recently able to show a narrow profit because of foreign sales growth.[5] Table 21.2 provides a list of the top ten U.S. exporters in 1987.

❑ **Table 21.2**   Top ten U.S. industrial exporters.

RANK 1986	RANK 1985	COMPANY	PRODUCTS	EXPORT SALES $ Thousands	EXPORT SALES Percent Change 1985–86	TOTAL SALES $ Thousands	TOTAL SALES Fortune 500 Rank	EXPORTS AS PERCENT OF SALES Percent	EXPORTS AS PERCENT OF SALES Rank
1	1	**General Motors** (Detroit)	Motor vehicles & parts, locomotives	8,366,100	−5.93	102,813,700	1	8.14	37
2	3	**Boeing** (Seattle)	Commercial & military aircraft	7,330,000	25.06	16,341,000	16	44.86	2
3	2	**Ford Motor** (Dearborn, Mich.)	Motor vehicles & parts	7,244,000	7.37	62,715,800	3	11.55	26
4	4	**General Electric** (Fairfield, Conn.)	Aircraft engines, medical systems	4,348,000	8.16	35,211,000	6	12.35	24
5	5	**International Business Machines** (Armonk, N.Y.)	Computers & related products	3,058,000	−12.30	51,250,000	4	5.97	45
6	8	**E.I. du Pont de Nemours** (Wilmington, Del.)	Specialty chemicals & energy products	2,960,000	14.95	27,148,000	9	10.90	28
7	6	**Chrysler** (Highland Park, Mich.)	Motor vehicles & parts	2,810,800	−5.61	22,513,500	11	12.48	23
8	7	**McDonnell Douglas** (St. Louis)	Aerospace & information systems	2,804,800	5.12	12,660,600	23	22.15	5
9	9	**United Technologies** (Hartford)	Jet engines, helicopters, cooling equip.	2,126,043	−0.05	15,669,157	17	13.57	20
10	11	**Eastman Kodak** (Rochester, N.Y.)	Photographic equipment & supplies	2,044,000	9.72	11,550,000	26	17.70	13

Source: From *Fortune,* July 20, 1987. © 1987 by *Time,* Inc. All rights reserved.

Marketing Foreign Products in the United States

Just as international marketing is profitable for American multinational corporations, it also pays other countries to manufacture or distribute in the United States. Foreign companies are not only investing in the United States, but they are seeking control of U.S. corporations. During the 1980s, foreign bids have been made to control F. W. Woolworth, National Steel, Foster Grant, Carnation, A&P, Firestone, CBS Records, Shell Oil, Peoples Drug, Inc., Federated Department Stores, and Marine Midland, among others.

In the United States, foreign multinational companies find a friendly environment in which to operate. This, in part, explains the successes of Honda, Panasonic, Sony, Unilever, Nestlé, and countless others. For example, the United States, unlike some other nations, does not require foreign multinationals to find domestic partners in order to operate. Nor does the United States limit the amount of profits that can be sent out of the country. Some companies, like Unilever, have captured large percentages of the market (20 to 25 percent in many categories). In one recent year, the United States accounted for 20 percent of Unilever sales.[6] It should be noted, however, that the U.S. Congress is considering legislation that would impose tough restrictions on U.S. trading partners who refuse to open their markets to U.S. goods.

Unilever products, sold through its U.S. subsidiary, Lever Brothers, account for 20 percent of the company's sales.

Source: Courtesy of Lever Brothers Company.

Marketing U.S. Products in International Markets

The decision for a U.S. company to become involved in international marketing is not an easy one. Many complex issues must be decided. This chapter examines the decision-making steps an organization must follow to resolve these issues. Figure 21.2 illustrates the decision-making process, which begins with an evaluation of international marketing environments. Once a decision has been made to sell in overseas markets, the company must organize its resources and develop its marketing plan. The final step is implementing the plan.

EVALUATING THE INTERNATIONAL MARKETING ENVIRONMENT

*M*ultinational companies must evaluate economic, sociocultural, political-legal, technological, and competitive international marketing environments.

When a company decides to consider the possibility of operating in an international market, it is essential that company personnel first thoroughly understand the marketing environment that exists in each country and among nations. The economic, sociocultural, political-legal, technological, and competitive environments must be examined.

❑ **Figure 21.2** Steps in international marketing decision making.

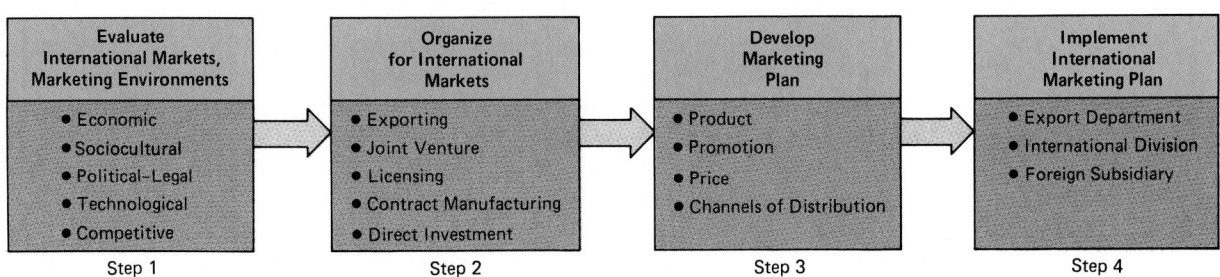

*I*n order to sell a product in some countries, it pays to take a creative approach to marketing. Coca-Cola discovered this fact quickly when attempting to expand its market for Coca-Cola into Yugoslavia.

In order to sell Coke, the company made a contract manufacturing arrangement with one of Yugoslavia's largest winemakers, Slovin. The deal was arranged so that Coca-Cola would export the Coke syrup and Slovin would bottle and market the product. Because Slovin lacked sufficient financial resources, they had to "pay" Coca-Cola in wine they made.

Unfortunately, there were only three problems with this proposal: Coca-Cola was stuck with a terrible wine, terrible bottle, and terrible label. Faced with these cold facts, Coca-Cola decided to use its advantages in manufacturing and marketing expertise to produce a better wine, that they could sell in the United States and in other global

THE REST OF THE STORY

Countertrade

markets. The company hired wine experts and changed the harvesting and manufacturing process of the

❑ Coca-Cola sold Avia wine in the United States in a countertrade move to sell Coke in Yugoslavia.

Yugoslavian wine. In addition, it renamed the wine Avia, after the last four letters of its country of origin. After Yugoslavian companies failed to come up with a high-quality label, an Italian firm was found to make one.

These efforts helped Coca-Cola sell 403,000 cases of Avia ($1.98 per bottle) in the United States. It made $25 million for Slovin, which in turn was able to use most of the money to pay Coca-Cola for the import of Coke. Thus, this unique countertrade deal had a happy ending for both companies.

Source: Adapted from Everett G. Marten and Thomas E. Ricks, "Countertrading Grows as Cash-Short Nations Seek Marketing Help," *The Wall Street Journal,* March 13, 1985, p. 1. Reprinted by permission of *The Wall Street Journal,* © Dow Jones & Company, Inc., 1985. All rights reserved.

Economic Environment

*S*tages of international economic development:
(1) underdeveloped,
(2) less-developed,
(3) developing,
(4) developed.

The economic environments of the world vary tremendously from one nation to another. Western nations offer the sophisticated marketplaces of London, Paris, and Montreal, whereas in countries such as Burma, Haiti, and Zaire people trade in street markets. How goods are distributed in a nation is just one factor in determining its level of economic development. Other factors include technology, literacy rate, population, income distribution, employment rates, and per capita income.

The least developed nations of the world are often described as **underdeveloped nations.** They frequently have economies based on the land and agriculture and are characterized by a low standard of living. Generally, these nations are not attractive to exporters. Examples include Nepal, Sudan, Guinea, and Bangladesh. Underdeveloped countries often engage in countertrade to avoid paying cash and thus minimize their debt burdens. **Countertrade** is a system of exchange that uses something other than money or credit as payment. Unfortunately, countertrade is often not enough to offset the high trade deficits and debts of these nations.

There are three types of countertrade: *barter, counterpurchase,* and *buyback.* Barter, the simplest form of countertrade, involves a buyer and a seller who exchange products directly, without dealing in currency or credit. In a counterpurchase, the supplier sells a plant or product for cash but agrees as a condition of the sale to enter into another contract with the customer to purchase unrelated products owned by the customer for cash to offset the cost to the buyer. A buyback occurs when, for instance, a seller builds a plant for a buyer and, under a separate agreement, agrees to buy some of the plant's output.[7]

The countertrade forms of barter, counterpurchasing, and buyback are seen most commonly in situations where buyers cannot or do not wish to pay cash for their purchases.

Until the early 1980s, countertrade was small in scale and was limited primarily to Eastern European foreign trade organizations. Third-World nations have recently joined the bandwagon with commodity trading. The U.S. Commerce Department estimates that 20 percent of world trade involves some form of countertrade (compared with 2 percent in 1975); however, estimates from other sources vary from 10 to 30 percent. Although most U.S. firms are not eager to engage in countertrade, many find it necessary in certain markets.

For example, 40 percent of East-West trade involves countertrade. The U.S.S.R. favors countertrade, which allows it to receive technology from the West, be guaranteed buyers for its products, and keep its currency in the Soviet Union. The accompanying feature provides an interesting commentary on countertrade and its effects on international marketing.

Less-developed nations, although characterized by unskilled labor and limited manufacturing, are often rich in one or more natural resources. Most of the revenues of such nations are generated by natural resource exports. For certain types of products, such as mining equipment, trucks, and related supplies, less-developed nations may offer excellent markets. Examples include Saudi Arabia (oil), Jamaica (bauxite), and Malaysia (rubber).

Brazil, Mexico, and South Korea are examples of **developing nations.** In these countries, the work force includes semiskilled and skilled labor. Developing nations are characterized by increased manufacturing and an upward shift in the population toward the middle and upper classes. As more and more businesses are successful, the need to export and import goods and services grows.

The United States, Japan, Canada, and most of the Western European nations are classified as **developed nations.** These countries engage in a complete variety of marketing activities. The exporting of manufactured goods, services, and investment funds are of major importance to the economies of these nations. Their large middle classes make them excellent markets for many goods and services.

THE CASE CONTINUES

*H*einz has established a goal of $1 billion in sales from third world operations by 1990. This will be quite a feat, considering that in 1983 sales were less than $100 million. In order to accomplish this goal, Heinz has developed a strategy that "isn't just for today or next year, but for ten years from now," according to Senior Vice-President, Richard B. Patton.

This strategy includes investing in local economies and aiding local farmers to become more productive. In part, this means introducing new crops such as tomatoes and beans. In the future, such agricultural developments could benefit both less-developed countries (LDCs) and Heinz. It is hoped that Heinz will have additional sources of raw materials for its many products.

Sociocultural Environment

*D*ifferences between cultures and between subcultures have a major impact on the marketing of international products.

Every nation has its own values, beliefs, and patterns of living. A closer look reveals that each of these factors, in turn, varies within each nation, creating separate subcultures. Culture is a major segmentation tool of the multinational company. International marketers cannot afford to underestimate the importance and variety

MARKETING IN ACTION

International Corporate Blunders

Chevrolet was puzzled when its Nova model, popular in this country, would not sell in Latin American markets. Firm officials finally figured out that in Spanish Nova means "does not go."

Pepsodent's promise of white teeth brought no new customers in a part of southeast Asia where people of status chew betel nuts and black, discolored teeth are a symbol of prestige.

Campbell soups languished on English shelves too long. The trouble was their Campbell condensed soup cans looked so small next to the English cans selling for the same price. In England, soup is sold with the water already added.

One firm tried selling refrigerators in the mostly Moslem Middle East with an ad picturing their appliance chock full of food, including a giant ham on the middle shelf. Since Muslems do not eat ham, this blunder was an insult to many potential Middle-East consumers.

Source: Adapted from David A. Ricks, *Big Business Blunders: Mistakes in Multinational Marketing* (Dow Jones Division, 1983). Copyright © Richard D. Irwin, Inc. Reprinted by permission.

*O*ver the past fifteen years, Ohio State University professor David Ricks has collected a list of over 200 documented corporate blunders that occurred in international markets. Ricks defines a blunder as "a mistake that could have been avoided, but because of carelessness it's not." It usually results in some type of loss. Most blunders we find are marketing and advertising mistakes.

Some examples which Ricks has uncovered include:

A baby food company tried unsuccessfully to peddle its product in a mostly illiterate African nation with a label showing a cuddly infant. It turned out Africans thought the jars contained ground babies.

---

of cultural differences that can directly or indirectly affect their marketing efforts. The accompanying Marketing in Action feature provides numerous illustrations of blunders made by companies that failed to recognize social and cultural differences.

An example of how cultural differences affect food consumption can be found in Japan. Few Americans enjoy soup for breakfast, but in Japan soup is a favorite in homes and at McDonald's alike. Because the Japanese have traditionally served miso shiru (fermented bean paste soup) for breakfast, McDonald's produced a Western version to cater to the Japanese culture.[8]

To market a product successfully, a firm often must modify the product's physical contents or its use. For example, to sell Tang in the Latin American market, General Foods altered the product's traditional breakfast positioning and urged consumers to drink Tang at any mealtime and throughout the day. Why? Because a breakfast of cornflakes, eggs, and juice is not part of the Latin culture. For the Brazilian market, General Foods added extra sweetener to the product and packaged it in a bright one-liter pouch. By making appropriate adjustments, the company gained an 80 percent share of the market for its product in some South American nations.[9]

Foreign competitors must understand the U.S. culture, too. To sell motorcycles in the United States, for example, Honda had to overcome the common, threatening stereotype of motorcycle riders. Honda was able to convince many Americans that "You meet the nicest people on a Honda." This marketing strategy was also successful in Europe.

Political-Legal Environment

Great extremes exist in the political-legal environments firms must face in foreign markets. Problems generated by nationalism, trade barriers, or legal complications, for instance, may arise within a host country, or they may arise within the firm's home country. Problems have arisen from both sources for U.S. multinationals operating within South Africa. Thirty-one of the top fifty companies on the *Fortune* 500 list did business in South Africa, and there are South Africans of all races who want these companies to continue doing business in their nation. Before divestiture, American firms controlled nearly 50 percent of South Africa's petroleum industry, 70 percent of its computer industry, and 33 percent of its auto industry, according to the Investor Responsibility Research Center.[10] Despite America's $2.3 billion stake in South Africa, however, U.S. politicians and civil rights groups, along with some South Africans, are increasing pressure on U.S. companies to withdraw from the nation because of its government's racial policies. Since 1985, 144 companies have withdrawn.

*P*olitical-legal environments include nationalism, trade barriers, and unfamiliar laws.

In assessing the political-legal environment, decision makers must consider many internal and external factors. They include nationalism, trade barriers of various sorts, and laws that are different from those of the home country.

NATIONALISM

*M*any nations view multinational companies with suspicion.

Initially, foreign nations may welcome multinational corporations. But a time usually comes when citizens of the host country begin to mistrust the multinationals' motives. For example, people in a less-developed country may view a particular multinational suspiciously because the GNP for the entire country is lower than the gross sales of the multinational. Eventually, people begin to wonder what kind of political influence a multinational enjoys when it has such economic power. Such was the case during the 1970s when people began to question the role of ITT in the internal politics of Chile, of the United Brands Fruit Company in Central American nations, and of Bell Helicopter in Iran.

This suspicion and fear of foreign nations may build slowly, or it may erupt violently, as it did against the U.S. in Iran, Cuba, and El Salvador. It is not uncommon for multinational executives to be held for ransom. For example, violence broke out in Argentina when Coca-Cola reportedly refused to pay $1 million demanded by leftist guerillas for a kidnapped executive. Often, the end result of such violence is the nationalization of multinational industries. Nationalization, or expropriation, occurs when the government of the host country takes over the multinational's facilities. Nationalization of U.S.-owned industries occurred first in Mexico in the 1930s and later in Cuba in 1959. In the 1970s American bauxite companies in Jamaica were nationalized by the pro-socialist administration.

TRADE BARRIERS

Although there are many reasons why nations do trade, there are also many reasons why countries favor a restriction of free trade. (See figure 21.3.) In Congress, there appears to be a growing belief that the U.S. government's advocacy of free trade in recent years has allowed Japan and some European nations to become stronger at the expense of the United States. Many U.S. industries and labor unions are pressing Congress for more restrictive trade barriers to protect them from foreign competition. The belief that free trade should be restricted for the protection of domestic industries is called **protectionism.** However, despite this growing pressure, many U.S. business executives oppose an end to free trade.

Several methods are used by governments to restrict trade, including both tariff and nontariff barriers.

*T*ariffs are popular trade barriers because they are both flexible and selective.

Tariffs are taxes or duties placed on imported goods. For instance, many European nations add a tax to goods imported into their countries. The purpose is to protect European producers from foreign competition. The United States places tariffs on automobiles, electronics equipment, specialty steel, clothing, carpets, and many other items. Tariffs are popular because they are both flexible and selective in nature. They can be aimed at any type of good or country and can provide both revenue and protection.

❑ **Figure 21.3**
When companies try to export.

Foreign Barriers against U.S. Products
Sampling of rules and policies in foreign nations that discourage U.S. imports.

Product	Country	Trade Barrier
Paperboard	Japan	Specifications require smoother board than the United States produces.
Drugs	Argentina, Brazil, Mexico, South Korea, Taiwan, Yugoslavia	Patents and trademarks are too weak to prevent copying of U.S. products.
Cosmetics	Brazil, Taiwan, South Korea	Extremely high tariff is aimed at reducing consumption.
Textile machinery	Brazil	Will not import machinery similar to any made in Brazil.
Wire, cable	Canada	Tariff is about three times the U.S. rate.
Machine tools	Argentina	Money from sales must remain in country for several months.
Machine tools	Japan	Government subsidizes the domestic industry.
Electronics	Brazil, Taiwan, South Korea	U.S. patents and trademarks are poorly protected.
Textiles and clothing	Brazil, India, Pakistan	Imports are banned.
Carbon steel	European Economic Community	Imports limited to 7 or 8 percent of the market.
Hogs	Canada	30-day quarantine period discourages sales by American farmers.
Pesticides	Canada	Residue standards ban some chemicals made in United States.

U.S. Barriers against Foreign Products
Some U.S. rules that discourage foreigners from selling in the United States.

Product	Barrier
Carbon steel	Imports limited to 1/5 of the market.
Sugar	Imports limited to 2.5 million short tons.
Peanuts	Imports limited to less than 1/10 of 1 percent of consumption.
Heavy motorcycles	Current tariff is 20 percent of sales price.
Clothes	26 percent tariff plus restrictions on volume.
Meat	Import levels vary with cattle-slaughter rate in U.S.

U.S. Barriers against U.S. Products
Three U.S. rules that limit exports to foreign countries.

Product	Barrier
Oil	Oil from Alaska's North Slope cannot be exported.
Timber	Timber from federal lands cannot be exported.
Computers, electronic equipment	Export licenses controlled for national security.

During the Great Depression of the 1930s, a trade war broke out. So many countries imposed tariffs that few could afford to sell their products abroad, and this situation helped to deepen the depression. In 1948, in order to prevent further trade wars, twenty-three nations formulated the **General Agreement on Tariffs and Trade (GATT).** A code covering four-fifths of world trade, GATT encouraged trade relations through the reduction and elimination of tariffs. Today eighty-five nations abide by the agreement.

Import quotas are used to combat dumping.

Quotas are quantitative limits on the amount of goods that can be legally imported into a country. A landmark case involving quotas in the United States came in 1968. U.S. television manufacturers complained to the U.S. Treasury that Japanese television manufacturers were **dumping** color televisions in the United States, which means they were selling the sets for less money in the United States than in Japan. Dumping allows a country to make a quick entry into another country's market and to capture a large market share with low prices.

For instance, Zenith sued in U.S. Customs Court to have a quota placed on Japanese color televisions. The end result was a three-year accord signed by the United States and Japan in mid-1977, which limited Japan's annual export of televisions to the United States to 1,560,000 sets, some 60 percent of the 1976 level. Japan also signed an accord in 1985 to limit the input of autos to 2.3 million. Japan estimated that without voluntary quotas, it could sell 2.8 million cars annually.

Whereas quotas limit the amount of a product that can be imported, **embargoes** prevent any amount of a particular good from entering or leaving a country. Embargoes are ordered by governments and can be directed at specific goods or countries. Usually embargoes are ordered for reasons of politics, health, or morality.

*E*mbargoes may be based on political, health-related, or moral concerns.

A politically motivated embargo bans the sale of South African gold Krugerrands in the United States.

Politically-Based Embargoes. In 1981 the U.S. government announced a cutoff of $300 million in annual sales of high-technology products, including computers and oil and gas equipment, to the U.S.S.R. in response to the Soviet military crackdown in Poland. This embargo caused many diplomatic problems with European allies of the United States when, in 1982, the U.S. government enforced the embargo and penalized two French firms for exporting gas-line equipment to the Soviet Union.

In 1985 the U.S. government ordered an embargo on products shipped to and from Nicaragua because of that nation's continuing attempt to export communism to neighboring Central American countries. Another set of sanctions was imposed on South Africa. President Reagan banned computer exports to South African law-enforcement agencies, halted the export of nuclear technology, prohibited loans to the South African government (except for programs benefiting blacks), and banned the importation of the Krugerrand, a South African gold coin. In addition, the U.S. in 1988 imposed sanctions against Panama in an effort to depose Panamanian leader General Manuel Noriega for alleged drug trafficking and government corruption.

Health-Based Embargoes. For health-related reasons, various pharmaceuticals, animals, plants, chemicals, fruits, and vegetables cannot be imported into the United States without being held in isolation for long periods by U.S. Customs. The U.S. Customs Service is authorized to hold any goods that might be harmful. For example, some toys from Hong Kong cannot be imported because they do not meet high U.S. standards for toxic paint content. In 1981, Japan refused to accept fruit from California because of an insect infestation.

Health concerns were also the basis of a boycott of the Nestlé company, a Swiss multinational. Boycotts are not government actions but involve organized refusals to buy certain products. Eighty-seven labor, religious, and health organizations from ten countries boycotted the Nestlé company's products for a seven-year period. Underlying the boycott was a campaign against high infant mortality rates in developing nations. Critics of Nestlé contended that the company had sold infant formula in poor countries without regard for whether it could be safely used. In 1984 an accord was reached after Nestlé agreed to change its marketing practices for infant formula in developing nations.[11]

Embargoes Caused by Moral Objections. What is considered moral in one country may not be considered so in another. For example, the U.S. government does not allow certain pornographic materials to be imported. But *Playboy* magazine is not considered pornographic in the United States and thus is not prohibited. In Australia, however, *Playboy* and similar sexually oriented magazines are considered immoral, and importing them is illegal. Similarly, Americans of legal age can purchase alcoholic beverages; however, in Saudi Arabia and other Muslim nations, alcoholic beverages cannot be imported or sold, for legal and religious reasons.

LEGAL DIFFICULTIES

*D*ifferences in the laws of different countries create legal complexities for multinationals.

Laws vary from country to country, a situation that creates legal complexities for multinational firms. For example, Kellogg recently wished to run a British-made commercial for its cornflakes in several European countries. After checking with the J. Walter Thompson advertising agency, Kellogg personnel discovered that use of the cute, cereal-loving kids featured in the ad was illegal in France. The added vitamins were forbidden in Belgium, and the hint of product superiority claimed in the jingle was in violation of German laws prohibiting comparative advertising. Fortunately, since Kellogg and JWT knew about these international laws, they made separate commercials for France, Belgium, and Switzerland.[12]

In Venezuela, the U.S.-based International Paper Company offered to build a badly needed $500 million pulp and paper-making facility in return for access to government-seeded timber plantations. After four years of negotiations, the government imposed new conditions: International Paper couldn't own more than 25 percent of the joint-venture project, and access to timber would be restricted more than initially expected.[13] (Joint ventures are discussed later in this chapter.) According to a recent Conference Board survey, more than one-third of surveyed corporations involved in international joint ventures had to meet laws mandating local participation (host firms usually maintain at least 51-percent control).

Local management participation does not absolve a multinational from legal responsibility. For example, in 1985 Union Carbide faced sixty-five lawsuits of well over $50 billion, which were filed on behalf of victims and their families who were accidentally gassed in Bhopal, India. The parent company (headquartered in Connecticut) tried to confine liability to its subsidiary, Union Carbide India, Ltd., which was managed by local employees. In the beginning, legal matters were so complex that two governments and hundreds of lawyers couldn't even agree on where a trial should occur.

Other types of legal problems also exist. For example, many nations do not recognize U.S. trademarks or copyrights. In such instances, movies, books, records, and brand names cannot be protected by law. At the 1984 Winter Olympics in Sarajevo, Yugoslavia, for example, a Yugoslavian entrepreneur offered a "Big Mek" on his menu and placed an arched "M" in front of his grill. The Yugoslavian government did nothing to stop this violation of McDonald's trademarks.

Technological Environment

*T*echnological factors can vary with stage of economic development.

Various technological factors may affect the way a company does business in a foreign nation. For example, in many nations, fewer than 50 percent of the population can read or write. A company that plans to set up technologically complex manufacturing facilities in a country with a high illiteracy rate may have to provide a great deal of training before its production systems can be installed and maintained by local workers. A high illiteracy rate also means many of the nation's consumers will not be able to read product instructions on labels.

Another potential problem is port facilities. It is very difficult to load or unload a containerized ship in a port that has not been equipped for advanced shipping technology. Another problem affects the export of products like air conditioners and electric shavers. Because Europe and the United States use different electrical standards, such products must be equipped with converters or similar devices when they are exported.

The United States also uses a system of measurement different from the one used in most other countries. U.S. firms have been voluntarily converting equipment to the metric system since the mid-1970s to facilitate trading with foreign nations. The failure of Congress to pass legislation on this subject has slowed down the conversion effort. Still, any U.S. company wishing to export its products must make the switch.

International Competitive Environment

Like any market analysis, an analysis of the international market must consider the competition. The international firm faces competitive influences that are beyond its normal influence, including cartels, orderly marketing agreements, and common markets.

CARTELS

*C*artels, such as OPEC, attempt to control the prices of the products they supply.

To improve their bargaining position with respect to the multinationals, some less-developed countries have developed **cartels**—groups of firms or countries that agree to act as monopolies. The most famous cartel is the Organization of Petroleum Exporting Countries (OPEC), which was founded in 1960. The purpose of OPEC is to control the price of petroleum throughout the world. By limiting production in its thirteen member countries, OPEC has managed to increase its export revenues from approximately $20 billion in the early 1970s to over $200 billion in 1986. Another famous producer cartel, DeBeers Central Selling Organization, markets industrial and gem-quality diamonds from South Africa, the U.S.S.R., and Botswana.

ORDERLY MARKETING AGREEMENTS (OMA)

The success of the OPEC cartel encouraged the development of similar arrangements called **orderly marketing agreements (OMA),** through which nations share markets. These agreements range from elaborate international accords, such as the forty-one-nation system that has carved up most of the world's major textile and garment markets, to shadowy European-Japanese "gentlemen's agreements." In every case, the purpose has been to restrict competition and, thus, to preserve shares in national markets for local manufacturers that would otherwise lose out to cheaper or better products from abroad.

*O*MAs are usually of limited duration and provide for some annual increase of imports.

Orderly marketing agreements are usually of limited duration and provide for some annual increase of imports. The exporting countries, by negotiating restrictions on their own products, forego the right to retaliate against the trading partners. In the United States, the 1974 Trade Act gives the president the option of negotiating such agreements instead of imposing tariffs, quotas, or other restrictions recommended by the International Trade Commission (ITC). Furthermore, when an agreement is made with a country that supplies 51 percent of U.S. imports of one product, the United States can unilaterally impose restrictions on other countries that supply that product. For example, the Ford Administration negotiated a specialty steel agreement with Japan and then imposed quotas on the European Community, Canada, Sweden, and other steel producers.

COMMON MARKETS

*C*ommon markets, such as EC, EFTA, LAFTA, and ASEAN, limit trade barriers among members but apply a tariff on imports from nonmembers.

Common markets, or regional trading blocks, are groups of geographically associated countries that agree to limit trade barriers among member nations and apply a common tariff on products from nonmember countries. The best-known common market is the twelve-member **European Community (EC),** founded in 1958. The EC includes 300 million people and has a combined gross domestic product (similar to GNP) comparable to the U.S. GNP. Better known as the Common Market, its membership consists of Italy, the Netherlands, Luxembourg, West Germany, Belgium, France, Ireland, the United Kingdom, Denmark, and Greece, plus Spain and Portugal, who joined in 1983. The EC (formerly called the European

Economic Community) is enacting some 300 new rules aimed at dismantling by 1992 virtually all trade barriers between members.

At present, fourteen other trading blocks exist around the world. Some major ones include the European Free Trade Association (EFTA), the Latin American Free Trade Association (LAFTA), the Caribbean Common Market, the Economic Community of West African States, the Council for Mutual Economic Assistance, the Asian Common Market, the Central American Common Market, and the Association of Southeast Asian Nations (ASEAN). These trading blocks, each having its own approach, play a significant role in international business development.

There is evidence that common markets will, in the next decade, force multinationals to comply with strict standards. For example, since 1968 the EC has increasingly tried to standardize corporate law and accounting procedures for companies with operations in member nations. Some economists speculate that in order for the United States to effectively market overseas, it may have to establish a North American common market with Mexico and Canada. Many see this as a possible route to lessening U.S. dependence on OPEC oil. Regardless, American companies must recognize that the protectionism inherent in common markets is altering the framework for international marketing.

THE CASE CONTINUES

*I*nternational marketing is very important to the H. J. Heinz Company. After all, one-third of its total sales comes from international markets. Heinz depends on other countries not only for sales, but also for their bountiful supplies of raw materials.

Operating in foreign countries can be risky business. Heinz has joined a relatively small (but fast growing)

group of U.S. food companies willing to market abroad. Company executives keep a constant watch on a long list of countries on their economic critical list. In addition, a separate list is kept on countries facing political upheaval. Its concern for stability has once kept Heinz out of

Latin America, where currency devaluations and political turmoil are common.

Other problems can exist as well. For example, Heinz was faced with English plant workers who shut down the entire canning line for tea breaks. Only recently has Heinz been able to increase productivity by staggering breaks and keeping the line going.

ORGANIZING THE MARKET ABROAD

*M*ultinationals can enter foreign markets by:
(1) exporting, (2) joint ventures, (3) licensing,
(4) contract manufacturing,
(5) direct investment.

After the decision has been made to sell goods and services to a foreign country, a company must decide on the best method of entry into that market. Choices include exporting, joint ventures, licensing, contract manufacturing, and direct investment.

Exporting

Exporting represents the simplest method of entering a foreign market. Companies can engage in exporting in two ways. First, they can use the services of international marketing middlemen. This is called **indirect exporting.** A second choice is **direct exporting,** by which a company handles its own exporting efforts.

Trading companies are a popular method of selling U.S. products in foreign markets.

Source: Mitsui & Co. (U.S.A.), Inc.

INDIRECT EXPORTING

*I*ndirect exporting is commonly used by companies just starting to export.

Many companies just beginning to export decide to use an indirect means of exporting. For example, Spectra Logic, a high-technology company of Sunnyvale, California, increased exports of its computer peripherals to 20 percent of annual sales in the first two years by using an export marketing consultant. Using indirect marketing requires less time and less initial investment than direct exporting.[14]

Trading companies provide an important means of exporting. In 1983, for example, Kmart established Kmart Trading Services (KTS) to export brand-name goods—from Jockey shorts to Thermos jugs—to wholesalers and retailers worldwide. Sears also opened six international trading offices in 1983 to market consumer goods and light industrial products. **Trading companies,** such as those established by Kmart and Sears, are organizations designed to expand exports. Their goal is to help foreign retailers design, build, and manage stores and to supply them with U.S. goods. For its services, KTS expects to match or exceed the typical trading company profit margin of 1 to 2 percent of sales.[15]

The **Export Trading Company Act** of 1982 granted U.S. companies the right to use trading companies to set prices abroad, provided access to Export-Import Bank financing and guarantees, and allowed banks to own and operate their own trading companies. The intent of the act was to allow small companies "one-stop shopping for everything from financing and insurance to freight handling forwarding and marketing services, which allow manufacturers to band together to export and achieve economies of scale."[16]

The **Export-Import Bank (Eximbank)** is an independent U.S. government agency established in 1934 to create jobs during the Great Depression. Today, the Eximbank finances loans to exporters who cannot find funds through commercial sources and to foreign countries that need money to purchase U.S. products. Besides the Eximbank, several states are helping to finance exporting ventures. For example, the Minnesota Export Finance Authority guarantees the commercial loans manufacturers obtain between the time an order arrives and the time the shipment leaves.

DIRECT EXPORTING

*D*irect exporting is more expensive and riskier than indirect exporting but offers greater rewards.

Although direct exporting is more expensive and riskier than indirect exporting, its potential rewards are greater, and it offers the exporter greater control over the distribution of its product. Often a firm starts with indirect exporting and then switches to direct exporting.

An example of a firm that has chosen to export directly is M & M Products of Atlanta, a manufacturer of hair-care products for blacks. Rather than use its own distributors overseas, M & M has formed relationships with foreign distributors to build export sales. In the company's first eighteen months of exporting, sales to distributors in Canada, England, France, West Germany, the Caribbean, and Nigeria accounted for $1 million in sales.[17]

Tax breaks can be achieved through the use of direct exporting. To provide an incentive for U.S. companies to export products, Congress in 1971 authorized tax-sheltered subsidiaries called Domestic International Sales Corporations (DISCs). This change in tax codes allowed certain U.S. exporters to defer federal income tax on one-half of their export profits.

The Tax Reform Act of 1984 replaced DISCs with **foreign sales corporations (FSCs).** Unlike DISCs, FSCs are required to maintain a foreign presence to qualify for a 15-to-32 percent tax exemption on foreign income. The changes were necessitated by pressure from countries belonging to GATT. These countries claimed that the DISC provisions represented an illegal export subsidy.[18]

Thus far, the IRS has approved twenty-three foreign countries and U.S. possessions as acceptable sites for FSCs. Any company maintaining such a business must have at least one non-U.S. resident as a director and must maintain a set of books of account, including invoices. An estimated 6,000 to 8,000 companies are expected to form FSCs.

Joint Ventures

*J*oint ventures are required by law for entry into some foreign markets.

International **joint ventures** are partnerships established between a domestic and a foreign company. This arrangement enables companies to operate production facilities in other countries. Often, in fact, foreign governments require firms entering their countries to form joint ventures with domestic companies. Joint ventures may include licensing, franchising, and contract manufacturing.

In 1988, McDonald's and the city of Moscow (U.S.S.R.) entered into a joint venture to open the first of a number of McDonald's restaurants in its downtown area in 1989. Similar McDonald's joint ventures exist in Hungary and Yugoslavia, where restaurants were opened in 1988.

Like McDonald's, many U.S. companies see joint ventures as a way to gain a global competitive edge. Usually the U.S. partner provides the technology and the foreign partner provides access to local customers. Other examples include Honeywell and L. M. Ericsson (Sweden), General Motors and Daervor Group (South Korea), Disney and the Oriental Land Company (Japan), CBS and Sony (Japan), and AT&T and N. V. Phillips (the Netherlands).[19] The accompanying Marketing in Action feature describes a successful joint venture between GM and the government of Kenya.

*A*t a General Motors plant, on land where tall Masai warriors once tended their cattle, Elijah Okonda checks a completed Isuzu Trooper for defects, marking for correction even the tiniest of air bubbles on the inside of a front-door frame.

Okonda, who has worked for GM Kenya Ltd. since the plant opened in 1977, is a stickler because quality control is a top priority in the plant and because GM has an unusual incentive program here for production and quality.

"Each month the best section gets a free lunch—a goat barbecue out in the loading area," said managing director Maury Dieterich. "There's great interest and lots of peer pressure."

"This is probably the smallest assembly facility that GM has," added Dieterich, who has run the plant for six years but still maintains a home in Troy, Mich. "Being small, we can do things as a family."

That togetherness has helped make GM Kenya Ltd. a success story. The plant, surviving tough economic times for the auto industry and this nation, has turned what Dieterich describes as a tidy profit and created a measure of goodwill between the automaker and the government of Kenya, which owns 51 percent of the plant.

MARKETING IN ACTION

GM and Kenya Team Up

"It's a shining example of how joint ventures can work," Dieterich said.

The GM plant was opened with an initial investment of about $4 million, officials said. Kenya's investment was paid off through dividends within four years.

Dieterich refused to quantify the company's profit, but said, "We've provided a very sufficient return on both GM and Kenya's investment."

The plant could make even more money, he said, if it could sell passenger cars. The government prohibits such sales because it wants its citizens to buy commercial vehicles that it believes can aid the nation's development.

More than a third of the vehicles produced by the plant are medium-duty trucks, such as the Isuzu TXD and Bedford J6; the rest are Isuzu light trucks, pickups, utility vehicles, and buses. The plant also puts together a ten-ton Bedford TL truck.

Isuzu Motors is a Japanese firm in which GM holds 42.4 percent interest. Bedford is a British company. They send the plant prepacked kits that are assembled by the Kenyan workers and then reassembled into motor vehicles.

Unlike U.S. autoworkers, employees at GM Kenya face no relentless, computer-fed, chain-driven assembly line. Working in small production units of about ten men, the Kenyans use small, flatbed carts to push the chassis from one assembly point to another.

The plant's 360 employees in 1987 produced about 2,300 vehicles. GM says production capacity for one shift is 3,500 units.

Dieterich said absenteeism is extremely low. "People like to work, and jobs are hard to get," he said. "If you're looking for a good, solid work force that puts out a quality product, this is it."

Dieterich also is proud that each of GM's twenty-two dealerships in Kenya is "owned and operated by an indigenous Kenyan." He said the automaker adopted that strategy so the dealers would be likely to stay in the country.

"It's a young dealer's organization, and they don't have much working capital, so we spend a lot of time making each one a professional company," he said.

Source: Adapted from Larry Olmstead, "GM and Kenya Team Up to Turn a Profit for Both," *Detroit Free Press,* January 6, 1985, p. 81, used with permission; and conversation with GM Public Relations Dept., May 1988.

Licensing

A licensee pays a licensor for permission to use a trademark, patent, copyright, or manufacturing process.

Licensing is a temporary agreement that allows a company (the licensee) to use a trademark, patent, copyright, or even manufacturing process that belongs to another company (the licensor), which is paid a fee or royalty. Licensing agreements tend to be shorter-lived than joint ventures.

Licensing offers another way to become involved in international marketing. For example, Calvin Klein, Gloria Vanderbilt, and Jordache have all entered licensing agreements with Brazilian manufacturers. Each of these U.S. companies hoped to capture a significant share of Brazil's $90 million market (the second largest in the world). In Hungary, Levi Strauss entered into a licensing agreement with a state-owned company to produce jeans.

A form of licensing is *international franchising,* which is very much like franchising in the United States. In the international franchise agreement, however, the foreign licensing partner maintains greater control over the company. International franchising has proven very successful in the fast-food industry. McDonald's, Wendy's, Kentucky Fried Chicken, Bonanza, and many others have international franchise operations from the Netherlands to Japan.

Although licensing has advantages—it requires only a small investment and provides easy entry into a foreign market—it also has disadvantages. For one, the licensor has little control over the decisions of the licensee. Often these decisions are based on government action. In 1982, the Indian government demanded that Coca-Cola give its Indian licensees the formula for Coke syrup. Needless to say, Coca-Cola is no longer produced in India.

Contract Manufacturing

U.S. companies may contract with foreign firms to manufacture products to exact specifications.

Contract manufacturing offers yet another way to trade abroad. In this case, the domestic company contracts with foreign manufacturers to produce products to its specifications and with its label. This method is very cost effective because it requires no investment costs and often takes advantage of inexpensive foreign labor. Several U.S. automakers use this method to manufacture auto parts in Mexico. Johnson & Johnson was forced to switch to contract manufacturing in Argentina when that nation banned U.S. imports because of the 1982 Falkland Islands War and a depressed economy.

Direct Investment

*D*irect investment offers maximum involvement in international markets.

For companies seeking maximum involvement in international markets, the direct investment option offers the best opportunity. **Direct investment** means that the company owns and operates manufacturing plants in foreign countries. Many foreign countries actively seek direct investment by U.S. companies. In Singapore, for example, the powerful Economic Development Board attracted Micro Peripherals to build an exact duplicate of its Chatsworth, California, plant. Singapore, like many other developing nations, offers inexpensive, trained labor and low taxes.[20]

Some companies, such as Procter & Gamble, invest directly by purchasing existing plants to manufacture their products. For example, in 1983 P&G bought 98 percent of a Chilean toothpaste manufacturer that claimed to be Chile's best-selling brand.

Despite earlier successes with direct investment, the early 1980s provided five consecutive years of near-zero growth in U.S. companies' foreign capital spending. In that period the total of U.S. direct investment grew by 1.6 percent—an actual decline if inflation is taken into account. Foreign investment in the United States has exceeded U.S. foreign investment every year since 1979, and in 1986 foreigners owned about $1 trillion in U.S. assets. Economists disagree on the meaning of such data. Some experts see the trend as a short-term one; however, it is likely to continue if the dollar remains weak. Only time will reveal the answer.

The potential political problems involved in direct investment are enormous. Besides the possibility of nationalization, a company might find itself in the unusual position of having to export products other than its own. Such is the case in Mexico, where foreign automakers are required by the Mexican government to export Mexican coffee, horsemeat, chick-peas, and honey, among others.[21]

CHAPTER 21   INTERNATIONAL MARKETING ❑ 595

H. J. Heinz built its first overseas factory in 1905 in Peckham, England. This is an example of direct investment. In the 1980s, Heinz invested $110 million to automate its largest plant in Great Britain. Production is expected to double as up to 800 cans per minute are processed, yet canning lines are being reduced from thirteen to five. In total, Heinz has twenty-four overseas plants (twelve in Great Britain).

THE CASE CONTINUES

The company has also entered into joint-venture arrangements such as the company's 51 percent purchase of Olivine Industries of Zimbabwe (manufacturer of cooking oils and margarines). Other acquisitions are pending in two other African nations, and Heinz has established Heinz Seoul Foods, a joint venture

with South Korea. In addition, Heinz is using a new fruit drink called Frutsi as a low-profile entry into other international markets.

Tomatoes and other crops grown in the United States and countries like Zimbabwe are made into ketchup, tomato paste, mustard, soup, and other products. These products are then exported to the United Kingdom, Australia, New Zealand, and a few other countries.

INTERNATIONAL MARKETS AND MARKET PLANNING

*M*arketers with a global approach view the world market as a set of integrated activities.

Once a decision has been made to market goods and services in foreign countries, the marketer must decide how the company's offerings will be marketed. International marketers must determine which parts of the marketing mix need to be modified or replaced to meet the requirements of the new market or markets.

Traditionally, multinational corporations have created tailor-made marketing strategies for each country in which they do business, providing individual packaging and advertising to appeal to the identified needs and wants of the local culture. Today, however, many multinational companies use a standardized approach to international marketing, or a **global marketing strategy.** Companies that take a global approach market their products in the same manner in each country. According to Theodore Levitt, professor at the Harvard Business School, the benefits from the global strategy "make the multinational corporation obsolete and the global corporation absolute."[22]

The standardized approach to international marketing is based on the belief that as international communication increases, consumer tastes become more similar around the world.[23] Many multinationals prefer a global strategy because of the larger economies of scale inherent in this nonsegmented approach—uniform production is less expensive. Thus, Levitt and many leading ad agencies counsel their clients to adopt a world brand concept.[24] Examples of global-centered industries include tractors and other farm equipment, watches, cigarettes, soft-drinks, aircraft, television sets, and heavy electrical equipment. Philip Morris, Coca-Cola, Seiko, Boeing, Sony, Panasonic, Westinghouse, and General Electric all have successful global marketing strategies.

But while the global marketing strategy is growing, the trend within multinationals appears to be *selective use* of this strategy. Thus, companies might have one portfolio of products that they market globally, and another set of products that are more successfully marketed on a *country-centered* basis.

*C*ountry-centered firms expect an independent return from each national profit center.

A **country-centered** approach to international marketing is a nonstandardized approach to the global market. Here, firms create different strategies and expect different returns for individual countries or world regions. The U.S. automobile

Ford uses a global marketing strategy to promote their Ford Escort.

Source: Courtesy of Ford Motor Company

industry initially sold their products globally, and then moved to a country-centered approach, with entries such as the GM Opel now sold exclusively in Europe. Ford is shifting back to the global market, with entries such as the Escort.

When considering whether or not to adopt a global marketing strategy, Grey Advertising suggests that companies should ask themselves the following questions.[25] According to Grey, a negative response to any one indicates that a global strategy would probably fail:

1. Has the market developed in the same way from country to country? Grey notes that Kellogg's Pop-Tarts failed in Great Britain because toasters are not widely used there. The continued popularity of clotheslines in Europe similarly meant there would likely be little demand for the type of fabric-softener sheets used in electric clothes dryers.
2. Does consumer reaction to a product differ from nation to nation? In its U.S. markets advertising preparations for its 35-millimeter cameras, Canon found that people were generally fearful of complex technological products. Many Japanese consumers of cameras, on the other hand, seek sophisticated, high-tech products. Thus Canon's advertising strategy in Japan, which stresses the complexity of its cameras, would likely fail in the United States.
3. Do consumers share the same wants and needs around the world? In the United States, General Foods Corporation successfully positioned Tang as a substitute for orange juice at breakfast. In France, however, the company discovered that people drink little orange juice in general and almost none at breakfast. General Foods had to create a totally different advertising approach in France, featuring Tang as a refreshment for any time of the day.

*M*ost multinationals use a combination of global and country-centered marketing strategies.

As noted, most multinationals will use a combination of global and country-centered approaches to their product lines. Although modifications in the marketing mix are critical, a standardized approach to planning is essential. This means that even though the price of advertising might be different from country to country or region to region, the process of determining these factors should remain the same. This allows for evaluative comparisons once sales results are tabulated.

Product

A survey of 120 senior marketing executives concluded that beer, household cleaners, toiletries, food, and clothing were the least suitable candidates for international marketing.[26] However, there are three basic alternatives. First, the existing product can be sold as it is. Coca-Cola (soft drinks), IBM (computers), Polaroid (cameras), and John Deere (farm equipment) sell their products in this way. A second possibility is to adapt the product. For example, Kentucky Fried Chicken offered smoked chicken and substituted french fries for mashed potatoes in Japan. Mattel slimmed Barbie's bustline and changed her hair style to market her in Japan, where she became the best-selling doll. The third alternative is to invent a new product for international distribution. Coca-Cola internationally markets a high-protein drink called Sampson, which is made of cheese. Sampson is not available in the U.S. market.

Promotion

Seldom is a multinational company lucky enough to be able to enter an international market with the same promotions it uses in the United States. Sometimes the U.S. promotions can be used in a nation like Canada, but the local environment usually requires some adjustments in language, colors and symbols, people, site locations (backgrounds), and other areas. For example, Procter & Gamble chose to use a promotion similar to its U.S. advertising when relaunching the Orange Crush soft drink in Peru. Television commercials featured a small boy who promised to save his soccer-playing brother's Crush drink but then succumbed to temptation and drank it. Basically only the sport and the language changed.[27]

Language can create unexpected message problems. For instance, McDonald's found their initial advertising for "Big Macs" embarrassing. It seems "big macs" is French-Canadian slang for big busts. A situation like this one often requires a company to change the name of a product. In another example, one airline advertised the "rendezvous lounger" on its 707 flights in Brazil and lost customers. *Rendezvous* in Portuguese is a place for sex. Companies can often avoid such problems by using local advertising agencies to develop their promotional campaigns. McDonald's, for instance, uses twenty-nine agencies outside North America.

Other promotional considerations include an analysis of media availability. In nations like India and the Philippines, where fewer people have television sets, promotions must be adapted for use in movie theaters, on billboards, and on radio. Newspapers and magazines are seldom used in some African and Asian nations because of their low literacy rates. Using these media to advertise products used by the masses would be inappropriate.

Even packaging plays a role. Ralston Purina, for example, is competing in China with Chinese producers of canned mushrooms. Since it can't charge a lower price than the local companies, Ralston Purina is exploiting a Chinese weakness by putting its mushrooms in fancy packages for display.[28]

Price

Many factors can affect the price of a product in an international market. These factors include local competition and transportation costs, as well as dumping, tariffs, currency devaluation, fluctuations in exchange rates, availability of duty-free trade zones, and inflation.

Some nations, in order to penetrate an international market, engage in dumping. As previously noted, *dumping* occurs when a product is sold in a foreign market

*D*evaluation of the dollar makes U.S. products more cost competitive. In contrast, a strong dollar raises the prices of U.S. products.

at less than the domestic price. One common retaliatory practice is to increase tariffs so that foreign products can't compete with local products. Thus, foreign products must often be priced high or not sold at all.

Devaluation of the dollar can also affect price. *Devaluation* is the reduction of a currency's value in relation to gold or other currencies. Devaluation of the dollar in the 1970s made U.S. products cost-competitive in international markets. The U.S. textile and garment industry, for example, was able to regain a foothold in Europe and Latin America when the dollar was weak. By contrast, when the dollar was strong in the mid-1980s, prices of U.S. goods and services increased. For instance, Coleman, a manufacturer of lanterns, ice chests, and other camping equipment and sporting goods, experienced a 40-percent drop in exports in 1983. The company's typical kerosene lamp sold wholesale in the United States for $20 and retailed for about $30 overseas. Foreign competitors charged $12 for similar lanterns. Coleman lowered its prices in Southeast Asia in order to keep its market share.[29]

The volatility of exchange rates causes special worries for the international marketer. Treasurers of multinationals often protect themselves by hedging. One such case involved Westinghouse, which in 1983 saved millions of dollars by hedging French franc receivables and royalties. To hedge, exporters like Westinghouse arrange to sell a foreign currency in the future (usually up to a year) to a bank at a set price. That price might be less than the current value of the currency, but more than the exporter expects the currency to be worth within several months of the time payment is due. Thus, the exporter is assured a certain exchange rate. In the process, the company protects its profits and makes planning, budgeting, and pricing much easier.[30]

A technique used to lower costs and thereby enable foreign products to compete is the use of duty-free trade zones. **Duty-free trade zones** are unique, designated areas set aside to allow businesses to store, process, and display products from abroad without first paying a tariff. Once a product leaves the zone and is delivered, a tariff must be paid, but not on the cost of assembly or on the profits. Duty-free trade zones in the United States were first established in 1934 by the Foreign Trade Zones Act. New York City opened the first zone, but few other localities followed suit. By 1970 only ten zones had been created. Today, however, because of the competition from foreign trade zones in other countries and because of increased labor costs, duty-free trade zones are booming in the United States. In 1987 there were 244 operating general purpose duty-free trade zones and subzones in forty-seven states and Puerto Rico. Figure 21.4 illustrates the location of major trade zones in the United States.

*W*orldwide, inflation is much higher than in the United States.

Inflation can also affect the price of goods. Although U.S. prices rose 56 percent from 1975 to 1980, this increase was far below the worldwide average increase of 79 percent. The U.S. average matched that of most industrial nations. Some nations, such as West Germany experienced less inflation; however, such countries as Israel, Turkey, Bolivia, and Argentina averaged over 100 percent. The average rise for non–oil producing countries was 243 percent. Needless to say, such increases can drastically affect pricing.[31]

Channels of Distribution

Apple Computer's initial entry into the Japanese market was less than a success. The company's distribution strategy relied on Japanese trading companies to import and distribute Apple personal computers in Japan. (According to the Japanese Trade Ministry, approximately 60 percent of all imports are channeled through such trading companies.) Today Apple operates its own subsidiary and hopes to gain a much larger market share. This change was essential in Japan because of the importance of service. When it did not distribute its own products, Apple could not control service, and its machines earned a reputation for working poorly. In addition, many

☐ **Figure 21.4**
Major U.S. duty-free
trade zones.

● Major Foreign Trade Zones

products in Japan must be sold through a complex network of five types of wholesalers before reaching the retail level.[32]

Multinational companies can use existing channels of distribution or develop new channels.

A multinational company can sell products through existing marketing channels, or it can develop new international marketing channels. In Europe, U.S. companies are trying to introduce American-style retailing and franchising operations. This effort is most evident in the development of fast-food restaurants and supermarkets. Europe currently has highly fragmented distribution and retail channels. Mass-marketing conglomerates like those popular in the United States do not exist in most of Europe. Instead, Europeans rely on medium-sized retailers and small outlets. Many such distributors do not have the financial resources to carry large inventories.

☐ **Figure 21.5**
Selected international
marketing channels.

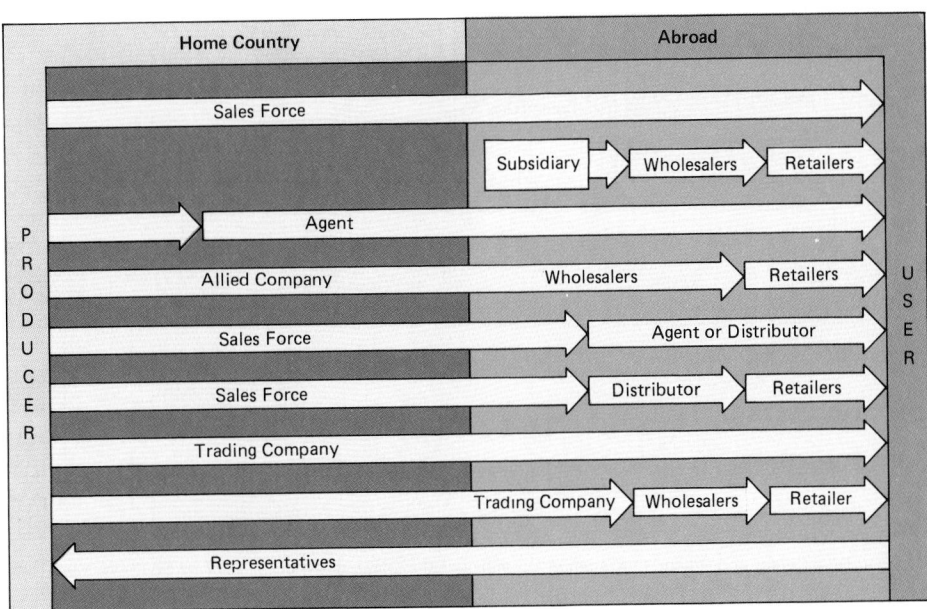

Source: Ruel Kahler and Roland
L. Kramer in *International
Marketing,* copyright © 1977 by
South-Western Publishing.

Marketing planners must give careful consideration to existing channels and physical distribution systems before developing a distribution strategy. Figure 21.5 gives an overview of selected international marketing channels.

IMPLEMENTING THE INTERNATIONAL MARKETING PLAN

*M*ultinationals can organize by using export departments, international divisions, or international subsidiaries.

In order to effectively and efficiently implement its marketing plan and manage its international operations, a firm must be organized in a manner suitable to the extent of its overseas commitments. Companies just beginning international trade normally choose to establish an export department (see figure 21.6). In order to obtain the necessary international marketing services, the sales manager and a small staff often work closely with a trading company.

A firm that enjoys marketing success and decides to expand often establishes an international division to implement the marketing plan. This is especially true if the company branches into joint ventures, contract manufacturing, or direct investments. Companies that establish international divisions may be organized in one of several ways. Coca-Cola uses an international subsidiary, Coke Export. This division of Coca-Cola accounts for approximately 55 percent of the company's total earnings. It markets Coke concentrate, other soft drinks, and dried coffee. General Motors is organized by product groups. CBS is organized by geographic region such as "Europe" and "Asia."

Although more and more companies are using centralized management, some companies, like Coca-Cola, GM, and CBS, are decentralized. Each international division has its own president, and decisions are made by managers down to the local level. Coca-Cola decided many years ago that local managers were best equipped to deal with their own problems. Most local managers are natives of the countries in which they operate.

❑ **Figure 21.6** Organization of a separate export department.

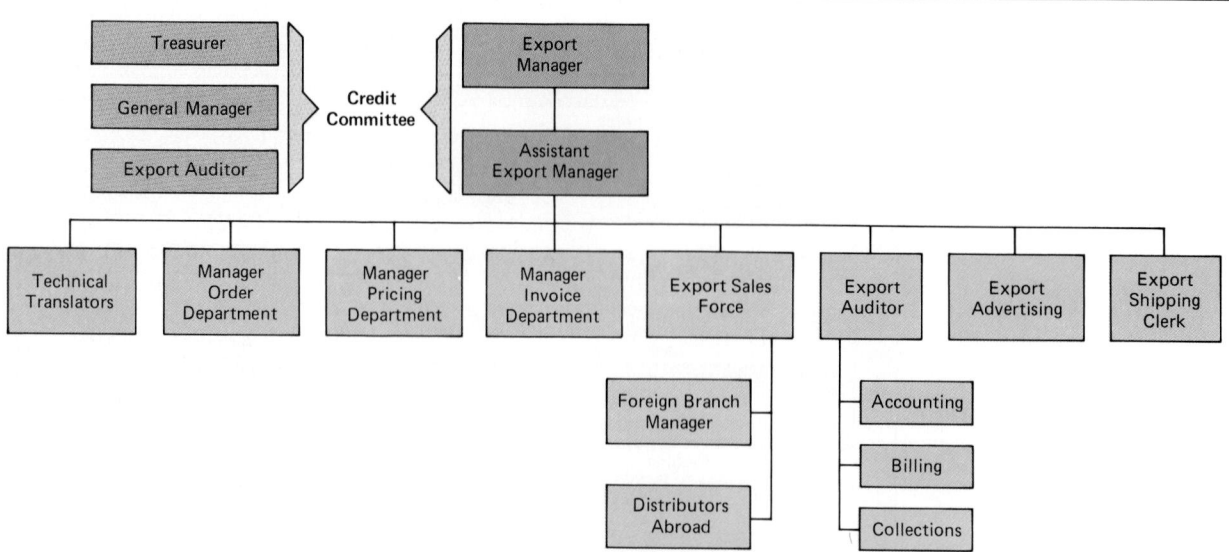

Source: Ruel Kahler and Roland L. Kramer in *International Marketing*, copyright © 1977 by South-Western Publishing.

Companies like Heinz must closely examine their marketing mix when deciding to market internationally. For example, the Ivory Coast and Cameroon were selected as excellent locations to market tomato paste, a popular ingredient in West African cooking. In Asia Heinz recognized an increasing desire for Western foods. The company is presently studying local taste habits and may modify the ketchup recipe to appeal to Asian tastes. Thus, because local

cooking customs vary widely, a global marketing strategy is not feasible for Heinz in many areas of the world.

Besides the product, other important considerations for Heinz include pricing, channels of distribution, and promotion. A key to success in countries like Japan will involve gaining access to complex distribution

systems and then promoting the product as "American- style," tailored to local tastes.

Finally, Heinz is organized along several product line divisions such as Ore-Ida, Star-Kist, Weight Watchers, and 9-Lives. These products are sold by Heinz international subsidiaries in other nations. Subsidiaries were chosen because many products are made in overseas plants and customized on a country-by-country basis for its consumers.

GOAL SUMMARY

1. **Explain why international marketing is important to the U.S. economy.** Not only does the United States import greatly needed goods and services, but it is also the world's largest exporter. Thus, international marketing has a huge impact on the employment of workers. It is estimated that 4.5 million workers hold export-related jobs. Furthermore, exporting accounts for approximately 24 percent of the U.S. GNP.

2. **Discuss factors a firm must evaluate when operating in an international environment.** When a company decides to consider marketing products on an international level, it must thoroughly understand the marketing environments of each nation and that among nations. Marketers must consider the economic, political-legal, sociocultural, and technological conditions in force.

3. **Explain why protectionism is a barrier to international marketing efforts.** Protectionism is the belief that free trade should be restricted. In order to increase exports and to protect domestic industries, countries around the world are dumping products and imposing tariffs. To protect themselves, other governments are imposing tougher trade barriers of their own—all in the name of protection from foreign competition.

4. **Compare the available alternatives for organizing an international marketing effort.** Several alternatives exist for companies that wish to market goods and services overseas. The choices include exporting directly or indirectly; entering joint ventures with foreign companies; making licensing agreements, that allow foreign companies to use trademarks, patents, copyrights, or manufacturing processes; engaging in contract manufacturing, through which the domestic company contracts with foreign companies to produce a product to its specifications and with its label; and directly investing in overseas plants.

5. **Modify a marketing plan for an existing good or service to be exported to an international market.** When developing or modifying a marketing plan for a good or service to be sold internationally, the marketer must study marketing research to learn whether parts of the marketing mix must be modified or whether a global marketing strategy can be utilized. Consideration must be given to the product, promotion, price, and channels of distribution.

6. **Identify the decision-making steps for determining whether to engage in international marketing.** The steps for determining whether to engage in international marketing are: (1) evaluating the international marketing environments of each nation and among nations, (2) organizing to market abroad, (3) developing a marketing plan, and (4) implementing the marketing plan.

KEY TERMS

International Trade, **p. 577**
International Marketing, **p. 577**
Balance of Payments, **p. 577**
Balance of Trade, **p. 578**
Imports, **p. 578**
Exports, **p. 578**
Absolute Advantage, **p. 578**
Comparative Advantage, **p. 579**
Multinational Corporation, **p. 579**
Underdeveloped Nation, **p. 582**
Countertrade, **p. 582**
Less-Developed Nation, **p. 583**
Developing Nation, **p. 583**
Developed Nation, **p. 583**
Protectionism, **p. 585**
Tariff, **p. 585**
General Agreement on Tariffs and Trade (GATT), **p. 586**
Quota, **p. 586**
Dumping, **p. 586**

Embargo, **p. 587**
Cartel, **p. 589**
Orderly Marketing Agreement (OMA), **p. 589**
Common Market, **p. 589**
European Community (EC), **p. 589**
Indirect Exporting, **p. 590**
Direct Exporting, **p. 590**
Trading Company, **p. 591**
Export Trading Company Act, **p. 591**
Export-Import Bank (Eximbank), **p. 591**
Foreign Sales Corporation (FSC), **p. 592**
Joint Venture, **p. 592**
Licensing, **p. 593**
Contract Manufacturing, **p. 594**
Direct Investment, **p. 594**
Global Marketing Strategy, **p. 595**
Country-Centered Marketing Strategy, **p. 595**
Duty-Free Trade Zone, **p. 598**

CHECK YOUR LEARNING

1. A nation's balance of trade is part of its balance of payments. **T/F**
2. The exchange of products between nations is called (a) international marketing, (b) international trade, (c) international business, (d) global marketing.
3. Companies with products in the (a) introductory, (b) growth, (c) maturity, (d) decline stage of the product life cycle find real advantages in marketing goods overseas.
4. Approximately 40 percent of U.S. trade involves countertrade. **T/F**
5. All of the following are developing nations except (a) Malaysia, (b) Brazil, (c) South Korea, (d) Mexico.
6. An evaluation of international marketing environments is the first step for companies trying to decide whether to market their products internationally. **T/F**
7. The United States has an absolute advantage in which of the following: (a) computers, (b) toys, (c) oil drill bits, (d) autos.
8. Protectionism is the belief that free trade should not be restricted. **T/F**
9. Which of the following is *not* a trade barrier? (a) tariffs, (b) joint ventures, (c) quotas, (d) embargoes.

10. Direct investment represents the simplest method of entering a foreign market. **T/F**
11. Which of the following granted U.S. companies Eximbank financing and guarantees? (a) Export Trading Company Act, (b) Export-Import Bank Act, (c) Domestic Sales Corporation Act, (d) none of the above.
12. Which of the following allows foreign companies to use domestic companies' trademarks, patents, copyrights, or manufacturing processes? (a) joint ventures, (b) licensing, (c) contract manufacturing, (d) direct investment.
13. FSCs allow U.S. exporters to defer federal income tax on one-half of their export profits. **T/F**
14. When entering a foreign market, a company can sell its existing product, adapt it, or invent a new product. **T/F**
15. Which of the following does *not* affect prices in international markets? (a) dumping, (b) currency devaluation, (c) inflation, (d) all affect prices.
16. Duty-free zones allow the storage of imports on a tariff-free basis if the products have not been assembled. **T/F**
17. GM and CBS use centralized management in making decisions regarding their foreign subsidiaries. **T/F**

QUESTIONS FOR REVIEW AND DISCUSSION

1. Define the key terms for this chapter that appear at the end of the goal summary.
2. What is the current status of the U.S. balance of trade and balance of payments?
3. Make a list of ten foreign products that are manufactured in the United States.
4. Explain the difference between absolute and comparative advantage and give examples of each.
5. Why is it important that a multinational corporation fully understand the marketing environment of each nation in which it sells?
6. Compare and contrast underdeveloped, less-developed, developing, and developed nations and give examples.
7. What types of trade barriers might U.S. companies face when marketing overseas?
8. Why is protectionism a threat to international trade and marketing?
9. Distinguish between political, health-related, and moral reasons for establishing embargoes.
10. Why is a strong U.S. dollar bad for U.S. companies trading overseas?
11. Besides the European Community (EC), what are some other regional trading groups?
12. Explain why joint ventures can be risky.
13. Explain how less-developed nations may be able to attract direct U.S. business investment.
14. If attempting to market hand soap in Latin America, what major considerations would you need to evaluate with respect to the marketing mix? Would you use a global or country-centered strategy?

NOTES

1. Alfred L. Malabre, Jr., "Trade Is Playing Fast-Growing Role in U.S. Economic Picture," *The Wall Street Journal,* November 13, 1980, p. 40.
2. Alan Murray, "Trade Cap of $30 Billion in First Quarter Indicates U.S. Is Now Debtor Nation," *The Wall Street Journal,* June 18, 1985, p. 60.
3. William J. Hampton, "The Long Arm of Small Business," *Business Week,* February 29, 1988, p. 64.
4. "The Import Bite, Product by Product," *U.S. News & World Report,* September 23, 1985, p. 50.
5. Hugh D. Menzies, "It Pays to Brave the New World," *Fortune,* July 30, 1979, p. 40.
6. Andrew C. Brown, "Unilever Fights Back in the U.S.," *Fortune,* May 26, 1986, pp. 32–38.
7. William F. Schoell and Joseph P. Guiltinan, *Marketing: Contemporary Concepts and Practices,* 3d ed., Boston: Allyn and Bacon, 1988, p. 708.
8. George Fields, "How to Scale the Cultural Fence," *Advertising Age,* December 13, 1982, pp. M11–12.
9. Laurel Wentz, "How General Foods Beat the Odds with Tang," *Advertising Age,* July 4, 1983, pp. M18–19.
10. Ellen Hume, "Furor on South Africa Makes Firms Question Value of Staying There," *The Wall Street Journal,* March 11, 1985, p. 1.
11. "Nestlé Boycott Being Suspended," *The New York Times,* January 27, 1984, p. A1.
12. Laurel Wentz, "Local Laws Keep International Marketers Hopping," *Advertising Age,* July 11, 1985, p. 20.
13. Art Pine, "Debt-Ridden Nations Impose Many Barriers on Foreign Investors," *The Wall Street Journal,* January 21, 1985, p. 1.
14. Clint Willis, "The Overlooked Market Overseas," *Venture,* April 1982, pp. 70–74.
15. "Kmart Is Peddling Its Know-How in the Third World," *Business Week,* August 22, 1983, pp. 45–46.
16. G. Thomas Gibson, "A New Way to Top Overseas Markets," *Venture,* February 1984, pp. 94–95.
17. Willis, "The Overlooked Market Overseas," p. 70.
18. Trepence Roth, "Smaller Firms Try to Master Export Plan," *The Wall Street Journal,* January 24, 1985, p. 9.
19. "U.S. Firms Plus Foreign Partners Equals Prosperity," *U.S. News & World Report,* March, 1983, pp. 51–52.
20. G. Thomas Gibson, "When Overseas Plants Make Sense," *Venture,* August 1982, pp. 82–85.
21. "How Carmakers Are Trimming an Import Surplus," *Business Week,* January 30, 1984, p. 36.
22. Theodore Levitt, "The Globalization of Markets," *Harvard Business Review,* May–June 1983, p. 92.
23. Alsop, "Efficacy of Global Ad Projects Is Questioned in Firm's Survey," *The Wall Street Journal,* September 14, 1985, p. 29.
24. George Anders, "Ad Agencies and Big Concerns Debate World Brand's Value," *The Wall Street Journal,* June 14, 1984, p. 29.
25. Ronald Alsop, "Efficacy of Global Ad Projects Is Questioned in Firm's Survey," p. 29.
26. "Global Marketing Candidates," *The Wall Street Journal,* June 20, 1985, p. 31.
27. Laurel Wentz, "P&G's Crush on Latin America Rekindled," *Advertising Age,* January 16, 1984, p. 4.
28. "Why Global Businesses Perform Better," *International Management,* January 1983, p. 10.

NOTES *(continued)*

29. "Where a Strong Dollar Has Cost American Jobs," *U.S. News & World Report,* January 16, 1984, pp. 74–75.

30. Michael R. Sesit, "Treasurers of Multinationals Plan Ways to Handle Currency Swings," *The Wall Street Journal,* January 24, 1984, p. 31.

31. Alfred L. Malabre, Jr., "Prices in Perspective: As Bad as Inflation May Be in the U.S., It's Far Worse in Most Other Places," *The Wall Street Journal,* December 30, 1980, p. 26.

32. "Apple Tries a Comeback in Japan," *Business Week,* April 11, 1983, pp. 53–55.

U.S. firms encounter many problems—as well as many rewards—when exporting overseas. On the problem side, probably no U.S. export effort is more frustrating than trying to sell cigarettes in Japan.

Prior to 1987, Japanese cigarette prices were fixed by Nihon Sembai Kosha (Japanese Monopoly Public Corporation), the state-owned tobacco company. The Monopoly Corporation, in business since 1904, was formed to raise funds for the Russo-Japanese War. The company annually purchases low-quality tobacco from Japanese farmers at triple the world market price for top quality tobacco. According to at least one U.S. official, this amounts to a subsidy.

To control the cigarette market, the Japanese combined taxes and tariffs to keep the price of American cigarettes high. U.S. cigarettes retailed for approximately 60 percent more than their Japanese competitor. In 1982 tariffs were reduced from 90 percent to 20 percent (same as the U.S. tariff rate); however, Japan's tariff was counted as a part of the foreign cigarettes' base price when the country's 56 percent tax was calculated. This made a pack of U.S. cigarettes approximately $1.25 versus a Japanese pack for 83 cents.

Over the years the Monopoly established a long list of restrictions for the marketing, advertising, and distribution of foreign cigarettes. For example, the Monopoly used a formula that allowed it to spend $70 million on advertising versus an average of $660,000 per American company. Another Monopoly rule permitted one-third of the cigarette budget to be spent on radio and TV advertising. This means that a company like Reynolds could spend its entire radio and TV budget in only eight weeks running spot commercials.

bution process. Until 1985, the Monopoly distributed all foreign and domestic cigarettes. The Monopoly requires that a brand be test marketed (only once per year) before it can go into general distribution. A brand must then pass fixed sales goals at stated intervals to pass the test. Currently, U.S. cigarette makers can sell to distributors. Often, however, these authorized distributors are located outside the prime selling areas of Tokyo and Osaka. Thus, American companies often find it too expensive to set up their own networks. Most still use the Monopoly.

In 1987, after a decade of steady political spadework culminating in a threat of sanctions by the Reagan Administration, foreign and U.S. tobacco manufacturers were finally able to set their own retail prices. U.S. cigarettes now sell for nearly the same price as their Japanese competitors. Thus, Philip Morris and other U.S. companies believe they can capture as much as 30 percent of the Japanese market. To illustrate this point, American companies in 1987 went from a 2.1 percent market share to 10 percent in six months. Now, however, the days of rapid growth are over and only smart marketing strategies will help U.S. companies achieve their goals.

Competition is fierce. Thirty-two million Japanese smoke over 300 billion cigarettes a year. Although Japan has the highest per-person cigarette consumption rate in the world, sales are dropping there as in the U.S. The 1 to 2 percent decrease per year is a result of a more health-conscious public and strong anti-smoking campaigns.

To combat these trends, rival companies are introducing niche

products. Japan Tobacco is introducing new brands at the rate of one per month. The majority of these new brands are targeted at young smokers and women smokers. For example, to capitalize on the strong cult image of James Dean, the brand "Dean" is packed 10 to a compact yellow-and-red box with a campaign that suggests Dean-style anger and rebellion.

For American companies this all means using strategies similar to the competition. Unfortunately for U.S. companies, they will be getting a late start and will have a fraction of the resources to accomplish the task. For example, Japan Tobacco uses a sales force of over 2,000 who can visit Japan's 250,000 newsstands at least once per month.

Issues for Discussion

1. If you were the marketing manager for a U.S. cigarette company, how would you propose that your firm further penetrate the Japanese market?

2. Make a list of various trade barriers that the Japanese used to keep American cigarette manufacturers and others from capturing significant market shares in their country.

3. Explain what role the international political environment plays in trading with nations like Japan.

Source: Adapted from Louis Kraar, "Japan Blows Smoke about U.S. Cigarettes," *Fortune,* February 21, 1983, pp. 99–111; Michael Doan, "Why U.S. Cigarettes Strike Out in Japan," *U.S. News & World Report,* September 23, 1985, p. 51; Damon Darlin, "Foreign Cigarette Firms Face Challenge of Further Growth in Japanese Market," *The Wall Street Journal,* October 19, 1987, p. 51; and Joel Dreyfus, "How to Beat the Japanese at Home," *Fortune,* pp. 80–83.

OUTLINE

CHAPTER

22

Marketing for Service and Nonprofit Organizations

LEARNING GOALS

After reading this chapter, you should be able to:

1. Define services and describe their importance to the U.S. economy.
2. Discuss important characteristics of services that influence their marketing.
3. Explain the environment's impact on service marketing.
4. Describe nonprofits and the environment that a marketer might face in working for a nonprofit.
5. List the types of nonprofit situations where marketing is employed.
6. Describe the marketing mix in a nonprofit situation.

In 1978, the federal government made a decision to deregulate several industries, including the airlines. Major airlines, such as United Airlines, underwent the change from an operations-orientation to a marketing-orientation. The change was forced partly by a new airline company, People Express (P/E), which was started when three people with administrative experience in the airline industry realized the opportunity deregulation offered. Donald Burr presented the idea for P/E to Bill Hambrecht, an investment banker who liked the idea, thought the company would be profitable, and agreed to handle a stock offering to raise capital.

In its early years, and before its eventual sale to Texas Air Corporation, People Express (P/E) grew faster than any other airline in the history of the United States. It rose from 250 to 3,000 employees, from three to thirty-three planes, and from a loss of $9 million to a gain of approximately $20 million in 1983. Donald Burr, CEO, commented, "We've designed a product that is so popular we can't satisfy the demand for it." The product, really a service, was a seat on an airliner traveling between major U.S. cities primarily on the East Coast.

What made this product so attractive to consumers? (After all, other airlines offer seats.) Price—cheap seats during peak hours, but even lower fares during off-peak hours. The passenger, however, did have to pay extra to have baggage checked and for snacks and drinks on board. Passengers were said to fit into one of two groups: those who had only a little money and those with a lot, but who preferred not to spend it.

P/E had no ticket counters. Reservations were made by phone or through travel agents, and tickets were paid for on-board. Burr's view was that air travel is a commodity business, that given safety, a convenient flight schedule, and clean aircraft, price is the most important thing to passengers. P/E's low fares generally hinged upon two factors: "Honest" pricing and People's people. Every employee owned at least one-hundred shares in the company and every employee had multiple responsibilities. For Burr, the real strength of the company was that it gave every employee the opportunity to use his or her creative talents.

What were P/E's best chances for continuing success? P/E is said to have altered strategies when the decision to serve Chicago was made. Some competitors were meeting—and sometimes beating—P/E's low fares. Northwest Airlines also started using comparative advertising, pointing out the differences in services provided. Previously P/E had competed, but not in the major markets. Some industry analysts believed P/E began to have difficulty maintaining control over its growth and finding enough qualified employees. P/E's phone reservation system seemed to have an endless busy signal.

Still, until they were absorbed by Texas Air Corp., P/E had a better load factor, revenue per passenger mile, and cost per available seat mile than the other major airlines.

Issues for Discussion

1. Why was P/E so successful in the early 1980s in the air travel market?
2. Did P/E take a marketing approach to providing a service?
3. Discuss some of the problems and opportunities that deregulation posed to P/E's marketers.

Sources: William Carley, "People Express's Newark-Chicago Entry Underscores Shift in Strategy of Carner," *The Wall Street Journal,* August 9, 1984, p. 4; Kurt Hoffman, "Airline Is Finding People Who Need People," *Advertising Age,* July 12, 1984, pp. 18–19; Lucien Rhodes, "That Daring Young Man and His Flying Machines," *Inc.,* January 1984, pp. 42–52; and "Marketing Efforts Sour at Airlines," *Advertising Age,* September 10, 1984.

◼ The marketing strategy and plan are very important to service firms also.

*M*uch of the discussion in the text has concentrated on business product companies and the strategies they use to market their goods. In this chapter, we turn to the service and nonprofit sectors of the economy. We define the nature of service organizations, examine the market for them, and look at how services use the marketing mix. Today, services—as opposed to manufacturing—represent the fastest-growing sector of our economy. In the second half of the chapter we look at nonprofit organizations, their target publics, and the marketing approaches they use. Many nonprofit organizations are service organizations that disperse profits differently than for-profit service and product companies. As you read through the chapter, the Introductory Case continues the People Express story of startling innovation in the transportation service industry. ■

MARKETING FOR SERVICES

*S*ervices are intangibles that we purchase.

Services are activities and benefits provided by an organization that satisfy the buyer's needs while providing little or no new ownership of physical or tangible goods. Physical items may or may not be involved in the production of the service; the primary customer benefit is from the usefulness or enjoyment derived from the service. It is possible for customers to purchase services that they will never be able to touch or even define clearly, as in the case of life insurance or inoculation against disease.

The process of marketing services and marketing tangible goods is fundamentally the same—the process of planning, implementing, and controlling the marketing mix are carried out in services as in products. However, because of their intangibility, services present special problems and challenges to the marketer. In marketing the service of a moving company, for example, it may be as important to stress the politeness, friendliness, and personal neatness of the employees as it is to emphasize

Day-care centers are an expanding service industry.

❑ **Figure 22.1**
Product-service
continuum.

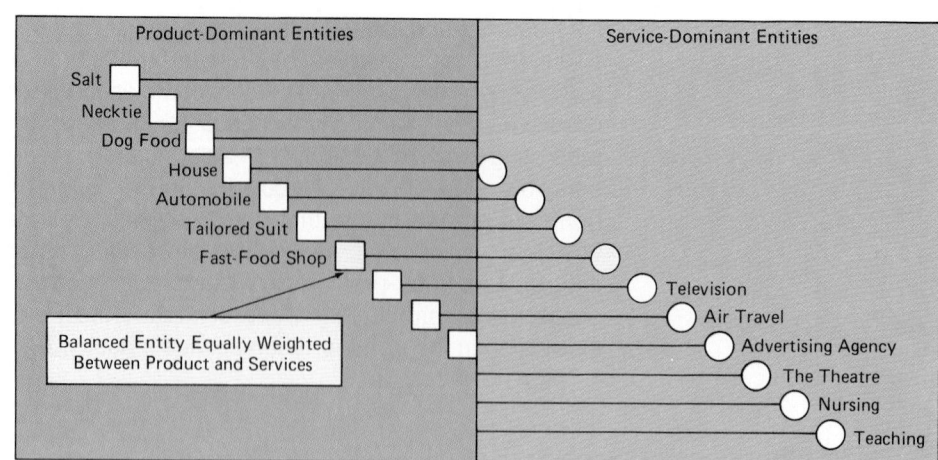

Source: Reprinted from G. Lynn
Shostak, "How to Design a
Service in Marketing of
Services." Proceedings of the
American Marketing Association,
Chicago, 1981, published by the
American Marketing Association.

their competence. The environment in which a service is sold and the image consumers have of service providers can be as important as the service itself in obtaining the acceptance of buyers.

Although services are intangible, they are frequently sold in conjunction with a physical product. For example, appliance stores are obviously in the business of selling goods, but the services they provide—in the form of information about upkeep or liberal delivery and repair policies—may be as important to their customers as more tangible considerations like brands and prices. A continuum exists, as shown in figure 22.1, from a total service to a total product offering.

The Market for Services

*S*ervices are increasingly
important to consumers,
job seekers, and
economies.

Services have increased in the last several years until they now total nearly 50 percent of the consumer's purchase dollar.[1] Services constitute a large proportion of expenditures made by industrial buyers also. Even in world trade, expenditures on services are estimated to be in the range of $400–$500 billion annually, about one-fourth of the amount of world trade in goods.[2]

In recent years, there has been a dramatic shift in the types of services exported. The traditional services of transportation and tourism remain important, but business services have gained significantly in sales. In many of the business services, like banking, insurance, consulting, franchising, and communication, the U.S. has a comparative advantage. The sales abroad in the business service sector would be even larger if regulations and barriers were removed.

Over two-thirds of the jobs in the United States are service-related, and the number is growing faster than the number of nonservice jobs. A major portion of economic growth and job creation in the industrial world is expected to originate in the service sector.

Service jobs have been characterized as menial and having lower pay and fewer benefits than manufacturing jobs. Like manufacturing jobs, however, they vary tremendously in the skill and knowledge they require and, therefore, in the pay and benefits they provide—from top corporate attorneys to short-order cooks.

*W*ant to start a business
of your own? Consider a
service.

The growth of the service sector has created new opportunities for the entrepreneurial spirit. Companies seemingly sprouted overnight in pursuit of a slice of the $40 billion dollar market in long-distance telephone business. In New York City a firm called Early Bird Messenger Service specializes in making quick deliveries on bicycles in the traffic-jammed midtown area. The bicycle rider can zigzag through stalled auto traffic, use the sidewalk, and occasionally even run a red light. A myriad of small, locally owned and operated firms provide services to communities—examples include real estate brokers, attorneys, beauty shop operators, accountants, printers, private detectives, and security bodyguards. Large and small firms alike see the marketing of services as potentially rewarding because of new types of services—such as satellite communication—and new ways of organizing existing services, such as H&R Block (tax accounting) and Century 21 (residential real estate). Competition and regulatory changes have also kindled an interest in marketing in some service industries. The airline and banking industries have been greatly influenced by deregulation and are paying increased attention to marketing details and strategy.

Characteristics of Services

Services may be less affected by the economy and more labor intensive than products.

Services are different from products in several ways. Service sales tend to be less affected by economic booms and recessions than goods sales. The production of services tends to require more labor and less capital than the production of manufactured goods. Partly as a result, increases in productivity have been lower in the service sector.[3] Four characteristics set services apart from products: intangibility, inseparability, quality variability, and perishability.

INTANGIBILITY

Because of the **intangibility** of services, our senses (sight, hearing, taste, smell, touch) cannot be used in the decision to purchase them. The purchaser comes to know the nature of the purchase—quality, dimensions, and benefits—only after the service is performed. The buyer of a service, therefore, must have faith in the ability and the willingness of the provider to deliver the service. The marketer should ask: Can this service be made tangible? How?

Increasing tangibility is an important strategy in service marketing.

Several strategies are available to improve the marketability of services by making them more tangible.[4] Suppliers use testimonials, being careful that the individuals are believable. Service establishments also develop brand names for themselves—One-Hour Martinizing (dry cleaning) and Avis Car Rental are examples. Public broadcasting stations offer bumper stickers and key chains to make their service tangible. Health maintenance organizations and some insurance companies provide their clients with plastic cards. They are really not necessary, but they create tangibility. Some hotels add tangible evidence of service performed by wrapping drinking glasses and leaving chocolate mints on turned-down beds.

The intangibility of services can make purchase decisions difficult, but this can be at least partially overcome. Beauticians display illustrations to help customers visualize the benefits of their service. Technology can be used to bring together as one picture the end result of a service. For example, a plastic surgeon could show a patient alternative results of the surgery. Instead of a "before" and only one "after" picture, there could be several "after" pictures showing all possible results of the surgery.

In general, service marketers should stress the benefits of the service instead of the service itself. American Express, for example, stresses that cardholders can be unknowns but still make purchases throughout the world through its "Do you know me?" campaign.

INSEPARABILITY

Separating a service from the individual supplier may be difficult if not impossible.

Inseparability means that a service cannot be separated from the person performing or selling it. There was only one Elvis Presley; to see any other performer, even the adept imitators, for Presley fans was not the same. Some customers have a personal physician, attorney, hair stylist, or other service supplier whom they know

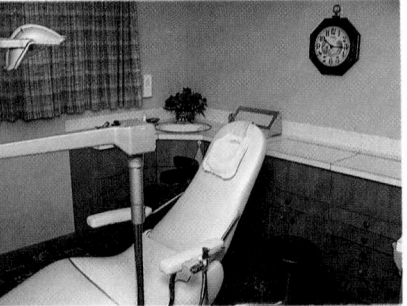

Artistic service is impossible to separate from the individual artist.

*M*aintaining quality is a key to successful service marketing.

*M*cDonald's is noted for consistent quality.

Empty appointment times represent lost opportunity for a dentist to provide a service.

*S*ervices cannot be stored.

and trust. Inseparability imposes certain limitations on the service supplier. The individual supplier has only so much time to devote to providing the service and obviously cannot be in more than one place at a time. To increase productivity, three possibilities exist. First, the supplier can work faster—physicians often have several examination rooms, thus allowing them to go directly from one room to another without the delay of patient preparation. Second, the supplier can see more than one buyer at a time. Providing a service to a group increases productivity. Third, the seller can detach the service from the individual supplier by training employees, franchisees, and others to perform the service at the same level of quality as the original supplier.

The close association between a service and its supplier means that the predominate channel of distribution for services is direct. Because services are created and dispensed simultaneously, the customer goes directly to the supplier to purchase a service. Buyers and sellers often interact during production and distribution. As the service is performed, the supplier can ask the buyer for information in order to customize the service to the buyer's specifications.

Even though direct distribution predominates in the marketing of services, intermediaries in the channel do exist. They represent the supplier and sell the supplier's service. Travel agents, for example, sell transportation and accommodation services and at the same time provide their own services.

QUALITY VARIABILITY

"Service quality is a measure of how well the service level delivered matches customer expectations. Delivering quality service means conforming to customer expectations on a consistent basis."[5] Because the provision of services is labor intensive, services vary in quality from one purchase to the next, even from the same supplier. A new bank teller probably supplies a different service from one who is more experienced. Either bank teller might perform differently at a branch location than at the main office. Both will probably give a different quality of service at the end of the day than at the beginning. Such **quality variability** poses special challenges to the marketer.

It is impossible to standardize services to the same degree as products, but marketers of services must work diligently to maintain consistent quality and standardize production and delivery as much as they can.[6] When employees in a service organization are selected and trained with care, the quality of their work is more dependable. McDonald's Corporation is known for the McDonald's system, which standardizes the preparation and delivery of food. Training is an important part of the system, which has enabled the company to establish a consistent level of service quality at its thousands of locations.

To maintain consistency, the quality of a service must be monitored constantly. This means that the ongoing supervision of employees is as important as their selection and training. In addition, service suppliers should pay close attention to the response of their customers. Surveys and suggestion boxes are both ways to collect data on customer complaints, satisfaction, and quality levels in general. Both ChemLawn and Holiday Inn have service guarantee programs to ensure that their customers are satisfied. The intent of these programs is to attract new business, but they also benefit the companies as effective quality control measures.

PERISHABILITY AND FLUCTUATING DEMAND

Services have high **perishability** since their production is based upon a time element and since they are intangible and cannot be stored. An empty theatre seat, dental chair, bus seat, or hotel room represent a lost opportunity to sell a service that cannot be recovered. Perishability and uneven demand for services call for creative strategy. If the resources for producing services are in place and if demand

*T*o level demand, reduce slack periods by lowering prices and promoting heavily.

levels exceed the ability to produce, sales are lost. If the service supplier builds facilities to meet peak demand, a portion of the facilities may sit idle during other periods. A solution to the problem of perishability is a key goal of the marketer. One strategy emphasizes leveling demand. Reducing fares during off-peak times, happy hour prices, weekend and evening long-distance telephone rates, and "red-eye" night flight fares on the airlines all represent examples of off-peak pricing attempts to level demand. Advertising more heavily for business during off-peak periods is another way of leveling demand. The objective to attract more business may only shift peak demand to off-peak times, a desirable feat if price reductions are not involved. Reservation systems, besides reducing consumer complaints over length of waiting times, also level demand by shifting some demand from peak times to other times.

Offering alternative services may also help solve the problems of perishability and uneven demand. When demand exceeds resources to provide the service, some suppliers have been very effective in offering complementary services. The restauranteur may shuffle people to the bar when the dining facilities are full. The racketball court manager may encourage people to use the weight or exercise room when all the courts are full. Some suppliers may be able to use their facilities for a different service during the off-peak times—using airplanes for passengers during the day but for packages and parcels at night.

*T*o level demand, handle peak periods by adding employees, focus on essential tasks, and contract out work.

Another strategy to overcome perishability and fluctuation of demand is to create a flexible production facility. The addition of temporary employees during periods of peak demand expands production when it is needed, yet it does not commit the service supplier to maintain the same level of production in slower periods. Concentrating on essential tasks during periods of high demand and housekeeping or maintenance tasks during periods of low demand is another way to increase flexibility. The fast-food industry is especially adept at both. A third solution to the problem of fluctuating demand is to contract out part of the task during peak periods. For example, electric utilities with different peak periods buy power from each other. Thus, they avoid constructing facilities that will duplicate resources in periods of lower demand.

THE CASE CONTINUES

*P*eople Express succeeded for many reasons, but its initial advantage came from cutting costs while developing a unique approach to the characteristics of a service industry. Every employee was a shareholder. Each had traits that exemplified the P/E organization philosophy. To the passenger, the employee embodied P/E. In this way, the service's *intangibility* was reduced. Because each

employee served in a variety of functions—baggage handler one day, ticket seller the next—the passenger had an opportunity to see employees in several roles. The resulting impression was of an airline interested

in the passenger's total traveling welfare. Because employees were so invested in the company, each one was more likely to be motivated and able to deliver a consistent *quality* of service on every occasion. P/E effectively dealt with the *perishability* of airline service by having a load factor of 80 percent, using off-peak prices and reservations to level demand.

Classification of Services

*H*ow a service is marketed may depend on whether it is people- or equipment-based.

Since many kinds of services are available, classifying the various types makes it easier to develop a marketing strategy. One way to classify services considers whether they depend on equipment or people. **Equipment-based services** require equipment for their production and delivery. A taxicab driver, for instance, obviously requires

☐ **Figure 22.2**
Equipment- and
people-based services.

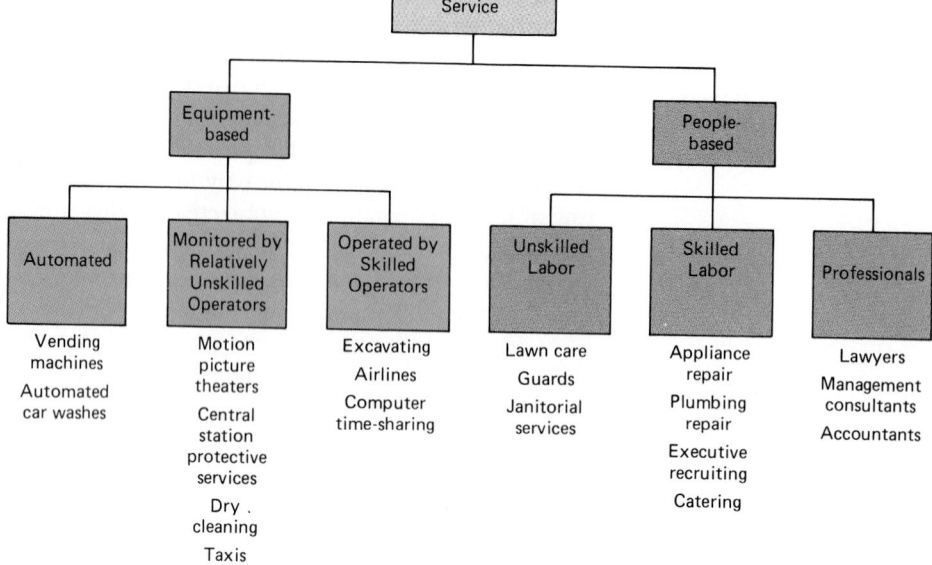

a car. **People-based services** can be produced and delivered without the aid of equipment. Legal services are an example. Within the primary categories of equipment-based and people-based services, there are secondary categories based on the skill level of the people involved: unskilled, skilled, or professional (see figure 22.2).

Skill level and amount of equipment indicate how a service might be marketed. If the service cannot be produced without a large investment in equipment, such as a CAT scan machine, the geographic market area served is likely to be large and the service high-priced. When equipment increases productivity, price usually becomes a competitive marketing tool. In the film processing industry, recent developments in film processing equipment have reduced the size of the equipment and lowered the price. The result has been new processing labs called minilabs that are rivaling the older, one-hour photo processors. Until recently, professional services have not been marketed aggressively; word-of-mouth and nonprice competition were typical promotional techniques. Attorneys are now advertising using TV, radio, newspapers, and magazines. A Baltimore law firm used the slogan, "If you have a phone, you have a lawyer," in its TV advertising campaign.

Another method of classifying services is by the type of purchaser—industrial or consumer. As with products, the marketing of services varies by the type of purchaser. Insurance programs for businesses are different from programs for individuals, and the marketing of the service differs as well. For instance, a business may be offered group rates for its employees and may receive more personal attention from the agency than an individual receives.

How much customer contact is needed to provide a service?

Client involvement in the service also serves as a basis for classification, which distinguishes between services where the client has to be present and services where the client does not have to be present. Usually, services are more highly customized when clients have to be present.

Services may also be classified according to whether they are provided by profit- or nonprofit-making organizations. Service organizations have generally not been marketing-oriented, especially the nonprofits. The second half of this chapter discusses nonprofit organizations.

❏ **Figure 22.3**
Examples of service
attributes.

```
Security
        Confidence in the airline pilot
        Double locks on hotel room doors
        Confidentiality of records by a tax preparation firm
Consistency
        TWA's on-time airline strategy
        Same flavor or quality of food at each visit to a restaurant
Attitude
        Recognition of regular customers at a restaurant
        Airline V.I.P. rooms
        Restaurant manager asking guests about the quality of their meals
Completeness
        American Airline's introduction of curb-side check-in service
        Acceptance of credit cards at a restaurant
        Holiday Inn's policy of providing a swimming pool at all their hotels
        Airport parking facilities
        Salad bar at a restaurant
Condition
        Clean restrooms at McDonald's
        Decor in theme restaurants
        Nonsmoking seating at Victoria Station restaurants
Availability
        Easy access to race track by public transportation
        Locations of service stations
        Convenient and frequent airline departures
Timing
        Serving of a meal at the "right" psychological moment in the dining experience
        Fast completion of tax reports by tax preparation firms
```

Source: W. Earl Sasser, R. Paul
Olsen, and D. Daryl Wyckoff,
*Management of Service
Operations: Text, Cases and
Readings,* © 1978. Reprinted by
permission of Allyn and Bacon.

The Marketing Mix for Services

Developing a marketing mix for services requires that many questions be answered. What services should be offered? What attributes of the service should be stressed? What price should be charged? How should the service be distributed and promoted?

SERVICE ATTRIBUTES

What attributes should the service include to encourage purchase? To answer this question, the marketer should understand what the consumer is actually buying when purchasing a service. Service attributes such as security, consistency, and completeness may be important factors in the purchase decision. Examples of attributes are given in figure 22.3. Correctly identified attributes can become the foundation for a customer-oriented service ethic throughout the firm. The attributes can be advertised, promoted, and marketed to customers and perhaps more importantly to employees of the firm.

*F*airness is the service attribute most desired by
Travelers' customers.

Attributes may be identified through basic research. Travelers Corporation in Hartford, Connecticut, commissioned the research firm of Yankelovich, Skelly and White to identify attributes important to Travelers' market. The research identified fairness as the most important attribute, and the Travelers' market defined fairness as responsiveness in customer service, good value for the money, and equal treatment. Travelers was able to use the identified attributes to differentiate the company from its competitors in a meaningful way.[7]

SERVICE MIX

*W*hat services should the
firm provide?

Service mix is a listing of all the services a supplier has to offer. Service firms, especially the smaller ones, often overlook mix considerations. Since no inventory exists, the request for a service slightly different from existing services often leads to an attempt to provide the requested service. Therefore, firms should develop a clear definition of what they offer.

❑ **Figure 22.4**
Service content
considerations.

Source: W. Earl Sasser, R. Paul
Olsen, and D. Daryl Wyckoff,
*Management of Service
Operations: Text, Cases and
Readings,* p. 13, © 1978.
Reprinted by permission of Allyn
and Bacon.

Prepackaging of Services
Direct mail order as prepackaged retailing Preprepared fast foods with specially designed "cooking" equipment Throw-away medical equipment—thermometers and syringes Do-it-yourself kits for such things as carpeting, paneling, and plumbing Self-instruction courses—language, occupational, and self-improvement Prepackaged insurance policies Tune-up kits and throw-away parts for automobile servicing
Increasing the Service Content of Goods and Services
"Have-it-your-way" fast foods Mix-and-match clothing Service centers and service warranties for autos, electronics, and appliances Specialty food departments (bakeries and delicatessens) in self-service groceries Decorator and other consumer "consultants" in department and discount stores
Consumerization of Production
Knock-down products requiring final assembly by the consumer Use of electronic tellers in banks Self-service retailers Self-service gasoline stations

Developing new services and deleting less requested services are a part of managing the service mix. A survey of Illinois hospitals, for example, indicates that hospitals are more adept at adding services than they are at gauging demand or pruning unwanted services.[8] Frequently added services include:

Birth Center	Mobile CAT Scanner
Home Health Nursing	Emergency Response System
Ambulatory Surgery	Health Education System
Infant Seat Loaner	Outpatient Clinics
Nutritional Support	Cardiac Rehabilitation
Satellite Facilities	Adult Alcohol and
Wellness Program	Drug Abuse Aid
Adolescent Sexual Abuse Program	Industrial Medicine

*T*he service level is the
percentage of service re-
quests that are fulfilled in a
specified time.

The chosen level of service affects the service mix. How many requests for services should the supplier attempt to satisfy, and how many should be turned away? Normally, none of the requests that are obviously in the range of the resources and abilities of the service firm will be turned away, but service should occur within a reasonable time and at a reasonable quality level. The marketer may establish the level of service as a percentage of requests, say 95 percent. This means that 95 percent of the requests for service should be satisfied within a specific period and at a specified quality level. Even with good promotion of what the firm has to offer, requests for variation in service will come that cannot and should not be fulfilled.

The marketing manager may also want to consider the amount of service content the firm will offer. Some of the possible options on service content appear in figure 22.4.

PRICING

*P*erishability of services
affects pricing.

Several characteristics of the service sector make pricing services different from pricing tangible products. If the service industry is regulated at all, price is very likely to be one of the features regulated, as with the utilities. Traditional pricing also may be more prevalent in services. Advertising agencies, for instance, traditionally receive an established percentage of the media from the media firm instead of from the client. Negotiation is more prevalent in service purchases than in product purchases. Market research, legal, financial, maintenance, and security services are often bought and sold at negotiated prices. When negotiating the service, the marketer will keep

THE REST OF THE STORY

Tax Preparation Takes a Timely Turn

Richard and Henry, recent university graduates, formed the United Business Company, a bookkeeping service for small businesses. To obtain business, they knocked on doors and offered to keep books for free to display their talents. The year was 1946.

By 1954, their excellent customer service helped them achieve the status of the largest bookkeeping service in Kansas City. The service included the preparation of clients' income tax forms for free. As clients told others of the tax service, the business grew to the point that United Business Company started charging for the preparation of tax forms. Still, the brothers were working seven days and nights a week. They made a decision in early 1954 to quit the tax business.

Clients protested loudly. By the end of 1954, the brothers had reversed their original decision, decid-

ing to discontinue bookkeeping and to devote the business to tax preparation. Tax preparation was a service that had not been proven as a money maker. No precedent had been established. Little perceived need existed and it was very seasonal. Nonetheless, on January 25, 1955, the concept was launched. On that very day, a Kansas City Star newspaper ad salesman insisted the firm run a small newspaper ad which read, "Income Taxes prepared, $5 and up." Both astute pricing and advertising have since been a part of the company's market plan.

The response to the tax preparation concept was overwhelming. In

1958 they decided to franchise. In 1965 they prepared one million returns in one year and in that year decided to use TV as their primary advertising medium. With office rental exceedingly high during the off-season, an arrangement with Sears and, eventually, other retailers was made for office space in their stores, but only during tax season. An attempt to have clients make appointments for tax form preparation was not accepted by clients.

H&R Block continues to seek ways of reducing the seasonality of its business. Now you know the rest of the story.

Sources: Adapted from Thomas Block, "Innovations in Service Marketing," in *Emerging Perspectives on Service Marketing;* Leonard Berry, G. Lynn Shostack, and Gregory D. Upah, eds. (Chicago: American Marketing Association, 1983), pp. 22–24, published by the American Marketing Association.

---

in mind the cost and the perishability characteristics. Since services are perishable, if demand for the firm's services are low, the price may be discounted in order to obtain the sale. As long as variable costs are covered, the marketer may be satisfied. Unfortunately, information on fixed, variable, average, and other costs may not be as readily available to the service firm as to the product company.[9] Offering a service at a reduced price can pose a problem. Because it is difficult for customers to evaluate a service, they may use price as a surrogate for quality. Thus, they may equate low or discounted prices with poor quality.

The service marketer should consider the following factors in establishing price: demand for service; production, marketing, and administrative costs; and competitive influences.[10]

DISTRIBUTION

Stimulating and leveling demand are a major part of service distribution.

Distribution channels for services tend to be shorter and simpler than for tangible products. Even when contact with the client is unnecessary, many clients prefer that a personal relationship be maintained. When intermediaries exist in the channel, they focus on stimulating and leveling demand rather than on inventory, transportation, or storage control.[11]

PROMOTION

Service contact personnel are a primary ingredient in service promotion.

Both the intangibility of services and the personal relationship that many customers desire influence promotional strategy. Promotional strategy may focus on increasing the tangibility of services. One technique is to highlight a particular feature of the firm, such as employees (Kroger Supermarkets' Employee of the Week), or

The Arizona Heart Institute in Phoenix is a clinic for the prevention and treatment of cardiovascular disease. Thanks in part to the prominence of its founder and director, cardiac surgeon Edward B. Diethrich, the institute already had achieved considerable name recognition from publicity generated by several breakthroughs in cardiac care.

Boosting name recognition was therefore a secondary marketing objective, with rapid expansion of the patient base being the primary one. The goal of increasing the number of new patients 30 percent was achieved in only six weeks; after ninety days of advertising, the number of patients treated was 95 percent greater than twelve months earlier.

The first step was to create a consistent and meaningful identity for the institute. The creative team developed the positioning headline, "The #1 defense against the #1 killer." That tag reinforced the image of the institute as *the* authority in preventing and treating cardiac problems. The positioning line was moved to the bottom of the ad in subsequent print ads. Rather than direct the ad to doctors who could make referrals, a consumer campaign was launched in the major morning and evening newspapers in the Phoenix market.

In the seventh week, a new creative execution was introduced that aggressively encouraged checkups for possible cardiovascular problems. The ad featured an illustration of a human heart, an erratic electrocardiogram (EKG) graph, and the headline, "Not everything is worth waiting for. Early detection can substantially reduce the risk of heart disease."

In addition to positioning the institute with consumer ads, direct mail was used to offer a package of several institute services coupled with price-off promotion.

MARKETING IN ACTION

Marketing a Heart Institute

Source: Excerpts reprinted from James A. Wichterman, "Packaged Goods Methods Click for Marketing of Heart Institute," *Marketing News,* January 18, 1985, p. 8, published by the American Marketing Association.

Room for Improvement

Some of us can get away with anything -- fudging on the income tax, buttering up the boss, or just being corny. But we can't cheat on our health and get away with it. Not for long, anyway.

We Are What We Eat

The laws of physiology, chemistry and physics aren't repealed just because we slide up to the table. We are, inescapably, what we eat. And for many Americans that can lead to heart disease-- still our number one killer. Heart disease is preventable, but that requires being honest with yourself. And it's reassuring to know we're in your corner.

When You Win, We Win

At the Arizona Heart Institute, we know a thing or two about prevention. In fact, we've blazed the trail. Our 15 years of clinical research and practice has led us to many victories in our battle against the ravages of heart disease. We've already helped over 40,000 Arizonans, and our national programs have helped tens of thousands more.

The Nation Looks to Us

PBS televised the first live open-heart operation nationally-- an operation by our team. ABC's "20/20 " program on our nationwide Heart Test generated a record 250,000 responses! And most recently, when we designed a testing program to make an entire eastern city more heart-healthy, PBS broadcasted a documentary about that, too. The bottom line? There are no easy answers for heart disease. But there are answers. And we've created many of them.

Your Life's Story

The more precise the diagnosis, the more precise the prescription-- for life Which is why some of our prescriptions for patients can run as many as 40 pages. And why not? Since human beings are one of the most complex systems

on the face of the earth, they are entitled to a prescription as unique as they are. That's why the prevention, diagnosis, and treatment of heart disease is so serious-- too important to be be taken casually. The answers aren't found in pills, diet drinks, fads, or health club memberships.

The State of the Heart

The answers come from professional heart teams-- the cardiovascular specialists, super-technicians, the physiologists, the psychologists, the researchers, the dietitians, even from the innovative diagnostic methods that you find here at the Heart Institute. Our methods and teams are so highly respected that they have been the model for programs in more than 60 American cities. Because we are nationally recognized innovators, you benefit from state-of-the-art technology and thinking. A step ahead of conventional wisdom.

Dr. Diethrich
To Be Alive
"Quality of Life"

Ask most people over 60 or 70 what is most important to them and they'll usually have the same answer. Good health. And that amazes me. Not because they realize it, but because it takes so many years to come to that conclusion.

Heart disease, for example, still runs rampant, flattening one in five Americans. Yet, it is preventable.

Maybe we need Surgeon General's warnings on packages of bacon, cheese, French fries, burgers, butter, eggs, and even ice cream. For many people, these products constitute a real and growing danger to their health.

These people know who they are. They don't own jogging shoes or sportswear, they don't regard their fork as a potentially lethal weapon, and they pollute the atmosphere with their cigarettes.

Their behavior affects all of us. And that's not just blowing smoke. Because they require proportionately more medical attention, they cause health insurance premiums to stay high.

One of these days the insurers will start offering less expensive health insurance to people who are dedicated to keeping themselves healthy. Like a "safe driver" discount. How's that for incentive?

Here's Help

If there's room for improvement in **your** life, and if you've made up your mind not to be the one in five stricken with heart disease, we can

AHI- widely imitated, but not equalled.

Call today: **955-1000.**

Arizona Heart Institute

4800 North 22nd Street
Phoenix , AZ 85016

86-2-SW-5x16

■ The marketing plan, even for a heart institute, should include promotion.
Source: VAS Communications/American Heart Institute.

architecture (McDonald's Golden Arches), or some other feature. The company's favorable image may become the tangible feature. Themes include friendliness, efficiency, progressiveness, and others.

Personal selling and contact with the customer are very important parts of the promotional program for service firms. Courtesy, diplomacy, and the resolution of customer problems by employees usually are desired features of service firms.

Publicity also occupies an important role in promotional strategy for service firms. Contribution of time and money to charitable organizations, sponsorship of athletic teams, and public events increase favorable public awareness if properly publicized.[12]

THE CASE CONTINUES

P/E utilized marketing extensively in its success. For instance, it developed a marketing strategy, at least initially, of not competing with the major airlines. The marketing mix was planned very carefully. Price was emphasized in the mix and low fares stressed as a major part of the strategy. Promotion, in the form of advertising, lets potential customers know about the low fares. The distri-

bution was the typical service distribution type—simple and direct. Reservations were phoned in to the company, and some ticket sales were made by travel agents. The service (product) was transportation, primarily between East Coast cities. Unlike other airline companies, P/E's

basic service included only the seat, not incidental items such as baggage checking or meals and drinks (except for an extra fee). A target market was selected—those travelers who are price-conscious. And finally, the whole marketing strategy was controlled and adjusted with collected information, such as load factor rate and cost per available passenger mile.

MARKETING FOR NONPROFIT ORGANIZATIONS

More and more administrators of nonprofit organizations have turned to marketing to achieve the objectives of their organizations. Planned Parenthood, the YMCA, the American Heart Association, the Peace Corps, and universities have all used marketing in varying degrees.

Why Is Nonprofit Marketing Different?

Diverse objectives characterize nonprofit organizations.

A **nonprofit organization** emphasizes goals other than returning a profit to owners. The objectives of nonprofit organizations vary widely. Some emphasize ecology and the environment, such as Greenpeace or the Sierra Club; some focus on governmental operations, such as Common Cause; and some emphasize health issues, such as the March of Dimes.

Nonprofit organizations are a considerable asset to U.S. society.

Nonprofit organizations represent a considerable part of the United States economy, and they contribute significantly to our quality of life. The exact value of their contribution is difficult to determine because money does not always enter into the marketing exchange when a nonprofit organization represents one side of the exchange. In fact, some would argue that many nonprofit organizations subtract from rather than contribute to the economy and the quality of life. Proponents and opponents of various affirmative action programs have been a case in point, each group arguing that the other's position represents a step backward for society. Nonprofit organizations do account for billions of dollars of value to the United States economy even if one does not include those that are controversial or that represent evaluation problems. Consider that government and governmental agencies at the federal, state, and local levels are nonprofit organizations as are institutions such as schools, universities, and hospitals.

CHARACTERISTICS OF NONPROFIT ORGANIZATIONS

The profit organization is the point of reference for defining the characteristics of nonprofit enterprises. Some nonprofit organizations differ little from the average profit organization, and some profit organizations vary little from the average nonprofit organization. Furthermore, the two types of organizations will probably grow more alike as organizational and management techniques are shared.

An obvious difference between profit and nonprofit organizations, is their primary objective—profit versus some other objective. Techniques have been developed for profit organizations that measure their success. Share of the market, return on investment, sales volume, and profit itself, all indicate how well the profit organization is satisfying the market and how efficiently it is using its resources. The objectives of nonprofit organizations are much more difficult to quantify, so results are more difficult to measure.

*N*onprofit organizations differ from profit organizations in objectives and often in organizational structure.

The organizational structures of nonprofit organizations are less clear than those of profit-oriented companies. Many nonprofit organizations have totally volunteer help. Because the office holders tend to change regularly the structure has less continuity. Lines of authority and responsibility never really become firm. Nonprofit organizations with salaried employees have more structure, but there also may be duplicate structures. For instance, a typical university has administrative, faculty, student, and alumni structures. Informal structures often predominate in nonprofit organizations, and there is less distinction between line and staff positions. Accountability in nonprofit organizations is less specific than in profit firms.[13]

TARGET PUBLICS

*N*onprofit organizations service many groups.

Whom does the organization benefit? That is, who are its **target publics**? Both profit and nonprofit organizations benefit a number of groups. The profit organization tends to focus on customers, owners, and employees. With the nonprofit organizations the list of those interested and benefitting may be longer. The publics receiving the most attention may or may not be the same as for profit organizations.

❑ **Figure 22.5**
Publics of a nonprofit organization.

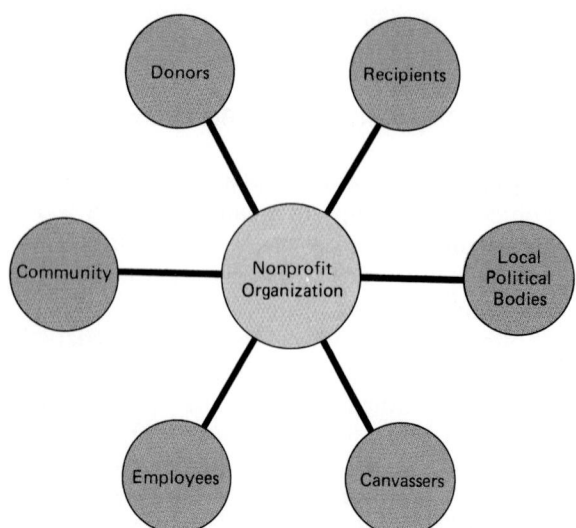

(See figure 22.5.) Nonprofit organizations, for instance, may emphasize contributors of resources as much as or more than clients.[14] Nonbusiness organizations may even have problems identifying their customers. Are Sierra Club clients its members, or are they everyone who might benefit from preserving the environment?

TANGIBILITY OF OFFERING

The offerings of nonprofit organizations are often intangible. Thus the nonprofit marketer faces the same challenge as the for-profit service marketer—defining the offering and making it more tangible.

Although nonprofit marketing like service marketing presents different challenges from product marketing, the basic marketing procedure is the same. Marketers must identify a need, select a target market, determine objectives, develop a strategy, and implement and control the plan. They must consider the environment, price, distribution, and promotion of the product. The nonprofit organization and its external environment are different enough from the profit organization to require different marketing strategies.[15]

ATTITUDES TOWARD MARKETING IN NONPROFIT ORGANIZATIONS

*I*s marketing appropriate in nonprofit organizations?

Marketing has been successful in nonprofit situations, but many people believe that marketing is not appropriate in nonprofit organizations. Opponents claim that marketing wastes resources. They concede that the time required to accomplish the objectives of a nonprofit may be longer without marketing, but they argue that the objectives will be obtained eventually, so marketing is a waste of money. Worse than waste, opponents believe, is the manipulative nature of marketing, especially advertising. Successful marketing means people have been led to behave in ways that they normally would not have considered—using services, accepting ideas, changing attitudes. Finally, marketing is sometimes thought of as an interfering activity. Individuals should have the right to make their own decisions and to clarify and satisfy their own needs without intrusion.

Administrators themselves may not hold the same views, but they hesitate to use marketing because they perceive, perhaps correctly, that some of the public the organization is attempting to satisfy hold marketing in low esteem. More and more, however, the attitude toward marketing as a useful tool for nonprofit organizations is gaining acceptance. Strategies for gaining such acceptance have also been developed and proposed.[16]

Nonprofit Marketing Strategies

Why do nonprofit organizations need marketing strategies? One reason is their vagueness. They have broad, general target markets and their objectives and offerings are often unclear. A good marketing strategy will help to clarify and limit alternatives and thus direct resources to achieve organizational goals more effectively.

TYPES OF NONPROFIT MARKETING

*T*here are four types of nonprofit marketing—organization, person, place, and idea.

Nonprofit organizations sell benefits. Products, services, and ideas are a means of conveying the benefit to the recipient. The marketing theorist Philip Kotler has classified nonprofit marketing by medium of conveyance: organization, person, place, and idea.[17]

Person Marketing.   A person or group of people can be marketed. Politicians, sports people, and performers are all marketed, many using a well-thought-out marketing strategy. Jimmy Conners is reported to have earned millions in endorsements of Converse, Robert Bruce, Wilson, McDonald's, and other company products. Politicians may hire market researchers to assess the market (voting public) and determine market segments where votes are most likely to be gained or lost. The campaign then can be based on such information.

Job seekers, salespeople, and individuals looking for mates also market themselves. Usually their marketing efforts are less formal than those of the politician or the celebrity. In **person marketing,** the objective is to "make" or "maintain" an impression of the person in the target market. The primary purpose of image consulting, which has become an entire industry, is marketing people. To make an impression means that awareness has been gained and an attitude has been created or altered. Generally, it is expected that the target market will take some action based on attitude: vote for the politicians, purchase concert tickets to see the celebrity perform, or hire the job seeker. Individuals take action because of some expected benefit: a politician in office with a philosophy and views closer to their own, a celebrity performance that entertains and diverts their minds from life's problems, or an employee who does the work efficiently and competently.

*I*f you believe the grading system should be changed, consider idea marketing.

*A*dvocacy advertising is paid advertising created to change ideas.

Idea Marketing. Another type of nonprofit marketing deals with social issues and causes. Convincing people of the need and benefits of wearing seat belts, of preserving their environments, of not smoking, of exercising regularly, of having regular health checkups are a few of the many examples of **idea marketing.** Idea marketing (also referred to as social marketing)[18] attempts to identify and gain acceptance of a practice, cause, philosophy, or way of thinking in a selected group.[19] As with other types of nonprofit marketing, seeking acceptance is usually only the initial step toward establishing a desired action or behavior.

Although idea marketers utilize the complete marketing planning process, a highly visual part of the marketing mix is advertising. Since most ideas and causes

An example of idea marketing—"Give to the college of your choice."

Support America's colleges. Because college is more than a place where young people are preparing for their future. It's where *America* is preparing for *its* future.

If our country's going to get smarter, stronger—and more competitive—our colleges and universities simply must become a national priority.

Government. Business. And you. We're all in this together. Because it's *our* future.

So help America keep its competitive edge with a gift to the college of your choice—and you'll know you've done your part.

Give to the college of your choice.

Source: Courtesy of Council for Aid to Education.

Places are marketed in much the same way as products.

Arkansas.
Where it's summer from
April 'til autumn.

Arkansas can stretch your summer and your horizons. You'll discover rivers running clear and clean. Scenery like you can't find anywhere else on earth. And new friends everywhere you stop. This is the season to jump in and get your feet wet, and it's a nice, long season. In The Natural State, summer's never over until the leaves start to turn. And that's another story.

Call or write today for the most complete visitor information kit in America. It's free.
Call toll-free 1-800-643-8383. IN ARKANSAS call 1-800-482-8999.
Mail to Arkansas Vacations, Dept. 1169, One Capitol Mall, Little Rock, Arkansas 72201

Name _____ Address _____

City _____ State _____ Zip _____

THE NATURAL STATE
Arkansas

Source: Arkansas Department of Parks and Tourism/Woods Brothers Agency.

have opposing views, idea marketing stimulates controversy, primarily through advocacy advertising. Advocacy advertising is paid for by an identified source placed in conventional media, but presents information or a viewpoint on a publicly controversial issue.[20]

Using marketing to increase the acceptance of a student organization is an example of organization marketing.

Organization Marketing. Marketing intended to gain, alter, or maintain acceptance of an organization's objectives and services is termed **organization marketing.** Churches, government agencies, schools, art galleries, museums, and labor unions are but a few of the many organizations using marketing. "For colleges and universities, sophisticated marketing strategies are becoming key to survival and prosperity."[21] Besides just accepting the organization's goals, most organizations desire the target audience to seek the services of the organization: fellowship at church, organized attempts to solve social problems by governmental agencies, acquisition of skills and knowledge from educational institutions, or representations by unions. Many organizations use organization marketing to encourage donations.

The acceptance of goals, the distribution of services, and the encouragement of donations all depend on the organization's positive public image with the desired groups. Changing an organization's image involves marketing. The Phoenix Symphony marketing consultant, for instance, surveyed the patrons of the symphony and found them to be older, better-educated people with higher incomes. To attract more young patrons, the symphony launched an advertising campaign using print media and direct mail. The campaign sought to change people's perceptions about the symphony.

Place marketing develops awareness of a geographic area.

Place Marketing. **Place marketing** tries to attract attention and create a positive attitude toward a particular place—including a county, state, region, city, neighborhood, industrial park, house, apartment site, warehouse, farm, terminal or resort. The benefits and advantages of the location are extolled. Advertising, publicity, and personal selling are all popular in promoting a place. Image is quite important, and all the marketing activities bearing on image receive attention. The other marketing elements besides promotion (product, distribution, and price) receive scant, if any, attention. Often product, distribution, and price have little relevance in place marketing, but sometimes they are ignored because of a limited perspective of marketing. Some place marketing programs attempt to lessen the appeal of a particular place. A few years ago, the state of Oregon attempted to discourage people and industry from moving to Oregon.

THE CASE CONTINUES

*A*lthough P/E's objective was to earn a profit, it marketed the idea and organization very much like a nonprofit organization. The need for financial and human resources encouraged Donald Burr to market both the idea for P/E's corporate mission and the organization itself. In idea marketing the attempt is to

identify and gain acceptance of a practice, cause, or philosophy. The cause for P/E was that people should have access to low cost air transportation. The investment banker Bill Hambrecht believed with Burr that it could be done at a profit.

Burr was also able to sell the idea and the organization to many experienced managers who were hired by P/E, and to hundreds of inexperienced (but evidently talented) people who became P/E employees. Business associates and friends, when speaking of Donald Burr, say that he could have been a preacher.

THE MARKETING MIX IN NONPROFIT ORGANIZATIONS

*E*ven in nonprofit organizations, marketing is more than promotion.

The environment within the nonprofit organization influences the marketing mix. The administrators of nonprofit organizations seem to be unaware of their own marketing efforts or at least reluctant to admit their existence.[22] Thus euphemisms tend to be used for marketing terms and activities: counselor for salesperson, service department for marketing department, and clients for target market. Nonprofit administrators also tend to overemphasize the importance and role of promotion—especially advertising—in the marketing mix, believing that advertising can overcome other problems.

*M*arket plans depend on knowledge of markets, competition, and the resources and mission of the organization.

Few nonprofit administrators understand the value of the organization's markets, resources, and mission—nor do they take the time to analyze them. All are essential to develop a comprehensive marketing approach. Mass market approaches are used more often than a market segmentation approach, either because of governmental edict or the mistaken belief that the nonprofit organization actually has an offering with mass appeal.[23] Many nonprofit organizations fail to consider their competition when designing marketing strategy and are generally unwilling to compete directly. The use of marketing research is viewed almost as a sign of weakness. Nonprofit administrators are supposed to know their publics. They fear that to analyze markets with marketing research will be interpreted to mean that they are not qualified for their positions. A notable exception is the U.S. Army. The Army's Program Analysis and Evaluation Directorate (PAE) functions much like a large corporation's marketing research department, monitoring sales, analyzing the effects of proposed programs, and recommending marketing changes. To increase recruiting effectiveness, marketing information is gathered, analyzed, and interpreted. The campaign theme, "Be all that you can be," was developed when marketing research indicated that the militaristic aspects of service should be de-emphasized and training opportunities, especially in high technology fields, emphasized.[24]

MARKETING IN ACTION

Marketing a Civic Group

Faced with declining membership, difficulty in attracting new members, waning volunteer involvement, rapid staff turnover, and confusion about its purpose, the Pensacola, Florida, Chamber of Commerce decided to try marketing itself. Promotion had been used previously but little attention was given to the product, price, and distribution. Furthermore, information to support the marketing decision was not available.

The cancellation of membership was occurring faster than new members could be recruited, even though recruiting new members was the focus of the chamber staff. Something had to be done. A survey was undertaken to find why memberships were cancelled and when the decision was made. Thirty-two percent returned the questionnaire, and one fourth of those expressed some dissatisfaction with the chamber, enough responses to provide in-

sights into what was happening at the chamber and to devise a marketing plan.

A majority of the membership cancellations were new members. The value of membership was measured in terms of direct benefits to the member's business and involvement in community business activities. In brief, camaraderie and pride were major reasons for membership. Most of the 300 active members were associated with large firms. To experience the camaraderie a high degree of participation in chamber activities and on committees was required. The small business members simply did not have the time.

The plan that was implemented was based on the research findings, and included the following concepts:

- Develop programs for inactive members so they could quickly meet other members without having to join a committee.
- Increase involvement with new members.
- Improve communication with members, particularly the inactive group.
- Increase member interaction.
- Improve service visibility.
- Continually monitor membership satisfaction levels.

At the end of the year, membership cancellations declined by 25 percent and volunteer participation was up.

Source: Reprinted from Janice R. Hall and Parks B. Dimsdale, "Civic Group Adopts Marketing Technique," *Marketing News*, June 21, 1985, p. 13, published by the American Marketing Association.

What benefits does the nonprofit offer?

Product.   Nonprofit organizations may deny that they are trying to sell something. Instead, they emphasize that they provide what the public obviously needs. Often, however, nonprofit organizations start with their own ideas of what the public needs, believing that, if only they can make the public aware of and knowledgeable about the idea, service, person, or place, the public will accept it. Increasingly, nonprofit administrators have realized they are faced with the same product decisions as profit-oriented organizations. They must develop the offering considering the needs that their publics perceive.[25] They have to decide on product mix, on identification, package, guarantees, and all product variables.

Price.   The price or cost factor in the nonprofit exchange may not always involve money. Instead, time, social, psychological, or other contributions may be a part of the exchange. A volunteer for a Legal Aid organization may contribute services for library research to help the cause; this will not involve direct costs as the organization "prices" what it can offer. However, as soon as computer-search equipment is part of the research effort, the organization will have to cope with a direct money cost for the computer time. This will eventually affect the price structure of their service.

Pricing in nonprofit organizations may have little relationship to cost or demand.

When money is involved, it may be used differently than in a profit-making situation. For instance, the profit-oriented organization frequently has an objective of maximizing profit. The nonprofit organization also sometimes seeks to maximize profit when pricing a specific activity. The difference in the two objectives exists in the time perspective of each. The profit organization usually attempts to maximize profit over the long run and for all of a firm's activities. A nonprofit organization may need to maximize profit for one short run activity, but does not want profit maximization on all its activities. An example of a nonprofit organization's profit maximization would be a concert performed by a well known musical group for the American Cancer Society's benefit. The Society seeks to keep the fixed and variable cost of the concert to a minimum and at the same time sell ticket prices at a level that will just fill the auditorium, thus maximizing the profits of the event. At the same time, the Society provides to the public free training sessions on how to detect breast cancer. This and other services may be provided by the Society either free or at a price that is intended just to recover the cost of the service provided. Price can also be a consideration for an organization devoted to discouraging consumption. Thus the American Cancer Society could lobby for a tax on cigarettes, as a way to create price barriers to cigarette smoking.

*D*istribution receives little attention in marketing nonprofit organizations.

Distribution. The channels for the offerings of most nonprofit organizations tend to be direct and simple. The channel intermediary organizations that do exist commonly act as agents. That is, they act on behalf of the nonprofit organization, usually in a sales capacity, and they do not have ownership or other responsibility. The intangible offerings typical of the nonprofit organization encourage the nonprofit organization to work directly with the client. Location for the nonprofit organization may, therefore, be very important. For instance, most churches locate conveniently for their congregations.

*T*he March of Dimes has effectively used promotion.

Promotion. We noted earlier that the administrators of nonprofit organizations are overconfident about the persuasive power of advertising, but some nonprofit organizations have shown exceptional insight into the use of promotion. For instance, personal selling generally is more effective if the salesperson has characteristics like the prospect and is a friend of the prospect. The March of Dimes solicits funds by requesting residents on each street (at given intervals) to ask the people who live on that street to contribute. When people become involved in the promotion, it has greater impact. The March of Dimes has used walkathons and other activities to entice people to become involved.

On the other hand, some nonprofit organizations tend not to use commercial advertising media but to rely on free and low-cost advertising (public service ads).

The March of Dimes uses brochures and advertisements to maintain a positive public image.

Source: March of Dimes.

The advertisements generally include the time and date of an event but little information on the benefits of attending.[26]

Nonprofit organizations do not ignore efficiency and productivity.

Control of Market Mix. Nonprofit organizations do not ignore cost efficiency and productivity. The organization has objectives that administrators and others want to achieve. On college campuses, for example, the goal is often "educational excellence." Organizational efforts and resources are evaluated with respect to the amount of excellence achieved.[27]

Nonprofit organizations often operate smoothly as long as revenues and expenses are at a consistent level. When one or both change radically the individuals in the organization rethink the goals. Turmoil and disagreements become more common until the organization regains a consensus. For instance, an especially successful fund-raising project often leaves individuals in the nonprofit organization fighting about what should be done with the funds. The marketing mix may also involve some disagreements. For instance, how much and what type of promotion should be used?

Standards, measurements, and research help nonprofit organizations to obtain objectives.

Although measurements and standards have not developed in nonprofit organizations to the same degree that they have in profit organizations, they do exist.[28] Surveys of a nonprofit organization's public can be conducted to assess changes in attitudes and behavior occurring from marketing programs. An example would be before-and-after surveys of changes in attitudes resulting from a campaign to reduce cigarette smoking. Total response measurements frequently provide a gross measurement of a nonprofit organization's success. For instance, how many total applications, ticket sales, or participants indicate success? The gross measure can then be compared to a forecast and even broken down into divisions, such as individuals over forty years of age or forty and under. Market share, cost per dollar of market response, and efficiency statistics, such as acceptance rates and number of donor contacts, also are employed to evaluate and control marketing mixes.

THE CASE CONTINUES

P/E probably would have operated quite differently if it were a nonprofit organization or, for instance, if it was state-run. The detail and depth of marketing plans would likely be different. As P/E operated, the marketing plan stressed a low-priced fare to a price-conscious target market. Usually nonprofit organizations have looser definitions of their target market. In addition, if P/E were a nonprofit organization, there probably would have been either a heavy reliance on advertising or little use of it at all. Although price was low as part of P/E's strategy, it still serves to maximize profit. In a nonprofit organization, price generally takes a different role—perhaps to encourage consumption, there would be no charge at all. Most likely there would also be a difference in the amount of control exercised over the marketing mix. Nonprofit organizations tend to be less accountability-oriented than profit organizations.

GOAL SUMMARY

1. **Define services and describe their importance to the U.S. economy.** A service is a deed, a performance, or an effort. Services are experiential. The purchase of a service results in no additional ownership in a tangible or physical item. In the U.S. economy over two-thirds of the jobs have a service orientation. Nearly 50 percent of the consumer's dollar goes for purchase of services. The growth of ser-

GOAL SUMMARY (continued)

vices and the smaller size of service firms offer entrepreneurial opportunities not found in manufacturing and product marketing.

2. **Discuss important characteristics of services that influence their marketing.** Several good strategies exist for reducing the problems people have in purchasing a service. Most of the strategies attempt to make the service more tangible. Services also present marketing challenges in that they suffer from quality variation, they have high perishability, and they cannot be separated from the producer. All these characteristics have led to innovative strategies. For instance, the problem of high perishability has been approached with efforts to equalize supply and demand—reservation systems are one such effort.

3. **Explain the environment's impact on service marketing.** One of the elements in the service market that changes marketing is type of service. Is the service equipment- or people-based? Does the service require skilled or unskilled people? When the service requires highly skilled people, marketing tends to be much more subdued—less promotion, product development, and concern for distribution. In fact, many professional service firms—attorneys, physicians, etc.—have traditionally ignored marketing. More recently, changes in regulations and competition have encouraged the use of marketing.

The relationship between customers and service organizations has a unique feature in that the customer may have to appear at the service organization to obtain the service. Thus, the environment at the service establishment must not only be cordial and inviting, it must also convey standards for acceptable customer behavior.

4. **Describe nonprofit organizations and the environment that a marketer might find in working for a nonprofit organization.** The objectives of nonprofit organizations usually emphasize creating awareness or changing attitudes, behavior, and

knowledge. They do not include making a profit over an extended period of time. Since profit serves profit organization as both an objective and a measurement of success, the absence of a profit orientation influences more than just objectives. Standards and techniques of measurement are also affected.

Individuals and organizations served by profit and nonprofit organizations also differ. Nonprofit organizations serve more publics. In addition, the nature of the publics is usually less clear. Targets of the nonprofit organization, therefore, are often vaguely defined.

5. **What are the types of nonprofit marketing?** Four primary types have been identified: person, idea, organization, and place. With *person marketing* the objective is to make or maintain an impression of a person. The goal of *idea marketing* is to identify and gain acceptance of a practice, cause, or philosophy. With *organization marketing* the aim is to gain, alter, or maintain acceptance of an organization's objectives or services. With *place marketing* the objective is to create, maintain, or change attitudes and behavior with regard to a place.

6. **How is the marketing mix of nonprofit organizations different from the marketing mix of profit organizations?** The same elements make up the marketing mix in both profit and nonprofit organizations. Price in nonprofit organizations can be expressed in other forms besides money. Time, social, and psychological prices may have more importance. Pricing strategies, even when money is involved, may be designed to accomplish objectives other than profit maximization—suppression of consumption, for example. Distribution has a minor role since channels tend to be simple and direct. "Product" is usually not well defined and often has an orientation other than satisfaction of a target market. Finally, promotion, if accepted, usually receives heavy emphasis in the mix.

KEY TERMS

Services, **p. 609**
Intangibility, **p. 611**
Inseparability, **p. 611**
Quality Variability, **p. 612**
Perishability, **p. 612**
Equipment-Based Services, **p. 613**
People-Based Services, **p. 614**
Client Involvement, **p. 614**

Service Mix, **p. 615**
Nonprofit Organization, **p. 619**
Target Publics, **p. 620**
Person Marketing, **p. 622**
Idea Marketing, **p. 622**
Organization Marketing, **p. 623**
Place Marketing, **p. 623**

CHECK YOUR LEARNING

1. Services are activities and/or benefits that satisfy buyer needs.   **T/F**
2. Less than half of the jobs in the U.S. are service oriented.   **T/F**
3. Uneven demand presents few problems for the service supplier.   **T/F**
4. The four characteristics of services are: (a) tangibility, inseparability, quality variation, and perishability, (b) intangibility, separability, quality variation, and perishability, (c) intangibility, inseparability, quality variation, and perishability, (d) intangibility, inseparability, quality variation, and imperishability.
5. The fundamental procedures for marketing services differ from those for marketing products.   **T/F**
6. An example of an equipment-based service is the CAT scan procedure that physicians in hospitals use to detect physical problems in patients.   **T/F**
7. Marketing has been well accepted in service establishments.   **T/F**
8. Service level is the level of use of a service facility.   **T/F**
9. In the marketing mix: (a) price is usually less regulated in service industries than in product industries, (b) service marketers should not attempt to fulfill all requests for services, (c) channels of distribution tend to be longer for services, (d) selling plays a minor role in service promotion.
10. Nonprofit organizations tend to have more formally organized structures and more highly defined ob-jectives than profit-making organizations.   **T/F**
11. The target publics of a nonprofit include all individuals interested in and/or benefitting from the organization.   **T/F**
12. Nonprofit administrators readily accept marketing as a valuable tool.   **T/F**
13. Most nonprofit managers overemphasize the "product" and the market mix.   **T/F**
14. Four types of nonprofit marketing have been identified—the marketing of: a) person, place, organization, and idea. b) person, place, service, and idea. c) place, person, task, and ideas. d) task, service, ideas, and person.
15. Marketing activities in nonprofit organizations are frequently called by other names.   **T/F**
16. Defining the target market to direct resources more efficiently is a common strategy of nonprofit administrators.   **T/F**
17. On specific products, events, or occasions, nonprofit organizations may attempt to maximize profit with their pricing strategy.   **T/F**
18. The March of Dimes has used walkathons to publicize the need for contributions and also to encourage people to become involved.   **T/F**
19. Controlling the marketing mix in nonprofits: a) does not occur, b) is almost always the sole concern of the accounting department, c) exists but not at the level of sophistication as in profit organization, d) is fairly simple since many nonprofits do not use marketing.

QUESTIONS FOR REVIEW AND DISCUSSION

1. Define the key terms for this chapter that appear at the end of the goal summary.
2. Compare and contrast services and products.
3. How important are services in the economy?
4. For a day, keep track of all the purchases you make and divide them into two groups, primarily service and primarily product. What percentage of the total dollar expenditure was each group?
5. List the characteristics of services.
6. How might a service marketer deal with the inseparability characteristic of services?
7. What are people-based services? Give examples.
8. Using the information you gathered in question 4, classify the services as people- or equipment-based.
9. Identify some of the important features of the service environment that a marketer should consider.
10. Is pricing a service different from pricing a product? How is it different?
11. Define the term nonprofit organization.
12. List all the nonprofit organizations or marketing activities you encounter during the next twenty-four hours.
13. How does nonprofit marketing differ, if at all, from other types of marketing?
14. Define the term "target public."
15. List the types of nonprofit marketing.
16. Describe the attitude toward marketing in nonprofit organizations.

NOTES

1. James Cook, "You Mean We've Been Speaking Prose All These Years?" *Forbes,* April 11, 1983, p. 143.
2. Helena Stolson, *U.S. Service Exports and Foreign Barriers: An Agenda for Negotiations* (Washington, D.C.: The National Planning Association, 1985), p. 1.
3. Thomas M. Stanback, Jr., *Understanding the Service Economy,* The John Hopkins University Press: Baltimore, MD, 1979, pp. 29–44.
4. Theodore Levitt, "Marketing Intangible Products and Product Intangibles," *Harvard Business Review* (May–June 1981): pp. 94–102.
5. Robert C. Lewis and Bernard H. Booms, "The Marketing Aspects of Service Quality," in *Emerging Perspectives on Service Marketing,* ed. Leonard L. Berry, G. Lynn Shostack, and Gregory Upah (Chicago: American Marketing Association, 1983), pp. 99–107.
6. Jeremy Main, "Toward Service Without a Snarl," *Fortune,* March 23, 1981, p. 58.
7. "Basic Research Uncovers Fairness As a Critical Component in Positioning of Financial Services," *Marketing News,* November 23, 1984, p. 9.
8. A. H. Kizilbash, "Hospitals Need Profitability and Need Analysis to Winnow Their Unwanted Products/Services," *Marketing News,* February 1, 1985, p. 3.
9. J. Dearden, "Cost Accounting Comes to Service Industries," *Harvard Business Review* 56 (September–October 1978): pp. 132–140.
10. Martin R. Schlissel, "Pricing in a Service Industry," *MSU Business Topics* (Spring 1977): pp. 37–48.
11. James H. Donnelly, Jr., "Marketing Intermediaries in Channels of Distribution for Services," *Journal of Marketing* (January 1976): pp. 55–57.
12. Christopher H. Lovelock and John A. Quelch, "Consumer Promotions in Services Marketing," *Business Horizons* (May–June, 1983): pp. 66–75.
13. Cecily Cannan Selby, "Better Performance from Nonprofits," *Harvard Business Review* (September–October 1978): p. 93.
14. Benson P. Shapiro, "Marketing for Nonprofit Organizations," *Harvard Business Review* (September–October 1973): pp. 123–132.
15. Michael L. Rothschild, "Marketing Communications in Nonbusiness Situations, or Why It's So Hard to Sell Brotherhood Like Soap," *Journal of Marketing* (Spring 1979): pp. 11–20.
16. Philip Kotler, "Strategies for Introducing Marketing into Nonprofit Organizations," *Journal of Marketing* (January 1979): pp. 40–44.
17. Philip Kotler, *Marketing for Nonprofit Organizations* (Englewood Cliffs, N.J.: Prentice-Hall, 1982), p. 481.
18. Philip Kotler and Gerald Zaltman, "Social Marketing: An Approach to Planned Social Change," *Journal of Marketing* (July 1971): pp. 3–12.
19. Sheth N. Jagdish and Gary L. Frazier, "A Model of Strategy Mix Choice for Planned Social Change," *Journal of Marketing* (Winter 1982): pp. 15–26.
20. *Controversy Advertising: How Advertisers Present Points of View in Public Affairs: A Worldwide Study by the International Advertising Association* (New York: Communication Arts Books, 1977), p. 18.
21. "Playing Hard Ball on Admissions," *Time,* May 28, 1984, p. 80.
22. Seymour H. Fine, *The Marketing of Ideas and Social Issues* (New York: Praeger, 1981), p. 53.
23. W. Wrey Buchanan, "The Marketing Concept in the Nonprofit Sector: Implemented or Ignored?" in *Marketing: Theories and Concepts for an Era of Change,* Southern Marketing Association Proceedings, 1983, pp. 5–9.
24. "Today's Army Relying on Marketing Research to Attain Recruitment Goals," *Marketing News,* July 6, 1984, p. 1.
25. Jay Nathan, *Marketing in a Nonprofit Organization: A Case Study,* Proceedings of the Annual Conference of the Academy of Marketing Science, 1983, pp. 388–390.
26. Buchanan, "The Marketing Concept in the Nonprofit Sector."
27. Lawrence H. Douglas, "In Search of Excellence on College Campuses: Academic Administrators Should Study the Characteristics of Successful Businesses," *Chronicle of Higher Education,* September 19, 1984, p. 72.
28. Philip Kotler, *Marketing for Nonprofit Organizations* (Englewood Cliffs, N.J.: Prentice-Hall, 1975), pp. 250–251.

The Metro Youth Soccer Association was established to promote soccer as a sport and to provide an opportunity for youth to play organized soccer in the metropolitan area. The board of directors is filled by individuals willing to serve—their election is perfunctory. It is not unusual during soccer season for a board member to receive five to ten telephone calls a day concerning soccer. The only people to receive payment for services are individuals who officiate games and the contractor who mows the grass on the fields. All others donate their time.

The association annually has about six-hundred to eight-hundred youth enrolled in the soccer program. Of these, the great majority play in house league teams, which always have games on the association fields.

To play on a house league team all a youth must do is have his or her parents sign up on one of the two sign-up weekends before each spring and fall season, be between the ages of six and nineteen, and pay $15 for each season. Before the start of last season, 125 youth signed up late due to confusion in administering sign-up arrangements.

About 100 youth also play on travel league teams, which play games in different cities in the state as well as on the association field. Once each spring and fall the travel teams enter a tournament out of state. To be on a travel league, an individual has to sign up on one of the sign-up weekends, be between the ages of ten and nineteen, try out for the team, pay $20 a season, and be willing to pay travel expenses to out-of-town games. Recently a split in the board of directors has developed over support of travel vs. house leagues; this has resulted in evening board meetings, continuing into the early morning hours, with tempers flaring.

None of the travel teams ever had a winning season or won a tournament. Since the house league teams play each other, some do have winning seasons. There is no tournament at the end of the house league season, however, because it is thought that a tournament would emphasize winning too much. Soccer could go the way of Little League Baseball, with irate and uncontrollable parents wanting to win at any cost.

Four of the house league teams in the most recent fall season did not have coaches until after the season started. Each team also has a company sponsor. The sponsor pays $200 and in return the company logo is placed on each player's shirt. Two teams did not have sponsors in the fall season.

To encourage spectators, the association does not charge for the games or for parking. However, in an attempt to raise money for the travel teams, the travel team commissioner has organized a tournament inviting out-of-state and out-of-town teams. The first year, in order to encourage teams to enter the tournament, the entry fee was intentionally set very low by the commissioner. The result was that many teams entered, but overall costs were higher than revenues and the Soccer Association absorbed the loss. The following and current year the entry fees were raised enough to cover anticipated costs and a small profit. More teams entered than expected, however, and more officials were needed; in order to obtain more game officials, their pay had to be increased. The result? Another loss, which the Soccer Association absorbed.

The Association now uses land owned by the county fairgrounds, a nonprofit organization not associated with county government, but formed for promoting youth in agriculture. Because of the location of the fairground the facility has a number of groups using it at any given time. Occasionally there is conflict between the groups.

As payment for using the land, the association agrees to maintain it by keeping the grass cut and the ground clean of trash. The association also has agreed to clean up the total fairground facility four times a year. Request for help to clean up, or to line and maintain the fields, has resulted in one or two parents and the person in charge showing up. No improvements are allowed on the land nor can any concessions be operated except by the Soccer Association itself.

There have not been any concessions at the fields for the last two years; somehow the concessions never get organized. Business and parent cooperation, active in the first years of the association, has waned in the last few years.

The association does have $12,000 in a Certificate of Deposit, but previous boards and some members on the current board want to see this money used for land for playing fields. In fact, a little money each year has been added to the amount, in the hope that enough would be available some day to purchase land.

Issues for Discussion
1. Who are the Metro Youth Soccer Association target publics?
2. What type of nonprofit market exists or should exist in this situation—person, idea, organization, or place?
3. If elected as the new president, what would you do to make Metro Youth Soccer Association more successful?

OUTLINE

CHAPTER

23

Ethics and Social Responsibility in Marketing

LEARNING GOALS

After reading this chapter, you should be able to:

1. Define ethics.
2. Describe the major ethical theories.
3. Describe today's conditions in business and society that influence our business ethics.
4. Explain marketing ethics.
5. Describe ethical behavior.
6. Know the key topics of the marketing code of ethics.
7. Explain how corporate ethics can be developed.
8. Describe social responsibility.
9. Evaluate and challenge our concepts of ethical behavior in business.

*R*JR Nabisco, Inc. is a diversified Fortune 500 corporation. It is the number one cigarette company (Camel, Winston, Salem, Vantage, More, Now, Doral), the number one fruit and vegetable packer (Del Monte), the number one Oriental food packager (Chun King), a beverage business (Heublein), and a major cookie producer (Nabisco).

In terms of social responsibility and ethics, how do you rate RJR? Probably your first thought is that it's bad because RJR is best known for its cigarettes produced by its R. J. Reynolds Tobacco Co. division. Cigarettes are just not the product that a company concerned with health and social responsibility manufactures today. On the other hand, RJR also markets fruits and vegetables, Oriental food, margarines, and Nabisco cookies—not all bad you say.

Let's take a closer look. On the good side, RJR can claim that over half of their sales are outside the tobacco area. However, tobacco accounts for 66 percent of their profits. Fewer than twenty-five American companies have higher profits than RJR.

RJR was the first cigarette company to make filtered cigarettes when the public began to suspect that smoking was harmful. The company is one of the nation's largest corporate contributors to colleges and universities. It was responsible for relocating Wake Forest University to Winston-Salem, North Carolina. They can also claim a $1,000,000

donation to citizens' coalitions to improve housing and transportation.

Other pluses include sponsoring one of the largest health maintenance organizations (HMO) in the nation. The HMO provides health care for 35,000 employees—of which 22 percent are minorities. RJR was the first corporation to provide religious counseling for its employees. In 1979, Reynolds was ranked eighth in the nation for the most purchases from minority-owned companies.

Perhaps, after learning of all the positive contributions of RJR, you may feel that the company is not so bad after all.

Issues for Discussion

1. At this point, how do you rate RJR as an ethical company? Why?
2. Why do you suppose RJR has so many varied operations?
3. Why does RJR donate so much to colleges, universities, and citizens' coalition groups?

Sources: Adapted from "The Burning Question at RJR: Now What?" *Business Week,* September 28, 1987, pp. 28–29; *Everybody's Business,* edited by Milton Moskowitz, Michael Katz, and Robert Levering (San Francisco: Harper & Row Publishers, 1980), pp. 359, 778–783, and 839; and *The Business Week Almanac,* edited by J. Robert Connor (New York: McGraw-Hill, Inc., 1982), pp. 841–843.

■ RJR Nabisco, Inc. is a food, beverage, and tobacco conglomerate.

*M*ost of us find it difficult to read abstract tracts about how corporations and businesses should or should not do business, especially since deciding what is and is not ethical can sometimes be hard—and even painful—to determine. In many instances we need to be confronted with actual circumstances in order to know what we would actually do. To help you begin to decide how as a marketer you might react to an ethical dilemma, we present numerous examples of real-life business situations where ethical problems arose. We hope that in reading this chapter, you will form some ideas of how to protect yourself in compromising situations.

Ultimately, our discussion revolves around being socially responsible, as you'll see in the pages ahead. ■

THE MEANING OF ETHICS

When Nestlé supplied infant formula to mothers in less-developed nations, its action was judged unethical because many mothers often were unable to properly prepare the formula, and, as a consequence, infants suffered from malnutrition and death. On the other hand, breweries are not considered unethical in marketing beer, which, consumed in excess, causes a substantial number of drunk driving accidents. How do we define ethics and how do we identify ethical behavior?

Historically, the Judeo-Christian ethic derived from the Bible provided the principles and standards by which human behavior was judged. Ethics is commonly identified as the branch of philosophy that studies what constitutes good and bad human conduct, including related actions and values.[1] This definition, however, is static and does not reflect the continuous changes taking place in business and in our society. A dynamic definition of ethics states that **ethics** is concerned with clarifying what constitutes human welfare and the kind of conduct necessary to promote welfare.[2]

The first part of this definition indicates a process of discussion that arrives at various accepted values.[3] Although certain values are shared by almost everyone, opinions on what constitutes human welfare vary widely. New technology, economic developments, altered value systems, and shifting political forces have altered our concept of human welfare. For example, the role of the government in furnishing benefits to the poor has changed this concept. During the 1960s and 1970s, the role of the government expanded, and our concept of human welfare came to include the idea that society had an obligation to assist its less fortunate citizens. During the 1980s, the role of the government contracted, and ideas about the role of self-sufficiency in human welfare developed.

The second part of this definition relates to the type of conduct that is necessary to affect human behavior. After we have determined the proper concept of human welfare, we must decide how we can attain this concept. For example, if we establish that part of our national income should be distributed on the basis of need, the income-tax rates can be adjusted to assess the wealthy in order to provide funds for the poor.

Ethical issues arise when our understanding of what constitutes human welfare requires clarification. One type of ethical conflict occurs when laws or judicial decisions are either unclear or in conflict with changing cultural values. The banning of cigarette advertising from TV has created this type of conflict. Although cigarette advertising was banned, the producers of small cigars began advertising extensively on TV. Because these cigars are packaged like cigarettes, many individuals feel that the producers were unethically confusing the public.

ETHICAL THEORIES

Before studying ethics in business and marketing, you should understand ethical theories and concepts. Figure 23.1 summarizes several of the major ethical theories. The theory that the same act may be morally right for one individual or society and morally wrong for another is called **ethical relativism.**[4] The usefulness of this concept

❏ **Figure 23.1**
Major ethical theories.

Ethical Relativism—the same act may be morally right for one group, but morally wrong for another.

Ethical Egoism—each individual should always act to promote the greatest balance of good over evil for himself or herself.

Utilitarianism—individuals should act so they promote the greatest good for the greatest number.

Kant's Categorical Imperative—you should take the right action—not necessarily because it produces good results—but because it is your duty to do so.

has been questioned because, if correct, we cannot state that any act or belief is morally better or worse than any other. Marketers who reject this theory believe that a particular action is either right or wrong; some marketers, however, accept ethical relativism. Several years ago, executives of the Lockheed Aircraft Corporation made illicit payments to Japanese government officials in order to obtain a large contract. Although these payments were considered unethical in our society, the executives believed that the only way for them to win the contract was to follow the practices that were common in Japan.

Another theory is **ethical egoism,** which states that each individual should always act to promote the greatest balance of good over evil for him- or herself. From the standpoint of ethical egoism any act that is contrary to one's self-interest is an immoral act. Egoists respect the interests of others because in the long run they benefit. By defining good as profits, marketers can identify with this concept. Marketers are aware that it is in their self-interest to render outstanding services to their customers in order to build loyalty and obtain long-run profits.

*U*nder act utilitarianism ethics, Lockheed executives could rationalize bribes to Japanese officials.

Utilitarianism ethics states that individuals should act to promote the greatest good for the greatest number. **Act utilitarians** believe that in every situation one should act to maximize the total good, even if it means breaking a rule. By following this principle Lockheed made total payments of about $12 million to the Japanese in order to obtain nearly $430 million in contracts. Lockheed executives rationalized their action by noting that it maintained employment, benefitted stockholders and suppliers, helped the U.S. balance of trade, and provided the Japanese with excellent aircraft.

The **rule utilitarian** believes that one should always follow the rules because in the long run they promote the general welfare. If Lockheed had followed the rule utilitarian principle, it would never have bribed the Japanese officials.

Another concept of ethics is **Kant's categorical imperative,** which states that you should take the right action—not necessarily because it produces good results—but because it is your duty to do so. The German philosopher Immanuel Kant (1724–1804), who formulated this concept, declared that in making an ethical decision you should determine whether you would be willing to have everyone take a similar action. Kant believed that the only moral actions were those that could be accepted as universal laws. Following Kant's categorical imperative, the Lockheed executives would have refused to pay the Japanese because they would have realized that the universal practice of bribery would undermine the operation of our business system.

*K*ant's categorical imperatives show certain limits that one should not go beyond even to attain the maximum good.

Each of these theories has its strengths and weaknesses. By drawing constructively on each theory, it is possible to develop a moral framework from which to make judgments in business and marketing. For example, utilitarianism can check each person's pursuit of his or her egotistic self-interest. Kant's categorical imperative indicates certain limits that one should not go beyond even to attain the maximum good. As you read on, you should keep in mind these four theories and note their application in the practice of marketing.

ETHICS IN BUSINESS TODAY

We are surrounded by those who behave unethically. It may involve your best friend from home or the girl sitting next to you in class. If someone mentions bad business ethics, we quickly think of older people who work for big corporations. This is not always so. Only a few years ago, several Tulane ballplayers were arrested for attempting to control the score of a Tulane-Southern Mississippi basketball game. Ken Turkle, a student just like you, and a business major, was the fifth undergraduate to be arrested in this case.[5] Turkle's point shaving differs little from General Electric's defrauding the government on missile-warhead contracts. We can pick up almost any daily newspaper or magazine and read about yet another person committing an unethical business practice.

These incidents do not always involve specific products. Advertising, which is a business service, is often criticized for fostering unethical practices. For example, cigarette makers are censured because they promote the pleasures of smoking even though medical research indicates that cigarettes are harmful to your health. In another instance, a Campbell's soup advertisement was declared unethical. The ad showed a bowl of chicken noodle soup with a large amount of chicken visible at the top. Because the pieces of chicken would ordinarily sink to the bottom of the bowl, marbles were placed in the dish—keeping the chicken at the top. Campbell claimed this was done only to permit the chicken in the bowl to be visible for photographic purposes. The Federal Trade Commission felt otherwise and issued a consent order to stop the practice.

Why is there so much talk today about business ethics? Are business ethics any different today than they were fifty years ago? To answer these questions let's look at where we are today in terms of business and society. Many aspects of our lives today are considerably different from what they were fifty years ago—or even yesterday. Some of the major changes result from the following factors: increased interest in resource conservation, increased concern about the environment, greater health consciousness, better informed consumers, growth of international markets with their different cultures, increase in the size of government and its regulations, an increasingly affluent society, and the stronger impact of the media.

Many aspects of our lives are considerably different today than they were fifty years ago—or yesterday.

Resources

One of the most significant changes we have experienced involves our attitude toward the earth's natural resources. We have finally come to the sad realization that these resources will not last forever unless we carefully monitor their use. In the past we thought that we could cut down whatever trees were needed, use as much gas as we wanted, and leave lights on to consume electricity at will. Today, however, we know that we must be far more careful with their use.

As consumers of these resources, we are trained to turn off the lights, to preserve trees, and to conserve gas. Basically, it has become unethical to abuse our natural resources. We are now **demarketing** resources. Demarketing means that instead of encouraging the demand for something, the seller discourages it. Marketers tell us it is good to conserve, ad agencies highlight how their client companies conserve natural resources.

Demarketing discourages the demand for products.

Environment

Closely related to resource conservation is the concern for the environment and a balanced ecological system. The smokestacks of the large industrial areas of the

Businesses are concerned with preserving resources.

Stan Blossom, Sun Company district engineer, with his son, Tony, fishing near Hillhouse oil rig in the Santa Barbara Channel.

SUN, OIL AND THE FISHERMAN'S SON. People get a lot of fish from the Santa Barbara Channel. And this is where Sun Company gets a lot of oil—more than three million barrels a year! Around here oil is our business. But Sun people like Stan Blossom can tell you it's not our only concern.

"I work for Sun, but I also fish in these waters. And I want my son's generation to fish here too. That's why precautions like our containment unit are so important. In case of a spill, it would quickly surround the oil and help prevent damage.

"This is just one of the ways we're helping to make sure there'll be many more years of fishing around here."

At Sun, we think putting energy back into the environment is as important as getting it out.

WHERE THERE'S SUN THERE'S ENERGY.

Source: Sun Company.

*C*orporate abuse of our environment still occurs.

Midwest have generated destructive acid rain in the Northeast and Canada. In major metropolitan areas such as Los Angeles and Phoenix even our cars—which are essential to a comfortable life—create pollution problems.

In order to halt this pollution, legislation has been passed requiring the use of unleaded gasoline. We have also imposed many regulations concerning the types of wastes the corporations can dump into the air, streams, and landfills. The Environmental Protection Agency (EPA) was created to see that businesses comply with these regulations.

Still, there is room for corporate abuse of our environment. For example, some believe that roadside billboards are not ethical because they pollute the landscape. On the other hand, the billboard can give the traveler very helpful information. On Interstate 75 in southern Florida you can admire the landscape and not be exposed to a series of billboards because very rigid rules control their use along the interstate. The signs must be set quite far back from the road, and they have to be so many yards apart. The problem is that the unprepared traveler may be lost when it comes to knowing what restaurants and gasoline stations are available and how far away they are. All retail operations are at least three miles off the highway, so the driver must rely on the small signs prepared by the highway department in order to learn about the availability of travelers' services. Other states, however, do not have the strict laws in force as in Florida.

Potential dangers at chemical companies brought mixed public reactions to the chemical industry. In West Virginia, the residents whose environment was affected by a spill from the Union Carbide Corporation reacted both positively and negatively. Some residents passed out "Carbide Kills" leaflets; others paraded in "I Love Carbide" T-shirts. Those supporting the chemical company—including the mayor—felt that the jobs Carbide provides are far more important than the hazards it poses to the environment.[6]

We have become a health-conscious society.

Standard equipment in the fight against heart disease.

Whatever activity you choose to help keep your heart fit, you need the right tools.

The same is true for the activity of eating. With Mazola® corn oil and Mazola® margarine as part of a healthy diet, your family is well

equipped to reduce cholesterol.

Naturally. Made from 100% pure corn oil, Mazola products contain no cholesterol, are low in saturated fat, and are high in polyunsaturates, which actually help lower blood cholesterol.

So if you want your heart to stay fit, follow all your doctor's recommendations.

And don't forget, keep a good pair of workout shoes in your locker. And Mazola in your cupboard.

Health Consciousness

A major change in our society has occurred because of medical advances.

Somewhat akin to our concern with the environment is our concern with our health. Advances in medicine have brought major changes. We have become much more conscious of the things that damage our health, such as poor nutrition, a contaminated environment, and stress.

We have learned that some things, long considered safe, are, indeed, harmful to our bodies. One of the most obvious is, of course, cigarettes. People smoked for many years and never thought much about it. Now, we realize that cigarettes are harmful to our health. Many are therefore questioning the ethics of marketing cigarettes. Likewise, is it also wrong to promote sugar-coated cereals on Saturday cartoon shows when we think those cereals injure children's teeth? Cigarettes were banned from TV commercials several years ago, but the commercials for sugar-coated cereal remain.

To combat the declining number of smokers, Philip Morris, Inc. now publishes *The Philip Morris Magazine,* a magazine for cigarette smokers.[7] Its purpose is to promote cigarette smoking and support for the industry and to help people feel it's alright to smoke. Other marketers and businesses have adapted strategies and products to our increased concern with being healthy. Campbell's Soup, for instance, recently introduced a new line of low-sodium soups.

Informed Consumers

*C*onsumers are better informed today.

Closely paralleling our health consciousness is our overall status of being better informed consumers. Due to today's rapid communications, consumers can be much more knowledgeable. Many purchasers know what products, such as phosphate-

Example of an ad message to the better-informed consumer.

If you want to quit smoking for good, see your doctor

New knowledge about the smoking habit

Two major factors in cigarette smoking have long been recognized—psychological and social factors. Now research has clearly revealed a third important link in the habit—*physical dependence on nicotine*, which slowly but surely develops in many smokers. When people first start smoking, their bodies must get used to the nicotine. After smoking becomes a habit, their bodies may *depend* on getting nicotine.

Why a total program approach is needed to break the habit

When smokers try to quit, the body often reacts to the withdrawal of nicotine. This can result in craving for tobacco, restlessness, irritability, anxiety, headaches, drowsiness, stomach upsets, and difficulty concentrating.

Because these effects can defeat even a strong willpower, your chances of quitting successfully are greater with a program that provides an alternative source of nicotine to help alleviate tobacco withdrawal while you concentrate on breaking the habit.

How your doctor and Merrell Dow can help you succeed

If you are determined enough to sustain a strong effort, your chances of breaking the smoking habit are better than ever. Now your doctor can provide a treatment to help control nicotine withdrawal symptoms, materials to help you overcome the psychological and social factors, plus valuable counseling and follow-up. Merrell Dow has conducted extensive research into the smoking problem and is providing a wide range of support to health professionals.

QUIT

Merrell Dow Pharmaceuticals Inc.
Dedicated to improving the health of Americans
LAKESIDE PHARMACEUTICALS Division of Merrell Dow Pharmaceuticals Inc., Cincinnati, Ohio 45215   ©1986, Merrell Dow Pharmaceuticals Inc.

Source: Lakeside Pharmaceuticals, A Division of Merrell Dow Pharmaceuticals, Inc.

based detergents and chemicals, or manufacturing procedures, such as steelmaking and asbestos production, are devouring our resources, polluting the air, or damaging our bodies. They realize what is fair in terms of finance charges or interest rates from financial institutions and retail establishments.

Because consumers are better informed, marketers have had to become very careful about truthful advertising. The old cliches that once sold many products are no longer creditable with large groups of consumers. Marketers have an ethical obligation to be responsible—to be truthful.

Merrell Dow Pharmaceuticals' quit smoking ad appeals to the consumer who wants to stop smoking. This ad suggests the need for a doctor to provide a treatment to help control nicotine withdrawal symptoms. The ad's message is to the better-informed consumers who care about their health.

International Markets

Gone are the days when farmers trudged to the general store five miles away to trade a gallon of milk for a bolt of fabric. Now, farmers are flying their prize bulls to Ireland for breeding and their wives are wearing dresses that were produced in Hong Kong or Taiwan.

*I*nternational markets have made our concept of business much more cosmopolitan.

Because we now participate in international markets, our whole concept of business must be much more cosmopolitan. Our businesspeople must deal with and

MARKETING IN ACTION

Nestlé

*T*he Nestlé Company became the focus of a bitter controversy over infant feeding in the Third World, and eventually Nestlé was boycotted by its critics. Controversy stemmed from the marketing practices of infant formula manufacturers (not just Nestlé) and from critics who believed that breast feeding should be promoted in underdeveloped countries. Ironically, Nestlé's reputation as an ethically oriented company rested on a product that was only 2.5 percent of its total business.

The accusers said that as a result of infant formula marketing, mothers were encouraged to cease breast feeding. Where manufactured formulas were substituted, often they were not prepared or administered correctly and this allegedly caused 10 million babies annually to suffer malnutrition or death. A report published in London about Nestlé's marketing

of infant formula was entitled "Baby Killer." Nestlé was portrayed as developing commercial gimmicks to gain market share.

This dilemma unfolded during the 1970s and Nestlé is just now recovering. Perhaps its marketing was a little too ambitious, but some observers believed that Nestlé was unfairly singled out while other manufacturers were also involved but not implicated. Nestlé, rightly or wrongly, attempted to respond to the problems and the misconceived ideas. The harder Nestlé worked to respond, however, the more people pointed the guilty finger only at them.

This is a classic case of marketing and ethical issues. The problem

remains—how to make products (infant formula) available to those who need them at a price they can afford, while ensuring that they are used correctly in widely differing environmental conditions.

As a result of all this controversy the WHO (World Health Organization) code was developed. This specifies international standards for information, education, advertising and promotion, product quality, marketing personnel, provisions for free samples and supplies, and product labeling.

Nestlé quickly endorsed the code and became aggressive in its efforts to counter the boycott with open discussions and modified policies. The company finally resolved its boycott, but worldwide the company still suffers from ten years of a tarnished reputation—deserved or undeserved?

---

understand cultures that are very different from ours. A business practice, such as black marketeering in scarce goods, or price haggling, both of which may be unacceptable to most Americans, may be perfectly acceptable to many foreign consumers.

One example of international business ethics involves the *gray market* (mentioned in Chapter 12). Gray market goods are usually high-ticket items imported to this country and sold below the fair market price of traditional retailers. For example, some cars are manufactured overseas in countries with fewer government regulations than the United States. Some of these cars may be sold on the gray market to unauthorized dealers at lower prices. The dealers make minimum modifications on the cars and pass on the lower price to the customer who purchases the car.

The wide range of businesses involved in international trade have made considerable changes in how we transact business. The American businessperson has had to learn new languages, new cultures, and new ways of doing business. In many cases our businesspeople have faced difficult ethical decisions when the values they hold as Americans are in conflict with the values held by the persons with whom they are doing business. For example, do American businesspeople attempt to skirt the Foreign Corrupt Practices Act of 1977 and provide "finder's fees" to the representatives of foreign governments who award them lucrative government contracts?

*A*mericans face difficult ethical decisions when their values clash with foreign values.

Government and Regulations

*U*nethical business practices have led to many government regulations.

The government has instituted many regulations for our businesses and industries. Some of these regulations protect our resources, some protect the environment,

☐ **Figure 23.2**
A pizza with the works—including 310 regulations.

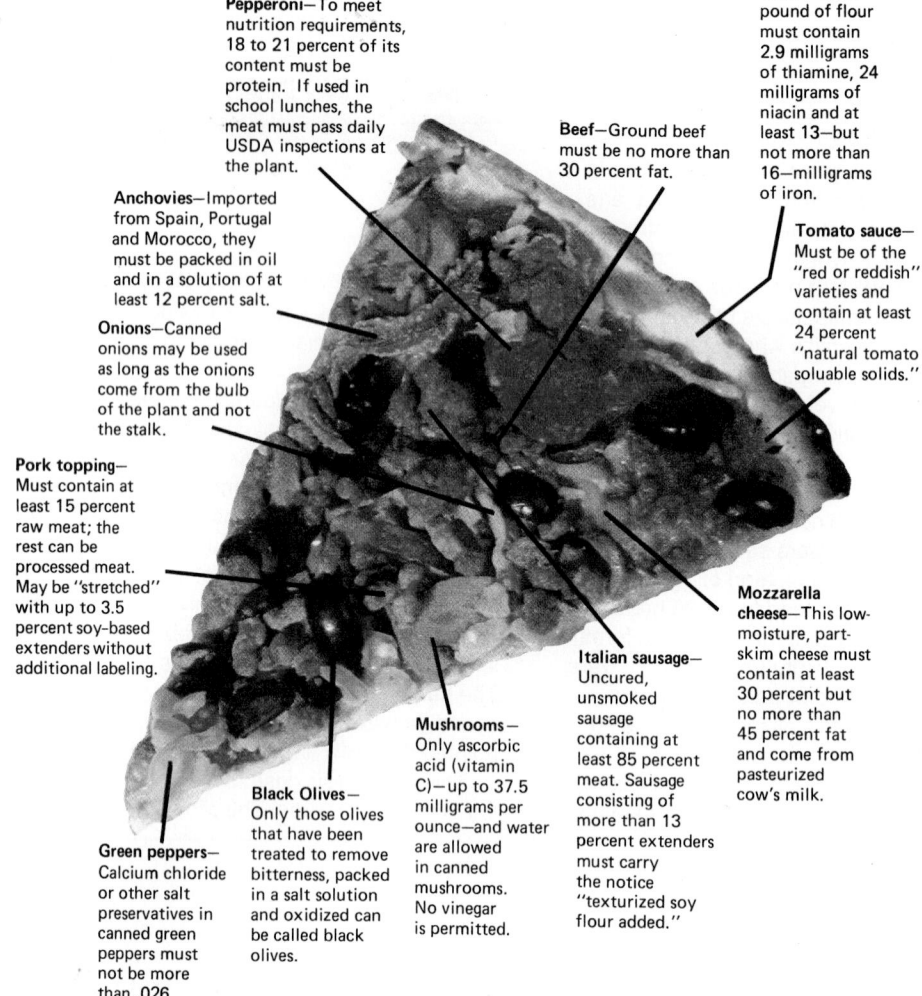

Pepperoni—To meet nutrition requirements, 18 to 21 percent of its content must be protein. If used in school lunches, the meat must pass daily USDA inspections at the plant.

Anchovies—Imported from Spain, Portugal and Morocco, they must be packed in oil and in a solution of at least 12 percent salt.

Onions—Canned onions may be used as long as the onions come from the bulb of the plant and not the stalk.

Pork topping—Must contain at least 15 percent raw meat; the rest can be processed meat. May be "stretched" with up to 3.5 percent soy-based extenders without additional labeling.

Green peppers—Calcium chloride or other salt preservatives in canned green peppers must not be more than .026 percent of the food's weight.

Black Olives—Only those olives that have been treated to remove bitterness, packed in a salt solution and oxidized can be called black olives.

Mushrooms—Only ascorbic acid (vitamin C)—up to 37.5 milligrams per ounce—and water are allowed in canned mushrooms. No vinegar is permitted.

Italian sausage—Uncured, unsmoked sausage containing at least 85 percent meat. Sausage consisting of more than 13 percent extenders must carry the notice "texturized soy flour added."

Beef—Ground beef must be no more than 30 percent fat.

Crust—Each pound of flour must contain 2.9 milligrams of thiamine, 24 milligrams of niacin and at least 13—but not more than 16—milligrams of iron.

Tomato sauce—Must be of the "red or reddish" varieties and contain at least 24 percent "natural tomato soluable solids."

Mozzarella cheese—This low-moisture, part-skim cheese must contain at least 30 percent but no more than 45 percent fat and come from pasteurized cow's milk.

Source: U.S. News & World Report chart by Ron Taylor and Carl Vansag—Basic data: U.S. Dept. of Agriculture, Food and Drug Administration.

others guard consumers' rights, and still others regulate international trade. Some laws even protect businesses from each other. Very few aspects of business and consumer life are not touched in some way by government regulation. Figure 23.2 illustrates the large number of regulations that monitor the production of even simple, everyday items like pizza. Figure 23.3 presents a detailed list of the federal departments and agencies with regulatory or administrative authority over businesses.

Some laws are deemed to be very beneficial to society; others are thought to be questionable. For example, the government required AT&T to break up because our judicial system ruled that the telephone enterprise was a monopoly. Many observers remain uncertain whether this breakup benefitted the consumer and the telephone industry. Whether regulations are perceived as good or bad, businesses, consumers, and industries must deal with them. Many of these regulations were developed to help eliminate unethical business practices.

☐ **Figure 23.3**
Some federal
departments and
agencies with
regulatory/
administrative
authority over
businesses.

Departments		
Department of Agriculture	Food and Drug Administration	Department of Labor:
Department of Commerce:	National Institute for	Office of Equal
Industry and Trade	Occupational Safety	Employment
Administration	and Health	Opportunity
Maritime Administration	Department of Housing and	Mine Safety and Health
National Bureau of	Urban Development	Administration
Standards	Department of Interior:	Pension and Welfare
National Fire Prevention	Geological Survey	Benefit Programs
and Control	Bureau of Land	Department of State:
Administration	Management	Office of Munitions
Patent and Trademark	Bureau of Mines	Control
Office	Bureau of Reclamation	Department of Transportation:
Bureau of East-West	Office of Surface Mining	Federal Aviation
Trade	and Reclamation	Administration
Department of Energy:	Enforcement	Federal Highway
Economic Regulatory	Department of Justice:	Administration
Administration	Antitrust Division	National Highway Traffic
Federal Energy	Land and Natural	Administration
Regulatory	Resources Division	Urban Mass
Commission		Transportation
Energy Information		Administration
Administration		Hazardous Materials
Department of Health,		Operations
Education and Welfare:		Department of Treasury:
Public Health Service		Internal Revenue Service
		U.S. Custom Service

Independent Agencies		
Consumer Product Safety Commission	Federal Reserve System	National Transportation Safety Board
Environmental Protection Agency	Federal Trade Commission	Nuclear Regulatory Commission
Equal Employment Opportunity Commission	General Services Administration	Pension Benefit Guaranty Corporation
Federal Communications Commission	Interstate Commerce Commission	Renegotiation Board
Federal Election Commission	National Labor Relations Board	Securities and Exchange Commission
Federal Maritime Commission	National Mediation Board	United States International Trade Commission
Federal Mediation and Conciliation Service		Water Resources Council

Affluent and Mobile Society

*I*n our society there is respect and awe for material
wealth.

Still another condition affecting business today is the increased wealth of the population. Most of us have access to or own material goods that our grandparents did
not even dream of. We can travel to and buy from foreign countries that, to our
elders, were only strange-sounding names in books and magazines. We drive sports
cars, fly hot air balloons, and sail our catamarans. We have labor-saving devices that
leave us with time on our hands. We live in a society where there is respect and awe
for material wealth. Some believe that the prospect of nuclear war has encouraged
an attitude of uncertainty about the future and a demand for immediate gratification
in the present.

Although all of our advances have provided us with many wonderful goods and
services, we are also left with many temptations and opportunities to cheat each
other. Even the most respected among us cannot escape the push to get ahead with
the hope that we don't get caught. In the financial market, for example, numerous
individuals, such as company officials, investment bankers, and accountants, have
inside information about impending security transactions. Under the security laws,
it is illegal for insiders to buy and sell stock before the official announcement to the
public of the transaction. The law requires that all investors have equal and timely

access to information that will affect a company's stock price. Investment banker Dennis Levine, a key player in the 1987 Ivan Boesky Wall Street insider trading scandal, became greedy and used inside information to make security trades that reaped $12.6 million in profits. Levine lowered his ethical standards and conducted the illegal trades in spite of possessing a million-dollar-a-year compensation package, an expensive apartment on upper Park Avenue, a rented house in fashionable South-ampton, and a new red Ferrari.[8]

Even the author of a book on ethics was unethical.

The following may be the ultimate in ethics violations. The author of *Telling Right From Wrong,* a philosophy book, admitted forging an endorsement letter from the head of the Harvard philosophy department.[9] The forger commented that he was proud of the letter because it got his book accepted for publication. However, the original publisher withdrew its agreement. After searching for another publisher, the author was able to market his work. In his eagerness to be a successful author, he was unethical in order to attain publication and the ensuing royalties.

Media

The media readily investi-gate the fair and unfair practices of companies.

The media and its vigilant investigative reporting is another aspect of our society that affects our lives considerably. In bygone days stories of unethical acts and corporate irresponsibility could be swept under the rug. Many examples of unsafe products and unfair business practices were hushed up or overlooked, or the news never reached the tiny hamlets in the far reaches of our country. Today, however, we all know almost instantly when deadly gas from a chemical plant pollutes the air or a mechanical defect in a particular model of a car results in a series of accidents. The media readily investigate the fair and unfair practices of companies.

The New York Times prepared a special report on the socially positive and negative activities of certain major corporations. On the positive side, major cor-porations were praised for:

1. pollution control,
2. refusing to buy advertising on excessively violent TV shows,
3. supporting legislation to require consumer representation at hearings,
4. funding ghetto neighborhood rehabilitation projects.

On the negative side, the corporations were admonished for:

1. manufacturing poorly designed products that had frequent breakdowns,
2. using leaded gas in company cars designed to use unleaded fuel,
3. overcharging and price fixing,
4. giving foreign payoffs,
5. killing dogs in order to train doctors and salespersons with new surgical instruments.[10]

The media can be as guilty of unethical behavior as any person or business.

In some instances, the media can be as guilty of unethical behavior as any person or business. This was illustrated by a TV movie, *The 11 O'Clock News,* which depicted the dilemma of the producers of TV newscasts. On the one hand, a station works hard to get good ratings by dramatizing topics and presenting them in the way that will be most appealing to audiences. On the other hand, the producer feels an obligation to be completely fair with the sources of information and the subjects of the news stories. Newspapers can also resort to sensationalism in an attempt to sell more papers. Other unethical media practices include not telling the whole story or not telling the truth.

*R*JR Nabisco, Inc. attempts to project itself as a good citizen of the corporate community. There are other factors to consider, however. In 1976, three of RJR's top executives were forced to resign when it was discovered that they had deposited between $65,000 and $90,000 in

THE CASE CONTINUES

corporate funds into a special account. It was found that the executives were using these funds to make illegal campaign contributions. In all, $190,000 had been given to domestic political campaigns illegally. Mat-

ters were made even worse when it was reported to the Securities and Exchange Commission by RJR that they had made questionable payments of some $25,000,000—of which $19,000,000 were unethical rebates. The company was fined $5,000 for this violation.

MARKETING AND ETHICS

*B*ecause marketers have more contact with the consumer, they are more subject to decisions involving ethical business practices.

Marketing and ethics influence each other. Marketers may be subject to many more decisions relative to ethical business practices than other businesspeople because they have more contact with the consumer. One of the classic ethical marketing dilemmas was the Nestlé case (see box on page 641). Nestlé's marketing of infant formula in Third World countries was questioned to the point that the corporate image was severely damaged and the company was boycotted. Nestlé suffered greatly but has regained a positive image.

Marketers must make product, promotion, distribution, and price decisions that have a wide-ranging impact in the marketplace (see figure 23.4). For this reason we

❑ **Figure 23.4**
Ethical dimensions of the marketing mix.

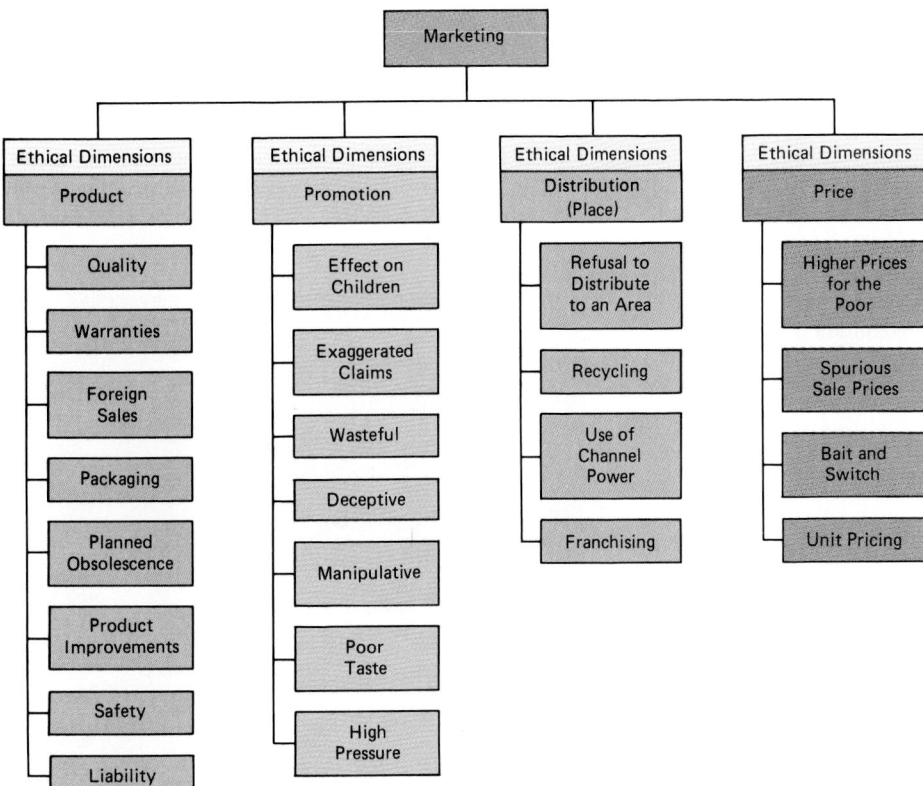

will take a close look at the relationships between ethics and the marketing mix. Because of the importance of marketing research in the marketing process, we will also examine the ethical aspects of this activity.

Product

There are two kinds of products—goods and services. Each should be marketed ethically. What are the ethical considerations related to the product in marketing goods and services? Two considerations involve quality control and warranties.

A firm that is concerned with quality control monitors the manufacturing of its product very carefully. The firm constantly tests the product to assure its quality. It hires inspectors to oversee production, run the tests, and make sure that certain standards are met. Hanes, a manufacturer of underwear, ran a notable advertising campaign featuring Inspector 12. She demonstrated some of the tests that Hanes uses to ensure quality control. No item carries the Hanes label until an inspector indicates that it meets Hanes's standards.

One of the most obvious assurances that the customer will obtain a reliable product is the warranty. Some warranties are very specific and limited. Cars have very specific warranties and usually have more than one.

Warranties protect the consumers and give them confidence in making purchases.

The warranties, of course, protect the consumers and give them confidence in making purchases. They also help the manufacturers sell more products. When the consumers know that they have recourse if they purchase faulty products, they will be more willing to make purchases. The Magnuson-Moss Warranty and Federal Trade Commission Improvement Act was passed to help consumers identify their warranty coverages. This act requires manufacturers of consumer products costing over $15 to use simple and concise language in their warranties and to state whether the coverages are full or limited.

Other ethical considerations relating to products involve selling products to foreign countries that do not meet our codes or regulations but are allowable in those countries. Another consideration involves packaging products in oversized containers or illustrating an oversized product so that the consumers think they are getting more or bigger merchandise. Manufacturers of health and beauty aids sometimes use elaborate, oversized packages that serve as strong promotional devices. Critics have charged that marketers seeking the sales of new products purposely plan for the phasing out of old products—a practice known as planned obsolescence.

Creative packaging for promotional purposes.

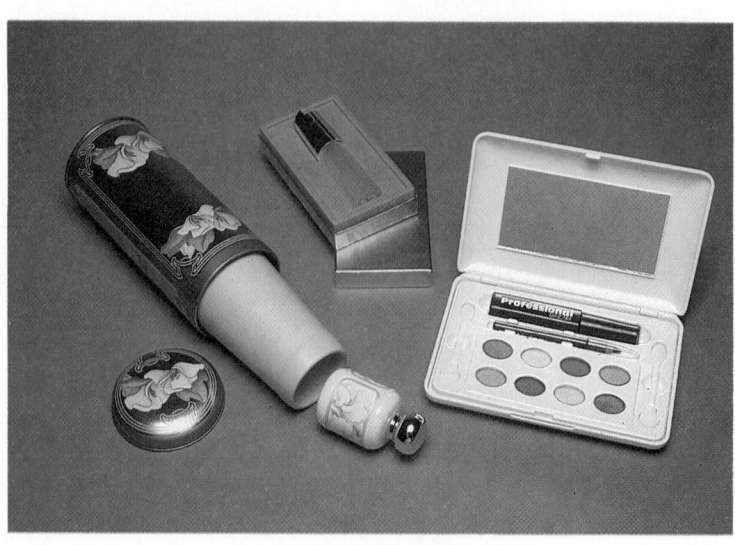

*W*ithholding product improvements from the market is an ethical consideration.

Product differentiation involves an ethical dimension. This is an effort by marketers to secure some control over the demand for a product by promoting distinctions—sometimes very minor—between their products and those of competing sellers. Another aspect of product ethics is withholding product improvements from the market. An implicit warranty that a product is safe is another ethical consideration. The amount of liability that a business assumes for the damage done by a product is an additional ethical factor.

We can all think of products that we question ethically. One which quickly comes to mind is the diet pill. We all realize that the pills cannot possibly do what they claim they can do—at least for most people. Yet, companies continue to make them, drugstores continue to stock them, and consumers obviously continue to buy them.

In some cases, a business service does not meet the ethical standards of the consumer. A well-known advertising agency offered to help a consortium of twenty New York City welfare agencies with overcrowded facilities for homeless children. The agencies needed help in getting the children out of the overcrowded institutions and into private (foster) homes. The ad agency drew up a campaign with the theme "Take two, they're small." For this clever theme, the agency won many creative awards, and the children's placement rate increased 400 percent! However, the welfare agency directors decided that the campaign was not putting the children in a good light. They said that the campaign was demeaning and undignified. Children, the agencies claimed, were being marketed like dog food.

*C*ompanies should value credibility and view ethical behavior as good business.

The ad agency felt that the ethical misgivings of the welfare agencies were misdirected, that they got in the way of doing good for the cause, and that the consortium of welfare agencies was self-destructive. An agency executive argued, "[this] spurious ethical issue should be dropped. It's strictly a mirage . . . and impedes productive development." Continuing, the agency person noted that the "amount of corruption in the marketplace is exaggerated." He felt strongly that businesses value credibility and view ethical behavior as good business.[11]

Promotion

Because marketers need to create unusual messages to attract attention and gain interest for their products, the promotional area is ripe for ethical conflicts. Both advertising and personal selling techniques often offend various groups of consumers. Some people are concerned about the impressions that TV commercials leave on the sensitive minds of children. In fact, a group of concerned citizens called Action for Children's Television (ACT) carefully evaluates the quality of commercials that are directed to children. Others are displeased about the exaggerated claims of some advertisements for health and beauty aids. The Federal Trade Commission ordered Listerine to run counter-advertising rebutting its original claim that the mouthwash killed millions of germs on contact.

Some critics of advertising state that it is wasteful, deceptive, manipulative, and in poor taste. When advertising is used to magnify minor differences between competing products—such as Budweiser beer and Miller beer—perhaps there is justification for stating that advertising is wasteful. An advertising message may occasionally deceive consumers. For example, in an effort to draw customers, some retailers and financial institutions advertise deceptively low interest rates. Some advertisements are criticized for being manipulative and causing people to buy things that they do not really need, for example, expensive TV sets or luxury cars instead of basic necessities. Advertisements that are in bad taste frequently offend the public. For example, an ad for Perry Ellis's Fragrance for men used a male model in a belligerent pose uttering an unprintable word. Because it offended certain groups, some publications would not print the ad.

*T*he tobacco companies' diversification has raised some ethical questions about their promotional activities.

Tobacco companies have recently diversified their interests and acquired a wide variety of businesses, raising some ethical questions about their promotional activities. We have already mentioned the product lines that are marketed by RJR Nabisco, Inc. American Brands' (Lucky Strike) revenues now come from life insurance, golf balls, and Chip-a-Roo cookies. Several years ago Philip Morris bought the Miller Brewing Company, and more recently it acquired the nation's largest food company, General Foods. Thus, the largest cigarette company also controls Jello, Maxwell House Coffee, Birds Eye, Post Cereals, Kool Aid, and numerous other valued consumer brands.

The cigarette companies argue that their diversification is a means of protecting themselves. Government regulations and changes in consumer attitudes are already shrinking the cigarette market. These companies can count on their other businesses to generate sales and earnings. There is another aspect to this, however. Consider that these companies now wield powerful advertising dollars—RJR controls $1 billion in advertising budgets; Philip Morris's is even bigger.

*S*ome publications give advance warnings to advertisers when negative cigarette articles are going to appear.

Let's think about what these cigarette giants might do with their advertising dollars in publications that write negative comments about cigarettes. Already, publications with large revenues from cigarette advertising have withheld newsworthy stories critical of cigarettes. Some publications notify advertisers before negative articles about cigarettes appear. This permits the advertisers to pull their ads. In the case of *Time* or *Newsweek,* it means the loss of $1 million per week in ad revenue. This could be construed as a form of blackmail. RJR ordered its Del Monte brand to retract funding of a TV show on nutrition because the station had aired negative shows about cigarettes. The amalgamation of the food and cigarette industries provides the latter with additional advertising muscle. Will it be flexed to curtail negative stories about cigarettes?

Distribution

In the marketing mix, distribution refers to the physical distribution of products or services. Distribution decisions provide numerous opportunities for unethical business practices. For example, a company may decide that it does not want to sell its products in remote areas even though there are no substitutes available. The company's reason is that it sells too few items in these areas and it cannot afford to deliver the goods and perform other marketing services economically. On the other hand, the lack of certain goods like plumbing supplies and home appliances may reduce the standard of living for residents in the area.

*T*he economic dimension generally overshadows ethics in making a decision regarding recycling.

The decision to recycle cans, bottles, and other waste involves an ethical dilemma. Should a company make a concerted effort to recycle its containers and reduce litter? Generally an economic dimension overshadows the ethical one in making a decision regarding recycling. When it is profitable to recycle, a company will do it; otherwise, it won't.

Large firms sometimes callously threaten their smaller suppliers with the loss of business. As mentioned in Chapter 12, channel captains wield channel power over the other members in a channel system. A large merchandiser like J.C. Penney or Sears can force a small supplier into bankruptcy by eliminating it as a supplier if it does not reduce its cost of goods.

Franchising arrangements often provide opportunities for unethical conduct by either the franchisor or the franchisee. Because franchisors sometimes make false claims and engage in deceptive practices, state and federal laws have been enacted to protect prospective franchisees. The major purpose of these laws is to force franchisors to make a complete disclosure of their franchise offers. In some cases, dishonest franchisees deceive franchisors by not disclosing their actual sales. Since the annual royalty fees are based on a percentage of the franchisee's sales, a fictitiously low sales figure reduces the franchisor's earnings.

Price

*R*etail businesses in poorer neighborhoods charge higher prices because of location.

The pricing policies of marketers frequently lead to ethical conflicts. For example, retail businesses operating in poorer neighborhoods often charge higher prices. Retailers in these locations claim that they are justified in charging higher prices because their costs are higher. Goods turn over more slowly, and higher crime rates increase the costs of maintaining inventory and insurance. On the other hand, there is less competition so prices can be kept high. Also, residents of poorer areas have less flexibility and find it more difficult to shop outside of their areas.

In some cases, consumers receive inadequate information about prices. They discover that many extra charges must be paid on top of a seemingly low price. For example, an advertised price of $39.95 for a replacement tire may not include additional costs for a necessary valve, or for balancing, tire removal, and taxes. To the disappointment of consumers, sale prices sometimes mean the sale of goods of inferior quality. Another unethical practice is the bait-and-switch tactic. The seller promotes a low-priced, stripped-down model. When consumers express interest in it, they are immediately switched to a higher-priced model with more features. Another questionable practice occurs when, without any announcement, a business reduces the quality or quantity of a product, indirectly reducing its price.

Unit pricing is an important ethical consideration in pricing. Unit pricing allows consumers to compare the prices of products per established units such as ounces or quarts. Without unit pricing, one study indicated that a group of homemakers who were sent to supermarkets to determine the best buys made the incorrect choice 40 percent of the time!

Marketing Research

*P*rivacy is an ethical issue in marketing research.

Marketing research raises important ethical issues. Research practices should be in line with the general ethical expectations of society. Marketing researchers must be very careful that in their aspiration to be successful researchers they do not violate the privacy of their subjects or put their subjects in embarrassing situations. Is it ethical, in the name of research, to use hidden eye-tracking equipment when respondents are viewing ads without informing them? On the other hand, not using this equipment might stifle the creation of effective ads. Is it fair to ask subjects very personal questions under the guise of performing research and then use the information for some personal gain?

Misleading and incomplete reporting create other ethical problems in marketing research. Research results can be reported in a way that leads consumers to draw incorrect conclusions. For example, an ad mentioned that in comparison tests "an amazing 60 percent" of a sample of consumers stated that Triumph cigarettes tasted as good as or better than Merit. Although this was a correct statement, a large number of the sample group indicated that the two cigarettes tasted the same. The ad does not indicate the percentage of respondents who actually said that Triumph tasted better so consumers could easily conclude that the percentage was much closer to 60 percent than it really was. Because so many respondents believed that the two cigarettes tasted the same, it is just as accurate to claim that 60 percent of the sample said that Merit tasted as good as or better than Triumph.[12] Other marketing research practices that have ethical implications are shown in figure 23.5.

Marketers must anticipate and react to the changing ethical expectations of consumers. The medicine man road shows of the 1880s are wholly unacceptable in the 1980s. Even the stereotypical high-pressure house-to-house salespeople characterized in the Dagwood comic strip must now abide by the legislated three-day cooling-off period that permits a consumer to break the sales contract.

To achieve the proper respect and recognition from the public, marketers should incorporate ethical behavior into all aspects of their decision making. Although most

❑ **Figure 23.5**
Research practices with ethical implications.

> 1. Research has consistently found that including a small amount of money in a mail survey will greatly increase the response rate. Promises of money for returning the questionnaire are much less effective. One explanation is that respondents experience guilt if they do not complete a questionnaire for which they have already been "paid," but find it not worth their while to complete a questionnaire for the amount of money usually promised. Based on this, a research firm puts 25¢ in all its mail surveys.
>
> 2 A research firm specializes in telephone surveys. It recently began using voice pitch analysis in an attempt to determine if respondents were distorting their answers to sensitive questions.
>
> 3. A mall intercept facility recently installed hidden eye-tracking equipment. Now, when respondents are asked to view advertisements or packages, they are not told that their eye movements are being recorded.
>
> 4. The research director of a large corporation is convinced that using the company's name in surveys with consumers produces (1) lowered response rates and (2) distorted answers. Therefore, the firm routinely conducts surveys using the title, Public Opinion Institute.
>
> 5. A company dramatically cuts the price of its products in a city where a competitor is test marketing a new product.
>
> 6. An insurance company uses a variety of projective techniques to assist in preparing advertisements for life insurance. Potential respondents are told that the purpose of the tests is to isolate factors that influence creativity.
>
> 7. A survey finds that 80 percent of the doctors responding do not recommend any particular brand of margarine to their patients who are concerned about cholesterol. Five percent recommend Brand A, four percent recommend Brand B, and no other brand is recommended by over 2 percent of the doctors. The company runs an advertisement that states: "More doctors recommend Brand A margarine for cholesterol control than any other brand."

Source: Donald S. Tull and Del I. Hawkins, *Marketing Research: Measurement and Method,* (3rd ed., New York: Macmillan Publishing Company, 1984), p. 681.

*O*f 250,000 corporations under the SEC, only 74 have been found guilty of illegal campaign contributions.

organizations function within a highly legal and ethical framework, marketing managers should take the lead in instilling the proper ethical conduct in their personnel. Throughout this country millions of marketing transactions occur daily, but there are only a few instances of complaints by consumers. Although political campaign support is only one area where the correct business behavior is often questioned, the following statement makes an important point: "Of 250,000 corporations under the Securities & Exchange Commission, 74 have been found guilty of illegal campaign contributions. That calculates out to 29/100 of 1 percent—purer than Ivory Soap's familiar claim of 99 and 44/100 percent pure."[13]

---

*A*lthough RJR Nabisco, Inc. is a highly respected organization in the business community, the spectre of unethical conduct continues to haunt it. One of the crusaders against the company is Patrick Reynolds, a grandson of the founder of the R. J. Reynolds Tobacco Co. When he reached age 21 in 1969, he inherited $2.5 million from his grandfather. He has been on TV talk shows and appeared before a congressional committee condemning cigarette advertising as immoral. Other mem-

THE CASE CONTINUES

bers of his family believe that he is overzealous and biting the hand that feeds him.

Reynolds is a reformed smoker who stridently claims that cigarettes have killed 10 million Americans since 1950 and smoking is costing our economy $65 billion annually in health care and lost wages. He advocates higher taxes on cigarettes and a complete ban on cigarette

advertising. Reynolds refuses to believe that RJR can be an ethical company as long as it markets cigarettes. At one time he had hoped to join RJR's board of directors and work from within the company to divest its tobacco holdings. In Winston-Salem, where RJR is the largest employer with 14,000 workers, Reynolds's crusade is virtually ignored. Because of the company's generosity and philanthropic effort, Winston-Salem residents hold the company in high esteem.

ATTENTION TO ETHICS

General Dynamics

When a well-known business engages in unethical practices, public attention focuses on business ethics. In the spring of 1985, the U.S. Navy banned contracts with the General Dynamics Corporation. Several problems led to the ban. Some of the company's executives had given presents to Admiral Hyman Rickover when he was director of the nuclear submarine program. General Dynamics' Vice President George Sawyer negotiated a contract while he was serving as Assistant Secretary of the Navy—a conflict of interest. The company improperly charged the Navy for such items as country club dues and dog kennel fees. The Navy withheld $437.8 million in payments to General Dynamics in an attempt to recover some of the losses for the improper charges.

General Dynamics prepared a 20-page ethics booklet which was given to all salaried employees.

The day after the Navy issued the ban against General Dynamics, the company contacted Gary Edwards, Director of the Ethical Resource Center in Washington. Edwards's nonprofit group helped General Dynamics prepare their twenty-page ethics booklet given to all salaried employees. The booklet opens with the comment, "Sometimes we take it for granted that our employees fully understand the importance of meeting the highest standards of business ethics."[14] Because the company instituted an ethics program, the Navy lifted its ban.

Business Majors and Ethics

A recent survey at an eastern university queried 131 business majors—93 MBAs, 15 seniors, 13 juniors, and 10 sophomores—about their attitudes concerning business ethics. The researcher's comment after studying the responses was that he had grave misgivings about whether students were prepared to make ethical decisions. He felt that they could only make ethical decisions under a legalistic system. A **legalistic system** is one in which rules and regulations spell out laws for behavior. Like General Dynamics, these students' future employers cannot afford to assume that they will meet high standards of business ethics.

Today's business students are not prepared to make ethical decisions.

The survey asked the students what they considered the current ethical climate in business to be, what direction they thought the business ethics climate would take, what ethics-related pressures they expected to encounter, and how they would respond to those pressures.

The responses indicated that today's business students are not prepared to improve the ethical climate in the firms they join. The students indicated that they felt businesses were quite unethical. They defined business as taking advantage of competitors before they can do it to you. To the students business means making a profit, and businesses will make that profit at anyone's expense, even if it means covering up mistaken or dangerous practices when the public cries out. Only one-third of the students considered businesses to be ethical.

Fear of failure motivated the students to respond that in certain situations they might behave unethically. They felt that most of the unethical behavior was a result of fear that one would not succeed. On the brighter side, almost half of the students thought that the ethical climate in business was improving. However, their reasons for thinking this were that government, society, and the media were forcing businesses to become more ethical. Most of the students were fatalistic in thinking that they would have no choice but to lower their ethical standards and go along with everyone else.[15]

REAL PEOPLE IN MARKETING

John Banzhaf: A Moral Conscience for Marketing

Although the consumer movement in the 1980s is showing signs of aging, John Banzhaf continues to display a fresh vigor for consumer causes. Through his crusading efforts and legal strategies, Mr. Banzhaf has greatly affected the marketing plans of numerous firms.

Although some may view him as an antithesis to sound marketing practices, he considers himself a moral conscience. After graduating from MIT in 1962, he entered Columbia Law School with the intent to become a wealthy patent attorney. He graduated from the school with a magna cum laude degree in law. As events unfolded, however, he became a strong opponent of cigarette smoking and of the advertisements for cigarettes. He thought that as an opponent of smoking, he could use the courts to create a better world. Believing that the legal system has been generally viewed as the tool of the privileged, he reasoned that it could be used just as effectively by the oppressed.

Mr. Banzhaf, who founded and is the executive director of Action on Smoking and Health (ASH), concluded that smoking had become a controversial issue of great public importance. Under the fairness doctrine of the Federal Communications Commission (FCC), Mr. Banzhaf insisted that opponents of smoking should be given rebuttal time by the broadcast media. Somewhat to his surprise, the FCC agreed with his position and ordered broadcasters who carried cigarette commercials to provide air time for antismoking messages.

In the late 1960s, the broadcasting industry was selling about $250 million worth of cigarette advertising time a year. Because the industry had to contribute millions of dollars worth of free radio and TV time for antismoking messages, Mr. Banzhaf's challenge to cigarette advertising posed a substantial economic loss for the industry. Although the tobacco and broadcasting industries appealed to the FCC to change its ruling, the commission held firm. Mr. Banzhaf successfully defended the FCC ruling before the United States Court of Appeals, and he later persuaded the United States Supreme Court that they should refrain from reviewing the decision.

Continuing to lash out against smoking, Mr. Banzhaf was the chief player in the effort to get all cigarette advertising banned from the airwaves in 1970. By demonstrating that cigarette smoke can be harmful to nonsmokers who inhale the smoke generated by smokers, he has been able to convince numerous public and private organizations to either prohibit smoking or provide individuals with nonsmoking areas.

Since 1968, Mr. Banzhaf has been a professor at the National Law Center of George Washington University. Through an experiential method of instruction, his students became involved in consumer crusades. They are divided into six-member teams, and each team is directed to select a public-service area in which it would engage in legal actions to correct certain wrongs. The types of student activities are indicated by the acronyms that identify the teams. These include: SOUP (Students Opposing Unfair Practices), CRASH (Citizens to Restrict Airline Smoking Hazards), CANDY (Candy Advertising Normally Directed Towards Youth), STORE (Students to Observe Retail Establishments), and PUMP (Protesting Unfair Marketing Practices).

Source: Adapted from John F. Banzhaf, III, *Current Biography,* 1973 (New York: The M. H. Wilson Company, 1973), pp. 30–33; John F. Banzhaf, III, *Marquis Who's Who,* 44th ed. (Wilmette, Ill.: Macmillan Directory Division, 1986–87), p. 139.

WHAT IS ETHICAL BEHAVIOR?

Ethical behavior results from either personal values or legislation.

Ethical behavior involves critical analysis of human acts to determine their rightness or wrongness in terms of two major criteria, truth and justice. The ethical behavior of individuals can result from the personal values that one has been trained to hold. If we are reared to value honesty and consideration for ourselves and others, then we probably have strong personal ethics. However, ethics can also be developed through laws.

Legalistic Ethics

One way to obtain ethical behavior is to legislate it. This is a legalistic approach in which rules are made about behavior, and people are punished if they don't obey the rules. The legalistic approach is sometimes necessary to *initiate* a change in ethical standards, but it is rarely sufficient to sustain one. To understand why this is so, ask yourself the following question: Would you rather develop your own rationale for what you consider to be a just decision or would you rather be told that you had to decide something in a certain way? Most of us would prefer to make up our own minds rather than be told what we had to do.

Personal Ethics

Quite obviously the better means of attaining ethical behavior is to have it be a personal choice rather than have it be imposed legally. But how do people develop the capacity to make ethical choices? We learn our code of ethics first from our parents and then from our schooling and our peers. We also learn ethics from the organizations with which we associate—churches, clubs, and businesses—and from the broader environment—government and the media.

Ethics encompasses what we hold to be culturally valuable. In American culture, some of these things are: (1) human life, (2) freedom, and (3) the right to pursue happiness.

Not all societies value the same things. In some heavily populated areas, human life is not so important. In some countries, such as Russia and China, where the government wants to attain certain goals, individual freedom is not valued because the government must have tight control. (The Russian policy of allowing greater personal freedom—glasnost—represents a significant loosening of state control.) However, in America, life, liberty, and the pursuit of happiness are highly cherished. When these values become unimportant, then our behavior becomes unethical. For example, if we place the value of money or profit above the worth of another human being, then we will probably behave unethically to make a profit. At that point we cease to care about our customers as people and are willing to cheat them in order to make our profit.

Business Ethics

People may appear ethical in their personal lives, but they behave unethically in business.

Sometimes people seem to be very ethical in their personal lives, but they behave unethically in their business dealings. Perhaps this is because a business is not a person, and with the personal aspect missing, we do not feel we are cheating anyone if we do something that is unethical. Individuals often view a business as an impersonal entity that has practically unlimited resources upon which to draw.

We closely connect ethics and goodness. "Good" is anything that promotes the well-being of others and ourselves. If we keep this concept in mind and let it override our personal, selfish interest, then we will experience fewer difficulties in making ethical decisions.

MAKING ETHICAL MARKETING DECISIONS

To qualify as a professional, a marketer should possess considerable integrity and broad vision.

Marketers should conduct themselves as professional individuals. Historically, the public has not considered many marketers to be professionals. To become a professional requires that the marketer possess considerable integrity and broad vision.

Marketers are constantly faced with situations in which they must determine right and wrong. Figure 23.6 indicates that the corporate and social environments affect the individuals who make ethical decisions. For example, the marketing vice

❏ **Figure 23.6**
Flow chart for ethical
decision making.

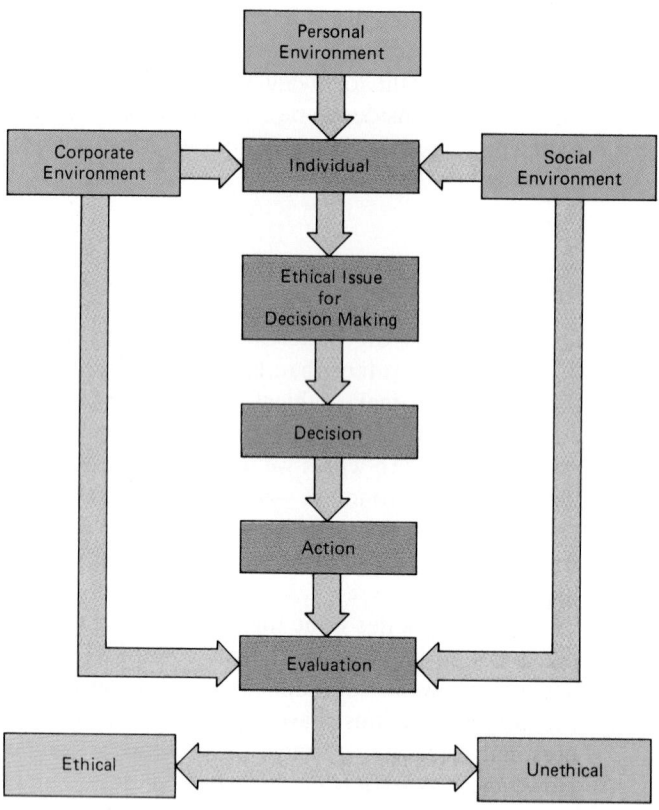

president of a toy company must determine not to go ahead with the production and sale of a toy that is potentially hazardous to children. Demand for the toy may be well established, and the marketer may be aware that a competitor is going to produce a similar toy. The marketer must go beyond the company's self-interest in making the decision not to market the toy.

Marketing could be made more ethical by the use of ethical consultants. Large firms might employ their own internal ethical consultants. Cummins, the diesel engine maker, follows this practice now. Small firms could use an outsider when an ethical decision is at stake. This might be a member of the clergy or a group of consumers. The point is that there should be someone, either inside or outside, who can more objectively look at a situation and evaluate it from an ethical perspective.

Finally, for marketers to become more professional, marketing must move beyond cost/benefit analysis to social analysis. In other words, the marketer should not think just in terms of how to market a particular product, but how the marketing effort could be turned into a positive social good.[16]

AMA Code

A marketer must be accountable, honest, knowledgeable, consumer oriented, and professional.

In order to help marketers make ethical decisions, a *Marketing Code of Ethics* was prepared by the American Marketing Association (see figure 23.7).[17]

This code encompasses several overall principles of professional conduct. As a marketer you accept responsibility for the consequences of your actions, you uphold and advance the integrity of the marketing profession. Your products, promotions, distribution methods, pricing, and marketing research are correctly represented without deception. If you violate the code you may have your Association membership suspended or revoked.

□ **Figure 23.7** American Marketing Association's Code of Ethics

CODE OF ETHICS
Members of the American Marketing Association (AMA) are committed to ethical professional conduct. They have joined together in subscribing to this Code of Ethics embracing the following topics:

Responsibilities of the Marketer
Marketers must accept responsibility for the consequences of their activities and make every effort to ensure that their decisions, recommendations, and actions function to identify, serve, and satisfy all relevant publics: customers, organizations, and society.
　　Marketers' professional conduct must be guided by:
1. The basic rule of professional ethics: not knowingly to do harm;
2. The adherence to all applicable laws and regulations;
3. The accurate representation of their education, training, and experience; and
4. The active support, practice, and promotion of this Code of Ethics.

Honesty and Fairness
Marketers shall uphold and advance the integrity, honor, and dignity of the marketing profession by:
1. Being honest in serving consumers, clients, employees, suppliers, distributors, and the public;
2. Not knowingly participating in conflict of interest without prior notice to all parties involved; and
3. Establishing equitable fee schedules, including the payment or receipt of usual, customary, and/or legal compensation for marketing exchanges.

Rights and Duties of Parties in the Marketing Exchange Process
Participants in the marketing exchange process should be able to expect that:
1. Products and services offered are safe and fit for their intended uses;
2. Communications about offered products and services are not deceptive;
3. All parties intend to discharge their obligations, financial and otherwise, in good faith; and
4. Appropriate internal methods exist for equitable adjustment and/or redress of grievances concerning purchases.

　　It is understood that the above would include, *but is not limited to,* the following responsibilities of the marketer:

In the area of product development and management,
- disclosure of all substantial risks associated with product or service usage;

- identification of any product component substitution that might materially change the product or impact on the buyer's purchase decision;
- identification of extra-cost added features.

In the area of promotions,
- avoidance of false and misleading advertising;
- rejection of high pressure manipulations, or misleading sales tactics;
- avoidance of sales promotions that use deception or manipulation.

In the area of distribution,
- not manipulating the availability of a product for purpose of exploitation;
- not using coercion in the marketing channel;
- not exerting undue influence over the resellers choice to handle a product.

In the area of pricing,
- not engaging in price fixing;
- not practicing predatory pricing;
- disclosing the full price associated with any purchase.

In the area of marketing research,
- prohibiting selling or fund raising under the guise of conducting research;
- maintaining research integrity by avoiding misrepresentation and omission of pertinent research data;
- treating outside clients and suppliers fairly.

Organizational Relationships
Marketers should be aware of how their behavior may influence or impact on the behavior of others in organizational relationships. They should not demand, encourage, or apply coercion to obtain unethical behavior in their relationships with others, such as employees, suppliers, or customers.
1. Apply confidentiality and anonymity in professional relationships with regard to privileged information;
2. Meet their obligations and responsibilities in contracts and mutual agreements in a timely manner;
3. Avoid taking the work of others, in whole, or in part, and represent this work as their own or directly benefit from it without compensation or consent of the originator or owner;
4. Avoid manipulation to take advantage of situations to maximize personal welfare in a way that unfairly deprives or damages the organization or others.

Any AMA members found to be in violation of any provision of this Code of Ethics may have his or her Association membership suspended or revoked.

Source: Reprinted with permission from the American Marketing Association.

Test Yourself

With the code in mind, test yourself to see how you would respond to these various marketing situations.[18]

PRODUCT POLICIES

If required government warnings are met, it is acceptable to market a harmful product.

It is ethical to release only the studies supporting a product that is under attack.

In designing products it is ethical to consider the product's effect on the environment.

It is unethical to have built-in obsolescence.

It is unethical to market harmful products even though consumers demand them.

PROMOTIONAL POLICY

It is ethical to approve ads promoting the use of unnecessary *combinations* of company products, when *one* would do.

Sexual overtones in advertising are taboo.

Appealing to fear in ads to increase sales is unethical.

If a marketing executive discovers a misleading ad, he or she should use remedial advertising.

Emotional appeals are unethical in advertising consumer products.

PRICING POLICIES

It is ethical to have an informal understanding of product pricing within an industry.

It is unethical to raise prices during a temporary shortage of a product.

It is ethical to raise prices in low-income areas to cover risk.

MARKETING RESEARCH CONCERNS

The ethical marketing researcher will inform participants of the true nature of a test.

Unsolicited telephone selling is ethical.

A marketing researcher can use a fictitious company name if using the real name will bias a survey.

It is unethical to release the names of survey respondents if they have been promised confidentiality—even to another department in the same company.

COMPETITION POLICIES

Would you always act ethically in a controversial marketing situation?

Ethical marketing researchers should not take jobs that will not benefit the client.

It is wrong to switch firms and give your new employer information about the old firm.

A marketing research firm is obligated to disclaim a client's misleading uses of its findings.

In international marketing it is alright to use tactics in the host country that would be considered wrong in the United States.

Using information about the competition is alright, no matter how the information is obtained.

SUPERIOR/SUBORDINATE RELATIONS

Survival of the firm is more important than ethical considerations.

If you discover that your firm has suppressed a bad report about one of its products, you should resign and go to the proper authority.

Social actions off the job are an ethical consideration for evaluating an employee.

You should quit your job before compromising your ethical standards to achieve company goals.

Ethics can be ignored if it means losing a long-term profit.

CONFLICT OF INTEREST

It is ethical for marketers to give a small gift at holiday time to a purchasing
    agent.
Most marketers feel it is alright to entertain legislators and government
    officials.
It is ethical to invest in firms with which you do business.
It is alright to accept small presents from other firms with which you do
    business.

CORPORATE ETHICS

An Ethics Resource Center has been established to help management make ethical decisions.

Ethical issues are so important in corporate life that an Ethics Resource Center has been established. The center is a nonprofit, tax-exempt, educational corporation formed to help improve public trust in business, government, and the other institutions of our society. Offering advisory services on ethical programs in business, labor organizations, professional groups, schools, and government, the center stresses practical applications in day-to-day business. It also publishes a free quarterly newsletter as well as other useful materials such as videos and pamphlets.

The ethical standards of the top management of an organization strongly determine the ethical thrust of its middle management and its entire moral climate. In order to extend the standards of top management throughout an organization, the company should develop a code of ethics, form an ethics committee, and initiate a training program in ethics.[19] In one study, 76 percent of the firms contacted had ethics codes and nearly 6 percent had an ethics committee of the board of directors.[20] Allied Corporation and Cummins are two firms that have included ethics in their management development programs.

An ethical code should reflect the current business environment and a company's uniqueness.

An ethics code should reflect the current business environment and the uniqueness of a company's operations. For example, the Norton Company, a multinational firm located in New England, revised its code during the 1960s to reflect the elimination of racial discrimination in employment and during the 1970s to express disapproval of any unethical conduct in international transactions.[21] A code should deal directly with the most frequent and most serious ethical issues facing a firm. The code of Cummins deals with questionable payments, meals, gifts, discounts, financial representations, supplier selection, and employee participation in political campaigns.[22]

Price Waterhouse, a "Big 8" accounting firm, has a "Corporate Policy With Respect to Ethics in Business Transactions." The firm encourages its managers to write policy statements and consider the following elements.[23]

1. General integrity
2. Compliance with laws and regulations
3. Political contributions
4. Fees to consultants and agents
5. Candor among members of management and in dealing with auditors
6. Proper accounting
7. Conflicts of interest
8. Fair competition
9. Acceptance of costly entertainment and gifts
10. Corporate hospitality of public officials

11. Discovery of violations of policy concerning corporate responsibility and integrity
12. Reporting to top management with respect to compliance with the policies

A special United Nations commission has been trying to develop a code of ethics for transnationals.

Ethical issues in international business have become so important that a special United Nations commission is trying to develop a code of ethics for transnationals. As of 1988, the commission still could not agree on the text. Basically, the problem seems to involve a difference of opinion between developing nations and socialist nations and member nations of the Organization for Economic Cooperation and Development (OECD), which are mostly Western market economies. They agree on how the transnationals should act in a host country but disagree on how the host should treat the transnational.[24]

The Ethics Committee

To see that a code of ethics is properly implemented and used, an ethics committee that consists of members of the board of directors is necessary. Internal and external directors should serve on this committee. The internal directors bring a knowledge of the operations of the firm to the committee; the external directors provide input from a variety of other areas. This committee should have the authority to apply penalties if it notes a breach of the ethical code. The committee should include individuals from both middle and top management.

DEVELOPMENT

Once the committee is established, it needs to develop the code in light of the particular circumstances of the company. For example, the code of a multinational company would have to contend with international cultures and the laws of other countries. Other considerations should include the ethical problems that the firm has faced in the past, the responses to those problems and their effectiveness, and future ethical issues that might be faced.

Let's look at two ethics statements. One is from World Book-Childcraft, a company that relies on personal selling (figure 23.8). The other is from the Ball Corporation, a multinational company with highly diversified product offerings (figure 23.9).

Most of the codes include a policy on accepting or giving gifts to business associates in other companies. Although most of the companies agree that token gift giving is acceptable, many put a limit on the amount that their companies consider appropriate.

A code of ethics should cover the areas of particular concern to a company.

Basically each code should cover areas of particular concern to the company. World Book is concerned with the interactions that take place between their representatives and potential customers. Ball, on the other hand, is more concerned with the handling of corporate assets.

COMMUNICATION

The ethics committee should be concerned with the way the code will be communicated to employees. The committee should develop a plan to ensure that employees know and understand what the code means.

ENFORCEMENT

The code should provide the ethics committee with some means of enforcement. If at all possible, the enforcement should be positive rather than negative. There

Figure 23.8
A corporate code of ethics.

Code of Ethics

For Managers and Independent Salespeople Representing World Book-Childcraft

As publishers of *The World Book Encyclopedia, Childcraft–The How and Why Library*, and other quality educational materials, WORLD BOOK-CHILDCRAFT is proud of its reputation for ethical business practices. Our Company's continued growth and leadership depend upon the integrity of the thousands of men and women who represent us. Each *World Book salesperson* subscribes to this Code of Ethics as an expression of personal commitment to these ethical selling practices.

1. *World Book salespeople* conduct themselves with courtesy and dignity and with respect for the rights and requests of a customer or prospective customer at all times. They avoid making calls at unreasonable hours without an appointment and do not overstay their welcome.

2. *World Book salespeople,* during the initial steps of a sales call, will disclose their name, their Company, and the products they represent, and will, upon request, present their Company identification card. They do not claim to be calling on a prospective purchaser in a nonselling capacity, nor do they otherwise misrepresent the purpose of the call or the amount of a prospect's time that is sought.

3. *World Book salespeople* may indicate that our products are widely used in schools and libraries and that *World Book* is approved by the appropriate state recommending bodies. However, they never falsely imply that the sales call is in any way connected with a school or that our products are required for school use, will guarantee school progress, or that they are approved by a particular school official.

4. *World Book salespeople* who are schoolteachers make it completely clear during the initial steps of a sales interview that they are presenting our products on their merits. They never imply that a student would receive any different treatment or consideration in school if parents do or do not purchase our products.

5. *World Book salespeople* base the sales presentation on the merit and quality of our products and do not disparage our competitors or their products. Nor do they seek the cancellation of any contracts that may exist between our competitors and their customers.

6. *World Book salespeople* make only Company-approved claims and use no form of coercion, sympathy appeal, or other high-pressure tactics in the sales presentation.

7. *World Book salespeople* always give clear and accurate information regarding the Company's products, prices, services, credit terms, quality and satisfaction guarantees, and policies. They avoid the use of false, misleading, half-true, or exaggerated statements.

8. *World Book salespeople* never imply that a prospective customer has been "specially selected" to receive certain benefits or that any offer is special or limited as to time when such is not the case. They do not falsely imply that our products are free nor do they misrepresent the savings available in the purchase of any product, alone or in combination. They do not offer any merchandise, price concession, or other special inducement to an individual customer that is not available to other parent or teacher customers at that time.

9. *World Book salespeople* observe the Company's policy of nondiscrimination by reason of race, creed, color, sex, age, or national origin. They also exercise due regard for a prospective customer's financial status and need for the products offered and never pay or advance any portion of a customer's initial deposit or monthly payment.

10. *World Book salespeople* take orders for the Company's products only on standard Company contract forms that must be signed by each customer. At the time such contracts are signed, the representative orally informs all customers of their cancellation rights and leaves with them the required copies of the contract and notice of cancellation with all pertinent blank spaces properly filled in.

Frank Gagliardi

Frank J. Gagliardi
President and Director
of North American Sales

I have read this Code of Ethics and agree to abide by it.

Signed: _____
Authorized Salesperson

Source: Courtesy of World Book, Inc.

could be incentives, recognition, commendation, or even monetary reward for positive ethical action.

IMPLEMENTATION

Once the code is written, the committee's job is to oversee its implementation. The committee should also monitor changes in the business environment and see that the company's code is up-to-date and applicable.

Ethics Programs

Companies should provide ethics training for employees.

Companies should provide programs for training in ethics. The sessions should encourage discussions of problem areas. They should include lower- and middle-management employees who are likely to be confronted with ethical problems. These sessions should not be lectures but should allow for plenty of open discussion.

❑ **Figure 23.9**
Ethics Policy
Statement of the Ball
Corporation.

**Corporate Policy Statements
of
Board of Directors
of
Ball Corporation**

Policy On Use Of Corporate Assets (Adopted April 22, 1976)

Introduction

There has been widespread publicity and public interest in recently disclosed uses of corporate assets for improper or illegal purposes on the part of a number of United States companies. This has lead management to conclude that a statement of policy on this subject should be disseminated to all employees to reaffirm our policies. This policy is applicable to Ball Corporation and all of its domestic and foreign subsidiaries.

Compliance with Laws and Regulations

The Company's policy is to comply with all laws and regulations that are applicable to its business—at all governmental levels in the United States and abroad. All employees, agents, and representatives acting for or on behalf of the Company or any subsidiary shall comply with all laws and regulations in any country in which they are so acting. The use of Company or subsidiary funds or assets for any unlawful or improper purpose, whether directly or through third parties is prohibited.

In some instances the laws and regulations may be ambiguous or difficult to interpret. Questions concerning interpretation or compliance should be referred to the Company's General Counsel, who may refer such questions to the Audit Committee for appropriate action.

Monitoring by Corporate Officers

The officers of the Company and of each subsidiary in the conduct of their area of responsibility will continue to monitor the activities of all Company or subsidiary employees, agents and representatives to assure that all such employees, agents and representatives are in compliance with all laws and regulations in any country in which they are operating on behalf of the Company or any subsidiary.

Policy On Conflicts Of Interest (As Restated April 25, 1978—Originally adopted April 26, 1973)

It is the policy of the Corporation that every employee, director and officer shall conduct himself with high ethical standards to avoid a conflict of interest with the Corporation or its stockholders.

A conflict of interest, in the broad sense, may arise where an individual's position or responsibilities on behalf of the Corporation present an opportunity for personal gain apart from the normal rewards of employment. It may also arise where an individual's personal interests are so inconsistent with the Corporation's interests that the latter become secondary, or otherwise conflict with his proper loyalties to the Corporation. Areas which require specific attention are:

- **Personal Financial Interest**
  Directors, officers, and employees should avoid any outside commercial interests which might influence their official decisions or actions. Such outside commercial interests could include (a) a financial interest in an enterprise which has business relations with the Corporation if such financial interest represents a significant part of the net worth of the individual or of the net value of such outside enterprise; and (b) an investment in another business which competes with any of the Corporation's interests if such investment represents a significant part of the net worth of the individual or of the net value of the other business. In short, financial activity in any form which would involve or suggest "self-dealing" should be avoided.

- **Inside Information**
  Directors, officers, and employees should refrain from the purchase or sale of the Corporation's securities or from involvement in any outside transaction which is influenced by confidential information or special knowledge of the Corporation's activities. Confidential information or special knowledge would be that which is not generally known or available to the public.

- **Gratuities**
  An individual must not place himself under actual or apparent obligation to anyone by accepting, or permitting those close to him to accept gifts or other favors where it might appear that they were given for the purpose of improperly influencing the individual in the performance of his duties.

- **Outside Activities**
  Officers and employees should avoid outside employment or activities which would impair the effective performance of their obligations to the Corporation, either because of excessive demands on their time, or because of their assumption of outside commitments obviously contrary to their legitimate commitments to the Corporation.

In many cases, outside participation on a board of directors or equivalent executive body is encouraged; however, serving in such a capacity for a profit-making organization requires the prior authorization of the appropriate Group Vice President, the President and Chief Operating Officer, or Chairman and Chief Executive Officer.

Finally, conflict of interest situations do occasionally present themselves, and those that do are hopefully inadvertent. Where only potential, they should be avoided by personal foresight and planning. Where actual, they should be eliminated promptly upon their discovery, and full disclosure should be made to the appropriate executive officer. Only in these ways can the individuals involved honor their special responsibilities of trust and good faith which are the lifeblood of the Corporation.

Policy On Political Contributions (Restated January 23, 1979—Originally adopted July 24, 1975)

Ball Corporation policy prohibits the use of corporate funds for political purposes, to the extent such use is prohibited by Federal, State or foreign legislation and regulations.

Ball Corporation policy prohibits exercise of any corporate action, or action by corporate officials, direct or implied, that infringes the right of any employee individually to decide whether, to whom and in what amount he or she will make political contributions.

Source: Ball Corporation, Muncie, IN.

In summary, the goal in establishing a corporate ethics policy should not be to write, teach, or enforce rigid rules of conduct. The goal is to develop within each employee a sensitivity to the ethical dimensions of business decisions.[25]

SOCIAL RESPONSIBILITY

One other aspect of ethical behavior is social responsibility. In some cases the two appear to intertwine, especially in companies whose products or services are essential to the health and well-being of the members of society. The drug companies are an example. The products developed in their research laboratories make major contributions by saving many lives. Consider, however, the dilemma that Johnson & Johnson faced when confronted with the cyanide contamination of its Tylenol capsules and the deaths which resulted. Johnson & Johnson determined that it was wiser to lose millions of dollars and remove all capsules from the market than to risk the death of another person. On the other hand, when Gerber was faced with glass slivers in its baby food, the company treated the problem as a series of isolated incidents. Gerber withdrew its product only from those regions of the country it determined to be affected.

The socially responsible deeds of business are often not obvious and receive little publicity. For example, few people probably know that ARMCO, IBM, FMC, and AT&T have agreed to combine forces and fund, to the tune of $12 million, hazardous waste-dump cleanups.[26]

Making a Commitment

A socially responsible company puts major emphasis on its role as a citizen.

A socially responsible company puts major emphasis on its role as a citizen. These companies make commitments to their employees and to the communities. In some cases, it may be donating large sums of money to charities (table 23.1). In other cases it may be building a day-care center for employees' children or purchasing noted art works for a local museum. Mobil has helped to fund an organization in New York with a national outreach—the Children of Alcoholics Foundation. McDonald's has gained a reputation for strong social programs such as the Ronald McDonald Houses where parents of hospitalized children can stay.

Keeping in Touch

Most corporations realize the need to respond to change in society. By keeping in touch with what is going on in the world, these corporations are able to adapt and market their products and services to meet the changing desires of their customers.

❑ **Table 23.1**   Total U.S. charitable contributions.

CONTRIBUTIONS (IN BILLIONS)		DISTRIBUTION (IN BILLIONS)			
Individuals	$71.72	Religion	$40.90	Arts, Culture & Humanities	$5.83
Bequests	$5.83	Education	$12.73	Public/Social Benefit	$2.38
Foundations	$5.17	Health	$12.26	Other	$3.99
Corporations	$4.50	Human Services	$9.13		

TOTAL CONTRIBUTION: $87.22 billion

Source: American Association of Fundraising Counsel

Socially responsible companies permit employees time away from their jobs to support community activities.

One way to keep in touch is by being socially responsible and ⊔ublicly involved. Many companies budget a significant amount of money for giving. The Dayton Hudson Corporation, a major retail chain, gives an amount equal to five percent of its federal taxable income to charities. Over a forty-year period the company has granted $120.4 million to communities where it has stores.[27]

There are many dimensions of corporate responsibility. Beginning at the smallest scale, the socially responsible company permitting employees some time away from their jobs to support community activities. On the large scale are the companies that donate millions of dollars for public service. Still another facet is the variety of projects that responsible companies undertake. Putting the company parking lot underground and landscaping the area are some examples.

Some people, however, criticize corporate philanthropy as a cover-up for other activities. For example, Philip Morris's support of the arts cannot, in some people's minds, substitute for the fact that it makes its money by selling cigarettes.[28] Philip Morris supports many public TV programs, but it does not allow its name to be identified with a particular program. The cigarette giant feels that it should respect the government's ban on cigarette advertising on TV.[29]

THE CASE CONTINUES

Although cigarette makers may attempt to act ethically, they appear to follow practices that create controversy. Perhaps this is because they are attempting to maintain and even increase product sales as cigarettes become more associated with health problems. In recent years several companies have begun selling cigarettes in packs of twenty-five rather than the standard twenty. RJR introduced its Century brand in 25-packs. The cigarette companies rationalize the use of the larger pack by citing research studies that indicate the average smoker consumes about twenty-three cigarettes a day. This size of pack is already popular in Canada and Australia. Of course, the price of the larger size pack is

greater than the standard pack.

Critics of the tobacco industry believe that the cigarette companies lack sincerity when they claim that the new packages are mainly for convenience. They contend that the actual intention of the companies is to sell more cigarettes. These critics point out that smokers think in terms of smoking a pack or two a day. By including more cigarettes in a pack, smokers will smoke more. The tobacco companies strongly deny that the bigger packs are meant to increase the number of cigarettes that a person smokes.

The tobacco companies are using a variety of promotions in order to generate more sales. Lorillard is offering discounts on vacations to London, Rome, Hawaii, the Orient, and other selected locations. Each empty pack of Kent is worth $3 toward one of the vacations with a maximum discount of 35 percent available. A spokesperson for Lorillard claimed that these promotions are necessary because of increased competition, the growth of discounted brands, and the greater use of coupons. Opponents of the tobacco industry are firmly opposed to these promotions by the companies. They declare that promotions just increase the likelihood that additional individuals will develop the nicotine habit.

GOAL SUMMARY

1. **Define ethics.** Ethics is concerned with clarifying what constitutes human welfare and the kind of conduct necessary to promote welfare.

2. **Describe the major ethical theories.** Ethical relativism states that the same act may be morally right in one instance and morally wrong in another. Ethical egoism is the belief that each individual should always act to promote the greatest balance of good over evil for himself or herself. Utilitarianism states that individuals should act to promote the greatest good for the greatest number. Kant's categorical imperative declares that you should take the right action not necessarily because it produces good results but because it is your duty to do so.

3. **Describe today's conditions in business and society that influence our business ethics.** Today's business conditions influence business ethics in many ways. These conditions include the following.
   a. Conservation of resources
   b. Environmental protection
   c. Health consciousness
   d. Informed customers
   e. International markets
   f. Government regulations
   g. Affluent mobile society
   h. Media

4. **Explain marketing ethics.** Marketing ethics involves marketers' making ethical decisions relative to product, promotion, place, price, and marketing research.

5. **Describe the sources of ethical behavior.** Ethical behavior derives from legal mandate and from personal choice.

6. **Know the key topics of the marketing code of ethics.** The marketing code of ethics involves:
   a. Responsibilities of the marketer
   b. Honesty and fairness
   c. Rights and duties of parties in the marketing exchange process
   d. Organizational relationships

7. **Explain how corporate ethics can be developed.** Corporate ethics can be developed through a code of ethics, an ethics committee, and ethics programs.

8. **Describe social responsibility.** Social responsibility involves putting major emphasis on your role as a citizen. Companies that are socially responsible make commitments to their employees and their communities.

KEY TERMS

Ethics, **p. 635**
Ethical Relativism, **p. 635**
Ethical Egoism, **p. 636**
Utilitarianism Ethics, **p. 636**
Act Utilitarians, **p. 636**

Rule Utilitarian, **p. 636**
Kant's Categorical Imperative, **p. 636**
Demarketing, **p. 636**
Legalistic System, **p. 651**

CHECK YOUR LEARNING

1. The ethical theory stating that the same act may be morally right for one group and morally wrong for another is called: (a) ethical egoism, (b) utilitarianism, (c) Kant's categorical imperative, (d) ethical relativism.

2. Because most of our resources are replenishable, we no longer have the great need we once thought we had to conserve them.   **T/F**

3. When the Detroit Edison electric utility attempts to persuade its consumers to use less electricity, it is said to be: (a) remarketing, (b) demarketing, (c) low-level marketing, (d) counteradvertising.

4. All of the following are significant aspects of business today except: (a) informed consumers and the media, (b) international marketing, (c) monopolistic business practices, (d) affluent, mobile society.

5. Although the marketing of tangible goods is subject to ethical considerations, the marketing of intangible services seldom generates ethical problems. **T/F**

6. The number of corporations found guilty of illegal political campaign contributions is: (a) less than 1 percent, (b) 3 percent, (c) 5 percent, (d) over 10 percent.

7. The ethical dimension is usually more important than the economic one in making a decision regarding the recycling of wastes.   **T/F**

8. Because of its mathematical focus, marketing research allows few opportunities for unethical behavior.   **T/F**

9. Today's business students are well prepared to improve the climate for making ethical decisions in the firms that they join.   **T/F**

10. The ethical thrust of an organization's middle man-

CHECK YOUR LEARNING *(continued)*

agement determines the ethics practiced by its top management. **T/F**
11. Ethical behavior that is mandated by the rules of the Federal Trade Commission is called:
(a) regulation ethics, (b) legalistic ethics, (c) rule

ethics, (d) code ethics.
12. An organization's ethical code is usually communicated to employees through: (a) top management, (b) middle management, (c) the board of directors, (d) the ethics committee.

QUESTIONS FOR REVIEW AND DISCUSSION

1. Define the key terms for this chapter that appear at the end of the goal summary.
2. What are the major ethical theories?
3. Explain the difference between "act" utilitarians and "rule" utilitarians.
4. What is unethical about a gray market?
5. Explain why marketers may be more subject than other businesspeople to facing ethical dilemmas in the course of making business decisions.
6. Can you identify some of the ethical decisions relative to promotions?
7. What are some of the unethical business practices that relate to place?
8. Pricing policies frequently lead to ethical problems. Can you identify some?
9. What are some ethical issues that arise in the context of marketing research?
10. What is a legalistic system of ethics as opposed to a personal system? Which is better?
11. How do we acquire ethical behavior?
12. Who or what influences the ethics practiced in a corporation?
13. How does an ethics committee function?
14. How does a company keep in touch and why?

NOTES

1. Vincent Barry, *Philosophy: A Text with Readings* (Belmont, Calif.: Wadsworth Publishing Co., 1980), p. 83.
2. C. Powans and D. Vogel, *Ethics in the Education of Business Managers* (Hastings-on-Hudson, N.Y.: The Hastings Institute of Society, Ethics, and the Life Sciences, 1980), p. 1.
3. Verna E. Henderson, "The Ethical Side of Enterprise," *Sloan Management Review,* vol. 23, no. 3 (1982): pp. 37–47.
4. W. Michael Hoffman and Jennifer Mills Moore, *Business Ethics, Readings and Cases in Corporate Morality* (New York: McGraw-Hill Book Company, 1984), pp. 3–10.
5. "Another Tulane Student Charged in Score Fixing," *Muncie Evening Press,* July 27, 1985, p. 7.
6. "March Supports Union Carbide Plant," *Muncie Star,* August 18, 1985, p. 2.
7. "Philip Morris, Inc.'s Magazine Promotes Pro-Smoking Issues," *The Wall Street Journal,* July 24, 1985, p. 23.
8. "Greed on Wall Street," *Newsweek,* May 26, 1986, p. 45.
9. "Ethics Book Author Confesses Forgery," *Muncie Evening Press,* October 5, 1984, p. 30.
10. "In Stocks, All the Saints Are Sinners," *The New York Times,* February 7, 1982, p. F15.
11. Richard M. Detwiler, "Fear of Trying: Why We Must Stop Being Squeamish About Mixing Marketing and Development," *Currents,* May 1985, p. 64.
12. S. A. Diamond, "Market Research Latest Target in Ad Claims," *Advertising Age,* January 25, 1982, p. 52.
13. James Weber, "Institutionalizing Ethics into the Corporation," *MSU Business Topics,* Michigan State University, vol. 29, no. 2 (Spring 1981): p. 48.
14. "General Dynamics Posts Ethics Code," *The Fort Wayne Journal-Gazette,* August 18, 1985, p. 8A.
15. "Notable and Quotable," *The Wall Street Journal,* December 16, 1977, p. 14.
16. Patrick E. Murphy and Gene R. Laczniak, "Some Prescriptions for Marketing," *National Forum,* vol. 61, no. 1 (Winter 1981): pp. 49–50.
17. "AMA Adopts New Code of Ethics," *Marketing Educator,* Fall 1987, pp. 1 and 6.
18. Fred Trawick and William R. Darden, "Marketers' Perceptions of Ethical Standards in the Marketing Profession: Educators and Practitioners," *Review of Business and Economic Research,* vol. XVI, no. 1 (Fall 1980): pp. 5–9 and 14.

NOTES *(continued)*

19. *Ethics Resource Center Report,* vol. 2, no. 2 (Winter 1986): p. 7.
20. Weber, "Institutionalizing Ethics into the Corporation," p. 48.
21. Weber, "Institutionalizing Ethics into the Corporation," p. 48.
22. Weber, "Institutionalizing Ethics into the Corporation," p. 48.
23. George A. Steiner and John F. Steiner, *Business, Government, and Society: A Managerial Perspective* (New York: Random House, 1980), p. 365.
24. "Corporate Policies With Respect to Ethics in Business Transactions," Price Waterhouse, October 15, 1975, p. 1.
25. Weber, "Institutionalizing Ethics into the Corporation," p. 48.
26. "Four Firms Agree to Fund $12 Million Dump Cleanup," *The Wall Street Journal,* August 5, 1985, p. 11.
27. Dayton Hudson Department Store Company, "Community Involvement," *1985 Annual Report,* p. 2.
28. "Philip Morris and the Arts," *The New York Times,* November 11, 1981, p. D1.
29. "Philip Morris and the Arts," p. 23.

*A*s traditional as motherhood and apple pie, the checkout lanes at supermarkets carry candy and gum. Supermarket retailers count on impulse buying to sell this sweet tooth merchandise. Most marketers agree that the racks at checkout lanes are invaluable territory. Wholesalers fight candy bar to candy bar for this space. It is estimated that in an average suburban shopping center a single checkout lane will in one month's time sell about $1,000 worth of candy.

For each square foot beside the supermarket cash register, the store can expect to take in $22.80 per week. The rest of the store averages $7.70 per square foot. The gross profits for candy at the checkouts are four times the gross profits for the rest of the store.

However, one gallant supermarket chain is ready to give up these sugarcoated profits. Kroger, in their Maderia, Ohio, store has removed the candy and other sweets from one checkout lane. A large sign hanging over the lane proclaims, "MOM! This is a no candy checkout lane. It's here to make your shopping more pleasant."

Why would the number two supermarket chain cease selling candy in checkout lanes? It all started when one patron at the midwestern Kroger store reached the end of her wrapper when her toddler grabbed a candy bar at the checkout while she was trying to pay the bill. Like many moms, she had been told by the dentist to limit her child's sweets. So she tracked down the manager who happened to be touring the store with a Kroger vice president. Both store officials agreed to try a candy-free checkout. Now, every Kroger in Cincinnati and St. Louis has a sweetless checkout lane.

The giant of candy bars, Hershey, refuses to comment. One candy wholesaler did say that discipline should begin with the parents and not the supermarket, and that the products should be available. But for Kroger customers in these midwestern cities, goodwill is winning over merchandising.

Issues for Discussion

1. What is the basis for Kroger acting socially responsible?

2. Would it be more socially responsible for Kroger to give 5 percent of their federal taxable income to charities than to employ candy-free checkouts?

3. Under each of the 4 P's of marketing, indicate an action that Kroger could take that would show more social responsibility.

Source: Adapted from "Taking Candy Out of Mouths of Babes," *The New York Times,* February 20, 1985, p. C3.

Comprehensive
Cases

*D*r. Charles Whalen, president of Western Technical College, was reviewing the enrollment and student recruitment situation at his institution. His concern was what the declining high school population would mean to the college in terms of staffing, funding, and proposed new programs.

THE COLLEGE
Western Technical College was created in 1962 by the Indiana General Assembly, and it is fully accredited by the Commission on Institutions of Higher Education of the North Central Association of Colleges. Since its inception, the college has offered courses through the following four administrative divisions: Business, Graphics and Media, Health Occupations, and Trade and Technical.

The college is located in west central Indiana and serves an eight-county area with a general population of approximately 278,000. The enrollment of Western Technical College has remained constant for the past three years at approximately 360 part-time students and almost 1,100 full-time students. The percentage of high school graduates in the state of Indiana enrolled in any kind of postsecondary institution is slightly above 44 percent, which is very low in relation to other states. In addition, the total number of high school students in the state is declining, and projections indicate a substantial drop during the next five-year period. It is also of concern to Dr. Whalen that the population of the eight-county area his institution serves has been steadily declining and will probably continue to decline in the foreseeable future.

The mission of Western Technical College is stated in the authorizing legislation: "There shall be a new post high school educational institution to be devoted to occupational training of a practical and technical nature for the citizens of West Central Indiana." A diversity of program offerings provides students with an

COMPREHENSIVE CASE 1

Western Technical College

opportunity to pursue a Technical Certificate or an Associate Degree (see figure 1).

A NEW PROMOTIONAL DIRECTION
During a weekly staff meeting, Dr. Whalen, his administrative officers, and several faculty representatives, were discussing enrollment trends, and the suggestion was made that W. T. C. should take a marketing approach to student recruitment. Some of the faculty representatives were

not too happy with this suggestion. To them, marketing meant a hard-sell approach full of gimmickry. However, the short-range objective of enhancing the recruitment situation at W. T. C. had been clearly stated and enrollment projections indicated that the objective would be difficult to meet. Considering the environmental factors and the present internally fragmented recruitment program, Dr. Whalen thought the best course of action was to interview a marketing consultant and discuss the situation.

A consultant was invited to campus to meet with the president and his executive staff. During the first meeting, the consultant asked questions that made everyone realize

❏ **Figure 1** Credit programs

	Minimum Required Credit Hours (Quarter Hours)	
	Technical Certificate	Associate Degree
Business Division		
Accounting Technology	47	94
Credit and Finance Technology		104
Small Enterprise Office Operations/ Entrepreneurship		92
Computer Programming Technology	60	100
Marketing Technology	45	90
Secretarial – Administrative	45	92
Secretarial – Word Processing		92
Secretarial – Legal	60	
Graphics and Media Division		
Commercial and Industrial Photography	45	
Printing Technology		102
Health Occupations Division		
Medical Laboratory Technician		99
Medical Assistant	71	
Practical Nursing	74	
Radiologic Technology		111
Trade and Technical Division		
Architectural Drafting Technology		106
Auto Body Repair Technology	61	
Automotive Service Technology	62	106
Electronics Communications Technology		107
Electronics Industrial Technology		105
Electronics/Instrumentation Technology		105
Electronics Digital Computer Repair Technology		105
Heating/Air Conditioning/Refrigeration Technology	60	
Industrial Maintenance Technology		105
Mining Operations Technology		109
Welding Technology	67	

there was a clear need for his services. Most members of the executive staff did not understand the broad scope of marketing activities. A week after the first meeting, the consultant met with President Whalen and presented a proposal that included a marketing audit, survey research, and the development of a marketing plan for student recruitment. The consultant was hired and charged with the responsibility of developing a marketing plan that would provide W. T. C. with both short-range and long-range recruitment strategies.

During the next few months, the consultant interviewed key members of the faculty and administrative staff. He was taking the first step toward developing a marketing plan by providing insight into the perceived value of the institution. The interviewees were asked to describe their perceptions of the weaknesses, strengths, opportunities, and threats (WOTS) that Western Technical College faced. In addition, all members of the faculty and staff were surveyed to provide an overall profile of the perceived value of the college (see figure 2).

The findings of the WOTS analysis provided in-depth perceptions of Western Technical College. The most significant results were as follows:

A. *Perceived Weaknesses*
   1. Lack of consistent message, especially in high school recruitment promotional efforts.
   2. Reluctance to abandon outdated program offerings.
   3. Lack of internal communication.
   4. Lack of awareness among local businesses and industries of quality of Western Technical College graduates.
   5. Lack of public relations efforts to make the most of positive aspects of college.
   6. Need to formalize job placement process.
   7. Need for better use and coordination of total institutional resources for recruitment.
B. *Perceived Strengths*
   1. Funding trend by state legislature.

   2. Faculty competence and loyalty.
   3. Leadership of institution.
   4. Innovativeness of institution and flexibility of programming.
   5. Progress in developing programs responsive to community business needs.
C. *Perceived Threats*
   1. Decreasing applicant pool.
   2. Weak economy (there is a positive relationship between a strong economy and increased enrollment).
   3. Competition from other institutions entering the market by providing training opportunities.
   4. Lack of coordinated promotional program for recruitment.

D. *Perceived Opportunities*
   1. Gain larger share of high school recruitment market.
   2. Increase involvement of academic departments in recruitment process.
   3. Develop training programs for military credit.
   4. Enhance relationships with high school guidance counselors.
   5. Market and promote institution to key selected publics.
   6. Enhance customized business and industrial training programs.
   7. Respond to needs of new industries in the eight-county area.

❑ **Figure 2** Survey to determine perceived value of college, by faculty and staff

Please use the response scale to indicate your agreement or disagreement with the following statements:

Western Technical College Offers:

		Strongly Agree	Agree	Neutral	Disagree	Strongly Disagree
(A)	Good Placement of Graduates	1	2	3	4	5
(B)	Competent Faculty	1	2	3	4	5
(C)	Successful Alumni	1	2	3	4	5
(D)	Affordable Tuition	1	2	3	4	5
(E)	Good Location	1	2	3	4	5
(F)	Good Curriculum	1	2	3	4	5
(G)	Good Facilities	1	2	3	4	5
(H)	Progressive Environment	1	2	3	4	5
(I)	Good Internal Communications	1	2	3	4	5
(J)	Beneficial Education	1	2	3	4	5

(K) Comments: _____

_____

_____

_____

_____

_____

Please check:

_____ Faculty   _____ Staff

The results of the faculty and staff survey were as follows (totals do not equal 100% because not everyone answered every question):

A. *Western Technical College offers good placement of graduates.*
   8.75% Strongly agree
   36.8% Agree
   28.0% Neutral
   22.8% Disagree
   0%   Strongly disagree

B. *Western Technical College offers competent faculty.*
   35.0% Strongly agree
   47.4% Agree
   14.0% Neutral
   3.5%   Disagree
   0%   Strongly disagree

C. *Western Technical College has successful alumni.*
   12.3% Strongly agree
   54.4% Agree
   28.0% Neutral
   0%   Disagree
   0%   Strongly disagree

D. *Western Technical College offers affordable tuition.*
   51.0% Strongly agree
   42.2% Agree
   3.5%   Neutral
   1.75% Disagree
   1.75% Strongly disagree

E. *Western Technical College offers a good location.*
   21.0% Strongly agree
   42.2% Agree
   22.8% Neutral
   5.25% Disagree
   1.75% Strongly disagree

F. *Western Technical College offers a good curriculum.*
   22.8% Strongly agree
   62.2% Agree
   11.4% Neutral
   3.5%   Disagree
   0%   Strongly disagree

G. *Western Technical College offers good facilities.*
   14.1% Strongly agree
   40.4% Agree
   40.4% Neutral
   5.2%   Disagree
   0%   Strongly disagree

H. *Western Technical College offers a progressive environment.*
   19.3% Strongly agree
   52.7% Agree
   26.3% Neutral
   1.7%   Disagree
   0%   Strongly disagree

I. *Western Technical College offers good internal communications.*
   1.75% Strongly agree
   31.6% Agree
   29.9% Neutral
   24.6% Disagree
   10.5% Strongly disagree

J. *Western Technical College offers a beneficial education.*
   43.8% Strongly agree
   49.1% Agree
   7.0%   Neutral
   0%   Disagree
   0%   Strongly disagree

The survey results were positive overall and suggested that the opportunity existed to enhance awareness and understanding through specific marketing actions. Also, it was suggested that the areas of job placement and internal communications receive in-depth evaluations.

The consultant identified a number of specific problem areas in admissions and recruitment procedures. The problems included publications that were dull and that did not project a consistent image; advertisements that used media without consideration for marketing targets; disorganized admissions procedures; poor training of admissions representatives; lack of any form of evaluation of recruitment activities; a poorly designed mailing program; ineffective use of alumni in the recruitment process; and a lack of communication between the admissions office staff and other members of the college community.

The design of the promotional literature mailed to prospects had not changed since the middle 1960s. The mailing program was grossly ineffective because the admissions office staff believed that the more literature they mailed, the greater the return would be. No target market had been identified, and no consideration was given to the prospects' needs at the various stages of the recruitment process. Indiscriminate mailings of outdated literature created a major negative factor for all recruitment functions.

The consultant provided examples of how other colleges had segmented their market and tailored their literature to meet the needs of each target group. He emphasized the idea that a college education represents a major product purchase that involves extensive decision making and substantial dollar expenditures. The choice involves both the program offerings and the institution. Consequently, college application and evaluation represent a long, carefully thought-out process, and each corresponding stage of the recruitment process must respond to different client needs.

After determining internal perceptions and identifying specific problem areas, the consultant asked the president to appoint a representative marketing committee. The committee, with the guidance of the consultant, would implement the total marketing recruitment program. Both the president and the consultant were pleased with the positive response of the internal college community. The faculty and staff members were becoming more aware of the opportunities a marketing approach would provide their college. The results of the WOTS analysis and the internal survey provided them with the necessary foundation for "getting their own house in order" before launching the college-wide recruitment campaign.

MARKETING COMMITTEE

The marketing committee for student recruitment was formed, and the director of admissions was appointed chairperson. The committee represented the total college community by including four administrators, four faculty members, and two student leaders.

The consultant and the committee discussed the ingredients of the marketing mix for the nonprofit institution. The *product* was identified as being everything students perceived as gains in exchange for their investment of time and money. It includes the curriculum, facilities, student services, counseling, job placement service, library, and the like. The *place* includes location, climate, scheduling of offerings, timing of classes, and so on. The *price* includes tuition, fees, discounts, scholarships, credit, and loans. Prices may vary with course offerings because of such factors as laboratory and equipment use. Furthermore, price differentiation may be based on enrollment of additional family members, sons and daughters of W. T. C. alumni, and so on. *Promotion* includes publications, direct mail, word of mouth, media coverage, publicity, public relations efforts, special events, display materials, and other public contacts.

The committee did not believe that the general environment—a declining population, fewer high school graduates, a slow-growth or no-growth economy, and competitive forces—particularly favored Western Technical College. The institution had much to offer in the way of an up-to-date, diversified curriculum, good placement, and successful alumni, but the committee had a difficult time identifying any of these assets as exclusive to W. T. C.

Competition came from two area four-year institutions that offered two-year Associate Degrees and the technical training offered by various labor unions. The committee agreed to determine early how students rated W. T. C. and its competition and to study the various ways in which the competitors communicated their offerings. It was essential, the committee determined, to analyze what advantages W. T. C. held over its competition.

W. T. C. maintained a high market share in three of the eight counties it serves, but a specific market share analysis had not yet been done. Determining W. T. C.'s share of the total market was a necessary early committee action, and plans called for a more detailed market share analysis to be conducted in the future.

The consultant surveyed students who had applied to W. T. C. but had not enrolled. The results indicated problems in the way prospective students perceived the benefits of enrollment. The perceived value of a degree from W. T. C. was not consistent with the reality of the situation. For example, W. T. C. had a much higher job placement rate than prospects perceived. Also, the projected image in the college's publications distorted the school's actual offerings. In fact, W. T. C. offered an

environment that was highly suitable for meaningful job placement and academic training appropriate to today's business needs.

The consultant wanted the committee to continue to examine what the institution had to offer with special attention to any exclusive offerings. It was determined that W. T. C. had an advantage over its competition in the area of faculty-student ratio. W. T. C. averaged one faculty member for every fourteen students, so students received much individualized attention. W. T. C. was cost-competitive, and its placement rate exceeded competitive efforts by more than 5 percent for each division.

The committee seemed to be making progress, and the consultant wanted to make sure the marketing orientation continued. He asked the committee members to respond to the following items:

1. Is the present mission of your college feasible in terms of resources and capabilities?
2. Who are your competitors?
3. How do your students rate your college and your competitors?
4. How do your competitors communicate their offerings?
5. What trends can be seen regarding future competition?
6. Conduct target market analysis to determine the following factors:
   a. Who uses your product?
   b. Who motivates the purchase or use?
   c. What is the image of your college among the various groups?
7. List the many publics your organization has and consider their wants and needs in relation to student recruitment.
8. What research is necessary to gather, analyze, store, and disseminate relevant marketing information?
9. Determine and assign priority to the opportunities that seem to have the greatest potential for student recruitment.
10. Determine the potential for total market penetration.
11. What is the potential for specific

market segment penetration for five-year and ten-year periods?
12. For the immediate term, develop a promotional plan to enhance recruitment efforts.

The list was meant to direct the committee toward a marketing approach similar to the approach a profit-oriented business might take. Many of the committee members began to realize that the marketing concept would offer more benefits if applied to the entire college—not just the recruitment functions. The consultant agreed but thought that action should first be focused on establishing a marketing foundation for the recruitment function.

The committee recommended the following short-term promotional ideas be implemented immediately while the total recruitment function was being organized under the marketing concept:

1. **Publicity**—provide high school newspapers with feature stories regarding various aspects of college life (for example, choosing a college).
2. **Promotion**—provide viewbooks, departmental brochures, and bookmarks that list important W. T. C. application dates, "on-campus days," and the like to all high school seniors. Distribute them through school guidance counselors.
3. **Publicity**—arrange for selected faculty and alumni to appear on radio and TV talk shows, especially on targeted stations and shows.
4. **Personal selling**—establish an 800 number for the W. T. C. Admissions Office and include the number on all promotional items and in college literature.
5. **Personal selling**—develop an alumni recruitment program.
6. **Promotion**—establish appropriate contests for high school students, for example, on auto technology, and maintain traveling trophies for the various events.
7. **Promotion**—establish "W. T. C. on Review Days" for all high school seniors, their parents, and guidance counselors.

8. **Publicity**—publish a list of faculty members and their particular areas of expertise and disseminate the list to appropriate media.

9. **Personal selling**—conduct strategically planned high school visits with admissions counselors and faculty members to sell W. T. C. in a consistent and coordinated fashion.

RESULTS

For the first time a genuine concern for students' satisfaction with the product was prevalent. The Admissions Office, with the cooperation of faculty and staff members, provided a consistent, carefully targeted projection of image and message. Internal communication was a high priority. Many other forms of the marketing strategy were incorporated, and the feeling of competitiveness with other schools was evident throughout the Admissions Office.

The actions of the marketing committee led to an evaluation of student retention and satisfaction with the product, since the committee believed that retention was as important as recruitment. Again, the needs of students were clearly being positioned in the center of the institutional offering.

After enrollment for the fall semester had closed, Dr. Whalen and the consultant met to review the enrollment figures. Western Technical College showed an 8 percent increase in new full-time students and a 15 percent increase in the part-time population. The president said, "I believe within a few years most colleges will understand the need to implement an effective strategic marketing process, and I want us now to consider a total institutional application of marketing management."

Discussion Questions

1. List all of the publics of Western Technical College.

2. What publics were surveyed, and what publics should have been surveyed?

3. What does the author mean when he says that "the results of the WOTS analysis and the internal survey provided them with the necessary foundation for 'getting their own house in order' "?

4. How would W. T. C. establish a total institutional marketing approach to management?

5. Discuss nonprofit organizations or institutions in your area that operate under the marketing concept, or discuss those that don't and how they could benefit if they did.

Source: Dr. Robert E. Thompson, Indiana State University. Case written for this text.

$\mathcal{B}$org-Warner, a manufacturer of industrial products, has employed strategic planning at the strategic business unit (SBU) level since 1974. The company has never had a central planning staff at the corporate level to dictate strategies to operating levels of the organization. Instead, operations people have been in charge of their own planning. As a result, Borg-Warner has been able to use systematic approaches such as the market attractiveness/business strength matrix approach popularized by the Boston Consulting Group. But the company has kept the process where it works best—in the hands of its SBU operating managers, who are close to their own plans and have a definite stake in successfully implementing them.

One SBU, the domestic operations of the Mechanical Seal Division of Borg-Warner Industrial Products, needs to devise a marketing plan to increase its sales in the domestic pulp mill industry.

A mechanical seal is a precision device used to control leakage in rotating machinery, such as centrifugal pumps. Borg-Warner sells its mechanical seals primarily to petroleum refineries, pipeline companies, petrochemical and chemical processing plants, and electric power utilities. The product category that offers the greatest competition is packing seals used in lieu of mechanical seals.

The business environment of the pulp and paper industry is expected to influence sales of Borg-Warner's mechanical seals. The following summary of this industry's environment helps to focus attention on the effects economic trends, environmental factors, and regulations may have on the division's future share of the market.

- Overall capacity growth in the pulp and paper industry will be moderate—2 percent next year and 1.5 percent the following year.
- Industry represents a growth market for mechanical seals. It has

COMPREHENSIVE CASE 2

Borg-Warner's Mechanical Seal Division: A Pulp Mill Market Plan

tended to use packing seals but is now moving to mechanical seals.

- Industry concerns related to energy, environment, and simplified maintenance provide a basis for long-term penetration of the market with mechanical seals.
- U.S. end users are now familiarizing themselves with mechanical seals.
- Approximately 20–25 percent of all new pumps are now purchased with mechanical seals.

The U.S. pulp mill market consists of 248 mill sites, 65 percent of which are in the southern United States. The estimated market shares of mechanical seal suppliers and of packing seals as a class are as follows:

Chesterton	12.0%
John Crane	6.0%
Durametallic	3.5%
Borg-Warner	0.1%
Sealol	3.5%
Packing seals	74.9%

The SBU needs much more information on the mill market, such as the number of plants per firm, the geographic concentration of plants, and the production level of companies in the industry, but this information has not yet been collected.

The mill market, with regard to seals, has three segments: severe service, general service, and off-stream service. The severe service segment requires seals that can withstand pressures up to 250 pounds per square inch, temperatures of 500 degrees Fahrenheit, and corrosives such as caustic chlorine and acids. In addition, the seals have to operate in various media: liquid, digestor (a semisolid), heat transfer material, and coating material (for

paper). Borg-Warner's Uniseal I, II, BXRH, and BX seals meet the requirements of this segment, which grows about 10 percent a year. Presently, the segment generates $8.5 million in annual sales. Mechanical applications account for 25 to 30 percent of seal use. Competitively, Chesterton and Crane are strong in this market, but Durametallic and Sealol also show strength.

Users in this segment consider price in making seal purchases, but price is only one of many factors. These buyers might benefit from training related to seal applications, specifications, installations, and maintenance. Large firms with central engineering departments, which would be good prospective buyers, include Georgia Pacific, Weyerhauser, and International Paper. Architectural and engineering firms that service the pulp and paper industry, and thus are potential buyers of Borg-Warner seals, include Fluor, Foster Wheeler, C. F. Braun, Brown and Root, and Bechtel.

The general service segment has grown about 5 percent in each of the last several years, and sales of $14.2 million make it the largest of the three segments. As in the severe service market, Chesterton and Crane are the strongest competitors, and Durametallic and Sealol are also factors. The importance of price in this market may cause some resistance to mechanical seals.

The seals must be able to handle fuel oil and white water on paper machines, as well as abrasive and solid materials. Temperatures typically are below 250 degrees Fahrenheit, and pressures can range from 0 to 200 pounds per square inch. Borg-Warner's Uniseal I, BX, Q, and QB seals all meet these conditions.

The off-stream service segment, a market primarily requiring seals for water pumping, is the smallest of the three segments, with annual sales of $5.6 million. Mechanical seals have obtained less than 1 percent of the off-stream segment. Yearly growth, at 3 percent, remains low. Competition comes primarily from packing seal suppliers. This segment has a high price resistance to mechanical seals. Furthermore, buyers in the market appear satisfied to continue using packing seals.

With respect to the pulp mill market, Borg-Warner has both strengths and weaknesses. In the severe service segment Borg-Warner's coverage is fair, with several types of seals for liquor and slurry services. Borg-Warner's general segment coverage is limited to one type of seal. The company has no products in the off-stream segment.

An evaluation of the company's marketing mix in the severe and general market segments shows that the price of its mechanical seals is competitive with the prices of other mechanical seal manufacturers. However, packing seals have a perceived price lower than that of mechanical seals. Borg-Warner's office and facilities in the field provide very limited coverage of the market. Likewise, account service has been limited to a few select accounts. Salespeople are very capable but have a low level of commitment to the mechanical seal products. Overall, a substantial sales coverage gap exists. Advertising promotion is poor. However, case histories are being developed for use in promotions. The company's reputation is generally unknown, although to a select few accounts, its reputation is well known and positive.

The market's attractiveness and Borg-Warner's strengths are summarized in figure 1.

Discussion Questions

1. What market segments would you emphasize in the U.S. pulp mill market plan? Why?
2. Identify market objectives, in dollars and in market share, if possible.
3. What products would you emphasize?
4. How would you use promotion?
5. What role would product education play in your market plan?

☐ **Figure 1**
Comparison of market attractiveness and Borg-Warner's strengths.

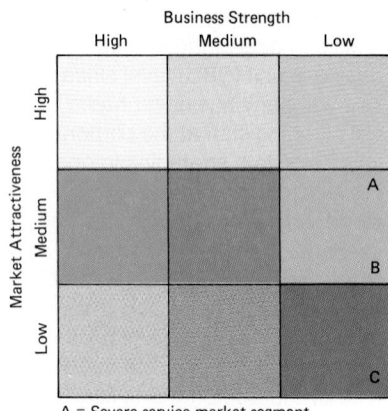

A = Severe service market segment
B = General service segment
C = Off-stream service segment

Source: Based on information from Todd M. Helmeke, "Strategic Business Unit Market Planning: An Industrial Case History," *Business Marketing,* November 1984, pp. 43–55.

The "Paws that refreshes" refers to Paws, Inc., a remarkable organization that produces one of the most widely read comic strips in the world—Garfield. This lovable, smart-aleck cat is the creation of Jim Davis, a skillful artist who tickles the funny bone of newspaper readers.

Jim Davis was born in Fairmount, Indiana, where he grew up with about twenty-five cats rambling in and out of his rural home. (Because of his wife's allergy, he no longer has a cat.) From 1963 through 1967, Jim studied art at Ball State University in Muncie, Indiana. After leaving college, he worked for an advertising agency, where he did paste ups and a variety of jobs. In 1969, he became an assistant to the cartoonist Tom Ryan, who draws the syndicated comic strip, Tumbleweeds. Although the pay was meager, Jim used the opportunity to perfect his drawing skills and obtain an introduction to the syndicated cartoon industry.[1] To supplement his income, Jim moonlighted as a freelance commercial artist, copywriter, radio personality, and political campaigner.

STARTING A NEW COMIC STRIP

After several restless but creative years with Ryan, Jim decided to initiate his own comic strip. Believing he had the perfect idea for a strip, Jim created a bug called Gnorm Gnat. His experience with comic strips had convinced him that nonhuman cartoon characters could be placed in many more interesting situations with more flexibility than humans, because animals are not perceived by readers as being white, black, male, female, young, or old. For the next six years, Jim tried to sell his strip to

*The authors are indebted to Jim Davis for his cooperation in providing the information for this case.
[1]A *syndicate* is a business concern that buys comic strips, articles, or other materials and sells them for simultaneous publication in many newspapers. A syndicate varies the selling price of its materials according to the circulation of the newspaper.

COMPREHENSIVE CASE 3

Paws, Inc.—
The Tale of Garfield*

the cartoon syndicates, but the response was overwhelmingly negative. One syndicate editor consoled him, "Your art is good, your gags are great, but bugs—nobody can identify with bugs!"

Nevertheless, Jim still had the entrepreneurial urge to develop his own strip. A thorough review of the successful strips revealed that dogs were popular. Snoopy®, Marmaduke®, Belvedere®, and Fred Bassett® were carried by many newspapers and enjoyed an immense audience. But there were very few cats in the comics at this time. Jim believed that there was a large group of cat lovers who, as readers, would sustain a comic strip about a cat. Based on this belief, Jim made a carefully calculated business decision to develop and market a strip featuring a cat. Jim reasoned that cat lovers would support a cat-centered strip even more than dog lovers would support a dog-centered strip. Dog owners are attracted to a certain breed of dog, such as German shepherd, boxer, or golden retriever, but cat lovers love all kinds of cats. In effect, cat fanciers own generic cats.

CREATING GARFIELD

In 1975, Jim's talented pen gave birth to an obstinate, overweight, and cynical cat called Garfield. As one writer commented, "The cat has all the Boy Scout virtues turned inside out." Garfield is named after Jim's paternal grandfather, James A. Garfield Davis, who was a large, cantankerous character. Other central personalities in the strip include Pooky, a teddy bear named after Jim's wife's childhood toy bear; Jon, Garfield's master, whose name is drawn from a vaguely recalled coffee commercial; Nermal, a cute little kitten whom Garfield jealously tries to upstage; and Odie, a not-too-smart slobbering dog who is usually overwhelmed by the shrewd Garfield.

In 1978, after spending nearly one and a half years painstakingly developing and perfecting the concept of the Garfield comic strip, Jim felt confident enough to attempt to peddle the strip to a syndicate. Much to his disappointment, the first two syndicates he contacted, King Features and the Chicago Tribune–New York News, refused to buy the strip. Happily, the third one—United Feature Syndicate, Inc.—signed him to a contract.

As Jim soon discovered, the life of an entrepreneur—whether illustrator or retailer—is not easy. After four months of test runs, Garfield was cancelled by the Chicago Sun-Times and major papers in Salt Lake City and Little Rock. Knowing that it takes from one to three years for a strip to attract and retain a loyal group of readers, Jim gloomily thought that the cancellations meant the end of his fledgling venture.

To the surprise of the newspapers, however, a legion of Garfield fans had already developed, and they strongly protested the removal of their favorite comic strip. Within a few days of the cancellation, the Sun-Times had heard from 1,300 angry readers who insisted that the strip be continued. As a result of this outpouring of sentiment for the roguish cat, the papers promptly reinstated Garfield. Turning what appeared to be certain failure into good fortune, Jim used the publicity and support to sell the strip to other newspapers. This breakthrough established the fiesty Garfield as a dominant comic strip personality. By 1986, the Garfield strip had become so popular that Jim decided to build on success and start another strip, U.S. Acres®, which features a runt piglet named Orson and his farm-animal friends.

Garfield, Pokie, and Odie. *Source:* © 1979 United Features Syndicate, Inc.

THE ADVANTAGES OF A LICENSING PROGRAM

While developing Garfield, Jim kept in mind the product development opportunities that would become available to a successful strip. Without a licensing program, a syndicated cartoonist's income is only a percentage of the fees that newspapers pay to the syndicate for the right to run the strip. Under a licensing program, however, the cartoonist can obtain considerable revenue. Most licensing agreements call for a percent royalty fee to be paid to the licensor (the copyright owner—in this case, United Feature Syndicate).

United Feature Syndicate has an outstanding track record in product development programs for its comic strip characters. (This syndicate handles Peanuts®, which has enjoyed an active licensing program for over twenty-five years.) Given United Feature Syndicate's experience in worldwide licensing, a coordinated marketing program could mean new-found opportunity to create a licensing system, not just art application of Garfield on products.

The sales of licensed products based on popular comic strips are fairly steady and not greatly affected by general economic conditions. In fact, there appears to be an inverse relationship between the sales of these products and economic conditions. For example, during the Great Depression of the 1930s, comic strips attained a high degree of popularity as people sought a psychological lift. Licensed products based on Popeye®, Mickey Mouse®, and

other comic strip characters sold very well during this period.

In retrospect, Jim's decision early in the Garfield era to initiate a strong product development program was masterful. The retail sales of licensed products climbed spectacularly during the early 1980s. By 1982, the retail sales of all licensed products were generating $20.6 billion. This was a 50 percent increase over 1981, more than twice the sales of 1980, and over three times the 1978 sales.[2]

A successful licensing arrangement benefits both the licensee and the licensor. When licensed popular characters appear on products, these products sell much more rapidly than similar products without a licensed character. The life spans of licensed characters vary greatly, however. One based on a movie may enjoy popularity for six months or a year. If the character is based on a Saturday morning TV cartoon, it may last for the duration of the cartoon series. Some licensed characters have very short lives, and others, such as Mickey Mouse (who is about 60) and Snoopy, endure for generations.

BUILDING THE FOUNDATION OF A LICENSING PROGRAM

To build the foundation for an active licensing program, Jim wanted to establish Garfield in as many newspapers as possible. However, for two reasons, it is often difficult for a new comic strip to obtain space in a newspaper. One reason is that every time a paper shortage occurs a newspaper eliminates some of its comic strips. When the shortage

[2]Marcie Lynn Avram, "Winning Characters," *Stores,* May 1983, p. 63.

ends, the comic strip section seldom returns to its original size. Another reason is that a large portion of a comic page is occupied by what the industry calls the "undroppables"— enduring features, such as Peanuts, Blondie®, and Beetle Bailey®, that are assured of space as long as they exist. A newspaper editor who wishes to add a new comic strip must drop a current one. Since a strip that has run in a paper for a period of time is viewed as an old friend by its readers, dropping it is a difficult decision to make.

Jim carefully estimated the time frame that would be necessary to gain reader acceptance and recognition of Garfield. He concluded that it would take from three to five years to establish a solid foundation on which to base a licensing program. In order to accelerate this timetable, Jim met with his staff and planned a strategic marketing move that significantly affected the Garfield program: publishing a horizontal Garfield book. As an avid comic book reader, Jim had never understood why all of the comic strip panels were stacked one on top of another and placed between the covers of a conventional vertical book. It seemed logical and more readable to print the strip on a horizontal format, as they appear in the newspapers. Another benefit from publishing a horizontal book is that it could not be displayed in the same area as the other books. Because of its odd shape, it would have to be displayed in its own area and, thus, would attract more attention.

To market the Garfield strips most effectively, Jim made the decision that in the books the strips would appear in chronological order—both daily and Sunday. They would be placed in a series of matching books with a bright new cover color for each edition. Jim's objective was to establish a subscription mentality for Garfield readers so that they instinctively would buy the next book as it was published. On the cover, each book would feature its number in the Garfield series spelled out in large letters. If a reader had the first book, the second book, and the fourth book, he or she would readily recognize the third book.

The Garfield crew swiftly developed a mock-up of a horizontal book. Then they designed and built a display that would hold the books. All of this activity was accomplished without advice from the printers, cutters, packagers, shippers, and rack jobbers who generally provide advice on the feasibility of such a project. Looking back, Jim believes that if these individuals had been consulted, the entire concept would have been dropped.

With the production and marketing concepts for the books worked out, Jim presented his idea to officials at United Feature Syndicate in New York. Their reaction was that it was unrealistic and unworkable. A disillusioned Jim Davis returned to his studio in Muncie, Indiana, on a Saturday. In the mail on the next Monday was a letter from Ballantine Books asking how it could obtain the publishing rights to Garfield. Jim immediately contacted United Feature Syndicate's licensing representative and took the mock-up to Ballantine, which accepted the entire concept.

Today in the publishing industry a book shaped like the Garfield books is said to have the Garfield format. Further evidence of the success of this venture is the fact that Davis had seven Garfield books on the prestigious *New York Times Best-Seller List* at one time—the only author ever to have accomplished this! By 1987, there were twenty-three Garfield books on the market.

As a result of the book sales, reader acceptance of Garfield increased greatly. To accelerate this momentum, in April 1980, Jim initiated a book tour of twenty major U.S. cities. At the start of Jim's travels, Garfield was being added to newspapers at the rate of about seven papers a month. Within two months after the tour had begun, the strip was being added to newspapers at the rate of one a day. During the book tour, Jim learned that bestsellers are self-perpetuating. When booksellers learn that a book is on the best-seller list, they immediately order it. This places the book in more stores and often in more advantageous displays, where additional sales keep it on the best-seller list.

DEVELOPING LICENSING PROGRAMS FOR GARFIELD PRODUCTS

With Garfield's popularity increasing, Jim decided to pursue licensing arrangements actively. In order to gain insight into the marketing of licensed products, Jim reviewed the marketing of the Kliban Cat® products. Although this character was still very popular on licensed items, its appeal was beginning to decline. Jim attributed this loss of appeal to the fact that the same cat was placed on every item without regard to the item's size, shape, printing process, or market. The artist's input had ceased years before, and repetition was beginning to take its toll.

Learning from the Kliban experience, Jim decided to take full creative and artistic control of the Garfield product development program. This would enable him to design an appropriate Garfield for each licensed item, taking into consideration the type of reproduction process and the target market for the item. He could readily check and maintain the quality of the licensed products, too. Jim discovered that this personalized approach was very demanding and difficult to achieve. The Garfield product development program involved working in the publishing, ceramics, textile, game, electronics, and other industries, each with its own requirements.

The success of the Gibson line of Garfield greeting cards provided an early gauge of consumer response to the Garfield products. Gibson test marketed the Garfield cards in several stores by placing them in regular display racks next to other cards. Gibson ordinarily test markets a new line of cards for three to six months. After a few weeks, it was evident that the Garfield cards were hot items.

As the licensing program in the United States took shape, a decision was made not to endorse a particular branded product, such as cereal or peanut butter. Jim believed that if Garfield were a commercial spokesperson—or spokescat—for a line of goods, he would receive too much exposure or possibly the wrong kind of exposure for his personality. (After Jim had been drawing the strip for three months, he had turned down a $50,000 offer from a cat food company.) Instead, the Garfield visage would be confined to products such as coffee mugs, T-shirts, and telephones. Garfield lines today include phones by Tyco, glassware by Anchor Hocking, and stationery by Mead. These are a notable few of the 335 licensees worldwide marketing Garfield goods.

An outstanding marketing advantage for Garfield is that he is seen daily by over 100 million readers in two thousand newspapers. For the Garfield licensees, this means two thousand advertisements a day in all of the major U.S. markets. Additional promotional exposure is obtained for the Garfield licensees through the Garfield television specials and a record album. The strong impact of TV on consumers ensures Garfield's credibility in the marketplace.

The Dakin Company, the world's largest manufacturer of plush dolls, was a licensee that discovered Garfield's power. During the development of the Garfield doll, eight versions of it were shipped back and forth in one year to the Dakin plant in Korea. When the design had finally been perfected, Dakin test marketed ten thousand dolls in stores in the San Francisco area. To determine the vigor of the doll's sales, Dakin representatives returned to the stores after forty-eight hours to check on the number of dolls on hand. To their surprise, all of the dolls had been sold. The brisk demand for these dolls was soon duplicated throughout the United States. Although Dakin began producing the dolls in four additional plants, it took over a year for supply to catch up with demand! At one plant, there were nearly two hundred Korean workers whose full-time pursuit was spray-painting stripes on Garfield dolls.

ESTABLISHING PAWS, INC.

As the product line began to grow, it became painfully obvious to Jim that he did not personally have the time to design each product. His working schedule—5:30 A.M. to late night—was already woefully overcrowded. As a result, Paws, Inc., was established. This closed corporation presently consists of fifteen creative workers and fifteen administrative employees who are responsible for the design and maintenance of the Garfield image throughout the world. On the creative side of the business are Jim and four other artists who work on the comic strips. This group dreams up the Garfield and U.S. Acres capers, with Jim doing the first pencil drawing of each strip himself. Another creative group consists of a production manager, a Garfield designer who prepares the initial design for Garfield's licensing ventures, a U.S. Acres designer, five artists who finalize the artwork for the Garfield and U.S. Acres licensing activity, a writer, and a technical engineer. The administrative area includes the vice-president of Paws, Inc., a business manager, a certified public accountant, an office manager and two assistants, a corporate pilot, three property managers who market Garfield to commercial enterprises, a product development manager, Jim's personal secretary, and three groundskeepers for his combined art studio and complex.

With the organization of Paws, Inc., Jim had the personnel to create original art for almost every item that was being licensed. Some licensees resisted this individualized approach because they did not want to pay for new artwork. These licensees were accustomed to using art from either the strips or the licensor's file. This resistance faded rapidly when their licensed products began selling briskly in the marketplace.

PAWS—STEPPING AHEAD

One of Jim's major concerns was to maintain a fresh and vibrant image for Garfield. Through 1980 and 1981, Garfield was depicted on licensed products in a sitting position against a bright red, blue, or yellow background. Because the Garfield items were selling well, some of the licensees were reluctant to alter this successful marketing formula. The Paws staff, however, believed that these licensees failed to understand the depth of readers' loyalty. Garfieldites would want the newest creations.

A decision was made to modify Garfield by using an airbrush treatment that would round him out and make him look a little more human. Fresh color combinations, such as powder blue, purple, rose, and lavender, were to be worked into Garfield creations. When informed of these changes, some of the licensees were aghast. They insisted that the original Garfield be continued; otherwise, the delicate combination of elements that created his success would be destroyed. To counter this opposition, Jim pointed out to the licensees that Garfield's long-term success depended on innovative approaches and new presentations. Although Jim believed Garfield could have been successfully continued as a fat orange cat on a red background for another two years, he knew that the public eventually would have become bored with Garfield. It was difficult to convince the licensees' product managers, whose jobs depend on Garfield's success, that this was the correct approach. Nevertheless, the more than 3,100 products bearing Garfield's visage provide evidence of the success of the Paws' program.

In competition with all other comic strips, the cartoon "Q" study by a marketing evaluation group ranked Garfield number one in recognition and appeal. This research involves the rating of 331 cartoon characters by a nationally representative sample made up of 1,746 people aged six and older. Through its research, the 21st century comics group came up with similar findings. In 1986, the National Cartoonist Society honored Jim as the "Best Humor Strip Cartoonist."

Several significant events demonstrate the enduring popularity of Garfield. Since 1984, Garfield's floating presence has been a favorite in the Macy's Thanksgiving Day Parade. In addition, Garfield is the spokescat for the Embassy Suites hotel chain. Because of the success of an American Express commercial featuring Jim, it was shown overseas to international TV audiences. Three Garfield television shows, "Garfield on the Town," "Garfield in the Rough," and "Garfield's Halloween Adventure," have won Emmy awards as outstanding animated programs of the year. Two others were nominated for Emmys.

With two thousand newspapers carrying Garfield, in early 1986 Jim launched U.S. Acres. This strip uses more sight gags and more physical humor than Garfield. It is positioned for the young reader; however, it has an adult appeal, too. Although United Feature Syndicate scoffed at Jim's prediction that U.S. Acres would debut in 500 newspapers, his forecast proved correct. It actually debuted in 505 papers! This record number of initial adopters made U.S. Acres the most successful new strip in comic history.

Discussion Questions

1. Explain how Jim Davis practices the marketing concept with Garfield.
2. How has Jim blended the four P's of the marketing mix in promoting Garfield?
3. Explain how the microenvironment and the macroenvironment affect the Garfield marketing program.
4. What groups are the target markets for Garfield's business ventures?
5. In what stage of the product life cycle is the Garfield comic strip? How can Jim keep Garfield from reaching the decline stage?
6. Develop a strategic marketing plan for Paws, Inc.

Source: Adapted from Richard D. Steade and James R. Lowry, *Business: An Introduction,* 11th ed. (Cincinnati: South-Western Publishing Co., 1987), Instructor's Manual. The authors are indebted to Jim Davis and his staff for their cooperation in providing the information for this case.

COMPREHENSIVE CASE 4

Marsh—Retail Food Distributor

One of the Midwest's largest food retailers, Marsh Supermarkets, Inc., has grown from a single store at its founding in 1931 to an operation encompassing 228 retail outlets in central Indiana and western Ohio. About eight thousand persons are employed in Marsh's 75 supermarkets, including Marsh Xtra combination stores and 175 Village Pantry convenience stores.

The supermarkets, with an average size of 26,500 square feet and average annual sales in excess of $7 million, are serviced from Marsh's own distribution centers. A specialized convenience store distribution center, in which Marsh is a partner, services the Village Pantry stores, 114 of which offer self-service gasoline.

In 1985, Don E. Marsh, president and chief executive officer, wrote in the Marsh annual report:

A year ago I reported to you on the severe price war among supermarket operators in our principal marketing area that began in the Summer of 1983. I advised you then that there appeared to be an easing of competitive pressures and an indication that the marketplace was returning to a more normal level of marketing practices. That assessment has proven to be correct. . . . [The easing of competitive pressures,] combined with a number of innovative steps taken by your management team, enabled us to produce net income of $4.7 million ($1.26 per share) in fiscal 1985 compared to $1.6 million ($.43 per share) for the preceding year. Sales increased to a record $628 million, an annual rate of growth of nearly 4 percent, while in our fourth quarter, sales gained over 9 percent. We are pleased with our profit and sales recovery in a marketplace which remains very competitive. However, we recognize many oppor-

tunities for further gains for Marsh, and you may be assured that your management team will continue to work aggressively to maintain the sales growth momentum of the fourth quarter and to improve your Company's profitability further.

Operating in an area of modest population growth, we cannot simply decide on the format of a supermarket, construct it, and enjoy an increasing volume of business as the population comes to us. Rather, our success depends upon using our skills as merchants to increase our market share. We must be able to *read* consumer preferences, to *influence* those preferences where possible and to *test* new concepts, judge consumer reaction and move quickly to implement those which receive customer acceptance. Many advances were made during the past year in the read, influence, and test merchandising philosophy which is the key to our future success.

● To better read consumer preferences and motivations, we have established a market research department and expanded our use of outside consumer attitude assessment professionals. Information coming from these sources influences the types of products and services we offer in our stores, and also influences the size, layout and design of each new or remodeled store.
● We have read evolving preferences for fresh, compared to processed, foods, for more product variety, more services and quick checkout, all of which are reflected in Marsh stores. We

have rapidly expanded service meat centers, full-service fresh seafood departments, salad bars, bulk displayed foods and, of course, our deli-bakery departments, which are considered to be the finest in the market. Our merchandise buyers have reemphasized our "open door" policy toward new products with the objective of offering products when first available and monitoring their movement carefully, permitting our customers to be the judge of our product line architecture. We have opened video cassette rental centers in 20 supermarkets, where customers enjoy the convenience of selecting a movie during their grocery shopping trip and plan to install 17 additional centers this year. Marsh is a leader in offering branch banking facilities, which are now available in 25 of our supermarkets. We currently are accepting major credit cards in 63 of our supermarkets and intend to offer this service in all of our supermarkets in the near future.

● Electronic scanning checkout systems are used in 44 supermarkets, providing not only increased customer convenience and productivity gains, but a wealth of raw data that, when properly summarized and interpreted, provides another valuable source for reading consumer preferences. Accordingly, we are continually upgrading our management information systems to utilize more effectively this data in our merchandising efforts.
● We also are making greater use of current technology in our efforts to influence consumer preferences. For example, we have found that fresh seafood sales are greatly increased through use of our point-of-sale video programs that address consumer uncertainties concerning preparation techniques . . .

and the opportunities to improve sales and margins by communicating our knowledge of food products to our customers through the video media are limitless.

● One of the most important factors in influencing consumers' decisions, particularly in our expanding service departments, is personal contact with the individual Marsh employee. We continue to place great emphasis on training and incentive programs to help our thousands of employees improve their personal selling skills. These efforts include extensive use of video training materials, which, along with the point-of-sale video programs, are developed in our production facilities.

● Marsh continues to test new concepts in our market. Last year, we conducted tests of CompuSave's automatic merchandising machine in five of our supermarkets. These computerized terminals permit shoppers to order from CompuSave's video-displayed menu of 1,500 very competitively priced, general merchandise items, including TV's, cameras, watches and other high quality, high ticket items. Our customer purchases the merchandise by check or credit card and receives the items directly from CompuSave's warehouse. Based on the success of this test and the dramatic growth predicted for this type of electronic shopping, we will be installing this unique service in 40 of our supermarkets during the current year. We will be the leader in our market in offering our customers this service, which will generate income for Marsh without large investments in inventory or overhead.

● We are in the early stages of developing a pilot program to test an electronic funds transfer system utilizing both "debit cards" and major credit cards with a view toward increasing convenience to our customers while reducing our expenses of check handling.

● We have selected two stores in which to test new products and merchandising innovations of our own creation as well as those which have had success in other market areas, and those which prove to be successful will be expanded to other stores.

Marsh has withstood the Indiana price war through its creative marketing skills and we are confident it will continue to grow and prosper by reading and influencing consumer preferences and testing new concepts designed to serve our customers better.

During the past year, we completed the relocation of the grocery warehousing operations to our highly automated facility in Indianapolis. With this facility and the state-of-the-art Perishable Products Handling Facility in Yorktown, we have a distribution system with the capacity to meet our needs more efficiently and cost effectively than was ever before possible. In addition, we are implementing a computerized standards and scheduling system at the Indianapolis warehouse which will provide the framework for even further productivity gains. With our investment in the most modern support systems having been made, with the most effective management tools currently available now in place, and with the enthusiastic support of our employees, which we continue to receive, we are ready to meet our objective of significantly reducing distribution costs in relation to sales volume.

Village Pantry had another outstanding year. The number of stores increased from 142 to 154 with two-thirds of the stores now offering gasoline service. Gasoline sales, an important traffic builder which leads to increased food sales, gained 29 percent to 22 million gallons, making Village Pantry one of the largest independent gasoline distributors in the Midwest. Our newer stores encompass 2,600 square feet

and include expanded deli and take-out food services as well as sit-down eating areas in some locations. Village Pantry enjoys a unique operating environment consisting of a highly concentrated geographic market in which few other convenience store chains operate, and can significantly increase the number of its stores without expanding its present market area and benefit from the increased efficiencies in advertising, distribution and supervision costs.

BEING A PART OF CUSTOMERS' LIVES

To its customers, Marsh represents more than convenient, contemporary supermarkets, each filled with over fifteen thousand products and staffed by seventy-five people. Marsh is part of customers' lives.

Knowing its customers and anticipating their needs are keys to Marsh's growth. A major influence among today's customers is that much-studied population segment known as the "baby boomers"—the 40 percent of the population between the ages of twenty-five and forty-five, whose lifestyles influence both those younger and older.

Baby boomers are known for high levels of education and affluence, which translate into sophisticated tastes and a demand for quality—and into success for Marsh innovations such as Prime Cut Service Meat Shops.

Today's baby boomers are credited, too, with the national search for fitness. They seek good price values, consider friendliness and caring service important, squeeze a multitude of interests into a twenty-four-hour day, and are concerned about their communities.

In responding to their needs, Marsh has introduced new services, policies, and products that also have been successes with both younger and older shoppers.

Marsh merchandisers, who are responsible for buying activities, recognize the need to please the customer. Therefore, they make sure every new item "earns" its place on Marsh's shelves by meeting or exceeding a high standard of quality.

When evaluating a new product, Marsh merchandisers talk one-on-one to manufacturers and growers and sometimes even travel many miles to evaluate production facilities. They look at product sources, such as pineapple plantations, hosiery mills, and shampoo laboratories, to be certain that suppliers can provide the promised product quality and to open personal communication lines that enhance business relationships with suppliers.

Marsh's concern for quality does not stop once the product has reached the supermarket shelf. Supervisors in each department are responsible for attractively displaying the freshest products possible. That means keeping freezers and coolers at the proper temperatures, checking code dates, and rotating stock. Close attention to customer service and to product quality, along with value pricing, conveys the message that is used as the company's slogan: at Marsh, "We Value You."

In addition to service, quality, and pricing, *variety* is a major concern of Marsh merchandisers. New products are constantly being introduced into the marketplace, and Marsh merchandisers carefully evaluate each one before and after it is first offered. In the vast majority of cases, the new products are introduced in Marsh stores so that customer demand can dictate whether the product will have a permanent display position.

Marsh receives quarterly reports on warehouse withdrawals of a variety of grocery items. The data included in these reports is useful for comparing the products available at Marsh with the products being offered by other supermarkets in the same market areas. Customer preferences for national brand name products can also be determined by analysis of these reports.

Marsh merchandisers recognize that local customer preferences may be different from those suggested by statistical analysis. If a customer wants an item that is not available in the Marsh store, it may be specially ordered; and when customer requests for an item are frequent, the product is added to the regular stock.

SERVICE IS IMPORTANT—TO MARSH AND ITS CUSTOMERS

The people who buy at Marsh are no different from those who participated in a national survey that asked how important service and friendliness are in selecting a supermarket. Of those responding, nearly half said it was the most important factor.

Assuring service and friendliness is a high priority with Marsh. Training is one tool used to provide employees with both the knowledge they need to answer questions and the skill to answer them in a friendly way.

Promptness is inherent in most customers' definition of service. Staff schedules and assignments are arranged to reduce waiting to a minimum. For example, in the larger stores' produce departments, attendants are assigned full time to weigh produce on weekends. Continuing attention is given to front-of-the-store staffing. That includes increasing the number of sackers and opening up additional checkout lanes. Additional express lanes to serve customers purchasing twelve items or less have been added in many stores, and more stores are being converted to this service. Groceries are carried to the customer's car by courteous service clerks.

The atmosphere of personal service in many stores is increased by a program prompted by another characteristic of today's customers—high interest in new foods. Demonstrators at sample tables on busy shopping days offer both new foods and pleasant interaction with customers.

DISTRIBUTING GOODS EFFICIENTLY

The link in the chain between the Marsh buyers and merchandisers and Marsh customers is the Marsh Distribution Center, located in Indianapolis, Indiana.

The distribution center is responsible for supplying produce and grocery items to the supermarkets. The methods of distribution and storage at the center are constantly being improved and modernized to keep the flow of "freshness" moving quickly into Marsh stores. Within the grocery warehouse, a system has been recently implemented to improve productivity by identifying some 1,300 slower-moving grocery items and segregating them from other, faster-moving items.

Another recently implemented system makes more efficient use of space in the distribution center as well as improving productivity. On arrival at the center, each pallet of product is dated and assigned a number by a computer. The number represents the best storage position for the pallet. As store orders are processed by the computer, the computer produces a schedule of the necessary replenishment activities. This enables stock to be used in proper rotation, enhances productivity, and improves the level of service to the Marsh stores and therefore to Marsh customers.

There are 44 tractor power units and 148 trailers in the Marsh fleet. This includes 16 new 45-foot refrigerated trailers. These new units are 5 feet longer and lighter in weight than the trailers being replaced and provide an additional 5,000-pound capacity per shipment.

A new inventory control system has also been implemented. This computerized system handles various categories of inventories by plotting each storage area in the warehouse according to location and cube capacity. Products are categorized by size, type of handling required, and velocity of movement. The computer coordinates this data and systematically assigns storage areas and provides retrieval instructions as merchandise is needed in a manner that maximizes efficiency and control. Programmed Item Retrieval (PIR) is a component of the new inventory control system that permits merchandise to be randomly stored instead of being placed in conventional fixed slots. The system finds the most efficient spot for storing merchandise and gives instruction on its selection for shipment in a manner that eliminates the need for any interim transfers and assures that products are shipped out in the order in which they were received.

PROMOTING THE MARSH IMAGE

Communicating with Marsh customers throughout Indiana and western Ohio and with eight thousand Marsh employees in various divisions is the responsibility of the Advertising and Public Relations Departments.

Weekly promotional programs are communicated to the public through newspaper ads and tabloid inserts, radio and TV commercials, and in-store posters and displays.

The Advertising Department works closely with Marsh merchandisers. Once the weekly merchandising plan has been established, the most effective and cost-efficient method of advertising and promoting the program is determined.

Television is a valuable and cost-effective medium for reaching a large number of customers. For example, the Indianapolis ADI (Area of Dominant Influence) reaches most of the cities and towns in Indiana where Marsh supermarkets are located. The total merchandising plan is much more effective when the weekly specials being offered in local newspapers are also seen on area TV.

Posters and displays are used to communicate with Marsh customers in the store. This method of promoting reminds customers of the specials they have seen advertised through other media and helps convey the "value" image that is the cornerstone of the Marsh merchandising program.

Because an informed employee is normally a happy employee, a company newspaper, the "General Store," is published monthly to keep Marsh's employees informed on important events. Coverage includes new store openings; employee awards for outstanding achievements, promotions, or involvement in community activities; and changes in employee benefit programs. Letters of thanks and appreciation from customers and community service organizations are also included.

MARSH AND ITS CUSTOMERS—IMPROVING COMMUNITY LIFE

Marsh affects its customers' lives beyond the supermarket shopping trip or Village Pantry stop. Throughout central Indiana and western Ohio, customers find Marsh playing a role in improving the quality of life in their communities.

Among the activities in which Marsh played a role during 1985 was the National Basketball Association All-Star game in the Hoosier Dome at Indianapolis. The Marsh All-Indiana college band played for the record-breaking crowd of over 43,000 people. Even larger crowds join Marsh each year at the Indianapolis Children's Museum, where the company annually sponsors the very popular Haunted House.

The Symphony on the Prairie, with Marsh as the sole sponsor, makes it possible for thousands of music lovers to combine enjoyment of the Indianapolis Symphony Orchestra with the serenity of Conner Prairie Pioneer Settlement.

Marsh's name also is prominent on the list of contributors to the Gleaners Food Bank for the needy and among the participants in the Partner 2000 program providing summer jobs for high school students. Marsh contributions help make possible the Sports Games for United Cerebral Palsy of Indiana.

In a look to the future, the company has made a major commitment to the new Indianapolis Zoo, which was opened during the summer of 1988 at White River State Park. It will cover expenses for the zoo's strollers for young children and for the stroller station and its maintenance as well.

Each year, Marsh contributes to many philanthropic programs to help care for individuals with cerebral palsy, muscular dystrophy, and other crippling birth defects and diseases. Junior Achievement, Boy Scouts, Girl Scouts, and many other youth programs are also supported by Marsh. This support includes donated merchandise, special discounts, and use of Marsh stores and parking lots, in addition to monetary contributions. More importantly, Marsh employees donate many hours of personal time in support of these activities in the communities in which they live.

Discussion Questions

1. Is the Marsh philosophy of read, influence, and test congruent with the marketing concept? Explain.

2. Discuss how Marsh uses scrambled merchandising to increase sales growth and profitability.

3. Explain how the Marsh marketing information system works.

4. How is the Marsh promotional plan integrated into the overall marketing strategy?

5. Identify the management decisions Marsh personnel had to make during the period of severe competitive pressures.

6. Explain how Marsh makes service as an integral part of its marketing plan.

Sources: Marsh Annual Reports for 1982, 1984, 1985, 1986.

Appendices

The text chapters concentrated on the foundations and principles of marketing. Many times, however, marketers need to know more in order to make effective marketing decisions. Decision making often requires mastery of basic marketing mathematics.

This appendix examines three areas of mathematics that marketers commonly use on the job: income, or profit and loss, statements; analytical ratios; and markups and markdowns.

THE INCOME STATEMENT

The *income statement,* sometimes called the profit and loss statement or operating statement, summarizes a firm's revenues and expenses over a specific period of time. Unlike the *balance sheet,* which shows assets, liabilities, and net worth at one particular point in time, the income statement consists of account totals for a specific period, such as a month, a quarter, or a year.

An income statement offers the marketer at least three specific advantages:

1. It allows an accurate determination of whether his or her investment in the business has increased or decreased and thus indicates how the business is progressing.
2. It provides an analytical statement that helps explain why more sales and profits were not realized. This allows changes in policy, management, or methods when needed.
3. If prepared in a standardized way, it allows stores (or other facilities) to exchange data and to determine by comparison their points of strength and weakness.[1]

Figure A.1 shows the 1989 income statement for the Robinwood Ski Touring Center, a small northern Michigan cross-country ski resort. An income statement such as the one shown is divided into five sections: revenues, cost of merchandise sold,

APPENDIX A

The Mathematics of Marketing

gross margin, expenses, and net income.

Revenue

The revenue section records total sales less merchandise returned by consumers and/or allowances given to consumers for damaged merchandise. By subtracting sales returns and allowances from gross sales, the owners of Robinwood arrive at net sales of $48,908.05. This is the amount from which expenses must be paid.

Cost of Merchandise Sold

The cost of goods (or merchandise) sold gives the total value of merchandise sold for the period covered by the statement. This figure, $8,024.44, will be subtracted from the net sales figure of $48,908.05. To calculate the cost of goods sold, Robinwood follows several steps. First, the total amount of inventory on hand on January 1 is recorded. Added to this amount are all purchases of additional merchandise, less purchase returns and allowances ($203.17) and purchase discounts ($158.21) for paying cash within a certain time. Net purchases of $960.76 are then added to the January 1 merchandise inventory to give the total cost of goods available for sale, $9,165.54. Finally, the value of any merchandise left at the end of the year, $1,141.10, is subtracted from the $9,165.54 to arrive at the cost of merchandise sold, $8,024.44.

Gross Margin

The gross margin gives the gross profit on operations before expenses are deducted. The gross margin for the Robinwood Touring Center is $40,883.61, the amount arrived at when the cost of merchandise sold ($8,024.44) is subtracted from net sales of $48,908.05.

Expenses

The expenses category summarizes the costs of selling and of operating the business. Expenses, which can be listed in any order, include such things as advertising, bad debts, credit card fees, depreciation, insurance, delivery costs, payroll taxes, salaries, rent, supplies, interest, and other miscellaneous expenses. Normally these figures are grouped and subtotaled. The total operating expenses for the touring center were $30,933.88.

Net Income

The final step in preparing the income statement is to arrive at the net income, or net profit, which we calculate by subtracting the total operating expenses and other expenses from the gross margin. Robinwood Ski Touring Center determines its net profit to be $9,219.73. From this figure, it must subtract federal income tax owed. In this case, $1,468.76 is owed, to yield a net profit after taxes of $7,750.97.

The statement we have just reviewed is for a small retail establishment, but the income statement format is essentially the same for all types of businesses. However, there are some differences in categories used among retailers, wholesalers, and manufacturers.

ANALYTICAL RATIOS

Analytical ratios are very important to management, for they are the key indicators of marketing success and efficiency. Using the income statement, management can calculate ratios such as the gross margin ratio, net profit ratio, operating expense ratio, returns and allowances ratio, and stock turnover rate. The return on investment, another important ratio, is based on figures from both the income statement and the balance sheet. Each of the ratios can be compared with industrywide ratios or with previous company performance.

Figure A.1 Income statement for a small retail establishment

ROBINWOOD SKI TOURING CENTER
Income Statement
For Year Ended December 31, 1989

Operating Revenue:			
Gross Sales		$49,432.17	
Less Sales Returns & Allowances		524.12	
Net Sales			$48,908.05
Cost of Merchandise Sold:			
Merchandise Inventory, January 1		$ 8,204.78	
Purchases	$1,322.14		
Less Purchase Returns & Allowances	$203.17		
Purchase Discounts	158.21	361.38	
Net Purchases		960.76	
Total Cost of Mdse. Avail. for Sale		$ 9,165.54	
Less Merchandise Inventory, December 31		1,141.10	
Cost of Merchandise Sold			8,024.44
Gross Profit on Operations (Gross Margin)			$40,883.61
Operating Expenses:			
Advertising Expense		1,372.34	
Bad Debts Expense		123.40	
Credit Card Fee Expense		64.21	
Depreciation Expense—Ski Rental Equipment		233.63	
Depreciation Expense—Office Equipment		1,321.18	
Depreciation Expense—Store Equipment		934.22	
Insurance Expense		781.56	
Payroll Tax Expense		1,005.10	
Rent Expense		4,800.00	
Salary Expense		17,952.00	
Supplies Expense		2,346.24	
Total Operating Expenses			30,933.88
Income from Operations			$ 9,949.73
Other Expenses:			
Interest Expense			730.00
Net Deduction			
Net Income before Federal Income Tax			$ 9,219.73
Less Federal Income Tax			1,468.76
Net Income after Federal Income Tax			$ 7,750.97

Gross Margin Ratio

The gross margin ratio expresses gross margin as a percentage of net sales. This ratio reveals the percentage of each dollar of sales available to cover operating expenses. We can calculate the gross margin percentage for the Robinwood Ski Touring Center by using the following formula and referring to figure A.1:

Gross Margin Ratio

$$= \frac{\text{Gross Margin}}{\text{Net Sales}}$$

$$= \frac{40,883.61}{48,908.05} = 83.6\%$$

Net Profit Ratio

The net profit ratio tells management the percentage of each sales dollar earned as profit before taxes. It should be noted that some firms calculate this figure after taxes.

Net Profit Ratio

$$= \frac{\text{Net Income (Profit)}}{\text{Net Sales}}$$

$$= \frac{9,219.73}{48,908.05} = 18.9\%$$

Operating Expense Ratio

Individual expense ratios can be calculated for each operating ex-pense. However, it is common prac-tice to figure the ratio for the total operating expense and then to deter-mine if total expenditures are too high. At that point, if necessary, indi-vidual expense ratios can be deter-mined and compared with ratios of businesses of similar size in the industry.

Operating Expense Ratio

$$= \frac{\text{Total Operating Expenses}}{\text{Net Sales}}$$

$$= \frac{30,933.88}{48,908.05} = 63.2\%$$

Returns and Allowances Ratio

The returns and allowances ratio expresses the relationship to net sales of the amount of merchandise that has been returned or for which an allowance has been given because of damage to the goods.

Returns and Allowances Ratio

$$= \frac{\text{Returns and Allowances}}{\text{Net Sales}}$$

$$= \frac{524.12}{48,908.05} = 1.1\%$$

Stock Turnover Rate

The stock turnover rate gives the number of times that an inventory is sold during a specified period of time (often one year). This ratio varies widely from industry to industry. For example, in the grocery industry the average turnover is close to fifty-two times per year, whereas the average for the furniture industry is two times per year.

The stock turnover rate can be calculated on the basis of cost or selling price. For Robinwood, we will use average inventory at cost, which we calculate by adding the beginning inventory of $8,204.78 to the ending inventory of $1,141.10 and dividing by 2. The result is divided into the cost of merchandise, or goods, sold, as follows:

Stock Turnover Rate

$$= \frac{\text{Cost of Goods Sold}}{\text{Average Inventory at Cost}}$$

$$= \frac{8,024.44}{(8,204.78 + 1,141.10)/2}$$

$$= 1.7 \text{ times}$$

Return on Investment (ROI)

The return on investment ratio provides a very important means of evaluating performance based on actual or projected sales and profits. ROI is a test of management's efficiency in using available resources. The question to be asked of managers is: What rate of return have you earned on the resources under your control?

In order to calculate ROI, as mentioned, management must take figures from two different financial statements. The sales and net income figures for the Robinwood Ski Touring Center come from the income statement. The investment, or total assets, figure can be found in the company's balance sheet. ROI is calculated as follows:

$$\text{ROI} =$$

$$\frac{\text{Net Income after Taxes}}{\text{Investment (Total Assets)}} \times 100$$

$$= \frac{9,219.73}{49,432.17} \times \frac{49,432.17}{78,000.00}$$

$$= 11.8\%$$

The company can raise ROI by reducing inventory (inventory is a part of the owner's investment), increasing sales, or increasing profit margins.

Managers must constantly evaluate the ROI, because if internal investments (reinvestments) are not earning profits higher than alternative outside uses, then funds should be shifted to earn more money. In other words, the ROI should be higher than the cost of borrowing money. In the case of the Robinwood Ski Touring Center, 11.8 percent is too low when compared with a current rate of borrowing of 14 percent.

To increase the ROI, Robinwood could cut back on its investment (assets) or borrow more money to increase its investments. The practice of borrowing is called *leveraging*. This practice increases the ROI, because only a firm's own money is considered when the rate is calculated. Because the ROI can be misleading for a firm that has borrowed heavily, many companies use a Return on Net Assets (RONA) or similar ratio to accurately measure the effective use of resources. RONA is an important test of management's ability to earn a return on funds supplied from *all* sources rather than solely from internal investment.

MARKUPS AND MARKDOWNS

Markups and markdowns are used to calculate the best selling price for a good or service.

Markups

The standard markup is the difference between the cost of an item and its selling price. The markup must cover all business expenses and a planned profit. There are two standard types of markup: markup in cost and markup in retail price.

First, consider an example of markup based on cost. If the Robinwood Ski Touring Center buys ski boots for $30.00 and sells them for $50.00, the markup is $20.00, and the percentage of markup is 66 percent based on cost. This is calculated as follows:

Markup percentage

$$= \frac{\text{Markup}}{\text{Cost}} = \frac{20}{30} = 66\%$$

Expressing markup as a percentage of cost is a simple approach to pricing. However, this method does not adjust for cost variations at different levels of output. If allowances are not made for variations and changes in costs, markup based on cost will fail.

Markup can also be expressed as a percentage of the retail price. If a retailer pays $5.50 for a ski cap and sells it for $8.98, the markup is $3.48, and the markup percentage is 38.8 percent, based on the retail price. This form of markup is the one most commonly used, because it equals the gross margin, which is very important in every business. It is calculated in this way:

Markup Percentage

$$= \frac{\text{Markup}}{\text{Selling Price}} = \frac{3.48}{8.98}$$

$$= 38.8\%$$

Markdowns

Markdowns are price reductions in the original selling price, which may be required when customers are not buying an item. Markdown analysis is an important tool to retailers who are trying to determine the size, number, and reason for various price reductions. This analysis will often reveal that a marked-down item was originally overpriced, became soiled or damaged, or was selected for a special sale.

Markdown percentages are calculated as follows for 280 pairs of cross-country skis originally priced at $125 and marked down to $100:

Markdown Percentage

$$= \frac{\text{Dollar Markdown and Allowances}}{\text{Net Sales}}$$

$$= \frac{4,700 + 400}{48,908.05} = 10.4\%$$

*M*arketing is one of the most exciting and fascinating career fields open to young people today. The field is huge and diverse. Today, nearly 28 million employees are engaged in marketing careers in retailing (16 million), wholesaling (3.8 million), and selected services (8 million). Added to this number are the workers in a variety of other marketing-related enterprises, ranging from United Parcel Service to the American Red Cross. If everyone engaged in some form of distribution activity is included, well over a third of the U.S. work force of over 110 million qualifies as marketing workers. The numbers employed in marketing and the variety of jobs available have grown recently because of the broadened concept of marketing. This is especially true in the service and nonprofit sectors.

This appendix examines some common careers in marketing and gives suggestions about how to select the right marketing career and how to get a job by writing an effective resume and conducting a successful interview. In 1988 the starting salary for a marketing or liberal arts major in a sales or marketing position was $22,920 (expect an annual increase in starting salary of approximately 4.2 percent).

TYPES OF MARKETING POSITIONS

In order to achieve their organizational goals, firms establish the necessary positions and define the relationships among those positions. Because the objectives of firms differ, their organizational structures differ, too. A marketing-driven institution should have the resources and organizational structure to implement the marketing concept.

The head of the marketing organization in a marketing-oriented firm is usually the **marketing manager** or vice president of marketing. This individual has the responsibility for fine-tuning the marketing mix and for

APPENDIX B

Careers in Marketing

creating the strategies that will accomplish the firm's marketing objectives. In contrast, a production-driven organization does not have a marketing manager but instead has a vice president of sales, whose activity is limited to directing the sales force.

The chief marketing executive is usually a line manager who directs other marketing personnel in a chain of command that ends with the salespersons in the field. In some organizations, however, marketing manager is a staff position. Here, the marketing manager advises, plans, and guides the line managers who oversee production of a good or service. Small production-oriented companies frequently have elected to change the name of their advertising manager to marketing manager. Some service organizations, such as hospitals and museums, believe that they are accepting the marketing concept by simply changing the title of a public relations director to marketing manager. In the absence of a total marketing commitment, these name changes do not alter the responsibilities associated with the positions.

In a marketing-oriented organization, the marketing manager usually supervises a sales manager, who is the key line figure in the marketing chain of command, as well as several staff or advisory personnel who directly support the selling function.

The degree of specialization in a marketing organization depends on its size. In a small organization, only a sales manager and an advertising manager may report to the chief marketing official. On the other hand, as shown in figure B.1, a large organization may engage in so many marketing activities that numerous marketing specialists are needed. The additional marketing staff may

include product managers, a product planning manager, a marketing research manager, a physical distribution manager, and a consumer relations manager. The **sales manager** is responsible for recruiting, training, and managing the sales force. The **advertising and promotion manager** generally works with an advertising agency to prepare the promotions that will create a favorable image for the company and sell its products. A large company may employ several product managers, who report to a general **product manager.** The product managers generally prepare the promotions, sales training programs, pricing policies, and overall marketing strategies for their product lines. The **product planning manager** is responsible for developing attractive new products and generally works closely with the design and engineering staffs. The **manager of marketing research** often supervises research analysts, sales analysts, market planners, and management information systems specialists. The role of the **physical distribution manager** (sometimes called an operations manager) is to minimize inventory and transportation costs while maintaining adequate inventories and moving the goods rapidly to their markets. A **consumer service manager** is responsible for resolving any problems arising from customers.

SELECTING THE RIGHT MARKETING CAREER: FORMULA FOR VOCATIONAL CHOICE[1]

When trying to choose a marketing career, it is essential that you approach the process systematically. One proven approach is to examine yourself first. Make sure before you start thinking about specific career possibilities that you have a clear understanding of your interests, aptitudes and abilities, and other factors that could affect your choices.

❏ **Figure B.1**
Marketing
organizations.

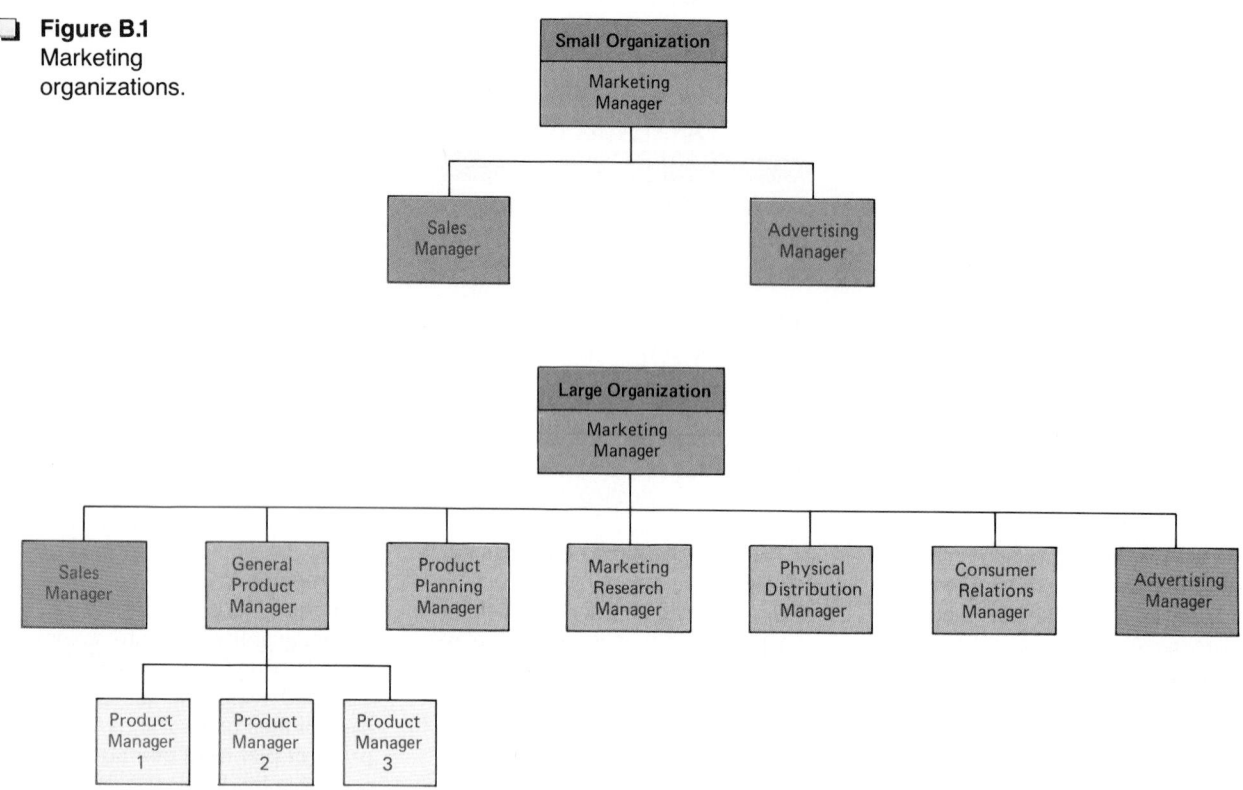

Next, you need to closely examine career clusters such as those illustrated in figure B.2. This exploration should include advantages and disadvantages, compensations, conditions for success, job requirements, projected annual openings, and prospects for career advancement.

The final step is to give serious thought to the relationship between your own characteristics and the characteristics of various careers. Matching up these elements should help you begin to make a career plan.

ASSESSING YOURSELF

Self-assessment isn't as easy as you may think, because most people either underrate or overrate themselves. However, being honest with yourself is a must if you are going to choose a satisfying career. Areas to explore in self-assessment include interests, aptitudes and abilities, values, and personality.

Interests

Interests are developed early as a result of heredity and experiences.

As people grow older, they pursue their interests for both self-satisfaction and reward. The pursuit of specialized interests often leads to the development of even more specialized competencies and the neglect of others.

Interests are very important components of career choices, for it is difficult to achieve success without enthusiasm. Furthermore, many vocational psychologists and personnel specialists believe that interests, wishes, and happiness play a larger role than intelligence, aptitudes, or skills in determining what people actually do well.

Interest surveys are one method of matching interests to specific occupational areas. The most common interest surveys are the Kuder Preference Record and the Strong Vocational Interest Blank. These surveys are administered at most college counseling offices.

Aptitudes and Abilities

Most of us have special aptitudes, which we often inherited from our parents. For example, some people have special athletic, artistic, mech-

anical, or musical aptitudes. As used here, an aptitude is an innate quality, whereas an ability is the development of an aptitude. A person can have an aptitude for music but not have the ability to play the piano.

The ability to reason and think quickly is often measured by IQ tests. Because many variables affect IQ scores, these scores should only be interpreted by qualified individuals, such as college psychologists or counselors. Aptitude is measured by such tests as the ACT and the SAT, which measure verbal and mathematical aptitude. Although IQ, ACT, and SAT scores will not tell you which career to choose, such tests can be useful in helping you to make general decisions about appropriate careers. Do you have any special aptitudes or abilities that would be considered strengths by an employer? Are there career choices you should avoid because of a lack of aptitude or ability?

Values

Your outlook on life is another important factor to consider when choosing a job. What do you value

Figure B.2
The twenty-six marketing occupations.

An invaluable career guide to marketing students is the book *Careers in Marketing*, coauthored by David Rosenthal, a professor of marketing at Miami University (Oxford, Ohio), and Michael Powell.

The book is sponsored by the American Marketing Association and the National Council of Physical Distribution Management, a professional organization.

As a result of two years of research and over 200 interviews, the authors developed a list of 26 marketing occupations. Here's the list, with paraphrased descriptions of what each job entails:

PRODUCT MANAGEMENT

1. **Product manager, consumer goods.** Develops new products that can cost millions of dollars, with advice and consent of management. A job with great responsibility.
2. **Administrative manager.** Oversees the organization within a company that transports products to consumers and handles customer service.
3. **Operations manager.** Supervises warehousing and other physical distribution functions; often directly involved in moving goods on the warehouse floor.
4. **Traffic and transportation manager.** Evaluates the costs and benefits of different types of transportation.
5. **Inventory control manager.** Forecasts demand for stockpiled goods, coordinates production with plant managers; keeps track of current levels of shipments to keep customers supplied.
6. **Administrative analyst planner.** Performs cost analyses of physical distribution systems.
7. **Customer service manager.** Maintains good relations with customers by coordinating sales staffs, marketing management, and physical distribution management.
8. **Physical distribution consultant.** Expert in the transportation and distribution of goods.

ADVERTISING

9. **Account executive.** Maintains contact with clients while coordinating the creative work of artists and copywriters. In full-service ad agencies, account executives are considered partners with clients in promoting the product and formulating marketing strategy.
10. **Media buyer analyst.** Deals with media sales representatives in selecting advertising media; analyzes the value of media being purchased.

11. **Copywriter.** Works with art director in conceptualizing advertisements; writes the text of print or radio ads or the storyboards of television ads.
12. **Art director.** Handles the visual component of advertisements.
13. **Sales promotion manager.** Designs promotions for consumer products; works at an ad agency or a sales promotion agency.
14. **Public relations manager.** Develops written or filmed messages for the public; handles contacts with the press.
15. **Specialty advertising manager.** Develops advertising for the sales staff and customers or distributors.

RETAILING

16. **Buyer.** Selects the products a store sells; surveys consumer trends and evaluates the past performance of products and suppliers.
17. **Store manager.** Oversees the staff and services at a store.

SALES

18. **Direct.** Engage in door-to-door or other personal selling. Compensation is based mostly on a commission.
19. **Sales to channel.** Sells to another member of the distribution channel (between the manufacturer and the store or customer). Compensation includes salary plus bonus.
20. **Industrial/semitechnical.** Sells supplies and services to businesses. Compensation is salary plus bonus.
21. **Complex/professional.** Sells complicated or custom-designed products to business. The job requires understanding of the technology of a product. Compensation is salary plus bonus.

MARKETING RESEARCH

22. **Project manager,** supplier. Coordinates and oversees market studies for clients.
23. **Account executive,** supplier. Serves as liaison between client and market research firm; similar to an advertising agency account executive.
24. **Project director,** inhouse. Acts as project manager for the market studies conducted by the firm itself (in contrast to 22, which performs this function for clients).
25. **Marketing research specialist,** advertising agency. Performs or contracts for market studies for agency clients.

NON-PROFIT

26. **Marketing manager,** performing arts. Develops and directs mail campaigns, fund raising, and public relations for arts organizations.

Source: Adapted from *Careers in Marketing* by David Rosenthal and Michael Powell by Prentice-Hall, Inc., 1984, for the Prentice-Hall-American Management Association series in marketing and *Business Week.*.

the most in life? Do you enjoy serving others? Would you like to make the most money possible? Do you enjoy the beauty of nature and life around you? Do you wish to be independent and do as you like? Often we find that our values conflict with our interests. For example, you may have an interest in travel but you may value time with your family. This might affect your evaluation of a career that required a great deal of travel.

Personality

Recent research has made it clear that the choice of a career is an expression of personality. Personality is the unique pattern of behavioral and mental processes that characterize a person and his or her interactions with the environment. It includes such traits as initiative, judgment, and emotional stability. College counseling centers often administer personality inventories,

such as the widely used Minnesota Multiphasic Personality Inventory (MMPI). Studies have shown that members of a particular profession often have similar personalities and similar histories of personal development. According to John L. Holland, a noted career theorist, "vocational satisfaction, stability, and achievement depend on the congruence between one's personality and the environment (composed largely of other people) in which one works."[2]

USING THE COLLEGE YEARS TO YOUR BEST ADVANTAGE

The foregoing discussion has outlined some elements of self-assessment. The career descriptions in figure B.2, together with the occupational outlook material for the 1990s in table B.1, should help you mesh your personal career preferences with opportunities in the changing job market. But once you have selected a career field, how do you go about gaining a place in it? You can take a number of steps while you are still in college, even before you start your job search.

First, companies and organizations are looking increasingly at college grades. Some colleges now require a grade point average of 2.5 or higher for entry to certain majors.

☐ **Table B.1** Marketing outlook in brief

MARKETING, SALES AND MANAGERIAL OCCUPATIONS	ESTIMATED 1984 EMPLOYMENT	PERCENT CHANGE IN EMPLOYMENT 1982–1995	NUMERICAL CHANGE IN EMPLOYMENT 1982–1995	EMPLOYMENT PROSPECTS
Buyers, retail and wholesale trade	229,000	30	76,000	Employment expected to grow about as fast as average. However, keen competition anticipated because merchandising attracts large numbers of college graduates.
Purchasing agents	189,000	27	52,000	Employment expected to grow about as fast as the average. Best opportunities for persons with master's degree in business administration; graduates of two-year programs in purchasing should find good opportunities in small firms.
Public relations specialists	95,000	29	26,000	Employment expected to grow much faster than average as corporations, associations, medical centers, and other large organizations expand public relations efforts. Competition for jobs is likely to be keen.
Insurance agents and brokers	371,000	25	90,000	Employment expected to grow more slowly than average. Opportunities will be best for ambitious persons who enjoy selling and developing expertise in many different types of insurance and investments.
Manufacturers' sales workers	547,000	15	64,000	Employment expected to grow more slowly than the average, as some manufacturers switch to wholesalers to sell their products.
Real estate agents and brokers	363,000	33	112,000	Employment expected to rise about as fast as average. However, the field is highly

Source: Occupational Outlook Handbook, U.S. Deptartment of Labor, 1986–1987.

These requirements reflect the recruiting practices of many companies and should be taken seriously by students.

Second, although organizations put college graduates in technical, entry-level positions (sales trainee, assistant, and so on), they look critically at employees for management potential. Here is where participation and leadership in campus organizations can be important. (You will note participation in campus organizations in your resume, discussed later in this appendix.) Such activities can contribute real-world experience to academic work in your chosen major. If you are a marketing major and belong to the marketing club, for example, you will hear speakers from companies in your area and go on

☐ **Table B.1** Marketing outlook in brief *(continued)*

MARKETING, SALES AND MANAGERIAL OCCUPATIONS	ESTIMATED 1984 EMPLOYMENT	PERCENT CHANGE IN EMPLOYMENT 1982–1995	NUMERICAL CHANGE IN EMPLOYMENT 1982–1995	EMPLOYMENT PROSPECTS
Real estate agents and brokers *(continued)*				competitive. Well-trained, ambitious people who enjoy selling should have the best chance for success.
Retail trade sales workers	4,000,000	27	898,000	Employment expected to grow about as fast as average. High turnover should create many openings for full-time, part-time, and temporary workers.
Securities sales workers	81,000	36	28,000	Employment has declined significantly since the 1987 crash and recent mergers of major brokerage firms. Future job employment depends on economic conditions and stability of the market; however, rising personal incomes could drive employment levels near or back to previous levels. The field will continue to be competitive, and many beginners may be unable to establish a sufficient clientele.
Travel agents	72,000	43	26,000	Employment expected to grow much faster than average. Because travel expenditures often depend on business conditions, job opportunities are sensitive to economic changes.
Wholesale trade sales workers	1,200,000	30	327,000	Employment expected to grow slightly faster than average as wholesalers sell a wider variety of products and improve customer services.
TOTALS	5,712,000		1,545,000	

Source: Occupational Outlook Handbook, U.S. Deptartment of Labor, 1986–1987.

field trips to local businesses. If you are elected vice president in charge of programming for the club, you will be contacting companies, arranging programs, leading committees, and taking part in other activities that develop your leadership skills; companies will be impressed with your motivation.

With college costs rising, more students work part-time and summers. If you work, say so in your resume, and be sure to note supervisory experience—managing a group of counselors at camp, waitresses in a lunchroom, labor in your lawn-mowing service, or the like. If you haven't time for activities in college because of your job, be honest. If you participated in activities in high school, you might mention them briefly.

Finally, investigate whether your college has a co-op or internship program that will allow you to work for a semester or summer in your chosen field. If your college doesn't have such a program, try to find a job in your chosen area of specialization, even if you have to take a pay cut. The experience will be worth it—both for a company to learn about your abilities and for you to decide whether you have made the correct initial career choice.

BEGINNING THE JOB SEARCH

The best place for a college student to begin a job search is on campus at the college placement office, which provides a variety of services to both students and alumni. Valuable assistance can often be found in areas such as career counseling, placement bulletins, job hunt workshops, free credentials services, and many others. Be sure to register with the placement office early in your last year, so you can take advantage of their many free services.

Review the weekly placement bulletin to find out what employers are interviewing on campus in future weeks. Screen these listings to identify employers seeking graduates in your major and your preferred geographic location.

Next, sign up for interviews and begin the important step of sizing up prospective employers. Your career

placement office will have literature describing many companies and employment opportunities. However, this information is often not enough. You should also seek information from such sources such as Dun & Bradstreet's *Million Dollar Directory* and *Half-Million Dollar Directory, Thomas' Register of American Manufacturers,* and various monthly publications that list vital information on various companies' plants, products, and financial performance.

Researching a firm thoroughly is important to you, because your future rests on whether you make the right job selection. In addition, research is important preparation for interviewing. When you interview, it will be to your advantage to ask probing questions about the company that reveal you have done your homework.

The following are some key questions your research should help you answer:

1. What is the history of the company? Has it shown substantial and continuing growth? What does the future have in store for the company?
2. What are its products or services, and who are its competitors?
3. How do employees feel about the company? Does it have a good reputation?
4. What is the potential for professional growth and promotion with the company? Does the company offer orientation, training, and seminars and encourage membership in business societies?
5. Where are its plants, branches, and headquarters? Where would you likely begin your career, and

❏ **Figure B.3** Sample content for a resume.

	Name	
Permanent Address Street City, State, ZIP Telephone: (AC) #		**School Address** Street City, State, Zip Telephone: (AC) #

Personal Data	May include marital status; birth date; health (physical limitations). May appear at top (after identification) or near bottom.
Job Objective	Should tell the reader clearly and concisely what kind of job you want. Should not be too broad (e.g., "challenging position with advancement potential"). This section is optional—depends on the use of the resume. May need to develop more than one resume to fit different job objectives.
Education	Begin with highest degree level attained. Tell what, when, where. Not usually necessary to include high school information. Cite academic awards, scholarships, scholastic achievements earned. List special skills or equipment used, grades, publications, special projects, independent study.
College Activities	May be placed after Education section or after Work Experience section. Should show memberships and offices in school organization, community activities, honors, and hobbies. Briefly tell what you did in any office you held. This section may be important, because it shows your out-of-class activities, which reflect your interests, abilities, values, and leadership potential.
Work Experience	List most recent first. Give name and location of employer, dates, job title, and brief description of duties. Stress those tasks and responsibilities related to the position you are seeking. Be specific. Include full time, part time, summer, volunteer, and self-employment experiences. Special academic projects of independent study may be listed here or under separate entry.
Skills & Interests	Optional. Cite any special skills, experience, projects, interests not listed elsewhere in resume.
Background	Optional. May include a brief sketch of your early background.
References	References furnished upon request.

Source: Adapted from Virginia Polytechnic Institute and State University Career Placement Office and Samuel C. Certo, Max E. Douglas, and Stewart W. Husted, *Business,* 2d ed. © 1987 by Allyn and Bacon, Boston. All rights reserved.

what kind of geographic mobility would be expected of you?

WRITING THE RESUME AND LETTER OF APPLICATION

Not all your interviews will take place on campus. You must develop a resume and a letter of application to accompany it for employers that do not visit your campus.

Resume

The resume is a vital part of the job search strategy. It is an orderly summary of your background and should be designed to contribute to your overall persuasive effort. Its main purpose is to get you an interview.

Each resume must be tailor-made for the person it describes. Ideally, a unique resume should be designed for each employer. The idea is to target the resume so the employer feels that the applicant's qualifications are a perfect match for the job requirements. However, for most recent college graduates, this may not be practical. The traditional chronological approach is recommended by the College Placement Council. (See figure B.3.)

Regardless of what style resume you use, there are some general rules that are universally accepted. They include the following:

- Develop separate sections to guide the reader. These sections should contain items such as career goals, education, honors, interests, work experience, and others that highlight your data.
- Type, space neatly, and use offset printing for reproduction. Make sure the resume is well balanced and attractive.
- Limit the resume to two pages. Remember to include your name on the second page as well as the first.
- Don't include a photograph. This is not a beauty contest, and if it were, you might lose.
- Don't automatically list references. It is a good idea to have accessible references on file at the placement office.

- Don't lie or distort. If you get the job based on misinformation, you may be fired later.
- Write short, concise statements. Use strong action verbs with short sentences. Economy is the key word here.
- Double-check spelling, punctuation, grammar, and dates.
- Give specific examples of your accomplishments. (See figure B.4.)

Letter of Application

Like the resume, the letter of application shouldn't be too long—usually three or four paragraphs is plenty. The letter of application is designed to introduce you to the reader and slants your background more precisely to a particular job than does the all-around, chronological resume. Because it is a reflection of you, it should be prepared with great care.

As a rule of thumb, you should always try to address your letter of application to the person most likely to make the hiring decision. Because most recent college graduates are recruited by the personnel department, you can address your letter to the personnel director. Call on the phone if necessary to ensure that you have the correct spelling of his or her name. Remember, always address your letter to a specific person unless you are answering a blind ad

Figure B.4 Sample resume.

Ryan S. Winthrop

Present Address (Until June 10, 1989)	Permanent Address
410 W. Main Street	1814 Bailey Place
Blacksburg, VA 24060	Greensboro, NC 27410
	(919) 524-3122

Job objective: Financial analysis, with opportunity to increase responsibility and ultimately move into corporate management.

Education: B.S., Marketing, June 1989,
Virginia Polytechnic Institute and State University,
Blacksburg, Virginia

GPA 2.72 (overall); 3.02 (in major); A = 4

Coursework related to job objective:
Marketing, 36 credits   Banking and Insurance,
Accounting, 15 credits   12 credits
Economics, 12 credits   Business Management,
                                  12 credits

Summer employment: Belk's Department Stores, Charlotte, NC, 1988
Interned as an assistant buyer for men's clothing; evaluated marketing research and consumer trends; assisted in selection of goods.

Cedar Point, Inc., Sandusky, OH, summers 1986, 1987.
Busboy, waiter, and bartender at various restaurants within the park.

Other skills: Experience in computer programming (COBOL, Basic, Fortran), familiar with basic hardware and several software packages; able to operate accounting and related office machines.

Activities: Vice president, Delta Sigma Pi; member of social fraternity; Representative to Student Government Association.

Hobbies: Water sports, snowskiing, chess, nonfictional reading.

Personal: Single, marriage planned for June, 22 years old, willing to relocate.

References: Available upon request.

❏ **Figure B.5** Contents of a letter of application.

> Your Street Address
> City, State, ZIP Code
> Month, Day, Year
>
> Name of person you are writing to
> Title
> Name or Organization
> City, State, Zip Code
>
> Dear (Name):
>
> Opening paragraph: State why you are writing. Identify the position or type of work for which you are applying. Mention how you heard of the opening.
>
> Second paragraph: Tell why you are particularly interested in the employer, location, and type of work. Mention one or two qualifications you think should be of interest to the employer. Be sure to mention your related experience, specialized training, and skills.
>
> Third paragraph: Refer the reader to your resume. This paragraph might also reemphasize your interest in the employer, your background, or both.
>
> Closing paragraph: If you want an interview, advise the employer of your desire to visit, or offer some similar suggestion to facilitate an immediate and favorable reply. For example, tell the employer you will be in town on a specific date and indicate your interest in a meeting.
>
> Sincerely,
>
> *(Your handwritten signature)*
>
> Your name, typed
>
> Enclosure

Source: Adapted from Virginia Polytechnic Institute and State University Career Placement Office and Samuel C. Certo, Max E. Douglas, and Stewart W. Husted, *Business,* 2d ed. © 1987 by Allyn and Bacon, Boston. All rights reserved.

(employer not named); and always ask for a job interview or some other type of specific response. (See figure B.5.)

INTERVIEWING FOR A JOB

The job interview may well prove to be twenty or thirty of the most important minutes of your life. This is your opportunity to show employers that you have the skills necessary to help them solve their problems. Preparing for the interview should enable you to reduce your anxiety and demonstrate competence and confidence in the interview.

Preparation

Being prepared for the job interview has two aspects: (1) anticipating what the interviewer will want from you and (2) knowing what you want from the interviewer. First, though, you should realize that there are several types of interviews. The most common type on the college campus is the screening interview. The purpose of this interview is to narrow choices so that the company can invite the most qualified candidates for a second, in-depth interview, which often takes place at the firm's offices. The most common mistake a candidate makes in a screening interview is getting into too much depth, such as "Who will I be working for?" or "What will my exact tasks be?"

The following specific guidelines should help you prepare for your interview:

- Practice makes perfect. Try role playing with a friend in a low-stress, dry-run interview. Videotape the practice interview if possible.
- Know the full name of the interviewer and how to pronounce it.
- Assemble all papers you may need, such as social security card, addresses of references, military records, and similar items.
- Review your research on the firm and your self-assessment of what you have to offer the company.
- Be prepared for questions that are illegal. Prospective employers shouldn't ask questions concerning race, nationality, religion or creed, age, marital status, or handicaps. You have three choices when asked such a question: (1) answer it without a fuss, (2) refuse to answer because of lack of relevance to the job, or (3) file a discrimination complaint with the Equal Employment Opportunity Commission.
- Allow yourself plenty of time to get to the interview early and to feel unhurried in the interview.
- Dress conservatively. Avoid either too-formal or too-casual attire. Be well-groomed.

The Interview

When the time comes for the interview, you should be ready and be enthusiastically anticipating the experience. If the interview doesn't yield a job, it should serve as a positive learning experience, which should improve your next interview. Some points to remember in the interview are as follows:

- Greet your interviewer by name and introduce yourself. Act as a guest and follow the interviewer's cues.
- Be enthusiastic about your accomplishments and what you can do, but don't act superior.
- Be frank and truthful and project self-respect. Don't exaggerate, "beg for a job," or criticize others.
- Be attentive and alert. Always ask for clarification of something you don't understand.
- Put the interviewer at ease by showing that you genuinely like him or her. Pursue areas in which the interviewer shows interest. Remember, though, to

let the interviewer control the interview.

- Be talkative and friendly but concise. Again, watch for cues from the interviewer.
- Be prepared to discuss salary, but don't introduce the subject. If necessary, give a general range.

Figure B.6 identifies some elements of a successful interview.[3]

Follow-Up Letter

After the interview, especially if a company still interests you, send a thank-you letter to the interviewer. This basic courtesy is often overlooked by people seeking jobs but it offers an excellent method of keeping your name fresh in the interviewer's mind and keeping your file active.

Thank-you letters should be relatively short and should show that you remember something about the interview.

Remember, this single expression of gratitude could decide the case in your favor.

☐ **Figure B.6** Elements of a successful interview.

What Made the Best Interviews?		
	%	Number
1. *Interviewee knew about company* ("had done homework," "knows the field")	66%	(174)
2. *Interviewee had specific career goals* ("knew what he/she wanted," "good fit between our need and his/hers," "well-thought-out career interests")	41%	(108)
3. *Interviewee knowledgeable* ("asked good questions," "knew what to ask")	29%	(76)
4. *Interviewee socially adept* ("rapport," "in tune with me," "outgoing and expressive")	28%	(74)
5. *Interviewee articulate* ("able to express ideas," "spoke well," "good with tricky questions")	19%	(50)

The Most Commonly Asked Questions: General Classification
1. Goals and purposes — Life purposes — Career objectives
2. Type of work desired — Kind of Job — Job expectations
3. Reasons for selection of company — Knowledge of company
4. Personal qualifications — Strengths and weaknesses
5. Career choice — Reasons for decisions
6. Qualifications for the job — How college education has prepared the candidate
7. Educational choices and plans — Choice of college — Choice of major
8. Geographical preferences — Willingness to relocate
9. Major achievements and accomplishments

Source: The Northwestern Endicott Report, the Placement Center, Northwestern University, Evanston, Illinois.

ACCEPTING OR REFUSING A JOB

When you receive a job offer you should be congratulated on your successful job search. Now the easiest part remains—accepting or rejecting the position.

In refusing a job, use an inductive approach. In other words, state your reasons first, then the refusal, then a pleasant ending. Reply as quickly as possible so that the job can be offered to someone else. Remember, you didn't like waiting for employers to notify you.

Acceptance letters should use a deductive approach. Begin by accepting the job in the first sentence, follow with any necessary details, and end with a pleasant closing.

There is one last important point to remember. Immediately inform your college placement office of your job acceptance so it will stop referring your name for possible placement.

Getting into the habit of attending to common courtesies such as these can start you on the right foot to a successful career in business.

GETTING OFF TO A GOOD START

According to several studies, your success on the job will often depend on your attitude and your ability to get along with others. It is assumed that you have the competence to perform your job skillfully.

Treat each new job as a challenge. Make a special effort to meet and get along with your fellow employees, and they will more readily make an effort to "show you the ropes." It is also important to relate to your supervisor and to try to understand exactly what is expected of you.

Finally, remember that just because you have a college degree

doesn't mean that you have all the answers. The world of business and industry isn't like the classroom environment. You must work hard at the transition and even harder at becoming a productive worker who is valuable to your employer. Be patient, tactful, and cooperative, and you'll find your chances of getting off to a good start will be greatly increased.

Notes

1. John W. Wingate, Elmer O. Schaller, and F. Leonard Miller, *Retail Merchandise Management* (Prentice-Hall, 1972), p. 36.
2. Adapted from Samuel C. Certo, Max E. Douglas, and Stewart W. Husted, *Business,* 2d ed. (Appendix A), Boston: Allyn and Bacon, 1988, pp. 586–597.
3. John Holland, *Making Vocational Choices: A Theory of Careers* (Englewood Cliffs, N.J.: Prentice-Hall, 1973).

Check-Your-Learning Answer Key

CHAPTER 1
1. T, 2. c, 3. F, 4. b, 5. b, 6. T, 7. a, 8. c, 9. T, 10. T

CHAPTER 2
1. F, 2. F, 3. T, 4. a, 5. F, 6. T, 7. F, 8. F, 9. T, 10. T, 11. F

CHAPTER 3
1. F, 2. d, 3. b, 4. b, 5. a, 6. T, 7. F, 8. d, 9. b, 10. F

CHAPTER 4
1. F, 2. F, 3. T, 4. d, 5. T, 6. T, 7. F, 8. b, 9. F, 10. T, 11. d, 12. F, 13. F, 14. F, 15. T, 16. F, 17. e

CHAPTER 5
1. F, 2. F, 3. T, 4. T, 5. T, 6. c, 7. F, 8. F, 9. F, 10. T, 11. a

CHAPTER 6
1. T, 2. F, 3. T, 4. d, 5. T, 6. F, 7. T, 8. F, 9. a

CHAPTER 7
1. d, 2. T, 3. b, 4. F, 5. F, 6. a, 7. F, 8. T, 9. c, 10. F, 11. e, 12. T, 13. d, 14. T, 15. T, 16. d, 17. F, 18. T, 19. F

CHAPTER 8
1. b, 2. c, 3. a, 4. b, 5. d, 6. a, 7. d, 8. b, 9. d, 10. b, 11. a 12. c, 13. d

CHAPTER 9
1. T, 2. F, 3. F, 4. T, 5. c, 6. F, 7. T, 8. F, 9. T, 10. F, 11. T, 12. T, 13. c, 14. T, 15. F, 16. T, 17. b

CHAPTER 10
1. T, 2. F, 3. F, 4. F, 5. a, 6. T, 7. F, 8. T, 9. F, 10. e, 11. F, 12. T, 13. F, 14. F, 15. a, 16. F

CHAPTER 11
1. F, 2. d, 3. F, 4. e, 5. F, 6. c, 7. F, 8. T, 9. F, 10. T, 11. F, 12. e, 13. T, 14. F, 15. F, 16. d, 17. T, 18. b

CHAPTER 12
1. F, 2. T, 3. a, 4. a, 5. b, 6. b, 7. F, 8. T, 9. d, 10. F, 11. a, 12. T, 13. b, 14. F, 15. c, 16. T

CHAPTER 13
1. d, 2. T, 3. a, 4. T, 5. F, 6. b, 7. T, 8. c, 9. a, 10. F, 11. b, 12. F, 13. T, 14. T, 15. d, 16. T

CHAPTER 14
1. c, 2. T, 3. T, 4. d, 5. b, 6. F, 7. F, 8. c, 9. F, 10. c, 11. F, 12. b, 13. b, 14. T, 15. a, 16. c

CHAPTER 15
1. a, 2. T, 3. c, 4. d, 5. F, 6. T, 7. a, 8. T, 9. d, 10. d, 11. F, 12. F

CHAPTER 16
1. F, 2. c, 3. d, 4. T, 5. F, 6. T, 7. d, 8. F, 9. a, 10. c, 11. T, 12. F, 13. c, 14. F, 15. c, 16. F

CHAPTER 17
1. F, 2. c, 3. d, 4. c, 5. F, 6. T, 7. c, 8. a, 9. F, 10. F, 11. T, 12. F

CHAPTER 18
1. T, 2. a, 3. T, 4. c, 5. T, 6. c, 7. F, 8. T, 9. b, 10. F, 11. b 12. T, 13. d, 14. b, 15. F

CHAPTER 19
1. F, 2. T, 3. F, 4. T, 5. T, 6. T, 7. T, 8. T, 9. a, 10. T, 11. c, 12. a, 13. T, 14. T, 15. F

CHAPTER 20
1. F, 2. T, 3. F, 4. T, 5. T, 6. b, 7. F, 8. F, 9. T, 10. F, 11. T, 12. T, 13. F, 14. F

CHAPTER 21
1. T, 2. b, 3. c, 4. F, 5. a, 6. T, 7. c, 8. F, 9. b, 10. F, 11. a, 12. b, 13. F, 14. T, 15. d, 16. T, 17. F

CHAPTER 22
1. T, 2. F, 3. F, 4. c, 5. F, 6. T, 7. F, 8. F, 9. b, 10. F, 11. T, 12. F, 13. F, 14. a, 15. T, 16. F, 17. T, 18. T, 19. c

CHAPTER 23
1. d, 2. F, 3. b, 4. c, 5. F, 6. a, 7. F, 8. F, 9. F, 10. F, 11. b, 12. d

Glossary

A

Absolute advantage
A trade advantage that exists when only one country can provide a product or can produce the product at a lower cost than any other country.

Accessory equipment
An industrial good that does not become a part of the finished product but does facilitate an organization's operation.

Accountability
Having to answer to higher-level management when objectives are not achieved, when budgets are exceeded, or when market share declines.

Act utilitarians
Those who believe that in every situation one should act to maximize the total good, even if it means breaking a rule.

Administered pricing
A condition under which the marketer has sufficient control within a market to set price and does.

Adoption process
The steps in an individual's evaluation of a product and decision to use that product. The stages in the adoption process are: awareness, interest, evaluation, trial, and adoption.

Advertising
Any paid form of nonpersonal presentation and promotion of ideas, goods, or services by an identified sponsor.

AIDA
An acronym that stands for attention, interest, desire, and action; signifies the sequence the consumer goes through in the persuasion process.

Allowance
A reduction in a product's list price.

Approach
A salesperson's initial contact with the customer.

Area sample
See *cluster sample*.

Assumptive close
Closely related to the trial close, except it takes for granted, through positive statements, that the customer is going to make a purchase.

Atmospherics
The blending of visual, aural, taste, and touch components that create the desired store atmosphere.

Attitude
Learned, enduring predisposition of cognitive feeling, action tendency, or evaluation set with regard to an object or idea.

Attitude tracking
Measurement of market satisfaction through the study of consumer attitudes.

Auction companies
Functional middlemen; important in selling tobacco, livestock, fur, and used cars; useful in the sale of goods that require physical inspection for an accurate evaluation of their qualities.

Average revenue
Total revenue divided by units sold.

Average total cost
Total cost divided by number of units.

B

Bait-and-switch pricing
Advertising a product at a very low price with no intention of selling the advertised product; an unethical, illegal type of promotional pricing.

Balance of payments
The difference between the expenditures made to foreign nations and the receipts taken in from foreign nations during a given time.

Balance of trade
The difference between the goods and services a nation buys from other countries (imports) and the goods and services a nation sells to other countries (exports).

Balance strategy
Strategy that focuses on maintaining the status quo and keeping profits at present levels by controlling costs and maintaining sales.

Bar-coding system
System to facilitate easy location, identification, and retrieval of a product. Bar codes can be read by hand-held or fixed-position scanners.

Base in segmentation
A set of variables with common characteristics, such as those related to demographics or psychographics, used to analyze market segments.

Base-point pricing
Pricing practice whereby the seller charges the buyer for transportation costs from the nearest designated base location even if the item is shipped from a different location.

Blitz
A scheduling strategy for advertising in which large sums of the advertising budget are spent in one campaign.

Bonded storage
A storage service through which merchandise is held in a duty-free zone until all state and federal taxes or U.S. Customs duties have been paid.

Brand
A name, term, sign, symbol, or design (or a combination of them) intended to identify the goods or services of one seller (or group) and to differentiate them from competitors' goods or services.

Break-even analysis
Procedure to identify the level of sales at which the firm has neither a profit nor a loss.

Broker
Functional middleman that represents either buyers or sellers on a transaction basis; does not take physical possession of the goods, has only limited pricing authority, and does not maintain a continuous contractual relationship with principals.

Business analysis
A step in product development; focuses on the viability of the product idea by forecasting sales revenues and costs.

Buyer
A member of the buying center with formal authority to make the purchase.

Buying center
All members of an organization involved in the purchasing process.

Buying committee
A group of individuals responsible for a purchase.

C

Canned presentation
A sales presentation prepared in advance that stops only to allow the customer to make directed responses. Also called a black-box approach.

Cartel
Group of firms or countries that agree to act as a monopoly.

CNash-and-carry wholesalers
Wholesalers that sell limited lines of warehoused goods on site for cash.

Cash cows
Successful products in the prime of their life cycle. Cash cows generate much more cash than they need, allowing the company to channel some funds to other SBUs.

Cash discount
Price reduction given to a buyer who pays the invoice within a specified number of days.

Cash flow
Cash funds generated minus expenses requiring cash funds.

Causal research
A research design permitting examination of the relationship between variables to provide evidence for the existence of a cause-and-effect relationship.

Census
Survey requiring contact with everyone in the population.

Central business districts
Areas where retailers are concentrated and where customer traffic is thereby strong.

Central market
A major marketplace for a line of goods, such as furniture or apparel.

Chain-store warehouse
A building that is owned by a retailer and operated as a wholesaling facility; enables chain-store organizations to perform the sorting process as economically as merchant wholesalers.

Channel captain
Managing or directing member of channel, who integrates and coordinates the objectives and policies of all the other members.

Channel of distribution
See *marketing channel.*

Channel of distribution sales analysis
The breakdown of sales by distribution channels when multiple channels are used.

Channel power
The ability of one channel member to strongly affect what another channel member does.

Channel system
A common technique for integrating the distribution communication network; often places computer terminals in customers' offices and assists in the management of inventory, analysis of cost, quality control, etc.

Client involvement
Describes a service that requires the client's presence.

Close
The point in a sales presentation at which the salesperson attempts to secure the customer's agreement to purchase.

Closed-end question
Question that requires the respondent to make choices among answers provided.

Cluster sample
A random sample of a population in which a census or a sample is taken from randomly selected geographic areas. Also called *area sample.*

Cognitive dissonance
The psychological conflict resulting from incongruous beliefs and attitudes held simultaneously.

Cold canvas
Describes an approach by which salespeople locate customers by calling on prospects without appointments or advance knowledge of their needs or financial status.

Commercialization
The last step in product development; involves the planning and launching of full-scale production and marketing programs for the new product.

Commission merchant
Functional middleman used by principals to sell specific lots of goods; deals mainly in agricultural commodities that must be sent from small local markets to large central ones.

Common carrier
Regular, scheduled transportation service available to the public, such as airlines, railroads, truck lines, and buses.

Common Market
Group of geographically associated countries that agree to limit trade barriers among member nations and to apply a common external tariff on products entering member countries.

Community shopping center
Shopping complex composed of twenty to fifty limited-line stores that handle a variety of convenience and shopping goods.

Comparison advantage
A trade advantage that a country takes advantage of when it specializes in those products that it can supply more efficiently and at a lower cost than other items.

Competitive advantage
What one firm can do better than competitors to satisfy customer needs.

Competitive pricing
The use of competitors' behavior as the basis for determining price.

Competitive stage
The growth and maturity stages of the product life cycle, when advertising is used to persuade consumers to purchase a specific brand.

Complementary pricing
Pricing of two products as a unit because they are used together.

Component parts
Industrial goods needing little if any additional processing to become a part of a physical product.

Composite of a line
The variety of products included in a line.

Concentrated strategy
Strategy by which the marketer approaches only one market segment.

Concept development
A step in product development that requires that the product idea be visualized in physical form.

Concept testing
A step in product development that determines customer reaction and preferences to the product concept features.

Consumer
A person buying for his or her own satisfaction.

Consumer behavior
All the activities in which people engage when buying products for personal and household use.

Consumer behavior model
Model that explains consumer behavior by identifying and relating variables that influence the purchase decision.

Consumer goods
Goods produced to provide pleasure or satisfaction to the ultimate consumer.

Consumer movement
A movement that seeks to increase the power of consumers in relation to the power of providers and sellers of goods and services.

Containerization
Consolidation of goods in containers that are sealed at origin and are not opened until they arrive at their destination.

Contingency plans
Alternative plans developed to deal with deviations that might occur because of environmental changes. Causes for deviations are anticipated in contingency plans.

Contract carrier
Company that offers transportation services for hire by individual contract.

Contract manufacturing
An agreement by which a domestic company contracts with a foreign manufacturer to produce products to the domestic company's specifications and with its label.

Contribution-margin analysis
Consideration of only traceable costs on the income statement to evaluate success.

Control
Process of analyzing results by measuring performance, comparing performance with objectives and, when necessary, making corrections.

Convenience goods
Consumer goods purchased frequently, with a minimum of effort, and immediately upon discovery of a need.

Convenience sample
Survey procedure that includes any population member who is readily available.

Convenience store
A store that is accessible to the consumer and offers frequently purchased goods, abundant parking, and rapid checkout.

Conversion cost method
Method of pricing that considers only direct labor and overhead costs.

Cooperative advertising
Procedure through which national advertisers share their advertising costs with local retailers who feature their products.

Copy testing
The tests and measurements used to evaluate the effectiveness of advertisements.

Corporate culture
An organization's traditions, values, unwritten norms, patterns of management thinking, and beliefs about and action toward customers, competitors, and the world.

Corporate strategic plan
Plan that details the objective of the larger corporation along with strategies for implementing and controlling these objectives.

Cost trade-off approach
An approach to physical distribution that seeks to minimize total cost while maximizing customer service; recognizes that changing the components of a physical distribution system can create conflicting cost structures.

Countertrade
A system of exchange that uses something other than money or credit as payment. The three types of countertrade include barter, counterpurchase, and buyback.

Country-centered marketing strategy
A nonstandardized marketing approach to the global market. Firms create different strategies and expect different returns for individual countries or world regions.

Coupon
A form of sales promotion, commonly distributed through newspapers, magazines, and direct mail, that offers cents off the retail price when redeemed at the point of purchase.

Creative selling process
A selling process whereby salespeople aggressively seek out customers and use a well-organized sales presentation to motivate a customer to make a purchase.

Credit
The ability to exchange something of value now in return for a promise to pay in the future.

Cross tabulation
The combination of responses from two or more questions to create a matrix.

Cue
A signal that stimulates an individual to think that a viable method for satisfying a need exists.

Culture
The abstract and material elements made by human beings that distinguish one society from another.

Customer segments sales analysis
Analysis of sales by customer segment to answer the question, "Who is buying and using the company's products?"

Customized research
Research service tailored to the needs of a client organization.

Cycle
A regularly recurring series of events.

D

Decider
Member of buying center who makes the final purchase decision.

Decline stage
The fourth stage in the product life cycle, in which sales continue the downward movement started in maturity.

Decoding
Conversion of a message into recognizable concepts and ideas.

Delaney Amendment
An amendment stating that the Food and Drug Administration must ban any product that shows a link with cancer.

Demand-backward pricing
Pricing method that starts with the consumer and works backward to the producer.

Demand schedule
The quantity of a product demanded at various prices.

Demarketing
A seller's attempt to discourage demand for its product, instead of encouraging it.

Demography
The study of vital and social statistics.

Derived demand
Demand for a product that depends on the sale of the purchaser's product.

Desk jobber
See *drop shipper.*

Developed nation
Nation that engages in a complete variety of marketing activities throughout its economy and is characterized by a large middle class.

Developing nation
Nation characterized by increased manufacturing, by a shift among the population toward the middle and upper classes, and by a generally semiskilled and skilled work force.

Dialectic hypothesis
Hypothesis of retail development that adapts the belief of the German philosopher G. W. Hegel that existing institutions are continually challenged by institutions of new and opposite kinds.

Differentiated strategy
Strategy by which the marketer attempts to serve two or more market segments.

Diffusion process
The spreading acceptance or rejection of a new product in a market.

Direct exporting
Arrangement by which a company handles its own exporting efforts.

Direct investment
Investment through which a domestic company owns and operates manufacturing plants in foreign countries.

Discounts
Reductions taken from the list price.

Discretionary income
The income left after expenditures for basic needs: food, shelter, and clothing.

Disposable personal income
The remainder of a person's income after taxes; represents the bulk of one's spending power.

Distribution
Refers to the means of bringing a product or service to the consumer.

Distribution center
A form of central warehousing through which goods are collected from other plants and suppliers and moved out as soon as possible.

Distributor's brand
A brand owned by a retailer, wholesaler, or other distributing channel member.

Dogs
Products with limited growth. Dogs do not generate positive cash flow.

Draw account
An account that enables people who sell seasonal products to draw advances against future commissions.

Drive
A basic or instinctual need.

Drop shipper
Limited-function wholesaler that generally operates from an office and does not take physical possession of the goods that it resells. Also called *desk jobber.*

Dumping
A situation in which a country makes a quick entry into another nation's market by selling a product in the foreign market at a price lower than that in its own market.

Duty analysis
A detailed account that focuses on the content of the sales call to improve sales effectiveness.

Duty-free trade zone
A designated area set aside to allow businesses to store, process, and display products from abroad without first paying a tariff.

E

Economic order quantity (EOQ)
The order size that minimizes the total cost of ordering and carrying inventory.

Economic utility
The capability of a product to provide satisfaction and value to consumers; includes utilities of form, place, time, information, and possession.

Effectiveness standards
Standards that are stated in terms of goals without consideration of the costs to obtain them.

Efficiency standards
Standards that focus on the use of company resources.

Embargo
The total prevention of a particular good's entering or leaving a country.

Emergency goods
Necessary goods purchased without prior planning.

Encoding
Putting a message into a transmittable form.

Engel's laws
A set of postulates that identify changes that occur in expenditure patterns as family incomes increase.

Environmental scanning
Procedures used to gather and examine environmental information to identify trends and predict their impact on the corporation and on marketing programs.

Equipment-based service
Service whose production or delivery requires equipment.

Erratic factor
Random variable that cannot be accounted for in forecasting.

Ethical egoism
A belief that each individual should always act to promote the greatest balance of good over evil for himself or herself.

Ethical relativism
A belief that the same act may be morally right for one individual or society and morally wrong for another individual or society.

Ethics
The discipline concerned with clarifying what constitutes human welfare and what kind of conduct is necessary to promote welfare.

European community (EC)
A twelve-member common market founded in 1958.

Evaluation criteria
The characteristics of a product or service used by the consumer in evaluating alternatives.

Evoked set
A group of brands, products, or stores from which a buyer normally makes his or her choice.

Exchange
A process in which something of value is given or received in return for something.

Exclusive dealing
An arrangement by which a producer prohibits its middlemen from handling competitive products.

Exclusive distribution
A marketing strategy whereby a middleman agrees to perform certain specific marketing activities for a producer in return for an exclusive sales territory.

Exclusive territory
A designated geographic area in which a single middleman handles the goods of a producer.

Executive summary
The part of the marketing plan that summarizes its major points; usually one page long, and written for the receiving executives.

Experience curve pricing
A pricing approach by which a firm initially establishes a low price to obtain volume in the expectation that it will eventually lower its average total costs through experience made possible by this large sales volume.

Experimental research
A research design through which the researcher manipulates a variable or variables and measures the change in other variables resulting from the manipulation.

Exploratory research
Research developed from initial hunches or insights and intended to provide direction for further research.

Export and import broker
Functional middleman that brings buyers and sellers together and represents either party; sells single lots of goods and often specializes in a particular line from a limited number of countries.

Export-Import Bank (Eximbank)
An independent U.S. government agency established in 1934 to create jobs during the depression. Today, it finances loans to exporters that cannot find funds through commercial sources and to foreign countries that need money to purchase American products.

Export management company (EMC)
Functional middleman that obtains goods from several small producers in order to offer foreign customers a complete line of goods in a specialized field.

Export Trading Company Act
A law that granted U.S. companies the right to use export trading companies (ETCs) to set prices in concert abroad, provided access to Export-Import Bank financing, and guaranteed and allowed banks the right to own and operate their own ETCs.

Exporting
Process by which goods and services are sold to foreign countries.

F

Face validity
A quality possessed by research results that seem by common sense and logic to be accurate.

Facilitating agency
A transportation firm, financial institution, or other organization that is not directly involved in the exchange process but assists in its accomplishment.

Fad
A product or idea that has a short life cycle.

Fair trade laws
Laws that granted manufacturers an exemption from antitrust legislation so that they could establish minimum resale prices for their goods.

Family brand
A single brand name applied to several related products.

Family household
Household made up of individuals living together who are related by blood or marriage.

Family life cycle
Cycle that traces the evolution of families from formation to dissolution or death.

Fashion
Popular style of product at a given time. Fashions have short *recurring* life cycles.

Feedback
Response by a receiver to a message.

Fishyback service
Transportation by ship of containerized trucks loaded with freight.

Fixed costs
Costs that do not change with changes in the volume of output.

Flexible pricing policy
Policy pursued by a seller willing to negotiate price.

Flighting
An advertising scheduling strategy similar to pulsing, except that the concentrated bursts of advertising are not regular.

Focus group
A small number (usually ten to twelve) of persons brought together to discuss their reactions to a product, either proposed or actual. Led by group leader.

Food broker
A functional middleman that represents both large and small producers in the grocery industry on a continuous contractual basis.

Forecast
Sales expectations for a company.

Forecast accuracy
Degree to which forecast sales match actual sales.

Forecast method requirement
A criterion that must be met for a forecast method to be considered valid.

Forecast precision
Refers to the width of the range of the forecast.

Forecast time horizon
Time period for which a forecast is made, e.g., short-term or long-term.

Foreign sales corporation (FSC)
A classification that allows a company maintaining a foreign presence to receive a tax exemption on foreign income of 15 to 32 percent.

Form utility
A type of benefit that results from the production function, which changes the

form of the starting material to a form more useful or desirable.

Franchise
A contractual relationship between an initiating organization and independent businesspersons, who are required to follow a carefully prescribed method of operation.

Franchisee
An independent businessperson who accepts the terms of a franchise agreement.

Franchisor
The initiating organization in a franchise agreement.

Free on board (FOB) pricing
Pricing method that makes buyer responsible for paying transportation costs after loading.

Freight absorption pricing
Seller meets delivery price of competitors and absorbs it; cost to seller is subtracted from profit margin.

Freight forwarder
A firm that acts as a common carrier or middleman to transport or provide for transport of small shipments assembled and consolidated into larger lots; this results in reduced rates for shippers.

Frequency
In advertising, the number of times an average person is exposed to the message of a campaign.

Full-cost analysis
An approach that requires that all costs be assigned in evaluating success.

Full-service agency
An advertising agency that offers a wide range of services, such as market research, media planning, package design, account management, and copy and art layout.

Functional cost account
Accounting of cost by specific reason for which the expenditure was made.

Functional discount
See *trade discount.*

Functional middleman
Wholesaling intermediary that does not acquire title to goods and seldom performs all of the wholesaling functions.

G

Gatekeeper
Individual within a buying center who exercises veto power in purchase decisions through possession of extensive product knowledge.

General Agreement on Tariffs and Trade (GATT)
An eighty-five nation accord signed in 1948 to encourage trade relations and to prevent price increases and trade wars.

General-line distributor
Merchant middleman in the industrial field that handles broad lines of industrial

products, such as chemicals or electrical supplies.

General-line wholesaler
Merchant middleman that limits its merchandise offering to a single line, such as groceries, hardware, drugs and beauty aids, or plumbing and heating equipment.

General merchandise wholesaler
Merchant middleman that handles a wide variety of unrelated goods.

General-specific-general hypothesis
Hypothesis that postulates that development in the retailing industry has moved from general merchandise assortments to specific or limited lines and then back to general merchandise lines.

Generic brands
Brand name that has become a part of public domain and can be legally used by anyone.

Generic product
Product without a brand name.

Generic strategy
Basic strategy that applies to a general and recurring marketing situation.

Geographic sales analysis
Breakdown of sales figures into geographic areas.

Global marketing strategy
A standardized approach to international marketing that views the world market as a set of integrated activities.

Gray market
A form of transshipping whereby goods are brought into the United States by importers who have not been appointed by foreign producers as their official distributors.

Growth stage
The second stage in the product life cycle; starts with rapidly increasing industry sales and ends with sales that continue to increase, but not so rapidly.

Growth strategy
An all-out effort to grow through expansion of markets, adaptation of products, and development of new products or markets.

Guarantee
A company's commitment that it will compensate customers if they are dissatisfied with a product or service.

H

Harvesting
A strategy of deliberately reducing expenditures on a product to increase that product's profit margin, even though the market share may decrease. Product quality, promotion, and other costs may be cut.

Hierarchy of needs
A ranking of human needs proposed by the psychologist Abraham Maslow; ranges from basic physiological needs

through needs for security, belonging, esteem, and self-actualization.

Horizontal marketing arrangement
Arrangement by which channel members on the same level of distribution form close working relationships to obtain the advantages associated with large operations.

Hypothesis
A guess, an assumption, or a tentative explanation offered as a possible solution to a problem; provides researchers with a guide as to what data to collect.

I

Iceberg principle
In evaluation, a principle whereby a deviation signals the need for closer examination of a situation to determine underlying causes; refers to those situations where 90 percent of the information pertaining to a situation lies beneath the surface.

Idea generation
The first step in product development; an ongoing search for product ideas.

Idea marketing
Marketing that attempts to identify and gain acceptance of a practice, cause, philosophy, or way of thinking.

Implementation
A management function that includes activities such as organizing, staffing, directing, and coordinating.

Importing
Process by which goods and services are purchased from foreign countries.

Impulse goods
Goods purchased without previous planning; "on-the-spot" purchases.

Incremental cost method
Pricing method using only the variable cost of direct labor and material to determine price.

Indirect exporting
Arrangement by which a company uses the services of international marketing middlemen to export goods.

Individual brand
A brand name that applies to only one item in a product line, rather than to the entire product line.

Industrial distributor
A middleman that purchases related product lines from many producers for resale to industrial users.

Industrial goods
Goods bought by organizations or individuals for the purpose of producing other products or services.

Industrial selling
The sale of products to business and industry; includes sales to middlemen, manufacturers, and institutions.

Inflation
An economic condition that reduces the purchasing power of money and thereby increases the price of goods to consumers.

Influencer
Individual, often technically oriented, within the buying center who controls some aspects of the purchase decision by defining the criteria the purchase must meet.

Information utility
A benefit provided by the selling function when it communicates the features and benefits of a good.

Inseparability (of services)
Quality common to services; they cannot be separated from the persons or sellers providing them.

Installation
Industrial good that represents a major capital investment used by a firm to produce its products and services.

Institutional advertising
Advertising designed to promote an image or goodwill message for a company, industry, organization, or government.

Intangibility (of services)
Quality common to services; they cannot be measured precisely because they lack physical characteristics.

Intensive distribution
A strategy whereby all possible types of outlets are used to sell goods.

Intermodal shipping system
A major advance in coastal and oceanic shipping by which ships handle containerized freight, or conex, containers.

International marketing
Marketing activities performed to facilitate the exchange of products among nations.

International trade
The exchange of products among nations.

Introductory stage
The first stage of the product life cycle; begins when the new product first becomes available for sale.

J

Joint demand
Demand for two or more products that depends on all the products being supplied.

Joint venture
In international commerce, a temporary partnership established between a domestic and a foreign company.

Judgment sample
Sample that includes any member of the population known to have a specific attribute.

Just-in-time concept (JIT)
Buying frequently and in small quantities just in time for use; reduces the size of inventory.

K

Kant's categorical imperative
A principle that states that one should take the right action—not necessarily because it produces good results but because it is one's duty to do so.

L

Label
Printed material on a product package that provides information to the buyer and others, satisfies legal requirements, and helps identify the brand owner.

Lanham Act
Federal law that allows a manufacturer to protect its brand or trademark.

Leading series factor
Factor that develops concurrently with current sales but actually has a closer relationship to future sales.

Legalistic system
A system in which rules and regulations spell out laws for behavior.

Less-developed nation
Nation characterized by unskilled labor and limited manufacturing; often rich in one or more natural resources.

Licensing
A temporary agreement that allows the licensee to use trademarks, patents, copyrights, or even manufacturing processes of another firm.

Lifestyle
A person's typical mode or manner of working and living.

Limited-function wholesaler
Merchant middleman that restricts its performance of marketing activities, passing them either backward to manufacturers or forward to retailers.

List price
Price quoted or announced to buyers and from which discounts and other adjustments are made.

Low cost marketing approach
A strategy used by organizations to achieve a competitive advantage; emphasizes low cost per unit and low price as an appeal to customers.

M

Macroenvironmental forces
Forces in the external environment that affect the firm, including economic factors, social and cultural values, technology, political and legal factors, and demographic conditions.

Macromarketing
Marketing that focuses on the overall economic processes that match the supply of goods and services produced

to demand and, in turn, satisfy the goals of the system.

Magnuson-Moss Act
Federal law empowering the Federal Trade Commission to regulate written warranty practices for products costing more than $15.

Mail-order wholesaler
Limited-function wholesaler that sells through catalogs and accepts both mail and telephone orders.

Majority fallacy
The false belief that selection of a large market segment will ensure high sales for a firm; other marketers may have the same thought; thus no firm will have high sales.

Manufacturer's agent
A functional middleman that generally establishes continuous contractual relationships with several noncompeting producers and handles the goods of these producers in certain designated territories. Also called *manufacturer's representative.*

Manufacturer's brand
Brand owned by the manufacturer of the product.

Manufacturer's export agent (MEA)
A functional middleman that provides a basic selling service in export markets for its principals and has only a short-term relationship with them.

Manufacturer's representative
Order getter who is usually employed by small manufacturing firms to sell to wholesalers, distributors, dealers, and sometimes ultimate consumers.

Manufacturer's sales branch
A wholesaling unit established by a manufacturer; represents a forward integration in the channel system.

Marginal analysis
Looks at the effects on total revenues and total costs of selling one additional unit.

Marginal cost
Cost associated with the last unit of output.

Marginal revenue
Revenue received from the last unit sold.

Markdown
The amount of reduction in price; stated as a percentage, original price minus the new price divided by the new price.

Market
All consumers and organizations that have both the need and the ability to make an exchange for the product, service, or idea offered.

Market factor
Any variable associated with the level of sales.

Market index
A combination of variables associated with sales level.

Market penetration
Strategy that seeks expansion by improvement in the market shares of existing products in markets presently served.

Market/product development
Strategy whereby the organization undertakes the development of a new product for the existing market or develops a new market for the existing product.

Market retention
Strategy that focuses on retaining the current market share. Similar to the balance strategy, but environmental conditions differ in that the desired product characteristics are subject to change and competitors are seeking to improve their positions in the market.

Market segmentation
Division of a larger market into smaller, more homogeneous markets.

Market share
The firm's sales divided by total industry's sales.

Market share analysis
Sales analysis to ascertain how the firm is performing compared with other firms in the industry.

Market share building
Strategy to increase market share; normally requires large outlays of money for promotion.

Marketing
The process of planning and executing the conception, pricing, promotion, and distribution of ideas, goods, and services to create exchanges that satisfy individual and organizational objectives.

Marketing audit
A systematic, unbiased examination of the organization's marketing philosophy, programs, and results.

Marketing channel
A group of organizations or individuals that assist in the flow of goods and services from producer to consumer. Also called *channel of distribution.*

Marketing communications
The exchange of information among those involved in the marketing process.

Marketing concept
A concept under which each department in an organization is responsive to consumer needs; affects decision making in every area of the organization.

Marketing-driven organization
Organization that understands consumer needs and develops and distributes products that satisfy those needs.

Marketing functions
Major economic activities that must be performed somewhere in the marketing system in order for the marketing task to be accomplished.

Marketing information system (MᴋIS)
Formalized procedure for collecting, storing, and retrieving information pertinent to routine decision making.

Marketing intermediary
Any of the specialists that aid in the performance of the marketing functions.

Marketing manager
Person who has the major management responsibility for marketing; usually a high-level position.

Marketing mix
Blend of product, price, promotion, and distribution elements that provides direction and structure to an organization's marketing program.

Marketing myopia
The failure of a firm to recognize the actual business that it is in.

Marketing opportunity
A circumstance in the market environment that provides the organization with a chance for advancement.

Marketing plan
Written document detailing a firm's marketing strategy and the time frames in which the strategy is to be implemented.

Marketing research
Systematic and objective process of gathering, recording, and analyzing data for marketing decision making.

Marketing strategy
A structured means of achieving the organization's marketing objectives within the context of the defined business, current trends, competition, and time frame.

Marketing threat
A circumstance in the environment that could harm the organization's marketing or general business goals.

Mass market approach
Marketers select the total market, such as industrial or consumer, assuming that all individuals in the market have the same needs and will respond similarly to a firm's offering. See also *undifferentiated strategy.*

Materials handling
All the activities involved in moving products short distances within a production facility.

Maturity stage
The third stage in the product life cycle, in which sales grow slowly at the beginning, peak, and then start to decline.

Media plan
A plan that includes the media to be used in a promotion and a time schedule for advertisements to appear; a crucial element in successful promotions.

Medium of transmission
The channel—verbal, nonverbal, written, or spoken—used to physically transmit a message.

Megamarketing
Marketing through which marketers attempt to persuade such audiences as government officials, public-interest groups, news media, and other opinion leaders.

Merchant wholesaler
An independent middleman that buys goods, takes title to them, assumes all risks for them, and resells them, mainly to retailers or industrial users.

Message
A series of coded signs or symbols that make up communications.

Microenvironmental forces
Smaller-scale environmental forces that can affect a company's marketing effort, such as its internal structure, suppliers, marketing intermediaries, competitors, and customers.

Micromarketing
Marketing activities performed within a particular organization in order to achieve the objectives of the organization.

Middlemen
Wholesalers or retailers that assist in the transfer of goods and their ownership rights.

Mission statement
Statement that defines the enduring purpose, vision, or aim of the organization in a way that makes the organization distinguishable from all others.

Missionary selling
Form of selling requiring periodic contact with wholesalers and retailers to check their stocks, arrange displays, provide advice on selling, and inform them about new products; used as a supplement to the personal selling of middlemen.

Modified rebuy
A purchase situation in which the buyer is somewhat familiar with the product but less than completely satisfied with the previous buy.

Monopolistic competition
Market structure in which many sellers trade slightly different products. Each seller varies its product's functions or features to differentiate the product from the competition.

Motive
The energizing force that directs behavior toward a need-satisfying object or goal.

Multinational corporation (MNC)
Corporation that operates in several countries and often has a substantial share of its total assets, sales, or labor force in foreign subsidiaries.

Multiple marketing channels
More than one marketing channel; multiple channels may be used to reach a single target market or different target markets.

Nationalism
A movement that, among other things, encourages the development of stronger domestic industries, which results in greater self-sufficiency.

Natural cost account
Usual records of expenditures, such as those for rent, salaries, promotion, and supplies. Purpose of the expenditure is not usually indicated in such accounts.

Need
An imbalance between the actual and desired states of being within the consumer.

Need-satisfaction approach
A sales approach that begins with completing a needs assessment for the customer; then selecting and recommending the product that will provide maximum satisfaction; and finally, communicating to the customer the satisfaction the product will give.

Neighborhood shopping center
Smallest type of retail center; often contains fewer than a dozen stores, which typically sell convenience goods.

Network of variables
An interrelated set of variables that must be considered when marketing decisions are made.

New product
A product that may be truly unique, satisfying a need that has gone unsatisfied; a substitute for existing products of considerably different nature; a replacement for existing but similar products; or an imitator new to the company but not to the market.

New product development department
Special department whose sole responsibility is to develop new products.

New task
A buying situation in which buying personnel initially lack the experience and knowledge necessary to make the required purchase.

New venture/diversification strategy
Situation in which both the market and the product are new to the organization.

Noise
Any influence outside the message that distracts the receiver or distorts the message.

Nonprobability sampling
Sampling procedure that uses an arbitrary technique, such as convenience or judgment, to select the sample.

Nonprofit organizations
Organizations that emphasizes goals other than returning a profit to owners.

Observation
Collection of data when the phenomenon occurs. Individual subjects may be aware or unaware of the research and do not directly interact with the researcher.

Odd pricing
Pricing the product so that its price ends in an odd number, as in $4.95.

Oligopolistic market
A market in which only a few sellers account for most of the sales.

One-price policy
Policy of offering the same price to all customers.

Open-end question
Question that allows the respondent to answer in his or her own words.

Opportunity requirement
The investment or expenditure needed to competitively take advantage of an opportunity.

Orderly marketing agreement (OMA)
Agreement by which nations share markets; the latest departure from free trade.

Organizational buyer
Buyer that has the formal authority to carry out the purchase function for an organization.

Organization market
Market in which an organization purchases goods and services so that it can produce a service, product, or idea for its customers.

Organizational marketing
Marketing intended to gain, alter, or maintain acceptance of an organization's objectives and services.

Organizational objectives
Aims that stress the benefits the organization wishes to obtain as a result of its actions.

Package
A product's container or wrapping.

Patronage motives
Factors that consumers perceive to be controlled by the retailer and that cause consumers to purchase at a particular retail establishment.

Penetration pricing
Pricing to gain market share by keeping the profit margin and the price low.

People-based services
Services that can be produced and delivered by a person or a group of people without the aid of equipment.

Percentage analysis
The evaluation of period-to-period percentage changes in assets and expenses.

Perception
The process of selecting, organizing, and interpreting stimuli received through the five senses.

Perceptual mapping
See *position mapping*.

Performance index
The reduction of data to a common base of 100.

Perishability (of services)
A quality possessed by services, since their production is based on a time element and they are intangible and cannot be stored.

Person marketing
Marketing aimed at making or maintaining an image or impression of a person.

Personal selling
A one-on-one promotional presentation by a seller to a prospective buyer.

Physical distribution
The handling and moving of goods from the point of production to the place of consumption.

Physical product development
The step in product development that requires that the physical product be made to determine if it fits the technological and production capabilities of the company.

Physiological test
Laboratory test designed to measure a consumer's involuntary responses to specific advertising elements.

Piggyback service
Service offered by railroads for hauling truck trailers on flatcars to locations close to customers.

PIMS (profit impact of marketing strategy)
A research program, provided by the Strategic Planning Institute, that reports on the products of firms that are members of the institute.

Pioneering stage
An introductory period during which the aim of advertising is to stimulate demand for a class of goods without particular regard to brand.

Place marketing
Marketing intended to create awareness or create, maintain, or change attitudes and behavior with regard to a geographic area or place.

Place utility
A benefit created by the transportation function when it moves a good to the place of need.

Planning
Process of determining the most efficient course of action for obtaining a desired objective.

Point-of-purchase (POP) display
Demonstration or other form of visual merchandising situated near the location at which the purchase is made.

Portfolio
The collection of SBUs in which the company has a managerial investment.

Portfolio analysis
The starting point in marketing strategy planning; the holdings in the portfolio are financially evaluated, and each SBU is usually visualized in product terms.

Portfolio test
A pretesting method in which an individual is asked to look at a folder of advertisements and then recall as much as possible about each advertisement.

Position mapping
A grid indicating a product's position in relation to competing brands. Also called *perceptual mapping.*

Positioning
The process of shaping the way customers perceive the firm's product.

Possession utility
Benefit created by the selling function, which gives rise to the exchange process, and the financing function, which facilitates this process through financing arrangements.

Posttesting
Tests conducted after a media campaign to measure campaign effectiveness; includes recognition and recall tests.

Potential
The possible short- and long-term net benefit to the organization from serving a market segment.

Premium
A piece of merchandise offered as a gift or sold for a small fee to provide an incentive for purchasing another product.

Prestige pricing
A type of psychological pricing that takes advantage of people's tendency to think that a product has to be expensive to be of high quality.

Pretesting
Testing done prior to a marketing campaign to help select the best appeals, advertisements, media, and to limit possible mistakes in the final campaign.

Price
The cost necessary to obtain ownership of a good or service.

Price discrimination
Condition that exists when a seller sells products of a like grade and quality to like buyers at different prices; the effect is to injure competition.

Price elasticity
An index measuring the effect of a change in price on the quantity of demand for a product.

Price objective
An objective that states what the firm wishes to accomplish with its prices.

Price skimming
Pricing the product high in order to have a high profit margin.

Primary data
Data collected from original sources specifically to achieve the research project's objectives.

Private brands
Brands of products sold to retailer, wholesaler, or other channel member (besides the manufacturer) for sale under their own name.

Private carrier
Company that has its own transportation fleet to move its products.

Private warehouse
Warehouse owned or leased by a company for its exclusive use.

Probability sampling
A sampling procedure that gives every member of a population a known, nonzero chance of being selected.

Problem children
Products with potential that do not do well. Also called *question marks.*

Problem definition
The first step in the research process; identifies a specific marketing decision area that will be clarified by answers to research questions.

Processed materials
Industrial goods that are used in production but that do not become an identifiable part of the product.

Producer
Firm that makes a profit primarily by creating and marketing form utility.

Producer cooperative
A middleman that accumulates, grades, processes, and distributes goods to cooperative members; used most frequently by farmers.

Product
The bundle of tangible and intangible benefits a buyer receives in exchange for currency or other forms of trade; a physical item and/or a service.

Product advertising
Advertising designed to promote a product or product line. It can be aimed at the ultimate consumer or a channel user.

Product development process
An organized and controlled process used to bring new products to the market.

Product differentiation
A marketing strategy whereby a company varies the function, style, quality, service, or packaging of its product from that of the competition.

Product item
Each unique product offered for sale by an organization.

Product life cycle
The time period over which a product is accepted and purchased by customers in a market; includes introductory, growth, maturity, and decline stages.

Product line
A group of products that are closely related by physical characteristics, customer need satisfaction, or other similarities and are therefore marketed in approximately the same way.

Product manager
The individual who plans and coordinates complete programs for a single brand, product, product line, or market.

Product mix
The combination of all product lines offered by an organization.

Product-planning committee
A committee that approves concepts, budgets, and development plans for new product ideas.

Product sales analysis
An analysis of sales figures that draws attention to products that have performed successfully as well as those that need attention.

Productivity
The relationship between output (results) and input (resources).

Profit maximization
A pricing technique that attempts to obtain the most possible profit.

Promotion
The communications means used by sellers to persuade or remind potential buyers that a product or service exists.

Prospecting
The systematic approach to developing new sales leads.

Protectionism
The belief that free trade should be restricted for the protection of domestic industries.

Psychographics
The study of consumers' attitudes and lifestyles. See also *VALS*.

Public relations
Communications process by which an organization maintains goodwill or promotes a positive image.

Public warehouses
Warehouses that are owned and operated by private contractors and are available to all users.

Publicity
Nonpaid commercially significant news or editorial comments about ideas, products, or institutions.

Pull strategy
A promotional strategy that tries to stimulate consumer demand for a product by using heavy advertising.

Pulsing
A scheduling strategy for advertising in which fairly regular intermittent bursts of advertising are used, followed by short periods of relative or complete inactivity.

Purchaser
The consumer who physically purchases the good.

Purchasing manager
The individual responsible for the acquisition of products and services.

Purchasing power
A measurement composed of income, wealth, and credit, with income being the most important factor.

Pure competition
A market consisting of many buyers and sellers exchanging products that vary little in physical characteristics.

Pure monopoly
A market supplied by one seller.

Push strategy
A promotional strategy that places primary emphasis on personal selling to all members of the marketing channel but supplements personal selling with advertising and other promotional efforts as needed.

Q

Qualifying
The procedure followed to determine if a prospect has a need for a product, the authority to buy it, and the money to pay for it.

Qualitative research
Research conducted with the intent of providing a better understanding of concepts and issues without regard for statistical accuracy.

Quality variability (of services)
The variation in a service's quality from one purchase to the next, even from the same supplier.

Quantitative research
Research based on data that can be statistically validated through measurement techniques.

Quantity discount
Discount offered to buyers who purchase large quantities.

Questionnaire
Standardized form used to guide the interviewer or respondent in the collection of the desired data.

Quota
Quantitative limit on the amount of goods that can be legally imported into a country.

Quota sample
A procedure that divides the population into subgroups and includes a certain number of individuals from each subgroup in the sample.

R

Raw materials
Goods, such as farm and natural products, that are used as input for industrial processing.

Reach
The number of potential viewers or readers an advertising campaign wishes to reach.

Rebate
Downward price change, also called reduction. Consumer pays the higher price and then applies for the rebate.

Recall test
Test similar to recognition test, except that respondents are not shown an advertisement but are asked to remember which advertisements they have previously read or viewed.

Receiver
Any person receiving a communication message.

Recognition test
A survey used to evaluate readership of advertisements. Respondents are interviewed and asked questions about advertisements they claim to have read.

Reference groups
All of the groups that influence the purchasing behavior of an individual.

Regional shopping center
The largest type of planned center; consists of at least fifty limited-line stores positioned between two or more department stores.

Reinforcement
A reward or punishment resulting from a response.

Research design
A master plan specifying the methods and procedures for collecting and analyzing the needed information; a framework for the research plan of action.

Reseller
Firm that makes a profit primarily by creating time, place, and possession utility.

Response
Behavior intended to satisfy a drive.

Response elasticity
People's reaction to marketing activities.

Retail buyer
A person responsible for buying and sometimes for selling merchandise in a department of a major store.

Retail establishment
A separate place of business from which sales are made, mainly to ultimate consumers.

Retail selling
The sale of products for personal nonbusiness use to ultimate consumers.

Retailer
A marketing intermediary who takes title to the goods and who sells primarily to ultimate consumers.

Retailer cooperative voluntary group
A group of retailers who join together and establish their own distribution center—which takes the place of a wholesaler in the channel system—in order to gain operating efficiencies and economies.

Retailing
A consumer-responsive business; includes all activities that involve selling to the ultimate consumer.

Retailing life cycle
Life cycle for a business; comprises the innovation, accelerated development, maturity, and decline stages.

Retentive stage
A stage of selective advertising that attempts to maintain the market share of a popular product.

Return on investment (ROI)
Profits divided by investments; measures profitability in terms of the amount of money invested.

Reverse marketing channel
A channel for reprocessed goods that move in reverse from consumer to middleman to producer.

Robinson-Patman Act
Federal act that makes most price discrimination illegal.

Rule utilitarian
One who believes that people should always follow the rules because in the long run they promote the general welfare.

S

Safety stock
Product inventory kept as insurance against variations in demand and lead time; held in addition to the basic stock kept to meet normal demand.

Sales analysis
Method of control whereby sales figures are broken down, most commonly at the level of geography, product, channel of distribution, and target market.

Sales force composite
A sales forecast developed from sales representatives' predictions.

Sales forecast
Estimated sales for a future period under anticipated environmental conditions by a firm employing a designated marketing plan.

Sales management
The process of planning, organizing, directing, and controlling the personal selling effort.

Sales presentation
A salesperson's attempt to make a sale by persuasively communicating with the customer.

Sales promotion
Those marketing activities, other than personal selling, advertising, and publicity, that stimulate consumer purchasing and dealer effectiveness.

Sales territory
The geographic area in which a salesperson works.

Sample
(1) A subset selected from a larger population.

(2) Small trial-size product distributed to consumers free of charge during the introductory stage of the product's development.

Sampling plan
A plan answering three questions: What are the sampling units, what is the sample size, and what is the sample selection procedure?

Scrambled merchandising
The strategy of adding nonrelated offerings to a traditional merchandise line.

Screening
The second step in product development; the separation of product ideas with sales potential from those lacking potential.

Seasonal discount
Discount offered to encourage out-of-season purchases when demand is low.

Seatrain
Containerized maritime shipping combined with railroad transport.

Secondary data
Data that has been collected previously, often for other purposes than current research effort.

Segmentation
(1) To divide the market into homogeneous groups.
(2) Process of identifying buyers that have similar needs and response elasticities.

Selective distribution
A marketing strategy whereby a limited number of carefully chosen middlemen within a particular trading area stock a line of goods.

Selectivity in perception
The perception of only some of the stimuli present in the environment.

Selling
The process through which consumers are persuaded to purchase the goods and services that an organization already has available.

Selling agent
Functional middleman who acts as the marketing arm of a producer and sells the producer's entire output.

Semantic differential
Rating scale technique commonly used to measure attitudes.

Sender
The source of a communication message.

Service
An activity and/or benefit that satisfies buyer needs but provides no ownership in a tangible or physical item. Also includes the intangibles needed and used by an organization in conducting its operation.

Service mix
The combination of services a supplier has to offer.

Shaping
The process of applying a series of rewards as reinforcement to develop complex behavior over time.

Shipper's association
Group of members that consolidate and distribute freight for themselves on a not-for-profit basis.

Shopping goods
Consumer goods that the customer, in the process of selection and purchase, characteristically compares on such bases as suitability, quality, price, and style.

Shopping store
A store patronized by consumers conducting a search process to compare the offerings of several stores.

Simple random sample
Basic type of probability sample; each member of the population has an equal chance of being selected.

Single-line store
Store that handles a broad assortment of goods in a basic line, such as men's apparel, women's apparel, hardware, or groceries.

Situation analysis
The process of gathering and examining information from the internal and external environment to determine the organization's past, present, and possible future position in the market.

Social class
A ranking based on authority, power, and social position.

Social pricing objective
Pricing to accomplish social goals.

Sorting process
A process that relies on the use of middlemen to resolve differences between the amounts and kinds of goods produced and purchased; establishes standards and places goods in classes based on these standards.

Specialty advertising
Articles of merchandise imprinted with an advertiser's message and distributed without obligation to the recipient.

Specialty distributor
Merchant middleman in the industrial field that restricts its line to a narrow product category, such as abrasives or power transmission equipment.

Specialty goods
Consumer goods about which buyers have strong preferences as to brand or some other feature; they will search extensively for the preferred product.

Specialty shop
Store that carries only a segment of a line of goods but provides many styles, colors, and sizes in this segment.

Specialty store
The preferred store of a loyal customer group that is willing to travel great distances to patronize it.

Specialty wholesaler
Merchant middleman that confines its offerings to a narrow group of goods in a general line.

Standard
The expected level of achievement.

Standard Industrial Classification System
A standardized data classification system used for collecting, recording, and analyzing data.

Stars
Products with high market share; the rapid growth of stars require that the company continuously allocate cash to keep ahead of demand.

Stock point
The level at which the inventory of stock is considered to be too low and stock is reordered.

Stockout
Condition in which the inventory of stock has completely run out; leads to lost sales.

Store image
A set of attitudes that result from the evaluation of store attributes important to consumers.

Strategic business unit (SBU)
A separate operating division that represents a major business area and operates with some autonomy within an organization.

Strategic marketing plan
Plan that matches the organization, its resources, and its abilities at the strategic business unit level with opportunities to achieve its objectives and fulfill its mission.

Strategic window
The time element associated with an opportunity; the time when the right combination of elements for success exists.

Stratified sampling
A sampling procedure that randomly selects individuals from subgroups into which the population has been divided.

Subculture
Homogeneous group within a culture whose members share some unique values, artifacts, and behaviors.

Subliminal perception
Perception that occurs at a subconscious level.

Substitute products
Alternative products that satisfy the same needs but differ slightly in some features.

Suggestion selling
A sales technique used to suggest additional items of merchandise that go with the product being purchased.

Summative close
A type of sales closing that attempts to review the main benefits the customer will gain from the product point by point.

Supplies
Industrial goods that facilitate the production of products and services but do not become a part of the finished product.

Survey
Means of gathering data by interviewing people; interviews may be conducted in person, by mail, or by phone.

Survey of buying power
A published source of information on the geographic distribution of income.

Symbiotic marketing
A process in which a low-cost, technically competent manufacturer produces a particular good and sells it to another manufacturer for resale under the second manufacturer's label.

Syncratic decision
Family purchase decision made jointly.

Syndicated service
Research firm that sells the same research results to several firms.

Systematic sample
A research sample that includes every nth item on a list.

T

Target margin on sales
Pricing that uses average total cost to determine selling price with the intent of obtaining a desired profit margin on sales.

Target market
The group of individuals that the marketer wants to satisfy.

Target public
Group of individuals that nonprofit organization benefits.

Target return on investment
A pricing method that seeks to obtain a desired return on investment. Uses both fixed and variable costs.

Tariff
Tax or duty on imported goods.

Technical selling
A form of selling often done by experienced scientists, who work with customers and/or their technical staffs; most valuable in specialized areas requiring great expertise.

Telemarketing
A marketing approach that uses advanced telecommunications technology to help companies maintain close contact with customers while reducing costs.

Test marketing
Introducing a new product in specific geographic areas to assess customer and dealer reaction.

Time analysis
A detailed account of how much time a salesperson allocates to each job activity.

Time utility
A benefit created by the storage function when it permits a good to be inventoried until needed.

Total average variable cost
Total variable cost divided by quantity.

Total cost
All costs associated with the product; must be exceeded by total revenue in order for a profit to be made.

Total cost approach
An approach to physical distribution that attempts to minimize total cost while maximizing customer service; considers components of the physical distribution system as a whole rather than individually.

Total revenue
The total money received from the sale of the product.

Trade discount
A reduction in list price that represents a payment for performance of marketing functions; intended to encourage channel members' participation in the distribution of a product. Also called *functional discount.*

Trade show
A relatively low-cost promotional method in which manufacturers or wholesalers display products; used as a pushing strategy and aimed primarily at channel middlemen.

Trading company
Any organization designed to expand exports.

Trading stamps
Stamps given to consumers by a retailer when merchandise is purchased as a sales promotion technique. The stamps can be exchanged at a redemption center for additional merchandise.

Training needs analysis
Study conducted by a sales manager to determine problem areas in a sales force.

Transaction
The transfer of either the ownership of a good or the right to use it from seller to buyer.

Transportation
The shipment of goods from one location to another.

Transshipper
Shipper that moves goods in an unauthorized manner from an area where they sell at low prices to another area where they can be sold at higher prices.

Trend
The long-term movement in a product's demand; it can be constant or move upward or downward.

Trial close
A part of a sales presentation in which the salesperson tests the readiness of the customer to buy.

Truck wholesaler
Limited-function wholesaler that combines the selling and transportation functions by using driver-salespersons to contact retailers and other institutions. Also called *wagon distributor.*

Tying contract
A contract that links the sale of one item with that of another; may be used by a manufacturer in an effort to obtain additional sales.

Underdeveloped nation
One of the least developed nations of the world; underdeveloped nations often have economies based on the land and agriculture and are characterized by a low standard of living.

Undifferentiated strategy
An approach that treats all buyers in the market as identical. Also called *mass market approach.*

Unfair trade legislation
Laws that prohibit retailers and wholesalers from selling either below their cost or below their cost plus a certain minimum markup.

Uniform delivered price
Price reflects the fact that seller pays all transportation costs in all cases.

Unit loading
Method of handling materials in which several items are grouped to permit efficient movement of loads; most commonly used forms of transportation are pallets and forklift trucks.

Unsought goods
Consists of (1) Goods for which consumers have no prior knowledge and (2) Goods for which consumers are unaware that they need.

User
Individual within the buying center who affects the purchase because he or she will actually use the product or service.

Utilitarianism
The belief that individuals should act so as to promote the greatest good for the greatest number.

Utility
The ability of a product to satisfy customer needs.

VALS
Stands for Values and Lifestyles, a system that attempts to define psychographic segments within the United States. Divides population into four comprehensive groups, which are subdivided into nine lifestyles. See also *Psychographics.*

Value-added consumer orientation
Company orientation that recognizes that the price a consumer is willing to pay depends on the benefits received from the product and not just the physical product itself.

Value pricing
A method of setting price that requires the marketer to assess how much the product is worth to the buyer.

Variable costs
Costs that change with a change in the volume of output.

Venture team
Select group of individuals within a company who devote all of their time to the development of a particular product concept.

Vertical marketing system
A system whereby channel members at different levels in the marketing process are tightly linked together in a centrally controlled marketing effort; types include administered, contractual, and corporate systems.

Wagon distributor
See *truck wholesaler.*

Warranty
A guarantee that the product is not defective or that it will not malfunction during a specified period of time.

Wealth
All of an individual's material possessions, including house, automobile, furniture, and all claims and rights, such as stock certificates and life insurance policies.

Web of relationships
The system of direct transactions that occur among producers and consumers when no middleman is present in the marketing process.

Wheel-of-retailing hypothesis
Hypothesis that deals with the life cycle of a retailing institution; states that new types of retailers emerge as low-price, limited-service, low-margin, low-status operators but eventually evolve into operations with the opposite characteristics.

Wheeler-Lea Act
An amendment to the Federal Trade Commission Act; gives the Federal Trade Commission the power to stop unfair or deceptive acts in commerce, especially pricing.

Wholesaler-sponsored voluntary chain
A group of independent retailers organized by a wholesaler into a centrally controlled channel system.

Wholesaler transaction
Transaction that has a business or profit motive.

Wholesaling
All transactions in which a buyer purchases goods either for resale or for use in making other products.

Willingness to purchase
A measurement of how much the strength of an individuals' needs outweighs that individual's resistance to satisfying those needs through an exchange.

Yuppie
A designation for the marketing segment comprising young professional consumers with discriminating buying habits.

Zone pricing
The seller pays actual transportation charge, billing the buyer the average amount that has been established for the buyer's zone.

Name Index

Subject Index